Lecture Notes in Artificial Intelligence 2143

Subseries of Lecture Notes in Computer Science
Edited by J. G. Carbonell and J. Siekmann

Lecture Notes in Computer Science
Edited by G. Goos, J. Hartmanis, and J. van Leeuwen

Springer
Berlin
Heidelberg
New York
Barcelona
Hong Kong
London
Milan
Paris
Singapore
Tokyo

Salem Benferhat   Philippe Besnard (Eds.)

Symbolic and Quantitative Approaches to Reasoning with Uncertainty

6th European Conference, ECSQARU 2001
Toulouse, France, September 19-21, 2001
Proceedings

Springer

Series Editors

Jaime G. Carbonell, Carnegie Mellon University, Pittsburgh, PA, USA
Jörg Siekmann, University of Saarland, Saarbrücken, Germany

Volume Editors

Salem Benferhat
Philippe Besnard
Université Paul Sabatier, IRIT-CNRS
118 route de Narbonne, 31062 Toulouse Cedex 4, France
E-mail: {benferha/besnard}@irit.fr

Cataloging-in-Publication Data applied for

Die Deutsche Bibliothek - CIP-Einheitsaufnahme

Symbolic and quantitative approaches to reasoning with uncertainty : 6th European conference ; proceedings / ECSQARU 2001, Toulouse, France, September 19 - 21, 2001. Salem Benferhat ; Philippe Besnard (ed.). - Berlin ; Heidelberg ; New York ; Barcelona ; Hong Kong ; London ; Milan ; Paris ; Singapore ; Tokyo : Springer, 2001
(Lecture notes in computer science ; Vol. 2143 : Lecture notes in artificial intelligence)
ISBN 3-540-42464-4

CR Subject Classification (1998): I.2, F.4.1

ISBN 3-540-42464-4 Springer-Verlag Berlin Heidelberg New York

Springer-Verlag Berlin Heidelberg New York
a member of BertelsmannSpringer Science+Business Media GmbH

http://www.springer.de

Printed in Germany

Typesetting: Camera-ready by author, data conversion by PTP-Berlin, Stefan Sossna
Printed on acid-free paper SPIN: 10840193 06/3142 5 4 3 2 1 0

Preface

These are the proceedings of ECSQARU 2001, the Sixth European Conference on Symbolic and Quantitative Approaches to Reasoning with Uncertainty held in Toulouse, France, on September 19-21, 2001. The series started ten years ago in Marseilles, host of ECSQARU 1991, and went to Granada (ECSQARU 1993), Fribourg (ECSQARU 1995), Bad Honnef (ECSQARU/FAPR 1997), and London (ECSQARU 1999).

In addition to the contributed papers (selected from over a hundred submissions from 23 countries), the scientific program of ECSQARU 2001 included three invited talks: H. Geffner, F. V. Jensen, and T. Schaub. We would like to thank Patrice Perny and Alexis Tsioukias for organizing a special session on decision, and Rui Da Silva Neves for organizing a session on studies about uncertainty from the point of view of psychology. All papers in these two sessions have gone through the regular reviewing process and are included in this volume.

Moreover, three workshops were held prior to the conference itself: "Management of uncertainty and imprecision in multimedia information systems" (Mohand Boughanem, Fabio Crestani, Gabriella Pasi), "Spatio-temporal reasoning and geographic information systems" (Robert Jeansoulin, Odile Papini), and "Adventures in argumentation" (Anthony Hunter, Simon Parsons). Also, ECSQARU 2001 was co-located with ESI 2001, the Euro Summer Institute on Decision Analysis and Artificial Intelligence.

We are most grateful to the members of the program committee and all the additional reviewers for their work. We are indebted to all the members of the organizing committee for their support, which included setting up and maintaining Web pages. We would especially like to thank Colette Ravinet, Jean-Pierre Baritaud, and Max Delacroix for their help.

June 2001

Salem Benferhat
Philippe Besnard

Conference Committee

ECSQARU 2001 was organized by IRIT (CNRS and Université Paul Sabatier, Toulouse, France).

Executive Committee

Program Chairs: Salem Benferhat and Philippe Besnard (CNRS, France)
Organizing Chair: Claudette Cayrol (Univ. Paul Sabatier, Toulouse, France)

Program Committee

Alain Appriou (France)
Ofer Arieli (Israel)
John Bell (United Kingdom)
Isabelle Bloch (France)
Gerd Brewka (Germany)
Claudette Cayrol (France)
Laurence Cholvy (France)
Giulianella Coletti (Italy)
Fabio Cozman (Brazil)
Luis M. de Campos (Spain)
Gert de Cooman (Belgium)
Adnan Darwiche (USA)
James P. Delgrande (Canada)
Thierry Denœux (France)
Patrick Doherty (Sweden)
Didier Dubois (France)
Peter A. Flach (United Kingdom)
Hector Geffner (Venezuela)
Angelo Gilio (Italy)
Lluís Godo (Spain)
Jean-Louis Golmard (France)
Michel Grabisch (France)
Petr Hajek (Czech Republic)
Andreas Herzig (France)
Anthony Hunter (United Kingdom)
Katsumi Inoue (Japan)
Jean-Yves Jaffray (France)
Finn V. Jensen (Denmark)
Robert Jeansoulin (France)
Uffe KjÊrulff (Denmark)
Jürg Kohlas (Switzerland)
Rudolf Kruse (Germany)
JérÙme Lang (France)
Daniel Lehmann (Israel)
Paolo Liberatore (Italy)
Thomas Lukasiewicz (Austria)
Christophe Marsala (France)
Khaled Mellouli (Tunisia)
Robert E. Mercer (Canada)
Aïcha Mokhtari (Algeria)
Serafín Moral (Spain)
Rui Da Silva Neves (France)
Ilkka Niemel" (Finland)
Odile Papini (France)
Simon Parsons (United Kingdom)
Luís Moniz Pereira (Portugal)
Ewa Orlowska (Poland)
Ramón Pino Pérez (France)
David Poole (Canada)
Henri Prade (France)
Alessandro Saffiotti (Sweden)
Ken Satoh (Japan)
Torsten Schaub (Germany)
Romano Scozzafava (Italy)
Prakash P. Shenoy (USA)
Philippe Smets (Belgium)
Milan Studeny (Czech Republic)
Leon van der Torre (Netherlands)
Mary-Anne Williams (Australia)
Cees Witteveen (Netherlands)

Additional referees

Bernhard Anrig
Blai Bonet
Christian Borgelt
Andrea Capotorti
Frédéric Cuppens
Stéphane Demri
Marek J. Druzdzel
Rim Faiz
Hélène Fargier
Christophe Garion
Joakim Gustafsson
Koji Iwanuma
Tomi Janhunen
Daniel Kayser
Gabriele Kern-Isberer
Fédia Khalfallah
Miyuki Koshimura
Ivan Kramosil
Philippe Lamarre
Helge Langseth
Norbert Lehmann
Gérard Ligozat
Thomas Linke
Weiru Liu
Mylène Masson
JérÙme Mengin
Yves Moinard
Kevin Murphy
Thomas D. Nielsen
David Over
Gabriella Pasi
Patrice Perny
Guy Politzer
M. Rahoual
Chiaki Sakama
Johan Schubert
Catherine Tessier
Rich Thomason
Jian Tian
Alexis Tsoukias
Carlos Uzcátegui
Barbara Vantaggi
Jiřina Vejnarová
Kewen Wang
Renata Wasserman
Emil Weydert

Organizing Committee

Salem Benferhat
Claudette Cayrol (chair)
Sylvie Doutre
Olivier Gasquet
Souhila Kaci
Marie-Christine Lagasquie-Schiex
Sylvain Lagrue
Jérôme Mengin
Thomas Polacsek
Vincent Vidal

Sponsoring Institutions

Conseil Régional Midi-Pyrénées, Toulouse, France
Fédération de Recherche en Informatique et Automatique, Toulouse, France
IRIT, Toulouse, France
Université Paul Sabatier, Toulouse, France

Table of Contents

Coherent Probabilities

Bayesian Networks

Learning Causal Networks

Graphical Representations of Uncertainty

Imprecise Probabilities

Belief Functions

Fuzzy Sets and Rough Sets

Possibility Theory

Applications

Merging

Belief Revision and Preferences

Inconsistency Handling

Causality, Events, Explanations

Logic Programming

Modal Logics for Information Systems

Satisfiability

Graphical Models as Languages for Computer Assisted Diagnosis and Decision Making

Finn Verner Jensen

Department of Computer Science, Aalborg University, Fredrik Bajers Vej 7E, DK-9220 Aalborg, Denmark
fvj@cs.auc.dk
http://www.cs.auc.dk/~fvj

1 Introduction

Over the last decade, graphical models for computer assisted diagnosis and decision making have become increasingly popular. Graphical models were originally introduced as ways of decomposing distributions over a large set of variables. However, the main reason for their popularity is that graphs are easy for humans to survey, and most often humans take part in the construction, test, and use of systems for diagnosis and decision making. In other words, at various points in the life cycle of a system, the model is interpreted by a human or communicated between humans. As opposed to machine learning, we shall call this activity human interacted modeling. In this paper we look at graphical models from this point of view. We introduce various kinds of graphical models, and the comprehensibility of their syntax and semantics is in focus.

2 Belief Graphs

We are faced with a particular part of the world. We already have some information that leads us to certain beliefs, and when we get new information, we update these beliefs. We organize the world into a set of *variables*. The possible values of variables are called *states*. The state set of variable A is denoted s_A.

Our belief is quantified as a set of real numbers. There are several belief calculi. Most prominent are probability calculus, fuzzy logic, and belief functions. The examples in this paper are taken from probability calculus, but the considerations are not restricted to this. The uncertainty calculus is expressed through *potentials* with sets of variables as their domains: for a set $\boldsymbol{X}$ of variables, the probability calculus defines a space, $sp(\boldsymbol{X})$, and a potential over $\boldsymbol{X}$ is a real-valued function over $sp(\boldsymbol{X})$. For probability calculus, $sp(\boldsymbol{X})$ is the Cartesian product of the state sets, and for belief functions, $sp(\boldsymbol{X})$ is the power set over this Cartesian product.

Definition 1. *A* belief graph *is a pair (Γ, Φ). Γ is a graph (Ω, Λ) with Ω being a set of variables and Λ a set of links. Links may be directed or undirected. Φ is a set of potentials. The domains of the potentials are subgraphs of Λ.*

S. Benferhat and P. Besnard (Eds.): ECSQARU 2001, LNAI 2143, pp. 1–15, 2001.

Definition 2. *The operations for potentials of belief graphs are* combination, $\otimes$, *and* projection, $\downarrow$. *The* joint potential *for a belief graph (Γ, Φ) with $\Gamma = (\Omega, \Lambda)$ is defined as $Bel(\Omega) = \otimes\Phi$, the combination of all potentials. For a set of variables $\boldsymbol{X}$, the marginal belief of $\boldsymbol{X}$ is defined as $Bel(\boldsymbol{X}) = Bel(\Omega)^{\downarrow \boldsymbol{X}}$.*

Evidence on a set of variables $\boldsymbol{Y}$ is a potential with the domain $\boldsymbol{Y}$. A particular kind of evidence is a potential identifying the state of a single variable.

A breakthrough for the application of belief graphs was the construction of efficient algorithms for the calculation of marginal beliefs with evidence included in the set of potentials. [16] and [6] give sets of axioms on combination and projection that ensure the correctness of these algorithms. The updating algorithms are not the issue in this paper.

For graphs, we use the following terminology: the parents $pa(A)$ denote the set of variables having a directed link to A, and the family $fa(A)$ is $pa(A)$ extended with A.

As mentioned above, there are several categories of belief graphs. Each category is characterized by type of graph and potentials permitted and with respect to the meaning of the various parts of the model.

Definition 3. *A* belief graph category *is a set of syntactic rules specifying a family of belief graphs.*

Example 1. Bayesian networks is a belief graph category meeting the following syntactic constraints:

- $\Gamma = (\Omega, \Lambda)$ is a directed acyclic graph.
- There is exactly one potential φ_A for each $A \in \Omega$.
- $dom(\varphi_A) = fa(A)$.
- $sp(\boldsymbol{X}) = \times_{A \in \boldsymbol{X}} s_A$.
- $\varphi_A(\underline{c}) \in [0, 1]$ for each $\underline{c} \in sp(fa(A))$.
- $\Sigma_A \varphi_A = \mathbf{1}_{pa(A)}$.

Figure 1 gives an example of a Bayesian network. The last five of the preceding rules ensure that the potentials to be specified for a Bayesian network are the conditional probabilities for each variable given its parents. In an axiomatic setting, the last rule is the *unit rule*

$$\varphi_A^{\downarrow pa(A)} = \mathbf{1}_{pa(A)},$$

where $\mathbf{1}_{\boldsymbol{X}}$ is the unit potential with domain $\boldsymbol{X}$.

Example 2. Markov networks is a belief graph category meeting the following syntactic constraints:

- $\Gamma = (\Omega, \Lambda)$ is an undirected graph.
- The domains of potentials are complete subgraphs of Γ.
- $sp(\boldsymbol{X}) = \times_{A \in \boldsymbol{X}} s_A$.

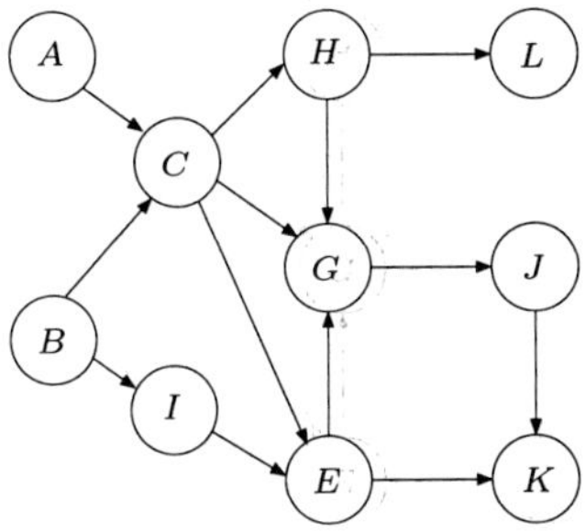

Fig. 1. A Bayesian network. The potentials to be specified are the following conditional probabilities: $P(A), P(B), P(C \mid A, B), P(I \mid B), P(H \mid C), P(G \mid C, H, E), P(E \mid C, I), P(L \mid H), P(J \mid G), P(K \mid E, J)$.

- Each pair of neighbours in the graph appears at least once in the same domain of a potential.
- The potentials have non-negative real values.

Figure 2 gives an example of a Markov network.

When a belief graph of a certain category is used for modeling, a domain expert will determine a graph Γ representing the domain in sufficient detail. Therefore, the semantics of the graph must be easy to understand and to communicate. Likewise, it must be evident from Γ what potentials to determine. In other words, when Γ has been determined, the number of potentials to be specified will be easily read from it, as will their domains. The strength of graphical models lies in this point. A graph is easy for humans to read and draw, and when the meaning of the variables and links is easy to understand, belief graphs are very well suited for interpersonal communication. When constructing and/or checking a model, we need comprehensible syntax to ensure easy determination of whether the model in question satisfies the syntax - with regard to structure as well as to potentials. This holds for both Bayesian networks and Markov networks.

Furthermore, we also require the semantics to be comprehensible. The semantics of a directed link in a belief graph is *causal impact* and the semantics of an undirected link is *covariance*. Although causality in many ways is a difficult concept to work with, we claim that it is much better understood than covariance and, from a practical point of view, it is much easier to have a meaningful dialogue with a domain expert on causal impact than on covariance. The semantic concepts causal impact and covariance are made operational through the concept of *observational independence*.

Definition 4. *Two variables A and B are observationally independent if no information on A will change the belief on B, and vice versa.*

We omit the term "observational" when obvious from the context. Observational independence is often conditioned on specific knowledge, and we talk of

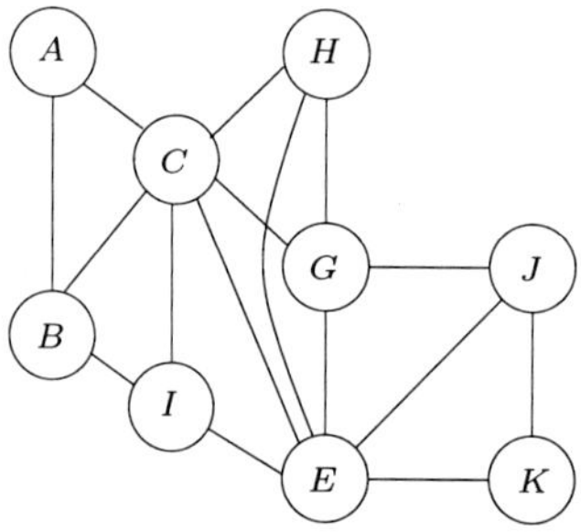

Fig. 2. A Markov network. The potential domains are subsets of the following sets: {A, B, C}, {B, C, I}, {C, E, I}, {C, E, G, H}, {E, G, J}, {E, J. K}.

conditional independence: A and B are independent given the set $\boldsymbol{X}$ if they are independent whenever the state of each variable in $\boldsymbol{X}$ is known.

The semantics of the graphical structure yields a set of conditional independence properties and this is the basis for the belief calculation algorithms. In general, these properties are called *Markov properties.* Thus, the request for comprehensible semantics has been transformed to a request for comprehensible Markov properties.

Markov Property for Markov Networks (Information Blocking)
Two distinct variables A and B are independent given $\boldsymbol{X}$ if all paths between A and B contain an intermediate variable from $\boldsymbol{X}$.

The Markov property for Markov networks is very easy to read and the questions to be asked the domain expert are usually comprehensible.

Markov Property for Bayesian Networks (d-separation)
Two distinct variables A and B are independent given $\boldsymbol{X}$ if all paths between A and B contain an intermediate variable C such that either

– the connection is serial or diverging and $C \in \boldsymbol{X}$

or

– the connection is converging and neither C nor any of its descendants are in $\boldsymbol{X}$.

The causal interpretation of directed links yields another property that can be used to test whether you agree with the model. If you force the state of a variable through an external intervention, this does not change your belief on its parents, nor does it introduce dependence among them. This kind of conditioning is called *conditioning by intervention.*

Note that the preceding Markov properties are consequences of the semantics of the structure and they are not related to the specific calculus for uncertainty.

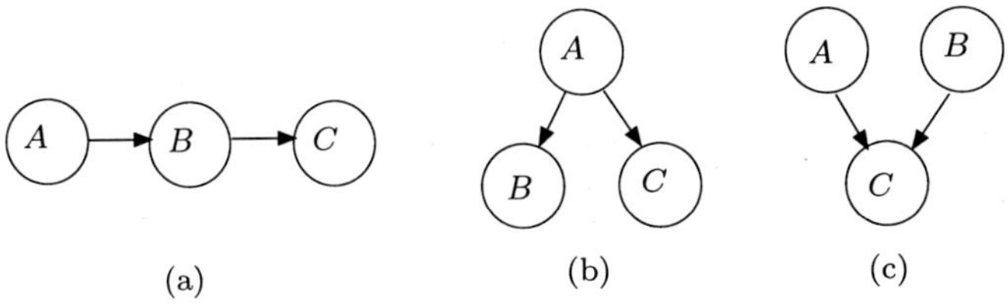

Fig. 3. Serial, diverging, and converging connections.

In an axiomatic setting, the basis for the rule on converging connections is the unit rule.

2.1 Chain Graphs

Bayesian networks and Markov networks represent two extreme types of graphs in which all links are either directed or undirected. We will now consider the more general class where we are allowed to mix the types of link.

Definition 5. *Let $\Gamma = (\Omega, \Lambda)$ be a graph. A* partially directed path *in Γ is a path with at least one directed link such that all directed links have the same direction. Γ is* acyclic *if it has no partially directed cycles.*

The *chain components* of Γ is the set of connected graphs obtained by removing all directed links from Γ. Let ϑ be a chain component, the parent set of ϑ, $pa(\vartheta)$, is the set of nodes with a directed link into a node in ϑ (see Figure 4). The *family graph* for chain component ϑ is the subgraph of Γ containing $\vartheta \cup pa(\vartheta)$. The *moral family graph* is the graph obtained from the family graph by introducing a link between all members of $pa(\vartheta)$ and removing all directions.

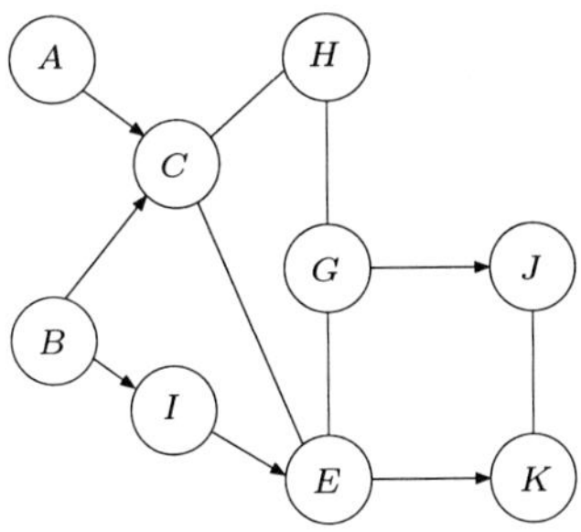

Fig. 4. A mixed graph. The non-singleton chain components are $\{C, E, H, G\}$ with parents $\{A, B, I\}$ and $\{J, K\}$ with parents $\{G, E\}$.

Let ϑ be a chain component with parents $pa(\vartheta)$. The cliques in the moral family graph we call *local factor domains.* Note that for a directed graph, the local factor domains are the families $fa(A)$.

Example 3. Chain graphs is a belief graph category meeting the following syntactic constraints:

- $\Gamma = (\Omega, \Lambda)$ is an acyclic graph.
- There is a potential φ_δ for each local factor domain δ in each moral family graph.
- $dom(\varphi_\delta) = \delta$.
- $\varphi_\delta(\underline{c}) \in [0, 1]$ for each $\underline{c} \in sp(\delta)$.
- Let Δ be the local factor domains of the chain component ϑ and let $\varphi_\vartheta = \Pi_{\delta\in\Delta}\delta$. Then $\Sigma_\vartheta\varphi_\vartheta = \mathbf{1}_{pa(\vartheta)}$.

In an axiomatic setting, the last rule should be the following version of the identity rule

$$(\otimes_{\delta\in\Delta}\delta)^{\downarrow pa(\vartheta)} = \mathbf{1}_{pa(\vartheta)}.$$

The chain graph category is nice and broad, encompassing both Bayesian networks and Markov networks. However, the syntax is hardly comprehensible. It is possible to test whether a graph is acyclic, but when it comes to the potentials, problems arise. The syntactic constraints on potentials may be interpreted so that the φ_ϑs are conditional probabilities $P(\vartheta \mid pa(\vartheta))$, but it is hard to imagine a domain expert being happy to provide the potentials for a chain graph.

Things do not get easier when considering the semantics. The causal interpretation of directed links is maintained and the interpretation of a family must generalise the causal interpretation. A possible interpretation of undirected links is that they are due to latent variables. A latent variable may have been *marginalized out* or it may have been *conditioned out* (see Figure 5).

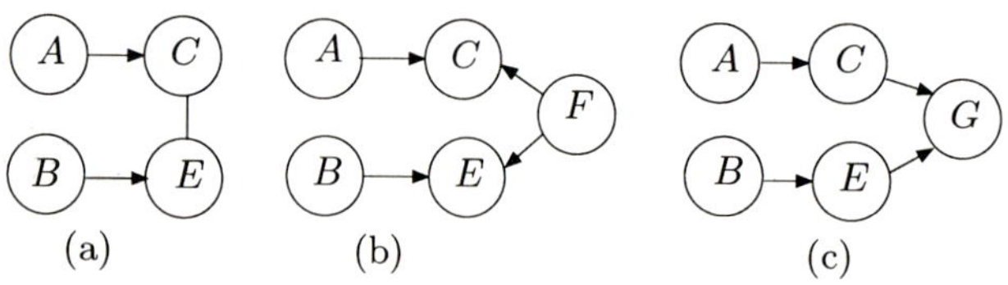

Fig. 5. (a) A mixed model that may be the result of marginalizing F out of (b) or conditioning G out of (c).

Unfortunately, this interpretation introduces ambiguity. As shown in Figure 5, the chain graph (a) can be the result of marginalizing F out from (b) or of conditioning G out from (c). The two possible origins will cause different conditional independence properties. If Figure 5 (a) is the result of marginalizing F out of Figure 5 (b), A and B will be independent, but this is not the case if the graph is the result of conditioning in Figure 5 (c). Accordingly, the potentials to be specified for (a) depend on the origin of the undirected link.

So, the chain graph category is not the appropriate one for representing causal models with latent variables. If the model builder is faced with covariance without causal direction, she has to analyse the situation in order to find out whether the covariance is due to latent variables and, if so, to include them temporarily in the model.

However, undirected covariance may also be caused by a feed-back mechanism. [7] gives an analysis of a causal interpretation of chain graphs where a chain component is interpreted as a feed-back complex. This interpretation yields the Markov properties proposed by [8] and [4].

Markov Property for Chain Graphs (The Global Chain Markov Property)
Let (X, Y, Z) be three disjoint sets of variables in a chain graph Γ and let G be the moral graph of the smallest ancestral set containing $X \cup Y \cup Z$.

Then X is independent of Y given Z if any path in G between X and Y contains a member of Z (see Figure 6).

[2] give a separation criterion in the style of d-separation, but this is too involved for this short presentation. We conclude that chain graphs will for several years stay a modeling language for specialists only as it has incomprehensible syntax and semantics.

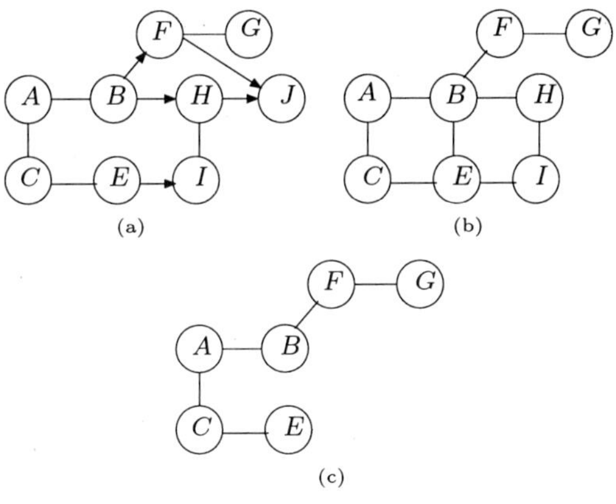

Fig. 6. (a) A chain graph; (b) The moral graph of the smallest ancestral set containing $\{A, E, G, I\}$; (c) The smallest ancestral set containing $\{A, E, G\}$. We see that E and G are independent given A, but they are not independent given A and I.

2.2 Computational Aspects

The focus of interest in this paper is on how well suited various categories of graphical models are for human interacted model building. As a model-builder, I may not at first care about the calculation. What is essential is to have a comprehensible language for specifying my problem in a precise manner. When the specification is finished, I "press a button" and the computer runs an algorithm made up by some smart guys, and this algorithm calculates the answer. In this way, the specification is also a kind of formal programming language. When the program has been constructed to meet the syntactic requirements, the computer can run it and will after a while give me an answer. If I have not been careful, the computer may run for too long. In the case of general programming languages, I risk never to get an answer, and I may have no prior idea on how much time or space the computer will require.

Belief updating is NP-hard, so the risk is that the task is too complicated for the computer. However, this can be analysed off-line. When the belief graph has been specified, I – or rather the computer – can pre-compile the program and report on how complex the task is.

3 Decision Graphs

Very often the reason for calculating beliefs is to utilize them in making a decision on some actions. This may also be represented in the graphical model. There are two types of actions, *interventions* and *observations*. An intervention is an action that may change the state of the world, whereas an observation only yields information on it. The crank for choosing actions is *utilities*. A utility is a real value expressing the value of a certain configuration of a set of variables. We assume that there is a way to combine beliefs and utilities in calculating expected utilities, and the task is to determine a strategy maximising the expected utility.

3.1 Influence Diagrams

In influence diagrams you do not distinguish between intervention decisions and observation decisions. An influence diagram is a DAG with three types of variables, *chance variables* (usually represented as circular or elliptic nodes), *decision variables* (usually represented as rectangular nodes), and *utility variables* (usually represented as diamond shaped nodes).

Apart from being a DAG, an influence diagram must satisfy two other structural constraints:

- utility nodes have no children.
- there is a directed path comprising all decision nodes (the *sequencing constraint*).

A chance node is said to be *barren* if none of its descendants are decision nodes or utility nodes. A barren node has no impact on the expected utility of any decision and plays no role in the decision analysis. Therefore, it is customary to add the following cosmetic syntactic constraint:

- there are no barren nodes

There are two types of potentials attached to influence diagrams, *chance potentials* and *utility potentials.* A utility potential for a utility node is a real valued function with domain $pa(U)$. The domain rules for chance potentials are similar to the rules for belief graphs, and apart from the operations for belief potentials, there is an operation for combining chance potentials and belief potentials. This is treated in more detail by [17] under the term *valuation networks.* The term "influence diagram" is reserved to valuation networks based on Bayesian networks, where the combination of probabilities and utilities is the usual expectation operation. Figure 7 gives an example of an influence diagram.

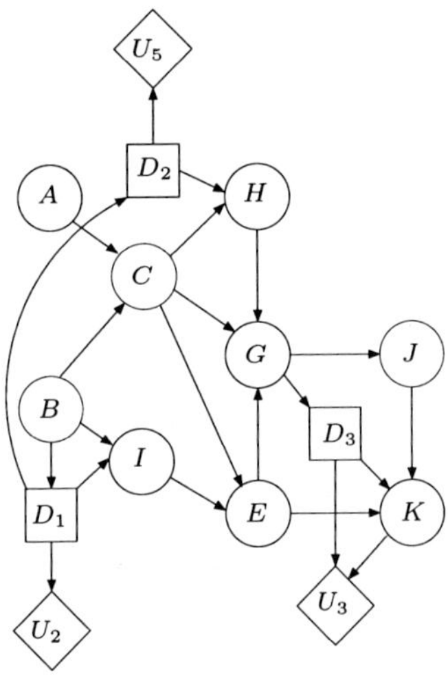

Fig. 7. An influence diagram. The utility potentials have the domains $\{D_1\}, \{D_2\}, \{D_3, K\}, \{L\}$, respectively. The probability potentials to be specified are for each variable A, $\mathrm{P}(A \mid \mathrm{pa}(A))$.

Altogether, the syntax for influence diagrams is comprehensible as is their semantics. Directed links into chance variables are causal, links into utility variables represent functional dependence, and links into decision variables represent temporal precedence. In other words, if the variable X is a parent of the decision variable D, the state of X is known at the time of deciding on D. Furthermore, *no-forgetting* is assumed. Everything known at some point of decision is also known later. The sequencing constraint provides a temporal sequencing of the decisions, and due to no-forgetting, an influence diagram specifies precisely what is known at each point of decision.

A *policy* for a decision variable D in an influence diagram is a function that for each configuration of the past yields a state of D. A *strategy* for an influence diagram is a set of policies, one for each decision variable. An optimal strategy is a strategy yielding maximal expected utility. We have algorithms well suited for calculating an optimal strategy for a specified influence diagram ([17], [5], [14]).

The algorithms exploit dynamic programming by passing through the influence diagram in reverse temporal order. For each decision, an optimal policy is determined and altogether these policies form an optimal strategy. The complexity of solving an influence diagram is in general higher than for a belief graph. One of the crucial complexity issues is the size of the domains for the optimal policies. The domain need not be the entire past, and the algorithms remove some irrelevant past.

A question of interest in connection with influence diagrams is the *relevant past* for a decision variable. A variable X belongs to the relevant past of the decision variable D if the state of A is known at the time of deciding on D and if the actual state may have an impact on the optimal decision. A variable X from the past is said to be *structurally irrelevant* for D if the actual state of X has no impact on the optimal decision for D, no matter the potentials attached. We have efficient algorithms for determining structural relevance for all decision variables in an influence diagram ([15], [10], [12]). For the influence diagram in Figure 7, the structurally relevant pasts for D_1, D_2 and D_3 are $\{B\}, \{B, D_1\}$ and $\{G, E\}$, respectively. The reason why both B and D_1 are relevant for D_2 is that all three variables influence the utility U_3.

3.2 Extensions of Influence Diagrams

The advantage of using influence diagrams when calculating optimal strategies is that the sequencing of decisions is determined. However, this constraint is unnecessarily strict. For example, two neighboring decisions with no intermediate observation can always be swapped – just like it happens that two decisions may be made independently of each other. So we can make the syntax less strict by removing the sequencing constraint. The ensuing category is called *partial influence diagrams* ([10]). Figure 8 shows an example of a partial influence diagram where D_1 and D_2 precede D_3, but nothing is specified concerning the order of D_1 and D_2.

Partial influence diagrams have comprehensible syntax and semantics, and it is easy to read the partial temporal order from the graph. However, they are defective in that their decision scenario may be *ambiguous.* A decision scenario is ambiguous if two extensions of the partial temporal order yield different optimal strategies. A partial influence diagram is accordingly said to be *well-defined* if all extensions of the partial temporal order yield the same optimal strategy. [10] provides what the authors claim to be the weakest set of structural syntactic rules ensuring a well-defined partial influence diagram. The rules consist of a systematic search through linear extensions of the partial order, for each of them investigating whether they yield the same set of relevant pasts. The syntactic definition of well-defined partial influence diagrams is not comprehensible, and these diagrams are not really candidates for human interacted model building.

If a partial influence diagram is well-defined, the classical algorithms from influence diagrams can be used. The ambiguity of partial influence diagrams

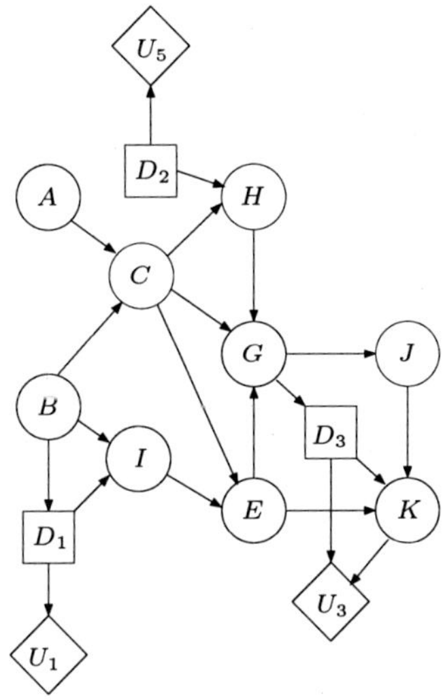

Fig. 8. A partial influence diagram.

refers to the use of dynamic programming algorithms yielding different strategies for different orders extending the partial order.

You may consider partial influence diagrams in a different way. A partial influence diagram specifies a decision scenario where the task not only is to calculate an optimal strategy, but an essential part of it is to calculate an optimal sequence as well. When considered this way, partial influence diagrams have comprehensible syntax and semantics. The problem is the computational complexity. When solving a partial influence diagram, there is a risk that you must solve an influence diagram for each linear extension of the partial temporal order. The work by [10] can be exploited to reduce the number of linear orders to be investigated. For example, a simple rule is that observations are placed as early as possible in the order. Not much work has been carried out in this direction, and certainly there are many simplifications to be found.

To represent decision scenarios with non-fixed temporal order, we propose another category that we call *D-models*. A D-model has as basis a Bayesian network and here we distinguish between intervention variables (rectangular) and observation variables (triangular). A D-model is a directed acyclic graph over chance variables, intervention variables, binary observation variables, and utility nodes, meeting the following constraints (see Figure 9):

- utility nodes have no children.
- observation variables have only chance variables as parents and utility nodes as children.
- intervention variables have no parents.

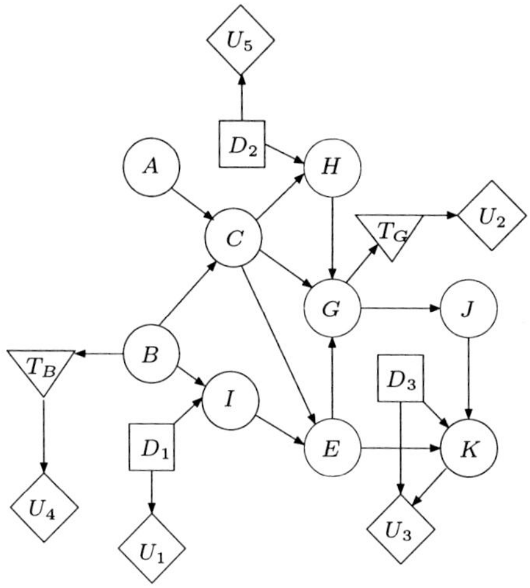

Fig. 9. A D-model.

The potentials for D-models are as for influence diagrams. There are no potentials attached to observation variables.

The semantics of observation nodes is the option of observing. By "observing" is meant that the state of each parent variable is determined. A non-perfect observation is represented through introduction of an intermediate chance variable (See Figure 10).

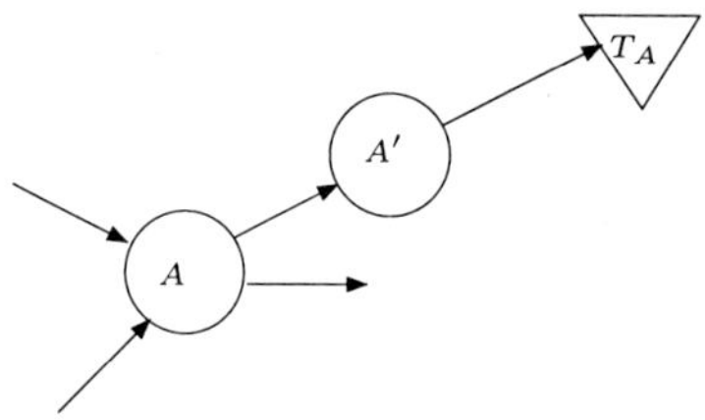

Fig. 10. Representation of a non-perfect observation of A.

There is one more issue to clear up. Consider, for example, the decision variable D_1 in Figure 9. It indicates that a decision can be made that together with B has an impact on I. What is not clear is whether the variable I exists before a decision on D_1 is made. D_1 may be a decision to fix the temperature, and in this case there will be a temperature influenced by B also before an action from D_1 has been performed. If, on the other hand, the decision is to start some process with a possible outcome represented by I, "the state of I" has no meaning before D_1 is instantiated.

The problem is resolved by also reading a temporal order into the model: a successor to a decision variable D cannot be observed until an action from D has been performed. For Figure 9, this means that decisions on D_1 and D_2 are made before an observation of G is possible.

As for belief graphs, we wish to use the semantics to derive rules for conditional independence for D-models.

Markov property for D-models
Two distinct variables Y and Z are independent given $\boldsymbol{X}$ if for all paths between them there is an intermediate variable I such that either

- the connection is serial or diverging and $I \in \boldsymbol{X}$

or

- the connection is converging and neither I nor any of its descendants are in $\boldsymbol{X}$.

Due to the direction of the link to an observation node, the Markov property for D-models reflects the difference between conditioning by observation and conditioning by intervention: if the state of a variable A is known due to an intervention, this has no impact on our belief of A's parents; but if the state is known due to an observation, then it may have an impact on our beliefs of the variable's parents.

The direct representation of observation decisions is not (yet) customary. Instead, observation nodes are transformed into intervention decisions. Let T_A be an observation on the variable A. Add a chance variable A' with a state $no-t$ and the states of A. Add an intervention action D_A. A' is a child of A and D_A. If $D_A = yes$, A' is in the same state as A, and if $D_A = no$, $A' = no - t$ (see Figure 11). Note that after the transformation, the Markov property does not hold.

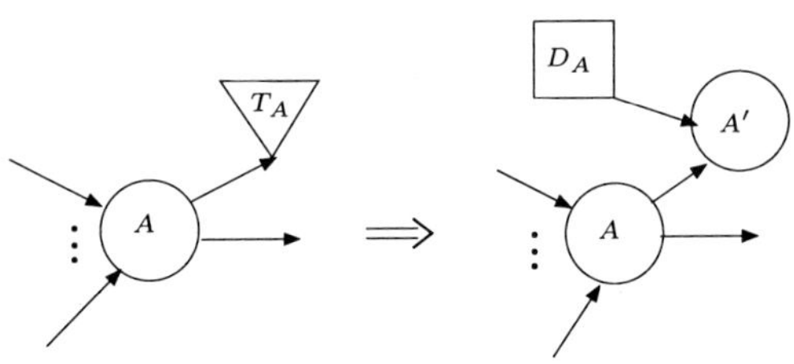

Fig. 11. Representation of observation decisions in influence diagrams.

A D-model represents a decision scenario for which the task is to find a sequencing with an optimal strategy. That is, a D-model can be expanded to a set of influence diagrams. For example, the sequence $\{T_B, D_1, D_2, T_G, D_3\}$ is represented by the influence diagram in Figure 7, and the sequence in which G is not observed is represented by the same influence diagram with the link from G to D_3 removed. Structure analysis similar to the one for partial influence diagrams can reduce the number of influence diagrams considerably. Also, the decomposition of influence diagrams presented by [9] can be exploited to save repeated computations, but not much work has been performed with respect to efficient algorithms for solving D-models. It should be noted that in general it is NP-hard to determine an optimal sequence ([19]).

D-models can be extended with precedence links analogous to information links in influence diagrams. Precedence links can indicate that some decisions must be made in a specific order and they reduce the search for an optimal sequence.

So far, the decision scenarios modelled have been symmetric: the decision variables and their states have been independent of the past. Various languages for representing asymmetric decision scenarios have been proposed ([13], [3], [1], [18], [11]), but we shall not go into this issue here.

References

1. C. Bielza and Prakash P. Shenoy. A comparison of graphical techniques for asymmetric decision problems. *Management Science*, 45(11):1552–1569, 1999.
2. Remco R. Bouckaert and Milan Studený. Chain graphs: Semantics and expressiveness. In Christine Froidevaux and Jürg Kohlas, editors, *Lecture Notes in Computer Science*, volume 946, pages 69–76. Springer, 1995. Proceedings of ECSQARU 1995, Fribourg, Switzerland.
3. Z. Covaliu and R. M. Oliver. Representation and solution of decision problems using sequential decision diagrams. *Management Science*, 41(12):1860–1881, 1995.
4. Morten Frydenberg. The chain graph Markov property. *Scandinavian Journal of Statistics*, 17:333–353, 1990.
5. Frank Jensen, Finn V. Jensen, and Søren L. Dittmer. From influence diagrams to junction trees. In Ramon Lopez de Mantaras and David Poole, editors, *Proceedings of the 10th Conference on Uncertainty in Artificial Intelligence*, pages 367–373, San Francisco, 1994. Morgan Kaufmann, San Francisco, CA.
6. Steffen L. Lauritzen and Finn V. Jensen. Local computation with valuations from a commutative semigroup. *Annals of Mathematics and Artificial Intelligence*, 21:51–69, 1997.
7. Steffen L. Lauritzen and T. S. Richardson. Chain graph models and their causal interpretation. Technical Report R-01-2003, Department of Mathematical Sciences, Aalborg University, 2001.
8. Steffen L. Lauritzen and Nanny Wermuth. Graphical models for associations between variables, some of which are qualitative and some quantitative. *The Annals of Statistics*, 17(1):31–57, 1989.
9. Thomas D. Nielsen. Decomposition of influence diagrams. 2001. In these proceedings.
10. Thomas D. Nielsen and Finn V. Jensen. Well-defined decision scenarios. In *Proceedings of the Fifteenth Conference on Uncertainty in Artificial Intelligence*, pages 502–511. Morgan Kaufmann Publishers, San Francisco, CA., 1999.

11. Thomas D. Nielsen and Finn V. Jensen. Representing and solving asymmetric Bayesian decision problems. In Craig Boutilier and Moises Goldszmidt, editors, *Proceedings of the Sixteenth Conference on Uncertainty in Artificial Intelligence*, pages 416–425. Morgan Kaufmann Publishers, San Francisco, CA., 2000.
12. Dennis Nilsson and Steffen L. Lauritzen. Evaluating influence diagrams using LIMIDs. In Craig Boutilier and Moises Goldszmidt, editors, *Proceedings of the Sixteenth Conference on Uncertainty in Artificial Intelligence*, pages 436–445. Morgan Kaufmann Publishers, San Francisco, CA., 2000.
13. Runping Qi, Lianwen Zhang, and David Poole. Solving asymmetric decision problems with influence diagrams. In R. Lopez de Mantaras and D. Poole, editors, *Proceedings of the Tenth Conference on Uncertainty in Artificial Intelligence*, pages 491–497. Morgan Kaufmann Publishers, San Francisco, CA., 1994.
14. Ross D. Shachter. Evaluating influence diagrams. *Operations Research*, 34(6):871–882, 1986.
15. Ross D. Shachter. Bayes-Ball: The rational pastime (for determining irrelevance and requisite information in belief networks and influence diagrams). In Gregory F. Cooper and Serafín Moral, editors, *Proceedings of the Fourteenth Conference on Uncertainty in Artificial Intelligence*, pages 480–487. Morgan Kaufmann Publishers, San Francisco, CA., 1998.
16. Glenn R. Shafer and Prakash Shenoy. Probability propagation. *Annals of Mathematics and Artificial Intelligence*, 2:327–352, 1990.
17. Prakash P. Shenoy. Valuation-based systems for Bayesian decision analysis. *Operations Research*, 40(3):463–484, 1992.
18. Prakash P. Shenoy. Valuation network representation and solution of asymmetric decision problems. *European Journal of Operations Research*, 121(3):579–608, 2000.
19. M. Sochorová and Jiří Vomlel. Troubleshooting: NP-hardness and solutions methods. In J. Vejnarová, editor, *Proceedings of Fifth Workshop on Uncertainty Processing*. Jindřichův Hradec, Czech Republic, 2000.

Planning with Uncertainty and Incomplete Information

Hector Geffner*

Depto de Computación, Universidad Simón Bolivar,
Caracas, Venezuela
hector@usb.ve

We consider the problem of planning in a general setting where actions can be deterministic or probabilistic, and their effects can be fully or partially observable. The task is to obtain a plan or closed-loop controller given a suitable description of the initial situation, actions, and goals.

We approach this problem by distinguishing three elements:

- models (that help us to make the tasks mathematically precise)
- languages (that help us to state problems in a convenient way), and
- algorithms (that compute the desired solutions: plans, controllers, etc.)

We show that the models - State Models, Markov Decision Processes (MDPs) and Partially Observable MDPs - can be conveniently described using suitable logical action languages, and in many cases can be solved by search algorithms that combine ideas from heuristic search and dynamic programming. We present empirical results over a number of domains and discuss limitations and challenges.

The talk is mostly self-contained and relevant material (papers, software, slides) can be found at: `http://www.ldc.usb.ve/ hector`

* This is joint work with Blai Bonet.

S. Benferhat and P. Besnard (Eds.): ECSQARU 2001, LNAI 2143, p. 16, 2001.

What's Your Preference? And How to Express and Implement It in Logic Programming!

Torsten Schaub*

Institut für Informatik, Universität Potsdam,
Postfach 60 15 53, D–14415 Potsdam, Germany
torsten@cs.uni-potsdam.de

We introduce a methodology and framework for expressing general preference information in logic programming under the answer set semantics. At first, we are interested in semantical underpinnings for existing approaches to preference handling in extended logic programming. To begin with, we explore three different approaches that have been recently proposed in the literature. Because these approaches use rather different formal means, we furnish a uniform characterizations that allows us to gain insights into the relationships among these approaches.

We then draw on this study for furnishing implementation techniques. In the resulting framework, an ordered logic program is an extended logic program in which rules are named by unique terms, and in which preferences among rules are given by a set of atoms of the form $s \prec t$ where s and t are names. Such an ordered logic program is transformed into a second, regular, extended logic program wherein the preferences are respected, in that the answer sets obtained in the transformed program correspond with the preferred answer sets of the original program. Our approach allows the specification of dynamic orderings, in which preferences can appear arbitrarily within a program. Static orderings (in which preferences are external to a logic program) are a trivial restriction of the general dynamic case. We develop a specific approach to reasoning with prescriptive preferences, wherein the preference ordering specifies the order in which rules are to be applied.

Since the result of our translation is an extended logic program, we can make use of existing implementations, such as dlv and smodels. To this end, we have developed the so-called plp compiler, available on the web at url `http://www.cs.uni-potsdam.de/~torsten/plp/`, as a front-end for these programming systems.

* Affiliated with the School of Computing Science at Simon Fraser University, Burnaby, Canada.

S. Benferhat and P. Besnard (Eds.): ECSQARU 2001, LNAI 2143, p. 17, 2001.

On Preference Representation on an Ordinal Scale*

Michel Grabisch**

LIP6, UPMC 8, rue du Capitaine Scott, 75015 Paris, France

Abstract. We present in this paper an attempt to deal with ordinal information in a strict ordinal framework. We address the problem of ranking alternatives in a multiple criteria decision making problem by the use of a compensatory aggregation operator, where scores are given on a finite ordinal scale. Necessary and sufficient conditions for the existence of a representation are given.

1 Introduction

In many practical problems, one has often to deal with non numerical, qualitative information, coming from human agents, decision makers, or any source providing information in natural language, etc. If this addresses in the large the problem of modelling knowledge, we address here more particularly the problem of dealing with *ordinal* information, that is, information given on some ordinal scale, i.e. a scale where only *order* matters, and not numbers. For example, a scale of evaluation of a product by a consumer such as

1=bad, 2=rather bad, 3=acceptable, 4=more or less good, 5=good

is an ordinal scale, despite the coding by numbers 1 to 5. In fact, these numbers are meaningless since one could have defined other numbers as well:

-23=bad, 2=rather bad, 31=acceptable, 49=more or less good, 50=good.

These numbers act more as labels than as true numbers, i.e. where usual arithmetical operations have a meaning. The consequence is that any manipulation of these numbers is forbidden, since meaningless, unless these manipulations involve only order: computing the arithmetic mean, the standard deviation over a population are forbidden operations, but the median, as well as any order statistic is permitted. These considerations pertains to *measurement theory* (see e.g. the book of Roberts [3]), and have influenced statistics, introducing the notion of *permissible* transformations of data (see however [5] for a criticism of this part of statistics).

* The long version of this paper with all proofs is available as a working paper.

** On leave from THALES, Corporate Research Laboratory, Domaine de Corbeville, Orsay, France

S. Benferhat and P. Besnard (Eds.): ECSQARU 2001, LNAI 2143, pp. 18–28, 2001.

If many powerful tools exist when information is quantitative (or cardinal), the practitioner is devoid of adequate tools in front of problems involving ordinal information. Most often, people perform an arbitrary mapping on a (true) numerical scale, to come back to the cardinal world, and then perform usual operations. But as it was said above, any operation which is not restricted to order manipulation is meaningless.

In this paper we focus on decision making under multiple criteria (MCDM): alternatives, or *acts*, are evaluated on some (ordinal) scale E with respect to several criteria. We assume here that the evaluations are done on the same common scale, representing the degrees of satisfaction (or *scores*) of the decision maker for the concerned act, with respect to the different criteria. The problem of interest is to represent the preference $\succcurlyeq$ of the decision maker over a set of acts A by some mapping u over A to some (again, ordinal) scale E', i.e., for any $a, b \in A$,

$$a \succcurlyeq b \text{ if and only if } u(a) \geq u(b)$$

where $\geq$ denotes the ordering on E'. In other words, we would like to mimic standard multiattribute utility theory in a purely ordinal framework.

Assuming mild conditions on the kind of mapping which are standard in multicriteria decision making, this paper gives necessary and sufficient conditions on E, A, and $\succcurlyeq$ to have such a representation.

A last remark is in order here. Although we have chosen the framework of multicriteria decision making, our work can be applied as well to decision under uncertainty with a finite set of states of the world, since a set of scores $a_1, \dots, a_n$ of a w.r.t. to n criteria can be assimilated to a set of utilities of a in different states of the world.

2 Multicriteria Decision Making in an Ordinal Context

Let $X_1, \dots, X_n$ be a set of attributes or *descriptors*, *criteria*, of a set of acts of interest. The Cartesian product $X = X_1 \times \cdots \times X_n$ represents the set of all possible acts, and we consider A a subset of X. We assume that we are able to assign to each $a \in A$ a vector of *scores* $(a_1, \dots, a_n)$, where a_i represents the degree of satisfaction of the decision maker for act a with respect to criterion i. These scores are all given on a common finite ordinal scale $E = \{e_1 < \cdots < e_k\}$. The assumption of *commensurateness* is made, i.e. if $a_i = e_l = a_j$, the satisfaction of the decision maker is the same for a_i and a_j, although a_i and a_j pertain to different criteria. This assumption is a strong one and should deserve a careful study. However, in this paper, we concentrate on aggregation of scores, leaving aside their construction. Anyway, in decision under uncertainty, this problem of commensurability vanishes. The ordering on E is denoted $\geq$.

We assume that the decision maker can express his/her preferences on A under the form of a binary relation $\succcurlyeq$ on $A \times A$, being reflexive, transitive and complete. We denote as usual $a \sim b$ if $a \succcurlyeq b$ and $b \succcurlyeq a$ hold, and $a \succ b$ if $a \succcurlyeq b$ and $\neg(b \succcurlyeq a)$.

The representation problem we address here is the following:

Find an ordinal scale E' with an order $\geq_{E'}$ and a mapping $u : A \longrightarrow E'$ such that for any $a, b \in A$, $a \succcurlyeq b$ if and only if $u(a) \geq_{E'} u(b)$.

We propose the following construction for u:

$$u = f \circ \mathcal{H} \tag{1}$$

where $\mathcal{H} : E^n \longrightarrow E$ is an *aggregation operator*, and $f : E \longrightarrow E'$ defines the scale E'. The aggregation operator assigns to every vector of scores $(a_1, \ldots, a_n)$ a global score on the same scale. Aggregation operators in the cardinal (numerical) case have been studied at length in the fuzzy logic community, for various applications in decision making (see a survey in e.g. [1]). Generally speaking, aggregation operators in the field of decision making should satisfy at least two fundamental properties, which leads to the following definition.

Definition 1. *An operator $\mathcal{H} : E^n \longrightarrow E$ is a* compensatory operator *if it satisfies:*

(i) *limit condition:*

$$\min_{i=1}^{n} a_i \leq \mathcal{H}(a_1, \ldots, a_n) \leq \max_{i=1}^{n} a_i, \quad \forall (a_1, \ldots, a_n) \in E^n.$$

(ii) *monotonicity: $\forall i \in \{1, \ldots, n\}, a_i > a'_i$ implies*

$$\mathcal{H}(a_1, \ldots, a_{i-1}, a_i, a_{i+1}, \ldots, a_n) \geq \mathcal{H}(a_1, \ldots, a_{i-1}, a'_i, a_{i+1}, \ldots, a_n).$$

The operator is said to be weakly compensative *if only (i) holds*[1].

The first property says that the global evaluation should not be beyond the scores on criteria, while the second one ensures that an improvement on one criterion cannot decrease the global score. In the sequel, with a slight abuse of notations, we will write $\mathcal{H}(a)$ instead of $\mathcal{H}(a_1, \ldots, a_n)$, for any $a \in A$.

We call $(A, \succcurlyeq, E)$ the *decision profile* of the decision maker, that is, the set of all vectors of scores $(a_1, \ldots, a_n), a \in A$, expressed on E, together with the preference relation.

Definition 2. *(i)* *The decision profile is* coherent *if for no pair of acts a, b, we have both $a \succ b$ and $a_i \leq b_i$ for all i in $\{1, \ldots, n\}$.*
(ii) *The decision profile is* weakly coherent *if there is no a, b in A such that $a \succ b$ and $\max_{i=1}^n a_i \leq \min_{i=1}^n b_i$.*

Obviously, coherence implies weak coherence.

Let us denote by $A_1, \ldots, A_{k'}$ the equivalence classes of $\succcurlyeq$, i.e. $\forall i$, $\forall a, b \in A_i$, $a \sim b$. We number them in such a way that $\forall a \in A_i, \forall a' \in A_j$, $a \succ a' \Longleftrightarrow i > j$. Obviously, we need at least k' degrees to represent this order, so that E' should have at least k' degrees.

[1] Usually, *min* and *max* are excluded from the class of compensative operators, so our definition is slightly different from the common one.

- If $k' = k$, we can choose $E' = E$, so that f must be the identity mapping.
- If $k' < k$, then several degrees of E will map on the same degree of E'. In other words, f is a surjective non decreasing mapping, which induces byf^{-1} a partition of E. E' can be then considered as the result of partitioning E.
- if $k' > k$, the original scale E is not enough fine to represent the preference, and some degrees have to be added.

Thus, the condition $k' \leq k$ appears as a first necessary condition to represent the preference *on the given fixed scale* E, i.e. we should have at least as many degrees on E than equivalence classes of $\sim$. In this paper, we look for additional necessary and sufficient conditions in order to represent the preference.

3 Preference Representation by a Compensatory Operator

In this section, we try to find necessary and sufficient conditions in order to have a representation of the preference relation by a compensatory operator, assuming $k' \leq k$.

3.1 Preliminary Definitions and Notations

Let us define a new scale $E' = \{e'_1, \ldots, e'_{k'}\}$, with $e'_1 < \cdots < e'_{k'}$, and e'_j corresponds to class A_j.

We introduce the following particular elements of E, for any class A_i:

$$\lfloor A_i := \min_{a \in A_i} \min_{i=1}^{n} a_i$$

$$A_i\rceil := \max_{a \in A_i} \max_{i=1}^{n} a_i.$$

The interval $\left[\lfloor A_i, A_i\rceil\right]$ is denoted $\lfloor A_i \rceil$ for simplicity. Note that this interval may reduce to a singleton. In order to avoid cumbersome conditions for some definitions, we introduce two (fictitious) additional elements e_0 and e_{k+1} on the scale, such that $e_0 < e_1$ and $e_k < e_{k+1}$, and the fictitious classes A_0 and $A_{k'+1}$ (worst and best possible classes), with $\lfloor A_0 \rceil = \{e_0\}$, and $\lfloor A_{k'+1} \rceil = \{e_{k+1}\}$.

Considering two intervals $[a, b], [c, d]$ (possibly reduced to singletons) of E, we say that $[a, b]$ is *to the left* (resp. *to the right*) of $[c, d]$ if $b < c$ (resp. $a > d$). This is denoted as $[a, b] \lessdot [c, d]$ (resp. $[a, b] \gtrdot [c, d]$). Lastly, for any interval $I = [a, b]$, we denote by $\sharp[a, b]$ or $|I|$ the number of elements in interval $[a, b]$, and denote the bounds by $\lfloor I := a$, and $I\rfloor := b$. This notation is extended to the supports of acts $a \in A$ (i.e. the interval $[\min_i a_i, \max_i a_i]$) by $\lfloor a := \min_{i=1}^{n} a_i$, and $a\rfloor := \max_{i=1}^{n} a_i$. By simplicity, the support is denoted $\lfloor a \rfloor$.

We state more precisely our problem using the following definition.

Definition 3. *Let $f : E \longrightarrow E'$ be a surjective non decreasing mapping defining a partition on E by $f^{-1}(\cdot)$. The mapping f is* compatible with a compensatory operator *(resp.* weakly compensatory*) with respect to $\succeq$ if it exists a compensatory operator $\mathcal{H} : E^n \longrightarrow E$ (resp. weakly compensatory), such that $f \circ \mathcal{H}$ represents $\succcurlyeq$, i.e.*

$$\forall a, b \in A, a \succcurlyeq b \Leftrightarrow f \circ \mathcal{H}(a) \geq f \circ \mathcal{H}(b).$$

In the sequel, we try to find necessary and sufficient conditions for the existence of a mapping compatible with a (weakly) compensatory operator.

3.2 Main Result

The following definition is useful [2].

Definition 4. *The* core *of A_j, for any j in $\{1, \ldots, k'\}$ is defined as:*

$$K_j := \emptyset, \text{ if } \min_{a \in A_j} \max_{i=1}^{n} a_i > \max_{a \in A_j} \min_{i=1}^{n} a_i$$

$$K_j := [\min_{a \in A_j} \max_{i=1}^{n} a_i, \max_{a \in A_j} \min_{i=1}^{n} a_i], \text{ otherwise.}$$

The core is non empty every time there exist two acts a, b in A_j with disjoint supports (or coinciding on only one point) for the scores, i.e. such that $\min_i a_i \geq \max_i b_i$ (see figure 1, where the support of three acts a, b, c is figured on a 7-degrees scale). In order that $f \circ \mathcal{H}$ with $\mathcal{H}$ being weakly compensatory can

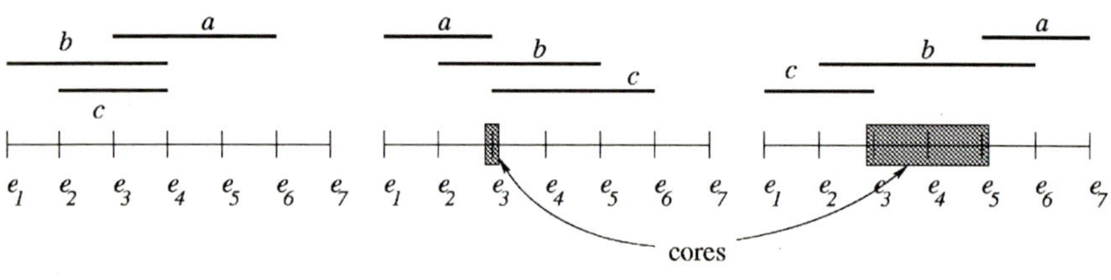

Fig. 1. The core of a class: (left) empty core, (center and right) non empty core

represent the preference, it is necessary that $f^{-1}(e'_j)$ contains K_j. Note that the existence of a non empty core is rather an abnormal situation. It means that no compensatory operator can represent the preference on E, since for $a, b \in A_j$ with disjoint supports we have both $a \sim b$ and $\mathcal{H}(a) \neq \mathcal{H}(b)$. But thanks to f, the evaluation on E' can be the same. This shows the usefulness of f.

Lemma 1. *If the decision profile $(A, \succcurlyeq, E)$ is weakly coherent, then the non empty cores (if any) are disjoint, and they are ordered the right way, i.e. $K_j \rhd K_{j'}$ whenever $j' < j$.*

We introduce another useful interval of $\lfloor A_j \rceil$.

Definition 5. *For any class* A_j, $j = 1, \dots, k'$,

$$A_{>j}\rfloor := \min_{j'>j} \min_{a^{j'} \in A_{j'}} a^{j'}\rfloor$$

$$\lfloor A_{<j} := \max_{j'<j} \max_{a^{j'} \in A_{j'}} \lfloor a^{j'}.$$

Defining the open interval (whenever non empty)

$$\langle A_j \rangle := \Big] \lfloor A_{<j}, A_{>j}\rfloor \Big[$$

the interior *of* A_j*, denoted by* $\lfloor \mathring{A}_j \rceil$*, is defined by:*

$$\lfloor \mathring{A}_j \rceil := \lfloor A_j \rceil \cap \langle A_j \rangle.$$

Figure 2 illustrates the definition, with three classes, and $a, b, c \in A_1$, d, e in A_2, and $f, g, h \in A_3$. Note that $A_{>k'}\rfloor$ and $\lfloor A_{<1}$ are properly defined thanks

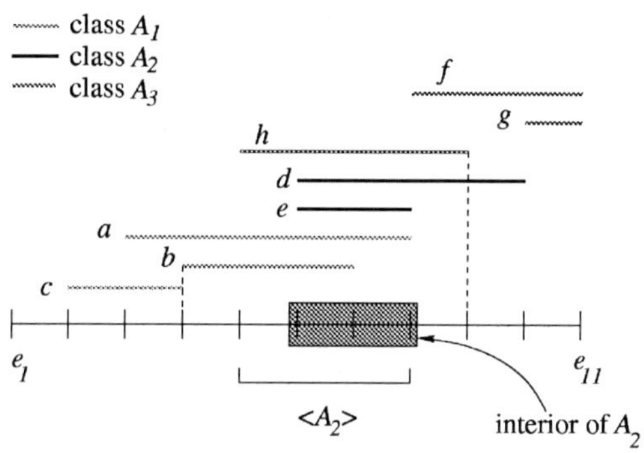

Fig. 2. Interior of class A_2

to the additional classes A_0 and $A_{k'+1}$. Indeed, $\langle A_1 \rangle = \Big[e_1, A_{>1}\rfloor \Big[$ and $\langle A_{k'} \rangle = \Big] \lfloor A_{<k'}, e_k \Big]$. Note also that the interior could be empty, even if the decision profile is coherent, as shown by the following simple example.

EXAMPLE 1: Let us consider $n = 3$ and 3 acts a, b, c such that $c \succ b \succ a$, denoted on a scale with $k = 7$, defined in the table below.

act	criterion 1	criterion 2	criterion 3
a	e_4	e_6	e_4
b	e_4	e_7	e_4
c	e_1	e_5	e_5

As it can be verified, the decision profile is coherent, but since $\lfloor A_{<2} = e_4$ and $A_{>2}\rfloor = e_5$, we have $\langle A_2 \rangle = \emptyset$ and thus the interior too is empty (see figure 3).

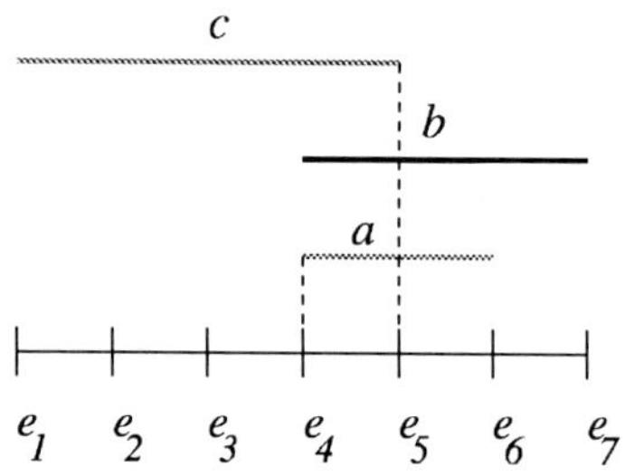

Fig. 3. Case of empty interior

We give some properties of the interior.

Lemma 2. *Let $(A, \succcurlyeq, E)$ be a decision profile. For any class A_j, the following properties hold.*

(i) $A_{>j}\rfloor$ *and* $\lfloor A_{<j}$ *are non decreasing with j, for $j = 1, \dots, k'$.*

(ii) the intervals $\lfloor \mathring{A}_j \rceil$, $j = 1, \dots, k'$, *whenever nonempty are such that* $\lfloor \mathring{A}_j$ *and* $\mathring{A}_j \rceil$ *are non decreasing with j, where* $\lfloor \mathring{A}_j, \mathring{A}_j \rceil$ *are respectively the left and right bounds of* $\lfloor \mathring{A}_j \rceil$.

(iii) $\forall j$, $\forall j' < j$ *such that* $K_{j'} \neq \emptyset$ *and* $\lfloor \mathring{A}_j \rceil \neq \emptyset$, $K_{j'}$ *and* $\lfloor \mathring{A}_j \rceil$ *are disjoint, and the latter is to the right of the former (and symmetrically for $j' > j$).*

(iv) if for some $j' < j$ such that $\lfloor \mathring{A}_j \rceil \neq \emptyset$, $\lfloor \mathring{A}_{j'} \rceil \neq \emptyset$, *and* $\lfloor \mathring{A}_j \rceil \cap \lfloor \mathring{A}_{j'} \rceil \neq \emptyset$, *then no $a \in A$ can be such that* $\lfloor a \rfloor \subset \lfloor \mathring{A}_j \rceil \cap \lfloor \mathring{A}_{j'} \rceil$.

Lemma 3. *Let $(A, \succcurlyeq)$ be a weakly coherent decision profile. For any class A_j, the following properties hold.*

(i) $\sharp\Big[\lfloor A_{<j}, A_{>j}\rfloor\Big] > 1$.

(ii) for any $a^j \in A_j$, *if* $\langle A_j \rangle \neq \emptyset$, *then necessarily* $\lfloor a^j \rfloor \cap \lfloor \mathring{A}_j \rceil \neq \emptyset$, *otherwise* $\sharp\Big(\lfloor a^j \rfloor \cap \Big[\lfloor A_{<j}, A_{>j}\rfloor\Big]\Big) = 2$.

(iii) if $\langle A_j \rangle \neq \emptyset$, *then* $\lfloor \mathring{A}_j \rceil \neq \emptyset$.

(iv) if $K_j \neq \emptyset$, *then* $\lfloor \mathring{A}_j \rceil \neq \emptyset$, *and* $\lfloor \mathring{A}_j \rceil \supset K_j$.

As we have seen, the weak coherence of the decision profile is not enough to ensure that the interior is non empty, although the above lemmas show that non empty interiors have many properties. We introduce the following definition, which is closely related to the non-emptiness of interiors.

Definition 6. $(A, \succeq, E)$ *satisfies the* condition of representability by a compensatory (resp. weakly compensatory) operator *if there are enough degrees in* E *for representing* $\succeq$ *by a compensatory (resp. weakly compensatory) operator* $\mathcal{H}$*, i.e., there exists a compensatory (resp. weakly compensatory) operator* $\mathcal{H}$ *such that:*

$$\forall a \in A_j, \forall a' \in A_{j'}, j' < j, \mathcal{H}(a') < \mathcal{H}(a).$$

Lemma 4. *Let* $(A, \succcurlyeq, E)$ *be a decision profile satisfying the condition of representability by a weakly compensatory operator. Then*

(i) $(A, \succcurlyeq, E)$ *is weakly coherent.*
(ii) $\forall j, j' \in \{1, \ldots, k'\}$ *such that* $j > j'$ *and* $K_j, K_{j'} \neq \emptyset$,

$$\sharp\Big[K_{j'}\rfloor, \lfloor K_j\Big] \geq j - j' + 1$$

and boundary conditions:

$$\sharp\Big[K_{j'}\rfloor, e_k\Big] \geq k' - j' + 1$$

where j' *is the index of the rightmost core,*

$$\sharp\Big[e_1, \lfloor K_{j'}\Big] \geq j'$$

where j' *is the index of the leftmost core.*
(iii) $\forall j, j', \quad j' < j, \sharp\Big[\lfloor \overset{\circ}{A}_{j'}, \overset{\circ}{A}_j\rceil\Big] \geq j - j' + 1.$
(iv) $\lfloor \overset{\circ}{A}_j\rceil \neq \emptyset$*, for* $j = 1, \ldots, k'$.
(v) *If, in addition,* $(A, \succcurlyeq, E)$ *satisfies the condition of representability by a compensatory operator, then the profile is coherent.*

Remark 1: Let $(A, \succcurlyeq, E)$ be a weakly coherent decision profile. If for some j, $\lfloor \overset{\circ}{A}_j\rceil = \emptyset$, then Lemma 4 (iv) implies that the profile is not representable. This is the case of Ex. 1. In fact, from Lemma 3 (iii), the condition $\langle A_j \rangle = \emptyset$ suffices.

Remark 2: If there exists a surjective non decreasing mapping $f : E \longrightarrow E'$ compatible with a (weakly) compensatory operator $\mathcal{H}$, then necessarily $(A, \succcurlyeq, E)$ is representable, precisely by $\mathcal{H}$. Indeed, let us take a, b such that $a \succ b$. Then $f \circ \mathcal{H}(a) > f \circ \mathcal{H}(b)$, which implies $\mathcal{H}(a) > \mathcal{H}(b)$.

Theorem 1. *Let $(A, \succcurlyeq, E)$ be a decision profile. It exists a non decreasing surjective mapping f defining a partition of E in k' elements, compatible with a weakly compensatory operator if and only if the following conditions are satisfied:*

(i) $(A, \succcurlyeq, E)$ *is weakly coherent*
(ii) $\forall j, j' \in \{1, \ldots, k'\}$ *such that* $j > j'$ *and* $K_j, K_{j'} \neq \emptyset$,

$$\sharp\Big[K_{j'}\rfloor, \lfloor K_j\Big] \geq j - j' + 1$$

and boundary conditions:

$$\sharp\Big[K_{j'}\rfloor, e_k\Big] \geq k' - j' + 1$$

where j' *is the index of the rightmost core,*

$$\sharp\Big[e_1, \lfloor K_{j'}\Big] \geq j'$$

where j' *is the index of the leftmost core.*

(iii) $\lfloor \overset{\circ}{A}_j \rceil \neq \emptyset$ *for* $j = 1, \ldots, k'$.
(iv) $\forall j, j' \in \{1, \ldots, k'\}$ *such that* $j > j'$,

$$\sharp\Big[\lfloor \overset{\circ}{A}_{j'}, \overset{\circ}{A}_j \rceil\Big] \geq j - j' + 1.$$

Remark 3: In condition (iii), $\lfloor \overset{\circ}{A}_j \rceil$ can be replaced by $\langle A_j \rangle$. Also, condition (iii) is a special case of (iv) if we allow $j = j'$.

Remark 4: Taking (iv) with $j = k'$, $j' = 1$, we get $\sharp\Big[\lfloor \overset{\circ}{A}_1, \overset{\circ}{A}_{k'} \rceil\Big] \geq k'$, which entails $k \geq k'$.

Remark 5: condition (iv) is sound since due to Lemma 2 (ii), interiors are ordered, so that $\Big[\lfloor \overset{\circ}{A}_{j'}, \overset{\circ}{A}_j \rceil\Big]$ is never empty.

The following can be easily obtained.

Theorem 2. *Let $(A, \succcurlyeq)$ be a decision profile. It exists a non decreasing surjective mapping f defining a partition of E in k' elements, compatible with a compensatory operator if and only if the following conditions are satisfied:*

(i) $(A, \succcurlyeq, E)$ *is coherent*
(ii) $\forall j, j' \in \{1, \ldots, k'\}$ *such that* $j > j'$ *and* $K_j, K_{j'} \neq \emptyset$,

$$\sharp\Big[K_{j'}\rfloor, \lfloor K_j\Big] \geq j - j' + 1$$

and boundary conditions:

$$\sharp\Big[K_{j'}\rfloor, e_k\Big] \geq k' - j' + 1$$

where j' is the index of the rightmost core,

$$\sharp\left[e_1, \lfloor K_{j'}\right] \geq j'$$

where j' is the index of the leftmost core.

(iii) $\lfloor \mathring{A}_j \rceil \neq \emptyset$ *for* $j = 1, \ldots, k'$.

(iv) $\forall j, j' \in \{1, \ldots, k'\}$ *such that* $j > j'$,

$$\sharp\left[\lfloor \mathring{A}_{j'}, \mathring{A}_j \rceil\right] \geq j - j' + 1.$$

3.3 Example

Figure 4 illustrates the preceding facts. We consider 8 acts a, b, c, d, e, f, g, h, 3 criteria and a scale E with 9 degrees. The decision profile is defined as follows.

act	criterion 1	criterion 2	criterion 3	class
a	e_1	e_2	e_2	A_1
b	e_4	e_3	e_3	A_1
c	e_1	e_1	e_6	A_2
d	e_3	e_5	e_4	A_3
e	e_4	e_4	e_6	A_3
f	e_8	e_7	e_7	A_3
g	e_9	e_8	e_7	A_4
h	e_5	e_9	e_7	A_5

Classes are such that $A_1 \prec A_2 \prec \cdots \prec A_5$. There are two cores K_1 and K_3. It can be verified that the profile is coherent, (E, A) is compatible, $k' \leq k$, and conditions (iii) and (iv) of the theorem are satisfied. Hence there exists a partition of E compatible with a compensatory operator, in the sense of theorem 2 (unique in this case).

4 Concluding Remarks

Our results tell if a given decision profile can be represented on a given scale E, by a compensatory or a weakly operator. We see that the necessary and sufficient conditions for doing this are of two kinds. The first kind involves only the inherent properties of the decision profile, regardless of E, while the second kind of conditions focuses on E only.

If the first kind of condition is not satisfied, then there is no hope for representing the decision profile by a (weakly) compensatory operator. By contrast, if some conditions of the second kind are not satisfied, this is only a matter of poorness of the scale, i.e. there is not enough degrees to represent properly the global preference. Thus, a corollary of our theorem could be to exhibit a new scale E'' containing E (i.e. a refinement of the original scale), which is just sufficient to fulfill all conditions of the second kind. This is of primary importance on a practical point of view. This problem is addressed in the long version of this paper.

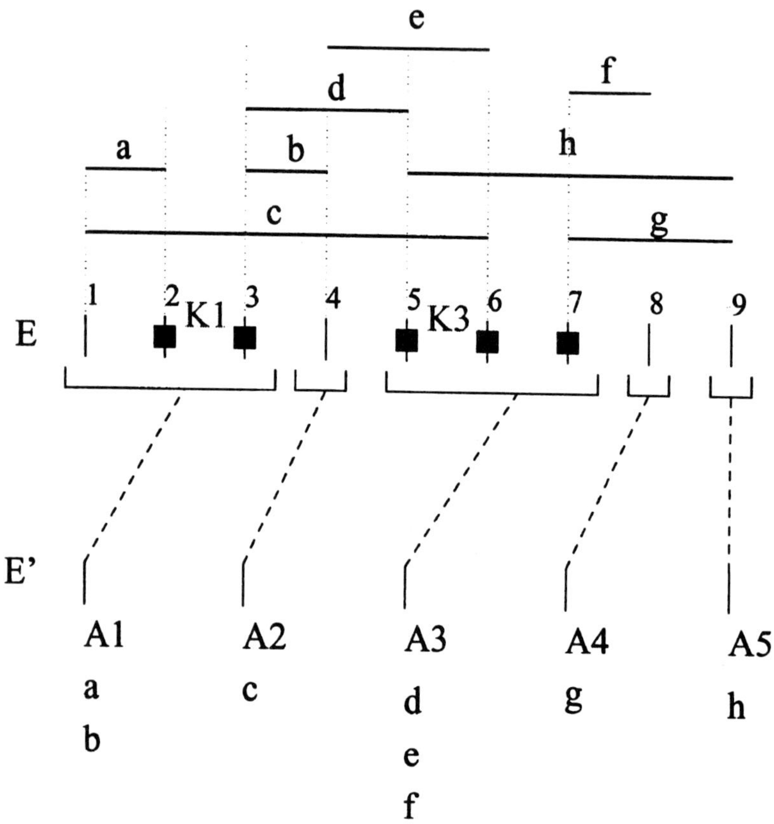

Fig. 4. An example of preference representation

References

1. M. Grabisch, S.A. Orlovski, and R.R. Yager. Fuzzy aggregation of numerical preferences. In R. Slowiński, editor, *Fuzzy Sets in Decision Analysis, Operations Research and Statistics*, The Handbooks of Fuzzy Sets Series, D. Dubois and H. Prade (eds), pages 31–68. Kluwer Academic, 1998.
2. M. Grabisch and M. Roubens. Probabilistic interactions among players of a cooperative game. In M.J. Machina and B. Munier, editors, *Beliefs, Interactions and Preferences*. Kluwer Academic, 1999.
3. F.S. Roberts. *Measurement Theory*. Addison-Wesley, 1979.
4. M. Sugeno. *Theory of fuzzy integrals and its applications*. PhD thesis, Tokyo Institute of Technology, 1974.
5. P.F. Velleman and L. Wilkinson. Nominal, ordinal, interval, and ratio typologies are misleading. *The American Statistician*, 47(1):65–72, 1993.

Rule-Based Decision Support in Multicriteria Choice and Ranking

Salvatore Greco[1], Benedetto Matarazzo[1], and Roman Slowinski[2]

[1] Faculty of Economics, University of Catania,
Corso Italia, 55, 95129 Catania, Italy

[2] Institute of Computing Science, Poznan University of Technology,
Piotrowo 3a, 60-965 Poznan, Poland

Abstract. Solving multicriteria decision problems, like choice and ranking, requires the use of DM's preference model. In this paper we advocate for the preference model in terms of "*if..., then...*" decision rules induced from decision examples provided by the DM. This model has two advantages over the classical models : (i) it is intelligible and speaks the language of the DM, (ii) the preference information comes from observation of DM's decisions. For a finite set A of actions evaluated by a family of criteria, we consider the preference information given in the form of pairwise comparisons of reference actions presented in a pairwise comparison table (PCT). In PCT, pairs of actions from a subset $B \subseteq A \times A$ are described by preference relations on particular criteria and by a comprehensive outranking relation. Using the dominance-based rough set approach to the analysis of the PCT, we obtain a rough approximation of the outranking relation by a dominance relation. Then, a set of "*if..., then...*" decision rules is induced from these approximations. The decision rules constitute the preference model which is then applied to a set $M \subseteq A$ of (new) actions. As a result, we obtain a four-valued outranking relation on set M. In order to obtain a final recommendation in the problem of choice or ranking, the four-valued outranking relation on set M is exploited using a net flow score procedure.

Keywords. Decision rules, Multicriteria decision analysis, Rough sets, Choice, Ranking.

1 Introduction

Construction of a logical model of behavior from observation of individual's acts is a paradigm of artificial intelligence and, in particular, of inductive learning. Solving multicriteria decision problems, such as choice and ranking, requires the use of DM's (Decision Maker's) preference model. It is usually a (utility) function or a binary relation – its construction requires some preference information from the DM, like substitution ratios among criteria, importance weights, or indifference, preference and veto thresholds. Acquisition of this preference information from the DM is not easy and, moreover, the resulting preference model is not intelligible for the DM. In this situation, the preference model in terms of "*if..., then...*" decision rules induced from

S. Benferhat and P. Besnard (Eds.): ECSQARU 2001, LNAI 2143, pp. 29–47, 2001.

decision examples provided by the DM has two advantages over the classical models : (i) it is intelligible and speaks the language of the DM, (ii) the preference information comes from observation of DM's decisions. The rule-based preference model and its construction are concordant with the above paradigm of artificial intelligence.

There is, however, a problem with inconsistency often present in the set of decision examples. These inconsistencies cannot be considered as simple error or noise – they follow from hesitation of the DM, unstable character of his/her preferences and incomplete determination of the family of criteria. They can convey important information that should be taken into account in the construction of the DM's preference model. Rather to correct or ignore these inconsistencies, we propose to take them into account in the preference model construction using the rough set concept [19,20,26]. For this purpose, we have extended the original rough sets theory in two ways : (i) substituting the classical indiscernibility relation by a dominance relation, which permits taking into account the preference order in domains (scales) of criteria (attributes), and (ii), substituting the data table by a pairwise comparison table, where each row corresponds to a pair of actions described by binary relations on particular criteria, which permits approximation of a comprehensive preference relation in multicriteria choice and ranking problems. The extended rough set approach is called dominance-based rough set approach [2,3,4,8,9,10].

Given a finite set A of actions evaluated by a family of criteria, we consider the preferential information in the form of a pairwise comparison table (PCT) including pairs of reference actions from a subset $B \subseteq A \times A$ described by preference relations on particular criteria and a comprehensive outranking relation. Using the rough set approach to the analysis of the PCT, we obtain a rough approximation of the outranking relation by a dominance relation. The dominance-based rough set approach answers several questions related to the approximation: (a) is the set of decision examples consistent? (b) what are the non-redundant subsets of criteria ensuring the same quality of approximation as the whole set of criteria? (c) what are the criteria which cannot be eliminated from the approximation without decreasing the quality of approximation? (d) what minimal "*if ..., then ...*" decision rules can be induced from the approximations? The resulting decision rules constitute a preference model. It is more general than the classical utility function or any relation.

Decision rules derived from rough approximations are then applied to a set $M \subseteq A$ of (new) actions. As a result, we obtain a four-valued outranking relation on set M. The definition of a suitable exploitation procedure in order to obtain a recommendation was an open problem. We proposed an exploitation procedure for multicriteria choice and ranking that is based on the net flow score and satisfies some desirable properties.

The paper is organized as follows. In section 2, we present the extension of the rough set concept on multicriteria decision problems, with particular emphasis on multicriteria choice and ranking problems. It is based on analysis of pairwise comparisons of actions, so the rough set approach concerns in this case approximation of a preference binary relation by specific dominance relations. These dominance relations can be multigraded, when the criteria have quantitative or numerical non-quantitative scales, or without degree of preference, when the criteria have ordinal scales. Section 3 presents an illustrative example and section 4 includes conclusions.

2 Extension of the Rough Set Concept on Multicriteria Decision Problems

In any multicriteria and/or multiattribute decision problem, no recommendation can be elaborated before the DM provides some preferential information suitable to the preference model assumed [16,23]. There are two major models used until now in multicriteria decision analysis: functional and relational. The functional model has been extensively used within the framework of multiattribute utility theory [15]. The relational model has its most widely known representation in the form of an outranking relation [24] and a fuzzy relation [22]. These models require specific preferential information more or less explicitly related with their parameters. For example, in the deterministic case, the DM is often asked for pairwise comparisons of actions, from which one can assess the substitution rates in the functional model or importance weights in the relational model. This kind of preferential information seems to be close to the natural reasoning of the DM. He/she is typically more confident exercising his/her comparisons than explaining them. The representation of this information by functional or relational models seems, however, less natural. According to Slovic [25], people make decisions by searching for *rules* that provide good justification of their choices. So, after getting the preferential information in terms of exemplary comparisons, it is natural to build the preference model in terms of "*if..., then...*" rules. Then, these rules can be applied to a set of potential actions in order to obtain specific preference relations. From the exploitation of these relations, a suitable recommendation can be obtained to support the DM in decision problem at hand.

The induction of rules from examples is a typical approach of artificial intelligence. It is concordant with the principle of posterior rationality by March [18] and with aggregation-disaggregation logic by Jacquet-Lagrèze [14]. The rules explain the preferential attitude of the DM and enable his/her understanding of the reasons for his/her preference. As pointed out by Langley and Simon [17], the recognition of the rules by the DM justifies their use for decision support. The preference model in the form of rules derived from examples fulfils both explanation and recommendation tasks.

In this section we are presenting the main extension of the rough set approach, resulting in a new methodology of modeling DM's preferences in terms of decision rules. The rules are induced from the preferential information given by the DM in the form of examples of decisions.

More precisely, for A being a finite set of actions (real or fictitious, potential or not) considered in a multicriteria problem, the examples of decisions are confined to a subset of actions $B \subseteq A$, relatively well known to the DM, called *reference actions*. Depending on the type of the multicriteria problem, the examples concern either assignment of reference actions to decision classes (sorting problem) or pairwise comparisons of reference actions (choice and ranking problems). As to relation of these examples to reality, they can be either *historical* or *simulated.* Historical examples represent actual decisions made by the DM in the past. Simulated examples represent decisions declared by the DM with respect to reference actions, but not really made. Selection of reference actions and exemplary decisions is a crucial issue for obtaining a robust preference model. The authors are currently working on this issue which is also linked to the problem of defining a proper interactive procedure for induction and acceptance of decision rules.

For algorithmic reasons, information about reference actions is represented in the form of a data *table*. The rows of the table are labeled by *reference actions*, whereas columns are labeled by *attributes* and entries of the table are *attribute-values*, called *descriptors*. Formally, by a data *table* we understand the 4-tuple **S=<B,Q,V,f>**, where B is a finite set of *reference actions*, Q is a finite set of *attributes*, $V=\bigcup_{q\in Q} V_q$ and V_q is a domain of the attribute q, and $f:B\times Q\rightarrow V$ is a total function such that $f(x,q)\in V_q$ for every $q\in Q$, $x\in B$, called an *information function.* A data table **S** can be seen as *decision table* if in the set of attributes Q there can be distinguished two disjoint sets: set C of *condition attributes* and set D of *decision attributes.*

As was already mentioned, the notion of *attribute* differs from that of *criterion* because the domain (scale) of a criterion has to be ordered according to a decreasing or increasing preference, while the domain of the attribute does not have to be ordered. Formally, for each $q\in C$ being a criterion there exists an outranking relation [23] S_q on the set of actions A such that xS_qy means "x is at least as good as y with respect to criterion q". We suppose that S_q is a total preorder, i.e., a strongly complete and transitive binary relation defined on A on the basis of evaluations $f(\cdot,q)$. If domain V_q for criterion q is quantitative and for each $x,y\in A$, $f(x,q)\geq f(y,q)$ implies xS_qy, then V_q is a scale of preference of criterion q. If, however, for criterion q, V_q is not quantitative and/or $f(x,q)\geq f(y,q)$ does not imply xS_qy, then in order to define a scale of preference for criterion q, one can choose a function $g_q:A\rightarrow\mathbf{R}$ such that for each $x,y\in A$, xS_qy if and only if $g_q(x)\geq g_q(y)$; to this aim it is enough to order the actions of A from the worst to the best on criterion q and to assign to $g_q(x)$ consecutive numbers corresponding to the rank of x in this order, i.e., for z being the worst, $g_q(z)=1$, for w being the second worst, $g_q(w)=2$, and so on. Then, the domain of function $g_q(\cdot)$ becomes a scale of preference for criterion q and the domain V_q is recoded such that $f(x,q)=g_q(x)$ for every $x\in A$.

Several attempts have already been made to use the rough sets theory to decision support [21,27]. The original rough set approach is not able, however, to deal with preference-ordered attribute domains and decision classes. Solving this problem was crucial for application of the rough set approach to multicriteria decision analysis (MCDA).

Let us explain shortly why the original rough set approach is not able to deal with inconsistencies coming from consideration of criteria, i.e. attributes with preference-ordered domains (scales), like product quality, market share, debt ratio. Consider, for example, two firms, *A* and *B*, evaluated for assessment of bankruptcy risk by a set of criteria including the "debt ratio" (total debt/total assets). If firm *A* has a low value while firm *B* has a high value of the debt ratio, and evaluations of these firms on other attributes are equal, then, from bankruptcy risk point of view, firm *A* dominates firm *B*. Suppose, however, that firm *A* has been assigned by a DM to a class of higher risk than firm *B*. This is obviously inconsistent with the dominance principle. Within the original rough set approach, the two firms will be considered as just discernible and no inconsistency will be stated.

In the case of multicriteria choice and ranking problems the decision table in its original form does not allow the representation of preference binary relations between actions. To handle binary relations within the rough set approach, Greco, Matarazzo and Slowinski [2] proposed to operate on, so called, *pairwise comparison table* (*PCT*), i.e., with respect to a choice or ranking problem, a decision table whose rows represent pairs of actions for which multicriteria evaluations and a comprehensive preference relation are known.

Using an indiscernibility relation on the PCT one cannot exploit properly the ordinal information present in the data. Indiscernibility permits handling *inconsistency* which occures when two pairs of actions have preferences of the same strength on considered criteria, however, the comprehensive preference relations established for these pairs are not the same. When dealing with criteria, there may arise also another type of inconsistency connected with the dominance principle: on a given set of criteria, one pair of actions is characterized by some preferences and another pair has all preferences of at least the same strength, however, for the first pair we have a comprehensive preference and for the other – an inverse comprehensive preference. This is why the indiscernibility relation is not able to handle all kinds of inconsistencies connected with the use of criteria. For this reason, another way of defining rough approximations and decision rules has been proposed, based on the use of *graded dominance relations*.

2.1 The Pairwise Comparison Table

Let C be the set of criteria used for evaluation of actions from A. For any criterion $q \in C$, let T_q be a finite set of binary relations defined on A on the basis of the evaluations of actions from A with respect to the considered criterion q, such that for every $(x,y) \in A \times A$ exactly one binary relation $t \in T_q$ is verified. More precisely, given the domain V_q of $q \in C$, if $v'_q, v''_q \in V_q$ are the respective evaluations of $x,y \in A$ by means of q and $(x,y) \in t$, with $t \in T_q$, then for each $w,z \in A$ having the same evaluations v'_q, v''_q by means of q, $(w,z) \in t$. Furthermore, let T_d be a set of binary relations defined on set A (comprehensive pairwise comparisons) such that at most one binary relation $t \in T_d$ is verified for every $(x,y) \in A \times A$.

The preferential information has the form of pairwise comparisons of reference actions from $B \subseteq A$, considered as exemplary decisions. The *pairwise comparison table* (PCT) is defined as data table $\mathbf{S}_{PCT} = \langle \mathcal{B}, C \cup \{d\}, T_C \cup T_d, g \rangle$, where $\mathcal{B} \subseteq B \times B$ is a non-empty *set of exemplary pairwise comparisons of reference actions*, $T_C = \bigcup_{q \in C} T_q$, d is a decision corresponding to the comprehensive pairwise comparison (comprehensive preference relation), and $g: \mathcal{B} \times (C \cup \{d\}) \rightarrow T_C \cup T_d$ is a total function such that $g[(x,y),q]\in T_q$ for every $(x,y)\in A\times A$ and for each $q\in C$, and $g[(x,y),d]\in T_d$ for every $(x,y)\in B$. It follows that for any pair of reference actions $(x,y)\in B$ there is verified one and only one binary relation $t\in T_d$. Thus, T_d induces a partition of B. In fact, data table $\mathbf{S}_{PCT}$ can be seen as decision table, since the set of considered criteria C and decision d are distinguished.

We assume that the exemplary pairwise comparisons made by the DM can be represented in terms of *graded preference relations* (for example "very weak preference", "weak preference", "strict preference", "strong preference", "very strong preference") P_q^h: for each $q\in C$ and for every $(x,y)\in A\times A$,

$$T_q = \{P_q^h,\ h\in H_q\},$$

where H_q is a particular subset of the relative integers and

$xP_q^h y$, $h>0$, means that action x is preferred to action y by degree h with respect to the criterion q,

$xP_q^h y$, $h<0$, means that action x is not preferred to action y by degree h with respect to the criterion q,

$x P_q^0 y$ means that action x is similar (asymmetrically indifferent) to action y with respect to the criterion q.

Within the preference context, the similarity relation P_q^0, even if not symmetric, resembles indifference relation. Thus, in this case, we call this similarity relation "asymmetric indifference". Of course, for each $q\in C$ and for every $(x,y)\in A\times A$, $[xP_q^h y,\ h\geq 0] \Leftrightarrow [yP_q^k x,\ k\leq 0]$.

The set of binary relations T_d may be defined in a similar way, but $x P_d^h y$ means that action x is comprehensively preferred to action y by degree h.

Technically, the modeling of the binary relation P_q^h, i.e. the assessment of h, can be organized as follows:

- first, it is observed that for any $q\in C$ there exists a function c_q: $A\rightarrow\mathbf{R}$ which is increasing with respect to the preferences on q (the evaluations of c_q depend on the evaluations of the total function f(x,q), more precisely f(x,q) = f(y,q) implies $c_q(x) = c_q(y)$),
- then, it is possible to define a function k_q: $\mathbf{R}^2\rightarrow\mathbf{R}$ which measures the *strength of the preference* (positive or negative) of x over y (e.g. $k_q[c_q(x),c_q(y)]=c_q(x)-c_q(y)$); it should satisfy the following properties for all $x,y,z\in A$:

$$c_q(x) > c_q(y) \Leftrightarrow k_q[c_q(x),c_q(z)] > k_q[c_q(y),c_q(z)], \qquad \text{(i)}$$

$$c_q(x) > c_q(y) \Leftrightarrow k_q[c_q(z),c_q(x)] < k_q[c_q(z),c_q(y)], \qquad \text{(ii)}$$

$$c_q(x) = c_q(y) \Leftrightarrow k_q[c_q(x),c_q(y)] = 0, \qquad \text{(iii)}$$

- next, the domain of k_q can be divided into intervals, using a suitable set of thresholds Δ_q, for each $q \in C$; these intervals are numbered such that positive strength intervals get numbers 1, 2, 3, …, while negative strength intervals, –1, –2, –3, …, starting symmetrically from interval no. 0 that includes $k_q[c_q(x),c_q(y)]=0$,
- the value of h in the relation $xP_q^h y$ is then equal to the number of interval that includes $k_q[c_q(x),c_q(y)]$, for any $(x,y) \in A\times A$.

Actually, property (iii) can be relaxed in order to obtain a more general preference model which, for instance, does not satisfy preferential independence [15].

We are considering a PCT where the set T_d is composed of two binary relations defined on A:

x outranks y (denoted by xSy or $(x,y) \in S$), where $(x,y) \in B$,

x does not outrank y (denoted by $xS^c y$ or $(x,y) \in S^c$), where $(x,y) \in B$,

and $S \cup S^c = B$, where "x outranks y " means "x is at least as good as y" [23]; observe that the binary relation S is reflexive, but neither necessarily transitive nor complete.

2.2 Multigraded Dominance

The graded dominance relation introduced in [2] assumes a common grade of preference for all the considered criteria. While this permits a simple calculation of the approximations and of the resulting decision rules, it is lacking in precision. A dominance relation allowing a different degree of preference for each considered criterion (*multigraded dominance*) gives a far more accurate picture of the preferential information contained in the pairwise comparison table $\mathbf{S}_{PCT}$.

More formally, given $P \subseteq C$ ($P \neq \emptyset$), $(x,y),(w,z) \in A\times A$, the pair of actions (x,y) is said to dominate (w,z), taking into account the criteria from P (denoted by $(x,y)D_P(w,z)$), if x is preferred to y at least as strongly as w is preferred to z with respect to each $q \in P$. Precisely, "at least as strongly as" means "by at least the same degree", i.e. $hq \geq kq$, where $hq,kq \in H_q$, $xP_q^{hq} y$ and $w P_q^{kq} z$, for each $q \in P$.

Let $D_{\{q\}}$ be the dominance relation confined to the single criterion $q \in P$. The binary relation $D_{\{q\}}$ is reflexive ($(x,y)D_{\{q\}}(x,y)$, for every $(x,y) \in A\times A$), transitive ($(x,y)D_{\{q\}}(w,z)$ and $(w,z)D_{\{q\}}(u,v)$ imply $(x,y)D_{\{q\}}(u,v)$, for every $(x,y),(w,z),(u,v) \in A\times A$), and complete ($(x,y)D_{\{q\}}(w,z)$ and/or $(w,z)D_{\{q\}}(x,y)$, for all $(x,y),(w,z) \in A\times A$). Therefore, $D_{\{q\}}$ is a complete preorder on $A\times A$. Since the intersection of complete preorders is a partial preorder and $D_P = \bigcap_{q \in P} D_{\{q\}}$, $P \subseteq C$, then the dominance relation D_P is a partial preorder on $A\times A$.

Let $R \subseteq P \subseteq C$ and $(x,y),(u,v) \in A\times A$; then the following implication holds:

$$(x,y)D_P(u,v) \Rightarrow (x,y)D_R(u,v).$$

Given $P \subseteq C$ and $(x,y) \in A \times A$, we define:

- a set of pairs of actions dominating (x,y), called P-*dominating set*, $D_P^+(x,y) = \{(w,z) \in A \times A: (w,z) D_P (x,y)\}$,
- a set of pairs of actions dominated by (x,y), called P-*dominated set*, $D_P^-(x,y) = \{(w,z) \in A \times A: (x,y) D_P (w,z)\}$.

The P-dominating sets and the P-dominated sets defined on *B* for all pairs of reference actions from *B* are "granules of knowledge" that can be used to express P-lower and P-upper approximations of comprehensive outranking relations S and S^c, respectively:

$$\underline{P}(S) = \{(x,y) \in B: D_P^+(x,y) \subseteq S\},$$

$$\overline{P}(S) = \bigcup_{(x,y) \in S} D_P^+(x,y).$$

$$\underline{P}(S^c) = \{(x,y) \in B: D_P^-(x,y) \subseteq S^c\},$$

$$\overline{P}(S^c) = \bigcup_{(x,y) \in S^c} D_P^-(x,y).$$

It has been proved in [2] that

$$\underline{P}(S) \subseteq S \subseteq \overline{P}(S), \quad \underline{P}(S^c) \subseteq S^c \subseteq \overline{P}(S^c).$$

Furthermore, the following complementarity properties hold:

$$\underline{P}(S) = B - \overline{P}(S^c), \quad \overline{P}(S) = B - \underline{P}(S^c),$$

$$\underline{P}(S^c) = B - \overline{P}(S), \quad \overline{P}(S^c) = B - \underline{P}(S).$$

The P-boundaries (P-doubtful regions) of S and S^c are defined as

$$Bn_P(S) = \overline{P}(S) - \underline{P}(S), \quad Bn_P(S^c) = \overline{P}(S^c) - \underline{P}(S^c).$$

From the above it follows that $Bn_P(S) = Bn_P(S^c)$.

The concepts of the quality of approximation, reducts and core can be extended also to the approximation of the outranking relation by multigraded dominance relations. In particular, the coefficient

$$\gamma_P = \frac{\mathrm{card}\left(\underline{P}(S) \cup \underline{P}(S^c)\right)}{\mathrm{card}(B)}$$

defines the *quality of approximation of* S and S^c by $P \subseteq C$. It expresses the ratio of all pairs of actions $(x,y) \in B$ correctly assigned to S and S^c by the set P of criteria to all the pairs of actions contained in *B*. Each minimal subset $P \subseteq C$, such that $\gamma_P = \gamma_C$, is called a *reduct* of C (denoted by $RED_{S_{PCT}}$). Let us remark that S_{PCT} can have more than one reduct. The intersection of all *B*-reducts is called the *core* (denoted by $CORE_{S_{PCT}}$).

Using the approximations defined above, it is then possible to induce a generalized description of the preferential information contained in a given $\mathbf{S}_{PCT}$ in terms of suitable decision rules. The syntax of these rules is based on the concept of *upward cumulated preferences* (denoted by $P_q^{\geq h}$) and *downward cumulated preferences* (denoted by $P_q^{\leq h}$), having the following interpretation:

- $xP_q^{\geq h}y$ means "x is preferred to y with respect to q by at least degree h",
- $xP_q^{\leq h}y$ means "x is preferred to y with respect to q by at most degree h".

Exact definition of the cumulated preferences, for each $(x,y)\in A\times A$, $q\in C$ and $h\in H_q$, is the following:

- $xP_q^{\geq h}y$ if $xP_q^k y$, where $k\in H_q$ and $k\geq h$,
- $xP_q^{\leq h}y$ if $xP_q^k y$, where $k\in H_q$ and $k\leq h$.

Using the above concepts, three types of decision rules can be considered:

1) $D_{\geq}$-*decision rules* with the following syntax:

   if $xP_{q1}^{\geq h(q1)}y$ *and* $xP_{q2}^{\geq h(q2)}y$ *and* ... $xP_{qp}^{\geq h(qp)}y$, *then* xSy,

   where $P=\{q1,q2,...,qp\}\subseteq C$ and $(h(q1),h(q2),...,h(qp))\in H_{q1}\times H_{q2}\times...\times H_{qp}$; these rules are supported by pairs of actions from the P-lower approximation of S only;

2) $D_{\leq}$-*decision rules* with the following syntax:

   if $xP_{q1}^{\leq h(q1)}y$ *and* $xP_{q2}^{\leq h(q2)}y$ *and* ... $xP_{qp}^{\leq h(qp)}y$, *then* xS^cy,

   where $P=\{q1,q2,...,qp\}\subseteq C$ and $(h(q1),h(q2),...,h(qp))\in H_{q1}\times H_{q2}\times...\times H_{qp}$; these rules are supported by pairs of actions from the P-lower approximation of S^c only;

3) $D_{\geq\leq}$-*decision rules* with the following syntax:

   if $xP_{q1}^{\geq h(q1)}y$ *and* $xP_{q2}^{\geq h(q2)}y$ *and* ... $xP_{qk}^{\geq h(qk)}y$ *and* $xP_{qk+1}^{\leq h(qk+1)}y$ *and* ... $xP_{qp}^{\leq h(qp)}y$, *then* xSy *or* xS^cy,

   where $O'=\{q1,q2,...,qk\}\subseteq C$, $O''=\{qk+1,qk+2,...,qp\}\subseteq C$, $P=O'\cup O''$, O' and O'' not necessarily disjoint, $(h(q1),h(q2),...,h(qp))\in H_{q1}\times H_{q2}\times...\times H_{qp}$; these rules are supported by actions from the P-boundary of S and S^c only.

2.3 Dominance without Degrees of Preference

The degree of graded preference considered above is defined on a quantitative scale of the strength of preference k_q, $q\in C$. However, in many real world problems, the existence of such a quantitative scale is rather questionable. Roy [23] distinguishes the following cases:

- preferences expressed on an ordinal scale: this is the case where the difference between two evaluations has no clear meaning;
- preferences expressed on a quantitative scale: this is the case where the scale is defined with reference to a unit clearly identified, such that it is meaningful to consider an origin (zero) of the scale and ratios between evaluations (ratio scale);
- preferences expressed on a numerical non-quantitative scale: this is an intermediate case between the previous two; there are two well-known particular cases:
  - interval scale, where it is meaningful to compare ratios between differences of pairs of evaluations,
  - scale for which a complete preorder can be defined on all possible pairs of evaluations.

The strength of preference k_q and, therefore, the graded preference considered in point 2.1, is meaningful when the scale is quantitative or numerical non-quantitative. If the information about k_q is non-available, then it is possible to define a rough approximation of S and S^c using a specific dominance relation between pairs of actions from A×A. This dominance relation is defined directly on an ordinal scale represented by evaluations $c_q(x)$ on criterion q, for all actions $x \in A$ [4]. Let us explain this latter case in more detail.

Let C^O be the set of criteria expressing preferences on an ordinal scale, and C^N, the set of criteria expressing preferences on a quantitative scale or a numerical non-quantitative scale, such that $C^O \cup C^N = C$ and $C^O \cap C^N = \emptyset$. Moreover, for each $P \subseteq C$, we denote by P^O the subset of P composed of criteria expressing preferences on an ordinal scale, i.e. $P^O = P \cap C^O$, and P^N the subset of P composed of criteria expressing preferences on a quantitative scale or a numerical non-quantitative scale, i.e. $P^N = P \cap C^N$. Of course, for each $P \subseteq C$, we have $P = P^N \cup P^O$ and $P^O \cap P^N = \emptyset$.

If $P = P^N$ and $P^O = \emptyset$, then the definition of dominance is the same as in the case of multigraded dominance (point 2.2). If $P = P^O$ and $P^N = \emptyset$, then, given $(x,y),(w,z) \in A \times A$, the pair (x,y) is said to dominate the pair (w,z) with respect to P if, for each $q \in P$, $c_q(x) \geq c_q(w)$ and $c_q(z) \geq c_q(y)$. Let $D_{\{q\}}$ be the dominance relation confined to the single criterion $q \in P^O$. The binary relation $D_{\{q\}}$ is reflexive ($(x,y)D_{\{q\}}(x,y)$, for every $(x,y) \in A \times A$), transitive ($(x,y)D_{\{q\}}(w,z)$ and $(w,z)D_{\{q\}}(u,v)$ imply $(x,y)D_{\{q\}}(u,v)$, for all $(x,y),(w,z),(u,v) \in A \times A$), but non-complete (it is possible that *not* $(x,y)D_{\{q\}}(w,z)$ and *not* $(w,z)D_{\{q\}}(x,y)$ for some $(x,y),(w,z) \in A \times A$). Therefore, $D_{\{q\}}$ is a partial preorder. Since the intersection of partial preorders is also a partial preorder and $D_P = \bigcap_{q \in P} D_{\{q\}}$, $P = P^O$, then the dominance relation D_P is also a partial preorder.

If some criteria from $P \subseteq C$ express preferences on a quantitative or a numerical non-quantitative scale and others on an ordinal scale, i.e. if $P^N \neq \emptyset$ and $P^O \neq \emptyset$, then, given $(x,y),(w,z) \in A \times A$, the pair (x,y) is said to dominate the pair (w,z) with respect to criteria from P, if (x,y) dominates (w,z) with respect to both P^N and P^O. Since the dominance relation with respect to P^N is a partial preorder on A×A (because it is a multigraded dominance) and the dominance with respect to P^O is also a partial preorder on A×A (as explained above), then also the dominance D_P, being the intersection of these two dominance relations, is a partial preorder. In consequence, all the concepts introduced in the previous points can be restored using this specific definition of dominance relation.

Using the approximations of S and S^c based on the dominance relation defined above, it is possible to induce a generalized description of the available preferential information in terms of decision rules. These decision rules are of the same type as the rules already introduced in the previous point; however, the conditions on criteria from C^O are expressed directly in terms of evaluations belonging to domains of these criteria.

Let $C_q=\{c_q(x), x\in A\}$, $q\in C^O$. The decision rules have then the following syntax:

1) $D_{\geq}$-*decision rules*:

   if $x P_{q1}^{\geq h(q1)} y$ *and* ... $x P_{qe}^{\geq h(qe)} y$ *and* $c_{qe+1}(x)\geq r_{qe+1}$ *and* $c_{qe+1}(y)\leq s_{qe+1}$ *and* ... $c_{qp}(x)\geq r_{qp}$ *and* $c_{qp}(y)\leq s_{qp}$, *then* xSy,

   where $P=\{q1,...,qp\}\subseteq C$, $P^N=\{q1,...,qe\}$, $P^O=\{qe+1,...,qp\}$, $(h(q1),...,h(qe))\in H_{q1}\times...\times H_{qe}$ and $(r_{qe+1},...,r_{qp})$, $(s_{qe+1},...,s_{qp})\in C_{qe+1}\times...\times C_{qp}$; these rules are supported by pairs of actions from the P-lower approximation of S only;

2) $D_{\leq}$-*decision rules*:

   if $x P_{q1}^{\leq h(q1)} y$ *and* ... $x P_{qp}^{\leq h(qp)} y$ *and* $c_{qe+1}(x)\leq r_{qe+1}$ *and* $c_{qe+1}(y)\geq s_{qe+1}$ *and* ... $c_{qp}(x)\leq r_{qp}$ *and* $c_{qp}(y)\geq s_{qp}$, *then* xS^cy,

   where $P=\{q1,...,qp\}\subseteq C$, $P^N=\{q1,...,qe\}$, $P^O=\{qe+1,...,qp\}$, $(h(q1),...,h(qe))\in H_{q1}\times...\times H_{qe}$ and $(r_{qe+1},...,r_{qp})$, $(s_{qe+1},...,s_{qp})\in C_{qe+1}\times...\times C_{qp}$; these rules are supported by pairs of actions from the P-lower approximation of S^c only;

3) $D_{\geq\leq}$-*decision rules*:

   if $x P_{q1}^{\geq h(q1)} y$ *and* ... $x P_{qe}^{\geq h(qe)} y$ *and* $x P_{qe+1}^{\leq h(qe+1)} y$ ... $x P_{qf}^{\leq h(qf)} y$ *and* $c_{qf+1}(x)\geq r_{qf+1}$ *and* $c_{qf+1}(y)\leq s_{qf+1}$ *and* ... $c_{qg}(x)\geq r_{qg}$ *and* $c_{qg}(y)\leq s_{qg}$ *and* $c_{qg+1}(x)\leq r_{qg+1}$ *and* $c_{qg+1}(y)\geq s_{qg+1}$ *and* ... $c_{qp}(x)\leq r_{qp}$ *and* $c_{qp}(y)\geq s_{qp}$,
   then xSy *or* xS^cy,

   where $O'=\{q1,...,qe\}\subseteq C$, $O''=\{qe+1,...,qf\}\}\subseteq C$, $P^N=O'\cup O''$, O' and O'' not necessarily disjoint, $P^O=\{qf+1,...,qp\}$, $(h(q1),...,h(qf))\in H_{q1}\times...\times H_{qf}$, $(r_{qf+1},...,r_{qp})$, $(s_{qf+1},...,s_{qp})\in C_{qf+1}\times...\times C_{qp}$; these rules are supported by pairs of actions from the P-boundary of S and S^c only.

Procedures for rule induction from rough approximations have been proposed in [10,28,29].

2.4 Exploitation Procedure

The decision rules, induced from a given $\mathbf{S}_{PCT}$ describe the comprehensive preference relations S and S^c either exactly ($D_{\geq}$- and $D_{\leq}$-decision rules) or approximately ($D_{\geq\leq}$-decision rules). A set of these rules covering all pairs of $\mathbf{S}_{PCT}$ represent a preference model of the DM who gave the pairwise comparison of reference actions. Application of these decision rules on a new subset $M \subseteq A$ of actions induces a specific preference structure on M.

In fact, any pair of actions $(u,v) \in M \times M$ can match the decision rules in one of four ways:

- at least one $D_{\geq}$-decision rule and neither $D_{\leq}$- nor $D_{\geq\leq}$-decision rules,
- at least one $D_{\leq}$ -decision rule and neither $D_{\geq}$- nor $D_{\geq\leq}$-decision rules,
- at least one $D_{\geq}$-decision rule and at least one $D_{\leq}$-decision rule, or at least one $D_{\geq\leq}$-decision rule, or at least one $D_{\geq\leq}$-decision rule and at least one $D_{\geq}$- and/or at least one $D_{\leq}$-decision rule,
- no decision rule.

These four ways correspond to the following four situations of outranking, respectively:

- uSv and *not* uS^cv, that is *true* outranking (denoted by uS^Tv),
- uS^cv and *not* uSv, that is *false* outranking (denoted by uS^Fv),
- uSv and uS^cv, that is *contradictory* outranking (denoted by uS^Kv),
- *not* uSv and *not* uS^cv, that is *unknown* outranking (denoted by uS^Uv).

The four above situations, which together constitute the so-called *four-valued outranking* [30], have been introduced to underline the presence and absence of *positive* and *negative* reasons for the outranking. Moreover, they make it possible to distinguish contradictory situations from unknown ones.

A final *recommendation* (choice or ranking) can be obtained upon a suitable exploitation of this structure, i.e. of the presence and the absence of outranking S and S^c on M. A possible exploitation procedure consists in calculating a specific score, called Net Flow Score, for each action $x \in M$:

$$S_{nf}(x) = S^{++}(x) - S^{+-}(x) + S^{-+}(x) - S^{--}(x),$$

where

$$S^{++}(x) = \text{card}\big(\{y \in M\text{: there is at least one decision rule which affirms } xSy\}\big),$$
$$S^{+-}(x) = \text{card}\big(\{y \in M\text{: there is at least one decision rule which affirms } ySx\}\big),$$
$$S^{-+}(x) = \text{card}\big(\{y \in M\text{: there is at least one decision rule which affirms } yS^cx\}\big),$$
$$S^{--}(x) = \text{card}\big(\{y \in M\text{: there is at least one decision rule which affirms } xS^cy\}\big).$$

The recommendation in ranking problems consists of the total preorder determined by $S_{nf}(x)$ on M; in choice problems, it consists of the action(s) $x^*\in M$ such that $S_{nf}(x^*)=\max_{x\in M}\{S_{nf}(x)\}$.

The procedure described above has been recently characterized with reference to a number of desirable properties [13].

3 An Example

Let us suppose that a company managing a chain of warehouses wants to buy some new warehouses. To choose the best proposals or to rank them all, the managers of the company decide to analyze first the characteristics of eight warehouses already owned by the company (reference actions). This analysis should give some indications for the choice and ranking of the new proposals. Eight warehouses belonging to the company have been evaluated by three following criteria: capacity of the sales staff (A_1), perceived quality of goods (A_2) and high traffic location (A_3). The domains (scales) of these attributes are presently composed of three preference-ordered echelons: $V_1=V_2=V_3=\{$sufficient, medium, good$\}$. The decision attribute (d) indicates the profitability of warehouses, expressed by the Return On Equity (ROE) ratio (in %). Table 1 presents a decision table with the considered reference actions.

Table 1. Decision table with reference actions

Warehouse	A_1	A_2	A_3	d (ROE %)
1	good	medium	good	10.35
2	good	sufficient	good	4.58
3	medium	medium	good	5.15
4	sufficient	medium	medium	-5
5	sufficient	medium	medium	2.42
6	sufficient	sufficient	good	2.98
7	good	medium	good	15
8	good	sufficient	good	-1.55

With respect to the set of criteria $C=C^N=\{A_1,A_2,A_3\}$ the following multigraded preference relations P_i^h, i=1,2,3, were defined:

- $x P_i^0 y$ (and $y P_i^0 x$), meaning that x is *indifferent* to y with respect to A_i, if $f(x,A_i)=f(y,A_i)$.
- $x P_i^1 y$ (and $y P_i^{-1} x$), meaning that x is *weakly preferred* to y with respect to A_i, if $f(x,A_i)$=good and $f(y,A_i)$=medium, or if $f(x,A_i)$=medium and $f(y,A_i)$=sufficient,
- $x P_i^2 y$ (and $y P_i^{-2} x$), meaning that x is *preferred* to y with respect to A_i, if $f(x,A_i)$=good and $f(y,A_i)$=sufficient,

- $x P_i^3 y$ (and $y P_i^{-3} x$), meaning that x is *strongly preferred* to y with respect to A_i, if $f(x,A_i)$=good and $f(y,A_i)$=medium, or if $f(x,A_i)$=medium and $f(y,A_i)$=sufficient.

Using the decision attribute, the comprehensive outranking relation was build as follows: warehouse x is at least as good as warehouse y with respect to profitability (xSy) if

$$\mathrm{ROE}(x) \geq \mathrm{ROE}(y) - 2\%.$$

Otherwise, i.e. if ROE(x) < ROE(y) - 2%, warehouse x is not at least as good as warehouse y with respect to profitability ($xS^c y$).

The pairwise comparisons of reference actions result in a PCT. The rough set analysis of the PCT leads to conclusion that the set of decision examples on reference actions is inconsistent. The quality of approximation of S and S^c by all criteria from set C is equal to 0.44. Moreover, $\mathrm{RED}_{S_{PCT}} = \mathrm{CORE}_{S_{PCT}} = \{A_1,A_2,A_3\}$; this means that no criterion is superfluous.

The C-lower approximations and the C-upper approximations of S and S^c, obtained by means of multigraded dominance relations, are as follows:

$\underline{C}(S)$ = {(1,2),(1,4),(1,5),(1,6),(1,8),(3,2),(3,4),(3,5),(3,6),(3,8),(7,2),(7,4),(7,5),(7,6),(7,8)},

$\underline{C}(S^c)$ = {(2,1),(2,7),(4,1),(4,3),(4,7),(5,1),(5,3),(5,7),(6,1),(6,3),(6,7),(8,1),(8,7)}.

All the remaining 36 pairs of reference actions belong to the C-boundaries of S an S^c, i.e. $Bn_C(S) = Bn_C(S^c)$.

The following minimal $D_{\geq}$-decision rules and $D_{\leq}$-decision rules can be induced from lower approximations of S and S^c, respectively (within parentheses there are the pairs of actions supporting the corresponding rules):

if $x P_1^{\geq 1} y$ *and* $x P_2^{\geq 1} y$, *then* xSy; ((1,6),(3,6),(7,6)),

if $x P_2^{\geq 1} y$ *and* $x P_3^{\geq 0} y$, *then* xSy; ((1,2),(1,6),(1,8),(3,2),(3,6),(3,8),(7,2),(7,6),(7,8)),

if $x P_2^{\geq 0} y$ *and* $x P_3^{\geq 1} y$, *then* xSy; ((1,4),(1,5),(3,4),(3,5),(7,4),(7,5)),

if $x P_1^{\leq -1} y$ *and* $x P_2^{\leq -1} y$, *then* $xS^c y$; ((6,1),(6,3),(6,7)),

if $x P_2^{\leq 0} y$ *and* $x P_3^{\leq -1} y$, *then* $xS^c y$; ((4,1),(4,3),(4,7),(5,1),(5,3),(5,7)),

if $x P_1^{\leq 0} y$ *and* $x P_2^{\leq -1} y$ *and* $x P_3^{\leq 0} y$, *then* $xS^c y$; ((2,1),(2,7),(6,1),(6,3),(6,7),(8,1),(8,7)).

Moreover, it was possible to induce five minimal $D_{\geq\leq}$-decision rules from the boundary of approximation of S and S^c:

if $x P_2^{\leq 0} y$ *and* $x P_2^{\geq 0} y$ *and* $x P_3^{\leq 0} y$ *and* $x P_3^{\geq 0} y$, *then* xSy *or* $xS^c y$; ((1,1),(1,3),(1,7),(2,2),(2,6),(2,8),(3,1),(3,3),(3,7),(4,4),(4,5),(5,4),(5,5),(6,2),(6,6),(6,8),(7,1),(7,3),(7,7),(8,2),(8,6),(8,8)), *if* x $P_2^{\le -1}$ y *and* x $P_3^{\ge 1}$ y, *then* xSy *or* xS^cy; ((2,4),(2,5),(6,4),(6,5),(8,4),(8,5)),

if x $P_2^{\ge 1}$ y *and* x $P_3^{\le -1}$ y, *then* xSy *or* xS^cy; ((4,2),(4,6),(4,8),(5,2),(5,6),(5,8)),

if x $P_1^{\ge 1}$ y *and* x $P_2^{\le 0}$ y *and* x $P_3^{\le 0}$ y, *then* xSy *or* xS^cy; ((1,3),(2,3),(2,6),(7,3),(8,3),(8,6)),

if x $P_1^{\ge 1}$ y *and* x $P_2^{\le -1}$ y, *then* xSy *or* xS^cy; ((2,3),(2,4),(2,5),(8,3),(8,4),(8,5)),

Using all above decision rules and the Net Flow Score exploitation procedure on ten other warehouses proposed for sale, the managers obtained the result presented in Table 2. The dominance-based rough set approach gives a clear recommendation:

- for the choice problem it suggests to select warehouse 2' and 6', having maximum score (9),
- for the ranking problem it suggests the ranking presented in the last column of Table 2:

$$(2',6') \rightarrow (8') \rightarrow (9') \rightarrow (1') \rightarrow (4') \rightarrow (5') \rightarrow (3') \rightarrow (7',10')$$

Table 2. Ranking of warehouses for sale by decision rules and the Net Flow Score exploitation procedure

Warehouse for sale	A_1	A_2	A_3	Net Flow Score	Ranking
1'	good	sufficient	medium	1	5
2'	sufficient	good	good	11	1
3'	sufficient	medium	sufficient	-8	8
4'	sufficient	good	sufficient	0	6
5'	sufficient	sufficient	medium	-4	7
6'	sufficient	good	good	11	1
7'	medium	sufficient	sufficient	-11	9
8'	medium	medium	medium	7	3
9'	medium	good	sufficient	4	4
10'	medium	sufficient	sufficient	-11	9

4 Conclusions

In this paper, we made a synthesis of the contribution of the extended rough sets theory to multicriteria choice and ranking problems. Classical use of the rough set approach, and more generally, of machine learning, data mining and knowledge discovery, is confined to problems of multiattribute classification, i.e. to problems where neither the values of attributes describing the actions, nor the classes to which the actions are assigned, are preference-ordered. On the other hand, MCDA deals with problems where descriptions (evaluations) of actions by means of criteria, as well as decisions in sorting, choice and ranking problems, are preference-ordered. The extension of the rough set approach to problems in which preference-order properties are meaningful is possible upon two important methodological contributions extensivelly discussed in this paper:

1) approximation of the comprehensive preference relation by dominance relations, which allows to deal with preference-order properties of criteria,
2) analysis of decision examples in a pairwise comparison table, which allows to represent preference relations for choice and ranking problems.

Let us point out the main advantages of the dominance-based rough set approach to MCDA in comparison with classical approaches:

- preferential information necessary to deal with a multicriteria decision problem is asked to the DM in terms of exemplary decisions,
- the rough set analysis of preferential information supplies some useful elements of knowledge about the decision situation; these are: the relevance of particular attributes and/or criteria, information about their interaction (from quality of approximation and its analyisi using fuzzy measures theory), minimal subsets of attributes or criteria (reducts) conveying an important knowledge contained in the exemplary decisions, the set of the non-reducible attributes or criteria (core),
- the preference model induced from the preferential information is expressed in a natural and comprehensible language of "*if..., then...*" decision rules; the decision rules concern pairs of actions and conclude either presence or absence of a comprehensive preference relation; conditions for the presence are expressed in "at least" terms, and for the absence in "at most" terms, on particular criteria,
- the decision rules do not convert ordinal information into numeric one but keep the ordinal character of input data due to the syntax proposed,
- heterogeneous information (qualitative and quantitative, ordered and non-ordered) and scales of preference (ordinal, quantitative and numerical non-quantitative) can be processed within the dominance-based rough set approach, while classical MCDM methods consider only quantitative ordered evaluations with rare exceptions,
- no prior discretization of the quantitative domains of criteria is necessary,
- the decision rule preference model resulting from the rough set approach is more general than all existing models of conjoint measurement due to its capacity of handling inconsistent preferences,
- the proposed methodology is based on elementary concepts and mathematical tools (sets and set operations, binary relations), without recourse to any algebraic or analytical structures; main ideas such us indiscernibility and dominance are very natural and difficult to contest.

As to axiomatic foundation of the decision rule preference model for multicriteria choice and ranking, it has been recently proposed by the authors in [11,12]. We proved the equivalence of preference representation by a general non-additive and non-transitive model of conjoint measurement and by "*if..., then...*" decision rules. Moreover, some well known multicriteria aggregation procedures (lexicographic aggregation, majority aggregation, ELECTRE I and TACTIC) were represented in terms of the decision rule model; in these cases the decision rules decompose the synthetic aggregation formula used by these procedures; the rules involve partial profiles defined for subsets of criteria plus a dominance relation on these profiles and pairs of actions. Such decomposition makes the preference model more understandable for the decision maker.

It is also worth noting that the rough set approach to information processing is complementary to the fuzzy set approach because roughness represents granularity of knowledge and fuzziness represents gradedness of similarity, uncertainty and preference. The proof of this complementarity was given in [1,5,6] where fuzzy similarity, fuzzy dominance and fuzzy multigraded dominance were considered in classification, sorting and choice/ranking problems, respectively. The dominance-based rough set approach has also been adapted to handle missing values in the decision table [7].

Acknowledgement. The research of the two first authors has been supported by the Italian Ministry of University and Scientific Research (MURST). The third author wishes to acknowledge financial support from State Committee for Scientific Research (KBN), research grant no. 8T11F 006 19, and from the Foundation for Polish Science, subsidy no. 11/2001.

References

1. Dubois, D., Prade, H.: "Putting Rough Sets and Fuzzy Sets Together". In: R. Slowinski (ed.): *Intelligent Decision Support, Handbook of Applications and Advances of the Rough Sets Theory*. Kluwer, Dordrecht 1992, 203-233
2. Greco S., Matarazzo, B., Slowinski, R., *Rough approximation of a preference relation by dominance relations*, ICS Research Report 16/96, Warsaw University of Technology, Warsaw, 1996, and in: *European Journal of Operational Research* 117 (1999) 63-83
3. Greco, S., Matarazzo, B., Slowinski, R.: "A new rough set approach to multicriteria and multiattribute classification" In: L. Polkowski, A. Skowron (eds.): *Rough sets and Current Trends in Computing*. Springer-Verlag, 1998, 60-67.
4. Greco, S., B. Matarazzo and R. Slowinski, "The use of rough sets and fuzzy sets in MCDM". Chapter 14 in: T. Gal, T. Stewart and T. Hanne (eds.), *Advances in Multiple Criteria Decision Making*. Kluwer Academic Publishers, Dordrecht, 1999, 14.1-14.59
5. Greco, S., Matarazzo, B., Slowinski, R., "A fuzzy extension of the rough set approach to multicriteria and multiattribute sorting". In: J. Fodor, B. De Baets and P. Perny (eds.), *Preferences and Decisions under Incomplete Knowledge*, Physica-Verlag, Heidelberg, 2000, 131-151

6. Greco, S., Matarazzo, B., Slowinski, R., "Rough set processing of vague information using fuzzy similarity relations". In: C.S. Calude and G. Paun (eds.), *Finite Versus Infinite – Contributions to an Eternal Dilemma*, Springer-Verlag, London, 2000, 149-173
7. Greco, S., Matarazzo, B., Slowinski, R., "Dealing with missing data in rough set analysis of multi-attribute and multi-criteria decision problems". In: S.H. Zanakis, G. Doukidis and C. Zopounidis (eds.), *Decision Making: Recent Developments and Worldwide Applications*. Kluwer, Dordrecht, 2000, 295-316
8. Greco, S., Matarazzo, B., Slowinski, R., "Extension of the rough set approach to multicriteria decision support". *INFOR* 38 (2000) no.3, 161-196
9. Greco, S., Matarazzo, B., Slowinski, R., "Rough sets theory for multicriteria decision analysis". *European J. of Operational Research* 129 (2001) no.1, 1-47
10. Greco, S., Matarazzo, B., Slowinski, R., "Multicriteria classification by dominance-based rough set approach". Chapter C5.1.9 in: W. Kloesgen and J. Zytkow (eds.), *Handbook of Data Mining and Knowledge Discovery*, Oxford University Press, New York, 2001 (to appear)
11. Greco, S., Matarazzo, B., Slowinski, R., "Conjoint measurement and rough set approach for multicriteria sorting problems in presence of ordinal criteria". In: Colorni, A., Parruccini, M., Roy, B. (eds.), *AMCDA – Aide Multicritère à la décision (Multiple Criteria Decision Aiding)*, EUR Report, Joint Research Centre, The European Commission, Ispra, 2001 (to appear)
12. Greco, S., Matarazzo, B., Slowinski, R., "Preference representation by means of conjoint measurement and decision rule model". In: *Book in honor of Bernard Roy*, Kluwer, Dordrecht, 2001 (to appear)
13. Greco, S., Matarazzo, B., Slowinski, R., Tsoukias, A.: "Exploitation of a rough approximation of the outranking relation in multicriteria choice and ranking". In: T.J.Stewart and R.C. van den Honert (eds.), *Trends in Multicriteria Decision Making*. LNEMS vol. 465, Springer-Verlag, Berlin, 1998, 45-60
14. Jacquet-Lagrèze, E.: *Systèmes de décision et acteurs multiples - Contribution à une théorie de l'action pour les sciences des organisations*, Thèse d'Etat, Université de Paris-Dauphine, Paris, 1981
15. Keeney, R. L., Raiffa, H.: *Decision with Multiple Actionives - Preferences and value Tradeoffs*. Wiley, New York, 1976
16. Krantz, D.M., Luce, R.D., Suppes, P., Tversky, A.: *Foundations of Measurements I*. Academic Press, New York, 1978
17. Langley, P., Simon, H. A.: "Fielded applications of machine learning". In: R.S. Michalski, I. Bratko, M. Kubat (eds.), *Machine Learning and Data Mining*. Wiley, New York, 1998, 113-129
18. March, J. G.: "Bounded rationality, ambiguity, and the engineering of choice". In: D.E. Bell, H. Raiffa, A. Tversky (eds.): *Decision Making, Descriptive, Normative and Prescriptive Interactions*. Cambridge University Press, New York 1988, 33-58
19. Pawlak, Z.: "Rough sets". *International Journal of Information & Computer Sciences* 11 (1982) 341-356
20. Pawlak, Z.: *Rough Sets. Theoretical Aspects of Reasoning about Data*. Kluwer, Dordrecht, 1991
21. Pawlak, Z., Slowinski, R.: "Rough set approach to multi-attribute decision analysis". *European Journal of Operational Research* 72 (1994) 443-459
22. Perny, P., Roy, B.: "The use of fuzzy outranking relations in preference modeling". *Fuzzy Sets and Systems* 49 (1992) 33-53
23. Roy, B.: *Méthodologie Multicritère d'Aide à la Décision*. Economica, Paris, 1985
24. Roy, B., Bouyssou, D.: *Aide Multicritère à la Décision: Méthodes et Cas*. Economica, Paris, 1993
25. Slovic, P.: "Choice between equally-valued alternatives". *Journal of Experimental Psychology: Human Perception Performance* 1 (1975) 280-287

26. Slowinski, R. (ed.): *Intelligent Decision Support. Handbook of Applications and Advances of the Rough Sets Theory*. Kluwer Academic Publishers, Dordrecht, 1992
27. Slowinski, R.: "Rough set learning of preferential attitude in multi-criteria decision making". In: J. Komorowski, Z. W. Ras (eds), *Methodologies for Intelligent Systems*, Lecture Notes in Artificial Intelligence, vol. 689, Springer-Verlag, Berlin, 1993b, 642-651
28. Slowinski, R., Stefanowski, J., Greco, S., Matarazzo, B.: "Rough sets based processing of inconsistent information in decision analysis". *Control and Cybernetics* 29 (2000) no.1, 379-404
29. Stefanowski, J.: "On rough set based approaches to induction of decision rules". In: A. Skowron and L. Polkowski (eds.): *Rough Sets in Data Mining and Knowledge Discovery*. Vol.1, Physica-Verlag, Heidelberg, 1998, pp 500-529
30. Tsoukias, A., Vincke, Ph.: "A new axiomatic foundation of the partial comparability theory". *Theory and Decision* 39 (1995) 79-114

Propositional Distances and Preference Representation

Céline Lafage and Jérôme Lang

IRIT - Université Paul Sabatier, 31062 Toulouse Cedex (France)
{lafage,lang}@irit.fr

Abstract. Distances between possible worlds play an important role in logic-based knowledge representation (especially in belief change, reasoning about action, belief merging and similarity-based reasoning). We show here how they can be used for representing in a compact and intuitive way the preference profile of an agent, following the principle that given a goal G, then the closer a world w to a model of G, the better w. We give an integrated logical framework for preference representation which handles weighted goals and distances to goals in a uniform way. Then we argue that the widely used Hamming distance (which merely counts the number of propositional symbols assigned a different value by two worlds) is generally too rudimentary and too syntax-sensitive to be suitable in real applications; therefore, we propose a new family of distances, based on Choquet integrals, in which the Hamming distance has exactly a position very similar to that of the arithmetic mean in the class of Choquet integrals for multi-criteria decision making.

1 Introduction

The specification of a decision making or a planning process necessarily includes the goals, desires and preferences of the agent (we will make use of the generic term "preference" for all of these notions – a goal will merely be a specific, strong form of preference). At the object level, the preference structure can be either a utility function assigning each possible consequence to a numerical value, or a weak order relation (possibly allowing for incomparibility in addition to indifference). Now, once it has been fixed what a preference structure is, the question of *how it should be represented*, or in other terms, how it should be encoded so as to be "computationally friendly", arises. A straightforward possibility consists in writing it down explicitly, namely by listing all possible consequences together with their utility values or by listing all pairs of consequences in the preference relation. Clearly, this explicit mode of representation is possible in practice only when the number of possible consequences is reasonably low with respect to the available computational resources. This is often not the case, in particular when the decision to take consists in giving a value to each of the variables of a set of n decision variables: here, the set of consequences is equal to the set of feasible assignments and thus grows exponentially with n.

S. Benferhat and P. Besnard (Eds.): ECSQARU 2001, LNAI 2143, pp. 48–59, 2001.

Therefore, it is obviously unreasonable to require from the agents the specification of an explicit utility function or preference ordering (under the form of a table or a list) on the set of all solutions. This argues for the need of a *compact* (or *succinct*) representation language for preferences. Furthermore, such a language for preference representation should be as *expressive* as possible, and as close as possible to the intuition (ideally, it should be easily translated from a specification in natural language of the preferences of an agent). Lastly, it should be equipped with decision procedures, as efficient as possible, so as to enable the automation of the search for an optimal collective decision.

The KR community has contributed a lot to the study of such succint and expressive languages for representing *knowledge* [1]. Now, for the last few years, there has been several approaches dedicated to the representation of *preferences* of an agent, to be used in a decision making process. They are briefly recalled in Section 2. We particularly focus on two families of representation languages, whose induced preference structure is a utility function: first, weighted logics, which consist in associating to each formula (representing an elementary goal) a positive weight representing the penalty for not satisfying this goal (together with a way of aggregating penalties coming from different violated goals); second, distance-based logics, where the violation of a goal is graded using a *distance* between worlds: given a goal (encoded as a propositional formula) G and given a distance d between worlds, then the closer a world w to a model of G, the better w (the optimal case being when w satisfies φ).

In [13] we showed that in some specific cases, a goal base written within the framework of distance-based logics could be translated into a goal base written within the framework of weighted logics and vice-versa. Here we go further by showing that this translation can be done independently of the chosen distance and aggregation function, and we propose an integrated logical framework which enables both the expression of weighted goals and distance-labelled goals in a uniform way. This is done in Section 3.

In Section 4 we focus on the practical choice of a distance between worlds. We first argue that the widely used distance in the Knowledge Representation community, namely the Hamming distance, is very poor with respect to expressivity and robustness to small changes in the propositional language. This leads us to propose alternative and more general families of propositional distances: we recast the specification or propositional distance in the framework of multicriteria decision making and we introduce the class of Choquet propositional distances, defined as a Choquet integral. We will show that the position of the Hamming distance in this family (to which is belongs) is the same as the position of the arithmetic mean in the family of Choquet integrals; namely, both are central but "degenerate" members of their respective families.

---

[1] Here we reserve the term "knowledge" for its restrictive meaning "information about the real world", excluding thus preferences, goals and desires.

2 Logical Representation of Preferences

2.1 Notations, Definitions, and Basic Assumptions

From now on, $\mathcal{L}$ denotes a propositional language built from a finite set of propositional symbols PS, the usual connectives, and two symbols $\top$ and $\bot$ denoting respectively tautology and contradiction. A *literal* is either a propositional symbol or its negation. A *clause* (resp. a *cube*) is a disjunction (resp. a conjunction) of literals. A formula is under CNF (resp. DNF) iff it is a conjunction of clauses (resp. a disjunction of cubes).

$\Omega = 2^{PS}$ is the set of truth assignments (called interpretations, or *worlds*) for $\mathcal{L}$. A world w on PS is denoted by listing the set of literals it satisfies: for instance, if $PS = \{a, b, c, d\}$, then the world in which a and c are false and b and d are true is written as $(\neg a, b, \neg c, d)$. If T is a nonempty subset of VAR, then $w^{\downarrow T}$ denotes the projection of w on T. For instance, $(\neg a, b, \neg c, d)^{\downarrow\{b,c\}}$ is the partial world in which b is true and c is false, written as $(b, \neg c)$.

$Diff(w, w')$ denotes the set of propositional symbols that are assigned a different value by w and w'. For instance, if $w = (\neg a, b, \neg c, d)$ and $w' = (\neg a, \neg b, c, d)$ then $Diff(w, w') = \{b, c\}$. $Mod(\varphi)$ is the set of all models of φ. We write $w \models \varphi$ when $w \in Mod(\varphi)$, i.e., φ is true in w, and $\varphi \models \psi$ when ψ is a logical consequence of φ, i.e., $Mod(\varphi) \subseteq Mod(\psi)$.

Throughout this paper we make the assumption that the set of feasible worlds is $Mod(K)$ where K is a propositional formula expressing integrity constraints. Therefore, the preference structure can be defined on $Mod(K)$. By default we assume $K = \top$.

Lastly, we introduce the notions of [weak][pseudo-] distances between propositional worlds.

Definition 1
A (propositional) weak distance *is a mapping* $d : \Omega \times \Omega \to \mathbb{N}$ *satisfying*

Sep $\forall w, w', d(w, w') = 0 \Leftrightarrow w = w'$
Sym $\forall w, w', d(w, w') = d(w', w)$

If d satisfies furthermore

TI $\forall w, w', w'', d(w, w'') \leq d(w, w') + d(w', w'')$

then d is a distance.

If φ is a formula and $w, w' \in \Omega$ then $d(w, \varphi) = \min_{w' \models \varphi} d(w, w')$ and $d(\varphi, \psi) = \min_{w \models \varphi, w' \models \psi} d(w, w')$

The *Hamming* distance d_H is defined as the number of propositional symbols that are assigned different values in the two worlds w, w', i.e., $d_H(w, w') = |Diff(w, w')|$. The choice of the propositional Hamming distance is by far the most frequent one in the Knowledge Representation community.

The *drastic* (or *Dirac*) distance d_δ is defined by $d_\delta(w, w') = \begin{cases} 0 \text{ if } w = w' \\ 1 \text{ if } w \neq w' \end{cases}$

2.2 Logical Representation of Preference: Brief Overview

A common way for an agent of specifying its preferences consists in listing a set of goals, each consisting of a propositional formula, and possibly some extra information such as weights, priorities, contexts or distances. How the preference relation or the utility function is determined from the set of goals depends on how these goals are understood. We list here (by increasing complexity) the most common constructions of preference structures from logical specifications. In the sequel, the G_i's and the C_i's denote propositional formulas, the α_i's denote numbers in a numerical scale (for example $\mathbb{N}$, or $\mathbb{R}$, or $[0, 1]$, or a finite scale etc.), and the d_i's denote weak distances. GB is a "goal base" (by analogy with "knowledge base") and u_{GB} (resp. $\geq_{GB}$) denotes the utility function (resp. the preference relation) induced by GB.

1. $GB = \{G_1, ..., G_n\}$ and $u_{GB}(w) = \begin{cases} 1 \text{ if } w \models G_1 \wedge \ldots \wedge G_n \\ 0 \text{ otherwise} \end{cases}$. This very rough representation assumption (the preference structure – a binary utility – cannot be more elementary) considers crisp goals, interpreted conjunctively and in a dependent way (i.e., the violation of any of the goals cannot be compensated by the satisfaction of another one).
2. $GB = \{G_1, ..., G_n\}$ and $u_{GB}(w) = |\{i | w \models G_i\}|$. This refinement of 1 considers crisp but independent goals and allows for compensation.
3. $GB = \{G_1, ..., G_n\}$ and $w \geq_{GB} w'$ if and only if $\{i | w \models G_i\} \supseteq \{i | w' \models G_i\}$. This (partial) preorder on worlds is nothing but the Pareto ordering.
4. $GB = \langle\{G_1, ..., G_n\}, >\rangle$ where $>$ is a priority order on $\{1, ..., n\}$; $\geq_{GB}$ is then computed in a way extending (2) and (3) so as to take the priority relation between goals into account. See for instance [5].
5. $GB = \{\langle\alpha_1, G_1\rangle, ..., \langle\alpha_n, G_n\rangle\}$ and

$$u_{GB}(w) = F_1(F_2(\{\alpha_i | w \models G_i\}, F_3(\{\alpha_j | w \models \neg G_j\}))$$

i.e., $u_{GB}(w)$ is a function of the weights of the goals satisfied by w and of the weights of the goals violated by w. When only relative utilities (i.e., differences of utilities between worlds) are important (which is usually the case), we can make the simplifying assumption that only the violated goals count(*negative* representation of preference [21] [12])[2], which leads to this simplified expression: $u_{GB}(w) = F(\{\alpha_i | w \models \neg G_i\})$. F should of course satisfy some specific properties (see [13]).
6. $GB = \{C_1 : G_1, ..., C_n : G_n\}$. C_i is the *context* of G_i (conditional goals).
7. $GB = \langle\{G_1, ..., G_n\}, d\rangle$ where d is a weak distance; and

$$u_{GB}(w) = F(d(w, G_1), ..., d(w, G_n))$$

where F is non-increasing in each of its arguments. The intuition is that ideally, the world w satisfies G, and when it is not the case, then the further

[2] Or, symetrically, that only the satisfied goals count (*positive* representation of preference).

to G the world w is, the less preferred it is w.r.t. the satisfaction of G. In a more general framework, the distances do not have to be constant, *i.e.*, we may start with $GB = \{\langle d_1, G_1\rangle, ..., \langle d_n, G_n\rangle\}$ and induce u by $u_{GB}(w) = F(d_1(w, G_1), ..., d_n(w, G_n))$.

In this paper we focus on items 5 (weighted logics) and 7 (distance-based logics). It has been shown in [13] that these two representation languages can be translated from one to each other (under some assumptions). Here we go a bit further and propose a representation language which integrate both, namely, where preference items are triples composed of a weight, a distance and a goal.

3 An Integrated Framework for the Logical Representation of Weighted and Distance-Graded Goals

In the sequel, we assume that individual goals are specified together with a weight and/or a distance.

Definition 2 *A* WD goal base *is a finite collection of triples* $GB = \{\langle \alpha_1, d_1, G_1\rangle,$ $..., \langle \alpha_n, d_n, G_n\rangle\}$ *where, for each* i, $\alpha_i \in \mathbb{N}$, d_i *is a weak propositional distance and* G_i *is a consistent propositional formula.*

We have now to choose how a preference structure should be induced from G. The preference structure will be numerical, i.e., a utility function. By convention, we will work with disutility functions on $\mathbb{N}$ (or equivalently, utility functions on $\mathbb{Z}^-$): elementary disutilities, or *penalties*, are induced by violation of goals, and ideal worlds, if any, have a null disutility, and therefore satisfy all goals. A disutility function will be denoted by $disu$, with the implicit assumption $disu(w) = -u(w)$.

Definition 3 *Let* $GB = \{\langle \alpha_1, d_1, G_1\rangle, ..., \langle \alpha_n, d_n, G_n\rangle\}$ *be a WD goal base. Then*

$$disu_{GB}(w) = F(H(\alpha_1, d(w, G_1)), ..., (H(\alpha_n, d(w, G_n))$$

where

- F *is a commutative, associative, non-decreasing operator on* $\mathbb{N}$ *, and has* 0 *as neutral element*[3]*;*
- $H : \mathbb{N} \times \mathbb{N} \rightarrow \mathbb{N}$ *is non-decreasing in both arguments and satisfies* $H(\alpha, x) = 0 \Leftrightarrow x = 0$.

Common choices for F are max and + (see [13], especially for an explanation why associativity is required). The operator H, whose role is to aggregate the weight of the goal (reflecting its importance) with the dissatisfaction stemming

[3] Note that F has the properties of *triangular conorms*, except that it is defined on $\mathbb{N}$ instead of $[0, 1]$.

from the distance to the goal, does not have to be commutative. Monotonicity is natural; the second property means that there is no penalty only if the goal is fully satisfied, i.e., w satisfies it. We consider three possible choices for H, which differ in their interpretation of the weight of a goal:

1. $H_1(\alpha, x) = \min(\alpha, x)$: α is an upper bound of the penalty; once the distance to the goal is at least α, the goal is considered as completely violated: no distinction is made between a distance of α and a larger distance.
2. $H_2(\alpha, x) = \begin{cases} 0 & \text{if } x = 0 \\ \alpha + x - 1 & \text{if } x > 0 \end{cases}$: α is the minimal penalty for a violation (even small) of the goal; after this penalty is taken into account, penalty grows linearly with distance to the goal;
3. $H_3(\alpha, x) = \alpha.x$: α determines the rate of growth of the disutility function.

The choice of H may be further guided by the following consideration: we would like our framework to degenerate (a) into the framework of weighted logics when all distances are taken to be the drastic distance δ and (b) into the framework of distance-based logics when all weights are 1. This imposes the further constraints (a) $H(\alpha, 1) = \alpha$ and (b) $H(1, x) = x$, and therefores excludes H_1. *From now on we assume (unless explicitly stated) that* $H \in \{H_2, H_3\}$.

The simultaneous presence of both weights and distances makes the framework somewhat complex. Furthermore, when GB is a simple base of weighted goals (without distances) $GB = \{\langle \alpha_1, G_1 \rangle, ..., \langle \alpha_n, G_n \rangle\}$, we know that $disu_{GB}(w)$ can be computed in polynomial time, whereas it is not the case with distance-based goals, because in general $d(w, G_i)$ cannot be computed in polynomial time.

In the sequel we show that a WD goal base can be translated into a base of weighted goals, while preserving the disutility function. This transformation is generally not polynomial; however, in some cases it is, especially when goals are expressed throw DNF formulas.

For this we start by giving a translation from distance-based weighted goals to standard weighted goals (thus getting rid of distances). We first need the following definitions of a *discs [13] and circles around a formula:*

Definition 4 *Let* $\varphi \in \mathcal{L}$, d *a weak distance and* $i \in IN$. *The* disc of radius i around G *is the formula (unique up to logical equivalence)* $D(G, i, d)$ *such that* $Mod(D(G, i, d)) = \{w \in \Omega | d(w, G) \leq i\}$ *and the* circle of radius i around G *is the formula (unique up to logical equivalence)* $C(G, i, d)$ *such that* $Mod(C(G, i, d)) = \{w \in \Omega | d(w, G) = i\}$

Clearly, we have (1) $D(G, 0, d) \equiv C(G, 0, d) \equiv G$; (2) $D(G, i, d) \models D(G, i+1, d)$; (3) $D(G, dmax, d) \equiv \top$, where $dmax = \max_{w, w' \in \Omega} d(w, w')$ (the latter quantity is defined because Ω is finite); (4) $D(G_1 \vee ... \vee G_p, k, d) \equiv D(G_1, k, d) \vee \ldots \vee D(G_n, k, d)$; (5) $C(G, i, d) \equiv D(G, i, d) \wedge \neg D(G, i-1, d)$. (6) $D(G, i, d) \equiv C(G, 0, d) \vee ... \vee C(G, i, d)$.

Proposition 1 *Let* $GB = \{\langle \alpha, d, G \rangle\}$ *be a singleton goal base, and let* $\Phi_1(GB)$, $\Phi_2(GB)$ *and* $\Phi_3(GB)$ *be the three distance-free goal bases defined as follows.*

- *let* $\Phi_1(GB) = \{\langle 1, \neg C(G,1,d)\rangle, \langle 2, \neg C(G,2,d)\rangle, \ldots, \langle \alpha, \neg C(G,\alpha,d)\rangle\}$. *If* $H = H_1$ *then* $disu_{GB} = disu_{\Phi_1(GB)}$.
- *let* $\Phi_2(GB) = \{\langle \alpha, \neg C(G,1,d)\rangle, \langle \alpha+1, \neg C(G,2,d)\rangle, \ldots, \langle \alpha + dmax, \neg C(G,\alpha,dmax)\rangle\}$. *If* $H = H_2$ *then* $disu_{GB} = disu_{\Phi_2(GB)}$.
- *let* $\Phi_3(GB) = \{\langle \alpha, \neg C(G,1,d)\rangle, \langle 2\alpha, \neg C(G,2,d)\rangle, \ldots, \langle dmax.\alpha, \neg C(G,dmax,d)\rangle\}$. *If* $H = H_3$ *then* $disu_{GB} = disu_{\Phi_3(GB)}$.

Thus, for $H \in \{H_1, H_2, H_3\}$, a WD goal base can be rewritten equivalently into a distance-free goal base. Unfortunately, there is no guarantee that the size of $\Phi_1(GB), \Phi_2(GB), \Phi_3(GB)$ should be polynomial, because in general $C(G,i,d)$ has a size exponential in $|G|$. However, if G is under DNF and $d = d_H$ then we have the following result:

Proposition 2 *[13]*
Let $d = d_H$ *and* $G = \gamma_1 \vee \ldots \vee \gamma_p$ *be a propositional formula under DNF, where, for each* i, $\gamma_i = l_1^i \wedge l_2^i \wedge \ldots \wedge l_{q_i}^i$ *is a consistent conjunction of literals. Then*

$$D(G,k,d_H) = \bigvee_{i=1\ldots p} \left(\bigvee_{I \subseteq \{1,\ldots,q_i\}, |I| = q_i - k} \left(\bigwedge_{i \in I} l_i \right) \right)$$

Note that, written this way, $D(G,k,d_H)$ still has an exponential size. However, it *does not have to be written this way*: enriching the syntax of propositional logic with so-called cardinality-formulas [4], the size of $D(G,k,d_H)$ is linear in the size of G. Therefore, if G is initially under DNF and d is taken to be the Hamming distance, computing $D(G,k,d_H)$, and therefore, computing $DC(G,k,d_H)$ and $d(w,G)$, can all be done in polynomial time. Moreover we get easily an upper bound of the $d_H(w,G)$ since $D(G,k,d_H) = \top$ as soon as k reaches the number of literals of the longest of the γ_i's, i.e. as soon as $k \geq \max_i |\gamma_i|$.

Unfortunately, what we gain by using the Hamming distance is lost in expressivity and sensitivity to the choice of the propositional symbols. In the following Section we discuss briefly the cons of the Hamming distance and propose a much more general family of weak distances (containing d_H) retaining this friendly computational properties of the Hamming distance.

4 Deconstructing Hamming: Topic-Decomposable and Choquet-Decomposable Weak Distances

4.1 Against Hamming

It is surprising to see how popular the Hamming distance is in the Knowledge Representation community[4] – not only it is widely used, but it is almost the only serious propositional distance considered. However, there are good reasons not to

[4] In this research community it is sometimes called Dalal's distance after it was used in [6] for belief revision; it was used as well by Forbus [9] for belief update, and by many authors for belief merging [15] [16] [10] [2].

choose it. The Hamming distance assumes not only that propositional symbols are *equally relevant* to determining a distance between worlds (which can be fixed easily by assigning weights to propositional symbols), but also that they are *independent from each other* and that *nothing else is relevant* to the determination of the distance between worlds. These assumptions are extremely compelling and give the Hamming distance very little flexibility. The more serious of its drawbacks is its extreme *sensitivity to the syntax*, or more precisely, to the choice of the propositional language. It is obvious that there is an infinity of possible choices for the set of propositional symbols to be used for representing a certain piece of knowledge. Now, the point with the Hamming distance is that it is extremely sensitive to this choice. Let us consider an example. Assume that we talk about a variable X which can take any integer value between 0 and 7. The most efficient propositional encoding of this variable uses 3 propositional variables x_1, x_2, x_3 being respectively the 1st, 2nd and 3rd bit of the binary representation of the value of X: for instance, $X = 6$ is represented by the propositional formula $x_1 \wedge x_2 \wedge \neg x_3$. The Hamming distance is extremely counterintuitive here: let w_1, w_2 and w_3 be three worlds where X takes respectively the values 3, 4 and 7, all other things being equal. Then $d_H(w_1, w_2) = 3$ while $d_H(w_1, w_3) = 1$. The introduction of weights on the symbols do not help much ($d_H(w_1, w_2)$ will be still be maximal). The less efficient choice of representing X with 8 propositional variables $X = 0$, ..., $X = 7$ is not better since it gives $d_H(w_1, w_2) = d_H(w_1, w_3) = 1$. Finding a representation such that $d_H(w, w') = |v - v'|$ if w and w' differ only in the values v and v' they assign to X is far from being obvious[5].

In the rest of this Section we propose much more general classes of distances containing the Hamming distance and its weighted variants, and which retain as much as possible its computationally friendly properties discussed in Section 3.

4.2 Topic-Decomposable Weak Distances

It is often the case that the set of propositional variables intuitively consists of the union of sets of variables, each of which corresponds to a specific *topic* (see e.g., [17]). It is not necessary to require that topics should be disjoint.

Definition 5 *Let $\mathcal{T} = \{T_1, ..., T_p\}$ be a collection of nonempty subsets of PS* (topics) *such that $\bigcup_i T_i = PS$. A weak distance d is $\mathcal{T}$-decomposable if and only if there exist p weak distances $d_1 : 2^{T_1} \times 2^{T_1} \rightarrow I\!N, \ldots, d_p : 2^{T_p} \times 2^{T_p} \rightarrow I\!N$, and an aggregation function $F : I\!N^p \rightarrow I\!N$, such that for all $w, w' \in \Omega$,*

$$d(w, w') = F(d_1(w^{\downarrow T_1}, w'^{\downarrow T_1}), \ldots, d_p(w^{\downarrow T_p}, w'^{\downarrow T_p}))$$

A topic can be considered as a criterion, hence for the choice of the function F it is relevant to make use of aggregation functions from the MCDM literature.

The simplest possible topic is a singleton and the "most" decomposable distances are those which are decomposable with respect to the set of singletons.

[5] Nevertheless, it is possible, but this representation is not intuitive at all.

Definition 6 *a weak distance d is* symbol-decomposable *if and only if (1) it is $\mathcal{ST}$-decomposable where $\mathcal{ST} = \{\{s_1\}, \{s_2\}, \ldots, \{s_n\}\}$ and (2) for each $i \in 1 \ldots n$, $d_i((s_i),(s_i)) = d_i((\neg s_i),(\neg s_i)) = 0$ and $d_i((s_i),(\neg s_i)) = 1$.*

More generally, a topic may be the set of propositional symbols used for encoding the possible values of a non-binary variable. For instance, if the domain of variable v is $\{1,2,3\}$ then we may use the propositional symbols $\{v=1, v=2, v=3\}$[6] together with the integrity constraint stating that one and only one among $v=1, v=2, v=3$ is true[7]. Still more generally, a topic may concern several variables and thus be the union of propositional symbols they generate.

In the definition of a topic-decomposable distance, nothing was said on the aggregation function F. Clearly, how d_1,...,d_p should be aggregated into d is a typical issue of multicriteria decision making. In this paper we focus on the particular class of topic-decomposable distances for which the aggregation function is a *Choquet integral* [19][18].

4.3 Choquet-Decomposable Weak Distances

Definition 7 (fuzzy measures) *A (unnormalized, integer-valued)* fuzzy measure *on $\mathcal{T} = \{T_1, ..., T_p\}$ is a mapping $\mu : 2^{\mathcal{T}} \rightarrow I\!N$ such that (1) $\mu(\emptyset) = 0$; (2) for any subsets A and B of $\mathcal{T}$, $A \subseteq B$ implies $\mu(A) \leq \mu(B)$*[8]. *A fuzzy measure is said* strictly positive *if and only if for all $X \subseteq \mathcal{T}$, $X \neq \emptyset$ implies $\mu(X) > 0$.*

Definition 8 (Choquet integrals) *[19][18]Let μ be a fuzzy measure on $2^{\mathcal{T}}$ and $\boldsymbol{x} = (x_1, ..., x_p)$ a vector of real numbers (with $p = |\mathcal{T}|$). Let σ be any permutation of $\{1, ..., p\}$ such that $x_{\sigma(1)} \leq ... \leq x_{\sigma(p)}$. The* Choquet integral *of $(x_1, ..., x_p)$ with respect to μ is defined as*

$$C_\mu(x_1, ..., x_p) = \sum_{i=1}^{p} (\mu(\{\sigma(i), ..., \sigma(p)\}) - \mu(\{\sigma(i+1), ..., \sigma(p)\}).x_{\sigma(i)}$$

Definition 9 *A weak distance d is a $\mathcal{T}$-*Choquet-decomposable *if and only if it is $\mathcal{T}$-decomposable and the associated aggregation function F is a Choquet integral.*

In other terms, a Choquet-decomposable weak distance d is defined by the collection of elementary weak distances d_i and a fuzzy measure $\mu : 2^{\mathcal{T}} \rightarrow [0,1]$ such that for any w, w', we have $d(w,w') = C_\mu(d_1(w,w'), ..., d_p(w,w'))$.

[6] Note that in spite of the symbol = appearing in them, they are atomic propositional symbols.

[7] Note that in practice, it would be more efficient to encode a 3-valued variable with two propositional symbols only: it is is well-known that a variable with a value domain of cardinality k requires $\lceil \ln_2(k) \rceil$, i.e., the upper integer part of the logarithm in base 2 of k.

[8] Usually fuzzy measures are also require to satisfy $\mu(\mathcal{T}) = 1$; however this requirement has little impact.

Note that if for all i, d_i is a weak distance on T_i, then it is not necessarily the case that the aggregated distance d is still a weak distance, because it may fail to be separable. The necessary and sufficient condition is that any nonempty subset of T has a non-null measure:

Proposition 3 *Let d_1, ..., d_p be weak distances on T_1, ..., T_p respectively, μ a fuzzy measure on T and d defined by $d(w, w') = C_\mu(d_1(w, w'), ..., d_p(w, w'))$. Then d is a weak distance if and only if μ is strictly positive.*

The problem of whether the triangular inequality (TI) is transferred from the d_i's to d is more complex. In general, it is not true. A sufficient (but non necessary) condition on μ under which d satisfies (TI) as soon as d_1, ..., d_p do is the following:

$$\forall(x_1, ..., x_p)\forall(y_1, ..., y_p),\ C_\mu(x_1, ..., x_p) + C_\mu(y_1, ..., y_p) \geq C_\mu(x_1 + y_1, ..., x_p + y_p)$$

We now focus on a particularly interesting class of weak distances.

4.4 SC-Decomposable Weak Distances

Intuitively, d is SC-decomposable iff it both symbol-decomposable and Choquet-decomposable.

Definition 10 *A weak distance d is a* SC-decomposable *if and only if (1) it is symbol-decomposable and (2) the associated aggregation function F is a Choquet integral.*

These weak distances can easily be characterized:

Proposition 4 *d is SC-decomposable if and only if there exists a fuzzy measure μ such that $d(w, w') = \mu(Diff(w, w'))$.*

From now on we denote by d_μ the STC-decomposable function defined by $d(w, w') = \mu(Diff(w, w'))$.

A special case of interest is when μ is *additive*. In this case we have $d_\mu(w, w') = \sum_{x_i \in Diff(w,w')} \mu(\{i\})$. Therefore, d_μ is a *weighted Hamming distance*. If furthermore we have $\mu(\{i\}) = \mu(\{j\}) = 1$ for all i, j, then $d_\mu(w, w') = |Diff(w, w')|$, i.e., d_μ is the Hamming distance d_H.

This sheds some light of what assumptions are implicitly done when choosing the Hamming distance, namely:

1. symbol-decomposability: criteria or topics are identified with single propositional symbols.
2. 1-additivity: propositional symbols are fully independent.
3. neutrality: propositional symbols have equal importance.

Therefore, the position of the Hamming distance in the set of distances is very similar to the position of the arithmetic mean in the set of aggregation functions: namely, it is central, but the choice of d_H assumes a lot of very strong assumptions without which it is far too arbitrary to be a good choice.

Apart of additive measures, another interesting subclass of measures is the set of measures μ such that $\mu(X)$ depends only on the cardinality of $|X|$. In this case, the Choquet integral associated with μ is an *Ordered Weighted Average* (OWA) [22]. This is equivalent to say that an (integer-valued, unnormalized) OWA is characterized by a vector $\boldsymbol{\alpha} = (\alpha_1, ..., \alpha_p)$[9] such that $C_\mu(x_1, ..., x_p) = \sum_{i=1}^{p} \alpha_i . x_{\sigma(i)}$[10] d_μ is a weak distance if and only if μ is strictly positive, which is equivalent to $\alpha_p > 0$.

The weak distances induced by OWAs include

- the drastic distance d_δ, associated with $\boldsymbol{\alpha} = (0, \ldots, 0, 1)$;
- the Hamming distance d_H, associated with $\boldsymbol{\alpha} = (1, \ldots, 1)$;
- the bounded Hamming distances d_H^k defined by $d_H^k(w, w') = \min(k, d_H(w, w'))$ where $k \in \{1, \ldots, p\}$ (remark that $d_H^1 = d_\delta$ and that $d_H^p = d_H$).

Proposition 5 *Let $d = d_\mu$ and $G = \gamma_1 \vee ... \vee \gamma_p$ be a propositional formula under DNF, where, for each i, $\gamma_i = l_1^i \wedge l_2^i \wedge \ldots \wedge l_{q_i}^i$ is a consistent conjunction of literals. Then*

$$D(G, k, d_\mu) = \bigvee_{i=1\ldots p} \left(\bigvee_{I \subseteq \{1, ..., q_i\}, \mu(T \setminus I) \leq k} \left(\bigwedge_{i \in I} l_i \right) \right)$$

Like discs around the DNF for d_H, $D(G, k, d_\mu)$ should not be explicitly written this way (or else it has an exponential size). Slightly generalizing cardinality-formulas by introducing the syntactical notation $(k, \mu) : \{l_1, ..., l_q\}$ – such a formula is satisfied if $\mu(\{s_1, ..., s_q\}) \leq k$, where s_i is the propositional symbol associated with l_i, $D(G, k, d_\mu)$ can be written with a size linear in the size of G.

5 Conclusion

The contribution of this paper to the logical representation of preference in twofold. First, we proposed a unified framework enabling the representation of weighted goals and distance-labelled goals, extending the approach first proposed in [13]. Second, we criticized the frequent use of the Hamming distance for the representation of preference and proposed a much more general family of distances based on Choquet integrals.

References

1. O. Bailleux, P. Marquis. DISTANCE-SAT : complexity and algorithms.Proceedings of *AAAI'99*, pages 642–647, 1999.

[9] Note that the usual normalization condition $\sum_{i=1}^{p} \alpha_i = 1$ is not required here.

[10] The weights α_i come directly from μ by the following relation: since $\mu(X)$ depends only on $|X|$, let $\mu(X) = f(|X|)$; then $\alpha_p = f(1)$; …; $\alpha_i = f(p - i + 1) - f(p - i)$; …; $\alpha_1 = f(p) - f(p - 1)$.

2. S. Benferhat, D. Dubois, S. Kaci and H. Prade. Encoding information fusion in possibilistic logic: a general framework for rational syntactic merging. *Proceedings of ECAI'2000*,3-7.
3. I. Bloch and J. Lang. Towards mathematical morpho-logics. *Proceedings of IPMU'2000.*
4. B. Benhamou, L. Sais and P. Siegel. Two proof procedures for a cardinality-based language in propositional calculus. *Proceedings of STACS'94.*
5. C. Cayrol. Un modèle logique pour le raisonnement révisable (in French). *Revue d'Intelligence Artificielle* 6, 255-284, *Hermès*, 1992.
6. M. Dalal. Investigations into a theory of knowledge base revision: preliminary report. Proceedings of *AAAI'88*, p. 475-479, 1988.
7. D. Dubois, J. Lang and H. Prade. Possibilistic logic. *Handbook of Logic in Artificial Intelligence and Logic Programming* (D.M. Gabbay, C.J. Hogger, J.A. Robinson, eds.), Vol. 3, 439-513, Oxford University Press. 1994.
8. F. Dupin de Saint-Cyr, J. Lang and T. Schiex., Penalty logic and its link with Dempster-Shafer theory, *UAI'94*, 1994.
9. K. D. Forbus. Introducing actions into qualitative simulation. *Proc. IJCAI'89*, 1273-1278.
10. S. Konieczny, R. Pino-Pérez, On the logic of merging. *Proceedings of KR'98*, 488-498, 1998.
11. S. Konieczny, R. Pino-Pérez. Merging with integrity constraints. *Proceedings of EC-SQARU'99*, 233-244, Lecture Notes in Artificial Intelligence 1638, Springer Verlag, 1999.
12. C. Lafage. *Représentation logique de préférences. Application à la décision de groupe.* Thèse de l'Unievsrté Paul Sabatier, Toulouse, 2001.
13. C. Lafage, J. Lang. Logical representation of preferences for group decision making. *Proceedings of KR'2000*, 457-468, 2000.
14. J.Lang. Conditional desires and utilities - an alternative approach to qualitative decision theory. *Proceedings of ECAI'96*, 318–322, 1996.
15. P. Liberatore and M. Schaerf. Arbitration: a commutative operator for belief revision. *Proceedings of the World Conference on the Fundamentals of Artificial Research* , 1995, 217-228.
16. J. Lin. Integration of weighted knowledge bases. *Artificial Intelligence* 83 (1996), 363-378.
17. P. Marquis and N. Porquet. Decomposing propositional knowledge bases through topics (extended abstract). Personal communication.
18. T. Murofushi and M. Sugeno. An interpretation of fuzzy measures and the Choquet integral as an integral with respect to a fuzzy measure, *Fuzzy Sets and Systems* 29 (1989), 201-227.
19. D. Schmeidler. Integral representation without additivity. *Proc. Americ. Math. Soc.* 97 (1986), 255-261.
20. S.-W. Tan and J. Pearl, Specification and evaluation of preferences for planning under uncertainty, *Proc. KR'94.*
21. L. van der Torre and E. Weydert. Parameters for utilitarian desires in a qualitative decision theory, *Applied Intelligence*, 2001, to appear.
22. R.R. Yager, On ordered weighted averaging aggregation operators in multi-criteria decision making. *IEEE Transactions on Systems, Man and Cybernetics* 18, p.183-190, 1988.

Value Iteration over Belief Subspace

Weihong Zhang

Department of Computer Science
Hong Kong University of Science & Technology
Clear Water Bay, Kowloon, Hong Kong, China
wzhang@cs.ust.hk

Abstract. Partially Observable Markov Decision Processes (POMDPs) provide an elegant framework for AI planning tasks with uncertainties. Value iteration is a well-known algorithm for solving POMDPs. It is notoriously difficult because at each step it needs to account for every belief state in a continuous space. In this paper, we show that value iteration can be conducted over a subset of belief space. Then, we study a class of POMDPs, namely informative POMDPs, where each observation provides good albeit incomplete information about world states. For informative POMDPs, value iteration can be conducted over a small subset of belief space. This yields two advantages: First, fewer vectors are in need to represent value functions. Second, value iteration can be accelerated. Empirical studies are presented to demonstrate these two advantages.

1 Introduction

Partially Observable Markov Decision Processes (POMDPs) provide a general framework for AI planning problems where effects of actions are nondeterministic and the state of the world is not known with certainty. Unfortunately, solving general POMDPs is computationally intractable(e.g., [12]). Although much recent effort has been devoted to finding efficient algorithms for POMDPs, there is still a significant distance to solve realistic problems.

Value iteration [13] is a standard algorithm for solving POMDP. It conducts a sequence of dynamic programming (DP) updates to improve values for each belief state in belief space. Due to the fact that there are uncountably many belief states, DP updates and hence value iteration are computationally prohibitive in practice.

In this paper, we propose to conduct DP updates and hence value iteration over a subset of belief space. The subset is referred to as *belief subspace* or simply *subspace*. It consists of all possible belief states the agent encounters. As value iteration is conducted over the subspace, each DP update accounts for only belief states in the subspace. The hope is that DP updates over a subset should be more efficient than those over the entire belief space. However, for general POMDPs, it is difficult to represent this subspace and perform implicit DP updates. Furthermore, occasionally the subspace could be as large as the original belief space. In this case, value iteration over subspace actually provides no benefits at all.

We study a class of special POMDPs, namely *informative POMDPs*, where any observation can restrict the world into a small set of states. For informative POMDPs,

S. Benferhat and P. Besnard (Eds.): ECSQARU 2001, LNAI 2143, pp. 60–71, 2001.

the subspace has clear semantics and can be represented in an easy way. Based on the subspace representation, we describe how to conduct implicit value iteration over subspace for informative POMDPs. Moreover, in informative POMDPs, the subspace is expected to be much smaller than the belief space. One expects value iteration over subspace can be more efficient than over belief space.

Informative POMDPs come to be a median ground in terms of informative degree of observations. In one extreme case, unobservable POMDPs assume that observations do not provide any information about world states and can not restrict the world into any range of states(e.g., [11]). In another extreme case, fully observable MDPs assume that an observation restricts the world states into a unique state.

The rest of the paper is organized as follows. In next section, we introduce background knowledge and conventional notations. In Section 3, we develop a procedure for explicitly conducting value iteration over subspace. In Section 4, we discuss problem characteristics of informative POMDPs and problem examples in the literature. In Section 5, we show how the problem characteristics can be exploited. Section 6 reports the experiments on comparing value iteration over subspace and the standard algorithm. Section 7 briefly examines related work. Finally, Section 8 concludes the paper with some future directions.

2 Background

A POMDP is a sequential decision model for an agent who acts in a stochastic environment with only partial knowledge about the states of the world. The environment is described by a set of states $\mathcal{S}$. The agent changes world states by executing one of a finite set of actions $\mathcal{A}$. At each point in time, the world is in one state s. Based on the information it has, the agent chooses and executes an action a. Consequently, it receives an *immediate reward* $r(s,a)$ and the world moves stochastically into another state s'. The *transition probability* is $P(s'|s,a)$. Thereafter, the agent receives an observation z from a finite set $\mathcal{Z}$ of observations randomly. The *observation probability* is $P(z|s',a)$. The process repeats itself.

Information that the agent has about the current state of the world can be summarized by a probability distribution over $\mathcal{S}$ [1]. The probability distribution is called a *belief state* and denoted by b. The set of all possible belief states is called the *belief space* and denoted by $\mathcal{B}$. If the agent observes z after taking action a in belief state b, its next belief state b' is updated as

$$b'(s') = kP(z|s',a)\sum_{s} P(s'|s,a)b(s) \tag{1}$$

where k is a re-normalization constant. Sometimes b' is denoted by $\tau(b,a,z)$.

A *policy* prescribes an action for each possible belief state. In other words, it is a mapping from $\mathcal{B}$ to $\mathcal{A}$. Associated with policy π is its *value function* V^{π}. For each belief state b, $V^{\pi}(b)$ is the expected total discounted reward that the agent receives by following the policy starting from b, i.e. $V^{\pi}(b) = E_{\pi,b}[\sum_{t=0}^{\infty} \lambda^t r_t]$, where r_t is the reward received at time t and λ ($0\leq\lambda < 1$) is the *discount factor*. It is known that there exists a policy π^* such that $V^{\pi^*}(b) \geq V^{\pi}(b)$ for any other policy π and any belief state b. Such a policy is called an *optimal policy*. The value function of an optimal policy is called the *optimal value function*. We denote it by V^*. For any positive number ϵ, a policy π is *ϵ-optimal* if $V^\pi(b) + \epsilon \geq V^*(b)$ for any belief state b.

The *dynamic programming(DP) update operator* T maps a value function V to another value function TV that is defined as follows: for any b in $\mathcal{B}$,

$$TV(b) = \max_a [r(b,a) + \lambda \sum_z P(z|b,a)V(\tau(b,a,z))] \tag{2}$$

where $r(b,a) = \sum_s r(s,a)b(s)$ is the expected immediate reward for taking action a in belief state b.

Value iteration is an algorithm for finding ϵ-optimal value functions. It starts with an initial value function V_0 and iterates using the formula: $V_n = TV_{n-1}$. Because T is a contraction mapping, V_n converges to V^* as n goes to infinity. Value iteration terminates when the *Bellman residual* $\max_b |V_n(b) - V_{n-1}(b)|$ falls below $\epsilon(1-\lambda)/2\lambda$. When it does, the value function $\mathcal{V}_n$ is ϵ-optimal.

Functions over the state space $\mathcal{S}$ are sometimes referred to as *vectors*. A set $\mathcal{V}$ of vectors *represents* a value function f in a subspace $\mathcal{B}'$ of belief states if $f(b) = \max_{\alpha \in \mathcal{V}} \alpha.b$ for any b in $\mathcal{B}'$. The notion $\alpha.b$ means the inner product of α and b. We will sometimes write $f(b)$ as $\mathcal{V}(b)$. A vector in a set is *extraneous in $\mathcal{B}'$* if, after its removal, the set represents that same value function. It is *useful in $\mathcal{B}'$* otherwise. If a value function f is representable by a set of vectors in $\mathcal{B}'$, there is a minimum set that represents f in $\mathcal{B}'$.

A value function that is representable as a set of vectors in the entire belief space is said to be *piecewise linear and convex (PLC)*. It is known that, if the initial value function is PLC, then value functions generated by value iteration are PLC and can be represented by a finite set of vectors [14].

3 Explicit Value Iteration over Subspace

In this section, we discuss the procedure of explicitly conducting value iteration over subspace. First, we study how it is possible to conduct DP updates over subspace. Second, we develop a stopping criterion for value iteration to terminate. Finally, we discuss the potential benefits of conducting value iteration over subspace and why it is difficult to conduct value iteration over subspace.

3.1 DP Updates over Subspace

We are interested in subspaces determined by pairs of actions and observations. To define a subspace, we assume that the agent can start from any belief state, executes a at previous time point and observes z. All possible belief states the agent can reach form a set. The set can be denoted by $\{\tau(b,a,z)|b \in \mathcal{B}\}$. For simplicity, we abuse our notation and denote it by $\tau(\mathcal{B},a,z)$. Obviously, it is a subset of $\mathcal{B}$. Next, we show how to relate this subset to DP updates.

In the right-hand side of DP equation (2), since $\tau(b,a,z)$ must belong to the set $\tau(\mathcal{B},a,z)$ for each $[a,z]$ pair, the notation $V(\tau(.,a,z))$ can be viewed as a value function over the subspace $\tau(\mathcal{B}, a, z)$. To make this explicit, we introduce a concept of *value function over subspace*. We use the notation $V_n^{\tau(\mathcal{B},a,z)}$ to denote a n-step value function over $\tau(\mathcal{B}, a, z)$. It maps any belief state in the subspace into the same value as V_n does.

With this notation, the DP Equation can be rewritten as: for any b in $\mathcal{B}$,

$$V_{n+1}(b) = \max_a \{r(b,a) + \lambda \sum_z P(z|b,a) V_n^{\tau(\mathcal{B},a,z)}(\tau(b,a,z))\}. \tag{3}$$

This equation means that the value function V_{n+1} over $\mathcal{B}$ can be represented by a set of value functions $\{V_n^{\tau(\mathcal{B},a,z)}\}$ over subspaces. If this fact is repetitively applied, we conclude that (1) for any n, in order to represent V_{n+1}, it suffices to maintain a set of value functions over subspaces; (2) in order to represent optimal or near optimal value function, it suffices to maintain a set of value functions over subspaces when n is sufficiently large.

The analysis suggests another way to formulate a DP update over a set of subspaces as follows.

> given a set of value functions $\{V_n^{\tau(\mathcal{B},a,z)}\}$ over subspaces, how to compute another set of value functions $\{V_{n+1}^{\tau(\mathcal{B},a,z)}\}$?

In this formulation, one need not to compute value function over belief space. Instead, one can compute a set of value functions over a set of subspaces.

Collectively, DP update over a set $\{\tau(\mathcal{B}, a, z)\}$ of subspaces can be regarded as that over a single belief subspace. For this purpose, we need to define the single subspace and value function over it.

- The union of subspaces $\cup_{a,z}\tau(\mathcal{B}, a, z)$ for all possible combinations of actions and observations consists of all the belief states the agent can encounter. To ease presentation, we denote this union by $\tau(\mathcal{B}, \mathcal{A}, \mathcal{Z})$. Since each subspace in it is a subset of $\mathcal{B}$, so is $\tau(\mathcal{B}, \mathcal{A}, \mathcal{Z})$.
- Given a set of value functions $\{V_n^{\tau(\mathcal{B},a,z)}\}$, we define value function $V_n^{\tau(\mathcal{B},\mathcal{A},\mathcal{Z})}$ over subspace $\tau(\mathcal{B}, \mathcal{A}, \mathcal{Z})$ as follows: for any b in $\tau(\mathcal{B}, \mathcal{A}, \mathcal{Z})$,

$$V_n^{\tau(\mathcal{B},\mathcal{A},\mathcal{Z})}(b) = V_n^{\tau(\mathcal{B},a,z)}(b) \tag{4}$$

  where $[a, z]$ is a pair such that b is in the set $\tau(\mathcal{B}, a, z)$. In fact, value function $V_n^{\tau(\mathcal{B},\mathcal{A},\mathcal{Z})}$ maps each belief state in $\tau(\mathcal{B}, \mathcal{A}, \mathcal{Z})$ to the same value as V_n.

With these two notations, DP update over subspace $\tau(\mathcal{B}, \mathcal{A}, \mathcal{Z})$ can be formulated as:

> given a value function $V_n^{\tau(\mathcal{B},\mathcal{A},\mathcal{Z})}$, how to compute $V_{n+1}^{\tau(\mathcal{B},\mathcal{A},\mathcal{Z})}$?

Under this formulation, at each iteration one needs to compute a value function over a subspace rather than the entire belief space.

3.2 Stopping Criterion

In value iteration over belief subspace $\tau(\mathcal{B},\mathcal{A},\mathcal{Z})$, since $V_{n+1}^{\tau(\mathcal{B},\mathcal{A},\mathcal{Z})}$ and $V_n^{\tau(\mathcal{B},\mathcal{A},\mathcal{Z})}$ specify the same values for belief states in $\tau(\mathcal{B},\mathcal{A},\mathcal{Z})$ as V_{n+1} and V_n, the Bellman residual between $V_{n+1}^{\tau(\mathcal{B},\mathcal{A},\mathcal{Z})}$ and $V_n^{\tau(\mathcal{B},\mathcal{A},\mathcal{Z})}$ becomes smaller over subspace $\tau(\mathcal{B},\mathcal{A},\mathcal{Z})$ as n increases. Therefore a nature criterion is: when the residual between $V_{n+1}^{\tau(\mathcal{B},\mathcal{A},\mathcal{Z})}$ and $V_n^{\tau(\mathcal{B},\mathcal{A},\mathcal{Z})}$ over $\tau(\mathcal{B},\mathcal{A},\mathcal{Z})$ falls below $\epsilon(1-\lambda)/2\lambda$, value iteration terminates.

When value iteration over subspace terminates, it outputs value function $V_n^{\tau(\mathcal{B},\mathcal{A},\mathcal{Z})}$. It can be used to represent value function V_{n+1} over $\mathcal{B}$ as in (3). Therefore the quality of $V_n^{\tau(\mathcal{B},\mathcal{A},\mathcal{Z})}$ can be measured by that of V_{n+1}. The following theorem gives a condition under which value iteration over subspace generates value functions of good quality. Note that the condition is more restrictive than the aforementioned one.

Theorem 1 *If value iteration over subspace terminates when* $\max_{b\in\tau(\mathcal{B},\mathcal{A},\mathcal{Z})} |V_n^{\tau(\mathcal{B},\mathcal{A},\mathcal{Z})}(b) - V_{n-1}^{\tau(\mathcal{B},\mathcal{A},\mathcal{Z})}(b)| \leq \epsilon(1-\lambda)/(2|\mathcal{Z}|\lambda)$, *value function* V_{n+1} *represented by* $V_n^{\tau(\mathcal{B},\mathcal{A},\mathcal{Z})}$ *is* ϵ*-optimal.* □

3.3 Benefits and Difficulties

In value iteration over subspace, DP update of computing $V_{n+1}^{\tau(\mathcal{B},\mathcal{A},\mathcal{Z})}$ needs to account for a subset $\tau(\mathcal{B},\mathcal{A},\mathcal{Z})$ of $\mathcal{B}$. If the subset $\tau(\mathcal{B},\mathcal{A},\mathcal{Z})$ is much smaller than $\mathcal{B}$, one expects: First, the set representing value function $V_n^{\tau(\mathcal{B},\mathcal{A},\mathcal{Z})}$ consists of much fewer vectors than the set representing V_n. Second, since there are fewer vectors representing $V_n^{\tau(\mathcal{B},\mathcal{A},\mathcal{Z})}$, fewer linear programs need to be solved for computing these vectors and determining their usefulness. This would lead to computational savings.

However, there are several difficulties before implementing these potential advantages for general POMDPs. First, we do not know how to represent subspace $\tau(\mathcal{B},\mathcal{A},\mathcal{Z})$. For now, it is just an abstract notation. Second, the subspace $\tau(\mathcal{B},\mathcal{A},\mathcal{Z})$ could be as large as $\mathcal{B}$ occasionally. In this case, value iteration over it does not provide more benefits than directly conducting standard DP updates.

In this regard, informative POMDPs have nice properties which can be explored. First, the subspaces have a clear representation. Second, the set $\tau(\mathcal{B},\mathcal{A},\mathcal{Z})$ is expected to be much smaller than belief space $\mathcal{B}$.

4 Problem Characteristics

In this section, we describe informative POMDPs and argue that they are suitable in modeling some realistic applications.

4.1 Informative POMDPs

In POMDP, the agent perceives the world via observations. Starting from any state, if the agent executes an action a and receives an observation z, the world states can be categorized into two classes by the observation model: states the agent can reach and states it cannot. Formally, the set of reachable states is $\{s|s \in \mathcal{S} \text{ and } P(z|s,a) > 0\}$. We denote it by $\mathcal{S}_{az}$.

An $[a, z]$ pair is said to be *informative* if the size $|\mathcal{S}_{az}|$ is much smaller than $|\mathcal{S}|$. Intuitively, if the pair $[a, z]$ is informative, after executing a and receiving z, the agent knows that the true world states are restricted into a small set. An observation z is said to be *informative* if $[a, z]$ is informative for every action a giving rise to z. Intuitively, an observation is informative if it always gives the agent an good idea about world states regardless of the action executed at previous time point. A POMDP is said to be *informative* if all observations are informative. In other words, any observation the agent receives always provides a good idea about world states. Since one observation is received at each time point, a POMDP agent always has a good albeit imperfect idea about the world.

4.2 Problem Class

Consider a robot navigation problem illustrated in Figure 1. In the figure, thick lines stand for walls and thin lines for nothing(open). At each time point, the robot reads from four sensors to determine its current locations. Each sensor informs the robot whether there is a wall or nothing along a direction(east, south, west and north). An observation is a string of four letters. For example, at location 2, the observation is `owow` where `o` means nothing and `w` means wall. We note that the same string is received at location 5. Also, the agent receives different strings when it is in any other locations. Accordingly, if the observation is `owow`, the agent knows that its location must be at 2 or 5. The following table summarizes the possible strings and the states they restrict the world into. We note that any observation can restrict the world into at most two locations although the world has ten.

observations	states	observations	states
`owww`	$\{1\}$	`owow`	$\{2, 5\}$
`owoo`	$\{3, 4\}$	`wwow`	$\{6\}$
`wowo`	$\{7, 8\}$	`woww`	$\{9, 10\}$

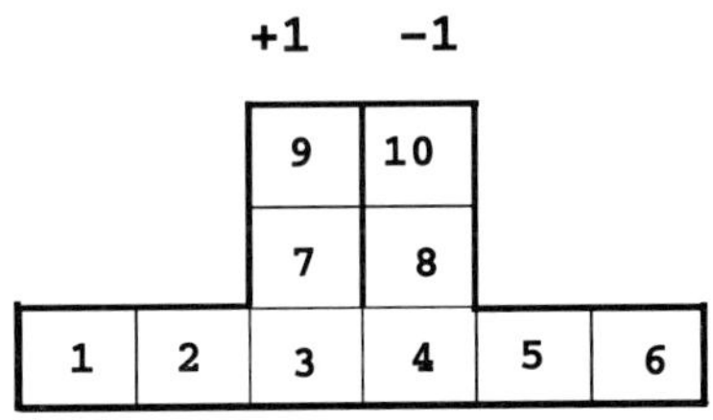

Fig. 1. A maze world

Informative POMDPs are especially suitable for modeling a class of problems. In these problems, a state is described by a number of variables (fluents). Some variables are observable and others are hidden. The possible assignments to observable variables form the observation space. A specific assignment to observable variables restricts the world states into a small range of them. A *slotted Aloha* protocol problem belongs to this class [2,5]. In this problem, a system state consists of the number of backlogged messages and the channel status. The channel status is observable and its possible assignments form the observation space. On the other hand, the system has no access to the number of the backlogged messages. If the maximum number of backlogged messages is set to m and there is n possible channel status, the number of states is $m \cdot n$. A particular assignment on channel status will restrict the system into m states out of $m{\cdot}n$. The similar problem characteristic also exists in a non-stationary environment model proposed for reinforcement learning [7].

5 Exploiting Problem Characteristics

In this section, we show how to carry out value iteration over subspace for informative POMDPs. We start from subspace representation.

5.1 Belief Subspace

A *belief simplex* is specified by a list of *extreme belief states*. The simplex with extreme points $b_1, b_2, ..., b_k$ consists of all belief states of the form $\sum_{i=1}^{k} \lambda_i b_i$ where $\lambda_i \geq 0$ and $\sum_{i=1}^{k} \lambda_i = 1$.

To reveal the relation between belief states in subspace $\tau(\mathcal{B}, a, z)$ and the set $\mathcal{S}_{az}$ for an $[a, z]$ pair, we define another belief subspace:

$$\{b| \sum_{s \in \mathcal{S}_{az}} b(s) = 1.0,\ \forall s \in \mathcal{S}_{az}, b(s) \geq 0\}. \tag{5}$$

It can be proven that for any b and $[a, z]$ pair, $\tau(b, a, z)$ must be in the above set. Due to this, from now on we abuse the notation $\tau(\mathcal{B}, a, z)$ to denote the above set [1]. It is easy to see that $\tau(\mathcal{B}, a, z)$ is a simplex in which each extreme point has probability mass on one state. The union $\tau(\mathcal{B}, \mathcal{A}, \mathcal{Z})$ of these simplexes consists of all possible belief states the agent can encounter.

One example on belief space and subspaces is shown in Figure 2. A POMDP has four states and four observations. Its belief space is the tetrahedron ABCD where A, B, C and D are extreme belief states. For simplicity, we also use these letters to refer to states. Suppose that $\mathcal{S}_{az}$ sets are independent of the actions. More specifically, $\mathcal{S}_{z_0} = \{A, B, C\}$, $\mathcal{S}_{z_1} = \{A, B, D\}$, $\mathcal{S}_{z_2} = \{A, C, D\}$, and $\mathcal{S}_{z_3} = \{B, C, D\}$. In this POMDP, belief simplexes are four facets ABC, ABD, ACD and BCD and belief subspace $\tau(\mathcal{B}, \mathcal{A}, \mathcal{Z})$ is the surface of the tetrahedron. We also note that the subspace $\tau(\mathcal{B}, \mathcal{A}, \mathcal{Z})$ is much smaller than $\mathcal{B}$ in size.

[1] As a matter of fact, $\tau(\mathcal{B}, a, z)$ is a subset of the set defined in (5). We mention this here but do not discuss it further.

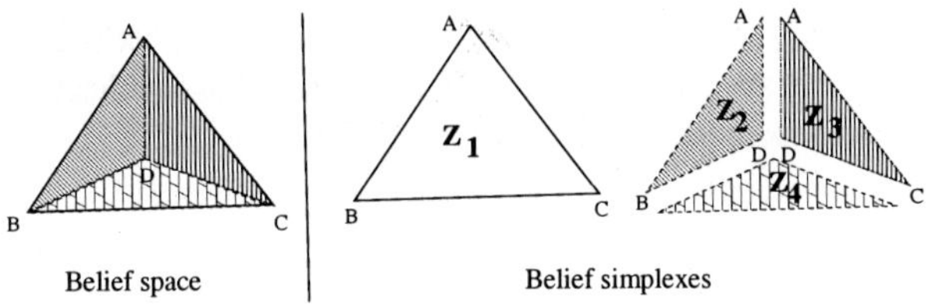

Fig. 2. Belief space, belief simplexes and belief subspace

5.2 Value Functions over Subspaces

Like value functions over $\mathcal{B}$, value functions over simplexes preserve the PLC property and can be represented by a set of vectors. For convenience, we use the notation $\mathcal{V}_n^{\tau(\mathcal{B},a,z)}$ to refer to the representing set of $V_n^{\tau(\mathcal{B},a,z)}$. In informative POMDPs, each vector in the set $\mathcal{V}_n^{\tau(\mathcal{B},a,z)}$ can be $|\mathcal{S}_{az}|$-dimensional because any belief state in $\tau(\mathcal{B},a,z)$ has zero beliefs for states outside the set $\mathcal{S}_{az}$.

Given a collection $\{\mathcal{V}_n^{\tau(\mathcal{B},a,z)}\}$ in which each set $\mathcal{V}_n^{\tau(\mathcal{B},a,z)}$ is associated with an underlying states set $\mathcal{S}_{az}$, we define a value function $\mathcal{V}_n^{\tau(\mathcal{B},\mathcal{A},\mathcal{Z})}$ over subspace $\tau(\mathcal{B},\mathcal{A},\mathcal{Z})$ as follows: for any b in $\tau(\mathcal{B},\mathcal{A},\mathcal{Z})$,

$$\mathcal{V}_n^{\tau(\mathcal{B},\mathcal{A},\mathcal{Z})}(b) = \mathcal{V}_n^{\tau(\mathcal{B},a,z)}(b) \tag{6}$$

where $[a,z]$ is a pair such that $b \in \tau(\mathcal{B},a,z)$. The set $\mathcal{V}_n^{\tau(\mathcal{B},\mathcal{A},\mathcal{Z})}$ can be regarded as a pool of sets over simplexes. When it needs to determine a value for a belief state, it (1) identifies a simplex containing the belief state and (2) computes the value using the corresponding set of vectors. The set $\mathcal{V}_n^{\tau(\mathcal{B},\mathcal{A},\mathcal{Z})}$ represents value function $V_n^{\tau(\mathcal{B},\mathcal{A},\mathcal{Z})}$.[2]

5.3 DP Update over Subspace

In this subsection, we show how to conduct implicit DP update over belief subspace. The problem is cast as: given a set $\mathcal{V}_n^{\tau(\mathcal{B},\mathcal{A},\mathcal{Z})}$ representing value function $V_n^{\tau(\mathcal{B},\mathcal{A},\mathcal{Z})}$ over subspace $\tau(\mathcal{B},\mathcal{A},\mathcal{Z})$, how to compute a set $\mathcal{V}_{n+1}^{\tau(\mathcal{B},\mathcal{A},\mathcal{Z})}$?

To compute the set $\mathcal{V}_{n+1}^{\tau(\mathcal{B},\mathcal{A},\mathcal{Z})}$, we construct one set $\mathcal{V}_{n+1}^{\tau(\mathcal{B},a',z')}$ for any possible pair $[a',z']$. Before doing so, we recall how DP update over belief space constructs a vector in set $T\mathcal{V}_n$. It is known that each vector in $\mathcal{V}_{n+1}$ can be defined by a pair of action and a mapping from the set of observations to the set $\mathcal{V}_n$. Let us denote the action by a and the mapping by δ. For an observation z, we use δ_z to denote the mapped vector in $\mathcal{V}_n$. Given an action a and a mapping δ, the vector, denoted by $\beta_{a,\delta}$, is defined as follows: for each s in $\mathcal{S}$,

$$\beta_{a,\delta}(s) = r(s,a) + \lambda \sum_z \sum_{s'} P(s'|s,a)P(z|s',a)\delta_z(s').$$

[2] Although we refer to $\mathcal{V}_n^{\tau(\mathcal{B},\mathcal{A},\mathcal{Z})}$ as a set, it can not be understood as $\cup_{az}\mathcal{V}_n^{\tau(\mathcal{B},a,z)}$. This union induces a different value function from (6).

By enumerating all possible combinations of actions and mappings, one can define different vectors. All these vectors form a set $\mathcal{V}_{n+1}$, i.e., $\{\beta_{a,\delta}|a \in \mathcal{A}, \delta : \mathcal{Z} \to \mathcal{V}_n\}$. It turns out that this set represents value function V_{n+1}.

We move forward to define a vector in $\mathcal{V}_{n+1}^{\tau(\mathcal{B},a',z')}$ given the set $\mathcal{V}_n^{\tau(\mathcal{B},\mathcal{A},\mathcal{Z})}$ represented as a pool of sets $\{\mathcal{V}_n^{\tau(\mathcal{B},a,z)}\}$ where vectors in set $\mathcal{V}_n^{\tau(\mathcal{B},a,z)}$ are $|\mathcal{S}_{az}|$-dimensional. Similar to the case in DP update $T\mathcal{V}_n$, a vector in set $\mathcal{V}_{n+1}^{\tau(\mathcal{B},a',z')}$ can be defined by a pair of action a and a mapping δ but with two important modifications. First, the mapping δ is from set of observations to the set $\mathcal{V}_n^{\tau(\mathcal{B},\mathcal{A},\mathcal{Z})}$. Moreover, for an observation z, δ_z is a vector in $\mathcal{V}_n^{\tau(\mathcal{B},a,z)}$. Second, the vector only need to be defined over the set $\mathcal{S}_{a'z'}$ because the beliefs are other states are known to be zero. To be precise, given a pair $[a', z']$, an action a and a mapping δ, a vector, denoted by $\beta_{a,\delta}$, can be defined as follows: for each s in $\mathcal{S}_{a'z'}$,

$$\beta_{a,\delta}(s) = r(s,a) + \lambda \sum_z \sum_{s' \in \mathcal{S}_{az}} P(s'|s,a)P(z|s',a)\delta_z(s').$$

If we enumerate all possible combinations of actions and mappings above, we can define various vectors. These vectors form a set

$$\{\beta_{a,\delta}|a \in \mathcal{A}, \delta : \mathcal{Z} \to \mathcal{V}_n^{\tau(\mathcal{B},\mathcal{A},\mathcal{Z})} \ \& \ \forall z, \delta_z \in \mathcal{V}_n^{\tau(\mathcal{B},a,z)}\}.$$

The set is denoted by $\mathcal{V}_{n+1}^{\tau(\mathcal{B},a',z')}$. Note that vectors in the set are $|\mathcal{S}_{a'z'}|$-dimensional. It can be proved that the set represents value function $V_{n+1}^{\tau(\mathcal{B},a',z')}$.

Proposition 1 *For any* $b \in \tau(\mathcal{B}, a, z)$, $\mathcal{V}_{n+1}^{\tau(\mathcal{B},a,z)}(b) = V_{n+1}(b)$. □

For now, we are able to construct a set $\mathcal{V}_{n+1}^{\tau(\mathcal{B},a,z)}$ for a pair $[a, z]$. A complete DP update over $\tau(\mathcal{B}, \mathcal{A}, \mathcal{Z})$ needs to construct such sets for all possible pairs of actions and observations. After these sets are constructed, they are pooled together to form a set $\mathcal{V}_{n+1}^{\tau(\mathcal{B},\mathcal{A},\mathcal{Z})}$. It introduces a value function as defined in (6).

Theorem 2 *For any* $b \in \tau(\mathcal{B}, \mathcal{A}, \mathcal{Z})$, $\mathcal{V}_{n+1}^{\tau(\mathcal{B},\mathcal{A},\mathcal{Z})}(b) = V_{n+1}(b)$. □

It is worthwhile mentioning that DP update often computes minimal representing sets in size. The set $\mathcal{V}_{n+1}^{\tau(\mathcal{B},\mathcal{A},\mathcal{Z})}$ is said to be *minimal* if each $\mathcal{V}_{n+1}^{\tau(\mathcal{B},a,z)}$ is minimal. Given a set $\mathcal{V}_{n+1}^{\tau(\mathcal{B},a,z)}$, its minimal set can be obtained by using normal prune procedure.

5.4 Complexity Analysis

DP update $T\mathcal{V}_n$ improves values for belief space $\mathcal{B}$, while DP update $\mathcal{V}_{n+1}^{\tau(\mathcal{B},\mathcal{A},\mathcal{Z})}$ from $\mathcal{V}_n^{\tau(\mathcal{B},\mathcal{A},\mathcal{Z})}$ improves values for belief subspace $\tau(\mathcal{B}, \mathcal{A}, \mathcal{Z})$. Since the subspace is much smaller than $\mathcal{B}$ in an informative POMDP, one expects:(1)fewer vectors are in need to represent a value function over a subspace;(2)since keeping useful vectors needs solve linear programs, this would lead to computational gains in time cost. Our experimental studies have confirmed these two expectations.

5.5 Value Iteration over Belief Subspace

Value iteration over subspace starts with a value function $\mathcal{V}_0^{\tau(\mathcal{B},\mathcal{A},\mathcal{Z})}$. Each $\mathcal{V}_0^{\tau(\mathcal{B},a,z)}$ can be set to be a zero vector. As the iterations proceed, the Bellman Residual becomes smaller between two consecutive value functions over $\tau(\mathcal{B},\mathcal{A},\mathcal{Z})$. In our experiments, the threshold for stopping criterion is set to be $\epsilon(1-\lambda)/2\lambda$.

6 Experiments

Experiments have been designed to test the performances of value iteration algorithms with and without exploiting problem characteristics. Here we report results on the maze problem in Figure 1. It has ten locations(states). At each time point, the agent can perform one of four "move" actions along different directions and a declare-goal action. The "move" actions are nondeterministic: they can achieve intended effect with probability 0.8 but lead to overshooting with probability 0.1. The declare-goal action does not change the agent's position. As mentioned previously, an observation is a string of four letters. At each time point, the robot receives one among six observations with certainty: `owww`, `owow`, `owoo`, `wwow`, `wowo` and `woww`. At location 9 and 10, the declare-goal action yields rewards of $+1$ and -1 respectively. Any other combinations of actions and states yield no reward.

This POMDP is informative since any observation can restrict the world into only one or two states. If value iteration is conducted without exploiting informativeness, one need to improve values over space $\mathcal{B}(=\{b|\sum_{i=1}^{10} b(s_i)=1.0,\ b(s_i)\geq 0\}$. Since the observations are independent of actions, DP update over subspace need to account for a union of six simplexes determined by observations. It is much smaller than $\mathcal{B}$.

Our experiments are conducted on a SUN SPARC workstation. The discount factor is set to 0.95. The precision parameter is set to 0.000001. The quality requirement ϵ is set to 0.01. In our experiments, incremental pruning [15,6] is used to compute sets of vectors representing value functions over belief space or subspace. For convenience, we use `VI1` and `VI` to refer to the value iteration algorithms with and without exploiting regularities respectively. We compare `VI` and `VI1` at each iteration along two dimensions: the size of set representing value function and time cost to conduct a DP update. The results are presented in Figure 3. Note that y-axis is drawn in log-scale in the figure.

The first chart depicts the number of vectors generated at each iteration for `VI` and `VI1`. In `VI`, at each iteration, we collects the size of minimal set representing value function. In `VI1`, we compute six sets representing value functions over six simplexes and report the sum of the sizes of these sets. For this problem, except first iterations, `VI` generates significantly more vectors than `VI1`. In `VI`, the number of vectors tends to grow severely for first iterations. At the 10th iteration, the number reaches its peak 2500. Afterwards, the number of vectors decrease slowly as value iteration proceeds. When value iteration terminates, it produces 121 vectors. In contrary, the number of vectors generated by `VI1` is much smaller. Our experiments show that the maximum number is below 28. After `VI1` terminates, the value function are represented by only 12 vectors. This suggests that much fewer vectors are in need to represent value functions over a belief subspace.

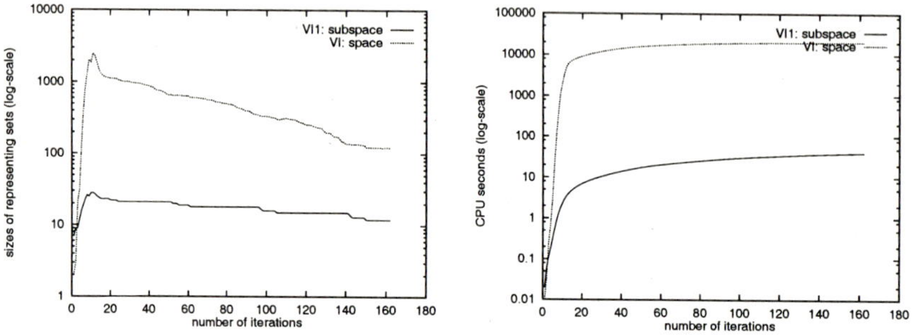

Fig. 3. Comparative study on value iterations over belief space and belief subspace

Due to the big difference between numbers of vectors generated by `VI1` and `VI`, `VI1` is significantly more efficient than `VI`. This is demonstrated in the second chart in Figure 3. When `VI1` terminates after 162 iterations, it takes around 40 seconds. On average, one DP update takes less than 0.25 seconds. For `VI`, it terminates after 162 iterations and takes time of 20,361 seconds. On average, each iteration takes around 125 seconds. Comparing with `VI`, we see that `VI1` is drastically efficient.

7 Related Work

In this paper, we provide a general framework for conducting value iteration over subspace and apply the principles to a special class of POMDPs. The subspace we considered here can be viewed as an application of reachability analysis (e.g. [8]). We also note that some work proposes to decompose value functions in order to reduce their complexity [4,10]. In connection to special classes of POMDPs, the assumption in informative POMDPs is very similar to that in regional observable POMDPs [15]. Both assume that observations can restrict the world into a set of handful of states. However, the motivations behind them are complementary rather than competitive. Regional observable POMDPs are proposed to approximate general POMDPs and our work show that their problem characteristic can be exploited to find solutions more efficiently. Some other POMDP classes have been examined in the literature. These include memory-resetting POMDPs in [9] and near-discernible POMDPs in [16].

8 Future Directions

As our preliminary experiments suggest, conducting value iteration over subspace seems to be a promising area. In informative POMDPs, the subspace containing all possible belief states an agent can encounter has a clear semantics. One future direction is to study how to describe such a subspace even the observations are non-informative. It is believable that such a subspace can be still much smaller than belief space under some circumstances.

Although our experiments are implemented for flat-space POMDPs, we note that the same idea is applicable to structural POMDPs(e.g. see [3]). Another direction is to combine the representational advantage in structural POMDPs and the computational advantage in conducting value iteration over belief subspace.

Acknowledgments. The author is grateful to Nevin L. Zhang for his valuable comments on an earlier version of this paper. This work has been supported by Research Grants Council of the Hong Kong Special Administrative Region, China (Project No. HKUST658 / 95E).

References

1. Aström, K. J.(1965). Optimal control of Markov decision processes with incomplete state estimation. *Journal of Mathematical Analysis and Applications*, 10, 403–406.
2. Bertsekas, D. P. and Gallagher, R. G.(1995). *Data Networks*. Prentice Hall., Englewood Cliffs, N. J..
3. Boutilier, C., Dearden, R. and Goldszmidt, M. (1995). Exploiting structures in policy construction. In *Proceedings of IJCAI-95*, 1104–1111.
4. Boutilier, C. and Poole, D.(1996). Computing optimal policies for partially observable decision processes using compact representations. In *Proceedings of AAAI-96*, 1168–1175.
5. Cassandra, A. R.(1998). *Exact and approximate algorithms for partially observable Markov decision processes*. PhD Thesis, Department of Computer Science, Brown University.
6. Cassandra, A. R., Littman, M. L. and Zhang, N. L.(1997). Incremental pruning: A simple, fast, exact method for partially observable Markov decision processes. *Proceedings of Thirteenth Conference on Uncertainty in Artificial Intelligence*, 54–61.
7. Choi, S.P.M., Yeung, D. Y. and Zhang, N.L. *An environment model for non stationary reinforcement learning*. Advances in Neural Information Processing Systems 12(NIPS-99), 987–993.
8. Dean, T. L., Kaelbling, L. P., Kirman, J. and Nicholson, A., (1995). Planning under time constraints in stochastic domains. Artificial Intelligence, Vol. 76(1–2), 35–74.
9. Hansen, E. A. (1998). *Finite-memory controls of partially observable systems*. PhD thesis, Depart of Computer Science, University of Massachusetts at Amherst.
10. Hauskrecht, M. and Fraser, H.(1998). Planning medical therapy using partially observable Markov decision processes. In *Proceedings of the 9-th International Workshop on Principles of Diagnosis,* Cape Cod, MA, 182–189, 1998.
11. Hauskrecht, M.(2000). Value-function approximations for partially observable Markov decision processes. *Journal of Artificial Intelligence Research,* 13, 33–94.
12. Papadimitriou, C. H. and Tsitsiklis, J. N.(1987). The complexity of Markov decision processes. *Mathematics of Operations Research,* Vol. 12, No. 3, 441–450.
13. Puterman, M. L. (1990), Markov decision processes, in Heyman, D. P. and Sobel, M. J.(eds.), *Handbooks in OR & MS,* Vol. 2, 331–434, Elsevier Science Publishers.
14. Sondik, E. J. (1971). The optimal control of partially observable decision processes. Ph D thesis, Stanford University, Stanford, California, USA.
15. Zhang, N. L. and Liu, W. (1997). A model approximation scheme for planning in stochastic domains. *Journal of Artificial Intelligence Research,* 7, 199–230.
16. Zhang, N. L. and Zhang, W. (2001). Space-progressive value iteration: an anytime algorithm for a class of POMDPs. To appear in *ECSQARU-2001*.

Space-Progressive Value Iteration: An Anytime Algorithm for a Class of POMDPs

Nevin L. Zhang and Weihong Zhang

Department of Computer Science
Hong Kong University of Science & Technology
Clear Water Bay, Kowloon, Hong Kong, China
{lzhang,wzhang}@cs.ust.hk

Abstract. Finding optimal policies for general partially observable Markov decision processes (POMDPs) is computationally difficult primarily due to the need to perform dynamic-programming (DP) updates over the entire belief space. In this paper, we first study a somewhat restrictive class of special POMDPs called almost-discernible POMDPs and propose an anytime algorithm called space-progressive value iteration(SPVI). SPVI does not perform DP updates over the entire belief space. Rather it restricts DP updates to a belief subspace that grows over time. It is argued that given sufficient time SPVI can find near-optimal policies for almost-discernible POMDPs. We then show how SPVI can be applied to more a general class of POMDPs. Empirical results are presented to show the effectiveness of SPVI.

1 Introduction

Partially observable Markov decision processes (POMDPs) provide a general framework for AI planning problems where effects of actions are nondeterministic and the state of the world is not known with certainty. Unfortunately, finding optimal policies for general POMDPs is computationally very difficult [8]. Despite of much recent progresses [6,4,5, 11], our ability to battle the computational complexity of general POMDPs is still limited. It is therefore advisable to study special classes of POMDPs and design special-purpose algorithms for them.

Several classes of special POMDPs have been previously investigated. For example, Hansen [4] has studied *memory-resetting* POMDPs, where there are actions that give perfect information about the current state of the world. Zhang and Liu [10] have examined *region-observable* POMDPs, where one always knows that the world must be in one set of a handful of possible states.

General POMDP problems are difficult to solve primarily due to the need to perform dynamic programming (DP) update over the entire belief space. Solving special POMDP problems is easier because they permit one to focus on a subspace. In fully observable Markov decision processes (MDPs), for instance, one needs to deal only with the set of extreme belief states. In memory resetting POMDPs, one needs to deal only with extreme belief states and those reachable from them within a limited number of steps.

This paper considers POMDPs where there are two types of actions that are informally said to be *information-rich* and *information-poor* respectively. An information-rich action, when executed, always gives one a good idea about the current state of the

S. Benferhat and P. Besnard (Eds.): ECSQARU 2001, LNAI 2143, pp. 72–83, 2001.

world. In other words, the possible belief states after an information-rich action comprise only a small subspace of the belief space. An information-poor action, on the other hand, provides little or no information. We call this class of POMDPs *near-discernible POMDPs* since one can get a good idea about the current state of the world by executing an information-rich action.

It is arguable that near-discernible POMDPs are general enough for many applications with a large flat state space. In some path planning problems, for instance, actions can be divided into those that gather information and those that affect the state of the world. Often actions in the first category are information-rich and those in the second are information-poor.

We propose an anytime algorithm for near-discernible POMDPs. The algorithm is called *space-progressive value iteration (SPVI)*. To avoid high complexity, SPVI does not perform DP updates over the entire belief space. Rather, it restricts DP updates and hence value iteration to a belief subspace and, when convergence is reached, expands the subspace if time permits. So, SPVI works in a fashion similar to the envelope algorithm for MDPs [3].

For technical reasons, we develop SPVI first for a subclass of near-discernible POMDPs called *almost-discernible* POMDPs. In this subclass, it is easier to discuss what initial belief subspace to begin with and how to expand a belief subspace. It is also possible to argue for optimality of the policies found.

SPVI has been evaluated on a number of test problems. Some of the problems are solvable by the exact algorithm described in [11], which is probably the most efficient exact algorithm. For those problems, SPVI was able to find near-optimal policies in much less time. For the other problems, SPVI was still able to find near-optimal policies within acceptable time.

2 Technical Background

A POMDP is a sequential decision model for an agent who acts in a stochastic environment with only partial knowledge about the state of the world. In a POMDP model, the environment is described by a set of states $\mathcal{S}$. The agent changes the states by executing one of a finite set of actions $\mathcal{A}$. At each point in time, the world is in one state s. Based on the information it has, the agent chooses and executes an action a. Consequently, it receives an *immediate reward* $r(s,a)$ and the world moves stochastically into another state s' according to a *transition probability* $P(s'|s,a)$. Thereafter, the agent receives an observation z from a finite set $\mathcal{Z}$ according to an *observation probability* $P(z|s',a)$. The process repeats itself.

Information that the agent has about the current state of the world can be summarized by a probability distribution over $\mathcal{S}$[1]. The probability distribution is called a *belief state* and is denoted by b. The set of all possible belief states is called the *belief space* and is denoted by $\mathcal{B}$. If the agent observes z after taking action a in belief state b, its next belief state b' is updated as

$$b'(s') = \frac{\sum_s P(z|s',a)P(s'|s,a)b(s)}{\sum_{s'}\sum_s P(z|s',a)P(s'|s,a)b(s)}.$$

We will sometimes denote this new belief state by $\tau(b, a, z)$. The dominator is the probability of observing z after taking action a in belief state b and will be denoted by $P(z|b, a)$.

A *policy* prescribes an action for each possible belief state. In other words, it is a mapping from $\mathcal{B}$ to $\mathcal{A}$. Associated with policy π is its *value function* V^π. For each belief state b, $V^\pi(b)$ is the expected total discounted reward that the agent receives by following the policy starting from b, i.e. $V^\pi(b) = E_{\pi,b}[\sum_{t=0}^{\infty} \lambda^t r_t]$, where r_t is the reward received at time t and λ ($0 \leq \lambda < 1$) is the *discount factor*. It is known that there exists a policy π^* such that $V^{\pi^*}(b) \geq V^\pi(b)$ for any other policy π and any belief state b. Such a policy is called an *optimal policy*. The value function of an optimal policy is called the *optimal value function*. We denote it by V^*. For any positive number ϵ, a policy π is *ϵ-optimal* if $V^\pi(b) + \epsilon \geq V^*(b)$ for any belief state b. Without explicitly referring to ϵ, we will sometimes say that such a policy is *near-optimal*.

The *dynamic programming(DP) update operator* T maps a value function V to another value function TV that is defined as follows: for any b in $\mathcal{B}$,

$$TV(b) = \max_a [r(b, a) + \lambda \sum_z P(z|b, a) V(\tau(b, a, z))]$$

where $r(b, a) = \sum_s r(s, a) b(s)$ is the expected immediate reward for taking action a in belief state b.

Value iteration is an algorithm for finding ϵ-optimal policies. It starts with an initial value function V_0 and iterates using the formula: $V_n = TV_{n-1}$. Because T is a contraction mapping, V_n converges to V^* as n goes to infinity. Value iteration terminates when the *Bellman residual* $\max_b |V_n(b) - V_{n-1}(b)|$ falls below $\epsilon(1 - \lambda)/2\lambda$. When it does, the so-called *V_n-improving* policy given below is ϵ-optimal: for any b in $\mathcal{B}$,

$$\pi(b) = \arg\max_a [r(b, a) + \lambda \sum_z P(z|b, a) V_n(\tau(b, a, z))].$$

Functions over the state space $\mathcal{S}$ are sometimes referred to as *vectors*. A set $\mathcal{V}$ of vectors *represents* a value function f in a subspace $\mathcal{B}'$ of belief states if $f(b) = \max_{\alpha \in \mathcal{V}} \alpha.b$ for any b in $\mathcal{B}'$. The notion $\alpha.b$ means the inner product of α and b. We will sometimes write $f(b)$ as $\mathcal{V}(b)$. A vector in a set is *extraneous in $\mathcal{B}'$* if, after its removal, the set represents that same value function in $\mathcal{B}'$. It is *useful in $\mathcal{B}'$* otherwise. If a value function f is representable by a set of vectors in $\mathcal{B}'$, then there is a minimum set that represents f in $\mathcal{B}'$. None of the vectors in this unique set are extraneous in $\mathcal{B}'$. A value function that is representable as a finite set of vectors in the entire belief space is said to be *piecewise linear and convex (PLC)*.

Since there are infinitely many possible belief states, value functions cannot be explicitly represented as a table. Sondik [9] has shown that if a value function V is PLC, then so is TV. Consequently, if the initial value function is PLC, every value function generated by value iteration is PLC and hence can be represented by a finite number of vectors.

3 Space-Progressive Value Iteration in Almost-Discernible POMDPs

In this section, we define almost-discernible POMDPs and outline space-progressive value iteration (SPVI). We also explain why SPVI is feasible and argue that given sufficient time it can find near-optimal policies.

3.1 Almost-Discernible POMDPs

For any action a, let $\mathcal{Z}_a$ be the set of observations that are possible after taking action a. For any z in $\mathcal{Z}_a$, define $\mathcal{S}_{az} = \{s : P(z|a, s)>0\}$. If z is observed after action a, the true state must be in the set $\mathcal{S}_{az}$ and one's belief state must be in $\mathcal{B}_{az} = \{b : b(s)=0 \ \forall s \notin \mathcal{S}_{az}\}$.

If there is an integer k such that $|\mathcal{S}_{az}| \leq k$ for every z in $\mathcal{Z}_a$, then executing a would narrow the true state down to no more than k possibilities. When this is the case, we say that the action is *k-focal*. For convenience, we will use the term *information-opulent actions* to refer to actions that are k-focal for some small integer k.

We say that a POMDP is *k-discernible* if it consists of one or more k-focal actions and all other actions are *information-void* in the sense that they do not yield any observations. For convenience, we will use that term *almost-discernible POMDPs* to refer to POMDPs that are k-discernible for some small k. To simplify exposition, we assume that there is only one information-opulent action and will denote it by d. Note that after executing d, one's belief state must be in $\cup_{z\in\mathcal{Z}_d}\mathcal{B}_{dz}$, where the union is taken over all possible observations that d might produce.

Almost-discernible POMDPs are obviously a generation of memory-resetting POMDPs. They also generalize region-observable POMDPs: An almost-discernible POMDP is region-observable if all actions are information-opulent.

3.2 Space-Progressive Value Iteration

SPVI starts with the belief subspace $\cup_{z\in\mathcal{Z}_d}\mathcal{B}_{dz}$. It performs value iteration restricted to the subspace and, when convergence is reached, expands the subspace. SPVI continues subspace expansions as long as time permits. When time runs out, SPVI returns the best policy found so far [1].

Belief Subspace Representation. In this paper, we consider only subspaces that are unions of belief simplexes. A *belief simplex* is specified by a list of *extreme points*. The simplex with extreme points $b_1, b_2, \ldots, b_k$ consists of all belief states of the form $\sum_{i=1}^{k} \lambda_i b_i$ where $\lambda_i \geq 0$ and $\sum_{i=1}^{k} \lambda_i = 1$.

The initial belief subspace $\cup_{z\in\mathcal{Z}_d}\mathcal{B}_{dz}$ is the union of belief simplexes. To see this, define, for any state s, χ_s to be the extreme belief state such that $\chi_s(s')=1$ if and only if $s'=s$. It is clear that $\mathcal{B}_{dz}$ is a simplex with the following set of extreme points: $\{\chi_s : s \in S_{dz}\}$.

[1] The quality of a policy can be determined by simulation.

In the rest of this subsection, we consider a belief subspace $\mathcal{B}'$ that consists of m simplexes $\mathcal{B}'_i, \mathcal{B}'_2, \ldots, \mathcal{B}'_m$. We explain how to restrict DP update to $\mathcal{B}'$, how to guarantee the convergence of value iteration when restricted to $\mathcal{B}'$, and how to expand the belief subspace $\mathcal{B}'$ when convergence is reached.

Restricted DP Update. DP update takes as input the minimum set of vector that represent a PLC value function V and computes the minimum set $\mathcal{U}$ of vectors that represents TV in the entire belief space. A simple and comparatively efficient algorithm for DP update is incremental pruning [10,2]. It solves a series of linear programs. Each linear program involves a vector α and a set of other vectors $\mathcal{W}$. The purpose of the linear program is to determine whether there is a belief state b where α *dominates* vectors in $\mathcal{W}$, i.e. $\alpha.b > \beta.b$ for all $\beta \in \mathcal{W}$. The linear program is as follows:

$$\begin{array}{l}\text{Maximize: } x.\\ \text{Constraints:}\\ \quad b.\alpha \geq x{+}b.\beta \ \forall \beta{\in}\mathcal{W}\\ \quad \sum_s b(s) = 1,\, b(s) \geq 0\ \forall s{\in}\mathcal{S}\end{array}$$

The vector α dominates vectors in $\mathcal{W}$ at some belief states if and only the optimal value of x is positive. We will refer to this linear program as $LP(\alpha, \mathcal{W}, \mathcal{B})$.

Restricting DP update to the belief subspace $\mathcal{B}'$ means to compute the minimum set $\mathcal{U}'$ of vectors that represents TV in that subspace. To do so, SPVI first does this in each belief simplex $\mathcal{B}'_j$, resulting in a set of vectors $\mathcal{U}'_j$. It then takes the union of those sets. Some vectors in the union might be extraneous in $\mathcal{B}'$. All such vectors can be identified and removed by checking for duplicates.

Restricting DP update to a simplex of belief states requires little change to incremental pruning. Let $\mathcal{B}'_j$ be the simplex with extreme points $b_1, b_2, \ldots, b_k$. To restrict DP update to $\mathcal{B}'_j$, all one has to do is to modify each linear program $LP(\alpha, \mathcal{W}, \mathcal{B})$ as follows:

$$\begin{array}{l}\text{Maximize: } x.\\ \text{Constraints:}\\ \quad \sum_{i=1}^{k} \lambda_i b_i.\alpha \geq x{+}\sum_{i=1}^{k} \lambda_i b_i.\beta \ \forall \beta{\in}\mathcal{W}\\ \quad \sum_{i=1} \lambda_i = 1,\, \lambda_i \geq 0\ \forall 1 \leq i \leq k\end{array}$$

We will refer to this linear program as $LP(\alpha, \mathcal{W}, \mathcal{B}'_j)$.

Restricting DP update to a subspace reduces computational complexity for two reasons. First, the number of variables in $LP(\alpha, \mathcal{W}, \mathcal{B}'_j)$ is $k{+}1$, while that in $LP(\alpha, \mathcal{W}, \mathcal{B})$ is $|\mathcal{S}|{+}1$. When solving near-discernible POMDPs, k is always much smaller than $|\mathcal{S}|$. Consequently, the numbers of variables in linear programs are reduced. Second, one needs fewer vectors to represents TV in a subspace than in the entire belief space. This implies fewer linear programs and fewer constraints in linear programs.

Restricted Value Iteration. Restricting value iteration to a belief subspace means to restrict DP update to the subspace at each iteration. Unlike unrestricted DP update, restricted DP update is not necessarily a contraction mapping. There is therefore an issue of ensuring the convergence of restricted value iteration. A simple solution is to start SPVI with a value function that is sufficiently small so that it is upper bounded by the optimal value function and to maintain monotonicity during restricted value iteration.

For each simplex $\mathcal{B}'_j$, let $\mathcal{V}_j$ be the minimum set of vectors that represents V in the simplex. This was computed in the previous iteration. After DP update in $\mathcal{B}'_j$, we get another set $\mathcal{U}'_j$ of vectors. To maintain monotonicity, SPVI takes the union $\mathcal{V}_j \cup \mathcal{U}'_j$ and then prunes vectors that are extraneous in $\mathcal{B}'_j$ by solving linear programs of the form $LP(\alpha, \mathcal{W}, \mathcal{B}'_j)$.

To determine whether to terminate restricted value iteration, SPVI considers the quantity $\max_{j=1}^{m} \max_{b \in \mathcal{B}'_j} [\mathcal{U}'_j(b) - \mathcal{V}_j(b)]$, which can be computed by solving linear programs of the form $LP(\alpha, \mathcal{V}_j, \mathcal{B}'_j)$. It terminates restricted value iteration when the quantity drops below a predetermined threshold. In our experiments, it is set at $0.1(1-\lambda)/2\lambda$ — the threshold for Bellman residual that exact value iteration would use in order to find 0.1-optimal policies.

Belief Subspace Expansion. When restricting value iteration to $\mathcal{B}'$, we are concerned only with values for belief states in $\mathcal{B}'$. However, values for some belief states in $\mathcal{B}'$ might depend on values for belief states outside $\mathcal{B}'$. Hence it is natural to, when convergence is reached in $\mathcal{B}'$, expand $\mathcal{B}'$ to include all such belief states.

Let V and U be the second last and the last value functions produced by restricted value iteration before it converges in $\mathcal{B}'$. Further let π be the V-improving policy. The value of U at a belief state b in $\mathcal{B}'$ depends on the values of V at belief states that are reachable from b be executing action $\pi(b)$.

For any belief simplex $\mathcal{B}'_j$, any action a, and any z in $\mathcal{Z}_a$, define $\tau(\mathcal{B}'_j, a, z) = \{\tau(b, a, z) : b \in \mathcal{B}'_j\}$. Suppose $\mathcal{B}'_j$ has k extreme points $b_1, b_2, \ldots, b_k$. It can be shown that $\tau(\mathcal{B}'_j, a, z)$ is a simplex with the following set of extreme points

$$\{\tau(b_i, a, z) : i \in \{1, 2, \ldots, k\} \text{ and } P(z|a, b_i) > 0)\}$$

Note that $\tau(\mathcal{B}'_j, a, z)$ has no more extreme points than $\mathcal{B}'_j$.

It is clear that $\cup_{z \in \mathcal{Z}_a} \tau(\mathcal{B}'_j, a, z)$ is the set of belief states reachable from inside $\mathcal{B}'_j$ by executing action a. Let $\mathcal{A}_j$ be the set of actions that π prescribes for belief states in $\mathcal{B}'_j$. Then $\cup_{j=1}^{m} \cup_{a \in \mathcal{A}_j} \cup_{z \in \mathcal{Z}_a} \tau(\mathcal{B}'_j, a, z)$ contains all the belief states whose values under V influence the values of U inside $\mathcal{B}'$.

SPVI expands $\mathcal{B}'$ by including more belief simplexes: for each j, each a in $\mathcal{A}_j$, and each z in $\mathcal{Z}_a$, it adds the simplex $\tau(\mathcal{B}'_j, a, z)$ to the collection of simplexes if it is not a subset of any existing simplexes.

3.3 Feasibility

SPVI would not be computationally feasible if the number of belief simplexes increases quickly. In this subsection, we argue that this is not the case thanks to the properties of almost-discernible POMDPs and the way the initial belief simplexes are chosen.

First note that when a is the information-opulent action d, the simplex $\tau(\mathcal{B}'_j, d, z)$ is a subset of $\mathcal{B}_{dz}$, which is in the collection to begin with. Consequently, it is not added to the collection. Second, each $\mathcal{B}'_j$ is small in size. The information-void actions that the V-improving policy prescribes for belief states are usually only a fraction of all information-void actions. Moreover, each information-void action has only one possible observation, namely the void observation. All those point to the conclusion that the number of belief simplexes does not increase quickly.

Although SPVI is proposed as an anytime algorithm, we argue below that, given sufficient time, SPVI will eventually *converge* in the sense that underlying belief subspace will stop growing. Define a *history* to be an ordered sequence of action-observation pairs. For any belief subspace $\hat{\mathcal{B}}$ and any history h, let $\tau(\hat{\mathcal{B}}, h)$ be the set of belief states that are possible when the history h is realized starting from inside $\hat{\mathcal{B}}$. Using this notation, we can rewrite each initial belief simplex $\mathcal{B}_{dz}$ as $\tau(\mathcal{B}, [d, z])$, where $[d, z]$ is the one step history where z is observed after taking action d. Similarly $\tau(\mathcal{B}'_j, a, z)$ can be rewritten as $\tau(\mathcal{B}'_j, [a, z])$.

It is easy to see that each belief simplex that SPVI encounters can be written as $\tau(\mathcal{B}, h)$ for some history h. As already pointed, each initial belief simplex $\mathcal{B}_{dz}$ can be written as $\tau(\mathcal{B}, [d, z])$. Now if $\mathcal{B}'_j$ is $\tau(\mathcal{B}, h)$, then $\tau(\mathcal{B}'_j, a, z)$ can be written as $\tau(\mathcal{B}, h')$, where $h'=h[a, z]$ is obtained by appending the pair $[a, z]$ to the end of h.

Let $\tau(\mathcal{B}, h)$ be a particular belief simplex that SPVI encounters. We claim that all actions in h are information-void except for the first one. This is trivially true if $\tau(\mathcal{B}, h)$ is an initial belief simplex $\tau(\mathcal{B}, [d, z])$. Suppose the statement is true if the length of h is k. Consider expanding $\tau(\mathcal{B}, h)$. For each action a and each $z \in \mathcal{Z}_a$, we get a new simplex $\tau(\mathcal{B}, h[a, z])$. When a is d, the new simplex is a subset of the initial belief simplex $\mathcal{B}_{dz}$ and hence is not added to the collection of simplexes. When a is d, all actions in $h[a, z]$ are information-void except for the first one. So the claim follows by induction.

Intuitively, after a long sequence of information-void actions, one should be quite uncertain about the current state of the world. As such, good policies should prescribe the information-opulent action for belief states in $\tau(\mathcal{B}, h)$ when h is long. The V-improving policy intuitively should be good as the underlying subspace grows large and hence should prescribe only the information-opulent action for belief states in $\tau(\mathcal{B}, h)$ when h is long. When this happens, no new belief simplexes will be produced from $\tau(\mathcal{B}, h)$. Consequently, SPVI should eventually stop introducing new belief simplexes and hence converge.

It should be noted that the foregoing arguments do not constitute proofs. The conclusions drawn might not be true in all cases. However, they are indeed found to be true in the problems used in our experiments.

3.4 Optimality

Assume SPVI does eventually converge. In this subsection, we argue that SPVI can find near-optimal policies.

Let $\mathcal{B}'$ be the final belief subspace, V and U be the second last and the last value functions, and π be the V-improving policy. The way that SPVI expands a subspace and the fact that $\mathcal{B}'$ is the final subspace imply that $\mathcal{B}'$ is *closed* under π in the following sense: Starting from inside $\mathcal{B}'$, the policy does not lead to belief states outside $\mathcal{B}'$. Let $\mathcal{P}_{\mathcal{B}'}$ be the set of all policies under which $\mathcal{B}'$ is closed. In the following, we prove that π

is near-optimal in $\mathcal{B}'$ among all policies in $\mathcal{P}_{\mathcal{B}'}$, i.e. $V^{\pi}(b)$ is close to $\max_{\pi' \in \mathcal{P}_{\mathcal{B}'}} V^{\pi'}(b)$ for any belief state b in $\mathcal{B}'$.

The POMDP under discussion can be transformed into an MDP over the belief space $\mathcal{B}$. Denote this MDP by $\mathcal{M}$. Define another MDP $\mathcal{M}'$ that is the same as $\mathcal{M}$ except that its state space is $\mathcal{B}'$ and possible actions for each belief state in $\mathcal{B}'$ include only those that do not lead to belief states outside $\mathcal{B}'$. Let V' and π' be respectively the restrictions of V and π onto $\mathcal{B}'$. Imagine carrying out value iteration for $\mathcal{M}'$ starting from V'. Let U' be the value function obtained after the first iteration. The fact that $\mathcal{B}'$ is closed under π implies that π' is a legitimate policy for $\mathcal{M}'$ and is V'-improving. It also implies that $U'(b)=U(b)$ for any b in $\mathcal{B}'$. Hence $\max_{b \in \mathcal{B}'} |V'(b) - U'(b)| = \max_{b \in \mathcal{B}'} |V(b) - U(b)|$. If restricted value iteration was terminated when the latter quantity is small, then π' is a near-optimal policy for $\mathcal{M}'$. Together with the fact all policies in $\mathcal{P}_{\mathcal{B}'}$, when restricted to $\mathcal{B}'$, are policies for $\mathcal{M}'$, this allows us to conclude π is near-optimal (for the original POMDP) in $\mathcal{B}'$ among policies in $\mathcal{P}_{\mathcal{B}'}$.

The intuition that near-optimal policies should prescribe the information-opulent action for belief state in $\tau(\mathcal{B}, h)$ when h is long gives us some reason to believe that the set $\mathcal{P}_{\mathcal{B}'}$ contains near-optimal policies. If this is the case, the policy π is near-optimal in $\mathcal{B}'$ among all policies. Since one can always get into $\mathcal{B}'$ be taking the information-opulent action, π is near-optimal in the entire belief space.

As in the previous subsection, we wish to note that some of the foregoing arguments rely strongly on intuitions. The conclusion drawn might not be true in all cases. However, our experiments do indicate that SPVI can find near-optimal policies after a few subspace expansions.

4 Empirical Results

We have tested SPVI on a number of problems. The results are encouraging. Due to space limit, we discuss only the results on a simple maze game. The layout of the maze is shown in Figure 1. There are 11 states: 10 locations plus one terminal state. An agent needs to move to location 9 and declare goal. There are six actions: four "move" actions plus `look` and `declare-goal`. The `look` action is information-opulent (2-focal) and all other actions are information-void.

The "move" actions allow the agent to move in each of the four nominal directions and have 80% chance of achieving their intended effects, i.e. moving the agent one step in certain direction. Moving against maze walls leaves the agent at its original location. These actions have no rewards. At locations 9 and 10, the `declare-goal` action yield rewards of +1 and -1 respectively and it moves the game into the terminal state. In all other states, it does not cause state transitions and has no reward. The `look` action does not have rewards and does not cause state transitions. It produces observations except in the terminal state. The observation it produces at a location is a sequence of four letters indicating, for each of the four directions, where there is a wall (w) or nothing (o). There are 4 pairs of locations that have the same observations. For example, locations 2 and 5 both have observation `owow`, meaning that there are walls in the South and North and the other two directions are open. Observations for the other 2 locations are unique.

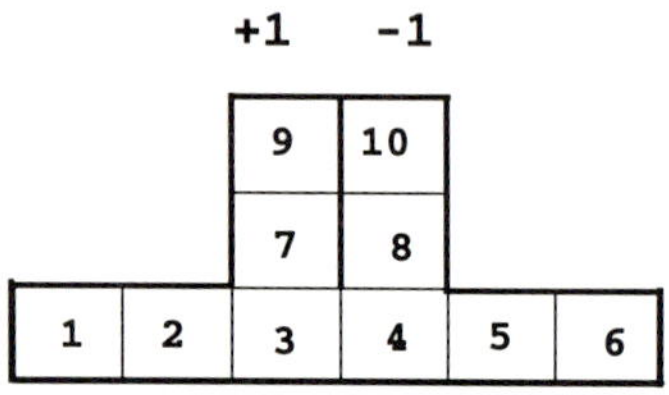

Fig. 1. Layout of test problem domain.

We have run SPVI on two versions of the maze problem: the original problem and a simpler version where locations 1 and 6 are deleted. The two versions will be referred to as Maze and Maze1 respectively. The point-based improvement technique described in Zhang and Zhang [11] is incorporated to speed up the convergence of restricted value iteration. The discount factor is set at 0.95. After restricted value iteration converges in a belief subspace, simulation is conducted to determine the quality of the policy found. The simulation consists of 1000 trials. Each trial starts from a random initial belief state and is allowed to run up to 20 steps. The average reward across all the trials is used as a measurement of policy quality.

The charts in Figure 2 depict quality of policies SPVI found in the belief subspaces against the time taken. Simulation time is not included. There is one data point for each belief subspace. What is shown for a subspace is not necessarily the quality of the policy found in that subspace. Rather, it is the quality of the best policy found so far. We present data this way for the following reason. As subspace grows, SPVI computes better and better value functions. However, as is well known, better value function does not necessarily imply better policy. In other words, the policy found in a larger subspace is not necessarily better than the one found in a smaller subspace. Knowing this fact, one naturally would want to keep the best policy so far.

In Maze1, SPVI converged after 11 expansions and the final number of simplexes is 100. In Maze, it converged after 22 expansions and the final number of simplexes is 432. These support our claims that the number of simplexes does not grow quickly and subspace expansion will eventually terminate.

Using the algorithm described in Zhang and Zhang [11], we were able to compute 0.1-optimal policies for Maze1 in 6,457 seconds. This provides us with a benchmark to judge how close the policies SPVI found are to the optimal. From Figure 2, we see that SPVI found a near-optimal policy for Maze1 in less than 50 seconds after two subspace expansions [2]. This is much less time than 6,457 seconds.

For Maze, the algorithm described in Zhang and Zhang [11] did not converge after 24 hours. On the other hand, SPVI was able to find a policy whose average reward is 0.46 in 13 seconds after only one subspace expansion and another policy whose average reward is 0.48 in 520 seconds after 6 subspace expansions. Since the optimal average

[2] One might notice that some of the policies found by SPVI appear to be better than the 0.1-optimal policy. This is probably due to randomness in simulation.

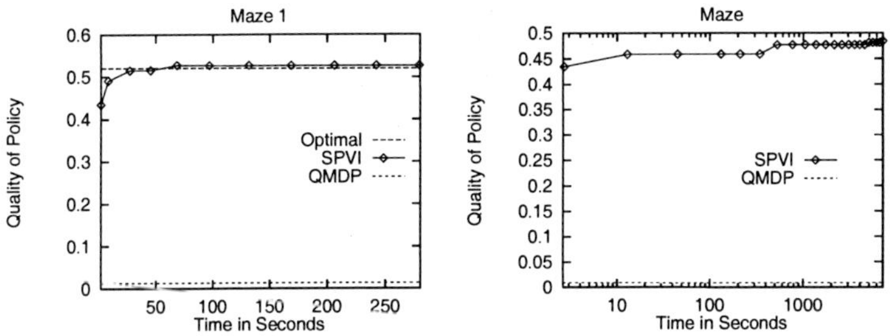

Fig. 2. Performance of SPVI in two almost-discernible POMDPs.

reward one can get in Maze should be less than that in Maze1 and the latter is 0.52, there are good reasons to believe the two policies found by SPVI are near-optimal.

QMDP [7] is a simple approximation method whose performance has been shown to be fairly good compared to other approximation methods [5]. It is computationally much cheaper than SPVI. Naturally, we are interested in how the two methods differ in terms of quality of policies they obtain. From Figure 2, it is clear that SPVI found much better policies than QMDP.

The poor quality of the QMDP approximation in our test problems can easily be explained. The symmetric nature of the domain mains that our agent can easily confuses the left and right halves. The only way to disambiguate the uncertainty is to move to either location 1 or location 6. Policies produced by QMDP simply do not have such sophisticated information-gathering strategy.

5 Near-Discernible POMDPs

The conditions that define almost-discernible POMDPs are rather restrictive. In this section, we relax those conditions to define a more general class of POMDPs called near-discernible POMDPs and show how SPVI can be adapted for such POMDPs.

We say that an action a is *information-rich* if, for each observation z in $\mathcal{Z}_a$, the probability $P(z|s,a)$ is close to zero except for a small number of states. On the other hand, if $P(z|s,a)$ is significantly larger than zero for a large number of states, then we say that a is *information-poor*. A POMDP is *near-discernible* if its actions are either information-rich or information-poor. To simplify exposition, we assume that there is only one information-rich action and we denote this action by d.

One difficulty of applying SPVI to near-discernible POMDPs is that the set $\mathcal{S}_{dz}$ can be large in cardinality. When this is the case, the belief simplex $\mathcal{B}_{dz}$ is also large and consequently the complexity of SPVI would be high if it starts with the belief subspace $\cup_{z\in\mathcal{Z}_d}\mathcal{B}_{dz}$. To overcome this difficulty, we introduce a number δ that close to zero and define $\mathcal{S}^{\delta}_{az} = \{s : P(z|a,s)>\delta\}$. By the definition of information-rich actions, the set $\mathcal{S}^{\delta}_{dz}$ should be small. We further define $\mathcal{B}^{\delta}_{az} = \{b : b(s)=0 \forall s \notin \mathcal{S}^{\delta}_{az}\}$ and let SPVI starts with the belief subspace $\cup_{z\in\mathcal{Z}_d}\mathcal{B}^{\delta}_{dz}$. In our experiments, δ is set at 0.1.

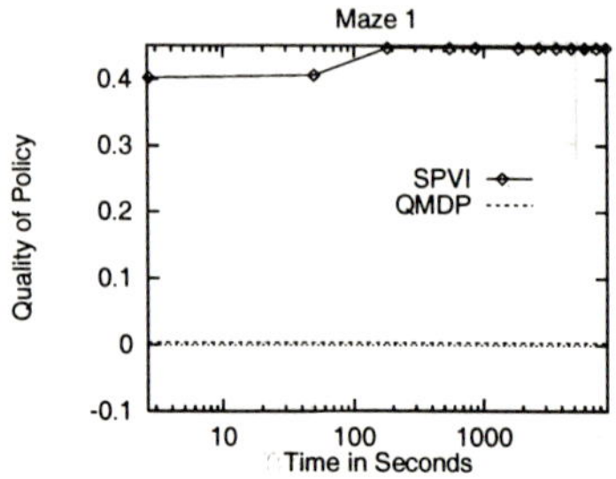

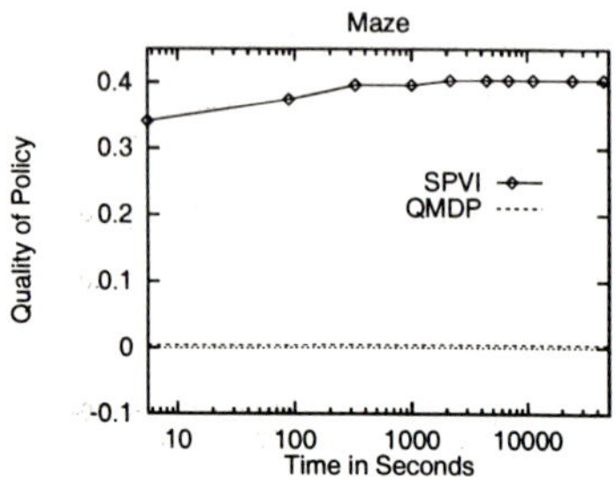

Fig. 3. Performance of SPVI in two near-discernible POMDPs.

The above way of choosing the initial belief subspace gives rise to another issue: new belief simplexes $\tau(\mathcal{B}'_j, d, z)$ generated by the information-rich action are not necessarily a subset of the initial belief simplex $\mathcal{B}^{\delta}_{dz}$. If belief subspaces are expanded in the same way as in almost-discernible POMDPs, the number of belief simplexes will increase quickly. To avoid this problem, new belief simplexes $\tau(\mathcal{B}'_j, d, z)$ generated by the information-rich action are simply discarded.

To evaluate the performance of SPVI in near-discernible POMDPs, we modified the two problems described in the previous section. The only changes are in the observation probability of the `look`. In the original problems, `look` produces, at each location, a string of four characters with probability 1. Let us say that the string is the ideal string for the location. In the modified problems, *look* produces, at each location, the ideal string for that location with probability around 0.8. With probability 0.05, it produces the void observation. Also with probability 0.05, it produces a string that is ideal for some other location and that differs from the ideal string for the current location by no more than 2 characters. After the modifications, `look` is no longer an information-opulent action. It produces the void observation with nonzero probability at all states.

The performance of SPVI in the two modified problems is shown in Figure 3. In modified Maze1, SPVI converged after 11 subspace expansions. In modified Maze, it was manually terminated after 9 subspace expansions. Intuitively, the maximum average rewards one can get in the modified problems should be less than those in the original problems. This and a quick comparison of Figures 2 and 3 suggest that the policies that SPVI found for the modified problems after two subspace expansions are near-optimal. They are much better than the policies found by QMDP.

6 Conclusions

Finding optimal policies for general partially observable Markov decision processes (POMDPs) is computationally difficult primarily due to the need to perform dynamic-programming (DP) updates over the entire belief space. In this paper, we first studied a somewhat restrictive class of special POMDPs called almost-discernible POMDPs and proposed an anytime algorithm called space-progressive value iteration (SPVI). SPVI does not perform DP updates over the entire belief space. Rather it restricts DP updates to a belief subspace that grows over time. It was argued that given sufficient time SPVI can find near-optimal policies for almost-discernible POMDPs. We then showed how SPVI can be applied to more a general class of POMDPs called near-discernible POMDPs, which is arguably general enough for many applications. We have evaluated SPVI on a number of test problems. For those that are solvable by previous exact algorithms, SPVI was able to find near-optimal policies in much less time. For the others, SPVI was still able to find, with acceptable time, policies that are arguably near-optimal.

Acknowledgements. The authors are grateful to the three anonymous reviewers for their helpful comments. This work has been supported by Research Grants Council of the Hong Kong Special Administrative Region, China (Project No. HKUST658/95E).

References

1. K. J. Astrom. Optimal control of Markov decision processes with incomplete state estimation. *Journal of Mathematical Analysis and Applications*, 10, 174-205, 1965.
2. A. R. Cassandra, M. L. Littman, and N. L. Zhang. Incremental pruning: a simple, fast, exact method for partially observable Markov decision processes. *Proceedings of Thirteenth Conference on Uncertainty in Artificial Intelligence*, 54-61, 1997.
3. T. Dean, L. P. Kaelbling, J. Kirman and A. Nicholson. Planning under time constraints in stochastic domains. *Artificial Intelligence*, Vol 76, Num 1-2, 35-74, 1995.
4. E. A. Hansen. Finite-memory controls of partially observable systems. PhD thesis, Depart of Computer Science, University of Massachusetts at Amherst, 1998.
5. M. Hauskrecht. Value-function approximations for partially observable Markov decision processes. *Journal of Artificial Intelligence Research*, 13, 33-94, 2000.
6. L. P. Kaelbling, M. L. Littman and A. R. Cassandra. Planning and acting in partially observable stochastic domains. *Artificial Intelligence*, 101, 99-134, 1998.
7. M. L. Littman, A. R. Cassandra and L. P. Kaelbling. Learning policies for partially observable environments: scaling up. *Proceedings of the Twelfth International Conference on Machine Learning*, 263-370, 1995.
8. C. H. Papadimitriou and J. N. Tsitsiklis(1987). The complexity of Markov decision processes. *Mathematics of Operations Research*, 12(3), 441-450, 1987.
9. E. J. Sondik. The optimal control of partially observable Markov processes. PhD thesis, Stanford University, 1971.
10. N. L. Zhang and W. Liu. A model approximation scheme for planning in stochastic domains. *Journal of Artificial Intelligence Research*, 7, 199-230, 1997.
11. N. L. Zhang and W. Zhang. Speeding up the convergence of value iteration in partially observable Markov decision processes. *Journal of Artificial Intelligence Research*, 14, 29-51, 2001.

Reasoning about Intentions in Uncertain Domains

Martijn Schut, Michael Wooldridge, and Simon Parsons

Department of Computer Science
University of Liverpool
Liverpool L69 7ZF, U.K.
{m.c.schut, m.j.wooldridge, s.d.parsons}@csc.liv.ac.uk

Abstract. The design of autonomous agents that are situated in real world domains involves dealing with uncertainty in terms of dynamism, observability and non-determinism. These three types of uncertainty, when combined with the real-time requirements of many application domains, imply that an agent must be capable of effectively coordinating its reasoning. As such, situated belief-desire-intention (BDI) agents need an efficient intention reconsideration policy, which defines when computational resources are spent on reasoning, i.e., deliberating over intentions, and when resources are better spent on either object-level reasoning or action. This paper presents an implementation of such a policy by modelling intention reconsideration as a partially observable Markov decision process (POMDP). The motivation for a POMDP implementation of intention reconsideration is that the two processes have similar properties and functions, as we demonstrate in this paper. Our approach achieves better results than existing intention reconsideration frameworks, as is demonstrated empirically in this paper.

1 Introduction

One of the key problems in the design of belief-desire-intention (BDI) agents is the selection of an *intention reconsideration policy* [3, 8]. Such a policy defines the circumstances under which a BDI agent will expend computational resources deliberating over its intentions. Wasted effort — deliberating over intentions unnecessarily — is undesirable, as is not deliberating when such deliberation would have been fruitful. There is currently no consensus on exactly how or when an agent should reconsider its intentions. Current approaches to this problem simply dictate the *commitment level* of the agent, ranging from *cautious* (agents that reconsider their intentions at every possible opportunity) to *bold* (agents that do not reconsider until they have fully executed their current plan). Kinny and Georgeff investigated the effectiveness of these two policies in several types of environments [3]; their analysis has been extended by others [8].

Our objective in this paper is to demonstrate how to model intention reconsideration in belief-desire-intention (BDI) agents by using the theory of Markov decision processes for planning in partially observable stochastic domains. We

S. Benferhat and P. Besnard (Eds.): ECSQARU 2001, LNAI 2143, pp. 84–95, 2001.

view an intention reconsideration strategy as a policy in a partially observable Markov decision process (POMDP): solving the POMDP thus means finding an optimal intention reconsideration strategy. We have shown in previous work [8] that an agent's optimal rate of reconsideration depends on the environment's *dynamism* – the rate of change of the environment, *determinism* – the degree of predictability of the system behaviour for identical system inputs, and *observability* – the extent to which the agent has access to the state of the environment. The motivation for using a POMDP approach here is that in the POMDP framework the optimality of a policy is largely based on exactly these three environmental characteristics.

The remainder of this paper is structured as follows. We begin by providing some background information on the BDI framework in which the problem of intention reconsideration arises. In Section 3 we discuss the Markov decision framework upon which our approach builds and present the implementation of intention reconsideration with a POMDP. In Section 4 we empirically evaluate our model in an agent testbed. Finally, in Section 5 we present some conclusions and describe related and future work.

2 Belief-Desire-Intention Agents

The idea of applying the concepts of beliefs, desires and intentions to agents originates in the work of Bratman [2] and Rao and Georgeff [6]. In this paper, we use the conceptual model of BDI agency as developed by Wooldridge and Parsons [10]. The model distinguishes two main data structures in an agent: a *belief* set and an *intention* set[1]. An agent's beliefs represent information that the agent has about its environment, and may be partial or incorrect. Intentions can be seen as states of affairs that an agent has committed to bringing about. We regard an intention as a simple unconditional plan. The behaviour of the agent is generated by four main components: a *next-state* function, which updates the agent's beliefs on the basis of an observation made of the environment; a *deliberation* function, which constructs a set of appropriate intentions on the basis of the agent's current beliefs and intentions; an *action* function, which selects and executes an action that ultimately satisfies one or more of the agent's intentions; and a *meta-level control* function, the sole purpose of which is to decide whether to pass control to the deliberation or action subsystems. On any given control cycle, an agent begins by updating its beliefs through its next-state function, and then, on the basis of its current beliefs, the meta-level control function decides whether to pass control to the deliberation function (in which case the agent expends computational resources by deliberating over its intentions), or else to the action subsystem (in which case the agent acts). As a general rule of thumb, an agent's meta-level control system should pass control to the deliberation function when the agent will change intentions as a result;

[1] Since desires do not *directly* contribute to our analytical discussion of intention reconsideration, they are left out of the conceptual BDI model in this paper. This decision is clarified in [10].

otherwise, the time spent deliberating is wasted. Investigating how this choice is made rationally and efficiently is the main motivation behind the work presented in this paper.

We have to consider that agents do not operate in isolation: they are situated in *environments*; an environment denotes everything that is external to the agent. Let P be a set of *propositions* denoting environment variables. In accordance with similar proposition based vector descriptions of states, we let environment states be built up of such propositions. Then E is a set *environment states* with members $\{e, e', \ldots\}$, and $e = \{p_1, \ldots, p_n\}$, where $p_i \in P$.

The internal state of an agent consists of beliefs and intentions. Let $Bel : E \to [0,1]$, where $\sum_{e \in E} Bel(e) = 1$, denote the agent's *beliefs*: we represent what the agent believes to be true of its environment by defining a probability distribution over the possible environment states. The agent's set of *intentions*, *Int*, is a subset of the set of environment variables: $Int \subseteq P$. An internal state s is a pair $s = \langle Bel, Int \rangle$, where $Bel : E \to [0,1]$ is a probability function and $Int \subseteq P$ is a set of intentions. Let S be the set of all internal states. For a state $s \in S$, we refer to the beliefs in that state as Bel_s and to the intentions as Int_s. We assume that it is possible to denote values and costs of the outcomes of intentions[2]: an *intention value* $V : Int \to \mathbb{R}$ represents the value of the outcome of an intention; and *intention cost* $C : Int \to \mathbb{R}$ represents the cost of achieving the outcome of an intention. The *net value* $V_{net} : Int \to \mathbb{R}$ represents the net value of the outcome of an intention; $V_{net}(i)$, where $i \in Int$, is typically $V(i) - C(i)$. We can express how "good" it is to be in some state by assigning a numerical value to states, called the *worth* of a state. We denote the worth of a state by a function $W : S \to \mathbb{R}$, and we assume this to be based on the net values of the outcomes of the intentions in a state. Moreover, we assume that one state has an higher worth than an other state if the net values of all its intentions are higher. This means that if $\forall s, s' \in S, \forall i \in Int_s, \forall i' \in Int_{s'}, V_{net}(i) \geq V_{net}(i')$, then $W(s) \geq W(s')$. In the empirical investigation discussed in this paper, we illustrate that a conversion from intention values to state worths is feasible, though we do not explore the issue here[3]. Finally, *Ac* denotes the set of physical actions the agent is able to perform; with every $\alpha \in Ac$ we identify a set of propositions $P_\alpha \subseteq P$, which includes the propositions that change value when α is executed.

In this conceptual model, the question of intention reconsideration thus basically boils down to the implementation of the meta-level control function. On every given control cycle, the agent must decide whether it acts upon its current intentions, or to adopt new intentions and this is decided by the meta-level

[2] We clearly distinguish intentions from their outcome states and we do not give values to intentions themselves, but rather to their outcomes. For example, when an agent *intends* to deliver coffee, an *outcome* of that intention is the state in which coffee has been delivered.

[3] Notice that this problem is the inverse of the utilitarian *lifting problem*: the problem of how to lift utilities over states to desires over sets of states. Discussing the lifting problem, and its inverse, is beyond the scope of this paper, and therefore we direct the interested reader to the work of Lang et al. [4].

control function. We continue with discussing how this implementation can be done by using Markov decision processes.

3 Implementing Intention Reconsideration as a POMDP

In this paper, the main point of our formalisation of intention reconsideration is the POMDP implementation of it. The fact that the optimality of a POMDP policy is based on the environment's observability, determinism and dynamism, renders the framework appropriate in the context of intention reconsideration. In this section, we explain what a POMDP is and how to use it for implementing intention reconsideration.

A partially observable Markov Decision Process (POMDP) can be understood as a system that at any point in time can be in any one of a number of distinct states, in which the system's state changes over time resulting from actions, and where the current state of the system cannot be determined with complete certainty [1]. Partially observable MDPs satisfy the Markov assumption so that knowledge of the current state renders information about the past irrelevant to making predictions about the future. In a POMDP, we represent the fact that the knowledge of the agent is not complete by defining a probability distribution over all possible states. An agent then updates this distribution when it observes its environment.

Let a set of states be denoted by S and let this set correspond to the set of the agent's internal states as defined above. This means that a state in the MDP represents an internal state of the agent. We let the set of actions be denoted by A. (We later show that $A \neq Ac$ in our model.) An agent might not have complete knowledge of its environment, and must thus *observe* its surroundings in order to acquire knowledge: let Ω be a finite set of observations that the agent can make of the environment. We introduce an *observation function* $O : S \times A \rightarrow \Pi(\Omega)$ that defines a probability distribution over the set of observations; this function represents what observations an agent can make resulting from performing an action $a \in A$ in a state $s \in S$. The agent receives rewards for performing actions in certain states: this is represented by a *reward function* $R : S \times A \rightarrow \mathbb{R}$. Finally, a *state transition* function $\tau : S \times A \rightarrow \Pi(S)$ defines a probability distribution over states resulting from performing an action in a state – this enables us to model non-deterministic actions.

Having defined these sets, we *solve* a POMDP by computing an *optimal policy*: an assignment of an action to each possible belief state such that the expected sum of rewards gained along the possible trajectories in the POMDP is a maximum. Optimal policies can be computed by applying dynamic programming methods to the POMDP, based on backwards induction; value iteration and policy iteration are the most well known algorithms to solve POMDPs [1]. A major drawback of applying POMDPs is that these kinds of algorithms tend to be highly intractable; we later return to the issue of computational complexity as it relates to our model.

Intention Reconsideration as a POMDP

We regard the BDI as a *domain dependent object level* reasoner, concerned directly with performing the best action for each possible situation; the POMDP framework is then used as a *domain independent meta level reasoning* component, which lets the agent reconsider its intentions effectively. We define a meta level BDI-POMDP as a tuple $\langle S, A, \Omega, O, R, \tau \rangle$. We have explained above that a state $s \in S$ in this model denotes an internal state of the agent, containing a belief part and intention part. As intention reconsideration is mainly concerned with states, actions and rewards, we leave the implementation of observations Ω, the observation function O and the state transition function τ to the designer for now.

Since the POMDP is used to model intention reconsideration, we are merely concerned with two possible meta level actions: the agent either performs an object level action (*act*) or the agent deliberates (*del*). The possible actions $A = \{act, del\}$ correspond to the agent either acting (*act*) or deliberating (*del*). Because the optimality criterion of policies depends on the reward structure of the POMDP, we define the rewards for action *act* and deliberation *del* in state $s \in S$ as follows:

$$R(s, a) = \begin{cases} W(s_{int}) & \text{if} \quad a = act \\ W(s) & \text{if} \quad a = del \end{cases}$$

where $s_{int} \in S$ refers to the state the agent intends to be in while currently being in state s. Imagine a robot that has just picked up an item which has to be delivered at some location. The agent has adopted the intention to deliver the item, i.e., to travel to that location and to drop off the item. The reward for deliberation is the worth of the agent's current state (e.g., 0) whereas the reward for action is the worth of the intented state (e.g., 10) for having delivered the item. The robot consequently acts, which brings it closer to its "correct" intentions. Intentions are correct in case the agent does not waste effort while acting upon them. An agent wastes effort if it is deliberating over its intentions unnecessarily. If an agent does not deliberate when that would have been necessary, the agent has wrong intentions. The reward for acting is thus the worth of the state that the agent intends to reach, whereas the reward for deliberation is the worth of the state as it currently is.

This structure of reward agrees with the intuition that the agent eventually receives a reward if it has correct intentions, it receives no reward if it has wrong intentions, and it receives no *direct* reward for deliberation. With respect to this last intuition, however, we must mention that the "real" reward for deliberation is indirectly defined, by the very nature of POMDPs, as the expected worth of future states in which the agent has correct intentions. As intentions resist reconsideration [2], the agent prefers action over deliberation and the implementation of the reward structure should thus favour action if the rewards are equivalent.

For illustrative purposes, consider the simple deterministic MDP in Figure 1. This Figure shows a 5×1 gridworld, in which an agent can move either right or left or stay at its current location. The agent's current location is indicated with

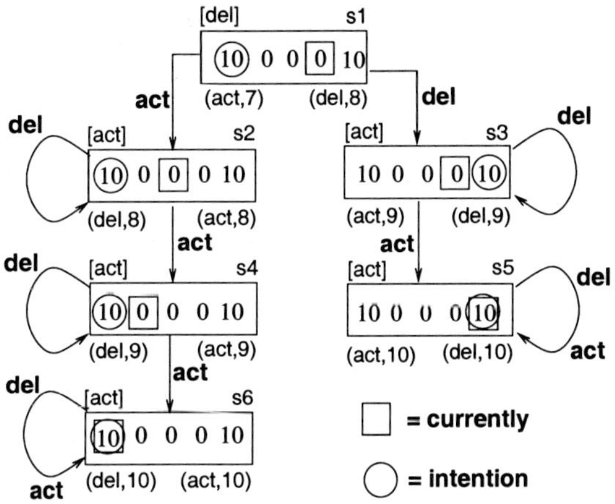

Fig. 1. A 5 × 1 gridworld example which illustrates the definition of rewards in a BDI-POMDP. Rewards, being either 0 or 10, are indicated per location. With each state we have indicated the expected reward for executing a physical action and for deliberation; the best meta action to execute is indicated in square brackets.

a square and the location it intends to travel to is denoted by a circle. Assume the agent is currently in state s_1: its location is cell 4 and it intends to visit cell 1. Action will get the agent closer to cell 1: it executes a move left action which results in state s_2. Deliberation results in dropping the intention to travel to cell 1, and adopting the intention to travel to cell 5 instead; this results in state s_3. Obviously, deliberation is the best meta action here and the expected rewards for the meta actions in s_1 reflect this: the expected reward for deliberation is higher than the one for action. In all other states, these expected rewards are equivalent, which means that the agent acts in all other states.

Solving a BDI-POMDP means obtaining an optimal intention reconsideration policy: at any possible state the agent might find itself in, this policy tells the agent either to act or to deliberate. The main contribution of our work is that our approach gives a well-founded means of establishing a domain dependent optimal reconsideration strategy. Thus the agent is programmed with a domain independent strategy, which it uses to compute a domain dependent strategy off-line, and then executes it on-line. Until now, empirical research on meta level reasoning aimed at efficient intention reconsideration has, to the best of our knowledge, involved hardwiring agents with domain dependent strategies.

It is important that deciding whether to reconsider intentions or not is computationally cheap compared to the deliberation process itself [10]; otherwise it is just as efficient to deliberate at any possible moment. Using a POMDP to determine the reconsideration policy satisfies this criterion, since it clearly distinguishes between design time computation, i.e., computing the policy, and run time computation, i.e., executing the policy. We recognise that the design time problem of computing a policy is very hard; this problem corresponds with the general problem of solving POMDPs and we do not attempt to solve this problem in this paper. However, the computation that concerns us most is the run time computation, and in our model this merely boils down to looking up the current state and executing the action assigned to that state, i.e., either to act or to deliberate. This is a computationally cheap operation and is therefore suitable for run time execution.

4 Experimental Results

In this section, we apply our model in the TILEWORLD testbed [5], and show that the model yields better results than were obtained in previous investigations of intention reconsideration in this testbed[4].

The TILEWORLD [5] is a grid environment on which there are agents and holes. An agent can move up, down, left, right and diagonally. Holes have to be visited by the agent in order for it to gain rewards. The TILEWORLD starts in some randomly generated world state and changes over time with the appearance and disappearance of holes according to some fixed distributions. An agent moves about the grid one step at a time[5]. The experiments are based on the methodology described in [8]. (We repeated the experiments described in [8] to ensure that our results were consistent; these experiments yielded identical results, which are omitted here for reasons of space.)

The TILEWORLD testbed is easily represented in our model. Let L denote the set of locations, i.e., $L = \{i : 1 \leq i \leq n\}$ represents the mutually disjoint locations, where n denotes the size of the grid. A proposition p_i then denotes the presence ($p_i = 1$) or absence ($p_i = 0$) of a hole at location i. An intention value corresponds to the reward received by the agent for reaching a hole, and an intention cost is the distance between the current location of the agent and the location that the agent intends to reach. An environment state is a pair $\langle \{p_i, \ldots, p_n\}, m \rangle$, where $\{p_i, \ldots, p_n\}$ are the propositions representing the holes in the grid, and $m \in L$ is the current location of the agent.

Combining the $2^n \times n$ possible environment states with n possible intentions means that, adopting explicit state descriptions, the number of states is $2^n \times n^2$, where n denotes the number of locations. Computations on a state space of such size is impractical, even for small n. In order to render the necessary computations feasible, we *abstracted* the TILEWORLD state space. In the TILEWORLD domain, we abstract the state space by letting an environment state e be a pair $\langle p_1, p_2 \rangle$, where p_1 refers to the location of the hole which is currently closest to

[4] Whereas until now we have discussed non-deterministic POMDPs, in the experimental section we restrict our attention to deterministic MDPs in order to compare our new results with previous results.

[5] Although it may be argued that the TILEWORLD is simplistic, it is a well-recognised testbed for evaluating situated agents. Because of the dynamic nature of the TILEWORLD, the testbed scales up to difficult and unsolvable problems.

the agent, and p_2 refers to the current location of the agent. Then an agent's internal state is $\langle\langle p_1, p_2\rangle, \{i_1\}\rangle$ where i_1 refers to the hole which the agent intends to visit. This abstraction means that the size of the state space is now reduced to n^3. However, the agent now has to figure out at run time what is the closest hole in order to match its current situation to a state in the TILEWORLD state space. This computation can be done in time $O(n)$, by simply checking whether every cell is occupied by a hole or not. Because the main purpose of this example is merely to illustrate that our model is viable, we are currently not concerned with this increase in run time computation.

In [8], the performance of a range of intention reconsideration policies was investigated in environments of differing structure. Environments were varied by changing the degree of dynamism (γ), observability (referred to by [8] as *accessibility*), and determinism. Dynamism is denoted by an integer in the range 1 to 80, representing the ratio between the world clock rate and the agent clock rate. If $\gamma = 1$, then the world executes one cycle for every cycle executed by the agent and the agent's information is guaranteed to be up to date; if $\gamma > 1$ then the information the agent has about its environment may not necessarily be up to date. (In the experiments in this paper we assume the environment is fully observable and deterministic.) The *planning cost* p was varied, representing the time cost of planning, i.e., the number of time-steps required to form a plan, and took values 0, 1, 2, and 4.

Three dependent variables were measured: effectiveness, commitment, and cost of acting. The *effectiveness* ϵ of an agent is the ratio of the actual score achieved by the agent to the score that could in principle have been achieved. An agent's *commitment* (β) is expressed as how many actions of a plan are executed before the agent replans. The agent's commitment to a plan with length n is $(k-1)/(n-1)$, where k is the number of executed actions. Observe that commitment defines a spectrum from a cautious agent ($\beta = 0$, because $k = 1$) to a bold one ($\beta = 1$, because $k = n$). The *cost of acting* is the total number of actions the agent executes.

Solving the TILEWORLD MDP off-line. To summarise, the TILEWORLD MDP that we have to solve off-line consists of the following parts. As described above, the state space S contains all possible internal states of the agent. Each state $s \in S$ is a tuple $\langle\langle p_1, p_2\rangle, \{i_1\}\rangle$, where p_1 refers to hole that is currently closest to the agent, p_2 refers to the current location of the agent, and i_1 denotes the hole which the agent intends to visit. The set of actions is $A = \{act, del\}$. (Note that the set of physical actions is $Ac = \{stay, n, ne, e, se, se, sw, w, nw\}$, but that is not of concern to us while specifying the TILEWORLD MDP.) Since we assume full observability, the set of observations is $\Omega = S$. Finally, state transitions are defined as the deterministic outcomes of executing an action $a \in A$. As the agent deliberates in state s resulting in state s' (i.e., $\tau(s, del) = s'$), then $Bel_s = Bel_{s'}$, but possibly $Int_s \neq Int_{s'}$; as the agent acts (i.e., $\tau(s, act) = s''$), then $Int_s = Int_{s''}$, but possibly $Bel_s \neq Bel_{s''}$. Thus deliberation means that the intention part of the agent's internal state possibly changes, and action

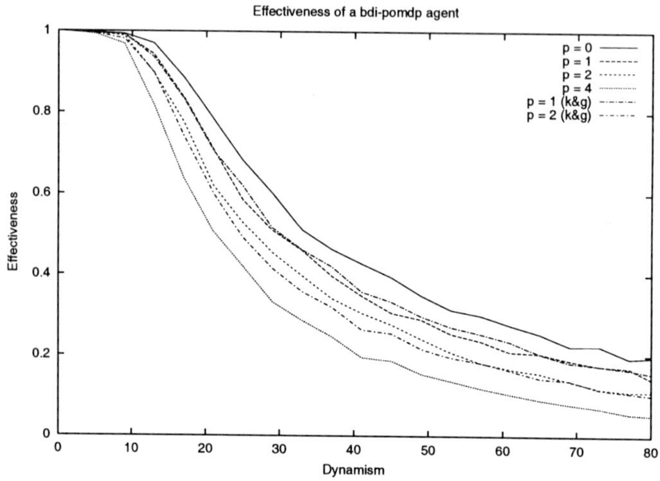

Fig. 2. Overall effectiveness of a BDI-POMDP agent. Effectiveness is measured as the result of a varying degree of dynamism of the world. The four curves show the effectiveness at a planning cost (denoted by p) from 0 to 4. The two other curves show the effectiveness at $p = 1$ and $p = 2$ of Kinny and Georgeff's best reconsideration strategy (from [3]).

means that the belief part of the agent's internal state possibly changes (both ceteris paribus with respect to the other part of the internal state). Although solving MDPs in general is computationally hard, we have shown above that by appropriate abstraction of the TILEWORLD state space, the computations for our TILEWORLD MDP become feasible.

Results. The experiments resulted in the graphs shown in Figures 2, 3(A) and 3(B). In every graph, the environment's dynamism and the agent's planning cost p (for values 0, 1, 2 and 4) are varied. In Figure 2, the overall effectiveness of the agent is plotted. In Figure 3(A) we plotted the agent's commitment level[6] and in Figure 3(B) the cost of acting.

Analysis. The most important observation we make from these experiments is that the results as presented in Figure 2 are overall better than results as obtained in previous investigations into the effectiveness of reconsideration (as

[6] The collected data was smoothed using a Bezier curve in order to get these commitment graphs, because the commitment data showed heavy variation resulting from the way dynamism is implemented. Dynamism represents the acting ratio between the world and the agent; this ratio oscillates with the random distribution for hole appearances, on which the commitment level depends.

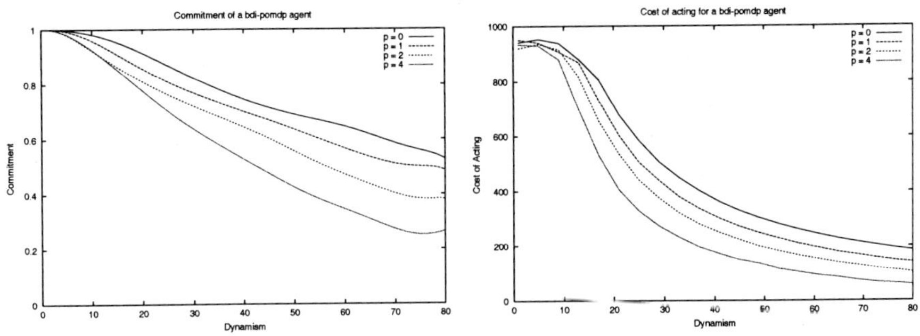

(A) (B)

Fig. 3. (A) Average commitment level for a BDI-POMDP agent. The commitment level is plotted as a function of the dynamism of the world with planning cost (denoted by p) of 0, 1, 2 and 4. (B) Average cost of acting for a BDI-POMDP agent. The cost of acting – the number of time steps that the agent moves – is plotted as a function of the dynamism of the world with planning cost (denoted by p) of 0, 1, 2 and 4.

elaborated below). Our explanation for this observation is that solving the BDI-POMDP for our TILEWORLD domain delivers an optimal domain dependent reconsideration strategy: the optimal BDI-POMDP policy lets the agent deliberate when a hole appears that is closer than the intended hole (but not on the path to the intended hole), and when the intended hole disappears. Kinny and Georgeff [3] concluded that it is best for an agent to reconsider when a closer hole appears or when the intended hole disappears. Besides this observation, we see in Figure 3(A) that our BDI-POMDP agent is able to determine its plan commitment at run time, depending on the state of the environment. This ability contributes to increasing the agent's level of autonomy, since it pushes the choice of commitment level from design time to run time.

Our experimental results confirm the results obtained in previous investigations on selecting an intention reconsideration strategy [3, 8, 9]: the agent's effectiveness and level of commitment both decrease as the dynamism or planning cost increases, and the cost of acting decreases as the dynamism or planning cost increases.

Whereas the focus of previous research was on investigating the effectiveness of *fixed* strategies in different environments, the aim of the investigation in this paper is to illustrate the applicability of our BDI-POMDP model. Kinny and Georgeff [3] have included empirical results for an agent that reconsiders based on the occurrence of certain events in the environment (see [3, p87] Figures 8 and 9 for $p = 2$ and $p = 1$, respectively). Their conclusion from these results was that it is best for an agent to reconsider when the agent observes that either a closer hole appears or the intended hole disappears, as mentioned above. We implemented this strategy for the agent in our testbed and yielded identical results. We observed that an agent using our BDI-POMDP model performs better than the agent using the mentioned fixed strategy with a realistic planning cost ($p \geq 2$). Having compared our results to the results of fixed strategies, we conclude that, as mentioned above, in effect, our agent indeed adopts the strategy that delivers maximum effectiveness.

In the context of *flexible* strategies, we compare our results to the results from [9], where the effectiveness of an alternative flexible strategy, based on discrete deliberation scheduling [7], is explored. The main conclusion we draw from comparing the results from the two strategies is that the empirical outcomes are analogous. Comparing the graphs from Figure 2 to the result graphs from [9], we observe that the agent's effectiveness is generally higher for our BDI-POMDP model; when we compare the graphs from Figure 3(B) to the cost of acting graphs from [9], we see that the cost of acting is lower overall in the discrete deliberation model. However, in our BDI-POMDP model, the level of commitment is more constant, since the BDI-POMDP agent's decision mechanism depends less on predictions of appearances and disappearances of holes.

5 Discussion

In this paper we presented a formalisation of the intention reconsideration process in BDI agents based on the theory of POMDP planning. The motivation for the formalism is that BDI agents in real world application domains have to reconsider their intentions efficiently in order to be as effective as possible. It is important that reconsideration happens autonomously, since an agent's commitment to its tasks changes depending on how its environment changes. The main contribution of our model is that we deliver a meta level and domain independent framework capable of producing optimal reconsideration policies in a variety of domains. The model *applies* POMDP planning to agents; in this paper we do not investigate how intentions can contribute to efficiently solving POMDPs, but regard such an investigation as important further work.

In the work presented, we show that the environmental properties of dynamism, observability and determinism are crucial for an agent's rate of intention reconsideration. Our formalism takes all mentioned environmental properties into account, and they form the basis of the decision mechanism of the BDI agent. A distinctive component in the BDI agent decides whether to reconsider or not, and we use the POMDP framework to determine an optimal reconsideration strategy that is used for implementing this component. We leave open the question whether a similar result can be achieved by the construction of complex sequential and conditional plans, since this defies the very nature of the BDI concept. A BDI agent is concerned with the management of simple plans over time, thus its intelligence is located in its meta-reasoning capabilities and not in its planning capabilities.

We have shown that an agent which is designed according to our formalism, is able to dynamically change its commitment to plans at run time, based on the current state of the environment. (In the experiments that are described in this paper, we assumed the environment to be fully observable and completely accessible, in order to compare our results with previous results.) This agent achieves better performance than existing planning frameworks, in which the level of plan commitment is imposed upon the agent at design time. The BDI-POMDP model has the advantage over the deliberation scheduling model (as used in [9]) that it computes a substantial part of the reconsideration strategy at design time, whereas all computations for deliberation scheduling are at run time. In contrast, the deliberation scheduling model is supposedly more flexible in changing the reconsideration strategy at runtime.

References

1. C. Boutilier, T. Dean, and S. Hanks. Decision-theoretic planning: Structural assumptions and computational leverage. *Journal of AI Research,* pages 1–94, 1999.
2. M. E. Bratman, D. J. Israel, and M. E. Pollack. Plans and resource-bounded practical reasoning. *Computational Intelligence,* 4:349–355, 1988.
3. D. Kinny and M. George. Commitment and effectiveness of situated agents. In *Proceedings of the Twelfth International Joint Conference on Artificial Intelligence (IJCAI-91),* pages 82–88, Sydney, Australia, 1991.
4. J. Lang, L. van der Torre, and E. Weydert. Utilitarian desires. *Journal of Autonomous Agents and Multi-Agent Systems,* 2001. To appear.
5. M. E. Pollack and M. Ringuette. Introducing the Tileworld: Experimentally evaluating agent architectures. In *Proceedings of the Eighth National Conference on Artificial Intelligence (AAAI-90),* pages 183–189, Boston, MA, 1990.
6. A. S. Rao and M. P. George. An abstract architecture for rational agents. In C. Rich, W. Swartout, and B. Nebel, editors, *Proceedings of Knowledge Representation and Reasoning (KR&R-92),* pages 439–449, 1992.
7. S. Russell and E. Wefald. Principles of metareasoning. *Artificial Intelligence,* 49(1-3): 361–395, 1991.
8. M. C. Schut and M. Wooldridge. Intention reconsideration in complex environments. In M. Gini and J. Rosenschein, editors, *Proceedings of the Fourth International Conference on Autonomous Agents (Agents 2000),* pages 209–216, Barcelona, Spain, 2000.
9. M. C. Schut and M. Wooldridge. Principles of intention reconsideration. In E. Andre and S. Sen, editors, *Proceedings of the Fifth International Conference on Autonomous Agents (Agents 2001),* Montreal, Canada, 2001.
10. M. Wooldridge and S. D. Parsons. Intention reconsideration reconsidered. In J. P. Müller, M. P. Singh, and A. S. Rao, editors, *Intelligent Agents V (LNAI Volume 1555),* pages 63–80. Springer-Verlag: Berlin, Germany, 1999.

Troubleshooting with Simultaneous Models

Jiří Vomlel[1] and Claus Skaanning[2]

[1] Department of Computer Science, Aalborg University
Fredrik Bajers Vej 7E, DK-9220 Aalborg, Denmark
jirka@cs.auc.dk

[2] Hewlett-Packard, Customer Support R&D
Fredrik Bajers Vej 7E, DK-9220 Aalborg, Denmark
claus_skaanning@hp.com

Abstract. The goal of decision-theoretic troubleshooting is to find a sequence of actions that minimizes the expected cost of repair of a device. If the device is complex then it is convenient to create several Bayesian Networks, each designed to solve a particular problem. At the beginning of a troubleshooting process, it is often necessary to help the user to select the proper model. Complications arise if the user is able to give only a vague description of the problem. In such a case we need to work simultaneously with many troubleshooting models. In this paper we show how models that were originally designed as independent models can be used together while memory space and computational time are kept low. We allow models to be overlapping, i.e., two or more models may contain equivalent troubleshooting steps and/or equivalent problem causes (device faults). We propose a troubleshooting procedure that can be used with many simultaneous models at once. The key that enables us to join the models together is the single fault assumption, which means that there is only one fault causing a device malfunction at a time.

1 SACSO Troubleshooting Approach

We start with a review of the SACSO troubleshooting approach proposed for troubleshooting with a single model. The approach was implemented in the HP BATS troubleshooter [2]. The goal of a troubleshooting task is to find and remove the cause of a device malfunction. In case of a complex device, such as for example a laser printer, it is convenient to create several models each designed to solve a particular problem. All original troubleshooting models $M_i, i = 1, 2, \ldots, N$ have similar structure. Each model M_i describes relations between a set of repair actions $\mathcal{A}_i$, a set of observations $\mathcal{O}_i$, and a set of causes $\mathcal{C}_i$ that can be solved within model M_i. Repair actions are actions that can directly solve the problem, while observations can not solve the problem directly, but may help identify the problem cause.

It is assumed that only one cause from $\mathcal{C}_i$ can be the cause of a device malfunction at a time. It is often referred to as the single fault assumption. This assumption is reasonable when troubleshooting printing systems and similar

S. Benferhat and P. Besnard (Eds.): ECSQARU 2001, LNAI 2143, pp. 96–107, 2001.

man-made devices. Therefore, each cause can be represented as a state $c_i \in \mathcal{C}_i$ of a single cause variable CM_i. The state space of each variable CM_i is extended by an additional state $n.a.$ This state corresponds to the case when the true cause of the problem is not addressed in model M_i. In other words, $CM_i = n.a.$ corresponds to the situation when model M_i does not solve the problem.

It is also assumed that actions and observations are independent given the cause. This assumption implies that if the cause of the problem is known then neither the fact that an action failed to solve the problem nor an outcome of a made observation affect the probability of any other action solving the problem. In Fig. 1 an example of two SACSO troubleshooting models is shown.

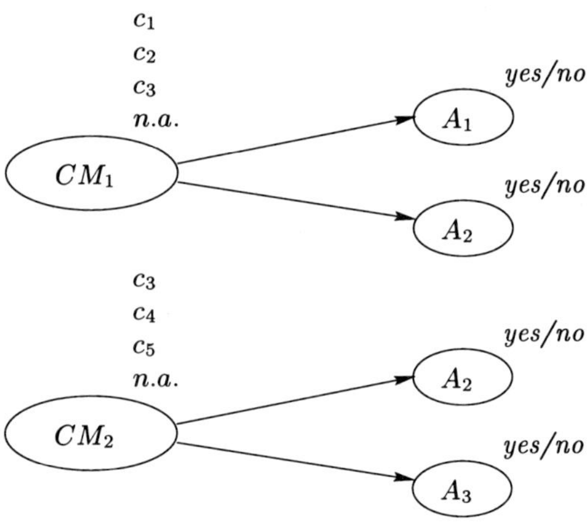

Fig. 1. Two SACSO troubleshooting models.

Remark 1. In the HP BATS troubleshooter both repair actions and observations are included. To keep the exposition simple we stick to actions only. However, the approach of this paper is suitable also for models containing both repair actions and observations.

For every action A and for each cause $c \in \mathcal{C}_i$ included in the model M_i the conditional probabilities $P_i(A = yes \mid CM_i = c)$ are provided by a domain expert and it is assumed that $P_i(A = yes \mid CM_i = n.a.) = 0$. We say that an action A can solve a cause c in a model M_i if $P_i(A = yes \mid CM_i = c) > 0$. The set of causes that can be solved by an action A in a model M_i is denoted by $pa_i(A)$, $pa_i(A) \subset \mathcal{C}_i$. The set of actions that can solve a cause c in a model M_i is denoted by $ch_i(c)$, $ch_i(c) \subseteq \mathcal{A}_i$.

Each action A has associated a cost $cost(A)$. It may correspond to the time needed to perform action A, money spent when performing action A, a combination of time and money, or another criteria. The troubleshooting task is to find a sequence of actions that minimizes the expected cost of repair, i.e., the expected total cost of all actions performed until the problem is solved.

It has been shown that in the case of actions $A \in \mathcal{A}$ with disjoint $pa_i(A)$ it suffices to order them decreasingly according to the ratio $P_i(A = yes)/cost(A)$ (see [4]). However, in [7] it was shown that in case of overlapping $pa_i(A)$ the troubleshooting task is NP-hard.[1] The heuristic algorithm that is the essence of the SACSO troubleshooting procedure [2, 5] consists of three basic steps that are repeated until the problem is solved:

1. Select a repair action of the highest efficiency
$$eff(A) = \frac{P_i(A = yes \mid h)}{cost(A)} ,$$
where h denotes evidence introduced by the troubleshooting history. This corresponds to the evidence that all performed actions failed to solve the problem.
2. Perform the chosen action and observe the result.
3. If the performed action did not solve the problem then enter the outcome of the troubleshooting step into the model and update the model.

The reader interested in details or in other approximate methods used to find a troubleshooting strategy is referred to [2, 5, 7].

In the rest of this paper we discuss how troubleshooting with simultaneous models can be performed. In Sec. 2 we describe how single troubleshooting models can be joined together. In Sec. 3 we apply the SACSO troubleshooting procedure to the troubleshooting with many simultaneous models. In Sec. 4 we propose how probabilities of causes can be initiated when only a vague description of a problem is provided.

2 Simultaneous Models

The current approach to multiple models, implemented in the HP BATS troubleshooter [2, 5], is, first, to use the authoring tool [6]. This creates dozens of models, with each model related to a particular problem. When troubleshooting with the HP BATS troubleshooter, the user selects one model with the help of a selection tree. Then she performs troubleshooting with the chosen model as described above. The problem of this approach is that as the user may not know what the problem exactly is, it may not be clear which model to select. Therefore we need a way to work with several models simultaneously.

In Fig. 2 a scheme for troubleshooting with simultaneous models is displayed. The troubleshooter consists of troubleshooting models $M_1, M_2, \ldots, M_N$ and a *supermodel.* The supermodel reflects dependencies between causes and problems. It uses the user's problem description and answers to certain questions that may help identify the problem, it communicates with the troubleshooting models,

[1] If $\forall A \in \mathcal{A} : |pa_i(A)| \leq 2$ then the complexity is still undecided.

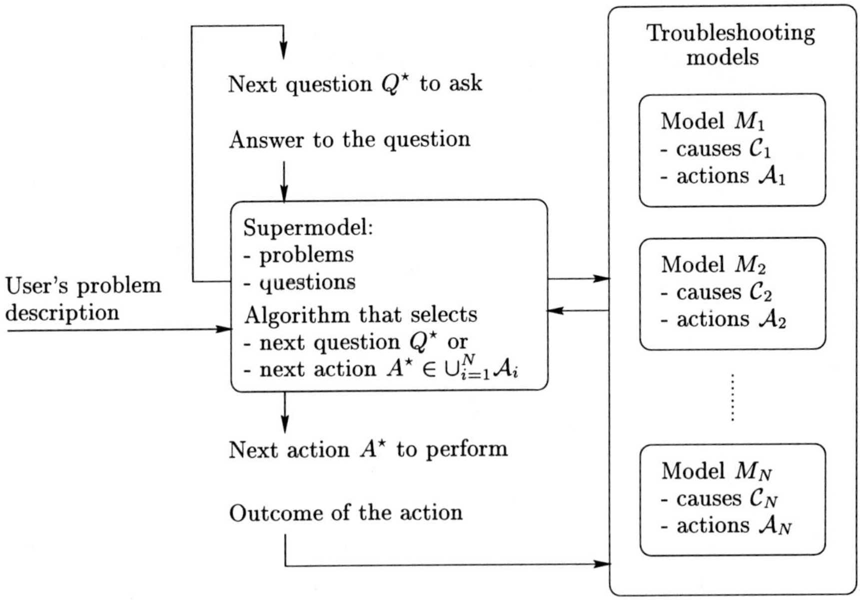

Fig. 2. A basic scheme for troubleshooting with simultaneous models

and it realizes the troubleshooting algorithm, i.e., it selects a best next action to perform and updates the troubleshooting models by the observed outcomes.

It will turn out that under assumptions discussed in this section we can join together all SACSO models and create a single Bayesian network which we will call the *joint model.* Then we can simply apply the algorithm used for troubleshooting with a single SACSO model to troubleshooting with simultaneous models. The supermodel is discussed in detail in Sec. 4.

Generally, there can be identical problem causes and actions that appear in more than one SACSO model. For example, "`Media out of specification`" can be a cause of "`Paper Jam`", "`Spots`", or "`Temporary problem solvable by cycling power`". For each of these three problems a single SACSO model is designed. If it is possible, we identify equivalent causes across all models automatically. Otherwise we need to consult a domain expert. We assign the same index to equivalent causes. Similarly, an automatic program or a domain expert should identify equivalent troubleshooting actions across all models. Again, we will assign the same index to equivalent actions. The joint model contains all problem causes and all troubleshooting actions from the individual SACSO models, i.e.,

$$\mathcal{C} = \bigcup_{i=1}^{N} \mathcal{C}_i \setminus n.a. \quad \text{and} \quad \mathcal{A} = \bigcup_{i=1}^{N} \mathcal{A}_i \ .$$

A question arises whether we can declare two causes $c \in \mathcal{C}_i, c' \in \mathcal{C}_j$ identical if $ch_i(c) \neq ch_j(c')$. For example in Fig. 1, cause c_3 of model M_1 is solved by action A_1 but action A_1 is not present in model M_2 where cause c_3 is present. A reason for this situation can be that an expert did not want to include the action that is part of the first model in the context of the second model, e.g., because the model would be too complex for the audience. We allow such situations and treat two identical causes solved by different actions as one cause solved by all actions that can solve that cause in any SACSO model. It means that for each cause $c \in \mathcal{C}$ the set of its children in the joint model

$$ch(c) = \bigcup_{i=1}^{N} ch_i(c) \ .$$

A similar question is whether two actions $A \in M_i, A' \in M_j$ can be declared identical if $pa_i(A) \neq pa_j(A')$. For example, in Fig. 1, action A_2 can solve cause c_4 in model M_2 but not in model M_1 since this model does not contain this cause. This situation will appear quite naturally, since no expert would like to list all possible causes that can be solved by an action no matter what the problem is. We treat two identical actions solving different causes as one action solving all causes solved in any SACSO model. It means that for each action $A \in \mathcal{A}$ the set of its parents in the joint model

$$pa(A) = \bigcup_{i=1}^{N} pa_i(A) \ .$$

Let us use the example of the two models from Fig. 1 to explain how to define the conditional distributions attached to actions present in more than one model. Action A_2 solves cause c_2 with probability $P_1(A_2 = yes \mid CM_1 = c_2)$ and c_3 with probability $P_1(A_2 = yes \mid CM_1 = c_3)$ in model M_1. In model M_2 it solves cause c_3 with probability $P_2(A_2 = yes \mid CM_2 = c_3)$ and cause c_4 with probability $P_2(A_2 = yes \mid CM_2 = c_4)$. It is natural to have the same conditional probabilities in the joint model. A question is what to do if for example $P_1(A_2 = yes \mid CM_1 = c_3) \neq P_2(A_2 = yes \mid CM_2 = c_3)$. We believe that the only reason for the difference can be that it is difficult for an expert to be 100% consistent. Therefore we either ask an expert to resolve this inconsistency or we simply take the average of the two numbers. In the rest of this paper we assume that for any two models $M_i \neq M_j$ containing an action A and a cause $c \in pa_i(A)$ and $c \in pa_j(A)$ it holds that

$$P_i(A \mid CM_i = c) = P_j(A \mid CM_j = c) \ .$$

In the individual SACSO models the basic assumption used is the single fault assumption. It is reasonable to keep this assumption in the joint model as well since it is a characteristics of the device and it can not be influenced by the fact that a user does not know what the problem is. The single fault assumption is encoded in the joint model using the node CA that has all possible causes as its states. We also keep the conditional independence of actions given the cause in the joint model.

The arguments provided above leads to a unique way of combining the SACSO models to a *joint model.* The joint model has a Naïve Bayes structure, whose conditional probability distributions are given by the following definition.

Definition 1. *Let $m(c \to A)$ define a function such that for any cause $c \in \mathcal{C}$ and any action $A \in \mathcal{A}$*

$$m(c \to A) = \begin{cases} i \text{ if } \exists M_i,\ A \in M_i\ \wedge\ c \in pa_i(A), \\ 0\ otherwise. \end{cases}$$

In the joint model the conditional probability of an action $A \in \mathcal{A}$ given a cause $c \in \mathcal{C}$ is defined as

$$P(A = yes \mid CA = c) = \begin{cases} 0 & \text{if } \ m(c \to A) = 0\ , \\ P_m(A = yes \mid CM_m = c) & \text{if } \ m = m(c \to A) \neq 0\ . \end{cases}$$

In Fig. 3 we give an example of a joint model, which is composed from two SACSO models of Fig. 1.

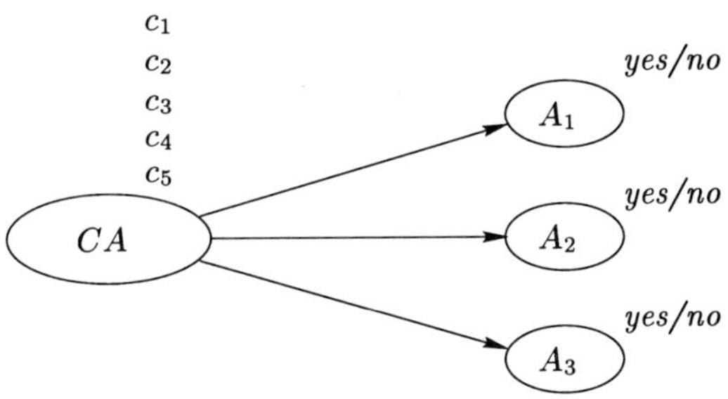

Fig. 3. The two SACSO troubleshooting models from Fig. 1 joined together.

3 A Troubleshooting Procedure

In Sec. 1 we sketched the SACSO troubleshooting procedure for an individual SACSO model. In Sec. 2 we described how the joint model is created from the SACSO models. In this section we propose an algorithm for troubleshooting with simultaneous models that is an application of the SACSO troubleshooting procedure to the joint model. We show that we need not even create the joint model since all information can be stored in and read from the SACSO models. We also demonstrate that a simple naïve approach to troubleshooting with simultaneous models ignoring the fact that different models may contain identical causes and actions may provide erroneous results.

We require $P_i(A = yes \mid CM_i = c)$ being equivalent for all models including both A and c and with $c \in pa_i(A)$. Therefore it does not matter which of these models is chosen by the function $m(c \to A)$. In fact, also after inserting a troubleshooting history h as evidence the function $m(c \to A)$ can be used to select a model for reading $P(A \mid CA = c, h)$.

Lemma 1. *For the conditional probability $P(A \mid CA = c, h)$ of A given a cause $c \in pa(A)$ and a troubleshooting history h in the joint model it holds that*

$$P(A \mid CA = c, h) = P_{m(c \to A)}(A \mid CM_{m(c \to A)} = c) \ .$$

Proof. By the conditional independence of actions given the cause in the joint model we get

$$P(A \mid CA = c, h) = P(A \mid CA = c) \ .$$

From Definition 1 we read that

$$P(A \mid CA = c) = P_{m(c \to A)}(A \mid CM_{m(c \to A)} = c) \ ,$$

which proves the assertion of the Lemma. □

The following lemma underlies the simple propagation scheme for Naïve Bayes models. It will be used in the troubleshooting procedure.

Lemma 2. *Consider the joint model with a troubleshooting history h. Let $L = |\mathcal{C}|$. Then the probabilities of causes $c \in \mathcal{C}$ of the joint model can be updated in the light of a new evidence $e = (A = no)$ by the following formula*

$$P(CA = c \mid e, h) := \frac{P(e \mid CA = c) \cdot P(CA = c \mid h)}{P(e \mid h)} \ ,$$

where $P(e \mid h) = \sum_{\ell=1}^{L} P(e \mid CA = c_\ell) \cdot P(CA = c_\ell \mid h)$.

Proof. Using Bayes' rule we can write

$$P(CA = c \mid e, h) = \frac{P(e, CA = c \mid h)}{P(e \mid h)} \ . \tag{1}$$

Since actions are independent given a cause in the joint model we get

$$P(e, CA = c \mid h) = P(e \mid CA = c) \cdot P(CA = c \mid h) \ . \tag{2}$$

The probability $P(e \mid h)$ can be computed as

$$P(e \mid h) = \sum_{\ell=1}^{L} P(e \mid CA = c_\ell) \cdot P(CA = c_\ell \mid h) \ . \tag{3}$$

Substituting $P(e \mid h)$ from (3) and $P(e, CA = c \mid h)$ from (2) into (1) we get the assertion of the lemma. □

Table 1. A troubleshooting procedure

1. Initiate h, $\mathcal{A}(h) := \mathcal{A}$, and $P(CA = c), c \in \mathcal{C}$.
2. For each action $A \in \mathcal{A}(h)$ compute

$$P(A = yes \mid h) := \sum_{c \in pa(A)} P(A = yes \mid CA = c) \cdot P(CA = c \mid h)$$

$$\mathit{eff}(A \mid h) := \frac{P(A = yes \mid h)}{cost(A)} \ .$$

3. Perform action $A^\star := \arg\max_{A \in \mathcal{A}(h)} \mathit{eff}(A \mid h)$.
4. If $A^\star$ solves the problem then quit otherwise set $e := \{A^\star = no\}$ and continue with step 5.
5. For each $c \in pa(A^\star)$ compute

$$f(c, e \mid h) := P(e \mid CA = c) \cdot P(CA = c \mid h) \ .$$

6. For each $c \in \mathcal{C} \setminus pa(A^\star)$ set $f(c, e \mid h) := P(CA = c \mid h)$.
7. Compute the normalization constant

$$P(e \mid h) := \sum_{c \in \mathcal{C}} f(c, e \mid h) \ .$$

8. Normalize, i.e., for each $c \in \mathcal{C}$

$$P(CA = c \mid e, h) := \frac{f(c, e \mid h)}{P(e)} \ .$$

Update $h := h \cup \{A^\star = no\}$ and $\mathcal{A}(h) := \mathcal{A}(h) \setminus A^\star$. If $\mathcal{A}(h) = \emptyset$ then quit. Otherwise, go to step 2.

Using Lemma 2 we establish a fast updating scheme. The full troubleshooting procedure based on this updating scheme is described in Table 1. We note that the procedure corresponds to the SACSO troubleshooting procedure [2, 5] applied to the joint model. This procedure does not provide optimal troubleshooting strategies. However, when troubleshooting printers, it was shown that the strategies provided by the SACSO troubleshooting procedure are very close to optimal strategies [2] .

Proposition 1. *The troubleshooting procedure described in Table 1 can be performed using the original SACSO models only, i.e., we need not create the joint model.*

Proof. Observe that $P(A = yes \mid CA = c)$, needed in step 2, can be read from model $M_i, i = m(c \to A)$ as $P_i(A = yes \mid CM_i = c)$ and $P(e \mid CA = c)$, needed in step 5, can be read from model $M_j, j = m(c \to A^\star)$ as $P_j(A^\star = no \mid CM_j = c)$

(Lemma 1). We only need to store repeatedly updated probabilities of causes $P(CA = c_\ell \mid h)$ somewhere. A convenient location can be the variables CM_i in the models $M_i, i = 1, 2, \ldots, N$, where, having new evidence e, we update the probability distribution $P_i(CM_i = c_\ell \mid h)$. Thus we keep all models updated and we can read the probability $P(CA = c_\ell \mid h)$ from any model containing the cause c_ℓ. □

The complexity of the proposed troubleshooting procedure if used to provide a full troubleshooting sequence is only $\mathcal{O}(|\mathcal{A}|^2 \times |\mathcal{C}|)$, where $|\mathcal{A}|$ is the number of different actions and $|\mathcal{C}|$ is the number of different causes over all models. Furthermore, we may substantially speed up the computations if we check for causes having $P(CA = c \mid h)$ equal or close to zero and disqualify such causes from further computations. Consequently we need not work with a great many models at the same time, since all models M_i having $P_i(CM_i = n.a. \mid h)$ equal or close to one can be disqualified from further computations.

In the following remark we show that if the probability of an action solving the problem was computed as the total sum over all SACSO models we would get erroneous results.

Remark 2. Note that each cause $c \in pa(A)$ is included in the sum of step 2 only once, which is generally different from the sum

$$\sum_{j \in \{1,2,\ldots N\}} P_j(A = yes \mid h) = \sum_{j \in \{1,2,\ldots N\}} \sum_{c \in pa_j(A)} \begin{array}{l} P_j(A = yes \mid CM_j = c) \\ \cdot P_j(CM_j = c \mid h) \end{array} ,$$

where each cause appear as many times as is the number of models it is contained in. Therefore, if this formula was used to estimate $P(A = yes \mid h)$, it would disproportionally favour actions solving causes that are contained in more models.

4 Initial probabilities of causes

The reader has probably realized that we have not discussed how the probabilities of the causes are defined when creating the joint model. Since this task requires a deeper discussion we have left it for an independent section.

In order to be able to reflect dependencies between causes and problems we create a Bayesian network model, which we call the *supermodel.* This model can use user's problem description and answers to certain questions that may help identify the problem. The problem variable PR has all possible problems $pr_1, pr_2, \ldots, pr_K$ as its states. The supermodel is connected to the joint model through variable CA. Expert knowledge of dependence between problems and causes is encoded in the conditional probability distribution

$$P(CA = c_\ell \mid PR = pr_k), \quad k = 1, 2, \ldots, K, \quad \ell = 1, 2, \ldots, L \ .$$

This means that for each problem pr_k the expert distributes the probability mass between the causes.

Remark 3. When building a single SACSO model M_i a domain expert provided the initial probabilities of causes assuming the problem being solved in that model, i.e. she provided the conditional probabilities $P_i(CM_i = c \mid problem_i)$, where $problem_i$ is the problem solved in model M_i (see [6] for details). If there is a one-to-one correspondence between models and problems, i.e., $problem_k \sim pr_k$, for $k = 1, 2, \ldots, K$ and $K = N$, then we can use the initial probabilities of causes from the SACSO models to define the conditional probability distribution $P(CA \mid PR)$, so that for $k = 1, 2, \ldots, K$

$$P(CA = c_\ell \mid PR = pr_k) = P_k(CM_k = c_\ell) \text{ if } c_\ell \in \mathcal{C}_k \;,$$
$$P(CA = c_\ell \mid PR = pr_k) = 0 \text{ otherwise.}$$

When starting with a particular troubleshooting process the model should reflect all the prior knowledge. Prior knowledge is summarized by means of the prior probability distribution of the variable PR:

$$P(PR = pr_1), \quad P(PR = pr_2), \quad \ldots, \quad P(PR = pr_K).$$

For example, these probabilities can be a result of a text mining task performed on the user's description of problem and observations the user made.

At the beginning of a troubleshooting process or during the process the user can be asked certain questions $Q_1, Q_2, \ldots, Q_J$ which may help identify the problem. For each question Q_j and for each problem pr_k, a conditional probability distribution $P(Q_j \mid PR = pr_k)$ is given. It is assumed that question Q_i is independent of Q_j given PR for any $i \neq j, i, j \in \{1, \ldots, L\}$. An example of a supermodel connected to a joint model is given in Fig. 4.

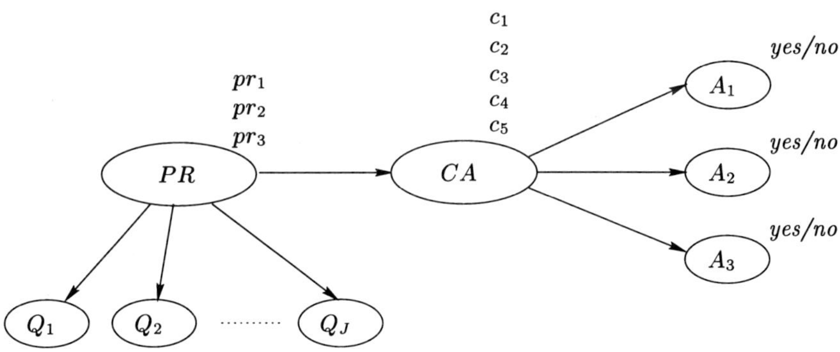

Fig. 4. The supermodel and the joint model joined together

In order to select the most informative question given a current probability distribution over problems $P(PR \mid h)$ we can use standard methods for value of information [1]. An overview of these methods can be found, e.g., in [3]. Methods used to select questions in the full version of the SACSO algorithm [2,5], i.e., the probability of a question identifying the problem and the expected cost of observation, are suitable here as well. These methods can be also used to decide whether we will ask the user more questions. In Table 2 the initialization of probabilities of causes is formally described.

Table 2. Initialization of the probabilities of causes.

1. For each problem $pr_k \in \mathcal{PR}$ and for each cause $c_\ell \in \mathcal{C}$, ask a domain expert to provide you $P(CA' = c_\ell \mid PR = pr_k)$.
2. Ask the domain expert to propose set of questions $\mathcal{Q}$. For all answers q_j to all questions $Q_j \in \mathcal{Q}$ and for all possible problems $pr_k \in \mathcal{PR}$ ask the domain expert to provide $P(Q_j = q_j \mid PR = pr_k)$. Use the knowledge acquisition methodology described in [6].

---

3. Set $h := \emptyset$.
4. Derive $P(PR = pr_k), k \in \{1, 2, \ldots, K\}$ from the user's problem description.
5. Ask the user the most informative question $Q_j \in \mathcal{Q}$ given the history h. Record the answer q_j.
6. For each $pr_k, k \in \{1, 2, \ldots, K\}$ compute

$$P(pr_k \mid h \cup \{Q_j = q_j\}) := \frac{P(Q_j = q_j \mid PR = pr_k) \cdot P(pr_k \mid h)}{\sum_{k=1}^{K} P(Q_j = q_j \mid PR = pr_k) \cdot P(pr_k \mid h)} \quad \text{and}$$

   set $h := h \cup \{Q_j = q_j\}$.
7. Use a criteria to decide whether you will ask the user more questions. If yes, go to step 5, else initialize $P(CA = c_\ell \mid h)$ for all $c \in \mathcal{C}$ as

$$P(CA = c \mid h) = \sum_{k=1}^{K} P(CA = c \mid PR = pr_k) \cdot P(PR = pr_k \mid h)$$

   and initiate $P_i(CM_i = c \mid h) = P(CA = c \mid h)$ in the individual SACSO models $M_i, i = 1, 2, \ldots, N$.

If we prefer to allow general questions from $\mathcal{Q}$ to be asked during a troubleshooting session then we need to communicate the probability distribution $P(CA \mid h)$ between the SACSO models and the supermodel. When necessary we can return to the supermodel and update it, i.e. in the supermodel we propagate

$$P(CA = c \mid h) = P_m(CM_m = c \mid h), \text{ for all } c \in \mathcal{C} \ ,$$

where m is the index of any model containing cause c. Then we use the algorithm of Table 2 starting with step 5 and using the updated probabilities to decide which questions we ask. Finally, when we decide to return back to the troubleshooting procedure we simply replace the values of $P_i(CM_i = c \mid h)$, $i = 1, 2, \ldots, N$ by the values computed in the supermodel as proposed in step 7.

5 Conclusions

We have presented a fast method that can be used to combine information from thousands of troubleshooting models that may share certain problem causes and solution actions. The single fault assumption, allowed us to derive a simple scheme for updating probabilities of causes in the models. Thus we were able to use the same troubleshooting methods as if we were working with a single joint model.

Acknowledgments

We would like to thank Finn V. Jensen, Helge Langseth, Thomas Nielsen, Kristian G. Olesen, Marta Vomlelová, and Ole-Christoffer Granmo for helpful comments and all other members of the Decision Support Group and Hewlett-Packard Laboratory for Normative Systems at Aalborg University for the friendly working environment they created.

References

1. R. A. Howard. Information value theory. *IEEE Transactions on Systems Science and Cybernetics*, pages 22–26, 1966.
2. Finn V. Jensen, Uffe Kjærulff, Brian Kristiansen, Helge Langseth, Claus Skaanning, Jiří Vomlel, and Marta Vomlelová. The SACSO methodology for troubleshooting complex systems. *Artificial Intelligence for Engineering Design, Analysis and Manufacturing (to appear)*, 2001.
3. F.V. Jensen. *An Introduction to Bayesian Networks.* Springer Verlag, 1996.
4. J. Kalagnanam and M. Henrion. A comparison of decision analysis and expert rules for sequential analysis. In P. Besnard and S. Hanks, editors, *The Fourth Conference on Uncertainty in Artificial Intelligence*, pages 271–281, New York, 1988.
5. Claus Skaaning, Finn V. Jensen, and Uffe Kjærulff. Printer troubleshooting using Bayesian Networks. In *the Thirteenth International Conference on Industrial & Engineering Applications of AI & Expert Systems*, 2000.
6. Claus Skaanning. A knowledge acquisition tool for bayesian-network troubleshooters. In C. Boutilier and M. Goldszmidt, editors, *Proceedings of the Sixteenth Conference on Uncertainty in Artificial Intelligence*, pages 549–557, San Francisco, 2000. Morgan Kaufmann Publisher.
7. Marta Sochorová and Jiří Vomlel. Troubleshooting: NP-hardness and solution methods. In *Proceedings of the Fifth Workshop on Uncertainty Processing WUPES'2000, Jindřichův Hradec, Czech Republic*, pages 198–212. University of Economics, Prague, 20-24th June 2000.

A Rational Conditional Utility Model in a Coherent Framework

Silvia Bernardi and Giulianella Coletti

Dipartimento di Matematica e Informatica, Università di Perugia,
via Vanvitelli 1, 06123 Perugia, Italy
{Bernardi, Coletti}@dipmat.unipg.it

Abstract. We present a decision model apt to handle preference relations among conditional acts, not necessarily satisfying transitivity and sure thing principle. We give also a characterization of preference relations agreeing with such a model, by means of rationality conditions interpretable in terms of betting scheme.

1 Introduction

Any expert system, devoted to help in decisions, has as grounds both a model for handling partial knowledge and a decision model of reference. On the other hand it is clear that any not static model must be based on conditioned objects and must possibly work with domains containing only the elements and the information of interest.

In the last years many results in this sense have been obtained for qualitative and quantitative function representing uncertainty, but not for decision models. A conditional decision model is in fact usually derived from an unconditional one (for a classical reference, see [19]). This is a very restrictive view of conditional decisions, corresponding trivially to just a modification of the "world" $\mathcal{S}$. It is instead essential to regard the events A_i conditioning the acts as "variables" or, in other words as uncertain events. This point of view gives to the decision maker the possibility to have "a priori" a plan of choice taking into account all the possible scenarios of interest, also those considered "infinitely less probable" than other ones. Similar aims are at the bottom of [16], but in this paper only acts conditioned on the same event can be compared.

We present a decision model for conditional acts which completely captures the instances expressed above. It is based on the concepts of coherent conditional probability and its relevant characterization in terms of classes of unconditional probabilities P_α (see for instance [2], [5]), representing in fact the different layers of degree of belief ([14] section 8 or [7]). For connections between layers and Spohn's theory see [8], in this issue.

The decision maker using this rational conditional model prefers an act f conditioned on an event A to an act g conditioned on an event B (f_A, g_B respectively), taking into account the utility which he attributes to the acts f_A and g_B and the degree of belief in the occurrence of A and B, when he supposes

S. Benferhat and P. Besnard (Eds.): ECSQARU 2001, LNAI 2143, pp. 108–119, 2001.

the occurrence of $A \vee B$. The preference relation among the conditional acts is in fact "locally" represented by a coherent conditional prevision which is the product of an utility function and a coherent conditional probability.

Precisely "locally" means that the strict monotonicity with the preference relation is assured only in the possible world of the events of the some probabilistic layer. For that the sure thing principle can be violated by the strict preference, and the transitivity is not assured for the symmetric part of the relation (indifference relation).

We present also conditions of rationality (both for finite and infinite framework), interpretable in terms of betting scheme. They are necessary and sufficient conditions for the existence of a rational conditional model agreeing with the preference relation. The sketched proof of the characterization Theorem, for the finite case, suggests the main steps for implementing an algorithm to actually build the conditional decision model, starting from a (possibly parsimonious) set of conditional acts and a (not necessarily complete) preference relation.

2 Coherent Conditional Previsions and Probabilities

In this section we recall some results related to the concept of coherence both for conditional previsions and conditional probabilities. Coherence conditions are essentially rules which permit to give a consistent definition of probability or prevision, avoiding any requirement of closure of the set of events or random quantities, with respect to logical or algebraic operations respectively.

2.1 Coherent Conditional Previsions

Given a random quantity X and an event $H \neq \emptyset$, $X|H$ denotes the random quantity conditioned on H, that is the random quantity assuming the same values of X, if H is true and undetermined when H is false. We denote by I_H the indicator function of the event H (that is the random quantity assuming values 1 or 0 according to H is true or false, respectively) and by XI_H the random quantity assuming the same value of X, if H is true and 0 if H is false.

Let $\mathcal{K} = \{X|H : X \in \mathcal{X},\ H \in \mathcal{H}\}$ be a set of conditional random quantities and $\mathbb{P}$ a real function defined on $\mathcal{K}$.

It is well known that if $\mathcal{K}$ satisfies:

a)$\mathcal{X}$ is a linear space containing a non-zero constant quantity

b)$\mathcal{H}$ is an additive set (i.e. closed with respect to finite disjunctions), containing I_H of any element $H \in \mathcal{H}$, and XI_H, for any $X \in \mathcal{X}$ and $H \in \mathcal{H}$, then $\mathbb{P}$ is a *conditional prevision* if the following conditions hold:

1)$\mathbb{P}(\cdot|H)$ is a linear function;

2)$\inf(X|H) \leq \mathbb{P}(X|H) \leq \sup(X|H)$;

3)$\mathbb{P}(I_{H_1}X|H_2) = \mathbb{P}(X|H_1 \wedge H_2) \cdot \mathbb{P}(I_{H_1}|H_2), \forall X, H_1, H_2$

Definition 1 *Let* $\mathcal{K} = \{X|H, X \in \mathcal{X}, H \in \mathcal{H}\}$ *be an arbitrary set of ¿conditional random quantities. A function* $\mathbb{P} : \mathcal{K} \to \mathbb{R}$ *is a* coherent conditional prevision *if,* *there exists a set* $\mathcal{K}' = \{X|H, X \in \mathcal{X}', H \in \mathcal{H}'\}$ *with* $\mathcal{X}'$ *satisfying (a), and* $\mathcal{H}'$ *satisfying (b),* $\mathcal{K}' \supseteq \mathcal{K}$*, such that there exists a conditional prevision* $\mathbb{P}' : \mathcal{K}' \to \mathbb{R}$ *extending* $\mathbb{P}$.

This definition of coherence is equivalent to that known as "de Finetti-coherence" (dF-coherence), expressed in terms of conditional bets" (see [15], [20] [13], [17]):

Definition 2 *Let* $\mathcal{K} = \{X|H : X \in \mathcal{X}, H \in \mathcal{H}\}$ *be a set of conditional random quantities. A real function* $\mathbb{P}$ *on* $\mathcal{K}$, *is a* dF-coherent conditional prevision *if:*

(CC) for every $X_1|H_1, \ldots, X_n|H_n \in \mathcal{K}$ *and* $r_1, \ldots, r_n \in \mathbb{R}$, *by putting* $H = \bigcup_1^n H_i$, *we have*

$$\sup_H \sum_{i=1}^{n} r_i(X_i - \mathbb{P}(X_i|H_i))I_{H_i} \geq 0.$$

2.2 Coherent Conditional Probabilities

Let $\mathcal{C} = \mathcal{G} \times \mathcal{B}^o$ be a set of conditional events $E|H$. If ¿$\mathcal{C}$ is such that $\mathcal{G}$ is a Boolean algebra and $\mathcal{B} \subseteq \mathcal{G}$ an additive set, $\mathcal{B}^o = \mathcal{B} \setminus \{\emptyset\}$ then a function $P : \mathcal{C} \to \mathbb{R}$ is a *conditional probability* in the sense of de Finetti [9], Dubins [11], Krauss [14], if it satisfies the following conditions:

(i) $P(H|H) = 1$, for every $H \in \mathcal{B}^o$,

(ii) $P(\cdot|H)$ is a (finitely additive) probability on $\mathcal{G}$ for any given $H \in \mathcal{B}^o$,

(iii) $P((E \wedge A)|H) = P(E|H) \cdot P(A|(E \wedge H))$, for every $A \in \mathcal{G}$ and E, H, $E \wedge H \in \mathcal{B}^o$.

Recall that properties *(i)* and *(iii)* are also in the definition by Rényi [18], where condition *(ii)* is replaced by the stronger one of σ-additivity (obviously, the two definitions are equivalent if the algebra $\mathcal{G}$ is *finite*).

Definition 3 *Given an arbitrary set of conditional events* $\mathcal{C}$, *a real function* $P(\cdot|\cdot)$ *on* $\mathcal{C}$ *is a* coherent conditional probability *assessment if, there exists* $\mathcal{C}' \supset \mathcal{C}$, $\mathcal{C}' = \mathcal{G} \times \mathcal{B}^o$, *with* $\mathcal{G}$ *Boolean algebra and* $\mathcal{B}$ *additive set, such that there exists a conditional probability* P' *on* $\mathcal{C}'$ *extending* P.

Definition 4 *Given an arbitrary set of conditional events* $\mathcal{C}$, *a real function* $P(\cdot|\cdot)$ *on* $\mathcal{C}$ *is a* dF-coherent conditional probability *assessment if satisfies condition (CC) in Definition 2, where* $X_i = I_{E_i}$, *for every* i.

Coherence and dF-coherence are equivalent (see [13], [17], [20]). A further characterization of coherence is given by the following theorem (see, [2],[5]).

Theorem 1 *Let* $\mathcal{C}$ *be an arbitrary family of conditional events. For* $\mathcal{F} = \{E_1|H_1, \ldots, E_n|H_n\} \subseteq \mathcal{C}$ *by* $\mathcal{A}_o(\mathcal{F})$ *we indicate the set of atoms* A_r *generated by the events* $E_1, H_1, \ldots, E_n, H_n$. *For a real function* P *on* $\mathcal{C}$ *the following statements are equivalent:*

(i) P *is a coherent conditional probability on* $\mathcal{C}$;

(ii) P is a dF-coherent *conditional probability on $\mathcal{C}$;*

(iii) for every finite $\mathcal{F} \subseteq \mathcal{C}$ there exists (at least) a class *of probabilities $\{P_0^{\mathcal{F}}, P_1^{\mathcal{F}}, \dots P_k^{\mathcal{F}}\}$, each probability $P_\alpha^{\mathcal{F}}$ being defined on a suitable subset $\mathcal{A}_\alpha(\mathcal{F}) \subseteq \mathcal{A}_0(\mathcal{F})$, such that for any $E_i|H_i \in \mathcal{F}$ there is a unique $P_\alpha^{\mathcal{F}}$ with*

$$\sum_{\substack{r \\ A_r \subseteq H_i}} P_\alpha^{\mathcal{F}}(A_r) > 0\,, \quad P(E_i|H_i) = \frac{\sum_{\substack{r \\ A_r \subseteq E_i \wedge H_i}} P_\alpha^{\mathcal{F}} > (A_r)}{\sum_{\substack{r \\ A_r \subseteq H_i}} P_\alpha(A_r)}\;;$$

moreover $\mathcal{A}_{\alpha'}(\mathcal{F}) \subset \mathcal{A}_{\alpha"}(\mathcal{F})$ for $\alpha' > \alpha"$ and $P_{\alpha"}^{\mathcal{F}}(A_r) = 0$ if $A_r \in \mathcal{A}_{\alpha'}(\mathcal{F})$.

3 A Conditional Decision Model

Let $\mathcal{X}$ be a set of real numbers (e.g. monetary payoffs), $\mathcal{S}$ a set of states of nature, and $\mathcal{A}$ a family of subsets of $\mathcal{S}$. Let $\mathcal{F}$ a family of acts or decisions i. e. random quantities ¿from $\mathcal{S}$ taking values in $\mathcal{X}$. Given $f \in \mathcal{F}$, $A \in \mathcal{A}, A \neq \emptyset$, we indicate by f_A the conditional act (or conditional random quantity).

For every $A, B \in \mathcal{A}, A \wedge B = \emptyset$, we can define the conditional act $f_A \cup g_B$ which assumes the same values of f if A is true, the same values of g if B is true, and is undetermined if $A \vee B$ is false.

Let $\mathcal{D}$ be a set of conditional acts: we denote by $\preceq$ a binary, reflexive, not necessarily complete, preference relation $\preceq$ in $\mathcal{D}$, expressing (as in [1]) the intuitive idea of "preferred or indifferent to". By $\prec$ and $\sim$ we denote the strict relation and the indifference relation, respectively.

We introduce the conditional decision model by a simple example:

Example 1:. Mister X is a billiards player. In the next weekend he can attend (only) one of three possible competitions $\mathbf{a_1}, \mathbf{a_2}, \mathbf{a_3}$, which will take place in three different cities. Both competitions $\mathbf{a_1}$ and $\mathbf{a_2}$ are organized in illegal gambling-houses and, taking into account confidential information, Mister X thinks that it is very probable that at the end both competitions will abort. On the contrary, $\mathbf{a_3}$ is a legal competition, but 20 is the fixed number of participants and moreover it is necessary to apply personally. Mister X estimates that he can arrive to apply on Friday at 9.30 and it is possible that at that moment it is too late.

Let now $p_1 < p_2 < p_3$ be the fees for $\mathbf{a_1}$, $\mathbf{a_2}$ and $\mathbf{a_3}$ respectively.

In both competitions $\mathbf{a_1}$ and $\mathbf{a_2}$ there is only one prize (for the winner), r_1, r_2 respectively, (with $r_1 = r_2$), while in competition $\mathbf{a_3}$ there are two prizes: r_3^1 for the first and r_3^2 for the second placed (with $r_3^2 = 1/4 r_3^1 < 1/2 r_1$).

Indicate by A_i the event *"The attendance at competition $\mathbf{a_i}$ is successful"*, by W_i the event *"one wins $\mathbf{a_i}$"*, $(i = 1, 2, 3)$ and by S_3 the event *"one is placed second in $\mathbf{a_3}$"*, it results that Mister X must choose among the following conditional acts:

$$f_{A_i}^i = \begin{cases} r_i - p_i & \text{if } A_i \wedge W_i \text{ is true} \\ -p_i & \text{if } A_i \wedge W_i^c \text{ is true} \qquad \text{(i=1,2)} \\ und. & \text{if } A_i^c \text{ is true} \end{cases}$$

$$f^3_{A_3} = \begin{cases} r^1_3 - p_3 \text{ if } A_3 \wedge W_3 \text{ is true} \\ r^2_3 - p_3 \text{ if } A_3 \wedge S_3 \text{ is true} \\ -p_3 \quad \text{ if } A_3 \wedge W^c_3 \wedge S^c_3 \text{ is true} \\ und. \quad \text{ if } A^c_3 \text{ is true} \end{cases}$$

Taking into account his information about the events and the consequences of the acts, Mister X gives the following preference relation among the conditional acts:

$$f^2_{A_2} \prec f^1_{A_1} \prec f^1_{A_1} \cup f^2_{A_2} \prec f^3_{A_3} \sim f^1_{A_1} \cup f^3_{A_3} \sim f^2_{A_2} \cup f^3_{A_3} \sim f^1_{A_1} \cup f^2_{A_2} \cup f^3_{A_3}$$

and the following relation expressing his comparative degree of belief (comparative probability) on the events:

$$\emptyset \prec A_1 \sim A_2 \prec A_1 \vee A_2 \prec A_3 \sim A_1 \vee A_3 \sim A_2 \vee A_3 \sim A_1 \vee A_2 \vee A_3.$$

Since we have $A_2 \prec A_1 \vee A_2$ and $A_1 \vee A_3 \sim A_1 \vee A_2 \vee A_3$ the comparative probability does not satisfy the well known additivity condition (introduced by de Finetti [10]), that, for an incomplete relation $\preceq$, is the following

(P) for every A, B, C, with $A \wedge C = B \wedge C = \emptyset$

$$A \preceq B \Rightarrow \neg(B \vee C \preceq A \vee C)$$

$$A \prec B \Rightarrow \neg(B \vee C \prec A \vee C).$$

Moreover, since $f^2_{A_2} \prec f^1_{A_1}$ and $f^1_{A_1} \cup f^3_{A_3} \sim f^2_{A_2} \cup f^3_{A_3}$, the preference relation does not satisfy the sure thing principle (ST), (introduced by Savage [19]), that, in this context, can be expressed as follows:

(ST) for every $f_A, g_B, h_C \in \mathcal{D}$ such that $A \wedge C = B \wedge C = \emptyset$ we have:

$$f_A \preceq g_B \Rightarrow \neg(g_B \cup h_C \prec f_A \cup h_C);$$

$$f_A \prec g_B \Rightarrow \neg(g_B \cup h_C \preceq f_A \cup h_C).$$

Therefore there exists neither probability representing the comparative probability (see [10]) nor linear utility representing the preference relation (see [19]).

We introduce now a conditional decision model apt to manage situations such as that described in the Example.

Given $\mathcal{D}$, we denote by $\mathcal{E}$ the set of events A such that at least one act in $\mathcal{D}$ is conditioned on A.

We call a triple $(\mathcal{E}, \mathcal{D}, \preceq)$ a *conditional structure* if satisfies the following properties:

(c1) $I_\emptyset \in \mathcal{D}$;
(c2) if $f_A, g_B \in \mathcal{D}$, then $I_A, I_B, I_{A \vee B} \in \mathcal{D}$;
(c3) $I_\emptyset \prec I_A$ for every $I_A \in \mathcal{D}, A \neq \emptyset$;
(c4) $I_A \preceq I_B$, for every $I_A, I_B \in \mathcal{D}, A \subseteq B$.

We note that a binary relation is induced on $\mathcal{E}$ by the restriction of $\preceq$ to the subset of $\mathcal{D}$ containing only the indicators of events. This relation (denoted in the following by the same symbol $\preceq$) can be viewed as a probability relation among events, expressing the subjective degree of belief (comparative probability) that is the idea of "no more probable than". It is trivial to see that it satisfies the following properties:

$(c3')$ $\emptyset \prec A$, for every $A \in \mathcal{E}, A \neq \emptyset$;
$(c4')$ $A \preceq B$, for every $A, B \in \mathcal{E}, A \subseteq B$.

Definition 5 *Let* $(\mathcal{E}, \mathcal{D}, \preceq)$ *a conditional structure. We say that* $(\mathcal{E}, \mathcal{D}, P, u)$ *is a* rational conditional utility model *for* $(\mathcal{E}, \mathcal{D}, \preceq)$ *if :*
• *u is a real function defined in $\mathcal{D}$;*
• *P is a coherent conditional probability defined on the set of conditional events* $\{E_i|E_i \vee E_j : E_i, E_j \in \mathcal{E}\}$;
• *the function w defined by putting for every $f_A \in \mathcal{D}$ and $C \in \mathcal{E}, C \supseteq A$,*

$$w(f_A, C) = u(f_A)P(A|C),$$

is a coherent conditional prevision for the acts $(fI_A)_C = (fI_A)|C$.
• *For every $f_A, g_B \in \mathcal{D}$ we have:*

$$\textit{if } f_A \preceq g_B \quad \textit{then} \quad u(f_A)P(A|A \vee B) \leq u(g_B)P(B|A \vee B)$$

$$\textit{if } f_A \prec g_B \quad \textit{then} \quad u(f_A)P(A|A \vee B) < u(g_B)P(B|A \vee B)$$

For a conditional structure admitting a rational conditional utility model, the relation $\preceq$ may be not-transitive and needs not satisfy the "sure thing principle" as proved by the following examples

Example 2: Let $A, B, C \in \mathcal{E}, f_A, g_B, h_C \in \mathcal{D}$. Let u be a utility function such that $u(g_B) = u(h_C) = 0,\ u(f_A) \neq 0$ and P a coherent conditional probability such that $P(A|A \vee C) \neq 0,\ P(A|A \vee B) = P(B|B \vee C) = 0$. Then $f_A \sim g_B$ and $g_B \sim h_C$, but $f_A \nsim h_C$.

Example 3: Let $A, B, C \in \mathcal{E}$ such that $A \wedge C = B \wedge C = \emptyset,$ and let P such that $P(A|A \vee B) = \frac{1}{3},\ P(B|A \vee B) = \frac{2}{3},\ P(A|A \vee B \vee C) = P(B|A \vee B \vee C) = 0$. Consider now $f_A, g_B, h_C \in \mathcal{D}$ and u such that $u(f_A) < u(g_B)$. Then $f_A \preceq g_B$ but $f_A \cup h_C \sim g_B \cup h_C$.

The Example 2 shows also that the relation induced on $\mathcal{E}$, need not satisfy condition (P).

However weaker principles of transitivity and independence are necessary for a conditional structure admitting a rational utility model, as the following Proposition proves:

Proposition 1 *A conditional structure admitting a rational conditional utility model necessarily satisfies the following conditions:*

D1) (weak transitivity). *For every $f_A, g_B, h_C \in \mathcal{D}$*
$(f_A \prec g_B$ *and* $g_B \prec h_C) \Rightarrow \neg(h_C \preceq f_A)$

$$(f_A \prec g_B, g_B \sim h_C \textit{ and } h_C \nsim I_\emptyset) \Rightarrow \neg(h_C \preceq f_A)$$

$$(f_A \sim g_B, g_B \sim h_C \textit{ and } g_B \nsim I_\emptyset) \Rightarrow \neg(h_C \prec f_A) \textit{ and } \neg(f_A \prec h_C)$$

D2) (weak ST). *For every $f_A, g_B, h_C \in \mathcal{D}$ such that $A \wedge C = B \wedge C = \emptyset$ we have:*

$$f_A \preceq g_B \Rightarrow \neg(g_B \cup h_C \prec f_A \cup h_C)$$

if moreover $(f_A \prec h_C$ *and* $g_B \sim h_C)$ *or* $g_B \cup h_C \nsim h_C$ *then*

$$f_A \prec g_B \Rightarrow \neg(g_B \cup h_C \preceq f_A \cup h_C).$$

Relation $\preceq$, *induced on* $\mathcal{E}$ *by* $\preceq$ *is a* weakly additive qualitative probability, *that is a reflexive binary relation which satisfies the following conditions:*
P1) $\emptyset \prec A$ *for every* $A \in \mathcal{E}, A \neq \emptyset$;
P2) $\preceq$ *has no intransitive cycles;*
P3) for every $A, B, C \in \mathcal{E}$ *with* $A \wedge C = B \wedge C = \emptyset$

$$A \preceq B \Rightarrow \neg(B \vee C \prec A \vee C)$$

moreover, if $B \prec B \vee C$ *or* $B \sim C$, *then*

$$A \prec B \Rightarrow \neg(B \vee C \preceq A \vee C).$$

Axioms $P1$–$P3$ essentially introduced in [3] are the natural generalization of those proposed in [4], for a complete binary relation defined on an algebra of events. As proved in [3] they are necessary (but not sufficient) conditions for the existence of a coherent conditional probability P defined on $\mathcal{E} \times \mathcal{E}^0$ locally representing $\preceq$, that is such that:

$$A \preceq B \Rightarrow P(A|B \vee A) \leq P(B|B \vee A)$$

$$A \preceq B \Rightarrow P(A|B \vee A) \leq P(B|B \vee A).$$

Moreover, as proved in [7] they are sufficient for the existence of a *conditional weakly* $(\oplus, \odot)$*-decomposable measure.*

In [16] a set of axioms to define a *generalized qualitative probability* is introduced. These axioms are implied by $P1$–$P3$ and then they are a necessary condition for the existence of a conditional probability locally representing. Nevertheless we may note that, if a *generalized qualitative probability* does not satisfy $P1$–$P3$, then it can not be locally represented either by a conditional probability nor by a *weakly* $(\oplus, \odot)$*-decomposable measure.*

For a weakly additive qualitative probability $\preceq$ on $\mathcal{E}$, we consider, for every event A of $\mathcal{E}$, the set $\mathcal{L}(A)$ of events *infinitely less probable* than it

$$\mathcal{L}(A) = \{B \in \mathcal{E} : \exists E_i \sim F_i \preceq A, \ F_i \subset E_i\},$$

with $i = 1, \ldots, n$ and $B \subseteq \bigvee_1^n (E_i \wedge F_i^c)$.

We note that if the relation $\preceq$ induced on $\mathcal{E}$ (which is a *weakly additive qualitative probability*), is *complete* and $\mathcal{E}$ is an *algebra*, then for every $A \in \mathcal{E}$ the set $\mathcal{L}(A)$ coincides with the set $\mathcal{L}_A$ (introduced in [4] and independently in

[16]), whose definition clearly expresses the meaning of the events *infinitely less probable* than A (for a proof see [3] or [7]):

$$\mathcal{L}_A = \{B \in \mathcal{E} : \ A \vee B \sim A \wedge B^c \sim A\}$$

Now we can define the set of events with the same order of probability of A

$$\mathcal{B}(A) = \{B \in \mathcal{E} : B \notin \mathcal{L}(A) \text{ and } A \notin \mathcal{L}(B)\}.$$

If the relation $\preceq$, induced on $\mathcal{E}$ (weakly additive qualitative probability satisfying ($c4'$)), is complete, and $\mathcal{E}$ is an algebra, the sets $\mathcal{L}(A)$ and $\mathcal{B}(A)$ satisfy many structural properties, as proved in ([4]).

We only recall here that $\{\mathcal{B}(A) : \ A \in \mathcal{E}\}$ is a partition of $\mathcal{E}$ (independently of the logical structure of $\mathcal{E}$). Moreover, we note that for every $A, B \in \mathcal{E}$, putting $G = \max_{\preceq}\{A, B\}$, we have that $A \vee B \in \mathcal{B}(G)$.

4 Rational Relations

We introduce now a rationality condition for a conditional structure $(\mathcal{E}, \mathcal{D}, \preceq)$. It is stated in terms of inequalities for sums of acts and then it is essentially an algebraic condition.

Definition 6 *Let $(\mathcal{E}, \mathcal{D}, \preceq)$ be a conditional structure. We say that the relation $\preceq$ is rational if satisfies the following condition*

(R) for every $n \in I\!N$ and $f^i_{A_i}, g^i_{B_i} \in \mathcal{D}$, with $f^i_{A_i} \preceq g^i_{B_i}$, $k_i \geq 0$, $(i = 1, \ldots, n)$

$$\sup \sum_{1}^{n}{}_{i} \, k_i(g^i I_{B_i} - f^i I_{A_i}) \leq 0$$

implies either of the following conditions:
1) $f^i_{A_i} \sim g^i_{B_i}$ *for every $i = 1, \ldots, n$*
2) *if ¿$f^j_{A_j} \prec g^j_{B_j}$ for some j, then $A_j \vee B_j \in \mathcal{L}(\bigvee_1^n (A_i \vee B_i))$*

It is possible to give an interpretation of (R) in terms of betting scheme. In fact we may regard $k_i(g^i I_{B_i} - f^i I_{A_i})$ as an exchange between a bookie and a gambler, which yields an amount $k_i g^i$ to the bookie if B_i happens, and the amount $k_i f^i$ to the gambler if A_i happens; if $A_i \vee B_i$ is false, the corresponding bet is annulling. This is betting even money on $g^i_{B_i}$ versus $f^i_{A_i}$. Suppose to have this rule: if $f^i_{A_i} \preceq g^i_{B_i}$, $i = 1, \ldots, n$, the bookie should accept any combination of bets, with $k_i \geq 0$, on $g^i_{B_i}$ versus $f^i_{A_i}$. The relation $\preceq$ is not rational if there exists one of these combinations, with a surely not positive gain and at least a pair of conditional acts $f^i_{A_i} \prec g^i_{B_i}$ such that the corresponding bet has an infinitesimal probability, than others, of not being annulled.

The following results focus the connections between rational relations and rational conditional utility models.

Proposition 2 *Let $(\mathcal{E}, \mathcal{D}, \preceq)$ be a conditional structure, and $\preceq$ satisfies (R). Then $\preceq$ satisfies (D1), (D2), and the relation $\preceq$, induced on $\mathcal{E}$, is a weakly additive qualitative probability.*

Theorem 2 *Let $\mathcal{D}$ be a finite set of conditional acts and $(\mathcal{E}, \mathcal{D}, \preceq)$ a conditional structure.*
The following statements are equivalent:
i) $\preceq$ satisfies (R);
ii) there exists a rational conditional utility model $(\mathcal{E}, \mathcal{D}, P, u)$.

Proof. We give here only a sketch of the proof, making in evidence the main steps for the actual construction of the numerical model.

Let $E_0^0 = \bigvee A, \forall A \in \mathcal{E}$, let $\mathcal{D}_0$ be the subset of $\mathcal{D}$ containing the acts conditioned on the elements of $\mathcal{B}(E_0^0)$. We denote by $\preceq_0$ the relation on $\mathcal{D}$ defined by putting: $f_A \preceq_0 g_B$ if $f_A \preceq g_B$ and $A \vee B \in \mathcal{B}(E_0^0)$, and $f_A \sim_0 I_\emptyset$ if $f_A \in \mathcal{D} \setminus \mathcal{D}_0$. $\mathcal{A}_0$ denotes the set of atoms generated by the events in which the conditional acts assume significant values ($\mathcal{A}_0$ is finite because $\mathcal{D}, \mathcal{X}$). Consider now the following linear system S_0, where the unknown is the m-vector $W_0 = (W_0^1, \ldots, W_0^m)$($m$ is the cardinality of the set $\mathcal{A}_0$); $*$ denotes the operation of scalar product, $f^i I_{A_i}$ denotes the act which assumes the same value of f^i if A_i is true, and is null if A_i is false:

$$(S_0) \begin{cases} W_0 * (g^i I_{B_i} - f^i I_{A_i}) > 0 & \text{if } f^i_{A_i} \prec_0 g^i_{B_i} \\ W_0 * (k^j I_{F_j} - h^j I_{E_j}) = 0 & \text{if } h^j_{E_j} \sim_0 k^j_{F_j} \\ W_0 \geq 0 \;\; W_0 \neq 0 \end{cases}$$

By using a well known theorem of alternative (see, for instance [12]), it is easy to prove that S_0 has a solution if (and only if) the following system S_0' has no solution:

$$(S_0') \begin{cases} \sum \alpha_i (g^i I_{B_i} - f^i I_{A_i}) + \sum \beta_j (k^j I_{F_j} - h^j I_{E_j}) \leq 0 \\ \alpha_i \geq 0, \; \sum \alpha_i > 0, \; \beta_j \in \mathbb{R} \end{cases}$$

Interchanging $h^j_{E_j}$ and $k^j_{F_j}$, if necessary, we can assume that all β_j's are not negative. It is easy to see that S_o' has a solution if (and only if) $\preceq$ does not satisfy condition (R).

The function $w_0 : \mathcal{D} \to \mathbb{R}$ defined by putting, for any $f_A \in \mathcal{D}$,

$$w_0(f_A) = \frac{W_0 * f I_A}{W_0 * I_{E_0^0}}$$

represents $\preceq_0$, since it satisfies system S_0.

The function $P_0 : \mathcal{E} \to \mathbb{R}$ defined by putting, for any $A \in \mathcal{E}$

$$P_0(A) = \frac{W_0 * I_A}{W_0 * I_{E_0^0}}$$

is a probability distribution.

We note that $w_0(I_A) = P_0(A)$, for every $A \in \mathcal{E}$. Now we inductively define $\mathcal{E}_k = \mathcal{L}(E^0_{k-1})$, $E^k_k = \bigvee A, \forall A \in \mathcal{E}_k$, for $k \geq 1$. Let $\mathcal{D}_k$ be the subset of $\mathcal{D}$ containing the acts conditioned on the elements of $\mathcal{E}_k$ and $\mathcal{D}'_k$ the subset of $\mathcal{D}_k$ containing the acts conditioned on the elements of $\mathcal{B}(E^0_k)$.

We denote by $\preceq_k$ the relation on $\mathcal{D}_k$ defined by putting: $f_A \preceq_k g_B$ if $f_A \preceq g_B$ and $A \cup B \in \mathcal{B}(E^0_k)$, and $f_A \sim_k I_\emptyset$, for every $f_A \in \mathcal{D}_k \setminus \mathcal{D}'_k$. Following the same procedure of $\preceq_0$, we obtain a function $w_k : \mathcal{D}_k \to \mathbb{R}$ defined by putting, for any $f_A \in \mathcal{D}_k$,

$$w_k(f_A) = \frac{W_k * fI_A}{W_k * I_{E^0_k}}$$

which represents $\preceq_k$. We also define the function $P_k : \mathcal{E}_k \to \mathbb{R}$ by putting, for every $A \in \mathcal{E}_k$,

$$P_k(A) = \frac{W_k * I_A}{W_k * I_{E^0_k}}$$

which is a probability distribution.

After a finite number h of steps, we get that $\mathcal{L}(E^0_h)$ contains only the impossible event $\emptyset$. Let $S_0, \ldots, S_h$ have a solution: if $\preceq$ does not satisfy (R), it is easy to see that there exists a subsystem of one among the systems $S_0, \ldots, S_h$ without solutions.

So $\preceq$ satisfies the condition of rationality if (and only if) $S_0, \ldots, S_h$ have a solution.

The existence of solution for $S_0, \ldots, S_h$ implies the existence of a rational conditional utility model for $(\mathcal{E}, \mathcal{D}, \preceq)$: for every $f_A \in \mathcal{D}$, we define

$$u(f_A) = \frac{w_k(f_A)}{w_k(I_A)}$$

where k is the natural number such that $A \in \mathcal{B}(E^0_k)$.

Then, for every $A|A \vee B$ with $A, B \in \mathcal{E}$, we define

$$P(A|A \vee B) = \frac{P_s(A)}{P_s(A \vee B)}$$

where s is such that $A \vee B \in \mathcal{B}(E^0_s)$. It is easy to see that u and P are well defined, and that, for every $A \in \mathcal{E}$, one has $u(I_A) = 1$. Moreover, by using Theorem 1 we can show that P is a coherent conditional probability. Following the same line it is possible to prove that function w defined by putting, for any $f_A \in \mathcal{D}, C \in \mathcal{E}$, with $C \supseteq A$

$$w(f_A, C) = u(f_A) \frac{P_\alpha(A)}{P_s(C)}$$

where α is such that $C \in \mathcal{B}(E^0_\alpha)$, is a coherent conditional prevision. It is immediate to prove that w locally represents $\preceq$.

Vice versa, if there exists a rational conditional utility model for $\preceq$, then any system S_α have a solution

$$W_\alpha = (w(I_{C_1}), \ldots, w(I_{C_m})) \quad (\alpha = 0, \ldots, n)$$

where $C_1, \ldots, C_m$ are the atoms of $\mathcal{A}_\alpha$.

We notice that the steps of construction of the model, given in the proof, single out in a natural way the steps of an algorithm to check rationality of a preference relation on a finite set of conditional acts.

5 Strongly Rational Relations

We notice that for infinite set of conditional acts, condition (R) is not sufficient to the existence of a rational conditional utility model $(\mathcal{E}, \mathcal{D}, P, u)$ for $(\mathcal{E}, \mathcal{D}, \preceq)$. We introduce now a condition of *strong rationality* (SR).

Definition 7 *Let $(\mathcal{E}, \mathcal{D}, \preceq)$ be a conditional structure. We say that the relation $\preceq$ is strongly rational if it satisfies the following condition*

(SR) for every $f^i_{A_i} \preceq g^i_{B_i}$ there exists a $\delta_i \geq 0, \delta_i > 0$ for $f^i_{A_i} \prec g^i_{B_i}$, such that for every $n \in I\!N$, $f^i_{A_i}, g^i_{B_i} \in \mathcal{D}$, $k_i > 0$, one has

$$\sup \sum_{i}{}_{1}^{n} k_i(g^i I_{B_i} - f^i I_{A_i} - \delta_i I_{A_i \vee B_i}) \leq 0$$

implies either of the following conditions:
1) $f^i_{A_i} \sim g^i_{B_i}$ *for every* $i = 1, \ldots, n$;
2) *if* $f^j_{A_j} \prec g^j_{B_j}$ *for some* j, *then* $A_j \vee B_j \in \mathcal{L}\big(\bigvee_1^n (A_i \vee B_i)\big)$

It is possible to give an interpretation of (SR) (in terms of betting scheme) similar to that for condition (R), by regarding δ_i as a penalty that one must pay to bet on a preferred conditional act.

It is immediate to prove the following result:

Proposition 3 *Let $(\mathcal{E}, \mathcal{D}, \preceq)$ be a conditional structure. If $\preceq$ satisfies (SR) then $\preceq$ satisfies (R).*

Strong rationality characterizes relations on an arbitrary set of conditional acts, which admit a rational conditional utility model:

Theorem 3 *Let $\mathcal{D}$ be an arbitrary set of conditional acts and $(\mathcal{E}, \mathcal{D}, \preceq)$ a conditional structure. The following statements are equivalent:*
i) $\preceq$ satisfies (SR);
ii) there exists a rational conditional utility model $(\mathcal{E}, \mathcal{D}, P, u)$.

The theorem can be proved by using a compactification theorem and the following

Lemma 1 *Let $\mathcal{D}$ be an arbitrary set of conditional acts and $(\mathcal{E}, \mathcal{D}, \preceq)$ a conditional structure. The following statements are equivalent:*
i) $\preceq$ satisfies (SR);
ii) for every finite set $\mathcal{F} \subseteq \mathcal{D}$, there exists a rational conditional utility model $(\mathcal{E}_{\mathcal{F}}, \mathcal{F}, P_{\mathcal{F}}, u_{\mathcal{F}})$, for $(\mathcal{E}, \mathcal{F}, \preceq_{\mathcal{F}})$ such that, for every $f_A, g_B \in \mathcal{F}$, with $f_A \prec g_B$ we have

$$u_{\mathcal{F}}(g_B) P_{\mathcal{F}}(B|A \vee B) - u_{\mathcal{F}}(f_A) P_{\mathcal{F}}(A|A \vee B) \geq \delta_i.$$

References

1. R.J. Aumann. Utility theory without the completeness axiom. *Econometrica*, 30 (3):445–461, 1962.
2. G. Coletti. Coherent numerical and ordinal probabilistic assessments. *IEEE Transactions on Systems, Man, and Cybernetics*, 24: 1747–1754, 1994.
3. G. Coletti. Non additive ordinal relations representable by conditional probabilities and its use in expert systems, *Proc. of IPMU'96*, Granada:43–48, 1996.
4. G.Coletti, G.Regoli. Probabilitá qualitative non archimedee e realizzabilitá *Riv. Mat. Sci. Economic. Soc.*, 6:79–99, 1983.
5. G. Coletti, R. Scozzafava. Characterization of coherent conditional probabilities as a tool for their assessment and extension. *International Journal of Uncertainty, Fuzziness and Knowledge-Based Systems*, 4: 103-127, 1996.
6. Coletti, G., Scozzafava, R.: Zero Probabilities in Stochastical Independence. In Information, Uncertainty, Fusion, Kluwer, Dordrecht (2000) 185–196. (Selected papers from IPMU '98, Paris)
7. G.Coletti, R.Scozzafava. Locally additive comparative probabilities *Proc. of 2nd International Symposium on Imprecise Probabilities and Their Applications*, Ithaca, New York, 2001.
8. Coletti, G., Scozzafava, R., Vantaggi, B.: Probabilistic Reasoning as a General Inferential Tool. *In this issue.*
9. B. de Finetti. Sul significato soggettivo della probabilità, *Fundamenta Matematicae*, **17**: 293-329, 1931.
10. B. de Finetti. Sull'impostazione assiomatica del calcolo delle probabilità. *Annali Univ. Trieste*, 19: 3–55, 1949. *Engl. transl.*: Ch.5 in *Probability, Induction, Statistics*, Wiley, London, 1972.
11. L.E. Dubins. Finitely additive conditional probabilities, conglomerability and disintegration. *Annals of Probability*, 3:89–99, 1975.
12. W. Fenchel. Convex cones, sets and functions. *Lectures at Princeton University*, Spring term, 1951.
13. S. Holzer. On coherence and conditional previsions, *Boll. U.M.I.*, **4-C** (1):441–460, 1985.
14. P.H. Krauss. Representation of conditional probability measures on Boolean algebras *Acta Mathematica Academiae Scientiarum Hungaricae*, 19:229-241, 1968.
15. R. S. Lehman. On confirmation and rational betting. *The Jour. of Symbolic Logic*, 20:251–262, 1955.
16. D. Lehmann. Generalized qualitative probability: Savage revisited. *Proc. UAI'96*, 381–388, 1996.
17. E. Regazzini. de Finetti's coherence and statistical inference. *Ann. Stat.*, 15:845–864, 1987.
18. A. Rényi. On conditional probability spaces generated by a dimensionally ordered set of measures. *Theor. Probab. Appl.*, 1: 61–71, 1956.
19. L.J. Savage, *The Foundations of Statistics,* Wiley, New York, 1954.
20. P.M. Williams. Notes on conditional previsions. *Technical Report, University of Sussex, School of Mathematical and Physical Siences,* 1975.

Probabilistic Reasoning as a General Unifying Tool

Giulianella Coletti[1], Romano Scozzafava[2], and Barbara Vantaggi[2]

[1] Dipartimento di Matematica, Università di Perugia,
Via Vanvitelli, 1 – 06100 PERUGIA (Italy)
coletti@dipmat.unipg.it

[2] Dipartimento Metodi e Modelli Matematici, Università "La Sapienza",
Via Scarpa, 16 – 00161 ROMA (Italy)
{romscozz, vantaggi}@dmmm.uniroma1.it

Abstract. Our starting point is the approach to probabilistic logic through *coherence*; but we give up de Finetti's idea of a conditional event $E|H$ being a 3–valued entity, with the third value being just an undetermined *common value* for all ordered pairs (E, H). We let instead the "third" value of $E|H$ suitably depend on the given pair. In this way we get, through a *direct* assignment of conditional probability, a general theory of probabilistic reasoning able to encompass other approaches to uncertain reasoning, such as *fuzziness* and *default reasoning*. We are also able to put forward a meaningful concept of *conditional independence*, which avoids many of the usual inconsistencies related to *logical* dependence. We give an example in which we put together different kinds of information and show how coherent conditional probability can act as a unifying tool.

1 Introduction

Our general aim is that of synthesizing our research in the field of probabilistic reasoning that has been published (going back to papers such as [15] and [2]) in diverse sources or that has been developed from diverse points of view. In fact this program will be fully pursued in a forthcoming paper [9]: so, with the limited space which is available here, we just try to convey some aspects of the main ideas and methodologies ruling our approach. A cornerstone is the concept of *coherence*, which allows to define *conditional probability* on an *arbitrary* family of conditional events. The starting point is a synthesis of the available information expressed by one or more events: to this purpose, the concept of *event* must be given its more general meaning, *i.e.* it must not looked on *just as a possible outcome* (a subset of the so–called "sample space"), but expressed by a *proposition*. Moreover, events play a two–fold role, since we must consider not only those events which are the direct object of study, but also those which represent the relevant "state of information": in fact *conditional* events are the tools that allow to manage specific (conditional) statements and to update (through *conditional probability*) degrees of belief on the basis of the evidence.

S. Benferhat and P. Besnard (Eds.): ECSQARU 2001, LNAI 2143, pp. 120–131, 2001.

What is usually emphasized in the literature – when a conditional probability $P(E|H)$ is taken into account – is only the fact that $P(\cdot|H)$ *is a probability for any given* H: this is a very restrictive (and misleading) view of conditional probability, corresponding trivially to just a modification of the "world" Ω.

It is instead essential to regard the conditioning event H as a "variable", *i.e.* the "status" of H in $E|H$ is not just that of something representing a given *fact*, but that of an (uncertain) *event* (like E) for which the knowledge of its truth value is not required (this means, using a terminology due to Koopman [19], that H must be looked on as being *contemplated*, even if *asserted*: similar terms are, respectively, *assumed* versus *acquired*). So, *even if beliefs may come from various sources, they can be treated in the same way* and can be measured by *probability*, since the relevant events (*including statistical data!*) can always be considered as being *assumed* propositions. In particular, the "statistical" concept of *likelihood* is nothing else that a conditional probability seen as a function of the *conditioning* event.

The concept of conditional event (as dealt with in this paper) plays a central role for the probabilistic reasoning. We generalize (or better, in a sense, we give up) the idea of de Finetti of looking at a conditional event $E|H$, with $H \neq \emptyset$ (the *impossible* event), as a 3–valued logical entity (*true* when both E and H are true, *false* when H is true and E is false, "undetermined" when H is false) by letting the third value *suitably depend on the given ordered pair* (E, H) and not being just an undetermined *common value* for all pairs: it turns out (as explained in detail in [5]) that this function can be seen as a measure of the degree of belief in the conditional event $E|H$, which under "natural" conditions reduces to the conditional probability $P(E|H)$, in its most general sense related to the concept of *coherence*, and satisfying the classic axioms as given by de Finetti [11], Rényi [28], Krauss [20], Dubins [12] (see Section 2). So, taking de Finetti's approach as starting point is not just a "semantic" attitude in favour of the subjectivist position. Rather it is mainly a way of exploiting the "syntactic" advantages of this view by resorting to an operational procedure (based on linear systems, see Section 4) which allows to consider, for example, *partial probability assessments* (numerical or comparative) on an *arbitrary* set of conditional events and to make inference with respect to any "new" event or information.

A relevant theory (but only for *unconditional* events) is the probabilistic logic by N.J. Nilsson [22], which is just a re-phrasing (with different terminology) of de Finetti's theory, as Nilsson himself acknowledges in [23].

We list some peculiarities (which entail a large flexibility in the management of any kind of uncertainty) of this concept of *coherent* conditional probability versus the usual one:

- due to its *direct* assignment as a whole, the knowledge (or the assessment) of the "joint" and "marginal" unconditional probabilities $P(E \wedge H)$ and $P(H)$ is not required;
- the *conditioning* event H (which *must* be a *possible* one) may have *zero probability*, so that (as shown for example in [3]) the class of admissible conditional probability assessments and that of possible extensions are larger (and the ensuing algorithms are more flexible). Moreover, in the assignment

of $P(E|H)$ we are driven by *coherence*, contrary to what is done in those treatments (for example, that by Frisch and Haddawy in [13]: see Section 3) where the relevant conditional probability is given an *arbitrary* value in the case of a conditioning event of zero probability;
- it allows a management of *stochastic* independence (conditional or not) which avoids many of the usual inconsistencies related to *logical* dependence. The latter situation may arise in the usual probabilistic approach which resort to graphical models (as, e.g., [10], [35], [21]);
- a suitable interpretation of its extreme values 0 and 1 for situations which are different, respectively, from the trivial ones $E \wedge H = \emptyset$ and $H \subseteq E$, leads to a "natural" treatment of the *default reasoning*;
- it is possible to represent and manage "vague" statements as those of fuzzy theory (but there is no room here to discuss these aspects: see [6], [8]).

2 Conditional Events and Conditional Probability

We shall refer to a definition of *conditional event* extensively discussed, e.g., in [5]. We just recall that a conditional event $E|H$ can be represented as a random variable (denoting by I_A the *indicator* of the event A)

$$X = 1 \cdot I_{E \wedge H} + 0 \cdot I_{E^c \wedge H} + t(E|H) \cdot I_{H^c} \,, \tag{1}$$

so that we have $X = 1$ when both E and H are true, $X = 0$ when H is true and E is false, and $X = t(E|H)$ when H is false (in particular, we have only *two* values, 1 and 0, when $H = \Omega$, the *certain* event).

By requiring the closure of suitable operations introduced inside this particular class of random variables (which is an *arbitrary* family $\mathcal{C}$ of conditional events), we get "automatically" (so to say) conditions on $t(E|H)$. Choosing as operations in $\mathcal{C}$ the *ordinary sum and product*, $t(E|H)$ satisfies the classic *axioms for a conditional probability*, which read (if the set $\mathcal{C} = \mathcal{G} \times \mathcal{B}^o$ of conditional events $E|H$ is such that $\mathcal{G}$ is a Boolean algebra and $\mathcal{B} \subseteq \mathcal{G}$ is closed with respect to (finite) logical sums (i.e., disjunctions) with $\mathcal{B}^o = \mathcal{B} \setminus \{\emptyset\}$) as follows:

(i) $P(H|H) = 1$, for every $H \in \mathcal{B}^o$,

(ii) $P(\cdot|H)$ is a (finitely additive) probability on $\mathcal{G}$ for any given $H \in \mathcal{B}^o$,

(iii) $P\big((E \wedge A)|H\big) = P(E|H) \cdot P\big(A|(E \wedge H)\big)$, for any $A, E \in \mathcal{G}$, $H, E \wedge H \in \mathcal{B}^o$.

Putting $P(\cdot|H) = P_H(\cdot)$, property *(iii)* can be written

$$P_H(E \wedge A) = P_H(E) \cdot P_{E \wedge H}(A) \,. \tag{2}$$

This means that a conditional probability $P_H(\cdot)$ is not singled–out by its *conditioning* event H, since its values are bound to suitable values of another conditional probability, *i.e.* $P_{E \wedge H}(\cdot)$. Then $P_H(\cdot)$ cannot be assigned (so to say) "autonomously" (recall the comments already made in Section 1 about the misleading way of looking at conditional probability).

On the other hand, if $P_\Omega(\cdot) = P(\cdot)$ is *strictly positive* on $\mathcal{B}^o$, we can write, putting $H = \Omega$ in (2),

$$P(E \wedge A) = P(E) \cdot P(A|E)\,.$$

Then – in this case – *all* conditional probabilities $P(\cdot|E)$, for any E, are uniquely determined by a single "unconditional" P (Kolmogorov approach), while in general – see Theorem 3 in Section 4 – we need a *class* of probabilities P_α's to represent the "whole" conditional probability.

3 Popper Measure

In the relevant literature there is no agreement in the definition of conditional measures *when the conditioning event has zero probability.* Also Popper in [25] (pp. 332–335) emphasizes the need for this more general view of conditional probability. He gives the following definition (we refer to the version presented in [17], p.84):

Definition 1 - A *Popper measure* P on $\mathcal{G} \times \mathcal{G}$ (where $\mathcal{G}$ is a Boolean algebra) is a function satisfying the following axioms:

1. $0 \leq P(B|A) \leq P(A|A) = 1$ for all $A, B \in \mathcal{G}$,
2. if $P(A|B) = 1 = P(B|A)$, then $P(C|A) = P(C|B)$ for all $C \in \mathcal{G}$,
3. if $P(C|A) \neq 1$, then $P(B^c|A) = 1 - P(B|A)$ for all $B \in \mathcal{G}$,
4. $P(A \wedge B|C) = P(A|C)P(B|A \wedge C)$ for all A, B, C in $\mathcal{G}$,
5. $P(A \wedge B|C) \leq P(B|C)$, for all A, B, C in $\mathcal{G}$,
6. there are two events A and B in $\mathcal{G}$ such that $P(A|B) < P(A|A)$.

Since a conditional probability P is defined on $\mathcal{G} \times \mathcal{B}^o$, to compare it with a Popper measure we need to extend P (with $\mathcal{B} = \mathcal{G}$) to $\mathcal{G} \times \mathcal{G}$, i.e. to allow also $\emptyset$ as conditioning event: notice that the only extension P^* (still dubbed "conditional probability") compatible with Popper measure (cf. axiom 1) is $P^*(A|\emptyset) = 1$ for any $A \in \mathcal{G}$. In [9] we prove the following

Theorem 1 - A conditional probability P^* on $\mathcal{G} \times \mathcal{G}$ is a Popper measure.

The following example shows that the converse is not true: in fact, when $P(H) = 0$, a Popper measure $P(\cdot|H)$ may not be a probability.

Example 1 - Let $\mathcal{E} = \{A_1, A_2, A_3\}$ be a partition of Ω and denote by $\mathcal{G}$ the algebra spanned by $\mathcal{E}$. Putting $P(A_1 \vee A_2|\Omega) = 0$, $P(A_3|\Omega) = 1$, define on $\mathcal{G}$ the measures $P(\cdot|A_1 \vee A_2)$, $P(\cdot|A_1)$, $P(\cdot|A_2)$, $P(\cdot|\emptyset)$ constantly equal to 1. Hence, the other values are uniquely determined by Popper axioms. This is a Popper measure, but $P(\emptyset|A_1 \vee A_2) = 1$ and $P(A_1 \vee A_2|A_1 \vee A_2) \neq P(A_1|A_1 \vee A_2) + P(A_2|A_1 \vee A_2)$.

Notice that this "unpleasant" consequence occurs, even more so, for all definitions that assign *arbitrary* values to $P(\cdot|H)$, as done, for example, by Frisch and Haddawy in [13]. The way–out is through the following modification of axiom 3, that should read: $P(B^c|A) = 1 - P(B|A)$ for all $B \in \mathcal{G}$ and $A \neq \emptyset$.

4 Coherent Conditional Probability and Extensions

In Section 2, conditional probability P has been defined on $\mathcal{G} \times \mathcal{B}^o$; however it is possible, through the concept of *coherence*, to handle also those situations where we need to assess P on an *arbitrary* set $\mathcal{C}$ of conditional events.

Definition 2 - The assessment $P(\cdot|\cdot)$ on $\mathcal{C}$ is *coherent* if there exists $\mathcal{C}' \supset \mathcal{C}$, with $\mathcal{C}' = \mathcal{G} \times \mathcal{B}^o$, such that $P(\cdot|\cdot)$ can be extended from $\mathcal{C}$ to $\mathcal{C}'$ as a *conditional probability.*

A characterization of coherence is given (see, e.g., [3]) by the following

Theorem 3 - Let $\mathcal{C}$ be an arbitrary finite family of conditional events $E_1|H_1, \ldots, E_n|H_n$ and $\mathcal{A}_o$ denote the set of atoms A_r generated by the (unconditional) events $E_1, H_1, \ldots, E_n, H_n$. For a real function P on $\mathcal{C}$ the following two statements are equivalent:

(i) P is a *coherent* conditional probability on $\mathcal{C}$;

(ii) there exists (at least) a *class* of probabilities $\{P_0, P_1, \ldots P_k\}$, each probability P_α being defined on a suitable subset $\mathcal{A}_\alpha \subseteq \mathcal{A}_o$, such that for any $E_i|H_i \in \mathcal{C}$ there is a unique P_α with

$$\sum_{A_r \subseteq H_i}^{r} P_\alpha(A_r) > 0\,, \quad P(E_i|H_i) = \frac{\sum_{A_r \subseteq E_i \wedge H_i}^{r} P_\alpha(A_r)}{\sum_{A_r \subseteq H_i}^{r} P_\alpha(A_r)}\;; \tag{3}$$

moreover $\mathcal{A}_{\alpha'} \subset \mathcal{A}_{\alpha''}$ for $\alpha' > \alpha''$ and $P_{\alpha''}(A_r) = 0$ if $A_r \in \mathcal{A}_{\alpha'}$.

According to Theorem 3, a coherent conditional probability gives rise to a suitable class $\{P_o, P_1, \ldots P_k\}$ of "unconditional" probabilities.

Where do the above classes of probabilities come from? Since P is coherent, there exists an extension P_o on $\mathcal{G} \times \mathcal{G}^o$, where $\mathcal{G}$ is the algebra generated by the set $\mathcal{A}_o$ of atoms: then, putting $\mathcal{B} = \{\Omega, \emptyset\}$, its restriction to $\mathcal{A}_o \times \mathcal{B}^o$ satisfies (3) with $\alpha = 0$ for any $E_i|H_i$ such that $P_o(H_i) > 0$. The subset $\mathcal{A}_1 \subset \mathcal{A}_o$ contains only the atoms $A_r \subseteq H_o^1$, the union of H_i's with $P_o(H_i) = 0$ (and so on: see the system below).

Conversely, given an *assessment* P on the family $\mathcal{C}$, let P_o be a probability on the algebra $\mathcal{G}$ agreeing with the conditional assessment (in the sense that, for every conditional event of $\mathcal{C}$, *(ii)* is satisfied for $H_i = \Omega$). Let $\mathcal{G}_1 \subset \mathcal{G}$ be the subalgebra of events $E \in \mathcal{G}$ such that $P_o(E) = 0$; we can define a new probability P_1 on $\mathcal{G}_1$, agreeing with the conditional assessment whose *conditioning* event is in $\mathcal{G}_1$, and consider $\mathcal{G}_2 \subset \mathcal{G}_1$ such that $P_1(E) = 0$, and so on. It is clear that in this process, given $\beta > \alpha$, the assignment of the probability P_β is in no way bound by the probability P_α (except for the domain), but the only constraints are given by the conditional assessments. So, starting from the class $\mathcal{P} = \{P_\alpha\}$, the function $P(\cdot|\cdot)$ on $\mathcal{G} \times \mathcal{G}^o$ defined by putting, for any $E|H \in \mathcal{G} \times \mathcal{G}^o$,

$$P(E|H) = \frac{P_\alpha(EH)}{P_\alpha(H)}\,,$$

where α is the index such that $P_\alpha(H) > 0$, is a *conditional probability* on $\mathcal{G} \times \mathcal{G}^o$ (as proved, for example, in [5]).

The proof of the equivalence between conditions (i) and (ii) gives rise to an algorithm to test the coherence of the assessment P, based on the equivalence between condition (ii) and the compatibility of a sequence of systems $(\mathcal{S}_\alpha)$ with unknowns $P_\alpha(A_r) \geq 0$, $A_r \in \mathcal{A}_\alpha$,

$$(\mathcal{S}_\alpha) \quad \begin{cases} \sum_{A_r \subseteq E_i \wedge H_i}^{r} P_\alpha(A_r) = P(E_i|H_i) \sum_{A_r \subseteq H_i}^{r} P_\alpha(A_r) & \left[\text{if } P_{\alpha-1}(H_i) = 0\right], \\ \sum_{A_r \subseteq H_0^\alpha}^{r} P_\alpha(A_r) = 1 \end{cases}$$

where $P_{-1}(H_i) = 0$ for all H_i's, and H_o^α denotes, for $\alpha \geq 0$, the union of the H_i's such that $P_{\alpha-1}(H_i) = 0$; so, in particular, $H_o^o = H_o = H_1 \cup \ldots \cup H_n$.

Any class $\{P_\alpha\}$ singled-out by the condition *(ii)* is said *to agree* with the conditional probability P. Notice that in general there are infinite classes of probabilities $\{P_\alpha\}$; in particular we have *only one class* in the case that $\mathcal{C}$ is a product of Boolean algebras.

Another fundamental result is the following, essentially due (for unconditional events, and referring to an equivalent form of coherence in terms of betting scheme) to de Finetti [11] (and extended to conditional events in [18], [26]).

Theorem 2 - Let $\mathcal{C}$ be a family of conditional events and P a corresponding assessment; then there exists a (possibly not unique) coherent extension of P to an *arbitrary* family $\mathcal{K} \supseteq \mathcal{C}$, *if and only if* P is coherent on $\mathcal{C}$.

In particular, given a "new" conditional event $E|H$, *i.e.* if $\mathcal{K} = \mathcal{C} \cup \{E|H\}$, then coherent assessments of $p = P(E|H)$ are all values of a suitable closed interval $[p', p''] \subseteq [0,1]$, with $p' \leq p''$. For a finite $\mathcal{C}$, in [3], [5] the two bounds p' and p'' have been *characterised* as infimum and supremum, respectively, of probabilities $P(E_*|H_*)$ and $P(E^*|H^*)$ of *suitable conditional events.* The relevant algorithm, based on linear programming technique, has been implemented in [1].

Notice that the problem of "updating" the priors $P(H_i)$ into the posteriors $P(H_i|E)$ (through Bayes' theorem, for a set of *exhaustive and mutually exclusive* hypotheses H_i) is just a very particular case of a coherent extension (see [7]): this Bayesian extension is unique and can be computed only if $P(E) > 0$.

5 Zero-layers and Spohn's ranking function

Given a class $\mathcal{P} = \{P_\alpha\}$, agreeing with a conditional probability, it is possible to define the *zero-layer* $\circ(H)$ of an event H as

$$\circ(H) = \alpha \quad \text{if } P_\alpha(H) > 0\,,$$

and the zero-layer of a conditional event $E|H$ as

$$\circ(E|H) = \circ(E \wedge H) - \circ(H).$$

Obviously, for the certain event Ω and for any event E with positive probability, we have $\circ(\Omega) = \circ(E) = 0$ (so that, if the class contains only an *everywhere positive* probability P_o, there is only one (trivial) zero-layer, *i.e.* $\alpha = 0$), while the zero-layer $\circ(\emptyset)$ is greater than that of any possible event (so that we put $\circ(\emptyset) = +\infty$).

For an example, see Section 6.2, where we will show the crucial role played by zero-layers for the concept of conditional independence.

On the other hand, Spohn (see, for example, [31], [32]) considers degrees of plausibility defined via a *ranking* function, that is a map κ that assigns to each *possible* proposition a natural number (its *rank*) such that

(a) either $\kappa(A) = 0$ or $\kappa(A^c) = 0$ (or both);
(b) $\kappa(A \vee B) = \min\{\kappa(A), \kappa(B)\}$;
(c) for all $A \wedge B \neq \emptyset$ the conditional rank of B given A is $\kappa(B|A) = \kappa(A \wedge B) - \kappa(A)$.

Ranks represent degrees of "disbelief". For example, A is *not* disbelieved iff $\kappa(A) = 0$, and it is disbelieved iff $\kappa(A) > 0$. Ranking functions are seen by Spohn as a tool to manage *plain belief* and *belief revision*, since he maintains that probability is inadequate for this purpose. In our framework this claim can be challenged, since our tools for belief revision are *coherent conditional probabilities* and the ensuing concept of *zero-layers*: it is easy to check that zero-layers have the same formal properties of ranking functions.

A brief discussion of *plain belief* is in Section 6.1.

6 Coherent Conditional Probability as Unifying Tool

In this Section we discuss briefly how to handle, by means of *coherent* conditional probability, some aspects of *default reasoning* (see, e.g., [27], [29]) and *conditional independence.*

In Section 6.3 we consider an example in which we put together different kinds of information and show how coherent conditional probability can act as a unifying tool.

6.1 On the default reasoning

First of all, we show that a sensible use of events whose probability is 0 (or 1) can be a more general tool in revising beliefs when new information comes to the fore.

We can challenge (see also [14]) a claim contained in [30] that probability is inadequate for revising plain belief: "I believe A is true *cannot be represented by* $P(A) = 1$ *because a probability equal to* 1 *is incorrigible, that is,* $P(A|B) = 1$ *for all* B *such that* $P(A|B)$ *is well defined. However, plain belief is clearly corrigible. I may believe it is snowing outside but when I look out the window and observe that it has stopped snowing, I now believe that it is not snowing outside".* In the usual framework, the above reasoning is correct, since $P(B) > 0$ implies that *there are no logical relations between* B *and* A (*i.e.*, in particular, $A \wedge B \neq \emptyset$) and $P(A|B) = 1$. Taking instead $P(B) = 0$, we may have $A \wedge B = \emptyset$ and so $P(A|B) = 0$. On the other hand, taking $B=$ "looking out the window, one observes that it is not snowing" (again assuming $P(B) = 0$), and putting $A=$"it is snowing outside", we can put $P(A) = 1$ to express a strong belief in A. Then it is clearly possible to assess coherently $P(A|B) = p$ for every $p \in [0, 1]$. So, contrary to the claim in [30], a probability equal to 1 *can be updated.*

Now we discuss briefly (exploiting the possibility of updating, in our setting, a probability equal to 1) the *default reasoning*, by referring to the classic example of Tweety. As recalled in Section 1, we may deal with the extreme value $P(E|H) = 1$ also for situations which are different from the trivial one $H \subseteq E$: the latter can be anyway useful to express that a penguin ($\mathcal{P}$) is *certainly* a bird ($\mathcal{B}$), i.e. $\mathcal{P} \subseteq \mathcal{B}$, by putting $P(\mathcal{B}|\mathcal{P}) = 1$; moreover we know that usually Tweety ($\mathcal{T}$) is a penguin, and this fact can be represented by $P(\mathcal{P}|\mathcal{T}) = 1$.

But we can express as well the statement "a penguin *usually* does not fly" (we denote by $\mathcal{F}^c$ the contrary of $\mathcal{F}$, the latter symbol denoting "flying") by writing $P(\mathcal{F}^c|\mathcal{P}) = 1$. Then the question "can Tweety fly?" can be faced through an assessment of the conditional probability $P(\mathcal{F}|\mathcal{T})$, which must be coherent with the already assessed ones: by Theorem 3, it can be shown that *any value* $p \in [0, 1]$ is a coherent value for $P(\mathcal{F}|\mathcal{T})$, so that no conclusion can be reached – *from the given premises* – on Tweety's ability of flying. In other words, interpreting an equality such as $P(E|H) = 1$ like a sort of *weak implication* (denoted by $\longmapsto$), which in particular (when $H \subseteq E$) reduces to the usual one, we have shown its *nontransitivity*: in fact

$$\mathcal{T} \longmapsto \mathcal{P} \text{ and } \mathcal{P} \longmapsto \mathcal{F}^c ,$$

but it *does not* necessarily follow that $\mathcal{T} \longmapsto \mathcal{F}^c$ (even if we *might* have that $P(\mathcal{F}^c|\mathcal{T}) = 1$, *i.e.* that "Tweety usually does not fly").

Notice the simplicity of this approach, which encompasses other well–known methodologies, such as that by Goldszmidt and Pearl [16].

6.2 Conditional Independence

In this Section, to avoid cumbersome notation, we will denote any conjunction $E \wedge H$ simply by EH.

It is well known that the classical definition of stochastic independence of two events A, B, *i.e.*

$$P(AB) = P(A)P(B) ,$$

gives rise to counterintuitive situations, in particular when the given events have probability 0 or 1. For example, an event A with $P(A) = 0$ or 1 is stochastically independent of itself, while it is natural (due to the intuitive meaning of independence) to require for *any* event E to be *dependent* on itself.

We recall some results from [4], extended to *conditional* independence in [33].

Definition 3 - Given a set $\mathcal{E}$ of events containing A, B, C, A^c, B^c, with $BC \neq \Omega$, $BC \neq \emptyset$, and a *coherent* conditional probability P, defined on a family $\mathcal{C} \subset \mathcal{E} \times \mathcal{E}^o$ and containing $\mathcal{D} = \{A|BC, A|B^cC, A^c|BC, A^c|B^cC\}$, we say that A is *conditionally independent* of B given C with respect to P (in symbols $A \perp\!\!\!\perp_{cs} B|C$) if *both* the following conditions hold:

(i) $P(A|BC) = P(A|B^cC)$;

(ii) there exists a class $\{P_\alpha\}$ of probabilities agreeing with the restriction of P to the family $\mathcal{D}$, such that

$$\circ(A|BC) = \circ(A|B^cC) \quad \text{and} \quad \circ(A^c|BC) = \circ(A^c|B^cC).$$

If condition *(i)* holds with $P(A|BC) = 0$, then the second equality under *(ii)* is trivially satisfied, so that conditional independence is ruled by the first one (in other words, *equality (i) is not enough to assure independence when both sides are null: it needs to be "reinforced" by the requirement that also their zero-layers must be equal*). Analogously, if condition *(i)* holds with $P(A|BC) = 1$ (so that $P(A^c|BC) = 0$), independence is ruled by the second equality under *(ii)*.

The symmetry property

$$A \perp\!\!\!\perp_{cs} B|C \Longrightarrow B \perp\!\!\!\perp_{cs} A|C$$

does not hold in general (see [33], [34]). For a "semantic" interpretation (in the case $C = \Omega$), we recall the following example given in [4].

Example 2 - Consider two events A, B, with

$$P(A) = 0\,,\; P(B) = \frac{1}{4}\,;$$

for instance, $B = \{4n\}_{n \in \mathbf{N}}$, $A = \{97, 44, 402\}$, which are among the possible answers that can be obtained by asking a mathematician to choose at his will and tell us a natural number n (a possible choice could be $n = [e^{427}]! + 1$, where $[x]$ denotes the maximum integer $\leq x$). Clearly, the probability distribution of the possible answers is a finitely additive one, with $P(n) = 0$ for any n. Assessing

$$P(B|A) = \frac{1}{3}\,,\; P(B|A^c) = \frac{1}{4}\,,$$

it turns out that $B \perp\!\!\!\perp_{cs} A$ does not hold, while $A \perp\!\!\!\perp_{cs} B$: in fact, assessing

$$P(B|A) = 0 = P(B|A^c)\,,$$

we need to find the relevant zero–layers, and system (S_o) gives easily $P_o(AB) = 0 < P_o(B)$ and $P_o(AB^c) = 0 < P_o(B^c)$, while system (S_1) gives $P_1(AB) > 0$ and $P_1(AB^c) > 0$, so that

$$\circ(A|B) = \circ(AB) - \circ(B) = 1 - 0 = \circ(AB^c) - \circ(B^c) = 1 = \circ(A|B^c).$$

This lack of symmetry means (roughly speaking) that the occurrence of the event B of *positive* probability does not "influence" the probability of A; but this circumstance does not entail, conversely, that the occurrence of the "unexpected" (zero probability) event A does not "influence" the (positive) probability of B.

Theorem 4 - Given the *possible* events AC, BC, with $AC \subset C$, if $A \perp\!\!\!\perp_{cs} B|C$, then A and B are *logically independent* (*i.e.*, none of the four events AB, A^cB, AB^c, A^cB^c is impossible).

In [4], [34] there are also theorems characterizing stochastic independence of two logically independent events A and B in terms of the probabilities $P(B|C)$, $P(B|AC)$ and $P(B|A^cC)$, *giving up any direct reference to the zero-layers.*

The usual definition [10] of conditional independence does not imply *logical* independence. For example Witthaker in [35] considers a probability distribution on the events A, B, C such that $P(ABC) + P(A^cB^cC^c) = 1$: hence the event A turns out to be conditionally independent of B given C, even if $A = B = C$ (so that A and B are *not* logically independent). This is counterintuitive: it is possible to show [33] that, with our definition, the conditional independence does not hold. Going back to Example 2 and checking all possible conditional independence statements, we always get different results from the usual theory, for which statements such as $A \perp\!\!\!\perp B|E$ and $B \perp\!\!\!\perp E|A$ cannot even be considered; moreover $E \perp\!\!\!\perp A|B$ holds in spite of the *logical* dependence between E and A, while $E \perp\!\!\!\perp_{cs} A|B$ *does not* hold (as can be easily checked taking the *coherent* assessment $P(E|AB) = 1 \neq P(E|A^cB) = 0$).

This more general concept of conditional independence has been studied (also for random variables) in [34]. The graphoid properties (see [24]) have been checked: in our framework, the set of conditional independence statements is closed with respect to the properties of *decomposition* and its reverse, *weak union*, *contraction* and its reverse, *intersection* (for which there is no need to require strict positivity of the relevant probability) and its reverse, while *the symmetric property does not hold* in general. Therefore our independence model is more general than a graphoid structure (which in the usual independence models is induced by a strictly positive probability).

The representation problem by means of graphs (also for models not closed with respect to the symmetric property) has been faced in [33].

6.3 Putting together different kinds of partial knowledge

Example 3 - This example extends Example 3 given in [7]. A patient arrives at the hospital showing symptoms of choking: the doctor considers the following hypotheses concerning the patient situation: H_1="cardiac insufficiency", H_2="asthma attack", $H_3 = H_2 \wedge H$, where H="cardiac lesion". The doctor does not regard them as mutually exclusive; moreover, he assumes the following natural logical relation: $H_3 \subset H_1 \wedge H_2$. The doctor makes the probability assessments

$$P(H_2) = \frac{1}{3}\,, \;\; P(H_3) = \frac{1}{5}\,, \;\; P(H_1 \vee H_2) = \frac{3}{5}\,,$$

and he expresses the *comparative* judgement $H_2 \prec H_1$, *i.e.* the asthma attack is "less probable" than cardiac insufficiency. It means that $P(H_1) = p$, where p must be a value strictly greater than $P(H_2) = \frac{1}{3}$. Its coherence is easily checked by referring to the system of Section 4, which has in this case the solution

$$P(H_1H_2H_3^c) = p - \frac{7}{15}\,, \;\; P(H_1^cH_2H_3^c) = \frac{9}{15} - p\,,$$

$$P(H_1H_2H_3) = \frac{1}{5}\,, \;\; P(H_1H_2^cH_3^c) = \frac{4}{15} = 2P(H_1^cH_2^cH_3^c)$$

under the constraint $\frac{7}{15} \le p \le \frac{9}{15}$.

Put now $E =$"taking the medicine M against asthma does not reduce choking symptoms". Since the *fact* E is incompatible with having asthma attack (H_2), unless the patient has cardiac insufficiency or lesion (recall that H_3 implies both H_1 and H_2), then for the doctor $H_2 \wedge H_1^c \wedge E = \emptyset$. Moreover, he believes that *usually* the medicine M does not reduce symptoms if the patient suffers from cardiac insufficiency, so – by the theory sketched in Section 7.1 – it follows $P(E|H_1) = 1$. A further information comes from his database, the "partial likelihood" $P(E|H_3^c) = \frac{1}{3}$. The whole "knowledge" is coherent, as can be proved by solving the relevant system, and we get

$$P(E^c H_1 H_2 H_3) = P(E^c H_1 H_2 H_3^c) = 0\,, \quad P(E^c H_1^c H_2 H_3^c) = \frac{2}{15}\,,$$

$$P(E^c H_1 H_2^c H_3^c) = 0\,, \quad P(E^c H_1^c H_2^c H_3^c) = \frac{2}{5}\,, \quad P(E H_1 H_2 H_3) = \frac{1}{5}\,,$$

$$P(E H_1 H_2 H_3^c) = 0\,, \quad P(E H_1 H_2^c H_3^c) = \frac{4}{15}\,, \quad P(E H_1^c H_2^c H_3^c) = 0$$

and $p = \frac{7}{15}$. Then the updating process allows to compute $P(H_i|E)$, $i = 1, 2, 3$, for example $P(H_2|E) = \frac{3}{7}$. For the sake of brevity, we omit other details.

References

1. Capotorti, A., Vantaggi, B.: Locally Strong Coherence in Inference Processes. Annals of Mathematics and Artificial Intelligence (2001), to appear
2. Coletti, G., Gilio, A., Scozzafava, R.: Conditional Events with Vague Information in Expert Systems. In: Lecture Notes in Computer Sciences, n.521, Springer-Verlag, Berlin (1991) 106–114
3. Coletti, G., Scozzafava, R.: Characterization of Coherent Conditional Probabilities as a Tool for their Assessment and Extension. International Journal of Uncertainty, Fuzziness and Knowledge-Based System **4** (1996) 103–127
4. Coletti, G., Scozzafava, R.: Zero Probabilities in Stochastical Independence. In: Information, Uncertainty, Fusion, Kluwer, Dordrecht (2000) 185–196. (Selected papers from IPMU '98, Paris)
5. Coletti, G., Scozzafava, R.: Conditioning and Inference in Intelligent Systems. Soft Computing **3** (1999) 118–130
6. Coletti, G., Scozzafava, R.: Conditional Subjective Probability and Fuzzy Theory. In: Proc. 18th Int. Conf. of NAFIPS, New York (1999) 77–80
7. Coletti, G., Scozzafava, R.: The Role of Coherence in Eliciting and Handling Imprecise Probabilities and its Application to Medical Diagnosis. Information Sciences **130** (2000) 41–65
8. Coletti, G., Scozzafava, R.: Fuzzy Sets as Conditional Probabilities: which Meaningful Operations can be Defined? In: Proc. 20th Int. Conf. of NAFIPS, Vancouver, Canada, (2001), to appear
9. Coletti, G., Scozzafava, R., Vantaggi, B.: The Role of Coherent Conditional Probability in Inferential Reasoning, in preparation
10. Dawid, A.P.: Conditional Independence in Statistical Theory. Journal of Royal Statistical Society B **41** (1979) 15–31

11. de Finetti, B.: Sull'impostazione assiomatica del calcolo delle probabilità. Annali Univ. Trieste **19** (1949) 3–55. (Engl. transl.: Ch.5 in: Probability, Induction, Statistics, Wiley, London, 1972)
12. Dubins, L.E.: Finitely Additive Conditional Probabilities, Conglomerability and Disintegration. Annals of Probability **3** (1975) 89–99
13. Frisch, A.M., Haddawy, P.: Anytime Deduction for Probabilistic Logic. Artificial Intelligence **69**, 1-2 (1993) 93–122
14. Gilio, A.: Conditional events and subjective probability in management of uncertainty. In: Uncertainty in Intelligent Systems, Elsevier, Amsterdam (1993) 109–120
15. Gilio, A., Scozzafava, R.: Le probabilità condizionate coerenti nei sistemi esperti. In: Ricerca Operativa e Intelligenza Artificiale, A.I.R.O., IBM Pisa (1988) 317–330
16. Goldszmidt, M., Pearl, J.: Qualitative probability for default reasoning, belief revision and causal modeling. Artificial Intelligence **84** (1996) 57–112
17. Harper, W.L.: Rational Belief Change, Popper Functions and Counterfactuals. In: Harper, Hooker (eds): Foundations of Probability Theory, Statistical Inference, and Statistical Theories of Sciences **1** (1976) 73–115
18. Holzer, S.: On Coherence and Conditional Prevision. Boll. Un. Mat. Ital. (6) **4** (1985) 441–460
19. Koopman, B.O.: The Bases of Probability. Bulletin A.M.S. **46** (1940) 763–774
20. Krauss, P.H.: Representation of Conditional Probability Measures on Boolean Algebras. Acta Math. Acad. Scient. Hungar. 19 (1968) 229–241
21. Lauritzen, S.L.: Graphical Models. Clarendon Press, Oxford (1996)
22. Nilsson, N.J.: Probabilistic Logic. Artificial Intelligence **28** (1986) 71–87
23. Nilsson, N.J.: Probabilistic Logic Revisited. Artificial Intelligence **59** (1993) 39–42
24. Pearl, J.: Probabilistic Reasoning in Intelligent Systems: Networks of Plausible Inference. Morgan Kaufmann, San Mateo CA (1988)
25. Popper, K.R.: The Logic of Scientific Discovery. Routledge, London and New York (1959)
26. Regazzini, E.: Finitely Additive Conditional Probabilities. Rend. Sem. Mat. Fis. Milano **55** (1985) 69–89
27. Reiter, R.: A Logic for Default Reasoning. Artificial Intelligence, **13**, 1-2 (1980) 81–132
28. Rényi, A.: On Conditional Probability Spaces Generated by a Dimensionally Ordered Set of Measures. Theory of Probability and its Applications **1** (1956) 61–71
29. Russel, S.J., Norvig, P.: Artificial Intelligence. A Modern Approach. Prentice-Hall, New Jersey (1995)
30. Shenoy, P.P.: On Spohn's Rule for Revision of Beliefs. International Journal of Approximate Reasoning **5** (1991) 149–181
31. Spohn, W.: On the Properties of Conditional Independence. In: Humphreys, P., Suppes, P. (eds): Scientific Philosopher **1**: Probability and Probabilistic Causality, Kluwer, Dordrecht (1994) 173–194
32. Spohn, W.: Ranking Functions, AGM Style. Research Group "Logic in Philosophy" Preprint **28** (1999)
33. Vantaggi, B.: Conditional Independence and Graphical Models in a Coherent Setting. PhD thesis, Università di Perugia, Italy (1999)
34. Vantaggi, B.: Conditional Independence in a Finite Coherent Setting. Annals of Mathematics and Artificial Intelligence (2001), to appear
35. Witthaker, J.: Graphical Models in Applied Multivariate Statistics. Wiley & Sons, New York (1990)

An Operational View of Coherent Conditional Previsions

Andrea Capotorti and Tania Paneni

Dip. di Matematica e Informatica
Università di Perugia,
via Vanvitelli 1 06123 Perugia - Italy capot@dipmat.unipg.it,
panenita@linux-aula.dipmat.unipg.it

Abstract. In this paper we propose a characterization theorem for coherent conditional previsions assessed on finite conditional random variables. The main feature is the direct applicability of the results to model practical problems. In fact the check of coherence and the inferential steps are reduced to the solvability of linear systems and of linear programming problems, respectively. The guideline of the procedure has been the already stated results for coherent conditional probabilities, so that now we have a unified theory for uncertainty represented by belief or synthesized by prevision. The procedure turns out to be helpful when the size of the relevant quantities strongly depend on the different scenarios in which they are considered. A simple example shows the potentiality of the entire machinery on a decision-aid problem.

1 Introduction

From applied areas in the treatment of uncertainty, the request of procedures that well "fuse" together large applicability, soundness in results and dynamic behaviour, are strongly demanded. For these reasons (but not only these) the approaches that go back to the more general interpretation of probability are having a wider and wider diffusion (as a representative, but not exhaustive, list see for example [3,4,5,6,7,11]). In fact, in the last decades several approaches have been developed adopting different uncertainty measure to escape from the "heavy and frozen" primordial probabilistic models. Anyhow, with a careful distinction between what are the logical and what the numerical components of the problem at hand, it is possible to stay within the "safe" probabilistic machinery, but requiring few information, just those really needed and available. This is possible by working with what are called "partial assessments", that means with numerical evaluations not given on fully specified framework (representable by mathematical structures with particularly nice properties), but on "macro situations" represented by arbitrary sets of quantities.

Obviously, mathematical structures will be adopted, but just as operational tools and will be generated by the information and not requested "a priori".

In these approaches, conditional evaluations, that well represent real phenomena whose entity strongly depends on the different scenarios in which they are studied, can be given directly and not as derived tools.

S. Benferhat and P. Besnard (Eds.): ECSQARU 2001, LNAI 2143, pp. 132–143, 2001.

When the uncertainty is numerically expressed by an assessment of previsions $\mathbb{P}$ on a set of (conditional) random variables $Y_i|H_i$, the principle that guides all these methodologies is that of coherence, introduced by de Finetti in [9] and later refreshed ([10,12]), developed for applied problems ([11]) and generalized ([7]). This principle is mainly based on a betting scheme, so that it could appear too abstract for practical applications. Anyhow, thanks to several alternative theorems, it has been shown it is possible to reduce it to linear programming problems, finding a good tool to deal with representation and analysis of real situations (once again, as reference points see for example [3,5,7,11])

On the subject of conditional probability assessments (i.e. when the Y_i's are $\{0,1\}$ random variables) and on that of unconditional previsions (i.e. when the H_i are the sure event), there are nowadays sound and well established results directly applicable. In particular, conditional probabilities have been characterized through *sequences* of unconditional probability distributions attainable solving *sequences* of linear systems. Once such distributions are obtained, any kind of inference step can be easily guided.

On the other hand, the results for conditional prevision assessments were almost theorical, so with this paper we "build a bridge" with the operational aspects.

In particular, in Sect.2 we will give the primary notions and the already known results about coherent conditional probabilities and previsions. In Sect.3 we propose a characterization theorem for conditional coherent previsions and inferential steps which use linear programming techniques, in analogy with what has been done for coherent conditional probabilities. Hence everything can be easily implemented for automatic decision-aid systems working on a finite framework, which is the natural choice for practical applications. And finally, to better understand all the "apparatus", we also describe in Sect.4 a simplified example of application of our results.

2 Preliminaries

First of all we need to introduce a suitable notation to adapt to our purpose the different (but strictly connected) approaches present in the literature (see for example [7,10]).

Given an arbitrary finite set $\mathcal{V}$ of finite random variables (r.v.) we denote by $< \mathcal{V} >$ the algebra spanned by the elementary events $\{V_i = v\}$, with $V_i \in \mathcal{V}$ [1]. Denoting by Ω the set of all the atoms A_r of $< \mathcal{V} >$, $r = 1, \dots, \#\Omega$ [2], any r.v. $V_i \in \mathcal{V}$ can be identified with a vector of $\mathbb{R}^{\#(\Omega)}$ (which we continue to designate with the same symbol). Its components v_{ir}'s represent the values taken by V_i on the different A_r's. In particular, if the r.v. V_i is an event E, its associated vector reduces to the indicator of the atoms $A_r \subseteq E$ (the sure event Ω coincide with the set of all the atoms and will have all components equal to 1, while

[1] Throughout all the paper we make the assumption to work in a finite framework so that, when not explicitly mentioned, it must be understood.

[2] With $\#(A)$ we denote the cardinality of any set A.

the impossible event ϕ coincide with the empty set of atoms and will have all components equal to 0).

In this way we can represent the logical connectives by arithmetic operations to apply component-wise to vectors, as shown in the following table

set repr.	vector repr.
$E \subseteq F$	$E \leq F$
$E \cap F$	EF (product)
$E \cup F$	$E \vee F$ (max)

These component-wise operations can be extended also to linear combinations of random variables, so that to $\sum_i \lambda_i V_i$ is associated the vector with r-th component $\sum_i \lambda_i v_{ir}$.

With such notation we can also easily represent the linear decomposition of the probability of an event $P(E)$ on its components $P(A_r)$. In fact, if $\mathbf{X}$ represents a vector whose components are $x_r = P(A_r)$, with P distribution of probability, then, for every event E, $P(E) = E \cdot \mathbf{X} = \sum_{A_r \leq E} x_r$, where $\cdot$ stands for the scalar product.

We will mainly deal with a set of conditional random variables $\mathcal{D} = \{Y_1|H_1, \ldots, Y_n|H_n\}$. A conditional r.v. $Y_i|H_i$ is usually understood as the restriction of the r.v. Y_i to the atoms in H_i,

To the set $\mathcal{D}$ we do not require any particular property (like to be a ring or to be closed under some operation) but we need to know the logical relations among both the events of the form $\{Y_i = y_i\}$ and the H_i's to be able to know (at least "potentially") the algebra $\mathcal{A} =< \{Y_i H_i : Y_i|H_i \in \mathcal{D}\} >$.

Very often we will refer to atoms $A_r \in \mathcal{A}$ with the further property to be inside some conditioning event H_i, so that we will denote by H_0 the union of all the conditioning ($H_0 = \bigvee_1^n H_i$) and by $\mathcal{A}_{|H_0}$ the subalgebra generated by such atoms.

The set $\mathcal{D}$ will be used to formalize the structure of quantities involved in a practical decision process together with their specific scenarios (the hypotheses H_i's). On the contrary, uncertainty about the possible values for the $Y_i|H_i$'s will be summarized by a n-vector $\mathbb{P}$ of real numbers, whose components $\mathbb{P}(Y_i|H_i)$ represent the previsions on the single $Y_i|H_i$'s expressed by a subject (an "expert" or more generally a decision maker). To obtain sound decisions, such values must be consistent and for this de Finetti [8] has introduced the Coherence Principle that later others ([7,10,11,12]) have refreshed, extended and found relevant application.

A full and detailed presentation of all the known properties and results is here impossible, so we limit to report the definitions and theorems introduced in the cited papers that we will use in the sequel. The notation is adapted to our framework, even if the vector notation is not always adopted because, even if it is more concise than others, sometimes it makes hard the understanding of the properties.

Definition 1. (The Principle of Conditional Coherence) *Let $\mathbb{P}$ be a map from $\mathcal{D}$ to $\mathbb{R}$. Then $\mathbb{P}$ is a* coherent conditional prevision *on $\mathcal{D}$ iff for all $Y_1|H_1, ..., Y_n|H_n \in \mathcal{D}$ and $\lambda_1, ..., \lambda_n \in \mathbb{R}$, the random number(random gain)*

$$G = \sum_{1}^{n} \lambda_i (Y_i - \mathbb{P}(Y_i|H_i))H_i$$

is such that $minG_{|H_0} maxG_{|H_0} \leq 0$, where $H_0 = H_1 \vee ..... \vee H_n$ and $minG_{|H_0}$, $maxG_{|H_0}$ are the minimum and the maximun, respectively, of the components associated to the atoms $A_r \leq H_0$ in the vector G.

The introduction of the random gain G (which has an its own interpretation in a betting scheme) is needed to introduce "interaction" among conditional random variables.

When the domain $\mathcal{D}$ has particular algebraic properties, the coherence is guaranteed by numerical conditions. One of these situation is:

Definition 2. *Let $\mathcal{Y}$ be the ring of all the random variables (including the constants and the indicator functions) with support on the finite algebra $\mathcal{A}$. Then a real function $\mathbb{P}$ on $\mathcal{Y}|(\mathcal{A} \setminus \{\phi\})$ is a* full *conditional prevision iff the following four properties hold (any time $\mathbb{P}$ appears its argument lies in $\mathcal{Y}|(\mathcal{A} \setminus \{\phi\})$):*
i) If $Y|H \geq 0$ then $\mathbb{P}(Y|H) \geq 0$ *(positivity)*
ii) $\mathbb{P}(\cdot|H)$ is a linear map *(linearity)*
iii) $\mathbb{P}(H|H) = 1$ *(normality)*
iv) $\mathbb{P}(YH|K) = \mathbb{P}(H|K)\mathbb{P}(Y|HK)$ *(multiplicative property)*

and in [10] it is shown that a full conditional prevision is coherent.

Anyhow, the relationship between *coherent* and *full* conditional prevision goes further, and in particular we have the following fundamental theorem (Th. 4.4 in [10], pag. 453):

Theorem 1. *Let $\mathcal{D} = \{Y_1|H_1, ..., Y_n|H_n\}$, $\mathcal{A} =< \mathcal{D} >$ and $\mathcal{Y}$ be the ring of all the random variables (including the constants and the indicator functions) with support on the finite algebra $\mathcal{A}$, then $\mathbb{P} = \{\mathbb{P}(Y_1|H_1), \ldots, \mathbb{P}(Y_n|H_n)\}$ is a* coherent prevision iff *there exists a* full conditional prevision *$\mathbb{P}'$, defined on $\mathcal{Y}|(\mathcal{A} \setminus \{\phi\})$, extension of $\mathbb{P}$.*

This principle is a direct consequence of the "Extension Property" and of the so called "Equivalence Principle" whose proofs in [10] are based on the betting scheme, involving the random gain G.

When, in particular, the domain $\mathcal{D}$ is actually a set of conditional events $\mathcal{E} = \{E_1|H_1, \ldots, E_n|H_n\}$ (i.e. the possible values for Y_i are only in $\{0,1\}$), instead of a general prevision we talk about a conditional probability assessment $P : \mathcal{E} \to [0,1]$. In this situation the Coherence Principle and the "fullness" are obtained by replacing in Def.1 and 2 the word "prevision" with "probability" and "the ring $\mathcal{Y}$" with "the Boolean algebra $\mathcal{A}$". Obviously we have that the existence of a full extension P' on $\mathcal{A}|(\mathcal{A} \setminus \{\phi\})$ of a conditional probability assessment P on $\mathcal{E}$ is a necessary and sufficient condition for the coherence of P.

Anyhow, for conditional probabilities assessment, in [3,5,7] a different (and more operative) kind of characterization of coherence has been introduced and widely adopted. We report one of their main results with an associated remark helpful for us in the sequel:

Theorem 2. *Let $P : \mathcal{E} = \{E_1|H_1, \dots, E_n|H_n\} \longrightarrow [0,1]$ be a numerical assessment. The following propositions are equivalent:*

- *P is a coherent conditional probability*
- *there exists at least one finite class of unconditional probabilities $\{P_0, P_1, \dots P_k\}$ each probability P_α being defined on a suitable subset $\mathcal{A}_\alpha \subseteq \mathcal{A}_\mathcal{E}$, such that for all $E_i|H_i \in \mathcal{E}$ there exists a unique P_α, with*

$$\sum_{A_r \leq H_i} P_\alpha(A_r) > 0$$

and

$$P(E_i|H_i) = \frac{\sum\limits_{A_r \leq E_i H_i} P_\alpha(A_r)}{\sum\limits_{A_r \leq H_i} P_\alpha(A_r)}.$$

Remark 1. The probabilities $P_\alpha(A_r)$ are precisely the solutions of the systems

$$\mathcal{S}_\alpha = \begin{cases} \sum\limits_{A_r \leq E_i H_i} x_r^\alpha = p_i \sum\limits_{A_r \leq H_i} x_r^\alpha, & \text{if } P_{\alpha-1}(H_i) = 0 \\ \sum x_r^\alpha > 0 \\ x_r^\alpha \geq 0 \end{cases} \tag{1}$$

where $p_i = P(E_i|H_i)$ and the x_r^α's are the unknowns associated to $P_\alpha(A_r)$, with A_r atom of $\mathcal{A}_{|H_0}$ for $\alpha = 0$ and of $\mathcal{A}_\alpha = < \{H_i : P_{\alpha-1}(H_i) = 0\} >_{|H_0^\alpha}$, for $\alpha \geq 1$.

Moreover, the restriction of the subalgebra to the atoms contained in H_0^α, for $\alpha \geq 1$, can be avoided taking subsets $\mathcal{A}_\alpha^*$ constituted by all the atoms A_r such that $P_{\alpha-1}(A_r) = 0$ (not only those contained in the relevant H_i's), extending each P_α on $\mathcal{A}_\alpha^*$ as

$$P_\alpha^* = \begin{cases} P_\alpha(A_r) & \text{if } A_r \in \mathcal{A}_\alpha \\ 0 & \text{if } A_r \in \mathcal{A}_\alpha^* \setminus \mathcal{A}_\alpha \end{cases}$$

If the set $\mathcal{A}_k^* \setminus \mathcal{A}_k$ is not empty, we can take an arbitrary probability distribution P^0 on these "remaining " atoms.

The operational lack of Theorem 1 is that it is just an existence theorem, while the powerfulness of the Characterization Theorem 2 is in the reduction of the problem of checking the coherence to a sequence of linear systems, whose solutions allow to build the necessary full conditional distribution. Note that, generally, the solution of one single system is not sufficient (see the examples reported in [3]) to ensure the coherence of P, in opposition with the definition where there is a single random gain G. Moreover, the possible presence of different "zero layers" (the α's) not only allows to deal with really general conditional assessments, but can also be skillfully used to reduce the computational complexity in implementations for automatic procedures, as already stated in [5,7] and later developed in [1,2]. Such a reduction is possible because it is not necessary to build all the atoms of the algebra $\mathcal{A}$ but only those that, at each layer, are really needed.

3 From Conditional Probabilities to Conditional Previsions

If the results about conditional *probability* assessments are nowadays well established, it is not the same for conditional *prevision* assessments. So, with the "guideline" of Theorem 2 and Remark 1, we propose the following characterization theorem:

Theorem 3. *Let $\mathcal{D} = \{Y_1|H_1, \ldots, Y_n|H_n\}$ be a finite set of conditional finite random variables. Then, the following assertions are equivalent:*

a) $\mathbb{P} = \{\mathbb{P}(Y_1|H_1), \ldots, \mathbb{P}(Y_n|H_n)\}$ *is a* coherent prevision
b) there exists (at least) a solution to a sequence of linear systems $\mathcal{S}_0, \mathcal{S}_1, \ldots, \mathcal{S}_{k+1}$ of the form

$$\mathcal{S}_\alpha = \begin{cases} \sum\limits_{A_r \le H_i} y_{ir}\, x_r^\alpha = \mathbb{P}(Y_i|H_i) \sum\limits_{A_r \le H_i} x_r^\alpha, \qquad \text{if } \sum\limits_{A_r \le H_i} x_r^{\alpha-1} = 0 \\ \sum\limits_{A_r \in \mathcal{A}_\alpha} x_r^\alpha > 0 \\ \sum\limits_{A_r \in \mathcal{A} \setminus \mathcal{A}_\alpha} x_r^\alpha = 0 \\ x_r^\alpha \ge 0 \end{cases} \qquad \alpha = 0, \ldots, k \tag{2}$$

and

$$\mathcal{S}_{k+1} = \begin{cases} \sum\limits_{A_r \in \mathcal{A}_{k+1}} x_r^{k+1} = 1 \\ x_r^{k+1} > 0 \quad \forall A_r \in \mathcal{A}_{k+1} \\ \sum\limits_{A_r \in \mathcal{A} \setminus \mathcal{A}_{k+1}} x_r^{k+1} = 0 \end{cases} \quad \text{if } \mathcal{A}_{k+1} \ne \phi \tag{3}$$

where the x_r^α's are the unknowns associated to each $A_r \in \mathcal{A}$, the y_{ir}'s are the values taken by the r.v. Y_i's on the A_r's, the sub-algebras $\mathcal{A}_\alpha \subseteq \mathcal{A}$, $\alpha = 0, \ldots, k$, *are identified by* $\mathcal{A}_\alpha =< \{Y_i H_i : \sum_{A_r \le H_i} x_r^{\alpha-1} = 0\} >_{|H_0^\alpha}$ *with* x_r^{-1} *set to 0 for all* $r = 1, \dots, \#\mathcal{A}$ *(so that* $\mathcal{A}_0 \equiv \mathcal{A}_{|H_0}$*) while* $\mathcal{A}_{k+1} = \{A_r \in \mathcal{A} : x_r^\alpha = 0 \ \forall \alpha = 0, \dots, k\}$.

Before we illustrate the proof, note that each solution of $\mathcal{S}_\alpha$, $\alpha = 0, \dots, k$, represented by a vector $\mathbf{X}^\alpha$ whose components are the x_r^α's, can be seen as a "mass" distribution on $\mathcal{A}$ with distinct constraints: in $\mathcal{A}_\alpha$ the assessed prevision must satisfy the multiplicative property while on $\mathcal{A} \setminus \mathcal{A}_\alpha$ the mass is forced to be 0. On the contrary, the last system $\mathcal{S}_{k+1}$ forces us to choose any probability mass function $\mathbf{X}^{k+1}$ with support $\mathcal{A}_{k+1}$ (when it is not empty) and it is needed to ensure each $A_r \in \mathcal{A}$ to have associated a positive mass x_r^α in some layer $\alpha \in \{0, \dots, k+1\}$. Obviously, whenever $\mathcal{A}_{k+1}$ turns out to be empty, $\mathcal{S}_{k+1}$ reduces to a vanishing system.

In the theorem we have chosen to explicitly denote, by the summations, all the elements involved in the constraints, on the contrary for its proof we will adopt the "lighter" vector notation.

Proof. (of Th.3)

First we prove the implication $b) \Rightarrow a)$.

By the class of solutions $\{\mathbf{X}^0, \dots, \mathbf{X}^{k+1}\}$ of the linear systems we can "directly" build a *full* conditional prevision $\mathbb{P}'$ on $\mathcal{Y}|(\mathcal{A} \setminus \{\phi\})$, extension of $\mathbb{P}$. In fact, for any $Y|H \in \mathcal{Y}|(\mathcal{A} \setminus \{\phi\})$ there is at least a $\mathbf{X}^\alpha$ such that $H \cdot \mathbf{X}^\alpha > 0$. Let l be the minimum of such indexes and define

$$\mathbb{P}'(Y|H) = \frac{YH \cdot \mathbf{X}^l}{H \cdot \mathbf{X}^l} \tag{4}$$

then it is easy to prove that $\mathbb{P}'$ is "full" (i.e. it satisfies conditions i)-iv) in Def.(2)):

- if $Y|H \ge 0$ then, by the non-negativity of the solutions $\mathbf{X}^\alpha$, the scalar product $YH \cdot \mathbf{X}^l$ is non-negative and so the fraction (4), proving i);
- ii) directly follows by linearity of the scalar product

$$\mathbb{P}'(\lambda Y + \mu Z|H) = \frac{(\lambda Y + \mu Z)H \cdot \mathbf{X}^l}{H \cdot \mathbf{X}^l} = \lambda \frac{YH \cdot \mathbf{X}^l}{H \cdot \mathbf{X}^l} + \mu \frac{ZH \cdot \mathbf{X}^l}{H \cdot \mathbf{X}^l} =$$

$$= \lambda \mathbb{P}'(Y|H) + \mu \mathbb{P}'(Z|H)$$

- condition iii) is trivially satisfied because we will have the same numerator and denominator in (4);
- for the multiplicative property iv) we have to distinguish two cases:
  1. if the same index l is associated to K and HK (i.e. $K \cdot \mathbf{X}^l > 0$ and $HK \cdot \mathbf{X}^l > 0$, while $K \cdot \mathbf{X}^\alpha = 0$ and $HK \cdot \mathbf{X}^\alpha = 0$ for all $\alpha < l$) then

$$\mathbb{P}'(YH|K) = \frac{YHK \cdot \mathbf{X}^l}{K \cdot \mathbf{X}^l} = \frac{HK \cdot \mathbf{X}^l \, YHK \cdot \mathbf{X}^l}{HK \cdot \mathbf{X}^l \, K \cdot \mathbf{X}^l} =$$

$$= \frac{HK \cdot \mathbf{X}^l}{K \cdot \mathbf{X}^l} \frac{YHK \cdot \mathbf{X}^l}{HK \cdot \mathbf{X}^l} = \mathbb{P}'(H|K)\mathbb{P}'(Y|HK)$$

2. if the two indexes, l associated to K and l' associated to HK, are different then we will have $l' > l$ (because $HK < K$) and, in particular, $HK \cdot \mathbf{X}^l = 0$. This last equality implies

$$\mathbb{P}'(YH|K) = \frac{YHK \cdot \mathbf{X}^l}{K \cdot \mathbf{X}^l} = 0 \quad , \quad \mathbb{P}'(H|K) = \frac{HK \cdot \mathbf{X}^l}{K \cdot \mathbf{X}^l} = 0$$

and hence property iv) is trivially satisfied as $0 = 0$.

Hence $\mathbb{P}'$ is a full conditional prevision which is sufficient, by Theorem 1, to guarantee the coherence of $\mathbb{P}$.

For the opposite implication $a) \Rightarrow b)$ we have, again by Th.1, the existence of a full extension $\mathbb{P}'$. Note that $\mathbb{P}'$ restricted to $\mathcal{A}|(\mathcal{A} \setminus \{\phi\})$ is a *full* conditional probability P' (i.e. properties i)-iv) in Def.2 are satisfied as probabilities). By the remark about characterization Theorem 2, there exists a class of probabilities $\{P_0^*, P_1^*, ...\}$ and an "arbitrary" probability distribution P^0 with the property that, for any $H_i \in H_0$, there is a unique index α such that $\sum_{A_r \leq H_i} P_\alpha^*(A_r) > 0$.

We denote now by $\mathbf{X}^\alpha$ the vectors with components $x_r^\alpha = P_\alpha^*(A_r)$ if $A_r \in \mathcal{A}_\alpha^*$ and $x_r^\alpha = 0$ if $A_r \in \mathcal{A} \setminus \mathcal{A}_\alpha^*$, for $\alpha = 0, \ldots, k$, while $x_r^{k+1} = P^0(A_r)$ if $A_r \in \mathcal{A}_{k+1}^*$ and $x_r^{k+1} = 0$ if $A_r \in \mathcal{A} \setminus \mathcal{A}_{k+1}^*$. Fix a conditional r.v. $Y_i|H_i \in \mathcal{D}$, with the previous choice for $\mathbf{X}^\alpha$ we have that, for any $\alpha \in \{0, \ldots, k\}$, if $H_i \cdot \mathbf{X}^\alpha = 0$ then the equation in $\mathcal{S}_\alpha$ associated to $Y_i|H_i$ is trivially satisfied as $0 = \mathbb{P}(Y_i|H_i)0$, otherwise, by the linearity property ii), it results (remember that $\mathbb{P}'$ extends $\mathbb{P}$)

$$\begin{aligned}
\mathbb{P}(Y_i|H_i) = \mathbb{P}'(Y_i|H_i) = \mathbb{P}'((\sum_{A_r \leq H_i} y_{ir} A_r)|H_i) &= \sum_{A_r \leq H_i} y_{ir} \mathbb{P}'(A_r|H_i) = \\
= \sum_{A_r \leq H_i} y_{ir} P'(A_r|H_i) \; &= \sum_{A_r \leq H_i} y_{ir} \frac{A_r \cdot \mathbf{X}^\alpha}{H_i \cdot \mathbf{X}^\alpha} = \\
= \sum_{A_r \leq H_i} y_{ir} \frac{x_r^\alpha}{H_i \cdot \mathbf{X}^\alpha} &
\end{aligned} \tag{5}$$

and hence the equation in $\mathcal{S}_\alpha$ associated to $Y_i|H_i$ is fulfilled.

Finally, by definition, it holds

$$\Omega \cdot \mathbf{X}^{k+1} = 1$$

hence the sequence $\{\mathbf{X}^0, \ldots, \mathbf{X}^{k+1}\}$ represents a solution of linear systems like $\{\mathcal{S}_0, \ldots, \mathcal{S}_{k+1}\}$. □

Note that the solution (if it exists) of the system $\mathcal{S}_\alpha$ could be not unique, so that the sub-algebra $\mathcal{A}_{\alpha+1}$ could be not uniquely determined. Anyhow, the result does not depend on this choice. In fact, if a system $\mathcal{S}_{\alpha+1}$ is not compatible, it means that the restriction of the assessment $\mathbb{P}$ to $\{Y_i|H_i \,:\, H_i \in \mathcal{A}_{\alpha+1}\}$ is not coherent, then also the whole assessment $\mathbb{P}$ is not coherent.

As already stressed for conditional probabilities, by the reduction of the problem to sequences of linear systems, it is possible to directly implement decision-aid systems. And also in this case we could profit from a skillful use of the layers to reduce the spatial complexity of such automatic procedures, but this will be deferred to a future work.

Once the coherence of $\mathbb{P}$ is ensured, the decision maker would like to find which are the coherent bounds for the prevision on a "new" conditional r.v. $Y|H$. In this paper, for the sake of simplicity, we allow only r.v. Y with support belonging to $\mathcal{A}$ and conditioning event $H \in (\mathcal{A} \setminus \{\phi\})$ (i.e. $Y|H$ must be *logically* dependent on $\mathcal{D}$), but the results could be generalized to any arbitrary discrete conditional random variable.

From the proof of Theorem 3 we can state that the coherence of $\mathbb{P}$ is equivalent to the existence of a set $\mathcal{P}$ of conditional probabilities on $\mathcal{A}|(\mathcal{A} \setminus \{\phi\})$ such that $\mathbb{P}(Y_i|H_i)$ coincides with the conditional expected value of $Y_i|H_i$ with respect to any $P \in \mathcal{P}$, for all $Y_i|H_i \in \mathcal{D}$, in formulae

$$\mathbb{P}(Y_i|H_i) \equiv E_P(Y_i|H_i) = \frac{Y_i H_i \cdot \mathbf{X}^\alpha}{H_i \cdot \mathbf{X}^\alpha} \quad \forall P \in \mathcal{P} \ \forall Y_i|H_i \in \mathcal{D}.$$

with $\mathbf{X}^\alpha$ vector of components $P^*_\alpha(A_r)$, $r = 1, ..., \#(\Omega)$ and α such that $H_i \cdot \mathbf{X}^\alpha > 0$. It follows that coherent bounds for $\mathbb{P}(Y|H)$ will be

$$\mathbf{p}_l = \inf_{P \in \mathcal{P}} E_P(Y|H) \qquad \mathbf{p}^u = \sup_{P \in \mathcal{P}} E_P(Y|H). \tag{6}$$

Anyhow, reasoning exactly as done in [7] for the extension of coherent conditional probabilities, it is possible to show that $\mathbf{p}_l$ and $\mathbf{p}^u$ can be computed, not with respect to the whole set $\mathcal{P}$, but just with respect to the conditional probability $P^e \in \mathcal{P}$ such that the number of relevant constraints $E_{P^e}(Y_i H_i) = \mathbb{P}(Y_i|H_i)\ P^e(H_i)$ is minimal (note that we judge such constraints "relevant" when they are not trivially satisfied as $0 = 0$, equivalently when H_i and H belongs to the same layer).

This is operationally reachable by choosing solutions $\mathbf{X}^\alpha$ for the $\mathcal{S}_\alpha$ such that, till possible, they respect the further constraint $H \cdot \mathbf{X}^\alpha = 0$ and only when at a layer $\overline{\alpha}$ this is not possible any more (note that by the definition of $\mathcal{S}_{k+1}$ such $\overline{\alpha} \leq k+1$ exists) the bounds in (6) can be computed by the two linear programming problems

$$\mathbf{p}_l = \min YH \cdot \mathbf{X}^{\overline{\alpha}} \quad \mathbf{p}^u = \max YH \cdot \mathbf{X}^{\overline{\alpha}} \text{ under constraints } \{\mathcal{S}_{\overline{\alpha}}\} \cup \{H \cdot \mathbf{X}^{\overline{\alpha}} = 1\} \tag{7}$$

Any value inside the range $[\mathbf{p}_l, \mathbf{p}^u]$ chosen for $\mathbb{P}(Y|H)$ is guaranteed to be coherent together with the initial assessment $\mathbb{P}$ and can guide the decision process.

4 A Simple Example

We present now a simple example with the purpose to illustrate all the theoretical steps already introduced. The example is "artificially" simplified for readability reasons. Obviously real practical applications would better show the potentiality of the procedure, on the other hand it would be much more difficult to analytically describe them.

Example 1. A farmer must decide if it will be more convenient to grow artichoke or fennel. His profit will strongly depend on the weather in the next winter season: if the season will be "cold" (e.g. with minimal temperatures always below 3^oC), then he will more likely get a good profit growing fennel. If the weather will be milder (e.g. with minimal temperatures always over 0^oC), then more likely the prices for artichokes will exceed those of fennel. Anyhow, inside the different kinds of season a variability on the profit is possible.

We can formalize this situation as the following:
the different (but "overlapping") kinds of season are represented by the events H_1 ="mild weather" and H_2 ="cold weather", while the different plantations are Y_1 ="artichokes" Y_2 ="fennel".

The pair (Y_1, Y_2) represents a random vector whose support we reduce to five discrete values (expressed in "thousands of euros/hectare"):

$$(Y_1, Y_2) \in \{(1,60); (10,45); (17,15); (20,5); (30,3)\}$$

Note that the single r.v. Y_1 and Y_2 are not independent but strongly negative correlated.

$\mathcal{A}$ is the algebra generated by the values taken by (Y_1, Y_2) and A_1, A_2, A_3, A_4, A_5 are the atoms.

In this way we can represent the different kinds of season as elements of $\mathcal{A}$, in particular $H_1 = A_1 \vee A_2 \vee A_3$ and $H_2 = A_2 \vee A_3 \vee A_4 \vee A_5$.

The farmer is not used to deal with probability but with his experience he can assess the following previsions:

$$\mathbb{P}(Y_1|H_1) = 24 \quad \mathbb{P}(Y_2|H_1) = 4.2 \quad \mathbb{P}(Y_1|H_2) = 2.8 \quad \mathbb{P}(Y_2|H_2) = 57$$

The support we can offer to the farmer before he takes any practical decision is, first of all, to check if his assessment is in some way "consistent", or if his strong non-monotone behaviour (legitimated by the negative correlation) is not justifiable with such an extent.

The answer is affirmative because, applying all the theoretical machinery we have described before, we obtain solutions for the following sequence of three linear systems:

$$\mathcal{S}_0 = \begin{cases} 10x_2^0 + 17x_3^0 + 20x_4^0 + 30x_5^0 = 24(x_2^0 + x_3^0 + x_4^0 + x_5^0) \\ 45x_2^0 + 15x_3^0 + 5x_4^0 + 3x_5^0 = 4.2(x_2^0 + x_3^0 + x_4^0 + x_5^0) \\ x_1^0 + 10x_2^0 + 17x_3^0 = 2.8(x_1^0 + x_2^0 + x_3^0) \\ 60x_1^0 + 45x_2^0 + 15x_3^0 = 57(x_1^0 + x_2^0 + x_3^0) \\ x_1^0 + x_2^0 + x_3^0 + x_4^0 + x_5^0 > 0 \\ x_i^0 \geq 0 \qquad i = 1, ..., 5 \end{cases}$$

The only normalized solution of this system is:
$x_4^0 = \frac{3}{5}, x_5^0 = \frac{2}{5} \quad x_1^0 = x_2^0 = x_3^0 = 0$ then $P(H_2) > 0$ and $P(H_1) = 0$

$$\mathcal{S}_1 = \begin{cases} x_1' + 10x_2' + 17x_3' = 2.8(x_1' + x_2' + x_3') \\ 60x_1' + 45x_2' + 15x_3' = 57(x_1' + x_2' + x_3') \\ x_1' + x_2' + x_3' > 0 \\ x_4' + x_5' = 0 \end{cases}$$

The only normalized solution of this system is:
$x'_1 = \frac{4}{5}, x'_2 = \frac{1}{5} \quad x'_3 = x'_4 = x'_5 = 0$ then $P(H_1) > 0$

$$\mathcal{S}_2 = \begin{cases} x''_1 = x''_2 = x''_4 = x''_5 = 0 \\ x''_3 = 1 \end{cases}$$

The farmer receives afterwards new information regarding the weather. According to the weather-forecast, the forthcoming winter will be neither too cold, nor too mild. For this reason he has to choose between the two new conditional r.v. : $Y_i|H \quad i = 1, 2$ with $H = H_1H_2$. We can apply what we have stated for the extension of $\mathbb{P}$ and, since solutions $\{\mathbf{X}^0, \mathbf{X}', \mathbf{X}''\}$ found are unique apart from a scale factor, the "highest" layer reachable by H is in $\mathcal{S}_1$. Hence coherent values for the extension in this case are uniquely determined as

$$\mathbb{P}(Y_1|H) = \frac{y_{12}\, x'_2}{x'_2} = y_{12} = 10 \quad \text{and} \quad \mathbb{P}(Y_2|H) = \frac{y_{22}\, x'_2}{x'_2} = y_{22} = 45$$

so that the farmer opts to grow fennel.

Note that in this example the different layers are strictly needed, because the first linear system $\mathcal{S}_0$ do not admit a solution that gives to both hypotheses positive probability. Hence, whenever one stops to look at the first system (as usually done), the assessment could seem inconsistent. Moreover, even if the different kinds of season could be modeled as fuzzy entities, in our approach they are "crisply" identified trough the different synthesized values of the random variables. In this way we avoid the crucial point of the choice of the membership functions, together with the robustness study that should be performed.

5 Conclusions

With this paper we have extended the fruitful results [3,4,5,6,7] of characterization of coherent conditional probabilities, and inferences based on them, to coherent conditional previsions. This operational results enlarge the applicability of partial assessments guided by coherence. In fact, conditional previsions allow to fully synthesize the behaviours on relevant quantities, contingently on different scenarios. Such syntheses can be easily performed and interpreted, and do not require to the user a deep probabilistic knowledge. Note that, even the decision maker does not express a probabilistic evaluation on the hypotheses $H_1, \ldots, H_n$, his conditional previsions $\mathbb{P}(Y_i|H_i)$ implicitly express his belief on the occurency of the different H_i's (this belief is obtainable by the set of admissible solutions $\mathbf{X}^0 \ldots, \mathbf{X}^{k+1}$ of the systems $\mathcal{S}_\alpha$'s).

With our results we give an operational tool to fruitfully use the generality and potentiality of partial conditional assessments, showing also in this case that in conditional frameworks it is absolutely needed to introduce different levels of interaction (represented by the layers α) among the quantities involved.

References

1. A. Capotorti and B. Vantaggi. An Algorithm for Coherent Conditional Probability Assessment. In *SIMAI'98*, Giardini Naxos, Italy, 2:144-148, 1998.
2. A. Capotorti and B. Vantaggi. Locally Strong Coherence in an Inference Process. To appear in *Annals of Mathematics and Artificial Intelligence.*
3. G. Coletti. Coherence Principles for Handling Qualitative and Quantitative Partial Probabilistic Assessments. *Mathware & Soft Computing*, 3, 159–172, 1996.
4. G. Coletti and R. Scozzafava. Characterization of Coherent Conditional Probabilities as a Tool for their Assessment and Extension. *Int. Journ. of Uncertainty, Fuzziness and Knowledge-Based Systems*, 4(2): 103-127, 1996.
5. G. Coletti and R. Scozzafava. Exploiting Zero Probabilities. *Proc. of EUFIT'97*, Aachen, Germany, ELITE Foundation, 1499–1503, 1997.
6. G. Coletti and R. Scozzafava. Conditional Measures: Old and New. In *New trends in Fuzzy Systems*, World Scientific: 107-120, 1998.
7. G. Coletti and R. Scozzafava. Conditioning and Inference in Intelligent Systems. *Soft Computing*, 3: 118-130, 1999.
8. B. de Finetti. Sull'Impostazione Assiomatica del Calcolo delle Probabilitá. *Annali Univ. di Trieste* 19: 29-81, 1949. (English translation in: (1972) Probability, Induction, Statistics. Ch. 5. London Wiley) .
9. B. de Finetti. *Theory of Probability*, vol. 1-2, Wiley, New York, 1974.
10. S. Holzer (1985) On coherence and conditional prevision. *Bull. Unione Matematica Italiana, Analisi funzionale e applicazioni.* 6(4): 441-460.
11. F. Lad. *Operational Subjective Statistical Methods: a Mathematical, Philosophical, and Historical Introduction.* Wiley, New York, 1996.
12. E. Regazzini (1985) Finitely additive conditional probabilities. *Rend. Sem. Mat. Fis. Milano*, 55: 69-89.

Decomposition of Influence Diagrams

Thomas D. Nielsen

Department of Computer Science
Aalborg University
Fredrik Bajers vej 7E, 9220 Aalborg Øst, Denmark
tdn@cs.auc.dk

Abstract. When solving a decision problem we want to determine an optimal policy for the decision variables of interest. A policy for a decision variable is in principle a function over its past. However, some of the past may be irrelevant and for both communicational as well as computational reasons it is important not to deal with redundant variables in the policies. In this paper we present a method to decompose a decision problem into a collection of smaller sub-problems s.t. a solution (with no redundant variables) to the original decision problem can be found by solving the sub-problems independently. The method is based on an operational characterization of the future variables being relevant for a decision variable, thereby also providing a characterization of those parts of a decision problem that are relevant for a particular decision.

1 Introduction

Influence diagrams (IDs) were introduced in [3] and serve as a powerful modeling tool for symmetric decision problems with a single decision maker. The ID supplies a natural representation for capturing the semantics of decision making "with a minimum of clutter and confusion for the non-quantitative decision maker" [12].

Given an ID representation of a decision problem, we can use the explicit structural information for analyzing relevance. For example, when analyzing the ID depicted in Figure 1 we find that knowledge of the states of D_1, A, D_2 and D_3 does not improve decision D_4 as long as the states of B and C are known. Hence, the variables D_1, A, D_2 and D_3 are not *required* for D_4, and having identified these irrelevant variables the domain of the policy for D_4 is reduced considerably; different operational characterizations of the required past for a decision variable have been found independently in [10,6].

Analogously to the possible occurrence of redundant variables in the past of a decision, there may also exist future variables which are irrelevant. By also identifying these variables, we obtain a complete specification of the parts of a decision problem that are relevant for a particular decision.

The advantages of being able to characterize the relevant parts of a decision problem are twofold. First of all, if some decision variable is of particular importance, then we can focus our attention on the parts relevant for that decision

S. Benferhat and P. Besnard (Eds.): ECSQARU 2001, LNAI 2143, pp. 144–155, 2001.

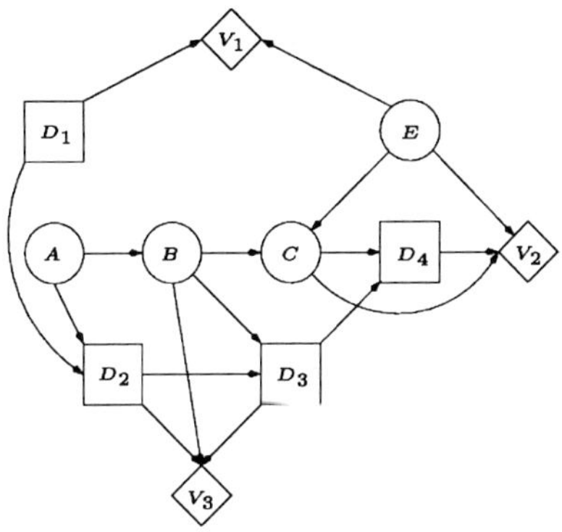

Fig. 1. The figure depicts an ID with four chance nodes A, B, C and E, four decision nodes D_1, D_2, D_3, D_4 and three value nodes; the total utility is the sum $V_1 + V_2 + V_3$.

variable when specifying the quantitative part (probabilities and utilities) of the model. Similarly, when using the ID as a tool for communication we can answer questions as to whether a variable X provides information which is relevant when deciding on a decision D. Being able to answer such questions is also useful in the context of *information filtering*, i.e., the problem of adjusting the configuration and quantity of information displayed to a decision maker (see e.g. [2]).

The second advantage has to do with the evaluation. When referring to the evaluation of an ID we usually mean computing an optimal policy for all decisions involved. This interpretation can, however, be slightly misleading as we might only be interested in a subset of the decisions; actually, in most cases we are only interested in the initial decision as this decision can be seen as generating a new decision problem. When only a subset of the decisions is of interest the ID may contain superfluous information, i.e., variables which has no impact on the solution for the decisions in question. By removing such irrelevant variables we can reduce the size of the problem and, thereby, the computational complexity of solving the decision problem.

In this paper we propose a method to decompose an ID into a collection of smaller IDs. The decomposition produces an ID for each decision variable of interest, and each of these IDs contains exactly the variables necessary and sufficient for determining an optimal policy for the associated decision variable; hence, the IDs can be solved independently of each other. The decomposition does not place any restrictions on the subsequent evaluation so we can use any evaluation scheme that we find suitable (see e.g. [11,13,4,5]). Additionally, since the IDs only include variables that are relevant for the associated decision variables, we are always given policies with no redundant variables. Note, that the methods cited above do not ensure this property themselves, i.e., solving an ordinary ID is not guaranteed to produce optimal policies with no redundant variables.

In Section 2 we formally introduce the ID and the terms and notation used throughout the paper. In Section 3 we give an operational characterization of the variables being relevant for a given decision variable. Based on this characterization we show how an influence diagram can be decomposed into a collection of smaller influence diagrams. Finally, the proposed method is illustrated by decomposing the influence diagram in Figure 1.

2 Preliminaries

An ID can be seen as a *Bayesian network* augmented with *decision nodes* and *value nodes*. Thus, an ID is a directed acyclic graph $G = (\mathcal{U}, \mathcal{E})$, where the nodes $\mathcal{U}$ can be partitioned into three disjoint subsets; *chance nodes*, decision nodes and value nodes.

The chance nodes $\mathcal{U}_C$ correspond to *chance variables*, and represent events which are not under the direct control of the decision maker. The decision nodes $\mathcal{U}_D$ correspond to *decision variables* and represent actions that are under the direct control of the decision maker. In the remainder of this paper we assume a total ordering of the decision nodes, indicating the order in which the decisions are made (the ordering of the decision nodes is traditionally represented by a directed path which includes all decision nodes.) Furthermore, we will use the concept of node and variable interchangeably if this does not introduce any inconsistency. We will also assume that no *barren nodes* are specified by the ID since they have no impact on the decisions (see [11]); a chance node or a decision node is said to be barren if it has no children, or if all its descendants are barren.

With each chance variable and decision variable X we associate a *state space* $sp(X)$ which denotes the set of possible outcomes/decision options for X. For a set $\mathcal{U}'$ of chance variables and decision variables we define the state space as $sp(\mathcal{U}') = \times\{sp(X) | X \in \mathcal{U}'\}$.

The uncertainty associated with a chance variable C is represented by a *conditional probability potential* $P(C|\pi_C) : sp(\{C\} \cup \pi_C) \rightarrow [0; 1]$, where π_C denotes the parents of C in the ID. The domain of a conditional probability potential $\phi_C = P(C|\pi_C)$ is denoted by $\text{dom}(\phi_C) = \{C\} \cup \pi_C$.

The set of value nodes $\mathcal{U}_V$ defines a set of *utility potentials*; value nodes have no descendants. Each utility potential indicates the local utility for a given configuration of the variables in its domain. The domain of a utility potential ψ_V is denoted by $\text{dom}(\psi_V) = \pi_V$, where V is the value node associated with ψ_V. The total utility is the sum or the product of the local utilities (see [14]); in the remainder of this paper we assume that the total utility is the sum of the local utilities. Analogously to the concepts of variable and node, we shall sometimes use the terms value node and utility potential interchangeably.

A *realization* of an ID I is an attachment of potentials to the appropriate variables in I, i.e., a realization is a set $\{P(C|\pi_C) : C \in \mathcal{U}_C\} \cup \{\psi_V(\pi_V) : V \in \mathcal{U}_V\}$. Hence, a realization specifies the quantitative part of the model, whereas the ID constitutes the qualitative part; we will sometimes use λ_X to denote the potential associated with the variable X if it is of no importance whether λ_X is a utility potential or a probability potential.

The arcs in an ID can be partitioned into three disjoint subsets, corresponding to the type of node they go into. Arcs into value nodes represent functional dependencies by indicating the domain of the associated utility potential. Arcs into chance nodes, termed *dependency arcs*, represent probabilistic dependencies, whereas arcs into decision nodes, termed *informational arcs*, imply information precedence; if there is an arc from a node X to a decision node D then the state of X is known when decision D is made.

Let $\mathcal{U}_C$ be the set of chance variables and let $\mathcal{U}_D = \{D_1, D_2, \dots, D_n\}$ be the set of decision variables. Assuming that the decision variables are ordered by index, the set of informational arcs induces a partitioning of $\mathcal{U}_C$ into a collection of disjoint subsets $\mathcal{C}_0, \mathcal{C}_1, \dots, \mathcal{C}_n$. The set $\mathcal{C}_j$ denotes the chance variables observed between decision D_j and D_{j+1}. Thus the variables in $\mathcal{C}_j$ occur as parents of D_{j+1}. This induces a *partial order* $\prec$ on $\mathcal{U}_C \cup \mathcal{U}_D$, i.e., $\mathcal{C}_0 \prec D_1 \prec \mathcal{C}_1 \prec \cdots \prec D_n \prec \mathcal{C}_n$.

The set of variables known to the decision maker when deciding on D_j is called the *informational predecessors* of D_j and is denoted pred(D_j). By assuming that the decision maker remembers all previous observations and decisions, we have pred$(D_i) \subseteq$ pred(D_j) for $i \leq j$, and pred(D_j) is the variables that occur before D_j under $\prec$. This property is known as *no-forgetting* and from this we can assume that an ID does not contain any no-forgetting arcs, i.e., $\pi_{D_i} \cap \pi_{D_j} = \emptyset$ if $D_i \neq D_j$.

The state configuration of pred(D_j) observed before deciding on D_j induces a set of independence relations on the variables in $\mathcal{U}$. These relations can be determined using the well-known *d-separation* criteria:

Definition 1 Let G be a directed acyclic graph. If $\mathcal{X}$, $\mathcal{Y}$ and $\mathcal{Z}$ are disjoint subsets of the nodes in G, then $\mathcal{X}$ and $\mathcal{Z}$ are said to be *d-separated* given $\mathcal{Y}$ if each path between a node in $\mathcal{X}$ and a node in $\mathcal{Z}$ contains a node Y s.t.:

- Y is an intermediate node in a converging connection (head-to-head), and neither Y nor any of its descendants are in $\mathcal{Y}$.
- Y is an intermediate node in a serial or a diverging connection (head-to-tail or tail-to-tail), and $Y \in \mathcal{Y}$.

If $\mathcal{X}$ and $\mathcal{Z}$ are not d-separated given $\mathcal{Y}$, then we say that $\mathcal{X}$ and $\mathcal{Z}$ are *d-connected* given $\mathcal{Y}$, and the paths connecting $\mathcal{X}$ and $\mathcal{Z}$ are called *active*.

[1] and [9] present efficient algorithms for detecting d-separation directly from the topology of the graph by examining the paths connecting $\mathcal{X}$, $\mathcal{Y}$ and $\mathcal{Z}$.

2.1 Evaluation

Solving an ID amounts to computing a policy for the decisions involved. A policy can be seen as a prescription of responses to earlier observations and decisions, and the set of policies for all the decision variables constitutes a strategy for the ID. The evaluation is usually performed according to the *maximum expected utility principle*, which states that we should always choose an alternative that maximizes the expected utility.

Definition 2 Let I be an ID and let $\mathcal{U}_D$ denote the decision variables in I. A *strategy* is a set of functions $\Delta = \{\delta_D | D \in \mathcal{U}_D\}$, where δ_D is a *policy* given by:

$$\delta_D : sp(\text{pred}(D)) \to sp(D) \ .$$

A strategy that maximizes the expected utility is termed an *optimal strategy*, and each policy in an optimal strategy is termed an *optimal policy*.

The optimal policy for decision variable D_n is given by*

$$\delta_{D_n}(\text{pred}(D_n)) = \arg\max_{D_n} \sum_{\mathcal{C}_n} P(\mathcal{C}_n | \mathcal{C}_0, D_1, \ldots, \mathcal{C}_{n-1}, D_n) \sum_{V \in \mathcal{U}_V} \psi_V$$

and the *maximum expected utility potential* for decision D_n is

$$\rho_{D_n}(\text{pred}(D_n)) = \max_{D_n} \sum_{\mathcal{C}_n} P(\mathcal{C}_n | \mathcal{C}_0, D_1, \ldots, \mathcal{C}_{n-1}, D_n) \sum_{V \in \mathcal{U}_V} \psi_V \ .$$

In general, the optimal policy for decision D_k is given by

$$\delta_{D_k}(\text{pred}(D_k)) = \arg\max_{D_k} \sum_{\mathcal{C}_k} P(\mathcal{C}_k | \mathcal{C}_0, D_1, \ldots, \mathcal{C}_{k-1}, D_k) \rho_{D_{k+1}} \ , \tag{1}$$

where $\rho_{D_{k+1}}$ is the maximum expected utility potential for decision D_{k+1}:

$$\rho_{D_{k+1}}(\text{pred}(D_{k+1})) = \max_{D_{k+1}} \sum_{\mathcal{C}_{k+1}} P(\mathcal{C}_{k+1} | \mathcal{C}_0, D_1, \ldots, \mathcal{C}_k, D_{k+1}) \rho_{D_{k+2}} \ .$$

By continuously expanding Equation 1, we get the following expression for the optimal policy for D_k:

$$\delta_{D_k}(\text{pred}(D_k)) = \arg\max_{D_k} \sum_{\mathcal{C}_k} \cdots \max_{D_n} \sum_{\mathcal{C}_n} P(\mathcal{C}_k, \ldots, \mathcal{C}_n | \mathcal{C}_0, \ldots, \mathcal{C}_{k-1}, D_1, \ldots, D_n) \sum_{V \in \mathcal{U}_V} \psi_V \ . \tag{2}$$

Not all the variables observed (i.e. $\text{pred}(D_k)$) do necessarily influence the optimal policy for D_k, hence we introduce the notion of a required variable:

Definition 3 Let I be an ID and let D be a decision variable in I. The variable $X \in \text{pred}(D)$ is said to be *required* for D if there exists a realization of I and a configuration $\bar{y}$ over $\text{dom}(\delta_D) \setminus \{X\}$ s.t. $\delta_D(x_1, \bar{y}) \neq \delta_D(x_2, \bar{y})$, where x_1 and x_2 are different states of X. The set of variables required for D is denoted $\text{req}(D)$.

* For the sake of simplifying notation, we shall assume that for all decision variables D_i there is always exactly one element in $\arg\max_{D_i}(\cdot)$.

Finally, when calculating an optimal strategy for an ID I, the variables in $\mathcal{C}_0 = \text{pred}(D_1)$ are never marginalized out; marginalizing out a chance variable corresponds to a summation over its state space. This allows us to define a *partial realization* $\mathcal{R}$ of I as a realization which does not necessarily include the potential λ_X if there does not exist a variable $Y \in \text{dom}(\lambda_X)$ s.t. $\mathcal{C}_0 \prec Y$. We allow a (partial) realization $\mathcal{R}$ to be extended with a set $\mathcal{R}'$ of potentials if there does not exist a potential in $\mathcal{R}'$ with the same domain as a potential in $\mathcal{R}$. That is, the extension is admissible if no variable is associated with more than one potential w.r.t. $\mathcal{R} \cup \mathcal{R}'$.

3 Decomposition of Influence Diagrams

In this section we describe a method for decomposing an ID I into a collection of smaller IDs s.t. an optimal strategy for I can be found by solving the smaller IDs independently. More precisely, the decomposition produces an ID for each decision variable D in I s.t. an optimal policy for D can be found by solving the associated ID independently of the other IDs produced by the decomposition.

Decomposing an ID I is essentially a question of identifying the potentials involved in the computation of δ_{D_i}, for all $1 \leq i \leq n$ and for any realization of I (see Equation 2). These potentials are uniquely identified by their associated variables. Thus, apart from the required variables we also need to identify the future variables that are *relevant* for the decisions in the ID, i.e., the variables that may influence the optimal policy for a decision variable:

Definition 4 Let I be an ID and let D be a decision variable in I. The variable $X(D \prec X)$ is said to be *relevant* for D if either:

- $X \in \mathcal{U}_C \cup \mathcal{U}_V$ and there exists two realizations $\mathcal{R}_1$ and $\mathcal{R}_2$ of I who only differ on the potential associated with X s.t. the optimal policies for D are different in $\mathcal{R}_1$ and $\mathcal{R}_2$, or
- $X \in \mathcal{U}_D$ and there exists a realization of I and two different policies δ_X^1 and δ_X^2 for X s.t. the optimal policies for D are different w.r.t. δ_X^1 and δ_X^2.

The set of variables relevant for D is denoted $\text{rel}(D)$.

The variables $\text{req}(D) \cup \text{rel}(D)$ determine the potentials involved in the computation of δ_D. Thus, we seek a decomposition scheme which produces a collection of IDs s.t. each of the IDs contains exactly the relevant and required variables for the associated decision and, furthermore, obeys the decision sequencing specified by the original ID. Note that the latter property may require the inclusion of informational arcs which are not part of the original ID.

Definition 5 Let I be an ID with nodes $\mathcal{U}^I$ and arcs $\mathcal{E}^I$, and let D be a decision variable in I. The ID I_D is said to *reflect the decision problem* D in I if:

- $\mathcal{U}^{I_D} = \text{rel}(D) \cup \text{req}(D) \cup \{D\}$, and

– $\mathcal{E}^{I_D} = \{(X,Y)|X,Y \in \mathcal{U}^{I_D} \text{ and } (X,Y) \in \mathcal{E}^I\} \cup$
$\{(X,Y)|X \in \mathcal{U}^{I_D}, Y \in \mathcal{U}_D^{I_D}, \text{ where } X \prec^I Y \text{ and } X \not\prec^{I_D} Y\}$.

Definition 3 and Definition 4 give semantic characterizations of both the variables being required and relevant for a particular decision variable. Different syntactical characterizations of the required variables have been found independently in [10,6]. In this paper we adopt the algorithm from [10], which is based on the notion of a *chance variable representation of a policy* (see [8] for further discussion on chance variable representations):

Definition 6 Let D be a decision variable and let $\delta_D(\text{req}(D))$ be an optimal policy for D. A chance variable D' with $\text{req}(D)$ as parents and with the potential $P(D'|\text{req}(D))$ defined as:

$$P(d|\bar{r}) = \begin{cases} 1 & \text{if } \delta_D(\bar{r}) = d \\ 0 & \text{otherwise} \end{cases}$$

is said to be the *chance variable representation of* δ_D.

The algorithm proposed in [10] works by visiting each of the decision variables in reverse temporal order. When a decision variable is visited the variables being required for that decision are identified, and the decision variable is replaced by its chance variable representation.

Algorithm 1 Let I be an ID and let $D_1, D_2, \ldots, D_n$ be the decision variables in I ordered by index. To determine the variables required for D_i ($\forall 1 \leq i \leq n$) do:

1) Set $i := n$.
2) **For** each decision variable not considered ($i > 0$)
   a) Let $\mathcal{V}_i$ be the set of value nodes to which there exists a directed path from D_i in I.
   b) Let $\mathcal{D}_{D_i}$ be a set of nodes s.t. $X \in \mathcal{D}_{D_i}$ if and only if X is d-connected to a node in $\mathcal{V}_i$ given $\{D_i\} \cup \text{pred}(D_i)\backslash\{X\}$.
   c) Set $\text{req}(D_i) := \mathcal{D}_{D_i} \cap \text{pred}(D_i)$ ($\text{req}(D_i)$ is the set of variables required for D_i).
   d) Replace D_i with a chance variable representation of the policy for D_i.
   e) Set $i := i - 1$.

The correctness of the algorithm is not proven in [10]. A proof can be found in [7], where it is also shown that the value nodes relevant for a decision variable D_i are exactly the value nodes $\mathcal{V}_i$ found by the algorithm above.

Example 1 Consider the ID depicted in Figure 1. By applying Algorithm 1 to this ID we start off by visiting decision D_4. As $\text{pred}(D_4) = \{D_1, A, D_2, B, D_3, C\}$ we find that only B and C are required for D_4; all other nodes $X \in \text{pred}(D_4)$ are d-separated from $\mathcal{V}_4 = \{V_2\}$ given $\{D_4\} \cup \text{pred}(D_4)\backslash\{X\}$. Note that from

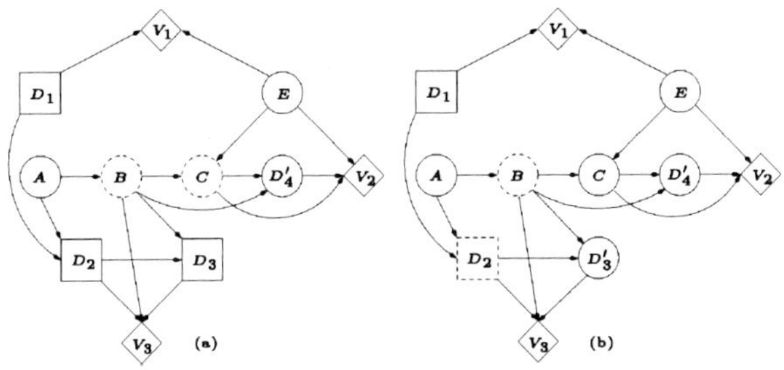

Fig. 2. The figures depict the IDs obtained from the ID in Figure 1, by applying the first two iterations of Algorithm 1. The dashed nodes in Figure (a) and (b) are the nodes required for D_4 and D_3, respectively.

Algorithm 1 (see [7]) we can also infer that V_2 is the only value node relevant for D_4. Decision D_4 is then replaced by its chance variable representation D'_4 having B and C as parents (see Figure 2a), and the algorithm proceeds to decision D_3.

Since $\mathcal{V}_3 = \{V_3\}$ in the ID produced by the previous step (see Figure 2a), we find that D_2 and B are the only variables required for D_3. Decision D_3 is then replaced by its chance variable representation (see Figure 2b), and the algorithm proceeds as above until all decision variables have been investigated. □

From Algorithm 1 we have a syntactical characterization of both the variables being required for a given decision variable D and the set of value nodes relevant for D. Moreover, from Definition 4 it is apparent that a decision variable $D'(D \prec D')$ is relevant for D if and only if there exist a utility function ψ relevant for both D and D' (see also [6]). Thus, we have narrowed our search for relevant variables down to the chance variables succeeding D under $\prec$.

Theorem 1 Let I be an ID and let D_i be a decision variable in I. Let I_i denote the ID obtained from I by replacing D_j with its chance variable representation, for $j = i+1, \ldots, n$. Then the chance variable $X(D_i \prec X)$ is relevant for D_i if and only if

- X is not barren in the ID formed from I_i by removing all value nodes that are not relevant for D_i, and
- there exists a utility potential ψ_V relevant for D_i s.t. X is d-connected to V in I_i given $\{D_i\} \cup \mathrm{pred}(D_i)$.

A proof of Theorem 1 is given in the appendix. Now, having found a syntactical characterization of the variables being required and relevant for a decision variable D, we have the following theorem which shows that performing a decomposition according to Definition 5 is sound w.r.t. the optimal policies.

Theorem 2 Let I be an ID and let $\mathcal{R}$ be a realization of I. If I_D reflects the decision problem D in I, then $\mathcal{R}$ is a (partial) realization of I_D and $\delta_D^{I_D} = \delta_D^I$.

Proof. From the construction of I_D we only need to show that for any realization of I, if λ_X is relevant for the computation of δ_D^I, then $\{X\} \cup \pi_X \subseteq \mathcal{U}^{I_D}$. That is, λ_X is contained in the (partial) realization of I_D. Now, consider $X \succ D$ and assume that λ_X is a probability potential. Since λ_X is relevant for the computation of δ_D we have that $X \in \mathcal{U}_{I_D}$ (see Theorem 1). Moreover, from the properties of d-separation it follows that for any $Y \in \pi_X$, $Y \in \text{req}(D)$ if $Y \in \text{pred}(D)$ and $Y \in \text{rel}(D)$ if $Y \notin \text{pred}(D)$. On the other hand, if X is required for D then there exists a variable $Y \in \pi_X$ which is relevant for D; if this was not the case λ_X would not be relevant for the calculation of δ_D. Thus, the variables in π_X are either required or relevant for D.

Finally, if X is a value node the proof follows immediately. □

Example 2 Consider the ID depicted in Figure 1. From Algorithm 1 we find that V_2 is the only value node relevant for D_4, and by Theorem 1 this implies that E is relevant for D_4. By Algorithm 1 we also have that B and C are required for D_4. These nodes define the potentials which are needed to compute an optimal policy for D_4, and by Definition 5 they constitute the nodes in the ID that reflects the decision problem D_4 (see Figure 3(D_4)). Note that i) the informational arc from B to D_4 ensures that the information constraints are consistent with the original ID, and ii) B is not associated with a probability potential as it is not marginalized out when calculating an optimal policy for D_4 (we work with a partial realization).

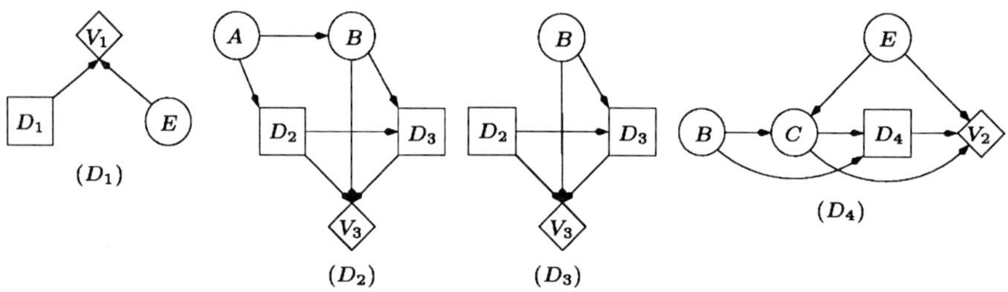

Fig. 3. The figure shows a decomposition of the influence diagram depicted in Figure 1 into four smaller influence diagrams.

Continuing to decision D_3, we start off by replacing D_4 with a chance variable D_4' having B and C as parents. From Algorithm 1 we have that B and D_2 are required for D_3 since V_3 is relevant for D_3. These nodes then constitute the nodes in the ID that reflects the decision problem D_3 (see Figure 3(D_3)); by Theorem 1 no future variables are relevant for D_3. The algorithm proceeds as above until all decision nodes have been considered, see Figure 3(D_2) and Figure 3(D_1). It should be noted though, that when investigating D_1 the chance node C is d-connected to V_1 which is relevant for D_1. However, C is not relevant for

D_1 since it is barren in the ID formed by removing the value nodes V_2 and V_3 which are not relevant for D_1. □

In addition to produce policies with no redundant variables, the decomposition of an ID may also yield a reduction in the computational complexity when calculating an optimal strategy. For instance, the *strong junction tree* representation (see [4]) of the original ID depicted in Figure 1 contains a *clique* consisting of five variables. On the other hand, the largest clique in the junction trees, for the IDs produced by the decomposition, contains only four variables.

It is easy to verify that the computational complexity of solving one subproblem is not larger than the computational complexity of solving the original decision problem. However, when working with overlapping subproblems we may need to repeat calculations previously performed. An immediate approach to overcome this problem is to cache/reuse some of the previous computations; this is subject to further research.

4 Conclusion

In this paper we have presented an operational characterization of the future variables being relevant for a decision variable. These variables, together with the variables of the required past, describe the parts of a decision problem which are necessary and sufficient to consider when calculating an optimal policy for a particular decision variable.

Moreover, based on this characterization we have presented a method for decomposing an ID into a collection of smaller IDs. A solution to the original ID can then be found by solving these smaller IDs independently. The decomposition ensures that no redundant variables are contained in the optimal strategy and, furthermore, it may also reduce the computational complexity of solving the original decision problem.

The proposed method may also provide a way to simplify the elicitation of the structure of a complex decision problem. For instance, it may be possible to characterize conditions that are necessary and sufficient to ensure the consistency of different subproblems based on the existence of a decision problem that decomposes into these subproblems.

Acknowledgement. The author would like to thank Finn V. Jensen for valuable discussions and helpful comments on earlier versions of this paper. The author would also like to thank the anonymous reviewers for constructive comments.

Appendix: Proofs

Before giving the proof of Theorem 1 we need the following lemma.

Lemma 1 Let X and Y be chance variables in a Bayesian network BN, and let $\bar{c}$ be a configuration over a set of variables $\mathcal{Z}$ not containing X or Y. If X is not barren, then X is d-separated from Y given $\bar{c}$ if and only if for any two realizations differing only on the potential $P(X|\pi_X)$ it holds that $P_1(Y|\bar{c}) = P_2(Y|\bar{c})$.

Proof. Consider the Bayesian network BN' obtained from BN by adding an artificial binary chance variable W as a parent for X. Let P_1 and P_2 be any two realizations differing only on the potential $P(X|\pi_X)$ in BN, and let the conditional probability distribution for X in BN' be specified s.t. $P'(X|\pi_X, W = 0) = P_1(X|\pi_X)$ and $P'(X|\pi_X, W = 1) = P_2(X|\pi_X)$. Recall that W and Y are d-separated given $\bar{c}$ if and only if for any realization of BN' the state of W has no impact on $P'(Y|\bar{c})$, i.e., $P'(Y|\bar{c}, W = 0) = P'(Y|\bar{c}, W = 1)$. Thus, W is d-separated from Y given $\bar{c}$ if and only if for any two realizations P_1 and P_2 of BN, differing only on $P(X|\pi_X)$, it holds that $P_1(Y|\bar{c}) = P_2(Y|\bar{c})$ in BN. However, from the construction of BN' we have that as X is not barren, W is d-separated from Y given $\bar{c}$ if and only if X is d-separated from Y given $\bar{c}$.

Based on the lemma above, we present the proof of Theorem 1.

Proof (Theorem 1). It is easy to verify that replacing D_j with its chance variable policy, for $j = i+1, \ldots, n$, does not change the optimal policy for D_i nor does it introduce any "false" structural dependencies (see also [10,7]).

So we can restrict our attention to the last decision variable in I. From Equation 2 we have:

$$\delta_{D_n}(\text{pred}(D_n)) = \arg\max_{D_n} \sum_{\mathcal{C}_n} P(\mathcal{C}_n|\mathcal{C}_0, \ldots, \mathcal{C}_{n-1}, D_1, \ldots, D_n) \sum_{V \in \mathcal{U}_V} \psi_V .$$

Without loss of generality we can assume that ψ_V is the only utility function relevant for D_n. Then by the distributive law we get:

$$\begin{aligned}\delta_{D_n}(\text{pred}(D_n)) &= \arg\max_{D_n} \sum_{\mathcal{C}_n} P(\mathcal{C}_n|\mathcal{C}_0, \ldots, \mathcal{C}_{n-1}, D_1, \ldots, D_n)\psi_V(\pi_V) \\ &= \arg\max_{D_n} \sum_{\mathcal{C}_n \cap \pi_V} \psi_V(\pi_V) \sum_{\mathcal{C}_n \setminus \pi_V} P(\mathcal{C}_n|\mathcal{C}_0, \ldots, \mathcal{C}_{n-1}, D_1, \ldots, D_n) \\ &= \arg\max_{D_n} \sum_{\mathcal{C}_n \cap \pi_V} \psi_V(\pi_V) P(\mathcal{C}_n \cap \pi_V|\mathcal{C}_0, \ldots, \mathcal{C}_{n-1}, D_1, \ldots, D_n) .\end{aligned}$$

So, X is relevant for D_n if and only if $P(X|\pi_X)$ has an effect on $P(\mathcal{C}_n \cap \pi_V|\text{pred}(D_n), D_n)$. By Lemma 1 we have that this holds if and only if X is d-connected to $\mathcal{C}_n \cap \pi_V$ given $\text{pred}(D_n) \cup \{D_n\}$. X is d-connected to $\mathcal{C}_n \cap \pi_V$ given $\text{pred}(D_n) \cup \{D_n\}$ if and only if X is d-connected to V given $\text{pred}(D_n) \cup \{D_n\}$, thereby completing the proof. □

References

1. Dan Geiger, Thomas Verma, and Judea Pearl. d-separation: From theorems to algorithms. In *Uncertainty in Artificial Intelligence 5*, 1990.
2. Eric Horwitch and Matthew Barry. Display of information for time-critical decision making. In Philippe Besnard and Steve Hanks, editors, *Proceedings of the Eleventh Conference on Uncertainty in Artificial Intelligence*, pages 296–305. Morgan Kaufmann Publishers, 1995.
3. Ronald A. Howard and James E. Matheson. Influence diagrams. In Ronald A. Howard and James E. Matheson, editors, *The Principles and Applications of Decision Analysis*, volume 2, chapter 37, pages 721–762. Strategic Decision Group, 1981.
4. Frank Jensen, Finn V. Jensen, and Søren L. Dittmer. From influence diagrams to junction trees. In Ramon Lopez de Mantaras and David Poole, editors, *Proceedings of the Tenth Conference on Uncertainty in Artificial Intelligence*, pages 367–373. Morgan Kaufmann Publishers, 1994.
5. Anders L. Madsen and Finn V. Jensen. Lazy evaluation of symmetric Bayesian decision problems. In Kathryn B. Laskey and Henri Prade, editors, *Proceedings of the Fifthteenth Conference on Uncertainty in Artificial Intelligence*. Morgan Kaufmann Publishers, 1999.
6. Thomas D. Nielsen and Finn V. Jensen. Welldefined decision scenarios. In Kathryn B. Laskey and Henri Prade, editors, *Proceedings of the Fifthteenth Conference on Uncertainty in Artificial Intelligence*. Morgan Kaufmann Publishers, 1999.
7. Thomas D. Nielsen and Finn V. Jensen. Welldefined decision scenarios. Technical Report R-01-5002, Department of Computer Science, Fredrik Bajers 7E, 9220 Aalborg, Denmark, 2001.
8. Dennis Nilsson and Finn V. Jensen. Probabilities of future decisions. In *Information, Uncertainty and Fusion*, pages 161–171. Kluwer Academic Publishers, 2000.
9. Ross D. Shachter. Bayes ball: The rational pastime (for determining irrelevance and requisite information in belief networks and influence diagrams). In Gregory F. Cooper and Serafin Moral, editors, *Proceedings of the Fourteenth Conference on Uncertainty in Artificial Intelligence*, pages 480–487. Morgan Kaufmann Publishers, 1998.
10. Ross D. Shachter. Efficient value of information computation. In Kathryn B. Laskey and Henri Prade, editors, *Proceedings of the Fifthteenth Conference on Uncertainty in Artificial Intelligence*, pages 594–601. Morgan Kaufmann Publishers, 1999.
11. Ross D. Shachter. Evaluating influence diagrams. *Operations Research Society of America*, 34(6):79–90, February 1986.
12. Ross D. Shachter and Mark A. Peot. Decision making using probabilistic inference methods. In Didier Dubois, Michael P. Wellman, Bruce D'Ambrosio, and Phillipe Smets, editors, *Proceedings of the Eighth Conference on Uncertainty in Artificial Intelligence*, pages 276–283. Morgan Kaufmann Publishers, 1992.
13. Prakash P. Shenoy. Valuation-based systems for Bayesian decision analysis. *Operations Research*, 40(3):463–484, 1992.
14. Joseph. A. Tatman and Ross. D. Shachter. Dynamic programming and influence diagrams. *IEEE Transactions on Systems, Man and Cybernetics*, 20(2):365–379, March/April 1990.

Mixtures of Truncated Exponentials in Hybrid Bayesian Networks

Serafín Moral[1], Rafael Rumí[2] and Antonio Salmerón[2]

[1] Dpt. Computer Science and Artificial Intelligence
University of Granada
Avda. Andalucía 38,
18071 Granada, Spain
smc@decsai.ugr.es

[2] Dpt. Statistics and Applied Mathematics
University of Almería
La Cañada de San Urbano s/n
04120 Almería, Spain
{rrumi,Antonio.Salmeron}@ual.es

Abstract. In this paper we propose the use of mixtures of truncated exponential (MTE) distributions in hybrid Bayesian networks. We study the properties of the MTE distribution and show how exact probability propagation can be carried out by means of a local computation algorithm. One feature of this model is that no restriction is made about the order among the variables either discrete or continuous. Computations are performed over a representation of probabilistic potentials based on probability trees, expanded to allow discrete and continuous variables simultaneously. Finally, a Markov chain Monte Carlo algorithm is described with the aim of dealing with complex networks.

Keywords: Hybrid Bayesian networks, MTE distribution, MTE networks, probability propagation, Markov chain Monte Carlo.

1 Introduction

Bayesian networks provide a framework for efficiently dealing with multivariate models. One important feature of these networks is that they allow to perform probabilistic inference taking advantage of the independence relationships among the variables. Probabilistic inference, commonly known as *probability propagation*, consists in obtaining the marginal distribution on some variables of interest given that the values of some other variables are known.

Much attention has been paid to probability propagation in networks where the variables are qualitative. Several exact methods have been proposed in the literature for this task [2, 7, 8, 13], all of them based on *local computation*. Local computation means to calculate the marginals without actually computing the joint distribution, and is described in terms of a message passing scheme over a structure called *join tree*. Also, approximate methods have been developed with the aim of dealing with complex networks [1, 10, 12].

S. Benferhat and P. Besnard (Eds.): ECSQARU 2001, LNAI 2143, pp. 156–167, 2001.

In mixed Bayesian networks, where both discrete and continuous variables appear simultaneously, it is possible to apply local computation schemes similar to those for discrete variables. However, the correctness of exact inference depends on the model.

The most deeply studied mixed model for which exact local computation is correct is based on the conditional Gaussian (CG) distribution [5,6,9]. In this model, networks where discrete variables have continuous parents are not allowed. To avoid this restriction, Koller et al. [3] model the distribution of discrete nodes with continuous parents by a mixture of exponentials, but then inference is carried out by means of Monte Carlo methods. In a more general setting, one way of using local computation is to discretize the continuous variables [4], and then they are treated as if they were quantitative.

In this paper, we study the use of mixtures of truncated exponentials to represent the distribution of the variables in the network. This model does not impose any restriction about the interactions among variables, either discrete or continuous (discrete nodes with continuous parents are allowed), and exact propagation can be performed using local computation algorithms. The main utility of this model is to provide an alternative to discretization. Discretization can be seen as approximating a density with a mixture of uniforms. We think that more accurate approximations can be obtained using exponential shaped functions instead of uniforms.

We introduce the notation used throughout the paper in section 2. The MTE model is presented in section 3, and the correctness of exact probability propagation on this model is shown in section 4; also, a data structure is proposed to represent MTE potentials based on probability trees. Section 5 is devoted to describe a Markov Chain Monte Carlo (MCMC) algorithm, useful when exact propagation is infeasible. The paper ends with conclusions in section 6.

2 Notation

A *Bayesian network* is a directed acyclic graph where each node represents a random variable, and the topology of the graph shows the independence relations among the variables, according to the d-separation criterion. Given the independences encoded by the graph, the joint distribution is determined giving a probability distribution for each node conditioned on its parents.

We will denote random variables by capital letters like X, Y and Z, while boldfaced capital letters will stand for multidimensional variables. A multidimensional variable will be denoted by $\mathbf{Y}$ if it is discrete, $\mathbf{Z}$ if it is continuous or $\mathbf{X}$ if its components may be discrete and continuous. If $\mathbf{X}$ is a variable, $\mathbf{x}$ will denote a value of that variable. The set of possible values of a variable $\mathbf{X}$ is denoted by $\Omega_{\mathbf{X}}$.

Given $\mathbf{x} \in \Omega_{\mathbf{X}}$ and $\mathbf{X}' \subseteq \mathbf{X}$, we denote by $\mathbf{x}^{\downarrow \Omega_{X'}}$ the element of $\Omega_{X'}$ obtained from $\mathbf{x}$ by dropping the coordinates corresponding to variables not in $\mathbf{X}'$.

A potential ϕ defined on $\Omega_{\mathbf{X}}$ is a mapping $\phi : \Omega_{\mathbf{X}} \mapsto \mathbb{R}_0^+$, where $\mathbb{R}_0^+$ is the set of non-negative real numbers. Probabilistic information (including 'a priori', conditional and 'a posteriori' distributions) will always be represented by means of potentials, as in [7]. If ϕ is a potential defined on $\Omega_{\mathbf{X}}$, $dom(\phi)$ will denote the set of variables for which ϕ is defined (i.e. $dom(\phi) = \mathbf{X}$). We will use letter ϕ to denote a generic potential, while letter f will be used for probability densities.

3 Mixtures of truncated exponentials

In this section we introduce a class of mixed distributions, which we will call *mixture of truncated exponentials*. Before defining the distribution itself, we study the concept of potential and the basic operations over them.

Definition 1. (MTE potential) *Let* $\mathbf{X}$ *be a mixed* n*-dimensional random variable. Let* $\mathbf{Y} = (Y_1, \ldots, Y_d)$ *and* $\mathbf{Z} = (Z_1, \ldots, Z_c)$ *be the discrete and continuous parts of* $\mathbf{X}$*, respectively, with* $c + d = n$*. We say that a function* $\phi : \Omega_{\mathbf{X}} \mapsto I\!R_0^+$ *is a* potential of class mixture of truncated exponentials (MTE potential) *if one of the next two conditions holds:*

i. ϕ *can be written as*

$$\phi(\mathbf{x}) = \phi(\mathbf{y}, \mathbf{z}) = a_0 + \sum_{i=1}^{m} a_i \exp\left\{ \sum_{j=1}^{d} b_i^{(j)} y_j + \sum_{k=1}^{c} b_i^{(d+k)} z_k \right\} \tag{1}$$

for all $\mathbf{x} \in \Omega_{\mathbf{X}}$*, where* a_i*,* $i = 0, \ldots, m$ *and* $b_i^{(j)}$*,* $i = 1, \ldots, m$*,* $j = 1, \ldots, n$ *are real numbers.*

ii. *There is a partition* $\Omega_1, \ldots, \Omega_k$ *of* $\Omega_{\mathbf{X}}$ *verifying that the domain of the continuous variables,* $\Omega_{\mathbf{Z}}$*, is divided into hypercubes, the domain of the discrete variables,* $\Omega_{\mathbf{Y}}$*, is divided into arbitrary sets, and such that* ϕ *is defined as*

$$\phi(\mathbf{x}) = \phi_i(\mathbf{x}) \quad \text{if} \quad \mathbf{x} \in \Omega_i \ ,$$

where each ϕ_i*,* $i = 1, \ldots, k$ *can be written in the form of equation (1) (i.e. each* ϕ_i *is an MTE potential on* Ω_i*).*

Example 1. The function ϕ defined as

$$\phi(z_1, z_2) = \begin{cases} 2 + e^{3z_1+z_2} + e^{z_1+z_2} & \text{if } 0 < z_1 \leq 1,\ 0 < z_2 < 2 \\ 1 + e^{z_1+z_2} & \text{if } 0 < z_1 \leq 1,\ 2 \leq z_2 < 3 \\ \frac{1}{4} + e^{2z_1+z_2} & \text{if } 1 < z_1 < 2,\ 0 < z_2 < 2 \\ \frac{1}{2} + 5e^{z_1+2z_2} & \text{if } 1 < z_1 < 2,\ 2 \leq z_2 < 3 \end{cases}$$

is an MTE potential since all of its parts are MTE potentials.

3.1 Operations over MTE potentials

Three basic operations are necessary for performing probabilistic inference over a distribution specified as a Bayesian network: *restriction, marginalization* and *combination (product).*

Definition 2. (Restriction) *Let ϕ be an MTE potential over $\mathbf{X} = (\mathbf{Y}, \mathbf{Z})$. Assume a set of variables $\mathbf{X}' = (\mathbf{Y}', \mathbf{Z}') \subseteq \mathbf{X}$, whose values $\mathbf{x}^{\downarrow \Omega_{\mathbf{X}'}}$ are fixed ($\mathbf{x}^{\downarrow \Omega_{\mathbf{X}'}} = \mathbf{x}' = (\mathbf{y}', \mathbf{z}')$). The* restriction *of ϕ to the values $(\mathbf{y}', \mathbf{z}')$ is a new potential defined on $\Omega_{\mathbf{X} \setminus \mathbf{X}'}$ according to the following expression:*

$$\phi^{R(\mathbf{X}'=\mathbf{x}')}(\mathbf{w}) = \phi^{R(\mathbf{Y}'=\mathbf{y}', \mathbf{Z}'=\mathbf{z}')}(\mathbf{w}) = \phi(\mathbf{x}) \tag{2}$$

for all $\mathbf{w} \in \Omega_{\mathbf{X} \setminus \mathbf{X}'}$ such that $\mathbf{x} \in \Omega_{\mathbf{X}}$, $\mathbf{x}^{\downarrow \Omega_{\mathbf{X} \setminus \mathbf{X}'}} = \mathbf{w}$ and $\mathbf{x}^{\downarrow \Omega_{\mathbf{X}'}} = \mathbf{x}'$. In other words, the restriction is the potential obtained replacing every occurrence of $\mathbf{X}'$ by value $\mathbf{x}'$.

Definition 3. (Marginalization) *Let ϕ be an MTE potential over $\mathbf{X} = (\mathbf{Y}, \mathbf{Z})$. The marginal of ϕ for a set of variables $\mathbf{X}' = (\mathbf{Y}', \mathbf{Z}') \subseteq \mathbf{X}$ is the potential computed as*

$$\phi^{\downarrow \mathbf{X}'}(\mathbf{y}', \mathbf{z}') = \sum_{\mathbf{y} \in \Omega_{\mathbf{Y} \setminus \mathbf{Y}'}} \left(\int_{\Omega_{\mathbf{Z}''}} \phi(\mathbf{y}, \mathbf{y}', \mathbf{z}', \mathbf{z}) d\mathbf{z}'' \right) , \tag{3}$$

where $\mathbf{Z}'' = \mathbf{Z} \setminus \mathbf{Z}'$. Observe that this function is defined on $\Omega_{\mathbf{X}'}$.

Example 2. Assume we want to obtain the marginal of the potential in example 1 for variable Z_2. This is achieved by integrating over Z_1 and simplifying afterwards:

$$\phi^{\downarrow z_2}(z_2) = \begin{cases} \frac{9}{4} + \frac{3e^4+2e^3-3e^2+6e-8}{6} e^{z_2} & 0 < z_2 < 2 \\ \frac{3}{2} + (e-1)e^{z_2} + 5(e^2-e)e^{z_2} & 2 \le z_2 < 3 \end{cases}$$

Definition 4. (Combination) *Let ϕ_1 and ϕ_2 be MTE potentials over $\mathbf{X}_1 = (\mathbf{Y}_1, \mathbf{Z}_1)$ and $\mathbf{X}_2 = (\mathbf{Y}_2, \mathbf{Z}_2)$ respectively. The combination of ϕ_1 and ϕ_2 is a new potential defined over $\mathbf{X} = \mathbf{X}_1 \cup \mathbf{X}_2$ computed as*

$$\phi(\mathbf{x}) = \phi_1(\mathbf{x}^{\downarrow \Omega_{\mathbf{X}_1}}) \cdot \phi_2(\mathbf{x}^{\downarrow \Omega_{\mathbf{X}_2}}) \quad \text{for all} \quad \mathbf{x} \in \Omega_{\mathbf{X}} . \tag{4}$$

Example 3. In order to illustrate this operation, we will combine the potential in example 1 with this one:

$$\phi'(x) = \begin{cases} 3 + e^x & 0 < x \le 2 \\ 2 + e^{-2x} & 2 < x < 4 \end{cases}$$

The result will be an MTE potential $\phi''(z_1, z_2, x) = \phi(z_1, z_2) \cdot \phi'(x)$ defined in 8 regions :

$$\phi''(z_1, z_2, x) = \begin{cases} 6 + 2e^x + 3e^{z_1+z_2} + 3e^{3z_1+z_2} + e^{z_1+z_2+x} + e^{3z_1+z_2+x} \\ \textit{if } 0 < z_1 \leq 1, 0 < z_2 < 2, 0 < x \leq 2 \\ 4 + 10e^{-2x} + 2e^{3z_1+z_2} + 2e^{z_1+z_2} + 5e^{3z_1+z_2-2x} + 5e^{z_1+z_2-2x} \\ \textit{if } 0 < z_1 \leq 1, 0 < z_2 < 2, 2 < x < 4 \\ 3 + e^x + 3e^{z_1+z_2} + e^{z_1+z_2+x} \\ \textit{if } 0 < z_1 \leq 1, 2 \leq z_2 < 3, 0 < x \leq 2 \\ 2 + 5e^{-2x} + e^{z_1+z_2} + 5e^{z_1+z_2-2x} \\ \textit{if } 0 < z_1 \leq 1, 2 \leq z_2 < 3, 2 < x < 4 \\ \frac{3}{4} + \frac{e^x}{4} + 3e^{2z_1+z_2} + e^{2z_1+z_2+x} \\ \textit{if } 1 < z_1 < 2, 0 < z_2 < 2, 0 < x \leq 2 \\ \frac{1}{2} + \frac{5e^{-2x}}{4} + 2e^{2z_1+z_2} + 5e^{2z_1+z_2-2x} \\ \textit{if } 1 < z_1 < 2, 0 < z_2 < 2, 2 < x < 4 \\ \frac{3}{2} + \frac{e^x}{2} + 15e^{z_1+2z_2} + 5e^{z_1+2z_2+x} \\ \textit{if } 1 < z_1 < 2, 2 \leq z_2 < 3, 0 < x \leq 2 \\ 1 + \frac{5e^{-2x}}{2} + 10e^{z_1+2z_2} + 25e^{z_1+2z_2-2x} \\ \textit{if } 1 < z_1 < 2, 2 \leq z_2 < 3, 2 < x < 4 \end{cases}$$

Proposition 1. *The class of MTE potentials is closed under restriction, marginalization and combination.*

Proof. This result can be proved relying of the fact that replacing a variable by one of its values, integrating over a variable, summing out a variable and multiplying two MTE potentials always result in a new MTE potential. For the sake of simplicity we omit the details of the proof.

3.2 MTE distributions

Based on MTE potentials, a probability distribution can be defined as follows.

Definition 5. (MTE distribution) *Let* $\mathbf{X} = (\mathbf{Y}, \mathbf{Z})$ *be an* n*-dimensional mixed random variable. We say that* $\mathbf{X}$ *follows an* MTE distribution, *if its density* f *verifies that* f *is an MTE potential and*

$$\sum_{\mathbf{y} \in \Omega_{\mathbf{Y}}} \int_{\Omega_{\mathbf{Z}}} f(\mathbf{y}, \mathbf{z}) d\mathbf{z} = 1 \ .$$

A potential verifying these conditions will be called an MTE density *for* $\mathbf{X}$.

In the framework of Bayesian networks, the model is specified as a set of conditional distributions rather than joint distributions. The conditional MTE distribution can be defined as follows:

Definition 6. (Conditional MTE density) *Let* $\mathbf{X}_1 = (\mathbf{Y}_1, \mathbf{Z}_1)$ *and* $\mathbf{X}_2 = (\mathbf{Y}_2, \mathbf{Z}_2)$ *be two mixed random variables. We say that an MTE potential* f *defined over* $\Omega_{\mathbf{X}_1 \cup \mathbf{X}_2}$ *is a* conditional MTE density *if for each* $\mathbf{x}_2 \in \Omega_{\mathbf{X}_2}$, *it holds that* $f^{R(\mathbf{X}_2 = \mathbf{x}_2)}$ *is an MTE density for* $\mathbf{X}_1$.

What makes the MTE distribution be worth of being studied is its versatility. Many models can be approximated by an MTE distribution, but also, some common models can be exactly represented; for instance, the uniform and the multinomial distributions are particular examples of this one.

Usually, when specifying a model as a Bayesian network, we give a set of conditional distributions that, according to the chain rule, corresponds to a factorization of the joint distribution of the variables in the network. If the conditional distributions are of class MTE, the next proposition shows that the joint distribution is also of class MTE.

Proposition 2. *Let G be a Bayesian network over an n-dimensional mixed variable $\mathbf{X} = (\mathbf{Y}, \mathbf{Z})$. If every conditional distribution associated with G corresponds to a conditional MTE density, then the joint distribution over $\mathbf{X}$ can be represented by an MTE density.*

Proof. This is a consequence of the facts that the product of the n densities in the network is the joint distribution over the n-dimensional variable $\mathbf{X}$ and the product of all the densities associated with the Bayesian networks is an MTE potential.

A Bayesian network representing an MTE distribution will be called an *MTE network.*

4 Probability propagation in MTE networks

Consider an MTE network defined for an n-dimensional variable $\mathbf{X}$. Let f denote the joint distribution of $\mathbf{X}$. If we denote by $f_i(x_i|\mathbf{x}_{pa(X_i)})$ the conditional MTE density of variable X_i, $i = 1, \ldots, n$, given its parents $\mathbf{X}_{pa(X_i)}$, then it holds that $f(\mathbf{x}) = \prod_{i=1}^{n} f_i(x_i|\mathbf{x}_{pa(X_i)})$.

Probability propagation consists in obtaining the marginal distribution on some variables of interest given some observations. An *observation* is the knowledge about the exact value $X_i = e_i$ of a variable. The set of observations will be denoted by $\mathbf{e}$, and called the *evidence set.* $\mathbf{E}$ will be the set of variables observed. Every observation, $X_i = e_i$, is represented by means of an MTE potential defined on Ω_{X_i} as $\delta_i(x_i; e_i) = 1$ if $e_i = x_i$, $x_i \in \Omega_{X_i}$, and $\delta_i(x_i; e_i) = 0$ if $e_i \neq x_i$.

Using this notation, probability propagation can be defined as calculating the 'a posteriori' probability function $f(x_i|\mathbf{e})$, for every unobserved variable $X_i \in \mathbf{X} \setminus \mathbf{E}$. Notice that

$$f(x_i|\mathbf{e}) = \frac{f^{\downarrow X_i}(x_i, \mathbf{e})}{f^{\downarrow \mathbf{E}}(\mathbf{e})} \;, \tag{5}$$

where $f^{\downarrow \mathbf{E}}(\mathbf{e})$ denotes the marginal of the joint distribution f evaluated for observations $\mathbf{e}$[1]. Thus, obtaining $f(x_i|\mathbf{e})$ is equivalent to compute $f(x_i, \mathbf{e})$ (observe that $\mathbf{e}$ is fixed) and normalize afterwards.

[1] From now on, whenever the term $\mathbf{e}$ is added to the argument of a function, we mean that if a variable in $\mathbf{E}$ is in the domain of the function, then that variable is fixed to its value in $\mathbf{e}$.

If we call $H = \{f_i(x_i|\mathbf{x}_{pa(X_i)})|i = 1,\ldots,n\} \cup \{\delta_i(x_i;e_i)|e_i \in \mathbf{e}\}$, then for any variable $X_i \in \mathbf{X}$

$$f^{\downarrow X_i}(x_i,\mathbf{e}) = \left(\prod_{\phi\in H} \phi(\mathbf{x}^{\downarrow \Omega_{dom(\phi)}})\right)^{\downarrow X_i} (x_i) \ . \tag{6}$$

The computation of $f^{\downarrow X_i}(x_i,\mathbf{e})$ is usually organized in a join tree. A *join tree* is a tree where each node V is a subset of $\mathbf{X}$, and such that if a variable is in two distinct nodes, V_1 and V_2, then it is also in every node in the path between V_1 and V_2.

Every density $\phi \in H$ is assigned to a node V_j such that $dom(\phi) \subseteq V_j$, in order to obtain an MTE potential ϕ_{V_j} defined over the set of variables V_j and that is equal to the product of all the densities assigned to it.

$f^{\downarrow X_i}(x_i,\mathbf{e})$ can be calculated by means of a propagation algorithm in a join tree. Afterwards, $f^{\downarrow X_i}(x_i,\mathbf{e})$ can be obtained from any node V_j containing variable X_i. One possibility is to use the Shenoy-Shafer propagation algorithm [13]. In the Shenoy-Shafer scheme, two mailboxes are placed on each edge of the join tree. Given an edge connecting nodes V_i and V_j, one mailbox is for messages V_i-outgoing and V_j-incoming, and the other mailbox is for the reverse. The messages allocated in both mailboxes will be MTE potentials defined on $V_i \cap V_j$. Initially, each mailbox is *empty*, and once a message has been placed on one of them, it is said to be *full*.

A node V_i in a join tree is allowed to send a message to its neighbour node V_j if and only if all V_i-incoming mailboxes are full except the one from V_j to V_i. Thus, initially only nodes corresponding to leaves can send messages. The message V_i-outgoing and V_j-incoming is computed as

$$\phi_{V_i\to V_j} = \left\{\phi_{V_i} \cdot \left(\prod_{V_k\in ne(V_i)\setminus\{V_j\}} \phi_{V_k\to V_i}\right)\right\}^{\downarrow V_i\cap V_j} , \tag{7}$$

where ϕ_{V_i} is the initial MTE potential on V_i, $\phi_{V_k\to V_i}$ are the messages in the mailboxes V_k-outgoing and V_i-incoming and $ne(V_i)$ are the neighbour nodes of V_i. Note that one message contains the information coming from one side of the tree and is sent to the other side of the tree. It can be shown [13] that there is always at least one node allowed to send a message until all mailboxes are full, and when the message passing ends, for every node V_i in the join tree it holds that the marginal of the joint distribution f on variables V_i is

$$f^{\downarrow V_i}(\mathbf{x},\mathbf{e}) = \phi_{V_i}(\mathbf{x},\mathbf{e}) \cdot \left(\prod_{V_k\in ne(V_i)} \phi_{V_k\to V_i}(\mathbf{x}^{\downarrow \Omega_{V_k\cap V_i}},\mathbf{e})\right) \quad \forall \mathbf{x}\in\Omega_{V_i} \ , \tag{8}$$

which is proportional to the conditional distribution of the variables in V_i given observation $\mathbf{e}$. $f^{\downarrow X_i}$ and the desired conditional probability for variable X_i can be calculated by marginalizing $f^{\downarrow V_i}$ over this variable and normalizing the result.

Observe that probability propagation just requires combinations and marginalizations of MTE potentials. Thus, any new potential resulting from an operation along the propagation is also of class MTE (see proposition 1). This fact is reflected in the next proposition.

Proposition 3. *The class of MTE potentials is closed under Shenoy-Shafer propagation.*

Proof. Initially, the potential stored in each node of the join tree is the product of some MTE densities. After propagation this fact still holds, since only combinations and marginalizations are performed, and these operations are closed for MTE potentials. Thus, the marginal densities computed in the Shenoy-Shafer propagation, $f^{\downarrow X_i}$ are also of class MTE, and so is the conditional density $f(x_i|\mathbf{e})$ in equation (5), since the division of an MTE potential by a real number is also an MTE potential.

According to this proposition, the entire propagation in an MTE network operates with MTE potentials.

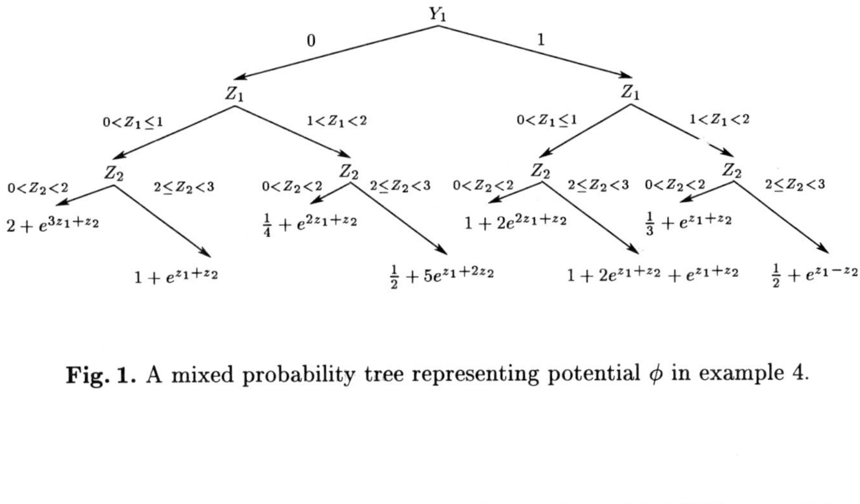

Fig. 1. A mixed probability tree representing potential ϕ in example 4.

As a data structure for representing and operating with MTE potentials, we propose the use of an extended version of probability trees [12], that we call *mixed probability trees.*

Definition 7. (Mixed probability tree) *We say that a tree $\mathcal{T}$ is a* mixed probability tree *if it meets the following conditions:*

i. *Every internal node represents a random variable (discrete or continuous).*
ii. *Every arc outgoing from a continuous variable Z is labeled with an interval of values of Z, so that the domain of Z is the union of the intervals corresponding to the arcs outgoing from Z.*

iii. *Every discrete variable has one outgoing arc for each of its states.*
iv. *Each leaf node contains an MTE potential defined on variables in the path from the root to that leaf.*

Mixed probability trees can represent MTE potentials defined by parts. Each entire branch in the tree determines one sub-region of the space where the potential is defined, and the function stored in the leaf of a branch is the definition of the potential in the corresponding sub-region.

Example 4. Consider the following MTE potential, defined for a discrete variable (Y_1) and two continuous variables (Z_1 and Z_2).

$$\phi(y_1,z_1,z_2)=\begin{cases} 2+e^{3z_1+z_2} & \text{if } \ y_1=0,\ 0<z_1\leq 1,\ 0<z_2<2 \\ 1+e^{z_1+z_2} & \text{if } \ y_1=0,\ 0<z_1\leq 1,\ 2\leq z_2<3 \\ \frac{1}{4}+e^{2z_1+z_2} & \text{if } \ y_1=0,\ 1<z_1<2,\ 0<z_2<2 \\ \frac{1}{2}+5e^{z_1+2z_2} & \text{if } \ y_1=0,\ 1<z_1<2,\ 2\leq z_2<3 \\ 1+2e^{2z_1+z_2} & \text{if } \ y_1=1,\ 0<z_1\leq 1,\ 0<z_2<2 \\ 1+2e^{z_1+z_2}+e^{z_1+z_2} & \text{if } \ y_1=1,\ 0<z_1\leq 1,\ 2\leq z_2<3 \\ \frac{1}{3}+e^{z_1+z_2} & \text{if } \ y_1=1,\ 1<z_1<2,\ 0<z_2<2 \\ \frac{1}{2}+e^{z_1-z_2} & \text{if } \ y_1=1,\ 1<z_1<2,\ 2\leq z_2<3 \end{cases}$$

A possible representation of this potential by means of a mixed probability tree is displayed in figure 1.

The operations of restriction, marginalization and combination over mixed probability trees can be carried out by means of algorithms very similar to those described by Kozlov and Koller [4] and Salmerón, Cano and Moral [12].

5 A Markov chain Monte Carlo propagation algorithm

In section 4 we showed that exact propagation can be carried out in MTE networks by means of Shenoy-Shafer algorithm, and suggested a possible representation of MTE potentials that allows to implement the propagation algorithm. However, during the propagation, the size of the potentials[2] involved in the calculations may grow so much that the propagation become infeasible. Instead, the posterior probabilities can be estimated using Markov chain Monte Carlo.

Markov chain Monte Carlo propagation [10] proceeds by generating a sample of the variables in the network, and then uses that sample to estimate the distribution of the variables of interest. The sample is generated from an initial

[2] By the *size* of a potential we mean the number of leaves of the mixed probability tree representing it.

configuration of the variables, where the observed variables **E** are instantiated to observation **e**. This initial configuration can be obtained by forward sampling.

Once we have a starting configuration, a new one is obtained by changing the value of the unobserved variables one by one. The new value for a variable X_i is obtained by simulating from the distribution function corresponding to the product of its conditional distribution $f_i(x_i|\mathbf{x}_{pa(i)})$ and the distribution of the variables in its Markov blanket (i.e. its parents, children and parents of its children except X_i) restricted to the values of all the variables but X_i in the current configuration.

The simulation procedure above described can be applied to MTE networks. The only aspect to clarify is how to simulate a value for a variable with MTE distribution.

5.1 Simulating from the MTE distribution

Observe that when we are going to simulate a variable X_i we simulate from a distribution that depends only on X_i and that distribution is of class MTE. If X_i is discrete, it is straightforward to simulate a value for it: a random number is generated and the inverse transform method is applied [11].

If X_i is continuous, we may find its density defined in several pieces, and besides, the inverse transform method, in general, cannot be applied to mixtures of exponentials. However, values can be obtained applying twice the composition method [11].

Assume that the density used to simulate a variable is defined as $f(x) = f_i(x)$ for $\alpha_i \leq x < \beta_i$, $i = 1, \ldots, k$, where each of the functions f_i are of the form

$$f_i(x) = a_0 + a_1 e^{k_1 x} + a_2 e^{k_2 x} + \cdots + a_n e^{k_n x} \quad \alpha_i \leq x < \beta_i \ . \tag{9}$$

The way to simulate from $f(x)$ by the composition method is to choose one of the f_i with probability equal to $\int_{\alpha_i}^{\beta_i} f_i(x)dx$ and then simulate a value inside interval (a_i, b_i) from a density f_i^* proportional to f_i:

$$f_i^*(x) = \frac{f_i(x)}{\int_{\alpha_i}^{\beta_i} f_i(x)dx} \quad \alpha_i \leq x < \beta_i \ ,$$

which is also a function of the form of equation (9).

In order to simulate from f_i^* we have to apply again the composition method. The steps to apply this method are:

1. Decompose density $f_i^*(x)$ as a weighted sum of densities
$$f_i^*(x) = p_1 f_1'(x) + \cdots + p_m f_m'(x) \tag{10}$$
with $\sum_{j=1}^{m} p_j = 1$.
2. Generate two random numbers u_1 and u_2.
3. Use u_1 to choose one f_j' with probability p_j, and use u_2 to obtain a value for variable X applying the inverse transform method to the distribution function corresponding to f_j'.

The decomposition in (10) must be such that the inverse of the distribution function corresponding to each f'_j can be computed.

We can obtain such decomposition as follows. Define $c_j = \int_{\alpha_i}^{\beta_i} e^{k_j x} dx$, $j = 1,\ldots,n$. Then $f'_j(x) = \frac{1}{c_j} e^{k_j x}$, $j = 1,\ldots,n$ is a density function in (α_i, β_i). For $j = 0$, $c_0 = \int_{\alpha_i}^{\beta_i} dx = \beta_i - \alpha_i$ and it holds that $f_0(x) = \frac{1}{c_0}$ is a density in (α_i, β_i). With this, multiplying and dividing each term by the corresponding c_j,

$$f_i^*(x) = a_0 c_0 \frac{1}{c_0} + a_1 c_1 \frac{1}{c_1} e^{k_1 x} + a_2 c_2 \frac{1}{c_2} e^{k_2 x} + \cdots + a_n c_n \frac{1}{c_n} e^{k_n x} , \quad \alpha_i \leq x \leq \beta_i ,$$

where we can take as weights $p_j = a_j c_j$, $j = 0,\ldots,n$. It can be easily verified that these weights sum up to one.

Finally, the inverse of the distribution function of each f'_j constructed as described here can be easily computed. If $j = 0$, the distribution is just the uniform in (α_i, β_i). If $j > 0$, for $x \in (\alpha_i, \beta_i)$, the distribution function is

$$F'_j(x) = \int_{-\infty}^{x} f'_j(t) dt = \int_{\alpha_i}^{x} \frac{1}{c_j} e^{k_j t} dt = \frac{1}{c_j k_j} \left(e^{k_j x} - e^{k_j \alpha_i} \right) .$$

To obtain the inverse, for a random number $0 < u < 1$ we take

$$u = \frac{1}{c_j k_j} \left(e^{k_j x} - e^{k_j \alpha_i} \right) \Rightarrow x = \frac{1}{k_j} \log \left(c_j k_j u + e^{k_j x} \right) .$$

Thus, for $j > 0$, $F_j'^{-1}(u) = \frac{1}{k_j} \log \left(c_j k_j u + e^{k_j x} \right) \quad 0 < u < 1$.

5.2 Estimating posterior probabilities from a sample

Once the sample is obtained, it can be used to estimate values such as $P(a < X_i < b)$ by counting configurations in the sample for which X_i falls into (a, b).

Another possibility is to give an estimation of the posterior density for variable X_i. Since we know that propagation is closed for MTE distributions, the sample could be used to estimate the parameters of the distribution. This is not a trivial task, and two problems must be addressed: into how many intervals the domain of variable X_i is to be divided and how many terms are added to the mixture of exponentials in each interval.

This estimation process can be seen as a particular case of a more general one: learning MTE networks from data, that we will address in forthcoming works.

6 Conclusions

We have introduced the MTE distribution as a model for dealing with hybrid Bayesian networks. We have shown how MTE networks allow local computation propagation algorithms, particularly the Shenoy-Shafer scheme. Any other scheme that involves the restriction, combination and marginalization operations is also valid for MTE networks.

Besides, we have described a Markov chain Monte Carlo algorithm for propagating in complex MTE networks.

Much more work must be done to complete the study of the MTE models. For instance, other simulation algorithms as *importance sampling* [12] could be applied. Our current work is concerned with the design of methods for learning MTE networks from data and we are also investigating the extension of the MTE model to allow incorporating distributions specified as mixtures of Gaussians.

References

1. A. Cano, S. Moral, and A. Salmerón. Penniless propagation in join trees. *International Journal of Intelligent Systems*, 15:1027–1059, 2000.
2. F.V. Jensen, S.L. Lauritzen, and K.G. Olesen. Bayesian updating in causal probabilistic networks by local computation. *Comput Stat Quarterly*, 4:269–282, 1990.
3. D. Koller, U. Lerner, and D. Anguelov. A general algorithm for approximate inference and its application to hybrid Bayes nets. In K.B. Laskey and H. Prade, editors, *Proceedings of the 15th Conference on Uncertainty in Artificial Intelligence*, pages 324–333. Morgan & Kauffman, 1999.
4. D. Kozlov and D. Koller. Nonuniform dynamic discretization in hybrid networks. In D. Geiger and P.P. Shenoy, editors, *Proceedings of the 13th Conference on Uncertainty in Artificial Intelligence*, pages 302–313. Morgan & Kauffman, 1997.
5. S.L. Lauritzen. Propagation of probabilities, means and variances in mixed graphical association models. *Journal of the American Statistical Association*, 87:1098–1108, 1992.
6. S.L. Lauritzen and F. Jensen. Stable local computation with conditional Gaussian distributions. *Statistics and Computing*, 11:191–203, 2001.
7. S.L. Lauritzen and D.J. Spiegelhalter. Local computations with probabilities on graphical structures and their application to expert systems. *Journal of the Royal Statistical Society, Series B*, 50:157–224, 1988.
8. A.L. Madsen and F.V. Jensen. Lazy propagation: a junction tree inference algorithm based on lazy evaluation. *Artif Intell*, 113:203–245, 1999.
9. K.G. Olesen. Causal probabilistic networks with both discrete and continuous variables. *IEEE Trans on Pattern Analysis and Machine Intell*, 15:275–279, 1993.
10. J. Pearl. Evidential reasoning using stochastic simulation of causal models. *Artificial Intelligence*, 32:247–257, 1987.
11. R.Y. Rubinstein. *Simulation and the Monte Carlo Method.* Wiley, 1981.
12. A. Salmerón, A. Cano, and S. Moral. Importance sampling in Bayesian networks using probability trees. *Computational Statistics and Data Analysis*, 34:387–413, 2000.
13. P.P. Shenoy and G. Shafer. Axioms for probability and belief function propagation. In R.D. Shachter, T.S. Levitt, J.F. Lemmer, and L.N. Kanal, editors, *Uncertainty in Artificial Intelligence 4*, pages 169–198. North Holland, Amsterdam, 1990.

Importance Sampling in Bayesian Networks Using Antithetic Variables

Antonio Salmerón[1] and Serafín Moral[2]

[1] Dpt. Statistics and Applied Mathematics
University of Almería
La Cañada de San Urbano s/n
04120 Almería, Spain
Antonio.Salmeron@ual.es

[2] Dpt. Computer Science and Artificial Intelligence
University of Granada
Avda. Andalucía 38,
18071 Granada, Spain
smc@decsai.ugr.es

Abstract. In this paper we introduce an improvement over importance sampling propagation algorithms in Bayesian networks. The difference with respect to importance sampling is that during the simulation, configurations are obtained using antithetic variables (variables with negative correlation), achieving a reduction of the variance of the estimation. The performance of the new algorithm is tested by means of some experiments carried out over four large real-world networks.

Keywords: Bayesian networks, probability propagation, importance sampling, antithetic variables.

1 Introduction

Bayesian networks provide a framework for efficiently dealing with complex multivariate models. One of the most common tasks performed over them is the so-called *probability propagation* or probabilistic inference, which consists in obtaining the probability distribution of some variables of interest given that the value of some other variables is known.

Exact probabilistic inference in Bayesian networks may be infeasible in large networks [2], which motivates the development of approximate algorithms, most of them based on Monte Carlo simulation.

Propagation algorithms based on Monte Carlo methods can be divided into two groups: those using Gibbs sampling [10,12] and those using importance sampling [4,6,8,9,16,17]. However, when dealing with very large networks with extreme probabilities, only the most sophisticated of them are able to provide accurate results, namely blocking Gibbs sampling [10] and importance sampling based on approximate pre-computation [8,9,16]. In both cases, the goal is to draw samples from a probability distribution that is difficult to manage, in the sense that its size is too big.

S. Benferhat and P. Besnard (Eds.): ECSQARU 2001, LNAI 2143, pp. 168–179, 2001.

It is known [3] that the problem of approximating probabilities in Bayesian networks is NP-hard in the worst case. More precisely, many simulation algorithms fail to provide good results in large networks with extreme probabilities, because it can be very difficult to get a sample with positive probability. This fact makes necessary the study of heuristic procedures to propagate over large networks with extreme probabilities.

A class of these heuristic procedures is composed by the importance sampling algorithms based on approximate pre-computation [9,16]. These methods perform first a fast but non exact propagation, following a node removal process [18]. In this way, an approximate 'a posteriori' distribution is obtained. In a second stage a sample is drawn using the approximate distribution and the probabilities are estimated according to the importance sampling methodology.

In this work we will rely on the basis of the importance sampling algorithm based on approximate pre-computation developed in [16]. One of the particularities of that algorithm is the use of *probability trees* to represent and approximate probabilistic potentials.

Probability trees use the regularities of the conditional distributions to reduce the space necessary to store them. The use of this representation instead of probability tables becomes more important when we cannot afford to compute exact values and we have to approximate the potentials. Probability trees have the possibility of approximating in an asymmetrical way, concentrating more resources (finer discrimination) where they are more necessary: higher values with more variability (see [16] for a deeper discussion on these issues).

In this paper we introduce a Monte Carlo algorithm that improves importance sampling based on approximate pre-computation by means of the use of antithetic variables during the simulation process. The performance of the new algorithm is compared to previous importance sampling in a series of experiments carried out over some large real-world networks.

The paper is organized as follows: in section 2 it is described how probability propagation can be carried out using the importance sampling technique. The use of antithetic variables is introduced in section 3, pointing out the modifications necessary to incorporate this new feature to the importance sampling algorithm. In section 4 the performance of the new algorithm is evaluated according to the results of some experiments where large networks have been used. The paper ends with conclusions in section 5.

2 Importance Sampling in Bayesian Networks

A *Bayesian network* is a directed acyclic graph where each node represents a random variable, and the topology of the graph shows the independence relations among the variables, according to the *d*-separation criterion [13]. Given the independences attached to the graph, the joint distribution is determined giving a probability distribution for each node conditioned on its parents.

Let $\mathbf{X} = \{X_1, \ldots, X_n\}$ be the set of variables in the network, each variable X_i taking values on a finite set Ω_i. If I is a set of indices, we will write $\mathbf{X}_I$

for the set $\{X_i|i \in I\}$, and Ω_I will denote the Cartesian product $\times_{i\in I}\Omega_i$. Given $\mathbf{x} \in \Omega_I$ and $J \subseteq I$, $\mathbf{x}_J$ is the element of Ω_J obtained from $\mathbf{x}$ by dropping the coordinates not in J.

A potential f defined on Ω_I is a mapping $f : \Omega_I \rightarrow \mathbb{R}_0^+$, where $\mathbb{R}_0^+$ is the set of non-negative real numbers. Probabilistic information will always be represented by means of potentials, as in [11]. The set of indices of the variables on which a potential f is defined will be denoted as $\text{dom}(f)$.

The conditional distribution of each variable X_i, $i = 1, \ldots, n$, given its parents in the network, $\mathbf{X}_{pa(i)}$, is denoted by a potential $p_i(x_i|\mathbf{x}_{pa(i)})$ where p_i is defined over $\Omega_{\{i\}\cup pa(i)}$.

If $N = \{1, \ldots, n\}$, the joint probability distribution for the n-dimensional random variable $\mathbf{X}$ can be expressed as

$$p(\mathbf{x}) = \prod_{i\in N} p_i(x_i|\mathbf{x}_{pa(i)}) \quad \forall \mathbf{x} \in \Omega_N \ , \tag{1}$$

An *observation* is the knowledge about the exact value $X_i = e_i$ of a variable. The set of observations will be denoted by $\mathbf{e}$, and called the *evidence set*. E will be the set of indices of the variables observed.

The goal of probability propagation is to calculate the 'a posteriori' probability function $p(x'_k|\mathbf{e})$, $x'_k \in \Omega_k$, for every not observed variable X_k, $k \in N \setminus E$. This probability can be obtained from the joint distribution (1), but in general, that joint distribution is not available for large networks, since the number of values necessary to specify it grows exponentially in the number of variables in the network.

Notice that the conditional probability $p(x'_k|\mathbf{e})$ is equal to $p(x'_k, \mathbf{e})/p(\mathbf{e})$, and, since $p(\mathbf{e}) = \sum_{x'_k\in\Omega_k} p(x'_k, \mathbf{e})$, we can calculate the *posterior* probability if we compute the value $p(x'_k, \mathbf{e})$ for every $x'_k \in \Omega_k$ and normalize afterwards.

Let $H = \{p_i(x_i|\mathbf{x}_{pa(i)})|i = 1, \ldots, n\}$ be the set of conditional potentials. Then, $p(x'_k, \mathbf{e})$ can be expressed as follows,

$$p(x'_k, \mathbf{e}) = \sum_{\substack{\mathbf{x}\in\Omega_N \\ \mathbf{x}_E=\mathbf{e} \\ \mathbf{x}_k=x'_k}} \prod_{i\in N} p_i(x_i|\mathbf{x}_{pa(i)}) = \sum_{\substack{\mathbf{x}\in\Omega_N \\ \mathbf{x}_E=\mathbf{e} \\ \mathbf{x}_k=x'_k}} \prod_{f\in H} f(\mathbf{x}_{\text{dom}(f)}) \tag{2}$$

If observations are incorporated by restricting potentials in H to the observed values, i.e. by transforming each potential $f \in H$ into a potential f_e defined on $\text{dom}(f) \setminus E$ as $f_{\mathbf{e}}(\mathbf{x}) = f(\mathbf{y})$, where $y_{\text{dom}(f)\setminus E} = \mathbf{x}$, and $y_i = e_i$, for all $i \in E$, then we have,

$$p(x'_k, \mathbf{e}) = \sum_{\substack{\mathbf{x}\in\Omega_N \\ \mathbf{x}_k=x'_k}} \prod_{f_e\in H} f_e(\mathbf{x}_{\text{dom}_{f_e}}) = \sum_{\mathbf{x}\in\Omega_N} g(\mathbf{x}), \tag{3}$$

where $g(\mathbf{x}) = \prod_{f_e\in H} f_e(\mathbf{x}_{\text{dom}_{f_e}})$.

Thus, probability propagation consists in estimating the value of the sum in (3), and here is where the *importance sampling* technique is used.

Importance sampling is well known as a variance reduction technique for estimating integrals by means of Monte Carlo methods (see, for instance, [14]), consisting in transforming the sum in (3) into an expected value that can be estimated as a sample mean. To achieve this, consider a probability function $p^* : \Omega_N \to [0,1]$, verifying that $p^*(\mathbf{x}) > 0$ for every point $\mathbf{x} \in \Omega_N$ such that $g(\mathbf{x}) > 0$. Then formula (3) can be written as:

$$p(x'_k, \mathbf{e}) = \sum_{\substack{\mathbf{x}\in\Omega_N, \\ g(\mathbf{x})>0}} \frac{g(\mathbf{x})}{p^*(\mathbf{x})} p^*(\mathbf{x}) = \mathrm{E}\left[\frac{g(\mathbf{X}^*)}{p^*(\mathbf{X}^*)}\right] ,$$

where $\mathbf{X}^*$ is a random variable with distribution p^* (from now on, p^* will be called the *sampling distribution*). Then, if $\{\mathbf{x}^{(j)}\}_{j=1}^{m}$ is a sample of size m taken from p^*,

$$\hat{p}(x'_k, \mathbf{e}) = \frac{1}{m} \sum_{j=1}^{m} \frac{g(\mathbf{x}^{(j)})}{p^*(\mathbf{x}^{(j)})} \tag{4}$$

is an unbiased estimator of $p(x'_k, \mathbf{e})$ with variance

$$\mathrm{Var}(\hat{p}(x'_k, \mathbf{e})) = \frac{1}{m}\left(\left(\sum_{\mathbf{x}\in\Omega_N} \frac{g^2(\mathbf{x})}{p^*(\mathbf{x})}\right) - p^2(x'_k, \mathbf{e})\right) .$$

Minimizing the error in unbiased estimation is equivalent to minimizing the variance, which is achieved using a sampling distribution proportional to $g(\mathbf{x})$, and this is the same as knowing the exact posterior distribution. Thus, in practical situations the best we can do is to obtain a sampling distribution as close as possible to the optimal one.

One characteristic of this method, as formulated above, is that it requires a different sample taken from a different sampling distribution for each value of each variable, which is very inefficient.

Salmerón, Cano and Moral [16] showed that it is possible to use a single sample to estimate all posterior distributions, if the sampling distribution is calculated as if it were going to be used to estimate $p(\mathbf{e})$ (see [16] for the details).

Once p^* is selected, $p(x'_k, \mathbf{e})$ for each value x'_k of each variable X_k, $k \in N \setminus E$ can be estimated with the following algorithm:

Importance Sampling

1. For $j := 1$ to m (sample size)
   a) Generate a configuration $\mathbf{x}^{(j)} \in \Omega_N$ using p^*.
   b) Calculate

$$w_j := \frac{\left(\prod_{i\in N} p_i(\mathbf{x}_i^{(j)}|\mathbf{x}_{pa(i)}^{(j)})\right) \cdot \left(\prod_{l\in E} \delta_l(\mathbf{x}_l^{(j)}; \mathbf{e}_l)\right)}{p^*(\mathbf{x}^{(j)})} . \tag{5}$$

2. For each $x'_k \in \Omega_k$, $k \in N \setminus E$, estimate $p(x'_k, \mathbf{e})$ as the average of the weights in formula (5) corresponding to configurations containing x'_k.
3. Normalize values $p(x'_k, \mathbf{e})$ in order to obtain $p(x'_k|\mathbf{e})$.

3 Using Antithetic Variables

The technique of importance sampling is based in a good selection of the sampling distribution p^* in order to achieve variance reduction with respect to plain Monte Carlo (in which the uniform distribution is used). However, there are other possibilities of reducing the variance of the estimation; some of them are reported in [14,15]. One of those possibilities is the use of antithetic variables.

A general setting for using antithetic variables is as follows: assume we want to estimate a parameter θ and we have two unbiased estimators of θ, $\hat{\theta}_1$ and $\hat{\theta}_2$. Then,

$$\hat{\theta}_3 = \frac{1}{2}(\hat{\theta}_1 + \hat{\theta}_2)$$

is an unbiased estimator of θ with

$$\mathrm{Var}(\hat{\theta}_3) = \frac{1}{4}\mathrm{Var}(\hat{\theta}_1) + \frac{1}{4}\mathrm{Var}(\hat{\theta}_2) + \frac{1}{2}\mathrm{Cov}(\hat{\theta}_1, \hat{\theta}_2) \ . \tag{6}$$

Then a variance reduction is achieved by using $\hat{\theta}_3$ instead of $\hat{\theta}_1$ or $\hat{\theta}_2$ if these estimators have a strongly negative correlation.

The point here is how to induce negative correlation between $\hat{\theta}_1$ and $\hat{\theta}_2$. One way to do this is to generate the sample in such a way that whenever a new value is generated from a random number U, another one is generated from $1 - U$. Then, one of the values is used to evaluate $\hat{\theta}_1$ and the other for $\hat{\theta}_2$. We say that *antithetic variables* are used when the sample is generated from negatively correlated pairs of random numbers U and $1 - U$.

This technique has been used for reducing the variance in Monte Carlo integration in Bayesian inference [7]. However, in that work antithetic variables are used with plain Monte Carlo instead of importance sampling, though the author considers promising the application of them together with importance sampling. We will describe here how it can be done within the context of probability propagation in Bayesian networks.

As described above, antithetic variables can be used to estimate just a single probability value:

1. Call θ the probability value to estimate.
2. Obtain a sampling distribution p^* in order to draw samples from the set of configurations of the variables in the network.
3. Generate a sample of configurations of the variables in the network where each two individuals in the sample are obtained from p^*, one by inversion of a random number U and the other by inversion of $1 - U$.
4. Estimate parameter θ from the sample obtained, as in importance sampling.

These four steps must be repeated for each state of each variable in the network, which may be very inefficient in large networks. Furthermore, usually it is not possible to obtain a complete configuration of the variables in the network from a single random number, since it would require a joint sampling distribution over all the variables in the networks, whose size would be equal to the size of the exact joint distribution in the network.

Because of that, importance sampling propagation algorithms based on approximate computation do not simulate directly using the inverse of the distribution function, but rather variables are simulated one at a time, using an individual sampling distribution and a different random number for each variable [16]. Also, the same sample is used to estimate the probability for each state of each variable in the network.

Thus, we have applied a modified version of the technique of antithetic variables: whenever a new variable is going to be simulated, use two numbers U and $1-U$. In this way, the configurations are not actually generated from antithetic variables, but nevertheless they are likely to be negatively correlated. Thus, it is reasonable to expect a variance reduction, but perhaps not as important as in the case of estimating the probability value of a single state of a single variable.

The sampling distribution for each variable can be obtained through a process of eliminating variables in the set H of potentials. An elimination order σ is considered and variables are deleted according to such order: $X_{\sigma(1)}, \dots, X_{\sigma(n)}$.

The deletion of a variable $X_{\sigma(i)}$ consists in combining all the functions in H which are defined for that variable, marginalizing afterwards in order to remove $X_{\sigma(i)}$, by adding on the different values of this variable. The potential obtained is inserted in H. More precisely, the steps are as follows:

- Let $H_{\sigma(i)} = \{f \in H | \sigma(i) \in \text{dom}(f)\}$.
- Calculate $f = \prod_{f \in H_{\sigma(i)}} f$ and f' defined on $\text{dom}(f) - \{\sigma(i)\}$, by $f'(\mathbf{x}) = \sum_{x_{\sigma(i)}} f(\mathbf{x}, x_{\sigma(i)})$.
- Transform H into $H - H_{\sigma(i)} \cup \{f'\}$.

Simulation is carried out in order contrary to the order in which variables are deleted. To obtain a value for $X_{\sigma(i)}$, we will use the function f obtained in the deletion of this variable. This potential is defined for the values of variable $X_{\sigma(i)}$ and other variables already sampled. Potential f is restricted to the already obtained values of variables in $\text{dom}(f) - \{\sigma(i)\}$ giving rise to a function which depends only of $X_{\sigma(i)}$. Finally, a value for this variable is obtained with probability proportional to the values of this potential.

The result of the combinations in the process of obtaining the sampling distributions may require a big amount of space to be stored, and therefore approximations are employed, either using probability tables [9] or probability trees [16] to represent the distributions.

The use of antithetic variables is independent of the representation used. In the experiments reported in this work, we will concentrate on implementations based on probability trees, since they provide more accurate sampling distributions. For a detailed discussion on the use of probability trees and the process of obtaining the sampling distributions using that representation we refer the reader to [16].

The propagation algorithm we propose, based on importance sampling using antithetic variables (denoted isav) can be formulated as follows:

Algorithm isav

1. Let $H = \{p_i \mid i = 1, \ldots, n\}$ be the set of conditional distributions in the network.
2. Incorporate observations $\mathbf{e}$ by restricting the functions in H to $\mathbf{e}$.
3. Select an order σ of variables in G, as described in [16].
4. For $i := 1$ to n, obtain a sampling distribution p_i^* for variable X_i.
5. For $j := 1$ to $m/2$ (to obtain a sample of size m),
   a) $wx_j := 1.0$.
   b) $wy_j := 1.0$.
   c) For $i := n$ to 1,
      i. Generate a random number U.
      ii. Simulate a value for $X_{\sigma(i)}$, $x_i^{(j)}$, using p_i^* as sampling distribution from U, and another value $y_i^{(j)}$ using $1 - U$ (before simulating, p_i^* is restricted to the configuration of the variables previously simulated).
      iii. Compute $wx_j := wx_j / p_i^*(x_i^{(j)})$ and $wy_j := wy_j / p_i^*(y_i^{(j)})$.
   d) Let $\mathbf{x}^{(j)}$ and $\mathbf{y}^{(j)}$ be the configurations obtained.
   e) Compute

$$wx_j := wx_j \cdot \left(\prod_{i=1}^{n} p_i(x_i^{(j)} | \mathbf{x}_{pa(i)}^{(j)}) \right) \cdot \left(\prod_{l \in E} \delta_l(x_l^{(j)}; e_l) \right).$$

   and

$$wy_j := wy_j \cdot \left(\prod_{i=1}^{n} p_i(y_i^{(j)} | \mathbf{y}_{pa(i)}^{(j)}) \right) \cdot \left(\prod_{l \in E} \delta_l(y_l^{(j)}; e_l) \right).$$

6. For each $x'_k \in \Omega_k$, $k \in N \setminus E$, estimate $p(x'_k, \mathbf{e})$ as the average of the weights wx_j and wy_j, $j = 1, \ldots, m/2$, corresponding to configurations containing x'_k.
7. Normalize values $p(x'_k, \mathbf{e})$ to obtain $p(x'_k | \mathbf{e})$.

4 Experimental Evaluation of the New Algorithm

The performance of the new algorithm has been evaluated by means of several experiments carried out over four large real-world Bayesian networks. The four networks are called pedigree (441 variables), munin1 (189 variables), munin2 (1003 variables) and water (32 variables).

The networks have been borrowed from the Decision Support Systems group at Aalborg University (Denmark) (`www.cs.auc.dk/research/DSS/misc.html`).

The performance of importance sampling using antithetic variables (isav) has been compared with importance sampling without this feature (is), using the same implementation as in [16].

The new algorithm has been implemented in Java, and included in the Elvira shell (`leo.ugr.es/~elvira`).

The four networks chosen for the experiments are difficult for simulation algorithms to be applied, since there are extreme probabilities, and obtaining a configuration from them may become hard. Extreme cases are the likelihood weighting method [17] and the bounded variance method [4]: these methods do not even get any result, since all the configurations in the sample get a zero weight.

We have carried out two experiments with each network (with and without observations), with different sample sizes (5000, 7500, 10000, 12500 and 15000). In all of the experiments the maximum potential size has been set to 1000 values. The only exception was made with network water for which a second experiment was carried out with a maximum potential size of 2500 values. The motivation of this second experiment is explained later. The threshold for pruning the probability trees has been set to $\epsilon = 0.01$ (see [16]). This value of ϵ indicates that values in the leaves of the tree whose difference with respect to a uniform distribution is less than a 1% are replaced by their average. Replacing values by the average of them may cause that some configurations whose probability is equal to zero have a positive probability after pruning. It means that it is possible to obtain a configuration in the sample whose exact probability is equal to zero, which implies that the configuration has to be discarded. Increasing the number of values used to represent a probabilistic potential (the potential size), the risk of discarding configurations decreases.

Each trial has been repeated 100 times to average the results. In each trial, we have calculated the computing time and error.

For a single variable X_l, the error is measured as follows (see [5]):

$$G(X_l) = \sqrt{\frac{1}{|\Omega_l|} \sum_{a \in \Omega_l} \frac{(\hat{p}(a|e) - p(a|e))^2}{p(a|e)(1 - p(a|e))}} , \tag{7}$$

where $p(a|e)$ is the true *posterior* probability, $\hat{p}(a|e)$ is the estimated value and $|\Omega_l|$ is the number of states of variable X_l. For a set of variables $\mathbf{X}_I$, the error is:

$$G(\mathbf{X}_I) = \sqrt{\sum_{i \in I} G(X_i)^2} . \tag{8}$$

This measure of error seems appropriate when we have extreme probabilities, since errors when estimating very low probability values are penalized.

The experiments have been carried out in an AMD K7 800MHz computer, with 512MB of RAM and operating system Linux 2.2.16. The Java virtual machine used was Java 2 version 1.3.

The results of the experiments are reported in figures 1 to 5 where error is represented versus computing time.

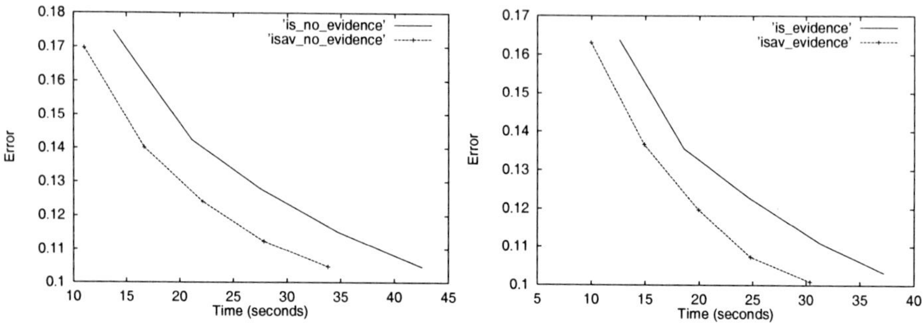

Fig. 1. Error vs. time for munin1 network without observed variables (left) and with observed variables (right)

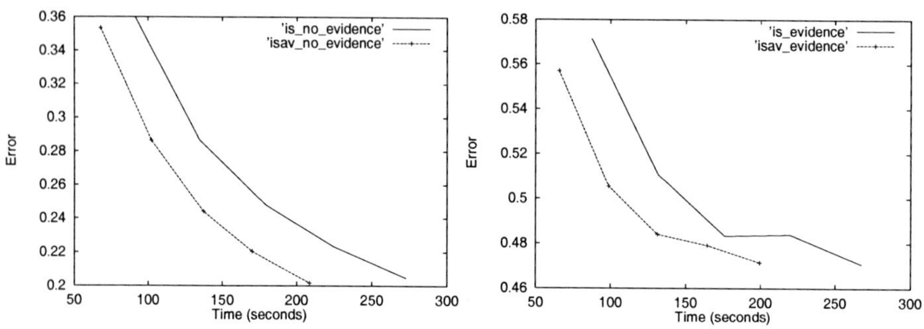

Fig. 2. Error vs. time for munin2 network without observed variables (left) and with observed variables (right)

4.1 Results Discussion

The experiments have shown a very good performance of algorithm isav, speeding up the convergence to the exact results in problems with observations and without observations. It must be pointed out that algorithm is also provides good approximations in all of the experiments, but adding the feature of using antithetic variables improves the behaviour of the algorithm. Part of the improvement is due to implementation aspects: generating two configurations simulateously is more efficient that simulating one after another.

However, there is an experiment in which the accuracy of isav decreases with respect to is. This is due to the difficulty of propagating in network water with the observations inserted. It happens that many configurations are not consistent with the evidence and then they have to be discarded, as we explained above. It has a double impact in the case of antithetic variables: in the process of simulating a pair of configurations, if one of them is found to be inconsistent with the evidence, then both configurations are discarded and the algorithm starts

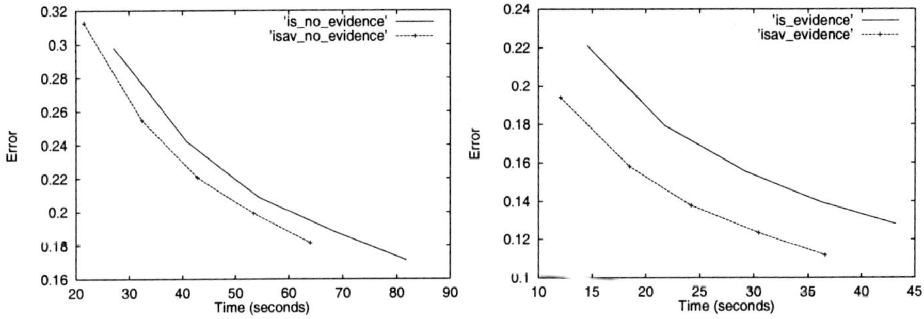

Fig. 3. Error vs. time for pedigree network without observed variables (left) and with observed variables (right)

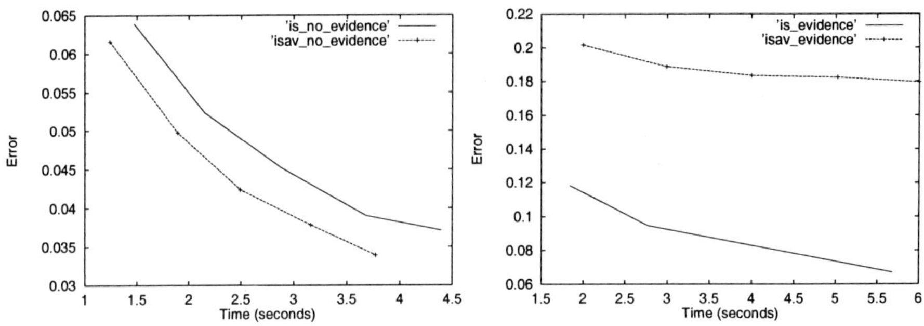

Fig. 4. Error vs. time for water network without observed variables (left) and with observed variables (right), taking a maximum of 1000 values for each potential

to look for a new pair of configurations, even if still the other configuration was consistent with the evidence.

One way of avoiding this problem is not to discard the two configurations, but continue with the valid one until it is completed.

We have not used this alternative in the experiments because we wanted to evaluate the impact of crude application of antithetic variables, in which the configurations should be always grouped in pairs of negatively correlated configurations.

Instead of it we have increased the maximum potential size up to 2500 values in order to reduce the amount of discarded configurations, obtaining the results shown in figure 5.

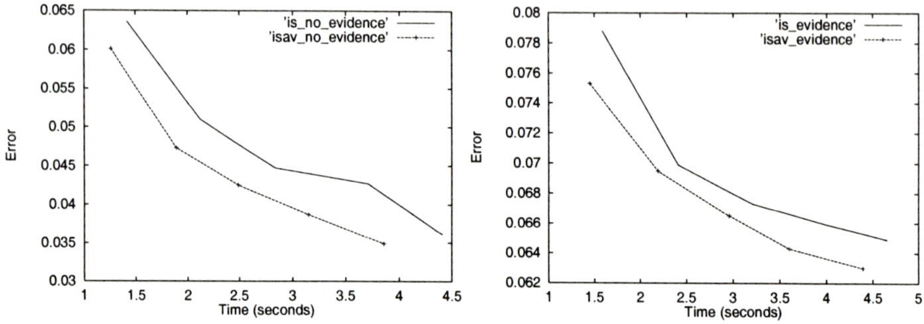

Fig. 5. Error vs. time for water network without observed variables (left) and with observed variables (right), taking a maximum of 2500 values for each potential

5 Conclusions

We have introduced a modification over importance sampling algorithms for probabilistic propagation in Bayesian networks, based on the use of antithetic variables.

The use of antithetic variables has been experimentally tested over four real-world large networks, showing an important increase of the performance of the algorithm: more accurate approximations are achieved in a lower time.

The use of variance reduction techniques as importance sampling [9,16], stratified sampling [1,9] and now antithetic variables, seems to be a good way of improving accuracy of Monte Carlo propagation algorithms for Bayesian networks.

Thus, we are planning to continue with the application of other variance reduction techniques (common variables, for instance) to obtain better propagation algorithms.

Acknowledgements. We are very grateful to Finn V. Jensen, Kristian G. Olesen and Claus Skaaning, from the Decision Support Systems group at Aalborg University for providing us with the networks used in the experiments reported in this paper.

References

1. R.R. Bouckaert, E. Castillo, and J.M. Gutiérrez. A modified simulation scheme for inference in Bayesian networks. *International Journal of Approximate Reasoning*, 14:55–80, 1996.
2. G.F. Cooper. The computational complexity of probabilistic inference using Bayesian belief networks. *Artificial Intelligence*, 42:393–405, 1990.
3. P. Dagum and M. Luby. Approximating probabilistic inference in Bayesian belief networks is NP-hard. *Artificial Intelligence*, 60:141–153, 1993.

4. P. Dagum and M. Luby. An optimal approximation algorithm for Bayesian inference. *Artificial Intelligence*, 93:1–27, 1997.
5. K.W. Fertig and N.R. Mann. An accurate approximation to the sampling distribution of the studentized extreme-valued statistic. *Technometrics*, 22:83–90, 1980.
6. R. Fung and K.C. Chang. Weighting and integrating evidence for stochastic simulation in Bayesian networks. In M. Henrion, R.D. Shachter, L.N. Kanal, and J.F. Lemmer, editors, *Uncertainty in Artificial Intelligence*, volume 5, pages 209–220. North-Holland (Amsterdam), 1990.
7. J. Geweke. Antithetic acceleration of Monte Carlo integration in Bayesian inference. *Journal of Econometrics*, 38:73–89, 1988.
8. L.D. Hernández, S. Moral, and A. Salmerón. Importance sampling algorithms for belief networks based on approximate computation. In *Proceedings of the Sixth International Conference IPMU'96*, volume II, pages 859–864, Granada (Spain), 1996.
9. L.D. Hernández, S. Moral, and A. Salmerón. A Monte Carlo algorithm for probabilistic propagation in belief networks based on importance sampling and stratified simulation techniques. *International Journal of Approximate Reasoning*, 18:53–91, 1998.
10. C.S. Jensen, A. Kong, and U. Kjærulff. Blocking Gibbs sampling in very large probabilistic expert systems. *International Journal of Human-Computer Studies*, 42:647–666, 1995.
11. S.L. Lauritzen and D.J. Spiegelhalter. Local computations with probabilities on graphical structures and their application to expert systems. *Journal of the Royal Statistical Society, Series B*, 50:157–224, 1988.
12. J. Pearl. Evidential reasoning using stochastic simulation of causal models. *Artificial Intelligence*, 32:247–257, 1987.
13. J. Pearl. *Probabilistic reasoning in intelligent systems.* Morgan-Kauffman (San Mateo), 1988.
14. R.Y. Rubinstein. *Simulation and the Monte Carlo Method.* Wiley (New York), 1981.
15. R.Y. Rubinstein and B. Melamed. *Modern simulation and modeling.* Wiley (New York), 1998.
16. A. Salmerón, A. Cano, and S. Moral. Importance sampling in Bayesian networks using probability trees. *Computational Statistics and Data Analysis*, 34:387–413, 2000.
17. R.D. Shachter and M.A. Peot. Simulation approaches to general probabilistic inference on belief networks. In M. Henrion, R.D. Shachter, L.N. Kanal, and J.F. Lemmer, editors, *Uncertainty in Artificial Intelligence*, volume 5, pages 221–231. North Holland (Amsterdam), 1990.
18. N.L. Zhang and D. Poole. Exploiting causal independence in Bayesian network inference. *Journal of Artificial Intelligence Research*, 5:301–328, 1996.

Using Recursive Decomposition to Construct Elimination Orders, Jointrees, and Dtrees

Adnan Darwiche and Mark Hopkins

Computer Science Department
University of California
Los Angeles, CA 90095
{darwiche,mhopkins}@cs.ucla.edu

Abstract. Darwiche has recently proposed a graphical model for driving conditioning algorithms, called a dtree, which specifies a recursive decomposition of a directed acyclic graph (DAG) into its families. A main property of a dtree is its width, and it was shown previously how to convert a DAG elimination order of width w into a dtree of width $\leq w$. The importance of this conversion is that any algorithm for constructing low-width elimination orders can be directly used for constructing low-width dtrees. We propose in this paper a more direct method for constructing dtrees based on hypergraph partitioning. This new method turns out to be quite competitive with existing methods in minimizing width. We also present methods for converting a dtree of width w into elimination orders and jointrees of no greater width. This leads to a new class of algorithms for generating elimination orders and jointrees (via recursive decomposition).

1 Introduction

Darwiche has recently proposed a graphical model, called a dtree, which specifies a recursive decomposition of a directed acyclic graph (DAG) into its families. The main application of dtrees is in driving a class of divide-and-conquer algorithms, called recursive conditioning, which can be used for anyspace probabilistic and logical reasoning [5, 3, 4]. Formally, a dtree is a full binary tree with its leaves corresponding to the DAG families (nodes and their parents). Figure 1(a) depicts a DAG and two corresponding dtrees.

The quality of a dtree is measured by a number of parameters. The main property of a dtree is its width. For example, if we have a belief network with n variables, and if we can construct a dtree of width w for the network, then we can answer probabilistic queries in $O(n \exp(w))$ space and time. A dtree has other important properties though. For example, if the height of a dtree is h, then we can reason about the network in $O(n)$ space and $O(n \exp(hw))$ time. Therefore, constructing dtrees with minimal width and height is quite important.

Existing methods for constructing dtrees for a DAG focus on initially constructing a good elimination order for the DAG. It was previously shown how to convert an elimination order of width w for DAG G into a dtree of width

S. Benferhat and P. Besnard (Eds.): ECSQARU 2001, LNAI 2143, pp. 180–191, 2001.

$\leq w$ for the same DAG [5], implying that any algorithm for constructing low-width elimination orders is immediately an algorithm for constructing low-width dtrees. It was also shown that any dtree can be balanced in $O(n \log n)$ time, giving it $O(\log n)$ height, while only increasing its width by a constant factor [5]. Therefore, to construct a dtree for linear-space reasoning, one can compute an elimination order of small width, convert it to a dtree of no greater width, and then balance the dtree to minimize its height.

We report in this paper on a new method for constructing balanced dtrees. The method is based on hypergraph partitioning, a well-studied problem with applications to many areas, including VLSI design, efficient storage of databases on disk, and data mining [11]—the goal here is to partition a hypergraph into equally-sized parts, while minimizing the hyperedges which cross from one part to another. Specifically, we show how the process of constructing balanced dtrees for a DAG can be reduced to the process of recursively partitioning a hypergraph based on the DAG.

Although the proposed method does not directly attempt to minimize the dtree width, our experimental results show that from a width standpoint, it generates dtrees that are competitive with those produced from elimination orders based on the min-fill heuristic. Furthermore, the generated dtrees are superior when considering other properties such as height.

A key point is that our algorithm for constructing dtrees has a much broader applicability, since any algorithm for producing low-width dtrees is immediately a good algorithm for producing low-width jointrees and elimination orders. It was shown previously that any dtree for a DAG can be immediately converted into a jointree for that DAG [5]. Therefore, our new method for constructing dtrees is immediately a method for constructing jointrees with similar properties, including width. We also show in this paper that each dtree of width w naturally determines a partial elimination order. Moreover, each (total) elimination order which is consistent with this partial order is guaranteed to have a width no greater than w. The implication of these results is that any method for recursively decomposing a DAG into a dtree can be used to produce elimination orders and jointrees for that DAG, with interesting guarantees on their qualities.

This paper is structured as follows. We start in Section 2 by reviewing dtrees and their applications. We then introduce the problem of hypergraph partitioning in Section 3, where we show how it can be used to obtain balanced dtrees. We then show in Section 4 how to convert dtrees of a certain width into elimination orders and jointrees of no greater width. We next present our experimental results in Section 5 and finally close with some concluding remarks in Section 6.

2 Dtrees

A dtree (decomposition tree) is a full binary tree which induces a recursive decomposition on a directed acyclic graph. A dtree is used to drive divide–and–conquer algorithms, such as the algorithm of recursive conditioning for inference in Bayesian networks [5]. The following is the formal definition of a dtree.

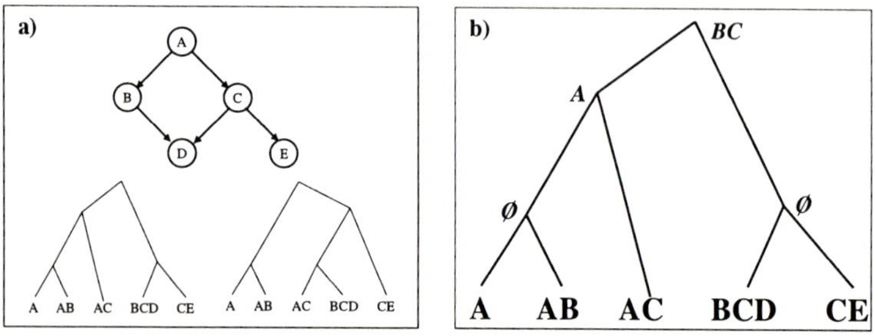

Fig. 1. (a) A DAG and two corresponding dtrees. (b) A dtree and its cutsets (in italic).

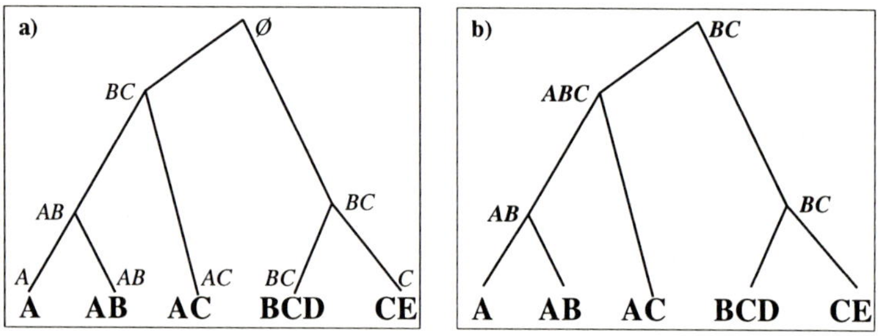

Fig. 2. (a) A dtree with its contexts (in italic). (b) A dtree with its clusters (in italic). The clusters of leaves are the families associated with these leaves .

Definition 1. *A* <u>*dtree*</u> *T for a DAG G is a full binary tree, the leaves of which correspond to the families of G.*[1] *If t is a leaf node in dtree T which corresponds to family F of DAG G, we define* $\mathsf{vars}(t) \stackrel{def}{=} F$.

Figure 1(a) depicts two dtrees for the DAG shown in the same figure. Examine the first dtree. The top level specifies a partition of the DAG families into two sets: $\{A, AB, AC\}$ and $\{BCD, CE\}$. The left subtree specifies a partition of families $\{A, AB, AC\}$, while the right subtree specifies a partition of families $\{BCD, CE\}$ (unique in this case).

We will use t_l and t_r to denote the left child and right child of node t in a dtree. Following standard conventions on binary trees, we will often not distinguish between a node and the dtree rooted at that node. We will next define a few more variable sets for each node in a dtree and then discuss their applications.

Definition 2. *[5] For an internal node t in a dtree:*

- *The* <u>*variables*</u> *of t are defined as* $\mathsf{vars}(t) \stackrel{def}{=} \mathsf{vars}(t_l) \cup \mathsf{vars}(t_r)$.
- *The* <u>*cutset*</u> *of t is defined as* $\mathsf{cutset}(t) \stackrel{def}{=} \mathsf{vars}(t_l) \cap \mathsf{vars}(t_r) - \mathsf{acutset}(t)$, *where* $\mathsf{acutset}(t)$ *is the union of cutsets associated with ancestors of t.*

[1] Recall that the *family* of node v in DAG G consists of v and its parents in G.

Moreover, for node t in a dtree:

- *The* <u>*context*</u> *of t is defined as* $\mathsf{context}(t) \stackrel{def}{=} \mathsf{vars}(t) \cap \mathsf{acutset}(t)$.
- *The* <u>*cluster*</u> *of t is defined as*

$$\mathsf{cluster}(t) = \begin{cases} \mathsf{vars}(t), & \textit{if } t \textit{ is leaf;} \\ \mathsf{cutset}(t) \cup \mathsf{context}(t), & \textit{otherwise.} \end{cases}$$

The <u>*width*</u> *of a dtree is defined as the size of its largest cluster minus 1.*

Figure 1(b) shows a dtree and its corresponding cutsets. Figure 2(a) shows the dtree contexts and Figure 2(b) shows its clusters.

The cutsets of a dtree are used by conditioning algorithms to recursively decompose a DAG-based model (such as a belief network) into smaller models that can be solved independently. The contexts are used to cache results obtained with respect to the smaller models, which reduces the running time of conditioning algorithms but at the expense of using more space.[2] The clusters are used to provide guarantees on the computational properties of conditioning algorithms based on dtrees.

The ways in which cutsets and contexts are used by conditioning algorithms are outside the scope of this paper, but we refer the reader to [5, 3, 4] for details. Here, we only focus on the significance of these sets from a complexity viewpoint. Specifically, suppose that we have a belief network with DAG G that contains n variables, and let T be a dtree for G. Let w_c be the size of the largest cutset in T (called the *cutset width* of T), w_x be the size of largest context in T (called the *context width* of T), w be the width of T, and h be the height of T. We can then use the algorithm of recursive conditioning given in [5] to compute the probability of some instantiation $\mathbf{e}$ according to the following complexity:

- $O(n \exp(w))$ time and $O(n \exp(w_x))$ space; or
- $O(n \exp(hw_c))$ time and $O(n)$ space.

The above complexity results represent two extremes on a time-space tradeoff spectrum. In general, we can use any amount of space we have available, and still be able to predict the average running time of recursive conditioning [5]. Moreover, we can always balance a dtree so that its height becomes $O(\log n)$ while only increasing the sizes of its cutsets, contexts and clusters by a constant factor.[3] Balanced dtrees are especially important if one wants to reason with belief networks under linear space as shown above.

The main existing method for constructing dtrees is to convert an elimination order of width w into a dtree of width $\leq w$ [5]. We discuss in Section 3 a different class of algorithms for constructing (balanced) dtrees based on hypergraph partitioning. This class of algorithms attempts to minimize the height and cutset width of dtrees. Yet, we shall present experimental results in Section 5 showing that it produces very competitive dtrees from the standpoint of width

[2] This is done using the technique of memoization from dynamic programming.

[3] The number of dtree nodes is always twice (minus one) the number of DAG nodes.

and context width, at least when compared with dtrees constructed based on elimination orders. Given that one can easily convert a dtree of width w into an elimination order or jointree of width $\leq w$, the proposed method has implications on the construction of elimination orders and jointrees. This is discussed in Section 4.

3 Dtree Construction as Hypergraph Partitioning

Previous methods for constructing low-width dtrees have focused on using existing heuristics to generate low-width elimination orders, then converting these elimination orders to dtrees [5]. An alternative approach is to generate the dtrees directly. The technique we now present uses hypergraph partitioning as a tool for directly generating low-width dtrees.

A *hypergraph* is a generalization of a graph, such that an edge is permitted to connect an arbitrary number of vertices, rather than exactly two. The edges of a hypergraph are referred to as *hyperedges.* The problem of *hypergraph partitioning* is to find a way to split the vertices of a hypergraph into k approximately equal parts, such that the number of hyperedges connecting vertices in different parts is minimized [11].

The problem of hypergraph partitioning is well-studied, as it applies to many fields, including VLSI design, efficient storage of databases on disk, and data mining [11]. Since solving the problem optimally is at least NP-hard [9], much energy has been devoted to developing approximation algorithms for hypergraph partitioning. A paper by Alpert and Khang [1] surveys a variety of the approaches taken to this problem.

For our purposes, we used hMeTiS, a hypergraph partitioning package distributed by the University of Minnesota [12]. Loosely speaking, hMeTiS collapses vertices and hyperedges of the original hypergraph to produce a smaller, aggregated hypergraph, then uses various specialized algorithms to partition the smaller hypergraph. After doing this, it uses specialized algorithms to construct a partition for the original, refined hypergraph using the partition for the smaller, aggregated hypergraph. Experimental results have shown that the partitions produced by hMeTiS are consistently better than those produced by other popular algorithms [12]. In addition, hMeTiS is between one and two orders of magnitude faster than other algorithms [12]. One of the useful features of hMeTiS is that the user can specify how balanced the partition will be. Concretely, the user can specify that each part must contain no less than $X\%$ of the vertices.

Generating a dtree for a DAG using hypergraph partitioning is fairly straightforward. The first step is to express the DAG G as a hypergraph H:

- For each family F in DAG G, we add a node N_F to H.
- For each variable V in DAG G, we add a hyperedge to H which connects all nodes N_F such that $V \in F$.

An example of this is depicted in Figure 3(a).

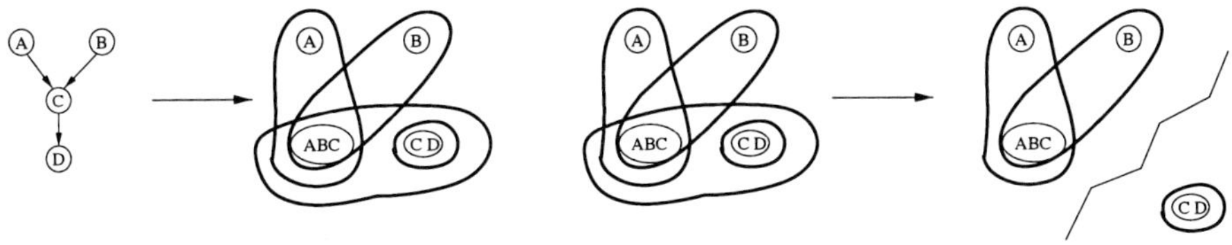

Fig. 3. (a) From a DAG to a hypergraph. (b) An example bipartitioning of the hypergraph into two subgraphs.

Notice that any full binary tree whose leaves correspond to the vertices of H is a dtree for our DAG. This observation allows us to design a simple recursive algorithm using hypergraph partitioning to produce a dtree. Figure 4 shows the pseudocode for this algorithm. HGR2BDT starts by creating a dtree node t at Line 01. Lines 02-05 correspond to the base case where hypergraph H contains a single vertex N_F (corresponding to family F) and, hence, leads to a unique dtree which contains the single leaf node t with $\mathsf{vars}(t) \leftarrow F$. Lines 06-08 correspond to the recursive step where hypergraph H has more than a single vertex. Here, we partition the hypergraph H into two subgraphs H_l and H_r, then recursively generate dtrees HGR2BDT(H_l) and HGR2BDT(H_r) for these subgraphs, and finally set these dtrees as the children of dtree node t.

HGR2BDT attempts to minimize the cutset of each node t it constructs at Line 01. To see this, observe that every time we partition the hypergraph H into H_l and H_r, we attempt to minimize the number of hyperedges that span the partitions H_l and H_r. By construction, these hyperedges correspond to DAG variables that are shared by families in H_l and those in H_r (which have not already been cut by previous partitions). Hence by attempting to minimize the number of hyperedges that span the partitions H_l and H_r, we are actually attempting to minimize the cutset associated with dtree node t. Notice that we do not make any direct attempt to minimize the width of the dtree. However, we shall see in Section 5 that cutset minimization is a good heuristic for dtree width minimization.

An advantage to this approach is that it also produces balanced dtrees, in the sense that for any node in the dtree, the ratio of the number of leaves in its left subtree to the number of leaves in its right subtree is bounded. This is a direct consequence of the fact that hMeTiS computes balanced hypergraph partitions. Thus the algorithm computes dtrees that have height of $O(\log n)$, where n is the number of nodes in the given DAG.

One can attach "weights" to edges in a hypergraph and then instruct hypergraph partitioning algorithms to minimize the sum of such weights in a hypergraph cut. This is important when building dtrees for DAGs where variables have different cardinalities. Specifically, suppose we have a variable V with N values in a DAG G. When defining the hypergraph for G, we can define the weight of the hyperedge representing variable V as $log(N)$. For each cut, the hypergraph partitioning algorithm will thus try to minimize the sum of the weights of the

Algorithm HGR2BDT

```
HGR2BDT(hypergraph H)
create dtreenode t
if H has only one vertex N_F,
    then vars(t) ← F
        t_l ← NULL
        t_r ← NULL
    else partition H into two subgraphs H_l and H_r
        t_l ← HGR2BDT(H_l)
        t_r ← HGR2BDT(H_r)
return t
```

Fig. 4. Pseudocode for producing dtrees using hypergraph partitioning.

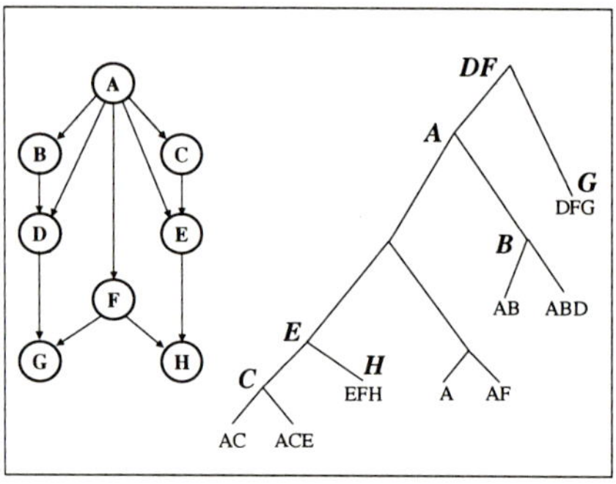

Fig. 5. Converting a dtree into an elimination order. The variables in bold/italic are eliminated at the corresponding dtree nodes.

cut edges, which translates to minimizing the product of variable cardinalities in the cut.

4 From Dtrees to Elimination Orders and Jointrees

In this section, we discuss width-preserving transformations from dtrees to elimination orders, and from dtrees to jointrees. The implication of such transformations is that any algorithm for constructing low-width dtrees is immediately an algorithm for constructing low-width elimination orders and jointrees. We will begin our discussion by reviewing the concept of an elimination order.

An *elimination order* of an undirected graph G is an ordering $\pi(1), \pi(2), \ldots$ of the nodes in G. One of the simplest ways for defining the *width* w of order π is constructively. Simply eliminate nodes $\pi(1), \pi(2), \ldots, \pi(n)$ from G in that order, connecting all neighbors of a node before eliminating it. The maximum number of neighbors that any eliminated node has is then the width of order

π.[4] The width of an elimination order with respect to a DAG G is defined as its width with respect to the moral graph of G–that is, the graph which results from connecting all parents of each node, and then dropping the directionality of edges.

Elimination orders are the basis of an important class of algorithms, known as variable elimination algorithms [7, 15]. They are also the basis for constructing jointrees [10, 14]. In both cases, the complexity of algorithms is exponential only in the width of given elimination order w. Hence, generating low-width elimination orders is critical for the efficiency of these algorithms.

An algorithm is presented in [5] for converting an elimination order of width w into a dtree of width $\leq w$. The method allows one to capitalize on algorithms for constructing low-width elimination orders in order to construct low-width dtrees. Here, we present a result which allows us to do the opposite. Specifically, we show how a dtree of width w can be used to induce elimination orders of width $\leq w$. In fact, we show that each dtree specifies a partial elimination order, and any total order consistent with it is guaranteed to have no greater width.

Definition 3. *Let T be a dtree for DAG G. We say that node v of G is eliminated at node t of T precisely when $v \in \mathsf{cluster}(t) - \mathsf{context}(t)$.*

Note that for an internal node t, $\mathsf{cluster}(t) - \mathsf{context}(t)$ is precisely $\mathsf{cutset}(t)$ [5]. Figure 5 depicts a dtree and the DAG nodes eliminated at each of its nodes.

It is actually not hard to prove that every DAG node is eliminated at some unique dtree node [6]. This allows us to define a partial elimination order, where for each DAG nodes v and u, we have $v < u$ if the dtree node at which v is eliminated is a descendant of the dtree node at which u is eliminated.

In the dtree of Figure 5, we have $C < E < A < \{D, F\}$. We also have $H < E$, $B < A$ and $G < \{D, F\}$. Any total elimination order consistent with these constraints is guaranteed to have no greater width than that of the dtree.

Theorem 1. *[6] Let T be a dtree of width w for DAG G and let π be a total elimination order for G which is consistent with the partial elimination order defined by T. The width of π is then $\leq w$.*

The following two orders are consistent with the dtree in Figure 5: $< C, H, E, B, A, G, D, F >$ and $< H, C, B, E, G, A, F, D >$. Each of these elimination orders has width 2. It is easy to generate an elimination order which is consistent with a given dtree through a post-order traversal of the dtree.

Therefore, if we have an algorithm for constructing low-width dtrees, then we immediately have an algorithm for constructing low-width elimination orders.

A similar result exists for converting a dtree of width w into a jointree of the same width [5]. We review the result here as it allows us to put the experimental

[4] If DAG variables have different cardinalities, we can also define the *weighted width* of an elimination order π. Specifically, for a set of variables $S = V_1, \ldots, V_m$ with cardinalities $N_1, \ldots, N_m$, the weight of S is defined as $\log_2 \prod_{i=1}^{m} N_i$. Let w_X be the weight of the set that contains X and its neighbors. The weighted width of an order is then defined as the maximum w_X that any eliminated node X has.

results of Section 5 in broader perspective. We start with the formal definition of a jointree.

A *jointree* for DAG G is a pair (T, C), where T is a tree and C labels each node in T with a subset of nodes in G such that

1. Each family of DAG G is contained in some label $C(v)$.
2. For every three nodes v, u and w in T, if w is on the path connecting v and u, then $C(v) \cap C(u) \subseteq C(w)$.

Each label $C(v)$ is called a *cluster*, and the *width* of a jointree is defined as the size of its largest cluster minus one. Another important aspect of a jointree is its separators: for each edges (u, v) in the jointree, one defines the *separator* as $C(u) \cap C(v)$. The running time of algorithms based on jointrees is exponential in the width. Their space complexity, however, can be only exponential in the size of the separators.

It is shown in [5] that if T is a dtree for a DAG G, and if C is a function that maps each node in dtree T to its cluster (as defined in Definition 2), then (T, C) is a jointree for DAG G (see Figure 2(b)). Moreover, the context of a node t in T is the separator on the edge connecting t to its parent in T (see Figure 2(a)). This means that one can easily convert a dtree into a jointree of the same width. It also means that if the dtree have small contexts, then the jointree will have small separators. Finally, if the dtree is balanced, then the jointree it induces will be also balanced in the following sense. We can choose a jointree node (call it the root) so that the distance from the root to any jointree leaf is $O(\log n)$, where n is the number of DAG nodes.

5 Experimental Results

We compare experimentally in this section two methods for constructing dtrees: one based on elimination orders and another based on hypergraph partitioning. The first method generates unbalanced dtrees, while the second generates balanced ones. As long as the two methods are comparable with regards to the width of dtrees they generate, we will prefer balanced dtrees. There are many heuristics for generating low-width elimination orders [13], but it is well accepted that the min-fill heuristic is among the best. This is the one we use in our experiments.

To build dtrees for our set of benchmark suites with HGR2BDT, we implemented HGR2BDT in C++ using the Standard Template Library, as well as the hMeTiS hypergraph partitioning package from the University of Minnesota [12]. Recall that hMeTiS allows the user to specify how balanced each partition will be. We varied this parameter such that hMeTiS could produce bipartitions of maximum ratio 51-49, 60-40, 70-30, 80-20, and 90-10. For example, for ratio 60-40, the larger part of the bipartition could be comprised of at most 60% of the vertices of the original hypergraph. Since hMeTiS is also nondeterministic, we ran 5 trials at each balance setting, and then took the best dtree (in terms of width) from the 25 total trials. This is the dtree that we report in our results.

Table 1. Statistics for ISCAS'85 Benchmark Circuits.

Circuit	hgr2bdt			Min-fill					
				Unbalanced			Balanced		
	Width	Context Width	Height	Width	Context Width	Height	Width	Context Width	Height
c432	27	23	11	27	23	16	27	23	12
c499	22	19	13	24	25	47	31	25	13
c880	23	22	13	25	24	42	29	25	16
c1355	22	19	24	24	25	49	31	25	16
c1908	44	32	13	50	43	23	51	46	16
c2670	33	29	22	37	32	39	37	29	19
c3540	74	61	15	97	81	73	97	81	19
c5315	52	49	16	45	44	79	53	51	19
c6288	46	38	35	53	43	48	53	43	19
c7552	42	35	17	48	37	41	51	42	21

Table 2. Results for Suite of Belief Networks.

Network	hgr2bdt		Min-fill				Weighted hgr2bdt	Unbalanced Min-fill
			Unbalanced		Balanced			
	Width	Height	Width	Height	Width	Height	Weighted Width	Weighted Width
barley	7	10	7	19	8	9	25.41	23.37
diabetes	7	11	4	53	9	14	24.70	17.23
link	16	17	15	33	19	17	27.00	24.00
mildew	5	7	4	13	7	8	24.50	20.74
munin1	11	10	11	31	12	12	25.19	28.03
munin2	9	13	7	47	9	17	22.16	18.10
munin3	8	16	7	35	10	17	21.84	17.25
munin4	9	13	8	37	10	18	23.75	21.38
pigs	11	11	10	38	14	14	19.02	17.43
water	10	7	10	12	10	9	20.34	20.75

Our first suite of DAGs is obtained from the ISCAS'85 benchmark circuits [2]. These circuits have been studied by El Fattah and Dechter in [8], wherein elimination orders were generated using several well-known heuristics. We found that min-fill produced better orders than any of the heuristics surveyed in [8]. Hence we used min-fill to construct elimination orders for these circuits, then constructed dtrees based on these orders in the manner described by [5]. We also constructed dtrees using HGR2BDT. The results are reported in Table 1. A third class of dtrees is also reported, which results from balancing the first class using a technique described in [5].

A number of observations are in order here. First, if all we care about is generating low-width elimination orders, then constructing a dtree using HGR2BDT and extracting an elimination order from it is almost always (much) better than using the min-fill heuristic. A particularly dramatic example of this is c3540, for which HGR2BDT was able to produce an elimination order of width 74. By contrast, min-fill produced an elimination order of width 97, while the best heuristic surveyed by El Fattah and Dechter in [8] produced an elimination order of width 114. Interestingly enough, these dtrees not only lead to better elimination orders, but are also balanced and tend to have smaller contexts. Therefore, HGR2BDT appears to be favorable for constructing dtrees and jointrees as well, for which other properties (beyond width) are of interest.

Our second class of DAGs is obtained from belief networks posted at http://www.cs.huji.ac.il/labs/compbio/Repository/; see Table 2. For these networks, the min-fill heuristic (without balancing) did better overall than either of the two methods that generate balanced dtrees. So we are paying a price here for balance, although it does not seem to be too high. The highest price appears

Table 3. Results for Randomly Generated DAGs.

Number of nodes	Edge prob.	Version	hgr2bdt			Min-fill					
						Unbalanced			Balanced		
			Width	Context Width	Height	Width	Context Width	Height	Width	Context Width	Height
200	.015	1	22	20	10	22	21	37	22	21	13
		2	34	28	10	32	31	42	33	31	13
		3	28	23	11	28	26	35	31	27	13
		4	29	25	10	29	28	42	30	28	13
		5	29	26	10	27	26	38	29	26	13
300	.008	1	29	25	11	31	30	47	31	30	14
		2	24	21	11	24	23	37	25	23	13
		3	33	29	11	33	33	50	35	32	14
		4	29	25	11	31	30	40	31	30	15
		5	30	27	11	31	30	49	32	31	14
400	.005	1	21	19	11	21	20	50	23	20	14
		2	20	18	11	20	19	45	21	20	15
		3	17	16	11	15	15	42	18	19	15
		4	18	16	11	18	19	42	21	19	15
		5	22	19	11	24	23	44	24	23	15
500	.004	1	16	15	11	16	14	39	16	14	15
		2	21	20	14	22	21	44	24	22	15
		3	23	21	12	24	22	51	24	22	14
		4	26	23	11	25	23	48	28	22	15
		5	23	22	11	23	22	32	23	22	16

to be for network *diabetes,* which has 413 nodes and whose dtree height went from 53 to 11 as a result of balancing. What is clear though is that generating balanced dtrees using HGR2BDT appears to be superior to generating dtrees using an elimination order and then balancing them.

This second suite of DAGs is our only testing suite with variables of differing cardinalities. Hence, we also ran the weighted version of our heuristic (as described at the end of Section 3) on this suite and compared the resulting elimination orders with min-fill. Again, min-fill generally does better on this suite with regards to this new evaluation criterion.

Our third suite of DAGs is generated randomly according to the given probabilities of edges; see Table 3. For this suite, the use of HGR2BDT for generating dtrees, jointrees and elimination orders seems to produce the best results overall, considering width, context width and height.

It is worth noting that the execution time of HGR2BDT is reasonable. For the largest network in our testing set, c7552 (a network with 7230 vertices), HGR2BDT takes approximately 5 minutes to produce a dtree on a Pentium II 266. For most of the smaller networks, the execution time of HGR2BDT is only a matter of seconds.

6 Conclusion

This paper rests on two contributions, one theoretical and another practical. Theoretically, we have shown how methods for recursively decomposing DAGs can be used to construct elimination orders, dtrees and jointrees. Practically, we have proposed and evaluated the use of a state-of-the-art system for hypergraph partitioning to recursively decompose DAGs and, hence, to construct elimination orders, dtrees and jointrees. The new method appears to be different from current tradition in automated reasoning, where elimination orders are the basis of constructing various graphical models. There are many heuristics for generating low-width elimination orders, and it is customary for automated reasoning systems to give the user a choice of which one to use since even a small reduction in width can be have a drastic practical effect. Our experimental results suggest that the construction of graphical models based on hypergraph partitioning should clearly be considered as one of these choices, whether one is interested in elimination orders, jointrees, or dtrees.

Refcrences

1. Charles J. Alpert and Andrew B. Kahng. Recent directions in netlist partitioning. *Integration, the VLSI Journal*, 19(1–81), 1995.
2. F. Beglez and H. Fujiwara. A neutral netlist of 10 combinational benchmark circuits and a target translator in FORTRAN. In *Proceedings of the IEEE symposium on Circuits and Systems*, 1985. http://www.cbl.ncsu.edu/www/CBL_Docs/iscas85.html.
3. Adnan Darwiche. Compiling knowledge into decomposable negation normal form. In *Proceedings of International Joint Conference on Artificial Intelligence (IJCAI)*, pages 284–289, 1999.
4. Adnan Darwiche. Utilizing device behavior in structure–based diagnosis. In *Proceedings of International Joint Conference on Artificial Intelligence (IJCAI)*, pages 1096–1101, 1999.
5. Adnan Darwiche. Recursive conditioning. *Artificial Intelligence*, 126(1-2):5–41, February, 2001.
6. Adnan Darwiche and Mark Hopkins. Using recursive decomposition to construct elimination orders, jointrees and dtrees. Technical Report D–122, Computer Science Department, UCLA, Los Angeles, Ca 90095, 2001.
7. Rina Dechter. Bucket elimination: A unifying framework for probabilistic inference. In *Proceedings of the 12th Conference on Uncertainty in Artificial Intelligence (UAI)*, pages 211–219, 1996.
8. Yousri El Fattah and Rina Dechter. An evaluation of structural paramters for probabilistic reasoning: Results on benchmark circuits. In *Proceedings of the 12th Conference on Uncertainty in Artificial Intelligence (UAI)*, pages 244–251, 1996.
9. Michael R. Garey and David S. Johnson. *Computers and Intractability: A Guide to the Theory of NP-Completeness.* W.H. Freeman, San Francisco, CA, 1979.
10. F. V. Jensen, S.L. Lauritzen, and K.G. Olesen. Bayesian updating in recursive graphical models by local computation. *Computational Statistics Quarterly*, 4:269–282, 1990.
11. George Karypis, Rajat Aggarwal, Vipin Kumar, and Shashi Shekhar. Multilevel hypergraph partitioning: Applications in vlsi domain. *IEEE Transactions on VLSI Systems*, 1998.
12. George Karypis and Vipin Kumar. Hmetis: A hypergraph partitioning package. *Available at http://www.cs.umn.edu/ karypis*, 1998.
13. U. Kjaerulff. Triangulation of graphs—algorithms giving small total state space. Technical Report R-90-09, Department of Mathematics and Computer Science, University of Aalborg, Denmark, 1990.
14. S. L. Lauritzen and D. J. Spiegelhalter. Local computations with probabilities on graphical structures and their application to expert systems. *Journal of Royal Statistics Society, Series B*, 50(2):157–224, 1988.
15. Nevin Lianwen Zhang and David Poole. Exploiting causal independence in bayesian network inference. *Journal of Artificial Intelligence Research*, 5:301–328, 1996.

Caveats For Causal Reasoning With Equilibrium Models

Denver Dash and Marek Druzdzel**

Intelligent Systems Program, University of Pittsburgh, Pittsburgh, PA 15260, USA,
{ddash,marek}@sis.pitt.edu

Abstract. In this paper[1] we examine the ability to perform causal reasoning with recursive equilibrium models. We identify a critical postulate, which we term the *Manipulation Postulate*, that is required in order to perform causal inference, and we prove that there exists a general class $\mathcal{F}$ of recursive equilibrium models that violate the Manipulation Postulate. We relate this class to the existing phenomenon of reversibility and show that all models in $\mathcal{F}$ display reversible behavior, thereby providing an explanation for reversibility and suggesting that it is a special case of a more general and perhaps widespread problem. We also show that all models in $\mathcal{F}$ possess a set of variables V' whose manipulation will cause an instability such that no equilibrium model will exist for the system. We define the *Structural Stability Principle* which provides a graphical criterion for stability in causal models. Our theorems suggest that drastically incorrect inferences may be obtained when applying the Manipulation Postulate to equilibrium models, a result which has implications for current work on causal modeling, especially causal discovery from data.

1 Introduction

Manipulation in causal models originated in the early econometrics literature [9, 12] in the context of structural equation models, and has recently been studied in artificial intelligence, building a sound theory from some basic axioms and assumptions regarding the nature of causality [10, 7]; work which has resulted in the development of the *Manipulation Theorem* [10] and in sound and complete axiomatizations for causality [3], including the development of a new language for causal reasoning [4].

Critical to these formalisms is the assumption that when some variable in the model is manipulated, the net result from a structural standpoint will be *the removal of arcs coming into that variable.* In this paper we label this fundamental assumption the *Manipulation Postulate.* The Manipulation Postulate, which will be formally defined in Section 2, is based on our conception of what a "causal model" is together with our conception of what it means to "manipulate" a variable. As intuitive as this idea is, there are a few simple physical examples that have been suggested [10, 1] which seem to violate the Manipulation Postulate; in particular, systems have been identified which appear to be reversible. Neither a formal analysis of why reversibility occurs nor an indication of how widespread the problem is has been presented in the

** Currently with ReasonEdge Technologies, Pte, Ltd, 438 Alexandra Road, #03-01A Alexandra Point, Singapore 119958, Republic of Singapore, mjdruzdzel@reasonedge.com.

[1] An extended version of this paper is being submitted to the Journal of Artificial Intelligence Research.

S. Benferhat and P. Besnard (Eds.): ECSQARU 2001, LNAI 2143, pp. 192–203, 2001.

causality literature. For these reasons the problem of reversibility has been widely ignored by researchers in causality.[2]

In this paper, we identify a class $\mathcal{F}$ of recursive equilibrium models that are guaranteed to violate the Manipulation Postulate; and in more complicated ways than merely reversing arcs under manipulation. Rather than relying on examples to demonstrate the existence of this class, this work is unique in that it provides a mathematical proof that $\mathcal{F} \neq \emptyset$ based on the existence of dynamic (time-dependent) models that possess recursive equilibrium counterparts. We show that the set of models which belong to $\mathcal{F}$ is surprisingly large, encompassing a wide array of the most common physical systems. We also show that every model in $\mathcal{F}$ displays reversibility, thereby providing a mathematical basis for this phenomenon and a set of sufficient conditions for it to occur, while at the same time indicating that it is a more general and perhaps widespread problem than previously suspected.

Our proofs rely on the results of Iwasaki and Simon [5] who apparently were the first to discuss the relationship between dynamic causal models and recursive equilibrium causal models. However, there has been other work relating dynamic models to non-dynamic models in general: Fisher [2] discusses the relationship between a time-varying model and its time-averaged counterpart; Kuipers [6] discusses temporal abstraction in dynamic qualitative models with widely varying time-scales; and Richardson [8] discusses the relationship between independencies in dynamic models and in *non*-recursive equilibrium causal models. Due to space limitations, some proofs are only sketched below; however, full proofs are available in an online appendix at: *http://www.sis.pitt.edu/~ddash/papers/caveats/appendix.ps.*

We will use the following notation throughout the remainder of the paper: If $G = \langle V, A \rangle$ is a directed graph with vertex set V and arc set A, we will use $\mathrm{Pa}(v)_G$ and $\mathrm{Ch}(v)_G$ to denote the parents and children, respectively, in G, for some $v \in V$. We will use $\mathrm{Anc}(v)_G$ and $\mathrm{Des}(v)_G$ to denote the ancestors and descendants of a variable v in graph G. If e is an equation then we use $Params(e)$ to denote the set of variables contained in e. If E is a set of equations, we use $Params(E)$ to represent $\bigcup_{e \in E} Params(e)$.

2 Causal Models

We are considering causal models, in the form of *structural equation models*, whereby a system is summarized by a set of feature variables V, relations are specified by a set of equations E which determine unique solutions for all $v \in V$, and each variable $v \in V$ is associated with a single unique equation $e \in E$:

Definition 1 (total causal mapping). *A total causal mapping over E is a bijection $\phi : V \rightarrow E$, where E is a set of n equations with $V \equiv \mathrm{Params}(E)$. Obviously ϕ can be written equivalently as a list of associations: $\{\langle v_1, e_1 \rangle, \langle v_2, e_2 \rangle, ..., \langle v_n, e_n \rangle\}$.*

The notion of a set of equations being "self-contained" is defined precisely in [9] and [5]. Roughly the term means that the set of equations are logically independent (no equation can be derived by other equations in the set) and all parameters are identifiable. We will use the terms "structural equation model" and "causal model" interchangeably:

[2] Galles and Pearl [3] and subsequently Halpern [4] prove a theorem which they label "reversibility"; however this concept of reversibility has nothing to do with our concept. In particular, their theorem assumes that the Manipulation Postulate holds.

e_1: $f_1(w, z, v, x) = 0$ (mapped to w)
e_2: $x = x_0$ (mapped to x)
e_3: $f_2(x, y, z) = 0$ (mapped to z)
e_4: $f_3(y, z) = 0$ (mapped to y)
e_5: $f_4(v) = 0$ (mapped to v)

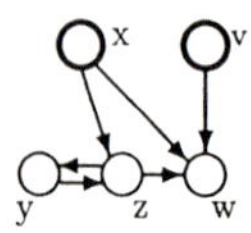

Fig. 1. An example causal model.

Definition 2 (structural equation model). *A structural equation model M is a triple $M = \langle V, E, \phi \rangle$, where E is a self-contained set of equations over parameters V, and $\phi : V \rightarrow E$ is a total causal mapping.*

A structural equation model can be used to represent a joint probability distribution over the variables by including in each equation dependence on an independent random variable that represents the external, non-modeled factors that may introduce noise into the system. It is sufficient for our purposes to consider only models such that any equation $e \in E$ can be freely inverted for any variable $v \in Params(e)$ so that v can be written as a function of the remaining parameters of e, e.g., $v = f(\mathrm{Pa}(v))$. An example of such a model is shown in Figure 1. Such a causal model defines a directed graph G by directing an edge, $p \rightarrow v$, for each $p \in Params(e) \setminus \{v\}$.

It will be sufficient for the purposes of this paper to consider recursive models only:

Definition 3 (recursive causal model). *A causal model $M = \langle V, E, \phi \rangle$ with a causal graph G is recursive if and only if G is acyclic.*

The following lemma shows that if M is a recursive model, then there exists exactly one mapping from equations to variables:

Lemma 1. *If $M = \langle V, E, \phi \rangle$ is a recursive structural equation model then any causal mapping $\phi' : V \rightarrow E$ must be identical to ϕ: i.e., $\phi(v) = \phi'(v)$ for all $v \in V$.*

Proof. (sketch) This can be proven by induction by ordering the variables according to the topological sort of the graph, and showing for any mapping that if all the parents of a variable x are assigned according to ϕ then x must be also. The base case corresponds to an exogenous variable x_0 which must be assigned to $\phi(x_0)$ since that equation must have x_0 as its only parameter. □

Causal inference may require the structure of the causal graph to be altered prior to performing probabilistic inference; in particular, it is made possible by a critical postulate which we call the *Manipulation Postulate.* All formalisms for causal reasoning take the Manipulation Postulate as a fundamental starting point:

Postulate 1 (Manipulation Postulate) *If $G = \langle V, E \rangle$ is a causal graph and $V' \subset V$ is a subset of variables being manipulated, then the causal graph, G', for the manipulated system is such that $G' = \langle V, E' \rangle$, where $E' \subseteq E$ and E' differs from E by at most the set of arcs into V'.*

In plain words, manipulating a variable can cause some of its incoming arcs to be removed from the causal graph, but can effect no other change in the graph. We say that a manipulation on v is *perfect* if all incoming arcs are removed from v in the manipulated graph. For the duration of this paper we will assume that all manipulations are perfect. This postulate is related to the well-known "do" operator of Pearl [7] in that a perfect manipulation on a system specified by a causal graph G will be correctly modelled by applying the do operator to G if and only if the Manipulation Postulate holds.

Manipulation inferences require only graphs (for qualitative inference), and maybe probability distributions (for quantitative predictions). This fact makes common tools used in causal modeling, for example causal discovery, useful from a causal inference perspective. It allows us to learn a causal graph from data and feel confident that such a graph can be used to predict the effects of manipulation, without detailed knowledge of equations underlying the graph. It is this fact which makes the Manipulation Postulate so important, because without it a causal graph and a probability distribution would not be sufficient to allow manipulation inferences.

3 Violating the Manipulation Postulate

Druzdzel [1], and Spirtes *et al.* [10] have pointed out that, contrary to the Manipulation Postulate, some systems appear to exhibit *reversibility* when manipulated. The standard example of a reversible system is the transmission of a bicycle. In normal operation, the rotation rate of the pedals is fixed and the wheels rotate in response. the following causal graph describes this system: *Pedal Rotation Rate* $\rightarrow$ *Wheel Rotation Rate;* however, if the bike is propped up on a bike rack and the wheel is directly rotated at some rate, then the pedals will rotate in response. The causal ordering of the system under these circumstances yields: *Wheel Rotation Rate* $\rightarrow$ *Pedal Rotation Rate.* The mere citing of physical examples, however, is not a completely satisfying demonstration that a correctly modeled system can violate the Manipulation Postulate. For example, perhaps there are hidden variables at play in our examples that, once included into the model, will produce a model that does not violate the Manipulation Postulate. Here we provide examples of systems which appear to violate the Manipulation Postulate in ways other than merely flipping arcs between manipulated children and their parents, suggesting that the problem of reversibility is a more general problem than originally supposed. All examples in this section possess recursive graphs, thus according to Lemma 1 their causal mappings are unique.

Reversibility is especially troubling from the point of view of automated causal discovery. It appears that manipulation inferences are possible only on models for which we have a strong understanding of the domain in the form of equations. Unfortunately, after learning a causal model from data, the only knowledge we have typically consists of an automatically discovered graph along with an automatically discovered probability distribution.

The Ideal Gas System Figure 2 displays one of the simplest physical systems. This system is comprised of an ideal gas trapped in a chamber with a movable piston, on top of which sits a mass, m. The temperature, T, of the gas is controlled externally by a temperature reservoir placed in contact with the chamber. Therefore, m and T can be controlled directly and so will be exogenous variables in our model of this system.

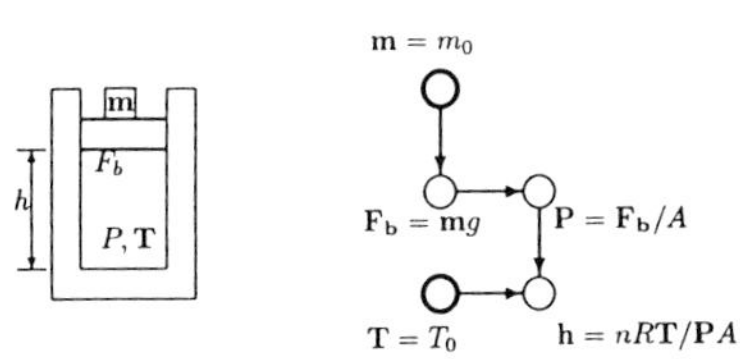

Fig. 2. Causal model of the ideal gas in equilibrium.

The equations presented in Figure 2 assume that the system is in equilibrium. That is, in a hypothetical experiment where m and T are set to some arbitrary values, there is an implicit time delay in measuring the remaining variables sufficient to allow all time-variation in their values to stabilize. Figure 2 shows the causal graph given by constructing a causal mapping for this system. In words: *"In equilibrium, the force applied to the bottom of the piston must exactly balance the mass on top of the piston. Given the force on the bottom of the piston, the pressure of the gas must be determined, which together with the temperature determines the height of the piston through the ideal gas law."*

Consider what happens when the height of the piston is set to a constant value: $h = h_0$. Physically this can be achieved by inserting pins into the walls of the chamber at the desired height, as shown in Figure 3. Applying the Manipulation Postulate to the model in Figure 2 yields the graph with the arcs $P \rightarrow h$ and $T \rightarrow h$ removed, as depicted in Figure 3 (b).

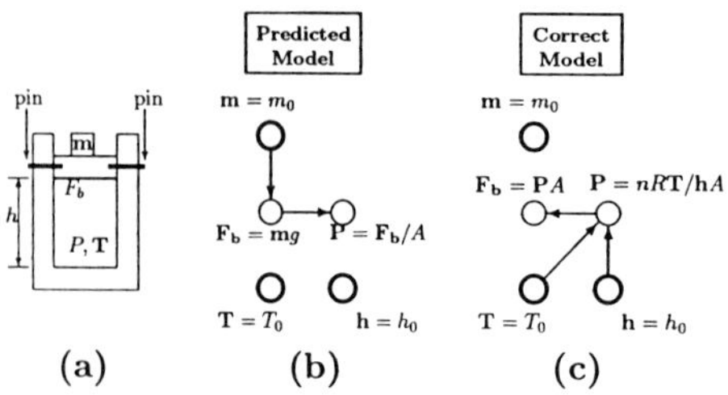

Fig. 3. The ideal gas model violates the Manipulation Postulate when h is manipulated.

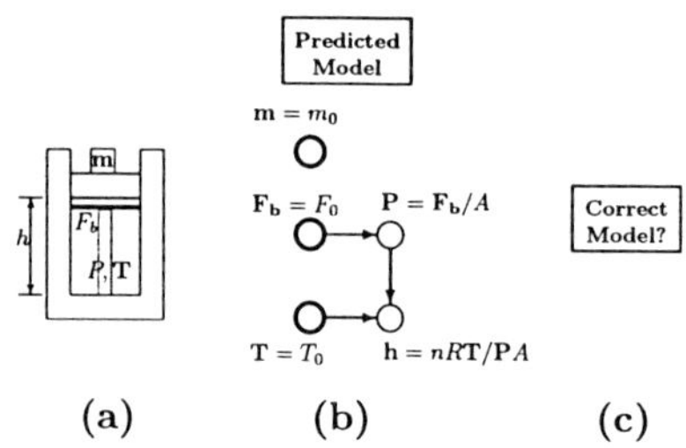

Fig. 4. No equilibrium model exists after manipulating F_b.

What is the true causal graph for this system? Fortunately since this is a simple system which we understand well, we are able to write down the governing equations, given in Figure 3 (c). Constructing the causal mapping (unique by Lemma 1) for these equations yields the graph shown. In words: *Since h and T are both fixed, P is determined by the ideal gas law, $P = kT/h$. Since the gas is the only source of force on the bottom of the piston, F_b is determined by P: $F_b = PA$.* Thus, P is no longer determined by F_b, and F_b becomes independent of m. It is clear that the true causal model differs from that predicted by the Manipulation Postulate. Furthermore, although some arcs have been reversed in the graph, one has been deleted ($m \rightarrow F_b$) and another has changed in an apparently arbitrary fashion ($T \rightarrow h$ changed to $T \rightarrow P$). This causal graph is exactly the one that would be learned from data using the *manipulated system* to generate the data, as can be verified by calculating the independencies between variables using the equations of Figure 3 (c) with independent error terms.

There are other, even more dramatic problems with manipulating variables in this model. Refer back to the original ideal gas model of Figure 2. Imagine that for some reason we want to minimize h; it would not be unreasonable, given the graph in Figure 2, to set the value of h by applying a manipulation to F_b, since F_b is a causal ancestor of h. In particular, in order to make h as small as possible, we would want to make F_b as large as possible according to Figure 2.

Consider what happens when F_b is manipulated in this way. In the real system, the force on the bottom of the piston can be set independently of the mass by raising a movable stage up through the chamber and directly applying the desired force to the piston with the stage, as shown in Figure 4 (a). Something very unexpected happens under this manipulation. Rather than getting the model of Figure 4 (b), expected by the Manipulation Postulate, unless by coincidence the force applied exactly balances the force due to the mass, the piston will continually be accelerated out of the cylinder, and h, which we intended to minimize, instead grows without bound. Not only does this manipulation violate the postulate, but even worse, we have discovered a *dynamic instability* in the system, i.e., there *is no* equilibrium model; a fact which a causal graph alone provides no indication of. If this example seems exaggerated it is only because we have some concrete understanding about the equations underlying this system. However, imagine applying manipulations to automatically learned models of complex socio-economic or medical systems, where our basic knowledge is at most fragmentary. Performing manipulations on such models could have unpredictable effects, to say the least.

4 Dynamic Causal Models

Manipulating the force in the ideal gas model led to an instability. This effect gives us a clue as to what is happening, namely, underlying the equilibrium ideal gas model is a dynamic system. When certain manipulations are made, this dynamic system may not possess an equilibrium point; the result is the hidden instability discovered in the ideal gas system. To understand the phenomenon, we must first discuss how to model this system on a finer time scale.

The issue of modeling a causal system on varying time scales and relating models on those time scales was addressed by Iwasaki and Simon [5]. The key points that we take from their work are the following: (1) It is possible to model dynamic systems on many different time scales, (2) The causal graphs will not necessarily be the same for different time scales, and (3) The causal models based on shorter time scales can be used to derive models on longer time scales by applying the *equilibration* operator.

Consider again the experiment we performed in Section 3. After we dropped a new mass on the piston and changed T, we waited some length of time for the piston to come to rest, then measured all of our variables. In this experiment, on the contrary, we will begin measuring our variables some time Δt after we have dropped the mass on the piston. If we repeated this experiment several times we would find that the independencies and the equations governing this dynamic behavior will in general be entirely different from those in equilibrium.

Structural equation models were used in [5] to handle time-dependent systems by modeling the system at fixed, discrete time intervals. This is accomplished by creating new variables for each time slice, and adding differential equations that may relate variables across time slices. From a modeling perspective, time-dependent models and graphs are thus no different in principle from equilibrium structural equation models. Finding a causal mapping over these sets of equations would again define a directed acyclic graph (in the recursive case), where some arcs might go across time slices.

We will illustrate the features of this technique by presenting the dynamic causal model of the ideal gas system. There are four physical laws: (1) Weight of a mass: $F_t = mg$, (2) Newton's second law: $\Sigma_i F_i = ma$, (3) the Ideal gas law: $P = kT/h$, and (4) the Pressure-force relationship: $P = F_b/A$, where a is the acceleration of the piston and all other variables are as defined in Figure 2. In addition to these physical laws, the system is constrained by the definition of acceleration and velocity of the piston (expressed in discrete form):

$$v_{(t)} = v_{(t-1)} + a_{(t-1)}\Delta t \quad \text{and} \quad h_{(t)} = h_{(t-1)} + v_{(t-1)}\Delta t$$

where we have used the notation that $x_{(t)}$ refers to the value of variable x at time slice t, and Δt is the (constant) time between slices. In order to specify a particular solution to these difference equations, initial conditions must be given for h: $h_{(0)} = h_0$ and for v: $v_{(0)} = v_0$, where h_0 and v_0 are constants. Finally, since m and T are exogenous, we have $m_{(t)} = m_0$ and $T_{(t)} = T_0$, for all t.

This model relates all the variables in our model at $t = 0$ with each other and with v and h at $t = 1$. Since $h_{(1)}$ and $v_{(1)}$ are now determined at $t = 1$, we can recursively iterate this procedure to generate causal graphs for arbitrary values of t.

Since this graph is Markovian through time i.e., the variables in the future are d-separated from variables in the past by variables in the present, it can be represented by a convenient shorthand graph for an infinite sequence of time steps. In this shorthand graph temporal subscripts can be dropped and we use special dashed links, labelled *integration links* [5], to denote that a causal relationship is really occurring through a time slice. The shorthand dynamic causal graph for the ideal gas system is shown later in Figure 5 (a). Since these shorthand graphs are based on differential equations, they always make the assumption that if x and $\dot{x}$ are present in the model then $\dot{x} \rightarrow x$ across time slices.

4.1 Deriving Equilibrium Models from Dynamic Models

The dynamic graph in Figure 5 (a) represents the causal graph for the system modelled over an infinitesimal time scale; whereas, the graph from Figure 2 is modelled over a time scale that is long enough for the system to come to equilibrium. Here we formally define dynamic models and we review how to use the equilibration operator to derive an equilibrium model from the dynamic model. We will use the notation that $\dot{v} \equiv dv/dt$ and that $v^{(0)} \equiv v$ and $v^{(i+1)} \equiv dv^{(i)}/dt$.

The shorthand dynamic graph presented in Figure 5 (a) adds some confusion to the concept of recursivity, since it possesses cycles itself although it really is meant to represent an acyclic graph that is unrolled in time. Thus to clear up confusion we generalize the concept of recursivity for a shorthand graph:

Definition 4 (recursive causal model). *A dynamic causal model $M = \langle V, E, \phi \rangle$ with a causal graph G is recursive if and only if the causal graph $G^{(0)}$, obtained by removing all integration links from G, is acyclic.*

Definition 5 (dynamic variable). *Given a causal model $M = \langle V, E, \phi \rangle$ with graph G, a variable $v \in V$ is a dynamic variable if and only if $\dot{v} \in \mathrm{Pa}(v)_G$.*

The operation of *equilibration* was presented in Iwasaki and Simon [5] whereby the derivatives of a dynamic variable x are eliminated from a model by assuming that x has achieved equilibrium:

Definition 6 ($\mathbf{V_{del}(x)}$, $\mathbf{E_{del}(x)}$). *Let $M = \langle V, E, \phi \rangle$ be a causal model with $x \in V$ and with $x^{(n)} \in V$ the highest order derivative of x in the model, then:*

$$V_{del}(x) = \{x^{(i)} \mid 0 < i \leq n,\, i \neq 0\} \text{ and } E_{del}(x) = \{\phi(x^{(i)}) \mid 0 \leq i < n\}$$

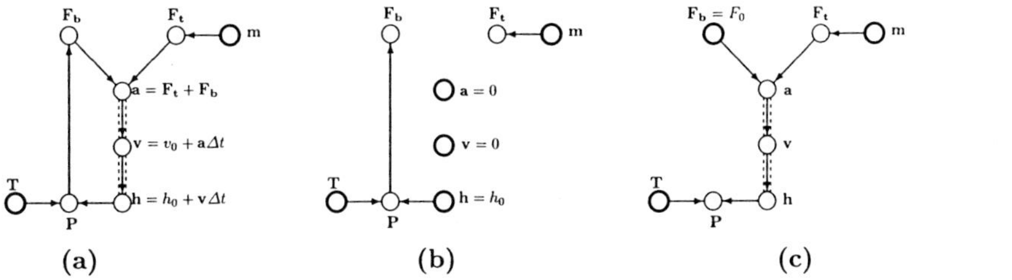

Fig. 5. (a) The dynamic ideal gas causal graph, (b) Manipulating h, (c) Manipulating F_b.

Note that $x \notin V_{del}(x)$ and $\phi(x^{(n)}) \notin E_{del}(x)$.

Definition 7 (equilibration). *Let $M = \langle V, E, \phi \rangle$ be a causal model and let $x \in V$ be a dynamic variable with $x^{(n)} \in V$ the highest order derivative of x in V. The model $M_{\tilde{x}} = \langle V_{\tilde{x}}, E_{\tilde{x}}, \phi_{\tilde{x}} \rangle$ due to the equilibration of x is obtained by the following procedure:*

1. *Let $V_{\tilde{x}} = V \setminus V_{del}(x)$,*
2. *Let $E_{\tilde{x}} = E \setminus E_{del}(x)$,*
3. *For each $e \in E_{\tilde{x}}$ set $v = 0$ for all $v \in V_{del}(x)$.*
4. *Construct a new mapping $\phi_{\tilde{x}} : V_{\tilde{x}} \rightarrow E_{\tilde{x}}$.*

Equilibration is equivalent to assuming that a dynamic variable x has achieved equilibrium. This implies that all of x's derivatives will be zero. Equilibration can cause the remaining set of equations to be non-self-contained. We call equilibration *well-defined* if this does not happen.

Definition 8 (equilibrium model). *A causal model $M = \langle V, E, \phi \rangle$ is an equilibrium model with respect to x for some $x \in V$ if and only if x is not a dynamic variable in M.*

Definition 9 (equilibrated model). *A causal model $M_{\tilde{x}} = \langle V_{\tilde{x}}, E_{\tilde{x}}, \phi_{\tilde{x}} \rangle$ is an equilibrated model with respect to x if and only if $M_{\tilde{x}}$ is derived from a dynamic model $M = \langle V, E, \phi \rangle$ by performing a well-defined equilibration on $x \in V$, and x is a dynamic variable in M.*

4.2 Manipulating Dynamic Models

We now examine the phenomena observed in the ideal gas system from the viewpoint of dynamics. Let us again fix the height of the piston, using the model of Figure 5 (a) to describe the ideal gas system. To fix the piston, we must set h to some constant value for all time, $h_{(t)} = h_0$. We also must stop the piston from moving so we must set $v_{(t)} = 0$ and $a_{(t)} = 0$. Thus, in the dynamic graph with integration links, we can think of this one action of setting the height of the piston as three separate actions. If we assume that the Manipulation Postulate holds on the dynamic model in Figure 5 (a), we obtain the graph depicted in Figure 5 (b). Since h is being held constant, this graph is already an equilibrium graph with respect to h (i.e., no equilibration operation is required). By comparing Figure 5 (b) to the manipulated equilibrium ideal gas system of Figure 3 (c), we can see that aside from the extra variables that were added to the dynamic model for clarity (F_t, a and v), Figure 5 (b) is identical to the expected manipulated model. Therefore, *the Manipulation Postulate holds for this model, and it produces precisely the graph that we originally expected to get but were unable to get from the equilibrium model.*

Dynamic models can also be used to predict when a manipulation will cause an instability. In order to demonstrate this, we first need to review a key result about stability in dynamic systems. If, within a dynamic model, a dynamic variable x possesses a fixed-point solution at, say, $x = x_0$, then that fixed-point will be a stable fixed-point if and only if the following stability relation [11] holds:

$$\left.\frac{\partial \dot{x}}{\partial x}\right|_{x_0} < 0, \text{ (Stability condition)}$$

where $\dot{x}$ is the time-derivative of x.

According to this stability condition, the variable $\dot{x}$ must somehow be a function of x for stability to occur. What does this imply about dynamic causal models? In order for stability to occur, there must exist some regulation process by which $\dot{x}_{(t)}$ can get information about $x_{(t')}$ for some $t' \leq t$. In our dynamic model, for example, this regulation takes place through the feedback loop: $h_{(t)} \rightarrow P \rightarrow F_b \rightarrow a_{(t)} \rightarrow v_{(t+1)}$. The stability condition thus suggests a structural condition for stability in a causal graph:

Definition 10 (The Structural Stability Principle). *Let G be a causal graph with dynamic variable v, and let* $\mathrm{Fb}(v)$ *denote the set* $\mathrm{Fb}(v) = \mathrm{Anc}(v)_G \cap \mathrm{Des}(v)_G$, *then v will possess a stable fixed-point only if* $\mathrm{Fb}(v) \neq \emptyset$.

Consider the implications of manipulating F_b in the dynamic model of the ideal gas system. If we again assume that the Manipulation postulate holds for the dynamic model, when F_b is manipulated in Figure 5 (a), the model shown in Figure 5 (c) is obtained. We can see immediately from the causal graph that this manipulation will break the only feedback loop for x in this system, and thus according to the Structural Stability criterion, there does not exist a stable equilibrium point for this model. Our second major observation is therefore that *the dynamic model, together with the Manipulation Postulate and the Structural Stability criterion correctly predict that some manipulations will cause an instability.*

5 Theorems

In this section we formalize the observations suggested by the examples in Section 3. For the remainder of this section, let $M = \langle V, E, \phi \rangle$ be an arbitrary dynamic causal model, let $x \in V$ be a dynamic variable in M and let $M_{\tilde{x}} = \langle V_{\tilde{x}}, E_{\tilde{x}}, \phi_{\tilde{x}} \rangle$ be the causal model obtained by performing a well-defined equilibration operation on x. Let G and $G_{\tilde{x}}$ be the causal graphs for M and $M_{\tilde{x}}$, respectively and $G_x^{(0)}$ be the graph corresponding to G with all of x's integration links removed. We define $\mathrm{Fb}(x)$ to be the set of feedback variables: $\mathrm{Fb}(x) = \{\mathrm{Anc}(x)_G \cap \mathrm{Des}(x)_G\}$, and let $V_{del}(x)$ and $E_{del}(x)$ be defined as in Definition 6.

Definition 11 (RFRE Model, $\mathcal{F}$). *$M_{\mathcal{F}}$ is a recursive feedback-resolved equilibrated (RFRE) model with respect to x if and only if the following conditions hold:*

1. **Equilibration:** *$M_{\mathcal{F}}$ is derived from a dynamic model M_d by equilibrating x in M_d,*
2. **Recursivity:** *$M_{\mathcal{F}}$ and M_d are both recursive, and*
3. **Feedback-resolution:**
   $\{\mathrm{Fb}(x) \setminus V_{del}(x)\} \cap \mathrm{Ch}(x)_{G_d} \neq \emptyset$.

We denote the class of all RFRE models as $\mathcal{F}$, and use $\mathcal{F}(x)$ to denote the set of RFRE models with respect to x.

Lemma 2. *If M is recursive, then there exists an ordering relation O on the associations of ϕ such that:*

1. *$O(\langle v_i, e_i\rangle) < O(\langle v_j, e_j\rangle)$ if $v_i \in \mathrm{Anc}(v_j)_{G_x^{(0)}}$, and*
2. *the pairs corresponding to $\mathrm{Fb}(x)$ form a contiguous sequence in O.*

Proof. In $G_x^{(0)}$, all $x^{(i)}$ such that $i \neq n$ are exogenous by construction (they are specified by the initial conditions in the model). Thus they can be ordered before all other $v \in \mathrm{Fb}(x)$. Define $\mathrm{Anc}(\mathrm{Fb}(x))_{G_x^{(0)}} \equiv \bigcup_{v\in \mathrm{Fb}(x)} \mathrm{Anc}(v)_{G_x^{(0)}}$ and $\mathrm{Des}(\mathrm{Fb}(x))_{G_x^{(0)}} \equiv \bigcup_{v\in \mathrm{Fb}(x)} \mathrm{Des}(v)_{G_x^{(0)}}$ to be the set of ancestors and descendants, respectively of $\mathrm{Fb}(x)$. By transitivity of the ancestor and descendant relationships, if there exists a $v \in \mathrm{Anc}(\mathrm{Fb}(x)) \cap \mathrm{Des}(\mathrm{Fb}(x))$ then $v \in \mathrm{Fb}(x)$. Thus an ordering can be defined such that $O(v_{anc}) < O(v_{fb}) < O(v_{des})$ for arbitrary variables $v_{anc} \in \mathrm{Anc}(\mathrm{Fb}(x)) \setminus \mathrm{Fb}(x)$, $v_{des} \in \mathrm{Des}(\mathrm{Fb}(x)) \setminus \mathrm{Fb}(x)$, and $v_{fb} \in \mathrm{Fb}(x)$. □

Lemma 3. *Let $\overline{F}$ denote the set $V_{\tilde{x}} \setminus \{\mathrm{Fb}(x) \cup \{x\}\}$. If M and $M_{\tilde{x}}$ are recursive then $\phi_{\tilde{x}}(v) = \phi(v)$ for all $v \in \overline{F}$.*

Proof. (sketch) Using Lemma 2 and a recursive proof similar to that of Lemma 1, it can be proven that it will always be possible to define a mapping ϕ' such that each $v \in \overline{F}$ gets mapped to $\phi(v')$ for some $v' \in \overline{F}$. It then follows by Lemma 1 that since $\phi_{\tilde{x}}$ is recursive, $\phi' = \phi_{\tilde{x}}$. □

The next lemma says, informally, that all ancestors of x in $\mathrm{Fb}(x)$ that are not dynamic variables in $G_x^{(0)}$ must pass through $x^{(n)}$:

Lemma 4. *The following relation holds:* $\mathrm{Fb}(x) \setminus V_{del}(x) \subseteq \mathrm{Anc}(x^{(n)})_{G_x^{(0)}}$.

Proof. First note that if v is a dynamic variable, then in $G_x^{(0)}$, by construction v must be given by initial conditions and so must be exogenous. Therefore, in the chain of derivatives: $x^{(n)} \to x^{(n-1)} \to \cdots \to x$, all $x^{(i)}$ such that $i \neq n$ must have a single parent which is connected by an integration link. Therefore, all $v \in \mathrm{Anc}(x)_G \setminus V_{del}(x)$ must be ancestors of $x^{(n)}$, i.e., $\mathrm{Fb}(x) \setminus V_{del}(x) \subseteq \mathrm{Anc}(x^{(n)})_{G_x^{(0)}}$. □

Lemma 5. *If $M_{\tilde{x}} \in \mathcal{F}(x)$ then there does not exist an $x^{(i)}$ such that $x^{(i)} \in \mathrm{Ch}(x)_G$.*

Proof. (sketch) First note that the result follows for all $x^{(j)}$ such that $j < n$, because by construction $\mathrm{Pa}(x^{(j)}) = \{x^{(j+1)}\}$ in M. Thus we only need to prove that $x^{(n)} \notin \mathrm{Ch}(x)$. $M_{\tilde{x}}$ is recursive by assumption; therefore, by Lemma 1 there only exists one causal mapping, $\phi_{\tilde{x}}$. However, if $x^{(n)} \in \mathrm{Ch}(x)$ then it can be shown by Lemma 3 that there exists a mapping ϕ' such that $\phi'(x) = \phi(x^{(n)})$, and all other variables in $V_{\tilde{x}}$ retain the associations specified by ϕ. By Lemma 4 it follows in such case that $\mathrm{Anc}(x) \cap \mathrm{Des}(x)$ is non-empty, which contradicts the recursivity of $\phi_{\tilde{x}}$. □

Lemma 6. *If $M_{\tilde{x}} \in \mathcal{F}(x)$, then there exists a $v \in V_{\tilde{x}}$ such that $v \in \mathrm{Pa}(x)_{G_{\tilde{x}}}$ and such that $v \in \mathrm{Ch}(x)_G$.*

Proof. Define an ordering O for ϕ and label the pairs $\langle v_l, e_l\rangle$ in ϕ according to O as in the proof of Lemmas 1 and 3. Let $\langle x, e_i\rangle$ be the association for x in $\phi_{\tilde{x}}$. By construction $x \neq v_i$, and by Lemma 3, $v_i \in \mathrm{Fb}(x)$. Since $x \in \mathit{Params}(e_i)$ and since $\langle v_i, e_i\rangle \in \phi$ it must be the case that $v_i \in \mathrm{Ch}(x)_G$. Since $x^{(l)}$ is exogenous in $G_x^{(0)}$ for all $l \neq n$ and since, by Lemma 5, $v_i \neq v^{(n)}$, it follows that $v_i \notin V_{del}(x)$. Therefore $v_i \in \text{Fb}(x) \setminus V_{del}(x)$, and since $v_i \in \mathit{Params}(e_i)$ it must be the case that $v_i \in \text{Pa}(x)_{G_{\tilde{x}}}$. □

Lemma 7. *If $M_{\tilde{x}} \in \mathcal{F}(x)$ and $M_{\hat{x}} = \langle V_{\hat{x}}, E_{\hat{x}}, \phi_{\hat{x}} \rangle$, with causal graph $G_{\hat{x}}$, is the causal model resulting when x is manipulated in M, then in $G_{\hat{x}}$ there will exist an edge $x \to v$ for all $v \in \text{Ch}(x)_G \cap V_{\hat{x}}$.*

Proof. Since M obeys the Manipulation Postulate, the only arcs that will be removed from M when x is manipulated will be the arcs coming into x and into x's derivatives $x^{(i)}$. Since by Lemma 5, x is not a parent of any $x^{(i)}$ the children of x must be preserved in $G_{\hat{x}}$. □

Finally, Theorem 1 presents conditions which are sufficient for $M_{\tilde{x}}$ to violate the Manipulation Postulate.

Theorem 1 (reversibility). *If $M_{\tilde{x}} \in \mathcal{F}(x)$ and the Manipulation Postulate holds for M, then the Manipulation Postulate does not hold for $M_{\tilde{x}}$.*

Proof. Manipulating x in M produces an equilibrium model with respect to x, $M_{\hat{x}}$, which must be the correct model that is obtained when x is manipulated, by definition of the Manipulation Postulate. Let $G_{\hat{x}}$ be the causal graph corresponding to $M_{\hat{x}}$. Since $M_{\tilde{x}} \in \mathcal{F}(x)$, by Lemma 6 there exists a $v \in \text{Ch}(x)_G$ such that $v \to x$ in $G_{\tilde{x}}$; however, according to Lemma 7, the edge $x \to v$ must exist in $G_{\hat{x}}$. Thus, manipulating x in $G_{\tilde{x}}$ by applying the Manipulation Postulate leads to an incorrect graph $G_{\tilde{x}}|_{\hat{x}}$, because it will not contain an edge between v and x. □

The theorem is labeled "reversibility" because its proof relies on the guaranteed reversal of an arc; nonetheless, it is clear by the examples given in Section 3 that there is more complex behavior being exhibited in these systems than mere reversibility.

The last theorem proves that hidden dynamic instabilities are a mathematical feature of some equilibrium causal models:

Theorem 2 (instability). *If $M_{\tilde{x}} \in \mathcal{F}(x)$, the Manipulation postulate holds for M and the Structural Stability condition holds then there exists a set of variables $V' \subset V_{\tilde{x}}$ such that if V' is manipulated in M, the variable x will become unstable.*

Proof. Define $V' \equiv \text{Fb}(x) \setminus V_{del}(x)$. It must be the case that $V' \neq \emptyset$ by definition of $\mathcal{F}(x)$. According to the Manipulation Postulate, manipulating V' in G will create a new graph $G_{\hat{V}'}$ with $\text{Fb}(x)_{G_{\hat{V}'}} = \emptyset$. Therefore, according to the Structural Stability principle, x will be unstable in $G_{\hat{V}'}$. □

6 Discussion

We have tried to emphasize the severity of our conclusions on the practice of causal discovery from equilibrium data. Because the examples we have presented are based on simple systems about which most readers are likely to have a good general understanding, the consequences of violating the Manipulation Postulate may not be fully appreciated. However, in domains where causal discovery procedures are used to elicit causal graphs from data, typically little or no background knowledge is present. After discovery, therefore, all knowledge that the modeler possesses is in the form of a causal graph and maybe a probability distribution. The theorems presented in this paper shed significant doubt on the usefulness of a graph so obtained for performing causal reasoning, because we would have no knowledge of the dynamics underlying this system. One obvious remedy is to use time-series data to learn dynamic causal graphs instead of equilibrium models when causal inferences are required. What then is the minimal information needed to insure that a model will support manipulation? Are there general relationships between dynamic models and equilibrium models that can allow us to answer these questions for arbitrary models? We believe these are hard questions but whose answers would be of significance to future work in causal reasoning.

Acknowledgments We would like to thank Greg Cooper, Clark Glymour, Richard Scheines, Herbert Simon, and Peter Spirtes for helpful and intense discussions, and Javier Díez and Nanny Wermuth for their comments and encouragement. The views expressed in this paper are not necessarily shared by any of those acknowledged above. Our work was supported by the National Aeronautics and Space Administration under the Graduate Students Research Program (GSRP), grant number S99-GSRP-085, the Air Force Office of Scientific Research under grant number F49620–00–1–0122, and by the National Science Foundation under Faculty Early Career Development (CAREER) Program, grant IRI–9624629.

References

1. Marek J. Druzdzel. *Probabilistic Reasoning in Decision Support Systems: From Computation to Common Sense.* PhD thesis, Department of Engineering and Public Policy, Carnegie Mellon University, Pittsburgh, PA, December 1992.
2. Franklin M. Fisher. A correspondence principle for simultaneous equation models. *Econometrica*, 38(1):73–92, January 1970.
3. D. Galles and J. Pearl. Axioms of causal relevance. *Artificial Intelligence*, 97(1–2):9–43, 1997.
4. Joseph Y. Halpern. Axiomatizing causal reasoning. *Journal of Artificial Intelligence Research*, 12:317–337, 2000.
5. Yumi Iwasaki and Herbert A. Simon. Causality and model abstraction. *Artificial Intelligence*, 67(1):143–194, May 1994.
6. Benjamin Kuipers. Abstraction by time-scale in qualitative simulation. In *Proceedings of the National Conference on Artificial Intelligence, AAAI–87*, pages 621–625, Seattle, WA, July 1987. American Association for Artificial Intelligence, Morgan Kaufmann Publishers, Inc., San Mateo, CA.
7. Judea Pearl and Thomas S. Verma. A theory of inferred causation. In J.A. Allen, R. Fikes, and E. Sandewall, editors, *KR–91, Principles of Knowledge Representation and Reasoning: Proceedings of the Second International Conference*, pages 441–452, Cambridge, MA, 1991. Morgan Kaufmann Publishers, Inc., San Mateo, CA.
8. Thomas Richardson. *Models of Feedback: Interpretation and Discovery.* PhD dissertation, Carnegie Mellon University, Department of Philosophy, 1996.
9. Herbert A. Simon. Causal ordering and identifiability. In William C. Hood and Tjalling C. Koopmans, editors, *Studies in Econometric Method. Cowles Commission for Research in Economics. Monograph No. 14*, chapter III, pages 49–74. John Wiley & Sons, Inc., New York, NY, 1953.
10. Peter Spirtes, Clark Glymour, and Richard Scheines. *Causation, Prediction, and Search.* Springer Verlag, New York, 1993.
11. Steven H. Strogatz. *Nonlinear Dynamics and Chaos with Applications to Physics, Biology, Chemistry, and Engineering.* Addison-Wesley, Publishers, Reading, MA, 1991.
12. Robert H. Strotz and H.O.A. Wold. Recursive vs. nonrecursive systems: An attempt at synthesis; part I of a triptych on causal chain systems. *Econometrica*, 28(2):417–427, April 1960.

Supporting Changes in Structure in Causal Model Construction

Tsai-Ching Lu and Marek J. Druzdzel

Decision Systems Laboratory
Intelligent Systems Program and School of Information Sciences
University of Pittsburgh Pittsburgh, PA 15260
{ching,marek}@sis.pitt.edu

Abstract. The term "changes in structure," originating from work in econometrics, refers to structural modifications invoked by actions on a causal model. In this paper we formalize the representation of reversibility of a mechanism in order to support modeling of changes in structure in systems that contain reversible mechanisms. Causal models built on our formalization can answer two new types of queries: (1) When manipulating a causal model (i.e., making an endogenous variable exogenous), which mechanisms are possibly invalidated and can be removed from the model? (2) Which variables may be manipulated in order to invalidate and, effectively, remove a mechanism from a model?

1 Introduction

Graphical probabilistic models, such as Bayesian networks, provide compact and computationally efficient representations of problems involving reasoning under uncertainty. Users can easily update their belief in the states of a modeled system by setting evidence in a model that reflect observations made in the real world. A related formalism of causal models, based on structural equations, in addition to observations, supports prediction of the effects of actions, i.e., external manipulation of modeled systems. Explicit representation of causality in causal models enables users to predict the effects of actions, which in turn allows users to perform counterfactual reasoning [8,12,16].

The problem of predicting the effects of actions was originally referred to in econometrics literatures as predicting the effects of *changes in structure* in simultaneous equation models. Assuming that a modeler has sufficient prior knowledge to predict the effects of changes in structure, researchers in econometrics modeled the effects of actions as "scraping" invalid equations and "replacing" them by new ones [10,13,17,18]. If we assume that the variable manipulated by an action is governed by an *irreversible* mechanism (for example, wearing sunglasses protects our eyes from the sun but it does not make the sun go away), the effect of an action amounts to an arc-cutting operation on the causal graph describing the situation [12,16]. However, there exist a large class of *reversible* mechanisms [4,12,13,15,16, 19,18] that are not amenable to this treatment. For example, a car engine causes the wheels to turn when going up hill, but wheels slow down the engine when going

S. Benferhat and P. Besnard (Eds.): ECSQARU 2001, LNAI 2143, pp. 204–215, 2001.

down hill with transmission being put in a lower gear. An action may reverse the direction of causal relations among variables and consequently have drastic effects on causal graphs.

There have been attempts to assist in predicting the effects of actions on systems containing reversible mechanisms. Bogers [1] developed theorems to support structure modifications when the equation being scraped by an action governs an exogenous variable. Druzdzel and van Leijen [6] studied the conditions under which a conditional probability table in a causal Bayesian network can be reversed when manipulating a reversible mechanism. Dash and Druzdzel [3] demonstrated how various equilibrium systems may violate the arc-cutting operation and further developed *differential causal models* to solve the problem by modeling systems dynamically.

Our approach to supporting changes in structure is based on our representation of reversibility of a mechanism. A mechanism asserts that there exists a relationship among a set of variables. We define the reversibility of a mechanism semantically on the set of possible effect variables of a mechanism. A set of mechanisms is a causal model only if the causal relations among the variables are consistent with the reversibility of its mechanisms. Similarly to STRIPS language [7], we conceptualized an action as consisting of three lists: *PRECONDITION* (a causal model), *ADD* (the set of mechanisms to be added), and *DELETE* (the set of mechanisms to be removed). Consequently, once an action is completely specified, the effect of an action is simply performing the modifications specified in *ADD* and *DELETE* lists on the causal model given in a *PRECONDITION*. Given the *PRECONDITION* and one of the *ADD* or *DELETE* lists of a partially specified action, we proved two theorems to assist modelers in answering two new types of queries: (1) When manipulating a causal model, which mechanisms are possibly invalidated and can be removed from the model? (2) Which variables may be manipulated in order to invalidate and, effectively, remove a mechanism from a model? As an extension of existing approaches [1,3,12,16], we formalize the representation of reversibility of a mechanism and assist modelers in predicting the effects of actions in systems consisting of mixtures of mechanisms.

2 Structural Equation Models and Causal Ordering

The work in simultaneous equation models (SEMs) is the root of the work on graphical causal models [8,12,16]. Given an equation e, we denote the set of variables appearing in e as $Vars(e)$. The set of variables appearing in a set of equations E is denoted as $Vars(E) = \bigcup_{e \in E} Vars(e)$. A structural equation model can be defined as a set of structural equations $E = \{e_1, e_2, \ldots, e_m\}$ on a set of variables $V = \{v_1, v_2, \ldots, v_n\}$ appearing in E, i.e., $V \equiv Vars(E)$. Each structural equation $e_i \in E$, generally written in its implicit form $e_i(v_1, v_2, \ldots, v_n) = 0$, describes a conceptually distinct mechanism active in a system.[1] A variable $v_j \in V$ is *exogenous* if it is determined by factors outside the model, i.e., if there exists a

[1] Every structural equation normally contains an error term to represent disturbance due to omitted factors. We will leave out error terms for the simplicity of exposition.

structural equation $e_i(v_j) = 0$ in E. A variable is *endogenous* if it is determined by solving the model. We denote the set of exogenous and endogenous variables in E as $ExVars(E)$ and $EnVars(E)$ respectively. E is *independent* if there is no $e_i \in E$ such that e_i is satisfied by all simultaneous solutions of any subset of $E \setminus e_i$. E is *consistent* if the solution set of E is not empty. In order to ensure that E is independent and consistent, Simon and Rescher [15] defined the concept of *structure*:

Definition 1. *A* structure *is a set of equations E where $|E| \leq |Vars(E)|$ such that in any subset $E' \subseteq E$: (1) $|E'| \leq |Vars(E')|$, and (2) If the values of any $|Vars(E')| - |E'|$ variables in $Vars(E')$ are chosen arbitrarily, then the values of the remaining $|E'|$ variables are determined uniquely.*

A SEM E is *self-contained* if E is a structure and $|E| = |V|$. E is *under-constrained* if E is a structure and $|E| < |V|$. E is *over-constrained* if E is not a structure. Whenever $|E| > |V|$, E is over-constrained. In general, we use a self-contained SEM to describe an equilibrium system since the set of equations is consistent and independent, and the values of variables are determined uniquely. A self-contained structure E is *minimal* if it does not contain any proper subset of equations in E which is self-contained. A minimal self-contained structure is a *strongly coupled component* if it contains more than one equation. A set of equations E can be represented qualitatively as a matrix, called *structure matrix* [5,13,15], with element $a_{ij} =$ x if $v_j \in V$ participates in $e_i \in E$, where x is a marker, and $a_{ij} = 0$ otherwise (see Fig. 1).

	v_1	v_2	v_3	v_4	v_5	v_6	v_7	v_8
e_1	x	0	0	0	0	0	0	0
e_2	0	x	0	0	0	0	0	0
e_3	0	0	x	0	0	0	0	0
e_4	0	x	0	x	x	0	0	0
e_5	0	x	x	x	x	0	0	0
e_6	0	0	x	0	x	x	0	0
e_7	0	0	0	x	0	0	x	0
e_8	x	0	0	0	0	0	x	x

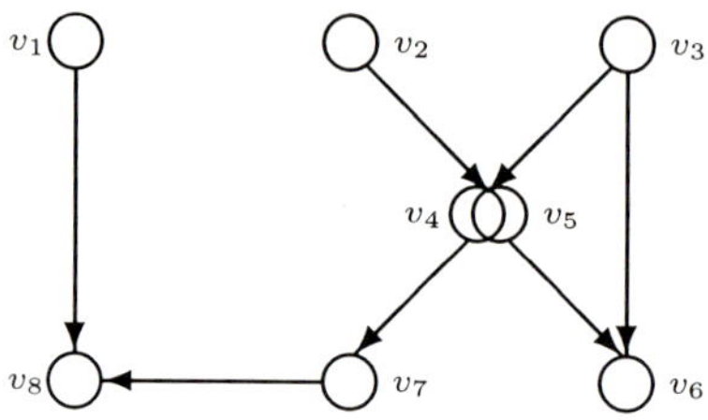

Fig. 1. COA takes a self-contained structure as input and outputs a causal graph.

As shown by Simon [13], a self-contained structure exhibits asymmetries among variables that can be represented by a special type of directed acyclic graph and interpreted causally. He developed a causal ordering algorithm (COA) that takes a self-contained structure E as input and outputs a *causal graph* $G_E = \langle N, A \rangle$ where $N = \{N_1, N_2, \ldots, N_r\}$ is a partitioning of V, consisting of pairwise disjoint sets such that $\bigcup_{i=1}^{r} N_i = V$, and A is a set of directed arcs $v \rightarrow N_i$ where $v \in V$, $N_i \in N$, and $v \notin N_i$. COA starts with *identifying* the minimal self-contained structures in E. These identified minimal self-contained structures, $C^0 = \{C_1^0, C_2^0, \ldots, C_l^0\}$, are called *complete structures of 0-th order* and a partition N_k^0 on V is created for $Vars(C_k^0)$ for each $C_k^0 \in C^0$. For each variable $v \in N_k^0$, a corresponding node is created. When a minimal self-contained structure is a strongly coupled component, i.e., $|C^0_k| > 1$, we draw the nodes created for variables in N^0_k as overlapping circles because their values need to be solved simultaneously. Next, COA *solves* for the values of $Vars(C^0)$ and *removes* C^0 from E. We denote the new structure $E \setminus C^0$ as $\widehat{E^1}$. COA then *substitutes* the solved values of $Vars(C^0)$ into $\widehat{E^1}$ to obtain the *derived structure of the first order* E^1. COA repeats the process of identifying, removing, solving, and substituting on the derived structure of p-th order until it is empty. In addition, whenever a partition N^p_k and corresponding nodes are created for a complete structure C^p_k in the complete structures of p-th order, COA refers C^p_k back to its equations before any substitutions in E, denoted as $\widehat{C^p_k}$, and add arcs from nodes representing variables in $Vars(\widehat{C^p_k}) \setminus Vars(C^p_k)$ to the nodes representing N^p_k. Notice that COA creates one-to-one mapping, denoted as $\langle \widehat{C^p_k}, N^p_k \rangle$, between the set of equations, $\widehat{C^p_k}$, and the set of variables, N^p_k, in a causal graph. We say that $\widehat{C^p_k}$ is *mapped to* N^p_k or vice versa in G_E (see Example 1).

Since the concept of *endogenous* and *exogenous* variables relative to the structure before substitutions of a complete structure of p-th order [13] plays an important role in the rest of the discussion, we introduce it formally as follows.

Definition 2. *Let C^p and C^q be complete structures of p-th and q-th order respectively in a self-contained structure E. Let $\widehat{C^p_k}$ be the structure before any substitutions of a complete structure $C^p_k \in C^p$ in E and $v \in Vars(\widehat{C^p_k})$. We say that v is endogenous in $\widehat{C^p_k}$, if $v \notin Vars(C^q)$ for* all *$q < p$, and v is exogenous in $\widehat{C^p_k}$, if $v \in Vars(C^q)$ for* some *$q < p$. We denote the sets of endogenous and exogenous variables in $\widehat{C^p_k}$ by $EnVars(\widehat{C^p_k})$ and $ExVars(\widehat{C^p_k})$ respectively.*

From Definition 2, we know that each variable v in a self-contained E can appear as an endogenous variable in only one $\widehat{C^p_k}$. We define the *necessary structure* for v in E to support changes in structure defined in Sect. 4.2.

Definition 3. *Let G_E be the causal graph generated by applying COA to a self-contained structure E. Let $v \in N^p_k$ and $Anc(N^p_k)$ be the ancestral set of N^p_k in G_E. The* necessary structure *for v, denoted as NS_v, is the set of equations that are mapped to $N^p_k \cup Anc(N^p_k)$ by COA.*

It is easy to see that a necessary structure is self-contained. In other words, NS_v consists of all equations in E that are necessary to determine v uniquely.

Example 1. In Fig. 1, COA takes the structure matrix as inputs and identifies $C^0 = \widehat{C^0} = \{\{e_1\},\{e_2\},\{e_3\}\}$, $\widehat{C^1} = \{\{e_4, e_5\}\}$, $\widehat{C^2} = \{\{e_6\},\{e_7\}\}$, and $\widehat{C^3} = \{\{e_8\}\}$ to generate the causal graph. The mapping between equations and variables are $\langle e_1, v_1\rangle$, $\langle e_2, v_2\rangle$, $\langle e_3, v_3\rangle$, $\langle\{e_4, e_5\},\{v_4, v_5\}\rangle$, $\langle e_6, v_6\rangle$, $\langle e_7, v_7\rangle$ and $\langle e_8, v_8\rangle$. From the causal graph, we may read off the causal relations among sets of variables. For example, $\{v_4, v_5\}$ is caused by v_2 and v_3, v_6 is caused by v_3 and v_5, and v_7 is caused by v_4. We may also read off indirect causal relations such as that v_3 is an indirect cause of v_7. However, the causal relations between v_4 and v_5 are undefined, since they are in a strongly-coupled component. Notice that v_4 is endogenous in $\widehat{C^1_1} = \{e_4, e_5\}$ but exogenous in $\widehat{C^2_2} = \{e_7\}$. The necessary structure for v_4 is $\{e_2, e_3, e_4, e_5\}$.

3 Reversible Mechanisms

Like any other scientific modeling, structural equation modeling requires us to clearly relate our definitions of variables and structural equations in a SEM to a system in the real world. In general, we start with identifying entities involved in a system. An entity can be a single object (e.g., a patient), a population of similar objects (e.g., male patients in a hospital), or a group of relevant objects (e.g., patients, doctors, and insurance company in a health system). We then define variables to refer to characteristics of entities (e.g., age of a patient) and define structural equations to describe the linkages among variables (mechanisms) in the system. Our prior domain knowledge serves as a guideline in hypothesizing which mechanisms are involved in a system. Therefore, the definitions of structural equations and variables in a SEM are a-priori [13,18]. Simon [14] suggested three classes of sources for specifying mechanisms: *experimental manipulation*, *temporal ordering*, and *"tangible" links*. In [12,18], researchers stressed that mechanisms should be *autonomous* in the sense that the external change on any one of the mechanisms does not imply the change of others. For the purpose of illustration, we define mechanisms as follows.

Definition 4. *A* mechanism *e, represented as a structural equation $e(v_1, v_2, \ldots, v_n) = 0$, asserts that there exists* autonomous *linkages among the set of variables $\{v_1, v_2, \ldots, v_n\}$.*

Simon [14] further pointed out that different *a-priori* assumptions for one mechanism may lead to different interpretations of causal relations among variables. For example, schooling helps to increase verbal ability in one experimental context, but verbal ability helps in getting higher schooling in another. He used the term *causal mechanisms* to refer to mechanisms considered under different a-priori assumptions. In other words, each causal mechanism represents a distinct theory that we hypothesized about the observation of a phenomena in the real world and is written as a function to explicitly describe the relation of the effect variable and its causes.

Definition 5. *Given a mechanism e, a* causal mechanism, *$v = f(Pa(v))$, describes a function f between the effect variable $v \in Vars(e)$ and its direct causes $Pa(v) = Vars(e) \setminus v$. We say that $v = f(Pa(v))$ is* instantiated *from e.*

Generally, there may be more than one causal mechanism instantiated from a mechanism as long as the functions formalized are consistent with the a-priori assumptions. In practice, we believe that people tend to first express a causal mechanism qualitatively as a specification of the effect variable and its causes, and later give it an explicit function. Assuming that the number of variables appearing in a mechanism is fixed, the number of possible effect variables for a mechanism is finite. Consequently, we can classify mechanisms into four categories according to their *reversibility*: (1) *completely reversible*: every variable in the mechanism can be an effect variable, (2) *partially reversible*: two or more of the variables in the mechanism can be effect variables, (3) *irreversible*: only one of the variables in the mechanism can be an effect variable, and (4) *unknown*: the reversibility of the mechanism is unspecified, i.e., the modeler only knows that variables in a mechanism are relevant, but does not know how they relate to each other causally.

Definition 6. *Given a mechanism e, let* $EfVars(e) \subseteq Vars(e)$ *be the set of all possible effect variables of all causal mechanisms instantiated from e. We say that e is (1)* completely reversible *if* $EfVars(e) = Vars(e)$ *and* $|EfVars(e)| > 1$*, (2)* partially reversible *if* $1 < |EfVars(e)| < |Vars(e)|$*, (3)* irreversible *if* $|EfVars(e)| = 1$*, and (4)* unknown *if* $|EfVars(e)| = \emptyset$.

We emphasize that the notion of reversibility of a mechanism is a semantic one since it is defined with respect to the set of effect variables of a mechanism. A functional relation may be reversible in *functional* sense (invertible), but may not be reversible in *causal* sense [18, footnote 6]. For example, ideal gas law and Ohm's law are given in [19, pp. 40] and [11, pp. 10] respectively as examples of partially reversible mechanisms, although their functional relations are invertible in general. Traditionally the reversibility of mechanisms is considered mainly applicable to mechanical and physical systems [19, pp. 325], since the concept is defined upon causal mechanisms, i.e., the invertibility of a function is a necessary condition for the reversibility. In our formalization, we define the concept of reversibility on the set of effect variables of a mechanism so that we can apply the reversibility to other domains. For example, it would be a mere coincidence that schooling, s, and verbal ability, a, can be described as $s = f(a)$ in one context and $a = f^{-1}(s)$ in another. However, it is more likely that $s = f(a)$ in one context and $a = g(s)$, where $g \neq f^{-1}$, in another.

Notice that the notion of entity plays an essential role in our modeling. We should not confuse the reversibility of a mechanism with *causal mixtures* [2] in which members of entities may not share the same causal relationships. For example, if the relation between schooling and verbal ability is modeled as a causal mixture, we may find that schooling helps to increase verbal ability in one subpopulation of students but verbal ability helps to getting higher schooling in another. However, reversible mechanisms model the same entities in different contexts. For example, the verbal ability helps some population of students to get higher schooling in one context, but in another context the schooling helps the same students to increase their verbal ability.

Taking the reversibility of mechanisms into account, we can define a *causal model* as follows.

Definition 7. *A causal model is a set of mechanisms* $E = \{e_1, e_2, \ldots, e_m\}$ *such that there exists a set of causal mechanisms* $F = \{f_1, f_2, \ldots, f_m\}$ *instantiated from* E*, where each* $f_i \in F$ *is an instantiation of* $e_i \in E$*, and* F *is a self-contained structure.*

Given a set of mechanisms E, we can test if E can form a causal model by checking whether there exists a self-contained F instantiated from E. The procedure, denoted as *IsCausalModel*(E), first checks if $|E| = |Vars(E)|$. If so, the procedure assumes that E is a self-contained structure and applies COA qualitatively on E's structure matrix to generate the graph G_E. For each node in G_E, the procedure checks if the mapped mechanisms have valid causal mechanisms to be instantiated, i.e., if there exists a causal mechanism whose effect variable is the same as the one depicted in G_E. If there exists a set of causal mechanism F, instantiated from E, whose effect variables are consistent with G_E, the procedure verifies that E is a causal model. In order to assist modelers in hypothesizing causal relations in a mechanism whose reversibility is unknown, the procedure treats its reversibility as completely reversible. Notice that for those E containing strongly coupled components, we may have several instantiations F from E. In other words, an irreversible mechanism cannot participate in a strongly coupled component.

Example 2. Assume that the set of mechanisms $E = \{e_1, e_2, \ldots, e_8\}$ for the set of variables $V = \{v_1, v_2, \ldots, v_8\}$ shown in Fig. 1 is stored in a knowledge base along with their causal mechanisms. In the knowledge base, e_6 and e_7 are irreversible where $EfVars(e_6) = \{v_6\}$ and $EfVars(e_7) = \{v_7\}$, e_4 and e_5 are completely reversible where $EfVars(e_4) = Vars(e_4)$ and $EfVars(e_5) = Vars(e_5)$, and e_8 is partially reversible where $EfVars(e_8) = \{v_1, v_8\}$. Consequently, E is a causal model since there exists a self-contained structure F that can be instantiated from E. However, if in the knowledge base we have $EfVars(e_7) = \{v_4\}$ instead of $EfVars(e_7) = \{v_7\}$, then E is not a causal model since there is no instantiation of e_7 that can make any instantiation F of E self-contained.

4 Actions in Causal Models

4.1 Representation of Actions

Given a causal model that describes a system of interest, we may easily hypothesize different manipulations, such as "raise interest rate" or "reduce tax," with the intention to influence the values of some target variables. Still, we may not know how other parts of the system may respond to these hypothetical manipulations. In other words, we suspect that our hypothetical manipulations will affect the variables of interest, which are the descendants of the manipulated variables in causal graph, but we are not certain how the equilibrium system will be disturbed by our hypothetical manipulations. Therefore, the process of policy making usually focuses on deliberating the side effects of a manipulation. How should we represent an action in causal modeling to facilitate this deliberation?

Pearl [12, pp. 225] suggested to use the notation $do(q)$, where q is a proposition (variable), to denote an action, since people use the phrases such as "reduce tax" in daily language to express actions. More precisely, an *atomic action*, denoted as $manipulate(v)$ in [2,16] and $do(v = \mathrm{v})$ in [12], is invoked by an external force or agent to manipulate the variable v by imposing on it a probability distribution or holding it at a constant value, $v = \mathrm{v}$, and replacing the causal mechanism, $v = f(Pa(v))$, that directly governs v in a causal model. The corresponding change in the causal graph is depicted as an arc-cutting operation in which all incoming arcs to the manipulated variable v are removed [12,16]. Notice that the implicit assumption behind the arc-cutting operation is that the manipulated variable is governed by an *irreversible* mechanism, i.e., only v can be an effect variable in mechanism $e(v, Pa(v)) = 0$. In order to ensure that the manipulated causal model is self-contained, the irreversible mechanism that governed the manipulated variable has to be removed from the original model. However, when the manipulated variable is governed by a *reversible* mechanism, the arc-cutting operation may lead to inconsistent results. We therefore argue that an action in causal modeling should be defined at the level of mechanisms, not propositions.

In econometric literature (e.g., [10,13,17,18]), a system is represented as a SEM, a set of structural equations, and actions are modeled as "scraping" invalid equations and "replacing" them by new ones. In STRIPS language [7], a situation is represented by a state, conjunctions of function-free ground literals (propositions), and actions are represented as *PRECONDITION*, *ADD*, and *DELETE* lists which are conjunctions of literals. There is a clear analogy between these two modeling formalisms, where the effects of actions are modeled explicitly as adding or deleting fundamental building blocks which are mechanisms in SEM and propositions in STRIPS. We therefore directly translate the "scraping" into *DELETE* and "replacing" into *ADD* and define an action in causal modeling as follows.

Definition 8. *An* action *in causal modeling is a triple ⟨PRECONDITION, ADD, DELETE⟩ where PRECONDITION is a causal model E and ADD and DELETE are the sets of mechanisms to be added and removed from E respectively when applying action to E.*

We consider the context and the effects of an action explicitly in Definition 8. This is consistent with our daily dialogue where we talk about an action and its possible effects under a certain context. For example, the phrase "reduce tax" is usually stated in an economic context with some expectations about how economic units would react.

Note that Definition 8 does not constrain us in what types of mechanisms and how many mechanisms can be specified in *ADD* and *DELETE* lists. There is also no guarantee that the manipulated model will be a self-contained structure. However, the atomic action defined in [12,16], which can be expressed explicitly as $\langle \{E\}, \{v = \mathrm{v}\}, \{e(v, Pa(v)) = 0\} \rangle$ using our definition, always derives a self-contained structure. We use the term *atomic addition*, denoted as $add(v)$, to refer to the *ADD* list of an action that consists of only one mechanism, $\{v = \mathrm{v}\}$, which expresses the manipulation on variable v in E. We use the term *atomic deletion*, denoted as $delete(e)$, to refer to the *DELETE* list of an action that consists of only one mechanism e in E. In order to account for systems with mixtures of different mechanisms, we say that an action is *atomic* if it consists of atomic addition and atomic deletion such that the manipulated model is self-contained.

4.2 Action Deliberation

Once we chose to represent an action explicitly including its effects and context, we shift the problem of predicting the effects of an action to which mechanisms should be specified in *ADD* and *DELETE* lists. We call the process of deciding which mechanisms should be in *ADD* and *DELETE* lists *action deliberation*. In this section, we develop theorems to facilitate the process of deliberating about an atomic action. Given a causal model E, we seek to answer two new types of queries (1) When making an endogenous variable exogenous, which mechanisms are possibly invalidated and can be removed from the model? (2) Which variables may be manipulated in order to invalidate and, effectively, remove a mechanism from a model? In other words, Query (1) assists modelers in modeling the effects of an action considering the manipulation alternatives at hand. Query (2), on the other hand, assists modelers in identifying the set of possible manipulation alternatives. We start by defining the set of *minimal over-constrained* equations that describes the situation where an atomic addition is added into a model.

Definition 9. *A set of over-constrained equations is* minimal *if it does not contain any over-constrained proper subsets itself.*

Lemma 1. *Let E be a self-contained structure and $add(v) \equiv \{v = \mathrm{v}\}$ be an atomic addition where $v \in EnVars(E)$. Let $E'_v = add(v) \cup E$. The set of equations $O'_v = NS_v \cup add(v)$ is minimal over-constrained where NS_v is the necessary structure of v in E.*

Lemma 1 states that an atomic addition makes a self-contained structure minimal over-constrained. Next, we prove Lemma 2 to identify the set of equations such that removing any one of them makes the set of minimal over-constrained equations self-contained again.

Lemma 2. *Given O'_v of E'_v, deleting any equation $e \in NS_v$ makes $O_v = O'_v \setminus e$ self-contained and consequently $E_v = E'_v \setminus e$ self-contained.*

Corollary 1. *Given $E'_v = add(v) \cup E$, E'_v will remain over-constrained if none of equations $e \in O'_v$ is removed.*

Example 3. Consider the self-contained structure E in Fig. 1. If we manipulate on variable v_7, i.e., $add(v_7)$, the resulting set of equations $E'_{v_7} = E \cup add(v_7)$ becomes over-constrained. From Lemma 1, we know that the set of equations $O'_{v_7} = \{e_2, e_3, e_4, e_5, e_7, add(v_7)\}$ is minimal over-constrained. From Lemma 2, we know that removing any equation $e \in \{e_2, e_3, e_4, e_5, e_7\}$ makes the remaining set of equations $E_{v_7} = E'_{v_7} \setminus e$ a self-contained structure. If we instead remove e_6, the set of equations $E'_{v_7} \setminus e_6$ remains over-constrained according to Corollary 1.

Notice that Lemmas 1 and 2 hold for sets of equations. As stated in Sect. 3, a self-contained structure is not necessarily a causal model unless it can be instantiated from a set of mechanisms. Therefore, in order to deliberate about an atomic action in a causal model, we need to verify that the manipulated set of mechanisms is a causal model. In general, we can simply enumerate each mechanism $e \in NS_v$ and use the procedure $IsCausalModel(E_v)$ outlined in Sect. 3 to check if the manipulated model E_v is a causal model. However, we observed that the irreversibility of mechanisms allows us to find the set of possible atomic deletions *locally*.

Consider an atomic addition $add(v)$ on a causal model $E = \{e_1, e_2, \ldots, e_m\}$ and $v \in EnVars(E)$. When all mechanisms governing $EnVars(NS_v)$ in NS_v are completely reversible or unknown, we may remove any one of the mechanisms in NS_v to have a manipulated causal model. When v is directly governed by an irreversible mechanism e, we have to remove e since v cannot be determined by $add(v)$ and e simultaneously in a manipulated model. In other words, the reversibility of mechanism governing the manipulated variable shrinks the set of possible atomic deletions from NS_v to e. We therefore learned that propagation of the effects of an atomic addition in a causal model can be blocked by irreversible mechanisms. Now, we prove Theorem 1 to answer Query (1).

Theorem 1. *Consider an atomic addition $add(v)$ in a causal model $E = \{e_1, e_2, \ldots, e_m\}$ and $v \in EnVars(E)$. There exists a non-empty set of possible atomic deletions $D \subseteq NS_v$ such that deleting any mechanism $d \in D$ derives the causal model $E_v = E \cup add(v) \setminus d$.*

Semantically, Theorem 1 identifies the set of manipulated systems that are self-contained. In other words, Theorem 1 assists modelers in hypothesizing a system's response toward a manipulation. Furthermore, we may find the set of possible atomic deletions *locally* with respect to the order of complete structures in NS_v. Namely, we perform $IsCausalModel(E_v)$ checking by enumerating from the mechanisms governing the manipulated variable and recursively up to those governing its ancestors in the causal graph until we reach irreversible mechanisms.

Considering a completely reversible mechanical system, such as the power train described in Sect. 1, a manipulation usually reflects the changes of the operational context as in from driving uphill to driving downhill, for example. The manipulated system normally responds with instantiating different causal mechanisms according to the current operational context. Consequently, the mechanism being removed is usually the one governing the exogenous variable in the system. However, if the mechanism being removed was governing endogenous variables, it means that the linkage among the set of variables is invalid in the manipulated system. For example, transmission or clutch between the engine and the wheels may be broken. Consequently, the link between engine and wheel is no longer valid. We therefore suggest modelers to use different enumeration orders to inspect the set of possible atomic deletions in different applications. When a system consists of irreversible mechanisms, Theorem 1 can further assists modelers in deliberating about the set of possible atomic deletions *locally.*

	v_1	v_2	v_3	v_4	v_5	v_6	v_7	v_8
$add(v_8)$	0	0	0	0	0	0	0	x
e_2	0	x	0	0	0	0	0	0
e_3	0	0	x	0	0	0	0	0
e_4	0	x	0	x	x	0	0	0
e_5	0	x	x	x	x	0	0	0
e_6	0	0	x	0	x	x	0	0
e_7	0	0	0	x	0	0	x	0
e_8	x	0	0	0	0	0	x	x

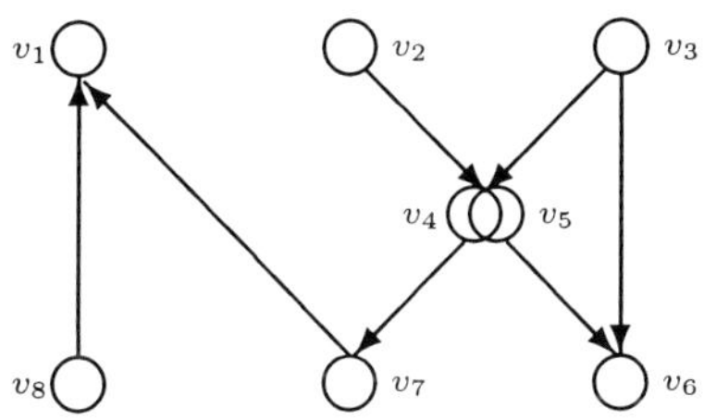

Fig. 2. The structure matrix and its corresponding graph after the atomic action $\langle E, add(v_8), delete(e_1)\rangle$.

Example 4. Consider the set of mechanisms in Fig. 1 and its reversibility assumed in Example 2. The set of possible atomic deletions for manipulating variable v_8, $add(v_8)$, is $\{e_1, e_8\}$ according to Theorem 1. Notice that the irreversibility of mechanisms allows us to find the set of possible atomic deletions in $\{e_1, e_7, e_8\}$ instead of NS_{v_8}. Moreover, $E_{v_8} = E \cup add(v_8) \setminus e_7$ is not a causal model since v_7 cannot be an effect variable in e_8 according to the reversibility of e_8 in the knowledge base. However, if we choose to remove e_1, $delete(e_1)$, the manipulated model is shown in Fig. 2.

The dual theorem to Theorem 1 is to identify the set of possible atomic additions given an atomic deletion, which answers Query (2).

Theorem 2. *Consider an atomic deletion* $delete(e)$ *for a causal model* $E = \{e_1, e_2, \ldots, e_m\}$ *where* $e \in E$. *Let* G_E *be the causal graph of* E. *Let* $e \in \widehat{C_k^p}$ *and* N_k^p *is mapped to* $\widehat{C_k^p}$ *in* G_E. *Let* $Des(N_k^p)$ *be the descendants of* N_k^p *in* G_E. *There exists a nonempty set of variables* $A \subseteq (Des(N_k^p) \cup N_k^p)$ *such that manipulating any variable* $a \in A$ *derives the causal model* $E_a = E \cup add(a) \setminus e$. *The set of mechanisms* $\bigcup_{a \in A} add(a)$ *is called the set of possible atomic additions.*

Example 5. Consider the set of mechanisms in Fig. 1 and its reversibility assumed in Example 2. The set of possible atomic additions for removing mechanism e_4, $delete(e_4)$, is $\{v_4, v_5\}$ according to Theorem 2.

5 Discussion

This paper formalizes the representation of reversibility of a mechanism to support modeling of changes in structure. We define the reversibility of a mechanism semantically on the set of possible effect variables. This definition allows us to extend the concept of reversible mechanisms from traditional mechanical and physical systems to other systems. We further draw the analogy between the action represented in SEM and STRIPS languages to argue that the context and the effects of an action should be represented explicitly in causal modeling. Our formalization allows us to answer two new types of queries: (1) When manipulating a causal model, which mechanisms are possibly invalidated and can be removed from the model? (2) Which variables may be manipulated in order to invalidate and, effectively, remove a mechanism from a model? In practical applications, it may be desirable to further encode domain knowledge, such as whether a variable is manipulatable ethically and what is the cost of such manipulation, along with each mechanism.

Acknowledgments. This research was supported by the Air Force Office of Scientific Research, grant F49620–00–1–0112 and by the National Science Foundation under Faculty Early Career Development (CAREER) Program, grant IRI–9624629. We thank Denver Dash, Hans van Leijen and Daniel Garcia Sanchez for their helpful comments on the early draft of this paper. We also thank anonymous reviewers for suggestions improving the clarity of the paper. Marek Druzdzel is currently with ReasonEdge Technologies, Pte, Ltd, http://www.reasonedge.com, mjdruzdzel@reasonedge.com.

References

1. Jeroen J.J. Bogers. Supporting the change in structure in a decision support system based on structural equations. Master's thesis, Department of Technical Mathematics and Informatics, Delft University of Technology, Delft, The Netherlands, August 1997.
2. Gregory F. Cooper. An overview of the representation and discovery of causal relationships using Bayesian networks. In Glymour and Cooper [8], chapter one, pages 3–62.
3. Denver Dash and Marek J. Druzdzel. Caveats for causal reasoning with equilibrium models. In *Sixth European Conference on Symbolic and Quantitative Approaches to Reasoning with Uncertainty*, 2001. In this proceeding.
4. Marek J. Druzdzel. *Probabilistic Reasoning in Decision Support Systems: From Computation to Common Sense.* PhD thesis, Department of Engineering and Public Policy, Carnegie Mellon University, Pittsburgh, PA, December 1992.
5. Marek J. Druzdzel and Herbert A. Simon. Causality in Bayesian belief networks. In *Proceedings of the Ninth Annual Conference on Uncertainty in Artificial Intelligence (UAI–93)*, pages 3–11, San Francisco, CA, 1993. Morgan Kaufmann Publishers.
6. Marek J. Druzdzel and Hans van Leijen. Causal reversibility in Bayesian networks. *Journal of Experimental and Theoretical Artificial Intelligence*, 13(1):45–62, Jan 2001.
7. Richard E. Fikes and Nils J. Nilsson. STRIPS: A new approach to the application of theorem proving to problem solving. *Artificial Intelligence*, 2(3-4):189–208, 1971.
8. Clark Glymour and Gregory F. Cooper, editors. *Computation, Causation, and Discovery.* AAAI Press, Menlo Park, CA, 1999.
9. William C. Hood and Tjalling C. Koopmans, editors. *Studies in Econometric Method. Cowles Commission for Research in Economics. Monograph No. 14.* John Wiley & Sons, Inc., New York, NY, 1953.
10. Jacob Marschak. Economic measurements for policy and prediction. In Hood and Koopmans [9], chapter I, pages 1–26.
11. P. Pandurang Nayak. Causal approximations. *Artificial Intelligence*, 70(1–2):1–58, 1994.
12. Judea Pearl. *Causality: Models, Reasoning, and Inference.* Cambridge University Press, Cambridge, UK, 2000.
13. Herbert A. Simon. Causal ordering and identifiability. In Hood and Koopmans [9], chapter III, pages 49–74.
14. Herbert A. Simon. The meaning of causal ordering. In Robert K. Merton, James S. Coleman, and Peter H. Rossi, editors, *Qualitative and Quantitative Social Research: Papers in Honor of Paul F. Lazarsfeld*, chapter 8, pages 65–81. The Free Press, A Division of Macmillan Publishing Co., Inc., 1979.
15. Herbert A. Simon and Nicholas Rescher. Cause and counterfactual. *Philosophy of Science*, 33(4):323–340, December 1966.
16. Peter Spirtes, Clark Glymour, and Richard Scheines. *Causation, Prediction, and Search.* Springer Verlag, New York, 1993.
17. Robert H. Strotz and H.O.A. Wold. Recursive vs. nonrecursive systems: An attempt at synthesis; part I of a triptych on causal chain systems. *Econometrica*, 28(2):417–427, April 1960.
18. Herman Wold. Causality and econometrics. *Econometrica*, 22(2):162–177, April 1954.
19. Herman Wold and Lars Jureen. *Demand Analysis. A Study in Econometrics.* John-Wiley and Sons, Inc., New York, 1953.

The Search of Causal Orderings: A Short Cut for Learning Belief Networks

Silvia Acid, Luis M. de Campos, and Juan F. Huete

Departamento de Ciencias de la Computación e I.A.
E.T.S.I. Informática, Universidad de Granada
18071 - Granada, SPAIN
{acid, lci, jhg}@decsai.ug.es

Abstract. Although we can build a belief network starting from any ordering of its variables, its structure depends heavily on the ordering being selected: the topology of the network, and therefore the number of conditional independence relationships that may be explicitly represented can vary greatly from one ordering to another. We develop an algorithm for learning belief networks composed of two main subprocesses: (a) an algorithm that estimates a causal ordering and (b) an algorithm for learning a belief network given the previous ordering, each one working over different search spaces, the ordering and dag space respectively.

1 Introduction

Belief Networks (also called Bayesian Networks or causal networks) are Knowledge-Based Systems that represent uncertain knowledge by means of both graphical structures and numerical parameters. In a belief network, the qualitative component is a directed acyclic graph (dag), where the nodes represent the variables in the domain, and the arrows represent dependence or causality relationships among the variables. The quantitative component is a collection of conditional probability measures, which measure our uncertainty [15]. The reasons for the success of belief networks are that they allow: (i) to represent the available information in a intelligible way (using causal relationships), (ii) to decompose and store the information efficiently (by means of independence relationships) and (iii) to perform inference tasks.

One of the most interesting problems when dealing with belief networks is that of developing methods capable of learning the network directly from data. As learning belief networks is NP-hard [12], then any kind of previous information about the model to be recovered may be quite useful, in order to facilitate the learning process. This information may be an ordering of the variables in the network [2,10,13,17] or knowledge about the (possible) presence of some causal or (in)dependence relationships [16]. Perhaps an expert may provide this kind of information, but the development of tools capable of obtaining this information as a first step to the learning process is clearly an interesting task.

In this work we focus on the problem of learning belief networks by first obtaining a good ordering on the set of variables. In general, if we look for

S. Benferhat and P. Besnard (Eds.): ECSQARU 2001, LNAI 2143, pp. 216–227, 2001.

an optimal ordering then obtaining it may require as much information as the learning of the complete structure itself, and the calculus may be quite complex as well [6,14]. So, we propose to use only partial (and easily available) information about the problem in order to get a 'good' approximation of the ordering. The type of partial information we use will be a subset of the set of dependence/independence relationships that could be represented in the network (more precisely, marginal and conditional (in)dependence relationships of order one), and the method to perform the search of the ordering will be simulated annealing. Once we have obtained an ordering, it will be supplied to an algorithm for learning belief networks that will use the ordering to reduce the search space. This algorithm, called BENEDICT-*step* [3], is based on a (hybrid) methodology which is a combination of the methods based on independence criteria and the ones based on scoring metrics.

The rest of the paper is organized as follows: in section 2 we briefly recall some general ideas about belief networks, and some basic concepts about simulated annealing. In the next two Sections we describe the components of our method: in Section 3 we present our algorithm to estimate an ordering and Section 4 describes the algorithm BENEDICT-step. Section 5 shows some experiments with the proposed method. Finally, Section 6 contains the concluding remarks.

2 Preliminaries

Given a belief network G, we can extract an ordering θ for its variables in the following way: if there is an arrow $x_j \rightarrow x_i$ in the graph then x_j precedes x_i in the ordering θ, i.e., $\theta(x_j) < \theta(x_i)$. Such an ordering θ is a *causal ordering* [6]. It is interesting to note that, given a dag, the causal ordering is not unique; for example $\theta_1 = \{x_1, x_2, x_3, x_4, x_5, x_6\}$ and $\theta_2 = \{x_1, x_4, x_2, x_3, x_5, x_6\}$ are two valid causal orderings for the first network in Figure 1.

Given any ordering θ, the Markov condition provides a systematic (but impractical) method to build a belief network [15]: for each node x_i, assign, as the parents of x_i in the dag, the minimal subset of predecessors of x_i in the ordering θ which makes x_i conditionally independent of the rest of its predecessors.

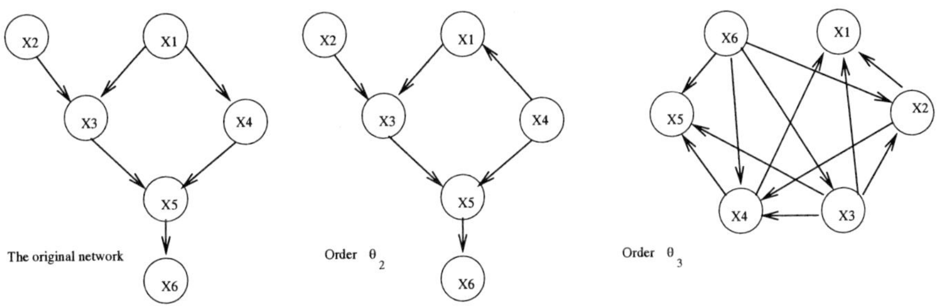

Fig. 1. Original dag and those obtained by using orderings θ_2 and θ_3

However, different orderings may give rise to different networks. For example, let us start from the network in the left hand side of Figure 1. Let $\theta_1 = \{x_1, x_2, x_3, x_4, x_5, x_6\}$, $\theta_2 = \{x_4, x_2, x_1, x_3, x_5, x_6\}$ and $\theta_3 = \{x_6, x_3, x_2, x_4, x_1, x_5\}$ be three different orderings. If we apply the previous process, for θ_1 we recover the original graph, for θ_2 we obtain the second graph, and for the ordering θ_3 we get the much more dense graph on the right hand side of the same figure.

After assigning the corresponding conditional probabilities to the nodes, the three models represent the same joint probability distribution. However, the set of independence relationships represented in these dags is not the same. In the graph associated to θ_3 only a few independences are preserved, whereas using θ_2 we get the same set of dependence/independence relationships as in the original model (the dags corresponding to θ_1 and θ_2 are equivalent according to [18]).

2.1 Learning belief networks

There are a big number of algorithms for learning belief networks from data. However, they can be grouped in two main approaches: methods based on conditional independence tests, and methods based on a scoring metric.

The algorithms based on independence tests (also called constraint-based) carry out a qualitative study on the dependence and independence properties among the variables in the domain, and then they try to find a network representing most of these properties. The number and complexity of the tests are critical for the efficiency and reliability of these methods. Some of the algorithms based on this approach can be found in [10,11,16].

The algorithms based on scoring metrics try to find a graph which has the minimum number of links that 'best' represents the data according to their own metric. They all use a function (the scoring metric) that measures the quality of each candidate structure and an heuristic search method to explore the space of possible solutions. The algorithms that use this approach when the search is in the space of general dags almost invariably use greedy searches. The scoring metrics are based on different principles, such as entropy, Bayesian approaches or Minimum Description Length [7].

2.2 Simulated Annealing

In this section we briefly recall some basic ideas about simulated annealing, the search method we shall use to find a good ordering for the variables in a belief network.

The idea behind simulated annealing [4] is to model numerically the physical annealing process of solids in order to solve optimization problems:

Consider a system composed of N variables and a function E to optimize (called the energy function). Our purpose is to find a configuration c of the N variables that minimizes (or maximizes) the function E. Starting from a random configuration (c_i), representing the current state, we can compute the energy $E(c_i)$ which measures the 'quality' of this configuration. A new configuration c_j can be obtained by applying a perturbation mechanism on c_i. Let $E(c_j)$ be the energy of this state, and ΔE be the difference of energy, i.e., $\Delta E =$

$E(c_j) - E(c_i)$. If the energy decreases, $\Delta E \leq 0$, we accept c_j as the new current state, otherwise c_j is only accepted with a probability given by $\exp\left(-\frac{\Delta E}{T}\right)$, being T the temperature, a control parameter that decreases with time. This criterion allows a 'uphill climb' from a configuration with a lower energy to another with higher energy, thus preventing the process from being trapped at local minima. The procedure continues the search until a stopping criterion is satisfied. This criterion may be based on considering the final temperature (close to zero), the value of the energy function or using a fixed number of iterations.

3 Approximating a Causal Ordering

We seek to find a good causal ordering for the variables in a (unknown) belief network. Given any ordering, it is possible to build a belief network representing the joint probability distribution, this network being an Independence map [15] of the underlying probabilistic model. However, the density of the resultant dag may change drastically depending on the selected ordering. Our goal is to find an ordering able to represent as much true independence relationships as possible. Given this ordering, the search space to find an optimal belief network reduces considerably.

Taking into account that for a network with n nodes, the size of the set of candidate orderings is $n!$, the task of finding an optimal ordering may be quite complex. Several approaches to deal with this problem can be found in the literature:

- *Singh and Valtorta* [17] use conditional independence tests to learn a draft of the network, which is then used to get an ordering. Next, they utilize the K2 algorithm [13] to learn the network.
- *Bouckaert* [6] proposes an algorithm which takes as the input a complete dependence model and an initial ordering, and gives as the output an optimal causal ordering.
- *Larrañaga et al.* [14] use a genetic algorithm to search for the best ordering. Each element of the population is a possible ordering, and their fitness function is the K2 metric.

Our approach is situated between the works of Singh and Valtorta and those of Larrañaga et al. The basic idea is to use only a subset of the (in)dependence relationships of the model to learn a draft of the network and next apply a combinatorial optimization tool to search for the ordering which preserves as much of these dependences and independences as possible.

When dealing with conditional independence relationships whose true values have to be estimated from a database by means of conditional independence tests, two problems appear: the number of tests and their order (i.e., the number of variables involved in the conditioning set). On one hand, the number of conditional independence tests that may be necessary to perform can increase exponentially with the number of variables; on the other hand, computing the truth value of a conditional independence test requires a number of calculations which grows exponentially with the order of the test. Moreover, another problem is not related with efficiency but reliability: conditional independence tests of high order are not reliable except if the size of the database is enormous. So, it may be interesting to restrict the kind of conditional independence tests that we are going to carry out to tests of low order.

We propose using only conditional independence tests of order zero and one (i.e. $I(x_i, x_j|\emptyset)$ and $I(x_i, x_j|x_k)$, respectively) for several reasons: i) these tests are quite reliable even for moderate datasets, ii) the number of tests is polynomial $O(n^3)$, and iii) this set of independences is quite expressive for sparse structures, as those we usually find in real applications. These independences are sufficient even for characterizing and learning some specific kinds of belief networks [8,9]. We shall call *0-1 Independences* to the set of conditional independence relationships of order zero and one which are true for a given model, also denoted as I^M_{0-1}.

Our algorithm will take the set I^M_{0-1} obtained from the data set as the input. In an initialization step, we build a undirected graph (denoted G_{0-1}) as a basic skeleton of the network: starting from the complete undirected graph, we remove those links $x_i - x_j$ such that there is a 0-1 independence between x_i and x_j in I^M_{0-1}. For example, let us suppose that the underlying model is isomorphic to the graph I) in Figure 2. In this case the set of 0-1 Independences is $I^M_{0-1} = \{I(x_2, x_3|x_1)\}$. The initialization step produces the undirected graph II) in Figure 2. In a second step we shall execute the search process, which tries to find an optimal ordering. For any ordering θ being considered, we direct the skeleton G_{0-1} as follows: if $x_i - x_j \in G_{0-1}$, and $\theta(x_j) < \theta(x_i)$ then we direct the link as $x_j \to x_i$. For the example in Figure 2, let us consider the following orderings: $\theta_1 = \{x_1, x_2, x_3, x_4\}$; $\theta_2 = \{x_2, x_3, x_4, x_1\}$; $\theta_3 = \{x_1, x_2, x_4, x_3\}$ and $\theta_4 = \{x_3, x_1, x_2, x_4\}$. Using these orderings we obtain the dags III), IV), V) and VI) respectively in Figure 2.

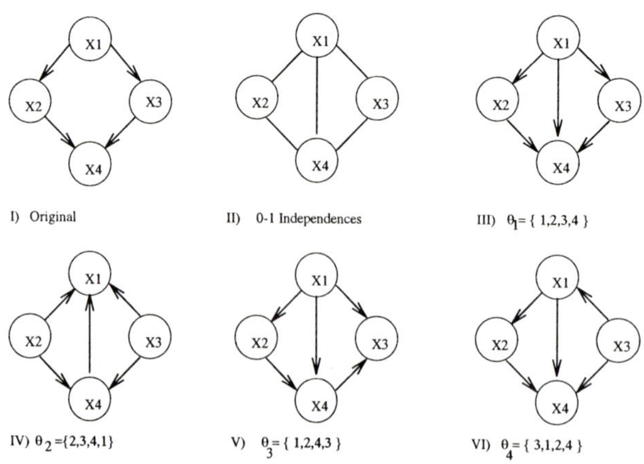

Fig. 2. Different orderings of G_{0-1}

Now, let us describe the different components of the search process:

• *Energy function*: For each configuration (ordering) θ we try to measure the degree $g(\theta)$ in which, after directing G_{0-1} according to the ordering θ (thus obtaining a dag G^{θ}_{0-1}), the dependence and independence relationships in I^{M}_{0-1} are preserved in the dag G^{θ}_{0-1}. Let us denote $I^{G^{\theta}}_{0-1}$ to the set of independence relationships of order zero and one that are valid in G^{θ}_{0-1} (using d-separation) and $\langle .,.|.\rangle$ to any d-separation statement in a dag. So, we count the number of dependence and independence relationships that are true in I^{M}_{0-1} but are not in $I^{G^{\theta}}_{0-1}$. Therefore, our energy function is:

$$g(\theta) = \sum_{x_i,x_j \wedge x_i \neq x_j} (I(x_i,x_j|\emptyset) \otimes \langle x_i,x_j|\emptyset\rangle) + \sum_{x_i,x_j,x_k \wedge x_i \neq x_j \neq x_k} (I(x_i,x_j|x_k) \otimes \langle x_i,x_j|x_k\rangle) \quad (1)$$

where we assume that an independence relationship takes on a binary value (1 for dependence, 0 for independence) and $\otimes$ corresponds to the exclusive-or operator[1]. A value $g(\theta) = 0$ represents that I^{M}_{0-1} and $I^{G^{\theta}}_{0-1}$ are equivalent, and the greater the value of $g(\theta)$ is, the greater number of dependence and independence relationships are not preserved. Obviously, we shall prefer those orderings giving a value of g as low as possible. For the example in Figure 2, we have $g(\theta_1) = 0$, $g(\theta_2) = 2$, $g(\theta_3) = 1$ and $g(\theta_4) = 0$, thus θ_1 and θ_4 are the preferred orderings.

• *Perturbation mechanism:* Each configuration representing an ordering θ is codified as a chain of variables, when x_j appears before x_i then x_j precedes x_i in θ. Given a configuration, the new configuration is obtained by modifying a randomly selected segment s in the current configuration. Two mechanisms (randomly selected with 0.5 probability) have been implemented. The first one, a *transportation* function that moves the segment toward a new random position p (interchanging the elements); the second one is the *inverse* function that inverts the ordering of the variables within the segment.

• *Temperature function:* A proportional decreasing function has been implemented, i.e., $T_k = \alpha T_{k-1}$, where $\alpha \in (0,1)$ and T_0 is a fixed initial temperature.

• *Stopping criterion:* The algorithm stops when: i) all the 0-1 independences have been captured by the current configuration θ, ii) the fitness is not modified after two consecutive iterations or iii) the process has been iterated 10 times.

4 Learning Belief Networks with a Given Ordering

The algorithm we are going to describe, BENEDICT-*step*, utilizes a hybrid methodology: it uses a specific metric and a search procedure (so, it belongs to the group of methods based on scoring metrics), although it also explicitly makes use of the conditional independences embodied in the topology of the network to elaborate the scoring metric and carries out independence tests to limit the search effort

[1] We also tried more quantitative ways of evaluating the goodness of the ordering. The idea is that a link may actually represent a very weak correlation, so its absence may not be so important as the absence of other links representing strong correlations. However, the best results were obtained by using the qualitative measure of eq.(1).

(hence it has also strong similarities with the algorithms based on independence tests). It is part of a family of algorithms [2,3] that share a common methodology for learning belief networks, which we have called BENEDICT.

Let us briefly describe the BENEDICT methodology. The basic idea is to measure the discrepancies between the conditional independences (d-separation statements) represented in any given candidate network G and the ones displayed by the database D. The lesser these discrepancies are, the better the network fits the data. The aggregation of all these (local) discrepancies will result in a measure $g(G, D)$ of global discrepancy between the network and the database.

To measure the discrepancy of each one of the independences in the graphical model and the numerical model (the database), BENEDICT uses the Kullback-Leibler cross entropy:

$$Dep(X, Y|Z) = \sum_{\mathtt{x},\mathtt{y},\mathtt{z}} P(\mathtt{x}, \mathtt{y}, \mathtt{z}) \log \frac{P(\mathtt{x}, \mathtt{y}|\mathtt{z})}{P(\mathtt{x}|\mathtt{z})P(\mathtt{y}|\mathtt{z})},$$

where x, y, z denote instantiations of the sets of variables X, Y and Z respectively, and P is a probability estimated from the database.

As the number and complexity of the d-separation statements in a dag G may grow exponentially with the number of nodes, we cannot use all the d-separations displayed by G, but some selected subset of 'representative' d-separation statements. Given any candidate network G, BENEDICT will take into account the conditional independencies for every two non-adjacent single variables, x_i and x_j given the set of minimum size, $S_G(x_i, x_j)$, that d-separates x_i and x_j [1]. Finding this set takes some additional effort, but it is compensated by a decreasing computing time of the corresponding dependence degree. Moreover, it also increases the reliability of the results, because less data is needed to reliably compute a conditional dependence measure of lower order. The method BENEDICT uses for efficiently finding the sets $S_G(x_i, x_j)$ is described in [1].

In order to give a score to a specific network structure G given a database D, BENEDICT uses the aggregation (the sum) of the local discrepancies, as the measure of global discrepancy $g(G, D)$ (which has to be minimized). Finally, the type of search method used by BENEDICT is a simple greedy search that allows to insert into the structure the candidate arc that produces a greater improvement of the score (removal of arcs is not permitted).

Let us describe more specifically the algorithm BENEDICT-*step*. It works under the assumption that the total ordering of the variables is known (this ordering θ is just the one obtained by the simulated annealing algorithm). BENEDICT-*step* consists in a process composed of n steps, where each step i represents the inclusion of a new node x_i (the i-th node in the ordering θ) in the (initially empty) structure and the inclusion of the necessary arcs to construct the best graph with i nodes, G_i.

At each step i only the d-separation relationships between x_i, the node just introduced, and the previous ones are considered, hence the metric used by BENEDICT-*step* is

$$g(G_i, D) = \sum_{x_j,\, x_j <_\theta x_i \wedge x_j \notin \pi_{G_i}(x_i)} Dep(x_i, x_j | S_{G_i}(x_i, x_j)) \quad (2)$$

Every step i is composed of a series of substeps. Each substep looks for the arc whose addition to the current graph results in a greater decrease of the discrepancy measure between the new graph (that one with the added arc) and the data. The process continues in this way, adding at each substep the single arc $x_j \rightarrow x_i$, $x_j <_\theta x_i$, which most decreases the discrepancy, until the stopping condition holds.

This condition is related with the fact that the algorithm also uses independence tests to remove candidate arcs; in this way, the process stops naturally when there is no more candidate arcs to consider (either because they are already inserted into the structure or because their extreme nodes are found to be independent). At the end of the algorithm a pruning process (also based on independence tests) is triggered (see [3] for details). This pruning partially overcomes some of the problems due to the use of an irrevocable search strategy.

5 Experimental Results

We will consider the performance of the proposed methodology to recover the so-called Alarm belief network (see Figure 3), which has been considered as a benchmark for evaluating learning algorithms. This network contains 37 variables and 46 arcs. The input data commonly used are subsets of the Alarm database which contains 20,000 cases, specifically we used the first 3,000 cases in our experiments.

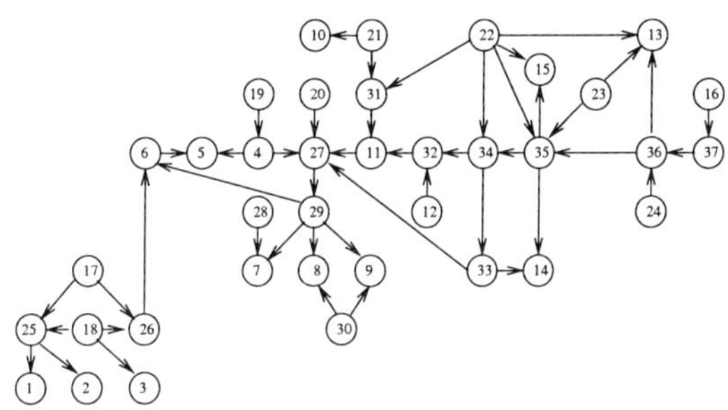

Fig. 3. The Alarm network

As we explained, the learning process is divided in two main processes. Let us first analyze the results of each one separately, and then the final results of the whole process.

The first subprocess consists on searching the 'best' ordering, θ, of the variables using a simulated annealing algorithm. The fitness value used was the number (in percentage) of 0-1 (in)dependences preserved by the current ordering. In order to measure the quality of the ordering we will compare with the Alarm 'correct' ordering. Due to the stochastic nature of the simulated annealing algorithm, we run several times the algorithm with the same training set. In every case the final fitness was 97.0%, resulting different indistinguishable orderings (one of these orderings is the 'correct' ordering). After analyzing the orderings obtained in our experiments we can extract some conclusions:

1. The degree in which the database reflects the set of 0-1 (in)dependences in the true model is important for getting a good output ordering.
2. For those subsets W of variables in the model with no 0-1 independence relationships, we do not have enough information to discriminate which partial orderings, involving the variables in W, are the correct ones. We found different orderings, involving changes in the relative ordering of variables in the set $\{35, 15, 34\}$, with the same fitness value. As we will see, the study of these orderings will be relevant in order to get a better network.
3. There are several orderings with the same fitness value that are indistinguishable even with more information. For example, considering the variables 4 and 19, regardless of the relative ordering used, we get equivalent structures.

The second subprocess consists on, using an ordering θ, let the algorithm BENEDICT-*step* to learn the structure of the network. In order to analyze its behaviour, we supply the BENEDICT-*step* algorithm with the 'correct' ordering and the same training data. From the topology of the learned network we observe: a) There are three missing edges, $11 \rightarrow 27$, $12 \rightarrow 32$ and $21 \rightarrow 31$. The last two arcs are not strongly supported by the data, as it was reported by several authors. b) There is one extra arc between variables 31 and 27 which has not been determined as independent by the independence tests; this arc is set while trying to compensate the loss of the arc $11 \rightarrow 27$ (a total of 4 different arcs from the original model). We have also computed several other measures to evaluate the quality of the learned network from different points of view. These measures are: 1.- the Kullback[2] distance between the probability distribution associated to the database and the probability distribution associated to the learned network. 2.- The K2 metric [13] (log version) and 3.- the BIC metric (Bayesian Information Criterion) which includes a penalty term. Finally we compare all these collected measures with those obtained by the K2 algorithm [13], running both algorithms on the same conditions. The results shown in the first row of Table 1 allow us to conclude that our algorithm is competitive and recovers a good model.

Now we are going to analyze the results obtained in the whole process. Usually when no ordering is known, the learning algorithm has to cope with the entire dag space to learn the network. We can make a comparison[3] between the two steps method proposed and the single searching process. For that purpose we have used a constraint based algorithm, BN Power Constructor (BNPC) [11] (we use the software package available at `http://www.cs.ualberta.ca/~jcheng/bnsoft.htm`). In Table 2 we show the results obtained by the BNPC algorithm which are worse than those obtained by any of the different orderings θ, used as entry to the algorithms BENEDICT-*step* and K2. All these orderings were score-equivalent for the simulated annealing process.

[2] Actually, we have calculated a decreasing monotonic transformation of the Kullback distance computed in a very efficient form [8]. The interpretation is: the higher this parameter the better is the network.

[3] We do not compare the running times because the three algorithms considered, run on different platforms and are implemented using different programming languages.

In order to focus on how some local misplacements in the ordering can modify the resulting learned network, we have studied the possible cases found by simulated annealing involving the relative orderings between 34, 35 and 15. As we said, simulated annealing is not capable to discriminate among these orderings, thus any configuration would be a possible input to the BENEDICT-*step* algorithm. As we could expect, they give rise to different networks. Table 1 presents the results obtained when we consider three orderings that differ only in the relative ordering of the variables 34, 35 and 15. As we can observe, some of the orderings are worse than others, and the output belief network structure depends on how lucky we were, in the first subprocess. As the ordering is obtained by using only partial information (0-1 Independences), its quality might be questioned. Hopefully, we do not have to reconsider the global ordering. In the general case, the set of 0-1 Independences is quite significant, so the learned structure is a 'good' representation of the model. Anyway, we thought about that BENEDICT-*step* with more information could detect some misplacements between variables in θ and could discriminate among indistinguishable orderings. Note that a 'bad' ordering (as for example the order θ_3 in Figure 1) tends to create cliques (we consider cliques having at least three nodes) among the variables involved.

Table 1. Comparison between the algorithms BENEDICT-*step* and K2

	BENEDICT-*step*				K2				Relative ordering
Ordering	Kullback	Hamming	BIC	K2	Kullback	Hamming	BIC	K2	
'correct'	9.20	4	-33919	-14425	9.23	2	-34351	-14424	
θ_1	9.11	14	-34830	-14624	9.21	12	-35697	-14520	$34 \prec 15 \prec 35$
θ_2	9.18	12	-34606	-14533	9.23	8	-36205	-14494	$34 \prec 35 \prec 15$
θ_3	9.21	8	-34358	-14479	9.23	5	-35203	-14450	$35 \prec 34 \prec 15$

Table 2. Performance measures for the network learned by BNPC

Kullback	Hamming	BIC	K2
9.12	7	-35197	-14541

We have developed a heuristic rule that, using the information stored in the output network, allows us to obtain a sparser representation of the same model. This refinement is carried out by determining local rearrangements in θ, giving rise to also local changes in the structure, but improving the quality of the output network. Basically the heuristics consists on selecting a variable x_i in a clique and generating a new ordering θ^*, where this variable changes its relative position with respect to some variables in the clique.

In Table 1, from the ordering θ_1 to θ_3, we can follow the steps of our heuristic focused on variables 34, 35 and 15. We make the comparisons taking as reference the structure obtained by BENEDICT-*step* when it uses the Alarm 'correct' ordering as the input (the initial erroneous arcs remain). Thus, taking the worst ordering, $34 \prec 15 \prec 35$, as the input, our first change involves the variables 15 and 35 (the last two variables in the clique), giving rise to a sparser network and also with a better fitness, which is accepted as the current one. Then, using the same reasoning, the change between variables 35 and 34 is performed. Note that the resulting ordering is the correct relative ordering. The algorithm stops at this point.

6 Concluding Remarks

We have addressed the problem of learning belief networks from data by means of a two steps process: estimating a good ordering of the variables (thus reducing the search space for the belief network learning algorithm) and then using a learning algorithm that exploits this ordering. The search for a good ordering is carried out by means of a simulated annealing method, which uses a function based on independence tests of order zero and one to measure the fitness. The algorithm that uses this ordering to learn the network is a member of the BENEDICT family, whose main characteristics are its hybrid nature and the use of d-separating sets of minimum size.

In addition to the specific algorithms that we use to develop our method, the main methodological difference with respect to other approaches [14,17] is that the two subprocesses are run independently on each other (this means that we carry out two 'simple' different search processes (over different spaces) instead of a single search process which intermingles the orderings and the graph structures).

In general, to obtain an optimal solution to the problem of finding a causal ordering, it would be necessary to learn the network (i.e., to have information about the complete set of valid conditional independence statements). Our experiments show that our approximate method (based on conditional independence tests of low order, for reasons of reliability, expressiveness and efficiency) is quite successful. Its combination with BENEDICT-*step* gives a very general and competitive algorithm for learning belief networks. However, a thorough experimental work, using networks of different complexity, is necessary in order to obtain definitive conclusions.

In future works we plan to continue the development of heuristic rules allowing the algorithm BENEDICT-*step* (or any other learning algorithm that requires an ordering) to make local rearrangements in the ordering to improve the quality of the learned network. We will also study methods that refine a given ordering (e.g., the output ordering provided by our algorithms) to obtain an optimal solution. These methods could be based on the idea of the reliability about the particular position of any given variable x_i in the ordering, which in turn is directly related to the number of 0-1 independences where this variable x_i is involved.

Acknowledgments. This work has been supported by the Spanish Comisión Interministerial de Ciencia y Tecnología under Project n. TIC2000-1351. We would like to thank the anonymous referees for their useful comments.

References

1. S. Acid and L.M. de Campos. An algorithm for finding minimum d-separating sets in belief networks. In *Proceedings of the Conference on Uncertainty in Artificial Intelligence*, E. Horvitz, F. Jensen (Eds.), pages 3-10 Morgan and Kaufmann, 1996.
2. S. Acid and L.M. de Campos. Benedict: An algorithm for learning probabilistic belief netwoks. In *Proceedings of Information Processing and Management of Uncertainty in Knowledge-Based Systems*, pages 979-984, 1996.
3. S. Acid and L.M. de Campos. An hybrid methodology for learning belief networks: Benedict. To appear in International Journal of Approximate Reasoning.
4. N. Ansari and E. Hou. *Computational Intelligence for Optimization.* Kluwer Academic Publishers, 1997.
5. I. Beinlich, H. Seurmondt, R. Chavez, and G. Cooper. The alarm monitoring system: a case study with two probabilistic inference techniques for belief networks. In *Proceedings of the Second European Conference on Artificial Intelligence in Medicine*, pages 247-256, 1989.
6. R. Bouckaert. Optimizing causal orderings for generating dag's from data. In *Proc. Conf. on Uncertainty in Artificial Intelligence*, pages 9-16. Morgan-Kaufmann, 1992.
7. W. Buntine. A guide to the literature on learning probabilistic networks from data. *IEEE Transaction on Knowledge and Data Engineering,* 8:195-210, 1996.
8. L.M. de Campos. Independency relationships and learning algorithms for singly connected networks. *Journal of Experimental and Theoretical Artificial Intelligence* 10:511-549, 1998.
9. L.M. de Campos and J.F. Huete. On the use of independence relationships for learning simplified belief networks. *Int. J. of Intelligent Systems*, 12:495-522, 1997.
10. L.M. de Campos and J.F. Huete. A new approach for learning belief networks using independence criteria. *International Journal of Approximate Reasoning*, 24(1)11-37, 2000.
11. J. Cheng, D.A. Bell and W. Liu. Learning belief networks form data: An information theory based approach In *Proc. of ACM CIKM'97*, pages 325-331, 1997.
12. D. Chickering, D. Geiger, and D. Heckerman. Learning Bayesian Networks is np-hard. Technical Report MSR-TR-94-17, Microsoft Research, 1994.
13. G.F. Cooper and E. Herskovits. A Bayesian method for the induction of probabilistic networks from data. *Machine Learning*, 9:309-347, 1992.
14. P. Larrañaga, C.M. Kuijpers, R.H. Murga, and Y. Yurramendi. Learning Bayesian network structure by searching for the best ordering with genetic algorithms. *IEEE Transactions on Systems, Man and Cybernetics- Part A: Systems and Humans*, 26(4):487-493, 1996.
15. J. Pearl. *Probabilistic Reasoning in Intelligent Systems: Networks of Plausible Inference.* Morgan and Kaufmann, 1988.
16. P. Spirtes, C. Glymour, and R. Scheines. *Causation, Prediction and Search.* Lecture Notes in Statistics 81. Springer Verlag, New York, 1993.
17. M. Singh and M. Valtorta. Construction of Bayesian networks structures from data: A survey and an efficient algorithm. *International Journal of Approximate Reasoning*, 12:111-131, 1995.
18. T. Verma and J. Pearl. Equivalence and synthesis of causal models. In *Proceedings of the Conference on Uncertainty in Artificial Intelligence*, pages 220-227, Mass, 1990.

Stochastic Local Algorithms for Learning Belief Networks: Searching in the Space of the Orderings

Luis M. de Campos[1] and J. Miguel Puerta[2]

[1] Dpto de Ciencias de la Computación e I.A.
Universidad de Granada
18071 - Granada, Spain
lci@decsai.ugr.es
[2] Dpto de Informática
Universidad de Castilla-La Mancha
02071 - Albacete, Spain
jpuerta@info-ab.uclm.es

Abstract. An important type of methods for learning belief networks from data are those based on the use of a scoring metric, to evaluate the fitness of any given candidate network to the data base, and a search procedure to explore the set of candidate networks. In this paper we propose a new method that carries out the search not in the space of directed acyclic graphs but in the space of the orderings of the variables that compose the graphs. Moreover, we use a new stochastic search method to be applied to this problem, Variable Neighborhood Search. We also experimentally compare our methods with some other search procedures commonly used in the literature.

Keywords: Belief Networks, Causal Orderings, Learning, Variable Neighborhood Search, Stochastic Hill-Climbing Search.

1 Introduction

Belief Networks (BNs), also known as Bayesian Networks or Causal Networks, are knowledge representation tools able to efficiently manage the dependence and independence relationships among the random variables that compose the problem domain we want to model. This representation has two components: a) a graphical structure, more precisely a directed acyclic graph (dag), and b) a set of parameters, which together specify a joint probability distribution over the random variables [20]. In belief networks, the graphical structure represents dependence and independence relationships. The numerical component is a collection of conditional probability measures, which shape the relationships.

Once we have the belief network specified, it constitutes an efficient device to perform inference tasks. However, there still remains the previous problem of building such a network. So, an interesting task is to develop automatic methods capable of learning the network directly from data, as an alternative or a complement to the method of eliciting opinions from experts.

S. Benferhat and P. Besnard (Eds.): ECSQARU 2001, LNAI 2143, pp. 228–239, 2001.

Nowadays, the problem of learning or estimating a belief network from data is receiving increasing attention within the community of researchers into uncertainty in artificial intelligence. Algorithms for learning (the structure of) BNs have been studied, basically from two points of view: Methods based on conditional independence tests [5,6,7,22,23] and methods based on a scoring metric optimization [12,16,17]. This classification is not exhaustive and/or strict, there also exist algorithms that use a combination of these two methods [1,2,13,21]. In this paper we only consider learning methods based on a scoring metric.

As learning belief networks is, in general, a NP-Hard problem [11], we have to solve it with heuristic methods. Most existing scoring-based learning algorithms apply standard heuristic search techniques, such as greedy hill-climbing, simulated annealing (local search), genetic algorithms, etc. In this paper we focus on local search methods, more precisely stochastic hill-climbing methods. These methods examine only possible local changes at each step, and apply the one that leads to the greatest improvement in the scoring function. When the search process is carried out in the space of dags, the usual choices for local changes are arc addition, arc deletion and arc reversal. Thus, there are $O(n^2)$ possible changes, where n is the number of variables.

However, several authors [18,14,8] have shown that the space of orderings of the variables is much 'smoother' than the space of dags. Moreover, it is also known that, by providing a good ordering of the variables, the learning algorithms become more efficient and accurate. In fact, there is a number of algorithms that need to use such an ordering [1,2,7,10,12]. Therefore, our proposal is to develop learning methods that carry out the search process in the space of the orderings instead of the space of dags.

The search method that we are going to adapt to our problem is, in addition to classical hill-climbing, the recently developed Variable Neighborhood Search (VNS) [15,19], which is a metaheuristic that uses a systematic change of neighborhood within a randomized local search algorithm.

The paper is structured as follows: we begin in Section 2 with the preliminaries. In Section 3 we formalize our proposal of learning belief networks by searching in the space of the orderings: we define our search space, the admissible local changes to move within this space and how to efficiently carry out the evaluation of the different orderings. In Section 4 we introduce the Variable Neighborhood Search. In section 5 we propose two learning algorithms based on orderings: one uses a hill-climbing search and the other uses VNS. In Section 6 we present the experimental evaluation. Finally, Section 7 contains the concluding remarks.

2 Preliminaries

In this section we briefly review BNs and how to learn them. A BN is a directed acyclic graph $G = (\boldsymbol{V}, E)$, where $\boldsymbol{V}$, a set of nodes, represents the system variables and E, a set of arcs, represents the dependence relationships among the variables. A set of parameters is also stored for each variable in $\boldsymbol{V}$, usually conditional probability distributions. For each variable $x_i \in \boldsymbol{V}$ we have a family of conditional distributions $P(x_i|Pa_G(x_i))$, where $Pa_G(x_i)$ represents the parent set of the variable x_i. From these conditional distributions we can recover the joint distribution over $\boldsymbol{V}$:

$$P(x_1, x_2, \ldots, x_n) = \prod_{i=1}^{n} P(x_i|Pa_G(x_i)) \tag{1}$$

This expression represents a decomposition of the joint distribution. The dependence/independence relationships which make possible this decomposition are graphically encoded (through the d-separation criterion [20]) by means of the presence or absence of direct connections between pairs of variables.

The problem of learning a BN can be stated as follows: given a *training set* $D = \{\mathbf{v}^1, \ldots, \mathbf{v}^m\}$ of instances of $\boldsymbol{V}$, find the BN that best matches D. The common approach to this problem is to introduce a scoring function, f, that evaluates each network with respect to the training data, and then to search for the best network according to this score. Different Bayesian and non-Bayesian scoring metrics can be used [1,4,12,16,17].

A desirable and important property of a metric is its decomposability in presence of full data, i.e, the scoring function can be decomposed in the following way:

$$f(G:D) = \sum_{i=1}^{n} f(x_i|Pa_G(x_i) : N_{x_i, Pa_G(x_i)}) \tag{2}$$

where $N_{x_i, Pa_G(x_i)}$ are the statistics of the variable x_i and $Pa_G(x_i)$ in D, i.e., the number of instances in D that match each possible instantiation of x_i and $Pa_G(x_i)$. The decomposition of the metric is very important for the learning task: a local search procedure that changes one arc at each move can efficiently evaluate the improvement obtained by this change. Such a procedure can reuse the computations made in previous stages. An example is a greedy hill-climbing method that at each step performs the local change that yields the maximal gain, until it reaches a local maximum. As this procedure is trapped in the first local maximum it reaches, several methods for avoiding this situation have been used, such as stochastic hill-climbing, simulated annealing, tabu search, etc. The main representative of stochastic hill-climbing is hill-climbing with random restart, which has been used by several authors with relative success (see [16] for more details). This fact has motivated us to try a new search method based on the same principles that the previous one, but with a systematic and reasonable random search in a larger neighborhood at each step if the current local search does not improve the best current maximum. This method, VNS [19], has been applied to solve optimization problems with successful results.

For a dag G, given a causal ordering θ (i.e., an ordering compatible with the topology of the dag[1]), the following independence relationships are true: x_i is conditionally independent of all the variables that precede it in the ordering,

[1] if there is an arc $x_i \rightarrow x_j$, then $\theta(x_i) < \theta(x_j)$.

given its parent set $Pa_G(x_i)$, for all x_i. This fact provides a systematic method to build belief networks: for each node x_i, the parents of x_i in the dag are the minimal subset of predecessors of x_i (in the ordering θ) which makes x_i conditionally independent of the rest of its predecessors.

However, different orderings may produce different networks. We would prefer those networks that are able to represent as much true independence relationships as possible (i.e., having as few arcs as possible). For that reason it makes sense to search for the best ordering.

3 Searching in the Space of the Orderings

Let us assume that we want to find a belief network for a problem having n variables, $\boldsymbol{V}=\{x_1, x_2, \ldots, x_n\}$, and we have a database of cases D. Although we are looking for a network, we are going to perform a main search process in the space of the orderings for the variables in $\boldsymbol{V}$, and this search will be guided by a scoring function, that evaluates the network obtained from the given ordering by means of a secondary search process (in the space of the dags compatible with this ordering).

So, our search space is the set of $n!$ orderings, θ, of the variables in $\boldsymbol{V}$ (i.e., the set of permutations of n elements). Now, we have to define the operator to move from one configuration to another neighboring configuration in this space. We propose to use the interchange between two positions i and j in the sequence defining an ordering. More precisely, if θ is the current configuration, then the $n(n-1)/2$ neighboring configurations of θ are those orderings θ_{ij}, where $i<j$, defined as follows:

Let x_u and x_v such that $\theta(x_u)=i$ and $\theta(x_v)=j$. Then

$$\theta_{ij}(x_k)=\begin{cases}\theta(x_k) & \text{if } x_k \neq x_u \text{ and } x_k \neq x_v\\ j & \text{if } x_k = x_u\\ i & \text{if } x_k = x_v\end{cases}$$

Now, we have to decide how to evaluate the quality of an ordering θ. Our proposal is to use a scoring metric, f, defined for dags and to perform a search process in the space of dags compatible with θ. The scoring value of the obtained dag G_θ, $f(G_\theta : D)$, will be the value of θ ($f(\theta : D) = f(G_\theta : D)$). For example, we can use a (deterministic) hill-climbing algorithm with operators of arc addition and arc removal (arc reversal has no sense because the ordering is fixed). In other words, we have to find the best parent set of each variable x_k among the variables that precede x_k in the ordering θ. The search of the parent set of a variable x_k can be done independently of the parent sets of the other variables.

However, if the metric f being used is decomposable, we should try to take advantage of this fact to reduce the complexity of evaluating an ordering θ_{ij}, by using as much information about the evaluation of θ as possible. As θ has been already evaluated, we know that

$$f(\theta : D)=\sum_{k=1}^{n} f(x_k|Pa_{G_\theta}(x_k) : N_{x_k,Pa_{G_\theta}(x_k)})$$

Therefore, for the nodes x_k such that $\theta(x_k) < i$ or $\theta(x_k) > j$, the set of predecessors of x_k will be the same for θ and for θ_{ij}, so that we can be sure that

$$Pa_{G_{\theta_{ij}}}(x_k) = Pa_{G_\theta}(x_k)$$

and we do not need to calculate $f(x_k|Pa_{G_{\theta_{ij}}}(x_k) : N_{x_k,Pa_{G_{\theta_{ij}}}(x_k)})$.

For the nodes x_k such that $i \leq \theta(x_k) \leq j$, their sets of predecessors change, so that we are forced to search again for their parent sets. For each one of these nodes x_k, we start from an empty parent set and, by applying the operators of arc addition and arc removal, perform a hill-climbing search.

With the aim of improving the efficiency of the search process, we are going to restrict, by means of a parameter, r (radius), the number of neighboring configurations. The only admissible neighbors of a given ordering θ are those orderings θ_{ij} such that the 'distance' between the variables to be interchanged is not greater than r, i.e., $|j-i| \leq r$. This will allow to speed up the search process, because each configuration has less neighbors (exactly $r(n-(r+1)/2)$), and the discarded neighbors are precisely the ones whose evaluation is more complex. A radius $r = n-1$ is equivalent to no restriction. If the starting point of the search process is a good ordering, we believe that a drastic change in this ordering (i.e., to interchange two very distant nodes) is not expected to produce an important improvement in the score. In any case, an interchange betwen two distant nodes x_u and x_v can also be obtained by performing successive interchanges involving x_u, x_v and some intermediate nodes (for example, an interchange of lenght $|j-i|$ may be obtained by means of three interchanges of lenght $|j-i|/2$).

4 Variable Neighborhood Search

In this section we review the rules of the basic VNS and apply them for learning belief networks.

Let us denote a finite set of pre-selected neighborhood structures with $\mathcal{N}_k$ ($k = 1, \ldots, k_{max}$), and let $\mathcal{N}_k(x)$ be the set of solutions in the kth neighborhood of x (heuristic local search usually uses one neighborhood structure, i.e., $k_{max} = 1$). The basic VNS heuristic comprises the following steps:

Initialization. Select the set of neighborhood structures $\mathcal{N}_k$, $k = 1, \ldots, k_{max}$, that will be used in the search; find an initial solution x; choose a stopping criterion.

Repeat the following until the stopping criterion is met:

(a) Set $k = 1$; Until $k = k_{max}$, repeat the following steps:

- (a.1) *Shaking.* Generate a solution x' at random from the kth neighborhood of x ($x' \in \mathcal{N}_k(x)$).
- (a.2) *Local search.* Apply some local search method with x' as the initial solution; denote with x'' the solution obtained as local optimum.
- (a.3) *Move or not.* If this local optimum is better than the incumbent, move there ($x \leftarrow x''$), and continue the search with $\mathcal{N}_1 (k = 1)$; otherwise, set $k = k + 1$.

The stopping condition may be based, for example, on maximum running time, maximum number of iterations (of step (a)), or maximum number of iterations (of step (a)) between two improvements. Note that point x' is generated at random in order to avoid cycling, which might occur if any deterministic rule were used.

Once we have an appropriate local search method for an optimization problem, it is easy to program steps (a.1) and (a.3) of the basic VNS. For example, if $\mathcal{N}_k$ is obtained by k-interchanges of solution attributes (as will be our case), only a few lines have to be added to an existing code for a local search method.

The basic VNS is a descent (ascent) first improvement method. Without much additional effort it could be transformed into a descent-ascent method (in step (a.3) set also $x \leftarrow x''$ with some probability even if the solution is worse than the incumbent). Of course, this variant is reminiscent of simulated annealing. Other variants of the basic VNS include:

- Introduce k_{min} and k_{step}, two parameters that control the movement between neighborhood structures, i.e., in the previous algorithm, instead of $k = 1$, set $k = k_{min}$ and instead of $k = k + 1$, set $k = k + k_{step}$. These parameters guide the intensification and diversification of the search.
- Remove the local search. This variant, which is denoted as Reduced VNS, is useful for very large problems for which local search is costly. This works in similar way to the Monte-Carlo method but in a more systematic way. Its relationship with the Monte-Carlo method is the same as that of VNS to multi-start methods.

When using more than one neighborhood structure in the search, as it is done in VNS, the following problem specific questions have to be answered:

- What $\mathcal{N}_k$ should be used and how many of them?
- What should be their order in the search?
- What search strategy should be used in changing neighborhoods?

Furthermore, we must decide what local search routine will be used in the local search step.

5 Learning Algorithms Based on Orderings

We have a database $D = \{\mathbf{v}^1, \ldots, \mathbf{v}^m\}$, containing m instances of $\boldsymbol{V}$. We assume a given decomposable scoring metric $f(G : D)$ for dags. Let Θ_n be the set of all the orderings of n elements and $\mathcal{G}_\theta$ be the family of all dags G whose set of vertices is $\boldsymbol{V}$ and whose arcs are compatible with the ordering θ. The problem considered is then:

$$\text{Find} \quad \theta^* = \arg\max_{\theta \in \Theta_n} f(\theta : D) \tag{3}$$

where

$$f(\theta : D) = f(G_\theta : D) = \max_{G \in \mathcal{G}_\theta} f(G : D) \tag{4}$$

Thus, we first find the best dag, G_θ (according to the selected metric f), compatible with an ordering θ, and next select the ordering θ^* that has produced the best dag. The dag G_{θ^*} is the desired solution of our learning problem. We tackle this problem from a heuristic point of view: the two optimization processes are solved using search methods.

The (approximate) solution to the problem in Equation (4) will be obtained by using the search process of dags described in Section 3 (i.e., a hill-climbing search of the best parent set of each node in $\boldsymbol{V}$).

To solve the problem in Equation (3), we propose two alternatives. The first one is to also use a hill-climbing search in the space of the orderings (with the operator of interchange of two positions described in Section 3, and a fixed radius). We call this algorithm HCSO (*H*ill-*C*limbing *S*earch based on *O*rderings).

The second alternative is to use a VNS. This algorithm will be called VNSO (*V*ariable *N*eighborhood *S*earch based on *O*rderings). To do this, we need to define the neighborhood structures $\mathcal{N}_k$. $\mathcal{N}_1$ will be the neighborhood defined by the operator of interchange of any two positions, i.e.,

$$\theta' \in \mathcal{N}_1(\theta) \Longleftrightarrow \theta'(x_u) = \theta(x_v),\ \theta'(x_v) = \theta(x_u) \text{ and } \theta'(x_k) = \theta(x_k)\ \forall x_k \neq x_u, x_v$$

$\mathcal{N}_2$ will be defined by the interchange of two pairs of positions, i.e.,

$$\theta'' \in \mathcal{N}_2(\theta) \Longleftrightarrow \theta'' \in \mathcal{N}_1(\theta') \text{ and } \theta' \in \mathcal{N}_1(\theta)$$

Similarly,

$$\theta'' \in \mathcal{N}_k(\theta) \Longleftrightarrow \theta'' \in \mathcal{N}_1(\theta') \text{ and } \theta' \in \mathcal{N}_{k-1}(\theta)$$

The search strategy between neighborhoods that we are going to use is the one used in the basic VNS ($k = 1$ and at each step $k = k + 1$). As stopping criterion we use the maximum number of iterations between two improvements, together with a maximum number of total iterations.

The local search chosen for the step (a.2) of VNSO is just HCSO. However, instead of using HCSO with a fixed radius r and, in accordance with the search strategy used by VNS, we propose an updating scheme for this parameter: when we move from $\mathcal{N}_k$ to a greater neighborhood $\mathcal{N}_{k+1}$, we also increase the radius (from r to $r + 1$), and when we move to $\mathcal{N}_1$, the radius is set to its initial value.

6 Experimental Evaluation of the Algorithms

In order to test the behavior of the methods proposed in the paper, we have selected the ALARM network [3]. This network has 37 nodes and 46 arcs and is used for diagnosis in a medical domain. It has been considered as a benchmark for evaluating learning algorithms. All the experiments have been carried out on the first 10000 cases of the ALARM database (and comparing the results with the true ALARM network). The scoring function used in all the experiments is the K2 metric [12].

We have run the HCSO with two different radii: $r = 36$ (the maximum radius in this case) and $r = 7$. For VNSO, we have used $k_{max} = 7$ and the initial radius is $r = 7$. We have also used three different options to obtain the initial solution:

- S-PC: Learning a network using the PC algorithm [22] and extracting a topological ordering.
- S-$\emptyset$: To start from an empty dag and an arbitrary ordering (in our case we used the ordering of the variables in the database).
- S-K2SN: To initialize the search with the result of the algorithm K2SN [9]. This algorithm is an extension of the algorithm K2 that does not require a given ordering: Starting from an empty graph, K2SN iteratively determines the best node to add, until all the nodes have been included in the graph. At each step, the best parent set for each node not previously introduced in the structure is selected (among the nodes already included in the graph, as the K2 algorithm does) and the node producing the best score is added to the graph, linking it to its corresponding parent set. In this way K2SN returns an ordering and a graph compatible with this ordering.

As stopping criterion, we have chosen a maximal number of two iterations without improvement, combined with a maximal number of three total iterations.

In order to compare our algorithms with the classical local search methods, we also use the classical hill-climbing in the space of dags (HCST), with operators of arc addition, arc removal and arc reversal, and the same three initialization methods.

6.1 Experimental Results

The information we have collected from each experiment is the following: the value of the K2 metric (log) of the best individual evaluated; the number of arcs added (A), deleted (D) and inverted (I), compared with the true ALARM network; the number of iterations carried out by the algorithm, i.e., the total number of hill-climbing searches carried out (nS); the total number of individuals evaluated during the search (nE); the total number of statistics (local scores) used (tS); the total number of different statistics calculated (tSC) (using a hashing method, we do not need to recalculate a local score already computed); the mean number of variables involved in the statistics (mV); finally, we also display the value (KL) of the best individual evaluated, which is defined as follows:

$$KL(G:D) = \sum_{\substack{i=1 \\ Pa(x_i)\neq\emptyset}}^{n} Dep(x_i, Pa(x_i)) \tag{5}$$

where:

$$Dep(\boldsymbol{X},\boldsymbol{Y}) = \sum_{\mathrm{x}_i,\mathrm{y}_j} P(\mathrm{x}_i,\mathrm{y}_j)\frac{P(\mathrm{x}_i,\mathrm{y}_j)}{P(\mathrm{x}_i)P(\mathrm{y}_j)} \tag{6}$$

Note that $KL(G:D)$ is a decreasing monotonic transformation of the Kullback distance between the probability distribution associated to the database and the probability distribution associated to the network G [5] (we use this transformation because it can be calculated very efficiently, whereas the computation of the Kullback distance has an exponential complexity). The interpretation of $KL(G : D)$ is: the higher this parameter the better is the network.

So, we have collected five measures of the quality of the learned networks (K2, KL, A, D and I) and five measures of the complexity of the search methods (nS, nE, tS, tSC and mV). nE represents the number of dags evaluated in the case of HCST, and the number of orderings evaluated for HCSO and VNSO. tSC is an interesting measure because computing a new local score (not previously stored) requires accessing to the database and it can be a time-consuming process. The complexity of the calculus of these local scores increases exponentially with the value of mV. Although the cost of accessing to the value of a stored local score is much smaller, it is also interesting to know the value tS, because all these local scores have been actually used to compute the (global) scoring values. The measures nE, tS and tSC do not include the cost of the initialization step in the S-PC case (which is quite high).

The results of the experiments are displayed in Tables 1, 2 and 3. For VNSO, the experiments have been carried out ten times. Table 2 displays the average value μ and the standard desviation σ of each item.

Table 1. Results for HCSO.

Radius = 36				Radius = 7			
	Empty	K2SN	PC		Empty	K2SN	PC
K2	-47080.22	-47076.20	-47109.89	K2	-47513.60	-47079.60	-47117.67
KL	9.2740	9.2740	9.2655	KL	9.2687	9.2762	9.2639
A	1	1	1	A	23	4	2
D	1	1	2	D	3	1	3
I	0	0	0	I	11	0	0
nS	1	1	1	nS	1	1	1
nE	17316	3330	3996	nE	7280	1300	3120
tSC	51609	20160	26263	tSC	18333	11384	17266
tS	1.39E7	2.52E6	2.96E6	tS	2.88E6	4.27E5	9.73E5
mV	4.83	4.35	4.39	mV	4.67	4.15	4.36

The best result found by the search algorithms is a network with a value of the K2 metric equal to -47076.20 (VNSO-S-∅, VNSO-S-K2SN and HCSO-S-K2SN are all able to obtain this network). Note that the K2 and KL values of the true ALARM network for the database being used are equal to -47086.57 and 9.2744, respectively.

First, we have to note that the initialization method used is quite relevant from the point of view of the quality of the obtained result (K2, A, D, and I values) and the efficiency of the search process (nS, nE, tSC and tS values) for all the methods (Table 4 displays the K2 and KL values for the different initial networks). The best initialization is always produced by the K2SN algorithm (particularly, a simple HCSO initialized with K2SN produces the best result). This is not surprising for VNSO and HCSO because K2SN is explicitly designed to work with orderings, but is somewhat surprising for HCST. Another interesting result is that the more informed initialization S-PC is not better than the 'vacuous' initialization S-∅ when searching in the space of the orderings (the exception is HCSO with a small radius). It seems to us that PC directs the process towards a suboptimal local maximum, which is difficult to offset by the search process.

Table 2. Results for VNSO.

	Empty		K2SN		PC	
	μ	σ	μ	σ	μ	σ
K2	-47087.39	12.26	-47076.49	0.90	-47110.08	0.41
KL	9.2731	0,004	9.2740	0.000	9.2655	0.000
A	4.5	3.03	1.8	0.42	1.9	0.32
D	1.6	0.52	1.0	0.0	2.0	0.0
I	0.8	1.03	0.0	0.0	0.0	0.0
nS	181.0	99.3	96.1	29.02	68.6	17.3
nE	327335	204091	179865	55924	99061	30844
tSC	68087	11680	49902	5664	54670	7832
tS	5.98E7	2.73E7	4.16E7	1.12E7	2.43E7	6.53E6
mV	4,96	0,06	4.79	0,08	4.85	0.1

The results obtained support the conclusion that searching in the space of the orderings is a good idea: Both VNSO and HCSO outperform HCST in all the cases (except HCSO-S-∅[2]).

Table 3. Results for HCST.

	Empty	K2SN	PC
K2	-47267.11	-47081.66	-47133.41
KL	9.2657	9.2761	9.2708
A	11	3	3
D	4	1	1
I	6	0	2
nS	1	1	1
nE	72335	15820	17901
tSC	3280	5384	1804
tS	1.47E5	5.56E4	3.65E4
mV	2.98	3.65	3.21

Focusing on the methods that search in the space of the orderings, restricting the search process by using a small radius produces results slighty worse than the unrestricted search, from the point of view of the solution quality, but with an important gain in efficiency. We conjecture that a radius of about a half of the maximum radius would be an optimal choice. On the other hand, VNSO is better than HCSO if we use the same radius, as we could expect. However, HCSO with maximum radius ($r = 36$) behaves even a bit better than VNSO

[2] remember that this initialization uses the ordering of the variables in the database, which is a particularly bad ordering.

with small radius ($r = 7$). We also conjecture that VNSO equipped with a radius of about one third of the maximum radius would produce excellent results.

Table 4. K2 and KL values for the three initial networks.

	Empty	K2SN	PC
K2	-86822	-47515	-51083
KL	0.0	9.2205	8.3170

With respect to the complexity of the search methods, although HCSO evaluates less individuals than HCST[3], the cost of evaluating each individual for HCSO is greater than for HCST. Overall, although HCSO gives results better than HCST, the latter is more efficient than the former. Obviously, the complexity of VNSO increases considerably. Nevertheless, we have observed that VNSO always finds the best individual in the first iteration (of step (a)), and due to the stopping criterion selected, it needs to perform another complete iteration to halt. So, the complexity of VNSO could be considerably reduced without compromising the quality of the result by performing only one iteration.

7 Concluding Remarks

In this work we have proposed a new strategy for learning belief networks based on searching for good orderings and searching for good networks compatible with a given ordering. Moreover, a new search method has been adapted to this problem. The proposed methods have improved the results obtained by other classical search methods that explore the space of dags. Nevertheless, a more systematic experimentation has to be done in order to confirm this conclusion. We also plan to study in the future other variants of VNS, as well as other operators for defining local changes in the space of the orderings.

Acknowledgements. This work has been supported by the Spanish Comisión Interministerial de Ciencia y Tecnología (CICYT), under project TIC 2000-1351.

References

1. Acid, S., Campos, L.M. de: BENEDICT: An algorithm for learning probabilistic belief networks. In: Proceedings of the Sixth International Conference of Information Processing and Management of Uncertainty in Knowledge-Based Systems (1996) 979–984
2. Acid, S., Campos, L.M. de: A hybrid methodology for learning belief networks: BENEDICT. Int. J. Approx. Reason., to appear
3. Beinlich,I.A., Suermondt, H.J., Chavez, R., Cooper, G.: The ALARM monitoring system: A case study with two probabilistic inference techniques for belief networks. In: Proceedings of the Second European Conference on Artificial Intelligence in Medicine (1989) 247–256

[3] This suggests that the space of the orderings is more 'smoother' than the space of dags.

4. Buntine, W.: A guide to the literature on learning probabilistic networks from data. IEEE T. Knowl. Data En. **8** (1996) 195–210
5. Campos, L.M. de: Independency relationships and learning algorithms for singly connected networks. J. Exp. Theor. Artif. In. **10** (1998) 511–549
6. Campos, L.M. de, Huete, J.F.: On the use of independence relationships for learning simplified belief networks. Int. J. Intell. Syst. **12** (1997) 495–522
7. Campos, L.M. de, Huete, J.F.: A new approach for learning belief networks using independence criteria. Int. J. Approx. Reason. **24** (2000) 11–37
8. Campos, L.M. de, Huete, J.F.: Approximating causal orderings for Bayesian networks using genetic algorithms and simulated annealing. In: Proceedings of the Eighth International Conference of Information Processing and Management of Uncertainty in Knowledge-Based Systems, Vol. I (2000) 333–340
9. Campos, L.M. de, Puerta, J.M.: Stochastic local and distributed search algorithms for learning belief networks. In: Proceedings of the Third International Symposium on Adaptive Systems (ISAS): Evolutionary Computation and Probabilistic Graphical Models (2001) 109–115
10. Cheng, J., Bell, D.A., Liu, W.: An algorithm for Bayesian belief network construction from data. In: Proceedings of AI and STAT'97 (1997) 83–90
11. Chickering, D.M.: Learning Bayesian networks is NP-complete. In: Fisher, D., Lenz, H.J. (eds): Learning from Data. Lectures Notes in Statistics, Vol. 112. Springer-Verlag (1996) 121–130
12. Cooper, G., Herskovits, E.: A Bayesian method for the induction of probabilistic networks from data. Mach. Learn. **9** (1992) 309–347
13. Dash, D., Druzdzel, M.: A hybrid anytime algorithm for the construction of causal models from sparse data. In: Proceedings of the Fifteenth Conference on Uncertainty in Artificial Intelligence (1999) 142–149
14. Friedman, N., Koller, D.: Being Bayesian about network structure. In: Proceedings of the Sixteenth Conference on Uncertainty in Artificial Intelligence (2000) 201–210
15. Hansen, P., Mladenović, N.: Variable neighborhood search: Principles and applications. Eur. J. Oper. Res. **130** (2001) 449–467
16. Heckemann, D., Geiger, D., Chickering, D.M.: Learning Bayesian networks: The combination of knowledge and statistical data. Mach. Learn. **20** (1995) 197–244
17. Lam, W., Bacchus, F.: Learning Bayesian belief networks. An approach based on the MDL principle. Comput. Intell. **10** (1994) 269–293
18. Larrañaga, P., Kuijpers, C.M., Murga, R.H., Yurramendi. Y.: Learning Bayesian network structure by searching for the best ordering with genetic algorithms. IEEE T. Syst. Man Cy. A **26** (1996) 487–493
19. Mladenović, N., Hansen, P.: Variable neighborhood search. Computer Oper. Res. **24** (1997) 1097–1100
20. Pearl, J.: Probabilistic Reasoning in Intelligent Systems. Morgan and Kaufman (1988)
21. Singh, M., Valtorta, M.: Construction of Bayesian network structures from data: A brief survey and an efficient algorithm. Int. J. Approx. Reason. **12** (1995) 111–131
22. Spirtes, P., Glymour, C., Scheines, R.: Causation, Prediction and Search. Lectures Notes in Statistics, Vol. 81. Springer-Verlag (1993)
23. Verma, T., Pearl, J.: Equivalence and synthesis of causal models. In: Uncertainty in Artificial Intelligence, Vol. 6. North-Holland (1991) 255–268

An Empirical Investigation of the K2 Metric

Christian Borgelt and Rudolf Kruse

Department of Knowledge Processing and Language Engineering
Otto-von-Guericke-University of Magdeburg
Universitätsplatz 2, D-39106 Magdeburg, Germany
{borgelt,kruse}@iws.cs.uni-magdeburg.de

Abstract. The K2 metric is a well-known evaluation measure (or scoring function) for learning Bayesian networks from data [7]. It is derived by assuming uniform prior distributions on the values of an attribute for each possible instantiation of its parent attributes. This assumption introduces a tendency to select simpler network structures. In this paper we modify the K2 metric in three different ways, introducing a parameter by which the strength of this tendency can be controlled. Our experiments with the ALARM network [2] and the BOBLO network [17] suggest that—somewhat contrary to our expectations—a slightly stronger tendency towards simpler structures may lead to even better results.

1 Introduction

Probabilistic inference networks—especially Bayesian networks [15] and Markov networks [14]—are well-known tools for reasoning under uncertainty in multidimensional domains. The idea underlying them is to exploit independence relations between the attributes used to describe a domain—an approach which has been studied extensively in the field of graphical modeling, see e.g. [12]—in order to decompose a multivariate probability distribution into a set of (conditional or marginal) distributions on lower-dimensional subspaces. Early efficient implementations include HUGIN [1] and PATHFINDER [9].

In this paper we focus on Bayesian networks. Formally, a Bayesian network represents a factorization of a multivariate probability distribution that results from an application of the product theorem of probability theory and a simplification of the factors achieved by exploiting conditional independence statements of the form $P(A \mid B, X) = P(A \mid X)$, where A and B are attributes and X is a set of attributes. Hence the represented joint distribution can be computed as

$$P(A_1, \ldots, A_n) = \prod_{i=1}^{n} P(A_i \mid \mathrm{par}(A_i)),$$

where $\mathrm{par}(A_i)$ is the set of parents of attribute A_i in a directed acyclic graph that is used to represents the factorization.

Bayesian networks provide excellent means to structure complex domains and to draw inferences. However, constructing a Bayesian network manually can

S. Benferhat and P. Besnard (Eds.): ECSQARU 2001, LNAI 2143, pp. 240–251, 2001.

be tedious and time-consuming. Considerable expert knowledge—domain knowledge as well as mathematical knowledge—is necessary to get it right. Therefore an important line of research is the automatic construction of Bayesian networks from a database of sample cases. Most algorithms for this task consist of two ingredients: a *search method* to traverse the possible network structures and an *evaluation measure* or *scoring function* to assess the quality of a given network.

In this paper we consider only the latter component, i.e., the scoring function. A desirable property of a scoring function is *decomposability*, i.e., that it can be computed by aggregating local assessments of subnetworks or even single edges. Intuitively, a decomposable scoring function assesses the significance of dependences between attributes in the database, in order to decide which edges between attributes are needed in the Bayesian network. An example for a decomposable scoring functions is mutual information [13,6]. Decomposable scoring functions are often used to select parents for each attribute, for example, in a greedy manner as in the K2 algorithm [7].

Due to the analogy of selecting parents for an attribute to the induction of a decision tree, there is a large variety of scoring functions [11,19,3]. Each of them exhibits a different sensitivity w.r.t. dependences in the data: Some scoring functions tend to select more edges/parents than others. Since in a cooperation with DaimlerChrysler, in which we work on fault diagnosis, it turned out that it is of practical importance to be able to control this sensitivity, we searched for parameterized families of scoring functions, where the parameter controls the sensitivity. In this paper we report the results of this research, which led us to certain variants of the K2 metric.

2 The K2 Metric

The K2 metric was derived first in [7], where it was used in the K2 algorithm, and later generalized in [10] to the Bayesian Dirichlet metric. It is the result of a Bayesian approach to learning Bayesian networks from data. The idea is as follows [7]: We are given a database D of sample cases over a set of attributes, each having a finite domain. It is assumed (1) that the process that generated the database can be accurately modeled as a Bayesian network, (2) that given a Bayesian network model cases occur independently, and (3) that cases are complete. Given these assumption we can compute from a given network structure B_S and a set of conditional probabilities B_P associated with it the probability of the database, i.e., we can compute $P(D|B_S, B_P)$. Adding an assumption about the prior probabilities of the network structures and the probability parameters and integrating over all possible sets of conditional probabilities B_P for the given structure B_S yields $P(B_S, D)$:

$$P(B_S, D) = \int_{B_P} P(D|B_S, B_P) f(B_P|B_S) P(B_S) \mathrm{d}B_P,$$

where f is the density function on the space of possible conditional probabilities and $P(B_S)$ is the prior probability of the structure B_S. $P(B_S, D)$ can be used to rank possible network structures, since obviously

$$\frac{P(B_{S_i}|D)}{P(B_{S_j}|D)} = \frac{P(B_{S_i}, D)}{P(B_{S_j}, D)}.$$

With the additional assumption that the density functions f are marginally independent for all pairs of attributes and for all pairs of instantiations of the parents of an attribute, we arrive at (see [7] for details):

$$P(B_S, D) = P(B_S) \prod_{k=1}^{n} \prod_{j=1}^{q_k} \int \cdots \int_{\theta_{ijk}} \left(\prod_{i=1}^{r_k} \theta_{ijk}^{N_{ijk}} \right) f(\theta_{1jk}, \ldots, \theta_{r_k jk}) \mathrm{d}\theta_{1jk} \ldots \mathrm{d}\theta_{r_k jk}.$$

Here n is the number of attributes of the network, q_k is the number of distinct instantiations of the parents attribute k has in the structure B_S, and r_k is the number of values of attribute k. θ_{ijk} is the probability that attribute k assumes the i-th value of its domain, given that its parents are instantiated with the j-th combination of values, and N_{ijk} is the number of cases in the database, in which the attribute k is instantiated with its i-th value and its parents are instantiated with the j-th value combination.

In the following we confine ourselves to single factors of the outermost product and thus drop the index k. That is, we consider only single attribute scores. This is justified because of the factorization property of Bayesian networks. Using a uniform prior density on the parameters θ_{ij}, namely $f(\theta_{1j}, \ldots, \theta_{rj}) = (r-1)!$, and assuming that the possible networks structures are equally likely yields as a scoring function [7]:

$$\mathrm{K2}(A|\,\mathrm{par}(A)) = \prod_{j=1}^{q} \frac{(r-1)!}{(N_{.j} + r - 1)!} \prod_{i=1}^{r} N_{ij}!,$$

where A is a child attribute and $\mathrm{par}(A)$ is the set of its parents. r is the number of values of the attribute A and q is the numbers of distinct instantiations of its parent attributes. N_{ij} is the number of cases in which attribute A is instantiated with its i-th value and its parents are instantiated with their j-th value combination; $N_{.j} = \sum_{i=1}^{r} N_{ij}$. Note that in the derivation of the above function the solution of Dirichlet's integral [8]

$$\int \cdots \int_{\theta_{ij}} \prod_{i=1}^{r} \theta_{ij}^{N_{ij}} \mathrm{d}\theta_{1j} \ldots \mathrm{d}\theta_{rj} = \frac{\prod_{i=1}^{r} N_{ij}!}{(N_{.j} + r - 1)!}$$

was used, which we need again below.

The higher the value of the above scoring function K2 (i.e., its product over all attributes), the better the corresponding network structure. To simplify the computation of this measure often the logarithm of the above function is used:

$$\log_2(\mathrm{K2}(A|\,\mathrm{par}(A))) = \sum_{j=1}^{q} \log_2 \frac{(r-1)!}{(N_{.j} + r - 1)!} + \sum_{j=1}^{q} \sum_{i=1}^{r} \log_2 N_{ij}!.$$

As already said above, the K2 metric was generalized to the Bayesian Dirichlet metric in [10]. This more general scoring function is defined as

$$\mathrm{BD}(A|\,\mathrm{par}(A)) = \prod_{j=1}^{q} \frac{\Gamma(N'_{.j})}{\Gamma(N_{.j} + N'_{.j})} \prod_{i=1}^{r} \frac{\Gamma(N_{ij} + N'_{ij})}{\Gamma(N'_{ij})},$$

where Γ is the well-known generalized factorial,

$$\Gamma(x) = \int_0^{\infty} e^{-t} t^{x-1} \mathrm{d}t, \qquad \forall n \in \mathbb{N} : \Gamma(n+1) = n!.$$

It is used to take care of the fact that N'_{ij} and $N'_{.j} = \sum_{i=1}^{r} N'_{ij}$, which represent a prior distribution (see [10] for details), may not be integer numbers. Obviously, the K2 metric results for the simple choice $\forall i, j : N'_{ij} = 1$, which very clearly signifies the assumption of a uniform prior distribution.

This representation also makes it plausible why the K2 metric has a tendency to select simpler network structures, i.e., why algorithms using it are somewhat reluctant to add parent attributes. By the prior $N'_{ij} = 1$ the frequency distributions are somewhat "leveled out" and the more so, the more parent attributes there are. The reason is that the number of cases in the database for a given instantiation of the parent attributes is the smaller, the more parents there are, simply because each parent introduces an additional constraint. Hence the influence of the data frequencies N_{ij} is smaller for a larger number of parents and consequently an attribute seems to be less strongly dependent on its parents. The result is an inclination to reject a(nother) parent.

Analogously, we can see why the Bayesian Dirichlet likelihood equivalent uniform (BDeu) metric [5,10], which has $\forall i, j : N'_{ij} = \frac{s}{r \cdot q}$, where s is a parameter called the *equivalent sample size*, has a tendency to select more complex network structures and tends to connect attributes with many possible values. Due to the product $r \cdot q$ in the denominator the influence of the prior is reduced by an additional parent and by parents with many possible values. The result is an increased influence of the data frequencies N_{ij} for more parents and thus a tendency to add a(nother) parent attribute.

3 Modifications of the K2 Metric

In this section we introduce three modifications of the K2 metric, all of which contain a parameter through which the strength of the tendency of the K2 metric towards simpler network structures can be controlled.

3.1 Weighted Data

The argument given above to explain the tendency of the K2 metric directly suggests an idea to control this tendency. Since the tendency depends on the relation of the data frequencies N_{ij} and the prior $N'_{ij} = 1$ one may consider weighting either of them. Due to the numerical properties of the Γ-function, especially its behavior for arguments less than 1, weighting the data frequencies seems to be preferable. That is, we simply multiply the data frequencies with a factor β, which we write as $\beta = (\alpha_1 + 1)^2$, since this form is advantageous for the presentation of our experimental results (see below).

This factor can also be made plausible as follows: Formally the factor β is equivalent to the assumption that we observed the data β times and thus we artificially increase or reduce the statistical basis of the network induction. Of course, a larger statistical basis allows us to justify a more complex structure, whereas a smaller basis allows us only to justify a simpler one. It should be noted, though, that we introduce this factor here only to study the properties of the K2 metric, not as a statistically justifiable correction factor.

With such a factor we get the following family of scoring functions:

$$\mathrm{K2}_{\alpha_1}^{(1)}(A|\,\mathrm{par}(A)) = \prod_{j=1}^{q} \frac{\Gamma(r)}{\Gamma((\alpha_1+1)^2 N_{.j} + r)} \prod_{i=1}^{r} \Gamma((\alpha_1+1)^2 N_{ij} + 1),$$

Obviously, for $\alpha_1 = 0$ we have the standard K2 metric as it was described above. For $\alpha_1 < 0$ we get a stronger, for $\alpha_1 > 0$ we get a weaker tendency to select simpler network structures.

3.2 Modified Prior

In the derivation of the K2 metric it is assumed that the density functions on the spaces of conditional probabilities are uniform. However, after we found the best network structure w.r.t. the K2 metric, we no longer integrate over all conditional probabilities (e.g. when we propagate evidence in the induced network). Although, of course, it is possible in principle to average over several network structures, a single network is often preferred. Hence we fix the structure and compute estimates of the probabilities using, for example, Bayesian or maximum likelihood estimation. Therefore the idea suggests itself to reverse these steps. That is, we could estimate first for each structure the best conditional probability assignments and then select the best structure based on these, then fixed, assignments. Formally, this can be done by choosing the density functions in such a way that the estimated probabilities have probability 1. Using maximum likelihood estimation of a multinomial distribution we thus get

$$f(\theta_{1j}, \ldots, \theta_{rj}) = \prod_{i=1}^{r} \delta\left(\theta_{ij} - \frac{N_{ij}}{N_{.j}}\right)$$

where δ is Dirac's δ-function (or, more precisely, δ-distribution, since it is not a classical function), which is defined to have the following properties:

$$\delta(t) = \begin{cases} +\infty & \text{for } t = 0, \\ 0 & \text{for } t \neq 0, \end{cases} \qquad \int_{-\infty}^{+\infty} \delta(t)\mathrm{d}t = 1, \qquad \int_{-\infty}^{+\infty} \delta(t)\varphi(t)\mathrm{d}t = \varphi(0).$$

Inserting this density function into the formula for $P(B_S, D)$ derived above, we get as a scoring function:

$$\begin{aligned}
\mathrm{K2}_\infty^{(2)}(A \,|\, \mathrm{par}(A)) &= \prod_{j=1}^{q} \int_{\theta_{ij}}^{\cdots}\!\!\int \left(\prod_{i=1}^{r} \theta_{ij}^{N_{ij}}\right) \left(\prod_{i=1}^{r} \delta\left(\theta_{ij} - \frac{N_{ij}}{N_{.j}}\right)\right) \mathrm{d}\theta_{1j} \dots \mathrm{d}\theta_{r_k j} \\
&= \prod_{j=1}^{q} \left(\prod_{i=1}^{r} \left(\frac{N_{ij}}{N_{.j}}\right)^{N_{ij}}\right)
\end{aligned}$$

An interesting thing to note about this function is that obviously

$$N_{..} \cdot H(A \,|\, \mathrm{par}(A)) = -\log_2 \mathrm{K2}_\infty^{(2)}(A \,|\, \mathrm{par}(A)),$$

where $N_{..} = \sum_{j=1}^{q} N_{.j}$ and $H(A \,|\, \mathrm{par}(A))$ is the expected entropy of the probability distribution on the values of attribute A given its parents. Note that we get the well-known *mutual information* (also called *cross entropy* or *information gain*) [13,6,16] if we relate the value of this measure to its value for a structure in which attribute A has no parents, i.e.,

$$N_{..} \cdot I_{\mathrm{gain}}(A, \mathrm{par}(A)) = \log_2 \frac{\mathrm{K2}_\infty^{(2)}(A \,|\, \mathrm{par}(A))}{\mathrm{K2}_\infty^{(2)}(A \,|\, \emptyset)}.$$

In other words, mutual information turns out to be equivalent to a so-called *Bayes factor* of this metric.

This Bayesian justification of mutual information as a scoring function may be doubted, since in it the database is—in a way—used twice to assess the quality of a network structure, namely once directly and once indirectly through the estimation of the parameters of the conditional probability distribution. Formally this approach is not strictly correct, since the density function on the parameter space should be a prior distribution whereas the estimate we used clearly is a posterior distribution (since it is computed from the database). However, the fact that mutual information results—a well-known and well-founded scoring function—is very suggestive evidence that this approach is worth to be examined.

The above derivation of mutual information as a scoring function assumes Dirac pulses at the maximum likelihood estimates for the conditional probabilities. However, we may also consider the likelihood function directly, i.e.,

$$f(\theta_{1j}, \dots, \theta_{rj}) = c_1 \prod_{i=1}^{r} \theta_{ij}^{N_{ij}}, \qquad c_1 = \frac{(N_{.j} + r - 1)!}{\prod_{i=1}^{r} N_{ij}!}.$$

where the value of the normalization constant c_1 results from the solution of Dirichlet's integral (see above) and the fact that the integral over $\theta_{1j}, \dots, \theta_{rj}$ must be 1 (since f is a probability density function).

With this consideration a family of scoring functions suggests itself, which can be derived as follows: First we normalize the likelihood function, so that the maximum value of this function becomes 1. This is easily achieved by dividing the likelihood function by the maximum likelihood estimate raised to the power N_{ij}. Then we introduce an exponent α_2, through which we can control the "width" of the function around the maximum likelihood estimate. Thus, if the exponent is zero, we get a constant function, if it is one, we get a function proportional to the likelihood function, and if it approaches infinity, it approaches Dirac pulses at the maximum likelihood estimate. That is, we get the family:

$$f_{\alpha_2}(\theta_{1j}, \ldots, \theta_{rj}) = c_2 \cdot \left(\left(\prod_{i=1}^{r} \left(\frac{N_{ij}}{N_{.j}} \right)^{-N_{ij}} \right) \left(\prod_{i=1}^{r} \theta_{ij}^{N_{ij}} \right) \right)^{\alpha_2} = c_3 \cdot \prod_{i=1}^{r} \theta_{ij}^{\alpha_2 N_{ij}}.$$

c_2 and c_3 are normalization factors to be chosen in such a way that the integral over $\theta_{1j}, \ldots, \theta_{rj}$ is 1. Thus we find, using again the solution of Dirichlet's integral,

$$c_3 = \frac{\Gamma(\alpha_2 N_{.j} + r)}{\prod_{i=1}^{r} \Gamma(\alpha_2 N_{ij} + 1)}.$$

Inserting the derived parameterized density into the function for the probability $P(B_S, D)$ and evaluating the formula using Dirichlet's integral yields the family of scoring functions

$$\mathrm{K2}_{\alpha_2}^{(2)}(A|\,\mathrm{par}(A)) = \prod_{j=1}^{q} \frac{\Gamma(\alpha_2 N_{.j} + r)}{\Gamma((\alpha_2 + 1) N_{.j} + r)} \prod_{i=1}^{r} \frac{\Gamma((\alpha_2 + 1) N_{ij} + 1)}{\Gamma(\alpha_2 N_{ij} + 1)}.$$

From the derivation above it is clear that we get the K2 metric for $\alpha_2 = 0$. Since α_2 is, like α_1, a kind of data weighting factor, we have a measure with a stronger tendency towards simpler network structures for $\alpha_2 < 0$ and a measure with a weaker tendency for $\alpha_2 > 0$. However, in order to keep the argument of the Γ-function positive, negative values of α_2 cannot be made arbitrarily large. Actually, due to the behavior of the Γ-function for arguments less than 1, only positive values seem to be useful.

3.3 Weighted Coding Penalty

It is well-known that Bayesian estimation is closely related to the minimum description length (MDL) principle [18]. Thus it is not surprising that the K2 metric can also be justified by means of this principle. The idea is as follows (see e.g. [11], where it is described w.r.t. decision tree induction): Suppose the database of sample cases is to be transmitted from a sender to a receiver. Both know the number of attributes, their domains, and the number of cases in the database[1], but at the beginning only the sender knows the values the attributes are instantiated with in the sample cases. Since transmission is costly, it is tried to code the values using a minimal number of bits. This can be achieved by exploiting

[1] A strict application of the MDL principle would assume that these numbers are unknown to the receiver. However, since they have to be transmitted in any case, they do not change the ranking and thus are neglected or assumed to be known.

properties of the value distributions to construct a good coding scheme. However, the receiver cannot know this coding scheme without being told and thus the coding scheme has to be transmitted, too. Therefore the total length of the description of the coding scheme and the description of the values based on the chosen coding scheme has to be minimized.

The transmission is carried out as follows: The values of the sample cases are transmitted attribute by attribute. That is, at first the values of the first attribute are transmitted for all sample cases, then the values of the second attribute are transmitted, and so on. Thus the transmission of the values of an attribute may exploit dependences between this attribute and already transmitted attributes to code the values more efficiently. Using a coding based on absolute value frequencies (for coding based on relative frequencies, see [11,3]) and exploiting that the values of a set $\text{par}(A)$ of already transmitted attributes are known, the following formula can be derived for the length of a description of the values of attribute A:

$$L(A|\,\text{par}(A)) = \log_2 S + \sum_{j=1}^{q} \log_2 \frac{(N_{.j} + r - 1)!}{N_{.j}!\,(r-1)!} + \sum_{j=1}^{q} \log_2 \frac{N_{.j}!}{\prod_{i=1}^{r} N_{ij}!}.$$

Here S is the number of possible selections of a set $\text{par}(A)$ from the set of already transmitted attributes. The lower the value of the above function (that is, its sum over all attributes), the better the corresponding network structure.

The above formula can be interpreted as follows: First we transmit which subset $\text{par}(A)$ of the already transmitted attributes we use for the coding. We do so by referring to a code book, in which all possible selections are printed, one per page. This book has S pages and thus transmitting the page number takes $\log_2 S$ bits. (This term is usually neglected, since it is the same for all selections of attributes.) Then we do a separate coding for each instantiation of the attributes in $\text{par}(A)$. We transmit first the frequency distribution of the values of the attribute A given the j-th instantiation of the attributes in $\text{par}(A)$. Since there are $N_{.j}$ cases in which the attributes in $\text{par}(A)$ are instantiated with the j-th value combination and since there are r values for the attribute A, there are $\frac{(N_{.j}+r-1)!}{N_{.j}!\,(r-1)!}$ possible frequency distributions. We assume again that all of these are printed in a code book, one per page, and transmit the page number. Finally we transmit the exact assignment of the values of the attribute A to the cases. Since we already know the frequency of the different values, there are $\frac{N_{.j}!}{\prod_{i=1}^{r} N_{ij}!}$ possible assignments. Once again we assume these to be printed in a code book, one per page, and transmit the page number.

It is easy to verify that it is

$$L(A|\,\text{par}(A)) = -\log_2 \text{K2}(A|\,\text{par}(A))$$

if we neglect the term $\log_2 S$ (see above). Hence minimizing the network score w.r.t. $L(A|\,\text{par}(A))$ is equivalent to maximising it w.r.t. $\text{K2}(A|\,\text{par}(A))$.

The above considerations suggests a third way to introduce a parameter for controlling the tendency towards simpler network structures. In the MDL view the tendency results from the need to transmit the coding scheme, the costs of which can be seen as a penalty for making the network structure more complex: If the dependences of the attributes do not compensate the costs for transmitting a more complex coding scheme, fewer parent attributes are selected. Hence the tendency is mainly due to the term describing the costs for transmitting the coding scheme and we may control the tendency by weighting this term. In order to achieve matching ranges of values for the parameters and thus to simplify the presentation of the experimental results (see below), we write the weighting factor as $\frac{1}{\alpha_3+1}$. Thus we get the following family of scoring functions:

$$L_{\alpha_3}(A|\,\mathrm{par}(A)) = \frac{1}{\alpha_3+1}\sum_{j=1}^{q}\log_2\frac{(N_{.j}+r-1)!}{N_{.j}!\,(r-1)!} + \sum_{j=1}^{q}\log_2\frac{N_{.j}!}{\prod_{i=1}^{r}N_{ij}!}.$$

Obviously, for $\alpha_3 = 0$ we have a measure that is equivalent to the K2 metric. For $\alpha_3 < 0$ we get a measure with a stronger tendency to select simpler network structures, for $\alpha_3 > 0$ we get a measure with a weaker tendency.

4 Experimental Results

We implemented all of the abovementioned families of scoring functions as part of INES (Induction of NEtwork Structures), a prototype program for learning probabilistic networks from a database of sample, which was written by the first author. With this program we conducted several experiments based on the well-known ALARM network [2] and the BOBLO network [17]. For all experiments we used greedy parent selection w.r.t. a topological order (the search method of the K2 algorithm). Of course, other search methods may also be used, but we do not expect the results to differ significantly.

The experiments were carried out as follows: For each network we chose three database sizes, namely 1000, 2000, and 5000 tuples for the ALARM network and 500, 1000, and 2000 tuples for the BOBLO network. For each of these sizes we randomly generated ten pairs of databases from the networks. The first database of each pair was used to induce a network, the second to test it (see below). For each database size we varied the parameters introduced in the preceding section from -0.95 to 1 (for α_1 and α_3) and from 0 to 1 (for α_2) in steps of 0.05.

The induced networks were evaluated in two different ways: In the first place they were compared to the original networks by counting the number of missing edges and the number of additional edges. Furthermore they were tested against the second database of each pair (see above) by computing the log-likelihood (natural logarithm) of this database given the induced networks. For this the conditional probabilities of the induced networks were estimated from the first database of each pair (i.e., the one the network structure was induced from) with Laplace corrected maximum likelihood estimation, i.e., using

$$\forall i,j: \hat{p}_{i|j} = \frac{N_{ij}+1}{N_{.j}+r},$$

in order to avoid problems with impossible tuples.

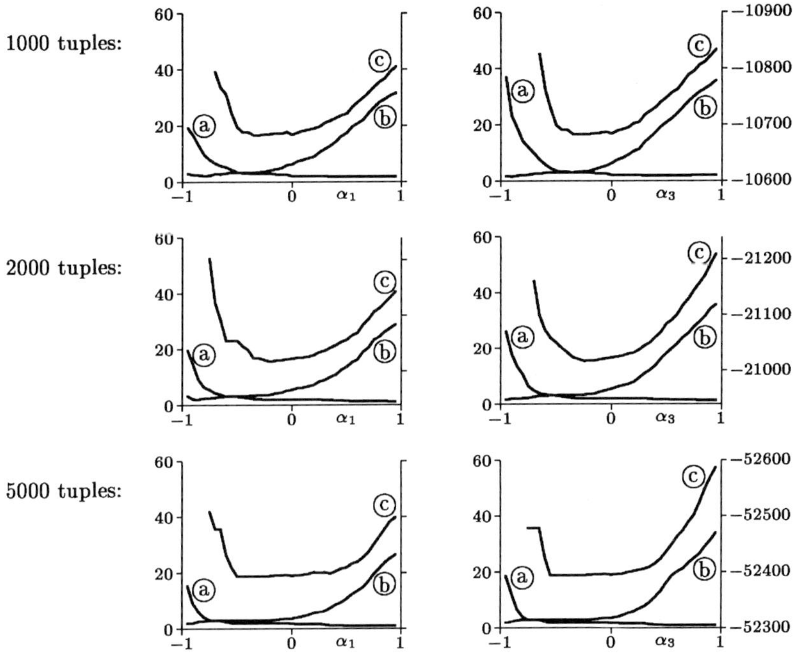

Fig. 1. Results for the ALARM network.

The results w.r.t. the parameters α_1 and α_3 are shown in figures 1 and 2. The results for α_2, which are less instructive, since this parameter should be positive, are very similar to the right halves of the diagrams for α_1 and α_3. Each diagram contains three curves, which represent averages over the ten pairs of databases:

a: the average number of missing edges,
b: the average number of additional edges,
c: the average log-likelihood of the test databases.

The scale for the number of missing/additional tuples is on the left, the scale for the log-likelihood of the test databases on the right of the diagrams.

All diagrams demonstrate that the tendency of the K2 metric (which corresponds to $\alpha_k = 0$, $k = 1, 2, 3$) is very close to optimal. However, the diagrams also indicate that a slightly stronger tendency towards simpler network structures ($\alpha_k < 0$) may lead to even better results. With a slightly stronger tendency some of the few unnecessary additional edges selected with the K2 metric can be suppressed without significantly affecting the log-likelihood of test data (actually the log-likelihood value is usually also slightly better with a stronger tendency, although this is far from being statistically significant).

It should be noted, though, that in some applications a weaker tendency towards simpler network structures is preferable. For example, in a cooperation

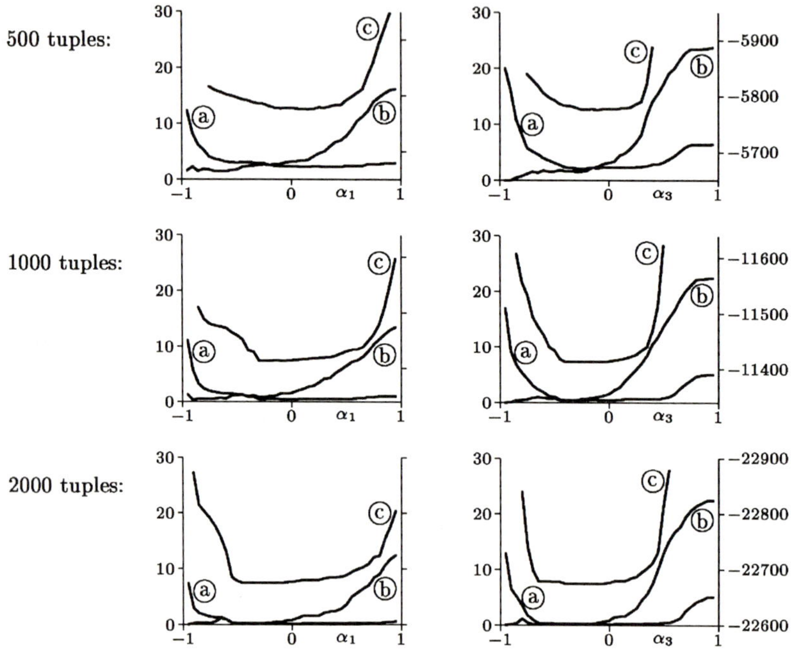

Fig. 2. Results for the BOBLO network.

with DaimlerChrysler, in which we work on fault diagnosis, we faced the problem that in tests against expert knowledge sometimes dependences of faults on the vehicle equipment, which were known to the domain experts, could not be found with the K2 metric. Usually this was the case if the dependence was restricted to one instantiation of the parent attributes. By adapting the parameters introduced above, however, these dependences were easily found. We regret that details of these results are confidential, so that we cannot present them here.

5 Conclusions

In this paper we introduced three modifications of the K2 metric, each of which adds a parameter to control the tendency towards simpler network structures. The resulting families of scoring functions provided us with means to explore empirically the properties of the K2 metric. Our experimental results indicate that the tendency strength of the K2 metric is a very good choice, but that a slightly stronger tendency towards simpler network structures may lead to even better results, although the improvement is only marginal.

References

1. S.K. Andersen, K.G. Olesen, F.V. Jensen, and F. Jensen. HUGIN — A Shell for Building Bayesian Belief Universes for Expert Systems. *Proc. 11th Int. J. Conf. on Artificial Intelligence (IJCAI'89, Detroit, MI, USA)*, 1080–1085. Morgan Kaufmann, San Mateo, CA, USA 1989
2. I.A. Beinlich, H.J. Suermondt, R.M. Chavez, and D.F. Cooper. The ALARM Monitoring System: A Case Study with Two Probabilistic Inference Techniques for Belief Networks. *Proc. Conf. on AI in Medical Care*, London, United Kingdom 1989
3. C. Borgelt and R. Kruse. Evaluation Measures for Learning Probabilistic and Possibilistic Networks. *Proc. 6th IEEE Int. Conf. on Fuzzy Systems (FUZZ-IEEE'97, Barcelona, Spain)*, Vol. 2:1034–1038. IEEE Press, Piscataway, NJ, USA 1997
4. L. Breiman, J.H. Friedman, R.A. Olshen, and C.J. Stone. *Classification and Regression Trees*, Wadsworth International Group, Belmont, CA, USA 1984
5. W. Buntine. Theory Refinement on Bayesian Networks. *Proc. 7th Conf. on Uncertainty in Artificial Intelligence (UAI'91, Los Angeles, CA, USA)*, 52–60. Morgan Kaufmann, San Mateo, CA, USA 1991
6. C.K. Chow and C.N. Liu. Approximating Discrete Probability Distributions with Dependence Trees. *IEEE Trans. on Information Theory* 14(3):462–467, IEEE Press, Piscataway, NJ, USA 1968
7. G.F. Cooper and E. Herskovits. A Bayesian Method for the Induction of Probabilistic Networks from Data. *Machine Learning* 9:309–347. Kluwer, Amsterdam, Netherlands 1992
8. P.G.L. Dirichlet. Sur un nouvelle methode pour la determination des integrales multiples. *Comp. Rend. Acad. Science* 8:156–160. France 1839
9. D. Heckerman. *Probabilistic Similarity Networks.* MIT Press, Cambridge, MA, USA 1991
10. D. Heckerman, D. Geiger, and D.M. Chickering. Learning Bayesian Networks: The Combination of Knowledge and Statistical Data. *Machine Learning* 20:197–243. Kluwer, Amsterdam, Netherlands 1995
11. I. Kononenko. On Biases in Estimating Multi-Valued Attributes. *Proc. 1st Int. Conf. on Knowledge Discovery and Data Mining (KDD'95, Montreal, Canada)*, 1034–1040. AAAI Press, Menlo Park, CA, USA 1995
12. R. Kruse, E. Schwecke, and J. Heinsohn. *Uncertainty and Vagueness in Knowledge-based Systems: Numerical Methods.* Springer, Berlin, Germany 1991
13. S. Kullback and R.A. Leibler. On Information and Sufficiency. *Ann. Math. Statistics* 22:79–86. Institute of Mathematical Statistics, Hayward, CA, USA 1951
14. S.L. Lauritzen and D.J. Spiegelhalter. Local Computations with Probabilities on Graphical Structures and Their Application to Expert Systems. *J. Royal Statistical Society, Series B*, 2(50):157–224. Blackwell, Oxford, United Kingdom 1988
15. J. Pearl. *Probabilistic Reasoning in Intelligent Systems: Networks of Plausible Inference (2nd edition).* Morgan Kaufman, San Mateo, CA, USA 1992
16. J.R. Quinlan. *C4.5: Programs for Machine Learning*, Morgan Kaufman, San Mateo, CA, USA 1993
17. L.K. Rasmussen. *Blood Group Determination of Danish Jersey Cattle in the F-blood Group System.* Dina Foulum, Tjele, Denmark 1992
18. J. Rissanen. Stochastic Complexity. *Journal of the Royal Statistical Society (Series B)*, 49:223-239. Blackwell, Oxford, United Kingdom 1987
19. L. Wehenkel. On Uncertainty Measures Used for Decision Tree Induction. *Proc. 7th Int. Conf. on Inf. Proc. and Management of Uncertainty in Knowledge-based Systems (IPMU'96, Granada, Spain)*, 413–417. Universidad de Granada, Spain 1996

Sequential Valuation Networks: A New Graphical Technique for Asymmetric Decision Problems

Riza Demirer and Prakash P. Shenoy

University of Kansas, School of Business
1300 Sunnyside Ave, Summerfield Hall
Lawrence, KS 66045-7585, USA
{riza, pshenoy}@ku.edu

Abstract. This paper deals with representation and solution of asymmetric decision problems. We describe a new graphical representation called sequential valuation networks, which is a hybrid of Covaliu and Oliver's sequential decision diagrams and Shenoy's asymmetric valuation networks. Sequential valuation networks inherit many of the strengths of sequential decision diagrams and asymmetric valuation networks while overcoming many of their shortcomings. We illustrate our technique by representing and solving a modified version of Covaliu and Oliver's Reactor problem.

1 Introduction

The goal of this paper is to propose a new graphical technique for representing and solving asymmetric decision problems. The new graphical representation is called a *sequential valuation network* and it is a hybrid of sequential decision diagrams (SDDs) [3] and asymmetric valuation networks (VNs) [13]. Sequential valuation networks adapt the best features from SDDs and asymmetric VNs and provide a fix to some of the major shortcomings of these techniques as identified by Bielza and Shenoy [1]. The algorithm for solving sequential valuation networks is based on the idea of decomposing a large asymmetric problem into smaller symmetric sub-problems and then using a special case of Shenoy's fusion algorithm to solve the symmetric sub-problems.

In a decision tree representation, a path from the root node to a leaf node is called a *scenario*. A decision problem is said to be *asymmetric* if there exists a decision tree representation such that the number of scenarios is less than the cardinality of the Cartesian product of the state spaces of all chance and decision variables.

There are three types of asymmetry in decision problems—chance, decision, and information. First, the state space of a chance variable may vary depending on the scenario in which it appears. In the extreme, a chance variable may be non-existent in a particular scenario. For example, if a firm decides not to test market a product, we are not concerned about the possible results of test marketing. Second, the state space of a decision variable may depend on the scenario in which it appears. Again, at the

S. Benferhat and P. Besnard (Eds.): ECSQARU 2001, LNAI 2143, pp. 252–265, 2001.

extreme, a decision variable may simply not exist for a given scenario. For example, if we decide not to buy a financial option contract, the decision of exercising the option on the exercise date does not exist. Finally, the information constraints may depend on the scenarios. For example, in diagnosing a disease with two symptoms, the order in which the symptoms are revealed (if at all) may depend on the sequence of the tests ordered by the physician prior to making a diagnosis. A specific example of information asymmetry is described in Section 5. Most of the examples of asymmetric decision problems have focused on chance and decision asymmetry. Information asymmetry has not been widely studied.

Several graphical techniques have been proposed for representing and solving asymmetric decision problems—traditional decision trees [11], combination of influence diagrams (IDs) and decision trees [2], contingent influence diagrams [5], influence diagrams with distribution trees [14], decision graphs within the ID framework [10], asymmetric valuation network representation with indicator valuations [13], sequential decision diagrams [3], configuration networks [7], asymmetric influence diagrams [9], and valuation networks with coarse valuations [8]. Each of these methods has some advantages and disadvantages. For a comparison of decision trees, Smith-Holtzman-Matheson's influence diagrams, Shenoy's asymmetric valuation networks, and Covaliu and Oliver's sequential decision diagrams, see [1].

Covaliu and Oliver's SDD representation [3] is a compact and intuitive way of representing the structure of an asymmetric decision problem. One can think of a SDD as a clustered decision tree in which each variable appears only once (as in influence diagrams and VNs). Also, SDDs model asymmetry without adding dummy states to variables. However, the SDD representation depends on influence diagrams to represent the probability and utility models. Also, preprocessing may be required in order to make the ID representation compatible with the SDD representation so that the formulation table can be constructed. One unresolved problem is that although a SDD and a compatible ID use the same variables, the state spaces of these variables may not be the same. The problem of exponential growth of rows in the formulation table is another major problem of this method. Finally, this method is unable to cope with an arbitrary factorization of the joint utility function. It can only handle either a single undecomposed utility function, or a factorization of the joint utility function into factors where each factor only includes a single variable.

Shenoy's asymmetric VN representation [13] is compact in the sense that the model is linear in the number of variables. It is also flexible regarding the factorization of the joint probability distribution of the random variables in the model—the model works for any multiplicative factorization of the joint probability distribution. However, this representation technique cannot avoid the creation of artificial states that lead to an increased state space for some variables in the model. Some types of asymmetry cannot be captured in the VN representation. Also, the asymmetric structure of a decision problem is not represented at the graphical level, but instead in the details of the indicator valuations.

This paper presents a new graphical representation called a *sequential valuation network* (SVN) that is a hybrid of SDDs and asymmetric VNs. This new graphical method combines the strengths of SDDs and VNs, and avoids the weaknesses of either. We use the graphical ease of SDD representation of the asymmetric structure of a decision problem, and attach value and probability valuations to variables as in VNs. The resulting SVN representation is able to address many of the shortcomings of VNs and SDDs as follows. The state spaces of the variables do not include artificial states, and all types of asymmetry can be represented. This is true for the Reactor problem and we conjecture that these aspects are true of all asymmetric problems. Most of the asymmetric structure of a decision problem is represented at the graphical level. A SVN does not need a separate graph to represent the uncertainty model. No pre-processing is required to represent a decision problem as a SVN, i.e., it is not necessary to construct a formulation table prior to solving a SVN. Finally, a SVN can easily represent any factorization of the joint utility function.

To solve SVNs, we identify different symmetric sub-problems as paths from the source node to the terminal node. Each such path represents a collection of scenarios. Finally, we apply a special case of Shenoy's [12] fusion algorithm for each sub-problem and solve the global asymmetric problem by solving smaller symmetric sub-problems. The strategy of breaking down an asymmetric decision problem into several symmetric sub-problems is also used by [7] and [9].

An outline of the remainder of the paper is as follows. In Section 2, we give a complete statement of a modified version of the Reactor problem of [3], and describe a decision tree representation of it. In Section 3, we represent the same problem using SVN representation and in Section 4, we sketch its solution. Finally, in Section 5, we conclude by summarizing some strengths of our representation as compared to the representations proposed so far.

2 The Reactor Problem

An electric utility firm must decide whether to build (D_2) a reactor of advanced design (a), a reactor of conventional design (c), or no reactor (n). If the reactor is successful, i.e., there are no accidents, an advanced reactor is more profitable, but it is also riskier. Past experience indicates that a conventional reactor (C) has probability 0.980 of being successful (cs), and a probability 0.020 of a failure (cf). On the other hand, an advanced reactor (A) has probability 0.660 of being successful (as), probability 0.244 of a limited accident (al), and probability 0.096 of a major accident (am). If the firm builds a conventional reactor, the profits are \$8B if it is a success, and –\$4B if there is a failure. If the firm builds an advanced reactor, the profits are \$12B if it is a success, –\$6B if there is a limited accident, and –\$10B if there is a major accident. The firm's utility function is assumed to be linear in dollars.

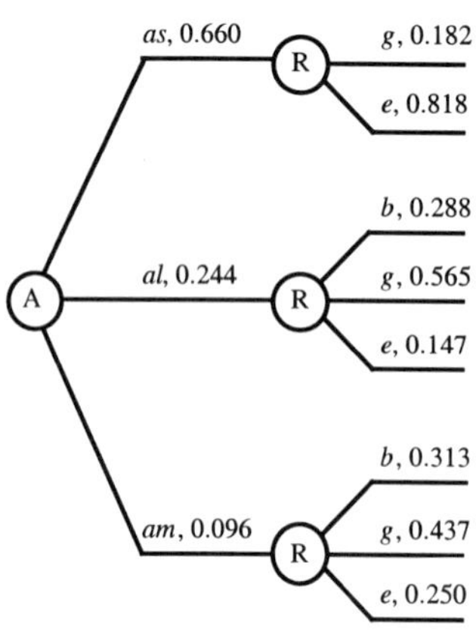

Fig. 1. A Probability Model for A and R in the Reactor Problem

Before making the decision to build, the firm has the option to conduct a test ($D_1 = t$) or not ($D_1 = \text{nt}$) of the components of the advanced reactor. The test results (R) can be classified as bad (b), good (g), or excellent (e). The cost of the test is \$1B. The test results are highly correlated with the success or failure of the advanced reactor (A). Figure 1 shows a causal probability model for A and R in the Reactor problem. Notice that if $A = as$, then R cannot assume the state b. If the test results are bad, then as per the probability model, an advanced reactor will result in either a limited or a major accident, and consequently, the Nuclear Regulatory Commission will not license an advanced reactor.

2.1 Decision Tree Representation and Solution

Figure 2 shows a decision tree representation and solution of this problem. The optimal strategy is as follows. Do the test; build a conventional reactor if test results are bad or good, and build an advanced reactor if test results are excellent. The maximum expected profit is \$8.13B.

The decision tree representation given in Figure 2 successfully captures the asym-

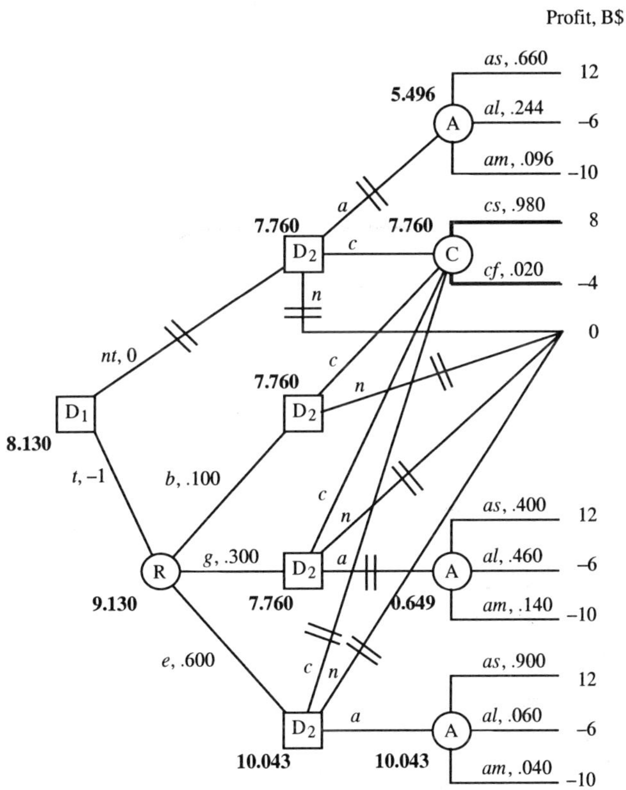

Fig. 2. A Decision Tree Representation and Solution of the Reactor Problem

metric structure of the Reactor problem. The product of the cardinalities of the state spaces of the decision and chance variables is 108, but there are only 21 possible scenarios in this problem. The decision tree is shown using coalescence, i.e., repeating sub-trees are shown only once. With coalescence, the number of endpoints is reduced to 12. Notice that before we can complete the decision tree representation, we need to compute the required probabilities, i.e. P(R) and P($A|R$).

3 Sequential Valuation Network Representation

In this section, we define a new hybrid representation, which we call a *sequential valuation network*. First we start with some notation.

Valuation Fragments. Suppose α is a utility valuation for h, i.e., $\alpha: \Omega_h \rightarrow R$, where Ω_h denotes the state space of the variables in h, and R denotes the set of real numbers. We shall refer to h as the *domain* of α. Suppose $g \subseteq h$, and suppose $\Gamma \subseteq \Omega_g$. Then $\alpha|\Gamma$ is a function $\alpha|\Gamma: \Gamma \times \Omega_{h-g} \rightarrow R$ such that $(\alpha|\Gamma)(\mathbf{x}_g, \mathbf{x}_{h-g}) = \alpha(\mathbf{x}_g, \mathbf{x}_{h-g})$ for all $\mathbf{x}_g \in \Gamma$, and all $\mathbf{x}_{h-g} \in \Omega_{h-g}$. We call $\alpha|\Gamma$ a *restriction* of α to Γ. We will also refer to $\alpha|\Gamma$ as a *fragment* of α. We will continue to regard the domain of $\alpha|\Gamma$ as h. Notice that $\alpha|\Omega_g = \alpha$.

Often, Γ is a singleton subset of Ω_g, $\Gamma = \{\mathbf{x}_g\}$. In this case, we write $\alpha|\Gamma$ as $\alpha|\mathbf{x}_g$. For example, suppose α is a valuation for $\{A, B\}$ where $\Omega_A = \{a_1, a_2\}$ and $\Omega_B = \{b_1, b_2, b_3\}$. Then, α can be represented as a table as shown in the left hand side of Table 1. The restriction of α to a_1, $\alpha|a_1$, is shown in the right hand side of Table 1. In practice, valuation fragments will be specified without specifying the full valuation. In the case of utility valuations, the unspecified values can be regarded as zero utilities (whenever the utility function decomposes additively), and in the case of probability valuations, the unspecified values can be regarded as zero probabilities.

A complete SVN representation of the Reactor problem is given in Figure 3, Table 2, and Table 3. The SVN graph consists of six types of nodes—chance, decision, terminal, indicator, utility and probability. Chance nodes are shown as circles and represent random variables. In the Reactor problem representation, there are three chance nodes, R, A, and C. Decision nodes are shown as rectangles and represent decision variables. In the Reactor problem representation, there are two decision nodes, D_1 and D_2. The terminal node is shown as an octagon and is a compact version of the end points of a decision tree. The terminal node is labeled T in the Reactor problem representation. Indicator valuations are shown as triangles with a double border, probability valuations are

Table 1. An Example of a Valuation Fragment

$\Omega_{\{A, B\}}$	α
a_1, b_1	$\alpha(a_1, b_1)$
a_1, b_2	$\alpha(a_1, b_2)$
a_1, b_3	$\alpha(a_1, b_3)$
a_2, b_1	$\alpha(a_2, b_1)$
a_2, b_2	$\alpha(a_2, b_2)$
a_2, b_3	$\alpha(a_2, b_3)$

$\{a_1\} \times \Omega_B$	$\alpha\|a_1$
a_1, b_1	$\alpha(a_1, b_1)$
a_1, b_2	$\alpha(a_1, b_2)$
a_1, b_3	$\alpha(a_1, b_3)$

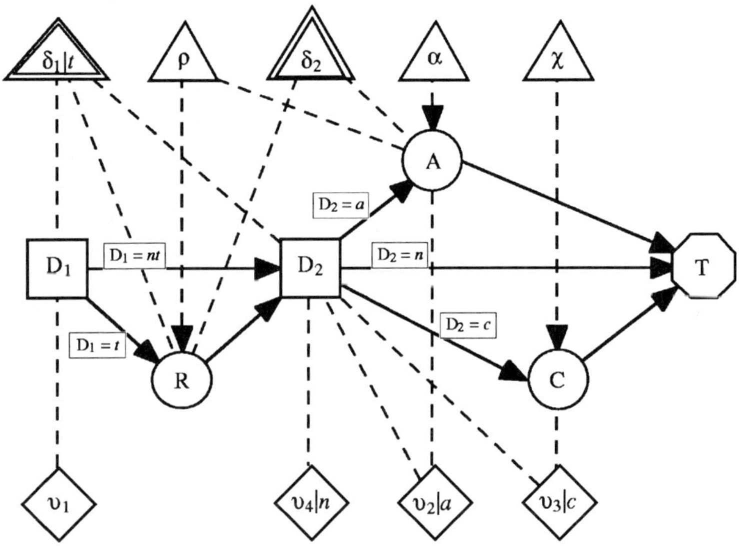

Fig. 3. A SVN Graphical Representation of the Reactor Problem

shown as triangles with a single border, and utility valuations are shown as diamonds. For further details, see [4].

The structure of the sub-graph is similar to the SDD graphical representation of [3] (with minor differences in the terminal node and the annotations associated with the directed edges) and the attached valuations have the same semantics as VNs [13].

In the qualitative part, we first define the state spaces of all chance and decision variables, and then specify the details of the indicator valuations. In the Reactor problem, $\Omega_{D_1} = \{t, nt\}$, $\Omega_R = \{b, g, e\}$, $\Omega_{D_2} = \{a, c, n\}$, $\Omega_A = \{as, al, am\}$, and $\Omega_C = \{cs, cf\}$. The indicator valuation $\delta_1|t$ with domain $\{t\}\times\{R, D_2\}$ is a constraint on the choices available to the decision-maker at D_2. This constraint can be specified by listing all states in $\{t\}\times\Omega_{\{R,\ D_2\}}$ that are allowed. Thus, the states that are allowed by $\delta_1|t$ are $\{(t, b, c), (t, b, n), (t, g, a), (t, g, c), (t, g, n), (t, e, a), (t, e, c), (t, e, n)\}$. Similarly, the indicator valuation δ_2 with domain $\{R, A\}$ can be regarded as a constraint on the state space $\Omega_{\{R,\ A\}}$. δ_2 rules out the state (b, as) that has zero probability. In this paper, we will regard an indicator valuation as a subset of the state space of its domain. For example, $\delta_1|t \subset \{t\}\times\Omega_{\{R,\ D\}}$, and $\delta_2 \subset \Omega_{\{R,\ A\}}$. During the solution phase, the computations in some sub-problems are done on the relevant state space (determined by the valuations that are being processed) constrained by the indicator valuations that are associated with the sub-problem.

In the quantitative part, we specify the numerical details of the probability and utility valuations as given in Tables 2 and 3. The numerical specifications have to be consistent with the graphical and qualitative specifications in the following senses. First, each valuation's domain is specified in the graphical part. For example, the domain of χ is C. Therefore, we have to specify the values of χ for each state in Ω_C. Second, since the edge from χ to C is directed, this means the probability valuation χ

Table 2. Utility Valuation Fragments in the Reactor Problem

Ω_{D_1}	υ_1
nt	0
t	–1

$\{a\}\times\Omega_A$	$\upsilon_2\|a$
a, as	12
a, al	–6
a, am	–10

$\{c\}\times\Omega_C$	$\upsilon_3\|c$
c, cs	8
c, cf	–4

$\{n\}\subset\Omega_{D_2}$	$\upsilon_4\|n$
n	0

Table 3. Probability Valuation Fragments in the Reactor Problem

Ω_C	χ
cs	0.98
cf	0.02

Ω_A	α
as	0.660
al	0.244
am	0.096

δ_2	ρ
b, al	0.288
b, am	0.313
g, as	0.182
g, al	0.565
g, a	0.437
e, as	0.818
e, al	0.147
e, am	0.250

is a conditional for C given the empty set, i.e., the marginal of χ for the empty set is a vacuous probability valuation. Third, if we have probability or utility valuations specified on domains for which we have indicator valuations, then it is only necessary to specify the values of the valuations for the states permitted by the indicator valuations. For example, probability valuation ρ has domain $\{R, A\}$. Since we have indicator valuation δ_2 with the same domain, it is sufficient to specify the values of ρ for the states in δ_2. Thus, we can regard ρ as a valuation fragment. Also, since the edge from ρ to R is directed, the values of ρ have to satisfy the condition $\rho^{\downarrow A} = \iota_A$ where ι_A is the vacuous probability valuation with domain $\{A\}$, i.e., a valuation whose values are identically one. Fourth, it is sufficient to specify values of utility or probability valuations for those states that are allowed by the annotations on the edges between variables. For example, consider the utility valuation fragment $\upsilon_2|a$. The domain of this valuation is $\{D_2, A\}$. However, the annotation on the edge from D_2 to A tells us that all scenarios that include variable A have $D_2 = a$. Therefore, it is sufficient to specify υ_2 for all states in $\{a\}\times\Omega_A$. Similarly, it is sufficient to specify $\upsilon_3|c$ for $\{c\}\times\Omega_C$, and sufficient to specify $\delta_1|t$ for $\{t\}\times\Omega_{\{R, D_2\}}$. Utility valuation $\upsilon_4|n$ is only specified for $D_2 = n$. Notice that when $D_2 = n$, the next node in the SVN is the terminal node T. Therefore, $\upsilon_4|n$ cannot include either A or C in its domain.

Utility valuations υ_1, $\upsilon_2|a$, $\upsilon_3|c$, and $\upsilon_4|n$ are additive factors of the joint utility function, and probability valuations χ, α, and δ are multiplicative factors of the joint probability distribution. In the Reactor problem, we have a factorization of the joint probability distribution into conditionals, i.e., a Bayes net model. But this is not a requirement of the sequential valuation network representation. As we will see in the next section, the SVN solution technique will work for any multiplicative factorization of the joint probability distribution.

4 Solving a SVN Representation

The main idea of the SVN solution method is to recursively decompose the problem into smaller sub-problems until the sub-problems are symmetric, then to solve the symmetric sub-problems, using a special case of the symmetric fusion algorithm [12]. Finally, the solutions to the sub-problems are recursively combined to obtain the solution to the original problem. We begin with some notation.

4.1 Combination

Consider two utility valuations ψ_1 for h_1 and ψ_2 for h_2. As defined in [12], we combine utility valuations using pointwise addition assuming an additive factorization of the joint utility function. In the SVN method, each sub-problem deals with valuation fragments that are relevant to the sub-problem. We start with defining combination of utility fragments.

Case 1. [*Combination of utility fragments*] Suppose $g_1 \subseteq h_1$, and $g_2 \subseteq h_2$, and consider two utility fragments $\psi_1|\Gamma_1$ and $\psi_2|\Gamma_2$ where $\Gamma_1 \subseteq \Omega_{g_1}$, and $\Gamma_2 \subseteq \Omega_{g_2}$. Let Γ denote $((\Gamma_1 \times \Omega_{h_1 \cup h_2 - g_1}) \cup (\Gamma_2 \times \Omega_{h_1 \cup h_2 - g_2}))^{\downarrow g_1 \cup g_2}$. The combination of $\psi_1|\Gamma_1$ and $\psi_2|\Gamma_2$, written as $(\psi_1|\Gamma_1) \otimes (\psi_2|\Gamma_2)$, is a utility valuation ψ for $h_1 \cup h_2$ restricted to Γ given by

$$
\begin{aligned}
(\psi|\Gamma)(\mathbf{y}) &= (\psi_1|\Gamma_1)(\mathbf{y}^{\downarrow g_1}, \mathbf{y}^{\downarrow h_1 - g_1}) + (\psi_2|\Gamma_2)(\mathbf{y}^{\downarrow g_2}, \mathbf{y}^{\downarrow h_2 - g_2}) && \text{if } \mathbf{y}^{\downarrow g_1} \in \Gamma_1 \text{ and } \mathbf{y}^{\downarrow g_2} \in \Gamma_2 \\
&= (\psi_1|\Gamma_1)(\mathbf{y}^{\downarrow g_1}, \mathbf{y}^{\downarrow h_1 - g_1}) && \text{if } \mathbf{y}^{\downarrow g_1} \in \Gamma_1 \text{ and } \mathbf{y}^{\downarrow g_2} \notin \Gamma_2 \\
&= (\psi_2|\Gamma_2)(\mathbf{y}^{\downarrow g_2}, \mathbf{y}^{\downarrow h_2 - g_2}) && \text{if } \mathbf{y}^{\downarrow g_1} \notin \Gamma_1 \text{ and } \mathbf{y}^{\downarrow g_2} \in \Gamma_2
\end{aligned}
$$

for all $\mathbf{y} \in \Gamma \times \Omega_{(h_1 \cup h_2) - (g_1 \cup g_2)}$.

Case 2. [*Combination of a utility fragment and a probability fragment*] Suppose $g_1 \subseteq h_1$, and $g_2 \subseteq h_2$, and consider utility fragment $\psi_1|\Gamma_1$ and probability fragment $\psi_2|\Gamma_2$ where $\Gamma_1 \subseteq \Omega_{g_1}$, and $\Gamma_2 \subseteq \Omega_{g_2}$. Let Γ denote $((\Gamma_1 \times \Omega_{h_1 \cup h_2 - g_1}) \cap (\Gamma_2 \times \Omega_{h_1 \cup h_2 - g_2}))^{\downarrow g_1 \cup g_2}$. The combination of $\psi_1|\Gamma_1$ and $\psi_2|\Gamma_2$, written as $(\psi_1|\Gamma_1) \otimes (\psi_2|\Gamma_2)$, is a utility valuation ψ for $h_1 \cup h_2$ restricted to Γ given by:

$(\psi|\Gamma)(\mathbf{y}) = (\psi_1|\Gamma_1)(\mathbf{y}^{\downarrow g_1}, \mathbf{y}^{\downarrow h_1 - g_1})(\psi_2|\Gamma_2)(\mathbf{y}^{\downarrow g_2}, \mathbf{y}^{\downarrow h_2 - g_2})$ if $\mathbf{y}^{\downarrow g_1} \in \Gamma_1$ and $\mathbf{y}^{\downarrow g_2} \in \Gamma_2$ and 0 otherwise, for all $\mathbf{y} \in \Gamma \times \Omega_{(h_1 \cup h_2) - (g_1 \cup g_2)}$.

Case 3. [*Combination of probability fragments*] Suppose $g_1 \subseteq h_1$, and $g_2 \subseteq h_2$, and consider probability fragments $\psi_1|\Gamma_1$ and $\psi_2|\Gamma_2$ for h_1 and h_2, respectively, where $\Gamma_1 \subseteq \Omega_{g_1}$, and $\Gamma_2 \subseteq \Omega_{g_2}$. Let Γ denote $((\Gamma_1 \times \Omega_{h_1 \cup h_2 - g_1}) \cap (\Gamma_2 \times \Omega_{h_1 \cup h_2 - g_2}))^{\downarrow g_1 \cup g_2}$. The combination of $\psi_1|\Gamma_1$ and $\psi_2|\Gamma_2$, written as $(\psi_1|\Gamma_1) \otimes (\psi_2|\Gamma_2)$, is a probability valuation ψ for $h_1 \cup h_2$ restricted to Γ given by

$(\psi|\Gamma)(\mathbf{y}) = (\psi_1|\Gamma_1)(\mathbf{y}^{\downarrow g_1}, \mathbf{y}^{\downarrow h_1 - g_1})(\psi_2|\Gamma_2)(\mathbf{y}^{\downarrow g_2}, \mathbf{y}^{\downarrow h_2 - g_2})$ if $\mathbf{y}^{\downarrow g_1} \in \Gamma_1$ and $\mathbf{y}^{\downarrow g_2} \in \Gamma_2$ and 0 otherwise for all $\mathbf{y} \in \Gamma \times \Omega_{(h_1 \cup h_2) - (g_1 \cup g_2)}$. The reactor problem described in this paper does not require this case of combination.

Note that, the combination of two utility valuations is a utility valuation; the combination of two probability valuations is a probability valuation; and the combination of a utility and a probability valuation is a utility valuation.

As for the marginalization and division operations, the SVN method uses the same marginalization and division operations as defined in [12]. For further details, see [4].

4.2 Tagging

The recursive algorithm of solving lower level sub-problems and sending the results to an upper level sub-problem requires the use of a concept that we call *tagging*. Suppose ψ is a utility valuation with domain h, and suppose $X \notin h$. Tagging ψ by $X = x$ is denoted by $\psi \otimes (\iota_X|x)$, where $\iota_X|x$ is the vacuous utility valuation with domain $\{X\}$ restricted to $X = x$. A vacuous utility valuation is a valuation that is identically zero. This operation basically extends the domain of ψ from h to $h \cup \{X\}$ without changing the values of ψ.

4.3 The Fusion Algorithm

The details of the fusion algorithm are given in [12]. In the context of sequential valuation networks, the fusion algorithm is the same as rollback in decision trees. Fusion with respect to decision variables is similar to the "folding back" operation in decision trees [11] and fusion with respect to chance variables is similar to the "averaging out" operation in decision trees [11]. Further details of the fusion algorithm for sequential valuation networks are found in [4].

4.4 Decomposition of the Problem

Starting from the SVN graphical representation, we decompose the decision problem into symmetric sub-problems. The symmetric sub-problems are identified by enumerating all distinct directed paths and sub-paths from the source node to the terminal node in the SVN graphical representation.

Variables. We start with the root node, say S. Next we identify all directed arcs in the SVN that lead out of the source node S. For each directed arc, say to variable *X*, we create a new sub-problem consisting of variables S and *X* on the path from the source node to variable *X*. We retain the annotation on the edges. We recursively proceed in this manner until all paths and sub-paths have been enumerated. Notice that the terminal node is not a variable and we do not include it in any sub-problem. The resulting directed tree is called a "decomposition tree." Figure 4 shows the decomposition tree that is constructed for the reactor problem.

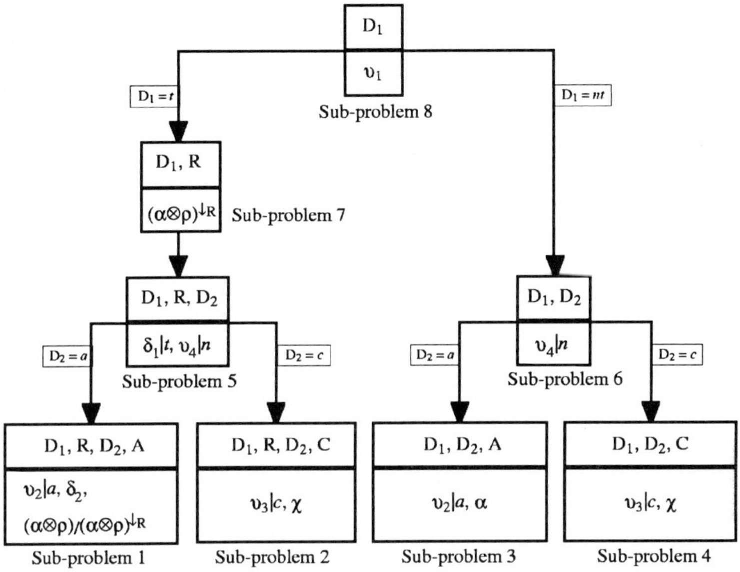

Fig. 4. The Decomposition Tree for the Reactor Problem

Utility and Indicator Valuations. We start at the root node, say S, of the decomposition tree with the set of all utility valuation fragments included in the SVN representation. All valuation fragments whose domains are included in the set of variables associated with the sub-problem are associated with this sub-problem. The valuations that are not are passed on to the child sub-problems suitably decomposed as per the annotation on the edges leading to the child sub-problems. This is recursively repeated.

In the Reactor problem, we start with utility and indicator valuations υ_1, $\upsilon_2|a$, $\upsilon_3|c$, $\upsilon_4|n$, $\delta_1|t$, and δ_2. Valuation υ_1 with domain $\{D_1\}$ is associated with sub-problem 8. Of the remaining valuations, only $\delta_1|t$ has D_1 in its domain. Since there is no fragment of $\delta_1|t$ that has $D_1 = nt$, Sub-problem 7 receives valuations $\upsilon_2|a$, $\upsilon_3|c$, $\upsilon_4|n$, $\delta_1|t$, and δ_2. Sub-problem 6 receives valuations $\upsilon_2|a$, $\upsilon_3|c$, $\upsilon_4|n$, and δ_2.

This process of associating utility and indicator valuations with sub-problems continues recursively as above. The resulting distribution of utility and indicator valuations in the sub-problems is shown in Figure 4.

Probability Valuations. We start by assuming that we have a factorization of the joint probability distribution for all chance variables in the problem. In the reactor problem, for example, the joint probability distribution τ for $\{C, A, R\}$ is given by $\tau = \chi \otimes \alpha \otimes \rho$.

We recursively compute the probability valuation associated with a leaf sub-problem that ends with a chance variable, say C_m, as follows. Let $\Gamma = \{C_1, \ldots, C_m\}$ denote the chance variables on a path from the source node to the leaf node whose last variable is C_m, and let $P = \{\pi_1, \ldots, \pi_k\}$ denote the set of probability potentials with domains $h_1, \ldots, h_k$, respectively, such that $(\pi_1 \otimes \ldots \otimes \pi_k)^{\downarrow \Gamma}$ is the joint distribution for the chance variables in Γ. The probability valuation associated with the leaf sub-problem whose last variable is C_m is given by $\pi^{\downarrow \Gamma} / \pi^{\downarrow \Gamma - \{C_m\}}$, where $\pi = \otimes\{\pi_j \mid C_m \in h_j\}$. Furthermore, the set of probability valuations associated with the set of chance variables $\Gamma - \{C_m\}$ is $\cup\{\pi_j \mid C_m \notin h_j\} \cup \{\pi^{\downarrow \Gamma - \{C_m\}}\}$, i.e., $(\otimes\{\pi_j \mid C_m \notin h_j\} \otimes \pi^{\downarrow \Gamma - \{C_m\}})^{\downarrow \Gamma - \{C_m\}}$ is the joint distribution for the chance variables in $\Gamma - \{C_m\}$. Thus, we can recursively compute the probability valuations associated with the other sub-problems whose last variable is a chance node. It follows from Lauritzen and Spiegelhalter [1988] that $\pi^{\downarrow \Gamma} / \pi^{\downarrow \Gamma - \{C_m\}}$ is the conditional probability distribution for C_m given the variables in $\Gamma - \{C_m\}$. For further details on how the sub-problems are populated with indicator, utility, and probability valuations, see [4].

4.5 Solving the Sub-problems

We start with solving the leaf sub-problems. After solving a sub-problem (as per the definition of fusion stated in [12]), we pass the resulting utility valuation fragment to its parent sub-problem and delete the sub-problem. In passing the utility valuation fragment to the parent sub-problem, if the domain of the utility valuation fragment does not include any variables in the parent sub-problem, we tag the utility valuation with the value of the last variable in the parent sub-problem that is in the annotation. We recursively continue this procedure until all sub-problems are solved.

Consider the decomposition of the Reactor problem into the eight sub-problems as shown in Figure 4. Consider Sub-problem 1 consisting of valuation fragments $\upsilon_2|a$, $(\rho \otimes \alpha)/(\rho \otimes \alpha)^{\downarrow R}$, and δ_2. We fuse the valuation fragments with respect to A using the definition of fusion from [12].

$$\mathrm{Fus}_A\{\upsilon_2|a, (\alpha \otimes \rho)/(\alpha \otimes \rho)^{\downarrow R}\} = \{[\upsilon_2|a \otimes (\alpha \otimes \rho)/(\alpha \otimes \rho)^{\downarrow R}]^{-A}\} = \{\upsilon_5|a\}.$$

The resulting utility valuation $\upsilon_5|a$ is sent to parent Sub-problem 5. Since $\upsilon_5|a$ includes D_2 in its domain, there is no need for tagging. All computations are done on relevant state spaces as constrained by indicator valuation δ_2. The details of the computation are shown in Table 4. The solutions to the remainder of the sub-problems are given in [4].

5 Summary and Conclusions

The main goal of this paper is to propose a new representation and solution technique for asymmetric decision problems.

The advantages of SVNs over SDDs are as follows. SVNs do not require a separate influence diagram to represent the uncertainty model. SVNs can represent a more general uncertainty model than SDDs, which like influence diagrams assume a Bayes net model of uncertainties. All asymmetries can be represented in SVNs. This is not true for SDDs. For example, in the Reactor problem, the impossibility of $R = b$ when $A = as$ is not represented in a SDD representation of the problem. SVNs do not require a separate formulation table representation as in SDDs. Finally, SVNs can handle any factorization of the joint utility function whereas SDDs as currently described can only

Table 4. The Details of Solving Sub-problem 1

$\{a\}\times\delta_2$	$\upsilon_2\|a$	$(\alpha\otimes\rho)/$ $(\alpha\otimes\rho)^{\downarrow R}$	$\upsilon_2\|a\otimes(\alpha\otimes\rho)$ $/(\alpha\otimes\rho)^{\downarrow R}=\varphi$	$\varphi^{-A}=$ $\upsilon_5\|a$
a, b, al	–6	0.700	–4.200	–7.200
a, b, am	–10	0.300	–3.000	
a, g, as	12	0.400	4.800	0.649
a, g, al	–6	0.460	–2.760	
a, g, am	–10	0.140	–1.400	
a, e, as	12	0.900	10.800	10.043
a, e, al	–6	0.060	–0.360	
a, e, am	–10	0.040	–0.400	

be used with either an undecomposed joint utility function or with a factorization of the joint utility function into singleton factors.

The advantages of SVNs over VNs are as follows. SVNs represent most of the asymmetry at the graphical level (some asymmetry is represented in the details of the indicator valuations) whereas in the case of VNs, all asymmetry is represented in the details of the indicator valuations. The state spaces of chance and decision nodes in SVNs do not include dummy states. All types of asymmetry can be represented in SVNs whereas VNs cannot represent some types of asymmetry. Finally, the modeling of probability distributions in SVNs is as intuitive as in influence diagrams (assuming we are given a Bayes net model for the joint probability distribution).

One main advantage of the SVN technique is that we do not need to introduce dummy states for chance or decision variables. To see why this is important, we will describe a simple example called Diabetes diagnosis. Consider a physician who is trying to diagnose whether or not a patient is suffering from Diabetes. Diabetes has two symptoms, glucose in urine, and glucose in blood. Assume we have a Bayes net model for the three variables—Diabetes (*D*), glucose in blood (*B*) and glucose in urine (*U*)—in which the joint distribution for the three variables P(*D, B, U*) factors into three conditionals, P(*D*), P(*B* | *D*), and P(*U* | *D*, *B*). Furthermore, assume that *D* has two states, *d* for Diabetes is present, and ~*d* for Diabetes is absent, *U* has two states, *u* for elevated glucose levels in urine, and ~*u* for normal glucose level in urine, and *B* has two states, *b* for elevated glucose levels in blood, and ~*b* for normal glucose level in blood. The physician first decides, *FT* (first test), whether to order a urine test (*ut*) or a blood test (*bt*) or no test (*nt*). After the physician has made this decision and observed the results (if any), she next has to decide whether or not to order a second test (*ST*). The choices available for the second test decision depend on the decision made at *FT*. If *FT* = *bt*, then the choices for *ST* are either *ut* or *nt*. If *FT* = *ut*, then the choices for *ST* are either *bt* or *nt*. Finally, after the physician has observed the results of the second test (if any), she then has to decide whether to treat the patient for Diabetes or not. As described so far, the problem has three chance variables, *D*, *U*, *B*, and three decision variables *FT* (first test), *ST* (second test), and *TD* (treat for Diabetes). Using the SVN technique, one can represent this problem easily without introducing any more variables or any dummy states. A SVN graphical representation is shown in Figure 5. In this figure, the indicator valuation fragment $\iota|FT = \{bt, ut\}$ represents a constraint on *ST* as described above, the utility valuations κ_1, κ_2, and κ_3 represents a factorization of the total cost of diagnosing and treating the patient for Diabetes, and the probability valuations δ= P(*D*), β= P(*B* | *D*), and υ= P(*U* | *B*, *D*) represent a factorization of the joint probability distribution into conditionals specified by the Bayes net model. Notice that the SVN graphical representation has several directed cycles. However, these directed cycles are disallowed by the annotations on the directed edges and the indicator valuation ι, which forbids, e.g., *FT* = *bt*, *ST* = *bt*, and also *FT* = *ut*, *ST* = *ut*.

Representing this problem using Smith-Holtzman-Matheson's asymmetric influence diagrams [14] or Shenoy's asymmetric valuation networks [13] is possible but only after either introducing additional variables or introducing dummy states for the existing variables. This is because if one uses the existing variables, the modeling of information constraints would depend on the *FT* decision. If *FT* = *bt*, then the true state of *B* is revealed prior to making the *ST* decision, and the true state of *U* is unknown when the *ST* decision is made. However if *FT* = *ut*, then the true state of *U* is known prior to making the *ST* decision and the true state of *B* is unknown when the *ST* decision is made. We call this aspect of the decision problem *information asymmetry*. Using either traditional influence diagrams or valuation networks, it is not possible to model this information asymmetry without either introducing additional variables or introducing dummy states for existing variables. In either of these cases, the modeling will need to adapt the Bayes net to a model that includes additional variables or dummy states or both. We leave the details of representing the Diabetes diagnosis problem using either influence diagrams or valuation networks or some other technique to the ingenuity of the reader.

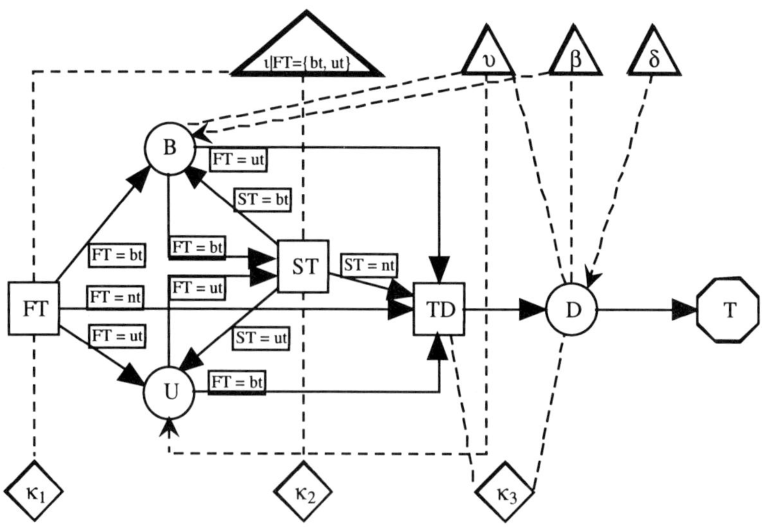

Fig. 5. A SVN Representation of the Diabetes Diagnosis Problem

Acknowledgements. The paper has benefited from comments and discussions with Concha Bielza, Finn Jensen, Thomas Nielsen, Zvi Covaliu, Liping Liu, and Kelli Wikoff.

References

1. Bielza, C. and P. P. Shenoy (1999), "A comparison of graphical techniques for asymmetric decision problems," *Management Science*, **45**(11), 1552–1569.
2. Call, H. J. and W. A. Miller (1990), "A comparison of approaches and implementations for automating decision analysis," *Reliability Engineering and System Safety*, **30**, 115–162.
3. Covaliu, Z. and R. M. Oliver (1995), "Representation and solution of decision problems using sequential decision diagrams," *Management Science*, **41**(12), 1860–1881.
4. Demirer, R. and P. P. Shenoy (2001), "Sequential Valuation Networks for Asymmetric Decision Problems," Working Paper No. 286, University of Kansas School of Business, Lawrence, KS. Available by anonymous ftp from <ftp://ftp.bschool.ku.edu/home/pshenoy/wp286.pdf>
5. Fung, R. M. and R. D. Shachter (1990), "Contingent influence diagrams," Working Paper Department of Engineering-Economic Systems, Stanford University, Stanford, CA.
6. Lauritzen, S. L. and D. J. Spiegelhalter (1988), "Local computations with probabilities on graphical structures and their application to expert systems" (with discussion), *Journal of Royal Statistical Society,* Series B, **50**(2), 157–224.
7. Liu, L. and P. P. Shenoy (1995), "A decomposition method for asymmetric decision problems," in *Proceedings of the 1995 Decision Sciences Institute Annual Meeting*, **2**, 589–591, Boston, MA.
8. Liu, L. and P. P. Shenoy (2000), "Representing asymmetric decision problems using coarse valuations," Working Paper No. 287, University of Kansas School of Business, Summerfield Hall, Lawrence, KS.
9. Nielsen, T. D. and F. V. Jensen (2000), "Representing and solving asymmetric decision problems," in C. Boutilier and M. Goldszmidt (eds.), *Uncertainty in Artificial Intelligence: Proceedings of the Sixteenth Conference*, 416–425, Morgan Kaufmann, San Francisco, CA.
10. Qi, R., L. Zhang and D. Poole (1994), "Solving asymmetric decision problems with influence diagrams," in R. L. Mantaras and D. Poole (eds.), *Uncertainty in Artificial Intelligence: Proceedings of the Tenth Conference*, 491–497, Morgan Kaufmann, San Francisco, CA.
11. Raiffa, H. (1968), *Decision Analysis: Introductory Lectures on Choices under Uncertainty*, Addison-Wesley, Reading, MA.
12. Shenoy, P. P. (1992), "Valuation-based systems for Bayesian decision analysis," *Operations Research*, **40**(3), 463–484.
13. Shenoy, P. P. (2000), "Valuation network representation and solution of asymmetric decision problems," *European Journal of Operational Research*, **121**(3), 2000, 579–608.
14. Smith, J. E., S. Holtzman and J. E. Matheson (1993), "Structuring conditional relationships in influence diagrams," *Operations Research*, **41**(2), 280–297.

A Two-Steps Algorithm for Min-Based Possibilistic Causal Networks

Nahla Ben Amor[1], Salem Benferhat[2], and Khaled Mellouli[1]

[1] Institut Supérieur de Gestion de Tunis, Tunisie,
{nahla.benamor, khaled.mellouli}@ihec.rnu.tn
[2] Institut de Recherche en Informatique de Toulouse (I.R.I.T),
France, benferhat@irit.fr

Abstract. In possibility theory, there are two kinds of possibilistic causal networks depending if the possibilistic conditioning is based on the minimum or the product operator. Product-based possibilistic networks share the same practical and theoretical features as Bayesian networks. In this paper, we focus on min-based causal networks and propose a propagation algorithm for such networks. The basic idea is first to transform the initial network only into a moral graph. Then, two different procedures, called stabilization and checking consistency, are applied to compute the possibility degree of any variable of interest given some evidence.

1 Introduction

Graphical models are knowledge representation tools commonly used by an increasing number of researchers, particularly from the Artificial Intelligence and Statistics communities. The reason for the success of graphical models is their capacity of representing and handling independence relationships, which are crucial for an efficient management and storage of the information.

In possibility theory there are two different ways to define the counterpart of Bayesian networks. This is due to the existence of two definitions of possibilistic conditioning : product-based and min-based conditioning. When we use the product form of conditioning, we get a possibilistic network close to the probabilistic one sharing the same features and having the same theoretical and practical results [1] [5] [6] which is not the case with min-based networks.
In this paper we focus on min-based possibilistic directed graphs and propose a *possibilistic inference* algorithm which allows to determine the possibility degree of any variable of interest given some evidence. Our aim is to avoid a direct adaptation of probabilistic propagation algorithms [7] [9] and especially the transformation of the initial network into a junction tree which is known to be a hard problem [2].
The proposed propagation algorithm works in two steps. First, the initial network is converted into a moral graph where cycles are easily handled, in the propagation algorithm, due to the idempotency of the minimum operator. Then,

S. Benferhat and P. Besnard (Eds.): ECSQARU 2001, LNAI 2143, pp. 266–277, 2001.

possibility degrees of variables of interest are computed via a message passes. More precisely, we first stabilize the moral graph then check its consistency.

Section 2 gives a brief background on possibilistic theory. Section 3 introduces the notions of *α-normalized min-based directed possibilistic graphs* and *α-normalized possibilistic moral graphs.* Section 4 develops the propagation algorithm when no evidence is available. Lastly, Section 5 considers the case of integrating the evidence.

2 Background on Possibility Theory

Let $V = \{A_1, A_2, ..., A_N\}$ be a set of variables. We denote by $D_A = \{a_1, .., a_n\}$ the domain associated with the variable A. By a we denote any instance of A. $\Omega = \times_{A_i \in V} D_{A_i}$ denotes the universe of discourse, which is the Cartesian product of all variable domains in V. Each element of $\omega \in \Omega$ is called a state of Ω. $\omega[A]$ denotes the instance in ω of the variable A.
In the following, we only give a very brief recalling on possibility theory (for more details see [3]).

Possibility distribution and possibility measure: The basic concept in the possibility theory is the notion of *possibility distribution* denoted by π which is a mapping from Ω to the unit interval [0, 1]. Possibility distribution aims to encode our knowledge about ill-known world: $\pi(\omega) = 1$ means that ω is completely possible and $\pi(\omega) = 0$ means that ω is impossible to be the real world. Given a possibility distribution π defined on the universe of discourse Ω, we can define a mapping grading the *possibility measure* of an event $\phi \subseteq \Omega$ by:

$$\Pi(\phi) = \max_{\omega \in \phi} \pi(\omega). \tag{1}$$

Definition 1 *A possibility distribution π is said to be α-*normalized, *if its normalization degree $h(\pi)$ is equal to α, namely:*

$$\alpha = h(\pi) = \max_{\omega} \pi(\omega) \tag{2}$$

If $\alpha = 1$, then π is simply said to be *normalized.*

Possibilistic conditioning: In the possibilistic setting conditioning consists in modifying our initial knowledge, encoded by the possibility distribution π, by the arrival of a new *sure* piece of information $\phi \subseteq \Omega$. The initial distribution π is then transformed into a new one denoted by $\pi' = \pi(. \mid \phi)$. In possibility theory there are two possible definitions of conditioning one based on the product and the other on the minimum. In this paper, given a *normalized* possibility distribution π, we use min-based conditioning proposed in [8][4] and defined by:

$$\Pi(\pi \mid \phi) = \begin{cases} \Pi(\pi \wedge \phi) \; if \; \Pi(\pi \wedge \phi) < \Pi(\phi) \\ 1 \qquad\qquad \text{otherwise} \end{cases} \tag{3}$$

When π is *subnormalized*, the degree 1 in (3) is replaced by $\alpha = h(\pi)$.

3 α-Normalized Possibilistic Graphs and α-Normalized Moral Graphs

We first need to introduce the notions of α-normalized possibilistic graphs and possibilistic moral graphs which will be used later.

3.1 α-Normalized Min-Based Directed Possibilistic Graphs

An *α-normalized min-based directed possibilistic graph* over a set of variables V, denoted by ΠG, is a DAG (Directed Acyclic Graph) where nodes represent variables and edges encode the link between the variables. Parents of a node A is denoted by U_A. For every root node A ($U_A = \emptyset$), uncertainty is represented by the a priori possibility degree $\Pi(a)$ of each instance $a \in D_A$, such that $\max_a \Pi(a) = \alpha$. For the rest of the nodes, ($U_A \neq \emptyset$), uncertainty is represented by the conditional possibility degree $\Pi(a \mid u_A)$ of each instances $a \in D_A$ and $u_A \in D_{U_A}$. These conditional distributions satisfy the following normalization condition: $\max_a \Pi(a \mid u_A) = \alpha$, for any u_A. When $\alpha = 1$, we recover classical possibilistic networks.

Given all the a priori and conditional possibilities, the joint distribution relative to the set V, denoted by $\pi_{\mathcal{D}}$, is expressed by the following *min-based chain rule*:

$$\pi_{\mathcal{D}}(A_1, .., A_N) = \min_{i=1..N} \Pi(A_i \mid U_{A_i}) \tag{4}$$

An important property of α-normalized graphs is:

Proposition 1 *Let ΠG be an α-normalized min-based possibilistic graph. Let $\pi_{\mathcal{D}}$ be the joint distribution computed from (4). Then, $\pi_{\mathcal{D}}$ is α-normalized (in the sense of Definition 1), namely $h(\pi_{\mathcal{D}}) = \alpha$.*

Example 1 *Let us consider the normalized min-based possibilistic graph ΠG composed by the DAG of Figure 1 and the following initial distributions:*

$$\Pi(A) = \begin{matrix} a_1 \\ a_2 \end{matrix} \begin{pmatrix} 1 \\ 0.9 \end{pmatrix}, \quad \Pi(B \mid A) = \begin{matrix} \\ b_1 \\ b_2 \end{matrix} \begin{matrix} a_1 & a_2 \\ \begin{pmatrix} 0.3 & 1 \\ 1 & 0.2 \end{pmatrix} \end{matrix}, \quad \Pi(C \mid A) = \begin{matrix} \\ c_1 \\ c_2 \end{matrix} \begin{matrix} a_1 & a_2 \\ \begin{pmatrix} 1 & 0 \\ 0.4 & 1 \end{pmatrix} \end{matrix},$$

$$\Pi(D \mid B, C) = \begin{matrix} \\ d_1 \\ d_2 \end{matrix} \begin{matrix} b_1 \wedge c_1 & b_1 \wedge c_2 & b_2 \wedge c_1 & b_2 \wedge c_2 \\ \begin{pmatrix} 1 & 1 & 1 & 1 \\ 1 & 0.8 & 0 & 1 \end{pmatrix} \end{matrix}.$$

These a priori and conditional possibilities encode the joint distribution relative to A, B, C and D using (4) as follows: $\forall a, b, c, d, \pi_{\mathcal{D}}(a \wedge b \wedge c \wedge d) = min(\Pi(a), \Pi(b \mid a), \Pi(c \mid d), \Pi(d \mid b \wedge c)$. For instance $\pi_{\mathcal{D}}(a_1 \wedge b_2 \wedge c_2 \wedge d_1) = min(1, 1, 0.4, 1) = 0.4$. Moreover we can check that $h(\pi_{\mathcal{D}}) = 1$.

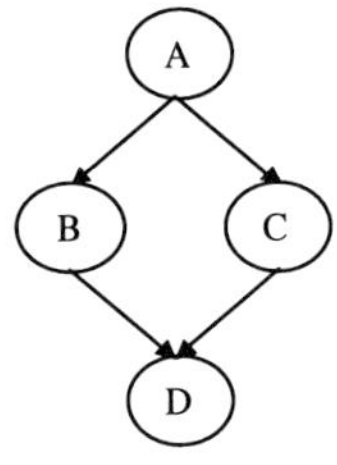

Fig. 1. Example of a Multiply Connected DAG

3.2 α-Normalized Possibilistic Moral Graphs

A *possibilistic moral graph* over a set of variables V, denoted by $\mathcal{MG}$ is a graphical representation where nodes are set of variables called *clusters* and denoted by C_i (in Section 4, each cluster is associated with a variable and its parents). Each edge in $\mathcal{MG}$ is labeled with the intersection of the adjacent clusters C_i and C_j called *separator* and denoted by S_{ij}. We denote by c_i and s_{ij} the possible instances of the cluster C_i and the separator S_{ij} respectively. $c_i[A]$ denotes the instance in c_i of the variable A.

For each cluster C_i (resp. separator S_{ij}) of $\mathcal{MG}$, we assign a local joint distribution relative to the variables in the cluster (resp. separator), called *potential* and denoted by π_{C_i} (resp. $\pi_{S_{ij}}$).

The joint distribution associated with $\mathcal{MG}$, denoted $\pi_{\mathcal{MG}}$ is expressed by:

$$\pi_{\mathcal{MG}}(A_1, .., A_N) = \min_{i=1..N} \pi_{C_i} \tag{5}$$

which is similar to the chain rule (4).

We now give some definitions regarding moral graphs:

Definition 2 *Let C_i and C_j be two adjacent clusters in a moral graph $\mathcal{MG}$ and let S_{ij} be their separator. The separator S_{ij} is said to be* stable *if:*

$$\max_{C_i \backslash S_{ij}} \pi_{C_i} = \max_{C_j \backslash S_{ij}} \pi_{C_j} \tag{6}$$

where $\max_{C_i \backslash S_{ij}} \pi_{C_i}$ is the marginal distribution of S_{ij} defined from π_{C_i}.

A moral graph $\mathcal{MG}$ is said to be stable *if all of its separators are stable.*

The following proposition shows that if a moral graph is stable, then the maximum value of all cluster's potentials is the same.

Proposition 2 *Let $\mathcal{MG}$ be a stabilized moral graph. Then $\forall C_i$, $\alpha = \max \pi_{C_i}$.*

In the following, a stabilized moral graph will be said to be *α-normalized moral graph* to make explicit the degree α. As we will see later, α-normalized moral graphs do not imply that $h(\pi_{MG}) = \alpha$. When this equality holds, we talk about *consistent* moral graphs.

Definition 3 *Let $\mathcal{MG}$ be a stabilized α-normalized moral graph and let $\pi_{\mathcal{MG}}$ be its joint distribution obtained by (5). $\mathcal{MG}$ is said to be* consistent *if $\alpha = h(\pi_{\mathcal{MG}})$.*

4 Possibilistic Propagation

4.1 Basic Ideas

Given a normalized possibilistic graph ΠG, our aim is to compute for any instance a of a variable of interest A the possibility distribution $\Pi_{\mathcal{D}}(a)$ inferred from ΠG. To compute $\Pi_{\mathcal{D}}(a)$, we first define a new possibility distribution π_a from $\pi_{\mathcal{D}}$ as follows:

$$\pi_a(\omega) = \begin{cases} \pi_{\mathcal{D}}(\omega) & \text{if } \omega[A] = a \\ 0 & \text{otherwise} \end{cases} \tag{7}$$

Then, from π_a, it can be checked that:

$$\Pi_{\mathcal{D}}(a) = h(\pi_a) = \max_{\omega} \pi_a(\omega). \tag{8}$$

Note that, in general, π_a is *subnormalized* i.e $h(\pi_a) < 1$.

The principle of the proposed propagation method is summarized in Figure 2 which explains how to compute in a local manner, the possibility distribution $\Pi_{\mathcal{D}}(a)$. Note that computing $\Pi_{\mathcal{D}}(a)$ corresponds to possibilistic inference with no evidence. The more general problem of computing $\Pi_{\mathcal{D}}(a \mid e)$ where e is the total evidence is advocated in Section 5.

The basic steps of the propagation algorithm are:

- *Initialization.* Transform the initial normalized graph into a moral graph, by marrying parents of each node. Then quantify the moral graph using the initial conditional distributions of the DAG. Lastly, incorporate the instance a of the variable of interest A. The resulting moral graph is, in general, neither stable nor consistent.
- *Stabilizing the Moral Graph.* Reach the stability of the moral graph by propagating potentials.
- *Checking and Recovering Consistency.* One way to check the consistency of an α-normalized moral graph is to construct its equivalent α-DAG. We proceed iteratively by adding successively new links to the moral graph and then by stabilizing it again until reaching the consistency.
- *Computing $\Pi_{\mathcal{D}}(a)$.* From a consistent α-normalized moral graph we can compute the possibility degree $\Pi_{\mathcal{D}}(a)$ by simply taking $\Pi_{\mathcal{D}}(a) = \alpha$.

In the following, we denote by $\pi^t_{C_i}$ the potential of the cluster C_i at a step t of the propagation. $t = 1$ (resp. $t = c$) corresponds to the initialization (resp. consistency) step.

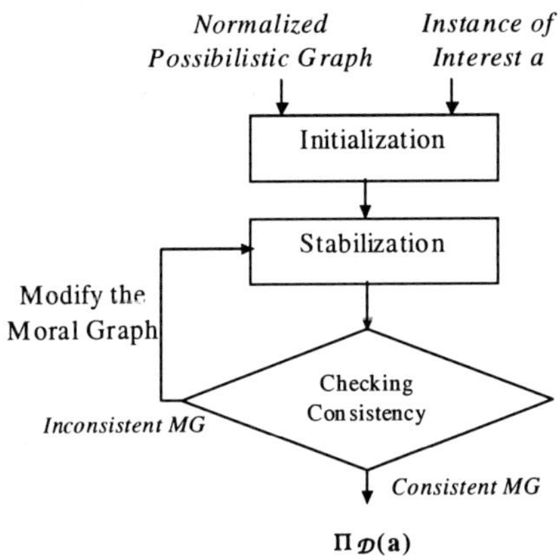

Fig. 2. Propagation Algorithm

4.2 Initialization

The first step of the propagation procedure is to transform the normalized possibilistic graph into a moral graph and to quantify it by transforming the initial conditional distributions into local ones. Once the transformation is done, the initialization procedure incorporates the instance a_i of the variable of interest A_i into the moral graph by considering that $A_i = a_i$. The outline of the initialization procedure is as follows:

1. Building the moral graph:
   1.0. For each variable $A_j \in V$:
   Form a cluster, denoted by C_j, containing $\{A_j\} \cup U_{A_j}$.
   1.1. $\pi^1_{C_j} \Pi(A_j \wedge U_{A_j}) \leftarrow \Pi(A_j \mid U_{A_j})$
   1.2. Between any two clusters with a non-empty intersection, add a link with their intersection as a separator. Potentials associated with separators are equal to 1.
2. Incorporating the instance a_i of the variable of interest A_i:

$$\pi^1_{C_i}(c_i) \leftarrow \begin{cases} \pi^1_{C_i}(c_i) & \text{if } c_i[A_i] = a_i \\ 0 & \text{otherwise} \end{cases}$$

Proposition 3 *Let ΠG be a min-based directed possibilistic graph. Let $\mathcal{MG}$ be the moral graph corresponding to ΠG given by the initialization procedure.*

Let π_a be the joint distribution given by (5) (which is obtained after incorporating the instance a of the variable of interest A). Let $\pi^1_{\mathcal{MG}}$ be the joint distribution encoded by $\mathcal{MG}$ (given by (5)). Then $\pi_a = \pi^1_{\mathcal{MG}}$.

Example 2 *Let us consider the ΠG given in Example 1. The moral graph corresponding to ΠG is represented in Figure 3. Suppose that we are interested with the value of $\Pi_D(D = d_2)$, then after the initialization step we obtain the potentials given in Table 1. We can check that the initialized moral graph is not stable. For instance, the separator A between AB and AC is not stable since* $\max_{AB \backslash A} \pi_{AB}(a_2) = 0.9 \neq \max_{AC \backslash A} \pi_{AC}(a_2) = 1$.

Table 1. Initialized potentials

a	π^1_A	a	b	π^1_{AB}	a	c	π^1_{AC}	b	c	d	π^1_{BCD}	b	c	d	π^1_{BCD}
a_1	1	a_1	b_1	0.3	a_1	c_1	1	b_1	c_1	d_1	0	b_2	c_1	d_1	0
a_2	0.9	a_1	b_2	1	a_1	c_2	0.4	b_1	c_1	d_2	1	b_2	c_1	d_2	0
		a_2	b_1	0.9	a_2	c_1	0	b_1	c_2	d_1	0	b_2	c_2	d_1	0
		a_2	b_2	0.2	a_2	c_2	1	b_1	c_2	d_2	0.8	b_2	c_2	d_2	1

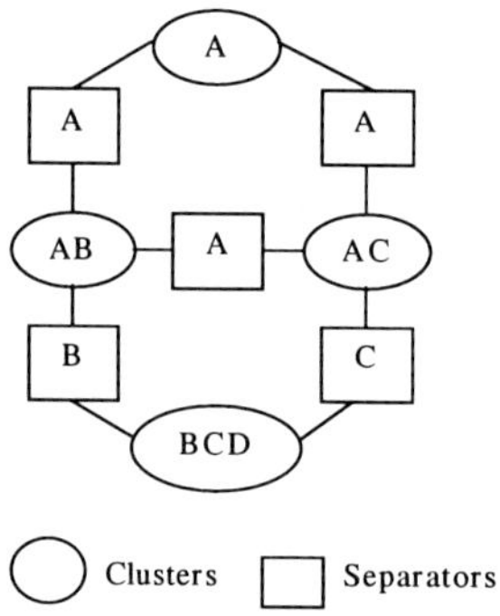

Fig. 3. Moral Graph of the DAG in Figure 1

4.3 Stabilizing the Moral Graph

The *stabilizing procedure* is performed via a *message passing* mechanism between different clusters where each separator *collects* information from its corresponding clusters, then *diffuses* it to each of them in order to update them by taking the minimum between their initial potential and the one diffused by their separator. This operation is repeated until there is no modification on the cluster's potentials.

At each level when $\mathcal{MG}$ is not stable, the potentials of any adjacent clusters C_i and C_j with separator S_{ij} are updated as follows:

– *Collect evidence (Update separators)*:

$$\pi_{S_{ij}}^{t+1} \leftarrow min(\max_{C_i \setminus S_{ij}} \pi_{C_i}^t, \max_{C_j \setminus S_{ij}} \pi_{C_j}^t) \tag{9}$$

– *Distribute evidence (Update clusters)*:

$$\pi_{C_i}^{t+1} \leftarrow min(\pi_{C_i}^t, \pi_{S_{ij}}^{t+1}) \tag{10}$$

$$\pi_{C_j}^{t+1} \leftarrow min(\pi_{C_j}^t, \pi_{S_{ij}}^{t+1}) \tag{11}$$

The outline of the stabilizing procedure is as follows:

1. While the moral graph is *not stable* repeat step 2
2. For each separator S_{ij}
   2.0. Collect evidence in S_{ij} from C_i and C_j using (9).
   2.1. Distribute evidence from S_{ij} to C_i and C_j using (10) and (11).

At each level of the stabilizing procedure (step 2) the moral graph encodes the same joint distribution:

Proposition 4 *Let $\pi_{\mathcal{MG}}^t$ and $\pi_{\mathcal{MG}}^{t+1}$ be the joint distributions computed, respectively, at level t and $t+1$. Then $\pi_{\mathcal{MG}}^t = \pi_{\mathcal{MG}}^{t+1}$.*

It can be shown that the stability is reached after a finite number of message passes of step 2 in the stabilizing procedure, and hence the stabilization procedure is polynomial.

From Propositions 3 and 4 we deduce that from the initialization to the stability level (s), the moral graph encodes the same joint distribution. More formally, at any level $t \in \{1, .., s\}$ we have:

$$\pi_a = \pi_{\mathcal{MG}}^t \tag{12}$$

Example 3 *Let us consider the moral graph initialized in Example 2. At stability level, reached after two message passes, we obtain the potentials given in Table 2. Note that, the maximum potential is the same in the four clusters i.e*
$max\pi_A = max\pi_{AB} = max\pi_{AC} = max\pi_{BCD} = 0.9$.

Table 2. Stabilized potentials (t=s)

a	π_A^s	a	b	π_{AB}^s	a	c	π_{AC}^s	b	c	d	π_{BCD}^s	b	c	d	π_{BCD}^s
a_1	0.9	a_1	b_1	0.3	a_1	c_1	0.9	b_1	c_1	d_1	0	b_2	c_1	d_1	0
a_2	0.9	a_1	b_2	0.9	a_1	c_2	0.4	b_1	c_1	d_2	0.9	b_2	c_1	d_2	0
		a_2	b_1	0.9	a_2	c_1	0	b_1	c_2	d_1	0	b_2	c_2	d_1	0
		a_2	b_2	0.2	a_2	c_2	0.9	b_1	c_2	d_2	0.8	b_2	c_2	d_2	0.9

In general, stability does not guarantee consistency. Indeed, it can be checked in our example that $h(\pi_{\mathcal{MG}}^t) = 0.8 \neq 0.9$.

4.4 Checking and Recovering Consistency

Given a stabilized α-normalized moral graph $\mathcal{MG}$, our aim is to check the consistency of $\mathcal{MG}$ in the sense of definition 3. First, we need a further definition:

Definition 4 *A cluster C_i relative to the variable A_i is said to be* consistent *if for any instance u_{A_i} of U_{A_i}:*

$$\max_{a_i} \pi^t_{C_i}(a_i \wedge u_{A_i}) = \alpha$$

Now, we provide a practical way to check the consistency of a moral graph.

Proposition 5 *A moral graph $\mathcal{MG}$ is consistent if all its clusters are consistent.*

The proof of this proposition is based on Proposition 1 and the following technical lemma:

Lemma 1. *Let $\mathcal{MG}$ be a stabilized α-normalized moral graph and let $\pi_{\mathcal{MG}}$ be its joint distribution. If all the clusters of $\mathcal{MG}$ are consistent, then there exists an α-DAG G' such that its joint distribution $\pi'_{\mathcal{D}}$ satisfies $\pi_{\mathcal{MG}} = \pi'_{\mathcal{D}}$.*

Case of consistency. In the case where the α-normalized moral graph is consistent, the computation of α is immediate with the help of Proposition 1 and Lemma 1. Namely, we can derive the following corollary:

Corollary 1 *Let $\mathcal{MG}$ be a consistent α-normalized moral graph and let a_i be any instance of the variable of interest A_i. Then,*

$$\Pi_{\mathcal{D}}(a) = max\pi^c_{C_i} = \alpha.$$

In other terms, we can compute the possibility degree $\Pi_{\mathcal{D}}(a)$ from the consistent α-normalized moral graph by simply taking the maximum potential of any cluster.

Case of inconsistency. If there exists a variable $A_i \in V$ where $\exists u_{A_i}$ s.t $\max_{a_i} \pi^t_{C_i}(a_i \wedge u_{A_i}) = \beta < \alpha$ then the moral graph is not yet consistent. In this case, we should drop the inconsistency from C_i by replacing for any instance u_{A_i} s.t $\max_{a_i} \pi^t_{C_i}(a_i \wedge u_{A_i}) = \beta < \alpha$, the potential β by α. However, we should not lose this degree.

Thus, the idea is to check if the parent variables of A_i are linked i.e it exists a cluster which contains U_{A_i}. If it is the case, the potential of this cluster is modified by incorporating the degree β.

If such cluster does not exist, we should create new links between variables in U_{A_i}. More precisely, we select any of the parents of A_i and we add to its parent set the remaining variables in U_{A_i}. Then, when quantifying these new links we can incorporate the degree β. The modifications of the moral graph are summarized as follows:

1. *Drop the inconsistency :*
   Let C_i be an inconsistent cluster. Let X be the set of all the instances u_{A_i} s.t $\max_{a_i} \pi^t_{C_i}(a_i \wedge u_{A_i}) = \beta < \alpha$.
   For any instance u_{A_i} in X, replace the potential β by α
2. *Add new links between parents* (If $\nexists$ a cluster containing U_{A_i}):
   Let A_j be any of the parents of A_i:
   - Add to C_j the variable set $T = U_{A_i} \setminus \{A_j\}$ as additional parents of A_j i.e $U_{A_j} \leftarrow U_{A_j} \cup T$
   - Update the separators associated with C_j (since the intersection between the other clusters and C_j is modified)
3. *Modify the parent cluster potential:*
   Let C_j be the cluster containing U_{A_i}:
   $\pi^{t+1}_{C_j} \leftarrow min(\pi^t_{C_j}, \pi_{new})$
   where $\pi_{new}(u_{A_i}) = \begin{cases} \beta \text{ if } u_{A_i} \in X \\ \alpha \text{ otherwise} \end{cases}$

Proposition 6 *Let $\mathcal{MG}$ be a stable moral graph and $\mathcal{MG}$' be the new moral graph obtained as result of the procedure above. Let $\pi^t_{\mathcal{MG}}$ be the joint distribution encoded by $\mathcal{MG}$ and $\pi^{t+1}_{\mathcal{MG}}$ be the joint distribution encoded by $\mathcal{MG}$'. Then, $\pi^t_{\mathcal{MG}} = \pi^{t+1}_{\mathcal{MG}}$.*

If step 3 in the modification procedure updates any of the parent cluster potentials, then we should restabilize the moral graph again and recheck the consistency. The algorithm stops when consistency is reached.

Example 4 *Let us consider the moral graph stabilized in Example 3. We can check that this moral graph is inconsistent since $max\pi_{AB} = 0.9$ while $h(\pi^t_{d_2}) = 0.8$. This is due to the cluster BCD corresponding to the variable D since $max(\pi^t_{BCD}(d_1 \wedge b_1 \wedge c_2), \pi^t_{BCD}(d_2 \wedge b_1 \wedge c_2)) = 0.8 < 0.9$ and $max(\pi^t_{BCD}(d_1 \wedge b_2 \wedge c_1), \pi^t_{BCD}(d_2 \wedge b_2 \wedge c_1)) = 0 < 0.9$.
Thus we should modify the potential of BCD and modify for instance the cluster AB by considering C as a new parent of B. This entails a modification of the moral graph by replacing the cluster AB by ABC and adding the corresponding separators.*

The new clusters's potentials after the modification and the restabilization are given in Table 3. Note that we get a 0.8-normalized moral graph, thus the possibility measure $\Pi_{\mathcal{D}}(d_2)$ corresponds to the maximum potential in clusters i.e $\Pi_{\mathcal{D}}(d_2) = 0.8$.

5 Handling the Evidence

The proposed propagation algorithm can be easily extended in order to take into account new evidence e which corresponds to a set of instanciated variables. The computation of $\Pi_{\mathcal{D}}(a \mid e)$ is performed via two calls of the above propagation algorithm in order to compute successively $\Pi_{\mathcal{D}}(e)$ and $\Pi_{\mathcal{D}}(a \wedge e)$. Then using the min-based conditioning, we get:

Table 3. Consistent potentials

a	π^c_A	a	c	π^c_{AC}	b	c	d	π^c_{ABC}	a	b	c	π^c_{BCD}
a_1	0.4	a_1	c_1	0.3	a_1	b_1	c_1	0.8	b_1	c_1	d_1	0
a_2	0.8	a_1	c_2	0.8	a_1	b_1	c_2	0.3	b_1	c_1	d_2	0.8
		a_2	c_1	0	a_1	b_2	c_1	0	b_1	c_2	d_1	0
		a_2	c_2	0.8	a_1	b_2	c_2	0.8	b_1	c_2	d_2	0.8
					a_2	b_1	c_1	0.8	b_2	c_1	d_1	0.8
					a_2	b_1	c_2	0.8	b_2	c_1	d_2	0.8
					a_2	b_2	c_1	0.8	b_2	c_2	d_1	0
					a_2	b_2	c_2	0.2	b_2	c_2	d_2	0.8

$$\Pi_{\mathcal{D}}(a \mid e) = \begin{cases} \Pi_{\mathcal{D}}(a \wedge e) & \text{if } \Pi_{\mathcal{D}}(a \wedge e) < \Pi_{\mathcal{D}}(e) \\ 1 & \text{otherwise} \end{cases}$$

The computation of $\Pi_{\mathcal{D}}(e)$ needs a slight transformation on the initialization procedure since the evidence can be obtained on several variables. More precisely, step 2 of Section 4.2 is replaced by:
Incorporating the instance $a_1 \wedge, .., \wedge a_M$ of the variables of interest $A_1, .., A_M$, i.e:
$\forall i \in \{1, .., M\}, \pi^1_{C_i}(c_i) \leftarrow \begin{cases} \pi^1_{C_i}(c_i) & \text{if } c_i[A_i] = a_i \\ 0 & \text{otherwise} \end{cases}$

Example 5 *Let us consider the ΠG given in Example 1. Suppose that we are interested with the value of $\Pi_{\mathcal{D}}(a_1 \mid d_2)$. In other terms, we want to compute the impact of the evidence $D = d_2$ on the instance a_1 of the variable A. Then we should first compute $\Pi_{\mathcal{D}}(d_2)$ then $\Pi_{\mathcal{D}}(a_1 \wedge d_2)$. The value $\Pi_{\mathcal{D}}(d_2)$ was already computed in Example 4, and is equal to 0.8. Then we will integrate $A = a_1$ in the consistent moral graph and apply again the propagation procedure. The new consistent potentials are given in Table 4. From these potentials we deduce that $\Pi_{\mathcal{D}}(a_1 \wedge d_2) = 0.4$, thus $\Pi_{\mathcal{D}}(a_1 \mid d_2) = 0.4$ since $\Pi_{\mathcal{D}}(a_1 \wedge d_2) < \Pi_{\mathcal{D}}(d_2)$.*

Table 4. Consistent potentials

a	π^c_A	a	c	π^c_{AC}	b	c	d	π^c_{ABC}	a	b	c	π^c_{BCD}
a_1	0.4	a_1	c_1	0.3	a_1	b_1	c_1	0	b_1	c_1	d_1	0.4
a_2	0	a_1	c_2	0.4	a_1	b_1	c_2	0.4	b_1	c_1	d_2	0.3
		a_2	c_1	0.4	a_1	b_2	c_1	0	b_1	c_2	d_1	0
		a_2	c_2	0.4	a_1	b_2	c_2	0.4	b_1	c_2	d_2	0.4
					a_2	b_1	c_1	0.4	b_2	c_1	d_1	0.4
					a_2	b_1	c_2	0.4	b_2	c_1	d_2	0.4
					a_2	b_2	c_1	0	b_2	c_2	d_1	0.4
					a_2	b_2	c_2	0.4	b_2	c_2	d_2	0.4

6 Conclusion

This paper has proposed an algorithm for computing the possibility degree of a variable of interest given some evidence e in min-based possibilistic graphs. Our algorithm is mainly based on two procedures: stabilization and checking consistency. These procedures are both polynomial. The weakness of our algorithm is that in a case of inconsistencies, some clusters are enlarged with additional variables. However, the maximum number of added variables, due to an inconsistent cluster, does not exceed the maximal cardinality of parents of the variable associated with the inconsistent cluster.
The algorithm proposed in this paper can be directly applied for revising a min-based possibilistic graph by integrating a new piece of knowledge (and not simply an evidence or observation). Namely, our algorithm can be used to construct a new DAG taking into account this new knowledge.
A further work will be to experimentally compare the proposed algorithm with a direct adaptation of the probabilistic propagation algorithms.

References

1. C. Borgelt, J. Gebhardt, and Rudolf Kruse, Possibilistic Graphical Models, In: Proc. ISSEK'98 (Udine, Italy), 1998.
2. G. F. Cooper, Computational complexity of probabilistic inference using Bayesian belief networks, Artificial Intelligence, 393-405, 1990.
3. D. Dubois and H. Prade, Possibility theory : An approach to computerized, Processing of uncertainty, Plenium Press, New York, 1988.
4. D. Dubois and H. Prade, An introductory survey of possibility theory and its recent developments. Journal of Japan Society for Fuzzy Theory and Systems, Vol.10, 1, 21-42, 1998.
5. P. Fonck, Conditional independence in possibility theory, Uncertainty in Artificial Intelligence, 221-226, 1994.
6. J. Gebhardt and R. Kruse, Background and perspectives of possibilistic graphical models, Qualitative and Quantitative Practical Reasoning: ECSQARU/FAPR'97, Lecture Notes in Artificial Intelligence, 1244, pp. 108-121, Springer, Berlin, 1997.
7. F. V. Jensen, Introduction to Bayesien networks, UCL Press, 1996.
8. E.Hisdal, Conditional possibilities independence and non interaction. Fuzzy Sets and Systems, Vol. 1, 1978.
9. S.L. Lauritzen and D. J. Spiegelhalter, Local computations with probabilities on graphical structures and their application to expert systems, Journal of the Royal Statistical Society, Vol. 50, 157-224, 1988.
10. J.Pearl, Probabilistic Reasoning in intelligent systems: networks of plausible inference. Morgan Kaufmman , Los Altos, CA, 1988.
11. L.A. Zadeh, Fuzzy sets as a basis for a theory of possibility. Fuzzy Sets and Systems, 1, 3-28, 1978.

Computing Intervals of Probabilities with Simulated Annealing and Probability Trees

Andrés Cano[1] and Serafín Moral[1]

Dpt. Computer Science and Artificial Intelligence. E.T.S. Ingeniería Informática.
University of Granada. Avda. de Andalucía 38. 18071 Granada. Spain.
{acu,smc}@decsai.ugr.es

Abstract. The paper shows a method to compute *a posteriori* intervals of probabilities when the initial conditional information is given also with intervals of probabilities. The right way of doing an exact computation is with the associated convex set of probabilities. Probability trees are used to represent these initial conditional convex sets, because they save enormously the required space. This paper proposes a simulated annealing algorithm, using probability trees as the representation of the convex sets, in order to compute the *a posteriori* intervals.

1 Introduction

Bayesian networks are graphical structures which are used to represent efficiently joint probability distributions, by taking advantage of the independence relationships [18] among the variables. Different problems can be solved using this graphical representation of the joint distribution. One of the most common tasks is the computation of posterior marginals given that the value of some of the variables is known. This task is called *probability propagation.*

One of the main problems faced when building Bayesian networks is the introduction of a large number of probabilities. Very often, an expert is more comfortable giving an interval of probability rather than a precise probability. Even if we use a learning algorithm to obtain probabilities, we may only have small samples for certain configurations of variables in a distribution. Therefore, it may also be more appropriate to estimate some kind of imprecise probabilities in this case.

In general, the use of imprecise probability models can be useful in many situations [26]. There are various mathematical models for imprecise probabilities [25,26]. Out of all these models, we think that convex sets of probabilities is the most suitable model for calculating with and representing imprecise probabilities, because there is a specific interpretation of numeric values [25]. They are powerful enough to represent the result of basic operations within the model without having to make approximations that cause loss of information, as in interval probabilities. Convex sets are a more general tool for representing unknown probabilities than intervals: there is always a convex set associated with a system of probabilistic intervals, but given a convex set there is not always a proper

S. Benferhat and P. Besnard (Eds.): ECSQARU 2001, LNAI 2143, pp. 278–289, 2001.

representation by using intervals. However, interval probabilities are the most natural way in which imprecise probabilities are given in practice. In this paper, therefore, we will assume that initial probability distributions are given with interval of probabilities, but computations are carried out by considering their associated convex sets.

Some authors have considered the propagation of probabilistic intervals in graphical structures [1,12,23,24]. However in the proposed procedures, there is no guarantee that the calculated intervals are always the same as those obtained by using a global computation. In general, it can be said that calculated bounds are wider than exact ones. The problem is that exact bounds need a computation with the associated convex sets of probabilities. This is the approach followed by Cano, Moral and Verdegay-López [10]. They assume that there is a convex set of conditional probabilities for each configuration of parent variables in the dependence graph. They give a model to obtain the exact bounds using local computations. However, working with convex sets may be very inefficient: if we have n variables and each variable, X_i, has a convex set with l_i extreme points as conditional information, the propagation algorithm is of the order $O(K. \prod_{i=1}^{n} l_i)$, where K is the complexity of carrying out a simple probabilistic propagation. This is so, because convex sets propagation is equivalent to the propagation of all the global probabilities that can be obtained by choosing an exact conditional probability in each of the convex sets.

Probability trees [9,20] can be used to represent probability potentials. The authors have used probability trees to propagate efficiently in Bayesian networks using a join tree when resources (memory and time) are limited, obtaining a greater or smaller error depending on the available time. Probability trees [8] can also be applied in order to propagate the convex sets associated to the interval of probabilities improving computing time, obtaining exact or approximated intervals, depending on the available computing time. Another solution to the problem of propagating the convex sets associated to intervals, is by using combinatorial optimization techniques such as simulated annealing [6], genetic algorithms [7], and gradient techniques [11].

In this paper, we propose adapting a simulated annealing algorithm in order to use probability trees. The rest of the paper is organized as follows. In section 2 we describe the basics of probability propagation in Bayesian networks; section 3 present basic notions about convex sets of probabilities and their relationships with probability intervals; section 4 studies probability trees as a tool to represent potentials in a compact way and also how they can be applied to represent convex sets of probabilities; section 5 describes the proposed simulated annealing algorithm; in section 6 we show some experimental work and finally section 7 gives some conclusions.

2 Probability Propagation in Bayesian Networks

Let $X = \{X_1, \ldots, X_n\}$ be a set of variables. Let us assume that each variable X_i takes values on a finite set U_i. For any set U, $|U|$ represents the number of elements it contains. If I is a set of indices, we will write X_I for the set $\{X_i | i \in I\}$. Let be $N = \{1, \dots, n\}$ the set of all the indices. The Cartesian product $\prod_{i \in I} U_i$ will be denoted by U_I. Given $x \in U_I$ and $J \subseteq I$, x_J will denote the element of U_J obtained from x dropping the coordinates which are not in J. In Shenoy and Shafer's [21] terminology, a mapping from a set U_I on $[0, 1]$ will be called a *valuation* h for X_I. Over valuations, Shenoy and Shafer define the operations of combination $h_1 \otimes h_2$ (multiplication) and marginalization $h^{\downarrow J}$ (adding in the removed variables). They give an abstract set of axioms to operate with valuations.

A *Bayesian network* is a directed acyclic graph where each node represents a random variable X_i, and the topology of the graph shows the independence relations between variables, according to the d-separation criterion [18]. Also, each node X_i has attached a conditional probability distribution $p_i(X_i | F(X_i))$ for the variable given its parents $F(X_i)$. Following Shafer and Shenoy terminology, these conditional distributions can be considered as valuations. In this way, taking into account the independence relations expressed by the graph, the Bayesian network determines an unique joint probability distribution:

$$p(x) = \prod_{i \in N} p_i(x_i | x_{F(X_i)}) \quad \forall x \in U_N \ . \tag{1}$$

An *observation* is the knowledge of the exact value $X_i = e_i$ of a variable. The set of observations will be denoted by e, and called the *evidence set*. E will be the set of indices of the observed variables. Every observation, $X_i = e_i$, is represented by means of a valuation which is a Dirac function defined on U_i as $\delta_i(x_i; e_i) = 1$ if $e_i = x_i$, $x_i \in U_i$, and $\delta_i(x_i; e_i) = 0$ if $e_i \neq x_i$.

The aim of probability propagation is to calculate the *a posteriori* probability function $p(x_k | e)$, for every $x_k \in U_k$, where $k \in \{1, \dots, n\} - E$. Given an evidence set e, $p(x_k | e) \propto \sum_{X_J, X_J \neq X_k} \left(\prod_i p_i(x_i | x_{F(X_i)}) \prod_{e_i \in e} \delta_i(x_i; e_i) \right)$. In fact, previous formula is the expression for $p(x_k \cap e)$. The vector of values $(p(x_k \cap e))$, $x_k \in U_k$, will be denoted as R_k.

A known propagation algorithm can be constructed transforming the directed acyclic graph in a *tree of cliques*. Basically there are two different schemes [17,21] to propagate on a tree of cliques. We will follow Shafer and Shenoy scheme [21] because we do not have to do divisions between valuations, which is an operation not defined for convex sets of probabilities. Every clique has attached a valuation Ψ_{C_i} initially set to the identity mapping. There are two messages (valuations) $M_{C_i \to C_j}$, $M_{C_j \to C_i}$ between every two adjacent cliques C_i and C_j. $M_{C_i \to C_j}$ is a message that sends C_i to C_j and $M_{C_j \to C_i}$ a message that sends C_j to C_i. Every conditional distribution p_i and every observation δ_i are assigned to one clique C_i that contains all its variables. If h_i (p_i or δ_i) is a valuation assigned to clique C_i then Ψ_{C_i} is transformed in the following way: $\Psi_{C_i} = \Psi_{C_i} \otimes h_i$. The algorithm of propagation is carried out by traversing the tree of cliques from leaves to root and then from root to leaves updating messages in the following way:

$$M_{C_i \to C_j} = (\Psi_{C_i} \otimes (\bigotimes_{C_k \in Ady(C_i, C_j)} M_{C_k \to C_i}))^{\downarrow C_i \cap C_j} \tag{2}$$

where $Ady(C_i, C_j)$ is the set of adjacent cliques to C_i except C_j.

Once the propagation is done, the *a posteriori* distribution R_k for variable X_k can be calculated looking for a clique C_i containing X_k and using the following expression:

$$R_k = (\Psi_{C_i} \otimes (\bigotimes_{C_j \in Ady(C_i)} M_{C_j \rightarrow C_i}))^{\downarrow X_k} \tag{3}$$

where $Ady(C_i)$ is the set of adjacent cliques to C_i.

3 Convex Sets of Probability Distributions

With imprecise probabilities, a piece of information for variables in a set I will be a closed, convex set, H, of mappings $p : U_I \longrightarrow \mathbb{R}_0^+$ with a finite set of extreme points. Every mapping is given by the vector of values $(p(x))_{x \in U_I}$.

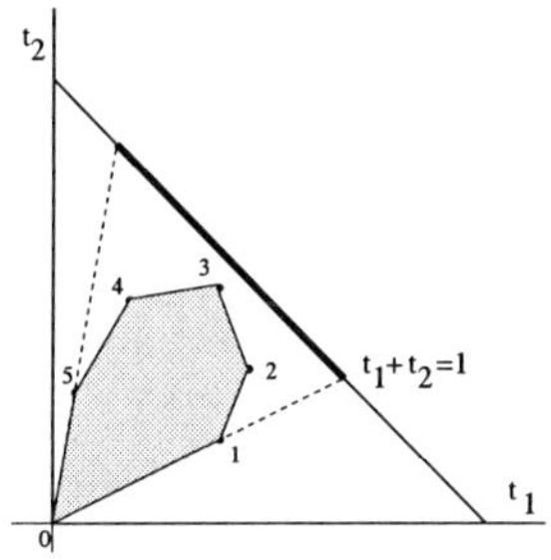

Fig. 1. Propagated Convex Set, R_k

The propagation of convex sets of probabilities [8,10] is completely analogous to the propagation of probabilities. The formulas are the same, but every valuation h_i is now a convex set with l_i extreme points. The operations of combination and marginalization are the same as in the probabilistic case repeated for all the extreme points of the operated sets. The result of the propagation for a variable, X_k, will be a convex set of mappings from U_k in $[0, 1]$. For the sake of simplicity, let us assume that this variable has two values: x_k^1, x_k^2. The result of the propagation is a convex set on $\mathbb{R}^2$ of the form of Figure 1 and that will be called R_k. The points of this convex set, R_k, are obtained in the following way: if P is a global probability distribution, formed by selecting a fixed probability for each convex set, then associated to this probability, we shall obtain a point $(t_1, t_2) \in R_k$ where, $t_1 = P(x_k^1 \cap e)$, $t_2 = P(x_k^2 \cap e)$, and e is the given evidence or family of observations. The projection of the point (t_1, t_2) on the line $t_1 + t_2 = 1$ is equivalent to dividing by $P(e)$ and gives rise to a normalized probability distribution: $P(x_k^i|e) = t_i/(t_1 + t_2), i = 1, 2$. So, the final intervals $[a, b]$ associated to x_k^i can be calculated with formula 4:

$$a = \inf\{t_i/(t_1+t_2) \mid (t_1,t_2) \in R_k\}$$
$$b = \sup\{t_i/(t_1+t_2) \mid (t_1,t_2) \in R_k\} \tag{4}$$

3.1 Convex Sets and Intervals

As it was mentioned in the introduction, we are trying to solve the problem of propagation in dependence graphs where each initial conditional information is given by an interval. We can obtain the convex sets associated to the initial informations (interval of probabilities), and then do computations using these convex sets and finally obtain the associated *a posteriori* intervals. The extreme points of the convex set associated to a set of probability intervals can be calculated in an efficient way with the algorithm presented in [4].

Suppose X_I is a set of random variables taking values on the finite set U_I and Y a random variable taking values on a finite set V. Then, if we have a conditional distribution $P(Y|X_I)$ given with probability intervals, we must apply the algorithm of Campos et al. [4] for each $x_I \in U_I$ to obtain the global convex set $H^{Y|X_I}$. That is to say, if Ext_{x_I} is the set of extreme points of the convex set associated to the distribution $P(Y|X = x_I)$, then the global convex set can be obtained with the following Cartesian product:

$$Ext(H^{Y|X_I}) = \prod_{x_I \in U_I} Ext_{x_I} \tag{5}$$

That it, a conditional extreme probability for Y given X_I is composed of an extreme probability conditioned to $X_I = x_I$ for each possible value x_I.

4 Probability Trees

Probability trees have been demonstrated to be useful to represent probability distributions in order to obtain more compact representations than tables. The size of a table is exponential in the number of parameters (number of variables in the distribution), while the size of a probability tree can be much smaller when there are regularities (asymmetrical independences) in the probability distribution. A *probability tree* $\mathcal{T}$ [3,5,9,13,16,19,20,22,27] for a set of variables X_I is a directed labeled tree, where each internal node represents a variable $X_i \in X_I$ and each leaf node represents a real number $r \in I\!R$. Each internal node will have as many outgoing arcs as possible values the variable it represents has. Let X_I, X_J, X_L and X_K be four disjoint sets of variables. X_I and X_J are *independent given* X_L *in context* $X_K = x_K$, noted as $I_c(X_I; X_J|X_L; X_K = x_K)$, if $P(X_I|X_L, X_J, X_K = x_K) = P(X_I|X_L, X_K = x_K)$ whenever $P(X_J, X_L, X_K = x_K) > 0$. When X_L is empty, it can be said that X_I and X_J are *independent in context* $X_K = x_K$.

Cano and Moral [5] present a methodology to build a probability tree from a probability table. They also propose a way of approximating potentials with probability trees of a given limited size. Also they give exact and approximated methods to calculate with probability trees. They show how to marginalize a probability tree to a set of variables, combine two probability trees and restrict a probability tree to a given configuration of variables.

4.1 Using Probability Trees in the Propagation of Probability Intervals

Probability trees are specially useful when dealing with the problem of propagating probability intervals. As we mentioned in section 3.1 a set of intervals is transformed into a set of extreme points to do the computations. Beside this, we transform the problem into an equivalent one. For each variable X_i, we originally give a valuation h_i for X_i conditioned to its parents $F(X_i)$. This valuation is a convex set of l conditional probability distributions, $h_i = \{p_1, \ldots, p_l\}$. To implement propagation algorithms we add to the domain of h_i a new variable, T_i, taking values on the set $\{t_1, \ldots, t_l\}$. This variable is made a parent node of X_i in the dependence graph. On this node we consider that all the probability distributions are possible, that is to say, the valuation for T_i is a convex set with l extreme points, each one degenerated in one of the possible cases of T_i. Now, the probability of X_i given its parents is an unique, determined probability distribution. Every extreme point p_i of the conditional convex set $H^{X_i|F(X_i)}$ can be recovered by fixing T_i to one of its possible values $\{t_1, \ldots, t_l\}$ in valuation h_i. We can verify that the structure of the problem does not change with this transformation. The only thing that has happened is that our lack of knowledge about the conditional probabilities is now explicit with the help of an additional node expressing all the possible conditional probability distributions. Nothing is known about this node. The idea is to keep the different values of T as parameters in the problem.

The previous way of representing conditional convex sets has a high required memory space that can be improved with probability trees (see Cano and Moral [8] for more details). Suppose we want to represent the global conditional convex set $H^{Y|X_I}$, and we know which are the extreme points of each one of the convex sets $H^{Y|X_I=x_I}$. This requires a set of extreme points given by expression 5. In general this leads us to a high cost representation. In [8] the authors use a transparent variable T_{x_I} for each $x_I \in U_I$. T_{x_I} will have as many cases as the number of extreme points which $H^{Y|X_I=x_I}$ has. The reduction in the representation is obtained by taking asymmetric independences among these transparent variables into account. It is obvious that $I_c(Y; T_{x_I}|X = x_J, x_I \neq x_J) : \forall x_I \in U_I$. Given $X_I = x_J$, Y does not depend on T_{x_I} for $x_I \neq x_J$. A compact probability tree can then be built if wet put the variables of X_I in the upper levels of the tree, then we put the transparent variables T_{x_I}, and finally we put variable Y in the lower level. With this probability tree, a point of the global convex set $H^{Y|X_I}$ can be found by fixing all transparent nodes T_{x_I} to one of its values. This corresponds with the operation of *restriction* (see for example [20]) in probability trees. In figure 2 we can see an example where a probability tree represents the global information $H^{Y|X}$ associated to the two convex sets $H^{Y|X=x_1}$ and $H^{Y|X=x_2}$.

The figure also shows the global information $H^{Y|X}$ by means of a table. In the probability tree of figure 2, we get the extreme points fixing T_{x_1} and T_{x_2} to one of its values. For example restricting the probability tree to $T_{x_1} = t_1^1$ and $T_{x_2} = t_2^2$ we get a new probability tree that gives us the extreme point r_2.

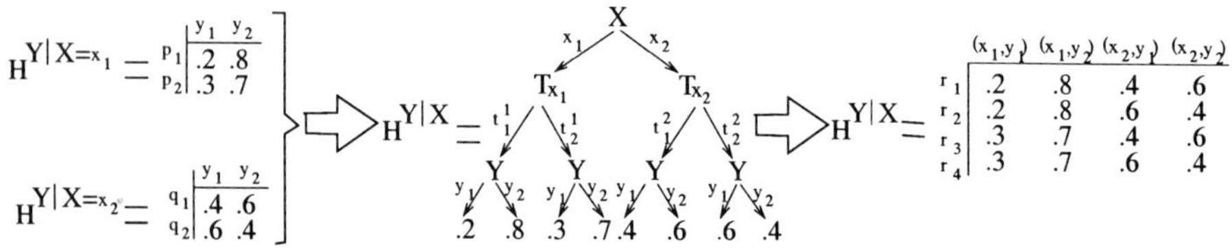

Fig. 2. A probability tree for $H^{Y|X}$

Let S_T be the set of all transparent variables on the tree of cliques. Using probability trees as valuations, the result R_k of the propagation algorithm described in section 2 for a variable X_k, will be represented with a valuation h_k (a probability tree) containing variable X_k and all variables in S_T. Selecting the different values for variables in S_T we can obtain the extreme points of the *a posteriori* convex set for X_k. Then, applying expression 4 we will obtain the intervals for the cases of X_k. This method is equivalent to do the following number of probabilistic propagations: $\prod |T_i| \, : \, T_i \in S_T$.

5 Propagating Convex Sets with Simulated Annealing and Probability Trees

The use of probability trees to represent convex sets of probabilities can reduce significantly the required space to maintain the convex sets of probabilities. But, the number of probabilistic propagations required to obtain *a posteriori* information is not reduced. Because of the big number of extreme points associated to each conditional information, the problem of calculating the *a posteriori* information could be unfeasible as we pointed in the introduction. In that case, a simulated annealing algorithm could be applied obtaining approximated results.

5.1 Simulated Annealing Algorithm

Simulated annealing [15] is an optimization technique to solve combinatorial optimization problems. Assume a cost function $C : \mathcal{S} \rightarrow I\!R^+$ defined on the search space $\mathcal{S}$ (a set of n variables). Our purpose is to find a configuration $s \in \mathcal{S}$ (a configuration of the n variables) that minimizes (or maximizes) the function C. This algorithm presupposes a *generation mechanism* to go from a configuration s_i to another one s_{i+1} by a small perturbation. The set of configurations that can be reached from a configuration s is called the neighbourhood of s, $\mathcal{N}(s)$. Simulated annealing is similar to hill climbing, but sometimes it accepts a configuration with higher cost. In this way it avoids being trapped at a local minimum. The possibility of going to a configuration of higher cost, depends on a parameter, t, called temperature. Initially t is high and the possibility of a cost increase is high. Like hill climbing, simulated annealing algorithm starts on an random configuration. When applying the generation mechanism to configuration s_i to obtain s_{i+1}, if $C(s_{i+1}) < C(s_i)$ then s_{i+1} is accepted. Otherwise, is only accepted with probability $Pr(s_i \rightarrow s_{i+1}) = e^{[-\frac{C(s_i)-C(s_{i+1})}{t}]}$ where t denotes the current temperature. Under an appropriate cooling procedure this algorithm converges to the global minimum.

A simple cooling procedure was introduced by Kirkpatrick, Gelatt and Vecchi [15]. With this procedure, at each step the temperature is decreased according to the formula: $t_{i+1} = \alpha . t_i$, where α is a given constant. This will be the procedure used in this paper. Another modification that can improve the efficiency was proposed by Green and Supowit, [14]. According to it, if we can calculate the cost of all neighbouring configurations of $N(s_i)$, then instead of randomly choosing a configuration of $N(s_i)$ and accepting it according to above procedure, it is better to choose a configuration, s_{i+1}, from $N(s_i)$, with a probability proportional to $e^{-(C(s_{i+1})-C(s_i))/t}$. This method will be also used in our algorithm.

5.2 Our Simulated Annealing Algorithm

We are trying to obtain the intervals $[a,b]$ in formula 4 for a given variable of interest X_k for all its cases x_k^i. For each x_k^i, this can be solved by selecting the configuration of transparent variables given rise to a minimum value for $a = P(x_k^i|e)$ (and the configuration for the maximum for b). We will use a simulated annealing algorithm to search those configurations of transparent variables. Now, the search space $\mathcal{S}$ is the set of transparent variables and a configuration s is a selection of one case for each one of the transparent variables. The algorithm starts obtaining the probability trees associated to each original conditional information $H^{Y|X_I}$ as described in section 4.1. Then, a tree of cliques is built as described in section 2, but now we need a double system of messages. For each pair of connected cliques, C_i and C_j, there are two messages going from C_i to C_j, $M^1_{C_i \rightarrow C_j}$ and $M^2_{C_i \rightarrow C_j}$, and two messages going from C_j to C_i, $M^1_{C_j \rightarrow C_i}$ and $M^2_{C_j \rightarrow C_i}$. Messages $M^1_{C_i \rightarrow C_j}$ are calculated as usual, according to formula 2. Messages $M^2_{C_i \rightarrow C_j}$ are also calculated as usual but it is assumed that the observation $X_k = x_k^i$ is added to the evidence e. Every probability tree $\mathcal{T}_i$ and every observation δ_i is associated to one clique C_i that contains all its variables. Then, the valuation Ψ_{C_i} is calculated for every clique C_i, and saved on a copy valuation $\Psi^c_{C_i}$. A random initial configuration s_0 is selected for the transparent variables, and the observation of these variables is appended to the evidence set e, and appended to the corresponding cliques modifying the valuations Ψ_{C_i}. These valuations Ψ_{C_i} are now probability trees with no transparent variables because all of them are observed and pruned in probability trees. After these initial steps, we carry out a probabilistic propagation, calculating the two types of messages, and we start the simulated annealing algorithm. To do that, we traverse the tree of cliques N times (the desired number of runs) from the root in such a way that we always go from one clique to one of its neighbours. This can be done building a sequence of the cliques $C_1, \ldots, C_n$ in such a way that C_1 is the root clique, and given two consecutive cliques in the sequence, then they are neighbours in the tree of cliques. A clique C_i can appear several times in the previous sequence. Every time a clique C_i is visited we simulate its transparent variables and then we send messages $M^1_{C_i \to C_j}$ and $M^2_{C_i \to C_j}$ to the next clique C_j (a neighbour of C_i). The scheme of the algorithm is the following:

1. For $r = 1$ to N
   a) Let be C the root clique.
   b) For all transparent variables T_j on the clique C
      i. Discard the observation of T_j from the evidence set.
      ii. Calculate $R^1_{T_j}$ and $R^2_{T_j}$ (a posteriori information for T_j) using expression 3 with the two system of messages.
      iii. Calculate the pointwise division $v = R^2_{T_j}/R^1_{T_j}$.
      iv. Select a new case c_j for T_j with a probability proportional to $e^{-v(c_j)/t}$.
      v. Add the observation $T_j = c_j$ to the evidence set.
   c) Let be C_j the next clique visited.
   d) Send messages $M^1_{C \to C_j}$ and $M^2_{C \to C_j}$ to C_j
   e) Let be $C = C_j$ the next clique to visit
   f) If C is not the root clique, go to step 1b
   g) Set $t = \alpha \cdot t$
2. The output of the algorithm will be the configuration of transparent variables with the minimum $R^2_{T_j}(c_j)/R^1_{T_j}(c_j)$ so far.

One point that must be clear in previous algorithm is how to do step 1(b)i, that is, how to discard previous observation of the variable T_j that we are going to simulate. This is easy to do because we have a copy $\Psi^c_{C_i}$ of the valuation Ψ_{C_i} of the clique C_i in which the transparent variable is. In the copy no transparent variable is instantiated. Then we calculate the new Ψ_{C_i} using $\Psi^c_{C_i}$ and instantiating all transparent variables in C_i except T_j. Another point that must be clear in step 1(b)ii is the meaning of $R^1_{T_j}$ and $R^2_{T_j}$. Both are vector of numbers. Each value in $R^1_{T_j}$ contains the probability of evidence $P(e)$ obtained in current configuration of transparent variables and each value in $R^2_{T_j}$ contains the *a posteriori* probability $P(x^i_k \cap e)$. Therefore $R^2_{T_j}/R^1_{T_j}$ is again a vector of values containing $P(x^i_k|e) = P(x^i_k \cap e)/P(e)$, that is, the target of our optimization algorithm.

A good property of previous algorithm is that it obtains a new candidate for the minimum every time a transparent variable is going to be simulated. This makes that with only one path in the tree of cliques we examine a big amount of possible candidates.

6 Experimental Work

To evaluate our simulated annealing algorithm we have applied it to several Bayesian networks available on Internet: Boerlage92 [2], Boblo, Car Starts and

Alarm. These graphs can be found in the literature for the probabilistic case, i.e. at each node we have a conditional probability distribution. Propagation on these networks is not very difficult from a probabilistic point of view. We have transformed each probability p into a randomly chosen probability interval. This makes the problem of exact propagation very difficult to solve, since it amounts to making a tremendous number of probabilistic propagations: 9.007199×10^{15} in Boerlage92, 4.529848×10^{8} in Boblo, 5.242888×10^{5} in Car Starts and 1.713495×10^{93} in Alarm. To transform each probability p into an interval we use the following procedure: for each p we select an uniform number r from the interval $[0, \max\{p, 1-p, d\}]$ with $d \leq 1$ being a given threshold (we have used $d = 0.1$). Then p is transformed into the interval $[p-r, p+r]$. This way of selecting the interval ensures that $p-r \geq 0$. Moreover, when $p = 0.0$ or $p = 1.0$ we will obtain $[0.0, 0.0]$ or $[1.0, 1.0]$ respectively.

Experiments have been carried out on an Intel Pentium II (400 MHz) computer with 384MB of RAM and the Linux RedHat operating system with kernel 2.0.36. Algorithms have been implemented in C language. We have used an initial temperature of $t_0 = 2.0$ and a cooling factor of $\alpha = 0.9$. Different numbers of iterations have carried out, getting the intervals for the first case of one of the variable of the network (the algorithm has been focused to optimize the lower limit of the first case of one of the variable of the network).

Here we only reproduced results for Boerlage92 network because of space limits. Similar results can be obtained for the other networks. Figure 3 shows the results obtained in three different instances of the problem. In situation (a) and (b) we apply the algorithm to get intervals for two different variables when there is not any observed variable. In situation (c) we apply the algorithm to another variable, but when one of the other variables is observed. Figures (a), (b) and (c) show intervals for each number of iterations (N) (the horizontal axis represents the number of iterations, and the vertical axis represents the probability). Figures (a) and (c) also show the exact intervals obtained with an exact method of propagation (we have used the variables elimination method [8] because it can exploit the d-separation criterion). In situations (a) and (c) the algorithm obtains an exact calculus of the lower interval with a few iterations. But we can see that the upper limit do not converge. This is because the simulated annealing algorithm has been run in order to minimize the lower limits, and not to maximize the upper limits. In situation (b) we cannot assure that exact results are reached because we were not able to obtain results with an exact method of propagation due to the high complexity of the problem. But looking at the figure (b) it seems that the lower interval is stable after 50 iterations.

7 Concluding Remarks

This paper has shown an approximate algorithm to obtain the *a posteriori* intervals for a given variable when the *a priori* conditional information is also given with intervals, and we suppose the independence among variables are represented with an acyclic directed graph as in a Bayesian network. The method uses prob-

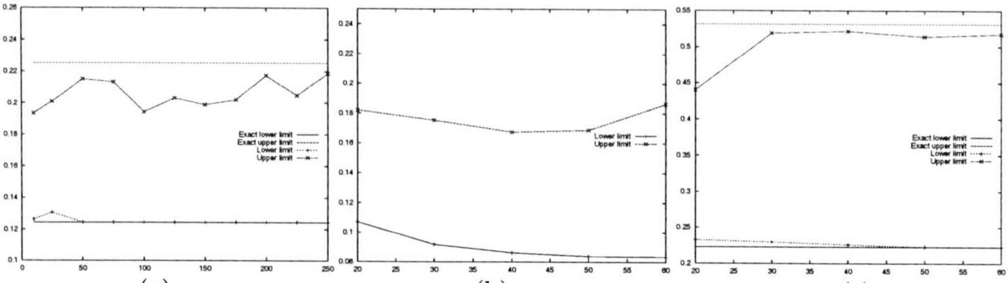

(a) (b) (c)

Fig. 3. Intervals for each number of iterations in Boerlage92 network

ability trees in order to reduce the size of the representation of the associated convex set, and it applies a simulated annealing algorithm to obtain approximate intervals. Experiments show that optimization techniques are promising in the propagation of intervals, when exact computations are unfeasible.

Acknowledgments. This work has been supported by the Spanish Comisión Interministerial de Ciencia y Tecnología (CICYT) under project TIC97-1135-C04-01.

References

1. S. Amarger, D. Dubois, and H. Prade. Constraint propagation with imprecise conditional probabilities. In B. D'Ambrosio, Ph. Smets, and P.P. Bonissone, editors, *Proceedings of the 7th Conference on Uncertainty in Artificial Intelligence*, pages 26–34. Morgan & Kaufmann, 1991.
2. B. Boerlage. *Link Strength in Bayesian Networks.* PhD thesis, Department of Computer Science, University of British Columbia., Canada., 1992.
3. C. Boutilier, N. Friedman, M. Goldszmidt, and D. Koller. Context-specific independence in Bayesian networks. In *Proceedings of the Twelfth Annual Conference on Uncertainty in Artificial Intelligence (UAI–96)*, pages 115–123, Portland, Oregon, 1996.
4. L. M. de Campos, J. F. Huete, and S. Moral. Probability intervals: a tool for uncertain reasoning. *International Journal of Uncertainty, Fuzziness and Knowledge-Based Systems*, 2:167–196, 1994.
5. L. M. de Campos and S. Moral. Removing partial inconsistency in valuation based systems. *International Journal of Intelligent Systems*, 12:629–653, 1997.
6. A. Cano, J. E. Cano, and S. Moral. Convex sets of probabilities propagation by simulated annealing. In *Proceedings of the Fith International Conference IPMU'94*, pages 978–983, Paris, 1994.
7. A. Cano and S. Moral. A genetic algorithm to approximate convex sets of probabilities. In *Proceedings of Information Processing and Management of Uncertainty in Knowledge-Based Systems Conference (IPMU' 96) Vol. 2*, pages 859–864, 1996.
8. A. Cano and S. Moral. Using probabilities trees to compute marginals with imprecise probabilities. *To appear in International Journal of Approximate Reasoning*, 2001.

9. A. Cano, S. Moral, and A. Salmerón. Penniless propagation in join trees. *International Journal of Intelligent Systems*, 15(11):1027–1059, 2000.
10. J. E. Cano, S. Moral, and J. F. Verdegay-López. Propagation of convex sets of probabilities in directed acyclic networks. In B. Bouchon-Meunier et al., editors, *Uncertainty in Intelligent Systems*, pages 15–26. Elsevier, 1993.
11. F. Cozman. Robustness analysis of Bayesian networks with local convex sets of distributions. In *Proceedings of the 13th Conference on Uncertainty in Artificial Intelligence*. Morgan & Kaufmann, San Mateo, 1997.
12. K. W. Fertig and J. S. Breese. Interval influence diagrams. In M. Henrion, R. D. Shacter, L. N. Kanal, and J. F. Lemmer, editors, *Uncertainty in Artificial Intelligence, 5*, pages 149–161. North-Holland, Amsterdam, 1990.
13. N. Friedman and M. Goldszmidt. Learning Bayesian networks with local structure. In *Proceedings of the Twelfth Annual Conference on Uncertainty in Artificial Intelligence (UAI-96)*, pages 252–262, Portland, Oregon, 1996.
14. J.W. Greene and K.J. Supowit. Simulated annealing without rejected moves. In *Proc. IEEE Int. Conference on Computer Design*, pages 658–663, Port Chester, 1984.
15. S. Kirpatrick, C.D. Gelatt, and M.P. Vecchi. Optimization by simulated annealing. *Science*, 220:671–680, 1983.
16. D. Kozlov and D. Koller. Nonuniform dynamic discretization in hybrid networks. In D. Geiger and P.P. Shenoy, editors, *Proceedings of the 13th Conference on Uncertainty in Artificial Intelligence*, pages 302–313. Morgan & Kaufmann, 1997.
17. S. L. Lauritzen and D. J. Spiegelhalter. Local computation with probabilities on graphical structures and their application to expert systems. *Journal of the Royal Statistical Society, Ser. B*, 50:157–224, 1988.
18. J. Pearl. *Probabilistic Reasoning with Intelligent Systems.* Morgan & Kaufman, San Mateo, 1988.
19. D. Poole. Probabilistic partial evaluation: Exploiting rule structure in probabilistic inference. In *Proceedings of the 15th IJCAI Conference (IJCAI' 97)*, pages 1284–1291, Nagoya, Japan, 1997.
20. A. Salmerón, A. Cano, and S. Moral. Importance sampling in Bayesian networks using probability trees. *Computational Statistics and Data Analysis*, 34:387–413, 2000.
21. P. P. Shenoy and G. Shafer. Axioms for probability and belief-function propagation. In Shachter et al., editors, *Uncertainty in Artificial Intelligence, 4*, pages 169–198. North-Holland, 1990.
22. S. E. Shimony and E. Santos Jr. Exploiting case-based independence for approximating marginal probabilities. *International Journal of Approximate Reasoning*, 14:25–54, 1996.
23. B. Tessen. Interval probability propagation. *International Journal of Approximate Reasoning*, 7:95–120, 1992.
24. H. Thöne, U. Güntzer, and W. Kießling. Towards precision of probabilistic bounds propagation. In *Proceedings of the 8th Conference on Uncertainty in Artificial Intelligence*, pages 315–322, 1992.
25. P. Walley. *Statistical Reasoning with Imprecise Probabilities.* Chapman and Hall, London, 1991.
26. P. Walley. General introduction to imprecise probabilities. http://ensmain.rug.ac.be/~ipp/documentation/introduction/introduction.html, 1997/98.
27. N. L. Zhang and D. Poole. Exploiting causal independence in Bayesian network inference. *International Journal of Intelligent Research*, 5:301–328, 1996.

Probabilistic Logic under Coherence, Model-Theoretic Probabilistic Logic, and Default Reasoning

Veronica Biazzo[1], Angelo Gilio[2], Thomas Lukasiewicz[3], and Giuseppe Sanfilippo[1]

[1] Dipartimento di Matematica e Informatica, Università degli Studi di Catania
Città Universitaria, Viale A. Doria 6, 95152 Catania, Italy
{vbiazzo,gsanfilippo}@dmi.unict.it

[2] Dipartimento di Metodi e Modelli Matematici, Università "La Sapienza"
Via A. Scarpa 16, 00161 Roma, Italy
gilio@dmmm.uniroma1.it

[3] Institut und Ludwig Wittgenstein Labor für Informationssysteme, TU Wien
Favoritenstraße 9-11, 1040 Vienna, Austria
lukasiewicz@kr.tuwien.ac.at

Abstract. We study probabilistic logic under the viewpoint of the coherence principle of de Finetti. In detail, we explore the relationship between coherence-based and model-theoretic probabilistic logic. Interestingly, we show that the notions of g-coherence and of g-coherent entailment can be expressed by combining notions in model-theoretic probabilistic logic with concepts from default reasoning. Crucially, we even show that probabilistic reasoning under coherence is a probabilistic generalization of default reasoning in system P. That is, we provide a new probabilistic semantics for system P, which is neither based on infinitesimal probabilities nor on atomic-bound (or also big-stepped) probabilities. These results also give new insight into default reasoning with conditional objects.

1 Introduction

The probabilistic treatment of uncertainty plays an important role in many applications of knowledge representation and reasoning. Often, we need to reason with uncertain information under partial knowledge and then the use of precise probabilistic assessments seems unrealistic. Moreover, the family of uncertain quantities at hand has often no particular algebraic structure.

In such cases, a general approach is obtained by using (conditional and/or unconditional) probabilistic constraints, based on the coherence principle of de Finetti and suitable generalizations of it [5,9,15,16]. Two important aspects in dealing with uncertainty are: (i) checking the consistency of a probabilistic assessment; and (ii) the propagation of a given assessment to further uncertain quantities.

Another approach for handling probabilistic constraints is model-theoretic probabilistic logic, whose roots go back to Boole's book of 1854 "The Laws of Thought" [8]. There is a wide spectrum of formal languages that have been explored in probabilistic logic, which ranges from constraints for unconditional and conditional events [2, 13,19,20,22,23] to rich languages that specify linear inequalities over events [12]. The

S. Benferhat and P. Besnard (Eds.): ECSQARU 2001, LNAI 2143, pp. 290–302, 2001.

main problems related to model-theoretic probabilistic logic are checking satisfiability, deciding logical entailment, and computing tight logically entailed intervals.

Coherence-based and model-theoretic probabilistic reasoning have been explored quite independently from each other by two different research communities. For this reason, the relationship between the two areas has not been studied in depth so far. The current paper and our work in [7] aim at filling this gap. More precisely, our research is essentially guided by the following two questions:

- Which is the semantic relationship between coherence-based and model-theoretic probabilistic reasoning?
- Can algorithms that have been developed for efficient reasoning in one area also be used in the other area?

Interestingly, it turns out that the answers to these two questions are closely related to default reasoning from conditional knowledge bases in system P.

The literature contains several different proposals for default reasoning and extensive work on its desired properties. The core of these properties are the rationality postulates of system P proposed by Kraus, Lehmann, and Magidor [18]. It turned out that these rationality postulates constitute a sound and complete axiom system for several classical model-theoretic entailment relations under uncertainty measures on worlds. More precisely, they characterize classical model-theoretic entailment under preferential structures [25,18], infinitesimal probabilities [1,24], possibility measures [10], and world rankings. They also characterize an entailment relation based on conditional objects [11]. A survey of all these relationships is given in [3].

Roughly speaking, coherence-based probabilistic reasoning is reducible to model-theoretic probabilistic reasoning using concepts from default reasoning. Crucially, it even turns out that *coherence-based probabilistic reasoning is a probabilistic generalization of default reasoning in system P*. That is, we provide a *new probabilistic semantics for system P*, which is neither based on infinitesimal probabilities nor on atomic-bound (or also big-stepped) probabilities [4,26].

The current paper deals with the semantic aspects of these findings, while [7] focuses on its algorithmic implications for coherence-based probabilistic reasoning.

The main contributions of the current paper can be summarized as follows:

- We define a coherence-based probabilistic logic. We define a formal language of logical and conditional constraints, which are defined on arbitrary families of conditional events. We then define the notions of generalized coherence (or *g-coherence*), g-coherent consequence, and tight g-coherent consequence for this language.
- We explore the relationship between g-coherence and g-coherent entailment, on the one hand, and satisfiability and logical entailment, on the other hand.
- We show that probabilistic reasoning under coherence is a probabilistic generalization of default reasoning from conditional knowledge bases in system P.
- We show that this relationship reveals new insight into Dubois and Prade's approach to default reasoning with conditional objects [11,3].

Note that detailed proofs of all results are given in the extended paper [6].

2 Probabilistic Logic under Coherence

In this section, we first introduce some technical preliminaries. We then briefly describe precise and imprecise probability assessments under coherence. We finally define our coherence-based probabilistic logic and give an illustrating example.

2.1 Preliminaries

We assume a nonempty set of *basic events* Φ. We use $\bot$ and $\top$ to denote *false* and *true*, respectively. The set of *events* is the closure of $\Phi \cup \{\bot, \top\}$ under the Boolean operations $\neg$ and $\wedge$. That is, each element of $\Phi \cup \{\bot, \top\}$ is an event, and if ϕ and ψ are events, then also $(\phi \wedge \psi)$ and $\neg\phi$. We use $(\phi \vee \psi)$ and $(\psi \Leftarrow \phi)$ to abbreviate $\neg(\neg\phi \wedge \neg\psi)$ and $\neg(\phi \wedge \neg\psi)$, respectively, and adopt the usual conventions to eliminate parentheses. We often denote by $\bar{\phi}$ the negation $\neg\phi$, and by $\phi\psi$ the conjunction $\phi \wedge \psi$. A *logical constraint* is an event of the form $\psi \Leftarrow \phi$. Note that $\bot \Leftarrow \alpha$ is equivalent to $\neg\alpha$.

A *world* I is a truth assignment to the basic events in Φ (that is, a mapping $I\colon \Phi \to \{\mathbf{false}, \mathbf{true}\}$), which is extended to all events as usual (that is, $(\phi \wedge \psi)$ is true in I iff ϕ and ψ are true in I, and $\neg\phi$ is true in I iff ϕ is not true in I). We use $\mathcal{I}_\Phi$ to denote the set of all worlds for Φ. A world I *satisfies* an event ϕ, or I is a *model* of ϕ, denoted $I \models \phi$, iff $I(\phi) = \mathbf{true}$. I *satisfies* a set of events L, or I is a *model* of L, denoted $I \models L$, iff I is a model of all $\phi \in L$. An event ϕ (resp., a set of events L) is *satisfiable* iff a model of ϕ (resp., L) exists. An event ψ is a *logical consequence* of ϕ (resp., L), denoted $\phi \models \psi$ (resp., $L \models \psi$), iff each model of ϕ (resp., L) is also a model of ψ. We use $\phi \not\models \psi$ (resp., $L \not\models \psi$) to denote that $\phi \models \psi$ (resp., $L \models \psi$) does not hold.

2.2 Probability Assessments

A *conditional event* is an expression $\psi|\phi$ with events ψ and $\phi \neq \bot$. It can be looked at as a three-valued logical entity, with values $\mathbf{true}$, or $\mathbf{false}$, or $\mathbf{indeterminate}$, according to whether ψ and ϕ are true, or ψ is false and ϕ is true, or ϕ is false, respectively. That is, we extend worlds I to conditional events $\psi|\phi$ by $I(\psi|\phi) = \mathbf{true}$ iff $I \models \psi \wedge \phi$, $I(\psi|\phi) = \mathbf{false}$ iff $I \models \neg\psi \wedge \phi$, and $I(\psi|\phi) = \mathbf{indeterminate}$ iff $I \models \neg\phi$. Note that $\psi|\phi$ coincides with $\psi{\wedge}\phi|\phi$. More generally, $\psi_1|\phi_1$ and $\psi_2|\phi_2$ coincide iff $\psi_1 \wedge \phi_1 = \psi_2 \wedge \phi_2$ and $\phi_1 = \phi_2$.

A *probability assessment* (L, A) on a set of conditional events $\mathcal{E}$ consists of a set of logical constraints L, and a mapping A that assigns each $\varepsilon \in \mathcal{E}$ a real number in $[0, 1]$. Informally, L describes logical relationships, while A represents probabilistic knowledge. For $\{\psi_1|\phi_1, \ldots, \psi_n|\phi_n\} \subseteq \mathcal{E}$ with $n \geq 1$ and n real numbers $s_1, \ldots, s_n$, let the mapping $G\colon \mathcal{I}_\Phi \to \mathbf{R}$ be defined as follows. For every $I \in \mathcal{I}_\Phi$:

$$G(I) \;=\; \sum_{i=1}^{n} s_i \cdot I(\phi_i) \cdot (I(\psi_i) - A(\psi_i|\phi_i)) \,.$$

In the previous formula, we identify the truth values $\mathbf{false}$ and $\mathbf{true}$ with the real numbers 0 and 1, respectively. Intuitively, G can be interpreted as the random gain corresponding to a combination of n bets of amounts $s_1 \cdot A(\psi_1|\phi_1), \ldots, s_n \cdot A(\psi_n|\phi_n)$ on $\psi_1|\phi_1, \ldots, \psi_n|\phi_n$ with stakes $s_1, \ldots, s_n$. In detail, to bet on $\psi_i|\phi_i$, one pays an amount of $s_i \cdot A(\psi_i|\phi_i)$, and one gets back the amount of s_i, 0, and $s_i \cdot A(\psi_i|\phi_i)$, when

$\psi_i \wedge \phi_i$, $\neg\psi_i \wedge \phi_i$, and $\neg\phi_i$, respectively, turns out to be true. The following notion of *coherence* now assures that it is impossible (for both the gambler and the bookmaker) to have *uniform loss*.

A probability assessment (L, A) on a set of conditional events $\mathcal{E}$ is *coherent* iff for every $\{\psi_1|\phi_1, \ldots, \psi_n|\phi_n\} \subseteq \mathcal{E}$ with $n \geq 1$ and for all real numbers $s_1, \ldots, s_n$, it holds $\max\{G(I) \mid I \in \mathcal{I}_\Phi,\, I \models L,\, I \models \phi_1 \vee \cdots \vee \phi_n\} \geq 0$.

An *imprecise probability assessment* (L, A) on a set of conditional events $\mathcal{E}$ consists of a set of logical constraints L and a mapping A that assigns each $\varepsilon \in \mathcal{E}$ an interval $[l, u] \subseteq [0, 1]$ with $l \leq u$. We say (L, A) is *g-coherent* iff there exists a coherent precise probability assessment $(L, A^\star)$ on $\mathcal{E}$ such that $A^\star(\varepsilon) \in A(\varepsilon)$ for all $\varepsilon \in \mathcal{E}$.

Let (L, A) be a g-coherent imprecise probability assessment on a set of conditional events $\mathcal{E}$. The imprecise probability assessment $[l, u]$ on a conditional event γ is called a *g-coherent consequence* of (L, A) iff $A^\star(\gamma) \in [l, u]$ for every g-coherent precise probability assessment $A^\star$ on $\mathcal{E} \cup \{\gamma\}$ such that $A^\star(\varepsilon) \in A(\varepsilon)$ for all $\varepsilon \in \mathcal{E}$. It is a *tight g-coherent consequence* of (L, A) iff l (resp., u) is the infimum (resp., supremum) of $A^\star(\gamma)$ subject to all g-coherent precise probability assessments $A^\star$ on $\mathcal{E} \cup \{\gamma\}$ such that $A^\star(\varepsilon) \in A(\varepsilon)$ for all $\varepsilon \in \mathcal{E}$.

2.3 Probabilistic Logic under Coherence

In the rest of this paper, we assume that Φ is finite. A *conditional constraint* is an expression $(\psi|\phi)[l, u]$ with real numbers $l, u \in [0, 1]$ and events ψ and ϕ. A probabilistic knowledge base $KB = (L, P)$ consists of a finite set of logical constraints L, and a finite set of conditional constraints P such that (i) $l \leq u$ for all $(\psi|\phi)[l, u] \in P$, and (ii) $\psi_1|\phi_1 \neq \psi_2|\phi_2$ for all distinct $(\psi_1|\phi_1)[l_1, u_1], (\psi_2|\phi_2)[l_2, u_2] \in P$.

Every imprecise probability assessment $IP = (L, A)$ with finite L on a finite set of conditional events $\mathcal{E}$ can be represented by the following probabilistic knowledge base:

$$KB_{IP} = (L, \{(\psi|\phi)[l, u] \mid \psi|\phi \in \mathcal{E},\ A(\psi|\phi) = [l, u]\})\,.$$

Conversely, every probabilistic knowledge base $KB = (L, P)$ can expressed by the following imprecise probability assessment $IP_{KB} = (L, A_{KB})$ on $\mathcal{E}_{KB}$:

$$\begin{aligned} A_{KB} &= \{(\psi|\phi, [l, u]) \mid (\psi|\phi)[l, u] \in KB\}\,, \\ \mathcal{E}_{KB} &= \{\psi|\phi \mid \exists\, l, u \in [0, 1]\colon (\psi|\phi)[l, u] \in KB\}\,. \end{aligned}$$

A probabilistic knowledge base KB is said *g-coherent* iff IP_{KB} is g-coherent. For g-coherent KB and conditional constraints $(\psi|\phi)[l, u]$, we say $(\psi|\phi)[l, u]$ is a *g-coherent consequence* of KB, denoted $KB \mathrel{|\!\sim} (\psi|\phi)[l, u]$, iff $\{(\psi|\phi, [l, u])\}$ is a g-coherent consequence of IP_{KB}. It is a *tight g-coherent consequence* of KB, denoted $KB \mathrel{|\!\sim}_{tight} (\psi|\phi)[l, u]$, iff $\{(\psi|\phi, [l, u])\}$ is a tight g-coherent consequence of IP_{KB}.

Example 2.1. The logical knowledge "all penguins are birds" and the probabilistic knowledge "birds have legs with a probability of at least 0.95", "birds fly with a probability between 0.9 and 0.95", and "penguins fly with a probability of at most 0.05" can be expressed by the following probabilistic knowledge base $KB = (\{\mathsf{bird} \Leftarrow \mathsf{penguin}\}, \{(\mathsf{legs}|\mathsf{bird})[.95, 1], (\mathsf{fly}|\mathsf{bird})[.9, .95], (\mathsf{fly}|\mathsf{penguin})[0, .05]\})$.

It is easy to see that KB is g-coherent and that $(\mathsf{legs}|\mathsf{bird})[.95,1]$, $(\mathsf{legs}|\mathsf{penguin})[0,1]$, $(\mathsf{fly}|\mathsf{bird})[.9, .95]$, and $(\mathsf{fly}|\mathsf{penguin})[0, .05]$ are tight g-coherent consequences of KB.

3 Relationship to Model-Theoretic Probabilistic Logic

In this section, we characterize the notions of g-coherence and of g-coherent entailment in terms of the notions of satisfiability and of logical entailment.

3.1 Model-Theoretic Probabilistic Logic

A *probabilistic interpretation* Pr is a probability function on $\mathcal{I}_\Phi$ (that is, a mapping $Pr\colon \mathcal{I}_\Phi \to [0,1]$ such that all $Pr(I)$ with $I \in \mathcal{I}_\Phi$ sum up to 1). The *probability* of an event ϕ in the probabilistic interpretation Pr, denoted $Pr(\phi)$, is defined as the sum of all $Pr(I)$ such that $I \in \mathcal{I}_\Phi$ and $I \models \phi$. For events ϕ and ψ with $Pr(\phi) > 0$, we use $Pr(\psi|\phi)$ to abbreviate $Pr(\psi \wedge \phi) \,/\, Pr(\phi)$. The *truth* of logical and conditional constraints F in a probabilistic interpretation Pr, denoted $Pr \models F$, is defined as follows:

- $Pr \models \psi \Leftarrow \phi$ iff $Pr(\psi \wedge \phi) = Pr(\phi)$.
- $Pr \models (\psi|\phi)[l,u]$ iff $Pr(\phi) = 0$ or $Pr(\psi|\phi) \in [l,u]$.

We say Pr *satisfies* a logical or conditional constraint F, or Pr is a *model* of F, iff $Pr \models F$. We say Pr *satisfies* a set of logical and conditional constraints $\mathcal{F}$, or Pr is a *model* of $\mathcal{F}$, denoted $Pr \models \mathcal{F}$, iff Pr is a model of all $F \in \mathcal{F}$. We say that $\mathcal{F}$ is *satisfiable* iff a model of $\mathcal{F}$ exists.

We next define the notion of logical entailment. A conditional constraint $F = (\psi|\phi)[l,u]$ is a *logical consequence* of a set of logical and conditional constraints $\mathcal{F}$, denoted $\mathcal{F} \models F$, iff each model of $\mathcal{F}$ is also a model of F. It is a *tight logical consequence* of $\mathcal{F}$, denoted $\mathcal{F} \models_{tight} F$, iff l (resp., u) is the infimum (resp., supremum) of $Pr(\psi|\phi)$ subject to all models Pr of $\mathcal{F}$ with $Pr(\phi) > 0$. Note that we define $l = 1$ and $u = 0$, when $\mathcal{F} \models (\phi|\top)[0,0]$. A probabilistic knowledge bases $KB = (L,P)$ is *satisfiable* iff $L \cup P$ is satisfiable. A conditional constraint $(\psi|\phi)[l,u]$ is a *logical consequence* of KB, denoted $KB \models (\psi|\phi)[l,u]$, iff $L \cup P \models (\psi|\phi)[l,u]$. It is a *tight logical consequence* of KB, denoted $KB \models_{tight} (\psi|\phi)[l,u]$, iff $L \cup P \models_{tight} (\psi|\phi)[l,u]$.

3.2 G-Coherence in Model-Theoretic Probabilistic Logic

The following theorem shows how g-coherence can be expressed through the existence of probabilistic interpretations. This result follows from a characterization of g-coherence in [15]. It shows that $KB = (L,P)$ is g-coherent iff every nonempty $P' \subseteq P$ has a model Pr such that $Pr \models L$ and that $Pr(\phi) > 0$ for at least one $(\psi|\phi)[l,u] \in P'$.

Theorem 3.1. *Let $KB = (L,P)$ be a probabilistic knowledge base. Then, KB is g-coherent iff for every nonempty $P_n = \{(\psi_1|\phi_1)[l_1,u_1], \ldots, (\psi_n|\phi_n)[l_n,u_n]\} \subseteq P$, there exists a model Pr of $L \cup P_n$ such that $Pr(\phi_1 \vee \cdots \vee \phi_n) > 0$.*

It then follows that g-coherence has a characterization similar to p-consistency in default reasoning. To formulate this result, we adopt the following terminology from default reasoning from conditional knowledge bases [3]. A probabilistic interpretation Pr *verifies* a conditional constraint $(\psi|\phi)[l,u]$, iff $Pr(\phi) > 0$ and $Pr \models (\psi|\phi)[l,u]$. A set of conditional constraints P *tolerates* a conditional constraint F under a set of logical constraints L, iff there exists a model of $L \cup P$ that verifies F. We say P is *under L in conflict* with F, iff no model of $L \cup P$ verifies F.

We are now ready to characterize g-coherence in a way similar to p-consistency by Goldszmidt and Pearl [17]. Note that in [7] we use this characterization to provide a new algorithm for deciding g-coherence, which is essentially a reformulation of a previous algorithm by Gilio [15] using terminology from default reasoning, and which is closely related to an algorithm for checking p-consistency given in [17].[1]

Theorem 3.2. *A probabilistic knowledge base $KB = (L, P)$ is g-coherent iff there exists an ordered partition $(P_0, \ldots, P_k)$ of P such that either*

(a) every P_i, $0 \leq i \leq k$, is the set of all $F \in \bigcup_{j=i}^{k} P_j$ tolerated under L by $\bigcup_{j=i}^{k} P_j$, or
(b) for every i, $0 \leq i \leq k$, each $F \in P_i$ is tolerated under L by $\bigcup_{j=i}^{k} P_j$.

3.3 G-Coherent Entailment in Model-Theoretic Probabilistic Logic

We next show how g-coherent entailment can be reduced to logical entailment.

For probabilistic knowledge bases $KB = (L, P)$ and events α, let $P_\alpha(KB)$ denote the set of all subsets $P_n = \{(\psi_1|\phi_1)[l_1, u_1], \ldots, (\psi_n|\phi_n)[l_n, u_n]\}$ of P such that every model Pr of $L \cup P_n$ with $Pr(\phi_1 \vee \cdots \vee \phi_n \vee \alpha) > 0$ satisfies $Pr(\alpha) > 0$.

The following theorem shows that the tight interval concluded under coherence can be expressed as the intersection of some logically entailed tight intervals.

Theorem 3.3. *Let $KB = (L, P)$ be a g-coherent probabilistic knowledge base, and let $\beta|\alpha$ be a conditional event. Then, $KB \mathrel{|\!\sim}_{tight} (\beta|\alpha)[l, u]$, where*

$$[l, u] = \bigcap \{[c, d] \mid L \cup P' \models_{tight} (\beta|\alpha)[c, d] \text{ for some } P' \in P_\alpha(KB)\}\,.$$

Clearly, this reduction of g-coherent entailment to logical entailment is computationally expensive, as we have to compute a tight logically entailed interval for each member of $P_\alpha(KB)$. In the following, we show that we can restrict our attention to the unique greatest element in $P_\alpha(KB)$. The following lemma shows that $P_\alpha(KB)$ contains indeed a unique greatest element with respect to set inclusion. This result can be proved by showing that $P_\alpha(KB)$ is nonempty and closed under set union.

Lemma 3.4. *Let $KB = (L, P)$ be a g-coherent probabilistic knowledge base, and let α be an event. Then, $P_\alpha(KB)$ contains a unique greatest element.*

The next theorem now shows the crucial result that *g-coherent entailment from KB can be reduced to logical entailment from the greatest element in $P_\alpha(KB)$.*

Theorem 3.5. *Let $KB = (L, P)$ be a g-coherent probabilistic knowledge base, and let $F = (\beta|\alpha)[l, u]$ be a conditional constraint. Let $KB^\star = (L, P^\star)$, where $P^\star$ is the greatest element in $P_\alpha(KB)$. Then,*

(a) $KB \mathrel{|\!\sim} F$ iff $KB^\star \models F$.
(b) $KB \mathrel{|\!\sim}_{tight} F$ iff $KB^\star \models_{tight} F$.

[1] Note that the relationship between the algorithms in [15] and [17] was suggested first by Didier Dubois (personal communication).

Thus, computing tight g-coherent consequences can be reduced to computing tight logical consequences from the greatest element $P^\star$ in $P_\alpha(KB)$. The following theorem shows how $P^\star$ can be characterized and thus computed. More precisely, it specifies some $P^\star$ by two conditions (i) and (ii). It can be shown that (i) implies that every member of $P_\alpha(KB)$ is a subset of $P^\star$, and that (ii) implies that $P^\star$ belongs to $P_\alpha(KB)$. In summary, this proves that the specified $P^\star$ is the greatest element in $P_\alpha(KB)$.

Theorem 3.6. *Let $KB = (L, P)$ be a g-coherent probabilistic knowledge base and α be an event. Let $P^\star \subseteq P$ and $(P_0, \ldots, P_k)$ be an ordered partition of $P \backslash P^\star$ such that:*

(i) every P_i, $0 \le i \le k$, is the set of all elements in $P_i \cup \cdots \cup P_k \cup P^\star$ that are tolerated under $L \cup \{\bot \Leftarrow \alpha\}$ by $P_i \cup \cdots \cup P_k \cup P^\star$, and
(ii) no member of $P^\star$ is tolerated under $L \cup \{\bot \Leftarrow \alpha\}$ by $P^\star$.

Then, $P^\star$ is the greatest element in $P_\alpha(KB)$.

In summary, by Theorems 3.5 and 3.6, a tight interval under g-coherent entailment can be computed by first checking g-coherence, and then computing a tight interval under logical entailment [7]. Semantically, Theorems 3.5 and 3.6 show that g-coherent entailment coincides with logical entailment from a smaller knowledge base. That is, under g-coherent entailment, we simply cut away a part of the knowledge base. Roughly speaking, we remove all those conditional constraints $(\psi|\phi)[l, u] \in P$ where ϕ is "larger" than α. Intuitively, g-coherent entailment does not have the property of inheritance, neither for logical knowledge nor for probabilistic knowledge, while logical entailment shows inheritance of logical knowledge but not of probabilistic knowledge. The following example illustrates this difference.

Example 3.7. Consider the following probabilistic knowledge base:

$$KB = (\{\mathsf{bird} \Leftarrow \mathsf{penguin}\},\ \{(\mathsf{legs}|\mathsf{bird})[1, 1],\ (\mathsf{wings}|\mathsf{bird})[.95, 1]\})\,.$$

Notice that KB is g-coherent and satisfiable. Moreover, we have:

$$KB \mathrel{|\!\sim}_{tight} (\mathsf{legs}|\mathsf{penguin})[0, 1] \text{ and } KB \models_{tight} (\mathsf{legs}|\mathsf{penguin})[1, 1]\,,$$
$$KB \mathrel{|\!\sim}_{tight} (\mathsf{wings}|\mathsf{penguin})[0, 1] \text{ and } KB \models_{tight} (\mathsf{wings}|\mathsf{penguin})[0, 1]\,.$$

That is, under g-coherent entailment, neither the logical property of having legs nor the probabilistic one of having wings is inherited from birds to penguins. Under logical entailment, however, the logical property is inherited, while the probabilistic one is not.

3.4 Coherence-Based versus Model-Theoretic Probabilistic Logic

We now describe the rough relationship between g-coherence and satisfiability, and between g-coherent entailment and logical entailment. The following theorem shows that g-coherence implies satisfiability. This result is immediate by Theorem 3.1.

Theorem 3.8. *Every g-coherent probabilistic knowledge base KB is satisfiable.*

In fact, g-coherence is strictly stronger than satisfiability, as the next example shows.

Example 3.9. Consider the probabilistic knowledge base $KB = (\emptyset, \{(\mathsf{fly}|\mathsf{bird})[.9, 1], (\neg\mathsf{fly}|\mathsf{bird})[.2, 1]\})$. It is easy to verify that KB is satisfiable, but not g-coherent.

The next theorem shows that logical entailment is stronger than g-coherent entailment. That is, g-coherent consequence implies logical consequence (or there are more conditional constraints logically entailed than entailed under g-coherence) and the tight intervals that are derived under logical entailment are subintervals of those derived under g-coherent entailment. This result follows immediately from Theorem 3.5.

Theorem 3.10. *Let* $KB = (L, P)$ *be a g-coherent probabilistic knowledge base, and let* $(\beta|\alpha)[l, u]$ *and* $(\beta|\alpha)[r, s]$ *be two conditional constraints. Then,*

(a) $KB \mathrel{|\!\sim} (\beta|\alpha)[l, u]$ *implies* $KB \models (\beta|\alpha)[l, u]$.
(b) $KB \mathrel{|\!\sim}_{tight} (\beta|\alpha)[l, u]$ *and* $KB \models_{tight} (\beta|\alpha)[r, s]$ *implies* $[l, u] \supseteq [r, s]$.

The following example now shows that logical entailment is in fact *strictly* stronger than g-coherent entailment (note that we identify $[1, 0]$ with the empty set).

Example 3.11. Consider the following probabilistic knowledge bases KB_1 and KB_2:

$$KB_1 = (\emptyset, \{(\mathsf{fly}|\mathsf{bird})[1, 1], (\mathsf{mobile}|\mathsf{fly})[1, 1]\}),$$
$$KB_2 = (\emptyset, \{(\mathsf{fly}|\mathsf{bird})[1, 1], (\mathsf{bird}|\mathsf{penguin})[1, 1], (\neg\mathsf{fly}|\mathsf{penguin})[1, 1]\}).$$

Some tight g-coherent and tight logical consequences of KB_1 and KB_2 are given by:

$$KB_1 \mathrel{|\!\sim}_{tight} (\mathsf{mobile}|\mathsf{bird})[0, 1] \text{ and } KB_1 \models_{tight} (\mathsf{mobile}|\mathsf{bird})[1, 1],$$
$$KB_2 \mathrel{|\!\sim}_{tight} (\neg\mathsf{fly}|\mathsf{penguin})[1, 1] \text{ and } KB_2 \models_{tight} (\neg\mathsf{fly}|\mathsf{penguin})[1, 0].$$

4 Relationship to Default Reasoning in System P

In this section, we show that consistency and entailment in system P are special cases of g-coherence and of g-coherent entailment, respectively. That is, probabilistic logic under coherence gives a new probabilistic semantics for system P, which is neither based on infinitesimal probabilities nor on atomic-bound (or also big-stepped) probabilities.

4.1 Default Reasoning in System P

We now describe the notions of consistency and of entailment in system P [18]. We define them in terms of world rankings.

A *conditional rule* (or *default*) is an expression of the form $\psi \leftarrow \phi$, where ϕ and ψ are events. A *conditional knowledge base* $KB = (L, D)$ consists of a finite set of logical constraints L and a finite set of defaults D.

A world I *satisfies* a default $\psi \leftarrow \phi$, or I is a *model* of $\psi \leftarrow \phi$, denoted $I \models \psi \leftarrow \phi$, iff $I \models \psi \Leftarrow \phi$. The world I *verifies* $\psi \leftarrow \phi$ iff $I \models \phi \wedge \psi$. The world I *falsifies* $\psi \leftarrow \phi$ iff $I \models \phi \wedge \neg\psi$ (that is, $I \not\models \psi \leftarrow \phi$). I *satisfies* a set of events and defaults K, or I is a *model* of K, denoted $I \models K$, iff I satisfies every member of K. We say K is *satisfiable* iff a model of K exists. A set of defaults D *tolerates* a default d *under* a set of classical formulas L iff $D \cup L$ has a model that verifies d. A set of defaults D is *under* L *in conflict* with a default $\psi \leftarrow \phi$ iff all models of $D \cup L \cup \{\phi\}$ satisfy $\neg\psi$.

A *world ranking* κ is a mapping $\kappa\colon \mathcal{I}_\Phi \rightarrow \{0, 1, \ldots\} \cup \{\infty\}$ such that $\kappa(I) = 0$ for at least one world I. It is extended to all events ϕ as follows. If ϕ is satisfiable, then $\kappa(\phi) = \min\{\kappa(I) \mid I \in \mathcal{I}_\Phi, I \models \phi\}$; otherwise, $\kappa(\phi) = \infty$. A world ranking κ is *admissible* with a conditional knowledge base (L, D) iff $\kappa(\neg\phi) = \infty$ for all $\phi \in L$, and $\kappa(\phi) < \infty$ and $\kappa(\phi \wedge \psi) < \kappa(\phi \wedge \neg\psi)$ for all defaults $\psi \leftarrow \phi \in D$.

A conditional knowledge base KB is *p-consistent* iff there exists a world ranking that is admissible with KB. It is *p-inconsistent* iff no such a world ranking exists. We say KB *p-entails* a default $\psi \leftarrow \phi$ iff either $\kappa(\phi) = \infty$ (that is, ϕ is unsatisfiable) or $\kappa(\phi \wedge \psi) < \kappa(\phi \wedge \neg\psi)$ for all world rankings κ that are admissible with KB.

A *default ranking* σ on $KB = (L, D)$ maps each $d \in D$ to a nonnegative integer. It is *admissible* with KB iff each $D' \subseteq D$ that is under L in conflict with some $d \in D$ contains a default d' such that $\sigma(d') < \sigma(d)$.

4.2 G-Coherence and P-Consistency

We now show that g-coherence is a generalization of p-consistency.

Recall first that the characterization of p-consistency by Goldszmidt and Pearl [17] corresponds to the characterization of g-coherence given in Theorem 3.2.

The following well-known result (see especially [14]) shows that p-consistency is equivalent to the existence of admissible default rankings.

Theorem 4.1. *A conditional knowledge base KB is p-consistent iff there exists a default ranking on KB that is admissible with KB.*

A similar result holds for g-coherence, which is subsequently formulated using the following concepts. A *ranking* σ on $KB = (L, P)$ maps each element of P to a nonnegative integer. It is *admissible* with KB iff each $P' \subseteq P$ that is under L in conflict with some $F \in P$ contains a conditional constraint F' such that $\sigma(F') < \sigma(F)$.

Theorem 4.2. *A probabilistic knowledge base KB is g-coherent iff there exists a ranking on KB that is admissible with KB.*

The following theorem finally shows the important result that g-coherence is a generalization of p-consistency.

Theorem 4.3. *Let $KB = (L, \{(\psi_1|\phi_1)[1,1], \ldots, (\psi_n|\phi_n)[1,1]\})$ be a probabilistic knowledge base. Then, KB is g-coherent iff the conditional knowledge base $KB' = (L, \{\psi_1 \leftarrow \phi_1, \ldots, \psi_n \leftarrow \phi_n\})$ is p-consistent.*

4.3 G-Coherent Entailment and P-Entailment

We now show that g-coherent entailment is a generalization of p-entailment.

The following result is essentially due to Adams [1], who formulated it for $L = \emptyset$.

Theorem 4.4 (Adams [1]). *A conditional knowledge base $KB = (L, D)$ p-entails a default $\beta \leftarrow \alpha$ iff $(L, D \cup \{\neg\beta \leftarrow \alpha\})$ is p-inconsistent.*

The following theorem shows that a similar result holds for g-coherent consequence, which is an immediate implication of the definition of g-coherent entailment.

Theorem 4.5. *Let $KB = (L, P)$ be a g-coherent probabilistic knowledge base, and let $(\beta|\alpha)[l, u]$ be a conditional constraint. Then, $KB \mathrel{|\!\sim} (\beta|\alpha)[l, u]$ iff $(L, P \cup \{(\beta|\alpha)[p, p]\})$ is not g-coherent for all $p \in [0, l) \cup (u, 1]$.*

The following related result for tight g-coherent consequence completes the picture.

Theorem 4.6. *Let $KB = (L, P)$ be a g-coherent probabilistic knowledge base, and let $(\beta|\alpha)[l, u]$ be a conditional constraint. Then, $KB \mathrel{|\!\sim}_{tight} (\beta|\alpha)[l, u]$ iff*

(i) $(L, P \cup \{(\beta|\alpha)[p, p]\})$ is not g-coherent for all $p \in [0, l) \cup (u, 1]$, and
(ii) $(L, P \cup \{(\beta|\alpha)[p, p]\})$ is g-coherent for all $p \in [l, u]$.

The next result finally shows that g-coherent entailment generalizes p-entailment.

Theorem 4.7. *Let $KB = (L, \{(\psi_1|\phi_1)[1, 1], \ldots, (\psi_n|\phi_n)[1, 1]\})$ be a g-coherent probabilistic knowledge base. Then, $KB \mathrel{|\!\sim} (\beta|\alpha)[1, 1]$ iff the conditional knowledge base $(L, \{\psi_1 \leftarrow \phi_1, \ldots, \psi_n \leftarrow \phi_n\})$ p-entails $\beta \leftarrow \alpha$.*

5 Relationship to Default Reasoning with Conditional Objects

In this section, we relate coherence-based probabilistic reasoning to default reasoning with conditional objects, which goes back to Dubois and Prade [11,3].

We associate with each set of defaults $D = \{\psi_1 \leftarrow \phi_1, \ldots, \psi_n \leftarrow \phi_n\}$, the set of conditional events $C_D = \{\psi_1|\phi_1, \ldots, \psi_n|\phi_n\}$. Given a nonempty set of conditional events $\mathcal{E} = \{\psi_1|\phi_1, \ldots, \psi_n|\phi_n\}$, the *quasi-conjunction* of $\mathcal{E}$, denoted $QC(\mathcal{E})$, is defined as the conditional event $(\psi_1 \Leftarrow \phi_1) \wedge \cdots \wedge (\psi_n \Leftarrow \phi_n) \mid \phi_1 \vee \cdots \vee \phi_n$.

We now define the notions of *co*-consistency and *co*-entailment as follows. A conditional knowledge base $KB = (L, D)$ is *co-consistent* iff, for every nonempty $D' \subseteq D$, there exists a model I of L such that $I(QC(C_{D'})) = \mathbf{true}$. We assume the total order $\mathbf{false} < \mathbf{indeterminate} < \mathbf{true}$. We say $KB = (L, D)$ *co-entails* a default $\beta \leftarrow \alpha$ iff either (i) $L \cup \{\alpha\} \models \beta$, or (ii) some nonempty $D' \subseteq D$ exists such that $I(QC(C_{D'})) \leq I(\beta|\alpha)$ for all models I of L.

The notions of *co*-consistency and *co*-entailment coincide with the notions of p-consistency and p-entailment, respectively [11,3]. We now show that our results in Sections 3 and 4 are naturally related to default reasoning with conditional objects.

It is easy to verify that the following counterpart of Theorem 3.1 for p-consistency formulates the above notion of *co*-consistency. Note that the notion of satisfiability used in this theorem is defined as in Section 4.1.

Theorem 5.1. *A conditional knowledge base $KB = (L, D)$ is p-consistent iff $L \cup D' \cup \{\phi_1 \vee \cdots \vee \phi_n\}$ is satisfiable for every nonempty $D' = \{\psi_1 \leftarrow \phi_1, \ldots, \psi_n \leftarrow \phi_n\} \subseteq D$.*

For conditional knowledge bases $KB = (L, D)$ and events α, let $D_\alpha(KB)$ be the set of all $D' = \{\psi_1 \leftarrow \phi_1, \ldots, \psi_n \leftarrow \phi_n\} \subseteq D$ such that $L \cup D' \cup \{\phi_1 \vee \cdots \vee \phi_n \vee \alpha\} \models \alpha$. Observe now that for $D' = \{\psi_1 \leftarrow \phi_1, \ldots, \psi_n \leftarrow \phi_n\}$, condition (ii) in the definition of the notion of *co*-entailment is equivalent to $L \cup D' \cup \{\phi_1 \vee \cdots \vee \phi_n \vee \alpha\} \models \alpha$ and $L \cup D' \models \beta \Leftarrow \alpha$. Thus, the following counterpart of Theorem 3.3 for p-entailment formulates the above notion of *co*-entailment.

Theorem 5.2. *Let $KB = (L, D)$ be a p-consistent conditional knowledge base. Then, KB p-entails the default $\beta \leftarrow \alpha$, iff $L \cup D' \models \beta \Leftarrow \alpha$ for some $D' \in D_\alpha(KB)$.*

Crucially, we can now also formulate counterparts to Lemma 3.4 and Theorems 3.5 and 3.6. To our knowledge, these results for system P are unknown so far. The following result shows that $D_\alpha(KB)$ contains a unique greatest element.

Lemma 5.3. *Let $KB = (L, D)$ be a p-consistent conditional knowledge base, and let α be an event. Then, $D_\alpha(KB)$ contains a unique greatest element.*

The next result shows that p-entailment from KB coincides with logical entailment from the greatest element in $D_\alpha(KB)$. That is, we can replace item (ii) in the definition of *co*-entailment by (ii') $I(QC(C_{D^\star})) \leq I(\beta|\alpha)$ for the greatest $D^\star$ in $D_\alpha(KB)$.

Theorem 5.4. *Let $KB = (L, D)$ be a p-consistent conditional knowledge base, and let $\beta \leftarrow \alpha$ be a default. Let $D^\star$ denote the unique greatest element in $D_\alpha(KB)$. Then,*

$$KB \text{ } p\text{-entails } \beta \leftarrow \alpha \text{ iff } L \cup D^\star \models \beta \Leftarrow \alpha.$$

The following theorem shows how $D^\star$ can be characterized and thus computed.

Theorem 5.5. *Let $KB = (L, D)$ be a p-consistent conditional knowledge base and α be an event. Let $D^\star \subseteq D$ and $(D_0, \ldots, D_k)$ be an ordered partition of $D \backslash D^\star$ such that:*

(i) every D_i, $0 \leq i \leq k$, is the set of all elements in $D_i \cup \cdots \cup D_k \cup D^\star$ that are tolerated under $L \cup \{\bot \Leftarrow \alpha\}$ by $D_i \cup \cdots \cup D_k \cup D^\star$, and

(ii) no member of $D^\star$ is tolerated under $L \cup \{\bot \Leftarrow \alpha\}$ by $D^\star$.

Then, $D^\star$ is the greatest element in $D_\alpha(KB)$.

6 Summary and Outlook

We explored the relationship between probabilistic logic under coherence, model-theoretic probabilistic logic, and default reasoning in system P. We showed that coherence-based probabilistic reasoning can be reduced to model-theoretic probabilistic reasoning by using concepts from default reasoning. Moreover, we showed that it is a probabilistic generalization of default reasoning in system P. That is, we gave a new probabilistic semantics for system P, which is neither based on infinitesimal probabilities nor on atomic-bound (or also big-stepped) probabilities. We finally showed that these results also give new insight into default reasoning with conditional objects.

Roughly speaking, the main difference between coherence-based and model-theoretic probabilistic reasoning is that the former generalizes default reasoning in system P, while the latter generalizes classical reasoning in propositional logic.

A very interesting topic of future research is to explore how other notions of coherence are related to model-theoretic probabilistic logic and to default reasoning. It would also be very interesting to develop coherence-based probabilistic extensions of notions of default reasoning different from system P (for example, in the spirit of [21]).

Acknowledgments. This work has been partially supported by a DFG grant and the Austrian Science Fund under project N Z29-INF. We are very grateful to the anonymous reviewers for their useful comments.

References

1. E. W. Adams. *The Logic of Conditionals*, volume 86 of *Synthese Library*. D. Reidel, Dordrecht, Netherlands, 1975.
2. S. Amarger, D. Dubois, and H. Prade. Constraint propagation with imprecise conditional probabilities. In *Proceedings UAI-91*, pp. 26–34. 1991.
3. S. Benferhat, D. Dubois, and H. Prade. Nonmonotonic reasoning, conditional objects and possibility theory. *Artif. Intell.*, 92(1–2):259–276, 1997.
4. S. Benferhat, D. Dubois, and H. Prade. Possibilistic and standard probabilistic semantics of conditional knowledge bases. *J. Logic Computat.*, 9(6):873–895, 1999.
5. V. Biazzo and A. Gilio. A generalization of the fundamental theorem of de Finetti for imprecise conditional probability assessments. *Int. J. Approx. Reasoning*, 24:251–272, 2000.
6. V. Biazzo, A. Gilio, T. Lukasiewicz, and G. Sanfilippo. Probabilistic logic under coherence, model-theoretic probabilistic logic, and default reasoning. Technical Report INFSYS RR-1843-01-03, Institut für Informationssysteme, TU Wien, 2001.
7. V. Biazzo, A. Gilio, T. Lukasiewicz, and G. Sanfilippo. Probabilistic logic under coherence: Complexity and algorithms. In *Proceedings ISIPTA-01*, Ithaca, New York, USA, June 26–29, 2001. To appear.
8. G. Boole. *An Investigation of the Laws of Thought, on which are Founded the Mathematical Theories of Logic and Probabilities.* Walton and Maberley, London, 1854. (Reprint: Dover Publications, New York, 1958).
9. G. Coletti and R. Scozzafava. Conditioning and inference in intelligent systems. *Soft Computing*, 3(3):118–130, 1999.
10. D. Dubois and H. Prade. Possibilistic logic, preferential models, non-monotonicity and related issues. In *Proceedings IJCAI-91*, pp. 419–424. 1991.
11. D. Dubois and H. Prade. Conditional objects as nonmonotonic consequence relationships. *IEEE Trans. Syst. Man Cybern.*, 24(12):1724–1740, 1994.
12. R. Fagin, J. Y. Halpern, and N. Megiddo. A logic for reasoning about probabilities. *Inf. Comput.*, 87:78–128, 1990.
13. A. M. Frisch and P. Haddawy. Anytime deduction for probabilistic logic. *Artif. Intell.*, 69:93–122, 1994.
14. H. Geffner. *Default Reasoning: Causal and Conditional Theories.* MIT Press, 1992.
15. A. Gilio. Probabilistic consistency of conditional probability bounds. In *Advances in Intelligent Computing, LNCS* 945, pp. 200–209. Springer, 1995.
16. A. Gilio. Precise propagation of upper and lower probability bounds in system P. In *Proceedings of the 8th International Workshop on Non-monotonic Reasoning*, 2000.
17. M. Goldszmidt and J. Pearl. On the consistency of defeasible databases. *Artif. Intell.*, 52(2):121–149, 1991.
18. S. Kraus, D. Lehmann, and M. Magidor. Nonmonotonic reasoning, preferential models and cumulative logics. *Artif. Intell.*, 14(1):167–207, 1990.
19. T. Lukasiewicz. Local probabilistic deduction from taxonomic and probabilistic knowledge-bases over conjunctive events. *Int. J. Approx. Reasoning*, 21(1):23–61, 1999.
20. T. Lukasiewicz. Probabilistic deduction with conditional constraints over basic events. *J. Artif. Intell. Res.*, 10:199–241, 1999.
21. T. Lukasiewicz. Probabilistic default reasoning with conditional constraints. In *Proceedings of the 8th International Workshop on Non-monotonic Reasoning*, 2000.
22. T. Lukasiewicz. Probabilistic logic programming with conditional constraints. *ACM Trans. Computat. Logic*, 2(3):289–337, July 2001. To appear.
23. N. J. Nilsson. Probabilistic logic. *Artif. Intell.*, 28:71–88, 1986.

24. J. Pearl. Probabilistic semantics for nonmonotonic reasoning: A survey. In *Proceedings KR-89*, pp. 505–516. 1989.
25. Y. Shoham. A semantical approach to nonmonotonic logics. In *Proceedings of the 2nd IEEE Symposium on Logic in Computer Science*, pp. 275–279, 1987.
26. P. Snow. Diverse confidence levels in a probabilistic semantics for conditional logics. *Artif. Intell.*, 113:269–279, 1999.

Belief Functions with Partially Ordered Values

Ivan Kramosil

Institute of Computer Science
Academy of Sciences of the Czech Republic
Pod vodárenskou věží 2, 182 07 Prague 8, Czech Republic
kramosil@cs.cas.cz

Abstract. Belief functions may be taken as an alternative to the classical probability theory, as a generalization of this theory, but also as a non-traditional and sophisticated application of probability theory. In this contribution, the idea of numerically quantified degrees of belief is abandoned in favour of the case when belief functions take their values in partially ordered sets perhaps enriched to lower or upper semilattices. Such structures seem to be the most general ones to which reasonable and nontrivial parts of the theory of belief functions can be extended and generalized.

1 Introduction, Motivation, Preliminaries

The degrees of belief quantified by belief functions, and the mathematical theory processing them and sometimes called the Dempster–Shafer theory, present an interesting mathematical model and tool for uncertainty quantification and processing. Belief functions may be taken, at the same time, as an alternative to the classical probability theory, as a generalization of this theory, but also as a non-traditional and sophisticated application of probability theory. The shortest way to the notion of belief function is the formalized combinatoric one: let m be a probability distribution on the power-set $\mathcal{P}(S)$ of all subsets of a finite set S, hence, $m : \mathcal{P}(S) \to [0,1]$ is such that $\sum_{A \subset S} m(A) = 1$ and m is called a *basic probability assignment* on S (b.p.a.) in this context. The *(non-normalized) belief function* $bel_m : \mathcal{P}(S) \to [0,1]$ is defined, given $A \subset S$, by

$$bel_m(A) = \sum_{\emptyset \neq B \subset A} m(B), \tag{1.1}$$

applying the convention according to which $bel_m(\emptyset) = 0$ for the empty subset $\emptyset$ of S. Keeping in mind the idea of possible generalization of belief functions to those taking also non-numerical values, only non-normalized belief functions will be considered below.

The following interpretation behind brings us to the idea of set-valued mappings important for our purposes. Let S be the set of all possible internal states of a system (a number of alternative interpretations being also possible) just one state $s_0 \in S$ being the actual one, let E be the space (perhaps a vector

S. Benferhat and P. Besnard (Eds.): ECSQARU 2001, LNAI 2143, pp. 303–315, 2001.

one) of empirical data which may result from some observations, experiments, measurements, etc. concerning the system in question. All what is known about the system is expressed by the so called *compatibility relation* $\rho : E \to \{0,1\}$ with the following intuition behind: if $\rho(s,x) = 0$ for some $s \in S$ and $x \in E$, then s cannot be the actual state of the system supposing that x was observed. If $\rho(s,x) = 1$, then s cannot be avoided from consideration when observing x, in other wording, s and x are compatible. Given $x \in E$, we can define the subset $U_\rho(x) = \{s \in S : \rho(s,x) = 1\}$ of states of S which are compatible with x.

The phenomenon of uncertainty enters our model supposing that the empirical data are of random nature. Namely, we shall suppose that x is the value taken by a random variable X defined on a fixed probability space $\langle \Omega, \mathcal{A}, P \rangle$ and with values in a measurable space $\langle E, \mathcal{E} \rangle$ generated by an appropriate nonempty σ-field of subsets of E. The composed mapping $U_\rho(X(\cdot)) : \Omega \to \mathcal{P}(S)$ is supposed to be measurable in the sense that for each $A \subset S$ its inverse image $(U_\rho(X))^{-1}(A)$ is in $\mathcal{A}$, so that the value

$$m(A) = P\left(\{\omega \in \Omega : U_\rho(X(\omega)) = A\}\right) \tag{1.2}$$

is defined. Hence, the mapping $U_\rho(X(\cdot))$ is supposed to be a *random set* or, more correctly, a (generalized set-valued) random variable which takes the probability space $\langle \Omega, \mathcal{A}, P \rangle$ into the measurable space $\langle \mathcal{P}(S), \mathcal{P}(\mathcal{P}(S)) \rangle$. S being finite, the relation (1.2) evidently defines a b.p.a. m on S and we can easily deduce that, given $A \subset S$,

$$bel_m(A) = P\left(\{\omega \in \Omega : \emptyset \neq U_\rho(X(\omega)) \subset A\}\right). \tag{1.3}$$

The approach to belief functions through compatibility relations and random sets has been already many times proposed, analyzed and investigated and we have repeated here the most basic idea just for the convenience of the reader perhaps not familiar with it (cf. some references in the list below).

Leaving aside a number of generalizations of the model just introduced (cf. [13], e. g., or some more special papers listed there), we shall focus our attention to the case when the degrees of belief are not quantified by real numbers, as it is the case in (1.1) and (1.3), but rather by elements of some non-numerical structures which may perhaps better reflect the nature of uncertainty in various particular cases. E. g., the degrees of belief need not be always dichotomic, i. e., some pairs of degrees of belief need not be comparable by the relation "greater than or equal to" without introducing some new and ontologically independent principles and accepting all the risks joined with such a step. Perhaps the first non-numerical structure arising in one's mind as a good tool for these sakes is a Boolean algebra, in particular, the Boolean algebra of all subsets of a fixed space with respect to the standard set-theoretic operations (cf. [11] and some papers listed there).

Going further with these reasonings we arrive at the key problem of this paper: which are the most general and most simple conditions which the structure over the degrees of uncertainty should meet in order to be able to develop a non-trivial fragment of the common theory of belief functions within the new framework? The aim of this contribution is to argue in favour of the idea that the degrees of belief should define a partially ordered set, perhaps enriched to an upper or lower (semi) lattice or to a lattice. This kind of results presented below implies that one should not expect some qualitatively new and perhaps surprising ones. On the other side, let us hope that the achieved results are still interesting enough to justify our effort.

Let us close this chapter by recalling some most elementary notions concerning the partially ordered sets. *Quasi-partially ordered* set is a pair $\langle T, \preceq \rangle$ where T is a nonempty set and $\preceq$ is a reflexive and transitive binary relation on T. If T is, moreover, antisymmetric, the pair $\langle T, \preceq \rangle$ is called a *partially ordered (p.o.) set* induced in T by the *partially ordering (relation)* $\preceq$. Each quasi-p.o. set $\langle T, \preceq \rangle$ can be easily converted into a partially ordered set over the equivalence classes $T| \approx$, here $x \approx y$ holds iff $x \preceq y$ and $y \preceq x$ hold simultaneously. Given a p.o. set $\langle T, \preceq \rangle$ and a nonempty subset $A \subset T$, the *supremum* $\bigvee_{x \in A} x$ and the *infimum* $\bigwedge_{x \in A} x$ ($\bigvee A$ and $\bigwedge A$, abbreviately) are defined in the standard way, even if these values need not be always defined. If $A = \{x_1, x_2, \ldots, x_n\}$, we shall write $x_1 \vee x_2 \vee \cdots \vee x_n$ and $x_1 \wedge x_2 \wedge \cdots \wedge x_n$ instead of $\bigvee A$ and $\bigwedge A$. If $\bigvee T$ ($\bigwedge T$, resp.) is defined, it is called the *unit* (*zero*, resp.) element of the p.o. set $\langle T, \preceq \rangle$ and denoted by $\mathbf{1}_T$ ($\mathbf{0}_T$, resp.). In this case the definition of supremum and infimum can be extended also to the empty subset $\emptyset$ of T, setting $\bigwedge \emptyset = \mathbf{1}_T$ and $\bigvee \emptyset = \mathbf{0}_T$. The definition of supremum and infimum can be extended also to quasi-p.o. sets, but in this case, if $\bigvee A$ and/or $\bigwedge A$ are defined, they are defined up to the equivalence relation $\approx$.

The reader is supposed to be familiar with the most elementary properties of p.o. set or she/he may consult [1,4] or other elementary textbook or monograph.

2 Set Structures over Partially Ordered Sets and Complete Upper Semilattices

In this chapter we shall build a structure of partial ordering over the power-set $\mathcal{P}(T)$ of all subsets of T, which extends conservatively the properties of partial ordering in T, and which can be totally embedded into the p.o. set $\langle T, \preceq \rangle$ supposing that this p.o. set is complete in the sense that $\bigvee A$ and $\bigwedge A$ are defined for all $A \subset T$. So, given a p.o. set $\langle T, \preceq \rangle$, let us define a binary relation $\sqsubseteq$ on $\mathcal{P}(T) = \{A : A \subset T\}$ in such a way that $A \sqsubseteq B$ holds for A, $B \subset T$ iff, for each $S_1 \subset A$ such that $\bigvee S_1$ exists, there exists $S_2 \subset B$ such that $\bigvee S_2$ is defined and the relation $\bigvee S_1 \preceq \bigvee S_2$ holds. The following assertion can be easily proved (cf. [12] for the details of the proofs of all the statements presented below).

Lemma 2.1. The relation $\sqsubseteq$ is a quasi-partial ordering on $\mathcal{P}(T)$ which extends conservatively the set-theoretic inclusion in $\mathcal{P}(T)$, i. e., $A \subset B \subset T$ implies that $A \sqsubseteq B$. □

Using the standard construction mentioned above, we introduce the equivalence relation $\sim$ on $\mathcal{P}(T)$, setting $A \sim B$ iff $A \sqsubseteq B$ and $B \sqsubseteq A$ hold simultaneously for A, $B \subset T$. Abusing the symbol $\sqsubseteq$, we may extend it to the equivalence classes $[A] \in \mathcal{P}(T)/\sim$, where $[A] = \{B \subset T : B \sim A\}$. So, $[A] \sqsubseteq [B]$ holds iff $A \sqsubseteq B$ holds; the validity of this relation clearly does not depend on the choice of representatives of the classes $[A]$ and $[B]$. As can be easily proved, for each $A \subset T$ such that $\bigvee A$ is defined the identity $[A] = [\{\bigvee A\}]$ holds, hence, the subsets of T which possess supremum in T are completely represented, up to the equivalence relation $\sim$, by this supremum value. Given a system $\mathcal{A} \subset \mathcal{P}(T)$ of subsets of T, we denote by $\bigsqcup \mathcal{A}$ ($\bigsqcap \mathcal{A}$, resp.) the supremum (infimum, resp.) of this system of sets with respect to the partial ordering $\sqsubseteq$ on $\mathcal{P}(T)$. In general, the values $\bigsqcup \mathcal{A}$ and $\bigsqcap \mathcal{A}$ need not be defined, but if they exists, they are defined uniquely up to the equivalence relation $\sim$. As can be easily seen, given $\mathcal{A} \subset \mathcal{P}(T)$ and denoting by $\bigcup \mathcal{A} = \bigcup_{A \in \mathcal{A}} A$ the union of all sets from $\mathcal{A}$, the relation $\bigsqcup \mathcal{A} \sqsubseteq [\bigcup \mathcal{A}]$ holds. If $\bigvee T = \mathbf{1}_{\mathcal{T}}$ is defined, then the relation $\emptyset \sqsubseteq A \sqsubseteq T$ holds for each $A \subset T$ (the relation $\emptyset \sqsubseteq A$ holds due to the trivial fact that there is no nonempty $S \subset \emptyset$, so that the antecedent of the corresponding relation is always false).

Definition 2.1. A partially ordered set $\mathcal{T} = \langle T, \prec \rangle$ is called *upper semilattice*, if for each $t_1, t_2 \in T$ their supremum $t_1 \vee t_2 \in T$ is defined. $\mathcal{T}$ is called *lower semilattice*, if for each $t_1, t_2 \in T$ their infimum $t_1 \wedge t_2 \in T$ is defined. $\mathcal{T}$ is called *complete upper semilattice*, if for each $\emptyset \neq A \subset T$ the supremum $\bigvee A \in T$ is defined. $\mathcal{T}$ is called *complete lower semilattice*, if for all $\emptyset \neq A \subset T$ the infimum $\bigwedge A \in T$ is defined. □

E. g., each complete Boolean algebra, hence, in particular, each power set over a nonempty set, together with the set-theoretic relations and operations of inclusion, union and intersection, is at the same time a complete upper semilattice and a complete lower semilattice. Every p.o. set which possesses this property, i. e., which is simultaneously a (complete) upper semilattice and a (complete) lower semilattice, is called the *(complete) lattice*. More generally, each Boolean algebra is an upper and lower semilattice, hence, a lattice.

Theorem 2.1. Let $\mathcal{T} = \langle T, \prec \rangle$ be a complete upper semilattice. Then

(i) for each $t \in T$, $[\{t\}] = \{A \subset T : \bigvee A = t\}$,
(ii) for each $A \subset T$, $[A] = [\{\bigvee A\}]$, hence $[A] = \{A \subset T : \bigvee B = \bigvee A\}$,
(iii) for each $A, B \subset T$, $[A] \sqsubseteq [B]$ holds iff $\bigvee A \prec \bigvee B$ holds,
(iv) for each $A, B \subset T$, $[A] \sqcup [B] = [A \sqcup B]$, if $[A] \sqcup [B]$ defined,
(v) for each $A, B \subset T$, $[A \sqcap B] \sqsubseteq [A] \sqcap [B]$, if $[A] \sqcap [B]$ defined,
(vi) if $\mathcal{T}$ is, moreover, a lower semilattice then, for each $A, B \subset T$, $[A] \sqcap [B] = [\{(\bigvee A) \wedge [\bigvee B]\}]$. □

Proof. The assertions are more or less evident, detailed proofs can be found in [12]. □

3 Belief Functions with Values in Partially Ordered Sets

Let S be a nonempty set, let $\mathcal{T} = \langle T, \prec \rangle$ be a.p.o. set, let $\vee$ and $\wedge$ denote the (partial, in general) supremum and infimum operations in T induced by the partial ordering relation $\prec$, let $\mathcal{B}_T = \langle \mathcal{P}(T), \cup, \cap, T - \cdot \rangle$ be the Boolean algebra induced in the power-set $\mathcal{P}(T)$ of all subsets of T by the standard set-theoretic operations of union ($\cup$), intersection ($\cap$) and complement ($T - \cdot$).

Definition 3.1. $\mathcal{B}_T$-valued basic possibilistic assignment on S ($\mathcal{B}_T$-b.poss.a. on S, abbreviately) is a mapping $\pi : \mathcal{P}(S) \to \mathcal{P}(T)$, i. e., $\pi(A) \subset T$ for all $A \subset S$, such that $\cup_{A \subset S} \pi(A) = T$. $\mathcal{B}_T$-b.poss.a. π is called *compact*, if there exists $A \subset S$ such that $\pi(A) = T$. $\mathcal{B}_T$-b.poss.a. π is called *$\mathcal{B}_T$-basic probabilistic assignment on* S, if $\pi(A) \cap \pi(B) = \emptyset$ for all A, $B \subset S$ such that $A \cap B = \emptyset$. The *$\mathcal{B}_T$-(valued) belief function defined by a $\mathcal{B}_T$-b.poss.a. π on* S is the mapping $BEL_\pi : \mathcal{P}(S) \to \mathcal{P}(T)$ ascribing to each $\emptyset \neq A \subset S$ the subset

$$BEL_\pi(A) = \cup_{\emptyset \neq B \subset A} \pi(B) \tag{3.1}$$

of T, by convention, $BEL_\pi(\emptyset) = \emptyset$ for the empty subset of S. □

The properties of belief functions taking their values (degrees of belief) in a Boolean algebra are at a more general level, and in more detail, investigated in [11], so that we shall refer to the corresponding results and statements without repeating their proofs. Here we shall take into consideration the fact that the values $\pi(A)$ and $BEL_\pi(A)$, $A \subset S$, are subsets of the p.o. set $\mathcal{T}$, so that they can be subjected to the quasi-partial ordering relation $\sqsubseteq$ defined on $\mathcal{P}(T)$ and extended to the equivalence classes from the factor-space $\mathcal{P}(T)/\sim$. Lemma 2.1 and Theorem 2.1 yield immediately that, for each $A \subset B \subset S$, the relation $BEL_\pi(A) \sqsubseteq BEL_{\pi(B)}$ holds. For every A, $B \subset S$ we can deduce that

$$[BEL_\pi(A)] \sqcup [BEL_\pi(B)] \sqsubseteq [BEL_\pi(A \cup B)] \tag{3.2}$$

holds supposing that $[BEL_\pi(A)] \sqcup [BEL_\pi(B)]$ is defined.

The mapping $BEL_\pi : \mathcal{P}(S) \to \mathcal{P}(T)$, defined by (3.1), easily induces the mapping $BEL_\pi^* : \mathcal{P}(S) \to \mathcal{P}(T)/\sim$, setting simply, given $A \subset S$

$$\begin{aligned} BEL_\pi^*(A) &= [BEL_\pi(A)] = \{R \subset T : R \sim BEL_\pi(A)\} = \\ &= \{R \subset T : R \sqsubseteq BEL_\pi(A) \text{ and } BEL_\pi(A) \sqsubseteq R\}. \end{aligned} \tag{3.3}$$

Similarly, the b.poss.a. $\pi : \mathcal{P}(S) \to \mathcal{P}(T)$ induces the mapping $\pi^* : \mathcal{P}(S) \to \mathcal{P}(T)/\sim$ such that, for each $A \subset S$,

$$\pi^*(A) = [\pi(A)] = \{R \subset T : R \sqsubseteq \pi(A) \text{ and } \pi(A) \sqsubseteq R\}. \tag{3.4}$$

The inclusion $\pi(C) \subset BEL_\pi(A)$, valid by definition for every $\emptyset \neq C \subset A$ implies immediately, using Lemma 2.1, that for each $A \subset S$ the relation

$$\sqcup_{\emptyset \neq C \subset A} \pi^*(C) \sqsubseteq BEL_\pi^*(A) \tag{3.5}$$

holds. The following lemma specifies the conditions under which the $\sqsubseteq$-inclusion in (3.5) can be replaced by equality.

Lemma 3.1. Let $\langle T, \prec \rangle$ be a complete upper semilattice, let $\pi : \mathcal{P}(S) \rightarrow \mathcal{P}(T)$ be a $\mathcal{B}_T$-valued b.poss.a. on S. Then for each finite $A \subset S$

$$BEL^*_\pi(A) = \sqcup_{\emptyset \neq C \subset A} \pi^*(C). \tag{3.6}$$

In particular, if whole the space S is finite, then

$$\sqcup_{A \subset S} \pi^*(A) = [T]. \tag{3.7}$$

□

Proof. The assertion follows from Theorem 2.1, (iv), supposing that this statement is easily extended to any finite nonempty system $\mathcal{A} \subset \mathcal{P}(T)$ of subsets of T. □

(3.7) may be taken also in such a way that the mapping π^* is a basic possibilistic assignment on S taking its values in the factor-space $\mathcal{P}(T)/\sim$. The relation (3.6) then enables to understand the mapping BEL^* as the belief function defined by the b.poss.a. π^*. The condition that $\langle T, \prec \rangle$ is a complete upper semilattice seems to be the weakest one imposed on the set of values of the b.poss.a. π^* under which the basic philosophy underlying the idea of belief functions can be applied.

4 Dempster Combination Rule for Partially Ordered Degrees of Belief

Within the framework of the classical Dempster–Shafer theory of belief functions, Dempster combination rule is defined as follows. Let S be a finite nonempty set, let m_1, m_2 be basic probability assignments on S, i. e., probability distributions on the power-set $\mathcal{P}(S)$ of all subsets of S. Let $m_{12} : \mathcal{P}(S) \rightarrow [0,1]$ be the mapping defined by

$$m_{12}(A) = \sum_{B,C \subset S,\, B \cap C = A} m_1(B)\, m_2(C) \tag{4.1}$$

for each $A \subset S$. As can be easily proved, m_{12} is also a basic probability assignment on S, denoted also by $m_1 \oplus m_2$ and called the *Dempster product* of m_1 and m_2. (4.1) is then called the *Dempster combination rule* for basic probability assignments. *(Non-normalized) belief function* defined by a basic probabilistic assignment m on S is the mapping $bel_m : \mathcal{P}(S) \rightarrow [0,1]$ such that

$$bel_m(A) = \sum_{\emptyset \neq B \subset A} m(B) \tag{4.2}$$

for all $A \subset S$, $bel_m(\emptyset) = 0$ by convention. Dempster product is defined also for (non-normalized) belief functions, setting simply

$$bel_{m_1} \oplus bel_{m_2} =_{\mathrm{df}} bel_{m_1 \oplus m_2}. \tag{4.3}$$

As analyzed in more detail in [8] or elsewhere, Dempster combination rule is legitimate supposing that the compatibility relations ρ_1, ρ_2 of the two subjects in question are composed by the operation of minimum, i.e., $\rho_{12}(s,x) = \min\{\rho_1(s,x), \rho_2(s,x)\}$ for every $s \in S$ and $x \in E$, and that the set-valued random variables (random sets) $U_{\rho_1}(X(\cdot))$ and $U_{\rho_2}(X(\cdot))$ are statistically (stochastically) independent (as the random variable X may be of vector character, we can suppose that it is common for both the subjects in spite of perhaps different nature of their empirical data).

For Boolean-valued basic probabilistic assignments and belief functions induced by them, Dempster combination rule can be rewritten in such a way that summations are routinely replaced by suprema and products by infima. Hence, for $\mathcal{B}_T$-valued b.poss.a.'s π_1, π_2 on S we obtain that

$$(\pi_1 \oplus \pi_2)(A) = \bigcup_{B,C \subset S,\, B \cap C = A}(\pi_1(B) \cap \pi_2(C)) \tag{4.4}$$

for each $A \subset S$. As can be easily proved,

$$\bigcup_{A \subset S}(\pi_1 \oplus \pi_2)(A) = T, \tag{4.5}$$

so that $\pi_1 \oplus \pi_2$ is also a $\mathcal{B}_T$-valued b.poss.a. on S.

Keeping in mind the interpretation introduced in Chapter 1, we arrive at the set-valued mapping $U_\rho(\cdot) : E \to \mathcal{P}(S)$, where $U_\rho(x) = \{s \in S : \rho(s,x) = 1\}$. In order to introduce Boolean-valued uncertainty degrees into our model, consider a complete Boolean algebra $\mathcal{B} = \langle B, \vee, \wedge, \neg \rangle$ and a B-valued complete possibilistic space $\langle \Omega, \mathcal{P}(\Omega), \Pi_0 \rangle$. Hence, Ω is a nonempty set, $\mathcal{P}(\Omega)$ is the power-set of all subsets of Ω and Π_0 is a $\mathcal{B}$-valued complete possibilistic measure on Ω, so that Π_0 takes $\mathcal{P}(\Omega)$ into B in such a way that $\Pi_0(\emptyset) = \mathbf{0}_{\mathcal{B}}$, $\Pi_0(\Omega) = \mathbf{1}_{\mathcal{B}}$, and

$$\Pi_0\left(\bigcup_{A \in \mathcal{R}} A\right) = \bigvee_{A \in \mathcal{R}} \Pi_0(A) \tag{4.6}$$

for every nonempty system R of subsets of Ω. Taking the empirical value $x \in E$ as that of a mapping $X : \Omega \to E$, the composed mapping $U_\rho(X(\cdot))$ takes Ω into $\mathcal{P}(S)$ so that, given $A \subset S$, we can define

$$\pi(A) = \Pi_0\left(\{\omega \in \Omega : U_\rho(X(\omega)) = A\}\right). \tag{4.7}$$

As can be easily proved, $\bigvee_{A \subset S} \pi(A) = \Pi_0(\Omega) = \mathbf{1}_{\mathcal{B}}$, so that π is a $\mathcal{B}$-valued basic possibilistic assignment S. If S is finite, the completeness of Π_0 is not necessary.

Consider two subjects operating over the same empirical space E and possibilistic complete space $\langle \Omega, \mathcal{P}(\Omega), \Pi_0 \rangle$, both using the same, possibly vector-like empirical value $x \in E$ taken by a variable $X : \Omega \to E$, but with perhaps different compatibility relations ρ_1 and ρ_2. Let

$$\rho_{12}(s,x) = \min\{\rho_1(s,x), \rho_2(s,x)\}, \tag{4.8}$$

so that

$$U_{\rho_{12}}(x) = U_{\rho_1}(x) \cap U_{\rho_2}(x) \tag{4.9}$$

holds for every $x \in E$. Applying (4.7) we obtain that

$$(\pi_1 \oplus \pi_2)(A) = \pi_{12}(A) = \tag{4.10}$$
$$= \bigvee_{B \cap C = A} \Pi_0 \left(\{\omega \in \Omega : U_{\rho_1}(X(\omega)) = B\} \cap \{\omega \in \Omega : U_{\rho_2}(X(\omega)) = C\}\right).$$

Hence, if Π_0 is a homeomorphism which takes the Boolean algebra $\mathcal{B}_\Omega = \langle \mathcal{P}(\Omega), \cup, \cap, \Omega - \cdot \rangle$ of all subsets of Ω on $\mathcal{B}$ in such a way that

$$\Pi_0 \left((U_{\rho_1}(X))^{-1} (B) \cap (U_{\rho_2}(X))^{-1} (C) \right) = \tag{4.11}$$
$$= \Pi_0 \left((U_{\rho_1}(X))^{-1} (B) \right) \wedge \Pi_0 \left((U_{\rho_2}(X))^{-1} (C) \right)$$

holds for all B, $C \subset S$, in particular, if $\Omega = T$ and Π_0 is the identity mapping, then

$$(\pi_1 \oplus \pi_2)(A) = \bigvee_{B \cap C = A} (\pi_1(B) \wedge \pi_2(C)), \tag{4.12}$$

introducing the $\mathcal{B}$-valued b.poss.a.'s π_1 and π_2 like as π is defined by (4.7). Using the terms similar to those in the classical probabilistic case, we can say that if (4.11) is valid, the set-valued mappings $U_{\rho_1}(X(\cdot))$ and $U_{\rho_2}(X(\cdot))$ are *possibilistically independent*. The notion of possibilistic independence is analyzed, compared with that of statistical (stochastical) independence, and discussed in more detail in [9].

Let us consider, again, a partially ordered set $\mathcal{T} = \langle T, \prec \rangle$, a nonempty set S, a $\mathcal{B}_T$-b.poss.a. π on S, the $\mathcal{B}_T$-valued belief function BEL_π defined by (3.1), and the induced b.poss.a. π^* and belief function BEL_π^* defined by (3.4) and (3.6). Using a more or less routine way of reasoning (cf. Theorem 7.1 in [12] for details), we arrive at the following statement.

Theorem 4.1. Let π_1, π_2 be $\mathcal{B}_T$-valued b.poss.a.'s, let their Dempster product $\pi_1 \oplus \pi_2$ be defined by (4.4). Let the Dempster product of the induced $\mathcal{P}(T)/\sim$-valued b.poss.a.'s π_1^*, π_2^* be defined by

$$(\pi_1^* \oplus \pi_2^*)(A) =_{\mathrm{df}} (\pi_1 \oplus \pi_2)^*(A) = [(\pi_1 \oplus \pi_2)(A)] \tag{4.13}$$

for all $A \subset S$. If $\mathcal{T} = \langle T, \prec \rangle$ is a complete upper semilattice and a lower semilattice, and if

$$\bigvee(\pi_1(B) \cap \pi_2(C)) = (\bigvee \pi_1(B)) \wedge (\bigvee \pi_2(C)) \tag{4.14}$$

holds for each B, $C \subset S$, then the relation

$$(\pi_1^* \oplus \pi_2^*)(A) = \bigsqcup_{B \cap C = A} [\pi_1^*(B) \sqcap \pi_2^*(C)] \tag{4.15}$$

is valid for all $A \subset S$. □

Remark. The relation (4.15) can be obtained also when adapting (3.1) routinely to the case of partially ordered set $\langle \mathcal{P}(T)/\sim, \sqsubseteq \rangle$ with its supremum ($\sqcup$) and infimum ($\sqcap$) operations. Theorem 4.1 then explicitates the conditions under which such a formal rewriting is legitimate. The relation

$$\bigvee(\pi_1(B) \cap \pi_2(C)) \prec (\bigvee \pi_1(B)) \wedge (\bigvee \pi_2(C)) \tag{4.16}$$

holds in general, so that the weakened version of (4.15), namely,

$$(\pi_1^* \oplus \pi_2^*)(A) \sqsubseteq \bigsqcup_{B\cap C=A} [\pi_1^*(B) \sqcap \pi_2^*(C)] , \tag{4.17}$$

can be proved without the assumption (4.14).

Let us introduce a particular case when (4.14) holds true. Let S and W be nonempty sets, let $\pi_0 : \mathcal{P}(S) \to \mathcal{P}(W)$ be a Boolean-valued b.poss.a., so that $\bigcup_{A\subset S}\pi_0(A) = W$. Set $\mathcal{T} = \langle \mathcal{P}(W), \subset \rangle$ and define a mapping λ: $\mathcal{P}(W) \to \mathcal{P}(\mathcal{P}(W))$ $(= \mathcal{P}(\mathcal{T}))$ in this way: for each $W_0 \subset W$,

$$\lambda(W_0) = \{\{w\} : w \in W_0\} \subset \mathcal{P}(W). \tag{4.18}$$

In particular, given $A \subset S$, set $\pi(A) = \lambda(\pi_0(A)) \subset \mathcal{P}(W) = \mathcal{T}$. An easy reasoning yield that $\bigvee \mathcal{A} = \bigcup \mathcal{A}$ and $\bigwedge \mathcal{A} = \bigcap \mathcal{A}$ for every $\mathcal{A} \subset \mathcal{P}(W)$. For the values $\pi(A)$ we obtain that $\bigvee \pi(A) = \pi_0(A)$ for every $A \subset S$, $\bigwedge \pi(A) = \pi_0(A)$, if $\pi_0(A)$ is a singleton, i. e., if $\pi_0(A) = \{w_0\}$ for some $w_0 \in W$, and $\bigwedge \pi(A) = \emptyset$ otherwise, as $\{w_1\} \cap \{w_2\} = \emptyset$ for every $w_1 \neq w_2$, w_1, $w_2 \in W$. An easy calculation yields that

$$\bigvee_{A\subset S}\pi(A) = \lambda(W) = \lambda\left(\mathbf{1}_{\langle \mathcal{P}(W),\subset\rangle}\right) , \tag{4.19}$$

as W is the unit element of the p.o. set $\langle \mathcal{P}(W), \subset \rangle$. Hence, in this sense π is a $\mathcal{P}(\mathcal{T})$-valued Boolean basic possibilistic assignment on S.

Let us consider two $\mathcal{P}(W)$-valued b.poss.a.'s π_{01}, π_{02} on S, let $\pi_1, \pi_2 : \mathcal{P}(S) \to \mathcal{P}(\mathcal{T})$ be defined by $\pi_i(A) = \lambda(\pi_{0i}(A))$ for both $i = 1, 2$ and for all $A \subset S$. Given B, $C \subset S$, we obtain that

$$\bigvee(\pi_1(B) \cap \pi_2(C)) = \pi_{01}(B) \cap \pi_{02}(C) = (\bigvee \pi_1(B)) \wedge (\bigvee \pi_2(C)) , \tag{4.20}$$

so that (4.14) holds in this particular case.

5 Nonspecificity Degrees and Dempster Rule

Leaving aside a number of perhaps more important and more deeply going problems concerning to the Dempster combination rule, let us focus our attention to the following quite legitimate question: whether, and in which sense and degree, the quality of a basic probability or basic possibilistic assignment is improved when combined with another such assignment?

Let S be a finite set, let $m : \mathcal{P}(S) \to [0, 1]$ be a basic probability assignment. The *nonspecificity degree* $W(m)$ is defined by

$$W(m) = \sum_{A\subset S} (\|A\|/\|S\|)\, m(A). \tag{5.1}$$

For two b.p.a.'s m_1, m_2 we can prove (cf. [8] together with a detailed discussion including the intuition behind) that the inequality

$$W(m_1 \oplus m_2) \leq W(m_1) \wedge W(m_2) \tag{5.2}$$

holds, where $\wedge$ denotes the (standard) infimum in $[0,1]$. For the dual Dempster rule $\otimes$, induced by the compatibility relation $\rho_{12}(s,x) = \rho_1(s,x) \vee \rho_2(s,x)$, where $\vee$ stands for supremum in $[0,1]$, we obtain that

$$W(m_1 \otimes m_2) \geq W(m_1) \vee W(m_2) \tag{5.3}$$

holds. These inequalities can be generalized to

$$W_\lambda(m_1 \oplus m_2) \leq W_\lambda(m_1) \wedge W_\lambda(m_2), \tag{5.4}$$
$$W_\lambda(m_1 \otimes m_2) \geq W_\lambda(m_1) \vee W_\lambda(m_2), \tag{5.5}$$

where

$$W_\lambda(m) = \sum\nolimits_{A \subset S} \lambda(A)\, m(A) \tag{5.6}$$

and λ is a fuzzy measure on S, i.e., $\lambda : \mathcal{P}(S) \to [0,1]$, $\lambda(\emptyset) = 0$, $\lambda(S) = 1$, and $\lambda(A) \leq \lambda(B)$ for every $A \subset B \subset S$.

The last approach can be shifted to the case of non-numerical b.poss.a.'s as follows. Let π_1, π_2 be Boolean-valued basic possibilistic assignments defined on S and taking their values in $\mathcal{P}(T)$, let for every $A \subset S$

$$(\pi_1 \oplus \pi_2)(A) = \bigcup_{B,C \subset S,\, B \cap C = A} (\pi_1(B) \cap \pi_2(C)), \tag{5.7}$$
$$(\pi_1 \otimes \pi_2)(A) = \bigcup_{B,C \subset S,\, B \cup C = A} (\pi_1(B) \cap \pi_2(C)). \tag{5.8}$$

Let $\lambda : \mathcal{P}(S) \to \mathcal{P}(T)$ be a $\mathcal{P}(T)$*-valued Boolean fuzzy measure* on S, i.e., $\lambda(\emptyset) = \emptyset$, $\lambda(S) = T$, and $\lambda(A) \subset \lambda(B)$ holds for each $A \subset B \subset S$. The $\mathcal{P}(T)$*-valued Boolean nonspecificity degree* $W_\lambda^b(\pi)$ of a Boolean-valued b.poss.a. π with values in $\mathcal{P}(T)$ is then defined by

$$W_\lambda^b(\pi) = \bigcup_{A \subset S} (\lambda(A) \cap \pi(A)). \tag{5.9}$$

The next assertion more or less immediately follows (cf. [12] for the details of the proof).

Theorem 5.1. For each Boolean-valued b.poss.a.'s π_1, π_2 on S the set inclusions

$$W_\lambda^b(\pi_1 \oplus \pi_2) \subset W_\lambda^b(\pi_1) \cap W_\lambda^b(\pi_2), \tag{5.10}$$
$$W_\lambda^b(\pi_1 \otimes \pi_2) \supset W_\lambda^b(\pi_1) \cup W_\lambda^b(\pi_2) \tag{5.11}$$

are valid. □

Lemma 2.1 immediately yields that, under the notation and conditions of Theorem 5.1, the relations

$$\left[W_\lambda^b(\pi_1 \oplus \pi_2)\right] \sqsubseteq \left[W_\lambda^b(\pi_1) \cap W_\lambda^b(\pi_2)\right], \tag{5.12}$$
$$\left[W_\lambda^b(\pi_1 \otimes \pi_2)\right] \sqsupseteq \left[W_\lambda^b(\pi_1) \cup W_\lambda^b(\pi_2)\right] \tag{5.13}$$

hold. If $\langle T, \prec \rangle$ is a complete upper semilattice, then Theorem 2.1 (iv) yields that

$$\left[W_\lambda^b(\pi_1 \otimes \pi_2)\right] \sqsupseteq \left[W_\lambda^b(\pi_1)\right] \sqcup \left[W_\lambda^b(\pi_2)\right], \tag{5.14}$$

if, moreover, $\langle T, \prec \rangle$ is a lower semilattice, then Theorem 2.1 (vi) yields that

$$[W_\lambda^b(\pi_1 \oplus \pi_2)] \sqsubseteq [W_\lambda^b(\pi_1)] \sqcap [W_\lambda^b(\pi_2)] \tag{5.15}$$

holds. Hence, under the conditions that $\langle T, \prec \rangle$ is a complete upper semilattice and, simultaneously, a lower semilattice, the mapping $[W_\lambda^b(\cdot)]$ seems to be a reasonable $\mathcal{P}(T)/\sim$-valued nonspecificity degree of $\mathcal{P}(T)/\sim$-valued basic possibilistic assignments, copying in a reasonable and nontrivial way some intuitive and acceptable properties of the nonspecificity degrees W, W_λ and W_λ^b. These conditions imposed to the partially ordered set $\langle T, \prec \rangle$ seem to be the weakest ones under which such a modification is possible and nontrivial.

6 Conclusions

When considering some possibilities of applications of non-numerical uncertainty degrees in general, and non-numerical basic possibilistic assignments and belief functions in particular, we can modify the basic paradigma used in the case of probabilistically quantified and processed degrees of uncertainty. In this case, elementary random events, mutually disjoint and defining a composition of the certain event, are supposed to be endowed by non-negative probability values summing to one. The assumption of additivity or σ-additivity, together with the assumption of statistical (stochastical) independence of at least some random events if they occur repeatedly, enable to compute probabilities for large collection of random events defining a very rich structure.

In the case of non-numerically quantified uncertainties we can start from a structure of events the degrees of uncertainty of at least some of them can be compared by the relation "greater than" or "greater than or equal to". The degrees of uncertainty of some events can be taken, by a subject, as acceptable as far as the risk following when taking them as surely valid is concerned, some other degrees of uncertainty are taken as too great to accept the same decision. In both the cases the subject's feelings are immediate, not being based on some numerical evaluations of these degrees of uncertainty by real numbers, in particular those from the unit interval. The events, when taken as sets, are structured by the relation of set-theoretical inclusion, perhaps with some more demands imposed to this structure, their degrees of uncertainty are structured by a partially ordering relations, and the aim is to compute the degree of uncertainty of some more sophistically defined events. Here "to compute" means to prove that the uncertainty degrees of these more complex events are comparable with those ascribed either to the elementary events supposed to be known a priori, or with degrees of uncertainty of events for which such a comparison has been already proved.

In particular, we can process, in this way, the non-numerical uncertainties ascribed to the events like "the actual state of the system in question is in an investigated subset of S", demanding answers of this kind: "the degree of uncertainty of this event is at least as great as the degree of uncertainty ascribed to an event A", or "the degree of uncertainty of this event is smaller than the degree of uncertainty ascribed to an event B", in both the cases A and B being events from the elementary basis so that the subject can take profit of the uncertainty degrees ascribed to them, in her/his decision making, thanks to her/his knowledge concerning the practical and extra-mathematical circumstances of the system and decision-making problem under consideration. E. g., a solution to a problem may be taken as good and fail-proof if we know that the uncertainty describing the possibility of its failure is not greater than the danger of a strong earthquake in our region, even if we perhaps do not know the precise probability value of the occurrence of the last catastrophe.

At least the three following problems or directions of further investigation would deserve being taken into consideration.

(I) We have chosen, in this paper, a rather general approach when degrees of uncertainty are subsets of a partially ordered set. Consequently, the set of uncertainty degrees can be endowed by two structures: the Boolean one, generated on the power-set $\mathcal{P}(T)$ of the partially ordered set $\langle T, \prec \rangle$ by the usual set-theoretic operations and relations (e. g., $\subset$, $\cap$, $\cup$), and the relations and operations defined through the partial ordering relation $\prec$ on T (e. g., $\sqsubset$, $\sqcap$, $\sqcup$). A question arises whether it is possible to obtain a similar model either with single-valued uncertainties, even if from a larger set than T, or with set-valued uncertainties, but structured only by usual set-theoretic operations and relations.

(II) In the author's opinion, the conditions imposed, in this paper, to the structure of the set of uncertainty degrees seem to be the weakest ones under which a non-trivial fragment of the theory of belief functions can be built up. Nevertheless, this conjecture should be re-written in a more formalized way to be either proved or rejected.

(III) It would be interesting and perhaps useful to seek for a non-artificial and rather practical structure of events charged by uncertainty such that this structure would meet the demands imposed in this paper, but would not meet some stronger demands requested by, say, probabilistic models of decision making under uncertainty.

Let us hope that at least some of these problems will be touched by a further investigative effort.

The items [4] and [16] listed below may serve as good sources of elementary knowledge concerning Boolean algebras, partial orderings and related structures. The monographs [6] and [14] then provide the basic pieces of information concerning measure theory in general and probability theory in particular, both in their most abstract and mathematically formalized settings. [15] represents one of the pioneering monograph in Dempster–Shafer theory of belief functions. Some more references, thematically very close to the subject of this paper, are also listed below.

Acknowledgement. This work has been sponsored by the grant no. A 1030803 of the GA AS CR.

References

1. Birkhoff, G.: Lattice Theory. Providence, Rhode Island (1967)
2. Dubois, D., Prade, H.: Théorie des Possibilités – Applications à la Représentation des Connaissances en Informatique. Mason, Paris (1985)
3. Dubois, D., Prade, H.: A note on measures of specificity for fuzzy sets. International Journal of General Systems **10** (1985) 4 279–283
4. Faure, R., Heurgon, E.: Structures Ordonnées et Algèbres de Boole. Gauthier–Villars, Paris (1971)
5. de Cooman, G.: Confidence relations and ordinal information. Information Sciences **107** (1997) 241–278
6. Halmos, P. R.: Measure Theory. D. van Nonstrand, New York – Toronto – London (1950)
7. Kramosil, I.: A probabilistic analysis of the Dempster combination rule. In: The LOGICA Yearbook 1997 (T. Childers, Ed.), Filosofia, Prague (1998) 175–187
8. Kramosil, I.: Nonspecificity degrees of basic probability assignments in Dempster–Shafer theory. Computers and Artificial Intelligence **18** (1999) 6 559–574
9. Kramosil, I.: On stochastic and possibilistic independence. Neural Network World **4** (1999) 275–296
10. Kramosil, I.: Elements of Boolean-valued Dempster–Shafer theory. Neural Network World **10** (2000) 5 825–835
11. Kramosil, I.: Boolean-valued belief functions. International Journal of General Systems (submitted)
12. Kramosil, I.: Degrees of belief in partially ordered sets. Neural Network World (submitted)
13. Kramosil, I.: Probabilistic Analysis of Belief Functions. Kluwer Publ. House (submitted)
14. Loève, M.: Probability Theory. D. van Nonstrand, New York (1960)
15. Shafer, G.: A Mathematical Theory of Evidence. Princeton Univ. Press, Princeton, New Jersey (1976)
16. Sikorski, R.: Boolean Algebras, 2nd Edit., Springer–Verlag, Berlin – Göttingen – Heidelberg – New York (1964)
17. Walley, P.: Statistical Reasoning With Imprecise Probabilities. Chapman and Hall, New York (1991)
18. Wang, Z., Klir, G. J.: Fuzzy Measure Theory. Plenum Press, New York (1992)
19. Wong, S. K. M., Bollmann, P., Yao, Y. Y.: Characterization of comparative belief structures. International Journal of Man–Machine Studies **37** (1992) 1 123–133
20. Wong, S. K. M., Yao, Y. Y., Bollmann, P., Bürger, H. C.: Axiomatization of qualitative belief structures. IEEE Transactions on Systems, Man, and Cybernetics **21** (1991) 726–734
21. Wong, S. K. M., Yao, Y. Y., Lingras, P.: Comparative beliefs and their measurements. International Journal of General Systems **22** (1993)1 68–89
22. Yager, R. R.: Entropy and specificity in a mathematical theory of evidence. International Journal of General Systems **9** (1983) 4 249–260

Dempster Specialization Matrices and the Combination of Belief Functions

Paul-André Monney

University of Fribourg, Seminar of Statistics, Beauregard 11, 1700 Fribourg
Switzerland
paul-andre.monney@unifr.ch

Abstract. This paper is a self-contained presentation of a method for combining several belief functions on a common frame that is different from a mere application of Dempster's rule. All the necessary results and their proofs are presented in the paper. It begins with a review and explanation of concepts related to the notion of non-normalized mass-function, or gem-function, introduced by P. Smets under the name basic belief assignment [1,6]. Then the link with Dempster's rule of combination is established. Several results in relation with the notion of Dempster specialization matrix are proved for the first time [2]. Based on these results, the method is then presented and a small application is considered.

1 Mass-Functions and Gem-Functions

In the Dempster-Shafer Theory of Evidence, it is well-known that a belief function on a finite frame Θ can be equivalently represented by its plausibility function, its commonality function or its basic probability assignment [4,5]. In this paper, the basic probability assignment, also called mass-function, will be used to represent a belief function. A mass-function is a mapping

$$m : \mathcal{P}(\Theta) \longrightarrow [0,1]$$

satisfying the two conditions

$$m(\emptyset) = 0$$
$$\sum \{m(A) : A \subseteq \Theta\} = 1.$$

This notion of mass-function has been generalized by P. Smets by allowing the possibility to assign a positive mass to the empty set, which leads to the concepts of basic belief assignment and non-normalized belief function [1]. In this paper, such a generalized mass-function will be called a gem-function :

Definition 1. *A gem-function g on a frame Θ is a mapping*

$$g : \mathcal{P}(\Theta) \longrightarrow [0,1] \tag{1}$$

such that

$$\sum \{g(A) : A \subseteq \Theta\} = 1. \tag{2}$$

S. Benferhat and P. Besnard (Eds.): ECSQARU 2001, LNAI 2143, pp. 316–327, 2001.

The difference with a mass-function is that a gem-function may assign a positive mass to the empty set, which is not possible for a mass-function. Of course, every mass-function is a gem-function but the converse is false. Also, a gem-function is called *proper* if the value assigned to the empty set is strictly smaller than 1. Note that a proper gem-function g can be transformed into a mass-function m by normalization :

$$m(A) = \begin{cases} \frac{g(A)}{1-g(\emptyset)} & if\ \emptyset \neq A \subseteq \Theta \\ 0 & if\ A = \emptyset. \end{cases}$$

The commonality function associated with a belief function or its mass-function m is the mapping

$$q : \mathcal{P}(\Theta) \longrightarrow [0,1] \tag{3}$$

given by

$$q(A) = \sum_{B \supseteq A} m(B). \tag{4}$$

Similarly, for a gem-function g, we define the commonality function of g as being the mapping

$$q : \mathcal{P}(\Theta) \longrightarrow [0,1] \tag{5}$$

given by

$$q(A) = \sum_{B \supseteq A} g(B). \tag{6}$$

The commonality function is also called the q-function. Obviously, the definitions given in equation (4) and (6) coincide if the gem-function g happens to be a mass-function.

Now recall the definition of the Dempster's rule of combination in terms of the mass-functions of the belief functions that are being combined :

Definition 2. *(Dempster's rule) Let $Bel_1, \ldots, Bel_n$ be a family of belief functions on the frame Θ. If m_i denotes the mass-function of Bel_i, then the combined belief function exists if the value*

$$k = \sum \{\prod_{i=1}^{n} m_i(A_i) : A_i \subseteq \Theta, \cap_{i=1}^{n} A_i = \emptyset\}$$

is strictly smaller than 1. If the combined belief function exists, then it is denoted by

$$Bel = Bel_1 \oplus \ldots \oplus Bel_n,$$

and its mass-function is

$$m(A) = \frac{\sum \{\prod_{i=1}^{n} m_i(A_i) : A_i \subseteq \Theta, \cap_{i=1}^{n} A_i = A\}}{1-k}$$

for all non-empty subsets $A \subseteq \Theta$ and of course $m(\emptyset) = 0$.

P. Smets [3] considers the combination of several gem-functions defined on a frame Θ. Since the present paper is placed in the classical framework of the Dempster-Shafer Theory of Evidence, the combination of gem-functions is considered here only as a technical tool, whereas for Smets it is an essential component of his Transferable Belief Model with its own meaning and interpretation. For this reason, we don't speak of the combination of several gem-functions, but we rather talk about the gem-function associated with a collection of gem-functions.

Definition 3. *Let*

$$\mathcal{C} = \{g_1, \ldots, g_n\}$$

be a collection of gem-functions on Θ that are not necessarily different, i.e. some gem-functions may appear several times in the collection. The gem-function associated with the collection $\mathcal{C}$ is the mapping

$$g : \mathcal{P}(\Theta) \longrightarrow [0, 1]$$

given by

$$g(A) = \sum \{\prod_{i=1}^{n} g_i(A_i) : A_i \subseteq \Theta, \cap_{i=1}^{n} A_i = A\}$$

for all subsets A of Θ. The gem-function g associated with $\mathcal{C}$ is denoted by $gem(\mathcal{C})$ and to simplify the notation we simply write $gem(g_1, \ldots, g_n)$ instead of $gem(\{g_1, \ldots, g_n\})$.

The mapping $gem(\mathcal{C})$ clearly satisfies conditions (1) and (2) and does not depend on the order in which the elements of $\mathcal{C}$ are considered. As the following definition shows, this allows us to speak about the gem-function associated with a collection of belief functions because every mass-function is a gem-function.

Definition 4. *For $i = 1, \ldots, n$, let m_i denote the mass-function of the belief function Bel_i on Θ. Then the gem-function associated with the collection of belief functions*

$$\mathcal{B} = \{Bel_1, \ldots, Bel_n\}$$

is

$$gem(\mathcal{B}) = gem(m_1, \ldots, m_n).$$

By definition of the Dempster's rule of combination (see definition 2), the combined belief function

$$Bel = Bel_1 \oplus \ldots \oplus Bel_n$$

exists if

$$gem(\mathcal{B})(\emptyset) < 1,$$

in which case its mass-function is obtained by normalization of the gem-function $gem(\mathcal{B})$. Therefore, to find a way of combining several belief functions that is different from a direct application of the definition of Dempster's rule, we need to find a method for computing $gem(\mathcal{C})$ that is different from its definition. For this purpose, the notion of Dempster specialization matrix is considered in the next section.

2 Dempster Specialization Matrices

From now on, let

$$\{B_1, B_2, \ldots, B_n\}$$

denote the set of all subsets of Θ and it is assumed that the following conditions are satisfied :

$$B_1 = \emptyset \quad and \quad (B_i \subseteq B_j \ \Rightarrow \ i \leq j). \tag{7}$$

Note that it is always possible to find such an ordering of the subsets of Θ. A gem-function g is then completely specified by a column vector

$$g = (g(B_1), \ldots, g(B_n))'$$

and, similarly, a commonality function q is completely specified by a column vector

$$q = (q(B_1), \ldots, q(B_n))',$$

where the prime denotes the transpose of the vector. The following notion of Dempster specialization matrix introduced by Klawonn and Smets [2] will be useful in the sequel.

Definition 5. *Let g be a gem-function on Θ. Then the Dempster specialization matrix of g is the square matrix S of order n given by*

$$S_{ij} = \sum \{g(K) : K \subseteq \Theta, K \cap B_j = B_i\}$$

for all i and j in $\{1, \ldots, n\}$.

If $U = B_i$ and $V = B_j$, then the element S_{ij} of the matrix S is also denoted by

$$S(U, V) = \sum \{g(K) : K \cap V = U\}.$$

Also, in order to keep the notation as simple as possible, it will be sometimes useful to simply write i instead of B_i and j instead of B_j. With this convention, the equation

$$S_{ij} = \sum \{g(k) : k \subseteq \Theta, k \cap j = i\}$$

still makes sense.

Basically, a special case of the following result is mentioned in Klawonn and Smets [2], but unfortunately no proof is given there. In the form given below, the following theorem is stated and proved here for the first time.

Theorem 1. *Let $\{g_1, \ldots, g_n, g_{n+1}\}$ be a collection of gem-functions on Θ. If S denotes the Dempster specialization matrix of g_{n+1}, then*

$$gem(g_1, \ldots, g_{n+1}) = S \cdot gem(g_1, \ldots, g_n).$$

Proof. For $k > 0$, let $\mathcal{P}(\Theta)^k$ denote the cartesian product of k copies of $\mathcal{P}(\Theta)$, i.e. an element of $\mathcal{P}(\Theta)^k$ is a k-dimensional vector whose components are subsets of Θ. Let A be a fixed subset of Θ. Then we define the set

$$\mathcal{M} = \{(A_1, \ldots, A_{n+1}) \in \mathcal{P}(\Theta)^{n+1} : \cap_{i=1}^{n+1} A_i = A\}$$

and for a subset L of Θ let

$$\mathcal{U}_L = \{(A_1, \ldots, A_n) \in \mathcal{P}(\Theta)^n : \cap_{i=1}^{n} A_i = L\}$$

and

$$\mathcal{V}_L = \{K \in \mathcal{P}(\Theta) : K \cap L = A\}$$

and

$$\mathcal{F}_L = \mathcal{U}_L \times \mathcal{V}_L$$

and

$$\mathcal{N} = \cup \{\mathcal{F}_L : L \subseteq \Theta\}.$$

First we prove that $\mathcal{M} = \mathcal{N}$. Indeed, let

$$x = (A_1, \ldots, A_{n+1}) \in \mathcal{M}.$$

If we define $A_0 = \cap_{i=1}^{n} A_i$, then we show that

$$x \in \mathcal{F}_{A_0} = \mathcal{U}_{A_0} \times \mathcal{V}_{A_0},$$

which proves that $x \in \mathcal{N}$. But $(A_1, \ldots, A_n) \in \mathcal{U}_{A_0}$, and $A_{n+1} \in \mathcal{V}_{A_0}$ because

$$A_{n+1} \cap A_0 = \cap_{i=1}^{n+1} A_i = A$$

since $x \in \mathcal{M}$. This implies that $x \in \mathcal{N}$ and hence $\mathcal{M} \subseteq \mathcal{N}$.

Conversely, let

$$x = (A_1, \ldots, A_{n+1}) \in \mathcal{N}.$$

Then there exists $A_0 \subseteq \Theta$ such that $(A_1, \ldots, A_n) \in \mathcal{U}_{A_0}$ and $A_{n+1} \in \mathcal{V}_{A_0}$. But then

$$\cap_{i=1}^{n+1} A_i = (\cap_{i=1}^{n} A_i) \cap A_{n+1} = A_0 \cap A_{n+1} = A,$$

which shows that $x \in \mathcal{M}$ and hence $\mathcal{N} \subseteq \mathcal{M}$, which finally implies that $\mathcal{M} = \mathcal{N}$.

Obviously, the union in the definition of $\mathcal{N}$ is a union of disjoint subsets because if $L \neq L'$, then

$$(\mathcal{U}_L \times \mathcal{V}_L) \cap (\mathcal{U}_{L'} \times \mathcal{V}_{L'}) = \emptyset.$$

The set $\mathcal{F}_L$ can be written as the disjoint union

$$\mathcal{F}_L = \cup \{\mathcal{U}_L \times \{K\} : K \in \mathcal{V}_L\}$$

and so if

$$\mathcal{G}_K = \mathcal{U}_L \times \{K\}$$

then

$$\mathcal{F}_L = \cup \{\mathcal{G}_K : K \in \mathcal{V}_L\}.$$

Now, let

$$g^* = gem(g_1, \ldots, g_{n+1}) \quad and \quad g = gem(g_1, \ldots, g_n).$$

Then, since $\mathcal{M} = \mathcal{N}$, we can write

$$g^*(A) = \sum_{(A_1,\ldots,A_{n+1})\in\mathcal{M}} (\prod_{i=1}^{n+1} g_i(A_i)) = \sum_{(A_1,\ldots,A_{n+1})\in\mathcal{N}} (\prod_{i=1}^{n+1} g_i(A_i)).$$

Then

$$g^*(A) = \sum_{L\subseteq\Theta} (\sum_{(A_1,\ldots,A_{n+1})\in\mathcal{F}_L} (\prod_{i=1}^{n+1} g_i(A_i)))$$

$$= \sum_{L\subseteq\Theta} (\sum_{K\in\mathcal{V}_L} (\sum_{(A_1,\ldots,A_n,K)\in\mathcal{G}_K} (g_{n+1}(K) \prod_{i=1}^{n} g_i(A_i))))$$

$$= \sum_{L\subseteq\Theta} (\sum_{K\in\mathcal{V}_L} (g_{n+1}(K)(\sum_{(A_1,\ldots,A_n)\in\mathcal{U}_L} \prod_{i=1}^{n} g_i(A_i)))).$$

But this implies

$$g^*(A) = \sum_{L\subseteq\Theta} (\sum_{K\in\mathcal{V}_L} (g_{n+1}(K)g(L))) = \sum_{L\subseteq\Theta} (g(L)(\sum_{K\in\mathcal{V}_L} g_{n+1}(K)))$$

$$= \sum_{L\subseteq\Theta} (g(L)S(A,L)) = \sum_{L\subseteq\Theta} (S(A,L)g(L)),$$

which means that the value of g^* on A is obtained by multiplying the row of the matrix S corresponding to A with the column vector g. But this simply means that $g^* = S \cdot g$ and the theorem is proved. ♢

3 A Representation of the Dempster Specialization Matrix

In this section it will be shown that the Dempster specialization matrix can be diagonalized.

Definition 6. *The incidence matrix of the ordering* $B_1, \ldots, B_n$ *is the square matrix* M *of order* n *given by*

$$M_{ij} = \begin{cases} 1 & if\ B_i \subseteq B_j \\ 0 & otherwise \end{cases}$$

for all i *and* j *in* $\{1, \ldots, n\}$.

The matrix M is an upper-triangular matrix because if $i > j$ then $M_{ij} = 0$ because $B_i \not\subseteq B_j$ by the second condition in (7). Also, M is a regular matrix because $M_{ii} = 1$ for all $i = 1, \ldots, n$. Now let g be a gem-function given by the column vector

$$g = (g(B_1), \ldots, g(B_n))'.$$

If the commonality function of g is given by the column vector

$$q = (q(B_1), \ldots, q(B_n))',$$

then we obviously have

$$Mg = q. \tag{8}$$

Definition 7. *Let q denote the commonality function of a gem-function g on the frame Θ. Then the commonality matrix of g is the square matrix Q of order n given by*

$$Q_{ij} = \begin{cases} q(B_i) & \text{if } i = j \\ 0 & \text{otherwise} \end{cases}$$

for all i and j in $\{1, \ldots, n\}$.

The following theorem states that the Dempster specialization matrix of a gem-function is diagonalizable. This result is mentioned in Klawonn and Smets [2], but unfortunately no proof is given there. A proof of this interesting and important result is published here for the first time.

Theorem 2. *Let S denote the Dempster specialization matrix and Q the commonality matrix of a gem-function g on the frame Θ. If M is the incidence matrix, then*

$$S = M^{-1}QM.$$

Proof. Let us define the matrices $A = MS$ and $C = QM$ and show that $A = C$, which will prove the theorem. But, using the notation convention explained in the previous section, we can write

$$A_{ij} = \sum \{M_{ik}S_{kj} : k \subseteq \Theta\} = \sum \{S_{kj} : k \supseteq i\} \tag{9}$$

$$= \sum \{(\sum \{g(t) : t \cap j = k\}) : k \supseteq i\}. \tag{10}$$

Now suppose first that $i \not\subseteq j$. Then there is an element x in Θ such that $x \in i$ and $x \notin j$. But $i \subseteq k$ implies that $x \in k$, and $t \cap j = k$ implies that $k \subseteq j$. On the other hand, since $x \in k$ and $x \notin j$, it follows that $k \not\subseteq j$, which is a contradiction to $k \subseteq j$. This shows that the double sum in equation (10) is empty when $i \not\subseteq j$, which implies that $A_{ij} = 0$ when $i \not\subseteq j$.

Now suppose that $i \subseteq j$. Then by equations (9) and (10)

$$A_{ij} = \sum \{g(t) : k \supseteq i, t \cap j = k\}.$$

Now we define the sets

$$E = \{(k,t) : k \supseteq i, t \cap j = k\}$$

and

$$F = \{(k,t) : i \subseteq k \subseteq j, t = k \cup x, x \subseteq j^c\}$$

and show that $E = F$. Indeed, if $(k,t) \in E$, then $k \supseteq i$ and $t \cap j = k$, which implies that $i \subseteq k \subseteq j$. But $k \subseteq j$ and $t \cap j = k$ implies that $t = k \cup x$ for some $x \subseteq j^c$, which shows that $(k,t) \in F$. Now suppose that $(k,t) \in F$. Then

$$t \cap j = (k \cup x) \cap j = (k \cap j) \cup (x \cap j) = (k \cap j) = k$$

because $x \subseteq j^c$ and $k \subseteq j$, which shows that $(k,t) \in E$. Therefore

$$\begin{aligned} A_{ij} &= \sum \{g(t) : i \subseteq k \subseteq j, t = k \cup x, x \subseteq j^c\} \\ &= \sum \{g(k \cup x) : i \subseteq k \subseteq j, x \subseteq j^c\}. \end{aligned}$$

We define the sets

$$U = \{k \cup x : i \subseteq k \subseteq j, x \subseteq j^c\}$$

and $V = \{l : l \supseteq i\}$ and show that $U = V$. Indeed, if $k \cup x$ is in U, then $i \subseteq k \subseteq k \cup x$ and hence $k \cup x \supseteq i$, which shows that $k \cup x \in V$. Conversely, let $l \in V$, i.e. $l \supseteq i$, and define

$$k = l \cap j \quad \textit{and} \quad x = l \cap j^c.$$

Then

$$l = l \cap (j \cup j^c) = (l \cap j) \cup (l \cap j^c) = k \cup x$$

and, in order to show that l is in U, we must prove

1. $i \subseteq k$, i.e. $i \subseteq l \cap j$, which is true because $i \subseteq l$, and $i \subseteq j$ by the general hypothesis.
2. $k \subseteq j$, i.e. $l \cap j \subseteq j$, which is clearly true.
3. $x \subseteq j^c$, i.e. $l \cap j^c \subseteq j^c$, which is also true.

But $U = V$ implies that

$$A_{ij} = \sum \{g(l) : l \supseteq i\} = q(i)$$

and therefore

$$A_{ij} = \begin{cases} q(i) & \textit{if } i \subseteq j \\ 0 & \textit{otherwise.} \end{cases}$$

On the other hand,

$$C_{ij} = \sum \{Q_{ik} M_{kj} : k \subseteq \Theta\} = \begin{cases} Q_{ii} & \textit{if } i \subseteq j \\ 0 & \textit{otherwise,} \end{cases}$$

which means that

$$C_{ij} = \begin{cases} q(i) & \textit{if } i \subseteq j \\ 0 & \textit{otherwise.} \end{cases}$$

This shows that $A_{ij} = C_{ij}$ for all i and j and hence $A = C$, which proves the theorem. ◇

4 Combining Several Belief Functions

In this section a method for computing the combination of several belief functions is presented. This method is different from the mere application of the definition of Dempster's rule.

Theorem 3. *For $i = 1, \dots, k$, let Q_i denote the commonality matrix of a gem-function g_i on the frame Θ. If M denotes the incidence matrix, then*

$$gem(g_1, \dots, g_k) = M^{-1}(\prod_{i=1}^{k-1} Q_i)Mg_k.$$

Proof. This theorem is proved by induction on k. For $k = 1$, we have

$$gem(g_1) = g_1 = M^{-1}IMg_1,$$

which proves the result when $k = 1$.

Now the induction step $(k-1) \longrightarrow k$ is proved. If S denotes the Dempster specialization matrix of g_k, then

$$gem(g_1, \dots, g_k) = S \cdot gem(g_1, \dots, g_{k-1})$$

by theorem 1. Then the induction hypothesis implies that

$$gem(g_1, \dots, g_{k-1}) = M^{-1}(\prod_{i=1}^{k-2} Q_i)Mg_{k-1}$$

and hence

$$gem(g_1, \dots, g_k) = SM^{-1}(\prod_{i=1}^{k-2} Q_i)Mg_{k-1}.$$

But by theorem 2

$$S = M^{-1}Q_kM$$

and therefore

$$gem(g_1, \dots, g_k) = M^{-1}Q_kMM^{-1}(\prod_{i=1}^{k-2} Q_i)Mg_{k-1} = M^{-1}(\prod_{i=1}^{k-2} Q_i)Q_kMg_{k-1}$$

because Q_k and $Q_1, \dots, Q_{k-1}$ are diagonal matrices and hence their product commute. If

$$e = (1, \dots, 1)'$$

denotes the column vector composed of ones only and if q_i denotes the commonality function of the gem-function g_i, then

$$Mg_i = q_i = Q_ie$$

for all $i = 1, \ldots, k$. Then, we can write

$$\begin{aligned} gem(g_1, \ldots, g_k) &= M^{-1}(\prod_{i=1}^{k-2} Q_i) Q_k Q_{k-1} e = M^{-1}(\prod_{i=1}^{k} Q_i) e \\ &= M^{-1}(\prod_{i=1}^{k-1} Q_i) Q_k e = M^{-1}(\prod_{i=1}^{k-1} Q_i) q_k \\ &= M\ ^{1}(\prod_{i=1}^{k-1} Q_i) M y_k, \end{aligned}$$

which proves the theorem. $\diamondsuit$

This result can be used to compute the combination of several belief functions on the same frame Θ.

Corollary 1. *For $i = 1, \ldots, k$, let m_i denote the mass-function of a belief function Bel_i on the frame Θ and let Q_i denote the commonality matrix of m_i. Furthermore, let M denote the incidence matrix. If the combined belief function*

$$Bel = Bel_1 \oplus \ldots \oplus Bel_k$$

exists, then its mass-function is obtained by normalization of the gem-function

$$g^* = M^{-1}(\prod_{i=1}^{k-1} Q_i) M m_k \tag{11}$$

Proof. This is a direct consequence of theorem 3. $\diamondsuit$

If q_k denotes the commonality vector of m_k, then the gem-function g^* in (11) can also be written as

$$g^* = M^{-1}(\prod_{i=1}^{k-1} Q_i) q_k \tag{12}$$

because

$$M m_k = q_k.$$

As a special case, this result can be applied to the situation where several copies of the same belief function must be combined by Dempster's rule.

Corollary 2. *Let m denote the mass-function of a belief function Bel on Θ and let Q denote the commonality matrix of m. Furthermore, let M denote the incidence matrix and define $Bel_i = Bel$ for all $i = 1, \ldots, k$. If the combined belief function*

$$Bel^* = Bel_1 \oplus \ldots \oplus Bel_k$$

exists, then its mass-function is obtained by normalization of the gem-function

$$g^* = M^{-1} Q^{k-1} M m.$$

Proof. This result is a direct consequence of corollary 1. ◇

In addition, if q denotes the commonality vector of m, then

$$g^* = M^{-1}Q^{k-1}q$$

according to equation (12).

5 Application

As a simple application of corollary 2, we consider the combination of k copies of a same belief function Bel on a frame $\Theta = \{\theta_1, \theta_2\}$. The ordering of the subsets of Θ is taken to be

$$B_1 = \emptyset,\ B_2 = \{\theta_1\},\ B_3 = \{\theta_2\},\ B_4 = \Theta.$$

The belief function Bel on Θ is specified by its mass-function m given by the column vector

$$m = \left(0,\ p,\ q,\ r \right)'$$

with $p + q + r = 1$. The commonality vector q of m is

$$q = \left(1,\ p+r,\ q+r,\ r \right)'$$

and the commonality matrix of m is

$$Q = \begin{pmatrix} 1 & 0 & 0 & 0 \\ 0 & p+r & 0 & 0 \\ 0 & 0 & q+r & 0 \\ 0 & 0 & 0 & r \end{pmatrix}.$$

The incidence matrix M is

$$M = \begin{pmatrix} 1 & 1 & 1 & 1 \\ 0 & 1 & 0 & 1 \\ 0 & 0 & 1 & 1 \\ 0 & 0 & 0 & 1 \end{pmatrix},$$

and its inverse matrix is

$$M^{-1} = \begin{pmatrix} 1 & -1 & -1 & 1 \\ 0 & 1 & 0 & -1 \\ 0 & 0 & 1 & -1 \\ 0 & 0 & 0 & 1 \end{pmatrix}.$$

Let Bel^* denote the combination of k copies of Bel by Dempster's rule of combination, i.e.

$$Bel^* = Bel \oplus \ldots \oplus Bel \qquad (k\ terms).$$

Then the mass-function m^* of Bel^* is obtained by normalization of the gem-function

$$\begin{aligned} g^* &= M^{-1}Q^{k-1}q \\ &= \Big(1-(p+r)^k-(q+r)^k+r^k,\ (p+r)^k-r^k,\ (q+r)^k-r^k,\ r^k\Big)', \end{aligned}$$

which yields

$$m^* = K^{-1}\Big(0,\ (p+r)^k-r^k,\ (q+r)^k-r^k,\ r^k\Big)'$$

where

$$K=(p+r)^k+(q+r)^k-r^k.$$

Acknowledgements. The author wants to thank the anonymous referees for their helpful comments.

References

1. P. Smets. The Nature of the Unnormalized Beliefs Encountered in the Transferable Belief Model. In Dubois D., Wellman M., D'Ambrosio B., and Smets P., editors, *Proceedings of the 8th Conference on Uncertainty in Artificial Intelligence,* pages 292–297. Morgan Kaufman Publishers, San Francisco, California, 1992.
2. P. Smets. The Transferable Belief Model for Quantified Belief Representation. In *Smets P. (Ed.) Quantified Representation of Uncertainty and Imprecision. Volume 1 in the Series Gabbay D., Smets P. (Eds.) Handbook of Defeasible Reasoning and Uncertainty Management Systems,* pages 267–301. Kluwer Academic Publishers, 1998.
3. F. Klawonn and P. Smets. The Dynamic of Belief in the Transferable Belief Model and Specialization-Generalization Matrices. In Dubois D., Wellman M., D'Ambrosio B., and Smets P., editors, *Proceedings of the 8th Conference on Uncertainty in Artificial Intelligence,* pages 130–137. Morgan Kaufman Publishers, San Francisco, California, 1992.
4. G. Shafer. *A Mathematical Theory of Evidence.* Princeton University Press, 1976.
5. J. Kohlas and P.A. Monney. *A Mathematical Theory of Hints. An Approach to the Dempster-Shafer Theory of Evidence,* volume 425 of Lecture Notes in Economics and Mathematical Systems. Springer Verlag, 1995.
6. P. Smets. The Combination of Evidence in the Transferable Belief Model. *IEEE Trans. PAMI,* 12:447–458, 1990.

On the Conceptual Status of Belief Functions with Respect to Coherent Lower Probabilities

Pietro Baroni[1] and Paolo Vicig[2]

[1] Dip. di Elettronica per l'Automazione, Univ. of Brescia, Via Branze 38, I-25123 Brescia, Italy
baroni@ing.unibs.it

[2] Dip. di Matematica Applicata "de Finetti", Univ. of Trieste, Piazzale Europa 1, I-34127 Trieste, Italy
{paolo.vicig}@econ.univ.trieste.it

Abstract. The interpretations of belief functins and their relationships with other uncertainty theories have been widely debated in the literature. Focusing on the interpretation of belief functions based on non-negative masses, in this paper we provide a contribution to this topic by addressing two questions concerning the relationships between belief functions and coherent lower probabilities. The answers we provide to both questions tend to exclude the existence of intuitively appreciable relationships between the two theories, under the above mentioned interpretation. While this may be regarded as a confirmation of the conceptual autonomy of belief functions, we also propose future research about an alternative characterization, based on the notion of independence.

1 Introduction

The conceptual status of belief functions with respect to other uncertainty theories has been extensively debated in the literature. This paper aims at providing a contribution to this topic, by considering the relationships with the theory of coherent lower probabilities [21], which encompasses belief functions as a special case. In particular, we focus on a distinguishing property of belief functions, namely non-negative masses. We analyze some examples and provide results showing that non-negative masses can hardly be given a meaningful interpretation in this context. On one hand, this result may be regarded as a confirmation of the absence of conceptual *liaisons* between belief functions and probability-based theories, as advocated for instance in [13], on the other hand, it evidences the opportunity of exploring alternative characterizations of belief functions.

The paper is organized as follows. In section 2 we recall some basic aspects of the original version of belief functions theory, pointing out the difficulties in its conceptual characterization. Section 3 briefly surveys interpretations and debates concerning Shafer's proposal, while section 4 analyzes its evolution in the Transferable Belief Model. In section 5 we pose two questions about the possibility of ascribing a meaningful interpretation to belief functions in the context of coherent imprecise probabilities and give a negative answer. Finally, in section 6 we summarize the results and point out future research directions.

S. Benferhat and P. Besnard (Eds.): ECSQARU 2001, LNAI 2143, pp. 328–339, 2001.

2 Shafer's Theory

In Chapter 1 of [10] it is stated that, given a finite set Ω and its powerset 2^Ω, if a function $Bel : 2^\Omega \to [0,1]$ satisfies the following conditions: i) $Bel(\emptyset) = 0$; ii) $Bel(\Omega) = 1$; iii) $Bel(A_1 \cup \ldots \cup A_n) \geq \sum_i Bel(A_i) - \sum_{i<j} Bel(A_i \cap A_j) + \cdots + (-1)^{n-1} Bel(A_1 \cap \ldots \cap A_n)$; then Bel is called a *belief function* over Ω.

A different conceptual framework is given in Chapter 2 of [10], where Shafer defines a basic probability assignment as a function $m : 2^\Omega \to [0,1]$ such that $m(\emptyset) = 0$; $\sum_{A \subseteq \Omega} m(A) = 1$. The values of the function m are supposed to measure probability *masses* associated with subsets. It is then stated that a function $Bel : 2^\Omega \to [0,1]$ is a belief function if, for some basic probability assignment $m : 2^\Omega \to [0,1]$, it is given by $Bel(A) = \sum_{B \subseteq A} m(B)$.

The duplication of belief function definition in Shafer's book indicates an ambiguity in its foundational part, which is reflected in subsequent presentations of the theory by other authors. For instance, in [5] belief functions are defined using the properties i)-iii). On the other hand, Smets [12] qualifies the definition based on these properties as unnatural, and defines belief functions starting from a slightly modified notion of mass function.

Later in his book, Shafer introduces another primitive concept, namely the weight of evidence, which represents a further source of complication about the conceptual foundations of belief functions. A weight of evidence is a real number in $[0, \infty]$: it is assumed that there is a relationship between weights associated with evidence items and belief degrees derived from them. In order to characterize this relationship, Shafer starts with the case of a *simple support function*, namely a belief function corresponding to a mass function assigning a non-zero mass value $m(A)$ to just one proper subset A of Ω and a mass value $1 - m(A)$ to Ω. A sequence of progressively more expressive classes of belief functions is then introduced. Each new class is provided with a characterization and an intuitive justification in terms of the previously defined ones.

The first idea is that of combining simple support functions using Dempster's rule: belief functions obtained by combining two or more simple support functions are called *separable support functions*. The dual process with respect to combination is decomposition, which consists of recovering from a separable support function a set of simple support functions generating it. Decomposition is, in general, not unique, however a single *canonical decomposition* can be identified by imposing some conditions on the simple support functions obtained.

The subsequent class of belief functions is related to the operations of coarsening and refinement: *support functions* are the belief functions that can be obtained from separable support functions by coarsening the frame of discernment. Shafer explicitly states that "they seem to constitute the subclass of belief functions appropriate for the representation of evidence". However, there exist belief functions which are not support functions: they are called *quasi support functions* and can be interpreted as limits of sequences of separable support functions or as restrictions of such limits. This interpretation, as Shafer admits, hardly has an intuitive counterpart: in summary, his book does not provide a satisfactory intuitive interpretation covering the whole set of belief functions.

3 Interpretations and Criticisms of Shafer's Theory

Several proposals have been formulated in order to provide a meaningful interpretation of belief function theory. Some of them rely on an underlying probabilistic model, such as the original notion of upper and lower probabilities introduced by Dempster [2], random codes [11], random sets [7], probabilities of provability [8]. An extension of evidence theory to the case of infinite frames of discernment, called hint theory, has been proposed in [6], where it is shown that considering inner and outer probability measures induced by a probability measure which, in hint theory, roughly corresponds to a basic probability assignment, one obtains an extended notion of belief and plausibility functions, which preserves some important properties, such as monotony of order ∞. A different kind of relationship between inner and outer probability measures and belief and plausibility functions for finite sets is pointed out in [3]. All these interpretations share the assumption that the notion of probability is given for granted.

Reasons for not sharing this assumption are given in several works (e.g. [14] [15]) proposing an alternative interpretation (and extension) of Shafer's theory: the Transferable Belief Model (TBM), which rejects any relationship with probability theory and will be discussed more extensively in next section. Another problem in the relationship between belief functions and probability has been pointed out in [23], where it is shown that some of the postulates introduced in [10] about the notions of chance, belief, weight of evidence, and evidence combination are altogether inconsistent. According to [23], the most reasonable solution to this inconsistency consists of rejecting Shafer's postulate that belief functions coincide with frequency limits, when they exist.

Leaving apart interpretation, Dempster's rule and its behavior are probably the most extensively debated issue in this theory. A large corpus of literature exists, including many examples of supposedly counterintuitive results produced by Dempster's rule and the relevant answers and/or counterexamples (see for instance [24] [9] [20] [14]). As a matter of fact, most of these works compare belief functions theory with precise probability theory and are focused on the so-called dynamic part of the model, involving conditioning and combination rules, while we are interested in the relationship with imprecise probabilities and in characterizing the static part of the model, namely the properties of belief functions as a representation formalism.

4 The Transferable Belief Model

Probably the most comprehensive attempt to provide a solid justification for the use of belief functions, both at the theoretical and intuitive level, is represented by the Transferable Belief Model (TBM) proposed by Smets and coauthors [12] [18]. Three complementary justifications have been proposed for this approach: i) axiomatic justification of belief functions representation; ii) axiomatic justification of Dempster's rule; iii) intuitive justification based on positive masses.

As far as point i) is concerned, in [17] a set of axioms is presented, which, however, is not completely satisfactory. In fact, the set of requirements is relatively large (actually eleven) and, most importantly, some of them are questionable. For instance, requirement 3 states that "Probability functions are credibility functions", however this contrasts with previous statements of Smets himself such as "the transferable belief model is built without ever introducing explicitly or implicitly any concept of probability" [13].

Turning to point ii), 8 axioms are used to prove the uniqueness of Dempster's rule of combination in [13]. Among the axioms, one requires that there are at least three elementary propositions (which is surely true in most cases, but sounds peculiar as a requirement). Another axiom, called autofunctionality, is provided without justification. Moreover, the fourth axiom postulates Dempster's rule of conditioning in order to derive Dempster's rule of combination. It is however worth remarking that Shafer regarded the notion of conditioning as substantially extraneous to his theory: after presenting Dempster's rule of conditioning, he says "since new evidence rarely occurs in the form of a certainty, these formulas are of little practical value"[10].

Finally point iii) is strictly related to the subject of this paper. It is postulated that there exists some finite amount of belief which is spread among the various propositions (the subsets of Ω) according to the available evidence [12]. In other words, evidence is assumed to be directly represented by mass functions: this is not in accordance with the original Shafer's view, as explained in section 2. An attempt to reconcile TBM with Shafer's notions of simple support function and canonical decomposition is proposed in [16] where the definition of simple support function is generalized to the cases where a negative mass value is assigned to a proper subset A of Ω. A simple support function with negative mass is supposed to represent a reason not to believe that the current state of the world is in A. It is then possible to define a generalized canonical decomposition of any non-dogmatic belief function (i.e. any belief function with $m(\Omega) > 0$) into generalized simple support functions. However, this proposal leaves some conceptual gaps open. In fact, in order to take into account the "reasons not to believe", a "latent belief structure" is introduced, which includes a confidence component and a diffidence component, both represented by belief functions. Then an apparent belief structure, which is again a belief function, is derived from the latent belief structure. The apparent belief structure is assumed to be the belief representation usually adopted in the TBM. However, as Smets points out, there are some latent belief structures that can not be represented by apparent belief structures, since the latter "are not rich enough to characterize every belief state". Moreover it is possible to point out that there are cases where the decomposition into generalized simple support functions does not seem to fit the interpretation of "reasons not to believe". Consider the following example with $\Omega = \{a, b, c\}$ and the mass assignment $m(\{a\}) = m(\{b\}) = m(\{c\}) = m(\Omega) = 0.25$. By applying the canonical decomposition proposed in [16], it easy to see that in this case one of the resulting generalized simple support functions assigns a negative mass to the empty set. The idea that there can be some evidence that gives reasons not to believe in the empty set is somehow difficult to accept from an intuitive point of view.

5 Belief Functions vs. Coherent Lower Probabilities

For the reasons explained in previous section, non-negative masses should be regarded as the intuitively most acceptable justification of the TBM framework. As well known, the mass function is biunivocally related with the corresponding belief function through the so-called Möbius inversion. Assuming non-negative masses entails that belief functions are capacities of order ∞: it has been observed that functions with weaker properties can also be considered for describing a state of partial information [1]. In particular, a theory of coherent imprecise probabilities has been developed in [21]. It is assumed that the following conjugacy relation holds between the lower ($\underline{P}$) and the upper ($\overline{P}$) probability of an event E: $\underline{P}(E) = 1 - (\overline{P}(\neg E))$. This enables one to consider lower probabilities only, whenever they are defined on a set of events closed under complementation.

Coherent lower probabilities(CLP) are defined as a special case of lower previsions in 2.5.1 (see also 2.7) of [21]: given an arbitrary (finite or not) set of events S, $\underline{P}(\cdot)$ is a *coherent lower probability* on S iff,

$\forall m, \forall E_0, \ldots, E_m \in S, \forall s_i \geq 0, i = 0, \ldots, m$, defining $I(E)$ as the indicator of E ($I(E) = 1$ if E is true, $I(E) = 0$ if E is false) and putting $\underline{G} = \sum_{i=1}^{m} s_i[I(E_i) - \underline{P}(E_i)] - s_0[I(E_0) - \underline{P}(E_0)]$ it is true that $max(\underline{G}) \geq 0$.

Coherent lower probabilities have a clear behavioral interpretation [21] and encompass several existing theories, including belief functions, as special cases [22]. In the sequel we shall exploit the characterization of CLP via envelope theorem, which assures, in particular, that the lower envelope of a family of precise probabilities is a coherent lower probability, thus giving a useful practical way to construct imprecise probabilities. Examples of CLP whose Möbius inverse yields negative mass values are provided in [21] [22]. As to our knowledge, little work has been done so far to investigate whether it is possible to characterize belief functions as a class of CLP, with intuitively appreciable features. Moreover, it is worth noting that belief functions have been most often compared with precise probabilities, where the most evident difference concerns the representation of ignorance, or with classes of so called upper and lower probabilities, where the existence of an ill-known precise probability is somehow assumed, which is instead rejected in the TBM approach [15]. In Walley's approach lower probabilities are not assumed to be an approximation of an underlying precise probability [22], therefore they do not seem to contrast with the basic assumptions of the TBM. Similarly, coherent imprecise probabilities are conceptually distinct from inner and outer measures mentioned in section 3, which represent the extension of a precise probability measure to nonmeasurable subsets. For these reasons, it seems that the relationships between CLP and TBM deserve some further investigation, that we start in this work, by examining the following questions:

1. Can mass sign be ascribed an intuitive meaning in the context of CLP ?
2. Independently of mass sign interpretation, do belief functions have distinct properties as a subclass of CLP ?

In order to provide a first answer to these questions, we restrict our analysis to a frame of discernment with three elements, namely we assume $\Omega = \{e_1, e_2, e_3\}$.

Even in this limited framework, it is easy to find examples of CLP where $m(\Omega) < 0$. We note that, for $\mid \Omega \mid = 3$, $m(\Omega)$ has the following optimal lower bound:

Proposition 1 *Let Ω be a set with $\mid \Omega \mid = 3$, $\underline{P}(\cdot)$ a coherent lower probability defined on 2^{Ω}, and m the mass function on 2^{Ω}, obtained from $\underline{P}$ by Möbius inversion, then $m(\Omega) \geq -1/2$.*

By Möbius inversion we have that

$$m(\Omega) = 1 \quad \underline{P}(e_1 \vee e_2) - \underline{P}(e_1 \vee e_3) - \underline{P}(e_2 \vee e_3) + \sum_{i=1}^{3} \underline{P}(e_i) \,. \tag{1}$$

Applying the coniugacy relation $\underline{P}(e_1 \vee e_2) = 1 - \overline{P}(e_3)$ and the analogous ones we obtain:

$$m(\Omega) = -2 + \sum_{i=1}^{3} (\underline{P}(e_i) + \overline{P}(e_i)) \,. \tag{2}$$

In order to minimize (2) let us recall the following necessary condition for coherence (see 2.7.4 of [21]):

$$1 - \underline{P}(e_i) \leq \overline{P}(e_j) + \overline{P}(e_k), \ i \neq j \neq k \,. \tag{3}$$

By summing the three inequalities corresponding to (3) we obtain:

$$3 - \sum_{i=1}^{3} \underline{P}(e_i) \leq \sum_{i=1}^{3} 2\overline{P}(e_i) \,. \tag{4}$$

By exploiting (4) we obtain

$$\sum_{i=1}^{3} (\underline{P}(e_i) + \overline{P}(e_i)) \geq 3/2 + \frac{\sum_{i=1}^{3} \underline{P}(e_i)}{2} \,. \tag{5}$$

We can derive the minimum value for the left part of (5) by assuming the equality and putting $\underline{P}(e_i) = 0, \forall i$: it can be easily seen that this entails $\overline{P}(e_i) = 1/2, \forall i$. This is a coherent imprecise probability assignment, which gives the actual minimal value of equation (2), yielding $m(\Omega) = -2 + 3/2 = -1/2$.

Finding an optimal lower bound for the mass function with $\mid \Omega \mid > 3$ is more complex. It is however significant to examine cases of imprecise probability assignments featuring a similar structure with a different cardinality of Ω. We consider therefore the lower probability assignments on a generic $\Omega = \{e_1, \ldots, e_n\}$, obtained as lower envelope of a set of n precise probabilities defined as follows:

$$\begin{array}{llll}
P_1(e_1) = 0; & P_1(e_2) = \frac{1}{|\Omega|-1}; & \cdots & P_1(e_n) = \frac{1}{|\Omega|-1}; \\
P_2(e_1) = \frac{1}{|\Omega|-1}; & P_2(e_2) = 0; & \cdots & P_2(e_n) = \frac{1}{|\Omega|-1}; \\
\cdots & \cdots & \cdots & \cdots \\
P_n(e_1) = \frac{1}{|\Omega|-1}; & P_n(e_2) = \frac{1}{|\Omega|-1}; & \cdots & P_n(e_n) = 0 \,.
\end{array} \tag{6}$$

The lower probability assignment minimizing (2) is recovered for $n = 3$. We are therefore interested in verifying whether the value of $m(\Omega)$ has a consistent characterization at the varying of n, i.e. of $\mid \Omega \mid$. The following result gives a negative answer: the sign of $m(\Omega)$ alternates at the varying of $\mid \Omega \mid$.

Proposition 2 *Let $\underline{P}_n$ be the lower probability obtained as lower envelope of the probabilities defined by (6) for a given n, and m_n the corresponding mass function obtained by Möbius inversion, then $m_n(\Omega)$ is positive when n is even and negative when n is odd.*

First of all, let us note that, in the considered case, we have $\forall A \subset \Omega, A \neq \emptyset$, $A \neq \Omega$, $\underline{P}_n(A) = \frac{|A|-1}{n-1}, \overline{P}_n(A) = \frac{|A|}{n-1}$ (these values are easily obtained as the maximum and minimum of the precise probability values $P_i(A)$ in the family defined by (6)). Recalling that $m_n(\Omega) = \sum_{A \subseteq \Omega} (-1)^{n-|A|} \underline{P}(A)$, we easily obtain:

$$m_n(\Omega) = \sum_{i=1}^{n} (-1)^{n-i} \binom{n}{i} \frac{i-1}{n-1} . \tag{7}$$

First, let us recall from combinatorial calculus that:

$$\sum_{i=0}^{n} (-1)^{i} \binom{n}{i} = \sum_{i=0}^{n} (-1)^{i+1} \binom{n}{i} = 0 . \tag{8}$$

Equation (7) can also be written as:

$$m_n(\Omega) = \frac{1}{n-1} \left[\sum_{i=1}^{n} (-1)^{n-i} \binom{n}{i} i - \sum_{i=1}^{n} (-1)^{n-i} \binom{n}{i} \right] . \tag{9}$$

As to the first summation in (9) we have:

$$\binom{n}{i} i = n \binom{n-1}{i-1} . \tag{10}$$

Putting $h = i - 1$ and recalling (8) we obtain:

$$\sum_{i=1}^{n} (-1)^{n-i} \binom{n}{i} i = n \sum_{i=1}^{n} (-1)^{n-i} \binom{n-1}{i-1} = n \sum_{h=0}^{n-1} (-1)^{n-(h+1)} \binom{n-1}{h} = 0 \tag{11}$$

As for the second summation in (9):

$$\sum_{i=1}^{n} (-1)^{n-i} \binom{n}{i} = \left(\sum_{i=0}^{n} (-1)^{n-i} \binom{n}{i} \right) - (-1)^{n} \binom{n}{0} = -(-1)^{n} . \tag{12}$$

Exploiting (11) and (12) in (9), we obtain the desired result:

$$m_n(\Omega) = \frac{(-1)^{n}}{n-1} . \tag{13}$$

Proposition 2 suggests a negative answer to the first question we posed. Starting from the lower probability corresponding to the minimal value of $m(\Omega)$ for $|\Omega|=3$, we have identified a family of CLP where the sign of $m(\Omega)$ varies with the cardinality of Ω itself. Apart from cardinality, it does not seem that, in this family, the cases where $m(\Omega)<0$ feature any significant difference with respect to the ones with $m(\Omega)>0$, nor the fact that cardinality of Ω is even or odd appears to be particularly meaningful. Given the lack of significance in these cases, we also tend to exclude that the mass sign can be ascribed any intuitively appreciable general meaning in the context of CLP.

Let us turn to the second question. We restrict our analysis to the case of $|\Omega|=3$ and analyze another generalization of the lower probability minimizing Ω in this case. We consider a family of lower probabilities obtained as lower envelope of three parametric precise probability assignments:

$$\begin{array}{lll} P_1(e_1)=k; & P_1(e_2)=\alpha(1-k); & P_1(e_3)=(1-\alpha)(1-k); \\ P_2(e_1)=(1-\alpha)(1-k); & P_2(e_2)=k; & P_2(e_3)=\alpha(1-k); \\ P_3(e_1)=\alpha(1-k); & P_3(e_2)=(1-\alpha)(1-k); & P_3(e_3)=k; \end{array} \qquad (14)$$

where $k\in[0,1]$; $\alpha\in[0,0.5]$ (note that this implies $\alpha(1-k)\leq(1-\alpha)(1-k)$). Given $|\Omega|=3$, (14) is a generalization of (6), which is recovered for $k=0$, $\alpha=0.5$.

The resulting parametric lower probability is as follows:

$$\underline{P}(e_i)= \quad min(k,\alpha(1-k)) \quad \forall i\in\{1,2,3\}; \qquad (15)$$
$$\underline{P}(e_i\vee e_j)=\alpha(1-k)+min(k,(1-\alpha)(1-k))\ \forall i,j\in\{1,2,3\},i\neq j\ . \qquad (16)$$

The corresponding mass function is:

$$m(e_i)= \quad \underline{P}(e_i) \quad \forall i\in\{1,2,3\}; \qquad (17)$$
$$m(e_i\vee e_j)= \quad \underline{P}(e_i\vee e_j)-2\underline{P}(e_i) \quad \forall i,j\in\{1,2,3\},i\neq j; \qquad (18)$$
$$m(\Omega)=1-3\underline{P}(e_i\vee e_j)+3\underline{P}(e_i)\ . \qquad (19)$$

Since the parametric family of CLP defined above includes both belief functions and non belief functions, we are interested in characterizing the subset of belief functions within it.

It is easy to see that at the varying of α and k, $m(e_i\vee e_j)\geq 0$, therefore we have just to characterize the couples (α,k) for which $m(\Omega)<0$. By applying (15) and (16) into (19) we obtain

$$m(\Omega)=1-3\alpha(1-k)-3(min(k,(1-\alpha)(1-k)))+3(min(k,\alpha(1-k)))\ . \qquad (20)$$

Several cases have to be considered:

1. for $k\leq\alpha(1-k)$, equation (20) yields:

$$m(\Omega)=1-3\alpha(1-k) \qquad (21)$$

in this case $m(\Omega)<0$ for $\alpha>\frac{1}{3(1-k)}$;

2. for $\alpha(1-k) \leq k \leq (1-\alpha)(1-k)$, equation (20) yields:

$$m(\Omega) = 1 - 3k \tag{22}$$

in this case $m(\Omega) < 0$ for $k > 1/3$;

3. for $k \geq (1-\alpha)(1-k)$, equation (20) yields:

$$m(\Omega) = 1 - 3(1-\alpha)(1-k) \tag{23}$$

in this case $m(\Omega) < 0$ for $\alpha < \frac{1}{3}\left(\frac{2-3k}{1-k}\right)$.

The equations above identify three regions of the space of the couples (α, k), each including both couples corresponding to belief functions and to non belief functions: this is graphically presented in Figure 1. As Figure 1 shows, belief functions do not represent a distinct region in the considered space: there are two different areas corresponding to belief functions. These areas intersect in a single point, corresponding to the only precise probability included in this family.

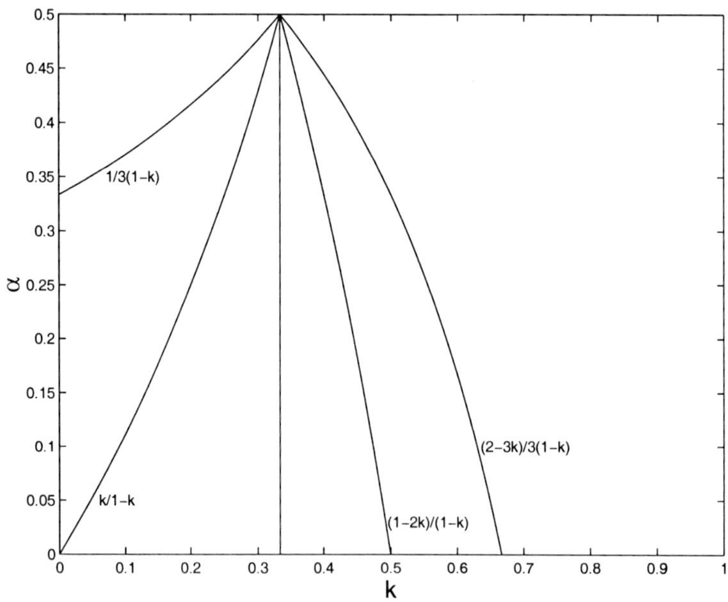

Fig. 1. Belief and non belief functions in the (α, k) space.

Figure 2 provides another view of the same result: the bold lines represent the values of $\underline{P}(e_i)$ and $\overline{P}(e_i)$ respectively, at varying of k for the case $\alpha = 0.4$ (a similar figure would be obtained for any $1/3 < \alpha < 1/2$, while other values of α give rise to simpler cases). Note that the values $\overline{P}(e_i)$ and $\underline{P}(e_i)$ completely define an imprecise probability assignment in the considered case. Vertical lines separate the regions with different sign of $m(\Omega)$, i.e. imprecise probabilities which are belief functions from those which are not. The position of the vertical lines derives directly from (21) - (23), the corresponding geometric constructions are not shown, since they would make the figure unreadable. Again, it does not seem that belief functions, which span on two separate regions, can be characterized as an intuitively meaningful subset. In particular, the borderlines between belief and non belief functions do not correspond to meaningful variations in the underlying upper-lower probability intervals. To put it in other words, it seems that belief functions can not be given a robust intuitive characterization as a class of imprecise probabilities, since infinitesimal (and not otherwise significant) variations of upper and lower probability values may make the difference.

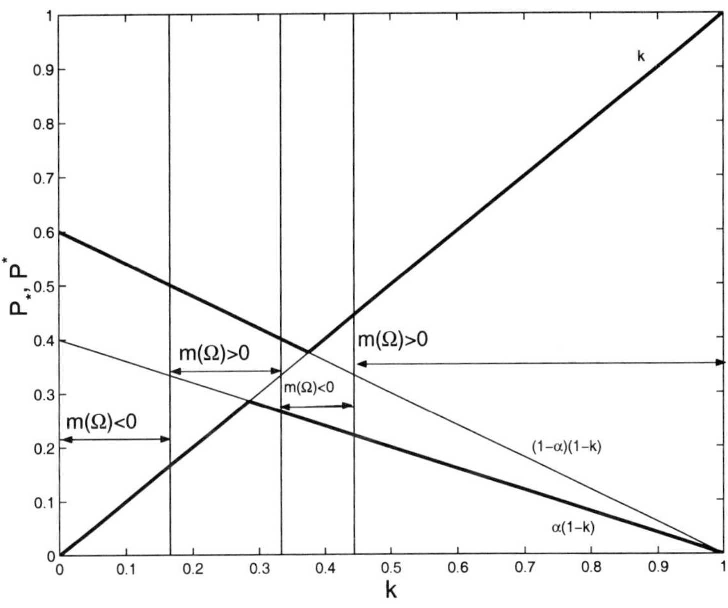

Fig. 2. $\underline{P}(e_i)$, $\overline{P}(e_i)$, and sign of $m(\Omega)$ for $\alpha = 0.4$

This result suggests a negative answer also to the second question we posed: the regions corresponding to belief functions do not seem to identify an intuitively sensible subclass within the set of coherent imprecise probabilities considered. While belief functions feature distinct mathematical properties, such as the mass sign, it does not seem that it is possible to point out any meaningful distinction between those imprecise probabilities which are belief functions and those which, possibly by an infinitesimal difference, are not. As pointed out by one of the referees, it has also to be noted that we have selected a specific cut, where the regions are not connected, while it may be the case that, in a higher dimensional space, they form a connected region, which may look nicely after some transformations. While we welcome this objection, we remark that the cut we used is a simple and "natural" one: alternative cuts and transformations in more complex spaces would in turn require an articulated (and possibly difficult to find) intuitive justification.

6 Conclusions

Though based on specific examples, the results of previous section provide reasonably justified answers to the questions we posed about the relationships between the interpretation of belief functions based on the notion of non-negative masses and coherent lower probabilities.

These answers can in turn be interpreted in two alternative ways:

- from a probability-oriented point of view, they tend to exclude the possibility of giving a meaningful interpretation of belief functions as an autonomous specialized theory in the framework of imprecise probabilities. In this sense, the results of this paper would accrue with other similar past criticisms.
- from a TBM-oriented point of view, they tend to confirm that the search for a common conceptual basis with any form of probability theory is doomed to fail, since the two theories have definitely different roots.

Grabisch has shown that the Möbius transform for a fuzzy measure yields the coefficients of its multilinear polynomial extension (see [4] for details). While this result supports an alternative mathematical interpretation of the mass values in a more abstract framework, which encompasses both uncertainty representation and multicriteria decision making, it does not seem to provide further hints for an intuitive interpretation of masses in the context of belief functions theory for the representation of uncertainty.

We propose a further perspective: the difficulties related to the notion of mass suggest that the search of alternative intuitive interpretations of belief functions should still be pursued. We believe that the more general theory of coherent imprecise probabilities may provide hints for this research goal. In particular, there is some evidence in the literature that the n-monotonicity property is somehow related to concepts of independence. We mention for this an example in 5.13.4 of [21], where lack of independence between two tosses of a coin naturally leads to a lower probability evaluation, which cannot be n-monotone. Further, it is shown in 4.1 of [19] that a general notion of epistemic independence is consistent with a concept of n-monotonicity, termed external n-monotonicity.

Acknowledgments. We thank the referees for their helpful comments.

References

1. Chateauneuf, A., Jaffray, J.-Y.: Some characterizations of lower probabilities and other monotone capacities through the use of Möbius inversion. Mathematical Social Sciences **17**(1989) 263–283

2. Dempster, A.: Upper and lower probabilities induced by a multivalued mapping. Annals of Mathematical Statistics **38**(1967) 325–339
3. Fagin, R., Halpern, J.Y.: Uncertainty, belief and probability. Proc. of IJCAI'89, Detroit, MI, (1989) 1161–1167
4. Grabisch, M.: k-Order additive discrete fuzzy measures. Proc. of IPMU 96, Granada, E, (1996) 1345–1350
5. Guan, J.W. and Bell, D.A.: Evidence theory and its applications. North Holland, Amsterdan, NL, (1991)
6. Kohlas, J., Monney, P.A.: Representation of Evidence by Hints. In: : Yager, R.R., Kacprzyk, J., Fedrizzi, M. (eds.): Advances in the Dempster-Shafer Theory of Evidence. John Wiley, New York, NY, (1994) 473–492
7. Nguyen, H.T.: On random sets and belief functions. Journal of Mathematical Analysis and Applications **65** (1978) 539–542
8. Pearl, J.: Bayesian and belief function formalisms for evidential reasoning: a conceptual analysis. In: Shafer, G., Pearl, J. (eds.): Readings in Uncertain Reasoning. Morgan Kaufmann, San Mateo, CA, (1990) 540–574
9. Pearl, J.: Reasoning with belief functions an analysis of compatibility. International Journal of Approximate Reasoning **4** (1990) 363–390
10. Shafer, G.: A mathematical theory of evidence. Princeton University Press, Princeton, NJ, (1976)
11. Shafer, G., Tversky, A.: Languages and designs for probability judgment. In: Shafer, G., Pearl, J. (eds.): Readings in Uncertain Reasoning. Morgan Kaufmann, San Mateo, CA, (1990) 40–54
12. Smets, P.: Belief functions. In: Smets, P., Mamdani, E.H., Dubois, D., Prade, H. (eds.): Non-Standard logics for automated reasoning. Academic Press, London, UK, (1988) 253–277
13. Smets, P.: The combination of evidence in the transferable belief model. IEEE Trans. on Pattern Analysis and Machine Intelligence **12**(1990) 447–458
14. Smets, P.: Resolving misunderstandings about belief functions. International Journal of Approximate Reasoning **6** (1992) 321–344
15. Smets, P.: What is Dempster-Shafer's model ? In: Yager, R.R., Fedrizzi, M., Kacprzyk, J.(eds.): Advances in the Dempster-Shafer Theory of Evidence. Wiley, London, UK, (1994) 5–34
16. Smets, P.: The canonical decomposition of a weighted belief. Proc. of IJCAI 95, Montreal, CA, (1995) 1896–1901
17. Smets, P.: The normative representation of quantified beliefs by belief functions. Artificial Intelligence **92** (1997)
18. Smets, P., Kennes, R.: The transferable belief model. Artificial Intelligence **66** (1994) 191–234
19. Vicig, P.: Epistemic Independence for Imprecise Probabilities. International Journal of Approximate Reasoning **24** (2000) 235–250
20. Voorbraak, F.: On the justification of Dempster's rule of combination. Artificial Intelligence **48** (1991) 171–197
21. Walley, P.: Statistical reasoning with imprecise probabilities. Chapman and Hall, London, UK, (1991)
22. Walley, P.: Measures of uncertainty in expert systems. Artificial Intelligence **83** (1996) 1–58
23. Wang, P.: A defect in Dempster-Shafer theory. Proc. of UAI 94, Seattle, WA, (1994) 560–566
24. Zadeh, L.A.: A mathematical theory of evidence (book review) AI Magazine **5** (1984) 81–83

About Conditional Belief Function Independence

Boutheina Ben Yaghlane[1], Philippe Smets[2], and Khaled Mellouli[1]

[1] AMID, Université de Tunis,
IHEC Carthage Présidence 2016 Tunisia
{boutheina.yaghlane,Khaled.mellouli}@ihec.rnu.tn

[2] IRIDIA, Université Libre de Bruxelles,
50, av. F. Roosevelt, CP 194/6 1050 Bruxelles Belgium
psmets@ulb.ac.be

Abstract. In this paper, we study different concepts of conditional belief functions independence in the context of the transferable belief model. We especially clarify the relationships between the concepts of conditional non-interactivity, irrelevance and doxastic independence. Conditional non-interactivity is defined by the 'mathematical' property useful for computation considerations and corresponds to decomposionality of the belief functions. Conditional irrelevance is defined by a 'common sense' property based on conditioning. Conditional doxastic independence is defined by a particular form of irrelevance, the one preserved under Dempster's rule of combination.

Keywords: Conditional Independence, Conditional Irrelevance, Conditional Non-interactivity, Belief functions, Transferable Belief Model.

1 Introduction

The essence of conditional independence (CI) can be identified with a common structure consisting of some basic properties of the CI relation, called '*graphoid axioms*' [5]. These axioms convey the simple idea that when we learn an irrelevant fact, the relevance relationships of all other facts remain unchanged [13].

The graphoid axioms have been initially developed by Dawid [5] for probabilistic conditional independence. In order to enhance the application of Probability Theory to Artificial Intelligence, Pearl and Paz [14] established the connections between probabilistic conditional independence and graphical representation. The graphoid axioms are also satisfied by other non-probabilistic models such as embedded multi-valued dependency models in relational databases [9], conditional independence in Spohn's theory of ordinal conditional functions [10], qualitative conditional independence in Dempster-Shafer theory of belief functions partitions [16], possibilistic conditional independence [8], [22], conditional independence and irrelevance in connection to the theory of closed convex sets of probability measures [4], and conditional independence in valuation-based systems representing many different uncertainty calculi [17].

S. Benferhat and P. Besnard (Eds.): ECSQARU 2001, LNAI 2143, pp. 340–349, 2001.

Unfortunately these axioms have not received a complete treatment when related to the theory of belief functions. For this purpose, we study the notion of conditional independence between sets of variables when uncertainty is expressed by belief functions as defined in the context of the transferable belief model (TBM) [20], [19]. We present the concepts of conditional non-interactivity, irrelevance and doxastic independence. We enhance the distinction between conditional irrelevance and conditional independence. Then, we show that, like in the marginal case [2], conditional irrelevance alone does not imply conditional non-interactivity. We also prove that conditional doxastic independence is equivalent to conditional non-interactivity. In this paper, all theorems are stated without proofs. The reader is referred to [3] for the proofs of these theorems.

The remainder of this paper is organized as follows. In section 2, we first introduce the necessary notations and terminologies. Then, after extending the definition of evidential and cognitive independence to the conditional case (section 3), we present our definitions of conditional non-interactivity (section 4), conditional irrelevance (section 5) and conditional doxastic independence (section 6) for belief functions. Finally, in section 7, we summarize the results achieved in this paper and point out some future directions.

2 Notations and Terminologies

The main purpose of the theory of belief functions, also known as Dempster-Shafer theory and theory of evidence, is to model someone's degree of belief. Since its introduction by Shafer [15], many interpretations have been proposed. Among them, we can distinguish: the lower probability model [23], the hint model [12] and the transferable belief model (TBM) [20]. In this paper, we are only concerned with the TBM.

Most needed definitions and properties have been previously given in our paper concerning the marginal belief function independence [2]. In this section, we just reproduce the important ones in order to help the reader.

2.1 Sets

When authors discuss about conditional independence, they begin with a set S of variables $X_1, X_2 ... X_n$, then consider pairwise disjoint subsets of variables U, V, W where $U \subseteq S$, $V \subseteq S$ and $W \subseteq S$. The concepts of non-interactivity, irrelevance and independence are then defined between U, V and W. We will not repeat systematically these preliminary definitions, and we will consider only three variables, denoted X, Y, Z, with the understanding that each one represents a variable which domain is the product space of its related X_i variables. We give here some essential set notations.

- By convention, indexed variables like x_i, y_j, z_k denote elements of their domain whereas x, y, z denote subsets of their domain.
- If X, Y, Z are three variables, XY denotes $X \times Y$ and XYZ denotes $X \times Y \times Z$.

- For $x \subseteq X, y \subseteq Y, (x, y)$ denotes the subset w of XY such that $w = \{(x_i, y_j) : x_i \in x, y_j \in y\}$.
- For $x \subseteq X, y \subseteq Y, z \subseteq Z, (x, y, z)$ denotes the subset w of XYZ such that $w = \{(x_i, y_j, z_k) : x_i \in x, y_j \in y, z_k \in z\}$.
- For $x \subseteq X$, $x^{\uparrow XY}$ is the cylindrical extension of x on XY: $x^{\uparrow XY} = (x, Y)$
- For $w \subseteq \Omega$, $w^{\downarrow X}$ is the projection of w on X: $w^{\downarrow X} = \{x_i : x_i \in X, x_i^{\uparrow \Omega} \cap w \neq \emptyset\}$.
- We assume that the variables X, Y, Z are 'logically independent', by what we mean that:

$$(x_i, Y, Z) \cap (X, y_j, Z) \cap (X, Y, z_k) \neq \emptyset, \ \forall x_i \in X, y_j \in Y, z_k \in Z.$$

2.2 Belief Functions

- We use the notation $m^{\Omega}[x]$ to represent the bba (shorthand for basic belief assignment) m defined on the domain Ω given the belief holder knows that x is true (i.e. x holds). The symbol m can be replaced by bel, pl, q in order to denote the belief function, the plausibility function and the commonality function. The values taken by these functions at $w \subseteq \Omega$ are denoted by $m^{\Omega}[x](w)$, $bel^{\Omega}[x](w)$, $pl^{\Omega}[x](w)$, $q^{\Omega}[x](w)$, respectively.

- In the TBM, none of these functions is necessarily normalized. When we want to get the normalized forms, we use the upper-cases notations M, Bel, Pl, Q. These normalized functions are obtained by dividing the unnormalized functions by the factor 1 - $m(\emptyset)$ (putting $M(\emptyset) = 0$, $Bel(\emptyset) = 0$ and $Q(\emptyset) = 1$).

- Let m^X be defined on the frame X. Then $m^{X\uparrow XY}$ is the bba defined on the frame $X \times Y$ with:

$$\begin{aligned} m^{X\uparrow XY}(w) &= m(x), \text{ if } w = (x, Y) \\ &= 0, \ otherwise. \end{aligned}$$

  $m^{X\uparrow XY}$ is called a *vacuous extension* of m^X.

- Let m^{XY} be defined on the frame $X \times Y$. Then $m^{XY\downarrow X}$ is the bba defined on the frame X with:

$$m^{XY\downarrow X}(x) = \sum_{w^{\downarrow X} = x} m^{XY}(w), \forall x \subseteq X$$

  $m^{XY\downarrow X}$ is called the *marginal* of m^{XY} on X.

- The $\oplus$ symbol represents Dempster's rule of combination in its normalized form and $\circledcirc$ represents the conjunctive combination, i.e., the same operation as Dempster's rule of combination except the normalization (the division by

$1-m(\emptyset))$ is not performed. The conjunctive combination rule can be written equivalently as:

$$m_{1\circledcirc 2}(w) = m_1 \circledcirc m_2(w) = \sum_{w_1,w_2 \subseteq \Omega, w_1 \cap w_2 = w} m_1(w_1)m_2(w_2)$$

The next formula is very useful (see Smets [18]):

$$f_{1\circledcirc 2}(w) = \sum_{w^* \subseteq \Omega} f_1[w^*](w)m_2(w^*), \ \forall w \subseteq \Omega \tag{1}$$

where $f \in \{m, bel, pl, q\}$ and $f_1[w^*]$ is the result of the unnormalized conditioning of f_1 on $w^* \subseteq \Omega$.

- Both $\oplus$ and $\circledcirc$ operations are extended, so that they can be applied to two bba's m_1 and m_2 not defined on the same frame (the frames being nevertheless compatibles), so $m_1^X \circledcirc m_2^Y$ is short for $m_1^{X\uparrow XY} \circledcirc m_2^{Y\uparrow XY}$.

- $pl_1 \circledcirc pl_2$ represents the plausibility function obtained from $m_1 \circledcirc m_2$ where m_1 and m_2 are the bba's related to pl_1 and pl_2, respectively (and similarly with bel and q).

- The set of belief functions defined on Ω is denoted by BF_Ω.

- By abuse of language, we may omit the Ω index and we will write statements like $m \in BF_\Omega$ to mean that the belief function associated with m belongs to BF_Ω.

- When convenient, bba's m on Ω are represented by the list of pairs (w, x) where w is a focal element of m (a subset of Ω with a non null bbm), and $x = m(w)$. So $((w_1, .4), (w_2, .6))$ represents the bba m^Ω on Ω with $m^\Omega(w_1) = .4$ and $m^\Omega(w_2) = .6$, and $w_1 \subseteq \Omega$ and $w_2 \subseteq \Omega$.

3 Evidential and Cognitive Independence

In the marginal case [2], we have presented the notions of evidential independence and cognitive independence for belief functions. These notions have been first introduced by Shafer [15] for the marginal case. In addition, it is shown in Shafer [15] that evidential independence implies cognitive independence, but not the reverse. In this section, we only consider evidential independence.

In the multivariate framework, Kong [11] studied the conditional case. He defined the notion of evidential conditional independence of belief functions, as follows (remember variables X, Y, and Z are always pairwise disjoint subsets of variables (see section 2.1):

Definition 1. ***Evidential Conditional Independence.*** *Let X, Y and Z be three variables. X and Y are (evidentially) conditionally independent given Z with respect to Bel^{XYZ} if and only if for all $x \subseteq X$, $y \subseteq Y$, $z_i \in Z$:*

$$Bel^{XYZ}[z_i]^{\downarrow XY}(x,y) = Bel^{XYZ}[z_i]^{\downarrow X}(x) Bel^{XYZ}[z_i]^{\downarrow Y}(y) \tag{2}$$

When Z is not specified this becomes marginal evidential independence of X and Y (Definition 3 in [2]).

Almond ([1], page 114) calls this independence a *strong* conditional independence and shows it is equivalent to:

Definition 2. ***Strong Conditional Independence.*** *Let X, Y and Z be three variables. X and Y are (strongly) conditionally independent given Z with respect to Bel^{XYZ} if and only if*

$$Bel^{XYZ} = Bel^{XYZ \downarrow XZ} \oplus Bel^{XYZ \downarrow YZ} \tag{3}$$

Note that these definitions are based on normalized belief functions. When we tolerate unnormalized belief functions, the term $Bel^{XYZ \downarrow Z}$ must be added and the definition becomes as follows:

Definition 3. ***Strong Conditional Independence.*** *Let X, Y and Z be three variables. X and Y are (strongly) conditionally independent given Z with respect to Bel^{XYZ} if and only if*

$$Bel^{XYZ} \oplus Bel^{XYZ \downarrow Z} = Bel^{XYZ \downarrow XZ} \oplus Bel^{XYZ \downarrow YZ} \tag{4}$$

This definition turns out to be equivalent to what we call hereafter conditional non-interactivity. In the following sections, we present our definition of conditional non-interactivity, conditional irrelevance and conditional doxastic independence.

4 Conditional Non-Interactivity

We focus now on the decompositional independence definition for belief functions. This definition is represented by the non-interactivity that is a mathematical property useful for calculus considerations.

For the definition of the conditional non-interactivity for belief functions, we start from the belief on the joint product space XYZ. We marginalize it on XZ and also on YZ. We combine these two marginal belief functions and we want it to be equal to the initial one (on XYZ) combined with its marginal on Z.

This last term results from the fact that the marginals on XZ and on YZ both contain the marginal on Z and this last is thus double counted when combining the marginals on XZ and on YZ. This term corresponds to the $pl^{XY}(X, Y)$ term encountered when defining marginal non-interactivity (see relation (6) in [2]). The formal definition is given as follows:

Definition 4. ***Conditional Non-interactivity.*** *Given three variables X, Y and Z, and $m^{XYZ} \in BF_{XYZ}$, X and Y are conditionally non-interactive given Z with respect to m^{XYZ}, denoted by $X \perp_{m^{XYZ}} Y|Z$, if and only if*

$$m^{XYZ} \circledcirc m^{XYZ\downarrow Z} = m^{XYZ\downarrow XZ} \circledcirc m^{XYZ\downarrow YZ} \tag{5}$$

This definition of conditional non-interactivity (5) corresponds to Shenoy' factorization (see [17], lemma 3.1 (5)). It can also be reformulated in terms of commonality functions as shown by Studeny [21].

Theorem 1. *$X \perp_{m^{XYZ}} Y|Z$ iff for all $w \subseteq XYZ$*

$$q^{XYZ}(w)\; q^{XYZ\downarrow Z}(w^{\downarrow Z}) = q^{XYZ\downarrow XZ}(w^{\downarrow XZ})\; q^{XYZ\downarrow YZ}(w^{\downarrow YZ}) \tag{6}$$

It is interesting to note that Studeny [21] has an objection about the definition of conditional non-interactivity[1] in the framework of Dempster-Shafer theory. Indeed, he notices that the definition based on equation (5) is *not consistent with marginalization*. It may happen that for two bba's $m_1 \in BF_{XZ}$ and $m_2 \in BF_{YZ}$ that share the same marginal on Z (i.e., $m_1^{\downarrow Z} = m_2^{\downarrow Z}$) there exists no bba m^{XYZ} on XYZ such that $m^{XYZ\downarrow XZ} = m_1$, $m^{XYZ\downarrow YZ} = m_2$ and $X \perp_{m^{XYZ}} Y|Z$.

Nevertheless the next theorem shows that, for any m^{XZ} and m^{YZ}, X and Y are non-interactive given Z under $m^{XYZ} = m^{XZ} \circledcirc m^{YZ}$. The only subtlety is that m^{XZ} and m^{YZ} are *not* the marginals of m^{XYZ} on XZ and YZ, respectively. This property provides in fact a convenient way to build belief functions that satisfy non-interactivity. Just take any pair of bba's m^{XZ} and m^{YZ} and combine them conjunctively, the result is a bba under which X and Y are conditionally non-interactive given Z.

Theorem 2. *Let m^{XZ} and m^{YZ} be two bba's on XZ and YZ, respectively. Let $m = m^{XZ} \circledcirc m^{YZ}$ then $X \perp_m Y|Z$.*

5 Conditional Irrelevance

Before presenting the definition of conditional irrelevance for belief functions, we explain the idea of two belief functions on XYZ that share the same marginals on Z after having been conjunctively combined with a given bba m on XYZ.

The underlying idea is a problem of belief state distinguishability. Suppose two agents who hold beliefs on XYZ. Suppose You can only observe the beliefs held by these two agents on Z (thus the marginal on Z of their bba's). If these two marginal bba's are equal, You cannot distinguish between the beliefs held by the two agents, even though their beliefs on XYZ may be different. One

[1] Studeny [21] uses the term 'conditional independence' rather than 'conditional non-interactivity'

way to distinguish them is to present to the two agents a new piece of evidence which induces the bba m on XYZ. This last m is then combined conjunctively with the initial bba's. The marginalization on Z can still be equal, or not, this depending on m. So one way to distinguish between belief states which can only be observed on Z is by producing various m, and comparing the marginals on Z.

For a given m on XYZ, we can consider all the belief functions on XYZ which are indistinguishable on Z. These bba's describe belief states that cannot be distinguished after having been conjunctively combined with m by only observing their marginals on Z. Thus m creates an *equivalence class* on the set of belief functions defined on XYZ.

5.1 Indistinguishability on Z under m

Let $R^Z(m)$ denote the set of belief functions on XYZ that are indistinguishable on Z under m. Its formal definition is as follows:

Definition 5. ***Indistinguishability on Z under m.*** *For any bba* $m, m_1, m_2 \in BF_{XYZ}$, $(m_1, m_2) \in R^Z(m)$ *iff* $(m \textcircled{\cap} m_1)^{\downarrow Z} = (m \textcircled{\cap} m_2)^{\downarrow Z}$.

In particular, we will use this concept of indistinguishability when $m \in BF_{XYZ}$ and $m_1, m_2 \in BF_{YZ}$ what is just a particular case of the definition. The reason will be that we will define conditional irrelevance as the fact that the belief on XZ is influenced by the belief on YZ only through the impact of this last belief on Z, and not on the details on how it is distributed on YZ.

5.2 Definition of Conditional Irrelevance

Let $m \in BF_{XYZ}$. Suppose that we study the impact of any bba $m_i \in BF_{YZ}$ on our belief on XZ, i.e., we study $(m \textcircled{\cap} m_i)^{\downarrow XZ}$. Suppose the impact of m_i on m is fully captured by its impact on Z. By that we mean that the impact of m_i defined on YZ and the impact of any other m_j defined on YZ with $(m_i, m_j) \in R^Z(m)$ are equal when it comes to the belief induced on XZ. Equivalently it means that all that counts for what regards our beliefs on XZ after we combine m with m_i is the belief induced by $m \textcircled{\cap} m_i$ on Z. Further details on the beliefs on YZ are irrelevant.

In that case, we say that Y is *conditionally irrelevant* to X given Z with respect to m. Formally, we have the following definition:

Definition 6. ***Conditional irrelevance.*** *Let* $m \in BF_{XYZ}$. Y *is conditionally irrelevant to* X *given* Z *with respect to* m, *denoted by* $IR_m(X, Y|Z)$, *if and only if for all* $m_1, m_2 \in BF_{YZ}$ *with* $(m_1, m_2) \in R^Z(m)$ *we have*

$$(m \textcircled{\cap} m_1)^{\downarrow XZ} = (m \textcircled{\cap} m_2)^{\downarrow XZ} \tag{7}$$

Notice that conditional irrelevance alone does not imply conditional non-interactivity between variables.

6 Conditional Doxastic Independence

In the probabilistic framework, it can be easily proved that independence and irrelevance concepts are equivalent. However, in the belief functions framework, the situation is not as simple, irrelevance alone does not imply independence.

In the marginal case [2], we have defined that two variables are *doxastically independent* when they are irrelevant and this irrelevance is preserved under Dempster's rule of combination. Then we have proved that non-interactivity and doxastic independence are equivalent.

In this section, we show that the notion of doxastic independence[2] defined in the marginal case can be extended to the conditional case. We also state the theorem establishing the equivalence between conditional doxastic independence and conditional non-interactivity.

6.1 Irrelevance Preservation under Conjunctive Combination

Just as in the marginal case, we feel that conditional doxastic independence requires not only the conditional irrelevance property, but that property should be preserved when combining two belief functions that satisfy it. The idea fits with the next scenario: if two agents claims that X and Y are conditionally doxastically independent given Z, then this conditional independence should be preserved when the belief functions representing the agents' beliefs are conjunctively combined.

So conditional doxastic independence is irrelevance plus irrelevance preservation under conjunctive combination, denoted $IRP\circledcirc$. Formally, the last property is defined as follows:

Definition 7. ***Irrelevance preservation under conjunctive combination.*** *Given $m_1, m_2 \in BF_{XYZ}$, we say that m_1 and m_2 satisfy $IRP\circledcirc$ if $IR_{m_1}(X,Y|Z)$ and $IR_{m_2}(X,Y|Z)$ imply $IR_{m_1 \circledcirc m_2}(X,Y|Z)$.*

6.2 Definition of Conditional Doxastic Independence

The notion of doxastic independence defined in the marginal case can be extended to the conditional case by the following definition.

Definition 8. ***Conditional Doxastic Independence.*** *Given three variables X, Y and Z, and $\in BF_{XYZ}$. The variables X and Y are doxastically independent given Z with respect to m, denoted by $X \perp\!\!\!\perp_m Y|Z$, if and only if m satisfies*

- $IR_m(X,Y|Z)$
- $\forall m_0 \in BF_{XYZ} : IR_{m_0}(X,Y|Z) \Rightarrow IR_{m \circledcirc m_0}(X,Y|Z)$

[2] We use here the term '*doxastic independence*' for making the distinction between probabilistic independence and belief function independence. In Greek, 'doxein' means 'to believe'.

6.3 Equivalence between $\perp$ and $\perp\!\!\!\perp$

We state the following theorem proving the equivalence between conditional doxastic independence and conditional non-interactivity. The proof of this theorem is in [3].

Theorem 3. *$X \perp_m Y|Z$ iff $X \perp\!\!\!\perp_m Y|Z$.*

7 Conclusion

We have studied the concept of conditional belief function independence in the context of the transferable belief model, pointing out different ways to tackle the problem leading to the following definitions:

- *Conditional non-interactivity*: the joint belief function can be rebuilt from its marginals.
- *Conditional irrelevance*: the belief on XZ depends on any belief over YZ only through the impact of the last belief function on Z.
- *Conditional irrelevance preservation under conjunctive combination rule*: if two belief functions satisfy conditional irrelevance, then their conjunctive combination satisfies also conditional irrelevance.
- *Conditional doxastic independence*: defined as conditional irrelevance that is preserved under conjunctive combination rule.

The major result of this study is that conditional non-interactivity and conditional doxastic independence are equivalent.

However, there remain a lot of future work to be done in this field such that the study of the properties of *conditional products* [7] for belief function theory, the links between our concept of conditional doxastic independence and the concept of *separoid* recently introduced by Dawid [6], and finally, the impact of conditional doxastic independence with respect to its graphical representation.

Acknowledgments
The authors are grateful to the referees for their helpful comments and suggestions.

References

1. G.A.R. Almond (1995), *Graphical Belief Modeling*, Chapman and & Hall.
2. B. Ben Yaghlane, Ph. Smets and K. Mellouli (2000), *Belief Function Independence: I. The Marginal Case*, Technical Report TR/IRIDIA/2000-13, Institut de Recherches Interdisciplinaires et de Développements en Intelligence Artificielle, Université Libre de Bruxelles (to be published at Int. J. of Approx. Reasoning).
3. B. Ben Yaghlane, Ph. Smets and K. Mellouli (2001), *Belief Function Independence: II. The Conditional Case*, Technical Report TR/IRIDIA/2001-8, Institut de Recherches Interdisciplinaires et de Développements en Intelligence Artificielle, Université Libre de Bruxelles.

4. F.G. Cozman (1999), *Irrelevance and Independence Axioms in Quasi-Bayesian Theory*, ECSQARU'99, London, Lecture Notes in AI 1638, A. Hunter and S. Parsons (Eds), Springer-Verlag, pp. 128-136.
5. A.P. Dawid (1979), *Conditional Independence in Statistical Theory*, Journal of the Royal Statistical Society, Series B, Vol. 41, pp. 1-31.
6. A. P. Dawid (2000), *Separoids: A general Framework for Conditional Independence and Irrelevance*, Technical Report 212, University College London.
7. A.P. Dawid and M. Studeny (1999), *Conditional Products: An Alternative Approach to Conditional Independence*, In Artificial Intelligence and Statistics 99, (Eds. D. Heckerman and J. Whittaker), Morgan Kaufmann Publishers, San Francisco, California, pp. 32-40.
8. L.M. deCampos, Huete J.F. and S. Moral (1995), *Possibilistic Independence*, Third European Congress on Intelligent Techniques and Soft Computing EUFIT'95, Germany, Vol. 1, pp. 69-73.
9. R. Fagin (1977), *Multivalued Dependencies and a New Form for Relational Databases*, ACM Transactions on Database Systems, Vol. 2(3), pp. 262-278.
10. D. Hunter (1991), *Graphoids and Natural Conditional Functions*, Int. Journal of Approximate Reasoning, Vol. 5, pp. 489-504.
11. C.T.A. Kong (1988), *A Belief Function Generalization of Gibbs Ensemble*, Joint Tech. report S-122 Harvard University and N239 University of Chicago, Departments of Statistics.
12. J. Kohlas and P.A. Monney (1995), *A Mathematical Theory of Hints. An Approach to Dempster-Shafer Theory of Evidence*, Lecture Notes in Economics and Mathematical Systems No. 425, Springer-Verlag.
13. J. Pearl (1988), *Probabilistic Reasoning in Intelligent Systems: Networks of Plausible Inference*, Morgan Kaufmman, Los Altos, CA.
14. J. Pearl and A. Paz (1987), *Graphoids: A Graph-based Logic for Reasoning about Relevance Relations*, In Advances in Artificial Intelligence (Eds. D. Hogg and L. Steels), North-Holland, Amsterdam, pp. 357-363.
15. G. Shafer (1976), *Mathematical Theory of Evidence*, Princeton University Press, Princeton.
16. G. Shafer, P.P. Shenoy, and Mellouli, K. (1987), *Propagating belief functions in qualitative Markov trees*, Int. J. of Approximate Reasoning, Vol. 1, pp. 349-400.
17. P.P. Shenoy (1994), *Conditional Independence in Valuation-Based Systems*, Int. J. of Approximate Reasoning, 10, pp. 203-234.
18. P. Smets (1993), *Belief Functions: The Disjunctive Rule of Combination and the Generalized Bayesian Theorem*, Int. J. of Approximate Reasoning, Vol. 1, pp. 349-400.
19. P. Smets (1998), *The Transferable Belief Model for Quantified Belief Representation.* In D.M. Gabbay and P. Smets (Eds.), Handbook of Defeasible Reasoning and Uncertainty Management Systems, Vol. 1, The Netherlands: Kluwer, pp. 349-400.
20. P. Smets and R. Kennes (1994), *The Transferable Belief Model*, Artificial Intelligence, 66, pp. 191-234.
21. M. Studeny (1993), *Formal Properties of Conditional Independence in Different Calculi of Artificial Intelligence*, ECSQARU'93, K. Clarke K., R. Kruse and S. Moral (Eds), Springer-Verlag, pp. 341-348.
22. J. Vejnarova (1999), *Conditional Independence Relations in Possibility Theory*, 1st International Symposium on Imprecise Probabilities and Their Applications ISIPTA'99, Ghent, pp. 343-351.
23. P. Walley (1991), *Statistical Reasoning with Imprecise Probabilities*, Chapman and Hall, London.

The Evaluation of Sensors' Reliability and Their Tuning for Multisensor Data Fusion within the Transferable Belief Model

Zied Elouedi[1], Khaled Mellouli[1], and Philippe Smets[2]

[1] Institut Supérieur de Gestion de Tunis,
41 Avenue de la liberté, cité Bouchoucha, 2000 Le Bardo, Tunis, Tunisia
{zied.elouedi@isg.rnu.tn}, {khaled.mellouli@ihec.rnu.tn}
[2] IRIDIA, Université Libre de Bruxelles,
50 av., F. Roosvelt, CP194/6, 1050 Brussels, Belgium
{psmets@ulb.ac.be}

Abstract. We develop a method to evaluate the reliability of a sensor in a classification task when the uncertainty is represented by belief functions as understood in the transferable belief model.
This reliability is represented by a discounting factor that minimizes the distance between the pignistic probabilities computed from the discounted beliefs and the actual values of the data in a learning set.
We then describe a method to tune the discounting factors of several sensors when their reports are merged in order to reach an aggregated report. They are computed so that together they minimize the distance between the pignistic probabilities computed from the combined discounted belief functions and the actual values of the data in a learning set.
The first method produces the reliability of a sensor considered alone. The second method considers a set of sensors, and weights each of them so that together they produce the best predictor.

1 Introduction

The belief function theory, in particular the Transferable Belief Model (TBM), is more and more used to represent and deal with uncertainty. It can be seen as a generalization of subjective probability theory. The TBM allows to handle data collected from partially reliable sensors. It can represent full, partial and even total ignorance. The conjunctive rule of combination provides the tool to aggregate the reports produced by several sensors in order to get their merged report. It seems to be perfectly adapted for multisensor data fusion [14].

Sensors use different approaches and types of measurements and work in different environments, and their reliability can vary from one to the other. One way to take in consideration the reliability and applicability of a sensor consists in weighing / discounting their reports.

In the TBM, a sensor reports about the actual value of a variable is represented by a belief function. The reliability of the sensor is represented by a

S. Benferhat and P. Besnard (Eds.): ECSQARU 2001, LNAI 2143, pp. 350–361, 2001.

discounting factor, i.e., a coefficient that 'weights' the belief function produced by the sensor. Reliability and discounting are linked by the idea that if a sensor is felt as unreliable by the user, he/she will discount what the sensor states. Discount can be understood as 'partially disregard'. The smaller the reliability, the larger the discounting. The discounting factor is a well defined concept in belief function theory (see section 2.3), whereas reliability will be used unformally hereafter.

This paper addresses the problem of assessing the discounting factor to be applied to the beliefs generated by the sensors. We develop two methods applicable in two contexts. The first consists in assessing the discounting factor to be applied to one sensor by comparing its report (represented by a belief function) with the actual values. The second consists in assessing the values of the discounting factor to be given to each of several sensors when their reports must be merged. It is obtained by comparing the merged discounted belief function with the actual values.

The first method concerns one sensor, the second concerns a group of sensors who jointly must produce an aggregated decision.

It may seem odd that we speak of 'beliefs held by a sensor', but the term belief is to be taken in a neutral way. No philosophical or psychological connotation is to be introduced. It is just a tradition that the functions that represent the sensor report are called 'belief function', hence the 'belief' term. Classically, sensors produce likelihoods. Here we just replace the term likelihood by beliefs, what enhances that we use belief functions and not probability functions.

This paper is composed as follows. We start by giving an overview of the basics of the TBM. Next, we present the multisensor data fusion within the belief function formalism. We then describe the two methods for assessing sensor reliabilities and for tuning them. Each method is illustrated by an example explaining its unfolding.

In this paper, we speak of sensors, but all we present here can be applied directly to other problems, like expert opinion pooling. An expert is just a sensor, and his/her opinion is equivalent to a sensor report. Data fusion and opinion pooling are analogous.

Experts differ in level of expertise, some of them are more reliable than others due to their better knowledge, training, experience, intelligence ... To express their opinions, experts may use different background, methodology and even knowledge. Hence, the necessity to consider the expert's reliability when receiving their opinions, and consequently these judgments must be appropriately 'discounted'.

Thus, the concepts of expert, opinion and expert opinion pooling are equivalent to those of sensor, report and data fusion. The methods presented in this paper can be applied directly to this other domain. Note that other researchers have proposed to assess experts' discounting factors within the belief function theory, we basically mention the one developed by Zouhal and Denoeux [15].

2 Belief Function Theory

In this section, we briefly review the basics of the belief function theory as interpreted in the Transferable Belief Model (TBM). For a more detailed explanation and other basics see [6,10,11].

2.1 Definitions

Let Θ be a finite set of elementary and mutually exclusive hypotheses related to a given problem domain. It is called the frame of discernment. One value of Θ, denoted θ_0, corresponds to the actual value of Θ. This actual value is not known by the belief holder (the sensor).

A basic belief assignment (bba) is a function m from the power set of Θ, denoted 2^Θ, to $[0,1]$ verifying:

$$\sum_{A \subseteq \Theta} m(A) = 1 \tag{1}$$

The basic belief mass (bbm) $m(A)$ given to $A \subseteq \Theta$ is the amount of belief specifically assigned to the event $\theta_0 \in A$ and that cannot support any subset of Θ more specific than A.

The belief function (bel) represents the belief assigned to an event $A \subseteq \Theta$. It is equal to the sum of bbm committed to the subsets of A. For each bba m, there corresponds a belief function bel such that: $bel : 2^\Theta \to [0,1]$, and defined by:

$$bel(A) = \sum_{\emptyset \neq B \subseteq A} m(B), \ \forall A \subseteq \Theta. \tag{2}$$

A vacuous belief function is such that $m(\Theta) = 1$ and $m(A) = 0, \ \forall A \subseteq \Theta, A \neq \Theta$. It represents a state of the total ignorance.

2.2 Combination

Consider two pieces of evidence on the same frame Θ represented by the two bbas m_1 and m_2, the joint bba quantifying the combined impact of these two pieces of evidence is obtained through the conjunctive combination rule as follows [8]:

$$(m_1 \circledcirc m_2)(A) = \sum_{B,C \subseteq \Theta : B \cap C = A} m_1(B).m_2(C) \tag{3}$$

where $\circledcirc$ denotes the operator of conjunction. The classical Dempster's rule of combination is the conjunctive combination rule where the result is normalized by dividing each term by $(1 - (m_1 \circledcirc m_2)(\emptyset))$. It is defined as:

$$(m_1 \oplus m_2)(A) = K. \sum_{B,C \subseteq \Theta : B \cap C = A} m_1(B).m_2(C) \tag{4}$$

where

$$K^{-1} = 1 - \sum_{B,C \subseteq \Theta : B \cap C = \emptyset} m_1(B).m_2(C) \tag{5}$$

and

$$(m_1 \oplus m_2)(\emptyset) = 0. \tag{6}$$

K is called the normalization factor.

The conjunctive combination rule and Dempster's rule of combination are commutative and associative, so we can combine several belief functions iteratively and in any order.

2.3 Discounting

Reliability, i.e. our opinion about the 'value' of a sensor, varies from sensor to sensor. The idea is to weight more heavily the reports produced by the 'best' sensors and conversely for the 'bad' ones. For $\alpha \in [0,1]$, let $(1-\alpha)$ be the degree of 'confidence' we assign to the sensor. It can be encoded into a bba defined on the set {reliable, not reliable} such that [9]:

$$m(reliable) = 1 - \alpha \qquad \text{and} \qquad m(not\ reliable) = \alpha \tag{7}$$

Suppose the bba m on Θ represents the sensor report about the actual value of Θ. The result of combining the sensor report with the bba given in (7) is a new bba, denoted m^α, defined as:

$$m^\alpha(A) = (1-\alpha).m(A) \text{ for } A \subset \Theta \tag{8}$$

$$m^\alpha(\Theta) = \alpha + (1-\alpha).m(\Theta) \tag{9}$$

This operation is called a discounting by Shafer [6] and the coefficient α is called the discounting factor. The larger α, the closer m^α is from the vacuous belief function.

2.4 Pignistic Transformation

To make decisions in the TBM, we build a probability function $BetP$ on Θ, called the pignistic probability function, by applying the pignistic transformation [10]. It is defined by:

$$BetP(A) = \sum_{B \subseteq \Theta} \frac{|A \cap B|}{|B|} \frac{m(B)}{1 - m(\emptyset)}, \ \forall A \subseteq \Theta \tag{10}$$

3 Multisensor Data Fusion with the TBM

Multisensor systems can be used for the detection, localization and recognition of objects in a given area [1]. Handling information collected by different sensors requires an evidence gathering process, called a multisensor data fusion process, in order to get, hopefully, a 'better' information. The TBM offers a formal way to combine sensor data what is achieved by the conjunctive combination rule.

As mentioned before, sensors do not usually have the same level of reliability, so before pooling sensor reports (hence combining their belief functions), each belief function should be discounted to take into account the sensor reliability represented by the discounting factor. When these discounting factors are not known, they must be assessed. We propose two methods for such an assessment which correspond to the two different contexts mentioned in the introduction.

4 Evaluating Sensor's Reliability

4.1 Introduction

Finding an 'automatic' method to assess the sensor's reliability relative to a given problem requires information regarding the judgments given previously by the sensor concerning 'past' events (related to the same problem) for which the truth is known by us and not by the sensor. Then, a comparison between the truth and the sensor's judgments allows to derive the reliability of the sensor.

In practice, one domain where we can get this kind of information is represented by classification problems[1]. In such problems, we can get the sensor's reports on the classes to which an object belongs, a class otherwise well known by us. In the following subsections, we focus on classification problems. The method can easily be adapted to other domains, the underlying schema being quite general.

4.2 The Framework

Let T be a set composed of n objects denoted by o_j ($j = 1, 2, ..., n$). Each object has to belong to one of the possible classes relative to the given problem. The set of classes is defined by $\Theta = \{\theta_1, \theta_2, ..., \theta_p\}$. For each object o_j, we know its class, denoted c_j with $c_j \in \Theta$, and the sensor produces a bba, denoted $m^\Theta\{o_j\}$ on Θ, that represents its opinion on the actual value of c_j.

4.3 Assessing the Discounting Factor

The first method considers one sensor for which we want to assess its reliability, thus its discounting factor. This is done by comparing the bba produced by the sensor about the class of each of the n objects with their actual classes.

[1] Several classification methods have been developed using belief function basics like the one proposed by Denoeux [2], and the one proposed by Elouedi and al. [3].

If we knew the discounting factor α applicable to a sensor we would discount the bba it generates by the discounting factor. So we would compute the bba $m^{\Theta,\alpha}\{o_j\}$ using relations (8) and (9).

If we had to decide which class objects o_j belongs to, we would then compute the pignistic probability from $m^{\Theta,\alpha}\{o_j\}$. Let the result be denoted by $BetP^{\Theta,\alpha}\{o_j\}$. This probability function is then to be compared with the actual value c_j of object o_j. Let the indicator function δ be defined as $\delta_{j,i} = 1$ if $c_j = \theta_i$ and 0 otherwise.

The distance between the pignistic probability computed from the discounted sensor's report and the indicator function δ is used as a measure of the reliability of the sensor for what concerns object o_j, and their sum over the n objects is used as a measure of the overall reliability of the sensor. It is denoted $TotalDist$ and defined as:

$$TotalDist = \sum_{j=1}^{n} \sum_{i=1}^{p} (BetP^{\Theta,\alpha}\{o_j\}(\theta_i) - \delta_{j,i})^2$$

We then define the reliability of the sensor as $(1-\alpha \in [0,1])$ where α minimizes $TotalDist$, i.e., the α that makes the discounted opinions of the sensor as good as possible, thus that makes the values of $BetP^{\Theta,\alpha}\{o_j\}$ as close as possible to $\delta_{j,i}$.

4.4 Explicit Computation with Normalized Belief Functions

In the special but common case where all bbas are normalized (thus $m(\emptyset) = 0$), it is possible to explicitate the value of α from the initial bba $m^{\Theta}\{o_j\}$. Let $BetP^{\Theta}\{o_j\}$ be the pignistic probability function computed from $m^{\Theta}\{o_j\}$, hence before discounting. The solution for α is given in the next theorem.

Theorem 1. *Let a set of normalized bbas $m^{\Theta}\{o_j\}$ defined on the set of classes $\Theta = \{\theta_1, \ldots, \theta_p\}$ for objects $o_j, j = 1, \ldots, n$. Let the indicator function $\delta_{j,i} = 1$ if the object o_j belongs to the class θ_i, and 0 otherwise. The discounting factor α that minimizes:*

$$TotalDist = \sum_{j=1}^{n} \sum_{i=1}^{p} (BetP^{\Theta,\alpha}\{o_j\}(\theta_i) - \delta_{j,i})^2$$

where $BetP^{\Theta,\alpha}\{o_j\}$ is the pignistic probability function computed from the discounted bba $m^{\Theta,\alpha}\{o_j\}$, is given by:

$$\alpha = \min(1, \max(0, \frac{\sum_{j=1}^{n} \sum_{i=1}^{p} (\delta_{j,i} - BetP^{\Theta}\{o_j\}(\theta_i)).BetP^{\Theta}\{o_j\}(\theta_i)}{n/p - \sum_{j=1}^{n} \sum_{i=1}^{p} BetP^{\Theta}\{o_j\}(\theta_i)^2}))$$

Proof. Given $m^{\Theta}\{o_j\}$, we have:

$$\begin{aligned} m^{\Theta,\alpha}\{o_j\}(\theta) &= (1-\alpha)m^{\Theta}\{o_j\}(\theta) && \text{if } \theta \subset \Theta \\ &= (1-\alpha)m^{\Theta}\{o_j\}(\Theta) + \alpha && \text{if } \theta = \Theta \end{aligned}$$

The pignistic probability $BetP^{\Theta,\alpha}\{o_j\}$ computed from $m^{\Theta,\alpha}\{o_j\}$ can be expressed as a function of the pignistic probability $BetP^{\Theta}\{o_j\}$ computed directly from $m^{\Theta}\{o_j\}$. For simplicity sake, we omit the $\{o_j\}$ index hereafter. One has:

$$BetP^{\Theta}(\theta_i) = \sum_{\theta_i \in \theta} \frac{m^{\Theta}}{|\theta|}$$

$$\begin{aligned} BetP^{\Theta,\alpha}(\theta_i) &= \sum_{\theta_i \in \theta} \frac{m^{\Theta,\alpha}(\theta)}{|\theta|} \\ &= \sum_{\theta_i \in \theta} \frac{(1-\alpha)m^{\Theta}(\theta)}{|\theta|} + \alpha/p = (1-\alpha)BetP^{\Theta}(\theta) + \alpha/p \end{aligned}$$

For simplicity sake, we write $P_{ij} = BetP^{\Theta}\{o_j\}(\theta_i)$. The term to be minimized becomes:

$$TotalDist = \sum_{j=1}^{n} \sum_{i=1}^{p} (BetP^{\Theta,\alpha}\{o_j\}(\theta_i) - \delta_{ji})^2 = \sum_{j,i} ((1-\alpha)P_{ij} + \alpha/p - \delta_{ji})^2$$

Its extremum is reached when its derivative is null, hence when:

$$\begin{aligned} 0 &= \frac{d\ TotalDist}{d\alpha} \\ &= 2\sum_{j,i}((1-\alpha)P_{ij} + \alpha/p - \delta_{ji})(-P_{ij} + 1/p) && (11) \\ &\propto \sum_{j,i} -(1-\alpha)P_{ij}^2 - \alpha n/p + \sum_{j,i} \delta_{ji}P_{ij} + (1-\alpha)n/p + \alpha n/p - n/p && (12) \\ &= \sum_{j,i} -(1-\alpha)P_{ij}^2 - \alpha n/p + \sum_{j,i} \delta_{ji}P_{ij} && (13) \end{aligned}$$

$$\text{Thus, } \alpha = \frac{\sum_{j,i}(\delta_{ji} - P_{ij})P_{ij}}{n/p - \sum_{j,i} P_{ij}^2}$$

□

Once the discounting factors are computed for several sensors, the observed values can be used to order several sensors: the smaller the value the better the sensor. It could be used to select optimal sensors. It can also be used to discount the reports produced by the sensor in the future.

4.5 The Simplified Equivalent

Usually, probabilities are easier to understand than discounting factors. So one way to get a feeling of what represents the value α of a discounting factor, we consider a highly simplified case where there are just 2 objects that can be either a or b. Both are a's. You are sure that object 1 is a, but have a probability

$\pi \leq 0.5$ that object 2 is a and $1-\pi$ that it is b. So you are right for object 1 and quite wrong with object 2 (with probability $1-\pi$). If π was known, we could compute its related discounting factor by applying the previous relations. When π is unknown but α is known, we can compute the value of π that underlies α in our simplified schema. We have: $\alpha \in [0,1]$, compute

$$\pi = \frac{3 - 2\alpha - \sqrt{1 + 4\alpha - 4\alpha^2}}{4 - 4\alpha}$$

This is the value π that would produce α in the simplified schema where we deal with only two objects and two classes and where the sensor is only uncertain about the class of one object. This π represents the probability that the sensor is correct and that would induced a discounting factor equals to α.

4.6 Example 1

Suppose there are two sensors S_1, S_2 applied to classify aerial targets. The possible classes are: $\Theta = \{Airplane, Helicopter, Rocket\}$. In order to find the degree of reliability of these two sensors, table 1 presents their reports on the classes of 4 objects where their classes are known by us (a part of a learning set), but not by the sensors S_1, S_2. At the first row of the table, we have the actual class of each object, then we present the two sensors' bbas on the classes of these objects (since they do not know the truth).

Table 1. The sensors' bbas and the truth

Truth	Airplane	Helicopter	Airplane	Rocket
S_1	o_1	o_2	o_3	o_4
$\emptyset$	0	0	0	0
Airplane	0	0	0	0
Helicopter	0	0.5	0.4	0
Rocket	0.5	0.2	0	0
Airplane ∪ Helicopter	0	0	0	0
Airplane ∪ Rocket	0	0	0.6	0.6
Helicopter ∪ Rocket	0.3	0	0	0.4
Airplane ∪ Helicopter ∪ Rocket	0.2	0.3	0	0

S_2	o_1	o_2	o_3	o_4
$\emptyset$	0	0	0	0
Airplane	0	0.3	0.2	0
Helicopter	0	0	0	0
Rocket	0	0	0	0
Airplane ∪ Helicopter	0.7	0.4	0	0
Airplane ∪ Rocket	0	0	0	0
Helicopter ∪ Rocket	0	0	0.6	1
Airplane ∪ Helicopter ∪ Rocket	0.3	0.3	0.2	0

Assume that the discounting factors assigned to the two sensors S_1 and S_2 are respectively α_1 and α_2.

Let's focus on the first sensor, we have to update the bbas relative to the objects o_1, o_2, o_3 and o_4 by taking into account α_1. We get:

$m_{S_1}^{\Theta,\alpha_1}\{o_1\}(Rocket) = 0.5(1-\alpha_1)$, $m_{S_1}^{\Theta,\alpha_1}\{o_1\}(Helicopter \cup Rocket) = 0.3(1-\alpha_1)$, $m_{S_1}^{\Theta,\alpha_1}\{o_1\}(\Theta) = 0.2 + 0.8\alpha_1$

$m_{S_1}^{\Theta,\alpha_1}\{o_2\}(Helicopter) = 0.5(1-\alpha_1)$, $m_{S_1}^{\Theta,\alpha_1}\{o_2\}(Rocket) = 0.2(1-\alpha_1)$, $m_{S_1}^{\Theta,\alpha_1}\{o_2\}(\Theta) = 0.3 + 0.7\alpha_1$

$m_{S_1}^{\Theta,\alpha_1}\{o_3\}(Helicopter) = 0.4(1-\alpha_1)$, $m_{S_1}^{\Theta,\alpha_1}\{o_3\}(Airplane \cup Rocket) = 0.6(1-\alpha_1)$, $m_{S_1}^{\Theta,\alpha_1}\{o_3\}(\Theta) = \alpha_1$

$m_{S_1}^{\Theta,\alpha_1}\{o_4\}(Airplane \cup Rocket) = 0.6(1-\alpha_1)$, $m_{S_1}^{\Theta,\alpha_1}\{o_4\}(Helicopter \cup Rocket) = 0.4(1-\alpha_1)$, $m_{S_1}^{\Theta,\alpha_1}\{o_4\}(\Theta) = \alpha_1$

The corresponding discounted $BetP$ relative to the first sensor is summarized in this following table:

Table 2. S_1's discounted BetPs

S_1	o_1	o_2	o_3	o_4
Airplane	$0.07 - 0.27\alpha_1$	$0.10 - 0.23\alpha_1$	$0.30 - 0.03\alpha_1$	$0.30 - 0.03\alpha_1$
Helicopter	$0.22 - 0.12\alpha_1$	$0.60 + 0.27\alpha_1$	$0.40 + 0.07\alpha_1$	$0.20 - 0.13\alpha_1$
Rocket	$0.72 + 0.38\alpha_1$	$0.30 - 0.03\alpha_1$	$0.30 - 0.03\alpha_1$	$0.50 + 0.17\alpha_1$

For example the computation of $BetP_{S_1}^{\Theta,\alpha_1}\{o_1\}(Helicopter)$ is done as follows: $BetP_{S_1}^{\Theta,\alpha_1}\{o_1\}(Helicopter) = \frac{0.3(1-\alpha_1)}{2} + \frac{0.2+0.8\alpha_1}{3} = 0.22 - 0.12\alpha_1$

Using the different values of $BetPs$, the whole distance relative to the sensor S_1 will be equal to:

$$TotalDist = \sum_{j=1}^{4} \sum_{i=1}^{3} (BetP^{\Theta,\alpha_1}\{o_j\}(\theta_i) - \delta_{j,i})^2$$

Hence

$$TotalDist = 0.41\alpha_1^2 - 0.56\alpha_1 + 2.81;$$

Minimizing $TotalDist$ under the constraint $0 \leq \alpha_1 \leq 1$ gives as a result $\alpha_1 = 0.68$. Hence, the discounting factor to be given to sensor S_1 by taking into account its opinions on the classes of the objects o_j, $j = 1, 2, 3, 4$, is equal to 0.68.

Applying the same procedure for the beliefs given by the second sensor (S_2), we get $\alpha_2 = 0.52$ as the discounting factor of this sensor. Thus sensor S_2 is (a little) better than sensor S_1.

Just to get an idea about what represents the two discounting factors (see section 4.5), their equivalent in the highly simplified schema of 2 objects produce

π values of 0.21 and 0.28, respectively, what can be understood as 'the sensors are really not good, and the second is just a little better then the first'. This is indeed what the data also show.

5 Tuning Sensors' Reports

Evaluating sensors within this second framework is based on taking into account the sensors' bbas together and not independently as we have done in the previous section.

The idea is to build the best predictor from a set of available sensors. Bad ones should be discounted more than good ones. The present method is applicable when the main objective is to get the best aggregated report induced from those given by the sensors.

This requires assessing the 'best' values of the discounting factors to be allocated to each sensor knowing that their discounted 'beliefs' will be merged.

The 'best' discounting factors are those that will make the pignistic probabilities induced by the conjunctive combination of the discounted bba's as close as possible from the actual values, just as done in the previous section. Such process is named tuning sensors' reports.

In order to derive the optimal set of discounting factors, we apply the following steps. Suppose we knew the discounting factors, we would then:

- For each bba $m^{\Theta}_{S_k}\{o_j\}$, discount it by its discounting factor α_k given to the sensor S_k. We get $m^{\Theta,\alpha_k}_{S_k}\{o_j\}$. This process will be applied for the bba given by the sensor for each object.
- For each object o_j $(j = 1, ..., n)$, combine the different discounted bba's by applying the conjunctive rule. We get:

$$m^{\Theta}\{o_j\} = m^{\Theta,\alpha_1}_{S_1}\{o_j\} \circledcap .... \circledcap m^{\Theta,\alpha_k}_{S_k}\{o_j\} \tag{14}$$

  $m^{\Theta}\{o_j\}$ is a joint bba representing the induced belief on the class to which object o_j belongs computed by taking into account the data collected from all the sensors.
- Compute the corresponding $BetP^{\Theta}\{o_j\}$ (relative to the bba $m^{\Theta}\{o_j\}$) representing the pignistic probability on the class of object o_j.
- For each object o_j, compute the distance between $BetP^{\Theta}\{o_j\}$ and the real class of o_j. This distance is defined by:

$$Dist\{o_j\} = \sum_{i=1}^{p} (BetP^{\Theta,\alpha}\{o_j\}(\theta_i) - \delta_{j,i})^2$$

  where $\delta_{j,i} = 1$ if $c_j = \theta_i$ and 0 otherwise.
- Compute $TotalDist$ as follows:

$$TotalDist = \sum_{j=1}^{n} Dist\{o_j\} \tag{15}$$

This variable depends on the discounting factors $\alpha_1, \alpha_2, \ldots, \alpha_k$.

- In order to find the optimal discounting factors, we have to minimize $TotalDist$ on the α's under the constraints $0 \leq \alpha_\nu \leq 1,\ \forall \nu \in \{1,..,k\}$

Example 2. Let's use the same data in the example 1 (see table 1). Let's apply our second method on the two sensors' reports by assuming that we want to get the merged report.

Once S_1'bbas and S_2'bbas are discounted, we get respectively $m_{S_1}^{\Theta,\alpha_1}\{o_j\}$ and $m_{S_2}^{\Theta,\alpha_2}\{o_j\}$ where $j = 1, 2, 3, 4$, which are linear functions of the discounting factors. For each object o_j,we compute the joint bba $m^\Theta\{o_j\}$:

$$m^\Theta\{o_j\} = m_{S_1}^{\Theta,\alpha_1}\{o_j\} \textcircled{\cap} m_{S_2}^{\Theta,\alpha_2}\{o_j\}$$

where the α terms are at most of the form $\prod_{i=1,\ldots,I} \alpha_i$ where I is the number of sensors ($I = 2$ in the present case).

The corresponding discounted $BetPs$ relative to the these bbas are also linear functions of the same product terms. The value of $Dist\{o_j\}$ relative to the objects, as wells as $TotalDist$ are quadratic functions of the previous product terms.

So its minimization on the α_i is very simple and can be achieved by any minimization program. Even when we work more than two sensors, any minimization program can give the different values of α.

In the present case, $\alpha_1 = 0.28$ and $\alpha_2 = 0.12$. It should be enhanced that the α coefficients computed in this second method should not be assimilated to those computed with the first one. Here we want the α so that the multisensor is 'optimal', whereas in the first method, we compute α in order to evaluate the individual sensor quality.

6 Conclusion

In the TBM, degrees of reliability to give to sensors are represented by discounting factors. In this paper, we have presented one method for assessing these discounting factors in a classification context where we to have at our disposal a learning set where the classes of the object are perfectly known and when each sensor is considered alone.

We have also present a tuning method by which each sensor in a group of sensors is partially discounted so that the overall set of sensors is optimal.

These methods are presented by studying a classification problem. They can easily be extended to other problems of prediction. All that is required is a learning set and a distance between the prediction and the actual values.

We have presented operational methods to assess the discounting factors in two contexts. It will be useful for any problem of multisensor data fusion [14].

References

1. Ayoun, A., Smets,P.: Data association in multi-target detection using the transferable model. Intern. J. Intell. Systems, (to appear) (2001)
2. Denoeux, T.: A k-nearest neighbor classification rule based on Dempster-Shafer theory. IEEE Transactions on Systems, Man, and Cybernetics, Vol 25, N5, May (1995) 804–813
3. Elouedi, Z., Mellouli, K., Smets, P.: Classification with belief decision trees. the proceedings of the Ninth International Conference on Artificial Intelligence: Methodology, Systems, Applications, AIMSA'2000 (2000) 80–90
4. Guan, J. W., Bell, D. A.: Discounting and Combination Operations in evidential Reasoning. Proceedings of the Ninth Conference on Uncertainty in Artificial Intelligence, (1993) 80–90.
5. Ling, X., Rudd, W. G.: Combining Opinions From Several Experts. Applied Artificial Intelligence **3** (1989), 439–452,
6. Shafer, G.: A mathematical theory of evidence. Princeton University Press (1976)
7. Shafer, G.: The Combination of Evidence. International Journal of Intelligent Systems **1**, (1986) 155–179
8. Smets, P.: The combination of evidence in the Transferable. Belief Model, IEEE Transactions on Pattern Analysis and Machine Intelligence **12**, (1990) 321–344
9. Smets, P.: The transferable belief model for expert judgments and reliability problems. Analysis and Management of uncertainty: Theory and Applications B.M. Ayyub, M.M. Gupta and L.N. Kanal (editors), Elsevier Science Publishers B.V. (1992)
10. Smets, P., Kennes, R.: The transferable belief model. Artificial Intelligence **66** (1994) 191–234
11. Smets, P.: The transferable belief model for quantified belief representation. D.M. Gabbay and Ph. Smets (eds.) Handbook of Defeasible Reasoning and Uncertainty Management Systems **1** Kluwer Doordrecht (1998) 267–301
12. Smets, P.: The Application of the transferable belief Model to Diagnostic Problems Int. J. Intelligent Systems **13** (1998) 127–158
13. Smets,P.: Practical Uses of Belief Functions. Laskey K. B. and Prade H. (eds.) Uncertainty in Artificial Intelligence **15** UAI99 (1999) 612–621
14. Waltz, E., Llinas, J.: Multisensor Data Fusion. Artech House, Boston, (1990)
15. L. M. Zouhal and T. Denoeux: An evidence-theoretic k-NN rule with parameter optimization. IEEE Transactions on Systems, Man and Cybernetics C, **28** (2) (1998) 263–271.

Coarsening Approximations of Belief Functions

Amel Ben Yaghlane[1], Thierry Denœux[2], and Khaled Mellouli[1]

[1] Institut Supérieur de Gestion de Tunis,
41 Avenue de la liberté, cité Bouchoucha, 2000 Le Bardo - Tunis - Tunisia
byaghlan@planet.tn, khaled.mellouli@ihec.rnu.tn
[2] Université de Technologie de Compiègne
UMR CNRS 6599 Heudiasyc
BP 20529 - F-60205 Compiègne cedex - France
Thierry.Denoeux@hds.utc.fr

Abstract. A method is proposed for reducing the size of a frame of discernment, in such a way that the loss of information content in a set of belief functions is minimized. This approach allows to compute strong inner and outer approximations which can be combined efficiently using the Fast Möbius Transform algorithm.

1 Introduction

The Dempster-Shafer theory of Belief Functions (BF's) is now widely accepted as a rich and flexible framework for representing and reasoning with imperfect information. The concept of belief function subsumes those of probability and possibility measures, making the theory very general. Situations of weak knowledge and heterogeneous information sources are easily modeled within this theory, making it quite suitable in many application domains such as medical diagnosis, sensor fusion and pattern recognition [14].

This generality, however, has a cost in terms of computational complexity. A BF (or, equivalently, a mass function) assigns a number to each of the 2^n subsets of the frame of discernment Ω (with $|\Omega| = n$), with $2^n - 1$ degrees of freedom, which is much larger that what is needed to specify a probability or a possibility measure. Although BF's as elicited from experts or inferred from observation data are usually constrained to be of a simple form, the fusion of several BF's using the Dempster's rule of combination almost inevitably increases the number of focal sets (i.e., subsets of Ω with a positive mass of belief), resulting in high storage and computational requirements for large-scale problems.

The algorithmic complexity of combining several BF's has been studied from a theoretical point of view by Orponen [10], who proved that the problem is $\#P$ complete. Recently, Wilson [16] provided a very complete review of algorithmic issues related to the manipulation of BF's. Currently, two algorithms exist for computing the conjunctive combination $m_1 \cap m_2$ of two mass functions m_1 and m_2 (similar methods hold for the disjunctive combination):

– the mass-based algorithm, initially sketched by Shafer, involves considering each focal set A of m_1, each focal set B of m_2, and assigning the mass

S. Benferhat and P. Besnard (Eds.): ECSQARU 2001, LNAI 2143, pp. 362–373, 2001.

$m_1(A)m_2(B)$ to the set $A \cap B$. Using this method, the combination can be performed in time proportional to $n|\mathcal{F}(m_1)||\mathcal{F}(m_2)|$, where $\mathcal{F}(m_i)$ denotes the number of focal sets of m_i $(i = 1, 2)$. The time needed for the combination of K BF's $m_1, \ldots, m_K$ depends on the particular structure of the mass functions, and is at worst roughly proportional to $n \prod_{i=1}^{K} |\mathcal{F}(m_i)|$, as shown by Wilson [16].
- the Fast Möbius Transform (FMT) method [8] converts each mass function m_i into its associated commonality function q_i; the product of these functions is computed, and the result is converted back into a mass function. The algorithm takes time proportional to $Kn^2 2^n$.

The choice of one of these methods depends on the structure of the mass functions. As remarked by Wilson, if the number of focal sets of the combined belief function is much small than 2^n, then the mass-based method is likely to be faster. However, this is generally not known in advance. If one of the BF's has a number of focal sets close to 2^n, then the FMT method is likely to be better. However, this method becomes impractical when Ω has more than 15 to 20 elements.

When the combination of several BF's cannot be computed exactly, one has to resort to stochastic or deterministic approximation procedures [16]. Since the mass-based method for combining BF's is the most widely used, most deterministic methods (which are exclusively considered here) have been designed with the aim of reducing the number of focal elements. This is true, in particular, for the summarization method initially introduced by Lowrance et al. [6], and for the more sophisticated methods proposed subsequently [15] [1] [5] [11] [2].

In this paper, a different approach is investigated. Instead of reducing the number of focal elements, we propose to reduce the size of the frame of discernment, which can be expected to drastically decrease the computing time of the FMT combination method, and can even make it applicable to find reasonable approximations in the case of large-size problems. Given a set of BF's, we propose to find a coarsening of the frame Ω that will preserve as much as possible of the information content of the belief functions. This approach allows to compute inner and outer approximations, from which lower and upper bounds for the combined belief values can be derived.

The following section summarizes the background definitions and results needed in the sequel. Our approximation method is then described in Section 3, and a simulation example is presented in Section 4.

2 Background

2.1 Basic Concepts

The main concepts of evidence theory are only summarized here. More details can be found in Refs. [12] and [13]. Let Ω denote a finite set called the frame of discernment. A mass function, or *basic belief assignment*(bba) is a function $m : 2^\Omega \to [0, 1]$ verifying:

$$\sum_{A \subseteq \Omega} m(A) = 1. \tag{1}$$

Each mass of belief $m(A)$ measures the amount of belief that is exactly committed to A. A bba m such that $m(\emptyset) = 0$ is said to be normal. This condition will not be imposed here. The subsets A of Ω such that $m(A) > 0$ are called *focal sets* of m. Let $\mathcal{F}(m) \subseteq 2^{\Omega}$ denote the set of focal sets of m.

The *belief function* induced by m is a function bel : $2^{\Omega} \rightarrow [0,1]$, defined as:

$$\mathrm{bel}(A) = \sum_{\emptyset \neq B \subseteq A} m(B) \tag{2}$$

for all $A \subseteq \Omega$. bel(A) represents the amount of support given to A.

The *plausibility function* associated with a bba m is a function pl : $2^{\Omega} \rightarrow [0,1]$, defined as:

$$\mathrm{pl}(A) = \sum_{\emptyset \neq B \cap A} m(B) \qquad \forall A \subseteq \Omega. \tag{3}$$

pl(A) represents the potential amount of support that could be given to A.

Given two bba's m_1 and m_2 defined over the same frame of discernment Ω and induced by two distinct pieces of evidence, we can combine them in two ways using the conjunctive or the disjunctive rules of combination [13] defined, respectively, as:

$$(m_1 \textcircled{\cap} m_2)(A) = \sum_{B \cap C = A} m_1(B) m_2(C) \tag{4}$$

$$(m_1 \textcircled{\cup} m_2)(A) = \sum_{B \cup C = A} m_1(B) m_2(C) \tag{5}$$

for all $A \subseteq \Omega$. The choice of one of these combination rules is related to the reliability of the two sources. In fact, if we know that both sources of information are fully reliable, then we combine them conjunctively. However, if we only know that at least one of the two sources is reliable, then we combine them disjunctively.

The conjunctive and disjunctive rules can be conveniently expressed by means of the commonality function q and the implicability function b, defined, respectively, as

$$q(A) = \sum_{A \subseteq B} m(B) \tag{6}$$

and

$$b(A) = \mathrm{bel}(A) + m(\emptyset) \tag{7}$$

for all $A \subseteq \Omega$. If $q_1 \textcircled{\cap} q_2$ denotes the commonality function associated to $m_1 \textcircled{\cap} m_2$, and $b_1 \textcircled{\cup} b_2$ denotes the implicability function associated to $m \textcircled{\cup} m_2$, we have the following simple relations:

$$q_1 \textcircled{\cap} q_2 = q_1 q_2 \tag{8}$$

$$b_1 \textcircled{\cup} b_2 = b_1 b_2 \tag{9}$$

The importance of this result arises from the fact that the functions m, q and b (as well as bel and pl) are equivalent representations, in the sense that, given any of these functions, it is possible to recover all the others. The conversion between these functions can be efficiently done using the FMT algorithm [8] in time proportional to $n^2 2^n$ [16]. Relations (8) and (9) provide the basis for the FMT-based method for combining BF's, which consists in transforming the BF's or the bba's to q or b, computing the product, and converting back the result into a mass or a belief function. In contrast, the more traditional mass-based approach relies exclusively on Eqs (4) and (5).

2.2 Coarsenings and Refinements

In applying the BF framework to a real-world problem, the definition of the frame of discernment is a crucial step. As remarked by Shafer [12], the degree of "granularity" of the frame is always a matter of convention, as any element ω of Ω representing a "state of nature" could always be split into several possibilities. Hence, it is fundamental to examine how a BF defined on a frame may be expressed in a finer or, conversely, in a coarser frame.

Let Ω and Θ denote two finite sets. A mapping $\rho : 2^\Theta \to 2^\Omega$ is called a *refining* if it verifies the following properties:

1. The set $\{\rho(\{\theta\}), \theta \in \Theta\} \subseteq 2^\Omega$ is a partition of Ω.
2. For all $A \subseteq \Theta$, we have

$$\rho(A) = \bigcup_{\theta \in A} \rho(\{\theta\}) \tag{10}$$

Following the terminology introduced by Shafer, the set Θ is then called a *coarsening* of Ω, and Ω is called a *refinement* of Θ.

Note that defining a coarsening of a frame Ω is formally equivalent to defining a partition of Ω. Let Θ be such a partition. The function $\rho : 2^\Theta \to 2^\Omega$ such that $\rho(\{\theta\}) = \theta$ for all $\theta \in \Theta$, and verifying (10) is a refining of Θ, and Θ is a coarsening of Ω.

A bba m^Θ defined on a frame Θ may easily be carried to a refinement Ω by means of the vacuous extension, which transfers the mass $m^\Theta(A)$ to $\rho(A)$, for all $A \subseteq \Theta$ (in the following, the superscript of a bba will always indicate its domain). The resulting bba m^Ω on Ω is then defined as

$$m^\Omega(B) = \begin{cases} m^\Theta(A), & \text{if } B = \rho(A) \quad \text{for some } A \subseteq \Theta \\ 0, & \text{otherwise.} \end{cases} \tag{11}$$

The inverse operation, i.e., carrying a bba m^Ω to a coarsening Θ of Ω is not so easy because a refining $\rho : 2^\Theta \to 2^\Omega$ is not, in general, onto; there are usually subsets A of Ω which are not "discerned" by Θ and, hence, are not equal to $\rho(B)$ for any $B \subseteq \Theta$ [12]. In order to associate a subset of Θ with each subset A of Ω, an *inner reduction* $\underline{\theta}$ and an *outer reduction* $\overline{\theta}$ may be defined, respectively, as functions from 2^Ω to 2^Θ, such that:

$$\underline{\theta}(A) = \{\theta \in \Theta | \rho(\{\theta\}) \subseteq A\} \tag{12}$$

$$\overline{\theta}(A) = \{\theta \in \Theta | \rho(\{\theta\}) \cap A \neq \emptyset\} \tag{13}$$

for all $A \subseteq \Omega$. Hence, the mass $m^\Omega(A)$ given to $A \subseteq \Omega$ by a bba m^Ω can be transferred either to $\underline{\theta}(A)$, or to $\overline{\theta}(A)$. This leads to the following definitions:

$$\underline{m}^\Theta(B) = \sum_{\{A \subseteq \Omega, B = \underline{\theta}(A)\}} m^\Omega(A) \quad \forall B \subseteq \Theta \tag{14}$$

$$\overline{m}^\Theta(B) = \sum_{\{A \subseteq \Omega, B = \overline{\theta}(A)\}} m^\Omega(A) \quad \forall B \subseteq \Theta. \tag{15}$$

The bba's $\underline{m}^\Theta$ and $\overline{m}^\Theta$ will be called, respectively, the inner and the outer reduction of m^Ω ($\overline{m}^\Theta$ is called the restriction of m^Ω par Shafer [12, p. 126]; the definition of $\underline{m}^\Theta$ is, to our knowledge, new).

To simplify the manipulation of expressions when changing frames, let us introduce the following definition.

Definition 1 *Let Ω_1 and Ω_2 be two finite sets, φ an application from 2^{Ω_1} to 2^{Ω_2}, m^{Ω_1} a bba on Ω_1, and m^{Ω_2} a bba on Ω_2. We say that m^{Ω_2} is the image of m^{Ω_1} by φ, and we note $m^{\Omega_2} = \varphi(m^{\Omega_1})$, if*

$$m^{\Omega_2}(A) = \sum_{\{B \subseteq \Omega_1, \varphi(B) = A\}} m^{\Omega_1}(B)$$

for all $A \subseteq \Omega_2$.

According to Def. 1, the vacuous extension of m^Θ in Ω may be noted $m^\Omega = \rho(m^\Theta)$, and Eqs (14) and (15) may be rewritten as $\underline{m}^\Theta = \underline{\theta}(m^\Omega)$ and $\overline{m}^\Theta = \overline{\theta}(m^\Omega)$.

2.3 Inclusion of Belief Functions

Another notion of interest is that of strong inclusion of bba's [3]. Let m and m' be two BS's with focal elements $\mathcal{F}(m) = \{F_1, \ldots, F_p\}$ and $\mathcal{F}(m') = \{F'_1, \ldots, F'_{p'}\}$. Then m is said to be strongly included in m', or to be a *specialization* of m' (noted $m \subseteq m'$), iff there exists a non-negative matrix W with entries w_{ij} ($i = 1, \ldots, p; j = 1, \ldots, p'$) such that

$$\sum_{j=1}^{p'} w_{ij} = m(F_i), \quad i = 1, \ldots, p, \tag{16}$$

$$\sum_{i=1}^{p} w_{ij} = m'(F'_j), \quad j = 1, \ldots, p' \tag{17}$$

and $w_{ij} > 0 \Rightarrow F_i \subseteq F'_j$. The relationship between m and m' may be seen as a transfer of mass from each focal element F_i of m to supersets $F'_j \supseteq F_i$, the quantity w_{ij} denoting the part of $m(F_i)$ transferred to F'_j. If $m \subseteq m'$, then we have (with obvious notations) $\mathrm{pl} \leq \mathrm{pl}'$ and $b' \leq b$, but the reverse is not true.

An approximation $\widehat{m}^-$ (resp. $\widehat{m}^+$) of a bba m is called a strong inner (resp. outer) approximation if $\widehat{m}^- \subseteq m$ (resp. $m \subseteq \widehat{m}^+$). Given strong inner and outer approximations of several BF's, it is possible to obtain lower and upper bounds for the belief and the plausibility values of the combined BF [3][2]. Methods for constructing such approximations were propose by Dubois and Prade [4] in a possibilistic setting, and by Denœux [2] using an approach based on the clustering of focal sets.

3 Coarsening Approximations of Belief Functions

In this section, we propose a new heuristic method for constructing strong inner and outer approximations of BF's. Our method consists in finding a coarsening Θ of the initial frame Ω such that the approximating BF can be represented exactly in Θ. We first present the basic principle and the algorithm in the case of a single BF, and then extend the method to the simultaneous approximation of several BF's.

3.1 Basic Principle

Main result. Let m^Ω denote a bba on Ω, Θ a coarsening of Ω, ρ the refining from 2^Θ to 2^Ω, and $\underline{\theta}$ and $\overline{\theta}$ the associated inner and outer reduction functions. Let $\underline{m}^\Theta$ and $\overline{m}^\Theta$ denote the inner and outer reductions of m^Ω as defined by Eqs (14) and (15), and let $\underline{m}^\Omega$ and $\overline{m}^\Omega$ be the vacuous extensions of $\underline{m}^\Theta$ and $\overline{m}^\Theta$, respectively, on Ω. We thus have

$$\underline{m}^\Omega = \rho(\underline{m}^\Theta) = \rho \circ \underline{\theta}(m^\Omega) \tag{18}$$

$$\overline{m}^\Omega = \rho(\overline{m}^\Theta) = \rho \circ \overline{\theta}(m^\Omega) \tag{19}$$

Theorem 1 *$\underline{m}^\Omega$ and $\overline{m}^\Omega$ are, respectively, strong inner and outer approximations of m^Ω: $\underline{m}^\Omega \subseteq m^\Omega \subseteq \overline{m}^\Omega$*

Proof: We have, by construction,

$$\underline{m}^\Omega(A) = \sum_{\{B \subseteq \Omega, A = \rho \circ \underline{\theta}(B)\}} m^\Omega(B) \quad \forall A \subseteq \Omega \tag{20}$$

$$\overline{m}^\Omega(A) = \sum_{\{B \subseteq \Omega, A = \rho \circ \overline{\theta}(B)\}} m^\Omega(B) \quad \forall A \subset \Omega \tag{21}$$

From Theorem 6.3 in [12, p.118], we have $\rho(\underline{\theta}(B)) \subseteq B$ for all $B \subseteq \Omega$. Hence, the mass $\underline{m}^\Omega(A)$ is the sum of masses $m^\Omega(B)$ initially attached to supersets of A, which implies that $\underline{m}^\Omega \subseteq m^\Omega$.

Similarly, $B \subseteq \rho(\overline{\theta}(B))$ for all $B \subset \Omega$, which implies that the mass $\overline{m}^\Omega(A)$ is the sum of masses $m^\Omega(B)$ initially attached to subsets of A, which implies that $m^\Omega \subseteq \overline{m}^\Omega$. QED

Matrix representation of bba's. A very simple construction of $\underline{m}^{\Omega}$ and $\overline{m}^{\Omega}$ for a given coarsening Θ can be obtained using the following representation. Let us assume that the frame $\Omega = \{\omega_1, \dots \omega_n\}$ has n elements, and the bba m^{Ω} under consideration has p focal sets: $\mathcal{F}(m^{\Omega}) = \{A_1, \dots, A_p\}$. One can represent the bba m^{Ω} by a pair $(\mathbf{m}^{\Omega}, \mathbf{F}^{\Omega})$ where $\mathbf{m}^{\Omega}$ is the p-dimensional vector of masses $\mathbf{m}^{\Omega} = (m^{\Omega}(A_1), \dots, (m^{\Omega}(A_p))$ and $\mathbf{F}^{\Omega}$ is a $p \times n$ binary matrix such that

$$\mathbf{F}^{\Omega}_{ij} = A_i(\omega_j) = \begin{cases} 1, & \text{if } \omega_j \in A_i \\ 0, & \text{otherwise.} \end{cases}$$

where $A_i(\cdot)$ denotes the indicator function of focal set A_i.

This representation is similar to an (objects $\times$ attributes) binary data matrix as commonly encountered in data analysis. Here, each focal set corresponds to an object, and each element of the frame corresponds to an attribute. Each object A_i has a weight $m^{\Omega}(A_i)$. Since a coarsening is inherently equivalent to a partition of Ω, finding a suitable coarsening is actually a problem of classifying the columns of data matrix $\mathbf{F}$, which is a classical clustering problem (see, e.g. [7]). Note that, in contrast, the clustering approximation method introduced by Denœux [2] is based on the classification of the lines of $\mathbf{F}$.

To see how the bba's $\underline{m}^{\Theta}$, $\overline{m}^{\Theta}$, $\underline{m}^{\Omega}$, $\overline{m}^{\Omega}$ can be constructed from $\mathbf{F}$, let us denote by $P = \{I_1, \dots, I_c\}$ the partition of $N_n = \{1, \dots, n\}$ corresponding to the coarsening $\Theta = \{\theta_1, \dots, \theta_c\}$, i.e.,

$$\theta_r = \{\omega_j, j \in I_r\} \qquad r = 1, \dots, c.$$

Let $(\underline{\mathbf{m}}^{\Theta}, \underline{\mathbf{F}}^{\Theta})$ denote the matrix representation of $\underline{m}^{\Theta}$. Matrix $\underline{\mathbf{F}}^{\Theta}$ may be obtained from $\mathbf{F}^{\Omega}$ by merging the columns $\mathbf{F}^{\Omega}_{\cdot j}$ for $j \in I_r$, and replacing them by their minimum:

$$\underline{\mathbf{F}}^{\Theta}_{i,r} = \min_{j \in I_r} \mathbf{F}^{\Omega}_{i,j} \quad \forall i, r \tag{22}$$

and we have $\underline{\mathbf{m}}^{\Theta} = \mathbf{m}^{\Omega}$. The justification for this is that the focal elements of $\underline{m}^{\Theta}$ are the sets $\underline{\theta}(A_i)$, and $\theta \in \underline{\theta}(A_i)$ iff $\rho(\theta) \subseteq A_i$, where ρ is the refining associated to Θ.

similarly, if $(\overline{\mathbf{m}}^{\Theta}, \overline{\mathbf{F}}^{\Theta})$ denotes the matrix representation of $\overline{m}^{\Theta}$, we have

$$\overline{\mathbf{F}}^{\Theta}_{i,r} = \max_{j \in I_r} \mathbf{F}^{\Omega}_{i,j} \quad \forall i, r \tag{23}$$

and $\overline{\mathbf{m}}^{\Theta} = \mathbf{m}^{\Omega}$.

The matrix representations of $\underline{m}^{\Omega}$ and $\overline{m}^{\Omega}$, the vacuous extensions of $\underline{m}^{\Theta}$ and $\overline{m}^{\Theta}$, are then obtained as:

$$\underline{\mathbf{F}}^{\Omega}_{i,j} = \underline{\mathbf{F}}^{\Theta}_{i,r} \quad \forall j \in I_r \tag{24}$$

$$\overline{\mathbf{F}}^{\Omega}_{i,j} = \overline{\mathbf{F}}^{\Theta}_{i,r} \quad \forall j \in I_r \tag{25}$$

and $\underline{\mathbf{m}}^{\Omega} = \overline{\mathbf{m}}^{\Omega} = \mathbf{m}^{\Omega}$.

3.2 Clustering Algorithm

As shown above, given a coarsening Θ of a frame of discernment Ω and a basic belief assignment m^Ω, we can define strong inner and outer approximations $\underline{m}^\Omega$ and $\overline{m}^\Omega$. It is clear that the quality of these approximations depends on the coarsenings considered, then how to choose these coarsenings so as to obtain good approximations of m^Ω?

To answer this question, we propose to use a measure of information allowing us to reduce the size of the frame of discernment while *retaining as much information as possible* from the original belief function. Several approaches have been proposed to measure the information contained in a piece of evidence [9]. Among these approaches, we will use the *generalized cardinality* [4,2] defined as:

$$|m| = \sum_{i=1}^{p} m(A_i)|A_i|, \tag{26}$$

where A_i, $i = 1, \ldots, p$ are the focal sets of m. The bba m is all the more imprecise (and contains all the less information) that $|m|$ is large.

It follows from Theorem 1 and the definition of strong inclusion that

$$|\underline{m}^\Omega| \leq |m^\Omega| \leq |\overline{m}^\Omega|$$

Hence, a way to keep $\underline{m}^\Omega$ and $\underline{m}^\Omega$ as "close" as possible to m^Ω is to minimize the increase of cardinality from m^Ω to $\overline{m}^\Omega$ (which correspond to a loss of information), and to minimize the decrease of cardinality from m^Ω to $\underline{m}^\Omega$ (corresponding to meaningless information).

More precisely, let us denote by $\mathcal{P}_c$ the set of all partitions of N_n in c classes ($c < n$). As shown above, each element of $\mathcal{P}_c$ corresponds to a coarsening of Ω with c elements. The coarsening yielding the "best" (least specific) inner approximation corresponds to the partition $\underline{P}_c$ defined as:

$$\underline{P}_c = \arg \min_{P \in \mathcal{P}_c} \Delta(m^\Omega, \underline{m}^\Omega)$$

with $\Delta(m^\Omega, \underline{m}^\Omega) = |m^\Omega| - |\underline{m}^\Omega|$. Similarly, the partition $\overline{P}_c$ yielding the best (most specific) outer approximation is defined as

$$\overline{P}_c = \arg \min_{P \in \mathcal{P}_c} \Delta(\overline{m}^\Omega, m^\Omega).$$

We are thus searching for the best coarsening over all possible partitions of Ω into c clusters. Unfortunately, the number of possible partitions is huge, and exploring all of them is not computationally tractable. Hierarchical clustering [7] is a heuristic approach for constructing a sequence of nested partitions of a given set. In our case, this approach will consist in aggregating sequentially pairs of elements of Ω until the desired size of the coarsened frame of discernment is reached. At each step, the two elements whose aggregation results in the best value of the criterion will be selected.

More precisely, let $(\mathbf{m}^\Omega, \mathbf{F}^\Omega)$ denote the matrix representation of m^Ω, and suppose that we are looking for the coarsening with $n-1$ elements corresponding to the "best" inner approximation. The aggregation of elements ω_j and ω_k of the frame corresponds to the fusion of columns j and k of $\mathbf{F}^\Omega$ using the minimum operator. In this process, the number of 1's in each line i of matrix $\mathbf{F}^\Omega$ is decreased by one if either $\omega_j \in A_i$ and $\omega_k \notin A_i$, or $\omega_k \in A_i$ and $\omega_j \notin A_i$. Hence, the decrease of cardinality is

$$\delta(\omega_k, \omega_l) = \Delta(m^\Omega, \underline{m}^\Omega) = \sum_{i=1}^{p} \mathbf{m}_i |\mathbf{F}^\Omega_{ij} - \mathbf{F}^\Omega_{il}| \tag{27}$$

Note that $\delta(\omega_k, \omega_l)$ can be interpreted as a degree of dissimilarity between ω_j and ω_l. The hierarchical clustering algorithm can then be described as follows:

- Given: the bba $(\mathbf{m}^\Omega, \mathbf{F}^\Omega)$
- Compute the dissimilarity matrix $D = (\delta(\omega_k, \omega_l)), k, l \in \{1, \ldots, n\}$
- $c \leftarrow n$
- Repeat
  - $c \leftarrow c - 1$
  - find k^* and l^* such that $\delta(\omega_{k^*}, \omega_{l^*}) = \min_{k,l} \delta(\omega_k, \omega_l)$
  - construct $\underline{\mathbf{F}}^\Theta$ with c columns by aggregating columns k^* and l^* using the minimum operator
  - update dissimilarity matrix D
- Until c has the desired value
- Compute $(\underline{\mathbf{m}}^\Omega, \underline{\mathbf{F}}^\Omega)$, the vacuous extension of $(\underline{\mathbf{m}}^\Theta, \underline{\mathbf{F}}^\Theta)$

The computation of outer approximations can be performed in exactly the same way, except that the minimum operator is replaced by the maximum operator. After aggregating columns k and l of matrix $\mathbf{F}^\Omega$, the number of 1's in each line i of matrix $\mathbf{F}^\Omega$ is now increased by one if either $\omega_j \in A_i$ and $\omega_k \notin A_i$, or $\omega_k \in A_i$ and $\omega_j \notin A_i$. Hence, the increase of cardinality is

$$\Delta(\overline{m}^\Omega, m^\Omega) = \sum_{i=1}^{n} \mathbf{m}_i |\mathbf{F}^\Omega_{ij} - \mathbf{F}^\Omega_{il}| = \delta(\omega_k, \omega_l) \tag{28}$$

We thus arrive at the same dissimilarity measure as in the previous case, although the resulting coarsening is, in general, different.

Remark 1 *Several lines of $\underline{\mathbf{F}}^\Omega$ or $\overline{\mathbf{F}}^\Omega$ computed by the above algorithm may be identical, which means that the number of focal sets has decreased. In this case, the binary matrix of focal sets and the mass vector have to be rearranged so that the line dimension becomes equal to the number of focal sets.*

Remark 2 *As remarked by Wilson [16], coarsening a frame may sometimes result in no loss of information. Two elements ω_j and ω_k can be merged without losing information if $\delta(\omega_j, \omega_k) = 0$. Hence, "lossless coarsenings" (using Wilson's terminology) will be found in the first steps of our algorithm, if such solutions exist. Our algorithm will even find the "coarsest lossless coarsening" as defined by Wilson [16].*

Remark 3 *Our algorithm is basically the classical hierarchical clustering algorithm applied to the binary matrix of focal sets. Hence, the time needed to compute an inner or outer coarsening approximation by this method is proportional to* n^3.

3.3 Inner and Outer Approximations of Combined Belief Functions

The approximation method proposed in the previous section can be generalized to compute inner and outer approximations of combined belief functions. Rather than computing the combination of the original belief functions defined on Ω, we will compute the combination of their approximations defined over a common coarsened frame of Ω using the FMT algorithm [8]. Then the vacuous extension defined above will be used to recover the combined belief function on the original frame Ω from its approximations defined over the coarsened frames.

Let $m_1^\Omega, ..., m_K^\Omega$ be K bba's defined over a frame of discernment Ω to be combined using either the conjunctive or the disjunctive rules of combination. Let $(\mathbf{m}_k^\Omega, \mathbf{F}_k^\Omega)$, $k = 1, \ldots, K$ denote their matrix representations. We wish to find a common coarsening $\Theta = \{\theta_1, ..., \theta_c\}$ of Ω that will preserve as much as possible of the information contained in each of the K bba's. For that purpose, let us define the following criterion to be minimized for the construction of an inner approximation: $\sum_{k=1}^K \Delta(m_k^\Omega, \underline{m}_k^\Omega)$, and for the construction of an outer approximation: $\sum_{k=1}^K \Delta(\overline{m}_k^\Omega, m_k^\Omega)$. To minimize these criteria, we may simply apply the same hierarchical clustering approach as above, to the matrix

$$\mathbf{F}^\Omega = \begin{bmatrix} \mathbf{F}_1^\Omega \\ \vdots \\ \mathbf{F}_K^\Omega \end{bmatrix}$$

and the weight vector $\mathbf{m}^\Omega = [\mathbf{m}_1^\Omega, \ldots, \mathbf{m}_K^\Omega]'$ (prime denotes transposition).

Determining Inner and Outer approximations of the Combined Belief Function. Given K bba's $\underline{m}_1^\Theta, \ldots, \underline{m}_K^\Theta$ and $\overline{m}_1^\Theta, \ldots, \overline{m}_K^\Theta$ defined over the common coarsened frame Θ of Ω, we shall proceed as follows to determine strong inner and outer approximations of their combination:

1. use the FMT algorithm to convert these approximated bba's to their related inner and outer commonality or implicability functions.
2. compute the approximated inner and outer combined commonality or implicability functions over the coarsened frame Θ. In the case of inner approximation they are given by: $\underline{q}^\Theta = \prod_{i=1}^K \underline{q}_i^\Theta$ and $\underline{b}^\Theta = \prod_{i=1}^K \underline{b}_i^\Theta$, and similarly for the outer approximations $\overline{q}^\Theta$ and $\overline{b}^\Theta$.
3. convert back these approximated combined commonality or implicability functions to their related inner and outer combined bba's $\underline{m}^\Theta$ and $\overline{m}^\Theta$ using the FMT algorithm.
4. use the vacuous extension to recover the inner and outer approximated combined belief function $\underline{m}^\Omega$ and $\overline{m}^\Omega$ from $\underline{m}^\Theta$ and $\overline{m}^\Theta$.

4 Simulations

As an example, we simulated the conjunctive combination of 3 bba's on a frame Ω with $n = |\Omega| = 30$, with 500 focal sets each. The focal sets were generated randomly in such a way that element ω_i of the frame had probability $(i/(n+1))^2$ to belong to each focal set. Hence, we simulate the realistic situation in which some single hypotheses are more plausible than others. The masses were assigned to focal sets as proposed by Tessem [15]: the mass given to the first one was taken from a uniform distribution on $[0,1]$, then a random fraction of the rest was given to the second one, etc. The remaining part of the unit mass was finally allocated to the last focal set. The conjunctive sum of the 3 bba's was approximated using the method described above, using a coarsening of size $c = 10$.

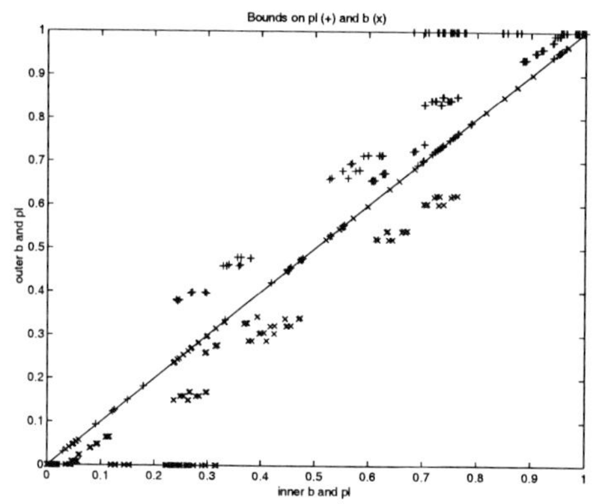

Fig. 1. Simulation results

A part of the results is shown in Fig. 1. The plausibilities and implicabilities $\underline{\mathrm{pl}}^{\Omega}(A)$ and $\underline{b}^{\Omega}(A)$ are plotted on the x axis against $\overline{\mathrm{pl}}^{\Omega}(A)$ and $\overline{b}^{\Omega}(A)$, for 1000 randomly selected subsets of Ω. As expected, we obtain a bracketing of the true plausibilities and implicabilities for any A, since $\underline{\mathrm{pl}}^{\Omega}(A) \leq \mathrm{pl}^{\Omega}(A) \leq \overline{\mathrm{pl}}^{\Omega}(A)$ and $\underline{b}^{\Omega}(A) \geq b^{\Omega}(A) \geq \overline{b}^{\Omega}(A)$. A bracketing of $\mathrm{bel}^{\Omega}(A)$ could also be obtained, as shown by Denœux [2].

5 Conclusion

A new method for computing inner and outer approximations of BF's has been defined. Unlike previous approaches, this method does not rely on the reduction of the number of focal sets, but on the construction of a coarsened frame in which combination can be performed efficiently using the FMT algorithm. Joint strategies aiming at reducing the number of focal sets or the size of the frame, depending on the problem at hand, could be considered as well, and are left for further study.

References

1. M. Bauer. Approximation algorithms and decision making in the Dempster-Shafer theory of evidence – an empirical study. *International Journal of Approximate Reasoning*, 17:217–237, 1997.
2. T. Denœux. Inner and outer clustering approximations of belief structures. In *Proceedings of IPMU'2000*, volume 1, pages 125–132, Madrid, July 2000.
3. D. Dubois and H. Prade. Representation and combination of uncertainty with belief functions and possibility measures. *Comput. Intell.*, 4:244–264, 1988.
4. D. Dubois and H. Prade. Consonant approximations of belief measures. *International Journal of Approximate Reasoning*, 4:419–449, 1990.
5. D. Harmanec. Faithful approximations of belief functions. In K. B. Laskey and H. Prade, editors, *Uncertainty in Artificial Intelligence 15 (UAI99)*, Stockholm, Sweden, 1999.
6. Lowrance J. D, T. D. Garvey, and T. M. Strat. A framework for evidential-reasoning systems. In T. Kehler et al., editor, *Proceedings of AAAI'86*, volume 2, pages 896–903, Philadelphia, August 1986. AAAI.
7. A. K. Jain and R. C. Dubes. *Algorithms for clustering data.* Prentice-Hall, Englewood Cliffs, NJ., 1988.
8. R. Kennes. Computational aspects of the Möbius transform of graphs. *IEEE Trans. SMC*, 22:201–223, 1992.
9. G. J. Klir and M. J. Wierman. *Uncertainty-Based Information. Elements of Generalized Information Theory.* Springer-Verlag, New-York, 1998.
10. P. Orponen. Dempster's rule of combination is # p-complete. *Artificial Intelligence*, 44:245–253, 1990.
11. S. Petit-Renaud and T. Denœux. Handling different forms of uncertainty in regression analysis: a fuzzy belief structure approach. In A. Hunter and S. Pearsons, editors, *Symbolic and quantitative approaches to reasoning and uncertainty (ECSQARU'99)*, pages 340–351, London, June 1999. Springer Verlag.
12. G. Shafer. *A mathematical theory of evidence.* Princeton University Press, Princeton, N.J., 1976.
13. P. Smets. The Transferable Belief Model for quantified belief representation. In D. M. Gabbay and P. Smets, editors, *Handbook of Defeasible reasoning and uncertainty management systems*, volume 1, pages 267–301. Kluwer Academic Publishers, Dordrecht, 1998.
14. P. Smets. Practical uses of belief functions. In K. B. Laskey and H. Prade, editors, *Uncertainty in Artificial Intelligence 15 (UAI99)*, pages 612–621, Stockholm, Sweden, 1999.
15. B. Tessem. Approximations for efficient computation in the theory of evidence. *Artificial Intelligence*, 61:315–329, 1993.
16. N. Wilson. Algorithms for dempster-shafer theory. In D. M. Gabbay and P. Smets, editors, *Hanbook of defeasible reasoning and uncertainty management. Volume 5: Algorithms for Uncertainty and Defeasible Reasoning*, pages 421–475. Kluwer Academic Publishers, Boston, 2000.

Label Semantics: A Formal Framework for Modeling with Words

Jonathan Lawry[1]

Department of Engineering Mathematics, University of Bristol, Bristol, BS8 1TR, UK
j.lawry@bris.ac.uk

Abstract. A framework for modeling with words is proposed based on the idea of selecting labels for values from a fixed finite set of terms. In this context membership degree is defined as the likelihood that a particular word is deemed appropriate as a label for a certain value. A calculus is described for evaluating linguistic expressions based on label semantics and this is compared with the more typical many-valued logic approaches. Reasoning with label semantics in specific contexts is then also considered.

1 Introduction

The phrase computing with words was introduced by Zadeh [11] to capture the idea of computation based not on numerical values, but on natural language terms and expressions. The applications of such methods are numerous and diverse. For instance, they would facilitate the incorporation of natural language rules, as might be provided by human experts, into formal mathematical models of complex systems. In addition, it would provide a framework for representing and inferring (pseudo) natural language rules from the information stored in potentially large databases as well as a means of evaluating hypothesis expressed in natural language on the basis of such data. These types of applications are of central importance to the area of data mining where a primary objective is the transparency of inferred models.

The general methodology for computing with words proposed by Zadeh [11] is that of fuzzy set theory or fuzzy logic [8] and in particular is based on the idea of linguistic variables (see [9]). A linguistic variable is defined as a variable that takes natural language terms such as *large, small*, *tall*, *medium* ..etc as values and where the meaning of these words is given by fuzzy sets on some underlying domain of discourse. Hence, a particular expression of the form *Bill is tall* can be taken as expressing the fact that the linguistic variable describing Bill's height has the value *tall*, and such a statement has a partial truth-value corresponding to the membership degree of Bill's actual height in the fuzzy set representing the meaning of *tall*. The truth-value of compound expressions such as *Bill is tall or medium* is then evaluated according to a fuzzy set calculus based on some choice of t-norm and co-norm.

In our view the principle problem with the above approach is that the semantics underlying standard fuzzy logic or indeed the notion of membership function itself is

[1] Partially supported by a grant from the Nuffield Foundation

S. Benferhat and P. Besnard (Eds.): ECSQARU 2001, LNAI 2143, pp. 374–384, 2001.

rather obscure. For instance, it is unclear exactly what information is conveyed by such statements as *Bill is tall.* According to Zadeh [10] the latter provides a flexible constraint on the variable representing Bill's height. More specifically, it tells us that the possibility distribution on Bill's height corresponds to the membership function of the fuzzy set *tall*. However, in our view, the semantics of possibility distributions as proposed in [10] are not themselves sufficiently clear for this to provide an adequate interpretation. Also, this association with possibility distributions does not, in itself, support the assumption of a truth-functional calculus for membership degrees. Now the above doubts about underlying meaning are of great importance given the goal of providing a framework to express transparent models of data. In order to understand rules or statements we must first be clear about their semantics. Furthermore, if such rules are going to be used for prediction in critical applications then some form of formal correctness is highly desirable. In the sequel we present an approach to modeling with words using the idea of label selection with a clear semantics based on random sets and mass assignments (see [5] for an exposition).

2 Label Semantics

The fundamental notion underlying label semantics is that when individuals make assertions of the kind described above they are essentially providing information about what labels are appropriate for the value of some underlying variable. For simplicity, we assume that for a given context only a finite set of words is available. This is a somewhat controversial assumption since it might be claimed that by applying hedges we can easily generate an infinite set of labels from an initially finite set of words. In other words, if *tall* is a possible label for Bill's height then so is *very tall*, *quite tall*, *very very tall* and so on. This claim is problematic, however, for a number of reasons. For instance, it would appear that the use of hedges in natural language is somewhat restricted. One might use the expressions *very tall* and *quite tall* but *very quite tall* or even *quite very tall* are never used. Also, there seems in practice to be a limit on the number of times hedges can be applied to a label before it becomes nonsensical. This latter point seems to suggest that in practice only a finite number of labels may be available even in natural language. Another related difficulty with the use of hedges is determining the relationship between the meaning of a word and the meaning of any new word generated from it by application of some hedge. In Zadeh [9] it is suggested that such relationships have a simple functional form. For example, if the meaning of *tall* is defined by a fuzzy set with membership function μ_{tall} then Zadeh [9] proposes that the meaning of *very tall* is the fuzzy set with membership function μ_{tall}^2. The choice of this particular function seems relatively arbitrary and indeed, perhaps more fundamentally, it is far from apparent that there should be any such simple functional relationship between the meaning of a word and a new word generated by application of a hedge. In other words, we would claim that while hedges are a simple syntactic device for generating new labels there is no equally simple semantic device for generating the associated new meanings.

Now let us return to the problem of interpreting natural language statements regarding, say, Bill's height as represented by variable H. Let us suppose then that there is a fixed finite set of possible labels for H, denoted LA, and that these labels are both known and completely identical for any individual who will make or interpret a statement regarding Bill's height. Given these assumptions how can we now interpret a statement such as *Bill is tall* as asserted by a particular individual I ? We claim that one natural interpretation is that it merely conveys the information that, according to I, *tall* is an appropriate label for the value of H. In order to clarify this idea suppose I knows that $H=h$ and that given this information he/she is able to identify a subset of LA consisting of those words appropriate as labels for the value h. This set is denoted D_h^I which stands for the description of h given by I. If we allow I to vary across some population of individuals V then we naturally obtain a random set D_h from V into the power set of LA such that $D_h(I)=D_h^I$. Given this we can obtain higher level information about the degree of applicability of a label to a value by defining, in this case, $\mu_{tall}(h)=\mathbf{Pr}\left(\left\{I\in V\middle|tall\in D_h^I\right\}\right)$ where the latter probability is calculated on the basis of some underlying prior distribution on V. This is similar to the voting model interpretation of fuzzy sets proposed by Black [1] and Gaines [4] although the latter required answering a binary yes/no question about whether or not h should be included in the set *tall* and made no explicit reference to other possible labels. Similarly we can determine a probability distribution (or mass assignment) for the random set D_h by defining $\forall S\subseteq LA\ m_{D_h}(S)=\mathbf{Pr}\left(\left\{I\in V\middle|D_h^I=S\right\}\right)$. Now suppose that I does not know the value of H (or alternatively we do not know the value assigned to H by I) then they (we) would naturally define a random set D_H^I from the universe of H into the power set of LA such that $D_H^I(h)=D_h^I$. The distribution of this random set will clearly depend on the prior information available regarding the distribution of H. Hence, the assertion by I that *Bill is tall* would in this context be interpreted as $\{tall\}\subseteq D_H^I$. Finally in the case when we have no information regarding I then we can define a random set D_H from the cross product of V and the universe of H into the power set of LA such that $D_H(I,h)=D_h^I$ and interpret the above statement as $\{tall\}\subseteq D_H$.

Example 2.1

Suppose the variable *SCORE* with universe $\{1,2,3,4,5,6\}$ gives the outcome of a single throw of a particular dice. Let $LA=\{low,\ medium,\ high\}$ and $V=\{I_1,I_2,I_3\}$ then a possible definition of D_{SCORE} is as follows:

$D_1^{I_1}=D_1^{I_2}=D_1^{I_3}=\{low\},\ D_2^{I_1}=\{low, medium\}, D_2^{I_2}=\{low\}, D_2^{I_3}=\{low\},$

$D_3^{I_1}=\{medium\}, D_3^{I_2}=\{medium\}, D_3^{I_3}=\{medium, low\},$

$D_4^{I_1}=\{medium, high\}, D_4^{I_2}=\{medium\}, D_4^{I_3}=\{medium\},$

$D_5^{I_1}=\{high\}, D_5^{I_2}=\{medium, high\}, D_5^{I_3}=\{high\}, D_6^{I_1}=D_6^{I_2}=D_6^{I_3}=\{high\}$

Now assuming a uniform prior on V then the appropriateness degree for each word is given by $\mu_{low}(1)=1, \mu_{low}(2)=1, \mu_{low}(3)=1/3$,

$\mu_{medium}(2)=1/3, \mu_{medium}(3)=1, \mu_{medium}(4)=1, \mu_{medium}(5)=1/3$,

$\mu_{high}(4)=1/3, \mu_{high}(5)=1, \mu_{high}(6)=1$ and also

$m_{D_1}=\{low\}:1,\ m_{D_2}=\{low, medium\}:1/3, \{low\}:2/3,$

$m_{D_3} = \{medium\}: 2/3, \{medium, low\}: 1/3$
$m_{D_4} = \{medium, high\}: 1/3, \{medium\}: 2/3$,
$m_{D_5} = \{high\}: 2/3, \{medium, high\}: 1/3$, $m_{D_6} = \{high\}: 1$
If we further assume that the dice is fair then the distribution of D_{SCORE} is given by
$m_{D_{SCORE}} = \{low\}: 5/18, \{low, medium\}: 1/9, \{medium\}: 2/9, \{medium, high\}: 1/9$
$, \{high\}: 5/18$

We now consider the problem of how to interpret expressions involving compound labels built up using some set of logical connectives. For the scope of this paper we consider only the three connectives $\wedge, \vee$ and $\neg$. This choice was based mainly on the fact that in the author's experience these are the most widely encountered connectives in the type of application discussed in the introduction. However, we freely admit that these are also the most straightforward connectives to define in the context of label semantics. Firstly let us consider the case of negation. How do we interpret expressions of the form *Bill is not tall*? We take the view here and in the sequel that negation is used in this case to express the non-suitability of a label. In other words the above statement means that *tall* is not an appropriate label for *H*, or $\{tall\} \not\subseteq \mathcal{D}_H$. Conjunction and disjunction are then taken as having the obvious meanings so that *Bill is tall and medium* is interpreted as saying that both *tall* and *medium* are appropriate labels for *H*, $\{tall, medium\} \subseteq \mathcal{D}_H$, and *Bill is tall or medium* is interpreted as saying that either *tall* is an appropriate label for *H* or *medium* is an appropriate label for *H*, $\{tall\} \subseteq \mathcal{D}_H$ or $\{medium\} \subseteq \mathcal{D}_H$. In the following section we introduce a formal framework based on the ideas described above.

3 Formal Framework

Consider a language *L* of the predicate calculus consisting of the set of unary predicate symbols $LA = \{L_1, \cdots, L_n\}$, a single variable *x*, a set of constants ranging across a domain of discourse Ω and connectives $\wedge, \vee$ and $\neg$.

Definition 3.1 (General Label Expressions)
The set of general label expressions of *L, GLE,* is defined recursively as follows:
1. $L_i(x) \in GLE$ for $i = 1, \cdots, n$
2. If $\theta, \phi \in GLE$ then $\neg\theta, \theta \wedge \phi, \theta \vee \phi \in GLE$

Definition 3.2 (Specific Label Expressions)
The set of specific label expressions for *L*, *SLE*, is defined by $SLE = \{\theta(a) | \theta(x) \in GLE, a \in \Omega\}$

Definition 3.3 (Appropriate Label Sets)
Every $\theta \in GLE$ is associated with a set of subsets of *LA* (i.e. an element of $2^{2^{LA}}$), denoted $\lambda(\theta)$, where $\lambda(\theta)$ is defined recursively as follows:

1. $\lambda(L_i(x))=\{S\subseteq LA|\{L_i\}\subseteq S\}$
2. $\lambda(\theta\wedge\phi)=\lambda(\theta)\cap\lambda(\phi)$
3. $\lambda(\theta\vee\phi)=\lambda(\theta)\cup\lambda(\phi)$
4. $\lambda(\theta)=\overline{\lambda(\theta)}$

Intuitively $\lambda(\theta)$ corresponds to those subsets of *LA* identified as being candidates for the set of appropriate labels for x (i.e. possible values for D_x) by expression θ.

We now introduce some basic notation. Let Val_a denote the set of valuations (i.e. allocations of truth values) on $\{L_1(a),\cdots,L_n(a)\}$ for $a\in\Omega$. For $v\in Val_a$ $v(L_i(a))=true$ can be taken as meaning that L_i is an appropriate label for a. Let $SLE_a=\{\theta(a)|\theta(x)\in GLE\}, SLE_a^0=\{L_1(a),\cdots,L_n(a)\}$ and
$SLE_a^{n+1}=SLE_a^n\cup\{\neg\varphi(a),\varphi(a)\wedge\phi(a),\varphi(a)\vee\phi(a)|\varphi(a),\phi(a)\in SLE_a^n\}$
Clearly we have that $SLE_a=\bigcup_n SLE_a^n$. From a valuation v on $\{L_1(a),\cdots,L_n(a)\}$ the truth-value, $v(\theta)$, for $\theta\in SLE_a$ can be determined recursively in the usual way by application of the truth tables for the connectives.

Definition 3.4
Let $\tau:Val_a\rightarrow 2^{LA}$ such that $\forall v\in Val_a\ \tau(v)=\{L_i|v(L_i(a))=t\}$ (Here *t=true* and *f=false*).
Notice that τ is clearly a bijection. Also note that for $v\in Val_a$ $\tau(v)$ can be associated with a Herbrand interpretation of the language L restricted to the single constant a (see [7])

Lemma 3.5
$\forall\theta(a)\in SLE_a\ \{\tau(v)|v\in Val_a, v(\theta(a))=t\}=\lambda(\theta)$

Proof
We prove this by induction on the complexity of $\theta(a)$.
Suppose $\theta(a)\in SLE_a^0$, so that $\theta(a)=L_i(a)$ for some $i\in\{1,\cdots,n\}$. Now as v ranges across all valuations for which $L_i(a)$ is true, then $\tau(v)$ ranges across all subsets of *LA* that contain L_i. Hence, $\{\tau(v)|v\in Val_a, v(L_i(a))=t\}=\{S\subseteq LA|\{L_i\}\subseteq S\}=\lambda(L_i)$ as required.

Now suppose we have $\forall\theta(a)\in SLE_a^n\ \{\tau(v)|v\in Val_a, v(\theta(a))=t\}=\lambda(\theta)$ and consider an expression $\theta(a)\in SLE_a^{n+1}$ then either $\theta(a)\in SLE_a^n$ in which case the result follows trivially or one of the following hold:

(1) $\theta(a)=\phi(a)\wedge\varphi(a)$ where $\phi(a),\varphi(a)\in SLE_a^n$. In this case
$\{v\in Val_a|v(\phi(a)\wedge\varphi(a))=t\}=\{v\in Val_a|v(\phi(a))=t\}\cap\{v\in Val_a|v(\varphi(a))=t\}$.

$\therefore\ \{\tau(v)|v \in Val_a, v(\phi(a) \wedge \varphi(a)) = t\} = \{\tau(v)|v \in Val_a, v(\phi(a)) = t\} \cap$ $\{\tau(v)|v \in Val_a, v(\varphi(a)) = t\} = \lambda(\phi) \cap \lambda(\varphi)$ (inductive hypothesis) = $\lambda(\phi \wedge \theta)$ by definition 3.3.

(2) $\theta(a) = \phi(a) \vee \varphi(a)$ where $\phi(a), \varphi(a) \in SLE_a^n$. In this case $\{v \in Val_a | v(\phi(a) \vee \varphi(a)) = t\} = \{v \in Val_a | v(\phi(a)) = t\} \cup \{v \in Val_a | v(\varphi(a)) = t\}$.
$\therefore\ \{\tau(v)|v \in Val_a, v(\phi(a) \vee \varphi(a)) = t\} = \{\tau(v)|v \in Val_a, v(\phi(a)) = t\} \cup$ $\{\tau(v)|v \in Val_a, v(\varphi(a)) = t\} = \lambda(\phi) \cup \lambda(\varphi)$ (inductive hypothesis) = $\lambda(\phi \vee \theta)$ by definition 3.3.

(3) $\theta(a) = \neg\phi(a)$ where $\phi(a) \in SLE_a^n$. In this case $\{\tau(v)|v \in Val_a, v(\neg\phi) = t\} = \overline{\{\tau(v)|v \in Val_a, v(\phi) = t\}} = \overline{\lambda(\phi)}$ (by the inductive hypothesis)= $\lambda(\neg\phi)$ by def. 3.3

Proposition 3.6
$\forall a \in \Omega\ \theta(a) \models \phi(a)$ iff $\lambda(\theta) \subseteq \lambda(\phi)$

Proof
($\Rightarrow$) For some arbitrary $a \in \Omega\ \ \theta(a) \models \phi(a) \Rightarrow \{v \in Val_a | v(\theta(a)) = t\}$
$\subseteq \{v \in Val_a | v(\phi(a)) = t\} \Rightarrow \{\tau(v)|v \in Val_a, v(\theta(a)) = t\}$
$\subseteq \{\tau(v)|v \in Val_a, v(\phi(a)) = t\} \Rightarrow \lambda(\theta) \subseteq \lambda(\phi)$ by lemma 3.5
($\Leftarrow$) Suppose $\lambda(\theta) \subseteq \lambda(\phi)$. For every $a \in \Omega\ \ \lambda(\theta) = \{\tau(v)|v \in Val_a, v(\theta(a)) = t\}$ and $\lambda(\phi) = \{\tau(v)|v \in Val_a, v(\phi(a)) = t\}$ by lemma 3.5. Therefore,
$\{\tau(v)|v \in Val_a, v(\theta(a)) = t\} \subseteq \{\tau(v)|v \in Val_a, v(\phi(a)) = t\}$
$\Rightarrow \{v \in Val_a | v(\theta(a)) = t\} \subseteq \{v \in Val_a | v(\phi(a)) = t\}$ since τ is a bijection.

Corollary 3.7
For $\theta(x), \phi(x) \in GLE\ \ \forall a \in \Omega\ \theta(a) \equiv \phi(a)$ iff $\lambda(\theta) = \lambda(\phi)$

We now introduce the notion of an interpretation in label semantics.

Definition 3.8 (Label Interpretation)
A Label Interpretation, *I*, of language *L* is defined as follows:

1. To each constant $a \in \Omega$, we assign a subset of *LA*, denoted D_a^I
2. To variable *x* we assign a random set D_x^I into 2^{LA}.

Given a label interpretation *I* the meanings of label expressions are then determined according to the following semantic rules.

Semantic Rules

For $\theta \in GLE$ then under I, θ is interpreted as meaning $D_x^I \in \lambda(\theta)$. For $\theta(a) \in SLE$ then under I, $\theta(a)$ is interpreted as meaning $D_a^I \in \lambda(\theta)$. Obviously this has a clear binary truth-value since both D_a^I and $\lambda(\theta)$ are precisely defined.

Proposition 3.9
If $\phi(a) \in SLE$ is inconsistent then it is false under all label interpretations.
Proof
If $\phi(a) \in SLE$ is inconsistent then $\phi(a) \equiv \theta(a) \wedge \neg\theta(a)$ so that by corollary 3.7 $\lambda(\phi) = \lambda(\theta \wedge \neg\theta)$ Let I be a label interpretation the under I, then $\phi(a)$ means $D_a^I \in \lambda(\theta \wedge \neg\theta) = \lambda(\theta) \cap \lambda(\neg\theta) = \lambda(\theta) \cap \overline{\lambda(\theta)} = \varnothing$ by definition 3.3
We now introduce higher-order functions describing the selection of labels across a set of label interpretations.

Definition 3.10 (Label Appropriateness Measure)
Let V be a set of label interpretations of L with associated prior distribution P_V then we define

$$\forall S \subseteq LA \; m_{D_a}(S) = P_V\left(\left\{I \in V | D_a^I = S\right\}\right)$$

In the case where V is finite and P_V is the uniform distribution this corresponds to

$$\forall S \subseteq LA \; m_{D_a}(S) = \frac{\left|\left\{I \in V | D_a^I = S\right\}\right|}{|V|}$$

From this mass assignment we define the appropriateness measure μ by

$$\forall \theta \in GLE, \forall a \in \Omega \; \mu_\theta(a) = \sum_{S \in \lambda(\theta)} m_{D_a}(S)$$

Trivially, by proposition 3.6 we have that if $\forall a \in \Omega \; \theta(a) \models \phi(a)$ then $\forall a \in \Omega \; \mu_\theta(a) \leq \mu_\phi(a)$ and similarly by corollary 3.7 we have that if $\forall a \in \Omega \; \theta(a) \equiv \phi(a)$ then $\forall a \in \Omega \; \mu_\theta(a) = \mu_\phi(a)$.

Proposition 3.11
$\forall \theta \in GLE, \forall a \in \Omega \; \mu_{\neg\theta}(a) = 1 - \mu_\theta(a)$
Proof

$$\mu_{\neg\theta}(a) = \sum_{S \in \lambda(\neg\theta)} m_{D_a}(S) = \sum_{S \in \overline{\lambda(\theta)}} m_{D_a}(S) = 1 - \sum_{S \in \lambda(\theta)} m_{D_a}(S) = 1 - \mu_\theta(a)$$

In order to consider the behavior of the μ operator on conjunctions and disjunctions of labels we introduce the notion of consonant mass assignments. More specifically, we will assume that m_{D_a} is consonant for all $a \in \Omega$. Here, consonance has the standard random set meaning (see [5]) that $\forall S, S' \subseteq LA$ if both $m_{D_a}(S) > 0$ and $m_{D_a}(S') > 0$ then either $S \subseteq S'$ or $S' \subseteq S$. This assumption may seem, on first inspection, very strong. However, if we think of each label interpretation as corresponding to a voter then consonance simply requires the restriction that voters in V differ regarding the composition of D_a^I, only in terms of its generality or specificity. In Lawry [6] it is proposed that voters decide on the truth-value of statements solely on the basis of some optimism parameter. In the current context this would mean that the higher the value of this parameter for I, the more likely that L_i for any particular i will be included in D_a^I. The framework presented in [6] is problematic since it assumes that truth-values are dependent only on the optimism parameter. Hence, for sentence θ, the most optimistic voters regarding θ will also be the most optimistic voters regarding $\neg\theta$. This is counterintuitive and requires the introduction of a weaker notion of negation. In label semantics the negation problem is avoided since for label expression θ, $\neg\theta$ is not interpreted as a positive assertion at all but rather as ruling out certain subsets of LA for the value description.

Proposition 3.12
If for all $a \in \Omega$ m_{D_a} is a consonant mass assignment (see [5]) then for $L_i, L_j \in LA$ we have that $\forall a \in \Omega$ $\mu_{L_i \wedge L_j}(a) = \boldsymbol{min}\left(\mu_{L_i}(a), \mu_{L_j}(a)\right)$

Proof
Notice $\lambda(L_i \wedge L_j) = \lambda(L_i) \cap \lambda(L_j) = \{S \subseteq LA | \{L_i\} \subseteq S\} \cap \{S \subseteq LA | \{L_j\} \subseteq S\}$ $= \{S \subseteq LA | \{L_i, L_j\} \subseteq S\}$. Hence, $\forall a \in \Omega$ $\mu_{L_i \wedge L_j}(a) = \sum_{S:\{L_i, L_j\} \subseteq S} m_{D_a}(S)$

For any a since m_{D_a} is a consonant mass assignment then it must have the form $m_{D_a} = M_1 : m_1, \cdots, M_k : m_k$ where $M_i \subset M_{i+1}$ for $i = 1, \cdots, k-1$
Now suppose w.l.o.g. that $\mu_{L_i}(a) \le \mu_{L_j}(a)$ then $\{L_i\} \subseteq M_i$ iff $\{L_i, L_j\} \subseteq M_i$ for $i = 1, \cdots, k$. Therefore, $\mu_{L_i \wedge L_j}(a) = \sum_{S:\{L_i\} \subseteq S} m_{D_a}(S) = \mu_{L_i}(a) = \boldsymbol{min}\left(\mu_{L_i}(a), \mu_{L_j}(a)\right)$

Proposition 3.13
If for all $a \in \Omega$ m_{D_a} is a consonant mass assignment then for $L_i, L_j \in LA$ we have that $\forall a \in \Omega$ $\mu_{L_i \vee L_j}(a) = \boldsymbol{max}\left(\mu_{L_i}(a), \mu_{L_j}(a)\right)$

Proof (Similar to proposition 3.12)

In order to compare and contrast label semantics with the many-valued logic approach to fuzzy reasoning we first give a formal definition of what is meant for a calculus to be fully truth-functional.

Definition 3.14 (Fully Truth-functional)
Let $\omega : GLE \times \Omega \to [0,1]$ then ω is said to be fully truth-functional if and only if there exist functions $f_\neg : [0,1] \to [0,1]$, $f_\wedge : [0,1]^2 \to [0,1]$ and $f_\vee : [0,1]^2 \to [0,1]$ such that $\forall \theta, \phi \in GLE$, $\forall a \in \Omega$ $\omega_{\neg\theta}(a) = f_\neg(\omega_\theta(a))$, $\omega_{\theta \wedge \phi}(a) = f_\wedge(\omega_\theta(a), \omega_\phi(a))$, $\omega_{\theta \vee \phi}(a) = f_\vee(\omega_\theta(a), \omega_\phi(a))$ where $\omega_\theta(a)$ is used as shorthand for $\omega(\theta, a)$.

Notice that propositions 3.12 and 3.13 do not imply that $\forall\theta,\phi\in GLE$, $\mu_{\theta\wedge\phi}(a)=\boldsymbol{min}(\mu_\theta(a),\mu_\phi(a))$ or that $\mu_{\theta\vee\phi}(a)=\boldsymbol{max}(\mu_\theta(a),\mu_\phi(a))$. For instance, assuming consonance, it can easily be seen from definition 3.10 that $\mu_{L_i\wedge\neg L_j}(a)=0$ if $\mu_{L_i}(a)\leq\mu_{L_j}(a)$ and $\mu_{L_i}(a)-\mu_{L_j}(a)$ otherwise. This is not generally equivalent to $\boldsymbol{min}(\mu_{L_i}(a),1-\mu_{L_j}(a))$. Nonetheless, if we assume consonance there is a sense in which the calculus of μ is functional, although not fully truth-functional, since for any $\theta\in GLE$ we have from definition 3.10 that $\mu_\theta(a)$ is completely determined by the mass assignment m_{D_a} and provided the latter is consonant then it in turn is completely determined by the values of $\mu_{L_i}(a)$ for $i=1,\cdots,n$ (i.e. this is due to the fact that a consonant mass assignment is completely determined by its fixed point coverage [5]). A pleasant consequence of this is that the meanings of all label expressions can be defined by a set of appropriateness measures $\mu_{L_i}:\Omega\to[0,1]$ for $i=1,\cdots,n$. One possible method for calculating $\mu_\theta(a)$ for general $\theta\in GLE$ is as follows: By the disjunctive normal form theorem we have that $\theta(a)$ is logically equivalent to a disjunction of atoms $\bigvee_{\alpha:\alpha\to\theta}\alpha$ where each atom is a conjunction of literals of the form $\alpha\equiv\bigwedge_i\pm L_i$. Now it can easily seen that $\lambda(\alpha)$ is a singleton consisting of the subset of LA made up from those labels appearing positively in α. Also by definition 3.3 and corollary 3.7 we have that $\lambda(\theta)=\bigcup_{\alpha:\alpha\to\theta}\lambda(\alpha)$ and hence $\mu_\theta(a)=\sum_{\alpha:\alpha\to\theta}m_{D_a}(\lambda(\alpha))$[2].

It should also be noted that μ satisfies the law of the excluded middle in the sense that $\forall a\in\Omega,\forall\theta\in GLE$ $\mu_{\theta\wedge\neg\theta}(a)=0$ as follows immediately from proposition 3.9. This does not contradicted the triviality result of Dubois and Prade [2] (later Elkan [3]) which states that any fully truth-functional logic, in the sense of definition 3.14, satisfying the law of the excluded middle can only be binary, since the calculus for μ is not fully truth-functional. More specifically, as we have seen there is no single binary function $f_\wedge$ such that $\forall\theta,\phi\in GLE,\forall a\in\Omega$ $\mu_{\theta\wedge\phi}(a)=f_\wedge(\mu_\theta(a),\mu_\phi(a))$.

It should be commented that we do not see the failure of label semantics to satisfy the fully-truth functional property as in anyway detrimental. The consonance assumption means that the μ function is completely determined by its values on the labels and hence computational feasibility is maintained. Furthermore, in our view, full truth-functionality is a somewhat naïve assumption since it does not take into account the logical structure of the expressions involved when combining them.

---

[2] We are abusing notation slightly here and taking $\lambda(\alpha)$ to correspond to the single element of 2^{LA} associated with α rather than the set containing that element.

4 Context Specific Reasoning with Label Semantics

In this section we discuss some of the issues associated with reasoning based on label semantics in a specific context. For instance, what additional information can be gained and utilised from specific knowledge of a particular μ function. In order to gain some insight into this issue consider the following observation. Suppose we have a set of label interpretations V together with an underlying distribution P_V , then let us refer to the pair $\langle V, P_V \rangle$ as a label frame. Now clearly from definition 3.10 m_{D_a} and μ are defined only relative to some fixed frame. In the specific context of such a frame we are likely to observe that only a proper subset of the set of label sets is in fact possible. For instance, given $LA = \{small, medium, large\}$ we may find that in some frame Ξ only the following occur as sets of possible labels: {*small*}, {*small, medium*}, {*medium*}, {*medium, large*}, {*large*}. We can formalize this observation by defining the set of focal elements for a frame Ξ as $F_\Xi = \left\{S \subseteq LA \middle| \exists a \in \Omega\ m_{D_a}(S) > 0\right\}$. Assuming consonance we can determine F_Ξ from examination of the associated μ function. We can now make the following natural definitions in the context of frame Ξ.

Definition 4.1
(i) (Universally follows from in Ξ) For $\theta, \phi \in GLE$ ϕ universally follows from θ in frame Ξ (denoted $\theta \models_\Xi \phi$) iff $\lambda(\theta) \cap F_\Xi \subseteq \lambda(\phi) \cap F_\Xi$
(ii) (Universally equivalent to in Ξ) For $\theta, \phi \in GLE$ ϕ is universally equivalent to θ in frame Ξ (denoted $\phi \equiv_\Xi \theta$) iff $\lambda(\phi) \cap F_\Xi = \lambda(\theta) \cap F_\Xi$ (e.g. in the frame mentioned above $small(x) \wedge medium(x) \equiv_\Xi small(x) \wedge medium(x) \wedge \neg large(x)$)
(iii) (Universally true in Ξ) For $\theta \in GLE$ θ is universally true in Ξ (denoted $\models_\Xi \theta$) iff $\lambda(\theta) \cap F_\Xi = F_\Xi$ (e.g. in the frame mentioned above $(small(x) \wedge \neg medium(x))$
$\vee (small(x) \wedge medium(x)) \vee (medium(x) \wedge \neg small(x)) \vee (medium(x) \wedge large(x))$
$\vee (large(x) \wedge \neg medium(x))$)

A common example of (i) in the above definition is when a certain label is conceptually implied by another label. For instance, we might say that whenever someone is described as being *very tall* then they can also be described as *tall*. In fuzzy set theory this would be captured by taking the fuzzy set for *very tall* as a fuzzy subset of the fuzzy set for *tall* (see [8]). In label semantics we would expect to have a frame Ξ in which whenever *very tall* was deemed an appropriate label so was *tall*. In other words, $very\ tall(x) \models_\Xi tall(x)$. In such a case it is not difficult to see that from definition 3.10 we have $\forall a \in \Omega\ \mu_{very\ tall}(a) \leq \mu_{tall}(a)$ so that in this instance fuzzy set theory and label semantics would coincide.

5 Conclusions

In this paper we have presented a formal framework for modeling with words based on the idea of label selection. In this framework label expressions give information about what words are appropriate to label a value. A higher level measure of label appropriateness can be defined based on the variation of the definition for the set of appropriate labels across a set of label interpretations. Given a consonance assumption the values of this measure can be determined completely from its values on the basic labels. We have also introduced the idea of a label frame and described how such a notion helps us to reason with label semantics within a specific context. Overall we would claim that label semantics provides a coherent and computationally feasible calculus for modeling with words.

References

1. Black, B.: "Vagueness: An Exercise in Logical Analysis", Philosophy of Science 4 (1937) 427-55
2. Dubois, D., Prade, H.: "An Introduction to Possibility and Fuzzy Logics" in Non-standard Logics for Automated Reasoning, Smets P., etal (ed.), Academic Press (1988) 742-755
3. Elkan, C.: "The paradoxical Success of Fuzzy Logic", Proceedings of the Eleventh National Conference on Artificial Intelligence, MIT Press (1993) 698-703
4. Gaines, B., R.: "Fuzzy and Probability Uncertainty Logics", Journal of Information and Control 38 (1978) 154-169
5. Goodman, I., R., Nguyen, H., T.: Uncertainty Models for Knowledge Based Systems, North-Holland, Amsterdam (1985)
6. Lawry, J.: "A Voting Mechanism for Fuzzy Logic", International Journal of Approximate Reasoning 19 (1998) 315-333
7. Lloyd, J., W.: Foundations of Logic Programming, Second Edition, Springer-Verlag, 1987
8. Zadeh, L., A.: "Fuzzy Sets", Information and Control 8 (1965) 338-353
9. Zadeh, L., A.: "The Concept of Linguistic Variable and its Applications to approximate Reasoning", Part 1: Information Sciences 8 (1975) 199-249, Part 2: Information Sciences 8 (1975) 301-357, Part 3: Information Sciences 9 (1976) 43-80
10. Zadeh, L., A.: "Fuzzy Sets as a Basis for a Theory of Possibility", Fuzzy Sets and Systems 1 (1978) 3-28
11. Zadeh, L., A.: "Fuzzy Logic = Computing with Words", IEEE Transactions on Fuzzy Systems 2 (1996) 103-111

Reasoning about Knowledge Using Rough Sets

Weiru Liu

School of ISE, University of Ulster at Jordanstown
Newtownabbey, Co. Antrim BT37 0QB, UK
w.liu@ulst.ac.uk

Abstract. In this paper, we first investigate set semantics of propositional logic in terms of rough sets and discuss how truth values of propositions (sentences) can be interpreted by means of equivalence classes. This investigation will be used to answer queries that involve general values of an attribute when the actual values of the attribute are more specific. We then explore how binary relations on singletons can be extended as set-based relations, in order to deal with non-deterministic problems in an information system. An example on test-case selection in telecommunications is employed to demonstrate the relevance of these investigations, where queries either contain values (concepts) at higher granularity levels or involve values of an attribute with non-deterministic nature or both.

1 Introduction

In rough sets, information and knowledge is usually represented using data tables or decision tables [9]. Each column in such a table is identified by an attribute, which describes one aspect of the objects being processed in an information system. Attribute values can be defined at different granularity levels, according to a specific requirement. In the past, most of the research work using rough sets has focused on how to use or manipulate or discover knowledge from the information carried by a table, under the assumption that attribute values in such a table have been chosen at the right granularity level (e.g., [10], and [11]).

Nevertheless, problems of granules of attribute values in query processing have been addressed by some researchers. In [5], a high level data table is derived from a lower level table when the concept required by the query is not matched by the values of the relevant attribute in the lower level table. In this case, the values of the attribute in the higher level table are replaced by more general values (concepts). In [12], approaches to answering non-standard queries in distributed information systems were explored. Values of an attribute at different granule levels are arranged as nodes in a tree structure, with the attribute name as the root and the most specific values of the attribute as the leafs. In contrast to the two approaches above, in [1], rough predicates are defined. These predicates associate user-defined lower and upper approximations with attribute values, or with logical combinations of values, to define a rough set of tuples for the result of the predicates. Each predicate, similar to the definition of a function on an

S. Benferhat and P. Besnard (Eds.): ECSQARU 2001, LNAI 2143, pp. 385–397, 2001.

entity in a functional data model, does not define an attribute as a function on a relation rather it chooses a possible value of an attribute as a function of the relation. For example, if relation *Horse* has an attribute *Age*, then a predicate *young(Horse)* is defined with the lower approximation containing those horses with age below 1, and the upper approximation consisting of those horses with ages in {2,3,4}.

Another common problem associated with attribute values in a data table is that an object has a set of possible values instead of just one value for a particular attribute. Although only one of the values is surely true but we cannot say (determine) precisely which value it is yet. When a data table involves this kind of attributes (non-determinictic), it is necessary to extend usual binary equivalence relations to be set-based relations (e.g., [13]).

In this paper, we aim at solving these two problems when a query either contains values (concepts) at higher granularity levels or involves values of an attribute with non-deterministic nature or both. We discuss how to reason about knowledge at different levels from a data table using the combination of logic and rough sets, when values of an attribute are given at the most specific level, in order to answer queries. To achieve this objective, we investigate set semantics of propositional logic first in rough sets and then explore the relationships between equivalence relations and propositions in terms of partitioning a data table. We then discuss how extended set-based binary relations can be applied to compute tighter bounds when the values of an attribute are non-deterministic (set-based) [6]. An example on test-case selection in telecommunications is employed to demonstrate the relevance of our research result. The paper is organized as follows. Section 2 introduces the basic notions of rough sets and set based computations in non-deterministic information systems. Section 3 explores the set semantic of propositional logic. Section 4 discusses how to apply the results to solve complex queries. Finally Section 5 summarizes the paper.

2 Deterministic and Non-deterministic Information Systems

Basics of rough sets: Let U be a set, also called a universe, which is non-empty and contains a finite number of objects (this assumption will not lose general properties of rough sets), and R be an equivalence relation on U. An equivalence relation is reflexive, symmetric and transitive. An equivalence relation R on U divides the objects in U into a collection of disjoint sets with the elements in the same subset indiscernible. We denote each partition set, known as an *equivalence class*, as W_l^R and an element in W_l^R as w_{lj}^R. The family of all equivalence classes $\{W_1^R, ..., W_n^R\}$ is denoted as U/R. W_l^R and w_{lj}^R are simplified as W_l and w_{lj} respectively when there is no ambiguity about which equivalence relation R we are referring to.

Given a universe, there can be several ways of classifying objects. Let R and R' be two equivalence relations over U, $R \cap R'$ is a refined equivalence relation.

$\cap$ can be understood as *and*. The collection of equivalence classes of $R \cap R'$ is

$$U/(R \cap R') = \{W_l^R \cap W_j^{R'} \mid W_l^R \in U/R, W_j^{R'} \in U/R', W_l^R \cap W_j^{R'} \neq \emptyset\}. \quad (1)$$

Equivalence relation $R_1 \cap R_2 \cap ... \cap R_n$, from $\mathcal{R} = \{R_1, ..., R_n\}$ on a universe U, is usually denoted as $IND(\mathcal{R})$ [9].

Definition 1. *Structure $(U, \Omega, V_a)_{a \in \Omega}$ is called an information system where:*
1. U is a finite set of objects,
2. Ω is a finite set of primitive attributes describing objects in U,
3. For each $a \in \Omega$, V_a is the collection of all possible values of a. Attribute a also defines a function, $a : U \to V_a$, such that $\forall u \in U$, $\exists x \in V_a$, $a(u) = x$.

Such an information system is also called a deterministic information system. For a subset $Q \in \Omega$, function R_Q defined by $u_1 R_Q u_2 \Leftrightarrow \forall a \in Q, a(u_1) = a(u_2)$ is an equivalence relation. When Q consists of only one attribute a, i.e., $Q = \{a\}$, R_Q is called an *elementary equivalence relation.* In [9], each equivalence class in an elementary equivalence relation is referred to as an *elementary concept.* Any other non-elementary equivalence relation R_Q can be represented by a set of elementary equivalence relations using the following expression, $R_Q = \cap_{a \in Q} R_{\{a\}}$.

Definition 2. *Let U be a universe and R be an equivalence relation on U. For a subset X of U, if X is the union of some W_l^R, then X is called R-definable; otherwise X is R-undefinable.*

Let $\mathcal{R} = \{R_1, ..., R_n\}$ be a collection of n equivalence relations. Then any subset $X \subseteq U$ obtained by applying $\cap$ and $\cup$ to some equivalence classes in any $U/\mathbf{R}$ (where $\mathbf{R} \subseteq \mathcal{R}$) is $IND(\mathcal{R})$-definable. This statement identifies all the concepts that are definable under equivalence relation $IND(\mathcal{R})$. For any subset X of U with a given R, we can also use two subsets of U to describe it as follows:

$$\underline{R}X = \cup\{W_l^R \mid W_l^R \subseteq X\}, \qquad \overline{R}X = \cup\{W_l^R \mid W_l^R \cap X \neq \emptyset\}.$$

When X is R-definable, $\underline{R}X = \overline{R}X = X$. Subsets $\underline{R}X$ and $\overline{R}X$ are called *R-lower* and *R-upper approximations* of X.

Set-based computation: In real world applications, not all attributes in a data table will be assigned with single values against individual objects (e.g., [6],[8]). The definition below defines those information systems where an attribute can have a set of values for a particular object.

Definition 3. *Structure $(U, \Omega, V_a)_{a \in \Omega}$ is called a non-deterministic information system where:*
1. U is a finite set of objects,
2. Ω is a finite set of primitive attributes describing objects in U,
3. For each $a \in \Omega$, V_a is the collection of all possible values of a. Attribute a also defines a function, $a : U \to 2^{2^{V_a}}$, such that $\forall u \in U$, $\exists S \subseteq 2^{V_a}$, $a(u) = S$.

Table 1. A sample data table

U	Manufactures	Color	Weight (g)	Age-Group
u_1	{{UK, France}, {UK, Japan}}	{grey, black}	{1,2}	{infant, Toddler}
u_2	{{Japan, Korea }, {UK, Japan}}	{grey}	{2,3,4}	{Toddler, Pre-school}
u_3	{{France, Germany}}	{grey}	{2,3,4}	{Pre-School}
u_4	{{Japan, Germany}}	{grey, brown}	{1}	{All}
u_5	{{UK, France}}	{brown}	{4,5}	{Teenager}

Table 1 shows a non-deterministic information system (also called an attribute system in [3]) with all attributes non-deterministic. Attribute *Manufactures* is even more complicated: each object is assumed to be manufactured jointly by two countries. When we don't know for sure which two countries manufactured a specific object, we assign several pairs of possible countries, such as for u_1. In [3], four possible explanations of the values in $a(u)$, a set assigned to an object against a particular attribute, are provided. We supplement 5th explanation on top of that to cover the situation as shown by attribute *Manufactures*. These five explanations are:

(1) $a(u)$ is interpreted disjunctively and exclusively: one and only one value is correct, such as the weight of an object (assume we use a closest integer to measure the weight of each object),

(2) $a(u)$ is interpreted disjunctively and non-exclusively: more than one value may be correct, such as the (suitability of) age groups of a toy,

(3) $a(u)$ is interpreted conjunctively and exclusively: all the correct values are included, such as the color of a toy (when we list all the colors involved),

(4) $a(u)$ is interpreted conjunctively and non-exclusively: all the values (but not limited to the values) in $a(u)$ are correct, such as the color of a toy (when we list main colors only),

(5) the combination of (1) and (3): one and only one value (subset) is correct and this value is the combination of individual values, such as the manufactures of a toy.

For the first 4 categories, set-based operations are enough to deal with attribute values. However, for category 5, we will need to use interval-based operations, since each value itself is again a set.

Definition 4. *(from [13]) Let r be a binary relation on V_a, a set of possible values of attribute a. A pair of extended binary relations (r_*, r^*) on $2^{V_a} \setminus \emptyset$ is defined as:*

$$Ar_*B \Longleftrightarrow (\forall a \in A, \forall b \in B)\, arb, \qquad Ar^*B \Longleftrightarrow (\exists a \in A, \exists b \in B)\, arb. \quad (2)$$

Let Q be a query that involves values in subset B of V_a, then retrieval sets

$$Ret_*(Q) = \{u_i \mid a(u_i) = A, Ar_*B\}; \qquad Ret^*(Q) = \{u_i \mid a(u_i) = A, Ar^*B\},$$

give the lower and upper approximations of a set of objects that support query Q under condition B. For example, if $Q =$ 'select grey objects', and we set $B =$

$\{grey\}$ and r be '$=$', then $Ret_*(Q) = \{u_2, u_3\}$ and $Ret^*(Q) = \{u_1, u_2, u_3, u_4\}$. However, Eqs. in (2) cannot be used to deal with values for attribute *Manufactures* because there may be several subsets of values assigned to an object. Therefore, we need to further extend the equations.

Given two sets $A_1, A_2 \in 2^{V_a}$ with $A_1 \subseteq A_2$, set $\mathcal{A}$ defined by $\mathcal{A} = [A_1, A_2] = \{X \in 2^{V_a}, A_1 \subseteq X \subseteq A_2\}$ is called a closed *interval set.*

Definition 5. *Let $\mathcal{A}$ and $\mathcal{B}$ be two interval sets from 2^{V_a}. A pair of extended binary relations $(\supseteq_*, \supseteq^*)$ on $2^{2^{V_a}} \setminus \emptyset$ is defined as:*
$\mathcal{A} \supseteq_* \mathcal{B} \Longleftrightarrow \forall X \in \mathcal{A}, \forall Y \in \mathcal{B}\ X \supseteq Y,$
$\mathcal{A} \supseteq^* \mathcal{B} \Longleftrightarrow \exists X \in \mathcal{A}, \exists Y \in \mathcal{B}\ X \supseteq Y.$

Let Q be a query that involves conditions described in interval set $\mathcal{B} = [B_1, B_2] \subseteq 2^{V_a} \setminus \emptyset$, then two retrieval sets $Ret_*(Q)$ and $Ret^*(Q)$ defined by

$$Ret_*(Q) = \{u_i, \mid a(u_i) = \mathcal{A}, \mathcal{A} \supseteq_* \mathcal{B}\};\ \ Ret^*(Q) = \{u_i, \mid a(u_i) = \mathcal{A}, \mathcal{A} \supseteq^* \mathcal{B}\}, \tag{3}$$

give the lower and upper approximations of a set of objects that support query Q. For instance, if query Q says 'select UK manufactures related objects' and we set $\mathcal{B} = [\{UK\}, \{UK\}] = \{\{UK\}\} \subseteq 2^{V_{manu}} \setminus \emptyset$, then $Ret_*(Q) = \{u_1, u_5\}$ and $Ret^*(Q) = \{u_1, u_2, u_5\}$.

3 Set Semantics of Propositional Logic

A deterministic information system can be best demonstrated using a data table in rough sets. Each data table contains a number of rows labelled by objects (or states, processes etc.) and columns by primitive attributes. Each primitive attribute is associated with a set of mutually exclusive values that the attribute can be assigned to. Each attribute also defines an elementary equivalence relation and each equivalence class of the relation is uniquely identifiable by an attribute value. When an attribute can choose values from different value sets, only one of the possible value sets will be used in a particular data table. Each equivalence class in a partition is also naturally corresponding to a concept which can be characterized by a proper proposition. In the following, if we take P, $P = \{q_1, q_2, ..., q_n\}$, as a finite set of atomic propositions, then as usual $\mathcal{L}(P)$ is used to denote the propositional language formed from P. $\mathcal{L}(P)$ consists of P, logical constants *true* and *false*, and all the sentences constructed from P using logical connectives $\{\neg, \wedge, \vee, \rightarrow, \leftrightarrow\}$ as well as parentheses (,).

Definition 6. *Let U be a non-empty universe with a finite number of objects, P be a finite set of atomic propositions. Function $val : U \times P \rightarrow \{true, false\}$ is called a valuation function, which assigns either true or false to every ordered pair (u, q) where $u \in U$ and $q \in P$.*

$val(u, q) = true$, denoted as $u \models_S q$, can be understood as *q is true with respect to object u in S*, where $S = (U, \Omega, V_a)_{a \in \Omega}$ is an information system. Based on val, another mapping function $v : P \rightarrow 2^U$ can be derived as:

$$v(q) = \{u \mid u \in U, u \models_S q\}, \tag{4}$$

where $u \in v(q)$ is interpreted as q holds at state u (or is proved by object u). Function v can be extended to a mapping $v : \mathcal{L}(P) \to 2^U$ as follows. For any $\phi, \psi \in \mathcal{L}(P)$,

$$v(\phi \wedge \psi) = \{u \mid u \in U, (u \models_S \phi) \ and \ (u \models_S \psi)\}, \tag{5}$$

$$v(\phi \vee \psi) = \{u \mid u \in U, (u \models_S \phi) \ or \ (u \models_S \psi)\}, \tag{6}$$

$$v(\neg\phi) = \{u \mid u \in U, u \not\models_S \phi\}. \tag{7}$$

Therefore, the subset of U containing those objects supporting formula ϕ (non-atomic proposition) can be derived through the initial truth assignment val. An atomic proposition can be formally defined as: there exists one and only one attribute $a \in \Omega$ in an information system $(U, \Omega, V_a)_{a \in \Omega}$, such that there exists only one x, $x \in V_a$, $v(q) = \{u \mid a(u) = x\}$.

Definition 7. *Let (U, R, P, val) be a structure where R is an elementary equivalence relation on U, P is a finite set of atomic propositions, and val is an valuation function on $U \times P$. If there is a subset $P' = \{q_1, ..., q_n\}$ of P such that $U/R = \{v(q_1), v(q_2), ..., v(q_n)\}$ holds, then subset P' is said to be equivalent to R, denoted as $U/R = v(P')$.*

$v(P')$ is defined as a collection of subsets of U, i.e., $v(P') = \{v(q_1), v(q_2), ..., v(q_n)\}$ for all $q_l \in P'$. This definition suggests that there can be a subset of a set of atomic propositions P which is functionally equivalent to an elementary equivalence relation in terms of partitioning a universe, regarding to a particular aspect (attribute) of the objects in the universe.

Table 2. A sample test case data table

U	ID	Engineer	Feature	Purpose
c_1	408	N Ross	STM-4o	
c_2	356	N Ross	STM-1o	Undefined
c_3	228	T Smith	Connections	Undefined
c_4	175	T Smith	Protection Switching	{{Forced Path Protection Switch is successful when Standby Path is faulty}, {Pass criteria: Path Protection to the Standby Path occurs}, {Fail criteria: Path Protection to the Standby Path} not occur}}
c_5	226	T Smith	Synchronisation	{{STM-N/ESI ports added to the SETG priority list, Ensure ports not logically equipped not added}}
c_6	214	none	2Mbit/s	Undefined
c_7	48	N Ross	STM-4o	
c_8	50	N Ross	STM-1o	{{Can configure Alarm Severity of Card Out, Default value of Severity is Minor}, {When Severity is changed Alarm should raise}}
c_9	72	N Ross	STM-1o	{{Can display card type, Card variant, and Unique serial No}, {Otherwise, Alarm should raise}}
c_{10}	175	P Hay	STM-1o	{{HP-UNEQ Alarm raised when C2=00 5 times}, {Alarm not raised when C2 is set 00}}

Example 1. Assume U is a universe containing 10 simplified snap-shot of test cases in telecommunications (Table 2). Let R be an equivalence relation on U which divides U into three disjoint sets, one with those cases for which the value of *Purpose* is empty, one with *Purpose Undefined*, and one with *Purpose Defined* (if the details of *Purpose* of an object are given, we say it is defined). Similarly, relation R', which divides U into six disjoint sets based on the names of Feature, is also an equivalence relation. The equivalence classes generated by R and R' are: $U/R = \{\{c_1, c_7\}, \{c_2, c_3, c_6\}, \{c_4, c_5, c_8, c_9, c_{10}\}\}$ and $U/R' = \{\{c_1, c_7\}, \{c_2, c_8, c_9, c_{10}\}, \{c_3\}, \{c_4\}, \{c_5\}, \{c_6\}\}$. $R = R_{\{Purpose\}}$ and $R' = R_{\{Feature\}}$ are elementary equivalence relations, but $R \cap R'$ is not. Let q_1, ..., q_6 be six atomic propositions, *'A test case has feature STM-4o'*, ..., *'A test case has feature 2Mbit/s'* respectively, these six atomic propositions divide U into six disjoint subsets: $v(q_1) = \{c_1, c_7\}$, $v(q_2) = \{c_2, c_8, c_9, c_{10}\}$, $v(q_3) = \{c_3\}$, $v(q_4) = \{c_4\}$, $v(q_5) = \{c_5\}$, and $v(q_6) = \{c_6\}$, where $v(q_i) = W_i^{R'}$ for $i = 1, ..., 6$. Therefore $v(P') = U/R$.

Definition 8. *Let (U, R, P, val) be a structure defined in Definition 7. For a formula ϕ in $\mathcal{L}(P)$, if $v(\phi)$ defined in Eq. (4) is R-definable then ϕ is said to be an R-definable formula. Otherwise, ϕ is R-underfinable. Formulae true and $false$ are always R-definable with $v(true) = U$ and $v(false) = \emptyset$.*

Theorem 1. *Let $(U, IND(\mathcal{R}), P, val)$ be a structure defined in Definition 7 with $\mathcal{R} = \{R_1, R_2, ..., R_n\}$ containing n elementary equivalence relations on U. When $U/R_i = v(P_i)$ holds for $i = 1, ..., n$ and $P_i \subseteq P$, every formula in $\mathcal{L}(P')$ ($P' = \cup_i P_i$) is an $IND(\mathcal{R})$-definable formula.*

Example 2. Let U be a set of objects containing a group of 10 test cases as given in Table 2. Let P_1 and P_2 be two subsets of a set of atomic propositions P as $P_1 = \{q_{11}, q_{12}, q_{13}\}$={Purpose is empty, Undefined, Defined} and $P_2 = \{q_{21}, q_{22}, q_{23}, q_{24}, q_{25}, q_{26}\}$={feature with STM-4o, STM-1o, Connections, protection-Switching, Synchronisation, 2Mbit/s}. These two subsets of atomic propositions are equivalent to the two elementary equivalence relations, R and R', in Example 1.

The following formulae:

ϕ =test cases with feature *STM-1o* and purpose given,

ψ =either test cases with feature *Connections* or with purpose undefined,

φ =test cases with feature is neither *STM-4o* nor *STM-1o* and purpose known,

which can be re-written into disjunctive normal forms:

$\phi = (q_{13} \wedge q_{22})$,

$\psi = (q_{12}) \vee (q_{23})$,

$\varphi = (q_{13} \wedge \neg(q_{12} \vee q_{22})) = (q_{13} \wedge (\neg q_{21} \wedge \neg q_{22}))$

are all $R_1 \cap R_2$-definable. The subsets of objects supporting these formulae, i.e., $v(\phi)$, $v(\psi)$, and $v(\varphi)$ are $\{c_8, c_9, c_{10}\}$, $\{c_2, c_3, c_6\}$, and $\{c_4, c_5\}$ respectively.

Valuation function *val* requires full information about every ordered pair (u, q) in the space $U \times P$. This is an ideal situation where for every formula

ϕ in $\mathcal{L}(P)$ it is possible to identify all the objects that support ϕ, and this set is $v(\phi)$ through Eq. (4). When a universe U is very large, it may not be practical to require function *val* being fully specified, but be quite reasonable to have information about a particular elementary equivalence relation (R) and its corresponding equivalent subset of a set of atomic propositions (P'). In this case, $v(\phi)$ can be determined only when $\phi \in \mathcal{L}(P')$, as $v(\phi)$ can be represented using elements in U/R.

Still, this is an unavoidable question that one may ask: is it realistic to assume that the relevant equivalence relations (hence equivalence classes) are given as prior knowledge? The answer may be 'No' for many applications, however, the answer is 'Yes' for the test-case selection scenario in telecommunications, because the feature or sub-feature of all already designed test cases must be given.

Definition 9. *Structure (U, R, P, P', val) is called a partial rough logic theory*

1. *U is a universe consisting of a finite number of objects,*
2. *P is a finite set of atomic propositions,*
3. *R is an elementary equivalence relation on U,*
4. *Valuation function val is only partially specified on space $U \times P$*
5. *$P' \subset P$. For each $q_l \in P'$, $v(q_l) = W_l$ and W_l is in U/R.*

Based on a partial rough logic theory (U, R, P, P', val), the following equations hold only for formulae ϕ, ψ in $\mathcal{L}(P')$.

$$v(\neg\phi) = U \setminus v(\phi), \qquad v(\phi \wedge \psi) = v(\phi) \cap v(\psi),$$
$$v(\phi \vee \psi) = v(\phi) \cup v(\psi), \qquad v(\phi \rightarrow \psi) = (U \setminus v(\phi)) \cup v(\psi).$$

Each partial rough logic theory defines the set of objects supporting a formula in $\mathcal{L}(P')$ precisely with the knowledge of relevant elementary equivalence relation R. That is, all formulae in $\mathcal{L}(P')$ are $R-$definable. For $\psi \in \mathcal{L}(P) \setminus \mathcal{L}(P')$ which is not R-definable, it is only possible to define the upper and lower approximations of $v(\phi)$.

$$\underline{v}(\phi) = \cup\{v(\psi) \mid \psi \models \phi, \psi \in \mathcal{L}(P')\} = \cup\{W_i \subseteq v(\psi) \mid \psi \models \phi, \psi \in \mathcal{L}(P')\}, \quad (8)$$

$$\overline{v}(\phi) = U \setminus \underline{v}(\neg\phi). \quad (9)$$

Eq. (8) defines the lower bound of the set of objects that make formula ϕ true and Eq. (9) gives the upper bound of that set. The algebraic properties of $(\underline{v}, \overline{v})$ can be found in [2]. All objects in the lower bound will definitely satisfy formula ϕ while an object in the upper bound is known not to satisfy $\neg\phi$, therefore, it may support ϕ. In terms of Dempster-Shafer theory of evidence, if a frame of discernment is defined as elements being the equivalence classes of R, then Eq.(8) will yield a belief function and Eq.(9) will produce a plausibility function ([7]).

4 Reasoning about Knowledge

From general concepts (values) to specific concepts (values) or vice versa: An information system, exemplified by a data table, provides the basic information to answer relevant queries. Since each attribute in a data table is confined to an exclusive set of values, some intermediate values cannot always be explicitly shown in this table. When a query involves in an intermediate value, a system has to have an approach to matching it with the more specific/general values available in the table. This process requires additional knowledge about the application domain that is being dealt with. We call the tables holding the domain knowledge as meta-level tables, such as Table 3.

Table 3. A meta-data table

$\rightarrow$	Feature-details	Feature
	T25 Alarm Reporting - Unterminated Through Connections	STM-4o
	T24 STM-4 Alarm Correlation - HP-REI masked by HP-RDI	STM-4o
	T20 Eqpt Alarms - ALS-Dis (STM-4)	STM-4o
	T19 Eqpt Alarms - Write Protect Jumper Fitted	STM-4o
	T12 Plug-in Unit Alarms - Unexpected Card	STM-4o
	T11 Plug-in Unit Alarms - Card Out	STM-4o
	T10 Loopback - Operation	STM-4o
	...	

Now we visit Example 1 again. In Table 2, one of the values of attribute *Feature* is *STM-4o*. In fact, *STM-4o* covers wide range of test activities, such as, *T20 Eqpt Alarms - ALS-Dis (STM-4)* or *T10 Loopback - Operation* (see Table 3 for more). Therefore, it is more useful to provide these details in a data table than just giving *STM-4o*. We now replace attribute *Feature* with *Feature-details* and update the values of *Feature-details* as appropriate as shown in Table 4. For instance, if feature *STM-4o* is not replaced by a set of detailed features, it is then difficult to answer the following query **Q1**: select test cases with features relevant to *Plug-in unit alarms*. With Table 4, it is easy to answer Q1. However, it raises problems when queries like Q2 below are issued, **Q2**: select test cases with *STM-4o* related *plug-in* tests.

To deal with the connections/relationships between general and specific concepts in a given domain, meta-level knowledge needs to be available. Meta-level tables can be used as supplements to data tables when answering queries. In this way, knowledge *"T25 Alarm Reporting $\rightarrow$ STM-4o"* is stored as a record in a meta-level table as shown in Table 3. There are in total 14 most general features, hence 14 meta-level tables are required. Now, let us assume that P is a set of atomic propositions with q_1 standing for *'A test case has feature T25 Alarm Reporting'*, q_2 for *'A test case has feature STM-1o'*, ..., , q_7 for *'A test case has feature Plug-in Unit Alarms'* respectively. Let us also assume that R is an elementary equivalence relation which partitions test cases according to their features. Based on Definition 7, subset $P' = \{q_1, q_2, .., q_7\}$ is equivalent to R and $U/R = v(P')$. Given the knowledge about P' and R, according to Theorem 1, every formula in $\mathcal{L}(P')$ is R−definable. Query Q1 above which can be re-written as a proposition, φ_1 = a test case has feature *Plug-in Unit Alarms* $= q_7$, can be answered based on knowledge R. Similarly, query Q2 which means 'a test case has feature *STM-4o* and feature *Plug-in*' can be expressed as $\varphi_2 = (q_1 \vee q_7 \vee q_8 \vee q_9 \vee q_{10} \vee q_{11} \vee q_{12}) \wedge q_7 = q_7$, is also R-definable, where q_8, ..., q_{12} stand for 5 atomic propositions that a test has feature with *T24, T20, T19, T11,* or *T10* respectively (see the details given above). Therefore test cases (objects) supporting it are obtained straightforwardly. However, query **Q3**: select test cases relevant to alarms (or alarm raise), is not R-definable, since test cases $c8$ and $c10$ are also relevant to alarms problems as shown in the column *Purpose* and they cannot be summarized into an equivalence class of R. If we use φ_3 to denote query Q3, we have $q_1 \models \varphi_3$ and $q_7 \models \varphi_3$, where $p_1 \models p_2$ means whenever an interpretation makes p_1 true, it must make p_2 true as well. According to Eqs. (8) and (9),

$$\underline{v}(\varphi_3) = \cup\{v(q) \mid q \models \varphi_3\} = v(q_1) \cup v(q_7) = W_1^R \cup W_7^R = \{c1, c7\},$$
$$\overline{v}(\varphi_3) = U \setminus \underline{v}(\neg\varphi_3) = U \setminus \emptyset = U.$$

$\underline{v}(\varphi_3)$ gives us those test cases which should be definitely selected while $\overline{v}(\varphi_3)$ covers those test cases that might be selected. For this query, $\overline{v}(\varphi_3)$ does not provide much useful information, since it contains all test cases. To further eliminate worthless test cases, we need to make use of other information in the database. Because values of attribute *Purpose* cannot be used to partition the universe due to its non-deterministic nature. When the details of Purpose of a test case are given, it usually contains several possible outcomes of a test, each of which may in turn consist of several symptoms simultaneously. To model this phenomena, we apply set-based computations discussed in Section 2.2.

Table 4. A set based sample test case data table

U	Purpose-key-word
c1	
c2	Undefined
c3	Undefined
c4	{{Forced Path Protection Switch, success, Standby Path faulty}, {Path Protection, Standby Path, occur}, {Path Protection, Standby Path, not occur}}
c5	{{Stm-N/ESI ports, Setg priority list, Ports not logically equipped, not added}}
c6	Undefined
c7	
c8	{{Alarm Severity, Card Out, Default value, Severity, Minor}, {Severity change, Alarm raise}}
c9	{{Card type, Card variant, Unique Serial No}, {Alarm raise}}
c10	{{HP-UNEQ, Alarm raised, C2=00 5 times}, {Alarm not raised, C2 set 00}}

Refining upper bounds using set-based computations: Equipped with Definition 5 and Eqs. in (3), we revise Table 2 *Purpose* to obtain Table 4 *Purpose-key-word* (we only include this attribute in Table 4). It is worth pointing out that when a test case has multiple values for attribute *Purpose*, each value is a possible outcome of that test case and the value cannot be decided until the test case is used in a specific test. In addition for each possible outcome, a set of joint descriptions is possible. In this situation, those descriptions should be read conjunctively. For example, value {*Can display card type; Card variant; Unique serial No*} means a user 'can read card type and card variant, and unique serial number'. In order to process the sentence descriptions in column *Purpose* more efficiently, we have identified a set of key-words used in all possibly purpose specifications. The sentence descriptions of *Purpose* of a test case are thus replaced by the combinations of these key-words, as shown in Table 4. Therefore, each possible outcome identified in column *Purpose-key-word* can be treated as a set of values[1]. This enables set-based computations applicable.

Let V_{purp} be the set of all key-word collections used for describing *Purpose*, and let p be a key-word appeared in a given query Q, logically expressed as formula q, then interval set $\mathcal{B} = [\{p\}, \{p\}] = \{\{p\}\} \subseteq 2^{V_{purp}} \setminus \emptyset$ is called a *base interval set.* Further more, let u_i be a test case in $\overline{v}(q)$, and let $\mathcal{A}_i = Purpose-key-word(u_i)$ be the set of subsets of purpose key-word collections of u_i. Then sets $\overline{v}(q)_*$ and $\overline{v}(q)^*$ defined by the following two equations are referred to as the *tighter upper bound* and the *looser upper bound* of $\overline{v}(q)$ respectively,

$$\overline{v}(q)_* = Ret_*(Q_\mathcal{B}) \cup \underline{v}(q) = \{u_i \mid purpose-k-w(u_i) = \mathcal{A}_i, \mathcal{A}_i \supseteq_* \mathcal{B}\} \cup \underline{v}(q), \quad (10)$$

$$\overline{v}(q)^* = Ret^*(Q_\mathcal{B}) \cup \underline{v}(q) = \{u_i \mid purpose-k-w(u_i) = \mathcal{A}_i, \mathcal{A}_i \supseteq^* \mathcal{B}\} \cup \underline{v}(q). \quad (11)$$

It is observed that the purpose of a test case may not be defined and it is also possible that the purpose of a test case in $\underline{v}(q)$ can either not be defined or not contain key-word p. Therefore, we will have to union $\underline{v}(q)$ to the selected set. Also, subscript $\mathcal{B}$ of Q can be omitted is there is no confusion about which base interval set we refer to.

When a query Q involves several key-words and generates multiple base interval sets, $\mathcal{B}_1, ..., \mathcal{B}_j$, Eqs. (10) and (11) will be repeatedly applied to all base interval sets. As for any two base interval sets $\mathcal{B}_i$ and $\mathcal{B}_j$ defined from two distinct key-words, the effect of conjunction or disjunction of the key-words in a query will be reflected by the computation of joint tighter/looser bounds using the following equations:

$$\overline{v}(q_{\mathcal{B}_i and \mathcal{B}_j})_* = \overline{v}(q_{\mathcal{B}_i})_* \cap \overline{v}(q_{\mathcal{B}_j})_*, \qquad \overline{v}(q_{\mathcal{B}_i and \mathcal{B}_j})^* = \overline{v}(q_{\mathcal{B}_i})^* \cap \overline{v}(q_{\mathcal{B}_j})^*;$$
$$\overline{v}(q_{\mathcal{B}_i or \mathcal{B}_j})_* = \overline{v}(q_{\mathcal{B}_i})_* \cup \overline{v}(q_{\mathcal{B}_j})_*, \qquad \overline{v}(q_{\mathcal{B}_i or \mathcal{B}_j})^* = \overline{v}(q_{\mathcal{B}_i})^* \cup \overline{v}(q_{\mathcal{B}_j})^*.$$

Now looking back at query Q_3, if we assume $\mathcal{B}$ =[{Alarm}, {Alarm}]={{Alarm}}, and apply Eqs. (10) and (11) to $\overline{v}(\varphi_3)$, we get $\overline{v}(\varphi_3)_* = \{c_8, c_{10}\} \cup \{c_1, c_7\}$ and $\overline{v}(\varphi_3)^* = \{c_8, c_9, c_{10}\} \cup \{c_1, c_7\}$.

5 Conclusion

In this paper, we have presented novel approaches to coping with two common problems usually involved in a query: general concepts that are not explicitly

[1] In fact, we rename the existing attribute *Purpose* as *Purpose-description* and add an additional attribute *Purpose-key-word.* In this way, we will be able to look at the detailed descriptions of test case purposes for those selected test cases.

defined in a data table and non-determinictic values among a set of possible choices. A logical based method is used to deal with the former while set based computations are applied to the latter.

The method in [5] is not applicable in test case selection problem, since there is a large number of attributes (24) involved in test case data table with thousands of records (test cases). It is not practical to re-generate the whole test case table every time a query is issued. The approach in [1] is also inadequate for this specific application because there are no user defined bounds available to generate possible predicates. However, our mechanism is very similar to the knowledge representation schema in [12], where a tree is used to represent all the possible values of an attribute at different levels. Instead of using trees, we use meta-level tables to do the same job. Each meta-level table, equivalent to a tree in [12], can have more than two columns, with the most specific values in the far-left column and the most general values at the far-right. The manipulation and maintenance of these tables are almost identical to any data table in an information system, so there is very little extra work involved in building these meta-level tables.

Acknowledgments. I would like to thank Andrzej Skowron and Ivo Düntsch for their valuable comments on an earlier version of the paper, and Alfons Schuster for providing the telecommunication database. This project (Jigsaw) is jointly supported by the Nortel Networks and the IRTU, Northern Ireland.

References

1. Beaubouef, T. and Petry, F. E., (1995) Rough querying of crisp data in relational databases. In [4], 85-88.
2. Düntsch, I., (1997) A logic for rough sets. *Theoretical Computer Science* **179**(1-2), 427-236.
3. Düntsch, I. et al, (2001) Relational attribute systems, *International Journal of Human Computer Studies*, To appear.
4. Lin, T.Y. and Wildberger, A.M. (eds), (1995) *Soft Computing. Proceedings of Third International Workshop on Rough Sets and Soft Computing.* San Jose State University, USA, November 10-12.
5. Lin, T.Y., (1998) Granular computing on binary relations I: Data mining and neighborhood systems. In [10], 107-121.
6. Lipski, W.J., (1981) On databases with imcomplete information. *J. of the ACM*, Vol 28, 41-70
7. Liu, W., (2001) *Propositional, Probabilistic and Evidential Reasoning: integrating numerical and symbolic approaches.* to appear in *Studies in Fuzziness and Soft Computing* series. Springer-Verlag (Physica-Verlag).
8. Pagliani, P., (1998) A practical introduction to the model-relational approach to approximation spaces. In [10], 207-232.
9. Pawlak, Z., (1991) *Rough Sets. Theoretical Aspects of Reasoning about Data.* Kluwer Academic Publishers,

10. Polkowski, L. and Skowron, A., (ed.) (1998a) *Rough Sets in Knowledge Discovery 1: methodology and applications.* In *Studies in Fuzziness and Soft Computing* Vol 18. Springer-Verlag (Physica-Verlag).
11. Polkowski, L. and Skowron, A., (ed.) (1998b) *Rough Sets in Knowledge Discovery 2: applications, case studies and software systems.* In *Studies in Fuzziness and Soft Computing* Vol 19. Springer-Verlag (Physica-Verlag).
12. Ras, Z.W., (1998) Answering non-standard queries in distributed knowledge based systems. In [11], 98-108.
13. Yao, Y.Y. and Noroozi, N., (1995) A unified model for set-based computations. In [4], 252-255.

The Capacity of a Possibilistic Channel

Andrea Sgarro

DSM, University , 34100 Trieste (Italy)
sgarro@units.it

Abstract. We put forward a model for transmission channels and channel coding which is possibilistic rather than probabilistic. We define a notion of possibilistic capacity, which is connected to a combinatorial notion called graph capacity. In the probabilistic case graph capacity is a relevant quantity only when the allowed decoding error probability is strictly equal to zero, while in the possibilistic case it is a relevant quantity for whatever value of the allowed decoding error possibility; as the allowed error possibility becomes larger the possibilistic capacity stepwise increases (one can reliably transmit data at a higher rate). We discuss an application, in which possibilities are used to cope with uncertainty as caused by a "vague" linguistic description of channel noise.

1 Introduction

The *coding-theoretic* approach to information measures was first taken by Shannon when he laid down the foundations of information theory in his seminal paper of 1948 [14], and has proved to be quite successful; it has lead to such important probabilistic functionals as *source entropy* or *channel capacity*. Below we shall adopt a model for transmission channels which is possibilistic rather than probabilistic; this will lead us to define a notion of *possibilistic capacity* in much the same way as one arrives at the corresponding probabilistic notion. We are confident that our coding-theoretic approach may be a contribution to enlighten, if not to disentangle, the vexed question of defining adequate information measures in possibility theory (non probabilistic, or "unorthodox", information measures are covered, e.g., in [11] or [12]). In [16] a general theory of possibilistic data transmission is put forward; both source coding and channel coding are covered; beside possibilistic capacity, in [16] also a notion of *possibilistic entropy* is defined; an interpretation of possibilistic coding is discussed, which is based on *distortion measures* as currently used in probabilistic source coding.

We recall that the capacity of a probabilistic channel is an *asymptotic* parameter; more precisely, it is the limit value for the *rates* of optimal codes, used to protect information from channel noise; the codes one considers are constrained to satisfy a reliability criterion of the type: the decoding error probability of the code should be at most equal to a tolerated value ϵ, $0 \leq \epsilon < 1$. A streamlined description of channel codes will be given below in Section 4; even from our fleeting hints it is however apparent that, at least *a priori*, the capacity of a channel depends on the value ϵ which has been chosen to specify the reliability criterion. If

S. Benferhat and P. Besnard (Eds.): ECSQARU 2001, LNAI 2143, pp. 398–409, 2001.

in the probabilistic models the mention of ϵ is usually omitted, the reason is that the asymptotic value for the optimal rates is the same whatever the value of ϵ, *provided however that ϵ is strictly positive.* A zero-error reliability criterion leads instead to quite a different quantity, called *zero-error capacity.* The zero-error problem of data protection in noisy channels is exceedingly difficult, and has lead to a new and fascinating branch of information theory and combinatorics, called *zero-error information theory*, which has been pretty recently overviewed in [13]. In particular, the zero-error capacity of a probabilistic channel is expressed in terms of a remarkable combinatorial notion called Shannon's *graph capacity.*

So, even in the case of *probabilistic* capacity one deals with a *step function* of ϵ, which assumes only two distinct values, one for $\epsilon = 0$ and the other for $\epsilon > 0$. We shall adopt a model of the channel which is possibilistic rather than probabilistic, and shall choose a reliability criterion of the type: the decoding error *possibility* should be at most equal to ϵ, $0 \leq \epsilon < 1$. As shown below, the possibilistic analogue of capacity exhibits quite a perspicuous stepwise behaviour as a function of ϵ, and so the mention of ϵ cannot be disposed of. As for the "form" of the functional one obtains, it is of the same type as in the case of the zero-error probabilistic case, even when the tolerated error possibility is strictly positive: the capacities of possibilistic channels are always expressed in terms of graph capacities. In the possibilistic case, however, as one loosens the reliability criterion by allowing a larger error possibility, the relevant graph changes and the capacity of the possibilistic channel increases.

We describe the contents of the paper. In Section 2, after some preliminaries on possibility theory, possibilistic channels are introduced. Section 3 contains simple lemmas, which are handy tools apt to "translate" probabilistic zero-error results into the framework of possibility theory. In Section 4, after giving a streamlined description of channel coding, possibilistic capacity is defined and a coding theorem is provided. Up to Section 4, our point of view is rather abstract: the goal is simply to understand what happens when one replaces probabilities by possibilities in the current models of data transmission. A discussion of the practical meaning of our proposal is instead deferred to Section 5; possibilities are seen as numeric counterparts for "vague" linguistic judgements.

In this paper we take the asymptotic point of view which is typical of Shannon theory, but one might prefer to take the constructive point of view of algebraic coding: as a first step in this direction, in [1] and [9] a possibilistic decoding strategy has been examined which is derived from minimum Hamming distance decoding. We deem that the need for a solid theoretical foundation of "soft" coding, as possibilistic coding basically is, is proved by the fact that several *ad hoc* coding algorithms are already successfully used in practice, which are not based on probabilistic descriptions of the source or of the channel; such descriptions, which are derived from statistical estimates, are often too costly to obtain, or even unfeasible, and at the same time they are uselessly detailed.

The paper aims at a minimum level of self-containment, and so we have shortly redescribed certain notions of information theory which are quite standard; for more details we refer the reader, e.g., to [3] or [4]. As for possibility theory, and in particular for a clarification of the elusive notion of *non-interactivity*, which is often seen as the natural possibilistic analogue of probabilistic independence (cf Section 2), we mention [5], [6], [8], [10], [11], [17].

2 Possibilistic Channels

We recall that a *possibility distribution* Π over a finite set $\mathcal{A} = \{a_1, \ldots, a_k\}$, called the *alphabet*, is defined by giving a *possibility vector* $\Pi = (\pi_1, \pi_2, \ldots, \pi_k)$ whose components π_i are the possibilities $\Pi(a_i)$ of the k singletons a_i ($1 \leq i \leq k$, $k \geq 2$); the possibility[1] of each subset $A \subseteq \mathcal{A}$ is the maximum of the possibilities of its elements:

$$\Pi(a_i) = \pi_i, \quad 0 \leq \pi_i \leq 1, \quad \max_{1 \leq i \leq k} \pi_i = 1, \quad \Pi(A) = \max_{a_i \in A} \pi_i \tag{2.1}$$

In particular $\Pi(\emptyset) = 0$, $\Pi(\mathcal{A}) = 1$. In logical terms taking a maximum means that event A is ϵ-possible when *at least* one of its elements is so, in the sense of a logical disjunction.

Instead, probability distributions are defined through a probability vector $P = (p_1, p_2, \ldots, p_k)$, and have an *additive* nature, rather than a *maxitive* one. With respect to probabilities, an empirical interpretation of possibilities is less clear. The debate on the meaning and the use of possibilities is an ample and long-standing one; the reader is referred to standard texts on possibility theory, e.g., those quoted at the end of Section 1; cf also Section 5, where the applicability of our model to real-world data transmission is discussed.

Let $\mathcal{A} = \{a_1, \ldots, a_k\}$ and $\mathcal{B} = \{b_1, \ldots, b_h\}$ be two alphabets, called in this context the *input alphabet* and the *output alphabet*, respectively. Probabilistic channels are usually described by giving a stochastic matrix W whose rows are headed to the input alphabet $\mathcal{A}$ and whose columns are headed to the output alphabet $\mathcal{B}$. The k rows of such a stochastic matrix are probability vectors over the output alphabet $\mathcal{B}$; each entry $W(b|a)$ is interpreted as the transition probability from the input letter $a \in \mathcal{A}$ to the output letter $b \in \mathcal{B}$. A *stationary and memoryless channel* W^n, or SML channel, extends W to n-tuples, and is defined by setting for each $\underline{x} = x_1 x_2 \ldots x_n \in \mathcal{A}^n$ and each $\underline{y} = y_1 y_2 \ldots y_n \in \mathcal{B}^n$:

$$W^n(\underline{y}|\underline{x}) \;=\; W^n(y_1 y_2 \ldots y_n | x_1 x_2 \ldots x_n) \;=\; \prod_{i=1}^{n} W(y_i|x_i) \tag{2.2}$$

Note that W^n is itself a stochastic matrix whose rows are headed to the sequences in $\mathcal{A}^n$, and whose columns are headed to the sequences in $\mathcal{B}^n$. The memoryless nature of the channel is expressed by the fact that the n transition probabilities $W(y_i|x_i)$ are multiplied.

We now define the possibilistic analogue of stochastic (probabilistic) matrices. The k rows of a *possibilistic matrix* Ψ with h columns are possibility vectors over

[1] The fact that the same symbol is used both for vectors and for distributions will cause no confusion; similar conventions will be tacitly adopted also in the case of matrices and channels.

the output alphabet $\mathcal{B}$. Each entry $\Psi(b|a)$ will be interpreted as the transition possibility[2] from the input letter $a \in \mathcal{A}$ to the output letter $b \in \mathcal{B}$; cf the example given below. In definition 2.1 Ψ is such a possibilistic matrix.

Definition 2.1. *A stationary and non-interactive channel, or SNI channel, $\Psi^{[n]}$, extends Ψ to n-tuples and is defined as follows:*

$$\Psi^{[n]}(\underline{y}|\underline{x}) = \Psi^{[n]}(y_1 y_2 \dots y_n|x_1 x_2 \dots x_n) = \min_{1\le i\le n} \Psi(y_i|x_i) \tag{2.3}$$

Products as in (2.2) are replaced by a minimum operation; this expresses the fact that the extension is non-interactive. Note that $\Psi^{[n]}$ is itself a possibilistic matrix whose rows are headed to the sequences in $\mathcal{A}^n$, and whose columns are headed to the sequences in $\mathcal{B}^n$. Taking the minimum of the n transition possibilities $\Psi(y_i|x_i)$ may be interpreted as a logical conjunction: only when *all* the transitions are ϵ-possible, it is ϵ-possible to obtain output $\underline{y}$ from input $\underline{x}$. We deem that Section 5 will vindicate the adequateness of the SNI model in situations of practical interest. If B is a subset of $\mathcal{B}^n$, one has in accordance with the last equality of (2.1):

$$\Psi^{[n]}(B|\underline{x}) = \max_{\underline{y}\in B} \Psi^{[n]}(\underline{y}|\underline{x})$$

Example 2.1. For $\mathcal{A} = \mathcal{B} = \{a, b\}$ we show a possibilistic matrix Ψ and its "square" $\Psi^{[2]}$ which specifies the transition possibilities from input couples to output couples. The possibility that a is received when b is sent is δ; this is also the possibility that aa is received when ab is sent, say ; $0 \le \delta \le 1$.

	a	b
a	1	0
b	δ	1

	aa	ab	ba	bb
aa	1	0	0	0
ab	δ	1	0	0
ba	δ	0	1	0
bb	δ	δ	δ	1

3 A Few Lemmas

Sometimes the actual value of a probability does not matter, what matters is only whether that probability is zero or non-zero, i.e., whether the corresponding event E is "impossible" or "possible". The *canonical transformation* maps probabilities to binary (zero-one) possibilities by setting $\text{Poss}\{E\} = 0$ if and only if

[2] Of course transition probabilities and transition possibilities are *conditional probabilities* and *conditional possibilities*, respectively, as made clear by our notation which uses a conditioning bar. We have avoided mentioning explicitly the notion of conditional possibilities because they are the object of a debate which is far from being closed (cf, e.g., Part II of [5]); actually, the worst problems are met when one starts by assigning a joint distribution and wants to compute the marginal and conditional ones. In our case it is instead conditional possibilities that are the starting point: as argued in [2], "prior" conditional possibilities are not problematic, or rather they are no more problematic than possibilities in themselves.

Prob$\{E\} = 0$, else Poss$\{E\} = 1$; this transformation can be applied to the components of a probability vector P or to the components of a stochastic matrix W to obtain a possibility vector Π or a possibilistic matrix Ψ, respectively. Below we shall introduce a more general notion called *ϵ-equivalence*. It will appear that a matrix Ψ obtained canonically from W is ϵ-equivalent to W for whatever value of ϵ (here and in the sequel ϵ is a real number such as $0 \leq \epsilon < 1$).

Definition 3.1. *A stochastic matrix W and a possibilistic matrix Ψ are said to be* ϵ-equivalent *when the following double implication holds $\forall a \in \mathcal{A}$, $\forall b \in \mathcal{B}$:*

$$W(b|a) = 0 \iff \Psi(b|a) \leq \epsilon$$

However simple, the following lemma 3.1 is the basic tool used to convert probabilistic zero-error results into possibilistic ones (the straightforward proofs of the two lemmas below are omitted).

Lemma 3.1. *Fix $n \geq 1$. The stochastic matrix W and the possibilistic matrix Ψ are ϵ-equivalent if and only if the following double implication holds $\forall \underline{x} \in \mathcal{A}^n$, $\forall B \subseteq \mathcal{B}^n$:*

$$W^n(B|\underline{x}) = 0 \iff \Psi^{[n]}(B|\underline{x}) \leq \epsilon$$

In Sections 4 and 5 on channel coding we shall need the following notion of *confoundability* between letters: two input letters a and a' are *confoundable* for the probabilistic matrix W if and only if there exists at least an output letter b such that the transition probabilities $W(b|a)$ and $W(b|a')$ are both strictly positive. Given matrix W, one can construct a *confoundability graph* $\mathbf{G}(W)$, whose vertices are the letters of $\mathcal{A}$, by joining two letters by an edge if and only if they are confoundable.

We now define a similar notion for possibilistic matrices. To this end we first introduce a *proximity index* σ_Ψ between any two input letters a and a':

$$\sigma_\Psi(a, a') = \max_{b \in \mathcal{B}} \left[\Psi(b|a) \wedge \Psi(b|a')\right]$$

Above the wedge symbol $\wedge$ stands for a minimum and is used only to improve readability. We observe that $\sigma_\Psi(a, a')$ is a *proximity relation* in the technical sense of fuzzy set theory.

Example 3.1. We re-take example 2.1 above. One has: $\sigma_\Psi(a, a) = \sigma_\Psi(b, b) = 1$, $\sigma_\Psi(a, b) = \delta$. With respect to $\Psi^{[2]}$, the proximity of two letter couples $\underline{x}$ and $\underline{x}'$ is either 1 or δ, according whether $\underline{x} = \underline{x}'$ or $\underline{x} \neq \underline{x}'$ (recall that $\Psi^{[2]}$ can be viewed as a possibilistic matrix over the "alphabet" of letter couples). Cf also example 4.1 and the application worked out in Section 5.

Definition 3.2. *Once a possibilistic matrix Ψ and a number ϵ are given ($0 \leq \epsilon < 1$), two input letters a and a' are defined to be* ϵ-confoundable *if and only if their proximity exceeds ϵ:*

$$\sigma_\Psi(a, a') > \epsilon$$

Given Ψ and ϵ, one constructs the *ϵ-confoundability graph* $\mathbf{G}_\epsilon(\Psi)$, whose vertices are the letters of $\mathcal{A}$, by joining two letters by an edge if and only if they are ϵ-confoundable for Ψ. If W^n and $\Psi^{[n]}$ are seen as matrices with k^n rows headed to $\mathcal{A}^n$ and h^n columns headed to $\mathcal{B}^n$, one can consider also the confoundability graphs $\mathbf{G}(W^n)$ and $\mathbf{G}(\Psi^{[n]})$ for the k^n input sequences of length n: as one soon checks, two "vertices" (two input sequences) $\underline{x} = x_1x_2 \ldots x_n$ and $\underline{u} = u_1u_2 \ldots u_n$ are joined by an edge if and only if for each component i either $x_i = u_i$, or x_i and u_i are adjacent; $1 \leq i \leq n$. Observe that this sort of extension to a "power-graph" $\mathbf{G}^n$ on vertex sequences of length n can be performed starting from *any* simple graph $\mathbf{G}$, i.e., from any graph without loops and without multiple edges; $\mathbf{G}^n$ is called the *strong power* of $\mathbf{G}$. If one uses strong powers, one can indifferently write $\mathbf{G}(W^n)$ or $\big(\mathbf{G}(W)\big)^n$, $\mathbf{G}_\epsilon(\Psi^{[n]})$ or $\big(\mathbf{G}_\epsilon(\Psi)\big)^n$, respectively.

Lemma 3.2. *If the stochastic matrix W and the possibilistic matrix Ψ are ϵ-equivalent the two confoundability graphs $\mathbf{G}(W^n)$ and $\mathbf{G}_\epsilon(\Psi^{[n]})$ coincide for each length $n \geq 0$.*

We still need a combinatorial notion; cf [4] and [13]. Take any simple graph $\mathbf{G}$ and let $\iota(\mathbf{G}^n)$ be the independence number[3] of the strong-power graph $\mathbf{G}^n$.

Definition 3.3. *The limit of $n^{-1}\log \iota(\mathbf{G}^n)$ when n goes to infinity is called the* graph capacity $C(\mathbf{G})$ *of the graph* $\mathbf{G}$.

The minimum value of Shannon's graph capacity, as it is also called, is zero: just take a *complete* graph. The maximum value of the capacity of a graph with k vertices is $\log k$: just take a graph without edges. It is rather easy to prove that

$$\log \iota(\mathbf{G}) \leq n^{-1}\log \iota(\mathbf{G}^n) \leq \log \chi(\overline{\mathbf{G}}) \tag{3.1}$$

and so whenever $\iota(\mathbf{G}) = \chi(\overline{\mathbf{G}})$ the graph capacity is very simply $C(\mathbf{G}) = \log \iota(\mathbf{G})$; here $\chi(\overline{\mathbf{G}})$ is the *chromatic number* of the *complementary graph* $\overline{\mathbf{G}}$, whose edges are exactly those which are lacking in $\mathbf{G}$. Unfortunately, a single-letter expression of graph capacity is so far unknown, at least in general ("single-letter" means that one is able to calculate explicitly the limit so as to get rid of the length n). E.g., let us take the case of a polygon $\mathbf{P}_k$ with k vertices. For $k = 3$, we have a triangle $\mathbf{P}_3$; then $\iota(\mathbf{P}_3) = \chi(\overline{\mathbf{P}}_3) = 1$ and the capacity $C(\mathbf{P}_3)$ is zero. Let us go to the quadrangle $\mathbf{P}_4$; then $\iota(\mathbf{P}_4) = \chi(\overline{\mathbf{P}}_4) = 2$ and so $C(\mathbf{P}_4) = 1$. In the case of the pentagon, however, $\iota(\mathbf{P}_5) = 2 < \chi(\overline{\mathbf{P}}_5) = 3$. It was quite an achievement of Lovász to prove in 1979 that $C(\mathbf{P}_5) = \log\sqrt{5}$, as conjectured for more than twenty years. The capacity of the heptagon $\mathbf{P}_7$ is still unknown.

[3] We recall that an independent set in a graph, called also a stable set, is a set of vertices no two of which are adjacent. The size of a maximal independent set is called the *independence number* of the graph.

4 The Capacity of a Possibilistic Channel

We start by the following general observation. The elements which define a code f, i.e., the encoder f^+ and the decoder f^- (cf below), do not require a probabilistic or a possibilistic description of the channel. One must simply choose the *input* alphabet $\mathcal{A}$ and the *output* alphabet $\mathcal{B}$; one must also specify a *length* n, which is the length of the codewords which are sent through the channel. Once these elements, $\mathcal{A}$, $\mathcal{B}$ and n, have been chosen, one can construct a code f, i.e., a couple encoder/decoder. Then one can study the performance of f by varying the "behaviour" of the channel: for example one can first assume that this behaviour has a probabilistic nature, while later one changes to a less committal possibilistic description.

We give a streamlined description of what a *channel code* is; for more details we refer to [3], [4], and also to [13], which is specifically devoted to zero-error information theory. The basic elements of a code f are the encoder f^+ and the decoder f^-. The encoder f^+ is an injective (invertible) mapping which takes uncoded messages onto a set of *codewords* $\mathcal{C} \subseteq \mathcal{A}^n$; the set $\mathcal{M}$ of uncoded messages is left unspecified, since its "structure" is irrelevant. Codewords are sent as input sequences through a noisy medium, or noisy channel. They are received at the other end of the channel as output sequences which belong to $\mathcal{B}^n$. The decoder f^- takes back output sequences to the codewords of $\mathcal{C}$, and so to the corresponding uncoded messages. This gives rise to a partition of $\mathcal{B}^n$ into *decoding sets*, one for each codeword $\underline{c} \in \mathcal{C}$. Namely, the decoding set $\mathcal{D}_{\underline{c}}$ for codeword $\underline{c}$ is $\mathcal{D}_{\underline{c}} = \{\underline{y} : f^-(\underline{y}) = \underline{c}\} \subseteq \mathcal{B}^n$.

The most important feature of a code $f = (f^+, f^-)$ is its *codebook* $\mathcal{C} \subseteq \mathcal{A}^n$ of size $|\mathcal{C}|$. The decoder f^-, and so the decoding sets $\mathcal{D}_{\underline{c}}$, are often chosen by use of some decision-theoretic principle, but we shall not need any special assumption. The encoder f^+ will never be used in the sequel, and so its specification is irrelevant. The *rate* R_n of a code f with codebook $\mathcal{C}$ is defined as

$$R_n = n^{-1} \log |\mathcal{C}|$$

The number $\log |\mathcal{C}|$ can be seen as the (not necessarily integer[4]) binary length of the uncoded messages, the ones which carry information; then the rate R_n is interpreted as a transmission speed, which is measured in information bits (bit fractions, rather) per transmitted bit. The idea is to design codes which are fast and reliable at the same time. Once a reliability criterion has been chosen, one tries to find the optimal code for each pre-assigned codeword length n, i.e., a code with highest rate among those which meet the criterion.

Let us consider a *stationary and memoryless* channel W^n, or SML channel, as defined in (2.2). To declare a code f reliable, one requires that the probability

[4] In Shannon theory one often incurs into the slight but convenient inaccuracy of allowing non-integer "lengths". By the way, the logarithms here and below are all to the base 2, and so the unit we choose for information measures is the *bit*. Bars denote size, i.e., number of elements. Notice that, not to overcharge our notation, the mention of the length is not made explicit in the symbols which denote coding functions and codebooks.

that the output sequence does *not* belong to the correct decoding set is acceptably low, i.e., below a pre-assigned threshold ϵ, $0 \leq \epsilon < 1$. If one wants to play safe, one has to insist that the decoding error should be low for *each* codeword $\underline{c} \in \mathcal{C}$ which might have been transmitted. The reliability criterion which a code f must meet is so:

$$\max_{\underline{c}\in\mathcal{C}} W^n\left(\neg\mathcal{D}_{\underline{c}}|\underline{c}\right) \;\leq\; \epsilon \tag{4.1}$$

The symbol $\neg$ denotes negation, or set-complementation; of course the inequality sign in (4.1) can be replaced by an equality sign whenever $\epsilon = 0$. Once the length n and the threshold ϵ are chosen, one can try to determine the rate $R_n = R_n(W, \epsilon)$ of an optimal code which solves the optimization problem:

Maximize the code rate R_n so as to satisfy the constraint (4.1)

The job can be quite tough, however, and so one has often to be contented with the asymptotic value of the optimal rates R_n, which is obtained when the codeword length n goes to infinity. This asymptotic value is called the *ϵ-capacity* of channel W. For $0 < \epsilon < 1$ the capacity C_ϵ is always the same, only the speed of convergence of the optimal rates to C_ϵ is affected by the choice of ϵ. When one says "capacity" one refers by default to the positive ϵ case[5]; cf [3] or [4].

Instead, when $\epsilon = 0$ there is a dramatic change. In this case one uses the *confoundability graph* $\mathbf{G}(W)$ associated with channel W; cf Section 3. As easily checked, for $\epsilon = 0$ the codebook $\mathcal{C} \subseteq \mathcal{A}^n$ of an optimal code is precisely a maximal independent set of $\mathbf{G}(W^n)$. Consequently, the zero-error capacity $C_0(W)$ of channel W is equal to the capacity of the corresponding confoundability graph $\mathbf{G}(W)$, as defined at the end of Section 3:

$$C_0(W) = C\big(\mathbf{G}(W)\big) \tag{4.2}$$

The paper [15] which Shannon published in 1956 and which contains these results inaugurated zero-error information theory. Observe however that the equality (4.2) gives no real solution for the problem of assessing the zero-error capacity of the channel, but simply re-phrases it in a neat combinatorial language; recall that a single-letter expression of graph capacity is so far unknown, at least in general.

We now pass to a *stationary and non-interactive* channel $\Psi^{[n]}$, or SNI channel, as defined in (2.3). The *reliability criterion* (4.1) is correspondingly replaced by:

$$\max_{\underline{c}\in\mathcal{C}} \Psi^{[n]}\left(\neg\mathcal{D}_{\underline{c}}|\underline{c}\right) \;\leq \epsilon \tag{4.3}$$

The optimization problem is now:

---

[5] The capacity relative to a *positive* error probability allows one to construct sequences of codes whose probability of a decoding error is actually infinitesimal; this point of view does not make much sense for possibilistic models, which are intrinsically "discrete".

Maximize the code rate R_n *so as to satisfy the constraint* (4.3)

The number ϵ is now the error *possibility* which we are ready to accept. Again the inequality sign in (4.3) is to be replaced by the equality sign when $\epsilon = 0$.

Definition 4.1. *The* ϵ*-capacity of channel* Ψ *is the limit of optimal code rates* $R_n(\Psi, \epsilon)$, *obtained as the codeword length* n *goes to infinity.*

The following lemma is soon obtained from lemma 3.1, and in its turn soon implies theorem 4.1 (use also lemma 3.2); it states that possibilistic coding and zero-error probabilistic coding are different formulations of the same mathematical problem.

Lemma 4.1. *Let the SML channel* W *and the SNI channel* Ψ *be* ϵ*-equivalent. Then a code* $f = (f^+, f^-)$ *satisfies the reliability criterion* (4.1) *at zero error for the probabilistic channel* W *if and only if it satisfies the reliability criterion* (4.3) *at* ϵ*-error for the possibilistic channel* Ψ.

Theorem 4.1. *The codebook* $\mathcal{C} \subseteq \mathcal{A}^n$ *of an optimal code for criterion* (4.3) *is a maximal independent set of* $\mathbf{G}_\epsilon(\Psi^{[n]})$. *Consequently, the* ϵ*-capacity of the possibilistic channel* Ψ *is equal to the capacity of the corresponding* ϵ*-confoundability graph* $\mathbf{G}_\epsilon(\Psi)$:

$$C_\epsilon(\Psi) = C\big(\mathbf{G}_\epsilon(\Psi)\big)$$

As for the decoding sets $\mathcal{D}_{\underline{c}}$ of an optimal code, their specification is straightforward: one decodes $\underline{y}$ to the unique codeword $\underline{c}$ for which $\Psi^{[n]}(\underline{y}|\underline{c}) > \epsilon$; if $\Psi^{[n]}(\underline{y}|\underline{c}) \leq \epsilon$ for all $\underline{c} \in \mathcal{C}$, then $\underline{y}$ can be assigned to any decoding set, this choice being irrelevant from the point of view of criterion (4.3). Below we stress explicitly the obvious fact that the graph capacity $C_\epsilon(\Psi)$ is a stepwise non-decreasing function of ϵ, $0 \leq \epsilon < 1$; the term "consecutive" refers to an ordering of the distinct components π_i which appear in Ψ (π_i can be zero even if zero does not appear as an entry in Ψ):

Proposition 4.1. *If* $0 \leq \epsilon < \epsilon' < 1$, *then* $C_\epsilon(\Psi) \leq C_{\epsilon'}(\Psi)$. *If* $\pi_i < \pi_{i+1}$ *are two consecutive entries in* Ψ, *then* $C_\epsilon(\Psi)$ *is constant for* $\pi_i \leq \epsilon < \pi_{i+1}$.

Example 4.1: *a "rotating" channel.* Take $k = 5$; the quinary input and output alphabet is the same; the possibilistic matrix Ψ "rotates" the row-vector $(1, \delta, \tau, 0, 0)$ in which $0 < \tau < \delta < 1$:

	a_1	a_2	a_3	a_4	a_5
a_1	1	δ	τ	0	0
a_2	0	1	δ	τ	0
a_3	0	0	1	δ	τ
a_4	τ	0	0	1	δ
a_5	δ	τ	0	0	1

After setting by circularity $a_6 = a_1$, $a_7 = a_2$, one has: $\sigma(a_i, a_i) = 1 > \sigma(a_i, a_{i+1}) = \delta > \sigma(a_i, a_{i+2}) = \tau$, $1 \leq i \leq 5$. Capacities can be computed as explained at the end of Section 3: $C_0(\Psi) = 0$ (the corresponding graph is complete), $C_\tau(\Psi) = \log\sqrt{5}$ (the pentagon graph pops up), $C_\delta(\Psi) = \log 5$ (the corresponding graph is edge-free). So $C_\epsilon(\Psi) = 0$ for $0 \leq \epsilon < \tau$, $C_\epsilon(\Psi) = \log\sqrt{5}$ for $\tau \leq \epsilon < \delta$, else $C_\epsilon(\Psi) = \log 5$.

Remark 4.1. In the probabilistic case a constraint of the type $\text{Prob}\{\neg C\} \leq \epsilon$ can be re-written in terms of the probability of *correct* decoding as $\text{Prob}\{C\} \geq 1-\epsilon$, because $\text{Prob}\{C\}+\text{Prob}\{\neg C\} = 1$. Instead, the sum $\text{Poss}\{C\}+\text{Poss}\{\neg C\}$ can be strictly larger than 1, and so $\text{Poss}\{C\} \geq 1 - \epsilon$ is a different constraint. This constraint, however, would be quite loose and quite uninteresting; actually, the possibility $\text{Poss}\{C\}$ of correct decoding and the error possibility $\text{Poss}\{\neg C\}$ can be both equal to 1 at the same time.

Remark 4.2. Theorem 4.1 has been solved by simply re-cycling a result already available in the probabilistic framework; in [16] we show that the introduction of possibility values which are intermediate between zero and one does enlarge[6] the probabilistic framework of zero-error coding. Namely, in [16] we solve a problem which is not encountered in the probabilistic theory, by proving that the capacity does not change when one relaxes criterion (4.3), and one uses the average possibility of error rather than the maximal one. We expect that more significant novelties will be obtained by the consideration of meaningful *interactive* models, i.e., by an "aggregation" of single transition possibilities different from (2.3).

5 An Application of the Possibilistic Model

We have examined a possibilistic model of data transmission and coding which is inspired by the standard probabilistic model: what we did is simply replacing probabilities by possibilities and independence by non-interactivity, a notion which is often seen as the "right" analogue of probabilistic independence in possibility theory. In this section we shall discuss an application. The reader is referred to [16] for a systematic interpretation of our possibilistic model of data transmission, which is based on *distortion measures*; here we shall only deal with a rather *ad hoc* example. Think of the keys in a digital keyboard, as the one of the author's telephone, say, in which digits from 1 to 9 are arranged on a 3×3 grid, left to right, top row to bottom row, while digit 0 is positioned below digit 8. It may happen that, when a telephone number is digited, the wrong key is pressed. We assume the following model of the "noisy channel", in which possibilities are seen as numeric labels for "uncertain linguistic judgements" (only the ordering of the labels counts, not the actual numeric values):

[6] The new possibilistic frame includes the traditional zero-error probabilistic frame: it is enough to take possibilities which are equal to zero when the probability is zero, and equal to one when the probability is positive, whatever its value.

1. it is *quite plausible* that the correct key is pressed (possibility 1)
2. it is *less plausible* that one inadvertently presses a "neighbour" of the correct key, i.e., a key which is positioned on the same row or on the same column and is contiguous to the correct key (possibility 1/2)
3. everything else is *quite unplausible* (possibility 0)

Using these values[7] one can construct a possibilistic matrix Ψ with the input and the output alphabet both equal to the set of the ten keys. As for the proximity $\sigma_\Psi(a,b)$, it is 1/2 whenever either keys a and b are neighbours, or there is a third key c which is a common neighbour of both. One has, for example: $\Psi(a|1) = 1/2$ for $a \in \{2,4\}$, $\sigma_\Psi(1,a) = 1/2$ for $a \in \{2,3,4,5,7\}$. When the wrong key is pressed, we shall say that a cross-over of type 2 or of type 3 has taken place, according whether its possibility is 1/2 or 0. A codebook is a bunch of admissible telephone numbers of length n; since a phone number is wrong whenever there is a collision with another phone number in a single digit, it is natural to assume that the "noisy channel" Ψ is non-interactive. If the allowed error possibility of the code is as large as 1/2 or more, the confoundability graph is edge-free and no error protection is required. If instead the error possibility is 0, the output sequence $\underline{y}$ is decoded to the single codeword $\underline{c}$ for which $\Psi^{[n]}(\underline{y}|\underline{c}) > 0$; so, error correction is certainly successful if there has been no cross-over of type 3. This example was suggested to us by J. Körner; however, at least in principle, in the standard probabilistic setting one would have to specify a stochastic matrix W such as to be 0-equivalent with Ψ. In W only the opposition zero/non-zero would count; unfortunately, the *empirical* meaning of W is not at all clear, and has nothing to do with the actual probabilities with which errors are committed by the hand of the operator; these probabilities would give one more stochastic matrix $W' \neq W$. So, the adoption of a "hard" probabilistic model is in this case pretty unnatural. Instead, in a "soft" possibilistic approach one specifies just *one* possibilistic matrix Ψ, which contains precisely the information which is needed and nothing more.

Unfortunately, the author's telephone is not especially promising. In this case one has $C_0(\Psi) = \log \iota\big(\mathbf{G}_0(\Psi)\big) = \log 3$; in other words the 0-capacity, which is an asymptotic parameter, is reached already for $n = 1$. To see this use inequalities (3.1). The independence number of $\mathbf{G}_0(\Psi)$ is 3, and a maximal independent set of keys, which are far enough from each other so as not to be confoundable, is $\{0,1,6\}$, as easily checked; however, one checks that 3 is also the chromatic number of the complementary graph. In practice, this means that an optimal codebook as in Theorem 4.1 may be constructed by juxtaposition of the input "letters" 0, 1, 6. If, for example, one digits number 2244 rather than 1111 a successful error correction takes place; actually, $\Psi^{[4]}(2244|\underline{c}) > 0$ only for $\underline{c} = 1111$. If instead one is so clumsy as to digit the "quite unplausible" number 2225, this is incorrectly decoded to 1116. The code is disappointing, since everything boils down to allowing only phone numbers which use keys

[7] We might have chosen a "negligible" positive value, rather than 0: this would have made no difference, save adding an equally negligible initial interval where the channel capacity would have been zero.

0, 1, 6. The design of convenient keyboards such that their possibilistic capacity is *not* obtained already for $n = 1$ is a graph-theoretic problem which may be of relevant practical interest in those situations when digiting an incorrect number may cause serious inconveniences.

References

1. Borelli, M., Sgarro, A.: A Possibilistic Distance for Sequences of Equal and Unequal Length. In *Finite VS Infinite*, ed. by C. Călude and Gh. Păun, Discrete Mathematics and Theoretical Computer Science (Springer, 2000) 27-38
2. Bouchon-Meunier, B., Coletti, G., Marsala, C.: Possibilistic Conditional Events. IPMU 2000, Madrid, July 3-7 2000, Proceedings, 1561-1566
3. Cover, Th.M., Thomas, J.A.: *Elements of Information Theory* (Wiley, 1991)
4. Csiszár, I., Körner, J.: *Information Theory* (Academic Press, 1981)
5. De Cooman, G.: Possibility Theory. International Journal of General Systems **25.4** (1997) 291-371
6. Dubois, D., Nguyen, H.T., Prade, H.: Possibility Theory, Probability and Fuzzy Sets: Misunderstandings, Bridges and Gaps. In *Fundamentals of Fuzzy Sets*, ed. by D. Dubois and H. Prade (Kluwer Academic Publishers, 2000)
7. Dubois, D., Ostasiewicz, W., Prade, H.: Fuzzy Sets: History and Basic Notions. In *Fundamentals of Fuzzy Sets*, ed. by D. Dubois and H. Prade (Kluwer Academic Publishers, 2000)
8. Dubois, D., Prade, H.: Fuzzy Sets in Approximate Reasoning: Inference with Possibility Distribution. Fuzzy Sets and Systems **40** (1991) 143-202
9. Fabris, F., Sgarro, A.: Possibilistic Data Transmission and Fuzzy Integral Decoding, IPMU 2000, Madrid, July 3-7 2000, Proceedings, 1153-1158
10. Hisdal, E.: Conditional Possibilities, Independence and Non-Interaction. Fuzzy Sets and Systems **1** (1978) 283-297
11. Klir, G.J., Folger, T.A.: *Fuzzy Sets, Uncertainty and Information* (Prentice-Hall, 1988)
12. Klir, G.J.: Measures of Uncertainty and Information. In *Fundamentals of Fuzzy Sets*, ed. by D. Dubois and H. Prade (Kluwer Academic Publishers, 2000)
13. Körner, J., Orlitsky, A.: Zero-error Information Theory. IEEE Transactions on Information Theory **44.6** (1998) 2207-2229
14. Shannon, C.E.: A Mathematical Theory of Communication. Bell System Technical Journal **27.3&4** (1948) 379-423, 623-656
15. Shannon, C.E.: The Zero-Error Capacity of a Noisy Channel, IRE Trans. Inform. Theory **IT-2** (1956) 8-19
16. Sgarro, A.: Possibilistic Information Theory: a Coding Theoretic Approach, 2001, preliminary version at: http://www.dsm.univ.trieste.it/~sgarro/possinfo.ps
17. Zadeh, L.: Fuzzy Sets as a Basis for a Theory of Possibility Fuzzy Sets and Systems **1** (1978) 3-28

New Semantics for Quantitative Possibility Theory

Didier Dubois[1], Henri Prade[1], and Philippe Smets[2]**

[1] IRIT, Université Paul Sabatier,
118 route de Narbonne, 31062, Toulouse, cedex 4, France
{dubois@irit.fr}, {prade@irit.fr}
[2] IRIDIA Université Libre de Bruxelles
50 av. Roosevelt, CP 194-6, 1050 Bruxelles, Belgium
{psmets@ulb.ac.be}

Abstract. New semantics for numerical values given to possibility measures are provided. For epistemic possibilities, the new approach is based on the semantics of the transferable belief model, itself based on betting odds. It is shown that the least informative among the belief structures that are compatible with prescribed betting rates is a possibility measure. It is also proved that the idempotent conjunctive combination of two possibility measures corresponds to the hyper-cautious conjunctive combination of the belief functions induced by the possibility measures. For objective possibility degrees, the semantics is based on the most informative possibilistic approximation of a probability measure. We show how the idempotent disjunctive combination of possibility functions is related to the convex mixture of probability distributions.

1 Introduction

Quantitative possibility theory has been proposed as a numerical model which could represent quantified uncertainty [32, 9, 3]. In order to sustain this claim, it is necessary to examine the representation power of possibility theory regarding uncertainty in both objective and subjective contexts. In the objective context, quantitative possibility can be devised as an approximation of upper and lower frequentist probabilities, due to the presence of incomplete statistical observations [6, 15]. In the subjective context, quantitative possibility theory somehow competes with the probabilistic model in its personalistic or Bayesian views and with the transferable belief model (TBM) [28, 24, 25], both of which also intend to represent degrees of belief. A major issue when developing formal models that represent psychological quantities (belief is such an object) is to produce an operational definition of what these degrees are supposed to quantify. Such an operational definition, and the assessment methods that can be derived from it, provide a meaning, a semantics, to the .7 encountered in statements like 'my

** This work was partially realized while the last author was Visiting Professor at IRIT, Université Paul Sabatier, Toulouse, France.

S. Benferhat and P. Besnard (Eds.): ECSQARU 2001, LNAI 2143, pp. 410–421, 2001.

degree of belief is .7'. Such an operational definition has been produced long ago by the Bayesians. They claim that any state of incomplete knowledge of an agent can be modeled by a single probability distribution on the appropriate referential, and that the probabilities can be revealed by a betting experiment in which the agent provides betting odds under an exchangeable bet assumption. A similar setting exists for imprecise probabilities [29], relaxing the assumption of exchangeable bets, and more recently for the TBM as well [28, 27], introducing several betting frames corresponding to various partitions of the referential. In that sense, the numerical values encountered in these three models are well defined.

Quantitative possibility theory (QPT) did not have such a wealth of operational definitions so far, despite an early proposal by Giles [17] in the setting of upper and lower probabilities, recently taken over by De Cooman and colleagues [30, 1]. One way to avoid the measurement problem is to develop a *qualitative* epistemic possibility theory where only ordering relations are used [11].

Nevertheless QPT seems to be a theory worth exploring as well, and rejecting it because of the current lack of convincing semantics would be unfortunate. The recent revival of a form of subjectivist QPT due to De Cooman and colleagues, and the development of possibilistic networks based on incomplete statistical data [16] suggests on the contrary that it is fruitful to investigate various operational semantics for possibility theory. This is due to several reasons: first possibility theory is a special case of most existing non additive uncertainty theories, be they numerical or not. Hence progress in one of these theories usually has impact in possibility theory. Another major reason is that possibility theory is very simple, certainly the simplest competitor for probability theory. Hence it can be used as useful approximate representation by other theories. A last reason is that previous works have suggested strong links between possibility theory and non-Bayesian statistics, especially the use of likelihood functions without prior [22], and confidence intervals. It is not absurd to think that, in the future, possibility theory may contribute to unify and shed some light on some aspects of non-Bayesian statistics.

The aim of this paper is to propose two new semantics for possibility theory: a subjectivist semantics and an objectivist one. We use the term 'subjectivist' to mean that we consider the concepts of beliefs (how much we believe) and betting behaviors (how much would we pay to enter into a game) without regard to the possible random nature and repeatability of the events. We use the term 'objectivist' to mean that we consider data generated by random processes where repetition is natural, and where histograms can summarize the data. The distinction is somehow similar to the one made between the personal and the frequential interpretations of probabilities. It also reflects that in the 'subjectivist' case, we start from a betting behavior, whereas in the 'objectivist' case we start from a histogram.

The subjective semantics differ from the upper and lower probabilistic setting of the subjective possibility proposed by Giles and followers, without questioning its merit. Instead of making the bets non-exchangeable, we assume that the exchangeable betting rates only imperfectly reflect the agent's beliefs. The objectivist semantics suggests a flexible extension of particular confidence intervals.

Moreover we show that the basic combination rules in possibility theory, minimum and maximum, can be interpreted in the proposed settings: the former using a minimal commitment assumption in the subjectivist setting; the latter using an information preservation principle in the frequentist setting.

This paper provides an overview of these semantics. Detailed theorems and proofs can be found in the long version of this paper, which pursues an investigation started in [26]. Up-to-date presentations of the TBM and possibility theory can be found in [25, 11], respectively.

2 Subjectivist semantics

2.1 The transferable belief model and bets

For long, it had been realized that possibility functions are mathematically identical to consonant plausibility functions [21], so using the semantics of the TBM for producing a semantics for quantitative epistemic possibility theory is an obvious approach, even if not explored in depth so far. This link had already been realized long ago. What was missing was to show that the analogy goes further.

Suppose You (the agent who holds the beliefs) consider what beliefs You should adopt on what is the actual value of a variable ranging on the frame of discernment Ω. You have decided that Your beliefs should be those produced by a fully reliable source, and the beliefs are represented by a belief function and its associated basic belief assignment (bba) . The basic belief mass assigned to each set is the weight given to the fact that all You may know from the source is that the value of the variable of interest lies somewhere in that set. A belief function (resp: plausibility function) is a set-function that assigns to each event (subset of the 'frame of discernment') the sum of the masses given to its subsets (resp: to the subsets that intersect it). It evaluates to what extent the event is implied by (resp. consistent with) the available evidence. When the sets with positive mass are nested, the plausibility function is called a possibility measure, and can be characterized, just like probability, by an assignment of weights to singletons, called a possibility distribution.

Should You know the beliefs of the source, they would be Yours. Unfortunately, it occurs that You only know the value of the 'pignistic' probabilities the source would use to bet on the actual value of Ω [23, 28]. The pignistic probability induced by a belief function is built by defining a uniform probability on each set of positive mass, and performing the convex mixture of these probabilities according to the mass function. The knowledge of the values of the probabilities allocated to the elements of Ω is not sufficient to construct a unique underlying belief function. Many belief functions can induce the same probabilities. So all You know about the belief function that represents the source's beliefs is that it belongs to the set of beliefs that induce the supplied pignistic probabilities.

Since several belief functions, lead to the same betting rates, You have to select one that most plausibility reflects the actual states of belief of the source.

A cautious approach is to obey a 'least commitment principle' that states that You should never presuppose more beliefs than justified. Then, You can select the 'least committed' element in the family of belief functions compatible with the pignistic probability function prescribed by the obtained betting rates. The first result of this paper is that the least committed belief function is consonant, that is, the corresponding plausibility function is a possibility function. This possibility function is the unique one in the set of belief functions having a prescribed pignistic probability, because the pignistic transformation is a bijection between possibilities and probabilities. So this possibility function turns out to be the least committed belief function whose pignistic transformation is equal to the pignistic probabilities supplied by the source.

More formally let $m(A)$ be the basic belief mass allocated to subset A. The function m is called a basic belief assignment (bba). The sum of these masses across all events is 1. The degrees of belief $bel(A)$ and plausiblity $pl(A)$ are defined for all $A \subseteq \Omega$, by:

$$bel(A) = \sum_{\emptyset \neq B \subseteq A} m(B) \qquad pl(A) = \sum_{B \cap A \neq \emptyset} m(B) = bel(\Omega) - bel(\overline{A}).$$

In order to enhance the fact that we work with non-normalized belief functions ($m(\emptyset)$ can be positive), we use the notation bel and pl, whereas Shafer uses the notation Bel and Pl. Another useful function that is also in one to one correspondence with any of m, bel and pl is the commonality function q such that: $q(A) = \sum_{B: A \subseteq B} m(B)$.

2.2 Consonant belief functions

A belief function is said to be *consonant* iff its focal elements are nested ([21], pg 219). By extension, we will speak of consonant basic belief assignments, commonality functions, plausibility functions, ...

Theorem 1. ***Consonant belief functions.*** *([21], Theorem 10.1, pg 220) Let m be a bba on Ω. Then the following assertions are all equivalent:*

1. *m is consonant.*
2. *$bel(A \cap B) = \min(bel(A), bel(B)),\ \forall A, B \subseteq \Omega$.*
3. *$pl(A \cup B) = \max(pl(A), pl(B)),\ \forall A, B \subseteq \Omega$.*
4. *$pl(A) = \max_{\omega \in A} pl(\omega)$, for all non empty $A \subseteq \Omega$.*
5. *$q(A) = \min_{\omega \in A} pl(\omega) = \min_{\omega \in A} q(\omega)$, for all non empty $A \subseteq \Omega$.*

Items 2 and 3 shows that consonant belief and plausibility functions are necessity and possibility functions, usually denoted by Π and N respectively, while the $pl(\omega)$'s define a possibility distribution, that contains all the necessary information for building the other set-functions. The fact that we work with unnormalized bba's does not affect these properties, being understood that we never require that possibility and necessity functions be normalized. The difference between $\Pi(\Omega)$ or $pl(\Omega)$ and 1, that equals $m(\emptyset)$, represents the amount of conflict between the pieces of evidence that were used to build these functions.

2.3 Least commitment

So far, what 'least committed' means has not been explained, and refers to the capability of comparing belief functions by their informational contents. Dubois and Prade [8] have made three proposals to order belief functions according to the 'specificity', or precision of the beliefs they represent. Let m_1 and m_2 be two bba's on Ω. The statement that m_1 contains at least as much information as, is at least as precise as m_2 is denoted $m_1 \sqsubseteq_x m_2$ corresponding to some x-ordering where we vary the subscript x. Then m_2 is said to be x-less committed than m_1. The proposed information orderings are:

- *pl-ordering.* If $pl_1(A) \leq pl_2(A)$ for all $A \subseteq \Omega$, we write $m_1 \sqsubseteq_{pl} m_2$
- *q-ordering.* If $q_1(A) \leq q_2(A)$ for all $A \subseteq \Omega$, we write $m_1 \sqsubseteq_q m_2$
- *s-ordering.* If m_1 is a specialization of m_2, we write $m_1 \sqsubseteq_s m_2$

where *pl* denotes the plausibility function and q denotes the commonality function.

The idea behind the pl-ordering is that a belief function is all the more specific as the intervals ranging from the belief degree to the plausibility degree of each event are small.

The idea behind the q-ordering is maybe less obvious. The commonality function of an event reflects the amount of support this event may received from its supersets. So, $q(A)$ represents the portion of belief that may eventually be assigned to A. The more amount of belief remains unassigned, i.e. the bigger the focal elements having a high mass assignment, the higher the commonality degrees and the less informative is the belief function. In particular, if $m(\Omega) = 1$, then $q(A) = 1$ for all sets. More generally, to consider $m(\Omega)$ as a rough measure of uninformativeness of a belief function seems reasonable. Suppose now we know that the actual world belongs to $A \subseteq \Omega$. Then $m[A](A)$ obtained by conditioning m with Dempster's rule of conditioning becomes the 'conditional measure of uninformativeness' in context A. It just happens that $m[A](A) = q(A)$, so the commonality function is the set of conditional measure of uninformativeness, and the fact that a measure of information content turns out to be a function of the q's becomes very natural.

The concept of specialization (s-ordering) [7, 31] is at the core of the transferable belief model [19]. The intuitive idea is that the smaller the focal elements, the more focused are the beliefs. Let $m_Y^\Omega[BK]$ be the basic belief assignment that represents Your belief on Ω given the background knowledge (BK) accumulated by You. The impact of a new piece of evidence Ev induces a change in Your beliefs characterized by a redistribution of the basic belief masses of $m_Y^\Omega[BK]$ such that $m_Y^\Omega[BK](A)$ is reallocated to the subsets of A. In a colloquial way, we say that 'the masses flow down'. The new belief function is said to be a specialization of the former one. More generally, m_2 is a specialization of m_1 if every mass $m_1(A)$ is reallocated to subsets of A in m_2. See [7] for the technical definition.

Dubois and Prade [7] prove that :

- $m_1 \sqsubseteq_s m_2$ implies $m_1 \sqsubseteq_{pl} m_2$ and $m_1 \sqsubseteq_q m_2$, but the converse is not true, and
- $m_1 \sqsubseteq_{pl} m_2$ and $m_1 \sqsubseteq_q m_2$ do not imply each other.

2.4 Pignistic probabilities

Suppose a bba m^Ω that quantifies Your beliefs on Ω. When a decision must be made that depends on the actual value ω_0 where $\omega_0 \in \Omega$, You must construct a probability function in order to make the optimal decision, i.e., the one that maximizes the expected utility. This is achieved by the pignistic transformation. Its nature and its justification are defined in [23, 28, 25].

Smets [23] has shown that the only transformation from m^Ω to $BetP^\Omega$ that satisfies some rationality requirements is the so-called pignistic transformation that satisfies:

$$BetP^\Omega(f) = \sum_{A:\omega\in A\subseteq\Omega} \frac{m^\Omega(A)}{|A|(1-m^\Omega(\emptyset))}, \qquad \forall\omega\in\Omega \tag{1}$$

where $|A|$ is the number of elements of Ω in A.

It is easy to show that the function $BetP^\Omega$ is indeed a probability function and the pignistic transformation of a probability function is the probability function itself. We call it pignistic in order to avoid the confusion that would consist in interpreting $BetP^\Omega$ as a measure representing Your beliefs on Ω.

The result showing that the least committed set of beliefs yielding a prescribed pignistic probability can be represented by a possibility function, has been formally obtained in two ways, depending on how belief functions are compared in terms of information contents. Comparing the belief functions having a prescribed pignistic probability, it can be proved that the least informed one in the sense of the q-ordering is a possibility function. The belief functions having a prescribed pignistic probability are called isopignistic. The following theorem has been obtained:

Theorem 2. *Let $BetP^\Omega$ be a pignistic probability function defined on Ω with the elements ω_i of Ω so labeled that :*

$$BetP^\Omega(\omega_1) \geq BetP^\Omega(\omega_2) \geq \ldots \geq BetP^\Omega(\omega_n)$$

where $n = |\Omega|$. Let $\mathfrak{B}isoP(BetP^\Omega)$ be the set of isopignistic belief functions induced by $BetP^\Omega$. The q-least committed element in $\mathfrak{B}isoP(BetP^\Omega)$ is the consonant belief function of mass $\widehat{m}$ whose only focal elements are the subsets $A_i = \{\omega_1, \omega_2, \ldots, \omega_i\}$ and:

$$\widehat{m}(A_i) = |A_i| \cdot (BetP^\Omega(\omega_i) - BetP^\Omega(\omega_{i+1}))$$

where $BetP^\Omega(\omega_{n+1})$ is 0 by definition.

The probability-possibility transformation described by the theorem was independently proposed by Dubois and Prade [13, 4] a long time ago, using a very different rationale. The other informational orderings do not lead to unique least informed solutions. However a scalar index for comparing belief functions in terms of specificity has been proposed in [5]. The idea is based on the fact that the level of imprecision of a set used to represent a piece of incomplete knowledge is its cardinality (or the logarithm thereof). A belief function is formally a random set, and the degree of imprecision of belief function is simply its expected cardinality (or expected logarithm of the cardinality). Let

$$I(m) = \sum_{A \subseteq \Omega} |A| \cdot m(A)$$

Comparing isopignistic belief functions in terms of expected cardinality, the same result as above obtains:

Theorem 3. *The belief function of maximal expected cardinality $I(Bel)$ among isopignistic belief functions induced by $BetP^{\Omega}$ is the unique possibility function having this pignistic probability.*

3 The minimum rule

The story goes on. Suppose we collect the pignistic probabilities about the actual value of Ω from two sources. From these two pignistic probabilities,You build two consonant plausibility functions, i.e., the two possibility functions induced by the observed betting rates as presented above. How to conjunctively combine the data collected from the two sources? Do we have to redo the whole betting procedure or can we get the result directly by combining the two possibility functions? We will show in this section that indeed the last idea is correct.

In possibility theory, there exists such a combination rule that performs the conjunction of two possibility functions. Let π_1 and π_2 be two possibility distributions on Ω that we want to combine conjunctively into a new possibility function π_{12}. The most classical conjunctive combination rule to build π_{12} consists in using the minimum rule: $\pi_{12}(\omega) = \min(\pi_1(\omega), \pi_2(\omega))$ for all $\omega \in \Omega$ and its related possibility measure is given by $\Pi_{12}(A) = \max_{\omega \in A \subseteq \Omega} \pi_{12}(\omega)$. Could it be applied in the present context? We will show here that it is indeed the case.

We must first avoid a classical trap. In belief function theory, the conjunctive rule of combination for the bba' produced by two distinct pieces of evidence is Dempster's rule of combination. It is well known that Dempster's rule of combination applied to two consonant plausibility functions does not produce a consonant plausibility function. So Dempster's rule of combination does not seem adequate to combine possibility measures. It seems thus that the analogy between consonant plausibility functions and possibility functions collapses here. This is not the case. Dempster's rule of combination requires that the involved pieces of evidence are 'distinct', a concept analogous to independence in random set theory. All we have here are the betting behaviors of the two sources, and 'distinctness' of the sources cannot be assumed.

In fact, other combination rules exist in the TBM, based on some kind of cautious approach and where 'possible correlations' between the involved belief functions are considered. How to combine two bba's conjunctively, when you cannot assume they are produced by two 'distinct' pieces of information? You may assume that the result of the combination must be a specialization of each of them (since the result of the combination should be a belief function at least as informative as the ones You start with). As said above, a specialization of a bba m_1 is a transformation of m_1 into a new bba m_2, both on the same frame of discernment, such that every mass $m_1(A)$ given by the first bba to a subset A of its frame is split and reallocated to the subsets of A so as to form the second bba.

So consider all belief functions that are specialization of *both* initial possibility functions derived from the pignistic probabilities produced by the two sources. In that family, apply again the 'cautious' approach and select as Your belief the least committed element of that family in the sense of specialization, which is the stronger notion of information comparison. The main result is that this procedure again yields a consonant plausibility function and it turns out to be exactly the result obtained within possibility theory when using the minimum rule.

Theorem 4. *Let m_1 and m_2 be two consonant belief functions on Ω with q_1 and q_2 their corresponding commonality functions. Let $\mathcal{SP}_1$ and $\mathcal{SP}_2$ be the set of specializations of m_1 and m_2, respectively. Let $q_{12}(A) = \min(q_1(A), q_2(A))$ for all $A \subseteq \Omega$, and m_{12} its corresponding bba. Then $m_{12} = m_{1 \circledwedge 2} = \min\{m : m \in \mathcal{SP}(m_1) \cap \mathcal{SP}(m_2)\}$ in the sense of s-ordering, and this minimally specific element is unique.*

We call the last combination the hyper-cautious conjunctive combination rule.

So the direct combination approach developed in possibility theory and the one derived using the TBM detour are the same (see Figure 1). This result restores the coherence between the two models, and thus using the TBM operational definition to explain the meaning of the possibility values is perfectly valid and appropriate.

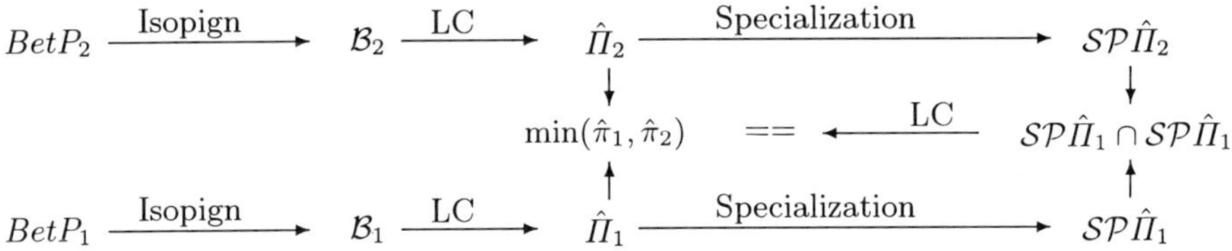

Fig. 1. Epistemic possibilities. Isopign = finding the set of belief functions that share the same pignistic probabilities. LC = least committed.

4 Objectivist semantics

Since possibility measures are special cases of plausibility functions, they are also, at the mathematical level envelopes of special families of probability functions (see, e.g. [10, 2]. Let Π be a possibility measure and $\mathfrak{P}(\Pi)$ be the set of probability functions dominated by Π.

Suppose a probability function P is obtained via some statistical experiment. Suppose that for some reason one wishes to use a possibilistic representation of this information, maybe because we just need an approximation of it, or because we want to compute a linear convex combination of them without knowing the weights (see section 5). The possibility measures Π that are candidates for representing P must clearly be such that $P \in \mathfrak{P}(\Pi)$. We shall say that Π covers P. Again there are many possibility measures obeying this constraint. It again makes sense to use an informational principle to pick the best Π induced by P. However the situation is different from the subjectivist setting. In the latter the pignistic probability is just what is revealed about the epistemic state of the agent by the betting experiments. So a principle of cautiousness prevails in order to be faithful to the incompleteness of the information. In the objectivist setting, P represents the information. Moving from a probabilistic to a possibilistic setting means losing information since we only get (special) probability bounds.

So the natural informational principle for picking a reasonable possibility distribution representing P is to preserve as much information as possible, hence picking the most informative possibility distribution (in the sense of any x-ordering above) in $\boldsymbol{\Pi}(P) = \{\Pi : P \in \mathfrak{P}(\Pi)\}$ by taking the possibility function that is pointwise minimal. It has been proved that generally this maximally informed possibility distribution exists and is unique. When P defines a total order of a finite referential. It is also true for "bell-shaped" unimodal distributions on the real line. When there are elements of equal probability, unicity is recovered if, due to symmetry, we also enforce equal possibility of these elements. See details in [12, 20].

5 The maximum rule

Again the story can be pursued considering the fusion of two probability distributions P_1 and P_2 coming from two statistical experiments pertaining to the same phenomena. If the fusion takes place on the data, it is usually enough to add the two sets of data, and derive the corresponding probability. It comes down to a linear convex combination of P_1 and P_2 whose weights reflect the relative amount of data of each source.

However if the original data sets are lost and only P_1 and P_2 are available, the relative weights of the data sets are unknown. The probability distribution resulting from merging the two data sets is of the form $\alpha P_1 + (1-\alpha)P_2$ where α is unknown. It gives a family of probability distributions F and the question is to find the most informative possibility distribution Π such that F is included in $\mathfrak{P}(\Pi)$ using the above principle of information preservation. Let Π_1 and Π_2

be the most informative possibility measures covering P_1 and P_2, respectively. Then $\Pi_1 \geq P_1$ and $\Pi_2 \geq P_2$, eventwise. Now it is obvious that

$$\max(\Pi_1, \Pi_2) \geq \max(P_1, P_2) \geq \alpha P_1 + (1-\alpha)P_2$$

It turns out that the set function $\Pi^{12} = \max(\Pi_1, \Pi_2)$ is also a possibility measure with possibility distribution $\max(\pi_1, \pi_2)$. So $\Pi^{12} = \max(\Pi_1, \Pi_2)$ encodes a family of probability measures that contains $\alpha P_1 + (1-\alpha)P_2$ for any α in the unit interval. However there are events A, B such that $P_1(A) = \Pi_1(A)$, and $P_2(B) = \Pi_2(B)$, basically the complements of the confidence sets. So $\Pi^{12} = \max(\Pi_1, \Pi_2)$ is actually the valid upperbound, i.e. it covers all the convex mixtures of P_1 and P_2. Now let Π_α be the most informative possibility measure covering $\alpha P_1 + (1-\alpha)P_2$. Obviously, the intersection over α of all sets of possibility measures less specific than Π_α has $\sup_\alpha \Pi_\alpha$ as a lower bound and it is the most specific possibility measure covering all the convex mixtures of P_1 and P_2. However it is clearly less than or equally specific as Π^{12}. Hence it is equal to it. It is thus proved that the most informative possibility distribution covering all the convex mixtures of P_1 and P_2 can be obtained as the idempotent disjunctive combination of the possibility measures Π_1 and Π_2 obtained from P_1 and P_2. Hence this setting justifies the maximum combination rule of possibility theory (see Figure 2).

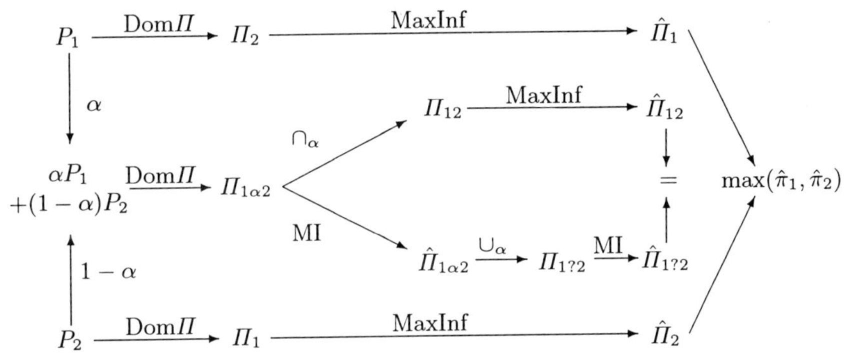

Fig. 2. Objective possibilities. DomΠ = dominating possibility measures. MI = MaxInf = maximally informative possibility measure. $\cap_\alpha$ = intersection over all α in [0,1]. $\cup_\alpha$ = union over all α in [0,1]. Other symbols as in text.

6 Conclusion

This paper studies two operational settings for the measurement of degrees of possibility. In the first one, Quantitative Epistemic Possibility theory can be viewed as a very cautious application of the TBM. It uses the operational definition of the TBM as an operational definition of the values of the possibility function whereby the betting rates provided by an agent only partially reflect beliefs. In a frequentist setting, a possibility measure can be induced from frequency observations as a consonant family of certain confidence sets. These operational settings shed light on well-known idempotent combination rules of possibility theory. The minimum and maximum rules are justified, one in each setting, based on opposite information principles. We provide a semantics for fuzzy set theory through quantitative possibility theory, based either on standard behavioral methods of subjective probability or as an extension of standard statistical practice. In both cases a probability measure is replaced by a possibility measure.

References

1. De Cooman, G., and Aeyels, D. Supremum-preserving upper probabilities. *Information Sciences 118* (1999), 173–212.
2. De Cooman, G., and Aeyels, D. A random set description of a possibility measure and its natural extension. *IEEE Trans on Systems, Man and Cybernetics 30* (2000), 124–131.
3. Dubois, D., Nguyen, H., and Prade, H. Possibility theory, probability theory and fuzzy sets: misunderstandings, bridges and gaps. In *The Handbook of Fuzzy Sets Series* (2000), D. Dubois and H. Prade, Eds., Kluwer Academic Publishers, Boston, pp. 344–438.
4. Dubois, D., and Prade, H. Unfair coins and necessity measures: a possibilistic interpretation of histograms. *Fuzzy Sets and Systems 10* (1983), 15–20.
5. Dubois, D., and Prade, H. A note on measures of specificity for fuzzy sets. *International Journal of General Systems 10*, 4 (1985), 279–283.
6. Dubois, D., and Prade, H. Fuzzy sets and statistical data. *Europ. J. Operations Research 25* (1986), 345–356.
7. Dubois, D., and Prade, H. A set-theoretic view of belief functions: logical operations and approximations by fuzzy sets. *International Journal of General Systems 12* (1986), 193–226.
8. Dubois, D., and Prade, H. The principle of minimum specificity as a basis for evidential reasoning. In *Uncertainty in Knowledge-based Systems* (1987), B. Bouchon and R. R. Yager, Eds., Springer Verlag, Berlin, pp. 75–84.
9. Dubois, D., and Prade, H. *Possibility theory : an approach to computerized processing of uncertainty.* Plenum Press, New York, 1988.
10. Dubois, D., and Prade, H. When upper probabilities are possibility measures. *Fuzzy Sets and Systems 49* (1992), 65–74.
11. Dubois, D., and Prade, H. Possibility theory: qualitative and quantitative aspects. In Gabbay and Smets [14], pp. 169–226.
12. Dubois, D., Prade, H., and Sandri, S. A. On possibility/probability transformations. In *Fuzzy Logic: State of the Art* (1993), R. Lowen, Ed., Kluwer Academic Publ., pp. 103–112.
13. Dubois, D., and Pradre, H. On several representations of an uncertain body of evidence. In Gupta and Sanchez [18], pp. 167–181.
14. Gabbay, D. M., and Smets, P., Eds. *Handbook of Defeasible Reasoning and Uncertainty Management Systems, Vol. 1* (1998), vol. 1, Kluwer, Doordrecht, The Netherlands.
15. Gebhardt, J., and Kruse, R. The context model - an intergating view of vagueness and uncertainty. *Int. J. Approximate Reasoning 9* (1993), 283–314.

16. GEBHARDT, J., AND KRUSE, R. Parallel combination of information sources. In *Handbook of Defeasible Reasoning and Uncertainty Management Systems, Vol. 3* (1998), D. M. Gabbay and P. Smets, Eds., vol. 3, Kluwer, Doordrecht, The Netherlands, pp. 393–440.
17. GILES, R. Foundations for a possibility theory. In Gupta and Sanchez [18], pp. 83–195.
18. GUPTA, M. M., AND SANCHEZ, E., Eds. *Fuzzy Information and Decision Processes* (1982), North Holland, Amsterdam.
19. KLAWONN, F., AND SMETS, P. The dynamic of belief in the transferable belief model and specialization- generalization matrices. In *Uncertainty in Artificial Intelligence 92* (1992), D. Dubois, M. P. Wellman, B. D'Ambrosio, and P. Smets, Eds., Morgan Kaufman, San Mateo, Ca, pp. 130–137.
20. LASSERRE, V., MAURIS, G., AND FOULLOY, L. A simple modelisation of measurement uncertainty: The truncated triangular possibility distribution. In *Information Processing and Management of Uncertainty* (1998), IPMU-98, Ed., pp. 10–17.
21. SHAFER, G. *A Mathematical Theory of Evidence.* Princeton Univ. Press. Princeton, NJ, 1976.
22. SMETS, P. Possibilistic inference from statistical data. In *Second World Conference on Mathematics at the Service of Man* (1982), A. Ballester, D. Cardus, and E. Trillas, Eds., Universidad Politecnica de Las Palmas, Spain, pp. 611–613.
23. SMETS, P. Constructing the pignistic probability function in a context of uncertainty. In *Uncertainty in Artificial Intelligence 5* (1990), M. Henrion, R. D. Shachter, L. N. Kanal, and J. F. Lemmer, Eds., North Holland, Amsterdam, pp. 29–40.
24. SMETS, P. The normative representation of quantified beliefs by belief functions. *Artificial Intelligence 92* (1997), 229–242.
25. SMETS, P. The transferable belief model for quantified belief representation. In Gabbay and Smets [14], pp. 267–301.
26. SMETS, P. Quantified possibility theory seen as an hyper cautious transferable belief model. In *Rencontres Francophones sur les Logiques Floues et ses Applications. LFA 2000, La Rochelle, France* (Toulouse, France, 2000), Cepadues-Editions, pp. 343–353.
27. SMETS, P. Decision making in a context where uncertainty is represented by belief functions. In *Belief Functions in Business Decisions*, R. P. Srivastava, Ed. Physica-Verlag, Forthcoming, 2001.
28. SMETS, P., AND KENNES, R. The transferable belief model. *Artificial Intelligence 66* (1994), 191–234.
29. WALLEY, P. *Statistical Reasoning with Imprecise Probabilities.* Chapman and Hall, London, 1991.
30. WALLEY, P. Statistical inferences based on a second-order possibility distribution. *International Journal of General Systems 26* (1997), 337–383.
31. YAGER, R. R. Arithmetic and other operations on Dempster-Shafer structures. *Int. J. Man-Machines Studies 25* (1986), 357–366.
32. ZADEH, L. Fuzzy sets as a basis for a theory of possibility. *Fuzzy Sets and Systems 1* (1978), 3–28.

Bridging logical, comparative and graphical possibilistic representation frameworks

Salem Benferhat, Didier Dubois, Souhila Kaci and Henri Prade

Institut de Recherche en Informatique de Toulouse (I.R.I.T.)–C.N.R.S.
Université Paul Sabatier, 118 route de Narbonne, 31062 TOULOUSE Cedex 4, FRANCE
E-mail:{benferhat, dubois, kaci, prade}@irit.fr

Abstract. Possibility theory offers a qualitative framework for representing uncertain knowledge or prioritized desires. A remarkable feature of this framework is the existence of three distinct compact representation formats which are all semantically equivalent to a ranking of possible worlds encoded by a possibility distribution. These formats are respectively: i) a set of weighted propositional formulas; ii) a set of strict comparative possibility statements of the form "p is more possible than q", and iii) a directed acyclic graph where links are weighted by possibility degrees (either qualitative or quantitative). This paper exhibits the direct translation between these formats without resorting to a semantical (exponential) computation at the possibility distribution level. These translations are useful for fusing heterogenous information, and are necessary for taking advantages of the merits of each format at the representational or at the inferential level.

1 Introduction

Usually, knowledge can be equivalently expressed in different formats. However, most of the approaches to reasoning under uncertain or incomplete information privilege a particular compact representation framework which is used both as a basis for communicating information and for performing inferences. However the interest of working with different representation modes has been pointed out recently in several works [4, 9]. Clearly, the use of several representation formats raise the issue of their representational equivalence, of their translation into another format, and of their respective merits (e.g., for elicitating knowledge, or for computational purposes).

In that respect, the possibility theory framework [10] offers different formats for representing knowledge either in terms of a possibilistic logic base [5] where classical formulas are associated with certainty weights, or in a graphical manner, using a possibilistic directed acyclic graphs (DAG) [7, 1] for exhibiting some independence structure, or also in comparative terms expressing (under the form of constraints) that some situations are more possible than others [2]. Each of these representations have been shown to be equivalent to a possibility distribution which rank-orders the possible worlds according to their level of plausibility. These formats can be used not only for representing knowledge, but also for modelling desires, then the possibilistic logic weights express priorities, and the possibility distribution encodes the levels of satisfaction of reaching each world. The framework can be made fully qualitative by referring

S. Benferhat and P. Besnard (Eds.): ECSQARU 2001, LNAI 2143, pp. 422–431, 2001.

only to a stratification of the formulas (where the distribution is replaced by a well ordered partition), or may use a symbolic discrete linearly ordered scales, or can as well be interfaced with numerical settings by using the unit interval as a scale. According to the chosen scale, a different type of conditioning should be used [6].

This paper offers an overview of the translations between the three representations by summarizing existing results and providing the remaining bridges between representations formats. The same example is used along the paper for illustrating the different transformations. The advantages of each format are briefly pointed out.

2 Background on possibility theory

A possibility distribution π is a function mapping a set of interpretations Ω into a linearly ordered scale, usually the interval $[0,1]$. $\pi(\omega)$ represents the degree of compatibility of the interpretation ω with the available beliefs about the real world in a case of uncertain information, or the satisfaction degree of reaching a state ω for modelling classical preferences. $\pi(\omega) = 1$ means that it is totally possible for ω to be the real world (or that ω is fully satisfactory), $1 > \pi(\omega) > 0$ means that ω is only somewhat possible (or satisfactory), while $\pi(\omega) = 0$ means that ω is certainly not the real world (or not satisfactory at all). A possibility distribution is said to be normalized if $\exists\omega$ s.t. $\pi(\omega) = 1$. Only normalized distributions are considered here.

Given a possibility distribution π, two measures are defined which rank order the formulas of the language. The *possibility* measure of a formula ϕ: $\Pi(\phi) = max\{\pi(\omega) : \omega \models \phi\}$, which evaluates the extent to which ϕ is consistent with the available beliefs expressed by π, and the *necessity* (or certainty) measure of a formula ϕ: $N(\phi) = 1 - \Pi(\neg\phi)$, which evaluates the extent to which ϕ is entailed by the available beliefs.

In a qualitative setting, the possibility distribution π can be represented by its well ordered partition $WOP(\pi) = E_1 \cup \cdots \cup E_n$ such that: $E_1 \cup \cdots \cup E_n = \Omega$, $E_i \cap E_j = \emptyset$, and $\forall\omega, \omega', \pi(\omega) > \pi(\omega')$ iff $\omega \in E_i, \omega' \in E_j$ and $i < j$.
Each possibility distribution has a unique well ordered partition, while the converse is false. However all numerical counterparts π of $WOP(\pi) = E_1 \cup \cdots \cup E_n$ are obtained by associating weights α_i to E_i such that $1 = \alpha_1 > \alpha_2 > \cdots > \alpha_n \geq 0$.

Conditioning in possibility theory depends if we use an in ordinal or a numerical scale. In an ordinal setting, *min-based conditioning* is used and is defined as follows: $\Pi(q \mid_m p) = 1$ if $\Pi(p \wedge q) = \Pi(p)$, and $\Pi(q \mid_m p) = \Pi(p \wedge q)$ if $\Pi(p \wedge q) < \Pi(p)$. In a numerical setting, the *product-based conditioning* is used: $\Pi(q \mid_\times p) = \frac{\Pi(p \wedge q)}{\Pi(p)}$. Moreover, if $\Pi(p) = 0$, then $\Pi(q \mid_\times p) = \Pi(q \mid_m p) = 1$.
Both conditioning satisfy an equation of the form: $\Pi(q) = \Box(\pi(q \mid p), \Pi(p))$, which is similar to Bayesian conditioning, for $\Box = min$ or $product$.

3 Compact representations

This section presents three compact representations of possibility distributions: a *possibilistic knowledge base* denoted by Σ, a *strict comparative possibility base* denoted by $\mathcal{P}$ and a *possibilistic graph* denoted by ΠG.

In the following we recall each of these compact representations and show their correspondencies with possibility distributions (or well ordered partitions). We will use the following example for illustrating the different transformations.

Example 1. Let r, s, w be three symbols which stand for " it rains", "sprinkler is on" and " the grass is wet" respectively. Let $\Omega = \{\omega_0 = \neg r \neg s \neg w, \omega_1 = \neg r \neg s w, \omega_2 = \neg r s \neg w, \omega_3 = \neg r s w, \omega_4 = r \neg s \neg w, \omega_5 = r \neg s w, \omega_6 = r s \neg w, \omega_7 = r s w\}$.
Let π be a possibility distribution defined as follows:
$\pi(\omega_0) = \pi(\omega_3) = 1$, $\pi(\omega_1) = \pi(\omega_2) = \pi(\omega_4) = \pi(\omega_5) = \frac{2}{3}$ and $\pi(\omega_6) = \pi(\omega_7) = \frac{1}{3}$.

In this example, we have only considered three levels of possibility degrees for simplicity. The most normal worlds are "it does not rain, and either sprinkler is on and the grass is wet or sprinkler is off and grass is dry". The most surprising worlds (having weight $\frac{1}{3}$) are encountered when it rains and sprinkler is on. However, one could refine this distribution more to better match the reality. For instance one could split the worst worlds by considering that "it rains and sprinkler is on and grass is wet" is less surprising than "it rains and sprinkler is on and the grass is dry". However, for keeping the example simple enough, we only consider three levels, here arbitrarily encoded as $\frac{1}{3}, \frac{2}{3}$ and 1.

3.1 Possibilistic knowledge bases

A possibilistic knowledge base is a set of weighted formulas of the form $\Sigma = \{(\phi_i, \alpha_i) : i = 1, n\}$ where ϕ_i is a classical formula and, α_i belongs to $[0, 1]$ in a numerical setting and represents the level of certainty or priority attached to ϕ_i.
In a qualitative setting, a possibilistic base Σ can be represented by a well ordered partition $WOP(\Sigma) = S_1 \cup \cdots \cup S_n$ where S_1 contains the most certain classical formulas in Σ, S_n contains the least ones, and more generally formulas in S_i are strictly more certain than formulas in S_j when $i < j$. For each well ordered partition $S_1 \cup \cdots \cup S_n$ we can construct a possibilistic base Σ by associating to each formula in S_i a weight α_i, such that $1 \geq \alpha_1 > \cdots > \alpha_n > 0$.
Given a possibilistic base Σ, we can generate a unique possibility distribution π_Σ, where interpretations will be ranked w.r.t. the highest formula that they falsify, [5]:

$$\forall \omega \in \Omega, \pi_\Sigma(\omega) = \begin{cases} 1 & \text{if } \forall (\phi_i, \alpha_i) \in \Sigma, \omega \models \phi_i \\ 1 - max\{\alpha_i : (\phi_i, \alpha_i) \in \Sigma \text{ and } \omega \not\models \phi_i\} & \text{otherwise.} \end{cases} \tag{1}$$

The converse transformation from π to Σ is straightforward. Let $1 > \alpha_1 > \cdots > \alpha_n \geq 0$ be the different weights used in π. Let ϕ_i be a classical formula whose models are those having the weight α_i in π. Let $\Sigma = \{(\neg\phi_i, 1 - \alpha_i) : i = 1, n\}$. Then, $\pi_\Sigma = \pi$.

3.2 Strict comparative possibility bases

A strict comparative possibility base $\mathcal{P}$ is a set of constraints of the form "in context p, q is more possible than $\neg q$" i.e., $\Pi(p \wedge q) > \Pi(p \wedge \neg q)$, denoted by $p \rightarrow q$. This can either express a general rule having exceptions, or the conditional desire of an agent. It encompasses the general case of constraints of the form $\Pi(r) > \Pi(s)$, which is equivalent to the default rule $r \vee s \rightarrow \neg s$ [2] since $\Pi((r \vee s) \wedge \neg s) >$

$\Pi((r\vee s)\wedge s) - \Pi(r\wedge\neg s) > \Pi(s) - \Pi(r) > \Pi(s)$ $(- max(\pi(r\wedge s), \pi(r\wedge\neg s)) > max(\pi(r \wedge s), \pi(\neg r \wedge s)))$.

Each strict comparative possibility base $\mathcal{P}$ induces a unique qualitative possibility distribution $WOP(\pi_{\mathcal{P}})$ obtained by considering the least specific solution satisfying:

$$\Pi(p_i \wedge q_i) > \Pi(p_i \wedge \neg q_i) \quad (2)$$

for all $p_i \rightarrow q_i$ of $\mathcal{P}$. The constraint (2) means that the most plausible situations where $p_i \wedge q_i$ is true, are preferred to the most plausible situations where $p_i \wedge \neg q_i$ is true.

In [2], an algorithm has been provided to compute $WOP(\pi_{\mathcal{P}}) = E_1 \cup \cdots \cup E_n$. Here we only recall its basic ideas, which consist in putting each interpretation in the lowest possible rank (or highest possibility degree) without violating constraints (2). The only case where we cannot put ω in some partition E_i, is when ω is in the right part of some constraint (where there is a rule $p_i \rightarrow q_i$ such that $\omega \models p_i \wedge \neg q_i$), and none of the interpretations of the left part of this constraint (i.e., $\omega \models p_i \wedge q_i$) is already classified in some E_j with $j < i$. Therefore $WOP(\pi_{\mathcal{P}})$ is computed as follows: for each step i, we put in E_i all interpretations which are not in the right part of any constraint, then we remove all rules $p_i \rightarrow q_i$ such that there exists at least ω in E_i such that $\omega \models p_i \wedge q_i$. The following example illustrates the steps of the algorithm:

Example 2. Let $\mathcal{P} = \{r \rightarrow \neg s, s \vee r \rightarrow w, \neg s \rightarrow \neg w, \}$. These rules stand for: " generally, if it rains, then the sprinkler is off", "generally, if either it rains or the sprinkler is on, then the grass is wet" and "generally, if the sprinkler is off, the grass is dry". Let $\mathcal{D}$ be the set of constraints associated with $\mathcal{P}$.
$\mathcal{D} = \{C_1 : \Pi(r \wedge \neg s) > \Pi(r \wedge s), C_2 : \Pi((s \vee r) \wedge w) > \Pi((s \vee r) \wedge \neg w),$
$C_3 : \Pi(\neg s\wedge\neg w) > \Pi(\neg s\wedge w)\}$. Let $\mathcal{C}_{\mathcal{D}} = \{(L(C_i), R(C_i)) : i = 1, 3\} = \{(\{\omega_4, \omega_5\}, \{\omega_6, \omega_7\})$ $(\{\omega_3, \omega_5, \omega_7\}, \{\omega_2, \omega_4, \omega_6\}), (\{\omega_0, \omega_4\}, \{\omega_1, \omega_5\})\}$, where the pair $(L(C_i), R(C_i))$ means $max\{\pi(\omega) : \omega \models p_i \wedge q_i\} > max\{\pi(\omega) : \omega \models p_i \wedge \neg q_i\}$.
At the first step, we put in E_1 the interpretations which do not belong to any $L(C_i)$ in $\mathcal{C}_{\mathcal{D}}$, we get $E_1 = \{\omega_0, \omega_3\}$. Then, we remove pairs in $\mathcal{C}_{\mathcal{D}}$ s.t. $L(C_i)$ contains at least one interpretation from E_1, we get $\mathcal{C}_{\mathcal{D}} = \{(\{\omega_4, \omega_5\}, \{\omega_6, \omega_7\})\}$. In a similar way, we get: $E_2 = \{\omega_1, \omega_2, \omega_4, \omega_5\}$ and $E_3 = \{\omega_6, \omega_7\}$. It can be checked that $\mathcal{P}$ induces the same distribution as in Example 1.

Let us now provide the converse transformation from π to $\mathcal{P}$. Again let $1 = \alpha_1 > \alpha_2 > \cdots > \alpha_n \geq 0$ be the different weights used in π, and ϕ_i be the classical formula whose models have a weight equal to α_i. Then, the comparative base associated to π is:
$\mathcal{P} = \{\rightarrow \phi_1, \neg\phi_1 \rightarrow \phi_2, \cdots,$
$\neg(\phi_1 \wedge \cdots \wedge \phi_{i-1}) \rightarrow \phi_i, \cdots, \neg(\phi_1 \wedge \phi_2 \wedge \cdots \wedge \phi_{n-2}) \rightarrow \phi_{n-1}\}$.
This strict comparative possibility base means that the most normal situation are ϕ_1, and then ϕ_2 if ϕ_1 is false, and so on. Let $\pi_{\mathcal{P}}$ be the possibility distribution associated with $\mathcal{P}$. Then, $WOP(\pi_{\mathcal{P}}) = WOP(\pi)$.

3.3 Possibilistic networks

The last compact representation is graphical and is based on conditioning. Symbolic knowledge is represented by DAGs, where nodes represent variables (in this paper, we assume that they are binary), and edges express influence links between variables. When

there exists a link from A to B, A is said to be a parent of B. The set of parents of a given node A is denoted by $Par(A)$. By the capital letter A we denote a variable which represents either the symbol a or its negation. An interpretation in this section will be simply denoted by $A_1 \cdots A_n$. Uncertainty is expressed at each node as follows:
– For root nodes A_i we provide the prior possibility of a_i and of its negation $\neg a_i$. These prior should satisfy the normalization condition: $max(\Pi(a_i), \Pi(\neg a_i)) = 1$,
– For other nodes A_j, we provide conditional possibility of a_j and of its negation $\neg a_j$ given any complete instantiation of each variable of parents of A_j, $\omega_{Par(A_j)}$. These conditional possibilities should also satisfy the normalization condition:

$$max(\Pi(a_j \mid \omega_{Par(A_j)}), \Pi(\neg a_j \mid \omega_{Par(A_j)})) = 1.$$

Due to the existence of two definitions of possibilistic conditioning, we get two kinds of possibilistic graphs, that we denote respectively by $\Pi \mathrm{G}_m$ and $\Pi \mathrm{G}_\times$, depending if we use min-based or product-based conditioning. A min or product-based possibilistic graph induces a unique joint distribution using the *chain rule* $\Box = min$ or $product$:

Definition 1 *Let ΠG be a direct possibilistic acyclic graph. The joint possibility distribution associated with ΠG is computed with the following equation (called chain rule):*

$$\pi(\omega) = \Box\{\Pi(a \mid \omega_{Par(A)}) : \omega \models a \text{ and } \omega \models \omega_{Par(A)}\}.$$

The converse transformation is straightforward. As said in Section 2.3, the two definitions of conditioning satisfy Bayesian rule. Hence, for $\omega = A_1 A_2 \cdots A_n$, we have:

$$\pi(A_1 \cdots A_n) = \Box(\pi(A_1 \mid A_2 A_3 \cdots A_n), \pi(A_2 A_3 \cdots A_n)).$$

Applying Bayesian rule repeatedly for any given ordering $A_1, \cdots, A_n$ yields:

$$\pi(A_1 \cdots A_n) = \Box(\pi(A_1 \mid A_2 \cdots A_n), \pi(A_2 \mid A_3 \cdots A_n), \cdots, \pi(A_{n-1} \mid A_n), \Pi(A_n)).$$

4 Logical bases and comparative bases

4.1 From a comparative base to a possibilistic base [2]

Algorithm **1.1** shows how to transform a comparative base $\mathcal{P}$ into a possibilistic base Σ.

Algorithm 1.1: From $\mathcal{P}$ to Σ

begin
  $m \leftarrow 1$;
  while $\mathcal{P} \neq \emptyset$ **do**
    $A = \{\neg p_i \vee q_i : p_i \rightarrow q_i \in \mathcal{P}\}$;
    $\mathcal{P}_m = \{p_i \rightarrow q_i \in \mathcal{P}$ and $A \cup \{p_i\}$ is consistent$\}$;
    $\mathcal{P} = \mathcal{P} - \mathcal{P}_m, m \leftarrow m + 1$;
  return $\Sigma = \{(\neg p_i \vee q_i, \frac{1}{m}) : p_i \leftarrow q_i \in \mathcal{P}_j\}$
end

The stratification in Σ reflects the specificity relation between elements of $\mathcal{P}$ when the letter encodes rules having exceptions. For instance, $\mathcal{P}_1$ contains only the most general rules. Indeed, if $p \rightarrow q$ is not considered in $\mathcal{P}_1$, then it means that $A \cup \{p\}$ is inconsistent, hence p would inherit its own property q, but also its negation property $\neg q$ from some superclass, hence it is not a general rule. This analysis is iterated in the algorithm. Let $\mathcal{P}$ be a comparative base, and Σ be its possibilistic counterpart given by the previous algorithm. Then, $WOP(\pi_{\mathcal{P}}) = WOP(\pi_{\Sigma})$.

Example 3. Let $\mathcal{P} = \{\neg s \to \neg w, s \vee r \to w, r \to \neg s\}$ considered in Example 2. We have $A = \{s \vee \neg w, \neg(s \vee r) \vee w, \neg r \vee \neg s\}$. Applying Algorithm 1, we get: $m = 3$, $\mathcal{P}_1 = \{\neg s \to \neg w, s \vee r \to w\}$ and $\mathcal{P}_2 = \{r \to \neg s\}$. Hence, $\Sigma = \{(s \vee \neg w, \frac{1}{3}), (\neg s \vee w, \frac{1}{3}), (\neg r \vee w, \frac{1}{3}), (\neg r \vee \neg s, \frac{2}{3})\}$. We can check that $WOP(\pi_\Sigma) = WOP(\pi_\mathcal{P})$. Moreover, Σ is such that $\pi_\Sigma = \pi$, where π is given in Example 1.

4.2 From a logical base to a comparative base

Let $\Sigma = S_1 \cup \cdots \cup S_n$ be a possibilistic knowledge base where formulas of S_i are prioritized over formulas of S_j for $i < j$. Let us denote $\neg S_j = \bigvee_{\phi_i \in S_j} \neg\phi_i$. Then, we can check that the set of strict comparative possibility $\mathcal{P}$ associated with Σ is given as follows: $\mathcal{P}_\Sigma = \{\to S_n, \neg S_{n-1} \vee \neg S_n \to S_{n-1},$
$\neg S_{n-2} \vee \neg S_{n-1} \to S_{n-2}, \cdots, \neg S_1 \vee \neg S_2 \to S_1\}$.
The rule $\neg S_i \vee \neg S_{i+1} \to S_i$ means that if S_i or S_{i+1} is false, then plausibly we prefer reject S_{i+1}, and accept S_i. This simply reflects the priorities between S_i's dictated by the possibilistic base Σ. It can be checked that: $WOP(\mathcal{P}_\Sigma) = WOP(\Sigma)$.

Example 4. Let $\Sigma = \{(s\vee\neg w, \frac{1}{3}), (\neg s \vee w, \frac{1}{3}), (\neg r \vee w, \frac{1}{3}), (\neg r \vee \neg s, \frac{2}{3})\}$. Then, $\Sigma = S_1 \cup S_2$ s.t. $S_1 = \{\neg r \vee \neg s\}$ and $S_2 = \{s \vee \neg w, \neg s \vee w, \neg r \vee w\}$.
Then, $\mathcal{P} = \{\to (s\vee\neg w)\wedge(\neg s\vee w)\wedge(\neg r\vee w), \neg(\neg r\vee\neg s)\vee\neg((\neg s\vee w)\wedge(\neg r\vee w)\wedge(s\vee\neg w)) \to \neg r \vee \neg s\}$ which is equivalent to $\{\to (sw \vee \neg r\neg s\neg w), rs \vee s\neg w \vee r\neg w \vee \neg sw \to \neg r \vee \neg s\}$. The comparative base obtained in this example apparently differs from the one of Example 2, even if all of them induce the same joint distribution. However, we could recover the syntactic equivalence between these default rules using System P and rational monotony.

Note that the same possibilistic base can be described by different strict comparative possibility bases. This is not surprising, as in classical logic, two different sets of formulas can have the same set of models. Rules used to show the syntactic equivalence between comparative possibility bases are System P and rational monotony [8]. Indeed, possibilistic logic is in full agreement with System P and rational monotony [2].

5 Possibilistic bases and possibilistic graphs

5.1 From graph to possibilistic bases

The basic idea is that a possibilistic base associated with a graph can be viewed as the result of fusing elementary bases. These elementary bases, associated with each variable (node) of the graph, are composed of all conditional possibilities, different of 1 attached to the node. More precisely, the elementary base associated with the variable A is:

$$\Sigma_A = \{(\neg a_i \vee \neg P_{a_i}, 1 - \alpha_i) : \Pi(a_i \mid P_{a_i}) = \alpha \in \Pi\text{G and } \alpha \neq 1\}.$$

Namely, each conditional possibility is transformed into a necessity formula which is the material counterpart of a conditional (remember that $N(p \mid q) = 1 - \Pi(\neg p \mid q)$).

The following proposition shows that applying the chain rule on the graph gives the same result if we combine the possibility distributions associated to elementary bases:

Proposition 1 *Let ΠG be a causal graph and $\pi_\Box$ the joint distribution obtained from ΠG using the chain rule. Let Σ_{A_i} be the possibilistic base associated with the node A_i, and π_{A_i} be its possibility distribution using Definition 1. Then, $\pi_\Box = \Box_{i=1,n} \pi_{A_i}$.*

Now to compute the global base associated with ΠG we use the results of [3] which provide syntactic counterparts of combining bases with minimum or product operators:

Proposition 2 *Let Σ_1 and Σ_2 be two bases, π_1 and π_2 their associated distributions.*
1. *Then, the possibilistic base associated with $min(\pi_1, \pi_2)$ is: $\Sigma_1 \cup \Sigma_2$.*
2. *The possibilistic base associated with $\pi_1 \times \pi_2$ is:*
$\Sigma_1 \cup \Sigma_2 \cup \{(\phi_i \vee \psi_j, \alpha_i + \beta_j - \alpha_i\beta_j) : (\phi_i, \alpha_i) \in \Sigma_1$ *and* $(\psi_j, \beta_j) \in \Sigma_2\}$.

Then, the base associated with a graph is obtained by the successive application of the previous proposition on the elementary bases Σ_{A_i}'s.

Example 5. Consider the following ΠG. The set of variables is $V = \{R, S, W\}$.

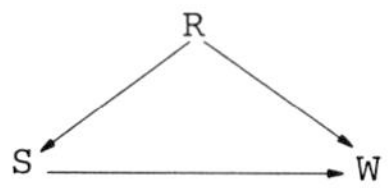

1- Let us consider ΠG_m where min-based conditional possibility degrees are computed from the distribution given in Example 1, $\Pi(R)$ $\Pi(S|R)$ $\Pi(W \mid SR)$

r	$\frac{2}{3}$
$\neg r$	1

	r	$\neg r$
s	$\frac{1}{3}$	1
$\neg s$	1	1

	$\neg s \neg r$	$\neg s r$	$s \neg r$	sr
w	$\frac{2}{3}$	1	1	1
$\neg w$	1	1	$\frac{2}{3}$	1

We have: $\Sigma_R = \{(\neg r, \frac{1}{3})\}$, $\Sigma_S = \{(\neg r \vee \neg s, \frac{2}{3})\}$ and $\Sigma_W = \{(r \vee s \vee \neg w, \frac{1}{3}), (r \vee \neg s \vee w, \frac{1}{3})\}$.
Then, the possibilistic base Σ_m associated with ΠG_m is:
$\Sigma_m = \Sigma_R \cup \Sigma_S \cup \Sigma_W = \{(\neg r, \frac{1}{3}), (r \vee s \vee \neg w, \frac{1}{3}), (r \vee \neg s \vee w, \frac{1}{3}), (\neg r \vee \neg s, \frac{2}{3})\}$.
2- Let us now consider $\Pi G_\times$ where product-based conditional possibilities are also computed from distribution of Example 1: $\Pi(R)$ $\Pi(S|R)$ $\Pi(W \mid SR)$

r	$\frac{2}{3}$
$\neg r$	1

	r	$\neg r$
s	$\frac{1}{2}$	1
$\neg s$	1	1

	$\neg s \neg r$	$\neg s r$	$s \neg r$	sr
w	$\frac{2}{3}$	1	1	1
$\neg w$	1	1	$\frac{2}{3}$	1

We have: $\Sigma_R = \{(\neg r, \frac{1}{3})\}$, $\Sigma_S = \{(\neg r \vee \neg s, \frac{1}{2})\}$ and $\Sigma_W = \{(r \vee s \vee \neg w, \frac{1}{3}), (r \vee \neg s \vee w, \frac{1}{3})\}$.
We first compute the combination of Σ_R and Σ_S. We get $\Sigma_{RS} = \{(\neg r, \frac{1}{3}), ((\neg r \vee \neg s, \frac{1}{2}), (\neg r \vee \neg s, \frac{2}{3})\}$ which is equivalent to $\{(\neg r, \frac{1}{3}), (\neg r \vee \neg s, \frac{2}{3})\}$. Combining Σ_{RS} and Σ_W. We get:
$\Sigma_\times = \{(\neg r, \frac{1}{3}), (\neg r \vee \neg s, \frac{2}{3}), (r \vee s \vee \neg w, \frac{1}{3}), (r \vee \neg s \vee w, \frac{1}{3})\}$.

We can easily check that the knowledge bases associated with the (slightly) different ΠG_m and $\Pi G_\times$ are equivalent, and even identical in this example. This is expected since both graphs are built from the same distribution.

5.2 Transforming a possibilistic base Σ into a min-based graph ΠG_m

The transformation from a possibilistic base Σ into ΠG_m has been given in [1]. We only illustrate the idea by an example. First, an ordering of variables $A_1, \cdots, A_n$ should be chosen. This ordering means that the parents of A_i should be among $A_{i+1}, \cdots, A_n$. Then we proceed into successive decompositions of Σ. At the first step, Σ is decomposed, in an equivalent way, into: $\Sigma_{A_1} \cup \Sigma_L$, where Σ_{A_1} allows to determine the parents of A_1 and the conditional possibilities attached to A_1. With the same procedure Σ_L is decomposed again into $\Sigma_{A_2} \cup \Sigma_{L'}$ and so on. The example only illustrates the decomposition process from Σ to $\Sigma_{A_1} \cup \Sigma_L$.

Example 6. Let Σ be the base of Example 4. Let $\{W, S, R\}$ be the ordering of the variables. The decomposition of Σ into $\Sigma_W \cup \Sigma_L$ follows three steps:
– The first step consists in putting in Σ_W all clauses of Σ containing W. We let $\Sigma_L = \Sigma - \Sigma_W$. We get $\Sigma_W = \{(s \vee \neg w, \frac{1}{3}), (\neg s \vee w, \frac{1}{3}), (\neg r \vee w, \frac{1}{3})\}$ and $\Sigma_L = \{(\neg r \vee \neg s, \frac{2}{3})\}$.
Then, we remove from Σ_W all strictly subsumed[1] formulas in Σ (since they are redundant and can induce fictitious dependence relations). Σ_W does not contain subsumed formulas, so it remains unchanged.
– The second step consists in determining the parents of W. They are the set of variables in $\{S, R\}$ (i.e., the set of parents of W) which are involved in at least one clause of Σ_W. Then, $Par(W) = \{S, R\}$.
– Lastly, the third step consists in computing conditionals $\Pi(W \mid \omega_{Par(w)})$. First, we replace Σ_W by its complete extension [2] w.r.t. $Par(W)$. Then, Σ_W becomes $\{(r \vee s \vee \neg w, \frac{1}{3}), (\neg r \vee s \vee \neg w, \frac{1}{3}), (r \vee \neg s \vee w, \frac{1}{3}), (\neg r \vee \neg s \vee w, \frac{1}{3}), (s \vee \neg r \vee w, \frac{1}{3})\}$.
Then, if $(a_1 \vee x, \alpha) \in \Sigma_W$ and $\Sigma \vdash x$, $(a_1 \vee x, \alpha)$ is removed from Σ_W and (x, α) is added to Σ_L where a_1 is either w or $\neg w$. Finally, we compute conditional possibilities from Σ_W as follows:

$\Pi(a_1 \mid P_W) = 1 - \alpha$ if $(\neg a_1 \vee \neg P_W, \alpha) \in \Sigma_W$, and $\Pi(a_1 \mid P_W) = 1$ otherwise.

For example $\Pi(w \mid \neg s \neg r) = \frac{2}{3}$ since $(s \vee r \vee \neg w, \frac{1}{3}) \in \Sigma_W$.

It can be checked [1] that the constructed graph is a DAG, and that $\pi_\Sigma = \pi_m$, where π_m is the possibility distribution obtained from the constructed ΠG using chaining rule.

5.3 Transforming a possibilistic base Σ into a product-based graph $\Pi G_\times$

Referring to the decomposition of a joint distribution, we have:

$$\pi_\Sigma(A_1 \cdots A_n) = \pi(A_1 \mid A_2 \cdots A_n) * \pi(A_2 \cdots A_n).$$

Therefore, the construction of the product-based graph is done in two different steps: one consists in computing conditional possibilities $\pi(A_1 \mid A_2 \cdots A_n)$, and the other consists in constructing a knowledge base Σ_L s.t. $\pi_{\Sigma_L} = \pi(A_2 \cdots A_n)$. Note that in the first step, the aim is to identify parents of A_1 since $\pi(A_1 \mid A_2 \cdots A_n) = \pi(A_1 \mid Par(A_1))$.
-*Step 1 :* **Computing parents of** A_1
The determination of parents of A_1 is done in an incremental way. First, we remove all subsumed formulas and tautologies from Σ. Then, we take $Par(A_1)$ as a set of variables from $\{A_2, \cdots, A_n\}$ which are involved at least in one clause containing A_1. $Par(A_1)$ are obvious parents of A_1. However, and contrary to the construction of ΠG_m it may exist other "hidden" variables, whose observation influences the certainty degree of A_1. To see if $Par(A_1)$ has to be extended or not, we proceed in the following way:
1- Take an instance of parent of A_1 which is consistent with Σ. Add it to Σ.
2- Compute the degree of inference α of a_1 (resp. $\neg a_1$) from Σ.
3- If $\alpha > 0$, then for each clause having a weight greater than α, add variables involved in this clause to $Par(A_1)$.

[1] (ϕ, α) is said to be strictly subsumed by Σ, if $\Sigma_{>\alpha} \vdash \phi$, where $\Sigma_{>\alpha}$ is composed of classical formulas of Σ having a weight strictly greater than α.
[2] For instance, if B and C are parents of A_1, if $(a \vee b, \alpha) \in \Sigma_{A_1}$, then we replace this clause by $\{(a \vee b \vee c, \alpha), (a \vee b \vee \neg c, \alpha)\}$ to extend the clause $(a \vee b, \alpha)$ to all of parents.

Now, once parents of A_1 are fixed, the determination of $\Pi(a_1 \mid_{\times} \omega_{Par(A_1)})$ is given as follows: Let $(x_1, \cdots, x_n)$ be an instance of $Par(A_1)$, and a_1 an instance of A_1. Recall that by definition: $\Pi(a_1 \mid x_1 x_2 \cdots x_n) = \frac{\Pi(a_1 x_1 \cdots x_n)}{\Pi(x_1 \cdots x_n)}$, and that $\Pi(a_1 \mid x_1 x_2 \cdots x_n) = 1$ if $\Pi(x_1 \cdots x_n) = 0$.

Syntactically, it can be checked that: $\Pi(\phi) = 1 - Inc(\Sigma \cup \{(\phi, 1)\})$, where $Inc(\Sigma) = max\{\alpha_i : \Sigma_{\geq \alpha_i}$ is inconsistent$\}$, where $\Sigma_{\geq \alpha_i}$ is the set of formulas in Σ whose weight is at least equal to α_i. (We recall that Σ is assumed to be consistent).

Therefore, to compute $\Pi(a_1 \mid x_1 \cdots x_n)$:

1. Add $\{(x_1, 1), \cdots, (x_n, 1)\}$ to Σ. Let Σ' be the result of this step.
2. Compute $h = 1 - Inc(\Sigma')$ (h represents $\Pi(x_1 \cdots x_n)$)
3. Add $\{(a_1, 1)\}$ to Σ'. Let Σ'' be the result of this step.
4. Compute $h' = 1 - Inc(\Sigma'')$ (h' represents $\Pi(a_1 x_1 \cdots x_n)$). Then,
$\Pi(a_1 \mid x_1 \cdots x_n) = 1$ if $h = 0$, and $\Pi(a_1 \mid x_1 \cdots x_n) = \frac{h'}{h}$ otherwise.

Example 7. Let us illustrate the computation of $\Pi(\neg w \mid s \neg r)$. We first assign the instance $\{(s, 1), (\neg r, 1)\}$ to Σ. We get $\Sigma' = \{(s, 1), (\neg r, 1), (s \vee \neg w, \frac{1}{3}), (\neg s \vee w, \frac{1}{3}), (\neg r \vee w, \frac{1}{3}), (\neg r \vee \neg s, \frac{2}{3})\}$. We have $Inc(\Sigma') = 0$. Then, $h = 1$.
We now add $(\neg w, 1)$ to Σ', we get $\Sigma'' = \{(\neg w, 1), (s, 1), (\neg r, 1), (s \vee \neg w, (s \vee \neg w, \frac{1}{3}), (\neg s \vee w, \frac{1}{3}), (\neg r \vee w, \frac{1}{3}), (\neg r \vee \neg s, \frac{2}{3})\}$. We have $Inc(\Sigma'') = \frac{1}{3}$. Then, $h' = \frac{2}{3}$. Hence, $\Pi(\neg w \mid s \neg r) = \frac{h'}{h} = \frac{2}{3}$. With a similar way, we get the following conditional possibilities:

$\Pi(W \mid SR)$

	$\neg s \neg r$	$\neg s r$	$s \neg r$	sr
w	$\frac{2}{3}$	1	1	1
$\neg w$	1	1	$\frac{2}{3}$	1

-Step 2: **Computing the marginal base Σ_L**
Let us first define the possibility distribution π_{a_1} as follows:
$\pi_{a_1}(\omega) = \pi(\omega)$ if $\omega \models a_1$ and $\pi_{a_1}(\omega) = 0$ otherwise.
$\pi_{\neg a_1}$ is similarly defined. Then, it can be checked that the possibilistic bases associated with π_{a_1} and $\pi_{\neg a_1}$ are $\Sigma_{a_1} = \Sigma \cup \{(a_1, 1)\}$ and $\Sigma_{\neg a_1} = \Sigma \cup \{(\neg a_1, 1)\}$. Σ_{a_1} (resp. $\Sigma_{\neg a_1}$) can be simplified by removing all clauses of the form $(a_1 \vee x, \alpha)$ (resp. $(\neg a_1 \vee x, \alpha)$) since they are subsumed by $(a_1, 1)$ (resp. $(\neg a_1, 1)$). Also, clauses of the form $(\neg a_1 \vee x, \alpha)$ (resp. $(a_1 \vee x, \alpha)$) are reduced into (x, α) since $(a_1, 1)$ and $(\neg a_1 \vee x, \alpha)$ (resp. $(\neg a_1, 1)$ and $(a_1 \vee x, \alpha)$) implies (x, α) which subsumes $(\neg a_1 \vee x, \alpha)$ (resp. $(a_1 \vee x, \alpha)$).
Our aim is to compute the base Σ_L associated with $\pi(A_2 \cdots A_n)$ since Σ_L will be used in place of Σ for computing the parents of A_2. Then, we can check that the possibilistic bases associated with the distributions $\pi_{a_1}^{A_1}$ and $\pi_{\neg a_1}^{A_1}$ resulting from the marginalization of π_{a_1} and $\pi_{\neg a_1}$ on $\{A_2 \cdots A_n\}$ are just $\Sigma_{a_1} - \{(a_1, 1)\}$ and $\Sigma_{\neg a_1} - \{(\neg a_1, 1)\}$ respectively. Then, Indeed, we are now able to provide the possibilistic base associated with $\pi(A_2 \cdots A_n)$ by noticing that:
$$\pi(A_2 \cdots A_n) = max(\pi_{a_1}^{A_1}(A_2 \cdots A_n), \pi_{\neg a_1}^{A_1}(A_2 \cdots A_n)).$$
Thus, Σ_L is the syntactic counterpart [3] of the max operation applied on $\pi_{a_1}^{A_1}$ and $\pi_{\neg a_1}^{A_1}$: $\Sigma_L = \{(\phi_i \vee \psi_j, min(\alpha_i, \beta_j)) \, (\phi_i, \alpha_i) \in \Sigma_{a_1}, (\psi_j, \beta_j) \in \Sigma_2\}$.
Example 7. (continued) Let us consider again the base given in Example 4. We start with the variable W. We first have $\Sigma_w = \{(s \vee \neg w, \frac{1}{3}), (\neg s \vee w, \frac{1}{3}), (\neg r \vee w, \frac{1}{3}), (\neg r \vee \neg s, \frac{2}{3}), (w, 1)\}$. We remove clauses containing w, we get $\Sigma_w = \{(s \vee \neg w, \frac{1}{3}), (\neg r \vee \neg s, \frac{2}{3}), (w, 1)\}$. Now, we replace the clause $(s \vee \neg w, \frac{1}{3})$ by $(s, \frac{1}{3})$. Hence, $\Sigma_w = \{(s, \frac{1}{3}), (\neg r \vee \neg s, \frac{2}{3}), (w, 1)\}$.

In a similar way, we get: $\Sigma_{\neg w} = \{(\neg s, \frac{1}{3}), (\neg r, \frac{1}{3}), (\neg r \vee \neg s, \frac{2}{3}), (\neg w, 1)\}$. Then, $\Sigma_L = \{(\neg r, \frac{1}{3}), (\neg r \vee \neg s, \frac{2}{3})\}$. Then, reapplying *Step 1* leads to

$\Pi(R)$

r	$\frac{2}{3}$
$\neg r$	1

$\Pi(S|R)$

	r	$\neg r$
s	$\frac{1}{2}$	1
$\neg s$	1	1

It is easy to check that we recover the same tables given in Example 5, point 2.

6 Concluding discussion

This paper has shown how to translate any of the three basic compact representations formats (logical, graphical, or comparative) into another, in the setting of qualitative or numerical possibility theory. Each translation guarantees that the underlying possibility distribution remains the same. These correspondences are useful if we have to combine pieces of information expressed in different formats, and to check their consistency. Each compact format has its interest for communication purposes, either for modelling expert knowledge, or for supplying information to the user. Besides, from an inference point of view, the logical and the graphical formats are the most interesting ones. There exists computational machineries of reasonable complexity [5] in possibilistic logic and local computational methods are under development for the graphical representation (which also extends to non-binary variables). However, each compact representation is not unique since there exists semantically equivalent logical (resp. graphical, comparative) bases which differ syntactically, as suggested by the example. Then, a procedure putting the resulting bases under some standard form may be needed. Moreover there exists another logical format (omitted here for the sake of brevity) which is also of interest: the logical description of the different sets of interpretations having the same possibility level. This can be easily derived from the distribution, and the direct computation from the possibilistic logic bases is left for further research.

References

1. S. Benferhat, D. Dubois, L. Garcia, and H. Prade. Possibilistic logic bases and possibilistic graphs. In *15th Conf. on Uncertainty in Artificial Intelligence, UAI'99, 57-64*, 1999.
2. S. Benferhat, D. Dubois, and H. Prade. Representing default rules in possibilistic logic. In *3rd Inter. Conf. of Principles of Knowledge Repres. and Reasoning (KR'92),673-684*, 1992.
3. S. Benferhat, D. Dubois, H. Prade, and M. Williams. A practical approach to fusing and revising prioritized belief bases. In *EPIA 99, LNAI 1695,222-236, Springer Verlag,*, 1999.
4. C. Boutilier, T. Deans, and S. Hanks. Decision theoric planning: Structural assumptions and computational leverage. In *Journal of Artificial Intelligence Research,11,1–94*, 1999.
5. D. Dubois, J. Lang, and H. Prade. Possibilistic logic. *Handbook of Logic in Artificial Intelligence and Logic Programming*, 3, Oxford Univ. Press:439–513, 1994.
6. D. Dubois and H. Prade. Possibility theory: qualitative and quantitative aspects. *Handbook of Defeasible Reasoning and Uncertainty Management Systems. Vol. 1, 169-226*, 1998.
7. J. Gebhardt and R. Kruse. Possinfer - a software tool for possibilistic inference. In *Fuzzy set Methods in Inf. Engineering. A Guided Tour of Applications*,Wiley, 1995.
8. D. Lehmann and M. Magidor. What does a conditional knowledge base entail? *Artificial Intelligence*, 55:1–60, 1992.
9. D. Poole. Logic, knowledge representation, and bayesian decision theory. In *Computational Logic - CL 2000*. LNAI 1861, Springer Verlag,70-86, 2000.
10. L. Zadeh. Fuzzy sets as a basis for a theory of possibility. *Fuzzy Sets Syst.*, 1:3–28, 1978.

Ellipse fitting with uncertainty and fuzzy decision stage for detection. Application in videomicroscopy.

Franck Dufrenois

Laboratoire d'Analyse des systemes du littoral,
50 rue Ferdinand Buisson,
62228 Calais, France
Franck.Dufrenois@lasl-gw.univ-littoral.fr

Abstract. The conic fitting from image points is a very old topic in pattern recognition. We propose here some new ideas of handling the difficult situations where the noised data span a small section of the conic. This new fitting process takes into account explicitly the maximum and minimum total arc length of the conic curves to constraint the conic search space. Our algorithm compared with some procedures of reference gives improved results. A confidence envelope is then estimated to direct the search for continuations of the ellipse. Considering the data organization resolved, we propose then a complete extraction scheme based on a fuzzy set representation of the fitting.

1 Introduction

One of basic tasks in pattern recognition and computer vision is a fitting of geometric primitives to a set of points. The use of primitive models allows reduction and simplification of data and, consequently, faster and simpler processing. A very important primitive is an ellipse, which, being a perspective projection of a circle, is exploited in many applications of computer vision like 3-D vision and object recognition, medical imaging, industrial inspections... Thanks to its many geometric properties and its different ways of representation, the elliptic model is an ideal experimentation field for estimation. In principle, two kind of approaches can be found : The voting/clustering and optimization methods.

·The most popular method belonging to the first group is the Hough transform. The HT is a robust method of parameter estimation, which doesn't require any spatial organization of the data beforehand. This method makes it possible to detect several overlapping and occluding ellipses (for a review see [1]). But, this approach has some drawbacks: it does not necessarily produce a unique solution as a) it can be difficult to detect the peak which can be spread across a high number of bins; b) the search space is multidimensional and hence sparse, which can make the search for the peak difficult unless a large number of data points are available; and c) choosing the sizes of the bins in the accumulator is problematic. More recently, the fuzzy clustering methods have been adapted to the problem of ellipse detection (see [2] for a review). Compared to the Hough based methods, these approaches require less computations and memory.

S. Benferhat and P. Besnard (Eds.): ECSQARU 2001, LNAI 2143, pp. 432–443, 2001.

·The least square based fitting methods have also received much attention especially the choice of the optimization criteria [3], [4],[5],[6]. However, there are very few works on global extraction methods. We can mention the works of P.L.Rosin and al [7] whose multistage algorithm is proposed to segment connected points into a combination of representations such as straight lines and conic sections. M.Li also develops a method of 2D-shape description in terms of straight and elliptic segments based on the Minimum Description Length criterion [8]. Most of these methods do not deal with the problem of fitting representations into disconnected pixels. T.Ellis and al tackle ellipse fitting as a three-stage process [9]. At first, contours are decomposed into straight and curved parts. Ellipses are initially fitted to detected arc segments. These initial fits are improved by extending the arcs, using existing edge connectivity information. Nevertheless, the performance of these methods is closely linked to the fact that they require data from a large proportion of the ellipse. The results of the fitting problem for short curve sections are generally unstable or inaccurate. It is necessary to add some information as T. Ellis does by exploiting connectivity of edges in the scene and initiating fitting on connected edges. Similarly, J. Porrill has developed a linear bias correction for the extended Kalman filter that allows him to predict a confidence region to direct the search for the ellipse continuations [10].
In this paper, we propose some new ideas to the ellipse fitting/detection problem. First, the fitting problem is resolved from the polar representation of the ellipse [11]. To the opposite of [11], we propose to estimate in a separated way the parameters and the parametrization. We show that the optimal parametrization is solution of a four degree equation with one unknow. If the parametrization seems to be a drawback to our method, its contribution is predominant to improve the parameter estimation in the case of short sections and in a noised context. Indeed, instability of the fit for short noisy conic segments is a serious practical problem. Integrating explicitly by the way of a scale factor, the maximum and minimum total arc length in the cost function, we constraint the conic search space. If we suppose that the image primitives have known bounded dimensions, we determine then an analyzing envelope taking into account uncertainty of the solution. In a second step, we propose a complete detection scheme based on a fuzzy decision stage. A last, our algorithm is applied to the detection of mushrooms in development on wheat leaves.

2 Ellipse fitting in parametric form

2.1 Principle

Let data points $X_i = (x_i, y_i)^T_{i\epsilon[1..N]}$ are given in the plane. These points describe an ellipse if they verify the parametric system :

$$X_i = X_0 + A.P(\theta_i) = X_0 + R(\alpha).F.P(\theta_i) \tag{1}$$

where $X_0 = (x_0, y_0)^T$ are the coordinates of the center, $A = \begin{pmatrix} a & b \\ c & d \end{pmatrix}$ is the matrix of the dimensional parameters and $P(\theta_i) = (\cos\theta_i, \sin\theta_i)^T$ the parameterization of the ellipse. A can be also expressed in fonction of the canonical parameters of the ellipse by the matrix $F = diag(\lambda_1, \lambda_2)$ where λ_1, λ_2 are the lengths of the semi-main axes $(\lambda_1 > \lambda_2)$ and the rotation matrix $R(\alpha)$ that represents its angular position α in the plane. To fit an ellipse, we need to estimate the parameters from the data points. This standard problem is classicaly resolved in the least square sense by minimizing the sum of the squares of the distances between the data points and the ellipse :

$$\Theta(X_i;\ \theta_i, A, X_0) = \sum_{i=1}^{N} \|G_i\|^2 = \sum_{i=1}^{N} \|X_i - X_0 - R(\alpha).F.P(\theta_i)\|^2 \quad (2)$$

This is equivalent to solving the nonlinear least squares problem :

$$G_i = X_i - X_0 - R(\alpha).F.P(\theta_i) \approx 0,\ \forall\, i \in [1, ..., N] \quad (3)$$

A classical way to resolve this nonlinear problem is to use the well known iterative Gauss-Newton method. Given that the Jacobian matrix is sparse, we can modify, as Gander and al do [11], its structure by using Givens transformations and compute the QR decomposition only on a block. Then the correction vector is given by backsubstitution. The initial values of the parameters and the parametrization are obtained by fitting a cercle to the data points. We propose in this section to estimate in a separated way the parameters and the parametrization. In (2), the product $R(\alpha)$F is replaced by the matrix A and the minimization of (2) is decomposed like that :

$$\min_{A,X_0,\theta_i} \Theta(X_i;\ \theta_i, A, X_0) = \min_{\theta_i}\{\min_{A,X_0}\Theta(X_i, \theta_i;\ A, X_0)\} = \min_{\theta_i}\Theta(X_i, A, X_0;\ \theta_i) \quad (4)$$

By considering the parametrization θ_i known and fixed, the problem is now linear and the minimization of (2) is direct:

$$\Theta(X_i, \theta_i;\ A, X_0) = \sum_{i=1}^{N} (x_i - h(\theta_i)\, q_x)^2 + (y_i - h(\theta_i)\, q_y)^2 \quad (5)$$

where $h(\theta_i) = [1, \cos\theta_i, \sin\theta_i]\,, q_x = [x_0, a, b]^T$ and $q_y = [y_0, c, d]^T$. Or in its matrix form :

$$\Theta = (X - Hq_x)^T (X - Hq_x) + (Y - Hq_y)^T (Y - Hq_y) \quad (6)$$

The estimation of the coefficients of A and X_0 is then resolved by computing two speudo-inverse, one on the x-component and the other on the y-component:

$$q_x = \left(H^T H\right)^{-1} HX, q_y = \left(H^T H\right)^{-1} HY \quad (7)$$

A and X_0 being fixed, we minimize (5) in relation to θ_i. The derivative of (5) leads us to look for the solutions of a quadratic equation with two unknowns:

$$(ab + cd)\, C_i^2 + \left(b^2 + d^2 - a^2 - c^2\right) C_i S_i - (ab + cd)\, S_i^2 - (bu + dv)\, C_i + (au + cv)\, S_i = 0 \quad (8)$$

Where $C_i = \cos\theta_i$, $S_i = \sin\theta_i$, u = x_i-x_0 $\neq 0$,v = y_i-y_0 $\neq 0$. To make the search of the solutions simpler, we replace the parameters (a, b, c, d) by the canonical parameters of the ellipse $(\lambda_1, \lambda_2, \alpha)$ (see eq. (1)). Then (8) is simplified and becomes :

$$US_i - VC_i + WC_iS_i = 0 \tag{9}$$

with $U = \lambda_1 (\text{u}\cos\alpha\text{-v}\sin\alpha), V = \lambda_2 (\text{u}\sin\alpha\text{+v}\cos\alpha)$ and $W = \lambda_2^2 - \lambda_1^2$. Then either dividing (9) by C_i or S_i and introducing the variable :

$$z_i = \tan(\theta_i mod(\pi)) = \frac{S_i}{C_i} = \frac{-S_i}{-C_i} \tag{10}$$

as unknown, we get a polynomial equation p (z_i) of degree four with one unknown :

$$z_i^4 - \frac{2U}{V}z_i^3 + \left(\frac{U^2+V^2-W^2}{V^2}\right)z_i^2 - \frac{2U}{V}z_i + \left(\frac{U}{V}\right)^2 = 0 \tag{11}$$

This equation gives four solutions (z_1, z_2, z_3, z_4) with at least two real zeros. The complex solutions are removed whereas we shall concentrate on the real solutions. We must also note that the solution θ_i according (10) is defined to within π. Then, the solution verifies one of these two conditions :$\pm US_i \mp VC_i + WC_iS_i = 0$. If (11) gives k real solutions $\theta_k = \tan^{-1}(z_k)$ (with k$\in$ [2..4]), we select the solution θ_{k*} that confirms : $\min\limits_k \|G_i(\theta_k)\|$. Then, we obtain an iterative least square fitting procedure :

· **Step 1:** *we compute* $\theta_i^{(0)}$. *In this case, a good starting values for the* $\theta_i^{(0)}$ *is obtained by fitting an ellipse by minimizing the algebraic distance.*

· **Step 2:** *we compute then* $X_O^{(t)}$ *and* $A^{(t)}$ *with (7).*

· **Step 3:** *we compute the real solutions* $z_i^{(t)}$ *of (11) and then* $\theta_i^{(t)}$.

· **Step 4:** *We set t* $\leftarrow$*t+1 and if* $|\Theta^t - \Theta^{t-1}| > \eta$ *then go to step 1 otherwise stop.*

Figure 1.a shows the obtained results witch are compared with the classical iterative Gauss-Newton algorithm (see [11]). 30 points (black dots) sample a high curvature section of an ellipse and a Gaussian noise with 2 pixels of standard deviation is added to each sample points. The ideal ellipse is represented in solid line, "–[]–" represents the algebraic fitting initialization, "–O– "represents our fitting (55 iterations) and "– * –", the Gauss-Newton fitting (32 iterations). Figure 1.a shows that the two geometric fits in parametric form converge to the ideal solution. Our approach seems to be more expansive than the Gauss-Newton approach. If the minimization of the parametrization seems to be a drawback to our method, we will see in the next section that is contribution is predominant to improve the parameter estimation in the case of short sections.

2.2 Constrained fitting

When data points are distributed on a short section of an ellipse, we can notice that most classical fitting methods are unstable or diverge. The density of data points being small, the problem is considered as badly conditioned. Generally, in that case it is necessary to obtain an acceptable solution, by adding some prior information about the data (noise) or about the criterion (dimensional constraint). If integrating the noise characteristics into the criterion will offer a distinct improvement on estimation, it is not a determining factor when the density of data points being to small. Besides, we can notice that statistical methods such as the re-normalization method with bias correction [3] diverge if we have not got enough data. Then, the only prior knowledge of the elliptical characteristics reduces the space of solution and then comes up the real solution. From this idea, we propose to modify the previous pattern to bring satisfactory results for short sections with distributed data points. We then consider that the elliptic shapes in images have known bounded dimensions. It is precisely the matter we encounter in the studied microscopic images. The classic use of least square fitting method based on the algebraic distance seems not to be appropriated to take this additional constraint into account. That is why it is difficult to find works on this subject in literature. One of the most essential reasons: the implicit parameters of an ellipse are correlated and have a large and different field of variations and then unusable to add a dimensional constraint. A fitting criterion based on the parametric representation of the ellipse seems to be more suitable to solve this problem. From this idea, we propose to introduce in the criterion a scale factor ν allowing to force the solution to stay in a choosen parametric space. To approach this optimal solution, the principle consists in weighting the parametrization θ by this scale factor. Then, we propose to minimize the following cost function :

$$\Theta(X_i;\, \theta_i, \nu, A, X_0) = \sum_{i=1}^{N} \left(x_i - h\left(\nu\theta_i\right) q_x\right)^2 + \left(y_i - h\left(\nu\theta_i\right) q_y\right)^2 \qquad (12)$$

Indeed, θ characterizes the following ratio of arc length :

$$\theta = \frac{2\pi l}{L} = \frac{2\pi}{L} \int_0^l \sqrt{x_l^2 + y_l^2}\, dl \qquad (13)$$

where l is an arc length along the curve from the starting point, and L is the total arc length of the curve. Then, given the arc length l of the analysed section known and if we alter the total arc length L by ν, we introduce implicitly a bias on the results of (12)(see fig. 1.b). The evolution of this bias is highlighted by observing the evolution of (λ_1, λ_2) solutions of (12) as a function of this parameter, we show that :

$$(\lambda_1, \lambda_2) \sim [\frac{1}{\nu^2}, \frac{1}{\nu}] \qquad \forall \ \frac{\lambda_2}{\lambda_1} \in]0, 1] \qquad (14)$$

This property is always true when the ratio $p = \frac{l}{L} < 0.5$. If $p > 0.5$, the density of data points is then sufficient to give a satisfactory estimation of the ellipse parameters. By analogy with the property of the similarity of the Fourier transform, we can see this term as a $\frac{1}{\nu}$ shrinking/dilatation factor of the harmonic (fig. 1.b). Then, it becomes possible by a good using of this factor in the minimisation process to constraint the solution to stay in a predefined aera.

Formulation of the problem*: if we consider the elliptic shapes in images have known bounded dimensions lying within the range [L_a, L_b] (L_a is the minimum total arc length of the ellipses and L_b is the maximum one) and that exist a reference ellipse parametrized by the pair (λ_1^*, λ_2^*), then we have to find in the interval [L_a, L_b] the* *length L^* which will give an optimal parametric solution close to $(\lambda_1^*, \lambda_2^*)$* (an example is given in figure 1.c).

Indeed, a restrictive solution close to $(\lambda_1^*, \lambda_2^*)$ avoid, with noisy data, having local minimum. The direct minimisation of (12) in function of ν seems to be difficult, then we propose a dichotomic process to approach this solution : given the interval $[L_a, L_b]$ and l known,

· **Step 1:** *initialization of the parametrization from (13). We put L =(La+Lb)/2.*

· **Step 2:** *we compute two scale factors $\nu_a=(L + L_a)/2L$ and $\nu_b=(L + L_b)/2L$.*

· **Step 3:** *we determine from (5) two elliptical candidates E_a and E_b :*

$$E_a \rightarrow \min_{A,X_0} \Theta(X_i, \nu_a\theta_i;\ A, X_0) \tag{15}$$

$$E_b \rightarrow \min_{A,X_0} \Theta(X_i, \nu_b\theta_i;\ A, X_0) \tag{16}$$

To avoid local minimum, we select the ellipse E_a or E_b which has closest dimensions of $(\lambda_1^*,\lambda_2^*)$. This can allow us to readapt the length interval by modifying bounds as follow:

If E_a is choosen then : La←La, Lb←(L+Lb)/2 *and* L←(La+Lb)/2 else : Lb←Lb, La←(L+La)/2 *and* L← (La+Lb)/2).

· **Step 4 :** *We thus compute in (11) the ellipse parameterization on the chosen ellipse and then back in step 1 if $|L^t - L^{t-1}| > \eta$.*

Results : we consider the discrete contour of the ideal ellipses with 70 percent of the boundary points missing. We consider also a very noised context by adding with a regular step (every 15 pixels) a zero-mean Gaussian noise with a standard deviation of 2. To analyse the quality and the stability of the method, this operation was repeated 50 times. The constraints are initialized : we suppose that the total arc length of the studied ellipses lies within the range [L_a=200, L_b=400] and the dimensions (λ_1^*=60, λ_2^*=30) of the reference ellipse are the same that the ideal ellipse. The figure 2 (top: high eccentricity section, bottom: low eccentricity section) present a visual comparison of the fitting results between our algorithm (fig. 2.a) and some methods of reference such as : Fitzgibbon (b), Taubin (c) and Gander (d). The continuous dark line represents the ideal ellipse, the noised dark short section is one of the 50 generated sections and the grey lines correspond to the fitting results of the 50 realizations. The table 1 collects the average values of the estimated parameters (standard deviation added) and the average computation time required. The NES column gives the number of the Non−Ellipse Solutions returned by the previous methods (among the 50 runs). As we can see on figure 2 and table 1, our approach and the Fitzgibbon's one are the most stable in a very noised context. In addition, the integration of dimensional constraints in the fitting of a short section improves obviously the estimation of the ellipse's parameters (see table 1 and the figure 2.a). The computation time given here is only for illustration, since I did not try to do any code optimization. All experiments were conducted using the Matlab system with a Sun Sparc 20 Workstation. We can however notice that our algorithm seems to be the most expensive. The most time-consuming part is the computation of the solutions of the polynomial equation (11).

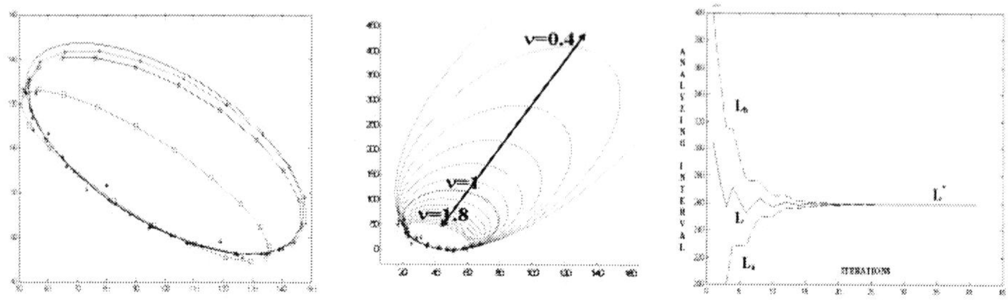

(a) (b) (c)

Fig. 1. Results of geometric fit in parametric form **(a)**. Evolution of the fitting result in function on ν **(b)**,(p= 0.4, zero-mean Gaussian noise (σ = 2)). Example of evolution of the analyzing interval **(c)**.

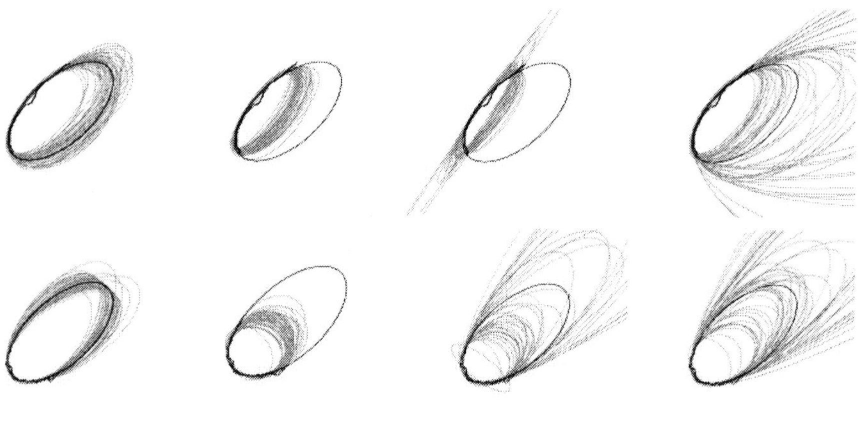

(a) (b) (c) (d)

Fig. 2. Stability comparison with the main conic-fitting algorithms. Fitting to a noised short section (top: high eccentricity section, bottom: low eccentricity section).

2.3 Dimensional uncertainty

Once this average solution, corresponding to the vector parameters (X_0^*,A^*,θ_i^*,L^*), is estimated, we can then determine a confidence region taking into account uncertainty on the result. Indeed, this envelope is obtained by least square fitting of two boundary ellipses E_m and E_M resulting respectively to the dilatation of the optimal parametrization θ_i^* by the scale factor ν' =L$_a/L^*$ and the contraction of the optimal parametrization by ν" =L$_b/L^*$:

$$E_m \rightarrow \min_{A,X_0} \Theta(X_i, \nu'\theta_i^*;\ A, X_0) \tag{17}$$

(ideal)	xo=100	yo=100	λ_1 = 60	λ_2 = 30	α = 45°	NES
CLSF cpu:5.5s	98.98 $\pm$5.04	99.11 $\pm$4.27	60.07 $\pm$4.88	28.56 $\pm$3.71	43.87 $\pm$3.85	0
Fitzigbon cpu:3.10^{-3}s	81.38 $\pm$2.92	100.15 $\pm$1.65	46.28 $\pm$2.13	16.04 $\pm$2.69	35.46 $\pm$2.37	0
Bookstein cpu:2.10^{-3}s	72.61 $\pm$6.07	102.37 $\pm$7.97	56.73 $\pm$24.76	9.20 $\pm$2.03	32.57 $\pm$6.07	18
Gander cpu:4.4s	175.40 $\pm$136.94	84.96 $\pm$45.94	137.24 $\pm$139.78	47.60 $\pm$34.09	41.86 $\pm$34.68	0

Table 1. Comparison of the average values of the ellipse parameters estimated by different approaches (high eccentricity section).

$$E_M \rightarrow \min_{A,X_0} \Theta(X_i, \nu'' \theta_i^*;\ A, X_0) \tag{18}$$

In order to observe the behaviour of this envelope according to the arc length, we have generated elliptic sections of increasing length. The experimental procedure was as follow : - We have considered the case of high eccentricity section. - The arc length was varied from 15 to 80% of the ideal total arc length in step of 10%. - These sections were corrupted with a zero mean Gaussian noise. We experiment a high noise level corresponding to standard deviation of 2 pixels. - The analyzing interval [L_a, L_b] is fixed as previously. The dimensions of the reference and ideal ellipses are defined by the pair (λ_1^*=70, λ_2^*=40) and (λ_1=60, λ_2=30) respectively. - The solution is obtained by the algorithm of the section 2.2. The envelope is deduced from the relations (17) and (18). The figure 3 presents the results of our fitting ('– * –') and its confidence envelope (grey aeras) estimated from two arc lengths (black noised sections)corresponding to 15% (left) and 42% (middle) of the total arc length of the ideal ellipse (solid line). For comparaison, we have added the ellipse estimated by the Fitzgibbon's procedure ('– o –'). As we can note in these two examples, the envelopes give us an optimal bound of the ideal solution even in the case of a very short section. However, in a very noised context (σ >1.5), the arc length between 10 and 30% of the total arc length may introduce a bias in the orientation of the envelope. So, we may "lose" the ideal solution. The figure 3.c illustrates the evolution of the estimates (λ_1, λ_2) (see the curves '– * –' on figure 4) and their corresponding envelopes (grey aeras). We observe these parameters in the whole interval, e.g. from 15 up to 80% of the total arc length. Some remarks can be deduced :

- The increase in the noise level decrease the regularity of the envelope's evolution. However, the bound on the ideal solution is always assured.
- More the arc length increases, more the bound of the ideal solution is optimized.
- Beyond that 50% of the total arc length, the width of the envelope plateaus and the estimate ('– * –') converge to the ideal solution (the effects of the arc length constraint is reduced).

The same observations may be expressed for the low eccentricity section. So, the estimation of an analysing envelope offers several interests: To make the search of further ellipse data easier and then refine the fitting process (see next section) - To reduce thus the time of computation in the detection procedure.

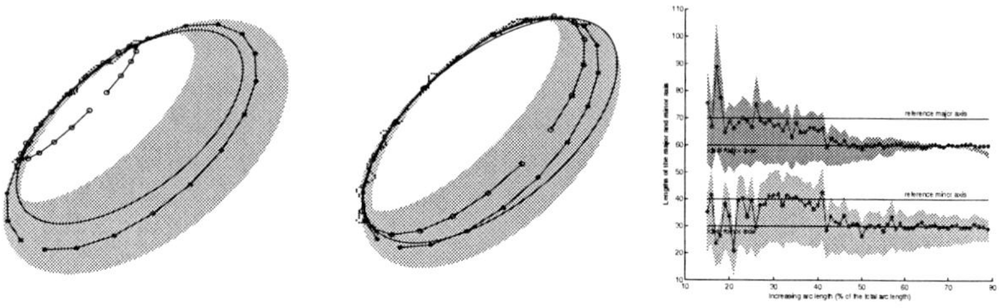

(a) (b) (c)

Fig. 3. Illustrations of the confidence envelopes (grey aeras) estimated on two arc lengths **(a)** and **(b)**. Evolution of the size of the confidence envelopes (grey aeras) estimated on increasing arc lengths **(c)**.

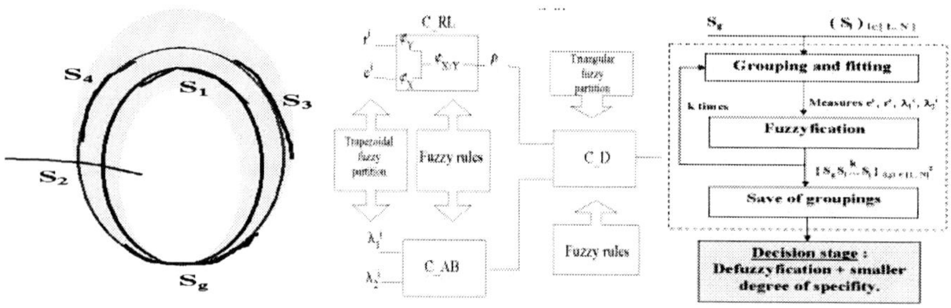

(a) (b) (c)

Fig. 4. Segments selected by an envelope (grey aera) **(a)**. Fuzzyfication of the fitting measures **(b)**. Strategy of decision **(c)**.

3 Decision scheme with fuzzy rules

So as to reduce the fitting process, we consider that the contours are classified in terms of "straight" and "curved" segments. This organisation step need a high level description including some elementary steps such as partitioning, grouping and classification. Then, the estimation of the envelopes is initialized on the "curved" segments. We must now refine the fitting process with the segments selected by the envelopes (fig. 4.a). However, several aspects must be considered : first, among the candidate edges selected in the analyzing envelope, some of these segments do not necessary belong to an elliptic boundary. And moreover, the space of shape in images is not only reduced to ellipses. Some "parasitical" structures with concave boundaries may exist. Then, it is necessary to exploit the unconnected neigbourhood in the fitting test and also clear up some ambiguities in the decision step. The incertainty of the data must be considered in the decision step in order to weight the result with a confidence degree. To minimize the wrong detections, we develop a decision scheme of the fitting results integrating four measures : the variance of the error of fit **e**, the ratio between the total length of the segments used in the fitting stage with the perimeter of the fitted ellipse **r**, and the two lengths of the semi-main axes (λ_1,λ_2). The measure e represents a distance between the fitted ellipse and the data. More this distance is small, more the model "fit" with the data. However, this measure is prone to noise in image that is characterized by irregular contours. Another factor biases the estimation : the shape are not perfectly elliptic. The incertainty attached to this quantity doesn't allow to specify exactly a threshold beyond which the data doesn't belong anymore to the ellipse. The parameter **r** weights the membership of an ellipse according to the quantity of data used in the fitting stage. In the same way, it is difficult to specify exactly the defined intervals for λ_1 and λ_2. Then, because of the incertain nature of the data, we propose to adopt a fuzzy representation of these measures. Every variable is described by a set of linguistic values representing by trapezoidal fuzzy sets. The support and the core of every set are determined in an experimental way. We also define three fuzzy controllers that provide the different rules between the input and the output (fig. 4.b). All these variables are represented by triangular and uniformly distributed fuzzy sets forming a strict fuzzy partition. The fuzzy controllers achieve a *fuzzyfication* φ_X of the input, a *vectorial fuzzyfication* $\varphi_{X\times Y}$ following with an *inference* operation ρ. In your application, the T-norm is the min operation and the T-conorm is the max. The controller C_RL made a fuzzy representation of the fitting with the measures **e** and **r** whereas the controller C_AB provide a fuzzy representation of the lengths λ_1 and λ_2 of the fitting ellipse. The outputs of these controllers are merging by the controller C_D that guarantees a symbolic description to the results. The general framework of decision is made up of the following steps (fig. 4.c) : - First an hierarchical and recursive procedure of grouping and fitting is realized with the set of the segments Si selected by the confidence envelope - Then, a symbolic description is associated with all the candidate ellipses generated previously. This fuzzy representation merges the fitting measures and provides to the result a degree of uncertainty - Lastly, a decision step extracts in all these candidates the most certain grouping. The decision rule retains the grouping which have a fuzzy representation belonging to some specific fuzzy sets and a smaller degree of specifity in these fuzzy sets.

4 Results

We have implemented our automatic extraction scheme to detect microscopic pathogenic mushrooms on a wheat leaf. As we can note on the figure 5.a, these cells, examined under an optical microscope, have shapes close to the ellipse (magnification 40). During its evolution, the dimensions of the mushroom lie between 10 and 15μm for the width (λ_2) and between 30 and 40 μm for the length (λ_1). These dimensional characteristics help us to initialize the different constraints of the procedure. But, we can constat also the difficulty of these images : First, the images are noised and blurred, and the light

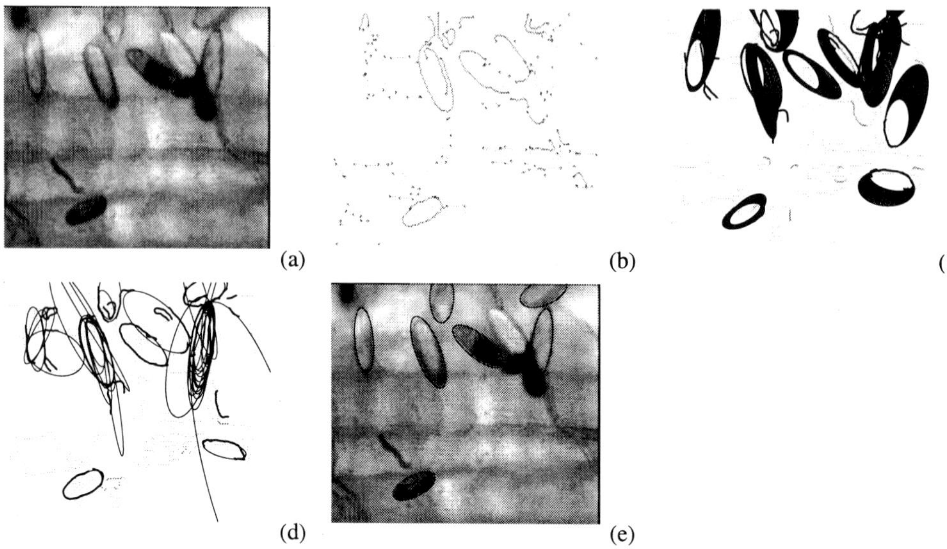

Fig. 5. Main steps of the detection procedure(see text).

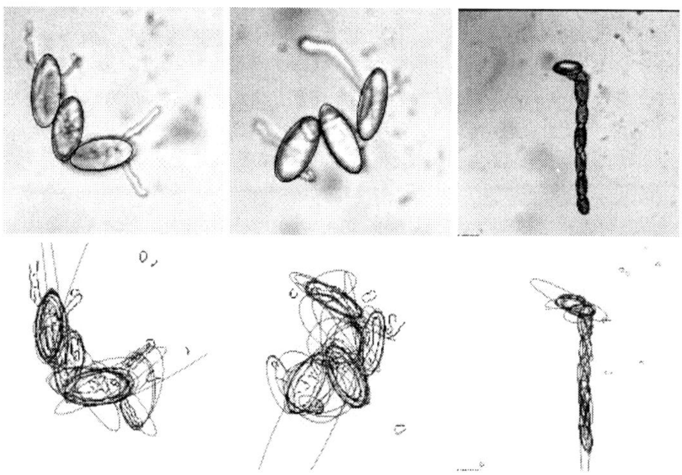

Fig. 6. Other examples. Results of the detection (top). All the candidate ellipses generated by the fitting combination stage (bottom).

is not homogeneous. Another constraints also can disturb the detection : most of the time mushrooms are grouped and overlapped and, parasitical structures (nervures, germination...) are present. The figure 5.b shows the result of the contour classification. Then, the confidence envelopes (gray aeras) are estimated from the significant "curved" segments (> 20 pixels)(see fig. 5.c). The figure 5.d shows all the candidate ellipses generated in the grouping and fitting stage. The final result of the decision stage is given on the figure 5.e. The degree of uncertainty is not illustrated. The another results presented in figure 6 confirm the robustness of our algorithm against noise and overlapping.

5 Discussion and conclusions

This article raises the difficult problem of the uncertainty handling in the ellipse fitting/detection process in complicated image data containing several overlapping and occluding elliptic shapes. First, we propose an iterative parametric fitting method incoporating implicitly the dimensional features of the image primitives. We estimate then a confidence envelope that gives information about the dimensional uncertainties of these shapes. A fuzzy decision step completes the detection procedure and gives a confidence degree to the results. it is a new reasoning in the framework of the ellipse detection, because most of the approaches gives hit or miss results. The generalization of our method to ellipses with different sizes is possible if we properly widen the analysing interval in the fitting step and ignore the controller C_AB in the decision scheme.

References

1. C. Daul, P. Graebling, and Ernest Hirsch., "From the hough transform to a new approach for the detection and approximation of elliptical arcs.," *Computer Vision and Image Understanding*, vol. 72, no. 3, pp. 215–236, 1998.
2. I.Gath and D. Hoory, "Fuzzy clustering of elliptic ring-shaped clusters.," *Pattern recognition letters.*, vol. 16, pp. 727–741, 1995.
3. K. Kanatani., "Renormalisation for unbiased estimation.," *In Proc. 4th Int'l Conf. Comput. Vision (Berlin)*, pp. 599–606, 1993.
4. F. Bookstein., "Fitting conic sections to scattered data.," *Computer Vision, Graphics and Image Processing.*, vol. 9, pp. 56–71, 1979.
5. A.W. Fitzgibbon, M. Pilu, and R.B. Fischer., "Direct least squares fitting of ellipses.," *IEEE Trans. on Patter Analysis and Machine Intelligence.*, vol. 21, no. 5, pp. 476–480, 1999.
6. G. Taubin., "Estimation of planar curves, surfaces, and nonplanar space curves defined by implicit equations with applications to edge and range image segmentation.," *IEEE Transactions on Pattern Analizis and Machine Intelligence.*, vol. 13, no. 11, pp. 1115–1138, 1991.
7. P.L. Rosin and G.A.W. West., "Nonparametric segmentation of curves into various representations.," *IEEE Trans. Patt. Anal. Mach. Intell.*, vol. 17, no. 12, pp. 1140–1153, 1995.
8. M. Li., "Minimum description length based 2d shape description.," *4th Proc. International Conference on Computer Vision.*, pp. 512–517, 1993.
9. T. Ellis, A. Abbood, and B. Billault., "Ellipse detection and matching with uncertainty.," *Image and Vision Computing*, vol. 10, no. 5, pp. 271–276, 1992.
10. J. Porrill., "Fitting ellipses and predicting confidence envelopes using bias corrected kalman filter.," *Image and Vision Computing*, vol. 8, no. 1, pp. 37–41, 1990.
11. W. Gander, G.H. Golub, and R. Strebel., "Least squares fitting of circles and ellipses.," *BIT*, vol. 34, pp. 558–578, 1994.

Probabilistic Modelling for Software Quality Control

Norman Fenton[1], Paul Krause[2], and Martin Neil[1]

[1] Queen Mary, University of London and Agena Ltd
Mile End Road, London E1 4NS
{norman, martin}@agena.co.uk
[2] Philips Research Laboratories, Crossoak Lane, Redhill RH1 5HA and
Department of Computing, University of Surrey, Guildford GU2 5XA
p.krause@surrey.ac.uk

Abstract. As is clear to any user of software, quality control of software has not reached the same levels of sophistication as it has with traditional manufacturing. In this paper we argue that this is because insufficient thought is being given to the methods of reasoning under uncertainty that are appropriate to this domain. We then describe how we have built a large-scale Bayesian network to overcome the difficulties that have so far been met in software quality control. This exploits a number of recent advances in tool support for constructing large networks. We end the paper by describing how the network was validated and illustrate the range of reasoning styles that can be modelled with this tool.

1 Introduction

Quality control for mechanical and electronic devices is now a well-developed science. However, as all computer users will be aware, the same is not true of quality control for software. There are a number of basic reasons for this. Firstly, the prerequisites for statistical process control, large sample sizes and repeatable processes, are not applicable to software development. Secondly, software failures are the result of design faults and not due to ageing of the software product. Consequently, very different techniques for quality control are needed for software development as compared to traditional manufacturing.

In this paper, we will discuss some of the difficulties with quality control approaches that have been tried so far. We will then identify a number of requirements that need to be satisfied by more robust models for software quality assessment and control. We will then describe the large-scale Bayesian network that we have built to meet these requirements, and discuss its validation using a number of real-world projects.

2 The Problem with Regression Models

In this section we will look at the general issues relating to quality control and assessment in software development. In subsequent sections we will primarily be focusing on software defect modelling. However, it is worth phrasing the problem in general terms to emphasise that the longer-term goal is to apply probabilistic graphical models to other quality characteristics, like reliability and safety [3, 7].

S. Benferhat and P. Besnard (Eds.): ECSQARU 2001, LNAI 2143, pp. 444–453, 2001.

There are two different viewpoints of software quality as defined by Fenton and Pfleeger [2]. The first, the external product view, looks at the characteristics and sub-characteristics that make up the user's perception of quality in the final product – this is often called quality-in-use. Quality-in-use is determined by measuring external properties of the software, and hence can only be measured once the software product is complete. For instance quality here might be defined as freedom from defects or the probability of executing the product, failure free, for a defined period.

The second viewpoint, the internal product view, involves criteria that can be used to control the quality of the software as it is being produced and that can form early predictors of external product quality. Good development processes and well-qualified staff working on a defined specification are just some of the pre-requisites for producing a defect free product. If we can ensure that the process conditions are

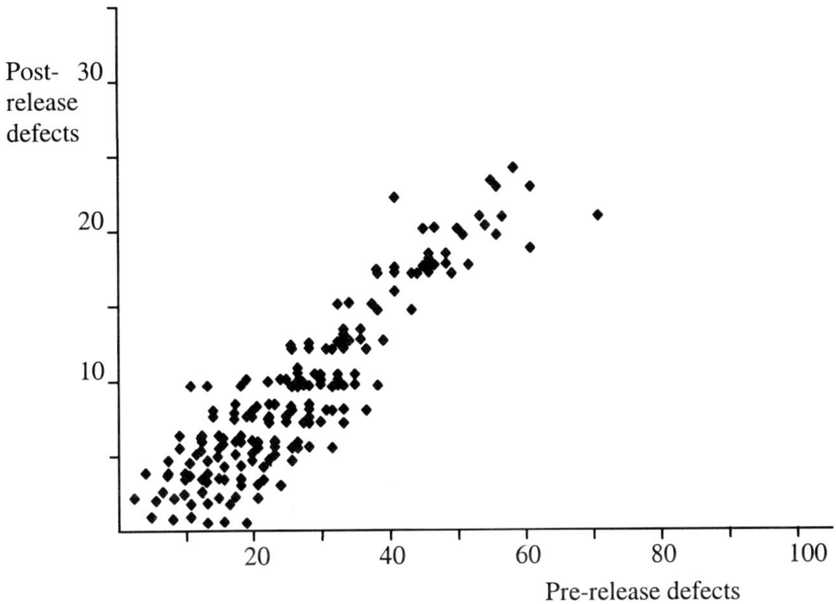

Fig. 1: A hypothetical plot of pre-release against post-release defects for a range of modules. Each dot represents a module.

right, and can check intermediate products to ensure this is so, then we can perhaps produce high quality products in a repeatable fashion.

Unfortunately the relationship between the quality of the development processes applied and the resulting quality of the end products is not deterministic. Software development is a profoundly intellectual and creative design activity with vast scope for error and for differences in interpretation and understanding of requirements. The application of even seemingly straightforward rules and procedures can result in highly variable practices by individual software developers. Under these circumstances the relationships between internal and external quality are uncertain.

Typically informal assessments of critical factors will be used during software development to assess whether the end product is likely to meet requirements:

- Complexity measures: A complex product may indicate problems in the understanding of the actual problem being solved. It may also show that the product is too complex to be easily understood, de-bugged and maintained.
- Process maturity: Development processes that are chaotic and rely on the heroic efforts of individuals can be said to lack maturity and will be less likely to produce quality products, repeatedly.
- Test results: Testing products against the original requirements can give some indication of whether they are defective or not. However the results of the testing are likely only to be as trustworthy as the quality of the testing done.

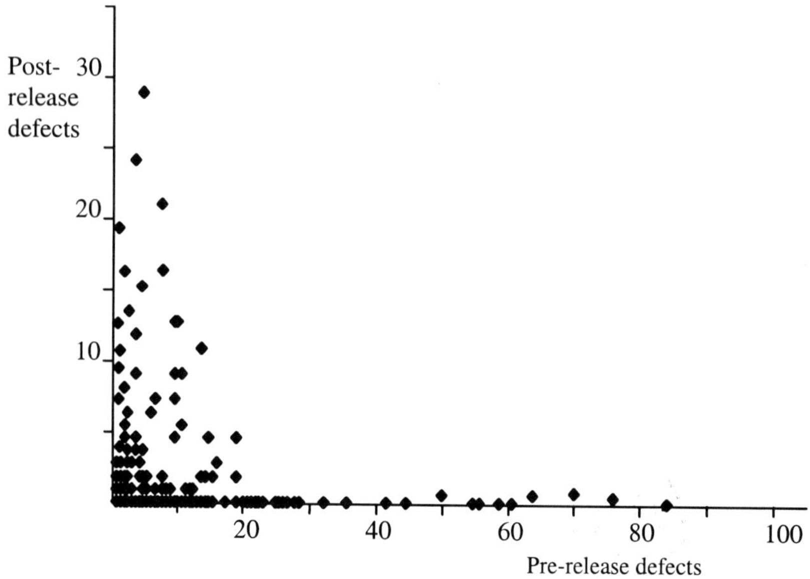

Fig. 2: Actual plot of pre-release against post-release defects for a range of modules.

The above types of evidence are often collected in a piecemeal fashion and used to inform the project or quality manager about the quality of the final product. However there is often no formal attempt, in practice, to combine these evidences together into a single quality model.

A holy grail of software quality control could be the identification of one simple internal product measurement that provides an advanced warning of whether or not the goals for the external product characteristics will be achieved. Unfortunately, in software engineering the causal relationships between internal and external quality characteristics are rarely straightforward. We will illustrate this with one simple example. More detailed analyses of naïve regression models for software engineering can be found in [3], and [4].

Suppose we have a product that has been developed using a set of software modules. A certain number of defects will have been found in each of the software modules during testing. Perhaps we might assume that those modules that have the highest number of defects during testing would have the highest risk of causing a failure once the product was in operation? That is, we might expect to see a relationship similar to that shown in figure 1.

What actually happens? It is hard to be categorical. However, two published studies indicate quite the opposite effect – those modules that were most problematic pre-release had the least number of faults associated with them post-release. Indeed, many of the modules with a high number of defects pre-release showed zero defects post-release. This effect was first demonstrated by [1], and replicated by [4]. Figure 2 is an example of the sort of results they both obtained.

So, how can this be? The simple answer is that faults found pre-release gives absolutely no indication of the level of residual faults unless the prediction is moderated by some measure of test effectiveness. In both of the studies referenced, those modules with the highest number of defects pre-release had had all their defects "tested out". In contrast, many of the modules that had few defects recorded against them pre-release clearly turned out to have been poorly tested – they were significant sources of problems in the final implemented system.

3 The Need for Causal Modelling

The fundamental difficulty with the use of naïve regression models for software quality assessment is that although they may be used to *explain* a data set obtained in a specific context, they cannot be used to *manage* a software development process. For this, we need to identify the causal influences on the attribute we are interested in. The example from the preceding section was a case in point. We cannot make management decisions about the quality of software from defect data alone. We must also take into account, at least, the effectiveness with which the software has been tested.

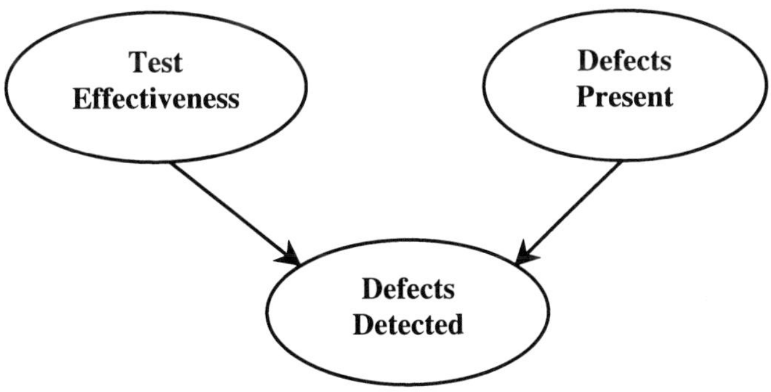

Fig. 3: A simple graphical model that provides greater explanatory power than a naïve regression model.

Figure 3 provides a slightly more comprehensive model. "Defects Present", is the attribute we are interested in. This will have a causal influence on the number of

"Defects Detected" during testing. "Test Effectiveness" will also have a causal influence on the number of defects detected and fixed. As we will see later, this will turn out to be a fragment of a much larger model, with the node representing defects present being a synthesis of a number of factors including, for example, review effectiveness, developer's skill level, quality of input specifications and resource availability.

4 A Probabilistic Model for Software Defect Prediction

These discussions lead us naturally to considering the use of Bayesian networks for quality control in software development. They have many advantages:

1. They can easily model causal influences between variables in a specified domain;
2. The Bayesian approach enables statistical inference to be augmented by expert judgement in those areas of a problem domain where empirical data is sparse;
3. As a result of the above, it is possible to include variables in a software reliability model that correspond to process as well as product attributes;
4. Assigning probabilities to reliability predictions means that sound decision making approaches using classical decision theory can be supported.

We have built a module level defect estimation model, and evaluated it against real project data. Since this was a research activity, resources were not available to perform extensive knowledge elicitation with the active and direct involvement of members of Philips' Lines of Businesses (LoBs). Philips Research Laboratory's experience from working directly with LoBs was used as a surrogate for this. Although this meant that the probabilistic network could be built within a relatively short period of time, the fact that the probability tables were in effect built from "rough" information sources and strengths of relations necessarily limits the precision of the model. However, as will be seen, the resulting model has proven to be quite accurate.

4.1 Overall Structure of the Bayesian Network

The probabilistic network is executed using the generic probabilistic inference engine Hugin (see http://www.hugin.com for further details). However, the size and complexity of the network were such that it was not realistic to attempt to build the network directly using the Hugin tool. Two of the authors (Fenton and Neil) have been actively developing tools and techniques to assist with the development of large-scale Bayesian networks [7]. As a result we were able to use two methods and tools, built on top of Hugin, to tackle effectively this otherwise intractable task:

- The SERENE method and tool [8], which enables: large networks to be built up from smaller ones in a modular fashion; and, large probability tables to be built using pre-defined mathematical functions and probability distributions.
- The IMPRESS method and tool [6], which extends the SERENE tool by enabling users to generate complex probability distributions simply by drawing distribution shapes in a visual editor.

The resulting network takes account of a range of product and process factors from throughout the lifecycle of a software module. Because of the size of the model, it is

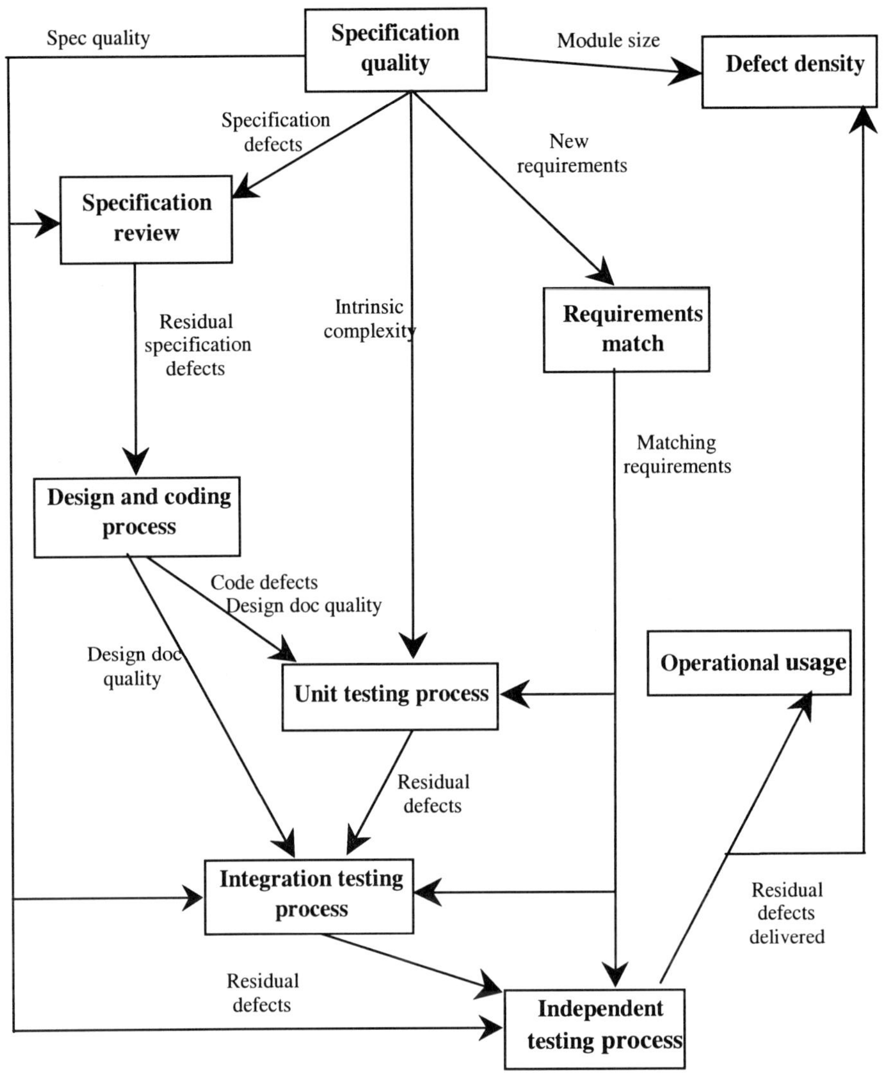

Fig. 4: Overall network structure.

impractical to display it in a single figure. Instead, we provide a first schematic view in terms of sub-nets (Figure 4). This modular structure is the actual decomposition that was used to build the network using the SERENE tool.

The arc labels in Figure 4 represent 'joined' nodes in the underlying sub-nets. This means that information about the variables representing these joined nodes is passed directly between sub-nets. For example, the specification quality and the defect density sub-nets are joined by an arc labelled 'Module size'. This node is common to both sub-nets. As a result, information about the module size arising from the specification quality sub-net is passed directly to the defect density sub-net. We refer to 'Module size' as an 'output node' for the specification quality sub-net, and an 'input node' for the defect density sub-net.

4.2 Some Comments on the Details of the Network

There is insufficient space to describe the details of all the sub-nets. However, we show the *Specification quality* sub-net in Figure 5 as an example. This can be explained as follows. *Specification quality* is influenced by three major factors:

- *intrinsic complexity* of the module (that is, the inherent complexity of the problem to be solved);
- the *internal resources* used, which are in turn factored into *staff quality* (or experience), the input *document quality*, and the *schedule* constraints;
- the *stability* of the requirements, which are in turn dependent on the extent of *stakeholder involvement* and the *novelty* of the problem.

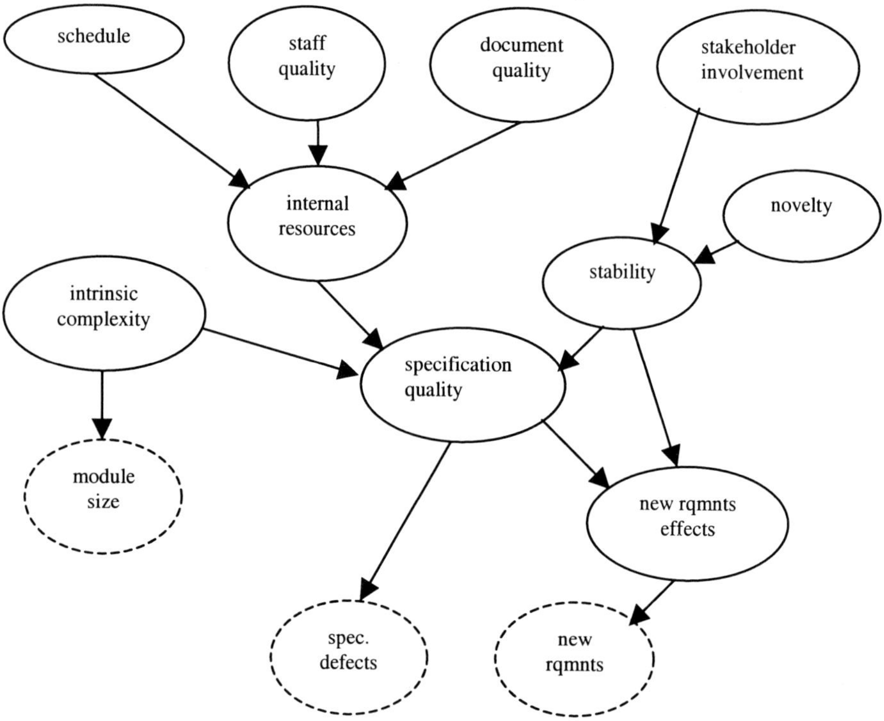

Fig. 5: Specification quality sub-net. A dashed border indicates a node that is shared with another sub-net.

The complete network models the entire development and testing life-cycle of a typical software module. We believe it contains all the critical causal factors at an appropriate level of granularity, at least within the context of software development within Philips. It contains 65 nodes, many with 3-5 ordinal values, but several having continuous scales.

The node probability tables (NPTs) were built by eliciting probability distributions based on experience from within Philips. Some of these were based on historical records, others on subjective judgements. For most of the non-leaf nodes of the network the NPTs were too large to elicit all of the relevant probability distributions using expert judgement. Hence we used the novel techniques that have been developed recently on the SERENE and IMPRESS projects [6, 8, 9], to extrapolate all the distributions based on a small number of samples.

Consider, for example, the node for *specification quality* in Figure 5. This has three parent nodes, two with 5 values and one with 4. Consequently, for each value of *specification quality* we need to define 100 probabilities. Instead of eliciting these directly, we elicit a sample of distributions (including 'extreme' values) and then extrapolate distributions for all intermediate values.

By applying numerous consistency checks we believe that the resulting NPTs are a fair representation of experience within Philips.

As it stands, the network can be used to provide a range of predictions and "what-if" analyses at any stage during software development and testing. It can be used both for quality control and process improvement. However, two further areas of work were needed before the tool could be considered ready for extended trials. Firstly and most importantly, the network needed to be validated using real-world data. Secondly a more user-friendly interface needed to be engineered so that (a) the tool did not require users to have experience with probabilistic modelling techniques, and (b) a wider range of reporting functions could be provided. The validation exercise will be described in the next section in a way that illustrates how the probabilistic network was packaged to form the AID tool (AID for "Assess, Improve, Decide").

5 Validation of the Defect Estimation Tool AID

The Philips Software Centre (PSC), Bangalore, India, made validation data available. We gratefully acknowledge their support in this way. PSC is a centre for excellence for software development within Philips, and so data was available from a wide diversity of projects from the various Business Divisions within PSC.

Data was collected from 31 projects from three Business Divisions: Mainstream Consumer Electronics, Philips Medical Systems and Digital Networks. This gave a spread of different sizes and types of projects. Data was collected from three sources:

- Pre-release and post-release defect data was collected from the "Performance Indicators" database.
- More extensive project data was available from the Project Database.
- Completed questionnaires on selected projects.

In addition, the network was demonstrated in detail on a one to one basis to five experienced quality/test engineers to obtain their reaction to its behaviour under a number of hypothetical scenarios.

The network was used to make predictions of numbers of defects found during unit test, integration test and independent testing of the module once it had been integrated into a product. These predictions were compared against the actual values obtained. Full data was only available from ten of the projects (that is, including data from independent testing). Consequently, insufficient data was available to perform a full statistical validation. However, with the exception of two projects the median value for the number of defects predicted at each testing phase was always within 10% of the actual value. The two exceptional projects involved significant elements of user interface design. These sorts of projects typically generate large numbers of change requests as the details of the UI design are clarified, so we feel that they fall outside of the scope of our model as it currently stands.

One of the major values of AID is as a tool for exploring the possible consequences of changes to a software process, or the constraints on a product's development. The ability of Bayesian networks to handle quite complex reasoning patterns is one of the reasons why the tool is proving so successful in this regard. We end with one example, which also illustrated how our model does handle the sort of effects that were discussed in Section 2.

Table 1 lists the median values of "Defects found at Unit Test" and "Defects Delivered" for a variety of values for the intrinsic problem complexity of the software module under development. Look at the first row first; the predictions for the number of defects found during unit test. For a very simple module, we get an increase in the number of defects found over the prior, and a decrease for a very complex module.

	Intrinsic Complexity of the Software Module		
	Prior	"Very Simple"	"Very Complex"
Defects found in Unit Test	90	125	30
Defects delivered	50	30	70

At first sight, this seems counter intuitive – we might expect simpler modules to be more reliable. The explanation is that the more complex modules are harder to test than the simpler modules. With their greater ability to "hide" faults, fewer faults will be detected unless there is a compensating increase in the effectiveness with which the module is tested. No such compensation has been applied in this case and the low prediction for defects detected and fixed for the "very complex" case indicates that typically such modules are relatively poorly tested.

This is borne out when we look at the respective figures for residual defects delivered, in the second row of the table. Now we see a reversal. The prediction for the "very complex" module indicates that it will contain more residual defects than the "very simple" module (a median of 70, compared to a median of 30). So our model naturally produces the qualitative behaviour of the real world data from our earlier experiment. That is, the better-tested modules yield more defects during unit test and deliver fewer defects. For the more poorly tested modules, the converse is the case. (Note that the table misses out data from the Integration and Independent Test Phases. When this is included the total number of defects – found plus delivered – is greatest for the "Very Complex" module).

6 Conclusion

We started with an introduction to the problem of quality control in software development. Our hypothesis was that this was a domain where use of state-of-the-art techniques for reasoning under uncertainty could provide significant added value. We have ended up with a remarkably accurate software defect prediction model that also has tremendous potential for exploring the consequences of diverse software development scenarios.

Due to space limitations, we have had to strike a balance between focussing on discussing the motivation for using advanced techniques for reasoning under uncertainty in the software engineering domain, and providing detail on our solution to this problem. An extended discussion of the method of construction of the network and the validation experiments so far performed can be found in [5], which can be obtained from any of the authors.

References

1. E. Adams, "Optimizing preventive service of software products", *IBM Research Journal*, **28**(1), 2-14, 1984.
2. N.E. Fenton and S.L. Pfleeger, *Software Metrics: A Rigorous and Practical Approach*, (2nd Edition), PWS Publishing Company, 1997.
3. N. Fenton and M. Neil "A Critique of Software Defect Prediction Research", *IEEE Trans. Software Eng.*, **25**, No.5, 1999.
4. N. Fenton and N. Ohlsson "Quantitative analysis of faults and failures in a complex software system", *IEEE Trans. Software Eng.*, **26**, 797-814, 2000.
5. N. Fenton, P. Krause and M. Neil "A Probabilistic Model for Software Defect Prediction", unpublished manuscript available from the authors, 2001.
6. IMPRESS (IMproving the software PRocESS using bayesian nets) EPSRC Project GR/L06683, http://www.csr.city.ac.uk/csr_city/projects/impress.html, 1999.
7. M. Neil, B. Littlewood and N. Fenton, "Applying Bayesian Belief Networks to Systems Dependability Assessment". *Proceedings of Safety Critical Systems Club Symposium*, Leeds, Published by Springer-Verlag, 6-8 February 1996.
8. M. Neil, N. Fenton and L. Nielson, "Building large-scale Bayesian Networks", *Knowledge Engineering Review*, **15**(3), 257-284, 2000.
9. SERENE consortium, "*SERENE (SafEty and Risk Evaluation using bayesian Nets): Method Manual*", ESPRIT Project 22187, http://www.dcs.qmw.ac.uk/~norman /serene.htm, 1999.

Spatial Information Revision: A Comparison between 3 Approaches

Éric Würbel[1], Robert Jeansoulin[1], and Odile Papini[2]

[1] LIM-CMI, Université de Provence,
39 avenue Joliot-Curie,
13453 Marseille Cedex 13, France
[2] SIS, Université de Toulon et du Var,
avenue de l'université, BP132,
83957 La Garde, France

Abstract. The present paper deals with spatial information revision in geographical information system (GIS). These systems use incomplete and uncertain information and inconsistency can result, therefore the definition of revision operations is required. Most of the proposed belief revision operations are characterized by a high complexity and since GIS use large amount of data, adjustments of existing strategies are necessary. Taking advantage of the specificity of spatial information allows to define heuristics which speed up the general algorithms. We illustrate some suitable adjustments on 3 approaches of revision: binary decision diagrams, preferred models and Reiter's algorithm for diagnostic. We formally compare them and we experiment them on a real application. In order to deal with huge amount of data we propose a divide and revise strategy in the case where inconsistencies are local.

1 Introduction

Geographic information systems (GIS) deal with incomplete and uncertain information. Since the data come from different sources characterized by various data qualities, these data may conflict and require belief revision operations.

In knowledge representation for artificial intelligence, one tries to represent a rational agent perceptions and beliefs. Since, most of the time, the agent faces incomplete, uncertain and inaccurate information, he needs a revision operation in order to manage his beliefs change in presence of a new item of information. The agent's epistemic state represents his reasoning process and belief revision consists in modifying his initial epistemic state in order to maintain consistency, while keeping new information and removing the least possible previous information. Most of the logical approaches have been developped at the theoretical level, except for a few applications [15] and it turns out that in the propositionnal case the theoretical complexity of revision is Π_2^p [6] [9]. In other respects, we deal with geographic information characterized by a huge amount of data and at first glance it seems to be no hope of performing revision in the context of GIS. However, we show in this paper that it is possible to identify a tractable class

S. Benferhat and P. Besnard (Eds.): ECSQARU 2001, LNAI 2143, pp. 454–465, 2001.

of problems for which revision can be performed with reasonable complexity. Effective implementation of revision operations requires a suitable ajustment of existing strategies and we have to take advantage of the spatial knowledge representation in order to define heuristics which speed up the general algorithms.

In this paper we propose three different approaches of revision in the context of GIS. The first one stems from the ROBDD[1], the second one is based on preferred models computation and the third one is an adaptation of Reiter's algorithm for diagnosis. We show that these three approaches formally give equivalent results and that the three defined revision operations verify KM postulates. We then conduct an experimental comparison. This experimental study is achieved on a real application developped by the CEMAGREF[2] about the flooding of the Herault river (France) in order to provide a better understanding of flooding phenomenon [11]. The aera is segmented into compartments, a compartment is a spatial entity in which the water height is considered to be constant. We first compare the three approaches on the maximal number of compartments they can deal with in reasonable time. Since the large size of the data, we then define divide and revise strategy and propose an algorithm in the case where the inconsistencies are supposed to be local.

The paper is organized as follows. After some preliminaries in Sect. 2, we first present in Sect. 3 the three approaches of revision, according to ROBDD, according to preferred models and according to Reiter's algorithm for diagnosis. We then show that these three revision operations are formally equivalent and satisfy the KM postulates. In Sect. 4 we perform an experimental study and describe the divide and revise strategy, before concluding in Sect. 5.

2 Preliminaries

In the following we use usual notations for propositional logic. $\mathcal{W}$ denotes the set of interpretations, we write $\omega \models \alpha$ for specifying that ω is a model of a propositional formula α and $Mod(\alpha)$ denotes the set of models of α.

Belief revision has been successfully characterized by Alchourron, Gärdenfors and Makinson [1] who provided a set of rationality postulates for epistemic states which consist in belief sets representing an agent's current beliefs. Katsuno and Mendelzon [7] reformulated these postulates for epistemic states represented by a single propositional formula ψ where any formula entailed by ψ is part of the belief set. Let ψ, ϕ and μ be propositional formulas, the postulates are:

(R1) $\psi \circ \mu$ implies μ.
(R2) If $\psi \wedge \mu$ is satisfiable, then $\psi \circ \mu \equiv \psi \wedge \mu$.
(R3) If μ is satisfiable, then so is $\psi \circ \mu$.
(R4) If $\psi_1 \equiv \psi_2$ and $\mu_1 \equiv \mu_2$, then $\psi_1 \circ \mu_1 \equiv \psi_2 \circ \mu_2$.
(R5) $(\psi \circ \mu) \wedge \phi$ implies $\psi \circ (\mu \wedge \phi)$.
(R6) If $(\psi \circ \mu) \wedge \phi$ is satisfiable, then $\psi \circ (\mu \wedge \phi)$ implies $(\psi \circ \mu) \wedge \phi$.

[1] Reduced Ordered Binary Decision Diagrams.
[2] French research center on water and forest management.

A revision operation satisfying the AGM postulates is equivalent to a set of total pre-orders between interpretations, of the propositional calculus. Katsuno and Mendelzon [7] define a *faithful assignment* with respect to ψ, a function that assigns to each formula ψ the total pre-order on $\mathcal{W}$, denoted $\leq_\psi$, satisfying the following properties: (1) If $\omega_1, \omega_2 \models \psi$ then $\omega_1 =_\psi \omega_2$; (2) if $\omega_1 \models \psi$ and $\omega_2 \not\models \psi$ then $\omega_1 <_\psi \omega_2$; (3) $\psi \equiv_s \phi$ iff $\leq_\psi = \leq_\phi$. They obtain a representation theorem:

Theorem 1. *A revision operator* $\circ$ *satisfies postulates (R1)–(R6) iff there exists a faithful assignment that maps each formula* ψ *to a total pre-order*$\leq_\psi$ *such that* $Mod\,(\psi \circ \mu) = min\,(Mod\,(\mu)\,, \leq_\psi)$.

3 Different Approaches

As mentionned in the introduction, we want to take advantage of the spatial knowledge representation. We consider an area which is segmented into regions, measurements on regions can be encoded in propositional mono-literal clauses (set S_1). Topological relations between regions produce binary clauses (set S_2^C). The fact that spatial entities are part of regions can be represented by domain constraints which are encoded in a n-ary clause and $n(n-1)/2$ mutual exclusion binary clauses (set S_2^D). Let $S_2 = S_2^D \cup S_2^C$. We suppose that S_1 and S_2 are consistent and that $S_1 \cup S_2$ is inconsistent. Since S_2 is more reliable than S_1 we revise S_1 by S_2. Our revision strategy stems from the determination of minimal subsets of clauses to drop out in order to restore consistency. More formally, we generalize the notion of *removed set* for a set of clauses revised by a set of clauses, previously introduced in [10] for a set of clauses revised by a unique clause.

Definition 1. *A* removed set R *for the revision operation* $S_1 \circ S_2$ *is the smallest subset of clauses to remove from* S_1 *such that* $((S_1 \cup S_2) \setminus R)$ *is consistent.*

Consequence 1. *If* R *is a removed set for the revision operation* $S_1 \circ S_2$*, then* $\forall c_i \in R$, $((S_1 \cup S_2) \setminus R) \models \neg c_i$.

Consequence 2. $R \subseteq S_1$ *is a removed set for the revision operation* $S_1 \circ S_2$*, iff* R *is a minimal set (according to cardinality) such that* $(S_2 \cup (S_1 \setminus R))$ *is consistent.*

3.1 Revision Using ROBDD

A BDD (Binary Decision Diagram),[4] represents a boolean function (or formula) ψ using a labeled direct acyclic graph. The graph has two sinks vertices labeled 0 and 1 representing the constant boolean function 0 and 1 respectively. Each non-sink vertex is labeled with a boolean variable v and has two out-edges labeled *then* and *else*. The *then* child corresponds to the case where $v = 1$ and the *else* child corresponds to the case where $v = 0$. Given an order on the variables, an ordered BDD is a BDD with the constraint that all paths from the source to a sink visit the variables in an ascending order. A reduced ordered or ROBDD is a OBDD which has been transformed by deleting some nodes, it may be viewed as a compressed decision tree for a propositional formula ψ. Each path from the source to a sink represents an interpretation of ψ and conversely each interpretation of ψ corresponds to a path from the source to a sink. A model, resp. a countermodel of ψ corresponds to a path from the source to the sink 1 resp.0.

The construction of a ROBDD associated with the set of clauses $S_1 \cup S_2$ leads to ROBDD with all paths to the sink 0 since $S_1 \cup S_2$ is inconsistent. In order to solve this problem, we use the transformation introduced by [8] and [3]. Each clause c of S_1 is replaced by the formula $\phi_c \rightarrow c$, where ϕ_c is a new variable. If ϕ_c is assigned true then $\phi_c \rightarrow c$ is true iff c is true, this enforces the clause c. On contrast, if ϕ_c is assigned false then $\phi_c \rightarrow c$ is true whatever the truth value of c, the clause c is not taken into account. More formally:

Definition 2. *Let C be a set of clauses, $\mathcal{H}(C)$ denotes the set of clauses resulting from the transformation described above, and H_C denotes the set of the newly introduced variables. We define a mapping σ from C to $\mathcal{H}(C)$ such that $\forall c \in C,\ \sigma(c) = \phi_c \rightarrow c$ and a mapping σ_{var} from $\mathcal{H}(C)$ to H_C such that $\forall (\phi_c \rightarrow c) \in \mathcal{H}(C),\ \sigma_{var}(\phi_c \rightarrow c) = \phi_c$.*

We construct a ROBDD associated with $(S_2 \cup \mathcal{H}(S_1))$ and minimizing the number of clauses to remove from S_1 amounts to minimize the number of new variables ϕ_c assigned false. To each path in the ROBDD we assign a cost as follows: for each variable in H_{S_1} the cost is 0 for the *then* branches, it is 1 for *else* branches and it is 0 for all the other variables. The cost of a path p is the sum of the costs of the visited branches. Minimizing the number of clauses to remove from S_1 amounts to find in the ROBDD representing $(S_2 \cup \mathcal{H}(S_1))$ a path p from source to sink 1 with minimal cost. More formally:

Definition 3. *Let C be a set of clauses and let the ROBDD representing $\mathcal{H}(C)$. Let p be a path. We define H_C^{p+} (resp. H_C^{p-}) as the set of new variables such that p starts from source to sink and visit the H_C^{p+} (resp. H_C^{p-}) variables in the* then *branch, (resp. the* else *branch).*

Theorem 2. *Let $R \subseteq S_1$. R is a* removed set *for the revision operation $S_1 \circ_{BDD} S_2$ iff there exists a complete path in the ROBDD representing $(S_2 \cup \mathcal{H}(S_1))$ to the sink 1 with minimal cost and such that $H_R = H_{S_1}^{p-}$.*

3.2 Revision Using Preferred Models (MPL)

[2], [5] provide an algorithm, called MPL, to compute the preferred models of a set of propositional formulas. This algorithm stems from the definition of a preference relation between models, in order to only compute the preferred models. The preference relation can be built on a subset of propositional variables and we use it to compute the *removed sets*. More formally:

Definition 4. *Let $\mathcal{D}$ be a set of propositional variables, $lit(\mathcal{D})$ denotes the set of literals of $\mathcal{D}$.*

- *A partial $\mathcal{D}$-interpretation IP is a set of non contadictory literals such that $IP \subset lit(\mathcal{D})$.*
- *A $\mathcal{D}$-interpretation is a partial $\mathcal{D}$-interpretation IP such that $\forall x \in \mathcal{D}$ either $x \in IP$ or $x \notin IP$ and $\mathcal{I}_{\mathcal{D}}$ denotes the set of $\mathcal{D}$-interpretations.*
- *Let IP be a partial $\mathcal{D}$-interpretation, $Ext(IP, \mathcal{D}) = \{I \in \mathcal{I}_{\mathcal{D}} \mid IP \subseteq I\}$ denotes the set of interpretation which extend IP.*
- *Let C be a set of clauses and let I be a $\mathcal{D}$-interpretation, I is a $\mathcal{D}$-model of C iff there exists M a model of C such that $I \subseteq M$.*

Definition 5. *Let $\mathcal{D}$ be a set of propositional variables, $lit(\mathcal{D})$ denotes the set of literals of $\mathcal{D}$.*

- *$lit(\mathcal{D}) = \mathcal{P} \cup \mathcal{NP}$ where $\mathcal{P}$ is the set of preferred literals and $\mathcal{NP}$ is the set of non-preferred literals.*
- *Let IP_1 and IP_2 be two partial $\mathcal{D}$-interpretations, IP_1 is preferred to IP_2 iff the set of non-preferred literals of IP_1 is included in the set of non-preferred literals of IP_2, this is denoted by $IP_2 \sqsubset IP_1$.*

The defined order $\sqsubset$ has a maximal element which is the $\mathcal{D}$-model $\mathcal{P}$ and a minimal element which is the $\mathcal{D}$-model $\mathcal{NP}$ [2].

Proposition 1. *Let IP be a partial $\mathcal{D}$-interpretation, $Ext(IP, \mathcal{D})$ represents the set of extensions of IP in $\mathcal{D}$ and $Ext(IP, \mathcal{D})$ only has one maximal element for $\sqsubset$ [5].*

The Davis and Putnam algorithm enumerates some of $\mathcal{D}$-interpretations, using the preference relation between literals these $\mathcal{D}$-interpretations are ordered, consequently the first $\mathcal{D}$-interpretation satisfying the set of clauses is a preferred $\mathcal{D}$-model, denoted M_p. In order to eliminate the non-preferred $\mathcal{D}$-model, the initial set of clauses is modified by the addition of a clause consisting of the negation of all the non-preferred literals of M_p.

We now show how we adapt the MPL algorithm. As in the previous approach, we construct a new set of clauses $\mathcal{H}(S_1)$ replacing each clause c of S_1 by the formula $\phi_c \rightarrow c$. The new variables ϕ_c of the set H_{S_1} play the same part as previously, they enforce the clause c. A preference relation is defined by the preference of literals of the clauses of H_{S_1}. Minimizing the number of clauses to remove from S_1 amounts to select among the preferred $lit(H_{S_1})$-models those of minimal cardinality. More formally:

Definition 6. *Let L be a finite set of literals. $n^-(L)$ (resp. $n^+(L)$) denotes the set of negative literals (resp. positive literals) of L.*

And the following theorem holds:

Theorem 3. *Let $R \subseteq S_1$ and MP[3] be the set of the preferred H_{S_1}-models of $(S_2 \cup \mathcal{H}(S_1))$. M_R denotes the H_{S_1}-interpretation such that $\forall c \in R$, $\neg\sigma_{var}(\sigma(c)) \in M_R$ and $\forall c \in S_1 \setminus R$, $\sigma_{var}(\sigma(c)) \in M_R$. R is a* removed set *for the revision operation $S_1 \circ_{MPL} S_2$ iff $M_R \in MP$ and $M' \in MP$ such that $M' \neq M_R$ $n^-(M') \geq n^-(M_R)$.*

3.3 Revision Using Reiter's Algorithm (REM)

In [17] Wurbel et al. presented a detailed description of the adaptation of Reiter's algorithm for diagnosis [12]. In order to perform the comparison with the two previous revision operations, we briefly recall the approach.

Definition 7. *Let F be a collection of sets. A* hitting set *of F is a set $H \subseteq \bigcup_{S \in F}$ such that $\forall S \in F$, $H \cap S \neq \emptyset$.*

H is a minimal hitting set *of F iff H is a hitting set of F and $\forall H' \subset H$ with $H' \neq \emptyset$, H' is not a hitting set of F.*

We denote by $\mathcal{N}(F)$ the set of minimal hitting sets of a collection of sets. Our revision strategy is to first compute the minimal hitting sets of the collection of inconsistent subsets of $S_1 \cup S_2$ denoted by $\mathcal{I}(S_1 \cup S_2)$, using an adaptation of Reiter's algorithm [12,14] and to then order the minimal hitting sets in order to only select one of them.

Proposition 2. *There exists $N \in \mathcal{N}(\mathcal{I}(S_1 \cup S_2))$ such that $N \cap S_2 = \emptyset$.*

We first establish the correspondance between minimal hitting sets and removed sets as follows:

Theorem 4. *Let $R \subseteq S_1$, R is a* removed set *for the revision operation $S_1 \circ_{REM} S_2$ iff R is a minimal hitting set of minimal cardinality for the collection of inconsistent subsets of $S_1 \cup S_2$ and $R \cap S_2 = \emptyset$.*

We recall the adaptation of Reiter's algorithm in order to compute the minimal hitting sets.

REM algorithm. Computation of $\mathcal{N}_{S_1}(\mathcal{I}(S_1 \cup S_2))$. Let $\mathcal{I}(S_1 \cup S_2)$ the collection of the inconsistent subsets of $S_1 \cup S_2$. The tree of the construction of the collection of minimal hitting sets, denoted T, is the smallest tree satisfying the following properties:

- its root is labeled by "$\surd$" if $\mathcal{I}(S_1 \cup S_2) = \emptyset$, otherwise its root is labeled by an element of $\mathcal{I}(S_1 \cup S_2)$.

[3] MP is obtained using the MPL algorithm with the set of clauses $(S_2 \cup \mathcal{H}(S_1))$ and the set of preferred literals $lit(H_{S_1})$.

– if n is a node in T we define $H(n)$ as the set of branches labels on the path from the root to n. If n is labeled by "$\surd$", it does not have any successor node in T. If n is labeled by a set $\Sigma \in \mathcal{I}(S_1 \cup S_2)$, then for each $\sigma \in \Sigma$ such as $\sigma \in S_1$ (according to Prop. 2) n has a successor node n_σ linked to n by a branch labeled by σ. n_σ is labeled by a set $S \in \mathcal{I}(S_1 \cup S_2)$ such that $S \cap H(n_\sigma) = \emptyset$ if such a set S exists. if there is no such S, n_σ is labeled by "$\surd$".

Consequence 3. *The maximum depth of the computing tree of minimal hitting sets of* $\mathcal{N}_{S_1}(\mathcal{I}(S_1 \cup S_2))$ *is* $\#S_1$.

We then provide a refinement of the REM algorithm, denoted by REM_R, which only computes the minimal hitting sets of minimal cardinality. This refinement stems from the following. In the tree construction, as soon as we find a minimal hitting set, we only continue the tree construction in breadth. Because if we continue the construction in depth we get a minimal hitting set which is not of minimal cardinality.

3.4 Properties of the Revision Operations

Proposition 3. *The revision operations* $\circ_{BDD}$, $\circ_{MPL}$ *and* $\circ_{REM}$ *give the same results.*

The proof follows from theorems 2, 3 and 4[16]. We then show that the defined revision operations satisfy the KM postulates. We first define a total pre-order corresponding to a propositional formula as follows:

Definition 8. *Let* ψ *be a formula, in conjunctive normal form (CNF). Let* $\omega \in \mathcal{W}$, $NS_\psi(\omega)$ *denotes the set of clauses appearing in the CNF* ψ *which are falsified by* ω *and* $\#NS_\psi(\omega)$ *the number of such clauses. We define the total pre-order* $\leq_\psi$ *by:* $\forall \omega_1, \omega_2 \in \mathcal{W}$, $\omega_1 \leq_\psi \omega_2$ *iff* $\#NS_\psi(\omega_1) \leq_\psi \#NS_\psi(\omega_2)$.

Proposition 4. *The function that assigns each formula* ψ *to the total pre-order* $\leq_\psi$, *defined in definition 8 is a faithful assignment.*

And the following theorem holds,

Theorem 5. *The revision operation* $\circ_{REM}$ *satisfies the KM postulates (R1)–(R6) and* $Mod(\psi \circ_{REM} \mu) = Min(Mod(\mu), \leq_\psi)$.

Since, by Prop. 3 the $\circ_{ROBDD}$ and $\circ_{MPL}$ operations give the same results than $\circ_{REM}$, they satisfy the KM postulates and theorem 5.

3.5 Comparison

The advantage of using the ROBDD lies in the good complexity in time in consistency checking. In our problem, using ROBDD amounts to look for the shortest path from the source to the sink 1. The drawback is that the incremental construction of a ROBDD can lead to a transitory binary decision diagram exponential in memory size. Moreover, we have to fix some parameters in order to provide a good ordering on the variables. The MPL and REM algorithms do not require this preliminary ordering on variables. Anyway, the REM_R algorithm gives best results since it uses a breadth first tree construction, and has the property to be "anytime" which allows to re-use some results before the end of the revision process.

4 Experimental Comparison

We now present the experimental study of a river flooding with the aim of assessing the water level.

4.1 The Application

The tests are conducted on data provided by CEMAGREF. The area is a valley segmented into 200 compartments. Aerial pictures provide the first source of information denoted by S_2, consisting of two kinds of hydraulic relations between adjacents compartments. A flow relation reflects the presence of a hydraulic link between two compartments with visible water flow. A hydrodynamic balance relation reflects the presence of a hydraulic link between two compartments but no visible flow. These relations are translated into constraints. Each constraint is encoded in propositional calculus by negative binary clauses representing the forbidden values of the constraint and the description of the variables is encoded by a n−ary clause for a domain of size n and $n(n-1)/2$ negative binary mutually exclusive clauses. The second source of information comes from land agricultural use, denoted by S_1, and consists of estimations on minimal and/or maximal submersion heights. These estimations are translated into a set of equalities. Each equality is encoded by means of monoliteral clauses. For an area of 200 compartments we deal with 37700 clauses and 3200 propositional variables.

The experimentation has been performed on a PC equipped with a Pentium II 233Mhz processor and 128Mo RAM. The algorithms have been implemented with C language and the egcs 1.0.2. compiler with -O2 optimizations activated. For the ROBDD approach the CUDD library has been used.

Since the ROBDD is very sensitive to the variables ordering, we first perform checks in order to provide the best variables ordering for our problem. In order to perform further comparison we then adopt the following methodology. We check the limits of each of the proposed algorithms, dealing with a certain number of compartments, and increasing this number as far as possible. When the limits are reached we propose "a divise and revise" strategy. We divide the problem into subproblems we solve them and we merge the solutions.

4.2 Experimental Results

We deal with an increasing number of compartments from three to twelve compartments. The CPU times shown in figure 1 only apply on 8 compartments because for a greater number of compartments some algorithms stop either for a limit in space (ROBDD, REM) or for a limit in CPU time (MPL). A refinement of REM algorithm denoted by REM_R which only computes the minimal hitting sets of minimal cardinality, gives much better results than the other algorithms, but it is not illustrated in the figure for the sake of legibility.

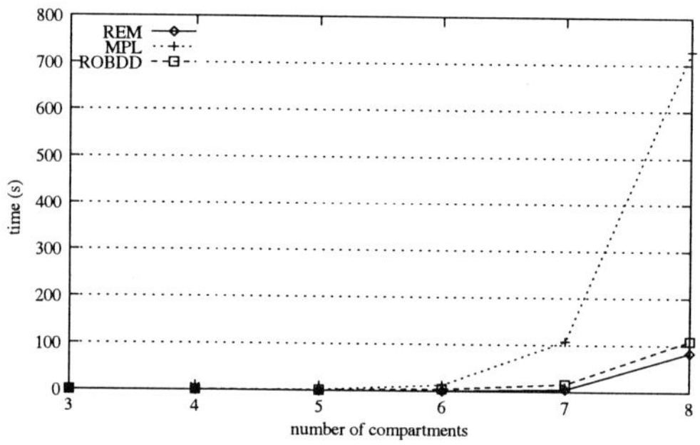

Fig. 1. Performance of the different approaches

As illustrated in the figures 2 (a) and (b), although the ROBDD, MPL and REM algorithms formally give equivalent results, the experimentation shows that the REM algorithm is faster than the others. Using the REM_R algorithm it is also possible to deal with twelve compartments in a reasonable time, which is not possible with the other algorithms.

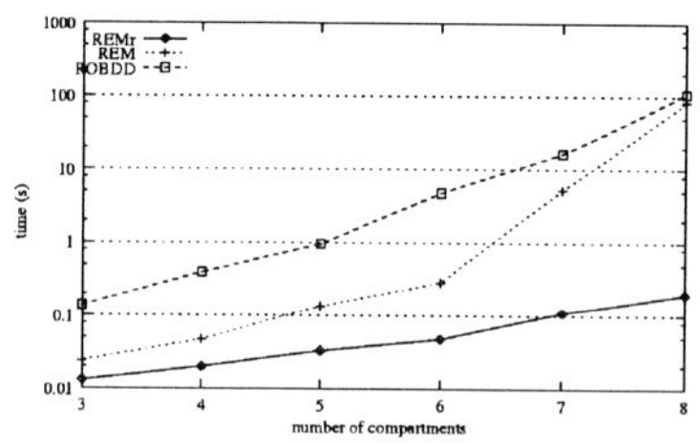

(a) performance gain for REM_R algorithm

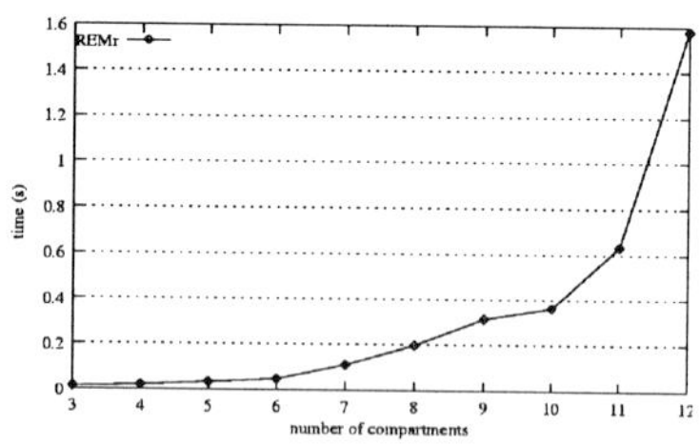

(b) performance of the REM_R algorithm

Fig. 2. Performance gain for REM_R algorithm

4.3 Divide and Revise

The experimental results show that it seems difficult, even using the REM_R algorithm, to deal with the 200 compartments at one and the same time. The experimentation underlines the fact that the untractable group of compartments corresponds to those which have numerous minimal hitting sets. Moreover, it turns out that the inconsistencies are not global but spatially localized. Therefore we divide the problem into subproblems with a reasonable number of compartments in order to solve the local inconsistencies. However several questions arise, how to partition the set of compartments, how to be sure that solving the subproblems and merging the solutions would restore the consistency of the initial problem, and how to perform the merging. The third question still is under investigation, anyway, in the case of local inconsistencies we propose a solution.

We divide the whole area, represented by S, into packets of compartments of tractable size. The computation of minimal hitting sets of S is achieved from the computation of minimal hitting sets of the packets, via REM algorithm, and we propose a merging algorithm stemming from the following considerations. Since the division of the whole area, is not necessarily a partition, some packets may overlap, the determination of minimal hitting sets R for the packets could not be sufficient to restore consistency. Therefore, we have to compute the minimal hitting sets for each $S \setminus R$ and the minimal hitting sets for S consist of elements from R and elements from $S \setminus R$. More formally, we now present some definitions in order to establish the algorithm computing the minimal hitting sets of S according to the divide and revise strategy.

Definition 9 (merging). *Let $S = S_1 \cup S_2$ be a set of clauses. Let $S' = S'_1 \cup S'_2$ and $S'' = S''_1 \cup S''_2$ be two subsets such that $S'_1 \subset S_1$, $S''_1 \subset S_1$, $S'_2 \subset S_2$, $S''_2 \subset S_2$. The merging operation $\sqcup$ is defined by: $(S' \sqcup S'') = S' \cup S'' \cup \{c \mid c \in S,\ lit(c) \cap (lit\,(S') \cup lit\,(S'')) \neq \emptyset\}$*

Definition 10. *Let $\mathcal{C}_1$ and $\mathcal{C}_2$ be two collections of sets. The operation $\otimes$ is defined by: $\mathcal{C}_1 \otimes \mathcal{C}_2 = \{S \mid S = S_1 \cup S_2,\ (S_1, S_2) \in \mathcal{C}_1 \times \mathcal{C}_2\}$*

Definition 11. *Let $\mathcal{C}$ be a collection of sets and E be a set. The operation $\bullet$ is defined by: $E \bullet \mathcal{C} = \{S \mid S = E \cup C,\ C \in \mathcal{C}\}$*

Definition 12. *Let $\mathcal{C}_1$ and $\mathcal{C}_2$ be two collections of sets. The operation $\bigtriangledown$ is defined by: $\mathcal{C}_1 \bigtriangledown \mathcal{C}_2 = \{S \mid S \in \mathcal{C}_1 \cup \mathcal{C}_2$ and $\forall S' \in \mathcal{C}_1 \cup \mathcal{C}_2,\ S' \neq S,\ S \not\subset S'\}$*

We now present the algorithm:

Function divrev $(TKB;\ TN)$
TKB: vector of $[1 \ldots n]$ bases of clauses ;
TN: vector of $[1 \ldots n]$ collections of minimal hitting sets;
TKB': vector of $[1 \ldots n']$ bases of clauses, with $n' < n$;
TN': vector of $[1 \ldots n']$ collections of minimal hitting sets;

LF: vector of $[1 \ldots n']$ tuples of size n giving the TKB to merge in order to construct the TKB';
$TmpC$, $TmpC'$: temporary collections of sets;

begin
  if $n = 1$ **then**
    return (TKB_1, TN_1);
  end if
  $LF :=$ get_merging_list (TKB);
  for all $(i_1, \ldots, i_m)_k \in LF$, $k \in [1..n']$ **do**
    $TKB'_k := (TKB_{i_1} \sqcup \ldots \sqcup TKB_{i_m})$;
    $TN'_k = \emptyset$;
    for all $R \in (TN_{i_1} \otimes \ldots \otimes TN_{i_m})$ **do**
      $TN'_k := TN'_k \bigtriangledown [R \bullet \mathrm{REM}\,(TKB'_k \setminus R)]$;
  end for
 end for
 return divrev(TKB', TN');
end

The completeness of the algorithm stems from the definition of the merging operation between subbases $\sqcup$, from the presence in the merged base of minimal hitting sets coming from the subbases and from the minimality of the hitting sets coming from $\bigtriangledown$ operation.

5 Conclusion

In this paper, we presented a comparison between three revision approaches stemming from a real application in the context of GIS. These approaches could be successfully applied to other applications in geophysics, demography, etc. Since the adaptation of Reiter's algorithm to revision gives the best experimental results, it could be fruitful to adapt other algorithms designed for diagnosis, particularly real time algorithms. In order to deal with the large size data we proposed a divise and revise strategy and gave an algorithm in case where the inconsistencies are assumed to be local, however how to partition the area is still an open question. And coming back from practice to theory, it is finally interesting to notice, as independently also shown in [13], that maxichoice revision operations give good results for the finite case while they are too restrictive for the deductively closed case.

Acknowledgements. This work was supported by European Community project IST-1999-14189 REVIGIS.

References

[1] Alchourrón, Gärdenfors, and Makinson. On the logic of theory change : Partial meet contraction and revision functions. *J. of Symbolic Logic*, 50(2):510–530, 1985.

[2] Daniel Le Berre. *Autour de SAT : le calcul d'implicants P-restreints, algorithmes et applications.* Thèse de doctorat, Université Paul Sabatier, Toulouse, France, January 2000.

[3] Fabrice Bouquet and Philippe Jégou. Solving over-constrained CSP using weighted OBDDs. In Michael Jampel, Eugene Freuder, and Michael Maher, editors, *Over-Constrained Systems*, volume 1106 of *Lecture Notes in Computer Science*, pages 293–308. Springer-Verlag, 1996.

[4] Randal E. Bryant. Graph-based algorithms for boolean function manipulation. *IEEE Transactions on computers*, C-35(8):677–691, August 1986.

[5] Thierry Castell, Claudette Cayrol, Michel Cayrol, and Daniel Le Berre. Using the Davis and Putnam procedure for an efficient computation of preferred models. In W. Wahlster, editor, *ECAI96*. John Wiley and Sons, Ltd, 1996.

[6] T. Eiter and G. Gottlob. On the complexity of propositional knowledge base revision, updates and counterfactual. *Artificial Intelligence*, 57:227–270, 1992.

[7] H. Katsuno and A. Mendelzon. Propositional knowledge base revision and minimal change. *Artificial Intelligence*, 52:263–294, 1991.

[8] Marie-Christine Lagasquie-Schiex. *Contribution à l'étude des relations d'inférence non-monotone combinant inférence classique et préférences.* PhD thesis, Université Paul Sabatier, Toulouse, IRIT, Université Paul Sabatier, 118 route de Narbonne, 31062 Toulouse Cedex, December 1995.

[9] Paolo Liberatore and Marco Schaerf. The complexity of model checking for belief revision and update. In *AAAI'96*, pages 556–561, 1996.

[10] Odile Papini. A complete revision function in propositionnal calculus. In B. Neumann, editor, *Proceedings of ECAI92*, pages 339–343. John Wiley and Sons. Ltd, 1992.

[11] Damien Raclot and Christian Puech. Photographies aériennes et inondation : globalisation d'informations floues par un système de contraintes pour définir les niveaux d'eau en zone inondée. *Revue internationale de gÈomatique*, 8(1):191–206, February 1998.

[12] Raymond Reiter. A theory of diagnosis from first principles. *Artificial Intelligence*, 32:57–95, 1987.

[13] Renata Wasserman. An algorithm for belief revision. In Anthony G. Cohn, Fausto Giunchiglia, and Bart Selman, editors, *Proceedings of the Seventh Internationnal Conference about Principles of Knowledge Representation and Reasoning, KR2000*, pages 345–352, Breckenridge, Colorado, USA, April 2000. KR, inc., Morgan Kaufmann.

[14] Ralph W. Wilkerson, Russel Greiner, and Barbara A. Smith. A correction to the algorithm in Reiter's theory of diagnosis. *Artificial Intelligence*, 41:79–88, 1989.

[15] M. A. Williams and D. Williams. A belief revision system for the world wide web. In *Proceedings of the IJCAI workshop of the Future of Artificial Intelligence and the Internet*, pages 39–51, 1997.

[16] Eric Würbel. *Révision de connaissances géographiques.* PhD thesis, UniversitÈ de Provence, LIM-CMI, 39 avenue Joliot-Curie 13453 Marseille cedex 13, December 2000.

[17] Eric Würbel, Robert Jeansoulin, and Odile Papini. Revision : An application in the framework of GIS. In Anthony G. Cohn, Fausto Giunchiglia, and Bart Selman, editors, *Proceedings of the Seventh Internationnal Conference about Principles of Knowledge Representation and Reasoning, KR2000*, pages 505–516, Breckenridge, Colorado, USA, April 2000. KR, inc., Morgan Kaufmann.

Social Choice, Merging, and Elections

Thomas Meyer[1], Aditya Ghose[1], and Samir Chopra[2]

[1] Decision Systems Laboratory
Department of Information Systems
University of Wollongong
Wollongong, NSW 2522, Australia
{tmeyer,aditya}@uow.edu.au
[2] Knowledge Systems Group
School of Computer Science and Engineering
University of New South Wales
Sydney, NSW 2052, Australia
schopra@cse.unsw.edu.au

Abstract. Intelligent agents have to be able to merge inputs received from different sources in a coherent and rational way. Recently, several proposals have been made for the merging of structures in which it is possible to encode the preferences of sources [5,4,12,13,14,1]. Information merging has much in common with the goals of social choice theory: to define operations reflecting the preferences of a society from the individual preferences of the members of the society. Given this connection it seems reasonable to require that any framework for the merging of information has to provide satisfactory ways of dealing with the problems raised in social choice theory. In this paper we investigate the link between the merging of *epistemic states* and two important results in social choice theory. We show that Arrow's well-known impossibility theorem [2] can be circumvented when the preferences of sources are represented in terms of epistemic states. This is achieved by providing a consistent set of properties for merging from which Arrow-like properties can be derived. We extend this to a consistent framework which includes properties corresponding to the notion of being *strategy-proof*. The existence of such an extended framework can be seen as a circumvention of the impossibility result of Gibbard and Satterthwaite [8,17,18] and related results [6, 3].

1 Introduction

Intelligent agents have to be able to merge inputs received from different sources in a coherent and rational way. Recently, several proposals have been made for the merging of structures in which it is possible to encode the preferences of sources. In [5,4] *information fusion* is described in terms of possibility distributions [7] and the κ-framework developed in [21]. In [13,14], *information merging* is described in terms of epistemic states; structures in the style of [20]. In [1] the *combination* of preferences is described in a framework where preferences are represented as arbitrary binary relations.

It has been pointed out that the merging of information is similar to the operations studied in social choice theory, where the aim is to provide fair and equitable methods

S. Benferhat and P. Besnard (Eds.): ECSQARU 2001, LNAI 2143, pp. 466–477, 2001.

for aggregating the preferences of the members of a society to produce a single relation reflecting the preferences of society [10,11]. It thus seems reasonable to expect any proposed framework for the merging of information to be able to deal satisfactorily with the problems raised in social choice theory. In this paper we investigate the link between the merging of epistemic states and two important impossibility results in social theory: the Arrow impossibility theorem and the Gibbard-Satterthwaite impossibility theorem. Arrow showed that there is no aggregation operation satisfying certain reasonable postulates [2]. We show that the Arrow result can be circumvented when preferences are represented in terms of epistemic states. Informally, epistemic states assign ranks to the valuations, or possible worlds, of the logic under consideration. We provide a list of properties to be satisfied by all rational merging operations and prove that the Arrow postulates, suitably modified to apply to this framework, can be derived from these properties. We show that these properties are consistent, thereby providing a circumvention of Arrow's result. Gibbard [8] and Satterthwaite [17,18] independently proved that, under certain conditions, every reasonable method to aggregate the preferences of members of a society is vulnerable to manipulation by the members of that society. One of the Gibbard-Satterthwaite conditions, single-valuedness, is quite restrictive, but similar impossibility results hold even in its absence [6,3]. We extend our framework for the merging of epistemic states by adding properties which disallow various forms of manipulation. In particular, we propose properties which force merging operations to be *strategy-proof*. The proof that the addition of these properties results in a consistent extension of the basic framework for merging can be seen as a circumvention of the Gibbard-Satterthwaite theorem and related results [6,3].

We assume a finitely generated propositional language L closed under the usual propositional connectives and with a classical model-theoretic semantics. V is the set of valuations of L and $M(\alpha)$ is the set of models of $\alpha \in L$. Classical entailment is denoted by $\models$. For $i \in \mathbb{N}$, we let $\mathcal{I}(i) = \{0, \ldots, i\}$ and $\mathcal{I}^+(i) = \{1, \ldots, i\}$.

2 Epistemic States

In *epistemic states* the preferences of sources are represented as plausibility rankings of natural numbers on the valuations of L; the lower the number assigned to a valuation, the more plausible it is deemed to be. This is along the lines of work initially proposed by Spohn [20]. It was used in [13,14] to define merging. Epistemic states are very similar to possibility distributions [7] and the κ-framework of Williams [21] and it is relatively easy to translate between these frameworks. It is possible to use epistemic states in various ways. In the context of merging our aim is to employ epistemic states *semi-qualitatively*. The intention is for the ranks assigned to valuations to serve merely as markers in order to define a notion of *relative distance* between valuations, and nothing more. This eliminates the typical problem with quantitative approaches in which it is usually difficult to justify a particular assignment of numbers. The advantage of the semi-qualitative approach is that it allows us to express the *strength* with which preferences are held; something that cannot be achieved with orderings on valuations. For example, in an epistemic state it is possible to express the information that I prefer u to v *more* than I prefer v to w.

Definition 1. *An* epistemic state Φ *is a (total) function from* V *to* $\mathbb{N}$.

It is possible to extract a consistent classical knowledge base from an epistemic state Φ by considering only those valuations with the best level of plausibility assigned to them. Let $M^i(\Phi) = \{v \in V \mid \Phi(v) = i\}$ and let $\min(\Phi) = \min\{\Phi(v) \mid v \in V\}$.

Definition 2. $\phi \in L$ *is a* knowledge base extracted from Φ *iff* $M(\phi) = M^{\min(\Phi)}(\Phi)$.

Observe that the knowledge bases extracted from Φ are all logically equivalent. We shall abuse notation by referring to $B(\Phi)$ as *the* knowledge base extracted from Φ. The intention is that $B(\Phi)$ is some canonical representative of *all* the knowledge bases extracted from Φ. By extracting knowledge from an epistemic state in this way we ensure that $B(\Phi)$ will always be satisfiable. This is in line with the stated intention of employing epistemic states semi-qualitatively; the choice of having 0 as the best plausibility rank which can be assigned to a valuation is purely for the sake of convenience.

Formally, we shall view merging as an operation in which the preferences of a *sequence* of sources, in the form of epistemic states, are combined to provide a new epistemic state representing the merged preferences of the sources. It is not sufficient to use finite *sets* of epistemic states, since different sources may have identical preferences, and the presence of more than one instance of an epistemic state may have a significant impact on the way in which merging takes places.

Definition 3. *An* epistemic list E *is a finite non-empty list, or sequence, of epistemic states. We let* $|E|$ *denote the size of* E.

In order for merging to be carried out at all it is crucial to make an assumption of *commensurability*; that all sources employ the same scale when they rank valuations. In practice this can be achieved by obtaining a worst level of plausibility P commonly agreed upon by all sources. Such a commitment does not mean that any of the sources *has* to rank at least one valuation at P; it simply means that this is the worst level of plausibility that a source would ever consider attributing to any valuation. We insist that P be a finite natural number. An agreement to use a particular worst level of plausibility means that all sources agree on a fixed level of *granularity*.

Definition 4. *An epistemic state* Φ *is* P-capped, *where* $P \in \mathbb{N}$, *iff* $\Phi(v) \leq P$ *for every* $v \in V$. *An epistemic list* E *is* P-capped *iff every epistemic state in* E *is* P*-capped. The set of all* P*-capped epistemic lists is denoted by* $\mathcal{E}^P$. *The set of* all *epistemic states is denoted by* $\mathcal{E}^\infty$.

This brings us to the formal definition of merging.

Definition 5. *A* P*-capped merging operation* Δ *is a function from* $\mathcal{E}^P$ *to* $\mathcal{E}^\infty$.

Observe that P-capped merging does not necessarily yield P-capped epistemic states. In general it seems reasonable to expect that, at least in some cases, attempts to merge the information contained in an epistemic list may increase the granularity level of information contained in the resulting epistemic state.

Definition 6. *For* $n \geq 1$ *a* P*-capped merging operation* Δ *is* Q-bound *for* n *iff for every* P*-capped epistemic list* E *s.t.* $|E| = n$, $\Delta(E)$ *is* Q*-capped and for some* P*-capped epistemic list* F *s.t.* $|F| = n$ *and some* $v \in V$, $\Delta(F)(v) = Q$. Δ *is* Q-bound *iff* *it is Q-bound for n for every $n \geq 1$. A P-capped merging operation which is Q-bound for n is referred to as (P, Q, n)-capped. Similarly, a P-capped merging operation which is Q-bound is referred to as (P, Q)-capped.*

For $n \geq 1$, P-capped merging operations are (P, Q, n)-capped for some Q, but, as will be seen in section 3.1, need not be (P, Q)-capped for some Q.

3 Basic Merging

We are now in a position to provide some basic properties with which all P-capped merging operations ought to comply. Our claim is not that these properties *define* merging. Indeed, in section 5 we shall consider more desirable properties for merging which cannot be derived from (Δ1)-(Δ6).

For the remainder of the paper we follow the convention that an epistemic list E has the form $[\Phi_1, \ldots, \Phi_{|E|}]$ and that an epistemic list F has the form $[\Psi_1, \ldots, \Psi_{|F|}]$.

(Δ1) $\forall E, F \in \mathcal{E}^P$ s.t. $|E| = |F|$, if $\Phi_i(v) = \Psi_i(v)\ \forall i \in \mathcal{I}^+(|E|)$, then $\Delta(E)(v) = \Delta(F)(v)$
(Δ2) $\forall n \geq 1$, if Δ is Q-bound for n, then $\forall q \in \mathcal{I}(Q)$ there is an $E \in \mathcal{E}^P$ and a $v \in V$ s.t. $\Delta(E)(v) = q$
(Δ3) If there is a bijection $\pi : \mathcal{I}^+(E) \to \mathcal{I}^+(F)$ such that $\Phi_i = \Psi_{\pi(i)}\ \forall i \in \mathcal{I}^+(|E|)$, then $\Delta(E) = \Delta(F)$
(Δ4) If $\Phi_i(v) \leq \Phi_i(w)\ \forall i \in \mathcal{I}^+(|E|)$, then $\Delta(E)(v) \leq \Delta(E)(w)$
(Δ5) If $\Delta(E)(v) \leq \Delta(E)(w)$, then $\Phi_i(v) \leq \Phi_i(w)$ for some $i \in \mathcal{I}^+(|E|)$
(Δ6) If $\Phi_i(v) = \Phi_j(v)\ \forall i, j \in \mathcal{I}^+(|E|)$, $\Phi_i(v) \leq \Phi_i(w)\ \forall i \in \mathcal{I}^+(|E|)$, and $\Phi_j(v) < \Phi_j(w)$ for some $j \in \mathcal{I}^+(|E|)$, then $\Delta(E)(v) < \Delta(E)(w)$

These properties need some explanation and motivation. (Δ1) states that the rank that Δ assigns to a valuation v is independent of the ranks assigned to any of the other valuations. This is similar in spirit to the property in social choice theory known as the *Independence of Irrelevant Alternatives* [2] and is intended to capture a similar intuition. This issue will be discussed in more detail in section 4. The adoption of (Δ1) enables us to define merging as an operation on sequences of natural numbers. Let $seq^P = \{s \mid s = s_1, \ldots, s_n$ where $n \geq 1$ and $s_i \in \mathcal{I}(P)\ \forall i \in \mathcal{I}^+(n)\}$. For $s \in seq^P$ we denote the size of s by $|s|$.

Proposition 1. *Let Δ be a P-capped merging operation satisfying (Δ1). Then there is a $\delta : seq^P \to \mathbb{N}$ such that, $\forall v \in V$, $\forall E \in \mathcal{E}^P$, $\forall s \in seq^P$, if $|s| = |E|$ and $s_i = \Phi_i(v)\ \forall i \in \mathcal{I}^+(E)$, then $\delta(s) = \Delta(E)(v)$.*

Merging operations on sequences thus have an indirect connection with the merging of epistemic states and it is only with the adoption of a property such as (Δ1) that this connection can be made explicit. (Δ2) is a convexity assumption. It ensures that, for a merging operation bound by Q for n, no rank from 0 to Q remains unused for epistemic lists of size n. (Δ3) ensures that the order in which epistemic states occur in an epistemic list does not affect the outcome of merging. In [13,14] this property was referred to as *commutativity* and in social choice theory it is known as *anonymity* [9].

($\Delta 3$) rules out any notion of *prioritised merging* in which some sources are seen to be more important, or trustworthy, than others. This does not mean that we deem prioritised merging to be undesirable, but rather that prioritised merging depends on the existence of rational merging operations in which all sources are equally reliable. Indeed, in [15] it is shown that there is a unique method of lifting non-prioritised merging operations into a prioritised setting. The adoption of ($\Delta 3$) means that it would be possible to define merging operations which receive inputs in the form of *multisets* or *bags*, instead of *lists*, of epistemic states. It is our position, however, that such assumptions should rather be made explicit, in the form of properties, instead of being encoded indirectly in the representational formalism. The intuitions associated with ($\Delta 4$), ($\Delta 5$) and ($\Delta 6$) have been discussed in [13,14].

The following useful properties follow easily from the above properties.

Proposition 2. *Let Δ be a P-capped merging operation.*

1. *If Δ satisfies ($\Delta 5$) or ($\Delta 6$) and Δ is Q-bound for n then $Q \geq P$*
2. *If Δ satisfies either ($\Delta 6$) or ($\Delta 4$) and ($\Delta 5$) then $\Delta(E)(v) \geq \min\{\Phi_i(v) \mid i \in \mathcal{I}^+(|E|)\}$.*
3. *If Δ satisfies ($\Delta 6$) and $\exists i, j, \in \mathcal{I}^+(|E|)$ s.t. $\Phi_i(v) \neq \Phi_j(v)$, then $\Delta(E)(v) > \min\{\Phi_i(v) \mid i \in \mathcal{I}^+(|E|)\}$.*

Part (1) of proposition 2 shows that the granularity level of information grows monotonically with merging. Parts (2) and (3) of proposition 2 provide lower bounds on the ranks assigned to valuations after merging. These results are all consistent with the intuition that more information leads to an increase in the level of granularity.

3.1 Constructing Merging Operations

In this section we briefly consider some methods for constructing merging operations on epistemic states. This is not an exhaustive survey of merging operations found in the literature. The intention is merely to show that there are constructions which satisfy ($\Delta 1$)-($\Delta 6$). We consider the following merging operations:

1. $\Delta_{\max}(E)(v) = \max\{\Phi_i(v) \mid i \in \mathcal{I}^+(|E|)\}$
2. $\Delta_{\text{min1}}(E)(v) = \begin{cases} \Phi_1(v) \text{ if } \Phi_i(v) = \Phi_j(v)\ \forall i, j \in \mathcal{I}^+(|E|), \\ \min\{\Phi_i(v) \mid i \in \mathcal{I}^+(|E|)\} + 1 \text{ otherwise} \end{cases}$
3. $\Delta_{\text{min2}}(E)(v) = \begin{cases} 2\Phi_1(E)(v) \text{ if } \Phi_i(v) = \Phi_j(v)\ \forall i, j \in \mathcal{I}^+(|E|), \\ 2\min\{\Phi_i(v) \mid i \in \mathcal{I}^+(|E|)\} + 1 \text{ otherwise} \end{cases}$
4. $\Delta_{\Sigma}(E)(v) = \sum_{i \in \mathcal{I}^+(|E|)} \Phi_i(E)(v)$

These operations have been proposed and discussed in [10,5,4,13,14,16], amongst others. Observe that $\Delta_{\max}$ and Δ_{min1} are (P, P)-capped, Δ_{min2} is $(P, 2P)$-capped, but that Δ_{Σ} is not (P, Q)-capped for any Q. We do know, however, that Δ_{Σ} is (P, nP, n)-capped for every $n \geq 1$.

Proposition 3. *$\Delta_{\max}$, Δ_{min1}, Δ_{min2} and Δ_{Σ} all satisfy ($\Delta 1$)-($\Delta 6$).*

4 Social Choice and Merging

Social choice theory [2,19] is a research area where the problems under scrutiny are similar to the problems encountered in merging. Social choice theory is concerned with the aggregation of preferences. An individual's preferences is usually represented as a total preorder $\preceq$ over a (finite) set of alternatives Ω. For $x, y \in \Omega$, $x \preceq y$ means that x is at least as preferred as y. The interest then lies in the description of an aggregation operation over the preferences of n individuals, $\preceq_1, \ldots, \preceq_n$ which produces a new preference ordering over Ω. The similarities between this setup and our framework for the merging of epistemic sets should be obvious. It is a matter of taking Ω to be V, the set of permissible valuations, and using the total preorder on V *induced* by an epistemic state. Observe that such an induced total preorder contains less information than the epistemic state from which it was induced.

One of the most important results in social choice theory is Arrow's impossibility theorem [2] which shows that there is no aggregation operation satisfying some intuitively desirable postulates. In this section we show that Arrow's result can be circumvented when recast into the framework of epistemic states.

Arrow's first postulate, dubbed *Restricted Range*, requires the result of an aggregation operation to be a total preorder on Ω. In our setup this translates to the requirement that a merging operation produce an epistemic state – something which is built into the definition of merging. The second Arrow postulate, known as *Unrestricted Domain*, states that one ought to be able to apply the aggregation operation to any n-tuple of total preorders on Ω. In our setup this translates to the requirement that merging may be applied to any (P-capped) epistemic set – again, something that is built into the definition of merging. The third Arrow postulate, known as the *weak Pareto Principle*, can be phrased as follows for epistemic sets:

(PP) If $\Phi_i(v) < \Phi_i(w)\ \forall i \in \mathcal{I}^+(|E|)$, then $\Delta(E)(v) < \Delta(E)(w)$

It is easily verified that (PP) is the contrapositive of ($\Delta 5$).

The fourth Arrow postulate, known as the *Independence of Irrelevant Alternatives*, translates to the following postulate:

(IIA) $\forall E, F \in \mathcal{E}^P$ s.t. $|E| = |F|$, $\Phi_i(v) \leq \Phi_i(w)$ iff $\Psi_i(v) \leq \Psi_i(v)\ \forall i, j \in \mathcal{I}^+(|E|)$ implies that $\Delta(E)(v) \leq \Delta(E)(w)$ iff $\Delta(F)(v) \leq \Delta(F)(w)$

When deciding on the relative ordering of valuations u and v, (IIA) requires of us to disregard all other valuations. At least, that is the intuition. It is easily seen that the intuition does not hold in our more structured setup in which it is possible to define degrees of relative plausibility between valuations.

Example 1. Let $E = [\Phi_1,\Phi_2]$, $F = [\Psi_1,\Psi_2]$ such that $\Phi_1(v) = \Psi_2(w) = 0$, $\Phi_1(w) = \Phi_2(w) = \Psi_1(v) = \Psi_2(v) = 1$, and $\Phi_2(v) = \Psi_1(w) = 2$. It is easily verified that $\Phi_1(v) \leq \Phi_1(w)$ iff $\Psi_1(v) < \Psi_1(w)$ and that $\Phi_2(v) \leq \Phi_2(w)$ iff $\Psi_2(v) \leq \Psi_2(w)$. Now consider the merging $\Delta_{\max}$ defined in section 3.1. It can be verified that $\Delta_{\max}(E)(w) = \Delta_{\max}(F)(v) = 1$, and $\Delta_{\max}(E)(v) = \Delta_{\max}(E)(w) = 2$. So it is not the case that $\Delta_{\max}(E)(v) \leq \Delta_{\max}(E)(w)$ iff $\Delta_{\max}(F)(v) \leq \Delta_{\max}(F)(w)$. $\Delta_{\max}$ therefore does not satisfy (IIA). Observe, however, that the ranks of v and w are obtained without reference to any of the other valuations. In fact, it is easy to see that the rank of any valuations obtained by applying $\Delta_{\max}$ is independent of all other alternatives, even though $\Delta_{\max}$ does not satisfy (IIA).

In the usual social choice theory framework, where only total preorders are used, it is necessary to define independence indirectly, in terms of the ordering between two valuations. In our more structured setup this independence can be described directly, in terms of the rank assigned to a valuation. Our contention, then, is that (Δ1) is an appropriate reformulation of (IIA).

The last of the Arrow postulates, known as *Non-Dictatorship*, states that one source should never be able to completely dominate. We can phrase this as follows.

(ND) There is no $i \in \mathcal{I}^+(|E|)$ such that, for every $E \in \mathcal{E}^P$, $\Phi_i(v) < \Phi_i(w)$ implies $\Delta(E)(v) < \Delta(E)(w)$ for every $v, w \in V$

It is easy to see that (ND) follows from (Δ3).

Proposition 4. *If a merging operation satisfies (Δ3) then it will also satisfy (ND).*

From the results above it follows that the modified Arrow postulates all follow from (Δ1)-(Δ6). And since proposition 3 shows that there are merging operations which satisfy (Δ1)-(Δ6), we have shown that the Arrow impossibility result can be circumvented. It is the move from the total preorders on V to epistemic states, which have more structure than mere total preorders, which makes this circumvention possible.

5 Strategy-Proof Merging

Strategy-proofness is an idea that has received a great deal of attention in social choice theory, where it is frequently discussed in the context of elections. The aim is to define an election procedure in which a winner is chosen in such a way that the outcome is immune to manipulation by voters, or groups of voters. The first impossibility result related to strategy-proofness is due to Gibbard [8] and Satterthwaite [17,18]. Given some basic conditions on the number of available alternatives and the size of the electorate, and the (strong) requirement that an election procedure should produce a unique winner, their result shows that every election procedure which is non-dictatorial cannot be strategy-proof. This result is, perhaps, not particularly surprising. Consider, for example, the case in which two voters, Jack and Jill, have to choose between two candidates, Al and George. If Jack strictly prefers Al to George and Jill strictly prefers George to Al then there simply is not enough information to declare either Al or George the unambiguous winner. However, even if the requirement of producing a unique winner is relaxed it seems that Gibbard-Satterthwaite type results still hold [6,3].

Our aim in this section is to investigate notions of strategy-proofness in the context of merging. Requiring merging operations to be strategy-proof seems as necessary, and as desirable, as is the case for election procedures, or indeed, for aggregation operations in general. Before formalising the notion of strategy-proofness we first consider two properties that allude to it. For $E, F \in \mathcal{E}^P$ s.t. $|E| = |F|$, and for $\mathcal{I} \subseteq \mathcal{I}^+(|E|)$, we denote by $rep(E, \mathcal{I}, F)$ the epistemic list obtained by replacing Φ_i with Ψ_i for every

$i \in \mathcal{I}$. Intuitively $rep(E, \mathcal{I}, F)$ produces a modified version of E in which the sources mentioned in $\mathcal{I}$ have changed their preferences. For example, if $E = [\Phi_1, \Phi_2, \Phi_3]$ and $F = [\Psi_1, \Psi_2, \Psi_3]$, then $rep(E, \{2,3\}, F) = [\Phi_1, \Psi_2, \Psi_3]$.[1]

(Mon↑) if $\Phi_i(v) \leq \Psi_i(v)$ then $\Delta(E)(v) \leq \Delta(rep(E, \{i\}, F))(v)$
(Mon↓) if $\Phi_i(v) \geq \Psi_i(v)$ then $\Delta(E)(v) \geq \Delta(rep(E, \{i\}, F))(v)$

(Mon↑) and (Mon↓) ensure that Δ exhibits monotonic behaviour. That is, (Mon↑) states that if a source worsens the rank it assigns to a valuation v, Δ will respond with a rank for v that is no better than the original. Similarly, (Mon↓) states that if a source improves the rank it assigns to a valuation v, Δ will respond with a rank for v that is no worse than the original.

Proposition 5. *If Δ satisfies (Δ4) then it also satisfies (Mon↑) and (Mon↓).*

These two properties do not guarantee strategy-proof behaviour, however, as will be shown in theorem 1. For a merging operation to be regarded as strategy-proof it must be the case that there is no incentive for any source to misrepresent its preferences. To be more precise, whenever a source provides an accurate representation of its preferences there should be a guarantee that the result of merging will be *no less compatible* with its true preferences than if it had misrepresented its preferences. Of course, the formalisation of such properties presupposes the existence of an appropriate *compatibility measure* between epistemic states. In the special case of two P-capped epistemic states there is an obvious way to measure compatibility.

Definition 7. *For $v \in V$, the* compatibility measure *between two P-capped epistemic states Φ and Ψ with respect to v is $\#^v(\Phi, \Psi) = |\Phi(v) - \Psi(v)|$.*

$\#^v(\Phi, \Psi)$ is a *local* compatibility measure in the sense that it measures compatibility between *valuations* contained in epistemic states. Below we provide two *global* measures in which compatibility is determined between *epistemic states*.

Definition 8. *1. The* compatibility measure *between two P-capped epistemic states Φ and Ψ is $\#(\Phi, \Psi) = \sum_{v \in V} \#^v(\Phi, \Psi)$.*
2. *An epistemic state Υ is* at least as compatible *with Φ as with Ψ, denoted by $\Upsilon \sqsubseteq_\Phi \Psi$, iff $\forall v \in V$, $\#^v(\Upsilon, \Phi) \leq \#^v(\Psi, \Phi)$. Υ is* more compatible *with Φ than with Ψ, denoted by $\Upsilon \sqsubset_\Phi \Psi$, iff $\Upsilon \sqsubseteq_\Phi \Psi$ and $\Psi \not\sqsubseteq_\Phi \Upsilon$.*

It is easy to see that $\sqsubseteq_\Phi$ provides a stronger form of compatibility than $\#(\Phi, \Psi)$.

Proposition 6. *If $\Upsilon \sqsubseteq_\Phi \Psi$ then $\#(\Upsilon, \Phi) \leq \#(\Psi, \Phi)$, but the converse does not hold.*

Definitions 7 and 8 make sense only when comparing P-capped epistemic states. Defining compatibility between P-capped and Q-capped epistemic states, where $Q \neq P$, is more problematic. We shall briefly address this issue in section 6. For the rest of this section, however, we focus on (P, P)-capped merging operations, thereby ensuring that we only need to compare P-capped epistemic states. This enables us to formalise strategy-proofness as follows.

[1] In the properties (Mon↑) and (Mon↓), the set $\mathcal{I}$ in $rep(E, \mathcal{I}, F)$ is the singleton set $\{i\}$, from which it might seem that the notation $rep(E, \mathcal{I}, F)$ is unnecessarily clumsy. However, in some of the properties later in the section we shall use this notation with $\mathcal{I}$ being any subset of $\mathcal{I}^+(|E|)$.

(IP) $\Delta(E) \sqsubseteq_{\Phi_i} \Delta(rep(E, \{i\}, F))\ \forall F \in \mathcal{E}^P$ s.t. $|E| = |F|$
(WIP) $\#(\Delta(E), \Phi_i) \leq \#(\Delta(rep(E, \{i\}, F)), \Phi_i)\ \forall F \in \mathcal{E}^P$ s.t. $|E| = |F|$

Both (IP) and (WIP) require of $\Delta(E)$ to be at least as compatible with the preferences of source i than $\Delta(F)$, where E is the epistemic state in which i's preferences are represented accurately and F is obtained from E by i misrepresenting its preferences in some way. Given these properties a rational source will realise that is in its own interests to represent its preferences accurately. Observe that (IP) implies (WIP).

Proposition 7. *A merging operation satisfying (IP) will also satisfy (WIP).*

(IP) and (WIP) define strategy-proofness only relative to single sources and do not exclude the possibility of groups of sources misrepresenting their preferences in such a way that *all* members of the group benefit from it. Groups of sources that are able to achieve this will be referred to as *strategy-coalitions*. The formal definition of a strategy-coalition depends on the compatibility measure that is used.

Definition 9. *Let $E \in \mathcal{E}^P$ and consider any group of sources $\mathcal{I} \subseteq \mathcal{I}^+(|E|)$.*

1. *$\mathcal{I}$ is a* strategy-coalition *in E iff $\exists F \in \mathcal{E}^P$ s.t. $|E| = |F|$, $\Delta(rep(E, \mathcal{I}, F)) \sqsubseteq_{\Phi_i} \Delta(E)\ \forall i \in \mathcal{I}$, and $\Delta(rep(E, \mathcal{I}, F)) \sqsubset_{\Phi_j} \Delta(E)$ for some $j \in \mathcal{I}$.*
2. *$\mathcal{I}$ is a* weak strategy-coalition *in E iff for some $F \in \mathcal{E}^P$ s.t. $|E| = |F|$, $\#(\Delta(rep(E, \mathcal{I}, F)), \Phi_i) \leq \#(\Delta(E), \Phi_i)\ \forall i \in \mathcal{I}$, and $\#(\Delta(rep(E, \mathcal{I}, F)), \Phi_i) < \#(\Delta(E), \Phi_i)$ for some $j \in \mathcal{I}$.*

The following *strategy-coalition proof* properties are intended to exclude the possibility of forming strategy-coalitions.

(SP) $\forall E \in \mathcal{E}^P$ there is no strategy-coalition in E
(WSP) $\forall E \in \mathcal{E}^P$ there is no weak strategy-coalition in E

The following proposition shows that there are connections between strategy-proofness and the various ways of forming strategy-coalitions.

Proposition 8. *Strategy-coalitions are also weak strategy-coalitions. Therefore (WSP) implies (SP). Furthermore (WSP) implies (WIP), but (SP) does not imply (IP).*

The reason for (SP) not implying (IP) is that $\sqsubseteq_\Phi$ is not a total preorder, unlike the weaker measure based on $\#(\Phi, \Psi)$.

In addition to misrepresenting preferences, it is conceivable that sources may stand to benefit by completely abstaining from providing information. For $E \in \mathcal{E}^P$ and for some $\mathcal{I} \subseteq \mathcal{I}^+(|E|)$ we denote by $rem(E, \mathcal{I})$ the epistemic list obtained by removing Φ_i from E for every $i \in \mathcal{I}^+(|E|)$. Intuitively, $rem(E, \mathcal{I})$ produces a modified version of E in which the sources mentioned in $\mathcal{I}$ abstain from providing information. For example, if $E = [\Phi_1, \Phi_2, \Phi_3]$ then $rem(E, \{1, 3\}) = [\Phi_2]$. We define a group of sources to be an *abstention-coalition* if, whenever all members of the group abstain, they *all* stand to benefit from doing so.

Definition 10. *Let $E \in \mathcal{E}^P$ and consider any group of sources $\mathcal{I} \subset \mathcal{I}^+(|E|)$.*

1. $\mathcal{I}$ *is an* abstention-coalition *in* E *iff* $\Delta(rem(E,\mathcal{I})) \sqsubseteq_{\Phi_i} \Delta(E)$ $\forall i \in \mathcal{I}$, *and* $\Delta(rem(E,\mathcal{I})) \sqsubset_{\Phi_j} \Delta(E)$ *for some* $j \in \mathcal{I}$.
2. $\mathcal{I}$ *is a* weak abstention-coalition *in* E *iff* $\#(\Delta(rem(E,\mathcal{I})),\Phi_i) \leq \#(\Delta(E),\Phi_i)$ $\forall i \in \mathcal{I}$, *and* $\#(\Delta(rem(E,\mathcal{I})),\Phi_i) < \#(\Delta(E),\Phi_i)$ *for some* $j \in \mathcal{I}$.

The next properties are intended to prevent sources from benefitting by abstaining.

(AP) $\forall E \in \mathcal{E}^P$ there is no abstention-coalition in E
(WAP) $\forall E \in \mathcal{E}^P$ there is no weak abstention-coalition in E

The notion of an abstention-coalition is stronger notion than that of a weak abstention-coalition.

Proposition 9. *Any abstention-coalition is also weak abstention-coalition and therefore (WAP) implies (AP).*

At present it is not clear whether an insistence on the absence of both strategy-coalitions and abstention-coalitions necessarily implies the absence of a combination of these notions. Thus, it seems necessary to provide properties forbidding the combination as well. Consider groups of sources $\mathcal{I},\mathcal{J} \subseteq \mathcal{I}^+(|E|)$ and $\mathcal{K} \subset \mathcal{I}^+(|E|)$ such that $\mathcal{I} = \mathcal{J} \cup \mathcal{K}$ and $\mathcal{J} \cap \mathcal{K} = \emptyset$. For $F \in \mathcal{E}^P$ s.t. $|E| = |F|$ we let $rr(E,\mathcal{J},F,\mathcal{K}) = rem(rep(E,\mathcal{J},F),\mathcal{K})$. That is, $rr(E,\mathcal{J},F,\mathcal{K})$ is the result obtained by first replacing Φ_j in E with Ψ_j for every $j \in \mathcal{J}$ and then removing Φ_k from the modified E for every $k \in \mathcal{K}$. For example, for $E = [\Phi_1,\Phi_2,\Phi_3,\Phi_4]$ and $F = [\Psi_1,\Psi_2,\Psi_3,\Psi_4]$, $rr(E,\{2\},F,\{1,4\}) = [\Psi_2,\Phi_3]$.

Definition 11. *Let* $E \in \mathcal{E}^P$ *and consider groups of sources* $\mathcal{I},\mathcal{J} \subseteq \mathcal{I}^+(|E|)$ *and* $\mathcal{K} \subset \mathcal{I}^+(|E|)$ *such that* $\mathcal{I} = \mathcal{J} \cup \mathcal{K}$ *and* $\mathcal{J} \cap \mathcal{K} = \emptyset$.

1. $\mathcal{I}$ *forms a* coalition *in* E *iff* $\exists F \in \mathcal{E}^P$ *s.t.* $|E| = |F|$, $\Delta(rr(E,\mathcal{J},F,\mathcal{K})) \sqsubseteq_{\Phi_i} \Delta(E)$ $\forall i \in \mathcal{I}$, *and* $\Delta(rr(E,\mathcal{J},F,\mathcal{K})) \sqsubset_{\Phi_j} \Delta(E)$ *for some* $j \in \mathcal{I}$.
2. $\mathcal{I}$ *forms a* weak coalition *in* E *iff for some* $F \in \mathcal{E}^P$ *such that* $|E| = |F|$, $\#(\Delta(rr(E,\mathcal{J},F,\mathcal{K}))\Phi_i) \leq \#(\Delta(E),\Phi_i)$ $\forall i \in \mathcal{I}$, *and* $\#(\Delta(rr(E,\mathcal{J},F,\mathcal{K})),\Phi_i) < \#(\Delta(E),\Phi_i)$ *for some* $j \in \mathcal{I}$.

So, a coalition, and a weak coalition, is a group of sources for which it is possible to either misrepresent their preferences or abstain from providing information in such a way that *all* members of the group stand to benefit. The next two properties forbid the existence of coalitions and weak coalitions respectively.

(CP) $\forall E \in \mathcal{E}^P$ there is no coalition in E
(WCP) $\forall E \in \mathcal{E}^P$ there is no weak coalition in E

There are close links between being strategy-proof and the various notions related to coalitions.

Proposition 10. *Any coalition is also a weak coalition and therefore (WCP) implies (CP). Also, (CP) implies (SP) and (AP) and (WCP) implies (WSP) and (WAP).*

Recall from section 3.1 that $\Delta_{\max}$ and $\Delta_{\min 1}$ are (P,P)-capped merging operations. It turns out that one of these satisfies all the properties related to strategy-proofness discussed here, and the other one doesn't.

Proposition 11. *Δ_{max} satisfies (WCP) and (IP). Δ_{min1} satisfies (AP) and (WAP), but it satisfies neither (WIP) nor (CP).*

The following result summarises the main contributions of this paper.

Theorem 1. *Δ_{max} satisfies (Δ1)-(Δ6), (WIP), (IP), (WSP), (SP), (WAP), (AP), (WCP) and (CP). Δ_{min1} satisfies (Δ1)-(Δ6), (AP) and (WAP), but does not satisfy (WIP), (IP), (WSP), (SP), (WCP) or (CP).*

Theorem 1 can be seen as a circumvention of Gibbard-Satterthwaite style impossibility results. It shows that, in the context of epistemic states, it is possible to define rational merging operations which are immune to manipulation by single sources and, indeed, by groups of sources. In addition, the fact that Δ_{min1} does not satisfy the properties related to strategies and coalitions shows that these properties cannot be derived from the basic properties for merging and that their addition constitutes a strict extension of (Δ1)-(Δ6). Our conjecture is that the same holds for the abstention-related properties, although we have not formally shown this to be the case.

6 Conclusion

In this paper we have drawn connections between information merging and social choice theory and shown that Arrow's impossibility result and versions of the Gibbard-Satterthwaite theorem disappear when recast in terms of epistemic states. The results described here need to be elaborated upon, though. In section 5 the focus was on the special case of (P, P)-capped merging operations since measures of compatibility between P-capped epistemic states are then easily obtained. In the general case, however, where we are dealing with a (P, Q)-capped merging operation, we are faced with the problem of comparing epistemic states with different levels of granularity. For example, Δ_{min2} defined in section 3.1 is a $(P, 2P)$-capped merging operation, making it necessary to define an appropriate way of comparing P-capped epistemic states with $2P$-capped ones. Currently it is unclear how to do so. One possible way to deal with this issue is to provide an appropriate method for mapping epistemic states with a high granularity level into epistemic states with the appropriate lower level of granularity. Such a mapping can be seen as a way to "convert" a Q-capped epistemic state to a P-capped one, thus making it possible to compare the two epistemic states. For example, for Δ_{min2} we need a suitable method for mapping the elements of $\mathcal{I}(2P)$ to $\mathcal{I}(P)$. In this case the appropriate mapping seems to be the function $\rho : \mathcal{I}(2P) \rightarrow \mathcal{I}(P)$ such that $\rho(i) = \lceil i/2 \rceil$ (where $\lceil i/2 \rceil$ denotes the smallest integer which is no smaller than $i/2$). However, it is not clear how to determine which mappings are appropriate in the general case. At present the best we can do is to insist that a mapping ρ which converts a Q-capped epistemic state to a P-capped one should be a surjective function from $\mathcal{I}(Q)$ to $\mathcal{I}(P)$ such that $\rho(i) \leq \rho(j)$ whenever $i \leq j$.

References

1. H. Andreka, M. D. Ryan, and P.-Y. Schobbens. Operators and laws for combining preference relations. *Journal of Logic and Computation (in print)*, 2001.

2. K. J. Arrow. *Social choice and individual values (2nd edition)*. Wiley, New York, 1963.
3. S. Barberá, B. Dutta, and A. Sen. Strategyproof Social Choice Correspondences. *Journal of Economic Theory (forthcoming)*, 2000.
4. S. Benferhat, D. Dubois, S. Kaci, and H. Prade. Encoding information in possibilistic logic: A general framework for rational syntactic merging. In Werner Horn, editor, *ECAI 2000. 14th European Conference on Artificial Intelligence*, Amsterdam, 2000. IOS Press.
5. S. Benferhat, D. Dubois, H. Prade, and M-A. Williams. A Practical Approach to Fusing Prioritized Knowledge Bases. In *Progress in Artificial Intelligence*, volume 1695 of *Lecture Notes In Artificial Intelligence*, pages 222–236, Berlin, 1999. Springer-Verlag.
6. Jean-Pierre Benoit. Strategyproofness for Lotteries and When Ties are Permitted. Unpublished manuscript, Department of Economics, New York University, January 2000.
7. Didier Dubois, Jerome Lang, and Henri Prade. Possibilistic logic. In *Handbook of Logic in Artificial Intelligence and Logic Programming*, volume 3, pages 439–513. 1994.
8. Allan Gibbard. Manipulation of Voting Schemes: A General Result. *Econometrica*, 41(4):587–601, 1973.
9. J. S. Kelly. *Arrow impossibility theorems*. Series in economic theory and mathematical economics. Academic Press, New York, 1978.
10. Sébastien Konieczny and Ramón Pino-Pérez. On the logic of merging. In A. G. Cohn, L. Schubert, and S. C. Shapiro, editors, *Principles of Knowledge Representation and Reasoning: Proceedings of the Sixth International Conference (KR '98)*, pages 488–498, San Francisco, California, 1998. Morgan Kaufmann.
11. Sébastien Konieczny and Ramón Pino-Pérez. Merging with Integrity Constraints. Unpublished manuscript, 1999.
12. C. Lafage and J. Lang. Logical representation of preferences for group decision making. In *Proceedings of the 7th International Conference on Principles of Knowledge Representation and Reasoning (KR 2000)*, San Mateo, CA, 2000. Morgan Kaufmann.
13. Thomas Meyer. Merging Epistemic States. In Riichiro Mizoguchi and John Slaney, editors, *PRICAI 2000: Topics in Artificial Intelligence*, volume 1886 of *Lecture Notes In Artificial Intelligence*, pages 286–296, Berlin, 2000. Springer-Verlag.
14. Thomas Meyer. On the semantics of combination operations. *Journal of Applied Non-Classical Logics (to appear)*, 2001.
15. Thomas Meyer, Aditya Ghose, and Samir Chopra. Context-based merging. In *Common Sense 2001: Fifth symposium on logical formalizations of commonsense reasoning*, 2001.
16. Thomas Meyer, Aditya Ghose, and Samir Chopra. Syntactic representations of semantic merging operations. In *IJCAI'01 Workshop on Inconsistency in Data and Knowledge*, 2001.
17. Mark Satterthwaite. *The Existence of a Strategy Proof Voting Procedure: a Topic in Social Choice Theory*. PhD thesis, University of Wisconson, 1973.
18. Mark Satterthwaite. Strategy-proofness and Arrow's Conditions: Existence and Correspondence Theorems for Voting Procedures and Social Welfare Functions. *Journal of Economic Theory*, 10(2):187–217, 1975.
19. Amartya Sen. Social choice theory. In K. J. Arrow and M. D. Intriligator, editors, *Handbook of Mathematical Economics*, volume III, chapter 22, pages 1073–1181. Elsevier Science Publishers, 1986.
20. Wolfgang Spohn. Ordinal conditional functions: A dynamic theory of epistemic states. In William L. Harper and Brian Skyrms, editors, *Causation in Decision: Belief, Change and Statistics: Proceedings of the Irvine Conference on Probability and Causation: Volume II*, pages 105–134, Dordrecht, 1988. Kluwer Academic Publishers.
21. Mary-Anne Williams. Iterated theory base change: a computational model. In *IJCAI-95. Proceedings of the 14th International Joint Conference on Artificial Intelligence*, volume 2, pages 1541–1547, San Francisco, CA, 1995. International Joint Conference on Artificial Intelligence, Morgan Kaufmann.

Data merging: Theory of Evidence vs knowledge-bases merging operators

Laurence Cholvy

ONERA Centre de Toulouse,
2 av Ed. Belin,31055 Toulouse, France
cholvy@cert.fr

Abstract. This paper addresses the problem of merging data provided by several sources of information. It aims at comparing two techniques of merging, one provided by Theory of Evidence and the other provided in the field of logic for merging knowledge-bases.
For doing so, it first presents a logical interpretation of Theory of Evidence, which is proved to be valid when the numbers are rational. Then, it shows the equivalence between the Maximum of Plausibility Decision Strategy of Theory of Evidence and a particular knowldege-bases merging operator, known to be a majority and also an arbitration operator.

Keywords: Data merging, Theory of Evidence, logic.

1 Introduction

Merging data is a problem which has received a lot of attention during these last years [2], [3], [4], [19], [13], [14], [16], [11], [10], [12]. This is due to the growing number of applications in which one needs to access several information sources to make a decision.

The many works which address this problem shows that there is not an unique method for merging information. Obvioulsy, the adequate merging process depends on the type of the information to be merged, which can be beliefs the sources have about the real world or preferences, i.e, descriptions of more or less ideal worlds. But the merging process also depends on the meta-information one has about the sources. For instance, in the case of merging beliefs provided by several sources, if the respective reliability of the sources is known, it obviously must be used in the merging process: the more reliable a source is, the more we trust it. But, if this meta-information is not known, some other types of merging processes must be defined. Konieczny and Pino-Perez's work, [11], [10] addresses this last case by defining two kinds of merging operators respectively called majority merging operators and arbitration merging operators. The first ones aim at implementing a kind of majority vote between the sources, and the second ones aim at reaching a consensus between the sources by trying to satisfy as much as possible all of them.

S. Benferhat and P. Besnard (Eds.): ECSQARU 2001, LNAI 2143, pp. 478–487, 2001.

Furthermore, in the case of beliefs merging, the sources may be more or less certain about the data they deliver. In that case, formalisms for reasoning about uncertainty must be used.

One of these formalisms is Theory of Evidence, which is a mathematical theory defined by Dempster [6] and Shafer [17], allowing one to reason with uncertainty and offering a rule for combining uncertain data provided by several information sources. In this theory, the uncertainty is represented by the fact that any proposition of the frame of discernment is associated with a real number, called its mass, which belongs to [0,1] and such that the mass of the contradiction is 0[1], and the sum of all the masses is 1. These numbers intend to represent *a measure of belief committed exactly to the proposition*. Given all the masses, one can define two other numbers: the degree of belief of a proposition, which is also a real number belonging to [0,1] and which represents *the degree of support a body of evidence provides for this proposition*, and the degree of plausibility of a proposition, which is also a real number belonging to [0,1] and which represents *the extend to which one fails to doubt the proposition*. Furthermore, this theory also focuses on the combination of masses through Dempster's rule of combination. This explains why Theory of Evidence is commonly applied in data fusion problems where data are uncertain. For instance, in object identification problems, (i.e, situation assessment [1], candidate assessment [7], decision from MRI images [8], data association [15]) the point is that several sources provide their own beliefs about an observed situation, and the problem is to decide which is the actual situation. For doing so, Theory of Evidence provides different decision strategies. For instance, the possible worlds may be ordered according to their degree of belief or to their degree of plausibility, and the associated decision strategy consists in selecting the maximal world according to this order. This comes to consider that the actual world is the one which has the highest degree of belief or the highest degree of plausibility.

This paper aims at establishing some relations between methods for combining data in Theory of Evidence and some methods provided in the field of logic, for merging knowledge-bases.

For doing so, it first presents Theory of Evidence in the light of classical propositional logic and establishes a relation between these two approaches to information representation. Then, it establishes some formal relations between the strategy of Maximum of plausibility and a merging operator defined by Konieczny and Pino-Perez.

This paper is organized as follows.

Section 2 presents an interpretation, in a logical setting, of the main concepts of Theory of Evidence. Section 3 and section 4 prove the formal equivalence between the Maximum of Plausibility Decision Strategy of Theory of Evidence and a particular knowledge-bases merging operator known to be a majority and an arbitration one. Finally, the last section lists some open questions.

---

[1] In some extensions of this theory, this constraint is relaxed. But we will focus on the initial version of Theory of Evidence

2 A logical interpretation of Theory of Evidence when numbers are rationals

In this section, we present an interpretation of Theory of Evidence[2] in logical terms. But before, we need to recall some definitions.

2.1 Preliminaries

Definition 1. A multi-set is a set where repeated occurrences of an element may exist. A **knowledge-set** is a multi-set of propositional formulas[3].

Example. If A and B are propositional letters, then $KS = [B, A \vee B, A, A \vee B, A \vee B]$ is a knowledge-set.

Definition 2. Let $KS_1 = [F_1, ..., F_{n_1}]$ and $KS_2 = [F_{n_1+1}, ..., F_p]$ be two knowledge-sets. Their union is: $KS_1 \sqcup KS_2 = [F_1, ..., F_{n_1}, F_{n_1+1}, ..., F_p]$.

Definition 3. Let $KS_1 = [F_1, ..., F_n]$ and $KS_2 = [G_1, ..., G_n]$ two knowledge-sets of the same size. KS_1 and KS_2 are equivalent, noted $KS_1 \leftrightarrow KS_2$ iff there exists a bijection f from KS_1 to KS_2 such that $\forall i \in \{1...n\} \models F_i \leftrightarrow f(F_i)$

2.2 Main concepts of Theory of Evidence

Theory of Evidence assumes the existence of **a frame of discernment** which is defined as a set Θ of N hypothesis : $\Theta = \{H_1, ..., H_N\}$. Hypothesis correspond to propositions one is dealing with. Their intuitive meaning depend on the context of application. For instance, in an identification problem, the hypothesis H_i will represent the fact "the object to be identified is H_i". The meaning given to hypothesis is out the Theory of Evidence. These hypothesis are supposed to be **exclusive**. This means for instance, that the object to be identified cannot be both H_i and H_j if $i \neq j$. Furthermore, in the initial version of Theory of Evidence (and we will focus on it), the hypothesis are supposed to be **exhaustive**. This means that the object to be identified is H_1 or ... H_n. This assumption is called Closed-World Assumption. Finally, in the Theory of Evidence, propositions are represented by **subsets of** Θ. The set 2^Θ is called Referential of definition.

Let $\Theta = \{H_1, ..., H_N\}$ be a frame of discernment. In the logical formulation, we will say that Θ is a propositional language whose propositional letters are $H_1 ... H_N$. Under the Closed-World Assumption and under the exhaustivity hypothesis, we will consider the axioms:

$$(CW) \;\; H_1 \vee ... \vee H_N \quad \text{and} \quad (EXCL) \;\; \neg(H_i \wedge H_j) \;\; if \;\; i \neq j$$

This implies that the possible worlds are the N worlds $w_1, ... w_N$ where w_i is the world in which only H_i is true. Thus, the problem of identification is the problem of *determining which, among these possible worlds, is the actual world.*

[2] Due to limitation space, we do not address conditioning nor discounting.

[3] One must notice that Konieczny and Pino-Perez define a knowledge-set as a multi-set of sets of formulas but, considering formulas is enough by assimilating a set of formulas as the conjunction of its formulas

We denote EV the theory whose proper axioms are (CW) and $(EXCL)$. As usual, the relation of logical consequences will be denoted by $\models$.

One can notice that in theory EV, any proposition is equivalent to a positive clause[4]. So here, the Referential of Definition is the set of positive clauses of Θ. This means that any subset of the frame of discernement is logically represented by a positive propositional clause. For instance, the subset $\{H_1, H_2, H_3\}$ of Θ is logically represented by the positive clause $H_1 \vee H_2 \vee H_3$.

The basic notions of the Theory of Evidence are the notion of basic probability assignment (or mass function), the notion of belief function, associated with an information source which, by this way, expresses its uncertainty about beliefs and the notion of plausibility function. They are mathematically defined by:

A **basic probability assignment** is a function $m : 2^\Theta \rightarrow [0,1]$ such that:

$$(i) \quad m(\emptyset) = 0 \quad \text{and} \quad (ii) \quad \sum_{A \subseteq \Theta} m(A) = 1$$

A **belief function** is a function $Bel_m : 2^\Theta \rightarrow [0,1]$ which associates any A of to $Bel_m(A)$ with:

$$Bel_m(A) = \sum_{B \subseteq A} m(B)$$

A **plausibility function** is a function $Pl_m : 2^\Theta \rightarrow [0,1]$ which associates any A to $Pl_m(A)$ with to $Pl_m(A) = 1 - Bel_m(\overline{A})$, where $\overline{A}$ is the complement of A in Θ.

Shafer gave the following informal interpretation of these numbers: *the basic probability number $m(A)$ is understood to be the measure of belief committed exactly to A (.... but) not the total belief that ones commits to A. To obtain the measure of the total belief committed to A, one must add to $m(A)$ the quantities $m(B)$ for all proper subsets B of A. Finally, the degree of plausibility represents the extend to which one fails to doubt the proposition.* So, the problem for us is to give, in logical terms, a meaning to these comments. This is done in the remainding of this section, for the case when the numbers are rational.

The logical representation of a basic assignment is given by the following definition:

Definition 4. Let m be a basic assignment defined on Θ by:
$m(P_1) = n_1/N, ..., m(P_k) = n_k/N$ with $n_1 + ... + n_k = N$.
The logical representation of m is the knowledge-set denoted $ks(m)$ defined by: $ks(m) = \{K_1, ..., K_N\}$ with: $K_1 = ... = K_{n_1} = \{P_1\}$, $K_{n_1+1} = ... = K_{n_1+n_2} = \{P_2\}$, ... $K_{N-n_k+1} = ... = K_N = \{P_k\}$

Notation. One must notice that, in this definition, the same symbol P_i is used to denote a subset of the Frame of discernment Θ and the propositional clause, of the propositional language associated with Θ, which logically represents it. However, it must be clear that m is defined on subsets while $ks(m)$ is a multi-set of propositional positive clauses.

---

[4] A positive clause is a disjunction of positive literals.

Example. Let $m(A) = 2/3, m(A, B) = 1/3$. The logical representation of m is the knowledge-set: $ks(m) = [A, A, A \vee B]$.

Proposition 1. Let m be a basic assignment. The mass of a proposition P, $m(P)$, is the proportion of formulas K_i in $ks(m)$ which are equivalent, under EV, to P. I.e, the proportion of K_i in $ks(m)$ such that: $EV \models K_i \leftrightarrow P$.

Proposition 2. Let m be a basic assignment. The degree of belief of a proposition P, $Bel_m(P)$, is the proportion of K_i in $ks(m)$ which, under EV, imply P. I.e, the proportion of K_i in $ks(m)$ such that: $EV \models K_i \rightarrow P$.

Example (continued). The three formulas of $ks(m)$ imply $A \vee B$, thus $Bel_m(A \vee B) = 1$. But only two formulas imply A so, $Bel_m(A) = 2/3$.

Proposition 3. Let m be a basic assignment. The degree of plausibility of a proposition P, $Pl_m(P)$, is the proportion of K_i in $ks(m)$ which do not, under EV, imply $\neg P$. I.e, the proportion of K_i in $ks(m)$ such that: $EV \wedge K_i \wedge P$ is consistent.

Example (continued). All the formulas in $ks(m)$ are consistent (under EV) with A, so $Pl_m(A) = 1$. Only one formula is consistent (under EV) with B, so $Pl_m(B) = 1/3$.

To sum up this section, we can say that *any basic assignment as defined by Shafer can, if the numbers are rational, be modelled by a knowledge-set as defined previously. Thus, the mass of a proposition A is the proportion of formulas in this knowledge-set which are equivalent, under EV, to A. The degree of belief of A is the proportion of formulas which imply, under EV, A. The plausibility degree of A is the proportion of formulas which are consistent, under EV, with A.*

2.3 Dempster's rule of combination

Dempster's rule of combination has been defined for combining several basic assignments. In the following, we focus on the case of two assignments only (the extension to the general case is obvious since the combination is commutative and associative) and we assume that the two assigments are defined on the same frame of discernment. Given two basic probability assignment m_1 and m_2 defined over a frame Θ, Dempster'rule of combination defines a third basic assignment denoted $m_1 \oplus m_2$ by the following equation:

$$m(A) = \frac{\sum_{A_i \cap B_j = A} m_1(A_i).m_2(B_j)}{N}$$

with

$$N = \sum_{A \neq \emptyset} \sum_{A_i \cap B_j = A} m_1(A_i).m_2(B_j)$$

Obviously, the fraction has a meaning only if $N \neq 0$. This assumption corresponds to the case when the two basic probability assignments are not totally in conflict. In the following, we give the correspondance, in terms of knowledge-sets, of this rule.

Definition 5 Let $KS_1 = \{K_1^1, ..., K_1^N\}$ and $KS_2 = \{K_2^1, ..., K_2^N\}$ be two knowledge sets of the same size. We say that they are **in total conflict** iff $\forall K_1^i \in KS_1 \ \ \forall K_2^j \in KS_2 \ \ EV \cup (K_1^i \wedge K_2^j)$ is inconsistent.

Proposition 4. $ks(m_1)$ and $ks(m_2)$ are in total conflict iff $N = 0$.

Let us now define an operator, also denoted $\oplus$, which combines two knowledge-sets which are not in total conflict.

Definition 6 Let $KS_1 = \{K_1^1, ..., K_1^N\}$ and $KS_2 = \{K_2^1, ..., K_2^N\}$ be two knowledge-sets of the same size which are not in total conflict. The operator $\oplus$ on knowledge-sets define a third knowledge-set by:

$$\begin{aligned} KS_1 \oplus KS_2 = [K : \ & \exists K_1^i \in KS_1 \ \ and \ \ \exists K_2^j \in KS_2 \quad such\ that : \\ & EV \cup \{K_1^i \wedge K_2^j\} \ \ is\ consistent\ \ and, \\ & EV \models (K_1^i \wedge K_2^j) \leftrightarrow K] \end{aligned}$$

Proposition 5. Let m_1 and m_2 be two basic assignments which are not in total conflict and let $ks(m_1)$ and $ks(m_2)$ be their logical representation. Then, $ks(m_1 \oplus m_2) \leftrightarrow ks(m_1) \oplus ks(m_2)$.

This proves that the operator $\oplus$ on knowledge-sets corresponds to the logical interpretation of Dempster's rule of combination.

Example. Let m_1 and m_2 be two basic assignments defined by: $m_1(A, B) = 1/2, m_1(B) = 1/2$ and $m_2(A) = 1/3, m_2(A, B) = 1/3, m_2(B) = 1/3$. Dempster's rule defines the basic assignment $m_1 \oplus m_2$ by: $m_1 \oplus m_2(A) = 1/5, m_1 \oplus m_2(A, B) = 1/5, m_1 \oplus m_2(B) = 3/5$. Besides, the logical interpretation of m_1 and m_2 are: $ks(m_1) = [A \vee B, B]$ and $ks(m_2) = [A, A \vee B, B]$. We can then compute $ks(m_1) \oplus ks(m_2)$ and get: $ks(m_1) \oplus ks(m_2) = [A, A \vee B, B, B, B]$. We can easily check that: $ks(m_1 \oplus m_2) \leftrightarrow ks(m_1) \oplus ks(m_2)$

To sum up this section, we can say that *the basic assignment $m_1 \oplus m_2$, provided by Dempster's rule on two assignments m_1 and m_2, can be logically interpreted by the knowledge-set denoted $ks(m_1) \oplus ks(m_2)$ previously defined, $ks(m_1)$ and $ks(m_2)$ beeing the knowledge-sets which logically interpret m_1 and m_2.*

2.4 Maximum of plausibility Decision Strategy

An assignment, obtained by combination or not, thus implicitly defines several orders between hypothesis of the frame of discernment. Indeed, one can order the hypothesis according to their degrees of belief, or to their degree of plausibility or to their pignistic probability [18].

Let us focus here on the Maximum of plausibility Decision Strategy (MPDS) which consists in selecting the hypothesis which are the most plausible (i.e, which have the greatest degree of plausibility).

We can show that, under EV, any hypothesis corresponds to only one world in $||EV||$[5], the one in which this hypothesis (and only this one) is true. So we can define the degree of plausibility of a model of EV by the degree of plausibility of

[5] $||E||$ denotes the set of interpretations which satisfy E i.e, the set of models of E

the only hypothesis which satisfies it. And thus, the MPDS is equivalent to select the models of EV, which are the most plausible. Let us denote $Maxpl(||EV||, m)$ the set of worlds in $||EV||$ which are selected by the MPDS defined by assignment m, i.e, the most plausible (for m) models of EV.

3 Maximum of plausibility vs merging operators

In this section we show that the MPDS is equivalent to a particular merging operator defined by Konieczny and Pino-Perez.

3.1 The merging operator *Sum*

Let us recall here some results given in [11] and [9]. Notice that we focus only on some results and change the notations.

Definition 7. Let w and w' be two interpretations of a propositional language. The drastic distance $d(w, w')$ between w and w' is defined by: $d(w, w') = 0$ iff $w = w'$ and $d(w, w') = 1$ iff $w \neq w'$. Let w be an interpretation and K a formula. The distance between w and K is defined by: $d(w, K) = Min_{w' \in ||K||} d(w, w')$. Let w be an interpretation and M a multi-set of formulas. One can define a distance, denoted here d_{sum} between w and M by: $d_{sum}(w, M) = \sum_{K_i \in M} d(w, K_i)$

Definition 8. Let M be a multi-set of formulas. One can define a pre-order on the propositional interpretations by:

$$w \leq_{d_{sum}(M)} w' \quad \text{iff} \quad d_{sum}(w, M) \leq d_{sum}(w', M)$$

Definition 9. Let M be a multi-set of formulas and IC a set of formulas considered as integrity constraints. A merging operator, denoted here Sum, is defined by:

$$Sum(M, IC) = Min_{\leq_{d_{sum}(M)}} ||IC||$$

In other terms, *the result of merging, under constraints IC, of the different formulas in M by the operator Sum, is semantically characterized by the models of IC whose distance to M, defined by d_{sum}, is minimal.*

Konieczny has shown that the operator Sum is both a majority merging operator and an arbitration one, and thus, satisfies the postulates which characterize such operators.

3.2 Relation between MPDS and *Sum*

The relation between the Maximum Plausibility Decision Strategy and the merging operator Sum is given by the following result:

Proposition 6. $Maxpl(||EV||, m) = Sum(ks(m), EV)$

Sketch of proof. We first prove the following lemma :

Let K be a propositional formula which is not a contradiction. Let $w_i \in ||EV||$ et H_i the unique propositional letter such that $||H_i|| = \{w_i\}$. Then:

(a) $d(w_i, K) = 0$ *iff* $EV \cup \{K \wedge H_i\}$ *is consistent*
(b) $d(w_i, K) = 1$ *iff* $EV \cup \{K \wedge H_i\}$ *is inconsistent*

Then we show that, if w_1 and w_2 are two models of EV. Then $d_{sum}(w_1, ks(m)) \leq d_{sum}(w_2, ks(m))$ iff $Pl_m(w_1) \geq Pl_m(w_2)$

This proposition shows that, given a basic assignment m, the Maximum of Plausibility Decision Strategy comes to merge, by the operator Sum, the knowledge-set which logically represents this assignment. I.e, the Maximum Plausibility Decision Strategy is a merging operator which is both a majority and an arbitration one and thus sastifies the postulates of this kind of operators. Due to space limitation, we cannot give the reformulation of these postulates in our setting, but this can be found in [5]

4 Merging operators vs Maximum of plausibility

In this section, we prove some symetrical results. We show that any knowledge-set KS can be represented, in Theory of Evidence, by a basic assignment m_{KS}. Then, we show that the merging operator Sum applied on KS under constraints IC, characterizes a formula which corresponds to what provides the MPDS when defined by m_{KS} and when considering IC.

4.1 Representation of a knowledge-set by a basic assignment

Let L be a finite propositional language and let $w_1, ..., w_N$ its interpretations.

We can define a frame of discernment Θ_L with n hypothesis denotes $H_1, ..., H_N$ which are exclusive and exhaustive. These hypothesis are defined by isomorphism from the interpretations $w_1, ..., w_N$, but for simplifying the presentation, we will omit this isomorphism: by convention, the world w_i is associated with the hypothesis H_i.

Definition 10. Let K be a consistent set of formulas of L and let $||K|| = \{w_{i_1}, ..., w_{i_k}\}$ the set of its models. We note $t(K)$, the set of hypothesis defined by $t(K) = \{H_{i_1}, ..., H_{i_k}\}$.

Example. Let L be a propositional language whose letters are a and b. The possible worlds are $w_1 = \{a, b\}$, $w_2 = \{a, \neg b\}$, $w_3 = \{\neg a, b\}$ and $w_4 = \{\neg a, \neg b\}$. Θ_L is thus the frame of discernment whose hypothesis are H_1, H_2, H_3, H_4. Let us now consider the formula $a \vee \neg b$. Then, $t(a \vee \neg b) = \{H_1, H_2, H_4\}$.

Definition 11. Let KS be a knowledge-set of L containing only consistent formulas. We denote m_{KS} the basic assignment, which associates any set of hypothesis A of Θ_L with the proportion of formulas K in KS such that $t(K) = A$.

One can check that definition 11 indeed characterizes a basic assignment.

Example. Let S be the knowledge-set made of the three formulas : $K_1 = a \wedge b, K_2 = a \wedge c, K_3 = \neg a$. The possible worlds are: $w_1 = \{a, b, c\}, w_2 = \{a, b, \neg c\}, ..., w_8 = \{\neg a, \neg b, \neg c\}$. Let $H_1...H_8$ the hypothesis of Θ_L. We have: $||K_1|| = \{w_1, w_2\}$. Thus, $t(K_1) = \{H_1, H_2\}$. $||K_2|| = \{w_1, w_3\}$, then $t(K_2) = \{H_1, H_3\}$. Finally, $||K_3|| = \{w_5, w_6, w_7, w_8\}$ and thus $t(K_3) = \{H_5, H_6, H_7, H_8\}$. This defines the following basic assignment: : $m_{KS}(H_1, H_2) = m_{KS}(H_1, H_3) = m_{KS}(H_5, H_6, H_7, H_8) = 1/3$.

4.2 Relation between *Sum* and MPDS

Proposition 7. $t(Sum(KS, IC)) = Maxpl(t(IC), m_{KS})$

Sketch of proof.

We first prove the following lemma: let w be an interpretation of L and let H be its associated hypothesis in Θ_L. Then, $Pl_{m_{KS}}(H)$ is equal to the proportion, in KS, of formulas whose w is a model.

Then we prove that, if w_1 and w_2 are two interpretations of L and if H_1 and H_2 are the hypothesis of Θ_L which are respectivly associated with them, then :

$d_{sum}(w_1, M) \leq d_{sum}(w_2, M)$ *iff* $Pl_{m_{KS}}(H_1) \geq Pl_{m_{KS}}(H_2)$

In other words, merging the knowledge-set KS under constraints IC with operator *Sum* is equivalent to selecting the most plausible hypothesis of $t(IC)$ according to the assignment m_{KS}.

Example. Let us take again the knowledge-set KS defined by the three formulas: $K_1 = a \wedge b, K_2 = a \wedge c, K_3 = \neg a$. Assume that $IC = \emptyset$. We have: $Sum(E, IC) = \{a, b, c\}$. And $t(Sum(E, IC)) = \{H_1\}$. The assignment associated with KS, m_{KS}, is defined by:

$m_{KS}(H_1, H_2) = m_{KS}(H_1, H_3) = m_{KS}(H_5, ..., H_8) = 1/3$.

Since $IC = \emptyset$, $||IC|| = \{w_1, ..., w_8\}$ and thus $t(IC) = \{H_1, ..., H_8\}$. Among these hypothesis, the most plausible according to m_{KS} is H_1. Thus,

$t(Sum(KS, IC)) = Maxpl(t(IC), m_{KS})$.

5 Conclusion

The contributions of this work are the following. First, it shows a possible way for interpreting in logical terms, the basic notions of Theory of Evidence when numbers are rational. In this case, it shows the equivalence between assignments and multi-sets of propositional formulas. Then, it shows the equivalence between the Maximum of Plausibility Decision Strategy provided by Theory of Evidence and the merging operator, here denoted *Sum*, provided for merging knowledge-bases.

The equivalence between the two theories being established, one consequence is that it is now possible to export some notions from one theory to the other.

In particular, the logical interpretation of Demspter's rule of combination, defines an operator on multi-sets of formulas, denoted $\oplus$ in section 2.3, which aims at combining two multi-sets of formulas. Such an operator has, as far as we know, never been studied and it would be interesting to study its properties and compare it to the other knowledge-base merging operators

Conversely, the multi-sets union operator suggests a new rule for combining two assignments. It can be shown that this rule is commutative and associative, and is always applicable, even if the two assignments are in total conflict which shows the interest of such of rule of combination. Studying the properties of this rule of combination is the subject of current research.

Finally, comparing other decision strategies (Maximum of Credibility and Maximum of Pignistic probability for instance) and other knowledge-bases merging operators remains to be done. And this constitutes another direction of research.

References

1. A. Appriou. Multi-sensor data fusion in situation assesment processes. In D. Gabbay, R. Kruse, A. Noncngart, and H. Ohlbach, editors, *Lectures Notes in AI 1244 : Proc of ECSQARU-FAPR'97*, 1997.
2. C. Baral, S. Kraus, J. Minker, and V.S. Subrahmanian. Combining multiple knowledge bases. *IEEE Trans. on Knowledge and Data Engineering*, 3(2), 1991.
3. C. Baral, S. Kraus, J. Minker, and V.S. Subrahmanian. Combining knowledge bases consisting of first order theories. *Computational Intelligence*, 8(1), 1992.
4. L. Cholvy. Proving theorems in a multi-sources environment. In *Proceedings of IJCAI*, pages 66–71, 1993.
5. L. Cholvy. Fusion de données pour l'analyse de situations : relation entre stratégie du maximu de plausibilité de la théorie de l'evidence et fusion logique majoritaire. Technical report, n° 1/04010/DTIM, ONERA, 2000.
6. A. Dempster. Upper and lower probabilities iduced by a multivalued mapping. *Annals of Mathematical Statistics*, 38:325–339, 1967.
7. D. Dubois, M. Grabbisch, H. Prade, and Ph. Smets. Assessing the value of a candidate. comparing belief functions and possibility theories. In *Proc. of* 15th *conf. on Uncertainty in AI*, 1999.
8. L. Gautier, A. Taleb-Ahmed, M. Rombaut, J. Postaire, and H. Leclet. Belief function in low level data fusion: Applications in mri images of vertebra. In *Proc of the* 3rd *International Conference on Information Fusion, Paris*, 2000.
9. S. Konieczny. *Sur la logique du changement : Révision et Fusion de bases de connaissances*. PhD thesis, Univ. des Sciences et Technologies de Lille, 1999.
10. S. Konieczny and R. Pino-Perez. Merging with integrity constraints. In *Proc. of ESCQARU'99*, 1999.
11. S. Konieczny and R. Pino-Perez. On the logic of merging. In *Proc. of KR'98*, Trento, 1998.
12. C. Liau. A conservative approach to distributed belief fusion. In *Proceedings of* 3rd *International Conference on Information Fusion (FUSION)*, 2000.
13. J.. Lin. Integration of weighted knowldege bases. *Artificial Intelligence*, 83:363–378, 1996.
14. J. Lin and A.O. Mendelzon. Merging databases under constraints. *International Journal of Cooperative Information Systems*, 7(1), 1998.
15. C. Royère, D. Gruyer, and V. Cherfaoui. Data association with believe theory. In *Proc of the* 3rd *International Conference on Information Fusion, Paris*, 2000.
16. S.Benferhat, D. Dubois, J. Lang, H. Prade, A. Saffiotti, and P. Smets. A general approach for inconsistency handling and merging information in prioritized knowledge bases. In *Proc. of KR'98*, Trento, 1998.
17. G. Shafer. *A mathematical theory of evidence.* Princeton University Press, Princeton and London, 1976.
18. P. Smets. The transferable belief model. *Artificial Intelligence*, 66:191–234, 1994.
19. V.S. Subrahmanian. Amalgamating knowledge bases. *ACM Transactions on Database Systems*, 19(2):291–331, 1994.

A Priori Revision

Florence Dupin de Saint-Cyr, Béatrice Duval, and Stéphane Loiseau

LERIA, Université d'Angers, 2 bd Lavoisier, 49045 ANGERS Cedex 01 France
{bannay, bd, loiseau}@info.univ-angers.fr

Abstract. The problem of revision is to find which formula ψ can be deduced from a formula φ, which has been added to a Knowledge Base KB. Since φ can bring inconsistency to KB, non-monotonic inference relations which are able to deal with inconsistency have been proposed; note that classical revision takes place after the arrival of φ. The aim of this paper is to propose a priori revision, that is to provide a way to "armor" the KB by suppressing some knowledge and by forbidding to accept some new information in such a way that adding any allowed formula φ to the revised KB will not bring inconsistency.

1 Introduction

A lot of researchers have studied inconsistency handling in knowledge bases (KB for short). The KB is used to describe a system and to deduce new information about it. The difficulty is to reason with an inconsistent KB because the possible deductions become trivial; if we do not want to throw away the whole KB we have to handle inconsistency. A particular problem is the insertion of a new formula in an initially consistent KB; reasoning with the KB after the arrival of this new formula is called *revision* [Alchourrón&al85, Winslett88, Katsuno-Mendelzon91]. So, the problem of revision is to find which formula ψ can be deduced from a formula φ that has been added to the KB. The inference must not be the classical inference since φ can bring inconsistency to the KB. This is why, many researchers have proposed, so called, *non monotonic inference relations* which are able to deal with inconsistency. Those non monotonic inference relations use some *preference relations* that select the most interesting consistent sub-theory(ies) of $\varphi \cup$ KB in which classical deduction can be applied. Note that classical revision takes place *after* the arrival of a new information φ, so this revision can be called *a posteriori revision*.

The aim of this paper is to propose a way to make *a priori revision*. In a priori revision, we want to provide a way to "armor" the KB by suppressing some rules and by forbidding to accept some new information in such a way that adding any allowed formula φ to the revised KB will not bring inconsistency. Consequently, in the revised KB, classical monotonic inference relation will always be usable. In this work, we distinguish between input variables, which can compose a new information, and other variables; we restrict also a new information to be a conjunction of input literals. We propose to examine the initial KB to provide a set of armored KB such that each one

S. Benferhat and P. Besnard (Eds.): ECSQARU 2001, LNAI 2143, pp. 488–497, 2001.

will be consistent with any conjunction φ of allowed input literals. A *diagnosis* is composed by a set of formulas that must be removed from the KB and a set of integrity constraints which define *valid new information* for the KB; those integrity constraints provide a way to eliminate some formulas from the set of possible arriving new formulas. Applying a diagnosis to a KB is called *armoring* the KB. One difficulty is that it can exist many such diagnoses. So, we propose to use a penalty preference relation [Dupin&all94] in order to select preferred diagnoses and so armored KB.

This paper is organized as follows. In a first part, we define a priori revision. In the second part, we present a preference relation on diagnoses, based on penalty theory, in order to provide a way to choose a best diagnosis, to obtain a best armored KB. In the last part we propose algorithms to compute the diagnoses and their associated penalty cost.

2 How to Armor a Knowledge Base?

In the following, we denote by L a finite propositional language. Elements of L, or *formulas*, are denoted by Greek letters. An *interpretation* in L is an assignment of a truth value in {T, F} to each formula of L in accordance with the classical rules of propositional calculus. A literal is an atomic variable p or its negation ¬p. An interpretation ω is a *model* of a formula α (ω"α) iff $\omega(\alpha)=T$. A formula β is called a logical consequence of α (α"β) iff each model of α is a model of β. A formula α is said to be consistent iff it has at least one model. Any inconsistent formula can be denoted by $\perp$. A knowledge base KB is a set of logical formulas. Non monotonic inference relation will be denoted by $\mid\!\sim$.

The problem of revision is to decide if, given a knowledge base KB composed by logical formulas and a new information φ, we can deduce ψ, denoted by $\varphi \mid\!\sim_{KB} \psi$. The a posteriori revision selects a set of consistent subsets $KB_{i\ (i=1\ \text{à}\ n)}$ of KB such for each subset KB_i, $KBi \cup \varphi \vdash \psi$, which is noted $\varphi \mid\!\sim_{KB} \psi$. The point is to define a preference relation which is able to select the most interesting preferred consistent subsets. In order to discriminate between the consistent subsets of KB, some approaches [Rescher64, Brewka89, Nebel91, Dubois&all92, Benferhat&al93, Lehmann92, Cayrol-Lagasquie95] consist in ranking the KB into priority levels and maximizing the set or the number of formulas satisfied at each level starting from the highest priority level. An important aspect of this kind of approach is that violating however many formulas at a given level is always more acceptable than violating only one formula at a strictly higher level; thus, these approaches are non-compensatory, i.e., levels never interact. An alternative approach, called *penalty* approach, [Pinkas91, Dupin&all94] is to weight the formulas of the KB with positive numbers called penalties. Intuitively, the penalty associated to a formula represents the importance of the formula, the higher it is, the more important is the formula and the more difficult it will be to reject this formula. Inviolable formulas are given an infinite penalty. Contrarily to priorities, penalties are compensatory since they are additive:

the cost associated to a subset of formulas of a KB is the sum of the penalties of the rejected formulas. The subsets having a minimum cost are preferred subsets of KB. Notice that in all these approaches, φ has a maximal priority.

We now present the framework we use in order to make a priori revision. We define a set of *input variables* which is a subset of the variables of L. An *input literal* is an input variable or its negation; we note I this set of input literals. The aim of a priori revision is to compute a revised KB, denoted by D(KB), so that for any valid conjunction of input literals φ which will be added in the future, D(KB) $\cup$ φ will be consistent; hence the classical monotonic inference relation will always be usable with φ. Such a revision of KB is made by defining a diagnosis. A diagnosis is composed of a set of formulas that must be removed from the KB and of a set of integrity constraints which define *valid new information* for the KB. An integrity constraint is a formula $(l_1\square\ldots\square l_n \rightarrow \bot)$, where each l_i is an input literal. Such a constraint means that $l_1\square\ldots\square l_n$ cannot be added to the KB. To simplify the notations, the constraint formula $(l_1\square\ldots\square l_n \rightarrow \bot)$ will be represented by its set of literals $\{ l_1, \ldots, l_n\}$.

We consider the following restrictions: the possible new information is a conjunction of input literals and the knowledge base is a set of *Horn clause* formulas where the positive literal in the clause is not an input literal (we can represent these Horn clauses by implicative formulas where input facts can only occur in the premises). This framework allows us to consider Modus Ponens as the unique inference relation (more formally, with our restrictions, if φ is a conjuction of input literals then $\varphi \cup$ KB infers classically ψ is equivalent to $\varphi \cup$ KB infers ψ by Modus Ponens).

Definition 1 – Diagnosis of a Knowledge Base

Let KB be a knowledge base; I a set of input literals. Let D be a pair $< E_D, r_D>$, where r_D is a subset of KB and E_D is a set of literal sets, $\{\{l_{1,1}; \ldots, l_{1,n}\}; \ldots;\{l_{p,1}; \ldots; l_{p,m}\}\}$ that represents a set of p integrity constraints, called R_{ED}.

D is a *diagnosis* for KB if for every conjunction j of input literals, consistent with the integrity constraints R_{ED}, $\{ j \} \cup$ KB $\setminus$ r_D is consistent

Example 1. Let us consider the following example: Quakers (Qua) are Pacifists (Pac), Republicans (Rep) are not pacifists, Republicans are American (Am), Americans like Baseball (Bball), and Republicans do not like Baseball. With this knowledge base KB_1, if a new information arrives and states that Nixon is both a Quaker and a Republican, it is possible to deduce that Nixon is both pacifist and not pacifist, a contradiction that we want to avoid.

r1: Qua $\rightarrow$ Pac r2: Rep $\rightarrow$ $\neg$Pac r3: Rep $\rightarrow$ Am

r4: Am $\rightarrow$ Bball r5: Rep $\rightarrow$ $\neg$Bball

If the set of input variables is {Rep, Qua}, then D_0= <{},{r1,r2,r3,r4,r5}>, D_1= <{}, {r1, r3}>, D_7= <{{Rep}}, {}> and D_9= <{{Rep, Qua}}, {r4}> for instance, are possible diagnoses. The computation of diagnoses will be explained in section 3.

An armored KB is a KB on which a diagnosis has been applied.

Definition 2 – Armoring a Knowledge Base
Let D(KB) be the *knowledge base KB armored* by D = < E_D, r_D> ; D(KB) corresponds to KB from which the rules of r_D have been deleted and to which the integrity constraints of R_{ED} are added: $D(KB) = R_{ED} \cup KB \setminus r_D$.

Example 1. If we consider D_9, $D_9(KB_1)$ = { Rep∧Qua→⊥} ∪ {r1, r2, r3, r5}. This means that, with $D_9(KB_1)$, the new information "Nixon is both pacifist and Quaker" represented by Rep∧Qua is forbidden; for any conjunction of input literals j that is not forbidden, j ∪ {r1, r2, r3, r5} is consistent.

3 How to Choose the Best Armoring ?

Definition 3 – A Priori Revision
A *priori revising* a KB consists in providing a preference relation on the possible diagnoses for a KB.

If there are several diagnoses with the same preference, then either we can define, as in a posteriori revision, that a formula ψ can be inferred from a formula φ if it can be inferred from all the preferred armored KB to which φ is added, or we select any preferred armored KB. A main difficulty is to choose among several possible diagnoses. We propose to use a preference ordering on diagnoses. First, we prefer and so only consider, minimal diagnosis. A minimal diagnosis is a diagnosis that leads to minimal change to the corresponding armored KB. Second, we use a penalty approach that provides criteria to prefer the diagnoses that reject or make useless the less important formulas of KB.

3.1 Minimal Change Diagnosis

Definition 4 – Minimal Diagnosis
A diagnosis <E_D, r_D> is *minimal* if there does not exist another diagnosis <E_D', r_D'> verifying: $r_D' \subseteq r_D$, and ($E_D' \subseteq E_D$ or $\forall F' \in E_D', \exists F \in E_D$ such that $F \subseteq F'$).

Examples. 1) For the preceding example KB_1, there are 10 minimal diagnoses:
D_1= <{ }, {r1, r3}>; D_2= <{ }, {r1, r4}>; D_3= <{ }, {r1, r5}>; D_4= <{ }, {r2, r3}>;
D_5= <{ }, {r2, r4}>; D_6= <{ }, {r2, r5}>; D_7= <{{Rep}}, { }>;
D_8= <{{Rep, Qua}}, {r3}>; D_9= <{{Rep, Qua}}, {r4}>; D_{10}= <{{Rep, Qua}}, {r5}>
2) Let us suppose that a knowledge base has the three following diagnoses: D1= <{{a,b},{a, c}}, {r1}>, D2=<{{a, b}}, {r1}>, D3=<{{a }}, {r1}>
D2 is minimal, D1 and D3 are not minimal. D1 is not minimal because it is not necessary to forbid the conjunction of the literals a and c to have a diagnosis; D3 is not minimal because D2 shows that it is not necessary to forbid all the interpretations satisfying a, it is sufficient to forbid the interpretations having a and b.
Note that the minimality principle is not interesting for comparing equivalent (in terms of models) diagnoses. For instance, between two diagnoses D1=<{a, b},{a,

¬b}}, {r1}> and D2=<{{a }}, {r1}>, the minimality criterion leads to prefer D1, but in fact the two sets of constraints are equivalent.

We have defined an order relation between diagnoses and the associated minimality criterion. However, this relation only defines a partial order that we propose to refine by using a penalty approach. The penalty approach can rank diagnoses by comparing the weights of the deleted or useless rules.

3.2. Uselessness of a Rule in an Armored KB

A diagnosis explicitly excludes some rules from the knowledge base. It may also happen that some rules become useless in the revised knowledge base because they can never be fired. A rule cannot be fired if its conditions correspond to an impossible conjunction of input literals or if some of its conditions cannot be proved after the deletion of rules of r_D. If a rule becomes useless after application of a diagnosis, we can consider that the information encapsulated in this rule is, in some way, suppressed from the knowledge base. So, in order to compare armored KB, it is important to know if the rules that are kept in the armored KB are useful.

Definition 5 – Useless Rule Set for a Diagnosis D
Let D = < E_D, r_D> be a diagnosis for KB.
A Horn clause r is *useless* for D iff there is no conjunction j of input literals, consistent with R_{ED}, such that the premises of r can be deduced from $\{ j \} \cup KB \setminus r_D$.
We call URS(D), useless rule set of D, the set of all useless rules of KB for D.

Example 1. D_1= <{}, {r1, r3}> D_1(KB)={r2, r4, r5}; URS(D_1)={r4}, r4 (Am $\rightarrow$ Bball) is useless because Am is not an input literal, and it cannot be deduced from {r2, r4, r5} with any input base.

Proposition : Minimality and Uselessness
If D = < E_D, r_D> is a diagnosis for KB, and if r_i in r_D is useless for D, then D is not minimal.

This property means that minimality and uselessness are complementary notions to evaluate diagnoses.

3.3 The Penalty Approach

For any formula φ_i of the KB, there is an associated penalty $\alpha(\varphi_i)$ that represents a degree of confidence in φ_i, it will be understood as the cost that the user must pay in order to discard the formula φ_i. Let us present the penalty preference on diagnosis. In the basic penalty approach, the philosophy consists in paying $\alpha(\varphi_i)$ when a formula φ_i of the initial knowledge base is discarded, we propose to extend this by taking into account formulas which become useless.

Definition 6 – Cost of a Diagnosis
Let D = < E_D, r_D> be a diagnosis for KB.
The *cost of the diagnosis* D, called C(D), is the sum of the penalties associated to the rules of KB which are deleted or brought useless by D, so C(D) = $\sum_{\varphi_i \in r_D \cup URS(D)} \alpha(\varphi_i)$

Definition 7 – Cost Preference
Let KB be a penalty knowledge base. Let D_1 and D_2 be two minimal diagnoses of KB. D_1 is *penalty-preferred* to D_2 iff $C(D_1) \leq C(D_2)$

Example 1. The set of input facts is {Qua, Rep}. We associate a penalty to each rule.
r1: Qua → Pac $\alpha_1 = 5$ r2: Rep → ¬Pac $\alpha_2 = 5$ r3: Rep → Am $\alpha_3 = 100$
r4: Am → Bball $\alpha_4 = 5$ r5: Rep → ¬Bball $\alpha_5 = 7$
The penalty associated to r3 means that this rule is very important.
For each of the minimal diagnoses presented before, we give its cost; the method for computing these costs will be presented in the next section.
D_1= <{ }, {r1, r3}> $C(D_1)$=110 (r4 is useless); D_2= <{ }, {r1, r4}> $C(D_2)$=10;
D_3= <{ }, {r1, r5}> $C(D_3)$=12; D_4= <{ }, {r2, r3}> $C(D_4)$=110 (r4 is useless);
D_5= <{ }, {r2, r4}> $C(D_5)$=10; D_6= <{ }, {r2, r5}> $C(D_6)$=12;
D_7= <{{Rep}}, { }> $C(D_7)$=117 (r2, r3, r4, r7 are useless);
D_8= <{{Rep, Qua}}, {r3}> $C(D_8)$=105 (r4 is useless);
D_9= <{{Rep, Qua}}, {r4}> $C(D_9)$=5; D_{10}= <{{Rep, Qua}}, {r5}> $C(D_{10})$=7.
So, the penalty-preferred minimal diagnosis is D_9, and the associated armored KB is :
Rep∧Qua→⊥ r1: Qua → Pac r2: Rep → ¬Pac
r3: Rep → Am r5: Rep → ¬Bball
It means that if a person is a Quaker then he is a pacifist, and if a person is a Republican then he is non pacifist, american and does not like baseball. But a person can not be both a Quaker and a republican.
Note that taking into account the uselessness of the rules avoids to prefer D_7. The D_7 constraint means that it cannot exist republican, which makes several rules useless.

To apply this approach, a difficulty is to obtain the penalties for all the rules. They can be given by an expert. If no penalty is given, each formula can be associated with a penalty 1, this approach is equivalent to count the number of formulas. An automatic approach can be to associate a penalty to each rule using heuristics. If the KB represents a default behavior of some components, penalties can be proportional to probabilities associated to a faulty component, as [de Kleer-Williams87].

4 Algorithms

Two algorithms are presented. The first one computes the minimal diagnoses of a knowledge base. The second one determines the cost of each diagnosis

4.1 Diagnosis Computation

The computation of diagnoses can be made in two steps using first an ATMS [deKleer86] and second an algorithm that extends [Reiter87]. The first step computes the minimal characterizations of the potential inconsistencies of the KB: such a characterization is a conjunction of input literals and a subset of rules sufficient to infer a contradiction. A conjunction of input literals is also called a fact base and will be represented as a set of literals. Let FB={f1,...,fn} and FB'={f'1,...,f'p} be two fact bases, in the following we denote FB $\models$ FB' the fact that f1 $\wedge$ ... $\wedge$ fn $\models$ f'1$\wedge$ ... $\wedge$ f'p. Notice that [Bouali-Loiseau95] proposes such an algorithm to debug a knowledge base and that [Bezzazi&al98] uses a very similar method for a posteriori revision.

Definition 8 – Characterization
Let KB be a knowledge base.
A *characterization* is a pair <FB, rb> where FB is a set of input literals, and rb is a subset of KB, such that FB $\cup$ rb $\models \bot$.
A characterization is *minimal* iff there does not exist another characterization <FB', rb'> such that rb' $\subseteq$ rb and FB $\models$ FB'

ATMS provides a way to compute for each literal a label that defines the necessary and sufficient condition, in terms of assumptions, that provides the deduction of the literal. ATMS provides also a mechanism to ensure that all parts of labels, called environments, are consistent.

Definition 9 – Environment and Label
An *environment* E is a conjunction of assumptions.
The *label* of a literal L is a disjunction of environments ($E_1 \vee .. E_i ... \vee E_n$) such that : $\forall$ E_i, $E_i \cup$ KB $\not\models \bot$ -the label is consistent with KB (except if L = $\bot$)-, $\forall$ E_i, E_j; $E_i \not\models E_j$ -the label is minimal-, $\forall$ E_i, $E_i \cup$ KB $\models$ L -the label is sound-, $\forall$ E and E $\cup$ KB $\models$ L then $\exists$ E_i / E $\models$ E_i -the label is complete-.

So given input literals and rules names as assumptions, and the set of rules KB (including for each rule its name as an additional premise), ATMS computes for each literal its label. We denote an environment Ei as composed of Ei_{Rules} the rules figuring in Ei, and Ei_{facts} the facts figuring in Ei. So, the minimal characterizations are composed of the Ei_{facts} part and the Ei_{Rules} part of the environments Ei of $\bot$.

Example 1. Assumptions: {Qua, Rep, r1, r2, r3, r4, r5}; Implications: { r1 $\wedge$ Qua $\rightarrow$ Pac, r2 $\wedge$ Rep $\rightarrow$ ¬Pac, r3 $\wedge$ Rep $\rightarrow$ Am, r4 $\wedge$ Am $\rightarrow$ Bball, r5 $\wedge$ Rep $\rightarrow$ ¬Bball}

BD_{atms} :

Label(Pac) = (Qua $\wedge$ r1)	Label(¬Pac) = (Rep $\wedge$ r2)
Label(Am) = (Rep $\wedge$ r3)	Label(Bball) = (Rep $\wedge$ r3 $\wedge$ r4)
Label(¬Bball) = (Rep $\wedge$ r5)	Label(Rep) = (Rep)
Label(Qua) = (Qua)	

Label($\bot$) = (Rep $\wedge$ r3 $\wedge$ r4 $\wedge$ r5)$\vee$ (Qua $\wedge$ Rep $\wedge$ r1 $\wedge$ r2). The environment E2 of label($\bot$) can be noted as $E2_{Rules}$ = {r1, r2} and $E2_{facts}$ = {Qua, Rep}. There exist two minimal characterizations, C1=<{Rep}, {r3, r4, r5}> and C2=<{Qua, Rep},{r1, r2}>.

The diagnoses for a rule base can be computed from the characterizations using the following theorem.

Theorem
Let KB be a rule base, and C = {C1, ..., Cn} the collection of minimal characterizations, D=<E_D, r_D> is a diagnosis w.r.t KB iff ∀ Ci=<E_{Ci}, r_{Ci}> of C, either $r_{Ci} \cap r_D \neq \{\}$ or ∃ {p1, .., pn} of E_D | E_{Ci} " {p1,..,pn}

The algorithm which computes the set of minimal diagnoses relative to a rule base from the minimal characterizations is an extension of the algorithm to compute diagnoses [Reiter87]. There are two important differences. First, in the data structure there are two different kinds of data taken into account: the rules and the input literals. A node corresponds to a *characterization*, to each node is associated for each rule it contains an arc labeled by the rule, and for each node is associated an arc labeled with the fact base part of the characterization. Second, the characterizations must be sorted. A diagnosis is obtained by keeping all the labels of arcs from root to a leaf V.

function MinDiag(C): a set of diagnoses
/* C = {C1,...,Cn} is the sorted collection of characterizations; let C_i = <FB_i, r_i>, C_j = <FB_j, r_j>, $C_i < C_j$ iff FB_j={p'1,...,p'm} ⊨ FB_i = {p1,...,pn}; the function makes a tree whose nodes are labeled by some C_i=<Fb_i, r_i>, and the arcs issued of Ci=<FB_i, r_i> are labeled by FB_i or a rule of r_i. *Hfb(N_i) is the set of FB that label the arcs that go from the root to N_i;. Hr(N_i) is the set of rules that label the arcs that are going from the root to N_i* */

```
MinDiag := {}
Label the root of the Tree with the first element of C
For each leaf Nk of Tree labeled by an element Ck=<FBk, rk>
   create a node Nj; create an arc from Nk to Nj labeled by FBk
   For each r of rk
      create node Nj; create an arc from Nk to Nj labeled by rk
   For each node Nj created with an arc from Nk to Nj
      If ∃ Ci=<FBi, ri> of C that verifies Hr(Nj) ∩ ri = {} and
       ∀ {f1,..,fn} of Hfb(Nj), FBi={f'1,...,f'm} |=/= {f1,..,fn}
        Nj := the first Ci verifying the preceding condition
      elseif ∃ Nj' = V, Hr(Nj') ⊆ Hr(Nj), and
       ∀ {f'1,..,f'm} of HFB(Nj'), ∃ {f1,..,fn} of HFB(Nj) /
         {f'1,..,f'm} |= {f1,..,fn}
        close Nj with X
      else close Nj with V, MinDiag:=MinDiag∪{<Hfb(Nj), Hr(Nj)>}
```

Example 1. The schema shows how we find the diagnoses: <{{Rep}}, {}>...

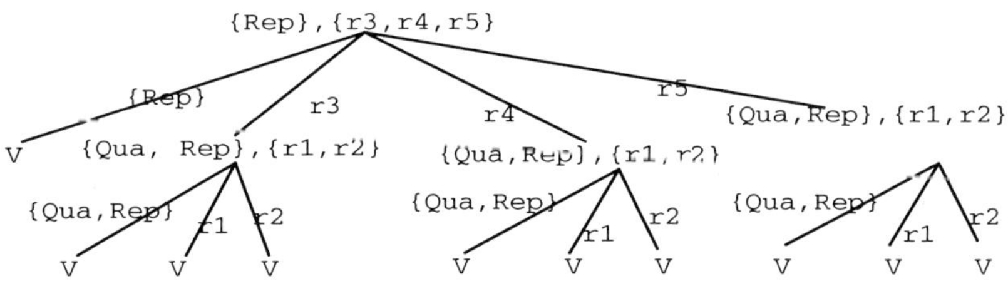

4.2 Diagnosis Cost Computation

The following algorithm computes the cost of a given diagnosis. It uses the labels (BD_{atms}) computed by ATMS during the diagnosis computation. The cost is composed of the cost of the rules of the diagnosis, plus the cost of the rules that are not useful when the integrity constraints are added and the rules of the diagnosis suppressed.

```
function Cost(D; BDatms) : integer/* Determine the cost of D */
Cost :=0
/* Cost of r of rD*/
For each r of rD
   Cost := Cost + C(r)
/*cost of useless rules*/
For each r of rD
   Suppress all environments of BDatms that contains r
Let RED be the set of the integrity constraints ∧j lij → ⊥
associated to ED
UpDate BDatms by adding the integrity constraints RED
For each r of KB \ rD
   If it does not exist a non contradictory environment in BDatms
   that contains r
      Then Cost := Cost + C(r)
```

Example 1 If we call Cost($D_1 = \langle\{\ \}, \{r1, r3\}\rangle$, BD_{atms}) /* Cost of r of r_D*/ Cost := c(r1) + c(r3) = 5 + 100 /*cost of useless rules*/ BD_{atms} modified: Label(Pac) = ~~($Qua \wedge r1$)~~; Label($\neg$Pac) = ($Rep \wedge r2$); Label(American) = ~~($Rep \wedge r3$)~~; Label(Bball) = ~~($Rep \wedge r3 \wedge r4$)~~; Label($\neg$Bball) = ($Rep \wedge r5$); Label(Rep) = (Rep); Label(Qua) = (Qua); Label($\perp$) = ~~($Rep \wedge r3 \wedge r4 \wedge r5$)~~$\vee$ ~~($Qua \wedge Rep \wedge r1 \wedge r2$)~~ . It does not exist a non contradictory environment in BD_{atms} modified that contains r4; Cost:=105+C(r4)=110

5 Conclusion

This paper presents a way to armor a knowledge base, by removing some rules and providing some integrity constraints. The adding, in the armored KB, of a new information, consistent with the constraints, does not provide inconsistency, consequently our approach avoids to make non monotonic inference when a new information is added to a KB. So a priori revision is clearly not a AGM revision. Nevertheless it could be interesting to study the links of our approach with contraction [Gärdenfors88].

In previous works [Dupin-Loiseau00], we compared validation versus revision. The validation approach attempts to measure the KB quality so that, if necessary, it can suggest to the expert to improve it. The KB refinement is supported by such a quality measurement. Our new approach for a priori revision extends the notion of diagnosis for validation [Bouali&al97] to diagnosis for revision. The computation of possible diagnoses led us to make restrictions about the syntactical form of the KB and about the new information, these restrictions are directly inspired from the validation field. A point to study is to see if considering any kind of formula as new information is of

any interest for a priori revision. If it is the case, we must study how the algorithms given for a priori revision can be extended in order to deal with any knowledge base in propositional logic.
We can remark that our minimality criterion is purely syntactic and does not recognize that different sets of constraints are equivalent. So further study can examine when it is interesting to propose a reformulation of the set of constraints.

References

[Alchourrón&al85] Alchourrón, Gärdenfors and Makinson. On the logic of theory change: partial meet contraction and revision functions. Symbolic Logic, vol 50, 510-530, 1985.

[Benferhat&al93] Benferhat, Cayrol, Dubois, Lang, Prade. Inconsistency management and prioritized syntax-based entailment. IJCAI, vol 3, 640-645, 1993.

[Benferhat&al95] Benferhat and Smets. Belief functions for logical problems: representing default rules in ε-beliefs logics. In Abstract of the Dagstuhl Seminar, 1993.

[Bezzazi&al98] Bezzazi H., Janot S., Konieczny S., Pino Perez R. Analysing Rational Properties of change operators based on forward chaining. In Transactions and Change in Logic Databases . LNCS Vol. 1472 , pp 317-339.

[Bouali-Loiseau95] Bouali, Loiseau. Rule Base Diagnosis for debugging. EUROVAV, 225-240, 1995.

[Bouali&al97] Bouali, Loiseau, Rousset. Revision of Rule Bases. EUROVAV, 193-204, 1997.

[Brewka89] G. Brewka. Preferred subtheories: an extended logical framework for default reasoning. IJCAI, 1043-1048, 1989.

[Cayrol-Lagasquie95]. Cayrol, Lagasquie-Schiex. Non-monotonic syntax-based entailment: a classification of consequence relations. Lecture notes in AI, 946, p. 107-114, 1995.

[Dubois&al92] Dubois, Lang, Prade. Inconsistency in possibilistic knowledge bases -To live or not live with it. Fuzzy Logic for the Management of Uncertainty, Wiley, 335-351, 1992.

[Dupin&al94] Dupin de Saint-Cyr, Lang and Schiex. Penalty logic and its link with Dempster-Shafer theory. In Proc. of the 10th Uncertainty in AI, p. 204-211, 1994.

[Dupin-Loiseau00] Dupin de Saint-Cyr, Loiseau. Validation et révision. 12ème Congrès Francophone AFRIF-AFIA de RFIA, Paris 1-3 février 2000, vol I, pages 175-183. 2000.

[Gärdenfors88] Gärdenfors P., Knowledge in Flux- Modeling the dynamic of epistemic states. The MIT Press, Cambridge, 1988.

[Katsuno-Mendelzon91] Katsuno, Mendelzon. On the difference between updating a knowledge base and revising it. Principles of Knowledge Representation, p. 387-394, 1991.

[deKleer86] de Kleer, J. An assumption-based truth-maintenance system. Artificial Intelligence, vol.28(2), p.127-224 1986.

[deKleer-Williams87] de Kleer, J. Williams, B.C. Diagnosing Multiple Faults. AI(32), 97-130 1987.

[Lehmann92] D. Lehmann. 1992. Another perspective on default reasoning. Tec. Report.

[Nebel91] B. Nebel. Belief revision and default reasoning: syntax-based approaches. In Proc. of the 2nd KR, p. 417-428. Cambridge, MA, 1991.

[Pinkas91] G. Pinkas. Propositional nonmonotonic reasoning and inconsistency in symmetric neural networks. In Prof. of the 12th IJCAI. p. 525-530. Sydney, Australia, 1991.

[Reiter87] Reiter, R. A theory of diagnosis from first principles. AI, vol 32, p. 57-95, 1987.

[Rescher64] N. Rescher. Hypothetical Reasoning. North-Holland, 1964.

[Winslett88] M. Winslett. Reasoning about action using a possible models approach. AAAI, p.89-93, 1988.

Some Operators for Iterated Revision

Sébastien Konieczny[1] and Ramón Pino Pérez[1,2]

[1] Centre de Recherche en Informatique de Lens
Université d'Artois
SP 16 - Rue de l'Université
62300 Lens - FRANCE
{konieczny,pino}@cril.univ-artois.fr
[2] Facultad de Ciencias
Universidad de Los Andes
Mérida, VENEZUELA
pino@ciens.ula.ve

Abstract. We propose a construction that allows to define operators for iterated revision from "classical" AGM revision operators. We call those operators *revision with memory operators*. We show that the operators obtained have nice logical properties. We illustrate this construction with the well-known Dalal revision operator. We also give two new particular revision operators based on the revision operators on OTP proposed by Ryan [20]. His operator do not satisfy a lot of logical properties. The two operators we give based on OTP satisfy all wanted revision properties.

1 Introduction

One of the predominant approaches to model belief change was proposed by Alchourrón, Gärdenfors and Makinson and is known as the AGM framework [1,10]. The core of this framework is a set of logical properties that a revision operator has to satisfy to guarantee a nice behaviour.

A drawback of AGM definition of revision is that it is a static one, that means that, with this definition of revision operators, one can have a rational one step revision but the conditions for the iteration of the process are very weak. The problem is that AGM postulates state conditions only between the initial knowledge base, the new evidence and the resulting knowledge base. But the way to perform further revisions on the new knowledge base does not depend on the way the old knowledge base was revised.

Numerous proposals have tried to state a logical characterization that adequatly models iterated belief change behaviour [8,7,5,13,17,16,12]. The more famous one seems to be [8]. The main idea that is common to all of those works is that the belief base framework is not sufficient to encompass iterated revision, since one needs some additional information for coding the revision policy of the agent. So the need of *epistemic states* to encode the agent "state of mind" is widely accepted. An epistemic state allows to code agent's beliefs but also to code its relative confidence in alternative possible states of the world. Epistemic states can be represented by several means: pre-orders on interpretations [8,13],

S. Benferhat and P. Besnard (Eds.): ECSQARU 2001, LNAI 2143, pp. 498–509, 2001.

conditionals [5,8], epistemic entrenchments [21,16], prioritized belief bases [2,3], etc. In this paper we will focus on the representation of epistemic states in terms of pre-orders on interpretations.

What we propose in this paper is not yet an other logical characterization, but the definition of a family of operators, that we call *revision with memory operators*, that aims to have good iteration properties.

Dalal-like revision operators are sometimes decry for their *a priori*, *extra-logical* information which represents the distance that they use to order interpretations. We give two operators derived from Ryan's OTP revision operator [20]. We will see that Ryan's operator does not satisfy the wanted logical properties and give two modifications of Ryan OTP revision operator that will. These three operators are interesting since, conversely to Dalal-like operators, there is no *a priori* distance. This information is provided by the formulae themselves in a very natural (syntactical) way.

In section 2 we recall the logical characterization of Darwiche and Pearl. In section 3 we give the definition of revision with memory operators and state the general logical results. Then, in section 4 we provide five examples of operators. Apart from Ryan operator (section 4.3), that is not a revision with memory operator, the four other operators have nice logical properties. Three of them are, as far as we know, new operators. We conclude in section 5 by some general remarks.

2 Iterated Revision Postulates

We give here a formulation of AGM postulates for belief revision *à la* Katsuno and Mendelzon [11]. More exactly we give a formulation of these postulates in terms of epistemic states [8]. The epistemic states framework is an extension of the belief bases one. Intuitively an epistemic state can be seen as a composed information: the beliefs of the agent, plus all information that agent needs about how to perform revision (preference ordering, conditionals, etc.). Then we give the additional iteration postulates proposed by Darwiche and Pearl [8].

2.1 Formal Preliminaries

We will work in the finite propositional case. A belief base φ is a set of formulae, which can be considered as the formula that is the conjunction of its formulae.

The set of all interpretations is denoted $\mathcal{W}$. Let φ be a formula, $Mod(\varphi)$ denotes the set of models of φ, *i.e.* $Mod(\varphi) = \{I \in \mathcal{W} : \ I \models \varphi\}$.

A pre-order $\leq$ is a reflexive and transitive relation, and $<$ is its strict counterpart, i.e $I < J$ if and only if $I \leq J$ and $J \not\leq I$. As usual, $\simeq$ is defined by $I \simeq J$ iff $I \leq J$ and $J \leq I$.

To each epistemic state Ψ is associated a belief base $Bel(\Psi)$ which is a propositional formula and which represents the objective (logical) part of Ψ. The models of Ψ are the models of its associated belief base, thus $Mod(\Psi) = Mod(Bel(\Psi))$. Let Ψ be an epistemic state and μ be a sentence denoting the new information. $\Psi \circ \mu$ denotes the epistemic state resulting of the revision of Ψ by μ. For reading convenience we will write respectively $\Psi \vdash \mu$, $\Psi \wedge \mu$ and $I \models \Psi$ instead of $Bel(\Psi) \vdash \mu$, $Bel(\Psi) \wedge \mu$ and $I \models Bel(\Psi)$.

Two epistemic states are equivalent, noted $\Psi \equiv \Psi'$, if and only if their objective parts are equivalent formulae, *i.e.* $Bel(\Psi) \leftrightarrow Bel(\Psi')$. Two epistemic states are equal, noted $\Psi = \Psi'$, if and only if they are identical. Thus equality is stronger than equivalence. In fact *equivalence* denotes a static equivalence, since after a belief change, the two epistemic states can lead to very different ones, whereas *equality* denotes a dynamic equivalence between epistemic states, since all sequences of belief change perform on these two epistemic states will lead to two equal epistemic states[1].

2.2 AGM Postulates for Epistemic States

Let Ψ be an epistemic state and μ and φ be formulae. An operator $\circ$ that maps an epistemic state Ψ and a formula μ to an epistemic state $\Psi \circ \mu$ is said to be a revision operator on epistemic states if it satisfies the following postulates [8]:

(R*1) $\Psi \circ \mu \vdash \mu$
(R*2) If $\Psi \wedge \mu \nvdash \bot$, then $\Psi \circ \mu \leftrightarrow \Psi \wedge \mu$
(R*3) If $\mu \nvdash \bot$, then $\Psi \circ \mu \nvdash \bot$
(R*4) If $\Psi_1 = \Psi_2$ and $\mu_1 \leftrightarrow \mu_2$, then $\Psi_1 \circ \mu_1 \equiv \Psi_2 \circ \mu_2$
(R*5) $(\Psi \circ \mu) \wedge \varphi \vdash \Psi \circ (\mu \wedge \varphi)$
(R*6) If $(\Psi \circ \mu) \wedge \varphi \nvdash \bot$, then $\Psi \circ (\mu \wedge \varphi) \vdash (\Psi \circ \mu) \wedge \varphi$

This is nearly the Katsuno and Mendelzon formulation of AGM postulates [11], the only differences are that we work with epistemic states instead of belief bases and that postulate (R*4) is weaker than its AGM counterpart. See [8] for a full motivation of this definition.

A representation theorem, stating how revisions can be characterized in terms of pre-orders on interpretations, holds. In order to give such semantical representation, the concept of faithful assignment on epistemic states is defined.

Definition 1. *A function that maps each epistemic state Ψ to a pre-order $\leq_\Psi$ on interpretations is called a faithful assignment over epistemic states if and only if:*

1. *If $I \models \Psi$ and $J \models \Psi$, then $I \simeq_\Psi J$*
2. *If $I \models \Psi$ and $J \not\models \Psi$, then $I <_\Psi J$*
3. *If $\Psi_1 = \Psi_2$, then $\leq_{\Psi_1} = \leq_{\Psi_2}$*

Now the reformulation of Katsuno and Mendelzon [11] representation theorem in terms of epistemic states is:

Theorem 1 *A revision operator $\circ$ satisfies postulates (R*1-R*6) if and only if there exists a faithful assignment that maps each epistemic state Ψ to a total pre-order $\leq_\Psi$ such that:*

$$Mod(\Psi \circ \mu) = \min(Mod(\mu), \leq_\Psi)$$

Notice that this theorem gives information only on the objective part of the resulting epistemic state.

[1] note that $\Psi = \Psi'$ implies $\Psi \equiv \Psi'$.

2.3 Darwiche and Pearl Postulates

A strong limitation of AGM revision postulates is that they impose very weak constraints on the iteration of the revision process. Darwiche and Pearl [7,8] proposed postulates for iterated revision. The aim of these postulates is to keep as much as possible of conditional beliefs[2] of the old belief base. So, besides postulates (R*1-R*6), a revision operator has to satisfy:

(C1) If $\varphi \vdash \mu$, then $(\Psi \circ \mu) \circ \varphi \equiv \Psi \circ \varphi$
(C2) If $\varphi \vdash \neg\mu$, then $(\Psi \circ \mu) \circ \varphi \equiv \Psi \circ \varphi$
(C3) If $\Psi \circ \varphi \vdash \mu$, then $(\Psi \circ \mu) \circ \varphi \vdash \mu$
(C4) If $\Psi \circ \varphi \nvdash \neg\mu$, then $(\Psi \circ \mu) \circ \varphi \nvdash \neg\mu$

These postulates can be explained as follows: (C1) states that if two pieces of information arrive and if the second implies the first, the second alone would give the same belief base. (C2) says that when two contradictory pieces of information arrive, the second alone would give the same belief base. (C3) states that an information should be retained after revising by a second information such that, when revising the current belief base by it, the first one holds. (C4) says that no piece of information can contribute to its own denial.

3 Building Memory Operators from "Classical" AGM Ones

A "classical" AGM revision operator is equivalent to a faithful assignment over belief bases as stated in the following theorem [11].

Definition 2. *A function that maps each* **belief base** φ *to a pre-order* $\leq_\varphi$ *on interpretations is called a faithful assignment over belief bases if and only if:*

1. *If* $I \models \varphi$ *and* $J \models \varphi$*, then* $I \simeq_\varphi J$
2. *If* $I \models \varphi$ *and* $J \not\models \varphi$*, then* $I <_\varphi J$
3. *If* $\varphi_1 \leftrightarrow \varphi_2$*, then* $\leq_{\varphi_1} = \leq_{\varphi_2}$

Theorem 2 *A revision operator* $\circ$ *satisfies "classical" AGM postulates (R1-R6)*[3] *if and only if there exists a faithful assignment (over belief bases) that maps each belief base* φ *to a total pre-order* $\leq_\varphi$ *such that:*

$$Mod(\varphi \circ \mu) = \min(Mod(\mu), \leq_\varphi)$$

So one can define a revision operator directly by defining the corresponding faithful assignment over belief bases. It is the case for most distance-based revision operators such as Dalal operator for example [6,11].

More precisely we say that a revision operator $\circ$ is defined from a distance d iff the following conditions hold:

---

[2] a conditional belief can be expressed as "if μ would be the case, then φ must be true"

[3] it is the same set of postulates than (R*1-R*6) but expressed for belief bases instead of belief states (*cf* [11]).

- d is a distance, that is d is a function $d : \mathcal{W} \times \mathcal{W} \mapsto \mathbb{R}^+$ that satisfies: $d(I, J) = d(J, I)$ and $d(I, J) = 0$ iff $I = J$.
- Then the distance between an interpretation I and a belief base φ is defined as: $d(I, \varphi) = \min\{d(I, J) : J \models \varphi\}$
- This distance induces a faithful assignment: $I \leq_\varphi J$ iff $d(I, \varphi) \leq d(J, \varphi)$
- And the revision operator is defined by $Mod(\varphi \circ \mu) = \min(Mod(\mu), \leq_\varphi)$

One can check that the assignment obtained like this is a faithful assignment and thus that all operators defined in this way satisfy AGM postulates. It can also be easily checked that operators defined in this way do not satisfy a lot of iterated revision postulates.

Now we will give a construction that allows, from a given faithful assignment (*i.e.* from a given "classical" revision operator), to define an other revision operator that satisfy AGM postulates but also most of iterated revision postulates.

First, let us notice that an epistemic state can be represented by a total pre-order on interpretations as suggested by theorem 1 and by several related works (*cf* e.g [8,3]). So, with this particular representation, that is if we identify the epistemic state Ψ with a pre-order $\leq_\Psi$, the belief base $Bel(\Psi)$ is simply the formula whose models are minimal for the pre-order, that is $Bel(\Psi) = \min(\mathcal{W}, \leq_\Psi)$. And the other interpretations are ordered according to their relative plausibility for the agent. For example $I \leq_\Psi J$ means that the agent that is in the epistemic state Ψ consider I as more plausible than J. It is this preferential information that can be used to encompass the iterated revision behaviour, by considering revision operators as functions that maps a pre-order (epistemic state) and a formula (new information) into a new pre-order (epistemic state). This idea is the mainstay in most of iterated revision works [21,8,16].

So using this representation by means of pre-orders on interpretations and theorem 1 we will define a familly of revision operators as follows:

Definition 3. *Suppose that we dispose of a function that maps each belief base φ to a pre-order $\leq_\varphi$. Then we define the epistemic state (the pre-order) $\Psi \circ \varphi$ result of the revision of Ψ by the new information φ as:*

$$I \leq_{\Psi \circ \varphi} J \text{ iff } I <_\varphi J \text{ or}$$
$$I \simeq_\varphi J \text{ and } I \leq_\Psi J$$

Then one can check that:

Theorem 3 *If the function that maps each belief base φ to a total pre-order $\leq_\varphi$ is a faithful assignment over belief bases, then the revision operator on epistemic states defined in definition 3 satisfies postulates (R*1-R*6). We will call* revision operators with memory *those operators.*

So with definition 3, one can start from any epistemic state (total pre-order over interpretations) and carry on iterated revisions. A particular epistemic state we can mention is the "empty" epistemic state, where the agent has no belief and no preferential information, that is such that $\forall I, J\ I \simeq J$. We will note Ξ this epistemic state. So the objective part of this epistemic state is $Bel(\Xi) = \top$. It can be considered as the epistemic state generalisation of $\top$ for the belief base framework, since they are both neutral elements for the corresponding operators:

$\Psi \circ \Xi = \Psi$ (as $\varphi \circ \top = \varphi$ in the belief base framework). One can consider that all agents start with this epistemic sate (we will consider this in the examples).

In fact the family defined is more specific than that, since there are more properties that are satisfied by those operators:

(H4) If $\Psi_1 = \Psi_2$ and $\mu_1 \leftrightarrow \mu_2$, then $\Psi_1 \circ \mu_1 = \Psi_2 \circ \mu_2$
(C) If $\varphi \wedge \mu$ is satisfiable, then $\Psi \circ \varphi \circ \mu \equiv \Psi \circ (\varphi \wedge \mu)$

(H4) is a strenghten of (R*4). (C) states that when one revises successively by two consistent pieces of information, it amounts to revise by their conjunction. It is close to a postulate proposed by Nayak and al. [17] called *Conjunction*, but (C) is weaker than *Conjunction*, since it requires only the equivalence of the two resulting epistemic states, not the equality. See [12] for a full logical characterization of revision with memory operators.

Concerning iteration postulates stated by Darwiche and Pearl [8]:

Theorem 4 *Revision operators with memory satisfy postulates (C1),(C3) and (C4).*

It can be also easily checked that (C2) is satisfied by a unique operator with memory, since it demands (in the presence of the other revision postulates), that the pre-order associated to a belief base by the faithful assignment on belief base used in definition 3 is a two-level pre-order with the models of the belief base at the lowest level and the counter-models at the higher one. This operator will be presented in the next section.

So most of our revision with memory operators do not satisfy (C2). But we do not consider this as a drawback. We rather think that it is (C2) that is not fully satisfactory.

In fact, in [7] the set of postulates (C1-C4) has first been given as a complement to usual "classical" AGM postulates. Freund and Lehmann [9] have shown that (C2) is inconsistent with those postulates. Furthermore Lehmann [13] has shown that (C1) plus AGM postulates imply (C3) and (C4). In [8] Darwiche and Pearl have rephrased their postulates (and AGM ones) in terms of epistemic states instead of belief bases, and thus have removed these logical contradictions.

But we do not think that it is enough to requalify (C2) and we think that satisfy (C2) can lead to counterintuitive results. Consider the following example:

Example 1 *Consider a circuit containing an adder and a multiplier. In this example we have two atomic propositions,* adder_ok *and* multiplier_ok, *denoting respectively the fact that the adder and the multiplier are working. We have initially no information about this circuit ($\Psi = \Xi$) and we learn that the adder and the multiplier are working ($\mu =$ adder_ok $\wedge$ multiplier_ok). Then someone tells us that the adder is not working ($\varphi = \neg$ adder_ok). There is, then, no reason to "forget" that the multiplier is working, which is imposed by (C2): $\varphi \models \neg\mu$ so by (C2) we have $\Psi \circ \mu \circ \varphi \equiv (\Psi \circ \varphi) \equiv \varphi$.*

This example is a slight modification of an example given in [8]. So, in some cases, postulates (C2) induces exactly the same kind of bad behaviour it tries to prevent.

4 Some Revision with Memory Operators

4.1 Basic Memory Operator

Let us define the assignment that maps each belief base to a pre-order in the following way:

Definition 4. *$I \le^b_\varphi J$ if and only if $I \models \varphi$ or*
$I \not\models \varphi$ and $J \not\models \varphi$

So we have what we shall call a basic order, which is a two-level order (at most), with the models of φ at the lower level and the other worlds at the higher level.

Definition 5. *The* basic memory operator *is the memory operator obtained from this assignment (i.e. the operator obtained by definitions 4 and 3).*

Even with this basic order on belief bases, one can build very complex epistemic states. This is due to revision memory. We illustrate the behaviour of this operator through some simple examples.

Example 2 *Consider a language $\mathcal{L}$ with only two propositional letters a and b. We will denote interpretations simply by the truth assignment, i.e 10 denotes the interpretation mapping a to true and b to false. Two interpretations are equivalent, with respect to the pre-order, if they appear at the same level. An interpretation I is better than another interpretation J ($I \le J$) if it appears at a lower level. Let us see some examples of epistemic states:*

$$\le^b_{\Xi\circ a\circ b} = \begin{array}{c} 00 \\ 10 \\ 01 \\ 11 \end{array} \quad \le^b_{\Xi\circ a\wedge b} = \begin{array}{c} 00\ 01\ 10 \\ 11 \end{array} \quad \le^b_{\Xi\circ(a\wedge b)\circ a} = \begin{array}{c} 00\ 01 \\ 10 \\ 11 \end{array} \quad \le^b_{\Xi\circ(a\wedge b)\circ a\circ\neg b} = \begin{array}{c} 01 \\ 11 \\ 00 \\ 10 \end{array}$$

$$\le^b_{\Xi\circ(a\wedge b)\circ\neg b} = \begin{array}{c} 01 \\ 11 \\ 00\ 10 \end{array} \quad \le^b_{\Xi\circ a\circ b\circ\neg(a\wedge b)} = \begin{array}{c} 11 \\ 00 \\ 10 \\ 01 \end{array} \quad \le^b_{\Xi\circ a\circ(a\wedge b)\circ\neg(a\wedge b)} = \begin{array}{c} 11 \\ 00\ 01 \\ 10 \end{array}$$

The assignment defined is a faithful assignment on belief bases, with theorems 3 and 4, it is easy to show that:

Theorem 5 *The only revision operator with memory that satisfies (R*1-R*6) and (C1-C4) is the basic memory revision operator.*

This operator has been already studied in the litterature under different particular representations: in [16] with epistemic entrenchments, in [2] with polynomials and syntactic belief bases. Finally, we can note that Liberatore has shown [15] that several problems are computationally simpler for the basic memory operator than for the other iterated belief revision proposals (including Boutilier's natural revision [4], Lehmann's ranking revision [13] and Williams' transmutations [21]).

4.2 Dalal Memory Operator

We use in this section the Hamming distance between interpretations[4] and then the Dalal distance between an interpretation I and a belief base φ is defined as $d(I, \varphi) = \min_{J \models \varphi}(dist(I, J))$.

Let's define the assignment that maps each belief base to a pre-order in the following way:

Definition 6. *$I \leq_{\varphi}^{d} J$ if and only if $d(I, \varphi) \leq d(J, \varphi)$.*

So we have a pre-order with the models of φ at the lowest level and the other worlds in the higher levels.

Definition 7. *The* Dalal memory operator *is the memory operator obtained from this assignment (i.e. the operator obtained by definitions 6 and 3).*

We can show on a toy example that this operator differs from classical Dalal revision operator [6,11]. Let a and b be two propositional letters and consider for example the sequence $\Psi = \Xi \circ a \circ b \circ \neg(a \wedge b)$. The classical Dalal operator gives $Bel(\Psi) = (a \wedge \neg b) \vee (\neg a \wedge b)$. Whereas Dalal memory operator gives $Bel(\Psi) = (\neg a \wedge b)$. This behaviour seems more natural since at the penultimate step we learnt that b was true, and it is normal to keep some credit for this evidence in the following step. It is in this way, that our operators use revision "memory".

4.3 Ryan OTP Operator

Mark Ryan has proposed to apply his *Ordered Presentations of Theories* (or OTP) to belief revision [20]. Very roughly, an OTP is a multi-set of formulae equipped with a partial pre-order. This pre-order represents the relative reliability of the sources of each formula. So, using a linear order, one can express the fact that the new information is more reliable than older ones and thus can simulate iterated revisions. To give the definition of OTP is not a subject of this work, the interested reader can see e.g [19]. We will simply introduce the notions needed to define the OTP revision operator.

First we have to define what the monotonicities of a formula are.

Definition 8. *Let I be an interpretation and p be a propositional letter, then $I^{[p]}$ (respectively $I^{[\neg p]}$) denotes the interpretation that is identical to I on each propositional letter except (maybe) on the propositional letter p that is assigned to true (resp. false).*

Definition 9. *Let φ be a consistent formula and p be a propositional letter.*

1. *φ is* monotonic in p *if $I \models \varphi$ implies that $I^{[p]} \models \varphi$.*
2. *φ is* anti-monotonic in p *if $I \models \varphi$ implies that $I^{[\neg p]} \models \varphi$.*

---

[4] the Hamming distance between two interpretations is the number of propositional letters on which the two interpretations differ

The set of symbols in which φ is monotonic (resp. anti-monotonic) is noted φ^+ (resp. φ^-). If $\varphi \leftrightarrow \bot$, then $\varphi^+ = \varphi^- = \emptyset$.

After this definition, Ryan defines an inference relation that he named *natural entailment*.

Definition 10. *φ naturally entails μ, written $\varphi \mid\!\sim_N \mu$, if $\varphi \vdash \mu$, $\varphi^+ \subseteq \mu^+$ and $\varphi^- \subseteq \mu^-$.*

This relation has some nice properties, in particular it does not allow to add irrelevant disjuncts in the conclusions (for example $p \mid\!\not\sim_N p \vee q$). See [19] for more details.

Finally, the preference relation associated with a formula φ is given by the set of natural consequences that the interpretations satisfy, that is:

Definition 11. *Let φ be a formula, and I, J two interpretations, the relation $\preceq_\varphi$ is defined as: $I \preceq_\varphi J$ if for each μ such that $\varphi \mid\!\sim_N \mu$, $(J \models \mu \Rightarrow I \models \mu)$ holds.*

So an interpretation is better than another if it satisfies more natural consequences. Note that the relation $\preceq_\varphi$ is a partial pre-order.

Definition 12. *The* Ryan operator *is the operator obtained from this assignment (i.e. the operator obtained by definitions 11 and 3).*

Because the starting assignment takes partial pre-orders as values, Ryan operator does not satisfy all the postulates. More precisely, one has the following result [20]:

Theorem 6 *The Ryan revision operator satisfies postulates (R*1), (R*3), (R*4), and (R*5), but does not satisfy (R*2) and (R*6).*

A counter-example to (R*2) and (R*6), given in [20], is the following:

Let $\varphi_1 = p \vee q \vee r$, $\varphi_2 = \neg p \wedge \neg q \wedge \neg r$ and $\varphi_3 = (p \leftrightarrow q) \wedge \neg r$. Then for (R*2), take $\Psi = \Xi \circ \varphi_1 \circ \varphi_2$ and $\varphi = \varphi_3$. Then $Mod(\Psi) = \{011, 101, 110\}$ and $Mod(\varphi) = \{000, 001, 010, 100, 110, 111\}$, so $Mod(\Psi \wedge \varphi) = \{110\}$ whereas $Mod(\Psi \circ \varphi) = \{110, 001\}$. The same counter-example holds for (R*6) also by putting $\Psi = \Xi \circ \varphi_1$, $\varphi = \varphi_2$ and $\mu = \varphi_3$.

These two violations of the rationality postulates seem to be very awkward. Especially (R*2) seems hardly debatable. The question is: how can we modify Ryan's definition in order to satisfy these properties ? In fact, the easiest way to modify this operator in order to obtain revision with memory operators is to "complete" the $\preceq_\varphi$ partial pre-orders in order to obtain total pre-orders. This can be achieved by two means that give the two following operators.

4.4 Closure of the Pre-order

First, following the construction of the rational closure of a conditional belief base [14] (see also Pearl's System Z [18]), we can figure out a lazy deformation of the pre-order, that is, the deformation that transforms the partial pre-order in a total pre-order with a minimal effort.

Definition 13. *Let $\rho_\varphi(I)$ be the "distance from I to φ" in the following sense:*

1. *If $I \in \min(\mathcal{W}, \preceq_\varphi)$ then $\rho_\varphi(I) = 0$,*
2. *Otherwise $\rho_\varphi(I) = a$, where a is the length of the longest chain of strict inequalities $I_0 \prec_\varphi \ldots \prec_\varphi I_n$ with $I_0 \in \min(\mathcal{W}, \preceq_\varphi)$ and $I_n = I$.*

This "distance" gives a total pre-order on interpretations:

Definition 14. *$I \leq_\varphi^{\mathrm{OTP}_1} J$ if and only if $\rho_\varphi(I) \leq \rho_\varphi(J)$.*

We illustrate this principle of "minimal effort" with an example: Let $\varphi = (\neg a \vee \neg b) \wedge \neg c$ be a belief base.

Fig. 1. Closure of the pre-order

The left hand side presents the partial pre-order $\preceq_\varphi$. Arrows $I \leftarrow J$ denote $I \prec_\varphi J$ (for reading convenience we do not represent transitivity, reflexivity and the equivalence between minimal interpretations). The right hand side presents the $\leq_\varphi^{\mathrm{OTP}_1}$ corresponding pre-order. It is clear that if $I \prec_\varphi J$ then $I <_\varphi^{\mathrm{OTP}_1} J$. Thus the only interpretation that is not straightforwardly placed is 110. The "minimal effort" is being illustrated here as follows: the first place where can be placed 001 is at the second level, so it is the chosen level. Conversely, for the interpretation 011 for example, the first "acceptable" level is the third one because there is an interpretation (001) that is strictly better than 011 which is occupying the second level.

It is easy to show that the function that maps each belief base φ to a total pre-order $\leq_\varphi^{\mathrm{OTP}_1}$ is a faithful assignement. Then we build our memory operator as usual:

Definition 15. *The* OTP$_1$ memory operator *is the memory operator obtained from this assignment (i.e. the operator obtained by definitions 14 and 3).*

4.5 Using Cardinalities

A second way to define a total pre-order from Ryan revision operator is to interpret it differently. The idea of the $\preceq_\varphi$ order, defining Ryan operator, is that an interpretation I is better than another J for a belief base φ if I satisfies all the natural consequences that J satisfies. In other terms I is better than J if I satisfies more natural consequences than J. Following this idea we can then focus uniquely on the number of natural consequences satisfied.

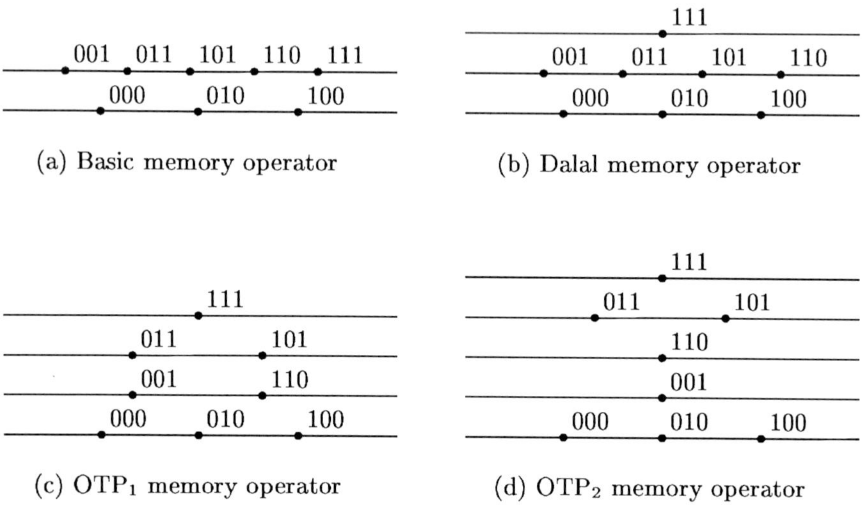

(a) Basic memory operator

(b) Dalal memory operator

(c) OTP_1 memory operator

(d) OTP_2 memory operator

Fig. 2. Behaviour differences between revision with memory operators

Definition 16. *$I \leq_{\varphi}^{\mathrm{OTP}_2} J$ if and only if $card(\{\mu \mid \varphi \mid\!\sim_N \mu$, and $J \models \varphi\}) \leq card(\{\mu \mid \varphi \mid\!\sim_N \mu$, and $I \models \varphi\})$.*

This definition is also a "completion" of the $\preceq_\varphi$ pre-order since if $I \preceq_\varphi J$, then $I \leq_{\varphi}^{\mathrm{OTP}_2} J$.

Then, as usual:

Definition 17. *The* OTP_1 memory operator *is the memory operator obtained from this assignment (i.e. the operator obtained by definitions 14 and 3).*

5 Conclusion

We will end by showing that the four revision with memory operators defined are differents. To show that, it is enough to show that the corresponding faithful assignments are differents. We will show that on the formula $\varphi = (\neg a \vee \neg b) \wedge c$. In figure 2 one can check that the four pre-orders obtained are different.

We have proposed in this paper a method to build revision operators that have interesting properties for iterated revision from any classical AGM operator.

This family of operators exhibits the fact that Darwiche and Pearl's (C2) postulate is certainly too demanding.

We have also introduced two new operators based on Ryan revision operator [20]. An open question is to know if those operators can be recovered from the definition of a classical distance-based revision operator.

We have mainly deal in this paper with the generic construction of iterated revision operators from classical AGM operators, but a full logical characterization of revision with memory operators can be found in [12].

References

1. C. E. Alchourrón, P. Gärdenfors, and D. Makinson. On the logic of theory change: Partial meet contraction and revision functions. *Journal of Symbolic Logic*, 50:510–530, 1985.
2. S. Benferhat, D. Dubois, and O. Papini. A sequential reversible belief revision method based on polynomials. In *Proceedings of the Sixteenth National Conference on Artificial Intelligence (AAAI'99)*, pages 733–738, 1999.
3. S. Benferhat, S. Konieczny and O. Papini and R. Pino Pérez, Iterated revision by pistemic states: axioms, semantics and syntax. In *Proceedings of the Fourteenth European Conference on Artificial Intelligence (ECAI'00)*, pages 13–17, 2000
4. C. Boutilier. Revision sequences and nested conditionals. In *Proceedings of the Thirteenth International Joint Conference on Artificial Intelligence (IJCAI'93)*, 1993.
5. C. Boutilier. Iterated revision and minimal change of conditional beliefs. *Journal of Philosophical Logic*, 25(3):262–305, 1996.
6. M. Dalal. Investigations into a theory of knowledge base revision: preliminary report. In *Proceedings of the National Conference on Artificial Intelligence (AAAI'88)*, pages 475–479, 1988.
7. A. Darwiche and J. Pearl. On the logic of iterated belief revision.In *Proc. of Theoretical Aspects of Reasoning about Knowledge (TARK'94)*, pages 5–23, 1994.
8. A. Darwiche and J. Pearl. On the logic of iterated belief revision. *Artificial Intelligence*, 89:1–29, 1997.
9. M. Freund and D. Lehmann. Belief revision and rational inference. Technical Report TR-94-16, Inst. of Comp. Science, Hebrew University of Jerusalem, 1994.
10. P. Gärdenfors. *Knowledge in flux.* MIT Press, 1988.
11. H. Katsuno and A. O. Mendelzon. Propositional knowledge base revision and minimal change. *Artificial Intelligence*, 52:263–294, 1991.
12. S. Konieczny and R. Pino Pérez. A framework for iterated revision. *Journal of Applied Non-Classical Logics*, 10 (3–4): 339–367, 2000.
13. D. Lehmann. Belief revision, revised. In *Proceedings of the Fourteenth International Joint Conference on Artificial Intelligence (IJCAI' 95)*, pages 1534–1540, 1995.
14. D. Lehmann and M. Magidor. What does a conditional knowledge base entail? *Artificial Intelligence*, 55:1–60, 1992.
15. P. Liberatore. The complexity of iterated belief revision. In *Proceedings of the Sixth International Conference on Database Theory (ICDT'97)*, pages 276–290, 1997.
16. A. C. Nayak. "iterated belief change based on epistemic entrenchment". *Erkenntnis*, 41:353–390, 1994.
17. A. C. Nayak, N. Y. Foo, M. Pagnucco, and A. Sattar. Changing conditional beliefs unconditionally. In *Proceedings of the Sixth Conference of Theoretical Aspects of Rationality and Knowledge (TARK'96)*, pages 119–135. Morgan Kaufmann, 1996.
18. J. Pearl. System z: a natural ordering of defaults with tractable applications to nonmonotonic reasoning. In *Proceedings of the Third Conference on Theoretical Aspects of Reasoning About Knowledge (TARK'90)*, 1990.
19. M. D Ryan. *Ordered Presentations of Theories.* PhD thesis, Imperial College, London, 1992.
20. M. D. Ryan. Belief revision and ordered theory presentations. In A. Fuhrmann and H. Rott, editors, *Logic, Action and Information.* De Gruyter Publishers, 1994.
21. M. A. Williams. Transmutations of knowledge systems. In *Proceedings of the Fourth International Conference on the Principles of Knowledge Representation and Reasoning (KR'94)*, pages 619–629, 1994.

On Computing Solutions to Belief Change Scenarios

James P. Delgrande[1], Torsten Schaub[2]*, Hans Tompits[3], and Stefan Woltran[3]

[1] School of Computing Science, Simon Fraser University,
Burnaby, B.C., Canada V5A 1S6
jim@cs.sfu.ca

[2] Institut für Informatik, Universität Potsdam,
Postfach 60 15 53, D–14415 Potsdam, Germany
torsten@cs.uni-potsdam.de

[3] Institut für Informationssysteme, Abteilung Wissensbasierte Systeme 184/3,
Technische Universität Wien, Favoritenstraße 9–11,
A–1040 Wien, Austria
[tompits,stefan]@kr.tuwien.ac.at

Abstract. Belief change scenarios were recently introduced as a framework for expressing different forms of belief change. In this paper, we show how belief revision and belief contraction (within belief change scenarios) can be axiomatised by means of quantified Boolean formulas. This approach has several benefits. First, it furnishes an axiomatic specification of belief change within belief change scenarios. Second, this axiomatisation allows us to identify upper bounds for the complexity of revision and contraction within belief change scenarios. We strengthen these upper bounds by providing strict complexity results for the considered reasoning tasks. Finally, we obtain an implementation of different forms of belief change by appeal to the existing system QUIP.

1 Introduction

In [3] a consistency-based framework for expressing belief change is developed. The essential idea with respect to revision is that, given a knowledge base K and a sentence for revision α, we express K and α in disjoint languages; coerce (via a maximisation process) the languages to agree on truth values of atoms wherever consistently possible; and finally re-express the result in a single language. The inherent non-determinism of the maximisation process gives rise to two notions of revision. In *choice revision* one such "extension" is selected for the revised state. In general (*skeptical*) *revision*, the revised state consists of the intersection of all such extensions. Belief contraction is defined similarly.

In this paper, we discuss a method to implement this approach to belief change, based on reductions to quantified Boolean formulas. By a quantified Boolean formula (or "QBF" for short) one understands a term which is constructed like an ordinary propositional formula, except that quantifiers ranging over propositional variables may also occur. Quantified Boolean formulas belong thus to the language of second-order logic and allow a compact representation of a large class of properties. Indeed, the

* Affiliated with the School of Computing Science at Simon Fraser University, Burnaby, Canada.

S. Benferhat and P. Besnard (Eds.): ECSQARU 2001, LNAI 2143, pp. 510–521, 2001.

latter is reflected by the fact that the evaluation problem of QBFs—i.e., the problem of determining the truth of a given QBF—is PSPACE-complete, whilst the evaluation problem of QBFs having prenex normal form with i alternating quantifiers is complete for the i-th level of the polynomial hierarchy [17; 18].

The general mechanism of our approach is to translate (in a polynomial way) a given reasoning task into the evaluation problem for QBFs and then using a sophisticated QBF-evaluator to compute the resultant instances. The existence of efficient QBF-solvers, such as the systems developed by Cadoli *et al.* [2], Kleine Büning *et al.* [12], Rintanen [16], or Feldmann *et al.* [8], makes such a rapid prototyping approach practically applicable.

A similar approach for solving various reasoning tasks belonging to the area of nonmonotonic reasoning have been realized in the system QUIP [7; 6; 5]. This prototypical implementation currently handles the computation of the main reasoning tasks for logic-based abduction, default logic, several types of modal nonmonotonic logics, and disjunctive logic programs under the stable model semantics. We implemented the translations for belief change problems by incorporating them into the system QUIP.

Reduction methods to QBFs naturally generalize similar approaches for problems in NP; these latter problems can in turn be solved by translating them (in polynomial time) to SAT, the satisfiability problem of classical propositional logic (see e.g., [11] for such an application in Artificial Intelligence). Besides the implementation of different nonmonotonic reasoning tasks as realized by the system QUIP, successful applications based on reductions to QBFs have also been applied to conditional planning [15].

The expression of belief change problems in terms of QBFs also allows the derivation of upper complexity bounds for the considered reasoning tasks. Moreover, we generalise and improve on the results in [3].

In the next section we briefly introduce QBFs, and describe the belief change scenarios that interest us. In Section 3 we give the polynomial-time constructible reductions of the relevant reasoning tasks into QBFs. Section 4 briefly sketches an implementation of the reductions, and Section 5 supplies some concluding remarks.

2 Background

2.1 Logical Prerequisites

We deal with propositional languages and use the logical symbols $\top$, $\bot$, $\neg$, $\vee$, $\wedge$, $\rightarrow$, and $\equiv$ to construct formulas in the standard way. We write $\mathcal{L}_{\mathcal{P}}$ to denote a language over an alphabet $\mathcal{P}$ of *propositional letters* or *atomic propositions*. Formulas are denoted by Greek lower-case letters (possibly with subscripts). *Knowledge bases*, or, equivalently, *belief sets*, are initially identified with deductively-closed sets of formulas (we use $K, K_1, \ldots$ to denote knowledge bases). So, we have $K = Cn(K)$, where $Cn(\cdot)$ is the deductive closure of the formula or set of formulas given as argument. Later we relax this restriction.

Given an alphabet $\mathcal{P}$, we define a disjoint alphabet $\mathcal{P}'$ as $\mathcal{P}' = \{p' \mid p \in \mathcal{P}\}$. Then, for $\alpha \in \mathcal{L}_{\mathcal{P}}$, we define α' as the result of replacing in α each atom p from $\mathcal{P}$ by the corresponding atom p' in $\mathcal{P}'$ (so implicitly there is an isomorphism between $\mathcal{P}$ and $\mathcal{P}'$). This is defined analogously for sets of formulas.

Quantified Boolean formulas (QBFs) generalize ordinary propositional formulas by the admission of quantifications over propositional variables (QBFs are denoted by Greek upper-case letters). Informally, a QBF of the form $\forall p\, \exists q\, \Phi$ means that for all truth assignments of p there is a truth assignment of q such that Φ is true. For instance, it is easily seen that the QBF $\exists p_1\, \exists p_2\, ((p_1$
$rightarrowp_2) \wedge \forall p_3 (p_3$
$rightarrowp_2))$ evaluates to true.

The precise semantical meaning of QBFs is defined as follows. First, some ancillary notation. An occurrence of a variable v in a QBF Φ is *free* iff it does not appear in the scope of a quantifier $\mathsf{Q}v$ ($\mathsf{Q} \in \{\forall, \exists\}$), otherwise the occurrence of v is *bound*. If Φ contains no free variables, then Φ is *closed*, otherwise Φ is *open*. Furthermore, $\Phi[v_1/\psi_1, \ldots, v_n/\psi_n]$ denotes the result of uniformly substituting the free variables v_i in Φ by formulas ψ_i ($1 \leq i \leq n$).

By an *interpretation*, M, we understand a set of variables. Informally, a variable v is true under M iff $v \in M$. In general, the truth value, $\nu_M(\Phi)$, of a QBF Φ under an interpretation M is recursively defined as follows:

1. if $\Phi = \top$, then $\nu_M(\Phi) = 1$;
2. if $\Phi = \bot$, then $\nu_M(\Phi) = 0$;
3. if $\Phi = v$ is a variable, then $\nu_M(\Phi) = 1$ if $v \in M$, and $\nu_M(\Phi) = 0$ otherwise;
4. if $\Phi = \neg\Psi$, then $\nu_M(\Phi) = 1 - \nu_M(\Psi)$;
5. if $\Phi = (\Phi_1 \wedge \Phi_2)$, then $\nu_M(\Phi) = min(\{\nu_M(\Phi_1), \nu_M(\Phi_2)\})$;
6. if $\Phi = (\Phi_1 \vee \Phi_2)$, then $\nu_M(\Phi) = max(\{\nu_M(\Phi_1), \nu_M(\Phi_2)\})$;
7. if $\Phi = (\Phi_1 \rightarrow \Phi_2)$, then $\nu_M(\Phi) = 1$ iff $\nu_M(\Phi_1) \leq \nu_M(\Phi_2)$;
8. if $\Phi = \forall v\, \Psi$, then $\nu_M(\Phi) = \nu_M(\Psi[v/\top] \wedge \Psi[v/\bot])$;
9. if $\Phi = \exists v\, \Psi$, then $\nu_M(\Phi) = \nu_M(\Psi[v/\top] \vee \Psi[v/\bot])$.

We say that Φ is *true under* M iff $\nu_M(\Phi) = 1$, otherwise Φ is *false under* M. If $\nu_M(\Phi) = 1$, then M is a *model* of Φ. Likewise, for a set S of formulas, if $\nu_M(\Phi) = 1$ for all $\Phi \in S$, then M is a model of S. If Φ has some model, then Φ is said to be *satisfiable*. If Φ is true under any model, then Φ is *valid*. Observe that a closed QBF is either valid or unsatisfiable, because closed QBFs are either true under each interpretation or false under each interpretation. Hence, for closed QBFs, there is no need to refer to particular interpretations.

In the sequel, we use the following abbreviations in the context of QBFs: Let $S = \{\phi_1, \ldots, \phi_n\}$ and $T = \{\psi_1, \ldots, \psi_n\}$ be indexed sets of formulas. Then, $S \leq T$ abbreviates $\bigwedge_{i=1}^{n} (\phi_i \rightarrow \psi_i)$, and $S \equiv T$ is a shorthand for $\bigwedge_{i=1}^{n} (\phi_i \equiv \psi_i)$. Furthermore, for a set $P = \{p_1, \ldots, p_n\}$ of propositional variables and a quantifier $\mathsf{Q} \in \{\forall, \exists\}$, we let $\mathsf{Q}P\, \Phi$ stand for the formula $\mathsf{Q}p_1 \mathsf{Q}p_2 \cdots \mathsf{Q}p_n\, \Phi$. Additionally, for each variable v occurring in some formula, v_{eq} denotes a globally new variable. Accordingly, for a set V of variables, we define $V_{eq} = \{v_{eq} \mid v \in V\}$. Finally, finite sets $T = \{\phi_1, \ldots, \phi_n\}$ of formulas are usually identified with the conjunction $\bigwedge_{i=1}^{n} \phi_i$ of its elements.

The operator $\leq$ is a fundamental tool for expressing tests on sets of formulas which are required to satisfy certain conditions. In particular, we use $\leq$ here in connection with the following task: Given finite sets T and $P = \{\phi_1, \ldots, \phi_n\}$ of formulas, we want to compute all subsets $R \subseteq P$ such that $T \cup R$ is consistent.

This problem can be expressed by the QBF

$$\Phi_{\leq} = \exists V(T \wedge (G \leq P)),$$

where V is the set of all variables occurring in T or P, and $G = \{g_1, \ldots, g_n\}$ is a set of new variables.

Note that G constitutes the set of free variables of $\Phi_{\leq}$. These variables facilitate the selection of those elements of P which determine the sets R such that $T \cup R$ is consistent. More precisely, we have the following properties:

- If M is a model of $\Phi_{\leq}$, then $T \cup \{\phi_i \mid g_i \in M, 1 \leq i \leq n\}$ is consistent.
- If $T \cup R$ is consistent, with $R \subseteq P$, then $\{g_i \mid \phi_i \in R, 1 \leq i \leq n\}$ is a model of $\Phi_{\leq}$.

Let us illustrate the first of these properties. Consider a model M of

$$\Phi_{\leq} = \exists V\Big(T \wedge (g_1 \rightarrow \phi_1) \wedge (g_2 \rightarrow \phi_2) \wedge \ldots \wedge (g_n \rightarrow \phi_n)\Big).$$

Clearly, under M, each conjunct $(g_i \rightarrow \phi_i)$ evaluates to true if $g_i \notin M$, and reduces to ϕ_i otherwise. Hence, $\Phi_{\leq}$ can be transformed into

$$\exists V\Big(T \wedge \bigwedge_{g_i \in M} \phi_i\Big). \tag{1}$$

Obviously, (1) is true under M iff $T \cup \{\phi_i \mid g_i \in M\}$ is consistent.

Note that $\Phi_{\leq}$ is constructed to express *all* subsets $R \subseteq P$ such that $T \cup R$ is consistent. To express, for example, all *maximal* such subsets, some additional elements are required. The computation of maximal sets satisfying certain criteria, using QBFs, is discussed in Section 3.

2.2 Belief Change Scenarios

Following Delgrande and Schaub [3], we define a *belief change scenario* in language $\mathcal{L}_\mathcal{P}$ as a triple $B = (K, U_1, U_2)$, where K, U_1, U_2 are sets of formulas in $\mathcal{L}_\mathcal{P}$. Informally, K is a knowledge base that will be changed such that the set U_1 will be true in the result, and the set U_2 will be consistent with the result. For a base approach to revision we take $U_2 = \emptyset$ and for a base approach to contraction we take $U_1 = \emptyset$.

In the definition below, "maximal" is with respect to set containment (rather than set cardinality). The following definition is central:

Definition 1. *Let $B = (K, U_1, U_2)$ be a belief change scenario in $\mathcal{L}_\mathcal{P}$. Define EQ as a maximal set of equivalences $EQ \subseteq \{p \equiv p' \mid p \in \mathcal{P}\}$ such that*

$$K' \cup EQ \cup U_1 \cup U_2 \nvdash \bot.$$

Then,

$$Cn(K' \cup EQ \cup U_1) \cap \mathcal{L}_\mathcal{P}$$

is a consistent definitional extension *of B.*

Table 1. (Skeptical) revision examples.

K'	α	EQ	$K\dot{+}\alpha$
$p' \wedge q'$	$\neg q$	$\{p \equiv p'\}$	$p \wedge \neg q$
$\neg p' \equiv q'$	$\neg q$	$\{p \equiv p',\ q \equiv q'\}$	$p \wedge \neg q$
$p' \vee q'$	$\neg p \vee \neg q$	$\{p \equiv p',\ q \equiv q'\}$	$p \equiv \neg q$
$p' \wedge q'$	$\neg p \vee \neg q$	$\{p \equiv p'\},\ \{q \equiv q'\}$	$p \equiv \neg q$

Hence, a consistent definitional extension of B is a modification of K in which U_1 is true, and in which U_2 is consistent. We say that EQ *underlies* the consistent definitional extension of B. In the sequel, we restrict the sets of equivalences to $\{p \equiv p' \mid p \text{ occurs in } K \cup U_1 \cup U_2\}$. Clearly, for a given belief change scenario there may be more than one consistent definitional extension.

In Definition 2 and 3 below, we make use of the notion of a *selection function*, c, that for any set $I \neq \emptyset$ has as value some element of I. These primitive functions can be regarded as inducing selection functions c' on belief change scenarios, such that $c'((K, U_1, U_2))$ has as value some consistent definitional extension of (K, U_1, U_2). This is a slight generalisation of selection functions as found in the AGM approach [10].

Definition 1 provides a very general framework for specifying belief change. In the next two definitions we give specific definitions for the belief-change operations *revision* and *contraction*.

Definition 2 (Revision). *Let K be a knowledge base and α a formula, and let $(E_i)_{i\in I}$ be the family of all consistent definitional extensions of $(K, \{\alpha\}, \emptyset)$. Then:*

1. $K\dot{+}_c\alpha = E_i$ *is a* choice revision *of K by α with respect to some selection function c with $c(I) = i$.*
2. $K\dot{+}\alpha = \bigcap_{i\in I} E_i$ *is the* (skeptical) revision *of K by α.*

Table 1 gives examples of (skeptical) revision. The first column gives the original knowledge base, but with atoms already renamed. The second column gives the revision formula, while the third gives the EQ set(s) and the last column gives the results of the revision. For the first and last column, we give a formula whose deductive closure gives the corresponding belief set.

In detail, for the last example, we wish to determine

$$\{p \wedge q\}\dot{+}(\neg p \vee \neg q)\ .$$

We find maximal sets $EQ \subseteq \{p \equiv p', q \equiv q'\}$ such that

$$\{p' \wedge q'\} \cup EQ \cup \{\neg p \vee \neg q\} \cup \emptyset$$

is consistent. We get two such sets of equivalences, namely $EQ_1 = \{p \equiv p'\}$ and $EQ_2 = \{q \equiv q'\}$. Accordingly, we obtain

$$\{p \wedge q\}\dot{+}(\neg p \vee \neg q) = \textstyle\bigcap_{i=1,2} Cn(\{p' \wedge q'\} \cup EQ_i \cup \{\neg p \vee \neg q\}) \cap \mathcal{L}_{\mathcal{P}}.$$

In addition to $(\neg p \vee \neg q)$, we get $(p \vee q)$, jointly implying $(p \equiv \neg q)$.

Contraction is defined similarly to revision.

Table 2. (Skeptical) contraction examples.

K'	α	EQ	$K\dot{-}\alpha$
$p' \wedge q'$	q	$\{p \equiv p'\}$	p
$p' \wedge q' \wedge r'$	$p \vee q$	$\{r \equiv r'\}$	r
$p' \vee q'$	$p \wedge q$	$\{p \equiv p',\ q \equiv q'\}$	$p \vee q$
$p' \wedge q'$	$p \wedge q$	$\{p \equiv p'\},\ \{q \equiv q'\}$	$p \vee q$

Definition 3 (Contraction). *Let K be a knowledge base and α a formula, and let $(E_i)_{i \in I}$ be the family of all consistent definitional extensions of $(K, \emptyset, \{\neg\alpha\})$. Then:*

1. $K\dot{-}_c\alpha = E_i$ *is a* choice contraction *of K by α with respect to some selection function c with $c(I) = i$.*
2. $K\dot{-}\alpha = \bigcap_{i \in I} E_i$ *is the* (skeptical) contraction *of K by α.*

Table 2 gives examples of (skeptical) contraction, using the same format and conventions as Table 1.

In detail, for the first example we wish to determine

$$\{p \wedge q\}\dot{-}q\ .$$

We compute the consistent definitional extensions of $(\{p \wedge q\}, \emptyset, \{\neg q\})$. We rename the propositions in $\{p \wedge q\}$ and look for maximal subsets EQ of $\{p \equiv p', q \equiv q'\}$ such that

$$\{p' \wedge q'\} \cup EQ \cup \emptyset \cup \{\neg q\}$$

is consistent. We obtain $EQ = \{p \equiv p'\}$, yielding

$$\begin{aligned} \{p \wedge q\}\dot{-}q &= Cn(\{p' \wedge q'\} \cup \{p \equiv p'\} \cup \emptyset) \cap \mathcal{L}_{\mathcal{P}} \\ &= Cn(\{p\}). \end{aligned}$$

2.3 Related Work

The approach of the previous subsection combines aspects of general (coherence-based) belief change with aspects of belief base revision [13]. In belief base revision, a knowledge base is an (arbitrary, syntactic) set of formulas that is to be modified, and that represents or characterises the logical closure of this set of formulas. Here, we allow such a syntactic characterisation of knowledge bases. As well, since belief change is phrased in terms of a set of syntactically-distinguished sentences, here the set of atomic sentences, it also resembles base revision. However, in [3] it is shown that this approach (essentially) satisfies the AGM revision and contraction postulates [1], with the exception of the revision postulate $(K\dot{+}8)$ and the contraction postulate $(K\dot{-}8)$. In particular, and in contrast to most approaches to belief base revision, it satisfies the postulate of *irrelevance of syntax*, in that the results of belief change do not depend on the syntactic expression of sentences in a belief change scenario.

We note also that the approach is capable of expressing *multiple contraction* [9] wherein, for belief change scenario (K, U_1, U_2), every element of U_2 would be individually consistent with the resulting knowledge base. However, we do not pursue this generalisation here; rather, we assume that the elements of U_2 will be *jointly* consistent in the resulting knowledge base.

3 Reductions

In this section, we present efficient (polynomial-time constructible) reductions of the relevant reasoning tasks in the context of belief change scenarios into QBFs. More specifically, we deal with the following basic reasoning tasks:

DEFEXT : Decide whether a given belief change scenario B has some consistent definitional extension.

CHOICE : Given a belief change scenario B and some formula ϕ, decide whether ϕ is contained in at least one consistent definitional extension of B.

SKEPTICAL : Given a belief change scenario B and some formula ϕ, decide whether ϕ is contained in all consistent definitional extensions of B.

For all of the above decision problems, we also treat the corresponding *search problems*.

Given a belief change scenario $B = (K, U_1, U_2)$, from now on we assume that K, U_1, and U_2 are finite; thus, these sets are also represented as the conjunction of its elements.

Consider B as above, and let V be the set of variables occurring in K, U_1, or U_2. We define the following basic module:

$$\mathcal{M}[B] = K' \wedge (V_{eq} \leq (V \equiv V')) \wedge U_1,$$

where $V_{eq} = \{v_{eq} \mid v \in V\}$ is a set of new variables.

The decision problem DEFEXT, together with the corresponding search problem, can be expressed as follows:

Theorem 1. *Let $B = (K, U_1, U_2)$ be a belief change scenario in $\mathcal{L}_\mathcal{P}$ and V the atoms occurring in B. Consider the following QBF:*

$$\begin{aligned}\mathcal{F}_{ext}[B] = {} & \exists V \exists V' (\mathcal{M}[B] \wedge U_2) \wedge \\ & \textstyle\bigwedge_{v \in V} \Big(\neg v_{eq} \rightarrow (\neg \exists V \exists V' ((v \equiv v') \wedge \mathcal{M}[B] \wedge U_2)) \Big). \end{aligned} \tag{2}$$

Then, B has a consistent definitional extension iff $\mathcal{F}_{ext}[B]$ is satisfiable. Moreover, the satisfying truth assignments of the free variables V_{eq} of $\mathcal{F}_{ext}[B]$ are in a one-to-one correspondence to the consistent definitional extensions of B. This correspondence is provided by the following two mappings:

1. *For a model M of $\mathcal{F}_{ext}[B]$, the corresponding consistent definitional extension of B is given by $Cn(K' \cup \{v \equiv v' \mid v_{eq} \in M\} \cup U_1) \cap \mathcal{L}_\mathcal{P}$.*
2. *For a consistent definitional extension $Cn(K' \cup EQ \cup U_1) \cap \mathcal{L}_\mathcal{P}$ of B, the set of atoms M with $\{v_{eq} \mid (v \equiv v') \in EQ\}$ is a model of $\mathcal{F}_{ext}[B]$.*

Note that V_{eq} constitutes the set of free variables of $\mathcal{F}_{ext}[B]$. Intuitively, V_{eq} guesses a set EQ of equivalences underlying a definitional extension of B. The first conjunct of $\mathcal{F}_{ext}[B]$ checks consistency, and the second conjunct checks whether EQ is maximal with respect to set containment.

For illustration, consider the belief change scenario $B = (\{p \wedge q\}, \{\neg p \vee \neg q\}, \emptyset)$ from Section 2.2, and the corresponding QBF $\mathcal{F}_{ext}[B]$. The free variables of $\mathcal{F}_{ext}[B]$ are given by $\{p_{eq}, q_{eq}\}$, so we get the following four interpretations serving as potential models of $\mathcal{F}_{ext}[B]$:

$$M_1 = \{\}; \qquad M_3 = \{q_{eq}\};$$
$$M_2 = \{p_{eq}\}; \qquad M_4 = \{p_{eq}, q_{eq}\}.$$

Since B has two consistent definitional extensions, generated by $EQ_1 = \{p \equiv p'\}$ and $EQ_2 = \{q \equiv q'\}$ (cf. Table 1), we expect M_2 and M_3 to be models of $\mathcal{F}_{ext}[B]$. Let us first look at the left conjunct $\exists V \exists V'(\mathcal{M}[B] \wedge U_2)$ of $\mathcal{F}_{ext}[B]$ in (2). For B as above, we obtain

$$\exists V \exists V'(\mathcal{M}[B] \wedge U_2) =$$
$$\exists pqp'q'\Big((p' \wedge q') \wedge (p_{eq} \rightarrow (p \equiv p')) \wedge (q_{eq} \rightarrow (q \equiv q')) \wedge (\neg p \vee \neg q)\Big). \tag{3}$$

This QBF has three models, viz. M_1, M_2, and M_3. Interpretation M_1 is a model because both conjuncts $(p_{eq} \rightarrow (p \equiv p'))$ and $(q_{eq} \rightarrow (q \equiv q'))$ of (3) evaluate to true (given that $p_{eq}, q_{eq} \notin M_1$), and since the remaining formula $(p' \wedge q') \wedge (\neg p \vee \neg q)$ is consistent. For M_2, we similarly get that $(q_{eq} \rightarrow (q \equiv q'))$ is true and that $(p' \wedge q') \wedge (p_{eq} \rightarrow (p \equiv p')) \wedge (\neg p \vee \neg q)$ is consistent, since $\{p', q', p\}$ is a model of $(p' \wedge q') \wedge (p \equiv p') \wedge (\neg p \vee \neg q)$. M_3 is a model by analogous arguments. However, M_4 is not a model of (3). The reason for this fact is that, under M_4, formula (3) can be reduced to

$$(p' \wedge q') \wedge (p \equiv p') \wedge (q \equiv q') \wedge (\neg p \vee \neg q), \tag{4}$$

which is not satisfiable.

Hence, we are left with three possible models of $\mathcal{F}_{ext}[B]$, viz. M_1, M_2, and M_3. Now we investigate the remaining conjuncts of $\mathcal{F}_{ext}[B]$, which are given by

$$\Phi_1 = \Big[\neg p_{eq} \rightarrow \neg \exists pqp'q'\Big((p \equiv p') \wedge (p' \wedge q') \wedge (p_{eq} \rightarrow (p \equiv p')) \wedge \\ \wedge (q_{eq} \rightarrow (q \equiv q')) \wedge (\neg p \vee \neg q)\Big)\Big]$$

and

$$\Phi_2 = \Big[\neg q_{eq} \rightarrow \neg \exists pqp'q'\Big((q \equiv q') \wedge (p' \wedge q') \wedge (p_{eq} \rightarrow (p \equiv p')) \wedge \\ \wedge (q_{eq} \rightarrow (q \equiv q')) \wedge (\neg p \vee \neg q)\Big)\Big].$$

First, consider interpretation M_2. Since $p_{eq} \in M_2$, conjunct Φ_1 evaluates to true, and it remains to analyse Φ_2. The latter formula evaluates to true if

$$\Big((q \equiv q') \wedge (p' \wedge q') \wedge (p_{eq} \rightarrow (p \equiv p')) \wedge (q_{eq} \rightarrow (q \equiv q')) \wedge (\neg p \vee \neg q)\Big) \tag{5}$$

is not satisfiable. However, given M_2, (5) reduces to (4), which is indeed unsatisfiable. Hence, M_2 is a model of Φ_2 and thus also a model of $\mathcal{F}_{ext}[B]$. By a similar argumentation it follows that M_3 is a model of $\Phi_1 \wedge \Phi_2$. It remains to see that M_1 is not a model of $\Phi_1 \wedge \Phi_2$. In fact, it holds that $\nu_{M_1}(\Phi_1) = \nu_{M_1}(\Phi_2) = 0$. We show the case of Φ_1 (the case of Φ_2 follows analogously). Since $M_1 = \{\}$, Φ_1 is false under M_1 iff

$$\exists pqp'q'\Big((p \equiv p') \wedge (p' \wedge q') \wedge (p_{eq} \rightarrow (p \equiv p')) \wedge (q_{eq} \rightarrow (q \equiv q')) \wedge (\neg p \vee \neg q)\Big)$$

is true under M_1. Given that both p_{eq} and q_{eq} are false under M_1, the previous condition holds iff

$$\Big((p \equiv p') \wedge (p' \wedge q') \wedge (\neg p \vee \neg q)\Big) \tag{6}$$

is satisfiable. Clearly, this is trivially the case, since $\{p, p', q'\}$ is a satisfying truth assignment for (6). Thus, M_1 is not a model of Φ_1. This concludes the proof that M_1 is not a model of $\mathcal{F}_{ext}[B]$.

We can also *directly* characterise the models of consistent definitional extensions, by means of the following construction:

Lemma 1. *Let $B = (K, U_1, U_2)$ be a belief change scenario in $\mathcal{L}_\mathcal{P}$, let V be the atoms occurring in B, and let $Cn(K' \cup EQ \cup U_1) \cap \mathcal{L}_\mathcal{P}$ be a consistent definitional extension. Define $\mathcal{M}^*[B]$ as the result of substituting all occurrences of v_{eq} in $\mathcal{M}[B]$ by $\top$ if $(v' \equiv v) \in EQ$ and by $\bot$ otherwise. Then, the models of $\exists V'\mathcal{M}^*[B]$ coincide with the models of $Cn(K' \cup EQ \cup U_1) \cap \mathcal{L}_\mathcal{P}$.*

Theorem 2. *Let B be as in Lemma 1 and consider the QBF*

$$\exists V_{EQ}(\mathcal{F}_{ext}[B] \wedge \exists V'\mathcal{M}[B]). \tag{7}$$

Then, an interpretation M of the free variables V of (7) is a model of (7) iff M is a model of some definitional extension of B.

Next, we discuss the translations of the reasoning tasks CHOICE and SKEPTICAL.

Theorem 3. *Let $B = (K, U_1, U_2)$ be a belief change scenario in $\mathcal{L}_\mathcal{P}$, ϕ a formula, and V the atoms occurring in B and ϕ. Consider the following QBFs:*

$$\mathcal{F}_{choice}[B, \phi] = \mathcal{F}_{ext}[B] \wedge \forall V(\exists V'\mathcal{M}[B] \rightarrow \phi);$$
$$\mathcal{F}_{skept}[B, \phi] = \mathcal{F}_{ext}[B] \wedge \neg\forall V(\exists V'\mathcal{M}[B] \rightarrow \phi).$$

Then:

1. *ϕ is contained in at least one definitional extension of B iff $\exists V_{eq}\, \mathcal{F}_{choice}[B, \phi]$ evaluates to true. Moreover, the satisfying truth assignments of the free variables V_{eq} of $\mathcal{F}_{choice}[B, \phi]$ are in a one-to-one correspondence to the definitional extensions of B containing ϕ.*
2. *ϕ is contained in all definitional extensions of B iff $\neg\exists V_{eq}\, \mathcal{F}_{skept}[B, \phi]$ evaluates to true. Moreover, the satisfying truth assignments of the free variables V_{eq} of $\mathcal{F}_{skept}[B, \phi]$ are in a one-to-one correspondence to the definitional extensions of B not containing ϕ.*

Theorems 1 and 3 provide encodings of reasoning tasks for *arbitrary* belief scenarios. In particular, they include the characterisation of the corresponding reasoning tasks associated with revision and contraction, as illustrated by the revision example discussed previously. For convenience, we list the tasks for revision:

RDEFEXT : Given a knowledge base K and some formula α, decide whether a consistent definitional extension of $B = (K, \{\alpha\}, \emptyset)$ exists.

RCHOICE : Given a knowledge base K and formulas α and ϕ, decide whether there is some choice revision $K \dot{+}_c \alpha$ containing ϕ.

RSKEPTICAL : Given a knowledge base K and formulas α and ϕ, decide whether ϕ is contained in the skeptical revision $K \dot{+} \alpha$.

The corresponding tasks for belief contraction, denoted by CDEFEXT, CCHOICE, and CSKEPTICAL, are defined accordingly.

From the reductions described above, we immediately obtain upper bounds for the computational complexity of the current belief change framework. This follows from the fact that our QBF encodings are polynomial and that the quantifier order of QBFs determines at which level of the polynomial hierarchy the associated evaluation problem lies. More specifically, the evaluation problem of QBFs having quantifier order $\exists\forall$ is complete for the class Σ_2^p, and, dually, the evaluation problem of QBFs having quantifier order $\forall\exists$ is complete for Π_2^p. Thus, since completeness of a decision problem D for a complexity class C implies membership of D in C, inspecting the quantifier order of the above translations yields the upper complexity bounds for the corresponding decision problems. In fact, for all of the above versions of CHOICE and SKEPTICAL, these bounds are *strict*, i.e., the completeness property is preserved for these tasks. This can be seen by providing polynomial mappings from the evaluation problem of QBFs having one quantifier alternation into the respective decision problems associated with belief change scenarios (these mappings represent in effect the inverse relations of the encodings described in Theorem 3). However, for DEFEXT and its variants we actually obtain lower complexity bounds than those for CHOICE and SKEPTICAL (providing the polynomial hierarchy does not collapse), because deciding whether a given belief change scenario $B = (K, U_1, U_2)$ has a consistent definitional extension is equivalent to checking whether $K' \cup U_1 \cup U_2$ is consistent.

Summarizing, we obtain the following complexity results, strengthening the complexity analysis discussed in [3]:

Theorem 4. *We have the following completeness results:*

1. DEFEXT, RDEFEXT, *and* CDEFEXT *are* NP*-complete.*
2. CHOICE, RCHOICE, *and* CCHOICE *are* Σ_2^p*-complete.*
3. SKEPTICAL, RSKEPTICAL, *and* CSKEPTICAL *are* Π_2^p*-complete.*

Let us remark that the NP-completeness of DEFEXT shows that this task can in principle be handled by an existentially quantified QBF, expressing a simple consistency check, as argued above. However, the circumstance that $\mathcal{F}_{ext}[B]$ is somewhat more involving (having quantifier order $\exists\forall$) is due to the fact that this QBF has been constructed to deal also with the corresponding *search problem* of DEFEXT, which is actually more complex than a simple yes-no-answer because of the inherent maximality-checks.

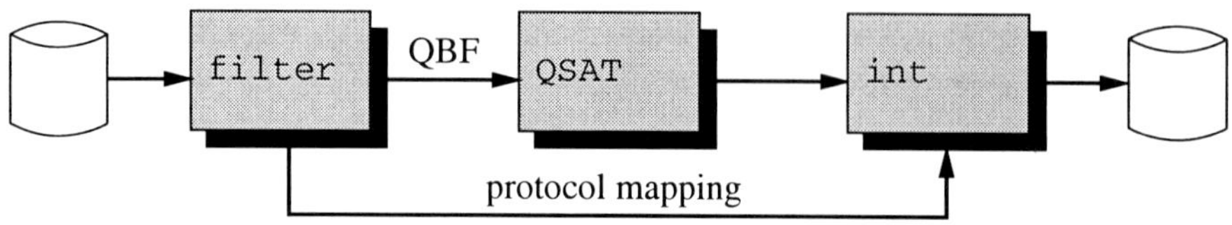

Fig. 1. Architecture to use different QBF-solvers.

4 Implementation

Our methodology for expressing reasoning tasks associated with belief change scenarios in terms of quantified Boolean formulas is motivated by the availability of several practicably efficient QBF-solvers. Among the different tools, there is a propositional theorem-prover, `boole`, based on *binary decision diagrams* (the system can be downloaded from the Web at http://www.cs.cmu.edu/~modelcheck/bdd.html), a system using a generalized resolution principle [12], several provers implementing an extended Davis-Putnam procedure [2; 8; 16], as well as a distributed algorithm running on a PC-cluster [8]. With the exception of `boole`, these tools do not accept arbitrary QBFs, but require the input formula to be in *prenex conjunctive normal form*. To avoid an exponential increase of formula size, *structure preserving normal form translations* [4; 14] can be used to translate a general QBF into the required normal form. In contrast to the usual normal form translation based on distributivity laws, structure preserving normal form translations introduce new labels for subformula occurrences and are polynomial in the length of the input formula.

The translations discussed in the previous section have been implemented as a special module of the reasoning system QUIP [7; 6; 5], which is a prototype tool for solving several nonmonotonic reasoning tasks based on reductions to QBFs. Currently, QUIP handles tasks for logic-based abduction, default logic, several types of modal nonmonotonic logics, and disjunctive logic programs under the stable model semantics.

The general architecture of QUIP is depicted in Figure 1. QUIP consists of three parts, namely the `filter` program, a QBF-evaluator, and the interpreter `int`. The input filter translates the given problem description (in our case, a belief change scenario and a specified reasoning task) into the corresponding quantified Boolean formula, which is then sent to the QBF-evaluator. The current version of QUIP provides interfaces to most of the sequential QBF-solvers mentioned above. For the solvers requiring prenex normal form, the QBFs are translated into structure preserving normal form. The result of the QBF-evaluator is interpreted by `int`. Depending on the capabilities of the employed QBF-evaluator, `int` provides an explanation in terms of the underlying problem instance (e.g., listing all consistent definitional extensions of a given belief change scenario). This task relies on a protocol mapping of internal variables of the generated QBF into concepts of the problem description which is provided by `filter`.

The system QUIP has been implemented in C using standard tools like LEX and YACC (comprising a total of 2000 lines of code, excluding the used QBF-solver); it runs currently in a Unix environment (Sun/Solaris and Linux), but is easily portable to other operating systems as well.

5 Conclusion

We have shown how belief revision and belief contraction within belief change scenarios can be axiomatised by means of quantified Boolean formulas. This approach has several benefits: First, the given axiomatics provides us with further insight about how belief revision and contraction work within belief change scenarios. Second, this axiomatisation allows us to furnish upper bounds for precise complexity results, going beyond those presented in [3]. Last but not least we obtain a straightforward implementation technique of belief change in belief change scenarios by appeal to the existing nonmonotonic reasoning framework QUIP [7; 6].

References

1. C. Alchourrón, P. Gärdenfors, and D. Makinson. On the Logic of Theory Change: Partial Meet Contraction and Revision Functions. *Journal of Symbolic Logic*, 50:510–530, 1985.
2. M. Cadoli, A. Giovanardi, and M. Schaerf. An Algorithm to Evaluate Quantified Boolean Formulae. In *Proc. AAAI-98*, pages 262–267, 1998.
3. J. Delgrande and T. Schaub. A Consistency-Based Model for Belief Change: Preliminary Report. In *Proc. AAAI-00*, pages 392–398, 2000.
4. E. Eder. *Relative Complexities of First Order Calculi*. Vieweg Verlag, Braunschweig, 1992.
5. U. Egly, T. Eiter, R. Feldmann, V. Klotz, S. .Schamberger, H. Tompits, and S. Woltran. On Mechanizing Modal Nonmonotonic Logics. In *Proc. DGNMR-01*, pages 44–53, 2001.
6. U. Egly, T. Eiter, V. Klotz, H. Tompits, and S. Woltran. Computing Stable Models with Quantified Boolean Formulas: Some Experimental Results. In *Proc. AAAI Spring Symposium-01*, pages 53–59, 2001.
7. U. Egly, T. Eiter, H. Tompits, and S. Woltran. Solving Advanced Reasoning Tasks Using Quantified Boolean Formulas. In *Proc. AAAI-00*, pages 417–422, 2000.
8. R. Feldmann, B. Monien, and S. Schamberger. A Distributed Algorithm to Evaluate Quantified Boolean Formulas. In *Proc. AAAI-00*, pages 285–290, 2000.
9. A. Fuhrmann and S. Hansson. A Survey of Multiple Contraction. *Journal of Logic, Language, and Information*, 3:39–74, 1994.
10. P. Gärdenfors. *Knowledge in Flux: Modeling the Dynamics of Epistemic States*. The MIT Press, Cambridge, MA, 1988.
11. H. Kautz and B. Selman. Planning as Satisfiability. In *Proc. ECAI-92*, pages 359–363, 1992.
12. H. Kleine-Büning, M. Karpinski, and A. Flögel. Resolution for Quantified Boolean Formulas. *Information and Computation*, 117(1):12–18, 1995.
13. B. Nebel. Syntax Based Approaches to Belief Revision. In P. Gärdenfors, editor, *Belief Revision*, pages 52–88. Cambridge University Press, 1992.
14. D. A. Plaisted and S. Greenbaum. A Structure Preserving Clause Form Translation. *Journal of Symbolic Computation*, 2(3):293–304, 1986.
15. J. Rintanen. Constructing Conditional Plans by a Theorem Prover. *Journal of Artificial Intelligence Research*, 10:323–352, 1999.
16. J. Rintanen. Improvements to the Evaluation of Quantified Boolean Formulae. In *Proc. IJCAI-99*, pages 1192–1197, 1999.
17. L. J. Stockmeyer. The Polynomial-Time Hierarchy. *Theoretical Computer Science*, 3(1):1–22, 1976.
18. C. Wrathall. Complete Sets and the Polynomial-Time Hierarchy. *Theoretical Computer Science*, 3(1):23–33, 1976.

"Not impossible" vs. "guaranteed possible" in fusion and revision

Didier Dubois, Henri Prade, Philippe Smets*

Institut de Recherche en Informatique de Toulouse, (I.R.I.T.)
Université Paul Sabatier, 118 route de Narbonne
31062 Toulouse cedex 4

* IRIDIA-CP 194/6, Université Libre de Bruxelles
50 av. Roosevelt
1050 Bruxelles, Belgium

Abstract. In daily life we have two kinds of knowledge at our disposal, pieces of information ruling out what is known to be impossible on the one hand, and case reports pointing out things which are indeed possible. The fusion of the first type of information is basically conjunctive, while it is disjunctive in the other case. The second type of information has been largely neglected by the logical tradition. Both types can be pervaded with uncertainty. The paper first describes how the two types of information can be accommodated in the possibility theory and in the evidence theory frameworks. Then it is shown how the existence of the two types of information can shed new light on the revision of a knowledge base when receiving new information.

1 Introduction

In the logical tradition, a piece of information delimits a set of possible worlds, and any interpretation which is not a model for the set of available pieces of information is regarded as impossible. The conjunctive combination of pieces of information represented in this framework amounts to performing the intersection of the sets of possible worlds representing these granules of information. Thus the more information we have, the more restricted is the corresponding set of possible worlds. This set may even become empty in case of inconsistent information.

But all the knowledge we have is not of this kind. We also accumulate information from observations or reports about particular cases, examples and so on. This information, which rather assesses the feasibility of possible worlds (in the sense that they can be done), is combined disjunctively (without ever leading to any inconsistency). Indeed the more information of this kind we have, the larger the set of possible worlds which is granted. Interestingly enough, the semantic entailment goes here in a way which is the opposite of the situation in the classical logical representation framework. Namely, if all the worlds in A are feasible, we can conclude from this piece of information that all the worlds in B are feasible only if the set inclusion $B \subseteq A$ holds, and nothing is said about the worlds outside A.

In fact, we may often have the two kinds of information at our disposal simultaneously. For instance, if we are interested in the price of a particular second hand car, we may know on the one hand that the laws of the market force the price to be in some range, while on the other hand the observation of similar cases may let us

S. Benferhat and P. Besnard (Eds.): ECSQARU 2001, LNAI 2143, pp. 522–531, 2001.

think that such and such prices are indeed feasible. The coexistence of the two kinds of information telling things which are not impossible, from things which are for sure possible, and their joint representation have been already recently discussed in various settings including modal logic by Dubois, Hajek, and Prade [3]. It has been also considered in the restricted setting of fuzzy rules by Ughetto *et al.*, [17].

Clearly, these two kinds of information can be pervaded with uncertainty. This is investigated in the frameworks of possibility theory and evidence theory in this paper. As we suggest in the second half of this paper, it contributes to shed new light on some belief revision problems, as first hinted in [10].

2 Incomplete information about classes and about objects

As already said, pieces of information about the value of an attribute for an object can be of two different types. In its simplest form this gives birth to a knowledge representation framework made of a pair of ordinary subsets (GP, NI) where GP stands for 'Guaranteed Possible', and NI for 'Not Impossible'; see [3]. When information is consistent, we should have GP $\subseteq$ NI, i.e. what is claimed to be feasible cannot be ruled out as being impossible. This framework enables us to capture incomplete information under two different forms, one pertaining to the description of *classes* of objects, and the other concerning the description of the *objects* themselves.

The range of *existing* values E for an attribute used in the description of a *class* of objects may be incompletely known. In other words, we may only know a lower bound GP, and an upper bound NI of the set E of attribute values existing in the class, i.e. GP $\subseteq$ E $\subseteq$ NI. When information *about the class* is complete for the considered attribute, we have GP = E = NI, i.e. for any value in the attribute domain, it is known if there exists or not, at least one object in the class whose attribute value is this one, in other words if the value is feasible or not. Thus, given the attribute domain U, incomplete information about the set of attribute values existing in the class can be modelled by the *twofold* set (GP, NI) with GP $\subseteq$ NI $\subseteq$ U. GP gathers attribute values which are known as possible for sure and which are said to have a *guaranteed possibility* (e.g., because such values have been encountered, or are known as feasible) on the one hand, while the set U – NI indicates what attribute values are known as impossible for the objects in the class (e.g., as the result of generic laws, principles,...) on the other hand. NI is thus the set of attribute values which are *not impossible* for the objects in the class, but which are not necessarily guaranteed as possible. For instance, we consider a class of cars and the attribute in which we are interested is the price. Then we may know that the price of all the cars in the class should be within some range NI, while some prices gathered in GP $\subseteq$ NI are surely possible ; the prices in NI – GP might be possible, since they are not forbidden although they have never been reported. Extreme situations are retrieved when either GP = $\varnothing$ (the situation captured by classical logic), or when NI = U (we only have a repertory of reported cases). GP = $\varnothing$ only indicates a total lack of observation-based information, while NI = $\varnothing$ means inconsistency (at least one value should be possible)! Thus NI $\neq$ $\varnothing$ is assumed.

Now if we are considering an *object* (a car in our example) which is just known to belong to the class (described as said above), we may wonder about the possible values of some attribute (here the price) for this object. The attribute is here supposed to be single-valued. Note that complete information *at the object level* not only means GP = NI *but also* that this set is a singleton. Then, in the general case, NI and GP play the role of {0,1}-valued distributions: in the above example, if $u \notin NI$ then u cannot be the price of the car; if $u \in GP$, u *can* indeed be the price of the car, while if $u \in (NI - GP)$ nothing forbids u from being the price of the car, but u does not belong to the kernel GP of values which are possible for sure (u *may* just be the price of the car).

More generally, given the statement s = 'the value of the attribute for the object is in S' and the complete information E about the class, the four standard modal situations (s is certainly true if $E \subseteq S$; s is possibly true if $E \cap S \neq \emptyset$; s is possibly false if $E \cap (U - S) \neq \emptyset$; s is certainly false if $E \cap S = \emptyset$) are now refined in a larger set of situations ($S \neq \emptyset$, $GP \neq \emptyset$ and $NI \neq U$ are assumed):

- s is certainly true (ct) if $NI \subseteq S$;
- s is accepted as true (at) if $GP \subseteq S$;
- s may be true (mat) if $GP \cap S \neq \emptyset$;
- s might be true (mit) if $NI \cap S \neq \emptyset$;
- s is guaranteed to be possible (gp) if $GP \supseteq S$ (all values in S have been reported);
- s might be false (mif) if $NI \cap (U - S) \neq \emptyset$;
- s may be false (maf) if $GP \cap (U - S) \neq \emptyset$ (s is guaranteed to be not certain);
- s is dubious (d) if $GP \cap S = \emptyset$;
- s is certainly false (cf) if $NI \cap S = \emptyset$.

Note that *ct* and *mif* are mutually exclusive, as well as *mit* and *cf*, while *ct* entails *at*, which entails *mat* (if $GP \neq \emptyset$), which entails *mit*; similarly *cf* entails *d*, which entails *maf*, which entails *mif*; lastly, *gp* entails *mat*.

3 The possibility theory setting

The information about the possible range of attribute values in a class can be pervaded with uncertainty. Different uncertainty frameworks which are compatible with the set-based representation of incomplete information can be used for refining the above view where laws and observations can both provide uncertain information. This is especially the case for belief function-based evidence theory and for possibility theory. Let us first consider this latter framework which is simpler.

3.1 Background

In possibility theory [2], the basic building element is the notion of a possibility distribution π which is defined from the considered attribute domain to a linearly ordered scale, finite or not (e.g., [0, 1]). Associated to π are a possibility measure and a necessity measure respectively denoted by Π and N, and defined by

$$\Pi(A) = \sup_{u \in A} \pi(u) \text{ if } A \neq \emptyset, \text{ and } \Pi(\emptyset) = 0;$$

$$N(A) = 1 - \Pi(A^c) = \inf_{u \notin A} (1 - \pi(u)) \text{ if } A \neq U, \text{ and } N(U) = 1;$$

where A^c denotes the complement of A ($u \in A^c \Leftrightarrow u \notin A$). As it can be seen, given the partition (A, A^c) of the attribute domain, the information represented by π is summarized by two numbers which are directly related to the maximum of π over A and over A^c. An event A is all the more possible as there is a model u of A which is highly possible; A is all the more necessarily true, or certain as there is no counter-model of A which is highly possible. Contradictions are impossible ($\Pi(\emptyset) = 0$) and tautologies are certain ($N(U) = 1$). Consistency requires to have π normalized, i.e. $\exists u \in U, \pi(u) = 1$, in order to have $\Pi(U) = 1$, $N(\emptyset) = 0$ and more generally $\forall A, N(A) \leq \Pi(A)$ where $N(A) = 0$ or $\Pi(A) = 1$. This expresses that an event A should be fully possible ($\Pi(A) = 1$) before being somewhat certain ($N(A) > 0$).

The possibility distribution π is not always directly available, but may be only implicitly defined through constraints of the form $N(A_i) \geq \alpha_i$ for some subsets A_i with $i = 1,k$, expressing that some events A_i are somewhat certain, as it is the case in possibilistic logic [4]. Then applying the *minimal specificity principle*, we can compute the less restrictive possibility distribution π^* which agrees with the constraints. π^* is given by

$$\pi^*(u) = \min_{i=1,k} \max(A_i(u), 1 - \alpha_i) \quad (1)$$

where $A_i(u) = 1$ if $u \in A_i$ and $A_i(u) = 0$ if $u \notin A_i$. π^* is the greatest distribution such that the constraints are satisfied (it can be checked that $N(A_i) \geq \alpha_i$ where N is computed from π^*).

Besides, a qualitative summarization of the information conveyed by π w.r.t. a partition (A, A^c) should also involve the minimal values of π over A, and over A^c. This is why two new set functions are worth introducing [7]. Namely

$$\Delta(A) = \inf_{u \in A} \pi(u) \; ; \; \nabla(A) = 1 - \Delta(A^c).$$

Δ is called guaranteed possibility function. $\nabla(A)$ estimates the potential certainty of A. Starting with a set of constraints of the form $\Delta(B_j) \geq \beta_j$ with $j = 1,n$, expressing that (all) the values in B_j are guaranteed to be possible at least at level β_j and applying a principle of *maximal* specificity, yields the smallest possibility distribution π_* such that the constraints are satisfied. Note that this principle is the converse of the one used in (1), and is in the spirit of a closed-world assumption: only what is said to be (somewhat) guaranteed possible is considered as so. Namely

$$\pi_*(u) = \max_{j=1,n} \min(B_j(u), \beta_j). \quad (2)$$

3.2 Possibilistic representation of the two types of information

Assume that we have at our disposal two collections of pieces of knowledge, $\{N(A_i) \geq \alpha_i, i = 1,k\}$ and $\{\Delta(B_j) \geq \beta_j, j = 1,n\}$, expressing respectively facts about which we are somewhat certain (the true state of the world cannot be outside the subsets A_i up to exceptional cases), and sets of values that are known as being feasible candidates for the true state of the world. Then we can derive the two distributions π^* and π_* defined in 3.1. These two distributions should be such that

$$\forall u, \pi_*(u) \leq \pi^*(u) \quad (3)$$

in order to guarantee the mutual consistency of the two sets of pieces of information, namely, which is known as being somewhat feasible should not be ruled out as being somewhat impossible. Thus, the pair (π_*, π^*) can be viewed as approximating an unknown possibility distribution π from above and from below, which is not completely defined from the available pieces of information and which would reflect the fuzzy range of existing attribute values for a class of objects, namely we have

$$\pi_* \leq \pi \leq \pi^*. \quad (4)$$

The normalization of π entails that π^* should be also normalized; π_* may not be normalized. Clearly, this generalizes the situation described in Section 2, where

$\pi(u) = E(u)$, $\pi_*(u) = GP(u)$ and $\pi^*(u) = NI(u)$ with $GP \subseteq NI$, and where $NI \neq \varnothing$ while we may have $GP = \varnothing$. Thus the possibilistic modelling provides a graded view of the feasibility and of the impossibility. Complete ignorance, i.e. absence of any information of any kind is modelled by $\forall u, \pi_*(u) = 0$ i.e. $GP = \varnothing$ (no observation reported) and by $\forall u, \pi^*(u) = 1$, i.e. $NI = U$ (no value is (even somewhat) impossible). The upper distribution is the basis for computing beliefs, i.e. what is held for somewhat certain since $N(A) = \inf_{u \notin A} (1 - \pi(u)) \geq \inf_{u \notin A} (1 - \pi^*(u))$ due to (4). Similarly, what is held as possible for sure can be estimated from $\Delta(A) = \inf_{u \in A} \pi(u) \geq \inf_{u \in A} \pi_*(u)$ due to (4). For instance, if $\forall u, \pi^*(u) = 1$, we have no (non-trivial) beliefs, although we may know that some values are indeed feasible.

Remarks

1. $GP(u_1) = GP(u_2) = 1$ means that both u_1 and u_2 are feasible for the objects in the class. In case we would only know that u_1 *or* u_2 is feasible, it would lead to work with disjunctions of distributions, namely $\pi_* \leq \pi$ *or* $\pi_*' \leq \pi$, where $\pi_*(u_1) = 1$ and $\pi_*(u_2) = 0$, $\pi_*'(u_1) = 0$ and $\pi_*'(u_2) = 1$.

2. Associated with π_* and π^*, we can build the possibility distribution $\underline{\pi}$ from 2^U to $[0,1]$, which estimates to what extent it is possible that a subset W be the exact range E of attribute values for the objects in the class. Namely,

$$\underline{\pi}(W) = \sup\{\min(\alpha, 1 - \beta), GP_\beta \subseteq W \subseteq NI_\alpha\} \quad (5)$$

where $GP_\alpha = \{u: \pi_*(u) > \alpha\}$ and $NI_\alpha = \{u: \pi^*(u) \geq \alpha\}$.

Note that is $\underline{\pi}$ normalized as soon as $GP_0 = \{u: \pi_*(u) > 0\} \subseteq NI_1 = \{u: \pi^*(u) = 1\}$, the support of GP (gathering the values which are somewhat feasible) is included in the core of NI (made of the values which are totally possible).

4 The evidence theory setting

The presentation follows what was done for the possibility theory setting in the previous section, and might provide a solution within belief function theory [12]. Let m be a basic belief assignment from 2^U to $[0,1]$, and the associated focal elements F_i such that $\Sigma_i\, m(F_i) = 1$, with possibly $m(\varnothing) \neq 0$. Then three set functions are classically associated with m, namely the belief, plausibility and commonality functions

$$bel(A) = \Sigma_{i:\ F_i \subseteq A \text{ and } F_i \neq \varnothing}\, m(F_i);$$

$$pl(A) = 1 - m(\varnothing) - bel(A^c) = \Sigma_{i:\ F_i \cap A \neq \varnothing}\, m(F_i);$$

$$q(A) = \Sigma_{i:\ F_i \supseteq A}\, m(F_i).$$

They generalize necessity, possibility and guaranteed possibility functions in the general case where the focal elements are not nested. Moreover $m(\varnothing) = 0$ is equivalent to the normalization of π in the nested case.

Given a collection of constraints $\{bel(A_i) \geq \alpha_i, i = 1,k\}$, choosing a particular solution among the belief functions satisfying these constraints is not an obvious matter, since the selected solution depends on the criterion which is used, or for some criterion which extends the idea of minimal specificity the solution may not

be unique. However, provided that $\Sigma_i \alpha_i < 1$, one noticeable solution maximizing the cardinality of the focal elements is to take $m^*(A_i) = \alpha_i$, and $m^*(U) = 1 - \Sigma_i \alpha_i$. If $\Sigma_i \alpha_i > 1$, masses should be allocated to the intersection of sub-families of A_i's. See Dubois and Prade [6] for further discussions.
Similarly, starting with a collection of constraints of the form $\{q(B_j) \geq \beta_j, j = 1,n\}$, if $\Sigma_j \beta_j < 1$, one obvious solution is $m_*(B_j) = \beta_j$, and $m_*(\emptyset) = 1 - \Sigma_j \beta_j$ obeying a minimal cardinality principle.

Thus, modelling the two types of information, in evidence theory amounts to using two basic belief assignments m_* and m^* (induced or not by such constraints). This is equivalent to have a collection of focal elements F_i together with pairs of weights $(m_*(F_i), m^*(F_i))$, where one of the elements of a pair may be equal to 0.

Mutual consistency between the two types of information also requires that m_* be "smaller" than m^*. Again several non-equivalent definitions are possible, e.g;, $bel_*(A) \leq bel^*(A)$ for any A, or the specialization (or random set inclusion) which generalizes $\forall u, \pi_*(u) \leq \pi^*(u)$; see Dubois and Prade [5] for detailed presentations.

5 Fusion of multiple-source information

Let us come back to the possibility theory setting first. As already explained, the distribution π_* represents the information reporting feasible values. π_* is the characteristic function of the set of observed interpretations (with their level of feasibility). $\pi_*(u) = 1$ means that u is totally *guaranteed to be possible*, while $\pi_*(u) = 0$ does not mean that u is impossible, but only that u has not been reported as *observed* (for the attribute value of an object in the class). Observations *accumulate*, the more observations we have, the larger π_*. This is why the elementary possibility distributions $\pi_{*j}(u) = \min(B_j(u), \beta_j)$ representing the constraints $\Delta(B_j) \geq \beta_j$, i. e. the pieces of information "the values in B_j are guaranteed to be feasible at level β_j", for j = 1,n are aggregated disjunctively by max operation in (2).

This is the *converse with* the upper distribution π^*. Indeed, $\pi^*(u) = 0$ means that u is impossible for sure, and $\pi^*(u) = 1$ means that u is not at all ruled out, not at all impossible. The more information we have, the smaller π^*. Indeed the pieces of information "the attribute value is in A_i is certain at level α_i" (i.e. $N(A_i) \geq \alpha_i$) represented by the elementary distribution $\pi^*_i(u) = \max(A_i(u), 1 - \alpha_i)$ are aggregated conjunctively by min operator in (1).

Thus given two epistemic states provided by two different sources of information, represented by the pair (π_{*1}, π^*_1), and a (π_{*2}, π^*_2) respectively, the fusion process yields $(\max(\pi_{*1}, \pi_{*2}), \min(\pi^*_1, \pi^*_2))$. As already explained, two consistency conditions should be preserved.
- First, $\min(\pi^*_1, \pi^*_2)$ should remain normalized.
- Second the mutual consistency condition (3) should still hold, namely

$$\max(\pi_{*1}, \pi_{*2}) \leq \min(\pi^*_1, \pi^*_2).$$

If one of these conditions is not satisfied, a revision process (discussed in the next section) should take place.

In the evidence theory setting, the situation is similar. Given two pairs (m_{*1}, m^*_1) and (m_{*2}, m^*_2) provided by two sources of information, m^*_1 and m^*_2 are to be combined by the (conjunctive) Dempster rule of combination, namely (in the non-normalized case)

$$m^*(C) = \Sigma_{i,j:\ F_i \cap G_j = C}\ m^*_1(F_i) m^*_2(G_j)),$$

while m_{*1} and m_{*2} are to be combined disjunctively (Dubois and Prade [5], Smets [14]), namely

$$m_*(C) = \Sigma_{i,j:\ F_i \cup G_j = C}\ m_{*1}(F_i) m_{*2}(G_j)).$$

Again mutual consistency condition has to be preserved here (see Section 4).

6 Revision

The upper distribution part of the representation, (π^*, or m^*) is the basis for computing beliefs, in terms of N or bel functions. Interestingly enough, this framework enables us to express not only beliefs but also *reasons for not being certain* about something when the lower distribution part of the representation, (π_*, or m_*) is not consistent with the upper distribution part.

Indeed first consider the *two-valued* case. Then, π^* restricts possible locations of the true state of the world according to the information we have. The two-valued *necessity measure* N, then defined by $N(A) = 1$ if $\{u: \pi^*(u) = 1\} \subseteq A$, and $N(A) = 0$ otherwise, enables us to describe our beliefs, i.e., the events A such that $N(A) = 1$.

The reasons not to believe A come from observations, reports, things we have experienced, that we know *for sure* as being possible. The distribution π_* can account for the reasons not to believe A. Indeed let us suppose that $\exists u_0\ \pi_*(u_0) = 1$ and $u_0 \notin A$. Then there is a conflict between statement A which rules out u_0 and the fact that u_0 has been observed. If the mutual consistency condition holds, namely $\{u: \pi_*(u) = 1\} \subseteq \{u: \pi^*(u) = 1\}$, nothing in π_* can provide reasons not to believe statements supported by π^*. Thus the set $\{u: \pi_*(u) = 1 \text{ and } \pi^*(u) = 0\}$, when it is not empty, provides reasons not to believe any statement A such that the inclusion A $\supseteq \{u: \pi_*(u) = 1 \text{ and } \pi^*(u) = 0\}$ fails.

This provides a basis for a natural way of *revising* π^* by π_* in case of conflict. Namely,

$$\pi^*_{\text{revised}}(u) = \max(\pi^*(u), \pi_*(u)). \quad (6)$$

This is a *contraction* of the belief set Gärdenfors [11]. It ensures, in a minimal way, the mutual consistency condition $\forall u, \pi_*(u) \leq \pi^*_{\text{revised}}(u)$. Note also that π^*_{revised} is still normalized if π^* is. This can be extended to *general* possibility measures to which formula (6) can be applied. Then we have reasons not to believe a statement A which is such that $N(A) \geq \alpha$ on the basis of π^*, if $\exists$ u such as $u \notin A$ and $\pi_*(u) > 1 - \alpha$, since we are then violating the consistency requirement between the observations and the belief set, expressed by the inclusion $\forall u\ \pi_*(u) \le \pi^*(u)$. This can be illustrated by the Ukalvia story Smets [16].

Here is the Ukalvia case. You are said that a newspaper reports that the economic situation was good last year in Ukalvia. If it's all you know about Ukalvia, you start to believe the information, let's denote it 'G', to some extent, i.e. $N(G) > 0$ or $bel(G) > 0$. But later you learn that the information is originated from the newspaper of the unique authorized party in Ukalvia. So you start to think that may be it is propaganda. So you would like to come back to a state close to total ignorance (as far as beliefs are concerned) about the economic situation in Ukalvia. Clearly, the idea is that the reasons not to believe A can somewhat inhibit the reasons to believe A, if any. There are two possibilities; either the situation is good (G) or it is not good ($\neg G$). Let U be the frame of discernment. $U = \{G, \neg G\}$. So $bel(G) > 0$ can be represented by the mass function $m(G) = \alpha$; $m(U) = 1 - \alpha$ which is a simple support function, still equivalent to a possibility distribution, i.e. $\pi^*(G) = 1$, $\pi^*(\neg G) = 1 - \alpha < 1$.

The state of total ignorance is represented by $m^{*\circ}(U) = 1$, or if we prefer by $\pi^{*\circ}(G) = \pi^{*\circ}(\neg G) = 1$. In evidence theory, we are apparently looking for a mass function m' such that $m \oplus m' = m^\circ$, where $\oplus$ is the Dempster rule of combination. But this equation has no solution. Note that $m^\neg(\neg G) = \alpha$; $m^\neg(U) = 1 - \alpha$, which corresponds to the opposite belief $bel^\neg(\neg G) = \alpha > 0$ is not a solution since $m \oplus m^\neg$ has G, $\neg G$, and U as focal elements. We are back to reasons to believe $\neg G$, rather than to representing reasons not to believe G. In possibility theory, the equation $\pi^\circ = \min(\pi^*, \pi') = 1$, has no solution either (if $\pi^* \neq 1$).

Since we are using simple support functions in this example, let us consider what the (π_*, π^*) - representation framework means here. In Ukalvia case, the fact that it is known from past experience that such article may be wrong can be represented by $\pi_*(G) = 0$ and $\pi_*(\neg G) = 1 - \beta \cong 1$, i.e. there is strong evidence that papers published in this newspaper often does not say the truth. Then applying (6), i.e. $\pi_{revised}(u) = \max(\pi^*(u), \pi_*(u))$ we get $\pi_{revised}(G) = 1$ and $\pi_{revised}(\neg G) = 1 - \beta$ which is close to ignorance.

Smets [16] has already proposed to deal with a confidence component and with a diffidence component separately, for representing belief states. It gives birth to a latent belief structure made of a pair of belief functions, one for the confidence part and the other for the diffidence part, which cannot be summarized into a unique structure of 'apparent' beliefs, without loss. Then apparent beliefs are obtained by subtracting the diffidence component from the confidence component, using the operation inverse of $\oplus$ for non-dogmatic[1] belief functions. This may however lead to belief structures with negative masses which are difficult to interpret. The important point (made in this paper) is that the two information components are not of the same nature and should be handled separately. Besides, a direct counterpart of (6) can be easily obtained in the belief function framework using the above rule of disjunctive combination.

It is important to notice that the revision process modelled by

---

[1] Non-dogmatic belief functions are such that $Pl(A) = 0 \Leftrightarrow A = \varnothing$ so that nothing is implausible, and nothing, except tautologies, is fully certain : $Bel(A) = 1 \Leftrightarrow A = X$ (since $Pl(A) = 1 - Bel(\neg A)$).

$$\pi^*_{\text{revised}}(u) = \max(\pi^*(u), \pi_*(u))$$

describes the revision of π^* by π_* once a new report has been fused with the current π_* using max operation. Thus priority is given to reports on observed values and it is a *belief* revision process. A dual type of revision which could be called "observation" revision would consist in changing π_* into $\pi_{*\text{revised}}$ when receiving information restricting π^* more (applying fusion based on min combination). Observation revision is defined by

$$\pi_{*\text{revised}}(u) = \min(\pi^*(u), \pi_*(u)). \quad (7)$$

Then beliefs are given priority w.r.t. observations, i.e, we keep our beliefs, and we forget some observations, which is unusual except perhaps for ostreiches!

Clearly there is another revision process in this framework, which deals with the upper distribution separately. It is well known and has been extensively considered in the literature. It is the revision of π^* when $\min(\pi^*, \pi^{*\text{new}})$ is no longer normalized, where $\pi^{*\text{new}}$ is the possibility distribution encoding the new belief (possibly uncertain) which is received (i.e. if we learn $N(A) \geq \alpha$ we have $\pi^{*\text{new}}(u) = \max(A(u), 1 - \alpha)$); see Dubois and Prade [9]. Note that the arrival of new information pertaining to π_* only leads to an expansion of π_* (via max combination) since observations just accumulate. The counterpart of (7) in the belief function framework is Dempster rule of conjunctive combination.

7 Concluding remarks

This paper has emphasized the interest of a twofold representation distinguishing between what is not impossible because not ruled out by our beliefs and what is known as feasible because it has been observed. In other words, it offers a framework for reasoning with rules and cases (or examples) in a joint manner. This representation framework has been discussed in a detailed way and its consequences on fusion and revision of knowledge have been outlined. Interestingly, one may consider subjective knowledge as the source of the description of " not impossible " states, while the " guaranteed possible " states stem from objective data. Our framework could thus contribute to the debate between objective and subjective probabilities.

There exist other situations where knowledge/ information of the two kinds takes place. Thus, in diagnostic problems, we encounter pieces of information of the kind "if you have a flu, then your temperature is between 38.5 and 40 °C; this means that *any* temperature *inside* this range is feasible, and can be explained by a flu for sure (while a temperature which is outside this range is impossible for a flu). Then assume a (very) imprecise observation, say 'temperature between 38 and 41', could not be explained here for sure by a flu, as pointed out by Besnard and Cordier [1] although knowing that the temperature is in the interval [38.5, 40], entails in the classical sense that it is also in the interval [38, 41]. Another informal example illustrating the distinction between the different types of information can be encountered when describing scenarii. Namely, in a scenario, we may have the following situations: 1) an event *j necessarily* follows another event *i* ; 2) an event *j can for sure f*ollow event *i* ; 3) an event *j may* follow event *i* (i.e. nothing forbids it). The difference between situation 2 and situation 3, is that in situation 2, the observation of *j* after *i* is a clue for this type of scenario (in the sense that *j* belongs to a set of feasible followers of *i*), while it is not the case in situation 3. The difference between situations 1 and 2 is that in the latter, *j* is among the events which are known as candidates for following *i*, while in situation 1 event *j* is not just a candidate, it should take place. The application of these ideas in diagnosis is an open issue.

References

1 Besnard Ph. and Cordier M. O. (1999) Explications causales. *Journées Nationales sur la Modélisation du Raisonnement (JNMR-1999)*, Paris, 22 - 23 mars 1999, http://www.irit.fr/GDRI3-ModRais/articlesJNMR.html.

2 Dubois D. and Prade H. (1998) Possibility theory: qualitative and quantitative aspects. In *Handbook of Defeasible Reasoning and Uncertainty Management Systems*, Vol. 1, D.M. Gabbay and Ph. Smets (series eds.), Kluwer, 169-226.

3 Dubois D., Hajek P., and Prade H. (2000) Knowledge-driven versus data-driven logics. *J. of Logic, Language and Information*, **9**, 65-89.

4 Dubois D., Lang J., and Prade H. (1994) Possibilistic logic. In: *Handbook of Logic in Artificial Intelligence and Logic Programming, Vol.3* (D.M. Gabbay, C.J. Hogger, J.A. Robinson, D. Nute, eds.), Oxford Univ. Press, 1994, 439-513.

5 Dubois D. and Prade H. (1986) A set-theoretic view of belief functions - Logical operations and approximation by fuzzy sets. *Int. J. General Systems*, **12**, 193-226

6 Dubois D. and Prade H. (1987) The principle of minimum specificity as a basis for evidential reasoning. In: *Uncertainty in Knowledge-Based Systems* (B. Bouchon, R.R. Yager, eds.), Springer Verlag, LNCS n° 286, 75-84.

7 Dubois D. and Prade H. (1992a) Possibility theory as a basis for preference propagation in automated reasoning. *Proc. of the 1st IEEE Inter. Conf. on Fuzzy Systems (FUZZ-IEEE'92)*, San Diego, Ca., March 8-12, 1992, 821-832.

8 Dubois D. and Prade H. (1992b) Belief change and possibility theory. In *Belief Revision.* (Gärdenfors P., ed.), 142-182.

9 Dubois D. and Prade H. (1998) A synthetic view of belief revision with uncertain inputs in the framework of possibility theory.*Int. J. Approx. Reas.*, **17**, 295-324.

10 Dubois D.*T.* and Prade H.*T.* (1999) Positive and negative evidence. A *fancy* IRIT report, 7 p., presented at Ph. Smets' retirement party day, Brussels, April 23.

11 Gärdenfors P. (1988) *Knowledge in Flux.*. The MIT Press.

12 Shafer G. (1976) *A Mathematical Theory of Evidence.* Princeton Univ. Press, N.J.

13 Smets Ph. (1990) The combination of evidence in the transferable belief model. *IEEE Pattern Analysis and Machine Intelligence*, **12**, 447-458.

14 Smets Ph. (1993) Belief functions: the disjunctive rule of combination and the generalized bayesian theorem. *Inter. J. of Approximate Reasoning*, **9**, 1-35.

15 Smets. Ph. and Kennes. R. (1994) The transferable belief model. *Artificial Intelligence*, **66**, 191-234.

16 Smets Ph. (1995) The canonical decomposition of a weighted belief. *Proc. of the 14th Inter. Joint Conf. on Artificial Intelligence* (IJCAI-95). Montréal, August 20-25, 1995, 1896-1901.

17 Ughetto L., Dubois D. and Prade H. (1999) Implicative and conjunctive fuzzy rules. A tool for reasoning from knowledge and examples. *Proc. 16th National Conference on Artificial Intelligence (AAAI-99)*, Orlando, July 18-22, 1999, Morgan and Kaufman, 214-219.

General Preferential Entailments as Circumscriptions

Yves Moinard

IRISA, Campus de Beaulieu, 35042 RENNES-Cedex FRANCE, tel.: (33) 2 99 84 73 13,
moinard@irisa.fr

Abstract. A (general) preferential entailment is defined by a "preference relation" among "states". States can be either interpretations or sets of interpretations, or "copies" of interpretations or of sets of interpretations, although it is known that the second kind and the fourth one produce the same notion. Circumscription is a special case of the simplest kind, where the states are interpretations. It is already known that a large class of preferential entailments where the states are copies of interpretations, namely the "cumulative" ones, can be expressed as circumscriptions in a greater vocabulary. We extend this result to the most general kind of general preferential entailment, the additional property requested here is "loop", a strong kind of "cumulativity". The greater vocabulary needed here is large, but only a very simple and small set of formulas in this large vocabulary is necessary, which should make the method practically useful.

1 Introduction

Preferential entailments are useful in knowledge representation. Four kinds are introduced in Kraus and al. [7], which in fact reduce to three. Till now, no system computing efficiently the most general kinds is known, but systems do compute circumscription, a particular case of the simplest kind of preferential entailment. Costello [4] has shown how, contrarily to an affirmation in [7], an important subclass of an intermediate kind can be translated into circumscription, by extending the vocabulary. We show that an important subclass of the most general kind can also be translated into circumscription by modifying the vocabulary. We begin with notations (§2), definitions (§3) and useful known results (§4). Then, we need two technical definitions: an auxiliary vocabulary in which the theories of the original language correspond to single interpretations in the new one (§5); and a simplified preference relation for a large class of preferential entailments (§6). Finally, we describe the translation (§7) and detail an example (§8).

2 Notations and Framework

• We work in a propositional language $\mathbf{L}$. As usual, $\mathbf{L}$ also denotes the set of all the formulas. $V(\mathbf{L})$, the vocabulary of $\mathbf{L}$, denotes a set of *propositional symbols*. Letters φ, ψ denote formulas in $\mathbf{L}$. A *formula* will generally be *assimilated to its equivalence class*. Letters such as $\mathcal{T}$ or $\mathcal{C}$ denote sets of formulas (i.e. subsets of $\mathbf{L}$). Two logical constants $\top$ and $\bot$ denote respectively the true and the false formulas.
• Letters μ, ν denote *interpretations for* $\mathbf{L}$, identified with subsets of $V(\mathbf{L})$. $\mu \models \varphi$ and $\mu \models \mathcal{T}$ are defined classically. If $\mathbf{M}_1 \subseteq \mathbf{M}, \mathbf{M}_1 \models \mathcal{T}$ means $\mu \models \mathcal{T}$ for any $\mu \in \mathbf{M}_1$. For

S. Benferhat and P. Besnard (Eds.): ECSQARU 2001, LNAI 2143, pp. 532–543, 2001.

a set E, $\mathcal{P}(E)$ denotes the set of the subsets of E. The set $\mathcal{P}(V(\mathbf{L}))$ of the interpretations for $\mathbf{L}$ is denoted by $\mathbf{M}$. A *model* of $\mathcal{T}$ is an interpretation μ such that $\mu \models \mathcal{T}$, $\mathbf{M}(\mathcal{T})$ and $\mathbf{M}(\varphi)$ denote respectively the sets of the models of $\mathcal{T}$ and φ.
• $\mathcal{T} \models \varphi$, $\mathcal{T} \models \mathcal{T}_1$ and $Th(\mathcal{T})$ are defined classically. A *theory* is a subset of $\mathbf{L}$ closed for deduction, $\mathbf{T}$ denotes the set $\{\mathcal{T} \subseteq \mathbf{L} \;/\; \mathcal{T} = Th(\mathcal{T})\}$ of the theories of $\mathbf{L}$. If $\mathcal{T}_1$ is a theory, we get $\mathcal{T} \subseteq \mathcal{T}_1$ iff $\mathcal{T}_1 \models \mathcal{T}$, for any $\mathcal{T} \subseteq \mathbf{L}$.
• A theory $\mathcal{C} \in \mathbf{T}$ is *complete* if $\forall \varphi \in \mathbf{L}$, $\varphi \in \mathcal{C}$ iff $\neg\varphi \notin \mathcal{C}$. We denote by $\mathbf{C}$ the set of all the complete theories of $\mathbf{L}$. $Th(\mu)$ denotes the set of the formulas satisfied by μ. For any subset $\mathbf{M}_1$ of $\mathbf{M}$, $Th(\mathbf{M}_1) = \{\varphi \;/\; \mathbf{M}_1 \models \varphi\} = \bigcap_{\mu \in \mathbf{M}_1} Th(\mu)$. This ambiguous use of Th and of $\models$ (for formulas or interpretations) is usual. For any $\mathcal{T} \in \mathbf{T}$, $\mathcal{T} = \bigcap_{\mathcal{C} \in \mathbf{C},\, \mathcal{C} \models \mathcal{T}} \mathcal{C}$. Th defines a one-to-one mapping between $\mathbf{M}$ and $\mathbf{C}$: $Th(\mu) \in \mathbf{C}$ for any $\mu \in \mathbf{M}$. If $V(\mathbf{L})$ is finite, Θ denotes the canonical one-to-one mapping from $\mathcal{P}(\mathbf{M})$ to $\mathbf{L}$: for any $\mathbf{M}_1 \subseteq \mathbf{M}$, $\Theta(\mathbf{M}_1)$ is the formula such that $\mathbf{M}(\Theta(\mathbf{M}_1)) = \mathbf{M}_1$.
• $\mathbf{T}, \mathbf{C}, \mathbf{M}, Th, \Theta$ and $\models$ should be indexed by $\mathbf{L}$. To keep the notations readable, we will denote two languages by say $\mathbf{L}$ and $\mathbf{L}'$, and all what concerns $\mathbf{L}$ will be denoted as above, while we will use $\mathbf{T}', \mathbf{C}', \mathbf{M}', Th', \Theta'$ and $\models'$ for what concerns $\mathbf{L}'$.

3 The Various Kinds of Preferential Entailments

Definition 3.1. A *pre-circumscription* f (in $\mathbf{L}$) is an extensive (i.e., $f(\mathcal{T}) \supseteq \mathcal{T}$ for any $\mathcal{T}$) mapping from $\mathbf{T}$ to $\mathbf{T}$. For any subset $\mathcal{T}$ of $\mathbf{L}$, we use the abbreviation $f(\mathcal{T}) = f(Th(\mathcal{T}))$, assimilating a pre-circumscription to a particular extensive mapping from $\mathcal{P}(\mathbf{L})$ to itself[1]. We write $f(\varphi)$ for $f(\{\varphi\}) = f(Th(\varphi))$. □

Definitions 3.2 1. A set of *states* $\mathbf{S}$ is a set of "copies" of elements of $\mathbf{T}$ (or equivalently [3] a set of "copies" of subsets of $\mathbf{M}$): there exists a mapping l from $\mathbf{S}$ to $\mathbf{T}$ and, for any $\mathcal{T} \in \mathbf{T}$, the subset $l^{-1}(\mathcal{T})$ of $\mathbf{S}$ is the set of the *copies of* $\mathcal{T}$.
2. As usual, we define $l(\mathbf{S}) = \{l(s)\}_{s \in \mathbf{S}} = \{\mathcal{T} \in \mathbf{T} \;/\; l^{-1}(\mathcal{T}) \neq \emptyset\}$. For any $\mathcal{T} \subseteq \mathbf{L}$, $\mathbf{S}(\mathcal{T})$ is the subset of $\mathbf{S}$ defined by $\mathbf{S}(\mathcal{T}) = \{s \in \mathbf{S} \;/\; l(s) \models \mathcal{T}\}$.
3. For any $\mathcal{T} \subseteq \mathbf{L}$ we define the subset of $\mathbf{T}$: $\mathbf{W}(\mathcal{T}) = \{\mathcal{T}_1 \in \mathbf{T} \;/\; \mathcal{T} \subseteq \mathcal{T}_1\}$. We write $\mathbf{W}(\varphi)$ for $\mathbf{W}(\{\varphi\})$. Notice that we get $\mathbf{S}(\mathcal{T}) = l^{-1}(\mathbf{W}(\mathcal{T}))$.

Definitions 3.3 1. A *general preference relation* $\prec_g$ is a binary relation over $\mathbf{S}$. For any $\mathcal{T} \in \mathbf{T}$, we define the subsets $\mathbf{S}_{\prec_g}(\mathcal{T})$ of $\mathbf{S}$ and $\mathbf{W}_{\prec_g}(\mathcal{T})$ of $\mathbf{T}$ as follows: $\mathbf{S}_{\prec_g}(\mathcal{T}) = \{s \in \mathbf{S}(\mathcal{T}) \;/\; s_1 \prec_g s \text{ for no } s_1 \in \mathbf{S}(\mathcal{T})\}$, and $\mathbf{W}_{\prec_g}(\mathcal{T}) = l(\mathbf{S}_{\prec_g}(\mathcal{T}))$.
2. The *general preferential entailment* $f_{\prec_g}$ is the pre-circumscription defined by $f_{\prec_g}(\mathcal{T}) = \bigcap_{\mathcal{T}_1 \in \mathbf{W}_{\prec_g}(\mathcal{T})} \mathcal{T}_1$ for any $\mathcal{T} \subseteq \mathbf{L}$.

This is the definition of [3, Definitions 3.1, 3.2], originating from [7, Definition 3.11]. Particular cases give the most classical kinds of preferential entailments:

Definitions 3.4 1. If $l(\mathbf{S}) \subseteq \mathbf{C}$ (instead of $l(\mathbf{S}) \subseteq \mathbf{T}$), let us call the general preference relation a *multi preference relation*, which we will denote by $\prec_m$ instead of $\prec_g$ and let us call $f_{\prec_m}$ a *multi preferential entailment*.

[1] For a reader familiar with [7], a pre-circumscription is an *inference operation* satisfying the full (or theory) versions of *reflexivity*, *left logical equivalence*, *right weakening* and *AND*.

2. If $\mathbf{S} = \mathbf{T}$ and $l = identity$, let us call $\prec_g$ a *simplified general preference relation.*
3. If $\mathbf{S} = \mathbf{C}$ and $l = identity$ (i.e. restrictions 1 and 2 apply), then the relation, defined in $\mathbf{C}$, is called a *preference relation* $\prec$ and $f_\prec$ is called a *preferential entailment.*

As we work in propositional logic, $\mathbf{C}$ can be replaced by $\mathbf{M}$ and $\mathbf{T}$ by $\mathcal{P}(\mathbf{M})$ (see e.g. [3]). Point 1 originates from [7, Definition 5.6] and point 3 from [18]. The notion of general preferential entailment has been qualified as "cumbersome" in the introducing paper [7]. Then, this notion has been tamed in various texts [1,2,3,6,13,10,14].

The best known kind of preferential entailment is circumscription:

Definition 3.5. $\mathbf{P}, \mathbf{Q}, \mathbf{Z}$ is a partition of $V(\mathbf{L})$. The symbols in $\mathbf{P}$, $\mathbf{Z}$ and $\mathbf{Q}$ are respectively *circumscribed, varying* and *fixed.* We define the preference relation $\prec_{(\mathbf{P},\mathbf{Q},\mathbf{Z})}$ in $\mathbf{M}$ by: $\mu \prec_{(\mathbf{P},\mathbf{Q},\mathbf{Z})} \nu$ if $\mathbf{P} \cap \mu \subset \mathbf{P} \cap \nu$ and $\mathbf{Q} \cap \mu = \mathbf{Q} \cap \nu$ ($\subset$: strict inclusion).

The *circumscription* $CIRC(\mathbf{P}, \mathbf{Q}, \mathbf{Z})$ is the preferential entailment $f_{\prec_{(\mathbf{P},\mathbf{Q},\mathbf{Z})}}$.

Definition 3.6. $\Phi \subseteq \mathbf{L}$, $V(\mathbf{L}) = \mathbf{Q} \cup \mathbf{Z}$ (disjoint union), $\mathbf{P}' = \{P'_\varphi\}_{\varphi \in \Phi}$ is a set of distinct propositional symbols not in $\mathbf{L}$. The *formula circumscription* of *the set of formulas* Φ, with $\mathbf{Q}$ *fixed* and $\mathbf{Z}$ *varying*, is defined as follows, for any $\mathcal{T} \subseteq \mathbf{L}$:

$$CIRCF(\Phi, \mathbf{Q}, \mathbf{Z})(\mathcal{T}) = CIRC(\mathbf{P}', \mathbf{Q}, \mathbf{Z})(\mathcal{T} \cup \{\varphi \Leftrightarrow P'_\varphi\}_{\varphi \in \Phi}) \cap \mathbf{L}.$$

$CIRC$ is defined in the greater language $\mathbf{L}'$: $V(\mathbf{L}') = V(\mathbf{L}) \cup \mathbf{P}'$.

Remark 3.1. $CIRCF(\Phi, \mathbf{Q}, \mathbf{Z})$ is the preferential entailment $f_\prec$ in $\mathbf{L}$ associated with the preference relation $\prec_{(\Phi;\mathbf{Q},\mathbf{Z})}$ defined in $\mathbf{M}$ by:

$\mu \prec_{(\Phi;\mathbf{Q},\mathbf{Z})} \nu$ if $Th(\mu) \cap \Phi \subset Th(\nu) \cap \Phi$ and $\mathbf{Q} \cap \mu = \mathbf{Q} \cap \nu$. □

These are the usual propositional adaptations [17,12,4] of the original predicate calculus versions [8,9,16]. Circumscription is a preferential entailment (Definition 3.4-3) and various systems make useful automatic computation for propositional circumscription[2]. Thus, it is interesting to express more complex formalisms in terms of circumscription. This has already been done for multi preferential entailments [4] (see also [13, 11]), what we do now is to extend this technique to general preferential entailments.

4 A Reminder: Characterization Results

Here are known results from [7,17] and other texts (see [13,14] for precise references).

We consider now that $V(\mathbf{L})$ *is finite.*

(Notice that in this case we can restrict our attention to finite sets $\mathbf{S}$ [7].)

Definition 4.1. A general preference relation $\prec_g$ is *safely founded (sf)*, if for any $s \in \mathbf{S}(\mathcal{T}) - \mathbf{S}_{\prec_g}(\mathcal{T})$, there exists $s_1 \in \mathbf{S}_{\prec_g}(\mathcal{T})$ such that $s_1 \prec_g s$.

Definitions 4.2 Here are various properties a pre-circumscription may possess. $\mathcal{T}_1, \mathcal{T}_2$ are in $\mathbf{T}$ (remind that intersecting theories corresponds to a disjunction $\vee$ of formulas):

Case reasoning:	$f(\mathcal{T}_1 \cap \mathcal{T}_2) \models f(\mathcal{T}_1) \cap f(\mathcal{T}_2)$.	**(CR)**
Disjunctive coherence:	$f(\mathcal{T}_1) \cup f(\mathcal{T}_2) \models f(\mathcal{T}_1 \cap \mathcal{T}_2)$.	**(DC)**

[2] Here are three examples: LWB (http://lwbwww.unibe.ch:8080/LWBtheory.html), SMODELS (http://www.tcs.hut.fi/Software/smodels/), and DLV (http://www.dbai.tuwien.ac.at/proj/dlv/).

Cumulative transitivity: If $\mathcal{T}'' \subseteq f(\mathcal{T})$, $f(\mathcal{T} \cup \mathcal{T}'') \subseteq f(\mathcal{T})$. **(CT)**

Cumulative monotony: If $\mathcal{T}'' \subseteq f(\mathcal{T})$, $f(\mathcal{T}) \subseteq f(\mathcal{T} \cup \mathcal{T}'')$. **(CM)**

Cumulativity: If $\mathcal{T}'' \subseteq f(\mathcal{T})$, then $f(\mathcal{T}) = f(\mathcal{T} \cup \mathcal{T}'')$. **(CUMU)**

If $\mathcal{T}_2 \subseteq f(\mathcal{T}_1), \cdots, \mathcal{T}_n \subseteq f(\mathcal{T}_{n-1}), \mathcal{T}_1 \subseteq f(\mathcal{T}_n)$, then $f(\mathcal{T}_1) = f(\mathcal{T}_n)$. **(LOOP$_n$)**

(Loop): For any integer $n \geq 2$, f satisfies (LOOP$_n$). **(LOOP)**

Preservation of consistency: If $f(\mathcal{T}_1) = Th(\perp) = \mathbf{L}$, then $\mathcal{T}_1 = \mathbf{L}$. **(PC)**

Proposition 4.1. *For pre-circumscriptions: 1. (CR) implies (CT).*
2. As (CUMU) is (CM) + (CT), in case of (CR), (CUMU) and (CM) are equivalent.
3. (LOOP$_2$) is equivalent to (CUMU), (LOOP$_{n+1}$) is stronger than (LOOP$_n$).
4. (CR) and (CUMU) imply (LOOP). □

Theorem 4.1. *1. For any general preferential entailment $f_{\prec_g}$, there exists a simplified general preference relation $\prec_{sg}$ such that $f_{\prec_g} = f_{\prec_{sg}}$.*
2. A pre-circumscription f satisfies (CT) iff it is a general preferential entailment.
3. A pre-circumscription f satisfies (CUMU) – respectively (LOOP) – iff it is a general preferential entailment defined by a relation $\prec_g$ satisfying (sf) – respectively a transitive and irreflexive relation (i.e. a strict order) $\prec_g$ satisfying (sf) (cf point 5).
4. A pre-circumscription satisfies (CR) iff it is a multi preferential entailment.
*5. A pre-circumscription satisfies (CR) and (CUMU) iff it is a multi preferential entailment defined in a finite set **S** by a relation $\prec_m$ which is a strict order (on a finite set this implies (sf) and, contrarily to 3 for (LOOP), (sf) alone suffices here).*
6. A pre-circumscription satisfies (CR) and (DC) iff it is a preferential entailment.
7. A preferential entailment satisfies (CUMU) and (PC) iff it is defined by a preference relation $\prec$ which is transitive and irreflexive, iff it is a formula circumscription. □

5 Modifying the Vocabulary

Definitions 5.1 $\mathbf{L}$ and $\mathbf{L}'$ are two languages, f is a mapping from $\mathbf{T}$ to $\mathbf{T}$ and f' is a pre-circumscription defined in $\mathbf{L}'$. We say that f is obtained from f' by (Def$\rightleftharpoons$) – respectively by (Def$\rightleftharpoons$4) – if there exist two mappings b_1 from $\mathbf{T}$ to $\mathbf{T}'$ and b_2 from $\mathbf{T}'$ to $\mathbf{T}$ such that the three conditions ($\rightleftharpoons$1–3) – respectively the four conditions ($\rightleftharpoons$1–4) – below are satisfied and such that we have, for any $\mathcal{T} \in \mathbf{T}$: $f(\mathcal{T}) = b_2(f'(b_1(\mathcal{T})))$.

1. b_1 preserves inclusion:
for any $\mathcal{T}_1, \mathcal{T}_2$ in $\mathbf{T}$, if $\mathcal{T}_1 \subseteq \mathcal{T}_2$, then $b_1(\mathcal{T}_1) \subseteq b_1(\mathcal{T}_2)$, ($\rightleftharpoons$1)

2. $b_1 \circ b_2$ is contractive on the set $f'(b_1(\mathbf{T}))$:
$b_1(b_2(f'(b_1(\mathcal{T})))) \subseteq f'(b_1(\mathcal{T}))$ for any $\mathcal{T} \in \mathbf{T}$, ($\rightleftharpoons$2)

3. $b_2 \circ f' \circ b_1$ is extensive: for any $\mathcal{T} \in \mathbf{T}$, $\mathcal{T} \subseteq b_2(f'(b_1(\mathcal{T})))$. ($\rightleftharpoons$3)

4. b_2 preserves inclusion on the set $f'(b_1(\mathbf{T}))$: For any $\mathcal{T}_1, \mathcal{T}_2$ in $\mathbf{T}$,
if $f'(b_1(\mathcal{T}_1)) \subseteq f'(b_1(\mathcal{T}_2))$, then $b_2(f'(b_1(\mathcal{T}_1))) \subseteq b_2(f'(b_1(\mathcal{T}_2)))$. ($\rightleftharpoons$4)

($\rightleftharpoons$3) means that $f = b_2 \circ f' \circ b_1$ is a pre-circumscription. Notice that we need only to know the value of b_2 on the subset $f'(b_1(\mathbf{T})) = \{f'(b_1(\mathcal{T})) \ / \ \mathcal{T} \in \mathbf{T}\}$ of $\mathbf{T}'$.

The following preservation results are immediate:

Proposition 5.1. *1. If f' is a pre-circumscription defined in a language $\mathbf{L}'$ which satisfies (CUMU) – resp. (LOOP) – and if f is defined from f' by (Def$\rightleftharpoons$), then f is a pre-circumscription defined in $\mathbf{L}$ which satisfies (CUMU) – resp. (LOOP).*
2. If f' is a pre-circumscription defined in a language $\mathbf{L}'$ which satisfies (CT) – respectively (CM) – and if f is defined from f' by (Def$\rightleftharpoons$4), then f is a pre-circumscription defined in $\mathbf{L}$ which satisfies (CT) – respectively (CM). □

6 A Useful Simplified General Preference Relation

Definition 6.1. [7] Let f be a pre-circumscription. We define the following general preference relation $\prec_f^{klm}$: 1. $\mathbf{S} = f(\mathbf{T}) = \{f(\mathcal{T}) \;/\; \mathcal{T} \in \mathbf{T}\}$,
2. l is the mapping from $\mathbf{S}$ to $\mathbf{T}$ defined by $l(f(\mathcal{T})) = f(\mathcal{T})$ for any $\mathcal{T} \in \mathbf{T}$.
3. $f(\mathcal{T}_1) \prec_f^{klm} f(\mathcal{T}_2)$ if $f(\mathcal{T}_1) \neq f(\mathcal{T}_2)$ and there exists $\mathcal{T}_3 \in \mathbf{T}$ such that
$f(\mathcal{T}_1) = f(\mathcal{T}_3)$ and $\mathcal{T}_3 \subseteq f(\mathcal{T}_2)$.

The set $f(\mathbf{T})$ is then the set denoted by $l(\mathbf{S})$ in Definition 3.3 for the general preference relation defined here. The relation $\prec_f^{klm}$ is introduced in [7, Theorem 3.25] in order to prove "the hard part" of Theorem 4.1-3 for (CUMU). The relation $\prec_f^{klm}$ can be replaced by a simplified general preference relation (see also [1,2]):

Definition 6.2. Let $\prec_g$ be a general preference relation (defining thus a set $\mathbf{S}$ and a mapping l). We define the following simplified general preference relation $\prec_s$: for any $\mathcal{T}_1, \mathcal{T}_2 \in \mathbf{T}$, $\mathcal{T}_1 \prec_s \mathcal{T}_2$ if 1. $\mathcal{T}_1 = Th(\bot)$ and $\mathcal{T}_2 \notin l(\mathbf{S}) \cup \{Th(\bot)\}$, or
2. $\mathcal{T}_1 = l(s_1)$, $\mathcal{T}_2 = l(s_2) \neq Th(\bot)$, and $s_1 \prec_g s_2$, for some s_1, s_2 in $\mathbf{S}$.

Proposition 6.1. *If a general preference relation $\prec_g$ is such that the mapping l is injective, we have, for any $\mathcal{T} \in \mathbf{T}$, $\mathbf{W}_{\prec_g}(\mathcal{T}) \cup \{Th(\bot)\} = \mathbf{W}_{\prec_s}(\mathcal{T}) \cup \{Th(\bot)\}$. Thus we have $f_{\prec_g} = f_{\prec_s}$ where $\prec_s$ is the simplified general preference relation defined from $\prec_g$ as in Definition 6.2.*

Proof: As l is injective, for any s_1, s_2 in $\mathbf{S}$, $s_1 \prec_g s_2$ iff there exist $\mathcal{T}_1$ and $\mathcal{T}_2$ in $l(\mathbf{S}) = f(\mathbf{S})$ such that $s_1 = l(\mathcal{T}_1)$, $s_2 = l(\mathcal{T}_2)$ and $\mathcal{T}_1 \prec_s \mathcal{T}_2$. Moreover $Th(\bot) \prec_s \mathcal{T}$ for any $\mathcal{T} \notin l(\mathbf{S})$, and $Th(\bot) \in \mathbf{W}(\mathcal{T})$ for any $\mathcal{T} \in \mathbf{T}$. Thus, for any $\mathcal{T} \in \mathbf{T}$, we have $\mathbf{W}_{\prec_g}(\mathcal{T}) \cup \{Th(\bot)\} = \mathbf{W}_{\prec_s}(\mathcal{T}) \cup \{Th(\bot)\}$. As $Th(\bot) \in \mathbf{W}(\varphi)$ for any $\varphi \in \mathbf{L}$, we get that if $\prec_1$ and $\prec_2$ are two general preference relations such that $\mathbf{W}_{\prec_1}(\mathcal{T}) = \mathbf{W}_{\prec_2}(\mathcal{T}) \cup \{Th(\bot)\}$, then $f_{\prec_1}(\mathcal{T}) = f_{\prec_2}(\mathcal{T})$. Thus we get here $f_{\prec_g} = f_{\prec_s}$. □

Definition 6.3. The mapping l of the relation $\prec_f^{klm}$ is injective. We can thus consider the simplified general preference relation, that we call $\prec_{nf}$, defined from $\prec_f^{klm}$ as in Definition 6.2. We call $\prec_{nf}$ the *normal general preference relation associated to* f. □

We get $f_{\prec_f^{klm}} = f_{\prec_{nf}}$ from Proposition 6.1.

As $V(\mathbf{L})$ is finite, we will now generally replace $\mathbf{T}$ by $\mathbf{L}$. $\mathbf{W}(\varphi)$ will be a set of formulas, any simplified general preference relation will be a binary relation in $\mathbf{L}$ and, if f is a pre-circumscription, $f(\varphi) = \psi$ will replace $f(\varphi) = Th(\psi)$.

Proposition 6.2. *If f satisfies (CT), the normal general preference relation $\prec_{nf}$ associated to f is the binary relation described as follows: for any φ_1, φ_2 in* **L**,
$\varphi_1 \prec_{nf} \varphi_2$ *iff* 1. $\varphi_1 = \bot$ *and* $\varphi_2 \neq \varphi$ *for any* $\varphi \in \mathbf{L}$, *or*
2. $\varphi_2 \neq \bot$, $\varphi_1 \neq \varphi_2$ *and there exist* φ_3, φ_4 *such that* $f(\varphi_3) = \varphi_1$, $f(\varphi_4) = \varphi_2$, $\varphi_2 \models \varphi_3$.

Proof: This is a consequence of Definitions 6.1 and 6.3, taking into account two peculiarities of $\prec_f^{klm}$. Firstly, the set $l(\mathbf{S}) = f(\mathbf{L})$ associated to the general preference relation $\prec_f^{klm}$ contains $\bot$: as f is a pre-circumscription, we have $f(\bot) = \bot$. Secondly, we have never $\bot \prec_f^{klm} \varphi$. Indeed, $\bot \prec_f^{klm} \varphi$ iff $f(\bot) \neq f(\varphi)$ and there exists $\varphi_1 \in \mathbf{L}$ such that $f(\varphi_1) = \bot$ and $f(\varphi) \models \varphi_1$. From (CT) we get then $f(f(\varphi)) = f(\varphi) \models f(\varphi_1)$, i.e. $f(\varphi) = \bot = f(\bot)$: a contradiction. □

These results show that all the general preference relations considered in [7] could have been replaced directly by a simplified general preference relation.

Proposition 6.3. *If f is a pre-circumscription satisfying (CUMU), then it is a general preferential entailment which can be defined by $\prec_{nf}$: $f = f_{\prec_{nf}}$.*
More precisely we have, for any $\varphi \in \mathbf{L}$: $\mathbf{W}_{\prec_{nf}}(\varphi) = \{f(\varphi), \bot\}$. □

We omit the proof, as it is an adaptation of a proof given in [7, proof of Theorem 3.25], establishing that we have in this case $\mathbf{W}_{\prec_f^{klm}}(\varphi) = \{f(\varphi)\}$. The fact that we use a simplified general preference relation simplifies even the matter. Notice also that, as in [7, proof of Theorem 3.25] for $\prec_f^{klm}$, we get that in this case $\prec_{nf}$ is (sf).

Here is another result extrapolated from [7], which will be useful in our translation of some general preferential entailments in terms of circumscription (cf the proof of [7, Theorem 4.9], which gives the result for what concerns $\prec_f^{klm}$ and its transitive closure):

Proposition 6.4. *A pre-circumscription f satisfying (CUMU) satisfies (LOOP) iff the transitive closure $\overline{\prec_{nf}}$ of the normal general preference relation $\prec_{nf}$ associated to f is irreflexive. In this case, i.e. if f satisfies (LOOP), we have $\mathbf{W}_{\prec_{nf}}(\varphi) = \mathbf{W}_{\overline{\prec_{nf}}}(\varphi) = \{f(\varphi), \bot\}$, thus $f = f_{\prec_{nf}} = f_{\overline{\prec_{nf}}}$.* □

7 Finite General Preferential Entailments as Circumscriptions

Theorem 7.1. *A pre-circumscription f in* **L** *satisfies (LOOP) iff it can be expressed by (Def⇄) — or by (Def⇄4) — from a formula circumscription $f' = CIRCF(\Phi', \emptyset, V(\mathbf{L}'))$ defined in a language $\mathbf{L}'$.*

By Proposition 6.4, "*A pre-circumscription f*" could be replaced by "*A general preferential entailment f*". Remind a similar result for multi preferential entailments satisfying (CM) ([11, Theorem 31], extrapolated from [4, Theorem 15]). The reason why we need (LOOP) here instead of just (CUMU) is that we must get a strict order relation in order to get a formula circumscription (see Theorem 4.1, points 3, 5 and 7).

Constructive proof: (if): Any formula circumscription f' satisfies (CUMU) and (LOOP) from Prop. 4.1-4 and Th. 4.1 (-6,7). Then f satisfies (LOOP) from Prop. 5.1-1.

(only if): $f = f_{\overline{\prec_{nf}}}$ from Proposition 6.4, $\prec_{nf}$ being described in Proposition 6.2. $\overline{\prec_{nf}}$ is a strict order from Proposition 6.4 and in fact this proof works for any simplified general preference relation $\prec_s$ such that $f = f_{\prec_s}$ and which is a strict order. We define (1) a language $\mathbf{L}'$ such that there exists a one-to one mapping p from $\mathbf{M}$ to $V(\mathbf{L}')$ and (2) a one-to one mapping b from $\mathcal{P}(\mathbf{M})$ to $\mathbf{M}' = \mathcal{P}(V(\mathbf{L}'))$:

$$\text{For any } \mu \subseteq V(\mathbf{L}), \quad p(\mu) = P'_\mu \in V(\mathbf{L}'). \tag{1}$$

$$\text{For any } \mathbf{M}_1 \subseteq \mathbf{M}, \quad b(\mathbf{M}_1) = p(\mathbf{M} - \mathbf{M}_1) = \{P'_\mu \in V(\mathbf{L}') \mathbin{/} \mu \in \mathbf{M} - \mathbf{M}_1\}. \tag{2}$$

Then, we define (3) a one-to-one mapping $\overline{b}$ from $\mathbf{L}$ to $\mathbf{L}'_C = \{\varphi' \in \mathbf{L}'/Th'(\varphi') \in \mathbf{C}'\} = \{\bigwedge_{P' \in \mathbf{P}'} P' \wedge \bigwedge_{P' \in V(\mathbf{L}') - \mathbf{P}'} \neg P / \mathbf{P}' \subseteq V(\mathbf{L}')\}$ ($\mathbf{L}'_C$ is the subset of $\mathbf{L}'$ corresponding to $\mathbf{C}'$, in the same way than $\mathbf{L}'$ corresponds to $\mathbf{T}'$) and (4) a mapping b_1 from $\mathbf{L}$ to $\mathbf{L}'$. For any $\varphi \in \mathbf{L}$:

$$\overline{b}(\varphi) = \left(\bigwedge_{P'_\mu \in V(\mathbf{L}') \,/\, \mu \in \mathbf{M} - \mathbf{M}(\varphi)} P'_\mu \right) \wedge \left(\bigwedge_{P'_\mu \in V(\mathbf{L}') \,/\, \mu \in \mathbf{M}(\varphi)} \neg P'_\mu \right). \tag{3}$$

$$b_1(\varphi) = \bigwedge_{\mu \in \mathbf{M} - \mathbf{M}(\varphi)} P'_\mu. \tag{4}$$

Thus, $\mathbf{M}'(\overline{b}(\varphi))$ is the singleton $\{b(\mathbf{M}(\varphi))\}$, where $b(\mathbf{M}(\varphi)) = \{P'_\mu \,/\, \mu \in \mathbf{M} - \mathbf{M}(\varphi)\} = \{P'_\mu \,/\, \mu \in \mathbf{M}(\neg\varphi)\}$. Here is a feature of these mappings, which greatly simplifies the translation: for any $\mathbf{M}_1, \mathbf{M}_2 \subseteq \mathbf{M}$: $\mathbf{M}_1 \subseteq \mathbf{M}_2$ iff $b(\mathbf{M}_2) \subseteq b(\mathbf{M}_1)$, i.e.,

$$\text{for any } \varphi, \psi \text{ in } \mathbf{L}, \quad \varphi \models \psi \text{ iff } b(\mathbf{M}(\psi)) \subseteq b(\mathbf{M}(\varphi)). \tag{5}$$

From (4), $b_1(\varphi)$ is the formula which has the set $\{\mu' \,/\, b(\mathbf{M}(\varphi)) \subseteq \mu' \subseteq V(\mathbf{L}')\}$ for set of models. Thanks to (5), we get that $b_1(\varphi)$ is the formula such that $\mathbf{M}'(b_1(\varphi)) = \{b(\mathbf{M}(\psi)) \,/\, \psi \in \mathbf{W}(\varphi)\}$: $b_1(\varphi)$ is an image of the set $\mathbf{W}(\varphi)$ in $\mathbf{L}'$. As b_1 is injective, it defines a one-to-one mapping between $\mathbf{L}$ and the set $b_1(\mathbf{L}) = \{b_1(\varphi) \,/\, \varphi \in \mathbf{L}\} = \{\bigwedge_{P' \in \mathbf{P}'} P' \,/\, \mathbf{P}' \subseteq V(\mathbf{L}')\}$ of all the *conjunctions of atoms of* $\mathbf{L}'$.

We must now come back from $\mathbf{L}'$ to the original language $\mathbf{L}$.

The one-to-one mapping b^{-1} from $\mathbf{M}'$ to $\mathcal{P}(\mathbf{M})$ can be described as follows (cf (2)):

$$b^{-1}(\mu') = \{b^{-1}(P'_\mu) \,/\, P'_\mu \in V(\mathbf{L}') - \mu'\} = \{\mu \,/\, P'_\mu \in V(\mathbf{L}') - \mu'\}.$$

We define the mapping b_2 from $\mathbf{L}'$ to $\mathbf{L}$ by the following two equivalent equations:

$$\text{for any } \varphi' \in \mathbf{L}', \quad b_2(\varphi') = b_1^{-1}\Big(\bigwedge_{P' \in V(\mathbf{L}'),\ \varphi' \models' P'} P' \Big). \tag{6}$$

$$\mathbf{M}(b_2(\varphi')) = b^{-1}(\{P'_\mu \,/\, \varphi' \models' P'_\mu\} = \{\mu \in \mathbf{M} \,/\, \varphi' \not\models' P'_\mu\}). \tag{7}$$

$$\text{From (4) and (6) we get, for any } \varphi \in \mathbf{L}: \ b_2(b_1(\varphi)) = \varphi. \tag{8}$$

The restriction of b_2 to the subset $\mathbf{L}'_C$ of $\mathbf{L}'$ is $(\overline{b})^{-1}$, a one-to one mapping from $\mathbf{L}'_C$ onto $\mathbf{L}$. Indeed we get, P' ranging over $V(\mathbf{L}')$:

$$\text{if } \varphi' \in \mathbf{L}'_C, \quad \text{then } \varphi' = \bigwedge_{\varphi' \models' P'} P' \wedge \bigwedge_{\varphi' \not\models' P'} \neg P'. \tag{9}$$

If $\varphi' \in \mathbf{L}'_C$, then $\mathbf{M}'(\varphi')$ is the singleton $\mathbf{M}'(\varphi') = \{\mu'\}$ for $\mu' = \{P' \in V(\mathbf{L}')/\varphi' \models' P'\}$, and we get: $\mathbf{M}(b_2(\varphi')) = b^{-1}(\mu')$.

It is convenient to introduce the "*exhaustive conjunction*" $\psi' = \bigwedge_{P' \in V(\mathbf{L}')} P'$.

We suppose here that $\varphi' = \varphi'_1 \vee \psi'$, with $\varphi'_1 \in \mathbf{L}'_C$. This means that there exists a subset $\mathbf{P}'$ of $V(\mathbf{L}')$ such that $\varphi' = \bigwedge_{P' \in V(\mathbf{L}') - \mathbf{P}'} P' \wedge (\bigwedge_{P' \in \mathbf{P}'} \neg P' \vee \bigwedge_{P' \in \mathbf{P}'} P')$.

$$\text{We get: if } \varphi' = \varphi'_1 \vee \psi' \text{ with } \varphi'_1 \in \mathbf{L}'_C, \quad \text{then } b_2(\varphi') = (\bar{b})^{-1}(\varphi'_1) \tag{10}$$

$$\text{From (7), we get that } b_2 \text{ preserves } \vee : b_2(\varphi'_1 \vee \varphi'_2) = b_2(\varphi'_1) \vee b_2(\varphi'_2). \tag{11}$$

We get then, reminding $b_2 = (\bar{b})^{-1}$ on $\mathbf{L}'_C$: $b_2(\varphi') = \bigvee_{\varphi'_c \in \mathbf{L}'_C, \varphi'_c \models' \varphi'} (\bar{b})^{-1}(\varphi'_c)$.

We define the following preference relation $\prec'$ on $\mathbf{M}'$ (remember section 2 for Θ):

$$\text{for any } \mu', \nu' \text{ in } \mathbf{M}', \ \mu' \prec' \nu' \text{ iff } \Theta(b^{-1}(\mu')) \prec_s \Theta(b^{-1}(\nu')). \tag{12}$$

Thus $\prec'$ is the image in $\mathbf{M}'$ of the relation $\prec_s$ on $\mathbf{L}$. It is a strict order and there exists a set Φ' of formulas in $\mathbf{L}'$ such that $f_{\prec'} = CIRCF(\Phi', \emptyset, V(\mathbf{L}'))$ (cf Theorem 4.1-7).

We know from (5) and (4) that $b_1(\varphi)$ has for set of models the set associated to the set $\mathbf{W}(\varphi)$ by b (or $\bar{b}$ if we consider $\mathbf{L}_C$ instead of $\mathbf{M}$). Thus, $\mathbf{W}_{\prec_s}(\varphi)$ is the reverse image of the set $\mathbf{M}'_{\prec'}(b_1(\varphi))$: $\mathbf{W}_{\prec_s}(\varphi) = (\bar{b})^{-1}(\Theta'(\mathbf{M}'_{\prec'}(b_1(\varphi)))) = \{(\bar{b})^{-1}(\varphi'_c)/ \ \varphi'_c \in \mathbf{L}'_C, \mathbf{M}'(\varphi'_c) = \{\mu'\} \text{ with } \mu' \in \mathbf{M}'_{\prec'}(b_1(\varphi))\}$. From Definition 3.3 we have, for any $\varphi \in \mathbf{L}$, $f_{\prec_s}(\varphi) = \bigvee_{\varphi_1 \in \mathbf{W}_{\prec_s}(\varphi)} \varphi_1$. We get thus, from the definition of $\prec'$: for any $\varphi'_c \in \mathbf{L}'_C$, the only model μ' of φ'_c is in $\mathbf{M}_{\prec'}(b_1(\varphi))$ iff the formula $(\bar{b})^{-1}(\varphi'_c)$ is in $\mathbf{W}_{\prec_s}(\varphi)$. As φ'_c is in $\mathbf{L}'_c$, we get (see (9)): $(\bar{b})^{-1}(\varphi'_c) = b_2(\varphi'_c)$. We get then $f_{\prec_s}(\varphi) = \bigvee_{\varphi_1 \in \mathbf{W}_{\prec_s}(\varphi)} \ \varphi_1 = \bigvee_{\varphi'_c \in \mathbf{L}'_C \text{ with } \mathbf{M}'(\varphi'_c) = \{\mu'\} \text{ and } \mu' \in \mathbf{M}'_{\prec'}(b_1(\varphi))} b_2(\varphi'_c)$.
From (11) we get $f_{\prec_s}(\varphi) = b_2(\bigvee_{\varphi'_c \in \mathbf{L}'_C \text{ with } \mathbf{M}'(\varphi'_c) = \{\mu'\} \text{ and } \mu' \in \mathbf{M}'_{\prec'}(b_1(\varphi))} \ \varphi'_c)$.

$$\text{We get then} \qquad f_{\prec_s}(\varphi) = b_2(f'_{\prec'}(b_1(\varphi))).$$

If we choose $\overline{\prec_{nf}}$ as our $\prec_s$, we get $\mathbf{W}_{\overline{\prec_{nf}}}(\varphi) = \{\bot, f(\varphi)\}$ from Proposition 6.4. Thus, $\mathbf{M}_{\prec'}(b_1(\varphi))$ as at most two elements, $V(\mathbf{L}')$ and the subset of μ' of $V(\mathbf{L}')$ which is the only other model of $f_{\prec'}(b_1(\varphi))$, if there is another model. As moreover we can apply (10) in this case, these peculiarities greatly simplify the effective computation.

It remains to check the conditions. ($\rightleftharpoons$1): $\varphi \models \psi$ iff $\mathbf{M}(\varphi) \subseteq \mathbf{M}(\psi)$ iff $\mathbf{M} - \mathbf{M}(\psi) \subseteq \mathbf{M} - \mathbf{M}(\varphi)$ and, from (4) we get that if $\mathbf{M} - \mathbf{M}(\psi) \subseteq \mathbf{M} - \mathbf{M}(\varphi)$, then $b_1(\varphi) \models' b_1(\psi)$.

($\rightleftharpoons$2): We prove that $b_1 \circ b_2$ is weakening on $\mathbf{L}'$. For any $\varphi' \in \mathbf{L}'$, we get $b_1(b_2(\varphi')) = \bigwedge_{P' \in V(\mathbf{L}'), \ \varphi' \models' P'} P'$ from (4) and (6), thus $\varphi' \models' b_1(b_2(\varphi'))$.

($\rightleftharpoons$3): For any $\varphi \in \mathbf{L}$, we get $\mathbf{M}(b_2(f'(b_1(\varphi)))) = \{\mu \in \mathbf{M} \ / \ f'(b_1(\varphi)) \not\models' P'_\mu\}$ from (7). As f' is a pre-circumscription, we have $f'(b_1(\varphi)) \models' b_1(\varphi)$, thus we get $\mathbf{M}(b_2(f'(b_1(\varphi)))) \subseteq \{\mu \in \mathbf{M} \ / \ b_1(\varphi) \not\models' P'_\mu\}$. Now we have $\mathbf{M}(b_2(b_1(\varphi))) = \{\mu \in \mathbf{M} \ / \ b_1(\varphi) \not\models' P'_\mu\}$. Thus we get $\mathbf{M}(b_2(f'(b_1(\varphi)))) \subseteq \mathbf{M}(b_2(b_1(\varphi)))$, i.e. $b_2(f'(b_1(\varphi))) \models b_2(b_1(\varphi))$, i.e., from (8): $b_2(f'(b_1(\varphi))) \models \varphi$.

($\rightleftharpoons$4): From $\mathbf{M}(b_2(\varphi')) = \{\mu \in \mathbf{M} \ / \ \varphi' \not\models' P'_\mu\}$ (7) we get that, if $\varphi' \models' \psi'$, then we have $b_2(\varphi') \models' b_2(\psi')$.

As the four conditions are satisfied, the translation preserves (LOOP) and also (CM) and (CT) (Proposition 5.1). The preservation of (CT) is interesting: from Theorem 4.1-2, if f' is a general preferential entailment, and if f is defined from f' as here, then f is a general preferential entailment. Thus this translation preserves the main properties which can be preserved in this case. Notice finally that, as the proof of the "if side" does not require condition ($\rightleftharpoons$4), we can formulate the theorem with or without ($\rightleftharpoons$4). □

A consequence of this proof is the following result:

Corollary 7.1. *A pre-circumscription satisfies (LOOP) iff it is a general preferential entailment defined by a simplified general preference relation which is a strict order.* □

We do not know what happens if $V(\mathbf{L})$ is infinite. A characterization of formula circumscription is known, but (sf) alone is not enough [12]. Moreover, b_1, b_2 should be defined for each $\mathcal{T} \in \mathbf{T}$ and not only for $\varphi \in \mathbf{L}$, which would complicate the matter.

Notice that we could use a slightly smaller vocabulary $\mathbf{L}'$, starting from the set $f(\mathbf{L})$ instead of the set $\mathbf{L}$, and from $\overline{\prec_f^{klm}}$ instead of $\overline{\prec_{nf}}$. However, this would complicate very seriously the definitions of b_1 and b_2 and we would loose the main advantage of our translation, the easy and natural definitions of b_1 and b_2.

The characterization result extends as follows to general preferential entailments:

Theorem 7.2. *A pre-circumscription f in $\mathbf{L}$ satisfies (CT) iff it can be expressed by (Def$\rightleftharpoons$4) from a preferential entailment $f' = f_{\prec'}$ defined in a language $\mathbf{L}'$.*

Proof: Notice that $V(\mathbf{L})$ must be finite, as for Theorem 7.1 and its corollary.

if: Preferential entailments satisfy (CT), thus f satisfies (CT) from Proposition 5.1, notice however that (Def$\rightleftharpoons$) would not suffice here.

only if: If f satisfies (CT), it is a general preferential entailment defined e.g. by the simplified relation $\prec_f$ introduced in [10, Definition 5.7]. We define $\mathbf{L}'$, b, b_1, b_2 and the preference relation $\prec'$ in $\mathbf{L}'$ as in the proof of Theorem 7.1, $\prec'$ being defined from $\prec_f$ exactly as in (12) from $\prec_s$. From the properties of b_1 and b_2 (mainly from (11)), we get then, as in the proof of Theorem 7.1: $f(\varphi) = b_2(f_{\prec'}(b_1(\varphi)))$ for any $\varphi \in \mathbf{L}$. □

This result adapts to finite general preferential entailment the characterization result [13, Theorem 4.8 and Preservation result 6.21] showing how to express any finite multi preferential entailment as a preferential entailment in a greater language.

8 A Detailed Example

Example 8.1. $V(\mathbf{L}) = \{P\}$, $f = f_{\prec_g}$ where $\prec_g$ is defined by $\bot \prec_g P$ and $\bot \prec_g \neg P$.

We get $f(\varphi) = \bot$ if $\varphi \in \{\bot, P, \neg P\}$ and $f(\top) = \top$ and also $\prec_g = \overline{\prec_g} = \prec_{nf} = \overline{\prec_{nf}}$. f falsifies (CR): $f(P \vee \neg P) \not\models f(P) \vee f(\neg P)$. Thus f is one of the simplest examples of a general preferential entailment which is not a multi preferential entailment. It is easy to check that f satisfies (LOOP) here, thus also (CUMU) (cf Theorem 4.1-3).

As f satisfies (LOOP), we apply Theorem 7.1, defining $\prec'$ from $\prec_s = \prec_g = \overline{\prec_{nf}}$. We define p and $V(\mathbf{L}')$ as follows: $p(\emptyset) = P'_0$, $p(\{P\}) = P'_1$, $V(\mathbf{L}') = \{P'_0, P'_1\}$, getting

Table 1. Computation of b_1 [and of $\mathbf{W}(\varphi)$ and $\mathbf{W}_{\prec_g}(\varphi)$] for each $\varphi \in \mathbf{L}$

$\mathbf{L}$ φ	$\mathcal{P}(\mathbf{M})$ $\mathbf{M}(\varphi)$	$\mathbf{M}'$ $b(\mathbf{M}(\varphi))$	$\mathbf{L}'_C$ $\bar{b}(\varphi)$	$b_1(\mathbf{L}) \subseteq \mathbf{L}'$ $b_1(\varphi)$	$[\in \mathcal{P}(\mathbf{L})]$ $\mathbf{W}(\varphi)$	$[\in \mathcal{P}(\mathbf{L})]$ $\mathbf{W}_{\prec_g}(\varphi)$
$\top$	$\{\emptyset, \{P\}\}$	$\emptyset$	$\neg P'_0 \wedge \neg P'_1$	$\top$	$\{\top, P, \neg P, \bot\}$	$\{\top, \bot\}$
P	$\{\{P\}\}$	$\{P'_0\}$	$P'_0 \wedge \neg P'_1$	P'_0	$\{P, \bot\}$	$\{\bot\}$
$\neg P$	$\{\emptyset\}$	$\{P'_1\}$	$\neg P'_0 \wedge P'_1$	P'_1	$\{\neg P, \bot\}$	$\{\bot\}$
$\bot$	$\emptyset$	$\{P'_0, P'_1\}$	$P'_0 \wedge P'_1$	$P'_0 \wedge P'_1$	$\{\bot\}$	$\{\bot\}$

$\mathbf{M}' = \{\emptyset, \{P'_0\}, \{P'_1\}, \{P'_0, P'_1\}\}$. Table 1 describes $\bar{b}$ and b_1. We get then $\prec'$ described as follows in $\mathbf{M}'$: $\{P'_0, P'_1\} \prec' \{P'_0\}$, $\{P'_0, P'_1\} \prec' \{P'_1\}$.

We get $\mathbf{W}_{\prec'}(\top) = \{\top, \bot\}$ and $\mathbf{W}_{\prec'}(\varphi) = \{\bot\}$ for $\varphi \in \{P, \neg P, \bot\}$.

Using the method given in [15], we get a set Φ' of formulas to circumscribe: We define the greatest pre-order (reflexive and transitive relation) $\preceq'$ on $\mathbf{L}'$, satisfying ($\mu' \prec' \nu'$ iff $\mu' \preceq' \nu'$ and not $\nu' \preceq' \mu'$): $\{P'_0, P'_1\} \preceq' \{P'_0\}$, $\{P'_0, P'_1\} \preceq' \{P'_1\}$, $\{P'_0\} \preceq' \{P'_1\}$, $\{P'_1\} \preceq' \{P'_0\}$ and $\mu' \preceq' \mu'$. Then for each $\mu' \in \mathbf{M}'$, we define the formula $\varphi'(\mu') \in \mathbf{L}'$ having for set of models μ' and its successors for $\preceq'$, getting a set $\Phi' = \{\varphi'(\emptyset), \varphi'(\{P'_0\}), \varphi'(\{P'_0, P'_1\})\}$ such that $f' = f_{\prec'} = CIRCF(\Phi', \emptyset, V(\mathbf{L}'))$ (Φ' is optimal in cardinality for describing f' as a formula circumscription):

$\varphi'(\mu')$	$\mathbf{M}'(\varphi'(\mu'))$
$\varphi'(\emptyset) = \neg P'_0 \wedge \neg P'_1$	$\{\emptyset\}$
$\varphi'(\{P'_0\}) = \varphi'(\{P'_1\}) = \neg(P'_0 \Leftrightarrow P'_1)$	$\{\{P'_0\}, \{P'_1\}\}$
$\varphi'(\{P'_0, P'_1\}) = P'_0 \vee P'_1$	$\{\{P'_0\}, \{P'_1\}, \{P'_0, P'_1\}\}$

As we get $\varphi'(\emptyset) = \neg\varphi'(\{P'_0, P'_1\})$, the formula $\varphi'(\emptyset)$ (or equivalently $\neg\varphi'(\emptyset)$) is "*fixed*" in the circumscription [5], which can help the computation. It is easy to check that this is always true (adding disjunctions of formulas to a set does not modify the circumscription of the set of formulas [15]): the formula associated to the set of models $\mathbf{M}' - \mathbf{M}'(b(f(\mathbf{L}))$ is always obtained by the construction, while the formula associated to the complementary set $\mathbf{M}'(b(\mathbf{L}))$ is the disjunction of the other formulas obtained.

Table 2 describes f' and b_2. Only the framed values are used by the method. The first column gives the formulas $\varphi' \in \mathbf{L}'$ (shortly framed when φ' is in the set $b_1(\mathbf{L})$, i.e. is a conjunction of atoms). The second column describes $f' = CIRCF(\Phi', \emptyset, V(\mathbf{L}'))$: in fact, we only need the (framed) values of $f'(\varphi')$ for the four values in $b_1(\mathbf{L})$. The next three columns give respectively $\mathbf{M}'(\varphi')$, $\mathbf{M}(b_2(\varphi'))$ and the formula $b_2(\varphi') \in \mathbf{L}$ (we need only to consider the two formulas φ' in the set $f'(b_1(\mathbf{L}))$, framed in the f' column, we have made this apparent by long frames in the φ' and b_2 columns).

From the values of $b_1(\varphi)$ for the four $\varphi \in \mathbf{L}$ (Table 1), we compute $b_2(f'(b_1(\varphi)))$, and check that we get indeed $b_2(f'(b_1(\varphi))) = f(\varphi)$ $[f(\varphi) = \bigvee_{\psi \in \mathbf{W}_{\prec_g}(\varphi)} \psi]$.

9 Conclusion and Perspective

We have extended the "expressive power of circumscription", by showing that not only cumulative multi preferential entailments as shown by Costello [4], but also general preferential entailments satisfying (LOOP), can be translated into circumscriptions in

Table 2. Theorem 7.1 applied to example 8.1 (only the six framed computations are used)

$\mathbf{L}'$ φ'	$[\in \mathbf{L}']$ $f'(\varphi')$	$\mathcal{P}(\mathbf{M}')$ $\mathbf{M}'(\varphi')$	$[\in \mathcal{P}(\mathbf{M})]$ $\mathbf{M}(b_2(\varphi'))$	$[\in \mathbf{L}]$ $b_2(\varphi')$
$\top$	$P'_0 \Leftrightarrow P'_1$	$\{\emptyset, \{P'_0\}, \{P'_1\}, \{P'_0, P'_1\}\}$	$\{\emptyset, \{P\}\}$	$\top$
$P'_0 \vee P'_1$	$P'_0 \wedge P'_1$	$\{\{P'_0\}, \{P'_1\}, \{P'_0, P'_1\}\}$	$\{\emptyset, \{P\}\}$	$\top$
$P'_0 \vee \neg P'_1$	$P'_0 \Leftrightarrow P'_1$	$\{\emptyset, \{P'_0\}, \{P'_0, P'_1\}\}$	$\{\emptyset, \{P\}\}$	$\top$
$\neg P'_0 \vee P'_1$	$P'_0 \Leftrightarrow P'_1$	$\{\emptyset, \{P'_1\}, \{P'_0, P'_1\}\}$	$\{\emptyset, \{P\}\}$	$\top$
$\neg P'_0 \vee \neg P'_1$	$\neg P'_0 \vee \neg P'_1$	$\{\emptyset, \{P'_0\}, \{P'_1\}\}$	$\{\emptyset, \{P\}\}$	$\top$
P'_0	$P'_0 \wedge P'_1$	$\{\{P'_0\}, \{P'_0, P'_1\}\}$	$\{\{P\}\}$	P
P'_1	$P'_0 \wedge P'_1$	$\{\{P'_1\}, \{P'_0, P'_1\}\}$	$\{\emptyset\}$	$\neg P$
$P'_0 \Leftrightarrow P'_1$	$P'_0 \Leftrightarrow P'_1$	$\{\emptyset, \{P'_0, P'_1\}\}$	$\{\emptyset, \{P\}\}$	$\top$
$P'_0 \not\Leftrightarrow P'_1$	$P'_0 \not\Leftrightarrow P'_1$	$\{\{P'_0\}, \{P'_1\}\}$	$\{\emptyset, \{P\}\}$	$\top$
$\neg P'_0$	$\neg P'_0$	$\{\emptyset, \{P'_1\}\}$	$\{\emptyset, \{P\}\}$	$\top$
$\neg P'_1$	$\neg P'_1$	$\{\emptyset, \{P'_0\}\}$	$\{\emptyset, \{P\}\}$	$\top$
$P'_0 \wedge P'_1$	$P'_0 \wedge P'_1$	$\{\{P'_0, P'_1\}\}$	$\{\emptyset\}$	$\bot$
$P'_0 \wedge \neg P'_1$	$P'_0 \wedge \neg P'_1$	$\{\{P'_0\}\}$	$\{\{P\}\}$	P
$\neg P'_0 \wedge P'_1$	$\neg P'_0 \wedge P'_1$	$\{\{P'_1\}\}$	$\{\emptyset\}$	$\neg P$
$\neg P'_0 \wedge \neg P'_1$	$\neg P'_0 \wedge \neg P'_1$	$\{\emptyset\}$	$\{\emptyset, \{P\}\}$	$\top$
$\bot$	$\bot$	$\emptyset$	$\emptyset$	$\bot$

another vocabulary. These various kinds of preferential entailment are introduced in Kraus and al. [7]. In order to achieve this translation, we needed two results. Firstly, the notion of general preferential entailment, as introduced in [7], is overly general [10]: we do not need copies of theories (or equivalently, of sets of interpretations). We can define the relation in the simpler set of the theories. Doing this, we have simplified some results in [7]: cumulative inferences correspond to general preferential entailment defined by a simplified relation satisfying (sf), also known as "smooth" (a result already given in [1,2] in much more complex ways). Secondly, we have described a modification of the vocabulary which allows to transpose any general preference relation among theories into a preference relation among complete theories (or among interpretations). This method needs a huge auxiliary vocabulary, however, only a very simple, and small, subclass of formulas in the new vocabulary (the conjunctions of atoms) needs to be considered. Moreover, the translation formulas from the old vocabulary to the new one and back are easy to compute. Thus, the method should be really applicable.

These results should have applications in helping the automatic computations of non monotonic formalisms. The modification of vocabulary introduced here could have other applications, as it is rather general, and relatively simple. Also, the simplification of the originally overly complex notion of general preferential entailment should help future studies on the subject: it is much easier to work with relations among theories that with relations among arbitrary sets of copies of theories. Finally, the translation results given here should also have real applications. This is obvious for the result allowing to translate any finite general preferential entailment satisfying (LOOP) into a circumscription. Indeed, the work on automatic computation of circumscription is still very active, and our work shows that any progress could be applied, not only to cumulative preferential entailments, as already known, but also to the strictly more general notion of general preferential entailment satisfying (LOOP). Also, the result showing how to express any finite cumulative general preferential entailment (a yet strictly more general notion) in terms of preferential entailment (where the relation is directly among interpretations) should have applications, since the notion of ordinary preferential entailment is simpler and more studied than the notion of general preferential entailment.

More studies are needed in order to apply these computations. Moreover, we are still waiting for efficient ways of computing ordinary preferential entailments, or even formula circumscriptions. At least we know now that not only multi, but also general, preferential entailments, would benefit from these demonstrators.

References

1. H.L Arlo-Costa and S.J. Shapiro, 'Maps between nonmonotonic and conditional logics.', in *KR'92*, pp. 553–564, Cambridge, (1992). Morgan Kaufmann.
2. Alexander Bochman. An Epistemic Representation of Nonmonotonic Inference. Unpublished manuscript, 1999.
3. Alexander Bochman, 'Credulous Nonmonotonic Inference', in *IJCAI-99*, ed., Thomas Dean, pp. 30–35, Stockholm, (August 1999). Morgan Kaufmann.
4. Tom Costello, 'The expressive power of circumscription', *Artificial Intelligence*, **104**(1–2), 313–329, (September 1998).
5. Johan de Kleer and Kurt Konolige, 'Eliminating the Fixed Predicates from a Circumscription', *Artificial Intelligence*, **39**(3), 391–398, (July 1989).
6. Joeri Engelfriet, 'Non-cumulative reasoning: rules and models', *Journal of Logic and Computation*, **10**(5), 705–719, (October 2000).
7. Sarit Kraus, Daniel Lehmann, and Menachem Magidor, 'Nonmonotonic Reasoning, Preferential Models and Cumulative Logics', *Artificial Intelligence*, **44**(1–2), 167–207, (July 1990).
8. John McCarthy, 'Circumscription–a form of non-monotonic reasoning', *Artificial Intelligence*, **13**(1–2), 27–39, (April 1980).
9. John McCarthy, ' Application of circumscription to formalizing common sense knowledge', *Artificial Intelligence*, **28**(1), 89–116, (February 1986).
10. Yves Moinard, 'Characterizing general preferential entailments', in *14th European Conference on Artificial Intelligence*, ed., Werner Horn, pp. 474–478, IOS Press, 2000.
11. Yves Moinard, 'Note about cardinality-based circumscription', *Artificial Intelligence*, **119**(1–2), 259–273, (May 2000).
12. Yves Moinard and Raymond Rolland, 'Propositional circumscriptions', TR INRIA 3538, Rennes, France, (October 1998). `http://www.inria.fr/RRRT/RR-3538.html`.
13. Yves Moinard and Raymond Rolland, 'Preferential entailments, extensions and reductions of the vocabulary', TR INRIA-IRISA 3787, Rennes, France, (October 1999).
14. Yves Moinard and Raymond Rolland, 'Characterizations of preferential entailments', TR INRIA-IRISA 3928, Rennes, France, (April 2000).
15. Yves Moinard and Raymond Rolland, 'Smallest Equivalent sets for Finite Propositional Formula Circumscriptions', in *CL-2000, in LNAI 1861*, pp. 897–911, 2000.
16. Donald Perlis and Jack Minker, 'Completeness results for circumscription', *Artificial Intelligence*, **28**(1), 29–42, (February 1986).
17. Ken Satoh, 'A Probabilistic Interpretation for Lazy Nonmonotonic Reasoning', in *AAAI-90*, pp. 659–664. MIT Press, (1990).
18. Yoav Shoham, *Reasoning about change*, MIT Press, Cambridge, 1988.

A Semantic Tableau Version of First-Order Quasi-Classical Logic

Anthony Hunter

Department of Computer Science
University College London
Gower Street
London WC1E 6BT
UK

Abstract. Quasi-classical logic (QC logic) allows the derivation of non-trivial classical inferences from inconsistent information. A paraconsistent, or non-trivializable, logic is, by necessity, a compromise, or weakening, of classical logic. The compromises on QC logic seem to be more appropriate than other paraconsistent logics for applications in computing. In particular, the connectives behave in a "classical manner" at the object level so that important proof rules such as modus tollens, modus ponens, and disjunctive syllogism hold. Here we develop QC logic by presenting a semantic tableau version for first-order QC logic.

1 Introduction

Paraconsistent reasoning is important in handling inconsistent information, and there have been a number of proposals for paraconsistent logics (for a review see [Hun98]). However, developing non-trivializable, or paraconsistent logics, necessitates some compromise, or weakening, of classical logic. Key paraconsistent logics such as C_ω [dC74] achieve this by weakening the classical connectives, particularly negation. However this results in useful proof rules such as disjunctive syllogism failing, and intuitive equivalences such as $\neg\alpha \vee \beta \equiv \alpha \rightarrow \beta$ failing.

An alternative, called quasi-classical (or QC) logic, is to restrict the proof theory [BH95,Hun00a]. In this restriction, compositional proof rules (for example, disjunction introduction) cannot be followed by decompositional rules (for example, resolution). Whilst this gives a logic that is weaker than classical logic, it does mean that the connectives behave classically at the object level. We believe the logic is appealing for reasoning with inconsistencies arising in applications such as systems development [HN98], and for reasoning with structured text [Hun00b].

In this paper, we present a first-order version of paraconsistent logic. First we give the semantics for the first-order language and then give a semantic tableau version of the proof theory.

S. Benferhat and P. Besnard (Eds.): ECSQARU 2001, LNAI 2143, pp. 544–555, 2001.

2 First-Order QC Logic

First-order QC logic is a development of QC logic as defined in [Hun00a]. We assume the usual classical definitions for the language including definitions for a free variable, a bound variable, a ground term, and a ground formula.

Definition 1. *The language of first-order QC logic is that of classical first-order logic. We let $\mathcal{L}$ denote a set of formulae formed in the usual way from a set of predicate symbols, a set of function symbols, a set of variable symbols, and the connectives*[1] $\{\neg, \vee, \wedge\}$. *We also assume there is at least one zero-place function symbol in the set of functions symbols.*

Definition 2. *Let α be an atom, and let $\sim$ be a complementation operation such that $\sim\alpha$ is $\neg\alpha$ and $\sim(\neg\alpha)$ is α. The $\sim$ operator is not part of the object language, but it makes some definitions clearer.*

Definition 3. *Let $\alpha_1 \vee .. \vee \alpha_n$ be a clause that includes a literal disjunct α_i. The focus of $\alpha_1 \vee .. \vee \alpha_n$ by α_i, denoted $\otimes(\alpha_1 \vee .. \vee \alpha_n, \alpha_i)$ is defined as the clause obtained by removing α_i from $\alpha_1 \vee .. \vee \alpha_n$. In the case of a clause with just one disjunct, we assume $\otimes(\alpha_1, \alpha_1) = \bot$.*

Example 1. Let $\alpha \vee \beta \vee \gamma$ be a clause where α, β, and γ are literals. Hence, $\otimes(\alpha \vee \beta \vee \gamma, \beta) = \alpha \vee \gamma$.

The notion of a model in first-order QC logic is based on a form of Herbrand interpretation.

Definition 4. *The* **Herbrand universe** *of $\mathcal{L}$ is the set of ground terms in $\mathcal{L}$ and is denoted $\mathcal{U}(\mathcal{L})$. The* **Herbrand base** *of $\mathcal{L}$ is the set of ground atoms in $\mathcal{L}$ formed using the Herbrand universe of $\mathcal{L}$ and is denoted $\mathcal{B}(\mathcal{L})$.*

Definition 5. *Let $\mathcal{B}(\mathcal{L})$ be the Herbrand Base of $\mathcal{L}$. Let $\mathcal{O}(\mathcal{L})$ be the set of objects defined as follows, where $+\alpha$ is a positive object, and $-\alpha$ is a negative object.*

$$\mathcal{O}(\mathcal{L}) = \{+\alpha \mid \alpha \in \mathcal{B}(\mathcal{L})\} \cup \{-\alpha \mid \alpha \in \mathcal{B}(\mathcal{L})\}$$

We call any $E \in \wp(\mathcal{O}(\mathcal{L}))$ a model. So E can contain both $+\alpha$ and $-\alpha$ for some ground atom α.

We can consider the following meaning for positive and negative objects being in or out of some model E,

$+\alpha \in E$ means α is "satisfiable" in the model
$-\alpha \in E$ means $\neg\alpha$ is "satisfiable" in the model
$+\alpha \notin E$ means α is not "satisfiable" in the model
$-\alpha \notin E$ means $\neg\alpha$ is not "satisfiable" in the model

[1] To provide a succinct presentation, we do not consider implication here.

Since we can allow both an atom and its complement to be satisfiable, we have decoupled, at the level of the model, the link between a formula and its complement. In contrast, in a classical model, if a model satisfies a literal, then it is forced to not satsify the complement of the literal.

We formalise the notion of satisfiability and extend it to the rest of the language using the following definitions.

Definition 6. *An assignment is a function from the set of variables used in $\mathcal{L}$ to $\mathcal{U}(\mathcal{L})$.*

Definition 7. *Given an assignment A, an X-variant assignment A' is the same as A except perhaps in the assignment for X.*

Definition 8. *For an assignment A, terms in $\mathcal{L}$ are interpreted as follows, where $[.]^A$ is a function from the terms in $\mathcal{L}$ to $\mathcal{U}(\mathcal{L})$.*

$$[c]^A = c \qquad \text{where } c \text{ is a constant symbol.}$$

$$[X]^A = A(X) \qquad \text{where } X \text{ is a variable symbol.}$$

$$[f(t_1, .., t_n)]^A = f([t_1]^A, .., [t_n]^A) \qquad \text{where } f \text{ is a function symbol and } t_1, .., t_n \text{ are terms.}$$

In this, each ground term in $\mathcal{L}$ is interpreted as the equivalent term in $\mathcal{U}(\mathcal{L})$. Hence the interpretation of terms is independent of the choice of model.

Definition 9. *For an assignment A, an atom $\alpha(t_1, .., t_n)$ in $\mathcal{L}$ is interpreted as follows, where $\models_h$ is a satisfiability relation called* **Herbrand satisfaction**.

$$(E, A) \models_h \alpha(t_1, .., t_n) \quad \textit{iff} \ +\alpha([t_1]^A, .., [t_n]^A) \in E$$

$$(E, A) \models_h \neg\alpha(t_1, .., t_n) \quad \textit{iff} \ -\alpha([t_1]^A, .., [t_n]^A) \in E$$

Using Herbrand satisfaction, we define two further satisfaction relations, namely strong satisfaction and weak satisfaction, that allow us to define an entailment relation. Essentially, the equivalences in strong satisfaction allow for any formula in $\mathcal{L}$ to be rewritten into a conjunctive normal form, and then into clauses, which can be evaluated with respect to the objects in the model. In addition, the definition for disjunction captures a form of resolution in the semantics. This is needed because the classical relationship between a positive and negative literal has been decoupled.

Definition 10. *Let $\models_s$ be a satisfiability relation called* **strong satisfaction**. *For a model E, and an assignment A, we define $\models_s$ as follows, where $\alpha_1, ..., \alpha_n$*

are literals in $\mathcal{L}$, and α is a literal in $\mathcal{L}$.

$$(E,A) \models_s \alpha \text{ iff } (E,A) \models_h \alpha$$

$$\begin{aligned}&(E,A) \models_s \alpha_1 \vee ... \vee \alpha_n\\ &\quad \text{iff } [(E,A) \models_s \alpha_1 \text{ or } ... \text{ or } (E,A) \models_s \alpha_n]\\ &\qquad \text{and } \forall i \text{ s.t. } 1 \leq i \leq n\\ &\qquad\quad [(E,A) \models_s {\sim}\alpha_i \text{ implies } (E,A) \models_s \otimes(\alpha_1 \vee ... \vee \alpha_n, \alpha_i)]\end{aligned}$$

For $\alpha, \beta, \gamma \in \mathcal{L}$, we extend the definition as follows,

$(E,A) \models_s \alpha \wedge \beta$ *iff* $(E,A) \models_s \alpha$ *and* $(E,A) \models_s \beta$
$(E,A) \models_s \neg\neg\alpha \vee \gamma$ *iff* $(E,A) \models_s \alpha \vee \gamma$
$(E,A) \models_s \neg(\alpha \wedge \beta) \vee \gamma$ *iff* $(E,A) \models_s \neg\alpha \vee \neg\beta \vee \gamma$
$(E,A) \models_s \neg(\alpha \vee \beta) \vee \gamma$ *iff* $(E,A) \models_s (\neg\alpha \wedge \neg\beta) \vee \gamma$
$(E,A) \models_s \alpha \vee (\beta \wedge \gamma)$ *iff* $(E,A) \models_s (\alpha \vee \beta) \wedge (\alpha \vee \gamma)$
$(E,A) \models_s \alpha \wedge (\beta \vee \gamma)$ *iff* $(E,A) \models_s (\alpha \wedge \beta) \vee (\alpha \wedge \gamma)$

$(E,A) \models_s (\exists X\alpha) \vee \beta$ *iff for some X-variant assignment* A', $(E,A') \models_s \alpha \vee \beta$
$(E,A) \models_s (\forall X\alpha) \vee \beta$ *iff for all X-variant assignments* A', $(E,A') \models_s \alpha \vee \beta$
$(E,A) \models_s (\neg\exists X\alpha) \vee \beta$ *iff for all X-variant assignments* A', $(E,A') \models_s \neg\alpha \vee \beta$
$(E,A) \models_s (\neg\forall X\alpha) \vee \beta$ *iff for some X-variant assignment* A', $(E,A') \models_s \neg\alpha \vee \beta$

The definition for weak satisfaction is similar to strong satisfaction. The main difference is that the definition for disjunction is less restricted. Note, distributivity is implied by the definition of weak satisfaction.

Definition 11. *Let $\models_w$ be a satisfiability relation called* **weak satisfaction**. *For a model E, and an assignment A, we define $\models_w$ as follows, where $\alpha_1, ..., \alpha_n$ are literals in $\mathcal{L}$ and α is a literal in $\mathcal{L}$.*

$$(E,A) \models_w \alpha \text{ iff } (E,A) \models_h \alpha$$

$$(E,A) \models_w \alpha_1 \vee ... \vee \alpha_n \text{ iff } [(E,A) \models_w \alpha_1 \text{ or } ... \text{ or } (E,A) \models_w \alpha_n]$$

For $\alpha, \beta, \gamma \in \mathcal{L}$, we extend the definition as follows,

$(E,A) \models_w \alpha \wedge \beta$ *iff* $(E,A) \models_w \alpha$ *and* $(E,A) \models_w \beta$
$(E,A) \models_w \neg\neg\alpha \vee \gamma$ *iff* $(E,A) \models_w \alpha \vee \gamma$
$(E,A) \models_w \neg(\alpha \wedge \beta) \vee \gamma$ *iff* $(E,A) \models_w \neg\alpha \vee \neg\beta \vee \gamma$
$(E,A) \models_w \neg(\alpha \vee \beta) \vee \gamma$ *iff* $(E,A) \models_w (\neg\alpha \wedge \neg\beta) \vee \gamma$

$(E,A) \models_w (\exists X\alpha) \vee \beta$ *iff for some X-variant assignment* A', $(E,A') \models_w \alpha \vee \beta$
$(E,A) \models_w (\forall X\alpha) \vee \beta$ *iff for all X-variant assignments* A', $(E,A') \models_w \alpha \vee \beta$
$(E,A) \models_w (\neg\exists X\alpha) \vee \beta$ *iff for all X-variant assignments* A', $(E,A') \models_w \neg\alpha \vee \beta$
$(E,A) \models_w (\neg\forall X\alpha) \vee \beta$ *iff for some X-variant assignment* A', $(E,A') \models_w \neg\alpha \vee \beta$

Example 2. Let $\Delta = \{\alpha(a), \gamma(b), \forall X(\neg\alpha(X) \vee \beta(X))\}$,
and let $\mathcal{B}(\mathcal{L}) = \{\alpha(a), \beta(a), \gamma(a), \alpha(b), \beta(b), \gamma(b)\}$.
Now let $A = \{X \mapsto a\}$ and $E = \{+\alpha(a), +\beta(a), +\gamma(b)\}$.
This gives the following.

$$(E, A) \models_s \alpha(a)$$
$$(E, A) \models_s \gamma(b)$$
$$(E, A) \models_s \forall X(\neg\alpha(X) \vee \beta(X))$$

Example 3. Let $\Delta = \{\exists X, Y\ \alpha(X, Y), \beta(f(a))\}$,
and let $\mathcal{B}(\mathcal{L}) = \{\alpha(a, a), \beta(a), \alpha(f(a), a), \beta(f(a)), \alpha(f(f(a)), a), \beta(f(f(a))), ...\}$.
Now let $A = \{X \mapsto a, Y \mapsto a\}$ and $E = \{-\alpha(a, a), +\beta(f(a))\}$.
This gives the following.

$$(E, A) \models_s \beta(f(a))$$
$$(E, A) \models_s \exists X \beta(X)$$
$$(E, A) \not\models_s \exists X, Y \alpha(X, Y)$$

Example 4. Let $\Delta = \{\forall X(\neg\alpha(X), \alpha(a))\}$,
and let $\mathcal{B}(\mathcal{L}) = \{\alpha(a)\}$.
Now let $A = \{X \mapsto a\}$ and $E = \{+\alpha(a), -\alpha(a)\}$.
This gives the following.

$$(E, A) \models_s \alpha(a) \qquad (E, A) \models_s \neg\alpha(a)$$
$$(E, A) \not\models_s \alpha(a) \vee \beta(b) \quad (E, A) \models_w \alpha(a) \vee \beta(b)$$

Definition 12. *We polymorphically extend strong satisfaction and weak satisfaction as follows*

$$E \models_s \alpha \textit{ iff for all assignments } A, (E, A) \models_s \alpha$$
$$E \models_w \alpha \textit{ iff for all assignments } A, (E, A) \models_w \alpha$$

In the following definition, we can see that QC entailment is of the same form as classical entailment except we use strong satisfaction for the assumptions and weak satisfaction for the inference.

Definition 13. *Let* $\models_Q$ *be an entailment relation, called the QC entailment relation, such that* $\models_Q \subseteq \wp(\mathcal{L}) \times \mathcal{L}$, *and defined as follows,*

$$\{\alpha_1, .., \alpha_n\} \models_Q \beta$$
$$\textit{iff for all } E \textit{ if } E \models_s \alpha_1 \textit{ and ... and } E \models_s \alpha_n \textit{ then } E \models_w \beta$$

We can consider the strong satisfaction relation as capturing the decomposition of the set of asumptions. Strong satisfaction forces each resolvent β of a clause $\alpha \vee \beta$ to hold if $\sim\alpha$ holds. In contrast, we can consider the weak satisfaction relation as capturing the composition of formulae from resolvents, allowing disjuncts to be introduced.

Example 5. The following illustrate QC entailment.

$$\{\alpha(a), \forall X(\neg\alpha(X) \vee \neg\alpha(X))\} \models_Q \neg\alpha(a)$$
$$\{\alpha(a), \forall X(\neg\alpha(X) \vee \beta(X))\} \models_Q \beta(a)$$
$$\{\alpha(a)\} \models_Q \exists X \alpha(X)$$

We can show that $\models_Q$ is non-trivializable in the sense that when Δ is classically inconsistent, it is not the case every formula in $\mathcal{L}$ is entailed by Δ.

Example 6. Let $\beta, \neg\beta$ and α be ground literals in $\mathcal{L}$. So $\{\beta \wedge \neg\beta\}$ is classically inconsistent. However it is not the case that $\{\beta \wedge \neg\beta\} \models_Q \alpha$ holds, since $E = \{+\beta, -\beta\}$ is a model where $E \models_s \beta \wedge \neg\beta$, but $E \not\models_w \alpha$.

However, many classical tautologies do not follow with $\models_Q$. In particular, the classical tautologies do not follow from an empty set.

Example 7. Let $\Delta = \emptyset$. Now consider the classical tautology $\alpha \vee \neg\alpha$. Here $\Delta \models_Q \alpha \vee \neg\alpha$ does not hold. Since $E = \emptyset$ strongly satisfies every formula in Δ, but E does not weakly satisfy $\alpha \vee \neg\alpha$.

This is one illustration of how QC logic is weaker than classical logic. A number of further features of classical logic such as left logical equivalence, conditionalization, cut, and right weakening also fail [Hun00a].

3 The QC Semantic Tableau

In order to provide an automated proof procedure, we adapt the tableau approach for classical logic that was developed by Smullyan [Smu 68]. For this adaptation, we need the following definitions.

Definition 14. *The set of signed formulae of $\mathcal{L}$ is denoted $\mathcal{L}^*$ and is defined as $\mathcal{L} \cup \{\alpha^* \mid \alpha \in \mathcal{L}\}$.*

We will regard the formulae in $\mathcal{L}^*$ without the $*$ symbol as satisfiable and the formulae in $\mathcal{L}^*$ with the $*$ symbol as unsatisfiable.

Definition 15. *We further extend the weak satisfaction and strong satisfaction relations as follows where $\alpha \in \mathcal{L}$.*

$$E \models_s \alpha^* \textit{ iff } E \not\models_s \alpha$$
$$E \models_w \alpha^* \textit{ iff } E \not\models_w \alpha$$

Definition 16. *For a formula $\alpha \in \mathcal{L}$ with free variable X, and a term $t \in \mathcal{U}(\mathcal{L})$, we let $\alpha[X/t]$ denote the substitution of all occurrences of X in α by t.*

In the definition of QC semantic tableau, there are two types of decomposition rule. The first type is represented by the S-rules given in Definition 17 and the second type is represented by the U-rules given in Definition 18. All the S-rules assume the formula above the line is satisfiable, and all the U-rules assume the formula above the line is unsatisfiable.

Definition 17. *The following are the S-rules for a QC semantic tableau, where t is in $\mathcal{U}(\mathcal{L})$ and t' is in $\mathcal{U}(\mathcal{L})$ but not occurring in the tableau constructed so far. The $|$ symbol denotes the introduction of a branch point in the QC semantic tableau.*

$$\frac{\alpha_1 \vee \ldots \vee \alpha_n}{(\sim \alpha_i)^* \mid \otimes(\alpha_1 \vee \ldots \vee \alpha_n, \alpha_i)} \quad \text{where } \alpha_1, .., \alpha_n \text{ are literals}$$

$$\frac{\alpha_1 \vee \ldots \vee \alpha_n}{\alpha_1 \mid \ldots \mid \alpha_n} \quad \text{where } \alpha_1, .., \alpha_n \text{ are literals}$$

$$\frac{\alpha \wedge \beta}{\alpha, \beta} \qquad \frac{\neg\neg\alpha \vee \gamma}{\alpha \vee \gamma}$$

$$\frac{\neg(\alpha \wedge \beta) \vee \gamma}{\neg\alpha \vee \neg\beta \vee \gamma} \qquad \frac{\neg(\alpha \vee \beta) \vee \gamma}{(\neg\alpha \wedge \neg\beta) \vee \gamma}$$

$$\frac{\alpha \vee (\beta \wedge \gamma)}{(\alpha \vee \beta) \wedge (\alpha \vee \gamma)} \quad \frac{\alpha \wedge (\beta \vee \gamma)}{(\alpha \wedge \beta) \vee (\alpha \wedge \gamma)}$$

$$\frac{(\forall X\alpha) \vee \gamma}{(\alpha[X/t]) \vee \gamma} \quad \frac{(\neg\exists X\alpha) \vee \gamma}{(\neg\alpha[X/t]) \vee \gamma} \quad \frac{(\exists X\alpha) \vee \gamma}{(\alpha[X/t']) \vee \gamma} \quad \frac{(\neg\forall X\alpha) \vee \gamma}{(\neg\alpha[X/t']) \vee \gamma}$$

We will refer to the first two rules as the disjunction S-rules, the next six rules as the rewrite S-rules, and the last four rules as the quantification S-rules.

Definition 18. *The following are the U-rules for a QC semantic tableau, where t is in $\mathcal{U}(\mathcal{L})$ and t' is in $\mathcal{U}(\mathcal{L})$ but not occurring in the tableau so far. The $|$ symbol denotes the introduction of a branch point in the QC semantic tableau.*

$$\frac{(\alpha \vee \beta)^*}{\alpha^*, \beta^*} \quad \frac{(\alpha \wedge \beta)^*}{\alpha^* \mid \beta^*} \quad \frac{(\neg\neg\alpha \vee \gamma)^*}{(\alpha \vee \gamma)^*}$$

$$\frac{(\neg(\alpha \wedge \beta) \vee \gamma)^*}{(\neg\alpha \vee \neg\beta \vee \gamma)^*} \quad \frac{(\neg(\alpha \vee \beta) \vee \gamma)^*}{((\neg\alpha \wedge \neg\beta) \vee \gamma)^*}$$

$$\frac{((\forall X\alpha) \vee \gamma)^*}{((\alpha[X/t']) \vee \gamma)^*} \quad \frac{((\neg\exists X\alpha) \vee \gamma)^*}{((\neg\alpha[X/t']) \vee \gamma)^*} \quad \frac{((\exists X\alpha) \vee \gamma)^*}{((\alpha[X/t]) \vee \gamma)^*} \quad \frac{((\neg\forall X\alpha) \vee \gamma)^*}{((\neg\alpha[X/t]) \vee \gamma)^*}$$

We will refer to the first rule as the disjunction U-rule, the second rule as the conjunction U-rule, the next three rules as the rewrite U-rules, and the last four rules as the quantification U-rules.

Definition 19. *A QC semantic tableau for a database Δ and a query α is a tree such that: (1) the formulae in $\Delta \cup \{\alpha^*\}$ are at the root of the tree; (2) each node of the tree has a set of signed formulae; and (3) the formulae at each node are generated by an application of one of the decomposition rules on a signed formula at ancestors of that node.*

The classical definition for semantic tableau incorporates a similar definition to that of Definition 19. The major difference is that in the classical definition, the root has $\Delta \cup \{\neg\alpha\}$ where $\neg\alpha$ is the negation of the query. The reason QC logic doesn't use this is that we have decoupled the classical relationship between a formula and its complement.

Definition 20. *A QC tableau is closed iff every branch is closed. A branch is closed iff there is a formula β for which β and β^* belong to that branch. A tableau is open if there is an open branch. A branch is open if there are no more rules that can be applied, and it is not closed.*

The classical form of tableau also incorporates the definitions given in Definition 20. In Proposition 8, below, we show that a database Δ implies a query α, by QC logic, if and only if a QC tableau for a database Δ and query α is closed. First we consider some examples in Figures 1, 2, and 3.

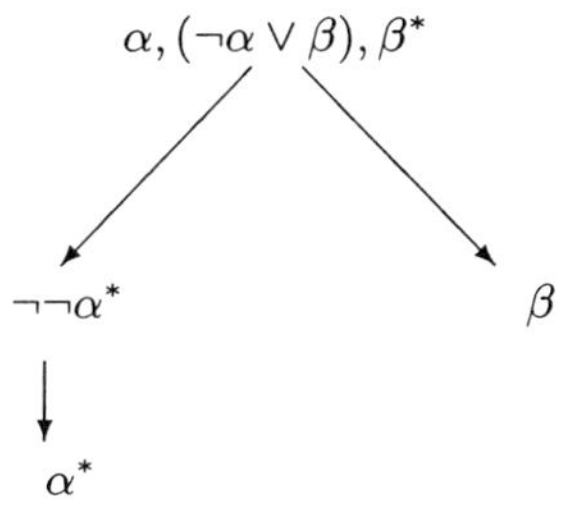

Fig. 1. Let Δ be $\{(\neg\alpha \vee \beta), \alpha\}$, and the query be β. This gives the root $\{\alpha, (\neg\alpha \vee \beta), \beta^*\}$, and the tableau is closed. In this tableau, $(\neg\alpha \vee \beta)$ is decomposed to $\sim\neg\alpha^*$ in the left branch, and $\otimes(\neg\alpha \vee \beta, \alpha)$ in the right branch, where $\sim\neg\alpha^* = \neg\neg\alpha^*$, and $\otimes(\neg\alpha \vee \beta, \neg\alpha)$ $= \beta$. The final step in the left branch is to obtain α^* from $\neg\neg\alpha^*$.

4 Some Properties of the QC Semantic Tableau

Each branch in a QC semantic tableau delineates a class of pairs of (E, A) where E is a model and A is an assignment. As we decompose the formulae in a branch, we refine the class of pairs (E, A).

Proposition 1. *Each tableau rule given in Definition 17 is sound in the following sense: If $\phi \in \mathcal{L}^*$ is the formula above the line, and $\psi \in \mathcal{L}^*$ is the formula below the line, and E is a model such that $E \models_s \phi$, then $E \models_s \psi$.*

Proof. For any formula $\phi \in \mathcal{L}$ at the root, if we assume that the formula is satisfiable according to the $\models_s$ relation, then we can also assume that any formula resulting from the decomposition of ϕ using the S-rules is also satisfiable using the

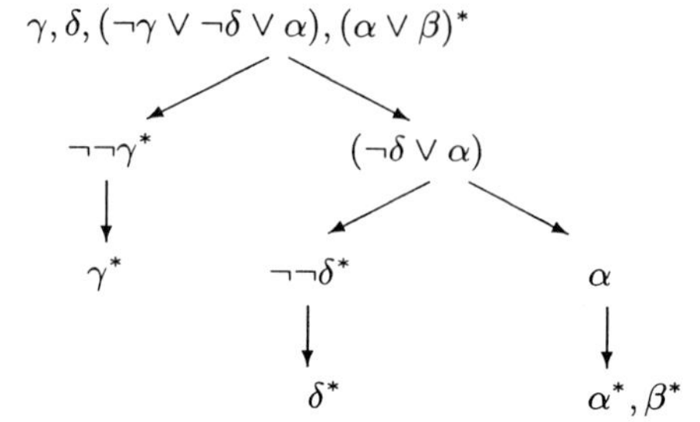

Fig. 2. Let Δ be $\{\gamma, \delta, (\neg\gamma \vee \neg\delta \vee \alpha)\}$ and let the query be $\alpha \vee \beta$. This gives the root $\{\gamma, \delta, ((\neg\gamma \vee \neg\delta) \vee \alpha), (\alpha \vee \beta)^*\}$, and the tableau is closed.

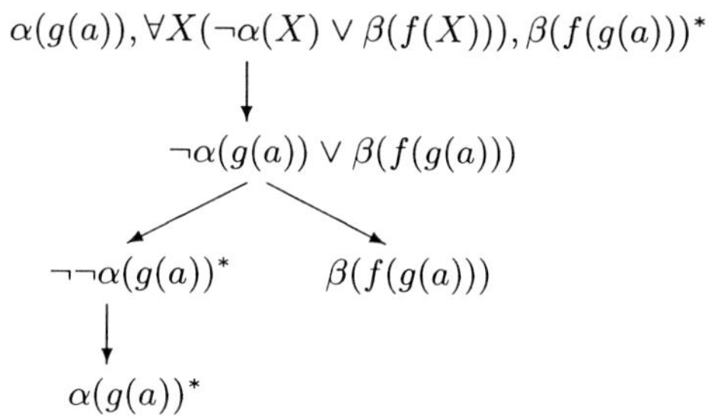

Fig. 3. Let Δ be $\{\alpha(g(a)), \forall X(\neg\alpha(X) \vee \beta(f(X)))\}$ and the query be $\beta(f(g(a)))$. This gives the root $\{\alpha(g(a)), \forall X(\neg\alpha(X) \vee \beta(f(X))), \beta(f(g(a)))^*\}$, and the tableau is closed.

$\models_s$ relation. We justify this for each of the S-rules as follows: (First disjunction S-rule) According to Definition 10, for all E,A, if $(E, A) \models_s \alpha_1 \vee .. \vee \alpha_n$, then for each α_i either $(E, A) \not\models_s \sim\alpha_i$, or $(E, A) \models_s \otimes(\alpha_1 \vee .. \vee \alpha_n, \alpha_i)$. (Second disjunction S-rule) According to Definition 10, for all E,A, if $(E, A) \models_s \alpha_1 \vee .. \vee \alpha_n$, then $(E, A) \models_s \alpha_1$ or ... or $(E, A) \models_s \alpha_n$. (Quantification S-rules) Consider the rule with $\forall X\alpha$ above the line. Here, for all E, A, if $(E, A) \models_s \forall X\alpha$, then for any A' that differs at most in X, and hence for any $t \in \mathcal{U}(\mathcal{L})$, $(E, A') \models_s \alpha[X/t]$. Now consider the rule with $\exists X\alpha$ above the line. Here, for all (E, A), if $(E, A) \models_s \exists X\alpha$, then for some A' that differs at most in X, and here for some t', $(E, A') \models_s \alpha[X/t']$. However, as we do not know which t', we remain impartial, and we select some t' that has not yet been used in the tableau so far. The other two quantification rules follow similarly. (Rewrite S-rules) The soundness for these follow directly from Definition 10.

Proposition 2. *Each tableau rule given in Definition 18 is sound in the following sense: If $\phi \in \mathcal{L}^*$ is the formula above the line, and $\psi \in \mathcal{L}^*$ is the formula below the line, and E is a model such that $E \models_w \phi$, then $E \models_w \psi$.*

Proof. For any formula ϕ^* at the root, if we assume that the formula is unsatisfiable according to the $\models_w$ relation, then we also assume that any formula resulting from the decomposition of ϕ^* using the U-rules is also unsatisfiable using the $\models_w$ relation. We justify this for each of the U-rules as follows: (Disjunction U-rule) According to Definition 11, for all E,A, if $(E, A) \not\models_w \alpha \vee \beta$, then $(E, A) \not\models_w \alpha$ and $(E, A) \not\models_w \beta$. (Conjunction U-rule) According to Definition 11, for all E,A, if $(E, A) \not\models_w \alpha \wedge \beta$, then $(E, A) \not\models_w \alpha$ or $(E, A) \not\models_w \beta$. (Quantification U-rules) Consider the rule with $(\exists X\alpha)^*$ above the line. Here, for all (E, A), if $(E, A) \not\models_w \exists X\alpha$, then for any A' that differs at most in X, and hence for any $t \in \mathcal{U}(\mathcal{L})$, $(E, A') \not\models_w \alpha[X/t]$. Now consider the rule with $(\forall X\alpha)^*$ above the line. Here, for all (E, A), if $(E, A) \not\models_w \forall X\alpha$, then there is a A' that differs at most in X, and hence a $t' \in \mathcal{U}(\mathcal{L})$, such that $(E, A') \not\models_w \alpha[X/t']$. However, we do not know which t', and so to remain impartial, we select some t' that has not yet been used in the tableau so far. The other two quantification rules follow similarly. (Rewrite U-rules) The soundness for these follow directly from Definition 11.

Proposition 3. *The set of decomposition rules given in Definition 17 is complete in the following sense: If $\phi \in \mathcal{L}$ is a formula in a branch of a QC semantic tableau, and there is a pair (E, A) such that $(E, A) \models_s \phi$, and according to Definition 10 there is a derivation of the form $(E, A) \models_s \phi$ implies $(E, A) \models_s \psi$, then ψ can be obtained as a formula in the branch using the S-rules in Definition 17.*

Proof. The strong satisfaction relation in Definition 10 is defined for non-literal formulae by eleven equivalences. The first, which is for disjunction, is captured by the two disjunction S-rules. The next six are captured by the six rewrite S-rules. The last four, which are the quantification rules, are captured by the four quantification S-rules.

Proposition 4. *The set of decomposition rules given in Definition 18 is complete in the following sense: If ϕ^* is a formula in a branch of a QC semantic tableau, and there is a pair (E, A) such that $(E, A) \models_w \phi^*$, and according to Definition 11 there is a derivation of the form $(E, A) \models_w \phi^*$ implies $(E, A) \models_w \psi^*$, then ψ^* can be obtained as a formula in the branch using the U-rules in Definition 18.*

Proof. The weak satisfaction relation in Definition 11 is defined for non-literal formulae by nine equivalences. The first, which is for disjunction, is captured by the disjunction U-rule. The second, which is for conjunction, is captured by the conjunction U-rule. The next three are captured by the three rewrite U-rules. The last four, which are the quantification rules, are captured by the four quantification U-rules.

Definition 21. *Let B be a branch of a QC semantic tableau where no further decomposition rules can be applied. $F(B) \subseteq \mathcal{L}^*$ is the set of all the formulae at the nodes in the branch. Also let $S(B) = F(B) \cap \mathcal{L}$ and let $U(B) = F(B) - S(B)$.*

Proposition 5. *For any set of formulae $\Delta \in \wp(\mathcal{L})$, and any formula $\alpha \in \mathcal{L}$, and any branch B of a QC semantic tableau for a database Δ and a query α, the branch B is closed iff there is no model E such that $E \models_s \phi$ for all $\phi \in S(B)$ and $E \models_w \phi^*$ for all $\phi^* \in U(B)$.*

Definition 22. *If $\Delta \in \wp(\mathcal{L})$ is of the form $\{\alpha_1, .., \alpha_n\}$, then $\bigwedge \Delta$ denotes the formula $\alpha_1 \wedge .. \wedge \alpha_n \in \mathcal{L}$.*

Proposition 6. *For any set of formulae $\Delta \in \wp(\mathcal{L})$, and any formula $\alpha \in \mathcal{L}$, there is a QC semantic tableau for a database Δ and a query α that is closed iff there is no model E such that $E \models_s \bigwedge \Delta$ and $E \models_w \alpha^*$.*

Proof. First, according to Propositions 1 and 2, each application of a decomposition rule is sound. Second, according to Propositions 3 and 4, the application of the decomposition rules is complete. Now let us consider a particular Δ and α. There is a QC semantic tableau for a database Δ and a query α that is closed $\Leftrightarrow$ Every branch of the semantic tableau with root $\Delta \cup \{\alpha^*\}$ is closed $\Leftrightarrow$ Every branch of the semantic tableau with root $\Delta \cup \{\alpha^*\}$ contains β and β^* for some ground literal $\beta \Leftrightarrow$ There is no model for each branch of the semantic tableau with root $\Delta \cup \{\alpha^*\} \Leftrightarrow$ There is no model E such that $E \models_s \bigwedge \Delta$ and $E \models_w \alpha^*$.

Proposition 7. *For any set of formulae $\Delta \in \wp(\mathcal{L})$, and any formula $\alpha \in \mathcal{L}$, there is an open branch B of a QC semantic tableau for a database Δ and a query α iff there is a model E such that $E \models_s \bigwedge \Delta$ and $E \models_w \alpha^*$.*

Proposition 8. *For any set of formulae $\Delta \in \wp(\mathcal{L})$, and any formula $\alpha \in \mathcal{L}$, a QC tableau for a database Δ and a query α is closed iff $\Delta \models_Q \alpha$ holds.*

Proof. This follows directly from Proposition 6. Let us consider a particular Δ and α. There is a QC semantic tableau for a database Δ and a query α that is closed $\Leftrightarrow$ There is no model E_i such that $E_i \models_s \bigwedge \Delta$ and $E_i \models_w \alpha^* \Leftrightarrow$ For all models E_j, $E_j \not\models_s \bigwedge \Delta$ or $E_j \models_w \alpha \Leftrightarrow$ For all models E_j, if $E_j \models_s \bigwedge \Delta$, then $E_j \models_w \alpha$. $\Leftrightarrow \Delta \models_Q \alpha$ holds

Proposition 9. *The QC semantic tableau collapses to a classical semantic tableau if the following rules are added to the decomposition rules,*

$$\frac{\alpha}{(\neg\alpha)^*} \qquad \frac{\neg\alpha}{\alpha^*} \qquad \frac{\alpha^*}{\neg\alpha} \qquad \frac{(\neg\alpha)^*}{\alpha}$$

and we can use the classical definition for closure of a branch (i.e. the branch contains both β and $\neg\beta$ for some ground atom).

5 Discussion

Developing a non-trivializable, or paraconsistent logic, necessitates some compromise, or weakening, of classical logic. The compromises imposed to give QC logic seem to be more appropriate than other paraconsistent logics for applications in computing. QC logic provides a means to obtain all the non-trivial resolvents from a set of formulae, without the problem of trivial clauses also following.

QC logic exhibits the nice feature that no attention needs to be paid to a special form that the formulae in a set of premisses should have, as long as each formula in the set is individually consistent and not a tautology. This is in contrast with other paraconsistent logics where two formulae identical by definition of a connective in classical logic may not yield the same set of conclusions.

Acknowledgements. The author would like to thank Ralph Miarka and the anonymous referees for some helpful comments.

References

[BH95] Ph Besnard and A Hunter. Quasis-classical logic: Non-trivializable classical reasoning from inconsistent information. In C Froidevaux and K Kohlas, editors, *Symbolic and Quantitative Approaches to Uncertainty,* volume 946 of *Lecture Notes in Computer Siences* pages 44–51, 1995.

[dC74] N C da Costa. On the theory of inconsistent formal systems. *Notre Dame Journal of Formal Logic,*15:497–510, 1974.

[HN98] A Hunter and B Nuseibeh. Managing inconsistent specifiations: Reasoning, analysis and action. *ACM Transactions on Software Engineering and Methodology,* 7:335–367, 1998.

[Hun98] A Hunter. Paraconsistent logics. In *Handbook of Defeasible Reasoning and Uncertainty Management Systems,* volume 2, pages 11–36. Kluwer, 1998.

[Hun00a] A Hunter. Reasining with conflicting information using quasi-classical logic. *Journal of Logic and Computation,* 10:677–703, 2000.

[Hun00b] A Hunter. Reasining with inconsistency in structured text. *Knowledge Engineering Review,* 15:317–337, 2000.

[Smu 68] R Smullyan. *First-order Logic.* Springer, 1968.

On Anytime Coherence-Based Reasoning

Frédéric Koriche

LIRMM, UMR 5506, Université Montpellier II CNRS
161, rue Ada. 34392 Montpellier Cedex 5, France
koriche@lirmm.fr

Abstract. A great deal of research has been devoted to nontrivial reasoning in inconsistent knowledge bases. Coherence-based approaches proceed by a consolidation operation which selects several consistent subsets of the knowledge base and an entailment operation which uses classical implication on these subsets in order to conclude. An important advantage of these formalisms is their flexibility : consolidation operations can take into account the priorities of declarations stored in the base, and different entailment operations can be distinguished according to the cautiousness of reasoning. However, one of the main drawbacks of these approaches is their high computational complexity. The purpose of our study is to define a logical framework which handles this difficulty by introducing the concepts of anytime consolidation and anytime entailment. The framework is semantically founded on the notion of resource which captures both the accuracy and the computational cost of anytime operations. Moreover, a stepwise procedure is included for improving approximations. Finally, both sound approximations and complete ones are covered. Based on these properties, we show that an anytime view of coherence-based reasoning is tenable.

1 Introduction

A great deal of research has been devoted to nontrivial reasoning from inconsistency. This problems arises in a number of areas in artificial intelligence, e.g., in merging knowledge bases [1,2], defeasible reasoning [16,5] and belief revision [13, 14]. Most of the research in this issue is influenced by work in nonmonotonic reasoning, in particular by Nebel [13,14], Pinkas and Loui [15], and Benferhat and his colleagues [3,4], who developed the so-called *coherence-based approaches*. The main idea of these techniques is to start with a knowledge base and to apply two successive mechanisms, namely, a *consolidation operation* which generates and selects several consistent subsets of the base and an *entailment relation* which uses classical logic on the consistent subsets in order to conclude.

As noticed by Nebel in [14], an important advantage of coherence-based approaches is their *flexibility*. Different classes of consolidation operations can be distinguished according to the importance or relevance of declarations stored in the knowledge base. For example, if priorities attached to declarations are available, then a preference ordering may be defined on the consistent subsets of the

S. Benferhat and P. Besnard (Eds.): ECSQARU 2001, LNAI 2143, pp. 556–567, 2001.

base and hence, the consolidation task has a more fined control over what declarations are discarded and what declarations are going to stay. In an orthogonal way, different classes of entailment operations can be distinguished according to the cautiousness of reasoning. For example, the following kind of entailment is considered in [2,5] : "a knowledge base A entails the declaration α if, and only if, α is classically inferred by all the preferred consistent subsets of A". A taxonomy of entailment operations, from credulous to skeptical ones, can be found in [15].

Unfortunately, one of the main drawbacks of coherence-based approaches is their high computational complexity. As stated in [7], the complexity of reasoning in the propositional case lies at least at the second level of the polynomial hierarchy. This is due to the interaction of two sources of complexity, namely, propositional satisfiability and the selection of preferred consistent subsets. For this reason, one cannot expect to arrive at a polynomial algorithm when eliminating only one source, e.g., by restricting the base to Horn logic.

Anytime reasoning is a technique which is used in many areas of artificial intelligence to deal with the computational intractability of problems [20]. This paradigm extends the traditional notion of reasoner by allowing it to return many possible answers to any given query. An original method, primarily due to Schaerf and Cadoli in [17], and recently generalized in [9], has received a great deal of interest in the knowledge representation community. The basic idea of the method is to define a family of inference relations by relaxing soundness or completeness of reasoning. The knowledge base can provide partial solutions even if stopped prematurely. The accuracy of the solution improves with the time used in computing the solution. Several extensions of this method have been proposed in the fields of modal logics [12] and first-order logic [10]. However, despite few exceptions (e.g. [6]), most of the studies in anytime reasoning have concentrated to the monotonic case. In particular, it is necessary to make formal steps in the direction of coherence-based reasoning.

The purpose of this paper is to develop a logic oriented framework for anytime coherence-based reasoning. Our formalism is based on a multi-modal propositional logic, presented in [9], and used to specify *anytime monotonic reasoners*. In this study, we extend our previous work in order to specify *anytime non-monotonic reasoners*. Starting from a knowledge base A and a preordering on A, we introduce the notion of *anytime consolidation*, an operation which generates and selects approximate preferred consistent subsets of A. Then, we define three classes of *anytime entailment relations*, which respectively incorporate the credulous principle, the skeptical principle and the argumentative principle. Based on these operations, we show that an anytime view of coherence-based reasoning is tenable. Specifically, our framework includes the following features:

- The logic is semantically founded on the notion of *resource* which reflects both the accuracy and the computational cost of the approximations.
- The framework enables *incremental reasoning*: the quality of approximations is a nondecreasing function of the resources that have been spent.
- The framework covers *dual reasoning*: both sound but incomplete and complete but unsound approximations are returned at any step.

The rest of the paper is organized as follows. Section 2 presents the logical machinery for anytime monotonic reasoners. Our main contribution lies in section 3 which is devoted to the formalization of anytime nonmonotonic reasoners. Finally, section 4 suggests some topics for future research.

2 Anytime Monotonic Reasoning

In this section, we focus on the formalization of anytime monotonic reasoners. For this purpose, we present a propositional logic, named **ARL**, for anytime reasoning. We begin to define its syntax, next we examine its semantics and then we present some interesting properties of the logic.

2.1 Syntax

Throughout this paper, we consider a nonempty and finite set of atomic propositions (atoms for short) P. The language of *declarations* is the smallest set built from P and closed off under the connectives $\wedge$, $\vee$ and $\neg$. The connective $\supset$ is defined in terms of $\neg$ and $\vee$; that is, $\alpha \supset \beta$ is an abbreviation of $\neg\alpha \vee \beta$. Given a declaration α, the set of atoms that occur in α is denoted $P(\alpha)$. A *literal* is an atom or its negation and a *clause* is a finite disjunction of literals. A *knowledge base* is a finite conjunction of clauses. When there is no risk of confusion, we shall model knowledge bases as sets of clauses.

Following [17], the concept of *computational resource* is captured by a parameter S, a subset of P. Intuitively, the parameter S corresponds to a limited and controlled exploration in the space of possibilities defined from P.

The main contribution of the logic relies on two families of modalities $\Box_S$ and $\Diamond_S$, defined for each subset S of P. The operator $\Box_S$ is to capture sound but incomplete inference and $\Diamond_S$ to capture complete but unsound inference. The language of **ARL** is defined by the smallest set of *sentences* built from the following rules: if α is a declaration then α is a sentence, if α and β are sentences then $\neg\alpha$, $\alpha \wedge \beta$ and $\alpha \vee \beta$ are sentences, and if α is a declaration and S is a subset of P then $\Box_S\,\alpha$ and $\Diamond_S\,\alpha$ are sentences. Intuitively, a sentence such as $\Box_S\,\alpha$ is read "the agent knows α given the resources S". Dually, $\Diamond_S\,\alpha$ is read "the agent considers α as possible given the resources S".

2.2 Semantics

In the context of limited reasoning, the four valued semantics first proposed by Belnap and notably studied in [11] meets our needs. The domain T of truth values is the powerset of $\{0,1\}$. So, in the logic **ARL**, sentences can be valued to be true, false, both, or neither. Based on this structure, we define a *valuation* as a total function v from P to T. The space of valuations generated from P is denoted V. A *possible world* is a valuation which maps every atom p of P into $\{1\}$ or $\{0\}$. The space of possible worlds generated from P is denoted W.

The notion of resource is semantically represented by an equivalence relation between valuations. Given a parameter S, we say that two valuations v and v'

are *S-equivalent* and write $v \sim_S v'$, iff for every atom $p \in P$, if $p \in S$ then $v(p) = v'(p)$. Intuitively, a relation of S-equivalence induces a partition of the set V into equivalence classes whose granularity captures the accuracy of approximation. When S increases, the partition becomes "finer" and the approximation more precise. The "coarsest" partition is obtained when S is the empty set; in this case, $\sim_S$ is the total relation over V. Conversely, the "finest" partition is given when S is the set P; in this case $\sim_S$ is the identity relation over V.

An *interpretation* of **ARL** consists of a *truth support relation* $\models_1$ and a *falsity support relation* $\models_0$ inductively defined by the following conditions:

$$\begin{aligned} &v \models_1 p \text{ iff } 1 \in v(p), \\ &v \models_0 p \text{ iff } 0 \in v(p), \end{aligned} \tag{1}$$

$$\begin{aligned} &v \models_1 \neg\alpha \text{ iff } v \models_0 \alpha, \\ &v \models_0 \neg\alpha \text{ iff } v \models_1 \alpha, \end{aligned} \tag{2}$$

$$\begin{aligned} &v \models_1 \alpha \wedge \beta \text{ iff } v \models_1 \alpha \text{ and } v \models_1 \beta, \\ &v \models_0 \alpha \wedge \beta \text{ iff } v \models_0 \alpha \text{ or } v \models_0 \beta, \end{aligned} \tag{3}$$

$$\begin{aligned} &v \models_1 \alpha \vee \beta \text{ iff } v \models_1 \alpha \text{ or } v \models_1 \beta, \\ &v \models_0 \alpha \vee \beta \text{ iff } v \models_0 \alpha \text{ and } v \models_0 \beta, \end{aligned} \tag{4}$$

$$\begin{aligned} &v \models_1 \Box_S\, \alpha \text{ iff } \forall v' \in V, \text{ if } v \sim_S v' \text{ then } v' \models_1 \alpha, \\ &v \models_0 \Box_S\, \alpha \text{ iff } v \not\models_1 \Box_S\, \alpha, \end{aligned} \tag{5}$$

$$\begin{aligned} &v \models_1 \Diamond_S\, \alpha \text{ iff } \exists v' \in V \text{ such that } v \sim_S v' \text{ and } v' \models_1 \alpha, \\ &v \models_0 \Diamond_S\, \alpha \text{ iff } v \not\models_1 \Diamond_S\, \alpha. \end{aligned} \tag{6}$$

A sentence α is *satisfiable* iff there exists a possible world w such that $w \models_1 \alpha$. We say that α is *valid*, and write $\models \alpha$, iff for every $w \in W$, $w \models_1 \alpha$ holds. Given two sentences α and β, we say that β is a *logical consequence* of α iff $\models \alpha \supset \beta$ holds. A sound and complete axiomatization for **ARL** can be found in [9].

2.3 Properties

After an excursion into the logic **ARL**, we now focus on its main properties. In this purpose, we specify an *anytime monotonic reasoner* as a function that takes in input a knowledge base A, parameter S and a declaration α, and returns in output "yes" if $\models \Box_S\,(A \supset \alpha)$, "no" is $\not\models \Diamond_S\,(A \supset \alpha)$ and "unknown" otherwise.

Interestingly, our model can be shown *incremental* and *dual*. Specifically, the reasoning process may be defined by an increasing sequence of parameters $S_0 = \emptyset \cdots \subset S_k \cdots \subset S_n = P$ that approximate the problem of deciding whether α is a logical consequence of A, or not, by means of two dual families of tests $\models \Box_{S_k}(A \supset \alpha)$ and $\models \Diamond_{S_k}(A \supset \alpha)$. If the reasoner returns "yes" using any operator $\Box_{S_k}$ then α is a consequence of A. Dually, if the reasoner answers "no" using any operator $\Diamond_{S_k}$ then α is not a consequence of A. This stepwise process has the important advantage that the iteration may be stopped when a confirming answer is already obtained for a small index k.

Theorem 1. *For any declaration α and any parameters S and S' s.t. $S \subseteq S'$,*

$$\text{if } \models \Box_S\,\alpha \text{ then } \models \Box_{S'}\,\alpha \text{ and hence } \models \alpha, \tag{1}$$

$$\text{if } \not\models \Diamond_S\,\alpha \text{ then } \not\models \Diamond_{S'}\,\alpha \text{ and hence } \not\models \alpha. \tag{2}$$

Lemma 1. *For any declaration α,*

$$\models \Box_S\,\alpha \text{ iff } \Diamond_S\,\neg\alpha \text{ is unsatisfiable,} \tag{1}$$

$$\not\models \Diamond_S\,\alpha \text{ iff } \Box_S\,\neg\alpha \text{ is satisfiable.} \tag{2}$$

Theorem 2. *For any declaration α and any S, there is an algorithm for deciding whether $\Box_S\,\alpha$ is satisfiable and $\Diamond_S\,\alpha$ is satisfiable which runs in $O(|\alpha| \cdot 2^{|S|})$.*
The above complexity result is just the worst case upper bound of an enumeration algorithm. Actually, in the case of clausal knowledge bases, one may conceive a two-phases procedure which first simplifies the initial knowledge base and next explores the resulting search space. The simplification phase proceeds as follows. In the scope of the modality $\Diamond_S$, the algorithm deletes all clauses of α that contain a literal whose atom occurs in S. Dually, in the scope of $\Box_S$, the algorithm eliminates in any clause of α all literals whose atom occurs in S. Since any atom in the resulting theory occurs in S, the exploration phase consists in a standard (two-valued) satisfiability algorithm. Systematic methods such as depth first search enumeration [19] can be used to compute at the same time the satisfiability of $\Box_S\,\alpha$ and the unsatisfiability of $\Diamond_S\,\alpha$. On the other hand, local search algorithms [18] can be exploited if we concentrate on the satisfiability of $\Box_S\,\alpha$. In a nutshell, the role of the simplification phase is to reduce the dimensions of the formula, thus gaining efficiency in the exploration phase.

The correct choice of S is crucial for the usefulness of deduction. Taking to the extreme, when S is chosen incorrectly, anytime reasoning may end up as expensive as classical reasoning. From this perspective, several heuristics have been proposed in the literature. For example, the atoms of S may be dynamically chosen using the *diversity heuristic* advocated in [8]. The diversity of an atom p is the product of the number of positive occurrences by the number of negative occurrences of p in the theory. This notion is based on the observation that an atom is a potential source of unsatisfiability only when it appears both positively and negatively in different clauses. Thus, in the scope of the modality $\Diamond_S$, the strategy consists in choosing atoms whose diversity is maximal. Dually, in the scope of $\Box_S$, the algorithm iteratively selects atoms whose diversity is minimal.

Example 1. Let $A = \{(\neg a \vee b \vee c), (a \vee b \vee \neg d), (a \vee \neg b \vee d), (\neg a \vee \neg b \vee c)\}$. We want to show that A is satisfiable. We need to find a subset S of $\{a, b, c, d\}$ s.t. $\Box_S\,A$ is satisfiable. Starting with $S = \varnothing$ and using the minimal diversity heuristic, we gradually add c and a to S. This is sufficient for proving that A is satisfiable.

Example 2. Suppose we want to show that $a \supset c$ is a logical consequence of the knowledge base A, defined above. We need to find a subset S such that the sentence $\Diamond_S\,(A \wedge a \wedge \neg c)$ is unsatisfiable. Using the maximal diversity strategy, we iteratively add a, b and c to S. This is sufficient for proving that $(A \wedge a \wedge \neg c)$ is unsatisfiable. So, $a \supset c$ is indeed a logical consequence of A.

3 Anytime Nonmonotonic Reasoning

In this section, we extend the concepts developed so far to the formalization of anytime nonmonotonic reasoners. In the setting suggested by our approach, these systems are defined in terms of *anytime consolidation* and *anytime entailment*. The quality of result of each operation depends on the computational resources that have been spent. We begin to define the concept of anytime consolidation, next we present three classes of anytime entailment, and then we examine the computational properties of our framework.

3.1 Anytime Consolidation Operations

As considered for instance in [13,14], a "standard" consolidation operation starts from a knowledge base and a priority ordering on this base and selects the preferred consistent subsets of the base. The purpose of "anytime" consolidation is to control the generation of these subsets by the notion of resource parameter.

To this end, we need some additional definitions. A *prioritized knowledge base* is a pair $(A, \leq)$ where A is a knowledge base and $\leq$ is a total preorder on A. It is equivalent to consider that A is stratified in a collection $(A_1, \cdots, A_n)$, where A_1 contains the declarations of highest priority and A_n those of lowest priority. Each knowledge base A_i is called a *stratum* of A. The structure $(A, \leq)$ is called *flat* if the relation $\leq$ is symmetric, or equivalently, if A contains an unique stratum. Different methods have been proposed to use the priority relation in order to select "preferred" consistent subsets (see e.g. [3]). In this study, we focus on the *inclusion-based preference ordering*, denoted $\preceq$, whose strict part is defined as follows: $B \prec C$ iff $\exists i : B \cap A_i \subset C \cap A_i$ and $\forall j : 1 \leq j < i, B \cap A_j = C \cap A_j$. By extension, $B \preceq C$ iff $B \prec C$ or $B = C$. Based on these considerations, the standard consolidation operation, denoted $\triangle$, is defined as follows:

$$\triangle(A, \leq) = max(\{B \subseteq A : B \text{ is satisfiable}\}, \preceq).$$

Now we incorporate the notion of computational resource. A parameter S is said *acceptable* for a prioritized knowledge base $(A, \leq)$ iff the following condition holds: if $\exists i : S \cap P(A_i) \neq 0$ then $\forall j : 1 \leq j < i$, $P(A_j) \subseteq S$. Intuitively, the acceptability condition imposes a restriction on the choice of computational resources: if an acceptable parameter contains at least one atom of any given stratum then it must contain all atoms of strata of higher priority. In particular, it is interesting to remark that if the structure $(A, \leq)$ is flat, then every subset of P is acceptable for $(A, \leq)$. The anytime view of consolidation is realized by parameterizing the operation $\triangle$ by means of two families of operations $\Box$ and $\Diamond$, the first one being sound, while the second one being complete with respect to standard consolidation. The corresponding *anytime consolidation operations* are defined as follows:

$$\Box(A, \leq, S) = max(\{B \subseteq A : \Box_S B \text{ is satisfiable }\}, \preceq),$$
$$\Diamond(A, \leq, S) = max(\{B \subseteq A : \Diamond_S B \text{ is satisfiable }\}, \preceq).$$

The following lemmas capture important properties of anytime consolidation. They will be frequently used in the remaining paper.

Lemma 2. *For any prioritized knowledge base $(A, \leq)$ and any acceptable parameters S and S' such that $S \subseteq S'$:*

$$\forall B \in \Box(A, \leq, S) \;\; \exists C \in \Box(A, \leq, S') \;\text{ such that } B \subseteq C, \tag{1}$$
$$\forall B \in \Diamond(A, \leq, S') \;\; \exists C \in \Diamond(A, \leq, S) \;\text{ such that } B \subseteq C. \tag{2}$$

Proof. Let us examine part (1). Assume that there exists a knowledge base $B \in \Box(A, \leq, S)$ such that for every base $C \in \Box(A, \leq, S')$, we have $B \not\subseteq C$. We show that this leads to a contradiction. If $B \in \Box(A, \leq, S)$ then $\Box_S B$ is satisfiable. By application of theorem 1 and lemma 1, it follows that $\Box_{S'} B$ is satisfiable. Since $B \notin \Box(A, \leq, S')$ there must exist a base $C \in \Box(A, \leq, S')$ such that $B \prec C$. Therefore, $\exists i : B \cap A_i \subset C \cap A_i$ and $\forall j : 1 \leq j < i, B \cap A_j = C \cap A_j$. By assumption, we know that $B \not\subset C$. So, $\exists k > i : B \cap A_k \not\subset C \cap A_k$. Thus, it follows that $B \cap A_k \neq \varnothing$. Since $\Box_S B$ is satisfiable, we must have $S \cap P(A_k) \neq \varnothing$. By acceptability condition, it follows that $\forall k' < k$, $P(A_{k'}) \subseteq S$. Let B' denotes the set $\bigcup\{C \cap A_{k'} : k' < k\}$. Obviously, $\Box_S B'$ is satisfiable. Moreover, it is clear that $B \prec B'$. Therefore, we obtain $B \notin \Box(A, \leq, S)$, but this contradicts the initial hypothesis. A dual argument applies to part (2).

Lemma 3. *For any knowledge base A, any clause α and any parameters S and S' such that $S \subseteq S'$,*

1. *if $\Box_{S'} A$ is satisfiable and $\Box_{S'} A \cup \{\alpha\}$ is unsatisfiable, then there exists a subset B of A such that $\Box_S B$ is satisfiable and $\Box_S B \cup \{\alpha\}$ is unsatisfiable.*
2. *if $\Diamond_S A$ is satisfiable and $\Diamond_S A \cup \{\alpha\}$ is unsatisfiable, then there exists a subset B of A such that $\Diamond_{S'} B$ is satisfiable and $\Diamond_{S'} B \cup \{\alpha\}$ is unsatisfiable.*

Proof. Let us examine part (1), If $\Box_S \alpha$ is unsatisfiable then $B = \varnothing$ and we have demonstrated the property. Now, suppose that $\Box_S \alpha$ is satisfiable. Thus, there exists a literal l in α such that its atom belongs to S. Moreover, since $\Box_{S'} A$ is satisfiable and $\Box_{S'} A \cup \{\alpha\}$ is unsatisfiable, there exists a clause β in A such that the negation of l belongs to β. So, $\Box_S \beta$ is satisfiable. Let γ denotes the resolvent of α and β. If $\Box_S \gamma$ is unsatisfiable, then $B = \{\beta\}$. Otherwise, there exists a literal l' in γ such that its atom belongs to S. Thus, there exists a clause β' in A that contains the negation of l'. Since γ does not contain any occurrence of l, it is clear that $P(l') \cap P(l) = \varnothing$. Therefore, $\Box_S \beta \wedge \beta'$ is satisfiable. Let γ' denotes the resolvent of γ and β'. If $\Box_S \gamma'$ is unsatisfiable then $B = \{\beta, \beta'\}$. Otherwise, we iteratively apply the same method until we obtain all the clauses of A. In this case, $\Box_S A$ is satisfiable. An analogous strategy applies to part (2).

Lemma 4. *For any prioritized knowledge base $(A, \leq)$ and any acceptable parameters S and S' such that $S \subseteq S'$:*

$$\forall B \in \Box(A, \leq, S') \;\; \exists C \in \Box(A, \leq, S) \;\text{ such that } C \subseteq B, \tag{1}$$
$$\forall B \in \Diamond(A, \leq, S) \;\; \exists C \in \Diamond(A, \leq, S') \;\text{ such that } C \subseteq B. \tag{2}$$

Proof. Let us examine part (1). Suppose we have $B \in \Box(A, \leq, S')$. If $B = A$ the demonstration is straightforward. Now, suppose that $B \subset A$. We know that $\Box_{S'} B$ is satisfiable. Moreover, for every clause β in A/B, $\Box_{S'} B \cup \{\beta\}$ is unsatisfiable. Let α denotes the clause $\bigvee\{\beta : \beta \in A/B\}$. Obviously, $\Box_{S'} B \cup \{\alpha\}$ is unsatisfiable. By application of lemma 3, there exists a subset B' of B such that $\Box_S B$ is satisfiable and $\Box_S B \cup \{\alpha\}$ is unsatisfiable. Clearly enough, B' can be extended to a set C such that $C \in \Box(B, \leq, S)$. Suppose that $C \notin \Box(A, \leq, S)$. Then, there must exist a set $C' \in \Box(A, \leq, S)$ such that $C \prec C'$. Therefore, $\exists i : C \cap A_i \subset C' \cap A_i$ and $\forall j : 1 \leq j < i, C \cap A_j = C' \cap A_j$. Clearly, $C \not\subset C'$. Suppose not. In this case, $\exists k > i$, such that $C \cap A_k \not\subset C' \cap A_k$. Thus, it follows that $C \cap A_k \neq \varnothing$. Since $\Box_S C$ is satisfiable, $P(A_k) \cap S \neq \varnothing$. Therefore, $\forall k' < k$, $P(A_{k'}) \subseteq S$. It follows that $\forall k' < k$, $C \cap A_{k'} = B \cap A_{k'}$. Thus, we obtain $B \cap A_i \subset C' \cap A_i$. So, $B \prec C'$. Since $\Box_{S'} C'$ is satisfiable, $B \notin \Box(A, \leq, S')$, but this contradicts the initial hypothesis. So, we can state that $C \subset C'$. Thus, $\exists \beta \in A/B$ such that $C \cup \{\beta\} \subseteq C'$. However, $\Box_S C \cup \{\beta\}$ is unsatisfiable. Therefore $C' \notin \Box(A, \leq, S)$. So, $C \in \Box(A, \leq, S)$. Moreover, since $C \in \Box(B, \leq, S)$, we obtain $C \subseteq B$, as desired. A dual argument applies to part (2).

3.2 Anytime Entailment Operations

In the setting of coherence based-reasoning, a "standard" entailment relation takes in input a collection of preferred consistent subsets and returns in output a set of cautious conclusions. A taxonomy of numerous entailment principles has been established in [15] according to their cautiousness. In this study, we are interested in three of them: the existential principle, the universal principle and the argumentative principle. We begin to present these different classes of entailment relations and next we examine their corresponding approximations.

The first two entailment principles, introduced by Rescher and Manor in [16], are the most commonly used in presence of contradictory knowledge bases (see e.g. [2,3]). They can be respectively described in the following way:

$$(A, \leq) \Vdash^{\exists} \alpha \ \text{ iff } \ \exists B \in \Delta(A, \leq) \text{ such that } \models B \supset \alpha,$$
$$(A, \leq) \Vdash^{\forall} \alpha \ \text{ iff } \ \forall B \in \Delta(A, \leq), \models B \supset \alpha.$$

Obviously, universal entailment is more cautious than existential entailment, since each conclusion obtained from $(A, \leq)$ using $\Vdash^{\forall}$ is also obtained by $\Vdash^{\exists}$. In fact, universal entailment is often too conservative and hence rather unproductive while existential entailment is often too permissive and may lead to pairs of mutually exclusive conclusions. The notion of argumentative entailment, suggested for instance in [4,15], is based on an intermediate principle which is more productive than universal entailment but does not lead to contradictory conclusions. It consists in keeping only the consequences obtained by the existential principle whose negation cannot be inferred. In formal terms:

$$(A, \leq) \Vdash^{\mathcal{A}} \alpha \ \text{ iff } \ (A, \leq) \Vdash^{\exists} \alpha \text{ and } (A, \leq) \nVdash^{\exists} \neg\alpha.$$

In the remaining paper, the symbol x will be used to refer to one of the entailment principles denoted by the symbols $\exists$, $\forall$ and $\mathcal{A}$.

We now turn to the anytime view of entailment relations. The idea is to approximate a standard nonmonotonic relation, say $\Vdash^x$, by means of two dual families of relations $\Vdash^x_\Box$ and $\Vdash^x_\Diamond$, the first one being sound, while the second one being complete with respect to $\Vdash^x$. The notions of *anytime existential entailment* and *anytime universal entailment* are defined as follows:

$$(A, \leq, S) \Vdash^\exists_\Box \alpha \text{ iff } \exists B \in \Box(A, \leq, S) \text{ such that } \models \Box_S (B \supset \alpha),$$
$$(A, \leq, S) \Vdash^\exists_\Diamond \alpha \text{ iff } \exists B \in \Diamond(A, \leq, S) \text{ such that } \models \Diamond_S (B \supset \alpha),$$

$$(A, \leq, S) \Vdash^\forall_\Box \alpha \text{ iff } \forall B \in \Box(A, \leq, S), \models \Box_S (B \supset \alpha),$$
$$(A, \leq, S) \Vdash^\forall_\Diamond \alpha \text{ iff } \forall B \in \Diamond(A, \leq, S), \models \Diamond_S (B \supset \alpha).$$

The notion of *anytime argumentative entailment* is defined as follows:

$$(A, \leq, S) \Vdash^A_\Box \alpha \text{ iff } (A, \leq) \Vdash^\exists_\Box \alpha \text{ and } (A, \leq) \not\Vdash^\exists_\Diamond \neg\alpha,$$
$$(A, \leq, S) \Vdash^A_\Diamond \alpha \text{ iff } (A, \leq) \Vdash^\exists_\Diamond \alpha \text{ and } (A, \leq) \not\Vdash^\exists_\Box \neg\alpha.$$

We are now in position to provide a specification tool for anytime nonmonotonic reasoning. From this perspective, we define an *anytime nonmonotonic reasoner* as a function that takes in input a prioritized knowledge base $(A, \leq)$, an acceptable parameter S, a declaration α (i.e. the query) and an entailment principle x, and returns in output "yes" if $(A, \leq, S) \Vdash^x_\Box \alpha$, "no" if $(A, \leq, S) \not\Vdash^x_\Diamond \alpha$, and "unknown" otherwise. As for monotonic deduction, the nonmonotonic reasoning process can be modeled by an increasing sequence of parameters $(S_0 = \varnothing \cdots \subset S_k \cdots \subset S_n = P)$ that approximate the problem of deciding whether $(A, \leq) \Vdash^x \alpha$ holds, or not, by means of two dual families of entailment tests $(A, \leq, S_k) \Vdash^x_\Box \alpha$ and $(A, \leq, S_k) \Vdash^x_\Diamond \alpha$. If the reasoner returns "yes" for a given index k, then $(A, \leq) \Vdash^x \alpha$ holds. On the other hand, if the reasoner answers "no" for a given k, then $(A, \leq) \Vdash^x \alpha$ does not hold. These considerations are clarified by the following properties.

Theorem 3. *For any prioritized knowledge base $(A, \leq)$, any declaration α and any acceptable parameters S and S' such that $S \subseteq S'$,*

$$\text{if } (A, \leq, S) \Vdash^\exists_\Box \alpha \text{ then } (A, \leq, S') \Vdash^\exists_\Box \alpha \text{ and hence } (A, \leq) \Vdash^\exists \alpha, \quad (1)$$
$$\text{if } (A, \leq, S) \not\Vdash^\exists_\Diamond \alpha \text{ then } (A, \leq, S') \not\Vdash^\exists_\Diamond \alpha \text{ and hence } (A, \leq) \not\Vdash^\exists \alpha. \quad (2)$$

Proof. Let us examine part (1). We begin to focus on the first implication. Suppose that $(A, \leq, S) \Vdash^\exists_\Box \alpha$ holds. Then, $\exists B \in \Box(A, \leq, S)$ such that $\models \Box_S (B \supset \alpha)$ holds. By lemma 2, we know that $\exists C \in \Box(A, \leq, S')$ such that $B \subseteq C$. By the monotonicity property of conjunction, it follows that $\models \Box_S (C \supset \alpha)$. By application of theorem 1, it follows that $\models \Box_{S'} (C \supset \alpha)$. Therefore, we obtain $(A, \leq, S') \Vdash^\exists_\Box \alpha$, as desired. Now we turn to the second implication of part (1). As before, we assume that $(A, \leq, S) \Vdash^\exists_\Box \alpha$ holds. Since $S \subseteq P$, it follows that $(A, \leq, P) \Vdash^\exists_\Box \alpha$. By using the semantical properties of $\sim_P$, we can easily verify that $\Box(A, \leq, P) = \Delta(A, \leq)$, and that $\models \Box_P (A \supset \alpha)$ holds iff $\models A \supset \alpha$ holds. So, $(A, \leq, P) \Vdash^\exists_\Box \alpha$ is logically equivalent to $(A, \leq) \Vdash^\exists \alpha$. Therefore, it follows that $(A, \leq) \Vdash^\exists \alpha$ holds, as desired. A dual strategy holds for part (2).

Theorem 4. *For any prioritized clausal knowledge base* $(A, \leq)$, *any declaration* α *and any acceptable parameters* S *and* S' *such that* $S \subseteq S'$,

$$\text{if } (A, \leq, S) \Vdash^{\forall}_{\Box} \alpha \text{ then } (A, \leq, S') \Vdash^{\forall}_{\Box} \alpha \text{ and hence } (A, \leq) \Vdash^{\forall} \alpha, \quad (1)$$
$$\text{if } (A, \leq, S) \nVdash^{\forall}_{\Diamond} \alpha \text{ then } (A, \leq, S') \nVdash^{\forall}_{\Diamond} \alpha \text{ and hence } (A, \leq) \nVdash^{\forall} \alpha. \quad (2)$$

Proof. We only examine the first implication of part (1). Suppose we are given $(A, \leq, S) \Vdash^{\forall}_{\Box} \alpha$ and $(A, \leq, S') \nVdash^{\forall}_{\Box} \alpha$. From the second assertion, $\exists B \in \Box(A, \leq, S')$ such that $\not\models \Box_{S'} (B \supset \alpha)$. By contraposition of theorem 1, it follows that $\not\models \Box_S (B \supset \alpha)$. Moreover, since $B \in \Box(A, \leq, S')$, by application of lemma 4, $\exists C \in \Box(A, \leq, S)$ such that $C \subset B$. By the monotonicity property of conjunction, it follows that $\not\models \Box_S (C \supset \alpha)$. Therefore $(A, \leq, S) \nVdash^{\forall}_{\Box} \alpha$, hence contradiction.

Theorem 5. *For any prioritized knowledge base* $(A, \leq)$, *any declaration* α *and any acceptable parameters* S *and* S' *such that* $S \subseteq S'$,

$$\text{if } (A, \leq, S) \Vdash^{A}_{\Box} \alpha \text{ then } (A, \leq, S') \Vdash^{A}_{\Box} \alpha \text{ and hence } (A, \leq) \Vdash^{A} \alpha, \quad (1)$$
$$\text{if } (A, \leq, S) \nVdash^{A}_{\Diamond} \alpha \text{ then } (A, \leq, S') \nVdash^{A}_{\Diamond} \alpha \text{ and hence } (A, \leq) \nVdash^{A} \alpha. \quad (2)$$

Proof. We only examine the first implication of part (1). Suppose that $(A, \leq, S) \Vdash^{A}_{\Box} \alpha$. Then, $(A, \leq, S) \Vdash^{\exists}_{\Box} \alpha$ and $(A, \leq, S) \nVdash^{\exists}_{\Diamond} \neg\alpha$. From the first assertion and by theorem 3(1), it follows that $(A, \leq, S') \Vdash^{\exists}_{\Box} \alpha$. From the second assertion and by theorem 3(2), it follows that $(A, \leq, S') \nVdash^{\exists}_{\Diamond} \neg\alpha$. Thus, $(A, \leq, S') \Vdash^{A}_{\Box} \alpha$.

3.3 Computational Properties

We now turn to computational considerations. To this very point, we recall that coherence-based reasoning is characterized by two interacting sources of complexity, namely, propositional satisfiability and the selection of preferred consistent subsets. The following theorem states that both sources of complexity are bounded by the same resource parameter S.

Theorem 6. *For any prioritized knowledge base* $(A, \leq)$, *any declaration* α *and any parameter* S, *there exists an algorithm for deciding whether* $(A, \leq, S) \Vdash^{x}_{\Box} \alpha$ *holds and* $(A, \leq, S) \Vdash^{x}_{\Diamond} \alpha$ *holds which runs in* $O((|A| + |\alpha|) \cdot 2^{|S|} \cdot 2^{|S|})$.

Proof. We focus on the complexity analysis of $(A, \leq, S) \Vdash^{\exists}_{\Box} \alpha$. The demonstration is analogous for the other entailment relations. We begin to prove that the size of $\Box(A, \leq, S)$ is bounded by $2^{|S|}$. Let B and B' be two sets of $\Box(A, \leq, S)$. Obviously, $\Box_S (B \cup B')$ is unsatisfiable. Let $V^{\Box}_S$ denotes the set of valuations v such that $\forall p \in P$, $v(p) = \{0\}$ or $v(p) = \{1\}$ if $p \in S$, and $v(p) = \{\}$ otherwise. Moreover, given a declaration β, let $V^{\Box}_S(\beta)$ denotes the set of valuations v in $V^{\Box}_S$ such that $v \models_1 \beta$. Clearly, $\Box_S (B \cup B')$ is unsatisfiable iff $V^{\Box}_S(B) \cap V^{\Box}_S(B') = \varnothing$. Since there exists $2^{|S|}$ valuations in $V^{\Box}_S$, the maximum number of bases being locally satisfiable and pairwise unsatisfiable under the scope of $\Box_S$ is $2^{|S|}$. Now, let us examine the main result. Suppose that if $(A, \leq, S) \Vdash^{\exists}_{\Box} \alpha$ holds then $\exists B \in \Box(A, \leq, S)$ such that $\models \Box_S (B \supset \alpha)$. By application of lemma 1 and theorem 2, the validity test of $\Box_S (B \supset \alpha)$ is in $O((|A| + |\alpha|) \cdot 2^{|S|})$. Since there are at most $2^{|S|}$ bases B, the entailment test is in $O((|A| + |\alpha|) \cdot 2^{|S|} \cdot 2^{|S|})$.

Several algorithms can be used for anytime nonmonotonic reasoning. The key difficulty lies in the consolidation operation. To this end, one may conceive an algorithm which takes in input a prioritized clausal base $(A, \leq)$ and computes $\Box(A, \leq, S_k)$ by means of an increasing sequence S_k. For $k = 0$ the procedure simply returns the empty base. For $k > 0$, the procedure proceeds into two steps. First, for each subset B of $\Box(A, \leq, S_{k-1})$, the procedure computes the satisfiable expansions of B that take clauses containing the literal p_k or its negation $\neg p_k$. Second, the procedure selects the maximal expansions and add them to $\Box(A, \leq, S_k)$. As far as $\Diamond(A, \leq, S_k)$ is concerned, dual considerations hold. Such an algorithm is indeed *incremental*; by exploiting lemmas 2 and 4, the procedure only needs to expand the maximal subsets generated in previous steps and does not require to perform all computations from scratch.

The correct choice of S is crucial for the usefulness of anytime consolidation. This choice may be guided by the priority ordering $\leq$. Following the acceptability condition, the parameter is constructed by selecting the atoms from the stratum of highest priority, then the atoms of the next important stratum are added, and so on. Alternatively, inside each stratum, the choice of S may be heuristic. In this case, the letters are iteratively selected to minimize the predicted number of consistent subsets, using a strategy such as the *minimal diversity heuristic*.

Example 3. Consider the flat base $A = \{a, b, c, \neg c, \neg a \vee \neg b, \neg a \vee c, \neg a \vee \neg c, \neg b \vee d\}$. We want to show that $A \Vdash^{\exists} d$. Hence, we need to find a set S such that $A \Vdash^{\exists}_{\Box} d$. Starting with $S = \varnothing$ and using the minimal diversity heuristic, we iteratively add d and b to S. Based on the following results, we observe that $A \Vdash^{\exists}_{\Box} d$.

S	$\Box(A, S)$
$\varnothing$	$\varnothing$
$\{d\}$	$\{\{\neg b \vee d\}\}$
$\{b, d\}$	$\{\{b, \neg b \vee d\}, \{\neg a \vee \neg b, \neg b \vee d\}\}$

Example 4. Suppose we are given the prioritized base $A = (A_1, A_2)$ where $A_1 = \{a, \neg a, e\}$ and $A_2 = \{c, \neg d, \neg a \vee b, \neg c \vee d\}$. We want to show that $(A, \leq) \Vdash^{A} b$. So, we need to find a set S such that $(A, \leq) \Vdash^{A}_{\Box} b$. Starting with $S = \varnothing$ and using the acceptability condition, we first add the atoms a and e and next we select b. Based on the following results, we indeed obtain $(A, \leq) \Vdash^{\exists}_{\Box} b$ and $(A, \leq) \nVdash^{\exists}_{\Diamond} \neg b$.

S	$\Box(A, \leq, S)$	$\Diamond(A, \leq, S)$
$\varnothing$	$\varnothing$	A
$\{a, e\}$	$\{\{a, e\}, \{\neg a, e, \neg a \vee b\}\}$	$\{\{a, e\} \cup A_2, \{\neg a, e\} \cup A_2\}$
$\{a, b, e\}$	$\{\{a, e, \neg a \vee b\}, \{\neg a, e, \neg a \vee b\}\}$	$\{\{a, e\} \cup A_2, \{\neg a, e\} \cup A_2\}$

4 Conclusion

In this paper, we have studied the problem of reasoning from inconsistency focusing on the so-called coherence-based approaches. One of the main drawbacks of these methods is their high computational complexity. Our aim was to provide a logical framework which tackles this difficulty through the paradigm of anytime computation. We have illustrated that the framework integrates several major features: resource-bounded reasoning, incrementality and dual reasoning. Some of the future directions of this work include the empirical study of anytime coherence-based reasoning. To this point, some benchmarks for coherence-based reasoning have recently been proposed in [7]. An important issue is to compare the performances of the standard methods with our anytime technique.

References

1. C. Baral, S. Kraus, and J. Minker. Combining multiple knowledge bases. *IEEE Transactions on Knowledge and Data Engineering*, 3(2):208–220, 1991.
2. C. Baral, S. Kraus, J. Minker, and V. S. Subrahmanian. Combining knowledge bases consisting of first order theories. *Comp. Intelligence*, 8(1):45–71, 1992.
3. S. Benferhat, D. Dubois, and H. Prade. How to infer form inconsistent beliefs without revising ? In *Proc. IJCAI'95*, pages 1449–1455, 1995.
4. S. Benferhat, D. Dubois, and H. Prade. Some syntactic approaches to the handling of inconsistent knowledge bases: a comparative study, part 1: the flat case. *Studia Logica*, 58:17–45, 1997.
5. G. Brewka. Preferred subtheories: An extended logical framework for default reasoning. In *Proc. IJCAI'89*, pages 1043–1048. Morgan Kaufmann, 1989.
6. M. Cadoli and M. Schaerf. Approximate inference in default reasoning and circumscription. In *Proc. ECAI'92*, pages 319–323, 1992.
7. C. Cayrol and M. C. Lagasquie-Schiex. Nonmonotonic reasoning: from complexity to algorithms. *Annals of Mathematics and Artificial Intelligence*, 22:207–236, 1998.
8. R. Dechter and I. Rish. Directional resolution: The Davis-Putnam procedure, revisited. In *Proc. KR'94*, pages 134–145, 1994.
9. F. Koriche. A logic for anytime deduction and anytime compilation. In *Logics in Artificial Intelligence*, volume 1489, pages 324–342. Springer Verlag, 1998.
10. F. Koriche. A logic for approximate first-order reasoning. In *Proc. CSL'01*, 2001. To appear.
11. H. J. Levesque. A logic of implicit and explicit belief. In *Proc. AAAI'84*, pages 198–202, 1984.
12. F. Massacci. Anytime approximate modal reasoning. In *Proc. AAAI'98*, pages 274–279, 1998.
13. B. Nebel. Belief revision and default reasoning: Syntax - based approaches. In *Proc. KR'91*, pages 417–428, 1991.
14. B. Nebel. Base revision operations and schemes: Semantics, representation, and complexity. In *Mathematical and Statistical Methods in Artificial Intelligence*, pages 157–170. Springer-Verlag, 1995.
15. G. Pinkas and R. P. Loui. Reasoning from inconsistency: A taxonomy of principles for resolving conflict. In *Proc. KR'92*, pages 709–719, 1992.
16. N. Rescher and R. Manor. On inference from inconsistent premises. *Theory and Decision*, 1:179–217, 1970.
17. M. Schaerf and M. Cadoli. Tractable reasoning via approximation. *Artificial Intelligence*, 74:249–310, 1995.
18. B. Selman, H. Levesque, and D. Mitchell. A new method for solving hard satisfiability problems. In *Proc. AAAI'92*, pages 440–446, 1992.
19. H. Zhang and M. E. Stickel. Implementing the Davis-Putnam method. *Journal of Automated Reasoning*, 24(1/2):277–296, 2000.
20. S. Zilberstein. Using anytime algorithms in intelligent systems. *AI Magazine*, 17(3):73–83, 1996.

Resolving Conflicts between Beliefs, Obligations, Intentions, and Desires

Jan Broersen, Mehdi Dastani, and Leendert van der Torre

Department of Artificial Intelligence
Vrije Universiteit Amsterdam
De Boelelaan 1081a
1081 HV Amsterdam, The Nederlands
{broersen,mehdi,torre}@cs.vu.nl
http://www.cs.vu.nl/~boid/

Abstract. This paper provides a logical analysis of conflicts between informational, motivational and deliberative attitudes such as beliefs, obligations, intentions, and desires. The contributions are twofold. First, conflict resolutions are classified based on agent types, and formalized in an extension of Reiter's normal default logic. Second, several desiderata for conflict resolutions are introduced, discussed and tested on the logic. The results suggest that Reiter's default logic is too strong, in the sense that a weaker notion of extension is needed to satisfy the desiderata.

1 Introduction

Various competing agent decision models have been proposed, and it is still unclear which type of model should be used in which type of application. For example, some decision models are based on goal-based planning or on variants of decision theory like qualitative decision theory [13,1], other models are based on cognitive models like belief-desire-intention models [5,14], and yet other models are based on social concepts like obligations and norms [6,20,19], as in deontic action programs [8]. Typically, the decision model is based on an attempt to reach goals, satisfy desires, or fulfill obligations. In the Belief-Obligation-Intention-Desire or BOID architecture [4] decision models are considered in which the main problem is not finding out how to reach goals, satisfy desires or fulfill obligations, but in which the main problem is to resolve conflicts between them.

The BOID logic discussed in this paper is an abstraction of the BOID architecture. For conflicts so-called extensions are constructed and one extension is selected, an idea adopted from Thomason's BDP logic [18], which is in turn based on Reiter's default logic [15]. In particular, BDP logic is based on conflict resolution for conditional beliefs and desires, which is extended in the BOID logic with conditional obligations and intentions borrowed from respectively deontic action programs [8] and BDI logic [5,14]. The BOID logic is an *abstraction* from the BOID architecture, in the sense that in the latter the components may not contain rules or be based on propositional logic, and in case of limited resources the extensions may not be fixpoints.

S. Benferhat and P. Besnard (Eds.): ECSQARU 2001, LNAI 2143, pp. 568–579, 2001.

The contributions of this paper are twofold:

1. We give a classification of conflict resolutions between *conditional* beliefs, obligations, intentions, and desires. Extending the BDP logic with obligations and intentions increases the number of possible conflicts dramatically. In all realistic conflict resolutions beliefs override obligations, intentions, and desires; in stable conflict resolutions intentions override desires and obligations; in unstable conflict resolutions desires and obligations override intentions; in selfish conflict resolutions desires override obligations; and in social conflict resolutions obligations override desires.
2. We propose several desired and undesired properties to analyze this overriding encoded in the BOID logic. As our running example we show how beliefs override desires to block wishful thinking. For example, assume that you believe that you get wet irrespective of your desire to stay dry. This would, according to Thomason, imply that the belief to get wet overrides the desire to stay dry, in the sense that in your planning you will assume that you will get wet.

The layout of this paper is as follows. In Section 2 different types of conflicts are introduced and a classification of conflict resolution types is discussed. In Section 3 the BOID logic and its extension calculation scheme are introduced. In Section 4 properties for wishful thinking are analyzed, and in Section 5 we discuss the properties of extensions provided by the BOID calculation scheme.

2 Beliefs, Obligations, Intentions, and Desires

Reasoning about beliefs, obligations, intentions and desires has been discussed in practical reasoning in philosophy [21,2], and its formalization to build intelligent autonomous agents has more recently been discussed in qualitative decision making in artificial intelligence [7,8,14,18]. On closer inspection each of these four concepts consists of related (though often quite distinct) concepts, for example respectively knowledge and defaults, prohibitions and permissions, commitments and plans, wishes and wants. All these concepts are grouped into these four classes due to their role in the decision making process: beliefs are informational states – how the world is expected to be – obligations and desires are the external and internal motivational states, and intentions are the deliberative states.

2.1 Conflict Resolutions

A conflict resolution type is an order of overruling. Given four attitudes, there are twenty-four possible total orders of overruling, and many more partial orders in which for example desires and obligations are equivalent. In this paper, we only consider those orders according to which beliefs overrule any other attitude. This reduces the number of possible total overruling orders to six. Some examples of conflict resolution are given below.

- A conflict between a belief and a prior intention means that an intended action can no longer be executed due to the changing environment. Beliefs therefore overrule the prior intention, which is retracted. Any derived consequences of this prior intention are retracted too. Of course, one may allow prior intentions to overrule beliefs, but this results in unrealistic behavior.
- A conflict between a belief and an obligation or desire means that a violation has occurred. As observed by Thomason [18], the beliefs must override the desires or otherwise there is wishful thinking; the same argument applies to obligations.
- A conflict between a prior intention and an obligation or desire means that you now should or want to do something else than you intended before. Here prior intentions override the latter because it is exactly this property for which intentions have been introduced: to bring stability. However, in cases of intention reconsideration such conflicts may be resolved otherwise. For example, if I intend to go to the cinema but I am obliged to visit my mother, then I go to the cinema unless I reconsider my intentions.

2.2 Detecting versus Resolving Conflicts

Further specifying and implementing the conflict types leads to several complications. It may seem that we can use one of the many approaches to conflict resolution developed in other areas of artificial intelligence like for example diagnosis [16], default reasoning or fusion of knowledge and databases. However, in these approaches a conflict is defined as a *minimal* set, in the sense that if two sets are conflict sets then one of the sets cannot be a strict subset of the other one. Whereas minimal sets may be useful to detect conflicts, it is not sufficient to resolve them.

An example has been given by Dignum *et. al.* [7], who discuss an extension of the BDI logic with obligations. In this example, there is a guy called Al who has an obligation to perform a task for Bob and another incompatible obligation to perform a task for Chris. Moreover, Al has the norm that he should tell Bob if he does not intend to meet this obligation. The problem discussed in the paper is that the existence of the norm should affect Al's decision on whether to intend to fulfill his obligation:

> "Consider Al's obligation above, until he actually commits to not meeting his obligation to Bob, the need to tell Bob does not exist, yet the *potential* for it may have a significant impact on his decision on whether to do the task for Bob. For example, imagine that the task is trivial (i.e., the direct consequences of not doing the task are small), but the social consequences of not informing Bob are very high (i.e., Al is perceived as unreliable)." [7, p.115]

The point is thus that to resolve the conflict we cannot restrict ourselves to the minimal set (the two obligations), but we have to consider the whole set. In general, agents should consider the effects of actions before committing to it. This is the reason why in the BOID logic complete extensions are constructed before one is selected, instead of solving a conflict as one is encountered.

3 BOID Logic

In this section we discuss the BOID logic. First, we consider Reiter's normal default logic and Thomason's BD logic.

3.1 Reiter's Normal Default Logic

Reiter defined extensions of normal default theories as follows, where we write $\alpha \hookrightarrow w$ for $(\alpha : Mw/w)$ and we write $\langle W, D\rangle$ instead of $\langle D, W\rangle$.

Definition 1. *[15, Def. 1] Let $\Delta = \langle W, D\rangle$ be a closed default theory, so that every default of D has the form $\alpha \hookrightarrow w$ where α and w are both closed wffs of a (first-order) language L, and let $Th_L(S)$ be the consequence set of S in L. For any set of closed wffs $S \subseteq L$ let $T(S)$ be the smallest set of closed formulas from L satisfying the following three properties:*

1. $W \subseteq T(S)$
2. $Th_L(T(S)) = T(S)$
3. *If* $\alpha \hookrightarrow w \in D$, $\alpha \in T(S)$ *and* $\neg w \notin S$, *then* $w \in T(S)$.

A set of closed wffs $E \subseteq L$ is an extension *for Δ iff $T(E) = E$, i.e. iff E is a fixed point of the operator T.*

A well-known theorem of Reiter's paper is the following more intuitive characterization of extensions.

Theorem 1. *[15, Th. 2.1.] Let $E \subseteq L$ be a set of closed wffs, and let $\Delta = \langle W, D\rangle$ be a closed default theory. Define*

$E_0 = W$

and for $i \geq 0$

$E_{i+1} = Th_L(E_i) \cup \{w \mid \alpha \hookrightarrow w \in D \text{ where } \alpha \in E_i \text{ and } \neg w \notin E\}$

Then E is an extension for Δ iff

$E = \cup_{i=0}^{\infty} E_i$.

3.2 Thomason's BD Logic

Thomason [18] proposes a so-called BDP-logic for beliefs, desires and planning which is capable of modeling a wide range of common-sense practical arguments, and which can serve as a more general and flexible model for the decision making process. Thomason first discusses the BD formalism and focuses on the interaction between beliefs and desires. The basic idea is to model beliefs and desires both as Reiter defaults [15], *without modalities for belief or desire*, such that the extensions contain all the derived atoms. That is, a BD-basis is a tuple $\langle Obs, NB, ND\rangle$ with Obs a set of formulas, NB a set of B-defaults 'if a then I believe x' written as $a \overset{B}{\hookrightarrow} x$, and ND a set of D-defaults 'if a then I desire x' written as $a \overset{D}{\hookrightarrow} x$. Extensions are built iteratively by applying default rules without distinguishing between beliefs and desires, so for example, the BD-basis $\langle\{a\}, \{a \overset{B}{\hookrightarrow} b\}, \{b \overset{D}{\hookrightarrow} c\}\rangle$ has as an extension $Th_L(\{a, b, c\})$. But then, there are two types of conflicts:

- Conflicts between a belief and a desire lead to overriding of desire by belief to block wishful thinking.
- Other conflicts, for instance, one between two desires or between two beliefs lead to multiple extensions.

Central in Thomason's iterative calculation of extensions is that belief and desire defaults are treated equally, except for the situations where a desire default conflicts with a subset of the belief defaults applied to the formulas derived in the sequence so far. In such a conflicting situation, the belief defaults are applied preferably.

3.3 BOID Logic

The BOID logic extends Thomason's idea with obligations and intentions (like [7]) resulting in the BOID logic. This logic consists of four sets of propositional logical formulae that represent the four attitudes *Beliefs*, *Obligations*, *Intentions*, and *Desires*. One reason for this extension is to incorporate elements of the social level, i.e. social commitments, to formalize for example social agents and social rationality. The BOID logic is parameterized in order to resolve conflicts between attitudes according to a complete conflict resolution type. This input parameter constrains the order in which derivation steps for different sets are undertaken and characterizes the type of conflict resolution.

The iterative procedure of the BOID calculation scheme is given as an extension of Reiter's more intuitive characterization of extensions in Theorem 1. As in [12] we assume that there is an order on the rules, which we represent by ρ. In order to define this calculation scheme, we first define an ordering function ρ that represents the conflict resolution type. In case of multiple applicable rules, one with the lowest ρ value is applied.

Definition 2. *Let L be a propositional language and S be a set of ordered pairs of L written as $\alpha \hookrightarrow w$ and called rules. An agent type is a set of functions ρ from S to the integers.*

The agent type is usually expressed as a constraint. For example, if S is the union of beliefs B and desires D, then the agent type 'realistic' is expressed by the constraint that for all $r_b \in B$ and $r_d \in D$ we have $\rho(r_b) < \rho(r_d)$. Given a specific agent type, the calculation scheme for building extensions is defined as follows.

Definition 3 (BOID Calculation Scheme). *Let L be a propositional language, let a tuple $\Delta = \langle W, B, O, I, D\rangle$ be a BOID theory with W a subset of L and B, O, I and D sets of ordered pairs of L written as $\alpha \hookrightarrow w$, let ρ be a function that assigns to each rule in $B \cup O \cup I \cup D$ a unique integer, and S a subset of L. Moreover, let*

$$\rho_{\min}(BOID, S) = \min\{\rho(\alpha \hookrightarrow w) \mid \alpha \hookrightarrow w \in B \cup O \cup I \cup D,\ \alpha \in S,\ \neg w \notin S\}$$

$$\min(BOID, S) = w \text{ s.t. } \alpha \hookrightarrow w \in B \cup O \cup I \cup D,\ \rho(\alpha \hookrightarrow w) = \rho_{\min}(BOID, S)$$

Define

$E_0 = W$
and for $i \geq 0$
$E_{i+1} = Th_L(E_i \cup \{\min(BOID, S)\})$ *if such a minimal element exists,*
$E_{i+1} = E_i$ *otherwise.*
Then $E \subseteq L$ *is an extension for* Δ *of agent type* A *iff* $\exists \rho \in A$ *s.t.* $E = \cup_{i=0}^{\infty} E_i$.

3.4 Discussion

Space does not permit us to compare the BOID logic in any detail with classical approaches to specification and verification of agent systems, based on for example modal and temporal logics like BDICTL [14,17]. We just make the following remarks:

- The analysis of conflicts in BDICTL is limited, in the sense that for example two conflicting desires cannot be represented in a consistent way.
- The representation of conditionals in BDICTL is not straightforward, whereas this is a central issue in BOID logics.
- To compare BDICTL and BOID logic the propositional base language of BOID logic must be replaced by BDICTL.[1]
- Each state in the BOID logic has the same logic, i.e. normal default logic, but it can be further developed such that for example for obligations and desires we do not have that inputs are included in the extensions, see [10, 11].

A second and more interesting issue is the comparison of BOID logic with extensions of default logic such as preferred answer sets [3]. One of the results obtained here is that a greedy approach as used in the BOID logic (always try to apply the rule with the highest priority) may lead to globally suboptimal results (e.g. by first applying a rule of priority 3 instead of one of priority 2 we can thereafter apply a rule of priority 1 - by convention the highest priority). The greedy approach is justified by the fact that the BOID logic is only an idealization. In reality fixpoints may never be reached due to limited resources.

4 No Wishful Thinking

Thomason [18] argues that beliefs override desires with the following example. If you think it is going to rain and you believe that if it rains, you will get wet, and you would not like to get wet, then you have to conclude that you get wet. Beliefs therefore prevail in conflicts with desires.

[1] This extension is not as interesting as it may seem at first sight, because the extensions are used in the agent's planning and to plan to achieve goal p it is irrelevant whether there is an intention, desire or obligation to see to it that p. Note that it is important in the implementation [4]. There have also been convincing philosophical arguments to do without modal operators, see [9]. Advantages of this extension are the formalization of more complex notions like permissions and ignorance.

How can we formulate this intuition as a property of extensions? In this section we consider three properties that guarantee that beliefs override desires. These properties are not restricted to one particular approach, but can be applied to any extension-based approach. To facilitate the definitions of the properties in this section we use the following definition.

Definition 4. *Let $\Delta = \langle W, B, D\rangle$ be a BD theory, where W is a set of propositional sentences and B and D ordered pairs of such sentences. We write $E_{BD}(\Delta)$ for the set of all extensions of a propositional BD theory, and for representational convenience we write $E_{BD}(W, B, D)$ for $E_{BD}(\langle W, B, D\rangle)$.*

4.1 Applied Desire Rules

The intuition behind Property 1 of no wishful thinking below is as follows. If in a conflict between a desire and a belief the desire rule is removed, then the extension cannot increase because the belief rule already had priority over the desire rule. In other words, the removal of desires can only decrease the extension, not increase it or remove it.

Property 1 (Applied D rules; first attempt). For each $E' \in E_{BD}(W, B, D')$ and $D \subseteq D'$ there is an $E \in E_{BD}(W, B, D)$ such that $E \subseteq E'$.

The following example illustrates that Property 1 is, unfortunately, too strong.

Example 1. Let $\Delta_1 = \langle \emptyset, \emptyset, \{\top \overset{D}{\hookrightarrow} p\}\rangle$ and $\Delta_2 = \langle \emptyset, \emptyset, \{\top \overset{D}{\hookrightarrow} p, \top \overset{D}{\hookrightarrow} \neg p\}\rangle$. Intuitively we have $E_{BD}(\Delta_1) = \{Th_L(p)\}$ and $E_{BD}(\Delta_2) = \{Th_L(p), Th_L(\neg p)\}$. But for $E' = Th_L(\neg p) \in E_{BD}(\Delta_2)$, there is no $E \in E_{BD}(\Delta_1)$ such that $E \subseteq E'$. This example contradicts Property 1.

Example 1 also illustrates where our first attempt goes wrong. The problem is that D may contain rules which have not been used to build E' of $E_{BD}(W, B, D')$, but they may be used when building E of $E_{BD}(W, B, D)$. In the example, this rule was $\top \overset{D}{\hookrightarrow} p$. We first introduce a definition to identify an extension with the set of rules which are applied in it (sometimes called its generators).

Definition 5 (Applied rules). *Let $\Delta = \langle W, B, D\rangle$ be a BD theory and let the set E be one of its extensions. The set of applied rules in extension E is $R_B(\Delta, E) = \{\alpha \overset{B}{\hookrightarrow} w \in B \mid \alpha \wedge w \in E\}$, $R_D(\Delta, E) = \{\alpha \overset{D}{\hookrightarrow} w \in D \mid \alpha \wedge w \in E\}$, and $R(\Delta, E) = R_B(\Delta, E) \cup R_D(\Delta, E)$.*

The following Property 2 is a weaker form of the Property 1, because we have $R_D(\langle W, B, D'\rangle, E') \subseteq D'$.

Property 2 (Applied D rules, second attempt). For each $E' \in E_{BD}(W, B, D')$ and $D \subseteq R_D(\langle W, B, D'\rangle, E')$ there is an $E \in E_{BD}(W, B, D)$ such that $E \subseteq E'$.

The following example reconsiders Example 1 and illustrates that Property 2 does not have the undesirable behavior.

Example 2. $\Delta_1 = \langle\emptyset,\emptyset,\{\top \overset{D}{\hookrightarrow} p\}\rangle$, $\Delta_2 = \langle\emptyset,\emptyset,\{\top \overset{D}{\hookrightarrow} p, \top \overset{D}{\hookrightarrow} \neg p\}\rangle$. As mentioned in Example 1, $E_{BD}(\Delta_1) = \{Th_L(p)\}$ and $E_{BD}(\Delta_2) = \{Th_L(p), Th_L(\neg p)\}$ contradict Property 1. However, it does not contradict Property 2, because for $E' = Th_L(\neg p)$ we have $R_D(\langle\emptyset,\emptyset,\{\top \overset{D}{\hookrightarrow} p, \top \overset{D}{\hookrightarrow} \neg p\}\rangle, E') = \{\top \overset{D}{\hookrightarrow} \neg p\}$, and this set is not a superset of the desire rules in Δ_1.

The following simple examples further illustrate Property 2.

Example 3. $\Delta_1 = \emptyset, \{\top \overset{B}{\hookrightarrow} p, q \overset{B}{\hookrightarrow} \neg p\}, \emptyset\rangle$, $\Delta_2 = \langle\emptyset, \{\top \overset{B}{\hookrightarrow} p, q \overset{B}{\hookrightarrow} \neg p\}, \{\top \overset{D}{\hookrightarrow} q\}\rangle$. If $E_{BD}(\Delta_1) = \{Th_L(p)\}$, then each element of $E_{BD}(\Delta_2)$ has to contain $Th_L(p)$, and $E_{BD}(\Delta_2)$ thus cannot contain for example $Th_L(q \wedge \neg p)$.

Example 4. $\Delta_1 = \langle\emptyset, \{\top \overset{B}{\hookrightarrow} p\}, \emptyset\rangle$, $\Delta_2 = \langle\emptyset, \{\top \overset{B}{\hookrightarrow} p\}, \{\top \overset{D}{\hookrightarrow} q, p \overset{D}{\hookrightarrow} \neg q\}\rangle$. If $E_{BD}(\Delta_1) = \{Th_L(p)\}$, then each element of $E_{BD}(\Delta_2)$ has to contain $Th_L(p)$, but $E_{BD}(\Delta_2)$ still can contain for example $Th_L(p, q)$ and $Th_L(p, \neg q)$.

Example 5. $\Delta_1 = \langle\emptyset, \{p \overset{B}{\hookrightarrow} \neg q\}, \{\top \overset{D}{\hookrightarrow} p\}\rangle$, $\Delta_2 = \langle\emptyset, \{p \overset{B}{\hookrightarrow} \neg q\}, \{\top \overset{D}{\hookrightarrow} p, \top \overset{D}{\hookrightarrow} q\}\rangle$. If $E_{BD}(\Delta_1) = \{Th_L(p, \neg q)\}$ then generalized no-wishful thinking based on applied desire rules implies $Th_L(p, q) \notin E_{BD}(\Delta_2)$. However, note that $Th_L(q)$ may be in $E_{BD}(\Delta_2)$ (verification left to the reader).

Example 6. $\Delta_1 = \langle\emptyset, \{p \overset{B}{\hookrightarrow} \neg q, r \overset{B}{\hookrightarrow} q\}, \{\top \overset{D}{\hookrightarrow} p\}\rangle$, $\Delta_2 = \langle\emptyset, \{p \overset{B}{\hookrightarrow} \neg q, r \overset{B}{\hookrightarrow} q\}$ $, \{\top \overset{D}{\hookrightarrow} p, \top \overset{D}{\hookrightarrow} r\}\rangle$. If $E_{BD}(\Delta_1) = \{Th_L(p, \neg q)\}$ then we have that the sets $Th_L(p, r, \neg q), Th_L(p, r, q) \notin E_{BD}(\Delta_2)$ but $Th_L(p, \neg q)$ and $Th_L(r, q)$ may be in $E_{BD}(\Delta_2)$ (analogous to the previous example, verification left to the reader).

A simple instance of this generalized no-wishful thinking property, which we call *Restricted no-wishful thinking*, is the case where D is the empty set. This property says that every BD extension extends a B extension.

Property 3 (Restricted Applied D rules). For each $E' \in E_{BD}(W, B, D')$ there is an $E \in E_{BD}(W, B, \emptyset)$ such that $E \subseteq E'$.

4.2 Applied Belief Rules

The second way to define no wishful thinking we consider is to look for a constraint on just the beliefs. The set of applicable belief rules of one extension cannot be a strict subset of the applicable belief rules of another extension.

Property 4 (Applied B rules, first attempt). For all $E_1, E_2 \in E_{BD}(\Delta)$ we have $R_B(\Delta, E_1) \subseteq R_B(\Delta, E_2)$ implies $R_B(\Delta, E_1) = R_B(\Delta, E_2)$.

Unfortunately, this property does not give intuitive results, as the following example illustrates.

Example 7. Let $\Delta = \langle \emptyset, \{p \overset{B}{\hookrightarrow} q\}, \{\top \overset{D}{\hookrightarrow} p, \top \overset{D}{\hookrightarrow} \neg p\}\rangle$. Intuitively we have $E_{BD}(\Delta) = \{Th_L(p,q), Th_L(\neg p)\}$, i.e. $R_B(\Delta, Th_L(\neg p)) \subset R_B(\Delta, Th_L(p,q))$. This example contradicts Property 4.

The following property is a variant of Property 1. The removal of desires can only decrease the set of applied belief rules, not increase it or remove it.

Property 5 (Applied B rules, second attempt). For each $E' \in E_{BD}(W,B,D')$ and $D \subseteq D'$ there is an $E \in E_{BD}(W,B,D)$ such that $R_B(\langle W,B,D\rangle, E) \subseteq R_B(\langle W,B,D'\rangle, E')$.

Property 5 gives the desired results for the rule sets in Example 1 and 7. However, Example 8 is a generalization of these two examples that shows why Property 5 has similar problems as Property 1.

Example 8. $\Delta_1 = \emptyset, \{p \overset{B}{\hookrightarrow} q\}, \{\top \overset{D}{\hookrightarrow} p\}\rangle$, $\Delta_2 = \langle \emptyset, \{p \overset{B}{\hookrightarrow} q\}, \{\top \overset{D}{\hookrightarrow} p, \top \overset{D}{\hookrightarrow} \neg p\}\rangle$. Intuitively we have $E_{BD}(\Delta_1) = \{Th_L(p,q)\}$ and $E_{BD}(\Delta_2) = \{Th_L(p,q), Th_L(\neg p)\}$. However, for $E' = Th_L(\neg p) \in E_{BD}(\Delta_2)$ there is no $E \in E_{BD}(\Delta_1)$ such that $R_B(\Delta_1, E) \subseteq R_B(\Delta_2, E')$.

The following property is analogous to Property 2.

Property 6 (Applied B rules, third attempt). For each $E' \in E_{BD}(W,B,D')$ and $D \subseteq R_D(\langle W,B,D'\rangle, E')$ there is an $E \in E_{BD}(W,B,D)$ such that we have $R_B(\langle W,B,D\rangle, E) \subseteq R_B(\langle W,B,D'\rangle, E')$.

The following example illustrates the distinction between Property 2 and 6.

Example 9. Let $\Delta_1 = \langle \emptyset, \emptyset, \{\top \overset{D}{\hookrightarrow} p\}\rangle$ and $\Delta_2 = \langle \emptyset, \emptyset, \{\top \overset{D}{\hookrightarrow} p, \top \overset{D}{\hookrightarrow} q\}\rangle$. If $E_{BD}(\Delta_1) = Th_L(p)$ then we cannot have $Th_L(\emptyset)$ in $E_{BD}(\Delta_2)$ according to generalized no wishful thinking based on applied desire rules, but it can be according to generalized no wishful thinking based on applied belief rules.

Intuitively we do not want $Th_L(\emptyset)$ in $E_{BD}(\Delta_2)$, but the reason for this is not the blocking of wishful thinking. Property 6 seems therefore a better characterization of no-wishful thinking than Property 2.

Property 7 is analogous to Property 3.

Property 7 (Restricted Applied B rules). For each $E' \in E_{BD}(W,B,D')$ there is an $E \in E_{BD}(W,B,\emptyset)$ such that $R_B(E) \subseteq R_B(E')$.

4.3 Abnormal Belief Rules

The third way to define no wishful thinking is not based on applied rules but on rules which could not be applied, which we call abnormal rules. These abnormal rules are defined analogously to applied rules in Definition 5.

Definition 6 (Abnormal rules). *Let $\Delta = \langle W, B, D \rangle$ be a BD theory and let the set E be one of its extensions. The set of abnormal rules is represented by $Ab_B(\Delta, E) = \{\alpha \overset{B}{\hookrightarrow} w \in B \mid \alpha \wedge \neg w \in E\}$.*

Generalized no wishful thinking based on abnormal belief rules is defined analogous to generalized no wishful thinking property based on applied rules in Property 2 and 6.

Property 8 (Abnormal B rules, first attempt). For each $E' \in E_{BD}(W, B, D')$ and $D \subseteq R_D(\langle W, B, D' \rangle, E')$ there is an $E \in E_{BD}(W, B, D)$ such that we have $Ab_B(\langle W, B, D \rangle, E) \supseteq Ab_B(\langle W, B, D' \rangle, E')$.

The following example illustrates that generalized wishful thinking based on abnormal belief rules is different from generalized wishful thinking based on applied desire or belief rules in Property 2 and 6.

Example 10. Let $\Delta_1 = \langle \{\neg q\}, \{p \overset{B}{\hookrightarrow} q\}, \emptyset \rangle$ and $\Delta_2 = \langle \{\neg q\}, \{p \overset{B}{\hookrightarrow} q\}, \{\top \overset{D}{\hookrightarrow} p\} \rangle$. If $Th_L(\neg q, p) \notin E_{BD}(\Delta_1)$ then according to generalized no wishful thinking based on abnormal belief rules $Th_L(\neg q, p) \notin E_{BD}(\Delta_2)$. However, according to generalized wishful thinking based on applied desire or belief rules, it may be that $Th_L(\neg q, p) \notin E_{BD}(\Delta_1)$ as well as $Th_L(\neg q, p) \in E_{BD}(\Delta_2)$.

5 BOID Properties

The first BOID property is called *Existence* and says that there is at least one BD extension, if the facts W are consistent. This is a very desirable and crucial property for decision making agents, because an agent needs an extension to act rationally. Otherwise the agent is stuck or starts to make random movements.

Property 9 (Existence). $E_{BD}(W, B, D) \neq \emptyset$ if $\bot \notin Th_L(W)$.

The second BOID property we discuss here is called BD maximality, and says that if a rule can be applied then it is applied. That is, we go as far as possible. This property implies that the set of BD extensions are a subset of the set of Reiter extensions where the set of rules consists of the union of belief and desire rules. We write $E_R(\Delta)$ for the set of all Reiter extensions of a propositional default theory, and if we consider Reiter extensions of BD theories consisting of $\alpha \overset{B}{\hookrightarrow} w$ and $\alpha \overset{D}{\hookrightarrow} w$, then we ignore the superscript above the arrows, i.e. we interpret $E_R(\langle W, BD \rangle)$ as $E_R(\langle W, \{\alpha \hookrightarrow w \mid \alpha \overset{B}{\hookrightarrow} w \in BD \text{ or } \alpha \overset{D}{\hookrightarrow} w \in BD\rangle)$.

Property 10 (BD maximality). $E_{BD}(W, B, D) \subseteq E_R(W, B \cup D)$

The following example reconsiders Example 10 and questions the BD maximality property.

Example 11. Let $\Delta = \langle\{\neg q\}, \{p \overset{B}{\hookrightarrow} q\}, \{\top \overset{D}{\hookrightarrow} p\}\rangle$ (we can also replace $\neg q$ by $\top \overset{B}{\hookrightarrow} \neg q$). We have $E_R(\Delta) = \{Th_L(\neg q, p)\}$, and thus with the existence property and the BD maximality property we can derive $E_{BD}(\Delta) = \{Th_L(\neg q, p)\}$. However, $\neg q \wedge p$ implies that to fulfill the desire for p we get into a situation in which something happens which we believe will not happen, namely the exception to the belief that p implies q.[2]

The following theorem and its corollary suggest that BD maximality is too strong (see [11] for an alternative notion of extension).

Theorem 2. *No-wishful thinking based on applied desire rules (Property 2), on applied belief rules (Property 6) or on abnormal belief rules (Property 8) conflicts with BD maximality (Property 10) together with Existence (Property 9).*

Proof. *For the applied rules, see Example 5 and 6. For the abnormal rules, see Example 10 and 11.*

Corollary 1. *The BOID logic does not satisfy any of the three notions of no-wishful thinking discussed in this paper.*

6 Concluding Remarks

We have discussed possible conflict types that may arise within or among informational and motivational attitudes and explained how these conflicts can be resolved within the BOID calculation scheme. The resolution of conflicts is based on Thomason's idea of prioritization, which is considered in the BOID logic as the order of derivations from different types of attitudes. We have shown that the order of derivations determines the type of conflict resolution method. For example, deriving desire before beliefs produces wishful thinking and deriving obligations before desires produces sociality. We have also introduced some desired and undesired properties, and checked whether some conflict resolution methods satisfied the properties.

Two issues for further research are the generalization of properties for overriding to multiple attitudes, and for other input/output logics [10,11] than Reiter's normal default logic. Although the properties are defined independent of the logic, both Definition 5 and 6 of applied and abnormal rules must be adapted if we allow for e.g. reasoning by cases (e.g. $E_{BD}(\emptyset, \{\alpha \overset{B}{\hookrightarrow} w, \neg\alpha \overset{B}{\hookrightarrow} w\}, \emptyset) = Th_L(w)$).

---

[2] Example 11 is not very convincing, because of the following two reasons. First, the behavior in Example 11 seems to be what is expected from *conditional* rules. If you do not like it, then you can formalize the belief rule with $\top \overset{B}{\hookrightarrow} p \rightarrow q$, where $\rightarrow$ is a material implication. Second, in the discussion in Example 11 the rules are used as a kind of causal rules. However, if the conditional $p \overset{B}{\hookrightarrow} q$ represents a causal relation, then the world will change such that $\neg q$ will turn into q.

Acknowledgment. Thanks to Salem Benferhat, Zisheng Huang and Joris Hulstijn for discussions on the issues discussed in this paper.

References

1. C. Boutilier. Toward a logic for qualitative decision theory. In *Proceedings of the KR'94*, pages 75–86, 1994.
2. Michael E. Bratman. *Intention, plans, and practical reason.* Harvard University Press, Cambridge Mass, 1987.
3. G. Brewka and T. Eiter. Preferred answer sets for extended logic programs. *Artificial Intelligence*, 109:297–356, 1999.
4. J. Broersen, M. Dastani, Z. Huang, J. Hulstijn, and L. van der Torre. The BOID architecture: Conflicts between beliefs, obligations, intentions, and desires. In *Proceedings of International Conference on Autonomous Agents (AA'01)*, 2001.
5. P.R. Cohen and H.J. Levesque. Intention is choice with commitment. *Artificial Intelligence*, 42:213–261, 1990.
6. F. Dignum. Autonomous agents and norms. *Artificial Intelligence and Law*, 7:69–79, 1999.
7. F. Dignum, D. Morley, E.A. Sonenberg, and L. Cavedon. Towards socially sophisticated BDI agents. In *Proceedings of the ICMAS 2000*, pages 111–118, 2000.
8. Thomas Eiter, V.S. Subrahmanian, and George Pick. Heterogeneous active agents I: Semantics. *Artificial Intelligence*, 108 (1-2):179–255, 1999.
9. D. Makinson. On a fundamental problem of deontic logic. In *Norms, logics and information systems*, pages 29–53. IOS Press, 1999.
10. D. Makinson and L. van der Torre. Input-output logics. *Journal of Philosophical Logic*, 29:383–408, 2000.
11. D. Makinson and L. van der Torre. Constraints for input-output logics. *Journal of Philosophical Logic*, 30(2):155–185, 2001.
12. V.W. Marek and M. Truszczynski. *Nonmonotonic logic: Context-dependent reasoning.* Springer, Berlin, 1993.
13. J. Pearl. From conditional oughts to qualitative decision theory. In *Proceedings of the UAI'93*, pages 12–20, 1993.
14. A. Rao and M. Georgeff. BDI agents: From theory to practice. In *Proceedings of the First International Conference on Multi-Agent Systems (ICMAS'95)*, pages 312–319, 1995.
15. R. Reiter. A logic for default reasoning. *Artificial Intelligence*, 13:81–132, 1980.
16. R. Reiter. A theory of diagnosis from first principles. *Artificial Intelligence*, 32:57–95, 1987.
17. K. Schild. On the relationship between BDI logics and standard logics of concurrency. *Autonomous Agents and Multi Agent systems*, 2000.
18. R. Thomason. Desires and defaults: a framework for planning with inferred goals. In *Proceedings of the KR'2000*, pages 702–713. Morgan Kaufmann, 2000.
19. L. van der Torre and Y. Tan. Contrary-to-duty reasoning with preference-based dyadic obligations. *Annals of Mathematics and Artificial Intelligence*, 27:49–78, 1999.
20. L. van der Torre and Y. Tan. Diagnosis and decision making in normative reasoning. *Artificial Intelligence and Law*, 7:51–67, 1999.
21. G.H. von Wright. *Norms, truth and logic. Practical Reason.* Blackwell, Oxford, 1983.

Comparing a Pair-wise Compatibility Heuristic and Relaxed Stratification: Some Preliminary Results

Robert E. Mercer[1], Lionel Forget, and Vincent Risch[2]

[1] Cognitive Engineering Laboratory, Dept. of Computer Science, The University of Western Ontario, London, Ontario, Canada
[2] InCA Team, LIM - ESA CNRS 6077, Centre de Mathématiques et d'Informatique, Marseille, France

Abstract. An extension-building heuristic is developed and a preliminary investigation of its computational properties is given by comparing its run times to those of DeReS which uses relaxed stratification, another extension-building heuristic. Heuristics which can take advantage of the structural properties of a default theory may provide the information about the theory so that divide-and-conquer-like techniques may be applied on those problems which exhibit appropriate structural properties. Structural properties of a default theory are defined in terms of properties of graphs that represent important features of default theories. Unlike the syntax-dependent heuristics used in previous extension-building algorithms, the heuristic developed here is consistency-based.

1 Introduction

The problem of building extensions for propositional default theories, although being straightforward from an algorithmic point of view, is in the complexity class Σ_2^P. [8] Heuristics that uncover appropriate structural properties of a default theory may allow divide-and-conquer-like techniques to be applied to reduce computation time. Few heuristics of this kind for the extension-building problem are known, with the noted exception of relaxed stratification [4]. In this paper we develop another extension-building heuristic and report on a preliminary investigation of its computational effects. Unlike relaxed stratification which is motivated by stratification in logic programming, our choice of structural property of a default theory has been motivated, in spirit, by work which relates graphs and default theories [5–7, 10].

The crucial piece of information to build an extension is its set of generating defaults. This feature has formed our principal goal: to discover potentially valuable, yet relatively easy to compute, information about sets of generating defaults. The proposed heuristic is an incremental method for generating the smallest possible supersets of generating defaults given only the currently known information about the defaults. More precisely, given a graph whose nodes represent defaults and whose edges represent pair-wise compatibility between defaults

S. Benferhat and P. Besnard (Eds.): ECSQARU 2001, LNAI 2143, pp. 580–591, 2001.

(that is, these defaults are not necessarily not in the same set of generating defaults), cliques in this graph represent supersets of sets of generating defaults. If the superset of a set of generating defaults is a proper subset of the default theory, the effort expended by an extension-building algorithm will be reduced.

We have chosen the complete (but brute force) extension-building method proposed in [12], because it is a clear and simple framework, to show this heuristic to be complete. We also discuss some preliminary results that we have obtained from an experimental study comparing the pair-wise compatibility heuristic and the relaxed stratification heuristic that has been implemented in DeReS [4].

2 Background

As defined by Reiter [11], a closed default theory is a pair (W, D) where W is a set of closed first order sentences and D a set of default rules. A default rule has the form $\frac{\alpha:\beta}{\gamma}$ where α, β and γ are closed first order sentences[1]. α is called the prerequisite, β the justification and γ the consequent of the default. $PREREQ(D)$, $JUST(D)$ and $CONS(D)$ are respectively the sets of all prerequisites, justifications and consequents that come from defaults in a set D. Whenever one of these sets is a singleton, we may identify it with the single element it contains. For instance, we prefer to consider $PREREQ(\{\frac{\alpha:\beta}{\gamma}\})$ as an element rather than a set. The following definition shows us how the use of a default is related to its prerequisite:

Definition 1. *[14] A set D of defaults is grounded in W iff for all $\delta \in D$ there is a finite sequence $\delta_0, \ldots, \delta_k$ of elements of D such that (1) $PREREQ(\{\delta_0\}) \in Th(W)$, (2) for $1 \leq i \leq k-1$, $PREREQ(\{\delta_{i+1}\}) \in Th(W \cup CONS(\{\delta_0, \ldots, \delta_i\}))$, and $\delta_k = \delta$.*

An *extension* of a default theory is usually defined as a smallest fixed point of a set of formulas. It contains W, is deductively closed, and the defaults whose consequents belong to the extension verify a property which allows their use. The manner in which this property is considered is related to the variant of default logic under consideration. In what follows, we consider the characterization previously obtained by [12, 13] for the extensions in the sense of [11].

Theorem 1. *[12, 13] Let $\Delta = (W, D)$ be a default theory. E is an R-extension for Δ iff there is D' a grounded subset of D such that $E = Th(W \cup CONS(D'))$, and for each default $\delta \in D$, of the form $\frac{\alpha:\beta}{\gamma}$: (i) if $\delta \in D'$ then $\alpha \in E$ and $\neg\beta \notin E$, (ii) if $\delta \notin D'$ then $\alpha \notin E$ or $\neg\beta \in E$. Each set D' is called* a set of generating defaults.

Definition 2. *For the default theory $\Delta = (W, D)$ and the potential set of generating defaults D', the default $\delta = \frac{\alpha:\beta}{\gamma} \in D$ is a* destroying default[2] *for D' if $\delta \notin D'$ but $\alpha \in E$ and $\neg\beta \notin E$, and $D' \cup \delta$ is not a set of generating defaults.*

[1] For simplicity, we restrict our attention to defaults with only one justification: the generalization to several justifications is straightforward, and is described in [1, 13].

[2] These defaults are called *selection defaults* in [4] (because they are viewed as filters) and *killing defaults* in [3].

A complete method for computing the R-extensions of a default theory is proposed by [13, 12] based on the characterization in Theorem 1. We refer to this method as Algorithm **E**. We have chosen Algorithm **E** because it is brute force; hence it is simple, clear, and not encumbered by superfluous detail such as other heuristics. Roughly speaking, an extension is the set of theorems over the union of W and a maximal set of default consequences (maximal in the sense that the addition of any other default consequence would falsify either the prerequisite or the justification condition). In other words, the default consequences that contribute to an extension come from a subset D' of D such that the prerequisite and justification conditions hold for every default of D. Thus, the central theme of the algorithm is to look for all subsets D' of D yielding extensions of Δ. Starting from D, the algorithm proceeds in three steps.

Algorithm ***E***

1. (Consistency condition)[3] All maximal consistent subsets of $W \cup CONS(D)$ that contain W are found. That is, a collection of subsets $D_1 \ldots D_n$ of D is found such that every $W \cup CONS(D_i)$ is maximally consistent for $1 \leq i \leq n$. For every D_i and every $\delta \in D \setminus D_i$, $W \cup CONS(D_i \cup \{\delta\})$ is inconsistent.

2. (Justification condition) The justification of every default δ of every previously computed D_i is checked. This procedure yields maximal subsets D_i^j of D_i such that $Th(W \cup CONS(D_i^j)) \cap \{\neg\beta\} = \emptyset$ for every $\beta \in JUST(D_i^j)$.

3. (Prerequisite condition) Maximal grounded sets of defaults are obtained by eliminating the defaults that are not grounded from the previously computed D_i^j. Testing groundedness for a default $\delta \in D_i^j$ consists of verifying that $PREREQ(\{\delta\}) \in Th(W \cup CONS(D_i^j \setminus \{\delta\}))$. If $PREREQ(\{\delta\}) \in Th(W)$ then $\{\delta\}$ is grounded; if $PREREQ(\{\delta\})$ is derived from the consequences of a subset D' of $D_i^j \setminus \{\delta\}$ then the groundedness of D' has to be checked. Thereby, a sequence of verifications is generated for the defaults of D_i^j such that

   - each default used for a verification is removed from D_i^j;
   - D_i^j is grounded iff every default of D_i^j belongs to a sequence that validates its prerequisite and the prerequisites of the first defaults of the sequence belong to $Th(W)$ (i.e. removing defaults from the sequence after each verification does not yield the empty set).

   Note that testing the groundedness of D_i^j costs no more than testing the prerequisite condition on the defaults of D_i^j.

At the end of the process, only the maximal computed sets of defaults are retained as good candidates for sets of generating defaults (note these sets are already sets of generating defaults with respect to Łukaszewicz's approach to default reasoning [9, 12]). Following Theorem 1, R-extensions are produced by the sets of defaults for which the complementary set of defaults satisfies *(ii)*. In other words, to obtain an extension, it is necessary to deal with the defaults that

[3] Step 1 is not necessary for Algorithm **E** to be complete. It will be ignored below.

are not involved in the construction of this extension, that is, it is necessary to check whether these defaults can be removed from the set of defaults that may yield an extension. It is only under this condition that this set of defaults can be called as a set of generating defaults under Reiter's approach.

Algorithms such as Algorithm **E** can be inefficient. On many problem instances, they rediscover extensions or they can rediscover that a certain subset of defaults lack an extension regardless of which other defaults are considered. These inefficiencies can oftentimes be removed with divide-and-conquer techniques that leave the completeness of Algorithm **E** intact. These techniques can reduce the number of times that an extension is discovered by limiting the number of permutations of the defaults and can reduce the rediscovery of failures by finding incompatibilities in sets of defaults early. The effect of the heuristic can also be pictured as pruning of the search tree that is generated by Algorithm **E**. We use this view in our presentation below.

3 Theoretical aspects

We first introduce the graph which represents pair-wise compatibility between defaults in a default theory.

Definition 3. *For all defaults* $\delta_1 = \frac{a:b}{c}$ *and* $\delta_2 = \frac{d:e}{f}$, *where* a, b, c, d, e, f *are propositional formulas,* δ_1 *and* δ_2 *are said to be* incompatible *iff* $a \wedge d \vdash \bot$, *or* $a \wedge e \vdash \bot$, *or* $a \wedge f \vdash \bot$, *or* $b \wedge d \vdash \bot$, *or* $b \wedge f \vdash \bot$, *or* $c \wedge d \vdash \bot$, *or* $c \wedge e \vdash \bot$, *or* $c \wedge f \vdash \bot$. *They are said to be* compatible, *otherwise.*

The incompatibility and compatibility relations are reflexive and symmetric. When referring to the (in)compatibility of a default and itself, we will say that a default is *self-(in)compatible*. It is noteworthy that W is not included on the left-hand side of $\vdash$. The compatibility relation that we have defined above is weaker (more defaults are compatible) than if W were added to the left-hand side of each $\vdash$. Initial experimentation using this compatibility relation will be followed by refinement of the heuristic.

All sets of generating defaults must be compatible with W. In the following, we will denote $w_1 = \{\frac{\top:\top}{W}\}$. Considering W as a default is only a convenience to make the definition of the compatibility graph simpler.

Definition 4. *The* compatibility graph, $G_\Delta(N_\Delta, E_\Delta)$, *for a default theory* $\Delta = (W, D)$, *is* $N_\Delta = D \cup w_1$, *the set of nodes, and* E_Δ, *the set of edges. There is an edge between two nodes* δ_1 *and* δ_2 *iff* δ_1 *and* δ_2 *are compatible.*

Definition 5. *A* clique *in a graph is a completely connected subgraph. The term is used throughout this paper to mean cliques which are maximal in the sense of subgraph containment.*

Cliques in the compatibility graph, which represents mutually pair-wise compatible defaults, are the structures which are at the heart of our heuristic. If these cliques are proper subgraphs of the compatibility graph the original problem has been successfully divided into simpler problems.

Because disjunctions in the components of the defaults can hide potentially useful incompatibility relations, the heuristic could benefit from information gained while the extension-building procedure is being done. We show how to propagate this information in the compatibility graph.

Definition 6. *Information, $i = i_1, \ldots, i_n$ is* propagated *in a graph by modifying the incompatibility relation to be $a \wedge d \vdash \perp$, or $a \wedge e \vdash \perp$, or $a \wedge (f \wedge \bigwedge i) \vdash \perp$, or $b \wedge d \vdash \perp$, or $b \wedge (f \wedge \bigwedge i) \vdash \perp$, or $c \wedge d \vdash \perp$, or $c \wedge e \vdash \perp$, or $c \wedge (f \wedge \bigwedge i) \vdash \perp$.*[4]

Algorithm $\boldsymbol{E}^*$

```
If W is inconsistent
      Then print "W is inconsistent"
      Else Generate the compatibility graph G
            Find cliques C_i in G
            For each clique C_i do E*(C_i)
E*(A)
For each possible order o (on nodes) of A do
     While the order o is not empty do
     % This is Step 2 of Algorithm E with information propagation added %
           If (w ∪ CONS(δ_i | δ_i ∈ A) ⊢ ¬just(o(1))
           Then Propagate ¬just(o(1)) in A
                 For each clique C' obtained do E*(C')
                 Empty the current order and erase all other orders with
                 the same beginning
           Else Remove the current node of the current order
     If all defaults in extension are grounded and no destroying defaults exist
     % This is Step 3 of Algorithm E with test for R-extension added %
           Then keep the extension
           Else delete the extension
```

Example 1.
Given the default theory: $\Delta = (\{A, D, G\}, \{\delta_1 = \frac{A:B}{C}, \delta_2 = \frac{D:E}{\neg F}, \delta_3 = \frac{G:H}{F}\})$, the compatibility graph has two cliques: $C_1 = \{w_1, \delta_1, \delta_2\}$ and $C_2 = \{w_1, \delta_1, \delta_3\}$. Having these two cliques indicates the impossibility of finding δ_2 and δ_3 in the same extension (their consequences are incompatible). Thus, the original problem of finding the correct D's in the original set $D = \{\delta_1, \delta_2, \delta_3\}$ has been turned into two simpler subproblems: finding the correct D's in $C_1 - w_1$ and $C_2 - w_1$.

Example 2.
Given the default theory: $\Delta = (\{A\}, \{\delta_1 = \frac{A:B}{C}, \delta_2 = \frac{C:D}{E}, \delta_3 = \frac{C:F}{G}\})$, the

[4] Propagating information into the prerequisite and justification of defaults is left to future work.

compatibility graph has only one clique because the graph is complete. Having one clique says that there it is no incompatibility relation in this default theory. So, no information is available to help Algorithm **E***. Moreover, when Algorithm **E*** discovers new information, propagating this information in the graph will only remove one default each time. So, Algorithm **E*** will not be any better than Algorithm **E** on this example. This is a very bad case for the heuristic, but in this case, applying the heuristic is very inexpensive because, it is easy to find all cliques in a complete graph.

Example 3.
We consider now the following example: $\Delta = (w = \{A, B \rightarrow \neg C, (C \vee D) \rightarrow \neg X, P\}, \{\delta_1 = \frac{A:C}{B}, \delta_2 = \frac{P:X}{C \vee D}, \delta_3 = \frac{P:\neg D}{C \vee E}\})$ This default theory has no extension. In this case, Algorithm **E** explores the complete search tree, and concludes, of course, that there is no extension, because all of the possible sets obtained are "destroyed" by the application of the default δ_1. When using Algorithm **E***, we have to look at two steps in particular. First, the compatibility graph is complete. So, there is only one clique. It is given to Algorithm **E***. Second, the first step of Algorithm **E*** is to try to entail $\neg C$. It succeeds. This new information is propagated in the graph. This propagation generates two cliques, because considering $\neg C$, δ_2 and δ_3 become incompatible because of D. Having two cliques allows Algorithm **E*** to study the two sub-problems $C_1 = \{w, \delta_2\}$ and $C_2 = \{w, \delta_3\}$. As in the previous example, Algorithm **E*** will conclude that there is no extension (because of the destroying default δ_1) without backtracking. Intuitively, propagating the new information says that considering this new information, δ_2 and δ_3 cannot appear in the same extension. Of course, it will be the same thing, if Algorithm **E*** tries to prove another justification instead of $\neg C$.

Algorithm **E*** is only Algorithm **E** with the new heuristic. Of course, if there exist cases where our heuristic is not applied, then only Algorithm **E** is used. So in the following, we will consider that Algorithm **E** is proved. Clearly, our method is a heuristic: It only helps Algorithm **E** by removing parts of the search tree which are redundant, given the knowledge gained by the heuristic. So, sometimes the heuristic just simplifies the problem for Algorithm **E**. Each time that Algorithm **E** discovers another piece of structural information about some defaults, the heuristic tries to propagate it in the current clique representation. If propagating the information divides the current clique, Algorithm **E** continues with these new cliques. If this is not the case, then Algorithm **E** continues. In each case Algorithm **E** finishes. So, we will prove that at each step, the heuristic makes only good problem reductions, and gives back to Algorithm **E** coherent subproblems.

Property 1. Every set of generating defaults is contained in a clique.

Proof. By definition, sets of generating defaults are sets of compatible defaults, so, these sets will be included in at least one clique.

Property 2. Every clique containing a set of generating defaults will be studied by **E***. It is then impossible to forget one clique representing an extension.

Proof. To prove this property it is sufficient to look at the algorithm. After generating the compatibility graph, we are looking for cliques, and for each clique we call the E^* function.

Property 3. If the $\mathbf{E}^*$ function is able to prove the negation of a justification, then propagating this new information in the clique cannot split a set of generating defaults.

Proof. Suppose that propagating a new piece of information, $\neg b$, in the clique splits the set of generating defaults. This means that the consequences $c_1, \ldots, c_n$ of a subset $\delta_1, \ldots, \delta_n$ of the set of generating defaults entails b (if $\neg b \wedge c_1 \wedge \ldots \wedge c_n \wedge w \vdash \bot$ then $c_1 \wedge \ldots \wedge c_n \wedge w \vdash \neg b$). So by monotonicity, the set of generating defaults entails b but does not entail $\neg b$ (by definition a set of generating defaults represents an extension and an extension is consistent). Therefore W and the set of consequences of generating defaults) is compatible with b, hence propagating $\neg b$ cannot split the set of generating defaults.

Theorem 2. *Algorithm* $\mathbf{E}^*$ *is complete.*

Proof. The algorithm is recursive, so we will prove that at each step Algorithm $\mathbf{E}^*$ is correct (each step is ultimately concluded by Algorithm **E**, a complete algorithm, if provided with supersets of generating defaults). We proved that the initial case is correct (Properties 1 and 2). Now, it is necessary only to prove that each time that a new piece of information is propagated in the $\mathbf{E}^*$ function, then propagating this new information in the clique we are considering cannot lead to false or lost extensions.

A : The clique contains no set of generating defaults. In this case
- If the propagated information only removes one or more defaults in the clique, then the set obtained using the clique is the same as the set obtained by Algorithm **E**. The algorithm continues as if it were Algorithm **E**, so it is correct.
- If the propagated information removes one or more defaults and splits the set of remaining defaults into two or more cliques, then since the previous clique contains no set of generating defaults, then the new ones contain no set of generating defaults, and then with each new set, Algorithm **E** will not find any extension, because it is complete.

B : The clique contains one or more sets of generating defaults. In this case
- If the propagated information only removes one or more defaults in the clique, then the set obtained using the clique is the same as the set obtained by Algorithm **E**. The algorithm continues as if it were Algorithm **E**, so it is correct.
- If the propagated information removes one or more defaults and splits the set of remaining defaults into two or more cliques, then by Property 3 every set of generating defaults is contained in one of these new cliques and Algorithm **E** continues with all of these new sets, so it is correct.

4 Description of DeReS

DeReS produces sets of generating defaults by searching a full binary tree representing all the subsets of the default rules in D. The binary tree is structured in the following way: The root is labelled as ϕ. The right child of each node is labelled with the same label as its parent. The left child of each node is labelled with the set that represents its parent unioned with the default that is being added by the current level. Of importance to the discussion that follows is that the complete default theory is represented by the tree's leftmost leaf node.

The heuristic used by DeReS is relaxed stratification, an idea influenced by Logic Programming.[5] Relaxed stratification uses a syntactically-based partition $\{D_1, \ldots, D_n\}$ of the default theory: propositional variables appearing in defaults from D_i do not appear in the consequence of defaults from D_j, for $i < j$, and no set D_i can be further partitioned preserving the constraint on variable occurrence. Also, formulas in W do not have common propositional variables with the consequents of the defaults. Extensions for the default theory are computed by letting $W_1 = W$ and incrementally finding extensions for the default theories (W_i, D_i), where $W_i = W_{i-1}$ unioned with the consequences of the generating defaults for (W_{i-1}, D_{i-1}). Three types of pruning are achieved by DeReS using relaxed stratification. Firstly, if a node in the binary tree represents an extension, the left and right subtrees can be pruned, since extensions are maximal. Secondly, relaxed stratification is a divide-and-conquer technique. It implicitly prunes the search tree by not considering combinations of defaults that are chosen from different strata. Thirdly, strategic location of destroying defaults in the strata can prune subtrees, preventing the rediscovery of extensions that would be destroyed by the destroying default.

5 Implementation of the Pair-wise Compatibility Heuristic

We are currently using a loosely-coupled hybrid system to obtain the preliminary results reported here. To produce the pair-wise compatibility graph we are using a simple inspection method, because the defaults in the problems that we have studied are simple enough to allow this. We are using the Bron and Kerbosch algorithm, known to be the best algorithm for finding all cliques in a graph [2]. It produces each clique in a small constant time and most importantly it produces each clique once. Given these two factors, the computation of the cliques adds almost nothing to the time to compute extensions. (This preprocessing time is not reported in any of the run times.) We also use the theorem prover and some other parts of the DeReS (Version 1.3) program for our timing of the pair-wise compatibility heuristic. Doing so means that the differences in run times is due solely to the effects of the heuristics on the extension-building. (Because

[5] The language used in [4] has a strong Logic Programming flavour — one section is titled "Programming with default logic".

Algorithm $\mathbf{E}^*$ builds from D to the sets of generating defaults and DeReS builds from ϕ to the sets of generating defaults, it is not clear what computational effects the two search strategies will ultimately have.)

To simulate the algorithm, with the pair-wise compatibility heuristic embedded properly, generating all of the extensions of a default theory, the hybrid method first calculates all of the cliques of the compatibility graph and then gives each clique to DeReS as a separate problem. The run times that we report are simply the sum of the times taken by all of the individual runs.

We have used this hybrid approach for a number of reasons. Firstly, as mentioned above, we didn't want any of the comparison to be biased due to parts of the implementation that have nothing to do with the heuristics. So, for the two heuristics, the extension-building engine is DeReS. Secondly, we are interested in studying the two heuristics combined. Using DeReS gives us access to relaxed stratification. (We currently can only conjecture that the two heuristics are independent so they can be used concurrently.) Thirdly, the University of Kentucky website described in [4] contains a number of default theories set up for use with DeReS. These publicly available test cases are a reasonable place to begin experimentation. Fourthly, we have only experimented with disjunction free theories. So, the incremental part of the compatibility heuristic is not being tested. When we move to this phase of the experimentation, we will need to move away from this hybrid approach.

6 Experiments and Results

6.1 Experimental Background

The University of Kentucky website described in [4] contains a number of default theories encoded for use by DeReS. We have used two sets of problems contained there to give us the preliminary results that we report below. The first problem set contains default theories that represent *maximum independent sets* (when the problem is represented as a graph, the maximum independent set problem is the dual of the clique problem). The representation is discussed in [4]. What makes this problem set interesting is that there are no self-incompatible defaults and no problem has a non-trivial stratification. The second problem set contains default theories whose extensions are precisely the *kernels in directed graphs.* What makes this problem set interesting is that the default theories include self-incompatible defaults (more than half of the defaults) and that the theories are finely stratified. W is the empty set for both problem sets.

6.2 Results

The four 'maximum independent sets' theories contain 10, 20, 30, and 40 defaults. Excluding the 10- and 20-default cases (the results are almost the same), a summary of the run times when using the pair-wise compatibility heuristic compared to using the relaxed stratification heuristic are in Table 1. The spread in running times increases with the number of defaults. The relaxed stratification heuristic does not modify the original default theories in any way. On the other hand, the 2101 and 15,380 cliques produced by the pair-wise compatibility heuristic for the 30- and 40-default theories, respectively, are precisely the sets of generating defaults for the extensions. This situation is the best possible for the pair-wise compatibility heuristic, and the worst possible for relaxed stratification. Because of the way that we have designed the experiment, only the heuristics account for the differences in run times[6].

The seven 'kernel' theories contain 80, 175, 252, 343, 448, 567, and 700 defaults. We studied only the first. It has 80 defaults, 48 being self-incompatible defaults. Each default theory consists of a number of prerequisite-free normal defaults, one whose consequence is a_i and one whose consequence is $\neg a_i$ for propositional letters, $a_1, \ldots, a_n$, where n depends on the theory. There are also a number of non-normal defaults which are self-incompatible defaults. The prerequisites of these self-incompatible defaults are conjunctions of some of the a_i and $\neg a_i$ found in the normal defaults. The 65,536 cliques are then just all possible maximal combinations of the normal defaults whose consequences are consistent. Six extensions result. The results are summarized in Table 1. DeReS with relaxed stratification performs very well (the theory is highly stratified). If the cliques[7] produced by the pair-wise compatibility heuristic are all blindly given to DeReS, the results are very poor. The results shown here use stratification also. However, if the cliques are pruned using the information provided by the self-incompatible defaults, (we simulate this pruning), then almost no search for the extensions is needed (the result in the table is shown as an approximation of the true run time). The last two columns show what happens to the run times if the self-incompatible defaults are moved so that they all follow the normal defaults, and if stratification is turned off.

6.3 Discussion of Results and Experiments

When interpreting these results it should be noted that W is empty and because the theories are disjunction-free and propositional we have been able to use table lookup methods instead of theorem proving since the representation allows this very simple form of proof procedure. Questions regarding the time to compute the cliques arise. At this time we are unable to answer this type of question with any authority. The overhead from the theorem prover is $O(n^2)$, where n is the number of defaults, and the times to compute the cliques is just the overhead of the clique algorithm itself. What to do with a non-empty W is a very interesting

[6] Times for the computation of the stratification and the compatibility graph are not included.

[7] Because we used the DeReS tree search engine, what is given to DeReS are the cliques unioned with the set of self-incompatible defaults, added in the same relative locations as in the original theory. Technically, all of the defaults not in the set of generating defaults are potentially destroying defaults, but because of the particular structure of all of the defaults in this theory, only the self-incompatible ones can possibly be destroying.

Table 1. Run times (in seconds) of various experiments on three default theories.

Theory	$\|D\|$	Relaxed Stratification	Cliques	Cliques (pruned)	Self-incompatible at end of theory	No Stratification
MaxIndSets	30	9.99	0.5	–	–	–
MaxIndSets	40	264.86	5.65	–	–	–
Kernel	80	0.022	3.78	≈ 0	1.97	36.19

problem. The compatibility relation has been defined purposefully without W, in order that the relation is easy to compute. Whether this is a good decision is left for future work.

During the testing of the 'maximum independent sets' theories, we discovered that DeReS does not make one very important prune.[8] If the complete default theory is an extension, DeReS continues to search the complete tree. Relaxed stratification requires the tree to be built from the empty set to sets of generating defaults, as described in Section 4. This means that if D is a set of generating defaults, the left-most leaf node in the tree represents an extension and no other nodes in the tree can represent an extension. So, the rest of the tree can be pruned. This prune generalizes to being able to prune any subtree whose left-most leaf is a set of generating defaults. Any method that constructs from the full default theory to sets of generating defaults at the leaves of the tree does this prune automatically.

We are no longer certain that some of the combinatorial graph problems make a good testbed for testing general heuristics. These problems have too much structure that can be taken advantage of by specialized heuristics. One outcome of these and future experiments may be that both general and specialized heuristics are desirable.

7 Conclusions and future work

Our contribution to improved default theory extension-building algorithms has been a heuristic which can divide the original problem into smaller problems by discovering structure in the default theory with less computational cost.

In this paper we have presented an initial comparison of two heuristics, the compatibility heuristic that we have introduced in this paper and the relaxed stratification heuristic found in the DeReS algorithm [4]. Although much remains to be done in such a comparison, we have indicated that these two heuristics take advantage of very different structural aspects of the default theories. The compatibility heuristic seeks out semantic relations (compatibility is defined in terms

[8] We have not confirmed with the authors of DeReS, but given the datasets on which their implementation was tested, this would have been an easy prune to have missed.

of consistency) among defaults, while relaxed stratification takes advantage of the syntactic presentation of the default theory.

Both heuristics seek to reduce the problem but in different ways. The compatibility heuristic reduces the number of defaults that need to be considered when constructing an extension by creating initial clusters of defaults which are the only clusters that can contain extensions. Relaxed stratification takes advantage of a reduced interaction among defaults to incrementally build parts of extensions which then form extensions by a simple union.

Acknowledgements

The presentation of our work has been improved by incorporating a number of the suggestions made by the referees. Some of our results were a direct result of using *atac*, a software profiling tool. Our thanks to Mike Katchabaw who suggested this tool to us. The first author was supported by NSERC Research grant 0036853.

References

1. Ph. Besnard. An introduction to default logic. *Springer Verlag*, 1989.
2. C. Bron and J. Kerbosch. Algorithm 457 - finding all cliques of an undirected graph. *Communications of the ACM*, 16:575–577, 1973.
3. P. Cholewiński, V. W. Marek, A. Mikitiuk, and M. Truszczyński. Experimenting with nonmonotonic reasoning. In *Proceedings of the 12th International Conference on Logic Programming*, pages 267–281, 1995.
4. P. Cholewiński, V. W. Marek, M. Truszczyński, and A. Mikitiuk. Computing with default logic. *Artificial Intelligence*, 112:105–146, 1999.
5. Y. Dimopoulos and V. Magirou. A graph-theoretic approach to default logic. *Information and Computation*, 112:239–256, 1994.
6. Y. Dimopoulos, V. Magirou, and C. H. Papadimitriou. On kernels, defaults and even graphs. *Annals of Mathematics and Artificial Intelligence*, 20:1–12, 1997.
7. Y. Dimopoulos and A. Torres. Graph theoretical structures in logic programs and default theories. *Theoretical Computer Science*, 170:209–244, 1996.
8. G. Gottlob. Complexity results for nonmonotonic logics. *Journal of Logic and Computation*, 2:397–425, 1992.
9. W. Lukaszewicz. Considerations on default logic — an alternative approach. *Computational Intelligence*, 4:1–16, 1988.
10. C. H. Papadimitriou and M. Sideri. Default theories that always have extensions. *Artificial Intelligence*, 69:347–357, 1994.
11. R. Reiter. A logic for default reasoning. *Artificial Intelligence*, 13:81–132, 1980.
12. V. Risch. Analytic tableaux for default logics. *Journal of Applied Non-Classical Logics*, 6:71–88, 1996.
13. V. Risch and C. Schwind. Tableau-based characterization and theorem proving for default logic. *Journal of Automated Reasoning*, 13:223–242, 1994.
14. C. Schwind. A tableau-based theorem prover for a decidable subset of default logic. *10th International Conference on Automated Deduction, CADE'10*, pages 541–546, 1990.

How to Reason Credulously and Skeptically within a Single Extension

James P. Delgrande[1] and Torsten Schaub[2]*

[1] School of Computing Science, Simon Fraser University, Burnaby, B.C., Canada V5A 1S6,
jim@cs.sfu.ca

[2] Institut für Informatik, Universität Potsdam, Postfach 60 15 53, D–14415 Potsdam, Germany,
torsten@cs.uni-potsdam.de

Abstract. Consistency-based approaches in nonmonotonic reasoning may be expected to yield multiple sets of default conclusions for a given default theory. Reasoning about such extensions is carried out at the meta-level. In this paper, we show how such reasoning may be carried out at the object level for a large class of default theories. Essentially we show how one can translate a (normal) default theory Δ, obtaining a second Δ', such that Δ' has a single extension that encodes every extension of Δ. Moreover, our translated theory is only a constant factor larger than the original (with the exception of unique names axioms). We prove that our translation behaves correctly. In the approach we can now encode the notion of *extension* from within the framework of standard default logic. Hence one can encode notions such as skeptical and credulous conclusions, and can reason about such conclusions within a single extension. This result has some theoretical interest, in that it shows how multiple extensions of normal default theories are encodable with manageable overhead in a single extension.

1 Introduction

In nonmonotonic reasoning, in so-called *consistency-based* approaches such as default logic [9] and autoepistemic logic [6], one typically obtains not just a single set of default conclusions, but rather multiple sets of candidate default conclusions. Consider the by-now hackneyed example wherein Quakers are normally pacifist, republicans are normally not, along with adults are normally employed. Assume as well that someone is a Quaker, republican, and an adult. In default logic (see Section 2) this can be encoded by: $(\{\frac{Q:P}{P}, \frac{R:\neg P}{\neg P}, \frac{A:E}{E}\}, \{Q, R, A\})$. This theory has two *extensions* or sets of default conclusions, one containing $\{Q, R, A, E, P\}$ and the other $\{Q, R, A, E, \neg P\}$. In autoepistemic logic the same example appropriately encoded yields two analogous *expansions* or possible belief sets.

Reasoning about these extensions (resp. expansions) is carried out at the meta-level: a default conclusion that appears in some extension (such as P) is called a *credulous* (or *brave*) default conclusion, while one that appears in every extension (such as E) is called a *skeptical* conclusion. Intuitively it might seem that skeptical inference is the more useful notion. However, this is not necessarily the case. In diagnosis from first

* Affiliated with Simon Fraser University, Burnaby, Canada.

S. Benferhat and P. Besnard (Eds.): ECSQARU 2001, LNAI 2143, pp. 592–603, 2001.

principles [10] for example, in one encoding there is a 1-1 correspondence between diagnoses and extensions of the (encoding) normal default theory. Hence one may want to carry out further reasoning to determine which diagnosis to pursue. More generally there may be reasons to prefer some extensions over others, or to somehow synthesize the information found in several extensions.

In this paper, we show how such reasoning can be carried out at the object level. For a default theory $\Delta = (D, W)$, we translate Δ to obtain a second theory $\Delta' = (D', W')$, such that Δ' has a single extension that encodes every extension of Δ. Given this, one can express in the theory what it means for something to be a skeptical or credulous default conclusion. Our result isn't completely general; however it applies to *normal* default theories. The translation has several desirable properties. The translated theory Δ' is only a constant factor larger than the original Δ, with the exception of introduced unique names axioms. As well, we *prove* that our translation behaves correctly.

We first show for a set of defaults D_m how, using an encoding, we can detect the case wherein all defaults in D_m apply. From this, for a default theory $(D \cup D_m, W)$ we show how to obtain a second theory wherein (informally) either all of the defaults in D_m are applied en masse (if possible) or none of them are. This is done by naming each of the defaults in D_m, and then expressing in default logic the applicability conditions for the defaults. We develop this in Section 3. In Section 4 we present our main result, where we show how a default theory can be translated into a second theory whose extension encodes the extensions of the original. Roughly we provide an axiomatisation that "locates" maximal sets of applicable defaults; for such a set, the set of default conclusions is "tagged" with the set name, to distinguish it from other instances. For example, in our original example, let $m_{1,3}$ be the name of the set $\{\frac{Q:P}{P}, \frac{A:E}{E}\}$ and $m_{2,3}$ be the name of $\{\frac{R:\neg P}{\neg P}, \frac{A:E}{E}\}$. These are maximal applicable sets of defaults, and from our translation we would obtain a single extension containing $\{Q(m_{1,3}), Q(m_{2,3}), R(m_{1,3}), R(m_{2,3}), A(m_{1,3}), A(m_{2,3}), E(m_{1,3}), E(m_{2,3}), P(m_{1,3}), \neg P(m_{2,3})\}$. As mentioned, we are able to prove that our translations in fact accomplish what is claimed.

The advantage of this approach is that we can encode the notion of extension within the framework of standard default logic. Hence one can reason about (skeptical and credulous) conclusions within the framework of a single extension of a default theory. Thus for example, in a diagnosis setting one could go on and axiomatise notions of preference among diagnoses having to do with, perhaps, number of faulty components, or based on components expected to fail first. This result has some theoretical interest, in that it shows (for theories that we consider) how multiple extensions are encodable, with no significant overhead in a single extension. The overall approach is similar to that of [2].

2 Default Logic

Default logic [9] augments classical logic by *default rules* of the form $\frac{\alpha : \beta}{\gamma}$. A default rule is *normal* if β is equivalent to γ; it is *semi-normal* if β implies γ. We sometimes denote the *prerequisite* α of a default δ by $PRE(\delta)$, its *justification* β by $JUS(\delta)$, and its *consequent* γ by $CON(\delta)$. Accordingly, $PRE(D)$ is the set of prerequisites of all defaults in D; $JUS(D)$ and $CON(D)$ are defined analogously. Empty components, such as no prerequisite or even no justifications, are assumed to be tautological. Semantically, defaults with unbound variables are taken to stand for all corresponding instances. A set of default rules D and a set of formulas W form a *default theory* (D, W) that may induce a single or multiple *extensions* in the following way [9].

Definition 1. *Let $\Delta = (D, W)$ be a default theory. For any set of formulas S, let $\Gamma_\Delta(S)$ be the smallest set of formulas S' such that*

1. $W \subseteq S'$,
2. $Th(S') = S'$,
3. *For any* $\frac{\alpha : \beta}{\gamma} \in D$, *if* $\alpha \in S'$ *and* $\neg\beta \notin S$ *then* $\gamma \in S'$.

A set of formulas E is an extension of Δ iff $\Gamma_\Delta(E) = E$.

Any such extension represents a possible set of beliefs about the world at hand. Further, define for a set of formulas S and a set of defaults D, the *set of generating default rules* as $GD(D, S) = \{\delta \in D \mid PRE(\delta) \in S \text{ and } \neg JUS(\delta) \notin S\}$.

3 Applying All, or None, of a Set of Defaults

In this section we consider the problem of how to apply all defaults in some set, or none in the set. We will thus work with default theories (D, W) having some distinguished finite subset $D_m \subseteq D$. For making the set D_m explicit, we denote such theories by $(D \cup D_m, W)$. The idea is that we wish to obtain extensions of $(D \cup D_m, W)$ subject to the constraint that *all* defaults in D_m are applied, or *none* are. For example, in the theory $(\{\frac{:A}{A}\} \cup \{\frac{:B}{B}, \frac{C:D}{D}\}, \emptyset)$ we would want to obtain an extension containing A, but not B (since both defaults in $\{\frac{:B}{B}, \frac{C:D}{D}\}$ cannot be jointly applied). For $(\{\frac{:A}{A}\} \cup \{\frac{:B}{B}, \frac{C:D}{D}\}, \{C\})$ we would want to obtain an extension containing A, B, and D.

We begin by associating a unique name with each default. This is done by extending the original language by a set of constants[1] N such that there is a bijective mapping $n : D \to N$. We write n_δ instead of $n(\delta)$ (and we often abbreviate n_{δ_i} by n_i to ease notation). Also, for default δ along with its name n, we sometimes write $n : \delta$ to render naming explicit. To encode the fact that we deal with a finite set of distinct default rules, we adopt a unique names assertion (UNA$_N$) and domain closure assertion (DCA$_N$) with respect to N. So, for a name set $N = \{n_1, \ldots, n_k\}$, we add axioms

$$\begin{aligned} \text{UNA}_N &: \neg(n_i = n_j) \ \text{ for all } \ n_i, n_j \in N \ \text{ with } \ i \neq j \\ \text{DCA}_N &: \forall x.\ name(x) \equiv (x = n_1 \vee \cdots \vee x = n_k)\ . \end{aligned}$$

We write $\forall x \in N.\ P(x)$ for $\forall x.\ name(x) \supset P(x)$.

We introduce a new constant m as the name of the designated rule set D_m. We relate the name of the rule set denoted by m with the names of its members by introducing a binary predicate in where $in(x, y)$ is true just if the default named by x is a member of

[1] [5] first suggested naming defaults using a set of *aspect* functions. See also [8,1].

the set named by y. In this section, instances of in will be of the form $in(\cdot, m)$. While we could get away with not using in (and m) here, this additional machinery is required in Section 4, and it is most straightforward to introduce it here. Note that we do not need a full axiomatization of in, representing set membership, since we use it in a very restricted fashion.

For applying all, or none, of the defaults in D_m, we need to be able to, first, detect when a rule has been applied or is blocked and, second, control the application of a rule based on other prerequisite conditions. There are two cases for a default $\frac{\alpha:\beta}{\gamma}$ to not be applied: the prerequisite is not known to be true (and so its negation $\neg\alpha$ is consistent), or the justification is not consistent (and so its negation $\neg\beta$ is derivable). For detecting this case, we introduce a new, special-purpose predicate $\mathsf{bl}/1$. Similarly we introduce a special-purpose predicate $\mathsf{ap}/1$ to detect when a rule has been applied. For controlling application of a rule we introduce predicates $\mathsf{ok}/1$ and $\mathsf{ko}/1$.

We are given a default theory $(D \cup D_m, W)$ over language $\mathcal{L}$ and its set of associated default names $N\dot{\cup}\{m\}$.[2] Let

$$D_m = \left\{ n_j : \tfrac{\alpha_j : \beta_j}{\gamma_j} \mid j = 1..k \right\}.$$

(For simplicity, we reuse the symbols j, k, m, n_j, α_j, etc. below.) We define $\mathcal{S}_m((D \cup D_m, W)) = (D', W')$ over $\mathcal{L}^*$, obtained by extending $\mathcal{L}$ to $\mathcal{L}^*$ with new predicates symbols $\mathsf{ok}/1$, $\mathsf{ko}/1$, $\mathsf{bl}/1$, $\mathsf{ap}/1$, and names $N\dot{\cup}\{m\}$, as follows

$$\begin{aligned} D' &= D \cup D_N \cup D_M \\ W' &= W \cup W_M \cup \{\mathrm{DCA}_N, \mathrm{UNA}_N\} \end{aligned}$$

where

$$D_N = \left\{ \frac{\alpha_j \wedge \mathsf{ok}(n_j) : \beta_j}{\gamma_j \wedge \mathsf{ap}(n_j)} \;\middle|\; j = 1..k \right\} \tag{1}$$

$$D_M = \left\{ \frac{: \neg\mathsf{ko}(m)}{\mathsf{ok}(n_1) \wedge \cdots \wedge \mathsf{ok}(n_k)} \right\} \tag{2}$$

$$\cup \left\{ \frac{: \neg\alpha_j}{\mathsf{bl}(m)}, \frac{(\gamma_1 \wedge \cdots \wedge \gamma_k) \supset \neg\beta_j :}{\mathsf{bl}(m)} \;\middle|\; j = 1..k \right\} \tag{3}$$

$$W_M = \{\forall x \in N. in(x, m) \equiv (x = n_1 \vee \ldots \vee x = n_k)\} \tag{4}$$

$$\cup \{\mathsf{bl}(m) \supset \mathsf{ko}(m)\} \tag{5}$$

$$\cup \left\{ \left(\forall x \in N.\, in(x, m) \supset \mathsf{ap}(x)\right) \supset \mathsf{ap}(m) \right\} \tag{6}$$

Clearly, D_N contains the images of the original rules in D_m. Each rule $\delta_j \in D_N$ is applicable, if $\mathsf{ok}(n_j)$ is derivable. In fact, we assert $\mathsf{ok}(n_j)$ for every $\delta_j \in D_m$, *unless* we cannot jointly apply all rules of D_m. That is, before activating the constituent rules, we have to make sure that none of them will be blocked. This is accomplished through the justification $\neg\mathsf{ko}(m)$ in (2) together with Axiom (5). We block Rule (2) (and with it the derivability of all $\mathsf{ok}(n_j)$) when we detect that one of $\delta_1, \ldots, \delta_k$ is blocked. That is, $\mathsf{ko}(m)$ will be an immediate consequence of $\mathsf{bl}(m)$.

Now, we have that D_m is blocked ($\mathsf{bl}(m)$) just if some rule in D_m is blocked. However, since we must control a whole set of defaults, we must check for the blockage

[2] We let $\dot{\cup}$ stand for disjoint union.

of one of the constituent default rules in the context of all other rules in the set applying. For detecting the failure of consistency, we verify for D_m and some set of formulas S (cf. Definition 1), whether $S \cup \{\gamma_1, \ldots, \gamma_k\} \vdash \neg\beta_j$ rather than $S \vdash \neg\beta_j$. This motivates the prerequisite of the second rule in (3). This context, $(\gamma_1 \wedge \cdots \wedge \gamma_k)$, is not needed for detecting the failure of derivability by means of the first rule in (3), since this test is effectuated with respect to the final extension E via $\neg\alpha_j \notin E$.

Finally, as given in (6), D_m is applied ($\mathsf{ap}(m)$) just if every rule in D_m is applied; it is only in this last case that the consequents of the constituent rules in D_m are asserted.

Consider theory $(D \cup D_m, W)$, where

$$D = \left\{\tfrac{:E}{E}\right\},\; D_m = \left\{n_1 : \tfrac{:P}{P},\; n_2 : \tfrac{:S}{S}\right\}. \tag{7}$$

For D_N and D_M, we obtain (after simplifying and removing redundant defaults):

$$\frac{\mathsf{ok}(n_1) : P}{P \wedge \mathsf{ap}(n_1)},\quad \frac{\mathsf{ok}(n_2) : S}{S \wedge \mathsf{ap}(n_2)},\quad \frac{: \neg\mathsf{ko}(m)}{\mathsf{ok}(n_1) \wedge \mathsf{ok}(n_2)},\quad \frac{(\neg P \vee \neg S) :}{\mathsf{bl}(m)}.$$

The in predicate has instances: $in(n_1, m)$ and $in(n_2, m)$. From (6) we can deduce $[\mathsf{ap}(n_1) \wedge \mathsf{ap}(n_2)] \supset \mathsf{ap}(m)$.

Let $W = \{\neg(P \wedge E \wedge S)\}$. We obtain two extensions, one containing $P, S, \neg E$ and the other containing $E, \neg(P \wedge S)$. For the first case, we obtain $\mathsf{ok}(n_1)$ and $\mathsf{ok}(n_2)$. If both δ_1 and δ_2 are applicable (which they are) then we conclude $P \wedge \mathsf{ap}(n_1)$ and $S \wedge \mathsf{ap}(n_1)$ as well as $\mathsf{ap}(m)$. From this we get P and S and so $\neg E$. For the other extensions, if the default $\frac{:E}{E}$ is applied, then $\neg P \vee \neg S$ is derivable, and so $\frac{(\neg P \vee \neg S) :}{\mathsf{bl}(m)}$ is applicable, from which we obtain $\mathsf{bl}(m)$, and so $\mathsf{ko}(m)$, blocking application of $\frac{: \neg\mathsf{ko}(m)}{\mathsf{ok}(n_1) \wedge \mathsf{ok}(n_2)}$. Consequently neither $\frac{\mathsf{ok}(n_1) : P}{P \wedge \mathsf{ap}(n_1)}$ nor $\frac{\mathsf{ok}(n_2) : S}{S \wedge \mathsf{ap}(n_2)}$ can be applied.

In the next example, defaults inside a set depend upon each other. Consider $(\emptyset \cup D_m, \emptyset)$ with

$$D_m = \left\{n_1 : \tfrac{:Q}{Q},\; n_2 : \tfrac{Q:R}{R}\right\}.$$

We get for D_N and D_M the following rules.

$$\frac{\mathsf{ok}(n_1) : Q}{Q \wedge \mathsf{ap}(n_1)},\quad \frac{Q \wedge \mathsf{ok}(n_2) : R}{R \wedge \mathsf{ap}(n_2)},\qquad \frac{: \neg\mathsf{ko}(m)}{\mathsf{ok}(n_1) \wedge \mathsf{ok}(n_2)},\quad \frac{(\neg Q \vee \neg R) :}{\mathsf{bl}(m)},\quad \frac{: \neg Q}{\mathsf{bl}(m)}.$$

We obtain $\mathsf{ok}(n_1)$, and $\mathsf{ok}(n_2)$, which allow us to apply default δ_1, yielding in turn $Q \wedge \mathsf{ap}(n_1)$. Given Q, we can now apply default δ_2, yielding $R \wedge \mathsf{ap}(n_2)$. This allows us to deduce $\mathsf{ap}(m)$. We thus get an extension containing Q and R.

The last example also shows why we cannot avoid the translation by replacing D_m by $\frac{\bigwedge_{\delta \in D_m} PRE(\delta) : \bigwedge_{\delta \in D_m} JUS(\delta)}{\bigwedge_{\delta \in D_m} CON(\delta)}$. As well, in Section 4, this replacement would result in an exponential blowup in the encoding.

The next theorem summarizes properties of our approach, and shows that rules are applied either en masse, or not at all.

Theorem 1. *Let E be a consistent extension of $S_m((D \cup D_m, W))$ for default theory $(D \cup D_m, W)$. We have that:*

1. $\mathsf{ap}(m) \in E$ *iff* $\{\mathsf{ap}(n_\delta) \mid \delta \in D_m\} \cup CON(D_m) \subseteq E$

2. $\mathsf{bl}(m) \in E$ *iff* $\{\mathsf{ap}(n_\delta) \mid \delta \in D_m\} \not\subseteq E$
3. $\mathsf{ok}(n_\delta) \in E$ *iff* $\mathsf{ap}(n_\delta) \in E$
4. $\mathsf{ok}(n_\delta) \in E$ *for all* $\delta \in D_m$ *iff* $\mathsf{ko}(m) \notin E$
5. $\mathsf{ap}(n_\delta) \in E$ *implies* $(\mathsf{ap}(m) \wedge in(n_\delta, m)) \in E$ *for some* $\delta \in D_m$
6. $\mathsf{ap}(n_\delta) \in E$ *for* $\delta \in D_m$ *iff* $\{\mathsf{ap}(n_\delta) \mid \delta \in D_m\} \subseteq E$.

Theorem 2. *For default theory* $(\emptyset \cup D, W)$*, we have that* $\mathcal{S}_m((\emptyset \cup D, W))$ *has extension* E *where either* $E \cap \mathcal{L} = Th(W \cup CON(D))$ *or else* $E \cap \mathcal{L} = Th(W)$.

The default theory $(\emptyset \cup \{\frac{:B}{\neg B}\},\ \emptyset)$ has an extension E where $E \cap \mathcal{L} = Th(\emptyset)$.

Theorem 3. *Let* (D, W) *be a (standard) default theory over* $\mathcal{L}$ *with extension* E *and (respective) set of generating defaults* $GD(D, E)$*. Then* $\mathcal{S}_m((\emptyset \cup GD(D, E), W))$ *has extension* E' *where* $E = E' \cap \mathcal{L}$.

4 Encoding Extensions Using Sets

For encoding extensions of a normal default theory (D, W), we use the machinery developed in the previous section to determine maximal (with respect to set inclusion) sets of applicable defaults. Names are introduced for each subset of D, and for each instance of a rule in each subset of D. As well, new predicate symbols are introduced to further control application of sets of rules. We then give a translation that yields a second default theory (D', W'). Viewed algorithmically, this second theory carries out the following: If the original set of defaults D constitutes the set of generating defaults of an extension, then a corresponding "ap"-literal is derived; all default consequences are obtained; and all subsets of the defaults are rendered inapplicable. If this isn't the case (and D isn't a set of generating defaults), we proceed along the partial order induced by set inclusion and consider every set $D \setminus \{\delta\}$ for every $\delta \in D$ to see whether it is a set of generating defaults. Crucially, default conclusions are "tagged" with the name of the set in which they appear so as to eliminate possible side effects.

To name sets of defaults, we take some fixed enumeration $\langle n_1, \ldots, n_k \rangle$ of N, and define m as a k-ary function symbol. Then, for $n_\perp \notin N$, define

$$\text{DCA}_M : \forall x_1, \ldots, x_k.\ \textit{set-name}(m(x_1, \ldots, x_k)) \equiv \\ (x_1 = n_1 \vee x_1 = n_\perp) \wedge \cdots \wedge (x_k = n_k \vee x_k = n_\perp).$$

Intuitively, $x_i = n_\perp$ tells us that n_i does not belong to the set at hand.

Accordingly, for $\boldsymbol{x} = x_1..x_k$ and $\boldsymbol{x}' = x'_1..x'_k$ define

$$\text{UNA}_M : \forall \boldsymbol{x}, \boldsymbol{x}'.\ \textit{set-name}(m(\boldsymbol{x})) = \\ \textit{set-name}(m(\boldsymbol{x}')) \equiv x_1 = x'_1 \wedge \cdots \wedge x_k = x'_k\ .$$

The advantage of this "vector-oriented" representation over a dynamic one including a binary function symbol (as with lists) is that each set has a unique representation. We write $\forall x \in M.\ P(x)$ instead of $\forall x.\ \textit{set-name}(x) \supset P(x)$. Further, we use M for denoting the set of all valid set-names, that is,

$$M = \{m \mid \text{DCA}_M \models \textit{set-name}(m)\}\ .$$

In order to ease notation, we write $m_{1,3}$ instead of $m(n_1, n_\perp, n_3, n_\perp, \ldots, n_\perp)$ when representing the set $\{\delta_1, \delta_3\}$. Also, we abbreviate $m(n_\perp, \ldots, n_\perp)$ by $m_\emptyset$ and $m(n_1, \ldots, n_k)$ by m_D. Note the difference between names n_i and m_i, induced by our notational convention.

We also rely on the "vector-oriented" representation for capturing set membership, denoted by $in/2$. Consider for instance $N = \{n_1, n_2\}$. Membership is then axiomatized through the formulas

$$\forall x_1, x_2.\ in(n_1, m(x_1, x_2)) \equiv (n_1 = x_1)$$
$$\forall x_1, x_2.\ in(n_2, m(x_1, x_2)) \equiv (n_2 = x_2).$$

While this validates $in(n_1, m_{1,2})$, it falsifies $in(n_1, m_2)$. See (15) for the general case.

We need to be able to refer to separate instances of the same default appearing in different sets. For this we introduce a function-symbol $\cdot/2$. For $\delta_j \in D_i$ we write $n_{\delta_j}{\cdot}m_i$ or $n_j{\cdot}m_i$ to name the instance of δ_j appearing in D_i. This results in name set $N{\cdot}M = \{n{\cdot}m \mid n \in N, m \in M\}$. Corresponding axioms, as $\mathrm{DCA}_{N\cdot M}$ and $\mathrm{UNA}_{N\cdot M}$, are obtained in a straightforward way. In what follows, we refer to the various domain closure and unique names axioms pertaining to N, M, and $N{\cdot}M$ as $Ax(N)$.[3]

Given language $\mathcal{L}$, we define a family of languages $\mathcal{L}(m)$ for $m \in M$ as follows. If P is an i-ary predicate symbol then $P(\cdot)$ is a distinct $(i+1)$-ary predicate symbol. If $\gamma \in \mathcal{L}$ then $\gamma(m) \in \mathcal{L}(m)$ is the formula obtained by replacing all predicate symbols in γ with predicate symbols extended as described, and with term m as the $(i+1)^{st}$ argument. This extra argument is used to index formulas by the (names of) sets in which they are used.

Lastly, we introduce special-purpose predicates for controlling the application of sets of defaults. These are summarised in the following table:

Name	Use/meaning
$m \sqsubset m'$	$D_m \subset D_{m'}$
$\mathsf{ok}(e)$	It is ok to try to apply set/rule e
$\mathsf{ap}(e)$	Set/rule e is applied
$\mathsf{bl}(m)$	Not all rules in set m can be applied
$\mathsf{ovr}(m)$	Some set named m' is applied and $m \sqsubset m'$
$\mathsf{ko}(m)$	For set m, $\mathsf{bl}(m) \vee \mathsf{ovr}(m)$ is true

Taking all this into account, we obtain the following translation, mapping default theories in language $\mathcal{L}$ onto default theories in the language $\mathcal{L}^+$ obtained by unioning all languages $\mathcal{L}(m)$ for $m \in M$ and using the aforementioned names and introduced predicates and functions:

Definition 2. *Given a finite default theory (D, W) over $\mathcal{L}$ and its set of associated default names N, define $\mathcal{E}((D, W)) = (D', W')$ over $\mathcal{L}^+$ by*

$$D' = D_N \cup D_M \cup D_\neg$$
$$W' = W_D \cup W_W \cup W_M \cup W_\sqsubset \cup Ax(N)$$

[3] Note that names in M and $N{\cdot}M$ are obtained from those in N.

where

$$D_N = \left\{ \frac{\alpha(x)\wedge in(n,x)\wedge \mathsf{ok}(n\cdot x) : \beta(x)}{\gamma(x)\wedge \mathsf{ap}(n\cdot x)} \;\middle|\; n : \frac{\alpha:\beta}{\gamma} \in D \right\} \tag{8}$$

$$D_M = \left\{ \frac{\mathsf{ok}(x) : \neg\mathsf{ko}(x)}{\forall y{\in}N.\ in(y,x) \supset \mathsf{ok}(y\cdot x)} \right\} \tag{9}$$

$$\cup \left\{ \frac{in(n,x)\wedge \mathsf{ok}(x) : \neg\alpha(x)}{\mathsf{bl}(x)} \;\middle|\; n : \frac{\alpha:\beta}{\gamma} \in D \right\} \tag{10}$$

$$\cup \left\{ \frac{([\forall y{\in}N.\ in(y,x)\supset c(y,x)]\supset\neg\beta(x))\wedge \mathsf{ok}(x) :}{\mathsf{bl}(x)} \;\middle|\; n : \frac{\alpha:\beta}{\gamma} \in D \right\} \tag{11}$$

$$D_\neg = \left\{ \frac{:\neg(x\sqsubset y)}{\neg(x\sqsubset y)}, \frac{:\neg in(x,y)}{\neg in(x,y)} \right\} \tag{12}$$

$$W_W = \{\forall x \in M.\, \alpha(x) \mid \alpha \in W\} \tag{13}$$

$$W_D = \{\forall x \in M.\, c(n_\delta, x) \equiv CON(\delta)(x) \mid \delta \in D\} \tag{14}$$

$$W_M = \{\forall x_1,\ldots,x_k.\ in(n_i, m(x_1,\ldots,x_k)) \equiv (n_i = x_i) \mid n_i \text{ in } \langle n_1,\ldots,n_k\rangle\} \tag{15}$$

$$\cup\, \{\forall x, x' \in M.[\exists y \in N.\neg in(y,x) \wedge in(y,x')] \wedge [\forall y.\ in(y,x) \supset in(y,x')] \supset x \sqsubset x' \} \tag{16}$$

$$W_\sqsubset = \{\mathsf{ok}(m_D)\} \tag{17}$$

$$\cup\, \{\forall x \in M\big[\forall y \in M.\, x \sqsubset y \supset \mathsf{bl}(y)\big] \supset \mathsf{ok}(x)\} \tag{18}$$

$$\cup\, \{\forall x \in M.\ \lfloor \mathsf{bl}(x) \vee \mathsf{ovr}(x)\rfloor \supset \mathsf{ko}(x)\} \tag{19}$$

$$\cup\, \{\forall x \in M\ \big[\forall y \in N.\, in(y,x) \supset \mathsf{ap}(y\cdot x)\big] \supset \mathsf{ap}(x)\} \tag{20}$$

$$\cup\, \{\forall x, x' \in M.\, \mathsf{ap}(x) \supset (x' \sqsubset x \supset \mathsf{ovr}(x'))\} \tag{21}$$

The rules in D_N and D_M directly generalise those in (1–3), from treating a single set named m to an arbitrary set referenced by variable x. The specific consequents used in the second rule in (3) are dealt with via the axioms in (W_D/14) that allows us to quantify over default consequents (via predicate c). This trick avoids the exponential blowup that would occur in (11) if we were to explicitly give the consequences of the rules.

The rules in ($D_\neg$/12) provide us with complete knowledge on predicates $\sqsubset$ and in. The axioms in ($W_W/13$) propagate the information in W to all possible contexts.

W_M takes care of what we need wrt set operations. That is, (15) formalises set membership, while (16) formalises strict set inclusion. $W_\sqsubset$ axiomatises the control flow along the partial order induced by $\sqsubset$. Axioms (17) and (18) tell us when it is ok to consider a certain set: we always consider the maximum set D; otherwise, via (18), we consider a set just when every superset is known to be blocked (and so inapplicable). (19) tells us when the consideration of a set is cancelled. This either happens because a set is inapplicable (given by bl) or because it has been explicitly cancelled (given by ovr). (20) asserts that a set is applied just if all of its member rules are. Once we have found an applicable set of rules (and hence a set of generating defaults) we need not consider any subset; (21) annuls the consideration of all such subsets.

For example, consider the following normal default theory:

$$\Delta_{22} = \left(\left\{n_1 : \frac{:A}{A}, n_2 : \frac{:B}{B}, n_3 : \frac{:\neg B}{\neg B}, n_4 : \frac{B:D}{D}\right\}, \emptyset\right). \tag{22}$$

From $\mathcal{E}(\Delta_{22})$ we get an extension, where the only "ap-literals" are $\mathsf{ap}(m_{1,2,4})$ and $\mathsf{ap}(m_{1,3})$. That is, Δ_{22} has two extensions with generating defaults, the first with δ_1, δ_2, δ_4, and the second with δ_1, δ_3. Among formulas in the extension of $\mathcal{E}(\Delta_{22})$ are $A(m_{1,2,4})$, $A(m_{1,3})$, $B(m_{1,2,4})$, $\neg B(m_{1,3})$, and $D(m_{1,2,4})$. To see this, let us take a closer look at the image of Δ_{22}, namely $\mathcal{E}(\Delta_{22})$. For D_N, we get

$$\frac{in(n_1,x)\wedge\mathsf{ok}(n_1\cdot x) : A(x)}{A(x)\wedge\mathsf{ap}(n_1\cdot x)} \qquad \frac{in(n_2,x)\wedge\mathsf{ok}(n_2\cdot x) : B(x)}{B(x)\wedge\mathsf{ap}(n_2\cdot x)} \tag{23}$$

$$\frac{in(n_3,x)\wedge\mathsf{ok}(n_3\cdot x) : \neg B(x)}{\neg B(x)\wedge\mathsf{ap}(n_3\cdot x)} \qquad \frac{B(x)\wedge in(n_4,x)\wedge\mathsf{ok}(n_4\cdot x) : D(x)}{D(x)\wedge\mathsf{ap}(n_4\cdot x)} \tag{24}$$

We get a single nontrivial rule in (10), namely

$$\frac{in(n_4,x)\wedge\mathsf{ok}(x) : \neg B(x)}{\mathsf{bl}(x)} \tag{25}$$

and four rules in (11)

$$\frac{([\forall y\in N.\ in(y,x)\supset c(y,x)]\supset\neg A(x))\wedge\mathsf{ok}(x) :}{\mathsf{bl}(x)} \tag{26}$$

$$\frac{([\forall y\in N.\ in(y,x)\supset c(y,x)]\supset\neg B(x))\wedge\mathsf{ok}(x) :}{\mathsf{bl}(x)} \tag{27}$$

$$\frac{([\forall y\in N.\ in(y,x)\supset c(y,x)]\supset\ B(x))\wedge\mathsf{ok}(x) :}{\mathsf{bl}(x)} \tag{28}$$

$$\frac{([\forall y\in N.\ in(y,x)\supset c(y,x)]\supset\neg D(x))\wedge\mathsf{ok}(x) :}{\mathsf{bl}(x)} \tag{29}$$

Given $\mathsf{ok}(m_D)$, we may consider any rule in D_M. However, given that $\forall y \in N.\ in(y, m_D)$ is true, we obtain that (14) and $\forall y \in N.\ in(y, m_D) \supset c(y, m_D)$ are inconsistent and thus imply any formula. Consequently, rules (26) to (29) are applicable and provide $\mathsf{bl}(m_D)$, yielding $\mathsf{ko}(m_D)$, which in turn blocks (9) for $x = m_D$. From (16), we obtain (among other relations) $m_{1,2,3} \sqsubset m_D$, $m_{1,2,4} \sqsubset m_D$, $m_{1,3,4} \sqsubset m_D$, and $m_{2,3,4} \sqsubset m_D$. From (18), we then get $\mathsf{ok}(m_{1,2,3})$, $\mathsf{ok}(m_{1,2,4})$, $\mathsf{ok}(m_{1,3,4})$, and $\mathsf{ok}(m_{2,3,4})$.

Now, consider $\mathsf{ok}(m_{1,2,4})$. From (9), we obtain

$$\forall y \in N.\ in(y, m_{1,2,4}) \supset \mathsf{ok}(y\cdot m_{1,2,4})$$

yielding $\mathsf{ok}(n_1\cdot m_{1,2,4})$, $\mathsf{ok}(n_2\cdot m_{1,2,4})$, and $\mathsf{ok}(n_4\cdot m_{1,2,4})$. This allows us to apply three of the four rules in (23/24) and we obtain $A(m_{1,2,4}) \wedge \mathsf{ap}(n_1\cdot m_{1,2,4})$, $B(m_{1,2,4}) \wedge \mathsf{ap}(n_2\cdot m_{1,2,4})$, and $D(m_{1,2,4}) \wedge \mathsf{ap}(n_4\cdot m_{1,2,4})$. From (20), we obtain $\mathsf{ap}(m_{1,2,4})$, from which we deduce with (21) in turn $\mathsf{ovr}(m_{1,2,4})$, $\mathsf{ovr}(m_{2,4})$, ... , $\mathsf{ovr}(m_4)$, and $\mathsf{ovr}(m_\emptyset)$.

Next, consider $\mathsf{ok}(m_{1,2,3})$. As with $\mathsf{ok}(m_D)$, we obtain an inconsistency among $in(n_1, m_{1,2,3})$, $in(n_2, m_{1,2,3})$, $in(n_3, m_{1,2,3})$, $\forall y \in N.\ in(y, m_{1,2,3}) \supset c(y, m_{1,2,3})$, and (14). This validates the prerequisites of Rule (26), (27), and (28), thus yielding $\mathsf{bl}(m_{1,2,3})$. As above, we then get from W_M that $\mathsf{ok}(m_{1,2})$, $\mathsf{ok}(m_{1,3})$, $\mathsf{ok}(m_{2,3})$. Note that we have already obtained $\mathsf{ovr}(m_{1,2})$ from $\mathsf{ap}(m_{1,2,4})$.

Given $\mathsf{ok}(m_{1,3})$, (9) provides us with $\mathsf{ok}(n_1\cdot m_{1,3})$ and $\mathsf{ok}(n_3\cdot m_{1,3})$. Using the two first rules in (23/24), we get $A(m_{1,3}) \wedge \mathsf{ap}(n_1\cdot m_{1,3})$ and $\neg B(m_{1,3}) \wedge \mathsf{ap}(n_3\cdot m_{1,3})$.

From (20), we then get $\mathsf{ap}(m_{1,3})$, from which we deduce with (21) in turn $\mathsf{ovr}(m_1)$, $\mathsf{ovr}(m_3)$, and $\mathsf{ovr}(m_\emptyset)$ (again).

Given $\mathsf{ok}(m_{2,3})$, along with the fact that $in(n_2, m_{2,3})$, $in(n_3, m_{2,3})$, $\forall y \in N. in(y, m_{2,3}) \supset c(y, m_{2,3})$, and (14) imply $B(m_{2,3})$ and $\neg B(m_{2,3})$, Rule (27) and (28) fire and we get $\mathsf{bl}(m_{2,3})$.

The next results show that our default theories resulting from $\mathcal{E}$ have appropriate properties.

Theorem 4. *Let E be a consistent extension of $\mathcal{E}((D, W))$ for normal default theory (D, W). We have for all $\delta \in D$ and for all $D_m, D_{m'} \subseteq D$ that:*

1. $(m \sqsubset m') \in E$ *iff* $\neg(m \sqsubset m') \notin E$
2. $in(n_\delta, m) \in E$ *iff* $\neg in(n_\delta, m) \notin E$
3. $\mathsf{ok}(m) \in E$ *if* $\mathsf{ovr}(m) \notin E$
4. $\mathsf{ok}(m) \in E$ *if* ($\mathsf{ap}(m) \in E$ *or* $\mathsf{bl}(m) \in E$)
5. $\mathsf{ap}(m) \in E$ *iff* $\mathsf{ko}(m) \notin E$
6. $\mathsf{ko}(m) \in E$ *iff* ($\mathsf{bl}(m) \in E$ *or* $\mathsf{ovr}(m) \in E$)
7. $\mathsf{ovr}(m) \in E$ *iff* $\mathsf{ap}(m') \in E$ *and* $m \sqsubset m' \in E$ *for some* $m' \in M$.
8. *If* $\mathsf{ap}(m) \in E$ *then* $\mathsf{bl}(m') \in E$ *for all* $m' \in M$ *with* $m \sqsubset m' \in E$.
9. *If* $\mathsf{ap}(m) \in E$ *then* $\mathsf{ovr}(m') \in E$ *for all* $m' \in M$ *with* $m' \sqsubset m \in E$.
10. *If* $\mathsf{ap}(m), \mathsf{ap}(m') \in E$ *for then* $\neg(m \sqsubset m') \in E$

Theorem 5. *If (D, W) is a normal default theory then $\mathcal{E}((D, W))$ has a unique extension.*

The next two theorems show that our translation captures an encoding of extensions of a normal default theory.

Theorem 6. *Let (D, W) be a normal default theory and let E be the extension of $\mathcal{E}((D, W))$.*

Then for any $\mathsf{ap}(m) \in E$ with $m \in M$, we have that $Th(\{\gamma \mid \gamma(m) \in E\})$ is an extension of (D, W).

Theorem 7. *Let (D, W) be a normal default theory with extensions $E_1, ..., E_n$ and E be the extension of $\mathcal{E}((D, W))$.*

Then, for any $i \in \{1, \ldots, n\}$, there is some $m \in M$ naming $GD(D, E_i)$ such that $\mathsf{ap}(m) \in E$.

Lastly, our claim that a translated theory is "almost" a constant factor larger than the original requires elaboration. UNA$_N$ yields a quadratic number of unique names assertions. In practice this is no problem, since any sensible implementation would not explicitly list such axioms. With the exception of unique names assertions, a translated theory is a constant factor larger than the original. To see this, it suffices to examine Definition 2. Each of (8, 10, 11, 14, 15) introduce $|D|$ axioms/rules; (13) introduces $|W|$ axioms. All remaining terms introduce a single axiom. Moreover, the size of individual axioms is similarly bounded. (For example, each instance of (8) is a constant factor larger than the original default.)

5 Discussion

We have shown how we can encode a normal default theory so that the extension from the encoding represents all extensions of the original theory. These results don't rely on the normal form of the defaults, but rather on the fact that normal default theories are *semi-monotonic*, that is on the fact that if E is an extension of (D, W), then there is an extension $E' \supseteq E$ of $(D \cup D', W)$. The results of the previous sections then extend to any such theory.

The fact that we encode all extensions of a theory within a single extension means that we can now encode phenomena of interest, usually dealt with at the metalevel, at the object level. Specifically we can now encode the notions of skeptical and credulous inference within a theory. In order to do this, we introduce two new constants $skep$ and $cred$, for "skeptical" and "credulous" respectively.

A formula is a skeptical inference if it is a member of every extension. In our approach, this means that it follows in every "ap-set". Hence we define skeptical inference within a theory, for a given formula γ, by

$$(\forall x \in M.\ \mathsf{ap}(x) \supset \gamma(x)) \supset \gamma(skep).$$

For credulous inference there are a number of possibilities. The simplest is to assert that a formula is a credulous inference if it is a member of some extension:

$$(\exists x \in M.\ \mathsf{ap}(x) \wedge \gamma(x)) \supset \gamma(cred).$$

With this definition, a formula and its negation may be credulous inferences. A stronger definition is to assert that a formula is a credulous inference if it is a member of some extension, and its negation is a member of no extension. We can define this notion of credulous inference (indicated by $cred'$) for a formula γ by means of the default:

$$\frac{\exists x \in M.\ \mathsf{ap}(x) \wedge \gamma(x)\ :\ \forall x \in M.\ \mathsf{ap}(x) \supset \gamma(x)}{\gamma(cred')}.$$

Hence in Example (22), we obtain that A is a $skep$tical inference, while D is a $cred'$ulous inference. B and $\neg B$ are $cred$ulous inferences.

We have suggested that the approach may be applicable in diagnosis programs, such as found in [10]. Similarly, the approach can be used to directly encode applications expressible in Theorist [8]. That is, there is a correspondence between so-called *Poole-type* theories and Theorist with constraints [3]. Since Poole-type theories are semi-monotonic, this means that our approach can encode any application encodable in Theorist.

Our approach relies on a first-order language. Despite this, the image of a theory over a finite language remains finite. As regards implementation, however, it is not advisable to use a bottom-up grounding approach, as done in many implementations of extended logic programming [4,7]. Instead, a query-oriented approach seems to be advantegous, because it may rely on unification rather than ground instantiation.

In Definition 2, sets of defaults were ordered based on the partial order given by set containment. This order represents one example of a *preference* order on sets of defaults. A natural avenue for future work would be to generalise our approach to address arbitrary preference orders on sets of defaults. In an arbitrary preference order on sets, one could represent desiderata as found in configuration, scheduling, or (generally) decision-theoretic problems. This could also be combined with the present approach yielding an encoding of preferences on extensions. Hence, for our diagnosis example, we might want to prefer extensions (diagnoses) on the basis of an ordering based on reliability of components.

6 Conclusion

We have described an approach for encoding default extensions within a single extension. Using constants and functions for naming, we can refer to default rules, sets of defaults, and instances of a rule in a set. Via these names we can, first, determine whether a set of defaults is its own set of generating defaults and, second, consider the application of sets of defaults ordered by set containment. The translated theory requires a modest increase in space: except for unique names axioms, only a contant-factor increase is needed. The translated theory is a (regular, Reiter) default theory. Hence we essentially axiomatise the notion of "extensions" for a class of default theories in a single extension. Further, we are able to prove that our translation behaves correctly.

Using the approach we can now express notions such as skeptical and credulous inference within a theory. Arguably this will prove beneficial in expressing at the object level problems and approaches generally expressed at the metalevel. Areas of application range from specific areas such as diagnosis, to broadly-applicable approaches such as Theorist. Lastly, we suggest that the approach may be easily extended to address arbitrary preferences over sets of defaults.

References

1. G. Brewka. Reasoning about priorities in default logic. In *Proceedings AAAI'94*, pages 940–945. The AAAI Press, 1994.
2. J. Delgrande and T. Schaub. Expressing preferences in default logic. *Artificial Intelligence*, 123(1-2):41–87, 2000.
3. J. Dix. On cumulativity in default logic and its relation to Poole's approach. In B. Neumann, editor, *Proceedings ECAI'92*, pages 289–293. Wiley, 1992.
4. T. Eiter, N. Leone, C. Mateis, G. Pfeifer, and F. Scarcello. A deductive system for nonmonotonic reasoning. In J. Dix, U. Furbach, and A. Nerode, editors, *Proceedings LPNMR'97*, pages 363–374. Springer, 1997.
5. J. McCarthy. Applications of circumscription to formalizing common-sense knowledge. *Artificial Intelligence*, 28:89–116, 1986.
6. R. Moore. Semantical considerations on nonmonotonic logics. *Artificial Intelligence*, 25:75–94, 1985.
7. I. Niemelä and P. Simons. Smodels: An implementation of the stable model and well-founded semantics for normal logic programs. In J. Dix, U. Furbach, and A. Nerode, editors, *Proceedings LPNMR'97*, pages 420–429. Springer, 1997.
8. D. Poole. A logical framework for default reasoning. *Artificial Intelligence*, 36:27–47, 1988.
9. R. Reiter. A logic for default reasoning. *Artificial Intelligence*, 13(1-2):81–132, 1980.
10. R. Reiter. A theory of diagnosis from first principles. *Artificial Intelligence*, 32(1):57–96, 1987.

Handling Conditionals Adequately in Uncertain Reasoning

Gabriele Kern-Isberner

FernUniversität Hagen, Department of Computer Science,
P.O. Box 940, D-58084 Hagen, Germany
gabriele.kern-isberner@fernuni-hagen.de

Abstract. Conditionals ("*if-then-rules*") are most important objects in knowledge representation, commonsense reasoning and belief revision. Due to their non-classical nature, however, they are not easily dealt with. This paper presents a new approach to conditionals, which is apt to capture their dynamic power peculiarly well. We show how this approach can be applied to represent conditional knowledge inductively. In particular, we generalize system-Z^* as an appropriate counterpart to maximum entropy-representations in a semi-quantitative setting.

1 Introduction

Relationships amongst propositions are crucial pieces of knowledge. Usually, they express plausible connections, bring isolated facts together and help us obtain a coherent image of the world. Such relationships may be represented in a most general form by *if-then-conditionals.* Conditionals are omnipresent, in everyday life as well as in scientific environments. We make use of conditional knowledge when we avoid puddles on sidewalks (being aware of "If you step into a puddle, then your feet might get wet"), and when we expect high wheat prices from observing cold and rainy weather in spring and summer (due to "If the growing weather is poor then there will be an increase in price of wheat"). Conditionals represent generic knowledge, acquired inductively from experience or learned from books. They tie a flexible and highly interrelated network of connections along which reasoning is possible and which can be applied to different situations. Moreover, as plausible yet defeasible conclusions, conditionals are intimately related to *nonmonotonic reasoning*, or, in general, to *uncertain reasoning.* In belief revision, they take the role of *revision policies*, guiding changes of beliefs when new (propositional) evidence becomes apparent. So, in contrast to factual knowledge which is mostly static, conditionals bear a clearly dynamic flavor.

The key to get conditionals right is to accept their non-classical nature – conditionals are not simply "true" or "false". In a particular situation, a conditional is *applicable* (you actually step into a puddle) or not (you simply walk around), it can be found *confirmed* (you step into a puddle and indeed, your feet get wet) or *violated* (you step into a puddle, but your feet remain dry because you are

S. Benferhat and P. Besnard (Eds.): ECSQARU 2001, LNAI 2143, pp. 604–615, 2001.

wearing rain boots). So the central problem in dealing with conditional knowledge is to handle adequately, on the one hand, inactive (or neutral, respectively) behavior, and, on the other hand, active as well as polarizing behavior.

The main object of this paper is

- to sketch a new theory for conditionals which captures their three-valued, dynamic nature peculiarly well,
- to show how it is realized in a semi-quantitative as well as in a probabilistic framework,
- to apply this theory to the problem of representing conditional knowledge inductively in both frameworks.

We will focus on the process of establishing conditional beliefs, considering conditionals as agents shifting possible worlds in order to establish relationships and beliefs. We will represent the effects (the learning of) conditionals have on worlds by *conditional structures*. Handling conditionals adequately then means to choose representations which are balanced with respect to the structures of the conditionals under consideration. In this way, highly complex interactions between different conditionals can be taken into account and maintained.

A well-known probabilistic method that follows this idea is the *principle of maximum entropy (ME-principle)* [Par94]. In a semi-quantitative setting, system-Z^* [GMP93] also realizes this approach, though it seems to be of restricted applicability. In this paper, we will generalize system-Z^* to make it applicable for any consistent set of conditionals. The generalized system-Z^*-approach will be shown to be theoretically justified, and will prove to handle even problematic examples adequately. Although this generalization of system-Z^* is important in itself, it should be taken as only one example of how the conditional approach presented in this paper can be used. Due to separating strictly between structural and numerical aspects of conditionals, the new conditional theory can be applied in any (semi-)quantitative framework that allows the representation of conditional beliefs. Therefore, it has also important consequences for possibility theory, which has seen a lot of important work on conditionals in the last decade (see e.g. [BDP97],[BSS00]). This connection to possibility theory is elaborated in [KI01b].

The following section summarizes fundamental facts about conditionals, ordinal conditional functions and probability distributions. Section 3 briefly sketches the ME-principle, as well as system-Z and system-Z^*. Section 4 presents the generalized system-Z^* approach. The new dynamic approach to conditionals is presented in Section 5, and is linked to (semi-)quantitative representation of knowledge in Section 6. An outlook on further results concludes this paper in Section 7.

2 Conditionals, Plausibility, and Probability

We consider a propositional language $\mathcal{L}$ over a finite alphabet $\mathcal{V} = \{a, b, c \ldots\}$. Let Ω be the complete set of interpretations of $\mathcal{L}$, where each $\omega \in \Omega$ is taken to be a *possible world* for $\mathcal{L}$. To simplify notation, we will write $\overline{A}$ instead of $\neg A$, and AB instead of $A \wedge B$, for formulas $A, B \in \mathcal{L}$. Conditionals $(B|A)$ represent statements of the form "*If A then B*", expressing a relationship between two (propositional) formulas A, the *antecedent* or *premise*, and B, the *consequent.* $(\mathcal{L} \mid \mathcal{L})$ denotes the set of all conditionals $(B|A)$ with $A, B \in \mathcal{L}$. A world $\omega \in \Omega$ is said to *verify* a conditional $(B|A)$, if $\omega \models AB$; it *falsifies* $(B|A)$, if $\omega \models A\overline{B}$; if $\omega \models \overline{A}$, then $(B|A)$ is not applicable to ω.

Epistemic states as representations of cognitive states of intelligent agents provide an adequate framework for conditionals. Two widely used types of epistemic states are *probability distributions* and *ordinal conditional functions, OCF's*, which are based on the notion of plausibility. In short, OCF's are functions $\kappa : \Omega \to \mathbb{N} \cup \{0, \infty\}$ from the set of worlds to the natural numbers, extended by 0 and ∞. They specify non-negative integers as degrees of plausibility – or, more precisely, as degrees of *disbelief* – for worlds. For propositional formulas $A, B \in \mathcal{L}$, we set $\kappa(A) = \min\{\kappa(\omega) \mid \omega \models A\}$. A proposition A is believed iff $\kappa(\overline{A}) > 0$, which is denoted by $\kappa \models A$. This may also be specified by degrees of plausibility (or of disbelief, respectively) by saying that $\kappa \models A[n]$ iff $\kappa(\overline{A}) > n$ $(n \in \mathbb{N} \cup \{0\})$. A conditional $(B|A) \in (\mathcal{L} \mid \mathcal{L})$ may be assigned a degree of plausibility via $\kappa(B|A) = \kappa(AB) - \kappa(A)$. κ *satisfies* $(B|A)$, $\kappa \models (B|A)$, iff $\kappa(AB) < \kappa(A\overline{B})$, i.e. iff AB is more plausible than $A\overline{B}$. We can also specify a numerical degree of plausibility of a conditional by defining $\kappa \models (B|A)\,[n]$ iff $\kappa(AB) + n < \kappa(A\overline{B})$ $(n \in \mathbb{N} \cup \{0\})$. OCF's are the qualitative counterpart of probability distributions (cf. [GMP93],[GP96]). For a probability distribution P, we have $P(B|A) = \frac{P(AB)}{P(A)}$ for $P(A) > 0$, and $P \models (B|A)\,[x]$ iff $P(B|A) = x$ $(x \in [0,1])$.

We will consider mostly measure-free conditionals, focusing on structural aspects, but also allow quantifications. If $\mathcal{R}^* = \{(B_1|A_1)\,[x_1], \ldots, (B_n|A_n)\,[x_n]\}$ is a set of (appropriately) quantified conditionals, then $\mathcal{R} = \{(B_1|A_1), \ldots, (B_n|A_n)\}$ denotes the set of unquantified conditionals, and vice versa. Throughout this paper, we will assume all OCF's to be finite, and all probability distributions to be positive. All results to be presented also hold in the general case, but then need some technical modifications (see [KI01a]).

3 Maximum Entropy and System-$Z^{(*)}$

In this section, we review briefly well-known model-based approaches to represent conditional knowledge inductively.

For a consistent set $\mathcal{R}^* = \{(B_1|A_1)\,[x_1], \ldots, (B_n|A_n)\,[x_n]\}$ of probabilistic conditionals, the *ME-representation of* $\mathcal{R}^*$, $ME(\mathcal{R}^*)$, is the unique distribution P that maximizes the entropy $H(P) = -\sum_\omega P(\omega) \log P(\omega)$ subject to $P \models \mathcal{R}^*$ (see e.g. [Par94],[KI98). $ME(\mathcal{R}^*)$ can be written as

$$ME(\mathcal{R}^*)(\omega) = \alpha_0 \prod_{\substack{1 \leqslant i \leqslant n \\ \omega \models A_i B_i}} \alpha_i^{1-x_i} \prod_{\substack{1 \leqslant i \leqslant n \\ \omega \models A_i \overline{B_i}}} \alpha_i^{-x_i}, \qquad (1)$$

with the α_i's being appropriately chosen so as to satisfy all conditionals in $\mathcal{R}^*$.

In a semi-quantitative framework, a well-known method to represent a (finite) set $\mathcal{R} = \{r_i = (B_i|A_i) \mid 1 \leqslant i \leqslant n\}$ of conditionals by an OCF is to apply the *system-Z* of Goldszmidt and Pearl [GMP93],[GP96]. A conditional $(B|A)$ is said to be *tolerated* by $\mathcal{R}$ iff there is a world ω such that ω verifies $(B|A)$ and ω does not falsify any of the conditionals in $\mathcal{R}$. $\mathcal{R}$ is consistent iff there is an ordered partition $\mathcal{R}_0, \mathcal{R}_1, \ldots, \mathcal{R}_k$ of $\mathcal{R}$ such that each conditional in $\mathcal{R}_m$ is tolerated by $\bigcup_{j=m}^k \mathcal{R}_j$, $0 \leqslant m \leqslant k$. The system-Z ranking function, κ^z, representing $\mathcal{R}$ is given by

$$\kappa^z(\omega) = \begin{cases} 0, \text{ if } \omega \text{ does not falsify any } r_i, \\ 1 + \max\limits_{\substack{1 \leqslant i \leqslant n \\ \omega \models A_i \overline{B}_i}} Z(r_i), \text{otherwise} \end{cases}$$

where $Z(r_i) = j$ iff $r_i \in \mathcal{R}_j$. κ^z assigns to each world ω the lowest possible rank admissible with respect to the constraints in $\mathcal{R}$.

A more sophisticated representation is obtained by combining the system-Z approach with the probabilistic ME-principle, yielding system-Z^* [GMP93]. The corresponding Z^*-rankings of the conditionals in $\mathcal{R}$ have to satisfy (see [GMP93])

$$Z^*(r_i) + \min_{\omega \models A_i \overline{B}_i} \sum_{\substack{j \neq i \\ \omega \models A_j \overline{B}_j}} Z^*(r_j) = 1 + \min_{\omega \models A_i B_i} \sum_{\substack{j \neq i \\ \omega \models A_j \overline{B}_j}} Z^*(r_j), \tag{2}$$

and κ^* is then calculated by

$$\kappa^*(\omega) = \sum_{\substack{1 \leqslant i \leqslant n \\ \omega \models A_i \overline{B}_i}} Z^*(r_i) \tag{3}$$

Z^*-entailment $\mid\!\sim^*$ is defined by $\mathcal{R} \mid\!\sim^* (B|A)$ iff $\kappa^*(AB) < \kappa^*(A\overline{B})$. System-$Z^*$ handles conditional knowledge quite appropriately (cf. [GMP93]). In particular, Z^*-entailment satisfies the crucial property of *irrelevance*: If d is an atomic proposition not appearing in any of the conditionals in $\mathcal{R}$, then

$$\mathcal{R} \mid\!\sim^* (B|A) \quad \text{iff} \quad \mathcal{R} \mid\!\sim^* (B|Ad) \tag{4}$$

In [GMP93], a procedure is given to calculate Z^*-rankings for so-called *minimal-core sets*, i.e. sets $\mathcal{R}$ of conditionals such that for each conditional $r \in \mathcal{R}$, there is a world $\omega \in \Omega$ that falsifies r and no other conditional in $\mathcal{R}$. Bourne and Parsons [BP99] presented an algorithm that computes the Z^*-ranking, whenever (2) possesses a unique solution. This algorithm is also able to take variable strength of conditionals into account, that is, to calculate solutions to

$$Z^*(r_i) + \min_{\omega \models A_i \overline{B}_i} \sum_{\substack{j \neq i \\ \omega \models A_j \overline{B}_j}} Z^*(r_j) = n_i + \min_{\omega \models A_i B_i} \sum_{\substack{j \neq i \\ \omega \models A_j \overline{B}_j}} Z^*(r_j), \tag{5}$$

so that $\kappa^* \models (B|A)[n_i]$. There are, however, sets of conditionals that do not specify unique solutions to (2), as the following example shows.

Example 1. For the set $\mathcal{R} = \{r_1 : (b|a), r_2 : (c|a), r_3 : (c|ab)\}$, (2) admits multiple solutions: $(Z^*(r_1), Z^*(r_2), Z^*(r_3))$ may be any one of, for instance, $(1, 0, 1), (1, 1, 0)$, or even $(2, -1, 2)$ (cf. [BP99]).

Bourne and Parsons argue that some examples may be too complex to be dealt with by a "flat" system-Z^* approach and advise to use variable strength conditionals to enforce unique solvability. This seems a bit strange – Example 1 does not look very complex, and the probabilistic ME-method yields a unique solution even if all three conditionals are assigned the same probability.

The problem with Goldszmidt & Pearl's and Bourne & Parsons' work is that, in order to use as much of the inferential power of the ME-method as possible, they cling too closely to *probabilistic* ME-techniques. The idea we will present and pursue here is to reveal the pattern that makes ME-methods a most adequate tool for handling conditional information and to transfer this pattern into the framework of semi-quantitative knowledge representation. This will bring forth a more general approach of which system-Z^* turns out to be a special instance.

4 Generalizing System-Z^*

System-Z^* suggests a straightforward generalization for representing a set $\mathcal{R} = \{r_i = (B_i|A_i) \mid 1 \leqslant i \leqslant n\}$ of conditionals by an OCF: Use approach (3) and determine the $Z^*(r_i)$ so that κ^* satisfies all of the conditionals r_i, i.e. such that

$$Z^*(r_i) > \min_{\omega \models A_i B_i} \sum_{\substack{j \neq i \\ \omega \models A_j \overline{B}_j}} Z^*(r_j) - \min_{\omega \models A_i \overline{B}_i} \sum_{\substack{j \neq i \\ \omega \models A_j \overline{B}_j}} Z^*(r_j) \qquad (6)$$

for $1 \leqslant i \leqslant n$. That means that condition (2) is weakened to be satisfied as an inequality constraint. Variable strengths of OCF-conditionals can be taken easily into account by adding them on the right-hand side of (6), thus generalizing (5). This generalization, however, seems to be quite ad hoc, leaving the ME-track and thus without theoretical justification.

Quite to the contrary – in the sequel, we will show that actually, this generalized approach emerged from a formal *principle of conditional indifference* that was formalized in [KI98] as one of four axioms apt to characterize the ME-techniques. This principle is based on observing *conditional structures* and provides a powerful methodology, not only to represent conditional knowledge appropriately, but even to guide the revision of epistemic states by conditional beliefs. In the next section, we will briefly develop the necessary theoretical background, which is purely algebraic and therefore can be applied in a probabilistic as well as in a semi-quantitative setting. Just as for the ME-methods, it will provide an intelligible and appealing scheme for the inductive representation of conditionals.

5 A Dynamic Approach to Conditionals

By observing the attitude of worlds with respect to it, each conditional $(B|A)$ can be considered as a generalized (three-valued) indicator function on worlds:

$$(B|A)(\omega) = \begin{cases} 1 & : \ \omega \models AB \\ 0 & : \ \omega \models A\overline{B} \\ u & : \ \omega \models \overline{A} \end{cases} \qquad (7)$$

where u stands for *unknown* or *indeterminate* (see, e.g., [Cal91]). Intuitively, representing or incorporating a conditional as a plausible conclusion in an epistemic state means to make – at least some – worlds verifying the conditional more plausible than the worlds falsifying it. In this sense, conditionals to be learned have effects on possible worlds, shifting them appropriately to establish the intended relationship. Which worlds will actually be shifted depends on the chosen inductive representation procedure – for the conditional $(B|A)$, all worlds in either of the partitioning sets $AB, A\overline{B}$ and $\overline{A}$ are indistinguishable.

When we consider (finite) sets of conditionals $\mathcal{R} = \{(B_1|A_1), \ldots, (B_n|A_n)\} \subseteq (\mathcal{L} \mid \mathcal{L})$, we have to modify the representation (7) appropriately to identify the effect of each conditional in $\mathcal{R}$ on worlds in Ω. To this end, we replace the numbers 0 and 1 by abstract symbols, $\mathbf{a}_i^+, \mathbf{a}_i^-$, that we associate to each conditional $(B_i|A_i)$ in $\mathcal{R}$. Moreover, we will make use of a group structure to represent the joint impact of conditionals on worlds.

So let $\mathcal{F}_\mathcal{R} = \langle \mathbf{a}_1^+, \mathbf{a}_1^-, \ldots, \mathbf{a}_n^+, \mathbf{a}_n^- \rangle$ be the free abelian group with generators $\mathbf{a}_1^+, \mathbf{a}_1^-, \ldots, \mathbf{a}_n^+, \mathbf{a}_n^-$, i.e. $\mathcal{F}_\mathcal{R}$ consists of all elements of the form $(\mathbf{a}_1^+)^{r_1}(\mathbf{a}_1^-)^{s_1} \ldots (\mathbf{a}_n^+)^{r_n}(\mathbf{a}_n^-)^{s_n}$ with integers $r_i, s_i \in \mathbb{Z}$ (the ring of integers). Each element of $\mathcal{F}_\mathcal{R}$ can be identified by its exponents, so that $\mathcal{F}_\mathcal{R}$ is isomorphic to $\mathbb{Z}^{2n}$. The commutativity of $\mathcal{F}_\mathcal{R}$ corresponds to the fact that the conditionals in $\mathcal{R}$ shall be effective simultaneously, without assuming any order of application. Note that, although we will speak of *multiplication* and *products* in $\mathcal{F}_\mathcal{R}$, the generators of $\mathcal{F}_\mathcal{R}$ are merely juxtaposed, like words.

For each $i, 1 \leqslant i \leqslant n$, we define a function $\sigma_i = \sigma_{(B_i|A_i)} : \Omega \to \mathcal{F}_\mathcal{R}$ by setting

$$\sigma_i(\omega) := \begin{cases} \mathbf{a}_i^+ & \text{if } (B_i|A_i)(\omega) = 1 \\ \mathbf{a}_i^- & \text{if } (B_i|A_i)(\omega) = 0 \\ 1 & \text{if } (B_i|A_i)(\omega) = u \end{cases}$$

$\sigma_i(\omega)$ represents the manner in which the conditional $(B_i|A_i)$ applies to the possible world ω. The neutral element 1 of $\mathcal{F}_\mathcal{R}$ represents the non-applicability of $(B_i|A_i)$ in case that the antecedent A_i is not satisfied, so the neutral group element corresponds to a neutral attitude with respect to the conditional. The function $\sigma_\mathcal{R} : \Omega \to \mathcal{F}_\mathcal{R}$,

$$\sigma_\mathcal{R}(\omega) := \prod_{1 \leqslant i \leqslant n} \sigma_i(\omega) = \prod_{\substack{1 \leqslant i \leqslant n \\ \omega \models A_i B_i}} \mathbf{a}_i^+ \prod_{\substack{1 \leqslant i \leqslant n \\ \omega \models A_i \overline{B}_i}} \mathbf{a}_i^- \tag{8}$$

describes the all-over effect of $\mathcal{R}$ on ω. $\sigma_\mathcal{R}(\omega)$ is called the *conditional structure of ω with respect to $\mathcal{R}$*. We will illustrate this notion of conditional structures in the following example which extends the well-known *Nixon diamond*:

Example 2. Let $\mathcal{R}$ consist of the following conditionals:
$r_1 : (p|q)$ *Quakers are pacifists.*
$r_2 : (\overline{p}|r)$ *Republicans are not pacifists.*
$r_3 : (a|q)$ *Quakers are Americans.*
$r_4 : (b|a)$ *Americans like baseball.*
$r_5 : (\overline{b}|q)$ *Quakers do not like baseball.*

The conditional structure of a possible world, say $pqrab$, is calculated in the following way: $pqrab$ verifies the first conditional r_1 ($pqrab \models pq$), so we have $\sigma_1(pqrab) = \mathbf{a}_1^+$. $pqrab$, however, falsifies the second conditional $r_2 = (\overline{p}|r)$, thus

$\sigma_2(pqrab) = \mathbf{a}_2^-$. In the same way, $\sigma_3(pqrab) = \mathbf{a}_3^+, \sigma_4(pqrab) = \mathbf{a}_4^+, \sigma_5(pqrab) = \mathbf{a}_5^-$. We obtain $\sigma_{\mathcal{R}}(pqrab) = \mathbf{a}_1^+\mathbf{a}_2^-\mathbf{a}_3^+\mathbf{a}_4^+\mathbf{a}_5^-$. In the table below, we list the conditional structures of all possible worlds with respect to $\mathcal{R}$:

ω	$\sigma_{\mathcal{R}}(\omega)$	ω	$\sigma_{\mathcal{R}}(\omega)$	ω	$\sigma_{\mathcal{R}}(\omega)$	ω	$\sigma_{\mathcal{R}}(\omega)$
$pqrab$	$\mathbf{a}_1^+\mathbf{a}_2^-\mathbf{a}_3^+\mathbf{a}_4^+\mathbf{a}_5^-$	$p\overline{q}rab$	$\mathbf{a}_2^-\mathbf{a}_4^+$	$\overline{p}qrab$	$\mathbf{a}_1^-\mathbf{a}_2^+\mathbf{a}_3^+\mathbf{a}_4^+\mathbf{a}_5^-$	$\overline{p}\,\overline{q}rab$	$\mathbf{a}_2^+\mathbf{a}_4^+$
$pqra\overline{b}$	$\mathbf{a}_1^+\mathbf{a}_2^-\mathbf{a}_3^+\mathbf{a}_4^-\mathbf{a}_5^+$	$p\overline{q}ra\overline{b}$	$\mathbf{a}_2^-\mathbf{a}_4^-$	$\overline{p}qra\overline{b}$	$\mathbf{a}_1^-\mathbf{a}_2^+\mathbf{a}_3^+\mathbf{a}_4^-\mathbf{a}_5^+$	$\overline{p}\,\overline{q}ra\overline{b}$	$\mathbf{a}_2^+\mathbf{a}_4^-$
$pqr\overline{a}b$	$\mathbf{a}_1^+\mathbf{a}_2^-\mathbf{a}_3^-\mathbf{a}_5^-$	$p\overline{q}r\overline{a}b$	$\mathbf{a}_2^-$	$\overline{p}qr\overline{a}b$	$\mathbf{a}_1^-\mathbf{a}_2^+\mathbf{a}_3^-\mathbf{a}_5^-$	$\overline{p}\,\overline{q}r\overline{a}b$	$\mathbf{a}_2^+$
$pqr\overline{a}\overline{b}$	$\mathbf{a}_1^+\mathbf{a}_2^-\mathbf{a}_3^-\mathbf{a}_5^+$	$p\overline{q}r\overline{a}\overline{b}$	$\mathbf{a}_2^-$	$\overline{p}qr\overline{a}\overline{b}$	$\mathbf{a}_1^-\mathbf{a}_2^+\mathbf{a}_3^-\mathbf{a}_5^+$	$\overline{p}\,\overline{q}r\overline{a}\overline{b}$	$\mathbf{a}_2^+$
$pq\overline{r}ab$	$\mathbf{a}_1^+\mathbf{a}_3^+\mathbf{a}_4^+\mathbf{a}_5^-$	$p\overline{q}\,\overline{r}ab$	$\mathbf{a}_4^+$	$\overline{p}q\overline{r}ab$	$\mathbf{a}_1^-\mathbf{a}_3^+\mathbf{a}_4^+\mathbf{a}_5^-$	$\overline{p}\,\overline{q}\,\overline{r}ab$	$\mathbf{a}_4^+$
$pq\overline{r}a\overline{b}$	$\mathbf{a}_1^+\mathbf{a}_3^+\mathbf{a}_4^-\mathbf{a}_5^+$	$p\overline{q}\,\overline{r}a\overline{b}$	$\mathbf{a}_4^-$	$\overline{p}q\overline{r}a\overline{b}$	$\mathbf{a}_1^-\mathbf{a}_3^+\mathbf{a}_4^-\mathbf{a}_5^+$	$\overline{p}\,\overline{q}\,\overline{r}a\overline{b}$	$\mathbf{a}_4^-$
$pq\overline{r}\,\overline{a}b$	$\mathbf{a}_1^+\mathbf{a}_3^-\mathbf{a}_5^-$	$p\overline{q}\,\overline{r}\,\overline{a}b$	1	$\overline{p}q\overline{r}\,\overline{a}b$	$\mathbf{a}_1^-\mathbf{a}_3^-\mathbf{a}_5^-$	$\overline{p}\,\overline{q}\,\overline{r}\,\overline{a}b$	1
$pq\overline{r}\,\overline{a}\overline{b}$	$\mathbf{a}_1^+\mathbf{a}_3^-\mathbf{a}_5^+$	$p\overline{q}\,\overline{r}\,\overline{a}\,\overline{b}$	1	$\overline{p}q\overline{r}\,\overline{a}\overline{b}$	$\mathbf{a}_1^-\mathbf{a}_3^-\mathbf{a}_5^+$	$\overline{p}\,\overline{q}\,\overline{r}\,\overline{a}\,\overline{b}$	1

Using this table, it is easy to see that $\mathcal{R}$ is consistent, with partition $\mathcal{R}_0 = \{r_2, r_4\}$ and $\mathcal{R}_1 = \{r_1, r_3, r_5\}$. $\mathcal{R}$, however, is not a minimal-core set, because each world falsifying r_1 (i.e. worlds with label $\mathbf{a}_1^-$ in the table) also falsifies at least one of r_3, r_4, r_5. In fact, Goldszmidt & Pearl's system-Z^* approach fails for $\mathcal{R}$. Bourne & Parsons' algorithm, however, computes $Z^*(r_1) = Z^*(r_2) = Z^*(r_4) = 1, Z^*(r_3) = Z^*(r_5) = 2$.

$\sigma_{\mathcal{R}}$ labels each world appropriately and makes conditional effects on worlds comparable and computable. For instance, from the table of Example 2 we see that $p\overline{q}\,\overline{r}ab$ and $\overline{p}\,\overline{q}\,\overline{r}ab$ have the same conditional structure (namely $\mathbf{a}_4^+$), and that forming the quotient $\dfrac{\sigma_{\mathcal{R}}(\overline{p}\,\overline{q}rab)}{\sigma_{\mathcal{R}}(\overline{p}\,\overline{q}ra\overline{b})} = \dfrac{\mathbf{a}_2^+\mathbf{a}_4^+}{\mathbf{a}_2^+\mathbf{a}_4^-} = \dfrac{\mathbf{a}_4^+}{\mathbf{a}_4^-}$ isolates the effect of the fourth conditional. Making calculations of conditional structures more convenient and more elegant, we take the worlds $\omega \in \Omega$ as formal generators of the free abelian group $\widehat{\Omega} := \langle \omega \mid \omega \in \Omega \rangle$. $\widehat{\Omega}$ consists of all products $\widehat{\omega} = \omega_1{}^{r_1} \ldots \omega_m{}^{r_m}$, with $\omega_1, \ldots, \omega_m \in \Omega$, and integers $r_1, \ldots r_m$. Introducing such a "multiplication between worlds" is nothing but a technical means to comply with the multiplicative structure the effects of conditionals impose on worlds. As in $\mathcal{F}_{\mathcal{R}}$, multiplication in $\widehat{\Omega}$ actually means juxtaposition. Now $\sigma_{\mathcal{R}}$ may be extended to $\widehat{\Omega}$ in a straightforward manner by setting $\sigma_{\mathcal{R}}(\omega_1{}^{r_1} \ldots \omega_m{}^{r_m}) = \sigma_{\mathcal{R}}(\omega_1)^{r_1} \ldots \sigma_{\mathcal{R}}(\omega_m)^{r_m}$, yielding a *homomorphism of groups* $\sigma_{\mathcal{R}} : \widehat{\Omega} \to \mathcal{F}_{\mathcal{R}}$.

Having the same conditional structure defines an equivalence relation $\equiv_{\mathcal{R}}$ on $\widehat{\Omega}$: $\widehat{\omega}_1 \equiv_{\mathcal{R}} \widehat{\omega}_2$ iff $\sigma_{\mathcal{R}}(\widehat{\omega}_1) = \sigma_{\mathcal{R}}(\widehat{\omega}_2)$. Those elements of $\widehat{\Omega}$ that are balanced with respect to the effects of conditionals in $\mathcal{R}$ are contained in the *kernel of* $\sigma_{\mathcal{R}}$, $\mathit{ker}\,\sigma_{\mathcal{R}} = \{\widehat{\omega} \in \widehat{\Omega} \mid \sigma_{\mathcal{R}}(\widehat{\omega}) = 1\}$. $\mathit{ker}\,\sigma_{\mathcal{R}}$ does not depend on the chosen representation of conditional structures by symbols in $\mathcal{F}_{\mathcal{R}}$ and thus, it is an invariant of $\mathcal{R}$ [KI01a]. In a semi-quantitative as well as in a probabilistic environment, implicit normalizing constraints have to be taken into account, namely, $\kappa(\top) = 0$ for OCF's, and $P(\top) = 1$ for probability distributions. This can be achieved by focusing on equivalence with respect to $\sigma_{(\top|\top)}$. Since $\sigma_{(\top|\top)}$ simply counts the worlds occurring in $\widehat{\omega}$, two elements $\widehat{\omega}_1 = \omega_1^{r_1} \ldots \omega_m^{r_m}, \widehat{\omega}_2 = \nu_1^{s_1} \ldots \nu_p^{s_p} \in \widehat{\Omega}$ are

$\sigma_{(\top|\top)}$-equivalent, $\widehat{\omega}_1 \equiv_\top \widehat{\omega}_2$, iff $\sum_{1 \leqslant j \leqslant m} r_j = \sum_{1 \leqslant k \leqslant p} s_k$. This means, $\widehat{\omega}_1 \equiv_\top \widehat{\omega}_2$ iff they both are a (cancelled) product of the same number of generating worlds, each generator being counted with its corresponding exponent.

The conditional structures of generalized worlds, $\sigma_{\mathcal{R}}(\widehat{\omega})$, can be considered as generalized, algebraic versions of the *interaction quotients* investigated by Good [Goo63]. $\sigma_{\mathcal{R}}(\widehat{\omega}) = 1$ (i.e. $\widehat{\omega} \in \mathit{ker}\, \sigma_{\mathcal{R}}$) indicates that the interactions between the conditionals in $\mathcal{R}$ are balanced in $\widehat{\omega}$. We will elaborate the consequences of this idea for representing conditionals adequately in the next section.

6 Conditional Indifference

To study conditional interactions, we now focus on the behavior of OCF's $\kappa : \Omega \to \mathbb{N} \cup \{0, \infty\}$ and probability functions $P : \Omega \to [0,1]$ with respect to the elements in $\widehat{\Omega}$. We extend each such function to a homomorphism, $\kappa : \widehat{\Omega} \to (\mathbb{Z}, +)$, or $P : \widehat{\Omega} \to \mathbb{R}^+$, respectively, by setting $\kappa({\omega_1}^{r_1} \cdot \ldots \cdot {\omega_m}^{r_m}) = r_1\kappa(\omega_1) + \ldots + r_m\kappa(\omega_m)$ and $P({\omega_1}^{r_1} \cdot \ldots \cdot {\omega_m}^{r_m}) = P(\omega_1)^{r_1} \cdot \ldots \cdot P(\omega_m)^{r_m}$. This allows us to analyze numerical relationships holding between different $\kappa(\omega)$, respectively $P(\omega)$, and to elaborate the conditionals whose structures these functions follow. In the sequel, let V denote an OCF or a probability function, i.e. $V = \kappa$ or $V = P$.

Definition 1. *Assume $\mathcal{R} \subseteq (\mathcal{L} \mid \mathcal{L})$ to be a set of conditionals. V is* indifferent *with respect to $\mathcal{R}$ iff $V(\widehat{\omega}_1) = V(\widehat{\omega}_2)$ whenever $\sigma_{\mathcal{R}}(\widehat{\omega}_1) = \sigma_{\mathcal{R}}(\widehat{\omega}_2)$ for $\widehat{\omega}_1 \equiv_\top \widehat{\omega}_2 \in \widehat{\Omega}$, i.e. iff $\mathit{ker}\, \sigma_{\mathcal{R}} \cap \mathit{ker}\, \sigma_{(\top|\top)} \subseteq \mathit{ker}\, V$.*

Note that we presupposed all OCF's to be finite and all probability functions to be positive in order to make this definition a very concise one. For the general case, cf. [KI01a].

V being indifferent with respect to $\mathcal{R}$ means that it does not distinguish between different elements $\widehat{\omega}_1, \widehat{\omega}_2$ with the same conditional structure with respect to $\mathcal{R}$. Normalizing constraints are taken into account by observing $\equiv_\top$-equivalence. Conversely, any deviation $\kappa(\widehat{\omega}) \neq 0$, respectively $P(\widehat{\omega}) \neq 1$, can be explained by the conditionals in $\mathcal{R}$ acting on $\widehat{\omega}$ in a non-balanced way. Conditional indifference captures interactions of conditionals of arbitrary depth by making use of the group homomorphism induced by V. The next theorem gives a simple criterion to check conditional indifference (for a proof, cf. [KI01a]):

Theorem 1. *Let $\mathcal{R} = \{(B_1|A_1), \ldots, (B_n|A_n)\}$ be a set of conditionals.*

A (finite) OCF κ is indifferent with respect to $\mathcal{R}$ iff there are rational numbers $\kappa_0, \kappa_i^+, \kappa_i^- \in \mathbb{Q}$, $1 \leqslant i \leqslant n$, such that for all $\omega \in \Omega$,

$$\kappa(\omega) = \kappa_0 + \sum_{\substack{1 \leqslant i \leqslant n \\ \omega \models A_i B_i}} \kappa_i^+ + \sum_{\substack{1 \leqslant i \leqslant n \\ \omega \models A_i \overline{B_i}}} \kappa_i^- \tag{9}$$

A (positive) probability function P is indifferent with respect to $\mathcal{R}$ iff there are positive real numbers $\alpha_0, \alpha_1^+, \alpha_1^-, \ldots, \alpha_n^+, \alpha_n^- \in \mathbb{R}^+$ such that for all $\omega \in \Omega$,

$$P(\omega) = \alpha_0 \prod_{\substack{1 \leqslant i \leqslant n \\ \omega \models A_i B_i}} \alpha_i^+ \prod_{\substack{1 \leqslant i \leqslant n \\ \omega \models A_i \overline{B_i}}} \alpha_i^- \tag{10}$$

Note that conditional indifference is a measure-free notion. In particular, it does not require the conditionals in $\mathcal{R}$ to be represented by κ or P, respectively. This qualitative or quantitative information is taken into account in a second step:

Definition 2. *Ordinal conditional functions, κ, and probability functions, P, representing a set $\mathcal{R}$ of (quantified) conditionals and being indifferent with respect to it, are called* c-representations.

Theorem 1 provides an intelligible schema to construct c-representations. For instance, for an OCF-c-representation, we simply set up κ according to (9) and choose the κ_i^+, κ_i^- appropriately to ensure that $\kappa \models \mathcal{R}^{(*)}$ holds, i.e. such that

$$\kappa_i^- - \kappa_i^+ > (n_i +) \min_{\omega \models A_i B_i} \Big(\sum_{\substack{j \neq i \\ \omega \models A_j B_j}} \kappa_j^+ + \sum_{\substack{j \neq i \\ \omega \models A_j \overline{B}_j}} \kappa_j^- \Big) - \min_{\omega \models A_i \overline{B}_i} \Big(\sum_{\substack{j \neq i \\ \omega \models A_j B_j}} \kappa_j^+ + \sum_{\substack{j \neq i \\ \omega \models A_j \overline{B}_j}} \kappa_j^- \Big) \quad (11)$$

where the optional addition of n_i on the right-hand side allows for variable strength conditionals. Furthermore, the normalizing constant κ_0 has to be chosen appropriately to ensure that actually an OCF is obtained. Once suitable numbers $\kappa_0, \kappa_i^+, \kappa_i^-$ are fixed, $\kappa(\omega)$ can easily be computed from the conditional structure $\sigma_{\mathcal{R}}(\omega)$ of ω by replacing each symbol $\mathbf{a}_i^+, \mathbf{a}_i^-$ by its numerical counterpart κ_i^+, κ_i^- (note the similarity of (8) with (9) and (10)).

By setting $\kappa_i^+ := 0$ for each conditional $r_i \in \mathcal{R}$, and determining $\kappa_i^- \geqslant 0$ according to (11), we recover the generalized system-Z^* (see (6)):

$$\kappa_i^- > (n_i +) \min_{\omega \models A_i B_i} \sum_{\substack{j \neq i \\ \omega \models A_j \overline{B}_j}} \kappa_j^- - \min_{\omega \models A_i \overline{B}_i} \sum_{\substack{j \neq i \\ \omega \models A_j \overline{B}_j}} \kappa_j^- \quad (12)$$

Note that, due to the consistency of $\mathcal{R}$, also $\kappa_0 = 0$ in this case. By choosing $\kappa_i^- \geqslant 0$ minimally, we obtain system-Z^*. As long as we do not have multiple minimal solutions κ_i^-, the algorithm of Bourne & Parsons can be used to calculate these numbers. We also recover the ME-distribution from (10) (see (1), with $\alpha_i^+ = \alpha^{1-x_i}$ and $\alpha_i^- = \alpha^{-x_i}$ for $1 \leqslant i \leqslant n$). So both ME-methods and system-Z^* obey the principle of conditional indifference.

In [BSS00], infinitesimal *lcd-plausibility functions* are introduced which are based (twofold) on the principle of least commitment (lc) and on the principle of auto-deduction (d) which simply states that the plausibility function should satisfy the conditionals in $\mathcal{R}$. The specific multiplicative structure of lcd-functions is motivated by using Dempster's rule of combination. These lcd-functions can be constructed directly from our approach: Instead of *proto-infinitesimals* introduced in [BSS00] to represent infinitesimals symbolically, we use the formal symbols $\mathbf{a}_1^-, \ldots, \mathbf{a}_n^-$ which can be assigned infinitesimals (or non-infinitesimal positive real numbers, in a non-infinitesimal framework) to give rise to plausibility functions of lcd-type. The specific form of lcd-functions is found to match the conditional structures of worlds – lcd-functions are indifferent with respect to $\mathcal{R}$. For a more detailed comparison in the framework of possibility theory, cf. [KI01b].

Example 3. We continue Example 2, the extended Nixon diamond. (12) yields $\kappa_2^-, \kappa_4^- > 0$. Therefore, we set $\kappa_2^- := \kappa_4^- := 1$. For determining $\kappa_1^-, \kappa_3^-, \kappa_5^-$, the table from Example 2 proves to be helpful. We calculate $\kappa_1^- > \min\{\kappa_3^-, \kappa_4^-, \kappa_5^-\} - \min\{\kappa_3^-, \kappa_4^-, \kappa_5^-\} = 0, \kappa_3^- > \min\{\kappa_4^-, \kappa_5^-\}, \kappa_5^- > \min\{\kappa_4^-, \kappa_3^-\}$. So we set $\kappa_1^- := 1, \kappa_3^- := \kappa_5^- := 2$. Because these numbers are minimal, they can also be obtained by applying the Bourne & Parsons-algorithm. Now, $\kappa_c(\omega) = \sum_{\substack{1 \leqslant i \leqslant 5 \\ \omega \models A_i \overline{B_i}}} \kappa_i^-$ can be computed easily. The table below shows κ_c-rankings for some worlds ω and compares them to system-Z-rankings.

ω	$\kappa_c(\omega)$	$\kappa^z(\omega)$	ω	$\kappa_c(\omega)$	$\kappa^z(\omega)$	ω	$\kappa_c(\omega)$	$\kappa^z(\omega)$	ω	$\kappa_c(\omega)$	$\kappa^z(\omega)$
$pqrab$	3	2	$pqr\overline{a}b$	5	2	$\overline{p}qrab$	3	2	$\overline{p}qr\overline{a}b$	5	2
$pqra\overline{b}$	2	1	$pqr\overline{a}\overline{b}$	3	2	$\overline{p}qra\overline{b}$	2	2	$\overline{p}qr\overline{a}\overline{b}$	3	2

It is clearly seen that a c-representation imposes a more finely grained structure on the possible worlds and thus establishes more conditionals. For instance, we have $\kappa^z \not\models (\overline{b}|pqr\overline{a})$, but $\kappa_c \models (\overline{b}|pqr\overline{a})$, that is, a republican, who is a pacifist and a quaker, but not an American, is supposed not to like baseball. To show that this is more than pure speculation, compare the conditional structures of the two worlds involved, $pqr\overline{a}b$ and $pqr\overline{a}\,\overline{b}$: They are the same, except for conditional r_5, and due to r_5, the person is supposed not to like baseball.

In general, system-Z appears to be too cautious to handle conditional interactions adequately. But the extended Nixon diamond also shows it to be too bold sometimes: Now we have $\kappa^z \models (p|qr)$, which seems to be quite unintuitive. This problem also holds for other well-known approaches to conditional reasoning, cf. [DP96]. Again, the c-representation κ_c proves to be more adequate: We have $\kappa_c(pqr) = 2 = \kappa_c(\overline{p}qr)$, so κ_c is completely indeterminate with respect to $(p|qr)$ – it preserves *ambiguity* (cf. [BSS00]).

In contrast to the limited applicability of system-Z^*, an OCF-c-representation can be calculated for any consistent set of conditionals:

Proposition 1. *$\mathcal{R} \subseteq (\mathcal{L} \mid \mathcal{L})$ is consistent iff a c-representation of $\mathcal{R}$ exists.*

It is already the approach (9) (or (3)) that guarantees a well-behavedness with respect to conditional interactions. In particular, all OCF-c-representations satisfy the property of irrelevance in the following sense (cf. (4)):

Lemma 1. *Suppose $\mathcal{R}$ is a set of conditionals, and d is an atomic proposition not appearing in any of the conditionals in $\mathcal{R}$. Then, for any OCF-c-representation κ_c of $\mathcal{R}$, and for any conditional $(B|A) \in (\mathcal{L} \mid \mathcal{L})$, $\kappa_c \models (B|A)$ iff $\kappa_c \models (B|Ad)$.*

An analogous quantified version of this lemma holds for probability functions, too. Furthermore, let $\mathrel{|\!\sim}^c$ be the (nonmonotonic) inference relation based on considering all c-representations:

$$\mathcal{R} \mathrel{|\!\sim}^c (B|A) \quad \text{iff} \quad \kappa_c \models (B|A) \text{ for all c-representations of } \mathcal{R} \tag{13}$$

where $\mathcal{R} \subseteq (\mathcal{L} \mid \mathcal{L}), (B|A) \in (\mathcal{L} \mid \mathcal{L})$. Then Lemma 1 yields

Corollary 1. *Let $\mathcal{R} \subseteq (\mathcal{L} \mid \mathcal{L}), (B|A) \in (\mathcal{L} \mid \mathcal{L})$, let d be an atomic proposition not appearing in any of the conditionals in $\mathcal{R}$. Then $\mathcal{R} \mathrel{|\!\sim}^c (B|A)$ iff $\mathcal{R} \mathrel{|\!\sim}^c (B|Ad)$.*

Moreover, it is easy to prove that $\mathrel{|\!\sim}^c$ also fulfills the basic inferential properties of system P (see, e.g., [BDP97]). But it does not suffer from the *drowning problem*, or, more specifically, from the *blocking of property inheritance problem* (see, e.g., [BDP97]), as the following example shows:

Example 4. Let $\mathcal{R}$ consist of the rules $(f|b)$ (*birds fly*), $(b|p)$ (*penguins are birds*), $(\overline{f}|p)$ (*penguins do not fly*) and $(w|b)$ (*birds have wings*). We will show $\mathcal{R} \mathrel{|\!\sim}^c (w|pb)$, that is, penguins inherit the property of having wings from their superclass *birds*, although they are non-typical birds.

Let κ_c be a c-representation of $\mathcal{R}$, with $\kappa_1^+, \kappa_1^-, \kappa_2^+, \kappa_2^-, \kappa_3^+, \kappa_3^-, \kappa_4^+, \kappa_4^-$ specifying the numerical effects of the conditionals, and with normalizing constant κ_0. For the fourth conditional $(w|b)$, (11) yields $\kappa_4^- - \kappa_4^+ > 0$ (this can be seen quickly by listing the conditional structures of all worlds involved), so that $\kappa_4^- > \kappa_4^+$. By checking the conditional structures of the worlds verifying, or falsifying, respectively, $(w|pb)$ we find that $\kappa_c(pbw) = \min\{\kappa_0+\kappa_1^+ +\kappa_2^+ +\kappa_3^- +\kappa_4^+, \kappa_0+\kappa_1^- + \kappa_2^+ +\kappa_3^+ +\kappa_4^+\}$ and $\kappa_c(pb\overline{w}) = \min\{\kappa_0+\kappa_1^+ +\kappa_2^+ +\kappa_3^- +\kappa_4^-, \kappa_0+\kappa_1^- +\kappa_2^+ +\kappa_3^+ +\kappa_4^-\}$. Due to $\kappa_4^- > \kappa_4^+$, we conclude $\kappa_c(pbw) < \kappa_c(pb\overline{w})$, that is, $\kappa_c \models (w|pb)$.

Suppose now that we also take the conditionals $(e|b)$ (*birds lay eggs*), $(\overline{w}|k)$ (*kiwis do not have wings*) and $(b|k)$ (*kiwis are birds*) into account.[1] Then it can be shown that any c-representation κ_c of this extended set of rules treats both penguins and kiwis as normal birds with respect to laying eggs: $\kappa_c \models (e|pb), (e|kb)$. If we further restrict our attention to c-representations with $\kappa_i^+ = 0$ (that is, the extended system-Z^* approach), then moreover, any such c-representation κ_c will also satisfy $(w|pb)$ and $(\overline{w}|kb)$. This shows, how most complicated interdependencies between conditionals are treated properly in our framework.

We described this example in detail to show that inference based on c-representations is largely qualitative and non-numerical. In fact, our argumentation used mainly structural information, provided by conditional structures.

7 Outlook

In this paper, we presented a new theory to handle conditionals most adequately in inductive knowledge representation and uncertain reasoning. This new theory is based on the algebraic notion of *conditional structures* of worlds. Its realization via group theory does not only provide an elegant methodological framework for representing conditional knowledge. The same machinery can be applied to guide the revision of epistemic states by sets of conditionals in a way that is compatible with the postulates for iterative belief revision of [DP97], and with their generalizations presented in [KI99] (cf. [KI01]a). Moreover, the new conditional theory sketched here can also be used for *knowledge discovery* (see [KI00],[KI01a]). It is there where the techniques introduced in this paper reveal

[1] I am grateful to an anonymous referee to raise this problem.

their full power by elaborating conditional structures from numerical relationships by group theoretical means.

So indeed, the conditional theory presented in this paper has important applications in the whole area of formal knowledge management – uncertain reasoning, belief revision and knowledge discovery. A comparison with conditional event theories can be found in [KI01b].

References

[BDP97] S. Benferhat, D. Dubois, and H. Prade. Nonmonotonic reasoning, conditional objects and possibility theory. *Artificial Intelligence*, 92:259–276, 1997.

[BP99] R.A. Bourne and S. Parsons. Maximum entropy and variable strength defaults. In *Proceedings Sixteenth International Joint Conference on Artificial Intelligence, IJCAI'99*, pages 50–55, 1999.

[BSS00] S. Benferhat, A. Saffiotti, and P. Smets. Belief functions and default reasoning. *Artificial Intelligence*, 122:1–69, 2000.

[Cal91] P.G. Calabrese. Deduction and inference using conditional logic and probability. In I.R. Goodman, M.M. Gupta, H.T. Nguyen, and G.S. Rogers, editors, *Conditional Logic in Expert Systems*, pages 71–100. Elsevier, North Holland, 1991.

[DP96] D. Dubois and H. Prade. Non-standard theories of uncertainty in plausible reasoning. In G. Brewka, editor, *Principles of Knowledge Representation.* CSLI Publications, 1996.

[DP97] A. Darwiche and J. Pearl. On the logic of iterated belief revision. *Artificial Intelligence*, 89:1–29, 1997.

[GMP93] M. Goldszmidt, P. Morris, and J. Pearl. A maximum entropy approach to nonmonotonic reasoning. *IEEE Transactions on Pattern Analysis and Machine Intelligence*, 15(3):220–232, 1993.

[Goo63] I.J. Good. Maximum entropy for hypothesis formulation, especially for multidimensional contingency tables. *Ann. Math. Statist.*, 34:911–934, 1963.

[GP96] M. Goldszmidt and J. Pearl. Qualitative probabilities for default reasoning, belief revision, and causal modeling. *Artificial Intelligence*, 84:57–112, 1996.

[KI98] G. Kern-Isberner. Characterizing the principle of minimum cross-entropy within a conditional-logical framework. *Artificial Intelligence,* 98:169–208, 1998.

[KI99] G. Kern-Isberner. Postulates for conditional belief revivion. In *Proceedings Sixteenth International Joint Conference on Artificial Intelligence, IJCAI-99,* pages 186–191, Morgan Kaufman, 1999.

[KI00] G. Kern-Isberner. Solving the inverse represenation problem. In *Proceedings 14th European Conference on Artificial Intelligence, ECAI'2000,* pages 581–585, Berlin, 2000. IOS Press.

[KI01a] G. Kern-Isberner. *Conditionals in nonmonotonic reasoning and belief revision.* Springer, Lecture Notes in Artificial Intelligence, 2001 (to appear).

[KI01b] G. Kern-Isberner. Representing and learning conditional information in possibility theory. In *Proceedings 7th Fuzzy Days, Dortmund, Germany.* Springer LNCS-Series, 2001 (to appear).

[Par94] J.B. Paris. *The uncertain reasoner's companion – A mathematical perspective.* Cambridge University Press, 1994.

Rankings We Prefer
A Minimal Construction Semantics for Default Reasoning

Emil Weydert

Max-Planck-Institute for Computer Science,
Saarbrücken, Germany, emil@mpi-sb.mpg.de

Abstract. We introduce a ranking construction semantics for graded defaults, formulate the principles of the minimal construction philosophy, from which we derive a preference order over ranking constructions. It defines a powerful rational default inference notion, JLX-entailment, which we are going to compare with system JZ.

1 Introduction

Since the beginning eighties, hundreds of formalisms have tried to capture our basic intuitions about default reasoning. However, a real consensus – e.g. comparable to the broad acceptance of the standard probabilistic framework – has not yet been reached, not even for particular application areas. The actual dominance of specific systems often merely reflects historical peculiarities rather than genuine superiority or the presence of stronger justifications. Nevertheless, independently from popularity considerations, some directions seem to be more promising than others. Of particular interest are the semantic-based conditional accounts, which may be seen as a qualitative counterpart to probabilistic reasoning. These approaches are theoretically and conceptually appealing because they provide a transparent model-theoretic semantics for default conditionals (defining the monotonic logic), as well as reasonable semantic-based default inference notions (defining the nonmonotonic logic).

The simplest and most prominent conditional default formalisms of acceptable strength are system Z [Pearl 90] and rational closure [Lehmann and Magidor 92], which are based on the normality maximization paradigm [Weydert 96]. They interpret defaults as constraints on plausibility rankings and prefer those rankings making more worlds more plausible. This procedure is quite successful, but it still fails to validate many desirable inheritance features. There have been several attempts to overcome these problems, e.g. [Geffner, Pearl 92, Lehmann 95], but most of them rely on more or less arbitrary – and probabilistically questionable – prioritization procedures, which sometimes derive their justification mainly from the handling of specific examples.

An important exception is default reasoning based on entropy maximization (ME-entailment) [Goldszmidt et al. 93]. Unfortunately, the associated ranking-based procedure only works for a very restricted class of suitably non-redundant default sets. There has been some progress, but no general solution [Bourne,

S. Benferhat and P. Besnard (Eds.): ECSQARU 2001, LNAI 2143, pp. 616–627, 2001.

Parsons 99, Kern-Isberner 01, Weydert 95,98]. Another exception is system JZ [Weydert 98], a powerful default inference relation which is based on a natural canonical ranking construction algorithm trying to implement the idea of information minimization directly within the ranking framework. It stands in the tradition of system Z but coincides with ME-entailment for a broad class of examples. In particular, system JZ defines a rational consequence relation and allows inheritance to exceptional subclasses. However, the corresponding minimal construction procedure, although well-motivated, is a bit cumbersome and opaque. In fact, a simple, purely semantic interpretation is still missing.

In this paper, we are going to take the direct preferential semantic road. The idea is to define a global preference order over ranking constructions, intended to implement the minimal construction and the normality maximization philosophy in a more reasonable and transparent way. The resulting JLX-ordering is motivated by three basic principles - minimizing evidence, minimizing surprise, and minimizing shifting. It guarantees the existence of a canonical minimal model for each consistent finite default base, which gives us a powerful rational default inference notion for graded default knowledge, JLX-entailment. Even more interesting, if we combine JLX-minimization with justifiable constructibility, the fourth minimal construction requirement, we get exactly system JZ.

The paper is built up as follows. First, we introduce the ranking construction semantics for defaults, as well as relevant transformation and description functions. After recalling our general semantic-based default entailment philosophy, we present our four minimal construction principles and use the first three to define a preference relation over ranking constructions, the JLX-order. It determines a rational default inference relation, JLX-entailment, which we illustrate with several examples. To conclude, we consider justifiable constructibility, the fourth minimal construction requirement, and investigate the relationship between JLX-entailment and system JZ.

2 Ranking Constructions

Our semantic framework is based on ranking measures, coarse-grained quasi-probabilistic valuations measuring the degree of disbelief, implausibility or surprise of propositions. More precisely, we consider standard $\kappa\pi$-measures, which generalize Spohn's discrete-valued κ-functions [Spohn 90] and are formally equivalent to real-valued possibility measures with multiplicative conditionalization [Dubois, Prade 88] (but without assuming a fuzzy-theoretic interpretation). Of particular interest is the probabilistic reading of $\kappa\pi$-measures. In fact, we may interpret each rank $R(A) = a$ as the order of magnitude of an infinitesimal probability $P(A) = \varepsilon^a$ (for an arbitrary but fixed infinitesimal $\varepsilon > 0$). This relationship allows us to exploit major tools and concepts from classical probability theory, like belief networks and entropy maximization.

Definition 21 (Standard $\kappa\pi$-measures)
Let $\mathcal{B} \subseteq 2^{\mathcal{W}}$ be a compact boolean algebra of propositions and $[0, \infty]$ be the set of positive reals and infinity. $R : \mathcal{B} \rightarrow [0, \infty]$ is a standard $\kappa\pi$-measure iff

- *1.* $R(\mathcal{W}) = 0$, *2.* $R(\emptyset) = \infty$, *3.* $R(A \cup B) = \min\{R(A), R(B)\}$.

The conditional $\kappa\pi$-measure $R(.|.)$ is defined by $R(B|A) = R(B \cap A) - R(A)$ for $R(A) \neq \infty$, else $R(B|A) = \infty$. R_0 is the uniform $\kappa\pi$-measure, with $R_0(A) = 0$ for $A \neq \emptyset$. If R satisfies only 2 and 3, we call it a $\kappa\pi$-pseudo-measure.

The domain $\mathcal{B}$ usually consists of the model/world sets over some classical compact background logic $(\mathcal{L}, \models)$. In what follows, we assume that $\mathcal{B}$ and $(\mathcal{L}, \models)$ have been fixed. In this context, let $Mod_{\kappa\pi}$ be the set of all $\kappa\pi$-measures over $\mathcal{B}$. For convenience, we use the sentences $A \in \mathcal{L}$ also to denote the corresponding model sets $Mod(A) \in \mathcal{B}$, e.g. abbreviating $R(Mod(A))$ by $R(A)$.

Following Spohn [Spohn 88], ranking measures – similar to subjective probability measures – can be used to model epistemic states. The idea is to identify the belief strength $Bel(A)$ with the degree of surprise of $\neg A$, namely $R(\neg A)$. That is, under the most liberal interpretation, A is believed iff $Bel(A) = R(\neg A) > 0$. It is believed with strength s (at least) iff $R(\neg A) \geq s$. This definition has the advantage that it supports full belief, i.e. belief closed under conjunction (and logical entailment).

We consider two basic transformations for $\kappa\pi$-pseudo-measures, shifting and normalization. Given a $\kappa\pi$-pseudo-measure S, shifting a proposition A by the amount a means uniformly increasing the ranks of A-worlds – more precisely, of A-subpropositions – by a. Normalization means uniformly downwards shifting until the $\kappa\pi$-pseudo-measure becomes a $\kappa\pi$-measure.

Definition 22 (Shifting, normalization)
Shifting is a ternary function $+ : (S, a, A) \mapsto S + aA$ (also written $S[A + a]$) defined on $\kappa\pi$-pseudo-measures S, $A \in \mathcal{B}$, and $a \in [0, \infty]$, such that for $B \in \mathcal{B}$,

- *$S + aA$ is a $\kappa\pi$-pseudo-measure,*
- *$(S + aA)(B|A) = S(B|A)$ and $(S + aA)(B|\neg A) = S(B|\neg A)$,*
- *$(S + aA)(A) = S(A) + a$ and $(S + aA)(\neg A) = S(\neg A)$.*

Normalization is a unary function mapping a $\kappa\pi$-pseudo-measure S to the $\kappa\pi$-measure $|S|$ defined by $|S|(A) = S(A) - S(\mathcal{W})$ $(\infty - \infty = 0)$.

With shifting and normalization, we can describe a simple and natural revision concept for $\kappa\pi$-measures which uses Jeffrey-conditionalization and goes back to Spohn. For consistent evidence (represented by) $A \in \mathcal{B}$ and $a \in [0, \infty]$, the parametrized Spohn-type revision procedure $\star^a_{sp}$ enforces a belief strength of at least a by shifting $\neg A$ as far as necessary, followed by a normalization step.

Definition 23 (Spohn-type revision)
We define $\star^a_{sp} : Mod_{\kappa\pi} \times \mathcal{B} \to Mod_{\kappa\pi}$ with $(R, A) \mapsto R \star^a_{sp} A$ s.t.

- *$R(\neg A) \geq a$ or $R(A) = \infty$: $R \star^a_{sp} A = R$.*
- *$R(\neg A) < a$ and $R(A) < \infty$: $R \star^a_{sp} A = |R + (a - R(\neg A) + R(A))\neg A|$.*

Given a prior $\kappa\pi$-measure R and a collection $\mathcal{I} \subseteq \mathcal{B}$ of possible consistent evidential inputs, we are interested in those $\kappa\pi$-measures which can be reached by iterated revision with $A_i \in \mathcal{I}$ starting at R. We present two perspectives.

Definition 24 (Epistemic accessibility, constructibility)
R' is epistemically accessible from R over $\mathcal{I}$ iff for some $a_i \in [0,\infty], A_i \in \mathcal{I}$,

- $R' = R \star_{sp}^{a_0} A_0 \star_{sp}^{a_1} \ldots \star_{sp}^{a_n} A_n$.

R' is epistemically constructible from R over $\mathcal{S}$ iff for some $a_i \in [0,\infty]$, $A_i \in \mathcal{S}$,

- $R' = |R + a_0A_0 + \ldots + a_nA_n|$.

$R \star_{sp} \mathcal{A}/R + \mathcal{A}$ is the class of $\kappa\pi$-measures epistemically accessible/constructible from R over $\mathcal{A}$.

Obviously, R' is epistemically accessible from R over $\mathcal{I}$ iff R' is epistemically constructible from R over $\neg\mathcal{I} = \{\neg A \mid A \in \mathcal{I}\}$, i.e. $R \star_{sp} \mathcal{I} = R + \neg\mathcal{I}$.

3 Default Semantics

On top of $\mathcal{L}$, we consider a graded default conditional language $\mathcal{L}(\Rightarrow)$ using positive rational strength-parameters s (with $\Rightarrow^1 \sim \Rightarrow$).

- $\mathcal{L}(\Rightarrow) = \{A \Rightarrow^s A' \mid A, A' \in \mathcal{L}, 0 < s \in Rat \cup \{\infty\}\}$.

The standard $\kappa\pi$-semantics for $\mathcal{L}(\Rightarrow)$ is based on the satisfaction relation $\models_{\kappa\pi}$.

- $R \models_{\kappa\pi} A \Rightarrow^s A'$ iff $R(A \wedge A') + s \leq R(A \wedge \neg A')$.

Monotonic entailment $\vdash_{\kappa\pi}$ is defined as usual. For each $\Delta \subseteq \mathcal{L}(\Rightarrow)$, let $Mod_{\kappa\pi}(\Delta) = \{R \in Mod_{\kappa\pi} \mid R \models_{\kappa\pi} \Delta\}$ be the set of $\kappa\pi$-models of Δ. Unfortunately, the usual ranking semantics for default conditionals conflicts, either with desirable inheritance features, or with basic nonmonotonic inference patterns. In fact, we know that any default formalism validating for all logically independent φ, ψ,

- **Exceptional inheritance:** $\{\neg\varphi\} \cup \{T \Rightarrow \varphi, T \Rightarrow \psi\} \mid\!\sim \psi$,

cannot be invariant under the substitution of $\kappa\pi$-semantically equivalent default sets. Otherwise, equivalent consistent premises could produce conflicting conclusions – consider e.g. $\{\neg\varphi\} \cup \{T \Rightarrow \varphi, T \Rightarrow (\varphi \leftrightarrow \psi)\} \mid\!\sim \neg\psi$ – which is inacceptable. In other words, the standard $\kappa\pi$-semantics is not fine-grained enough to capture relevant independency information implicitly encoded in the choice of defaults and affecting our intuitions about admissible default conclusions. Therefore, we may want to extend our default semantics so as to sensibilize it for this sort of structural information. More concretely, we are going to introduce refined semantic entities exploiting the epistemic construction perspective. The idea is to consider not the $\kappa\pi$-measures, but the collections of shifting steps, i.e. the $\kappa\pi$-constructions, summarizing their update history. This allows a closer match of the default knowledge structure.

Definition 31 ($\kappa\pi$-construction semantics)
A $\kappa\pi$-construction σ is a sequence $(a_i, A_i \mid i \leq n)$, written $a_0A_0 + \ldots + a_nA_n$, where $A_i \in \mathcal{B}$, $a_i \in [0,\infty]$, and $R_\sigma = R_0 + a_0A_0 + \ldots + a_nA_n$ is a proper $\kappa\pi$-measure. Let $\mathcal{S}_\sigma = \{A_i \mid i \leq n\}$. The $\kappa\pi$+-semantics for $\kappa\pi$-constructions over $\mathcal{L}(\Rightarrow)$ is given by the satisfaction relation

- $\sigma \models_{\kappa\pi+} A \Rightarrow^s A'$ *iff* $R_\sigma \models_{\kappa\pi} A \Rightarrow^s A'$ *and* $Mod(A \wedge \neg A') \in \mathcal{S}_\sigma$.

As before, we set $\sigma \models_{\kappa\pi} A \Rightarrow^s A'$ *iff* $R_\sigma \models_{\kappa\pi} A \Rightarrow^s A'$.

This immediately neutralizes the exceptional inheritance paradox. An important fact is the equivalence of $\kappa\pi$- and $\kappa\pi$+-consistency. Let $\Delta = \{A_i \Rightarrow^{s_i} A'_i \mid i \leq n\}$ and $\Delta^{\rightarrow}_{mod} = \{Mod(A \rightarrow A') \mid A \Rightarrow^s A' \in \Delta\}$. If Δ has a $\kappa\pi$-measure model, we may find a $\kappa\pi$+-model of Δ of the form $\sigma = a_0(A_0 \wedge \neg A'_0) + \ldots + a_n(A_n \wedge \neg A'_n)$.

Theorem 32 (Model accessibility)
$Mod_{\kappa\pi}(\Delta) \neq \emptyset$ *iff* $Mod_{\kappa\pi}(\Delta) \cap (R_0 \star_{sp} \Delta^{\rightarrow}_{mod}) \neq \emptyset$ *iff* $Mod_{\kappa\pi+}(\Delta) \neq \emptyset$.

Our specification of default entailment relations within the $\kappa\pi$+-framework uses several auxiliary functions to evaluate the characteristics of $\kappa\pi$-constructions, e.g. the amount of surprise or the shifting efforts associated with $\sigma = \Sigma_{i \leq n} a_i A_i$.

Definition 33 (Active rank)
The active rank function $r_\sigma : \mathcal{B} \rightarrow [0, \infty]$ *for* σ *is given by*

- $r_\sigma(A) = sup(\{s \geq 0 \mid A \subseteq \cup\{A_j \mid R_\sigma(A_j) \geq s, a_j > 0\}\})$.

The active rank $r_\sigma(A)$ of a proposition A is the maximal rank s so that A is covered by actively shifted propositions A_j of rank at least s. Obviously, we have $r_\sigma(A) \leq R_\sigma(A)$. For instance, if $A, B, P \in \mathcal{B}$ are logically independent and $\sigma = 1A + 1B + 0(A \wedge B \wedge P)$, then $r_\sigma(A \wedge B \wedge P) = 1 < 2 = R_\sigma(A \wedge B \wedge P)$.

Definition 34 (Cumulative surprise)
The cumulative surprise functions $sur_\sigma, sur^+_\sigma : [0, \infty] \rightarrow 2^{\mathcal{B}}$ *for* σ *are*

- $sur_\sigma(s) = \{A_i \mid i \leq n, s \leq r_\sigma(A_i)\}$.
- $sur^+_\sigma(s) = \{A_i \mid i \leq n, s < r_\sigma(A_i)\}$.

$sur_\sigma(s)/sur^+_\sigma(s)$ is the set of all those shiftable propositions getting at least active rank s/active rank higher than s. For instance, if $\sigma = 1A{+}2B{+}0P$, the weak cumulative surprise function for σ is characterized by $sur_\sigma(0) = \mathcal{S}_\sigma$, $sur_\sigma(1) = sur''_\sigma(]0,1]) = \{A, B\}$, $sur_\sigma(2) = sur''_\sigma]1,2] = \{B\}$, $sur_\sigma(\infty) = sur''_\sigma]2,\infty] = \emptyset$. If $\sigma = 1A + 2(A \vee B)$, the relevant sets and values are $sur_\sigma(2) = \{A, A \vee B\}$ and $sur_\sigma(3) = \{A\}$. Obviously, it is enough to know $sur_\sigma(s)$ or $sur^+_\sigma(s)$ for $s \in \{R_\sigma(A) \mid A \in \mathcal{B}\}$. Whereas sur_σ, sur^+_σ indicate the active surprise structure of σ, the binary function sh_σ describes the fine-grained local shifting structure.

Definition 35 (Shifting effort)
The shifting effort $sh_\sigma : [0, \infty]^2 \rightarrow 2^{\mathcal{B}}$ *for* σ *at rank* s *and shifting length* h *is*

- $sh_\sigma(s, h) = \{A_i \mid i \leq n, r_\sigma(A_i) = s, a_i = h\}$.

$sh_\sigma(s, h)$ collects those effectively shifted propositions of active rank s which are shifted by the amount h. For instance, if $\sigma = 1A + 1B + 2(A \vee B)$, we have $sh_\sigma(1, x) = sh_\sigma(2, x) = \emptyset$, $sh_\sigma(3, 1) = \{A, B\}$, and $sh_\sigma(3, 2) = \{A \vee B\}$.

4 Default Entailment Philosophy

Default reasoning in the context of a plausibility semantics $\models_{pl}$ for default conditionals usually takes the following form. For a fact base $\Sigma \subseteq \mathcal{L}$, a default base $\Delta \subseteq \mathcal{L}(\Rightarrow)$, and a potential conclusion $\psi \in \mathcal{L}$, we first collect the corresponding plausibility models – e.g. plausibility orders, $\kappa\pi$-measures or $\kappa\pi$-constructions – of Δ in $Mod_{pl}(\Delta)$. Using a suitable choice criterion – e.g. minimizing surprise or construction efforts – we determine the preferred plausibility models of Δ and put them into $Pref(\Delta) \subseteq Mod_{pl}(\Delta)$. Then we accept ψ as a default conclusion of Σ and Δ iff in each distinguished model of Δ, ψ is sufficiently plausible given Σ. More precisely, if $\Sigma = \{\varphi_1, \ldots, \varphi_p\}$ and $\varphi_\Sigma = \varphi_1 \wedge \ldots \wedge \varphi_p$, there should be a conditional $\varphi_\Sigma \Rightarrow^s \psi$ valid in each preferred plausibility model. Within the $\kappa\pi$-framework, this amounts to require $R(\neg\psi|\varphi_\Sigma) > 0$. Being the weakest possible condition, this maximizes the set of defeasible conclusions. The default entailment notion is thus fixed by the plausibility semantics $\models_{pl}$, the preferred model function $Pref$, and the sufficient plausibility requirement.

- $\Sigma \cup \Delta \mathrel{|\!\sim}^{Pref} \psi$ iff $\Sigma \mathrel{|\!\sim}^{Pref}_{\Delta} \psi$ iff $\exists s > 0\ Pref(\Delta) \models_{pl} \varphi_\Sigma \Rightarrow^s \psi$.

From this definition, the preferential nature of plausibility models, and the closure of preferential conditional theories under intersections, it automatically follows that $\mathrel{|\!\sim}^{Pref}_{\Delta}$ is a preferential consequence relation [Kraus et al. 90]. Consequently, we may describe it by a pre-order over $\mathcal{L}$-worlds, which of course depends on Δ. A different question is whether $Pref$ itself is preferential in the sense that it results from a pre-order $\prec$ over plausibility models, i.e. whether $Pref(\Delta) = Min_{\prec}(Mod_{pl}(\Delta))$. This would give us a preferential consequence relation over $\mathcal{L}(\Rightarrow)$ extending $\vdash_{pl}$.

Of particular interest are of course those powerful approaches singling out a canonical preferred ranking model, e.g. like rational closure/system Z [Lehmann, Magidor 92, Pearl 90], or lexicographic closure [Lehmann 95]. For each consistent, finite Δ, we then obtain a rational consequence relation $\mathrel{|\!\sim}_{\Delta}$. System JZ [Weydert 98], a well-behaved default inference notion anchored in the epistemic construction framework, also belongs to this category. It is based on the minimal effort construction of a canonical $\kappa\pi$-measure model of Δ. However, system JZ encodes the minimal construction philosophy through a somewhat more opaque – although well-motivated – algorithm. We would certainly prefer a more flexible, semantic-oriented approach, based for instance on the explicit comparison of construction efforts. Accordingly, we are going to look for preferred model functions resulting from suitable preference orderings $\prec$ over $\kappa\pi$-constructions.

- $Pref(\Delta) = Min_{\prec}(Mod_{\kappa\pi^+}(\Delta))$.

The idea is to prefer those $\kappa\pi$-constructions with the highest inherent plausibility and requiring the lowest construction efforts. To determine appropriate preference relations $\prec$, we are going to exploit four intuitive informal guidelines which reflect different faces of this *minimal construction philosophy.* The first principle restricts the collection of shiftable propositions, the second one maximizes the plausibility of R_σ lexicographically, the third one minimizes at each level the local shifting efforts, and the fourth one attacks shifting redundancy. So, let $\{R(A'_i) + s_i \leq R(A_i) \mid i \leq n\}$ be the set of constraints resulting from a finite default base Δ and σ be a $\kappa\pi$-construction. In the examples, we assume that the propositions A, A', B are logically independent.

P1. Minimizing evidence.
The set of shiftable propositions S_σ should be minimized, i.e. restricted to the exceptional areas from the defaults given in Δ ($P \wedge \neg P' \in S_\sigma$ iff $P \Rightarrow^s P' \in \Delta$).

This is a simple structural parsimony principle. For instance, $\sigma_1 = 2A$ is preferable to $\sigma_2 = 1A{+}0B$, although $R_{\sigma_2}(A) < R_{\sigma_1}(A)$. Furthermore, $\sigma_1 = 1\neg A{+}1\neg B$ is a better model of $\Delta = \{T \Rightarrow A, T \Rightarrow B\}$ than $\sigma_2 = 0.5\neg A{+}0.5\neg B{+}0.5(\neg A \wedge B) + 0.5(A \wedge \neg B)$. In fact, without this requirement, our approach would be indistinguishable from pure normality maximization, i.e. mishandle exceptional inheritance.

P2. Minimizing surprise.
$\kappa\pi$-constructions making more propositions less surprising should be preferable. This means minimizing the set of shiftable – or at least effectively shifted ($a_i \neq 0$) – propositions A_i arriving at any given rank s, i.e. verifying $R_\sigma(A_i) \geq s$. Because increasing the degree of surprise of more plausible propositions has a higher informational impact than doing so for less plausible ones, we should start minimization at the bottom and proceed lexicographically.

For instance, we should prefer $\sigma_1 = 1(A \vee B) + 0A + 2(A \wedge B)$ to $\sigma_2 = 1(A \vee B) + 1A + 0(A \wedge B)$ because $sur_{\sigma_1}(2) = \{A \wedge B\} \subset \{A, A \wedge B\} = sur_{\sigma_2}(2)$. This principle strengthens and adapts the classical normality maximization philosophy to the epistemic construction framework.

P3. Minimizing shifting.
The length of shifting moves aimed at pushing propositions to a given rank should be minimized, starting with the longest, most costly ones, before proceeding lexicographically towards the shorter ones.

For instance, we should prefer $\sigma_1 = 1A{+}1B{+}1(A{\vee}B)$ to $\sigma_2 = 2A{+}2B{+}0(A{\vee}B)$. Although $R_{\sigma_i}(A) = R_{\sigma_i}(B) = R_{\sigma_i}(A \vee B) = 2$, σ_2 should be rejected because it uses longer shifting moves (of length $2 > 1$) to reach rank 2. This requirement reflects the minimal effort philosophy locally. It takes into account that the evaluation of efforts is best done relative to a specific task in a specific context, here to build up a particular ranking level. It supports uniqueness, which would fail if we maximized the shorter moves.

P4. Justifiable constructibility (w.r.t. Δ).
There should be no unjustified, redundant shifting moves w.r.t. the satisfaction of the ranking constraints from Δ. That is, a shifting of A_i may only occur – in other words $0 < a_i$ – if there is no oversatisfaction, i.e. if we do not only have $R_\sigma(A'_i) + s_i \leq R_\sigma(A_i)$, but even $R_\sigma(A'_i) + s_i = R_\sigma(A_i)$. Note that justifiable constructibility has to be evaluated w.r.t. a specific Δ.

For instance, if $\Delta = \{T \Rightarrow A, T \Rightarrow^2 A \wedge A'\}$, we get the constraints $\{R(\neg A) \geq 1, R(\neg A \vee \neg A') \geq 2\}$. Then $\sigma_1 = 2(\neg A \vee \neg A') + 0\neg A$ is preferred to $\sigma_2 = 2(\neg A \vee \neg A') + 1\neg A$. In fact, because $R_{\sigma_1}(A \wedge A') + 2 = R_{\sigma_2}(A \wedge A') + 2 = 2 = R_{\sigma_1}(\neg A \vee \neg A') = R_{\sigma_2}(\neg A \vee \neg A')$, whereas $R_{\sigma_1}(A) + 1 = 1 < 2 = R_{\sigma_1}(\neg A)$ and $R_{\sigma_2}(A) + 1 = 1 < 3 = R_{\sigma_2}(\neg A)$. That is, the shifting of $\neg A$ is redundant and only σ_1 is justifiably constructible.

5 JLX-Entailment

In this section, we exploit the first three principles to build a $\kappa\pi$-construction ordering $\prec_{jlx}$. Starting with S_σ (**P1**), the general idea is to proceed lexicographically and bottom-up, minimizing at any given rank s, first the set of shiftable propositions arriving at s, secondly the local shifting efforts directed at reaching s. More precisely, when comparing two $\kappa\pi$-constructions σ_1, σ_2, we look for the first rank s where the shifting moves diverge and pick up the one with the smaller cumulative surprise set $sur_{\sigma_i}(s)$ (**P2**). If the $sur_{\sigma_i}(s)$ don't differ, we concentrate on the common active rank s part, i.e. $sur_{\sigma_i}(s) - sur^+_{1,2}$, where $sur^+_{1,2} = sur^+_{\sigma_1}(s) \cup sur^+_{\sigma_2}(s)$. In this context, we choose the σ_i with the set-theoretically smallest set of shifts $sh^+_{\sigma_i}(s,h) = sh_{\sigma_i}(s,h) - sur^+_{1,2}$ at the largest shifting length h where they split, i.e. where $sh^+_{\sigma_1}(s,h) \neq sh^+_{\sigma_2}(s,h)$ (**P3**).

Definition 51 (Construction order)
Let σ_1, σ_2 be $\kappa\pi$-constructions and $\mathcal{S}_{\sigma_1}, \mathcal{S}_{\sigma_2}$ be the corresponding sets of shiftable propositions. Then $\sigma_1 \prec_{jlx} \sigma_2$ iff

- $\mathcal{S}_{\sigma_1} \subset \mathcal{S}_{\sigma_2}$, *or*
- $\mathcal{S}_{\sigma_1} = \mathcal{S}_{\sigma_2}$ *and for* $s = Min\{s' \in [0,\infty] \mid \exists h\ sh^+_{\sigma_1}(s',h) \neq sh^+_{\sigma_2}(s',h)\}$,
  - $sur_{\sigma_1}(s) \subset sur_{\sigma_2}(s)$, *or*
  - $sur_{\sigma_1}(s) = sur_{\sigma_2}(s)$, $s \neq \infty$ *and for*
    $h = Max\{h' \mid sh^+_{\sigma_1}(s,h') \neq sh^+_{\sigma_2}(s,h')\}$, $\quad sh^+_{\sigma_1}(s,h) \subset sh^+_{\sigma_2}(s,h)$.

It is clear that $\prec_{jlx}$ is a partial order. To see how it works, we may illustrate its specification with some examples (**P1**: 1, **P2**: 2, 3, **P3**: 4).

1. $3(A \vee B) \prec_{jlx} 1A + 1B + 1(A \vee B)$ – because $\{A \vee B\} \subset \{A, B, A \vee B\}$.
2. $1A + 3B \prec_{jlx} 2A + 2B$ – because $sur_{\sigma_1}(2) = \{B\} \subset \{A, B\} = sur_{\sigma_2}(2)$.
3. $1A + 2B$, $2A + 1B$ are incomparable – because $\{A\} \not\subset \{B\}, \{B\} \not\subset A$.
4. $2A + 2B + 2(A \vee B) \prec_{jlx} 3A + 3B + 1(A \vee B)$ – for $2 < 3$, $\emptyset \subset \{A, B\}$.

What makes the $\kappa\pi$-construction-ordering $\prec_{jlx}$ particularly attractive is the existence of a canonical minimal $\kappa\pi$+-model for each consistent finite default base.

Theorem 52 (Canonicity)
Let $\Delta \subseteq \mathcal{L}(\Rightarrow)$ be finite and consistent. Then there is a single $\prec_{jlx}$-minimum $\sigma \models_{\kappa\pi+} \Delta$. We set $JLX[\Delta] = R_\sigma$.

This gives us the following preferential default entailment relation.

Definition 53 (JLX-entailment)
Let $\Sigma \cup \{\psi\} \subseteq \mathcal{L}$, $\varphi_\Sigma = \wedge\Sigma$, and $\Delta \subseteq \mathcal{L}(\Rightarrow)$ be finite and consistent.

- $\Sigma \cup \Delta \mid\!\sim^{jlx} \psi$ *iff* $JLX[\Delta](\neg\psi|\varphi_\Sigma) > 0$.

Obviously, $\mid\!\sim^{jlx}_{\Delta}$ is a rational inference relation in the sense of Lehmann. Its main strengths are the existence of a transparent preferential semantics, its adherence to the minimal construction philosophy, its combination of the epistemic construction paradigm with normality maximization, and its verification of relevant inference patterns. Let us discuss some examples. As a warm-up, we consider the exceptional inheritance pattern. So, let Δ_1 be a default base telling us that birds normally fly and that birds are normally small (big = non-small).

- $\Delta_1 = \{B \Rightarrow F, B \Rightarrow S\}$.

We want to determine JLX[Δ_1]. Obviously, the set of shiftable propositions is $\mathcal{S}_1 = \{B \wedge \neg F, B \wedge \neg S\}$. Accordingly, the JLX-construction has the form

- $x(B \wedge \neg F) + y(B \wedge \neg S)$ for some $x, y \geq 0$.

The corresponding ranking constraints are $R(B \wedge F) + 1 \leq R(B \wedge \neg F)$ and $R(B \wedge S) + 1 \leq R(B \wedge \neg S)$. It is clear that for $s \in]0,1]$, $sur_1(s) = \{B \wedge \neg F, B \wedge \neg S\}$. Obviously, the best possible solution is then to have $sur_1(s) = \emptyset$ for all $s \in]1, \infty]$, i.e. shifting minimization becomes obsolete.

- $\text{JLX}[\Delta_1] = R_0 + 1(B \wedge \neg S) + 1(B \wedge \neg F)$.

It follows that $\{B \wedge \neg S\} \cup \Delta_1 \mid\!\sim^{jlx} F$. A more sophisticated example is the big birds hammer (BBH), where we add to Δ_1 the default that unusual – non-flying or big – birds normally don't fly.

- $\Delta_2 = \{B \Rightarrow F, B \Rightarrow S, B \wedge (\neg F \vee \neg S) \Rightarrow \neg F\}$.

What we want to know is whether big birds normally fly and non-flying birds are normally small. The intuitive answer seems to be that big birds normally don't fly, whereas we cannot assume that non-flying birds are normally small. That is, we would expect from a suitable $\mid\!\sim$ that

- $\{B \wedge \neg S\} \cup \Delta_2 \mid\!\sim \neg F$ and $\{B \wedge \neg F\} \cup \Delta_2 \not\mid\!\sim S$.

Interestingly, the traditional proposals either satisfy the big birds hammer (system Z) or the exceptional inheritance requirement (Lehmann's lexicographic closure, Geffner's conditional entailment), but not both. Fortunately, our minimal construction strategy is more successful. So, let us compute JLX[Δ_2]($F|B \wedge \neg S$) and JLX[Δ_2]($\neg S|B \wedge \neg F$). The set of shiftable propositions is $\mathcal{S}_2 = \{B \wedge \neg F, B \wedge \neg S, B \wedge \neg S \wedge F\}$. Thus, the JLX-construction takes the form

- $x(B \wedge \neg F) + y(B \wedge \neg S) + z(B \wedge \neg S \wedge F)$.

The ranking constraints resulting from Δ_2 include those from Δ_1 together with $R(B \wedge \neg F) + 1 \leq R(B \wedge \neg S \wedge F)$. For $s \in]0,1]$, we have $sur_2(s) = \{B \wedge \neg F, B \wedge \neg S, B \wedge \neg S \wedge F\}$. It is easy to see that we realize the best surprise minimization if $sur_2(s) = \{B \wedge \neg S \wedge F\}$ for $s \in]1,2]$ and $sur_2(s) = \emptyset$ for $s \in]2,\infty]$. This requires $R(B \wedge \neg F) = R(B \wedge \neg S) = 1$ and $R(B \wedge \neg S \wedge F) = 2$, which entails $x = 1, y = 0, z = 2$ and

- $\mathrm{JLX}[\Delta_2] = R_0 + 1(B \wedge \neg F) + 2(B \wedge \neg S \wedge F)$.

That is, $\mathrm{JLX}[\Delta_2](F|B \wedge \neg S) = 1$ and $\mathrm{JLX}[\Delta_2](\neg S|B \wedge \neg F) = 0$, which meets our expectations. To see shifting minimization in action, we may consider the following example, which will also shed light on justifiable constructibility.

- $\Delta_3 = \{T \Rightarrow^2 A \wedge B, T \Rightarrow A, T \Rightarrow B\}$.

Δ_3 induces the constraints $\{R(\neg A \vee \neg B) \geq 2, R(\neg A) \geq 1, R(\neg B) \geq 1\}$. The best possible cumulative surprise scenario is given by $sur_3(s) = \{\neg A \vee \neg B, \neg A, \neg B\}$ for $s \in]0,2]$ and $sur_3(s) = \emptyset$ for $s \in]2,\infty]$. In this context, the unique $\kappa\pi+$-model minimizing the shifting lengths is $1(\neg A \vee \neg B) + 1\neg A + 1\neg B$. That is

- $\mathrm{JLX}[\Delta_3] = R_0 + 1(\neg A \vee \neg B) + 1\neg A + 1\neg B$.

For instance, $\{\neg A\} \cup \Delta_3 \mid\!\sim^{jlx} B$. Like system JZ, JLX-entailment also validates basic inferential invariance features [Weydert 98].

Theorem 54 (Inferential invariance)
JLX verifies representation independence and minimum irrelevance.

6 JLX and JZ

Our fourth minimal construction principle is justifiable constructibility, which was first discussed, in a slightly different formal context, in [Weydert 96]. This is an important notion, which is also backed by the information-minimization philosophy [Weydert 98].

Definition 61 (Justifiable constructibility)
σ is a justifiably constructible $\kappa\pi+$-model w.r.t. $\Delta = \{A_i \Rightarrow^{s_i} A'_i \mid i \leq n\}$ iff

- $\sigma = \Sigma_{i \leq n} a_i (A_i \wedge \neg A_i) \models_{\kappa\pi+} \Delta$,
- $0 < a_i$ *implies* $R_\sigma(A_i \wedge A'_i) + s_i = R_\sigma(A_i \wedge \neg A'_i)$.

$JMod_{\kappa\pi+}(\Delta)$ is the set of justifiably constructible models w.r.t. Δ .

The JZ-construction procedure sanctions the following result.

Theorem 62 (Existence)
$Mod_{\kappa\pi}(\Delta) \neq \emptyset$ implies $JMod_{\kappa\pi+}(\Delta) \neq \emptyset$.

Justifiable constructibility and $\prec_{jlx}$-minimization represent different faces of the minimal construction philosophy. To clarify their relationship, consider our earlier example $\Delta_3 = \{T \Rightarrow^2 A \wedge B, T \Rightarrow A, T \Rightarrow B\}$. It is not difficult to see that $R(\neg A \vee \neg B) \geq 2$ has to be satisfied as an equality constraint, whereas $R(\neg A) \geq 1$ and $R(\neg B) \geq 1$ are necessarily oversatisfied, i.e. they do not sanction shiftings of $\neg A$ and $\neg B$. Consequently, $2(\neg A \vee \neg B) + 0\neg A + 0\neg B$ is the only justifiably constructible $\kappa\pi$+-model of Δ_3, which therefore corresponds to the JZ-model. It clearly differs from the JLX-model $1(\neg A \vee \neg B) + 1\neg A + 1\neg B$. So we see that $\prec_{jlx}$-minimality does not guarantee justifiable constructibility.

In fact, this example illustrates another interesting peculiarity of justifiable constructibility. Consider $\Delta_4 = \{T \Rightarrow A \wedge B, T \Rightarrow^2 A, T \Rightarrow^2 B\}$. Although Δ_4 has exactly the same $\kappa\pi$+-models as Δ_3, we have

- $JMod_{\kappa\pi+}(\Delta_4) = \{0(\neg A \vee \neg B) + 2\neg A + 2\neg B\} \neq$
  $JMod_{\kappa\pi+}(\Delta_3) = \{2(\neg A \vee \neg B) + 0\neg A + 0\neg B\}$.

That is, we cannot always determine $JMod_{\kappa\pi+}(\Delta)$ from $Mod_{\kappa\pi+}(\Delta)$, we may have to exploit Δ itself. Our construction semantics is not fine-grained enough to fully grasp justifiable constructibility. It follows that system JZ cannot be defined by minimizing a global preference order over $\kappa\pi$-constructions, which could only exploit $Mod_{\kappa\pi+}(\Delta)$. Although system JZ and JLX-entailment share standard structural and inferential features, we see that there are also substantial differences. So, we may distinguish at least two major minimal construction traditions in default reasoning. One possibility to bridge the gap between these approaches would be to combine them by restricting $\prec_{jlx}$-minimization to justifiably constructible $\kappa\pi$+-models. Surprisingly, this doesn't bring us anything new.

Theorem 63 (Equivalence JZ - JJLX)
Let $\Delta \subseteq \mathcal{L}(\Rightarrow)$ be a finite consistent default base. Then the JZ-construction is the unique $\prec_{jlx}$-minimal justifiably constructible $\kappa\pi$+-model of Δ.

This result gives us a transparent – although not $\kappa\pi$+-invariant – (partial) preferential semantics for system JZ. The main conclusion of this paper is that there are – at least but presumably not more than – two major implementations of the minimal construction philosophy, JLX-entailment and system JZ. Thus, system JZ is slightly less hegemonial than we have thought. Both represent natural powerful rational default entailment notions exhibiting nice features. Further research will show which one offers the most reasonable default conclusions.

References

Bourne, Parsons 99 R. Bourne, S. Parsons. Maximum entropy and variable strength defaults. In *Proc. of IJCAI 99.* Morgan Kaufmann, 1999.

Goldszmidt et al. 93 M. Goldszmidt, P. Morris, J. Pearl. A maximum entropy approach to nonmonotonic reasoning. *IEEE Transactions of Pattern Analysis and Machine Intelligence*, 15:220-232, 1993.

Dubois, Prade 88 D. Dubois, H. Prade. *Possibility Theory*. Plenum Press, New York 1988.

Geffner, Pearl 92 H. Geffner, J. Pearl. Conditional entailment : bridging two approaches to default reasoning. In *Artificial Intelligence*, 53: 209 - 244, 1992.

Kern-Isberner 01 G. Kern-Isberner. *Conditionals in nonmonotonic reasoning and belief revision*. Springer LNAI, 2001.

Kraus et al. 90 S. Kraus, D. Lehmann, M. Magidor. Nonmonotonic reasoning, preferential models and cumulative logics. *Artificial Intelligence*, 44:167-207, 1990.

Lehmann 95 D. Lehmann. Another perspective on default reasoning. *Annals of Mathematics and Artificial Intelligence*: 15(1), 1995.

Lehmann, Magidor 92 D. Lehmann, M. Magidor. What does a conditional knowledge base entail? *Artificial Intelligence* 55:1-60, 1992.

Pearl 90 J. Pearl. System Z: a natural ordering of defaults with tractable applications to nonmonotonic reasoning. In *Proc. of the Third Conference on Theoretical Aspects of Reasoning about Knowledge*. Morgan Kaufmann, 1990.

Spohn 88 W. Spohn. Ordinal conditional functions: a dynamic theory of epistemic states. In *Causation in Decision, Belief Change, and Statistics*, W.L. Harper, B. Skyrms (eds.), Kluwer, 1988.

Spohn 90 W. Spohn. A general non-probabilistic theory of inductive reasoning. In *Uncertainty in Artificial Intelligence 4*, North-Holland, 1990.

Weydert 95 E. Weydert. Defaults and infinitesimals. Defeasible inference by non-archimdean entropy maximization. In *Proc. of UIA 95*. Morgan Kaufmann, 1995.

Weydert 96 E. Weydert. System J – Revision entailment. In *Proc. of FAPR 96*, Springer, 1996.

Weydert 98 E. Weydert. System JZ – How to build a canonical ranking model of a default knowledge base. In *Proc. of KR 98*. Morgan Kaufmann, 1998.

Formalizing Human Uncertain Reasoning with Default Rules: A Psychological Conundrum and a Pragmatic Suggestion

Jean-François Bonnefon and Denis J. Hilton

Dynamiques Socio-Cognitives et Vie Politique, Université Toulouse-2,
5 allées Antonio Machado, 34058 Toulouse Cedex, France
{bonnefon, hilton}@univ-tlse2.fr

Abstract. The suppression of Modus Ponens by the introduction of a second conditional is introduced as a result relevant both to psychologists and to AI researchers interested in default reasoning. Some psychological considerations on the explanation of this effect, together with (a) their tentative formalisation within the framework of default logic, and (b) recent experimental results from the present authors, lead to the conclusion that our understanding of ordinary human default reasoning would benefit from considering the existence of a specific class of conditional statements, with the pragmatic status of "preconditionals".

1 Introduction

Whereas default rules and the handling of their exceptions have long been central issues for Artificial Intelligence researchers interested in formalizing human reasoning, psychologists have only recently embraced the task of investigating human default reasoning: Psychologists used to consider that human reasoners may treat a conditional either as a material implication or as a biconditional, but neglected the default, exception-flawed nature of most everyday conditionals (see [1] for a review). Things have changed, however, and during the past 10 years many studies have addressed human reasoning with exception-flawed conditionals. Yet, one paradoxical aspect of this situation is that (a) many notions that have flourished in the psychology of default reasoning straightforwardly stem (perhaps unsurprisingly) from one of the best established exception-handling formalism, Reiter's default logic [2], whereas (b) most of these notions were introduced in order to explain a rather intriguing result that default logic would have difficulty in accounting for, the so-called "suppression of Modus Ponens".

In the first section hereafter, this result is introduced first in its original form, which is more closely related to non-monotonic reasoning, then in later forms which highlight its relevance to uncertain reasoning. It is argued that a satisfying formalisation of human reasoning should be able to reflect such a robust and general inferential behaviour.

Next, some psychological accounts of the suppression of Modus Ponens are briefly (and partially) summarised: It is argued that a formalisation of these accounts in the

S. Benferhat and P. Besnard (Eds.): ECSQARU 2001, LNAI 2143, pp. 628–634, 2001.

framework of default logic (as the formalism from which these accounts have the most acquaintance) clearly demonstrate that the effect cannot be accounted for without appealing to some pragmatic considerations on the way people interpret conditional assertions. Then, building on recent results by the present authors, the case is made for the existence of a very specific class of conditional assertions (dubbed preconditionals) which function is to unconditionally suggest that the justification (in Reiter's sense) of a default is not met, which in turn inhibits the derivation of a Modus Ponens inference.

2 The Suppression of Modus Ponens

Modus Ponens is certainly one of the most basic, automatic inferences the human mind can draw (on this subject, see [3]). Generations of participants in reasoning experiments have been proposed premises like "if the ignition key is turned, then the car will start ; the ignition key is turned" – and these participants have always almost unanimously declared that what followed was "the car will start".

However, Byrne [4] first discovered that this very basic inference could be "suppressed" (blocked, inhibited...) by the introduction of an additional, seemingly innocuous premise. Consider the following set of premises:

"If the ignition key is turned, then the car will start;
If there is gas in the tank, then the car will start;
The ignition key is turned."

When presented with this set of premises, less than 40% of reasoners would derive the conclusion that the car will start: Without any sound logical reason, but in an intuitively appealing way, people refrain from applying Modus Ponens to the first and third premises of the set when, as we shall see in the next section, the antecedent of the second conditional is a justification of the first (default) conditional.

This result may seem more closely related to nonmonotonic reasoning than to uncertain reasoning per se, but it has been quickly reframed in the field of uncertain reasoning: Various authors (e.g., [5], [6], [7], [8]) demonstrated that while reasoners rated the conclusion of the standard Modus Ponens argument as highly certain, they rated this same conclusion significantly less certain when presented with the 3-premise set.

The suppression of Modus Ponens, either in its nonmonotonic framing or in its uncertainty framing, has proven impressively robust trough a large number of replications using different thematic contents. The suppression of Modus Ponens by the introduction of an additional conditional is undoubtedly robust, general, and routinely observed. Moreover, people that refrain from applying Modus Ponens have strong confidence in the fact that they are not committing any reasoning mistake. Indeed, there is strong intuitive appeal in refraining from applying Modus Ponens to the 3-premise set above. Anyway, whether this inferential behaviour is desirable or not, one would expect a satisfying formalisation of human reasoning to be able to account for such a general and robust psychological observation.

In the following, the symbols α, β, and γ will be used to designate the predicates involved in the premise set that leads to the suppression of Modus Ponens. Thus, the complete premise set will be noted:

If α (x) then γ (x) ,
If β (x) then γ (x) ,
α (x) .

The car-starting example above will be noted:

If Turn key (car) then Start (car) ,
If Gas (car) then Start (car) ,
Turnkey (car) .

3 Psychological Accounts and Their Possible Formalisation

Whatever their subsequent theoretical options, most reasoning researchers interested in the suppression of Modus Ponens could be said to agree on at least one point, namely the peculiar nature of the antecedent of the second conditional. In brief, β is such that were β (x) to be false, γ (x) could not be true whatever the truth-value of α (x), although the occurrence of α (x) is usually considered sufficient to lead to the occurrence of γ (x).

In order to illustrate this agreement, it is briefly outlined below how this point is made in two of the most recent contending accounts of the suppression of Modus Ponens. Then, a straightforward formalisation of this claim in the framework of default logic is proposed.

3.1 The Nature of the Second Antecedent

[5] and [9] have in common a pragmatic approach of the suppression of Modus Ponens, some details of which are presented in Section 4. Suffice it to say for now that they consider β (x) as a requirement for γ (x) to be possible, to the difference of α (x): In other words, β (x) is a necessary condition of γ (x), whereas α (x) is one of the potential causes of γ (x). (No car will start without gas in its tank, and fortunately cars do not start just because there is some gas in their tank, but when there is gas in the tank, one may start the car either by turning the ignition key or, e.g., by hotwiring.) The occurrence of α (x) is typically said to lead to the occurrence of γ (x) because the necessary condition β (x) is usually part of the background assumptions that hold when it is asserted that “if α (x) then γ (x)”. (When one asserts that “if you turn the key, then the car will start”, everybody would usually assume that there is gas in the tank.) In [9] β (x) is called a “Complementary Necessary Condition” of γ (x). Much to the same effect, the term “precondition” is used in [5] to designate β (x).

Although the view that is adopted in [10] to the suppression of Modus Ponens is very different to the one advocated independently in [5] and [9], the key suggestion in [10] seems to imply the same assumption about the peculiar nature of β (x). It is suggested in [10] that Modus Ponens is blocked because the second conditional make readily available to reasoners a counterexample situation to the first conditional, namely the situation where α (x) is true but γ (x) is false because β (x) is false. Clearly, this only makes sense if reasoners consider that the falsity of β (x) leads to the falsity of γ (x) whatever the truth-value of α (x). One has reasons to consider that the situation where a car has no gas in its tank provides a counterexample to the rule "if the ignition key is turned, then the car will start" only if one believes that the lack of gas makes it impossible to start a car whatever actions are taken regarding turning the key.

3.2 Default Logic and the Suppression of Modus Ponens

Keeping in mind the nature of the second antecedent as considered in Section 3.1., what would be a satisfying formal transcription of the 3-premise set? Like most everyday conditionals, the rule "if the ignition key is turned, then the car will start" is flawed with exceptions. Without the need to specify what these exceptions could be, we can take into account their possible occurrence by expressing the first premise as a normal default:

$$\frac{\text{Turnkey (car) : Start (car)}}{\text{Start (car)}} \tag{1}$$

Such a transcription would be inappropriate for the second premise, since the second conditional does not express a default. Yet, one striking feature of the psychological suggestions in Section 3.1. is that the characteristics assigned to β (x) precisely make it the *justification* of a default that would have α (x) as its prerequisite and γ (x) as its consequent. Hence, the most straightforward way to translate these suggestions might be to consider that the second premise, rather than expressing a new default, is introducing variation of the first, a general default of the form:

$$\frac{\text{Turnkey (car) : Gas (car)}}{\text{Start (car)}} \tag{2}$$

The 3-premise set:
If α (x) then γ (x) ,
If β (x) then γ (x) ,
α (x) ,
would then turn into the three formulas:

$$\frac{\alpha(x) : \gamma(x)}{\gamma(x)} \tag{3}$$

$$\frac{\alpha(x) : \beta(x)}{\gamma(x)} \tag{4}$$

$$\alpha(x)\,. \tag{5}$$

Is the suppression of Modus Ponens accounted for by such a formal transcription? It is not, for $\gamma(x)$ is still a conclusion that follows from the three formulas above. The second conditional has been taken as specifying a counterexample situation to the first, i.e., as replacing the "normal" justification $\gamma(x)$ in the first default by the newly-specified justification $\beta(x)$. However, the two defaults make no other restriction on the derivation of $\gamma(x)$ from $\alpha(x)$ than to ensure that nothing in the knowledge base is inconsistent with either $\gamma(x)$ or $\beta(x)$. Were there any reason to consider that $\beta(x)$ is untrue, the conclusion $\gamma(x)$ would be blocked. Since there is no information represented here about $\beta(x)$, $\beta(x)$ has to be considered true, hence the derivation of $\gamma(x)$.

The derivation of $\gamma(x)$ would only be blocked if some information was available that would hint at the non-satisfaction of the justification $\beta(x)$. As a consequence, if the suppression of Modus Ponens is to be explained in the general framework of default logic, what is needed is some insight on how some information regarding the falsity of $\beta(x)$ could be conveyed by the 3 premise-set. Are there any experimental results that would support the view that some information regarding the falsity of $\beta(x)$ is indeed embedded in the 3-premise set? This issue is dealt with in the next section.

4 Recent Empirical Results : Preconditional Statements

Whereas common world knowledge makes it obvious that the presence of gas in the tank is a necessary (and not a sufficient) condition for the car to start, the assertion "if there is gas in the tank, then the car will start" seems to give the presence of gas a different status: one of sufficiency, one of causality. This discordance between the ordinary role of gas (as a background necessary condition for the car to start) and the specific role the conditional syntax seems to grant it (as a sufficient factor for the car to start, a factor that would explain the starting of the car) is important because empirical research has demonstrated that people usually avoid explaining events by appealing to their necessary conditions : Necessary conditions (e.g., presence of gas) are ordinarily considered infelicitous explanations of an event (e.g., a car starting). (See e.g., [11] and [12].)

Yet there is one particular situation where necessary conditions are considered relevant explanations of an event: Situations where the necessary condition is not readily available, cannot be presupposed, or is not easily satisfied (as demonstrated in [13] and [14]). For example, saying that "Mr X. ate because there was food available" is more felicitous than to say "Mr X. ate because he was hungry" in the situation where Mr X. is a refugee who had been starving for three weeks due to lack of food. As a consequence, it is conceivable that asserting "if there is gas in the tank then the car will start" (i.e., explaining the starting of the car by the satisfaction of a background requirement) would only make sense if the presence of gas was not readily available, or could not be presupposed.

From these considerations together with some elements of conversational pragmatics, two experimental predictions are derived in [5]. First, that most people, if the 3-premise set was presented to them as a conversation, would recognise the intention of the second conditional: that is, conveying doubts on the satisfaction of the requirement $\beta(x)$. Second, that those people that did recognise the intention would manifest low confidence in the conclusion $\gamma(x)$, whereas those people that did not recognise the intention would not decrease their certainty in $\gamma(x)$ as compared to the certainty they would grant it from a standard Modus Ponens argument.

It is reported in [5] that 60 students were presented with different Modus Ponens premises (either in standard form or within 3-premise set). The students had to (a) rate on a 7-point scale (from "no chance to be true" to "certainly true") the confidence they had in the occurrence of $\gamma(x)$, and (b) to say if, in their opinion, the locutor asserting the second conditional wished to convey the idea that chances were for $\beta(x)$ not to be true.

When asked if the second conditional of a 3-premise set was intended to convey the idea that chances were for $\beta(x)$ not to be true, almost 80% of participants answered affirmatively. More importantly, participants that recognised this intention granted the conclusion $\gamma(x)$ a mean certainty of 3.62 (on a 7-point scale), whereas participants that did not recognize the intention granted this conclusion a certainty of 5.46. As a standard to compare those ratings with, the mean certainty granted to conclusions of standard Modus Ponens arguments was 5.57.

People that did not see any specific information regarding the truth-value of $\beta(x)$ in the second conditional applied Modus Ponens as they would have done without the second conditional. But most people take the second conditional not only as specifying a justification $\beta(x)$ to the default rule "if $\alpha(x)$ then $\gamma(x)$", but also to convey some information hinting at the non-satisfaction of the justification $\beta(x)$. Thus, this majority of reasoners seems to interpret the 3-premise set the following way:

$$\frac{\alpha(x) : \gamma(x)}{\gamma(x)} \tag{3}$$

$$\frac{\alpha(x) : \beta(x)}{\gamma(x)} \tag{4}$$

$$\neg\beta(x)\,. \tag{6}$$

$$\alpha(x)\,. \tag{5}$$

From this set of formulas, the conclusion $\gamma(x)$ is no longer derivable. Thus, the suppression of Modus Ponens could be explained, and this explanation formalised, if it was agreed on the existence of a specific class of conditional assertions that will be called here "preconditional statements".

Preconditionals are statement of conditional syntax like "if $\beta(x)$ then $\gamma(x)$", where $\beta(x)$ is known from implicit knowledge to be a requirement for $\gamma(x)$ to happen. Despite their conditional syntax, preconditionals do not make any conditional claim: They unconditionally suggest that their antecedent $\beta(x)$ is untrue. Indeed, preconditionals do not serve the same function as regular conditionals, nor do they obey the same rules: They form a class of assertions that is pragmatically distinct from the class of regular conditionals. To consider their existence could be the decisive step into solving the logical riddle of the suppression of Modus Ponens by lay reasoners, and a promising step into formalising ordinary human default reasoning.

References

1. Evans, J. St.B. T., Newstead, S. E., & Byrne, R. M. J. : Human Reasoning. Hillsdale, NJ: Lawrence Erlbaum Associates (1993)
2. Reiter, R. : A logic for default reasoning. Artificial Intelligence 13 (1980) 81-132
3. Smith, E. E., Langston, C., & Nisbett, R. : The case for rules in reasoning. Cognitive Science 16 (1992) 1-40
4. Byrne, R. M. J. : Suppressing valid inferences with conditionals. Cognition 31 (1989) 61-83
5. Bonnefon, J.F., & Hilton, D. J. : The suppression of Modus Ponens as a case of pragmatic preconditional reasoning. Accepted subject to revision, Thinking & Reasoning (2001)
6. Liu, I., Lo, K., & Wu, J. : A probabilistic interpretation of "If-then". Quarterly Journal of Experimental Psychology 49A (1996) 828-844
7. Politzer, G. & Bourmeau, G. : Deductive reasoning with uncertain conditionals. Manuscript submitted for publication (2001)
8. Stevenson, R. J., & Over, D. E. : Deduction from uncertain premises. Quarterly Journal of Experimental Psychology 48A (1995) 613-643
9. Politzer, G. : Premise Interpretation in Conditional Reasoning. To appear in : D. Hardman and L. Macchi (Eds.): Reasoning and Decision Making: A Handbook. Chichester: Wiley (2001)
10. Byrne, R. M. J., Espino, O., et Santamaria, C. : Counterexamples and the suppression of inferences. Journal of Memory and Language 40 (1999) 347-373
11. Leddo, J., Abelson, R. P., & Gross, P. H. : Conjunctive explanations: When two reasons are better than one. Journal of Personality and Social Psychology 47 (1984) 933-943
12. McClure, J. L., Lalljee, M., Jaspars, J., & Abelson, R. P. : Conjunctive explanations of success and failure: The effects of different types of causes. Journal of Personality and Social Psychology 56 (1989) 19-26
13. McClure, J. L., & Hilton, D. J. : For you can't always get what you want: When preconditions are better explanations than goals. British Journal of Social Psychology 36 (1997) 223-240
14. McClure, J. L., & Hilton, D. J. : Are goals or preconditions better explanations? It depends on the question. European Journal of Social Psychology 28 (1998) 897-911.

Statistical Information, Uncertainty, and Bayes' Theorem: Some Applications in Experimental Psychology

Donald Laming

University of Cambridge, Department of Experimental Psychology, Downing Street, Cambridge, England CB2 3EB.
E-mail: drjl@cus.cam.ac.uk

Abstract. This paper contains, first, a brief formal exploration of the relationships between information (statistically defined), statistical hypothesis testing, the channel capacity of a communication system, and uncertainty. Thereafter several applications of these ideas in experimental psychology are examined. The applications are grouped under "Mathematical theories that are not matched to the psychological task", "The human observer treated as a physical system", and "Bayes' theorem".

1 Introduction

The notion of information has entered experimental psychology through two, quite distinct, points of entry. The first was a paper by Miller and Frick [20] that introduced Shannon's [25] communication theory to a psychological audience. Garner [2, p. 8 *et seq.*] has charted the explosive impact that those ideas had within psychology. The second was through signal detection [29]. Without using the label 'information', these authors transposed the "Theory of signal detectability" [24] into sensory discrimination, and the "Theory of signal detectability" stands in a direct line of intellectual descent from the Neyman-Pearson Lemma [21; see 15].

Notwithstanding that within psychology these two traditions have evolved in complete independence from each other, their intellectual foundations are closely related. The first task of this account is to bring out that interrelationship as simply as possible. I then examine a number of applications within experimental psychology, some successful, others misconceived, with a view to some general conclusions, how the idea of information might profitably be exploited and what mistakes need to be guarded against.

2 Information and Uncertainty

Suppose I do an experiment and record a matrix of data X. Because this particular configuration of data will play a pivotal role in what follows, I cite, as an example in Table 1, one set of data from Experiment 4 by Braida & Durlach [1]. In this experiment 1 kHz tones of various intensities were presented for 0.5 s, one at a time,

S. Benferhat and P. Besnard (Eds.): ECSQARU 2001, LNAI 2143, pp. 635–646, 2001.

and the subject asked to identify each one in turn. The matrix in Table 1 shows the number of times each stimulus value was presented and the given identification made.

Table 1. Absolute identification of 1kHz tones with 2 dB spacing of stimulus values from Braida & Durlach [1, Expt. 4, Subj. 7]

Stimuli (dB)	Responses (dB)									
	68	70	72	74	76	78	80	82	84	86
68	120	37	8	1	0	0	0	0	0	0
70	33	74	42	15	0	0	0	0	0	0
72	8	47	76	33	10	2	0	0	0	0
74	0	8	38	73	48	10	1	0	0	0
76	0	1	9	43	108	45	9	0	0	0
78	0	0	1	9	61	77	36	3	1	0
80	0	0	0	0	7	48	58	29	1	0
82	0	0	0	0	0	5	38	74	38	1
84	0	0	0	0	0	1	6	25	115	29
86	0	0	0	0	0	0	0	3	32	123

Suppose I have a particular hypothesis about my experiment. Call that hypothesis H_0. I cannot tell whether H_0 fits my data absolutely, but I can ask whether it fits better than some other hypothesis H_1. The Neyman-Pearson Lemma [21] tells us that the optimum statistic for distinguishing H_0 from any other state of nature (H_1) is the likelihood ratio $\lambda = P(X|H_1)/P(X|H_0)$, ultimately on the principle of choosing that hypothesis which is the more likely in the light of the data.

If my experiment is not sufficiently decisive, I can repeat it to obtain two independent data matrices, X_1 and X_2. Then

$$\begin{aligned}\lambda &= P(X_1\&X_2|H_1)/P(X_1\&X_2|H_0) \\ &= [P(X_1|H_1)/P(X_1|H_0)][P(X_2|H_1)/P(X_2|H_0)],\end{aligned} \tag{1}$$

because independent probabilities multiply. Taking logarithms in Eq. 1,

$$\ln\lambda = \ln[P(X_1|H_1)/P(X_1|H_0)] + \ln[P(X_2|H_1)/P(X_2|H_0)],$$

and the expression splits into two independent parts, one for each replication of the experiment. Accordingly, it is convenient to define

$$\ln\lambda = \ln[P(X|H_1)/P(X|H_0)] \tag{2}$$

to be the information in the data matrix X in favour of hypothesis H_1 and against H_0 [9, p. 5]. Note the involvement of two hypotheses. Information is information about *something*. Data is absolute, but information is relative to the two hypotheses to be distinguished.

2.1 Testing Statistical Hypotheses

Suppose hypothesis H_0 is a special case of H_1 (some otherwise free parameters are set to zero or equal to each other). Then $\ln\lambda = \ln[P(X|H_1)/P(X|H_0)]$ is the optimum statistic for testing H_0 against all the possible states of nature encompassed by H_1. The statistic $2 \ln \lambda$ is distributed asymptotically as χ^2 [35]. Most parametric statistical tests (the analysis of variance, for example) fall out of this formulation [9], simply by inserting appropriate hypotheses H_0 and H_1 in Eq. 2. The best-known exception is Pearson's X^2.

The statistical tests in use are those for which it is feasible to calculate the distribution of the statistic when H_0 is true. As an example, suppose that H_0 asserts that the row and column classifications in Table 1 are independent; (this is manifestly false, but this is the H_0 for which the distribution of the likelihood-ratio is readily calculable). Let p_{ij} stand for the probability of some particular combination of stimulus (i) and response (j); let $p_{i\cdot}$ be the marginal probability of stimulus i, and $p_{\cdot j}$ the marginal probability of response j. Then, the hypothesis of independence is

$$H_0: \qquad p_{ij} = p_{i\cdot} \times p_{\cdot j},$$

while the alternative hypothesis (H_1) allows the probabilities of individual cells (p_{ij}) to assume any set of values that sum to unity. The probability ratio attaching to a trial in which stimulus i is presented and response j occurs is $(p_{ij}/p_{i\cdot}p_{\cdot j})$ and the average information, averaged over all combinations of stimulus and response, is

$$\Sigma_{ij}\, p_{ij} \ln(p_{ij}/p_{i\cdot}p_{\cdot j}). \tag{3}$$

In practice, the unknown probabilities (p_{ij}, $p_{i\cdot}$, and $p_{\cdot j}$) are estimated from the data and the resultant statistic gives us Wilkes' [34] likelihood-ratio test of independence in two-way contingency tables.

2.2 Channel Capacity in a Communication System

Suppose now that my experiment consists of sending messages through a communication system. As in Table 1, I record the number of times message (stimulus) i is sent and received as message (response) j. Given the resultant matrix of data (X), I ask: Is this communication channel working (with some degree of reliability, H_1) or is the line open-circuit (H_0)? The appropriate statistical test is Wilkes' [34] likelihood-ratio test of independence. If the transmission takes T s, then $\Sigma_{ij}\ p_{ij}\ln[p_{ij}/p_{i\cdot}p_{\cdot j}]/T$ is an estimate of the information transmitted per second. Depending on my choice of message ensemble (that is, of my experimental design), the information transmitted might take various values. But there is an upper limit, achieved when the experiment is optimally matched to the statistical characteristics of the channel. This upper limit is known as the *channel capacity*. Shannon [25] showed that, given an arbitrary message source, a system of encoding could always be found that afforded transmission at a rate arbitrarily close to the limiting capacity of the channel, but that this capacity limit could never be exceeded.

2.3 Uncertainty

Suppose I send a single message, selected with probability $\{p_{i\cdot}\}$ from a set of possible messages. This is received as message j. The mean information transmitted with an arbitrary selection of the message is given by Eq. 3, and that expression has a maximum value when the message received (j) identifies the message sent (i) uniquely. This happens when $p_{ij} = p_{\cdot j}$, and the maximum value is then

$$-\Sigma_i\, p_i \ln p_{i\cdot} \tag{4}$$

This expression is the uncertainty of the choice of message. But if I know that message j was received, the posterior probabilities attaching to the different inputs, calculated from Bayes' theorem, are $p_{ij}/p_{\cdot j}$, and the uncertainty (now *residual uncertainty*) is reduced to $-\Sigma_i\,(p_{ij}/p_{\cdot j})\ln(p_{ij}/p_{\cdot j})$. The residual uncertainty averaged over the different messages received is

$$-\Sigma_{ij}\, p_{ij} \ln(p_{ij}/p_{\cdot j}). \tag{5}$$

But

$$\Sigma_{ij}\, p_{ij}\ln[p_{ij}/p_{i\cdot}p_{\cdot j}] = -\Sigma_i\, p_i \ln p_i + \Sigma_{ii}\, p_{ij} \ln(p_{ij}/p_{\cdot j}); \tag{6}$$

so the information transmitted is equal to the difference between the initial (stimulus) uncertainty (Eq. 4) and the residual uncertainty (Eq. 5) given the message received.

One might, for this reason, be tempted to suppose that uncertainty is fundamental and information derivative. But suppose the input message is a normally distributed voltage (zero mean, variance σ^2) and the output similar, with correlation ρ. The information transmitted is then $-½\ln(1-\rho^2)$ [9, p. 8], irrespective of the value of σ^2, but the input uncertainty is $-½\ln(2\pi\sigma^2)-1$, which depends on the choice of σ^2. When information is calculated as a difference of uncertainties (as in Eq. 6), the scale factor (σ^2) drops out of the reckoning. Uncertainty therefore stands in relation to information as velocity potential stands in relation to velocity or voltage to current flow in an electrical circuit. Only differences in potential or voltage are significant.

3 Mathematical Theory Not Matched to the Psychological Task

It is not sufficient merely for an equation to agree with an observed result; the assumptions from which that equation is derived must also match the details of the psychological experiment.

3.1 Hick's Law

There are n equally probable stimuli (pea bulbs) arranged in a somewhat irregular circle. The subject responds as quickly as possible with a corresponding response. Hick [5] fit his own data and some historic data from Merkel [19] to the equation

$$\text{Mean R.T.} = a \ln(n+1) \tag{7}$$

in which the possibility of "no signal" was treated as an $(n+1)$th alternative. The quality of the fit is shown in Figure 1, where the abscissa is scaled according to $\ln(n+1)$. Now put $p_{i\cdot}$ equal to $1/(n+1)$ in formula 4. The stimulus uncertainty is $\ln(n+1)$, and Eq. 7 is equivalent to

$$\text{Mean R.T.} = a(\text{Stimulus uncertainty})$$

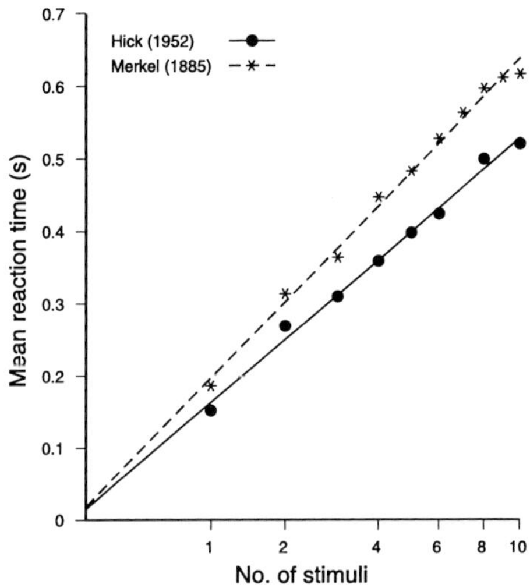

Fig. 1. Mean choice reaction times from [5] and Merkel [19] plotted against ln(n+1).

The idea here is that mean reaction time is equal to the time taken to pass a message through an ideal communication system to specify the response that needs to be made. This result, above all others, was influential in encouraging the idea that the human operator was analogous to a communication channel operating at maximum capacity. It has given us such terms as "(channel) capacity" and "encoding". But this idea will not wash. A choice-reaction experiment involves the transmission of single stimuli, one at a time, a condition that affords no opportunity for the sophisticated coding on which Shannon's theorem depends. Shannon's theory applies only to the limiting rate at which messages from a continuous source can be passed through a channel, and those messages might suffer an arbitrary delay before transmission to allow for encoding. The logarithmic formula relates only to the *length* of encoded signal required to carry the message, not to the *delay* it might suffer in transmission.

This mismatch between the assumptions of the mathematical theory and the circumstances of the experimental task has this consequence. The task becomes much more difficult if the subject is instructed to respond to the signal one, or two, or three places back in the series, notwithstanding that the task then approximates more closely the condition under which a communication channel operates efficiently; and performance collapses altogether when the response has to be produced four stimuli in arrear [7].

3.2 Wason's Selection Task

There are four cards, each of which has a letter on one side and a number on the other. Given the cards with 'A', 'K', '2', and '7' uppermost, which of them need to be turned over to discover whether it is true that "If a card has a vowel on one side, it has an even number on the other"? Only about four per cent of subjects select 'A' and '7' [6].

Oaksford and Chater [22] proposed that subjects consider these two hypotheses with respect to an imagined population of cards of which the four are but a sample:

H_0: P(vowel & odd number) = 0
H_1: Number (even or odd) independent of letter (vowel or consonant).

But statistical methodology requires that H_0 (the rule to be tested) be compared to *all* alternative states of nature, that is to

H_2: P(vowel & odd number) ≠ 0,

not just to the special case H_1. Oaksford and Chater have surreptitiously assumed that all possibilities alternative to H_0 and H_1 are seen by the subjects to have probability zero, and that assumption is slipped in without even an attempt at justification. The comparison between H_0 and this particular H_1 does not, in fact, generate a model of Wason's selection task. It does, however, generate the so-called 'ravens paradox' [18, 23].

Oaksford and Chater [22] next proposed that subjects select amongst the four cards according to the expected yield of information measured according to

$$\Sigma_i\, p_{ij} \ln[p_{ij}/p_{i\cdot}p_{\cdot j}], \tag{8}$$

where *i* indexes the hypothesis (H_0 or H_1) and *j* the choice of card. They believed that such a sampling strategy would be optimal, but Klauer [8] has shown otherwise. Formula 8 is the Shannon measure of information transmitted conditional on selecting Card *j*. Now, the underside of Card *j* may well tell the subject that the rule does not hold, but that is not what formula 8 measures. It compares, instead, the hypotheses

H_1': Underside of card independent of whether H_0 or H_1 holds, and
H_2': Underside of card related to the distinction between H_0 and H_1.

That is, it measures the extent to which the underside of Card *j* is relevant to the discrimination between H_0 and H_1. While this might appear a plausible basis for choice, even more relevant would be the expected yield of information in favour of H_0 and against H_1 (or, more correctly, H_2).

However, if the information is correctly evaluated with respect to H_0 and H_2 (P(vowel & odd number) = 0 and P(vowel & odd number) ≠ 0), it delivers the conventional logical prescription, 'A'and '7' [16], This is just what one should expect from a valid mathematical theory.

4 The Human Observer as a Physical System

Kullback [9, p. 22] proved a fundamental theorem that says, in words, "There can be no gain of information by statistical processing of data." This theorem has a profound application.

4.1 Signal Detection

Think of the human observer as a purely physical system and the stimulus as a datum. Sensory analysis of that input equates to "statistical processing of data" and human performance is limited by the information implicit in the stimulus. The signal-detection operating characteristic provides a direct estimate of the distribution of the information transmitted [see 12, pp. 98–103]; in fact, the logarithm of the gradient of the operating characteristic *is* the information random variable in favour of 'signal' and against 'noise alone'. This provides a basis for comparing the information implicit in the observer's responses with the information supplied by the stimulus.

Signal detection theory has been revolutionary in the field of sensory discrimination. It distinguishes between the information available to the observer and the partitioning of values of that information between the available responses (the choice of criteria). Looking solely at information throughput, and disregarding the criteria, it can be shown that the information available to the observer is derived from a sensory process that is differentially coupled to the physical stimulus, because the component of information derived from the stimulus mean is entirely absent from the information implicit in the observer's performance [13, pp. 169–172]. This provides an explanation of Weber's Law and of many other related phenomena [see 13, 14].

5 Bayes' Theorem

Bayes' theorem specifies how posterior probabilities may be calculated from the combination of prior probabilities and a probability ratio calculated from experimental data. If the result of the first replication of the experiment in Eq. 1 be taken as defining a prior probability ratio, $[P(\mathrm{H}_1)/P(\mathrm{H}_0)]$, for the second replication,

$$[P(\mathrm{H}_1|X)/P(\mathrm{H}_0|X)] = [P(\mathrm{H}_1)/P(\mathrm{H}_0)][P(X|\mathrm{H}_1)/P(X|\mathrm{H}_0)].$$

On taking logarithms,

$$\ln[P(\mathrm{H}_1|X)/P(\mathrm{H}_0|X)] = \ln[P(\mathrm{H}_1)/P(\mathrm{H}_0)] + \ln[P(X|\mathrm{H}_1)/P(X|\mathrm{H}_0)] \quad \mathbf{(9)}$$

or

Posterior information = Prior information + Information in data *X*.

Probability ratios are exponents of information values and a simple transformation relates Eq. 9 to the usual form of Bayes' theorem. Human performance is manifestly influenced in many experiments by the probabilities of the different stimuli (e.g. Fig. 1). The present question is whether such effects are accurately described by Eq. 9.

5.1 Two-Choice Reaction Experiments

There are two alternative signals. One of two responses is to be made "as quickly as possible". One interesting idea is that reaction time is the time taken to collect sufficient information to make a response to some prescribed level of accuracy.

Imagine the experiment of Eq. 1 to be repeated many times; if i indexes successive replications,

$$\ln[P(H_1|\Sigma_i X_i)/P(H_0||\Sigma_i X_i)] = \ln[P(H_1)/P(H_0)] + |\Sigma_i \ln[P(X_i |H_1)/P(X_i |H_0)]. \quad \textbf{(10)}$$

The sequence of replications $\{X_i\}$ continues until the posterior information (on the left) reaches some desired bound, which guarantees that Response 1 (H_1), rather than Response 0 (H_0), is correct to within some small degree of error. The subject chooses a desired level of accuracy and the reaction times follow stochastically from that error-criterion. The mathematics required to develop the idea is the sequential probability ratio test [33], and the idea itself was first suggested by Stone [27]. In effect, Bayes' theorem is continuously and repeatedly applied to test the validity of the accumulated evidence and one can hardly get more Bayesian than that.

This idea does not work. While my own data [10] might suggest otherwise, there are further unpublished results that show it to be hopeless. I explain why it will not work.

5.2 The Choice of Criterion in Signal-Detection Experiments

If signal detection data conform accurately to the normal, equal variance, model, there is a particular location of the criterion, varying with signal probability, which minimises the total number of errors [3]. Figure 2 compares two sets of calculations, 'Bayes' theorem' from [4, p. 90] using data from one subject in the experiment by Tanner, Swets, & Green [30] and 'Probability matching' based on a suggestion by Thomas & Legge [31]. The abscissa coordinate is the criterion value of likelihood ratio specified by 'Bayes' theorem' (asterisks) and by 'Probability matching' (open circles) respectively. The ordinate is the criterion value (the same in both calculations) estimated from the data. If the predictions were accurate, then the estimated criterion values would be equal to the calculated values. The diagonal dashed 45° line tracks those estimates of criterion placement that would match the predictions (either set) exactly. It can readily be seen that the actual likelihood ratio at the estimated criterion is always conservative, too close to unity, relative to the predictions from Bayes' theorem. But suppose, instead of minimizing the number of errors, the subject merely adjusts the frequency of "Yes" responses to match the frequency of signals (i.e., 'probability matching', [31]). The concordance between the open circles and the dashed line shows that idea to work well. But why?

In this experiment [30] the subject had feedback at the end of each trial and so knew immediately when he had made an error. Under such circumstances, subjects effect a large shift in criterion following an error, shifting in the direction that reduces the risk of a similar error in future (but increasing the risk of an error of the opposite kind; [28]). The signal-detection criterion is not a fixed parameter, but evolves from trial to trial in a dynamic equilibrium, driven by re-adjustments following each error. It drifts towards a value where the absolute numbers of errors of each kind are equal. That equality means that the numbers of "Yes" responses lost through a mistaken "No" equate to the number gained through a mistaken "Yes" and, overall, the frequency of "Yes" matches the frequency of the signals.

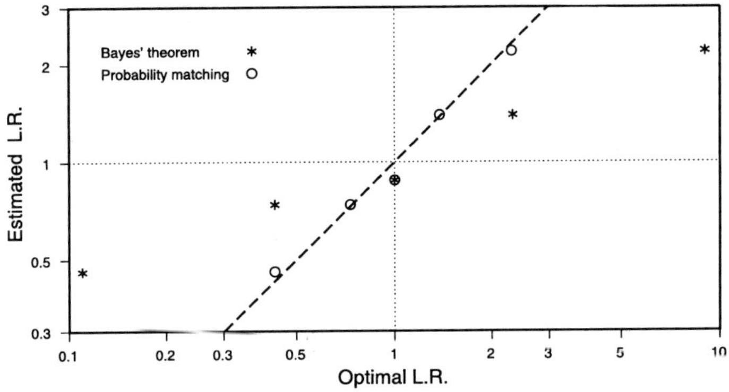

Fig. 2. Calculations of likelihood ratio at optimal criterion ('Bayes' theorem') from [4, p. 90], and of likelihood ratio given probability matching [31] using data from one subject in the experiment by Tanner, Swets, & Green [30].

Table 2. Numbers of all combinations of signal and response for two subjects in the experiment by Tanner, Swets, & Green [30].

P(signal)	"No"| noise	"Yes"| noise	"No"| signal	"Yes"| signal
Observer 1				
0.10	521	19	37	23
0.30	365	55	75	105
0.50	194	106	84	216
0.70	90	90	72	348
0.90	12	48	22	518
Observer 2				
0.10	492	48	40	20
0.30	334	86	89	91
0.50	180	120	87	213
0.70	86	94	90	330
0.90	18	42	43	497

Table 2 sets out the relevant data in more detail, showing the actual numbers of errors (Cols 3 & 4), both for the subject in Fig. 2 and for another subject in the same experiment [4, p. 95]. The numbers in Cols 3 and 4, are approximately the same, even though the corresponding numbers of correct responses (Cols 2 & 5), and therefore the absolute probabilities of each kind of error, vary widely.

In an experiment where many people expected prior probabilities to enter into a rational calculation based on Bayes' theorem, that failed to happen. Instead, performance was driven by successive shifts of the criterion, oscillating around a dynamic equilibrium where the numbers of errors of each sort were approximately equal. To performance in this kind of experiment Bayes' theorem does not apply.

5.3 Absolute Identification

Analysis of two-choice reaction times [10, Ch. 8; 11] shows that both latencies and errors are subject to a similar series of trial-to-trial adjustments. That is, Bayes' theorem does not apply, either, to the involvement of prior probabilities in choice-reaction times. But what about the aggregation of information (Eq. 10) during a single trial? The sequential probability ratio test is isomorphic to a random walk and can also be modelled as a diffusion process in continuous time. Is that idea applicable to the human operator? To see why not, I turn to an experiment on absolute identification [1, Expt 4].

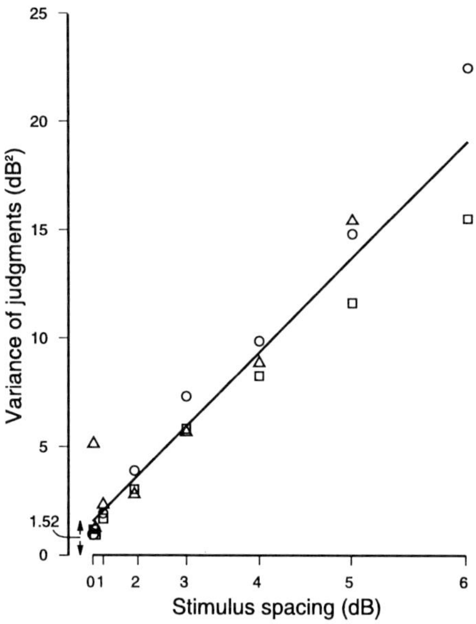

Fig. 3. Estimates of the variance of identification judgments in each condition (different stimulus spacings) in Experiment 4 by Braida and Durlach [1]. Differently shaped symbols show estimates from three different subjects. (From "Reconciling Fechner and Stevens?" by D. Laming, Behavioral and Brain Sciences, 1991, vol 14, p. 191. Reproduced by permission.)

The stimuli were ten 1 kHz tones of different amplitudes. The subjects were required to identify individual tones in isolation. In different sessions the tones were spaced at 0.25, 0.5, 1, 2, 3, 4, 5, 6 dB intervals. (Table 1 sets out the data for one session from this experiment). Figure 3 plots estimates of the variability of the identifications calculated in this manner. Torgerson's [32] Law of Categorical Judgment with equal variances (Class 1C) was used as model, but with the means set equal to the decibel values of the stimuli. The one free parameter was the standard deviation, σ. Figure 3 plots the values of the variances, σ^2, for three individual subjects, against (the square of) the stimulus spacing. The estimated variances increase in proportion to the square of the spacing, with a small intercept, 1.52 dB^2.

The point here is that, except for the declining influence of the intercept, resolution does not improve with wider spacing of the stimulus values. Identification of the stimuli is tied to the geometric ladder of stimulus magnitudes and is no better than ordinal [17, Ch. 10]. That is, the judgment of one stimulus relative to another is no better than <greater, about the same, less> and the aggregation of such crude ordinal comparisons cannot support a sequential probability ratio test procedure of the kind I envisaged in my study of two-choice reaction times [10].

6 Conclusions

(i) There are some simple interrelationships between the notions of statistical information, statistical hypothesis testing, and their applications in psychology, that are less well understood than they need to be. Under the influence of Shannon's theory, psychologists are wont to suppose that information is an absolute. Not so! Data is absolute, but information is always relative to the two hypotheses between which it distinguishes.
(ii) If the human operator be viewed as a purely physical system, then Kullback's [9, p. 22] theorem applies unconditionally. Analysis of information flow provides a 'model-independent' technique for identifying the 'information-critical' operations involved. In this way information theory provides, as it were, a 'non-parametric' technique for the investigation of all kinds of systems without the need to understand the machinery, to model the brain without modeling the neural responses.
(iii) But Bayes' theorem fails to describe the contribution of prior information. In signal detection and two-choice reaction-time experiments performance fluctuates from trial to trial about a dynamic equilibrium that does not correspond to the optimal combination of information from different sources.

References

1. Braida, L.D., Durlach, N.I.: Intensity perception. II. Resolution in one-interval paradigms. J. Acoust. Soc. of Am. 51 (1972) 483–502
2. Garner, W.R.: Uncertainty and Structure as Psychological Concepts. Wiley, New York (1962)
3. Green, D.M. Psychoacoustics and detection theory. J. Acoust. Soc. of Am. 32 (1960) 1189-1203
4. Green, D.M., Swets, J.A.: Signal Detection Theory and Psychophysics. Wiley, New York (1966)
5. Hick, W.E.: On the rate of gain of information. Quart. J. Exp. Psychol. 4 (1952) 11–26
6. Johnson-Laird, P.N., Wason, P.C.: A theoretical analysis of insight into a reasoning task. Cog. Psychol. 1 (1970) 134-148
7. Kirchner, W.K.: Age differences in short-term retention of rapidly changing information. J. Exp. Psychol. 55 (1958) 352–358.
8. Klauer, K.C.: On the normative justification for information gain in Wason's selection task. Psychol. Rev. 106 (1999) 215–222
9. Kullback, S.: Information Theory and Statistics. Wiley, New York (1959)
10. Laming, D.R.J.: Information Theory of Choice-Reaction Times. Academic Press, London (1968)

11. Laming, D.R.J.: Subjective probability in choice-reaction experiments. J. Math. Psychol. 6 (1969) 81-120
12. Laming, D.R.J.: Mathematical Psychology. Academic Press, London (1973)
13. Laming, D.: Sensory Analysis. Academic Press, London (1986)
14. Laming, D.: Précis of Sensory Analysis. and A reexamination of Sensory Analysis. Behav. Brain Sci. 11 (1988) 275–96 & 316–39
15. Laming, D.: The antecedents of signal-detection theory. A comment on D.J. Murray, A perspective for viewing the history of psychophysics. Behav. Brain Sci. 16 (1993) 151-152
16. Laming, D.: On the analysis of irrational data selection: A critique of Oaksford & Chater (1994). Psychol. Rev. 103 (1996) 364-373
17. Laming, D.: The Measurement of Sensation. Oxford University Press, Oxford (1997)
18. Mackie, J.L.: The paradox of confirmation. Brit. J. Philos. Sci. 13 (1963) 265–277
19. Merkel, J.: Die zietlichen Verhältnisse der Willensthätigkeit. Philos. Stud. 2 (1885) 73–127
20. Miller, G.A., Frick, F.C:. Statistical behavioristics and sequences of responses. Psychol. Rev. 56 (1949) 311–324
21. Neyman, J., Pearson, E.S.: On the problem of the most efficient tests of statistical hypotheses. Trans. Royal Soc. London, Ser. A, 231 (1933) 289–337
22. Oaksford, M., Chater, N.: A rational analysis of the selection task as optimal data selection. Psychol. Rev. 101 (1994) 608-631
23. Oaksford, M., Chater, N.: Rational explanation of the selection task. Psychol. Rev. 103 (1996) 381–391
24. Peterson, W.W., Birdsall, T.G., Fox, W.C.: The theory of signal detectability. Trans. IRE PGIT 4 (1954) 171-212
25. Shannon, C.E.: A mathematical theory of communication. Bell System Tech. 27 (1948) 379–423, 623–656
26. Shannon, C.E.: Communication in the presence of noise. Proc. IRE 37 (1949) 10-21
27. Stone, M.: Models for choice-reaction time. Psychometrika 25 (1960) 251–260
28. Tanner, T.A., Rauk, J.A., Atkinson, R.C.: Signal recognition as influenced by information feedback. J. Math. Psychol. 7 (1970) 259-274
29. Tanner, W.P. Jr, Swets, J.A.: A decision-making theory of visual detection. Psychol. Rev. 61 (1954) 401–409
30. Tanner, W.P., Swets, J.A., Green, D.M.: Some general properties of the hearing mechanism. University of Michigan: Electronic Defense Group, Tech. Rep. 30 (1956)
31. Thomas, E.A.C., Legge, D.: Probability matching as a basis for detection and recognition decisions. Psychol. Rev. 77 (1970) 65–72
32. Torgerson, W.S.: Theory and Methods of Scaling. Wiley, New York (1958)
33. Wald, A.: Sequential Analysis. Wiley, New York (1947)
34. Wilkes, S.S.: The likelihood test of independence in contingency tables. Ann. Math. Statist. 6 (1935) 190–196
35. Wilkes, S.S.: The large-sample distribution of the likelihood ratio for testing composite hypotheses. Ann. Math. Statist. 9 (1938) 60-62

Polymorphism of Human Judgment under Uncertainty

Rui Da Silva Neves* and Eric Raufaste**

Centre d'Etude et de Recherche en Psychopathologie (CERPP)*
Laboratoire Travail et Cognition (LTC)**
Université Toulouse-Le Mirail, 5 allées Antonio Machado
31038 Toulouse cedex
{neves, raufaste}@univ-tlse2.fr

Abstract. The aim of this paper is to test if conjunctive and disjunctive judgments are differently accounted for possibility and probability theories depending on whether (1) judgments are made on a verbal or a numerical scale, (2) the plausibility of elementary hypotheses is low or high. 72 subjects had to rate the extent to which they believe that two characters were individually, in conjunction or in disjunction, involved in a police case. Scenarios differed on the plausibility of the elementary hypotheses. Results show that the possibilistic model tends to fit the subjects' judgments in the low plausibility case, and the probabilistic model in the high plausibility case. Whatever the kind of scale, the possibilistic model matches the subjects' judgments for disjunction, but only tends to do it for conjunction with a verbal scale. The probabilistic model fits the subjects' judgments with a numerical scale, but only for disjunction. These results exhibit the polymorphism of human judgment under uncertainty.

1 Introduction

Uncertainty is a constitutive aspect of human cognition, and to some extent, the human cognitive system is specialized in processing uncertainty. This contrasts with the old idea in psychology that people permanently try to avoid or to reduce uncertainty [6]. However, such a reduction or avoidance is not always possible. In that case, in order to make sense of internal or external events or states, and in order to make decisions, people must combine uncertain information efficiently. This leads to some questions. How does one represent feelings of knowing, beliefs, doubts, and expectancies… accurately? Is there a unique set of formal rules sufficient to describe uncertainty combinations by the human cognitive system precisely? Numerous psychological studies have been devoted to the search for answers to such questions. Not surprisingly, most of them have focused on a probabilistic representation of uncertainty. For example, Kahneman, Slovic and Tversky [7] have conducted a vast research program in order to test human intuitions and performances about probabilities. The very important amount of obtained data exhibited a contrasted panorama: people succeed in some classes of problems and fail in others (see [5] and [7]). A subsequent purpose has been to establish the factors or the conditions under which people behave normatively. In particular, studies of judgment under uncertainty have exhibited the general result that judgments of probability are influenced by contextual features that are unrelated to a problem's formal structure

S. Benferhat and P. Besnard (Eds.): ECSQARU 2001, LNAI 2143, pp. 647–658, 2001.

[12]. Another strong result is that people commit two kinds of fallacies: the conjunction and disjunction fallacies. The former is committed when the estimated probability of a conjunction exceeds the probability of either constituent [17], the latter when the probability of a disjunction is lesser than the probability of at least one of its constituents [9]. These two biases are of particular interest because they are directly related to crucial rules of uncertainty composition, whatever the considered normative framework. Another line of research has consisted in testing human judgment under uncertainty given non-classical probabilistic models of uncertainty. Several models studied by artificial intelligence present interesting properties from a psychological point of view. These models include at least the Bayesian approach, probabilistic logics, belief functions, upper and lower probability systems, and possibility theory. Except for the Bayesian approach, only few or no psychological studies have focused on these models. Possibility theory has been considered by Zimmer [20] and Raufaste and Da Silva Neves [11].

This paper extends Raufaste and Da Silva Neves's previous study, and pursues the objective to gain insight into the conditions under which human judgment under uncertainty follows basic rules of either probability theory or possibility theory. It leaves apart other frameworks like belief functions. In order to achieve this objective, an experiment has been conducted that tests the convergence of human conjunctive and disjunctive judgments with the possibilistic and the probabilistic models, given two kinds of factors. The first one depends on the kind of scale designed to measure the subjects' uncertainty about single, conjunctive and disjunctive hypotheses. Two scales have been tested: an ordinal one and a numerical one. The second factor is the relative plausibility of competing hypotheses. Three conditions were studied. In the first one both hypotheses were unlikely, in the second one only one hypothesis was unlikely and the other one was very likely, and in the last condition both hypotheses were very likely. Moreover, the way each model fits subjects' judgments was compared for conjunctive and disjunctive judgments when judgments produce a high level of plausibility on the one hand, and a low level on the other hand.

Section 2 introduces the probabilistic and possibilistic frameworks, some previous empirical results, and our objectives based on these results. Section 3 presents the experimental apparatus, the method for the test of our hypotheses and results. Some concluding remarks are made in section 4.

2 Formal Apparatus, Previous Empirical Findings, and Objectives

According to Zadeh ([19] p. 4) "Contrary to what has become a widely accepted assumption –much of the information on which human decisions are based is possibilistic rather than probabilistic in nature". In a previous study, Raufaste and Da Silva Neves [11] have shown that human experts might behave in a way that is much closer to possibilistic predictions than to probabilistic ones. However, a significant correlation between possibilistic measures and probability measures has been found, and possibilistic and probabilistic predictions have been differentiated statistically for conjunction only, but neither for simple disjunction nor for exclusive disjunction. Thus, if it can be concluded that under some conditions "subjective probabilities" could be reinterpreted as "subjective possibilities", these conditions are not clear. This section introduces the two frameworks and some empirical results related to their empirical validity with regard to human subjective degrees of confidence. Next, critical results are outlined and our experimental questions are formulated.

2.1 A Brief Recall of Probability Theory and Possibility Theory

Probability Theory

A probability measure P is defined on a family of events, each one construed as a set of possibilities so that (1) for any event A, $P(A) \geq 0$; (2) for an event A' certain to occur, $P(A') = 1$; (3) the probability of an event equals the sum of the probabilities of its disjoint outcomes (additivity). In addition, consider two independent events A and B, according to mathematical probability theory,

$$P(A \cap B) = P(A) * P(B) \tag{1}$$

where $P(A \cap B)$ is the probability of occurrence of both A and B and $P(A)$ and $P(B)$ are the probabilities of occurrence of A and B considered separately. In case of dependent events,

$$P(A \cap B) = P(A) * P(B/A) = P(B) * P(A/B) \text{ with } P(B/A) = P(A \cap B)/P(A) \tag{2}$$

The probability of occurrence of A or B or both ($P(A \cup B)$) is

$$P(A \cup B) = P(A) + P(B) - P(A \cap B) \tag{3}$$

Probability theory has traditionally been used to analyze repetitive chance processes, but the theory has also been applied to essentially unique events where probability is not reducible to the relative frequency of "favourable" outcomes [17].

Possibility Theory

Let X be an ill-known variable, and Ω_X the set of all the values ω that X can take. Zadeh defined a "possibility distribution" $\pi_x(\omega)$: $\Omega \rightarrow [0, 1]$ which expresses the level of plausibility of ω, that is the degree to which it is possible that the actual value of an ill-known variable X is ω. The interval [0, 1] is taken as a set of ordinal values, not necessarily numeric. Now, if A is an event (i.e., a subset of Ω, e.g. a particular diagnostic hypothesis), the "possibility measure" that A is correct is $\Pi(A)=\sup_{\omega \in A} \pi_x(\omega)$. Possibility measures satisfy the property of max-decomposability for disjunction,

$$\Pi(A \vee B)=Max(\Pi(A), \Pi(B)) \tag{4}$$

The dual measures of possibility measures are certainty measures defined in such a way that

$$N(A)=1-\Pi(\neg A) \tag{5}$$

Certainty measures satisfy Min-decomposability for conjunction

$$N(A \wedge B) = Min\ (N(A), N(B)) \quad (6)$$

Moreover, according to [4] under the dependence hypothesis,

$$\Pi(A \wedge B) = Min(\Pi(B/A), \Pi(A)) \text{ with, when } \Pi(A) > 0 \quad (7)$$

$$\Pi(B/A) = 1 \text{ if } \Pi(A \wedge B) = \Pi(A); = \Pi(A \wedge B) \text{ otherwise.}$$

2.2 Empirical Results

Generally, psychologists have cast a substantial doubt on the generality of the hypothesis that the subjects' probability estimates are related in a way described by the laws of mathematical probability theory. However, it has been found that while there was not a perfect conformity between the subjects' judgments and the proper combinations of the probabilities for elementary events, rules from probability theory yielded better descriptions than some alternate improper rules did [1]. More recently, [12] have found differences in probabilistic reasoning as a function of whether problems were presented in a frequentist or case-specific form. These different forms influence the likelihood of subjects committing the conjunction and disjunction fallacies. Furthermore, it has been found that verbal probabilities do not simply reflect the objective level of uncertainty, but are also determined by how this degree of uncertainty is brought about [14]. In everyday life, uncertainties are most commonly expressed through verbal phrases, like "possibly", "perhaps"... although some numerical estimates, usually given as percentages also have become a part of lay vocabulary of probability and risk. Attempts to quantify verbal expressions of uncertainty have demonstrated that different terms typically refer to different levels of probability [8] [2] [10]. For example, at the group level, several different studies conclude that the expression *probable* is used to express a mean subjective probability in the range of .70-.80, whereas *improbable* typically refers to a probability in the range of .12-.20. However, a large variability has been found in individual numerical estimates of verbal probability phrases [16]. When alternatives are defined to be approximately equivalent, high probability terms can be used to characterize low-probability outcomes whereas such usage is less frequent when a dominant alternative is available.

Another issue of particular interest is related to the verbal versus numerical presentation mode. Research on this topic exhibits contradictory results. On the one hand, no significant main effect (or very small differences) of the presentation mode of expressed probabilities has been found [3]. On the other hand, it is conceivable that information is processed differently when the final output is to be linguistic rather than numeric [18]. In addition, Zimmer [20] presented some data suggesting that linguistic information is actually processed more optimally in reasoning than direct numerical expressions, even if the tasks performed rely on frequency information. Interestingly, Zimmer used possibility theory as a framework for modeling the individual usage of verbal categories for grades of uncertainty. Also, it must be noticed that he obtained empirical evidence that, in verbal judgments, people are not prone to the conjunction fallacy. Zimmer's results agree with Raufaste and Da Silva Neves's finding that possibilistic and probabilistic predictions can be differentiated statistically for conjunction [11]. However, It must be remembered that this result has not been found with disjunction. This last result can be explained a posteriori by contextual characteristics and by the properties of possibility measures. Indeed, Raufaste and Da Silva Neves's experiment has been conducted with practitioner radiologists who had to provide and to rate plausible hypotheses about the pathologies suggested by the radiological film. As a consequence, the mean plausibility of subjective judgments was quite high (the mean values were around 80 with scales that ranged from 0 to 100). Now, recall that maximizing occurs always with possibility measures only, but not with certainty measures. Thus, it cannot be excluded that maximizing should occur with less plausible hypotheses. This hypothesis is strengthened by questions of relevance in the use of possibility and necessity measures. Indeed, intuitively, when some hypotheses to be evaluated are already known as plausible, reasoning in terms of degrees of possibility does not appear to be very informative. Conversely, when some hypotheses to be evaluated are already known as unlikely, reasoning in terms of degrees of necessity no longer appears to be very relevant.

2.3 Objectives

At least two questions emerged from this review of previous empirical results:
(1) Are conjunctive and disjunctive judgments differently accounted by possibility theory and probability theory depending on whether judgments are made on a verbal or a numerical scale?
(2) Is the degree of adjustment between the subjects' judgments and both possibilistic and probabilistic models dependent on the plausibility of the hypotheses?

The next section presents the experimental device which is constructed to explore these questions.

3 Experiment

In order to answer the questions above, an experiment was conducted where the subjects' confidence judgments about direct, conjunctive and disjunctive hypotheses were compared to the values computed from the possibilistic and the probabilistic models. The latter were computed from the subjects' confidence judgments. Then, the experiment dedicated to data collection, and the principles of data analyses are described. Next, the results of this experiment are presented and discussed.

3.1 Subjects

The subjects were 72 first-year psychology students at the University of Toulouse-Le Mirail, all native speakers in French.

3.2 Material

The material consisted of 3 short scenarios randomly presented in booklets. In each scenario (see Table 1), a detective inspector investigates a murder case and retains

Table 1. An example of the kind of scenario presented to the subjects (translated from the French original).

Scenario 1 (condition -/-)

A little bank of the district has been burgled. At the end of his investigation, the detective inspector focused on two suspects, well known to the police, Aurélien and Boris. However, both Aurélien and Boris had a good alibi: several persons attested they had seen them at the very moment of the burglary. In addition, the detective knew that it was not impossible that the burglar or burglars be someone else independent from Aurélien and Boris, but he knew no more.

In addition, the material involved the following 5 questions:

Q1: To what extent do you believe that Aurélien is involved in the burglary?

Q2: To what extent do you believe that Boris involved in the burglary?

Q3: To what extent do you believe that Aurélien and Boris are both involved in the burglary?

Q4: To what extent do you believe that Aurélien or Boris or both are involved in the burglary?

Q5: To what extent do you believe that Aurélien or Boris but not both is involved in the burglary?

two main suspects. The 3 scenarios differ mainly in the intuitive plausibility of the suspects' culpability. In scenario 1, the two hypotheses are weakly plausible (-/- condition). In scenario 2, they are strongly plausible (+/+ condition). In scenario 3, one hypothesis is strongly plausible and the other is unlikely (+/- condition).

3.3 Design and Procedure

The subjects were informed that they had to read the three scenarios carefully, in the given order, and to answer to the 4 questions of each scenario (see above). They were also informed that they had to answer the questions in checking the point (in the verbal condition, the square) of the scale that best matched their judgment. Two kinds of scales were randomly assigned to subjects (with only one kind of scale by subject): a numerical scale and a verbal scale (see figure 1).

3.4 Predictions and Analysis

In order to study the effects of the response format (verbal versus numerical) and of the relative plausibility of both hypotheses on subjective judgments with regard to the possibilistic and the probabilistic conjunctive and disjunctive rules of composition, the subjects' responses on the verbal scale were encoded in a numerical format and the subjects' responses on the numerical scale were encoded in a verbal form according to the rules given in table 2. Numerical encoding values of the verbal response modalities were obtained in dividing a scale ranging from 0 to 1 in 6 equivalent intervals between 0 and 1. The interval bounds provided the numerical modalities associated with the verbal modalities. The verbal encoding values of numerical responses were obtained in a more sophisticated manner. Indeed, to apply such an encoding makes sense if we suppose that when checking the verbal scale, subjects make use of some implicit *metric* representation so that a check on the left part of the square of a given verbal descriptor indicates a lesser degree of confidence than a check in its right part. Moreover, following the same logic, some correspondence should exist between the bounds of the squares and corresponding values projected on the numerical scale. These values provided the bounds of the numerical intervals that encode verbal modalities. Because the comparison with direct numerical judgments supposes only one value by modality, the choice has been made to apply the same encoding rule as for ordinal modalities.

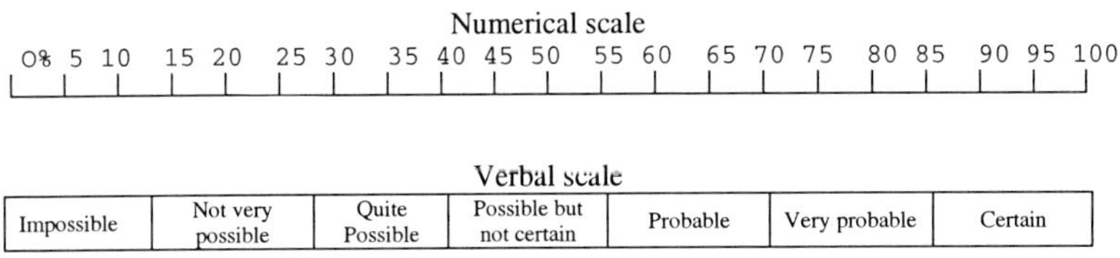

Fig. 1. Scales for the subjects' answers

Given the hypothesis that subject's judgments conform to the possibilistic framework, basic combinatorial relations (see section 2.1.) should predict subjects' estimates and it should be observed that:

P1: When subject's estimates of the conjunctive hypothesis (question 3) are over .5 (entirely possible), under the independence hypothesis, the possibilistic model ($N(A \wedge B) = Min\ (N(A), N(B))$ should fit better the subjects' conjunctive judgments than the probabilistic model do ($P(A \cap B) = P(A) * P(B)$).

Values of $\Pi(A \wedge B)$ and $P(A \cap B)$ are mean values. $N(A)$ and P(A) have the same value, which is the mean value of the subjects' answer to the question 1 (see table 1). N(B) and P(B) have also the same value computed from the answer to question 2.

P2: When subject's estimates of the conjunctive hypothesis (question 3) are over .5 (entirely possible), under the non independence hypothesis, the possibilistic model ($\Pi(A \wedge B) = Min\ (\Pi(B/A), \Pi(A))$ should fit better the subjects' conjunctive judgments than the probabilistic model do ($P(A \cap B) = P(A) * P(B/A)$).

$\Pi(A)$ and P(A) are computed according to the same rule as above. For the computation of P(B/A), the mean value of the subjects' answer to the question 3 is divided by the mean value of the answer to the question 1. For the computation of $\Pi(B/A)$, the mean value of the answer to the question 4 is subtracted to the mean value of the answer to the question 5. The same is made with respectively questions 4 and 2. Then, the result of the first subtraction is divided by the result of the second one.

P3: When subject's estimates of the disjunctive hypothesis (question 4) are under .5 (not entirely possible), the possibilistic model ($\Pi(A \vee B) = Max(\Pi(A), \Pi(B))$) should fit better the subjects' disjunctive judgments than the probabilistic model do ($P(A \cup B) = P(A) + P(B) - P(A \cap B)$).

These tests have been made for each scenario given the two kinds of transformation applied to subjects' judgments. In order to compute the fit of the models with the subjects' estimates, two kinds of statistical tests have been applied. The first is the computation of a correlation coefficient between the direct subjects' responses and the predicted value. The second is the test of the equality of the mean values computed over the subjects' responses on the one hand and computed over the predicted values on the other hand. The applied tests were the *rho* Spearman test of correlation and the Wilcoxon rank test (see Siegel and Castellan [14]).

Table 2. Rules of encoding

Numerical encoding of verbal measures		Ordinal encoding of numerical measures		
1- Impossible	→ .00	[0 .14]	→ 1	→ .00
2- Not very possible	→ .16	[.14 .28]	→ 2	→ .16
3- Quite possible	→ .33	[.28 .42]	→ 3	→ .33
4- Possible but not certain	→ .50	[.42 .58]	→ 4	→ .50
5- Probable	→ .66	[.58 .72]	→ 5	→ .66
6- Very probable	→ .83	[.72 .86]	→ 6	→ .83
7- Certain	→ 1.00	[.86 1.00]	→ 7	→ 1.00

3.5 Results

Fifteen ANOVA (Analysis of Variance) have been computed for each of the 5 questions crossed with each scenario in order to test a potential effect of the presentation order of the scenarios. No order effect has been found. In order to test the effect of the conjunctive and disjunctive hypotheses' plausibility on the fit of the possibilistic and probabilistic models, two kinds of analyses have been made. The first one consisted in comparing the fit of the models with the subjects' judgments for each scenario (C-/-, C+/- and C+/+, see section 3.2). In order to conduct the second kind of analysis, subjects first have been attributed two conditions, Pl^* (high plausibility) and Pl_* (low plausibility), according to the following criteria: (1) when plausibility judgments are under or equal to .5 (i.e. from impossible to possible but not certain), subjects have been attributed the Pl_* condition, (2) when plausibility judgments are over .5 (i.e. from probable to certain), subjects have been attributed the Pl^* condition. Next, the fit of the models with the subjects' judgments under Pl^* and Pl_* have been compared for conjunction and disjunction according to the rules given in section 3.4. Table 3 summarizes the main results needed for the relevant comparisons. Of particular interest are the comparisons labeled *Data/Π* (vs. *N*) and *Data/P*, where *Data* represents the subjects' judgments; *Π*(vs. *N*) represents the mean computed by the possibilistic model (*N* for min composition and *Π* for max composition, and *P* represents the mean computed by the probabilistic model. The *sig* value (placed between brackets in the table) computed from the *z* coefficient (Wilcoxon test) represents the probability of rejecting by error the null hypothesis that the two means are equal. When the *sig* value is under the .05 level, the difference is judged significant. It is not so in the other case. In addition, The *sig* value (equally placed between brackets) computed from the *rho* coefficient of correlation (Spearman test) represents the probability of rejecting by error the null hypothesis that the two distributions are correlated. The same decision criterion is applied. In order to conclude that one model fits the data better than the other one, it must be found that the *rho* coefficient value is significant at least for the former model (whatever the latter) and that the *z* value is not significant for the former and is significant for the latter.

Table 3. Correlations (*rho*) and differences (*z*) between the subjects' judgments (*Data)* and possibility theory (*N* for conjunction and Π for disjunction), and between *Data* and probability theory *(P)*, under Pl^* and Pl_*. N represents the sample size and *sig* represents the probability that the hypothesis of no difference between the mean values be rejected by error.

Under the independence assumption

Conjunction			C-/-	C+/-	C+/+
Pl^*	Data/N	Z (sig.)	-1.34 (.18)	-3.43 (.001)	-2.94 (.003)
		Rho (sig.)	.81 (.18)	.04 (.86)	.44 (.12)
	Data/P	Z (sig.)	-.1.84 (.07)	-3.73 (.000)	-3.18 (.001)
		Rho (sig.)	.81 (.18)	.11 (.67)	.32 (.26)
	N		4	18	14
Disjunction			**C-/-**	**C+/-**	**C+/+**
Pl_*	Data/Π	Z (sig.)	-1.14 (.25)	-2.38 (.02)	-.75 (.45)
		Rho (sig.)	.81 (.000)	.57 (.000)	.36 (.04)
	Data/P	Z (sig.)	-5.37 (.000)	-4.71 (.000)	-4.29 (.000)
		Rho (sig.)	.81 (.000)	.62 (.000)	.52 (.002)
	N		66	39	33

Under the non independence assumption

Conjunction			C-/-	C+/-	C+/+
Pl^*	Data/Π	Z (sig.)	--.65 (.52)	-.06 (.95)	-2.37 (.02)
		Rho (sig.)	.92 (.000)	.83 (.000)	.85 (.000)
N			68	68	68
	Data/P	Z (sig.)	-.1.19 (.24)	-0.02 (.98)	-2.51 (.012)
		Rho (sig.)	-.28 (.24)	.26 (.07)	.37 (.004)
N			14	51	59

The comparisons between scenarios of the mean values of the subjects' judgments for elementary hypotheses have shown that the subjects endorsed the a priori plausibility of the hypotheses.

Test of the Plausibility Level

Examination of table 3 shows that, for disjunction, the possibilistic model fits the subject's disjunctive judgments in C-/- and C+/+ scenarios but not in the C+/- scenario. The probabilistic model never fits the subjects' data. These results are consistent with Raufaste and Da Silva Neves's findings. Indeed, in the previous study, no model fit the subjects' disjunctive judgments, but the latter were highly plausible (> .80). In the present study, the disjunctive hypothesis which significantly received the highest plausibility (C+/-: mean = .62; σ = .25; the difference with the second more plausible hypothesis is significant at the .05 level) was precisely that which did not fit any model. For conjunction, table 3 shows that under the independence assumption and under Pl*, whatever the scenario, none of the models fits the subjects' conjunctive judgments. Under the non independence assumption, the probabilistic model didn't fit the data whatever the scenario, whereas the possibilistic model fits data in the C-/- and C+/-. The fact that the condition that is not fitted is the C+/+ one is consistent with the hypothesis that it applies better with the less plausible hypothesis. On the whole, These results suggest that the possibilistic model tends to fit the subjects' judgments when they produce a low or only a "fair" plausibility.

Table 4.. Correlations (*rho*) and differences (*z*) between the subjects' judgments (*Data*) and possibility theory (*N* for conjunction and *Π* for disjunction), and between *Data* and probability theory *(P)*, in the verbal and numerical conditions. *sig* represents the probability that the hypothesis of no difference between the mean values be rejected by error. N = 36

Under the independence assumption				
Conjunction		C-/-	C+/-	C+/+
Verbal				
Data/N	Z (sig.)	-.05 (.96)	-.40 (.69)	-3.18 (.001)
	Rho (sig.)	.76 (.000)	.25 (.14)	.37 (.02)
Data/P	Z (sig.)	-5,05 (.000)	-3.55 (.000)	-2.17 (.03)
	Rho (sig.)	.76(.000)	.26 (.13)	.36 (.03)
Numerical (n = 36)				
Data/N	Z (sig.)	-.21 (.83)	-1.15 (.25)	-.15 (.88)
	Rho (sig.)	82 (.000)	.41 (.01)	.65 (.000)
Data/P	Z (sig.)	-3.49 (.000))	-2.53 (.01)	-3.16 (.002
	Rho (sig.)	.82 (.000)	.48 (.003)	.67 (.002)
Disjunction		C-/-	C+/-	C+/+
Verbal				
Data/Π	Z (sig.)	-.71 (.48)	-.22 (.82)	-.38 (.71)
	Rho (sig.)	.86 (.000)	.46 (.004)	.51 (.002)
Data/P	Z (sig.)	-4,55 (.000)	-4.16 (.000)	-4.54 (.002)
	Rho (sig.)	.86(.000)	.42 (.01)	.48 (.003)
Numerical (n = 36)				
Data/Π	Z (sig.)	-1.02 (.31)	-.69 (.49)	-1.81 (.07)
	Rho (sig.	84 (.000)	.65 (.000)	.79 (.000)
Data/P	Z (sig.)	-2.98 (.003)	-1.73 (.08)	-1.4 (.16)
	Rho (sig.)	.84 (.000)	.60 (.000)	.83 (.000)

Test of the Presentation Scale (Verbal vs. Numerical)

The examination of table 4 shows that, for conjunction (computed only under the independence assumption), with the numerical scale, the possibilistic model fits the subjects' judgments whatever the scenario, whereas it fits only the C-/- condition with the verbal scale. Data did not fit any model in the C+/- and C+/+ scenario. For disjunction, with the verbal scale, the possibilistic model fits the subjects' judgments whatever the scenario, and not the probabilistic model. With the numerical scale, the possibilistic model fits the C-/- scenario, the probabilistic model fits the C+/+

scenario, and both models competed for the fit with the C-/- scenario. These results exhibit an interaction effect between the kind of scale (verbal vs. numerical) and of the kind of judgment (conjunctive vs. disjunctive). With a verbal scale, the probabilistic model does not fit the subjects' judgments, while with a numerical scale, it tends to fit the subjects' judgments only for disjunction. On the other hand, whatever the kind of scale, the possibilistic model fits the subjects' judgments for disjunction and only tends to do it for conjunction with a verbal scale.

4 Conclusion

The aim of this study was (1) to test if conjunctive and disjunctive judgments were differently accounted for possibility theory and probability theory depending on whether judgments are made on a verbal or a numerical scale, and (2) to test if the degree of adjustment between the subjects' judgments and both possibilistic and probabilistic models dependent on the relative plausibility of the combined hypotheses. An experiment has been conducted in which 72 subjects had to rate in 3 different scenarios the extent to which they believe that two characters were (i) each one, (ii) both, (iii) only one or both, (iv) only one, involved in an police case. The scenarios differed on the plausibility level of the hypotheses that each character be involved in the case. Our results appeared to be consistent with previous findings. In addition, it has been found that the possibilistic model tends to fit the subjects' judgments when they produce a low plausibility. On the contrary, given additional results not presented here, probabilistic judgments tend to fit the subjects' judgments when they produce a high plausibility. Moreover, an interaction effect between the kind of scale (verbal vs. numerical) and the kind of judgment (conjunctive vs. disjunctive) has been found. In particular, whatever the kind of scale, the possibilistic model fits the subjects' judgments for disjunction but only tends to do it for conjunction with a verbal scale. Finally, the probabilistic model fits the subjects' judgments with a numerical scale, but only for disjunction. These results remain to be explained, but emphasize the psychological plausibility of the possibilistic model. They suggest also that several models are needed in order to describe the rules that underlie the subject's judgments formally. Probability theory is such a model. Because part of the subjects' judgments have not been accounted for neither by possibility nor probability theory, further work should focus on other frameworks like, for example, the Dempster-Shafer one [see 13].

References

[1] Barclay, S., & Beach, L.R.: Combinatorial properties of personal probabilities. Organizational Behavior and Human Performance, 8 (1972) 176-183.

[2] Budescu, D.V., Wallsten, T.S.: Processing Linguistic Probabilities: General Principles and Empirical Evidence. In: The Psychology of Learning and Motivation, Vol. 32, Academic Press, (1995) 275-317.

[3] Budescu, D.V., Weinberg, S., Wallsten, T.S.: Decisions Based on Numerically and Verbally Expressed Uncertainties. Journal of Experimental Psychology: Human Perception and Performance, 14 (1988) 281-294.

[4] Dubois, D., Lang, J., Prade, H.: Possibilistic Logic. In...

[5] Evans, St. J.: Bias in human reasoning. Causes and Consequences. Lawrence Erlbaum Associated, Publishers. Hove and London (UK) (1989).

[6] Festinger, L.: A theory of Cognitive Dissonance. Evanston, IL: Row Peterson (1957).

[7] Kyburg, H.E.: Uncertainty Logics. In: D.M. Gabbay, C.J. Hogger, J.A. Robinson, D. Nute, (eds.): Handbook of Logic in Artificial Intelligence and Logic Programming, Vol. 3, Oxford University Press (1994) 439-513.

[8] Lichtenstein, S., Newman, J.R.: Empirical Scaling of Common Verbal Phrases Associated with Numerical Probabilities. Psychonomic Science, 9 (1967) 563-564.

[9] Morier, D.M., Borgida, E.: The Conjunction Fallacy: A task Specific Phenomenon ? Personality and Social Psychology Bulletin, 10 (1984) 243-252.

[10] Rapoport, A., Wallsten, T.S., Cox, J.A.: Direct and indirect scaling of membership functions of probability phrases. Mathematical Modelling, 9 (1987) 6, 397-417.

[11] Raufaste, E., Da Silva Neves, R.: Empirical evaluation of possibility theory in human radiological diagnosis. In H. Prade Ed., Proceedings of the 13th Biennal Conference on Artificial Intelligence, ECAI'98 (1998) pp. 124-128. London: John Wiley & Sons.

[12] Reeves, T., Lockhart, R.S.: Distributional Versus Singular Approaches to Probability and Errors in Probabilistic Reasoning. Journal of Experimental Psychology: General. (1993) Vol. 122, n°2, 207-226.

[13] Shafer, G.: A Mathematical Theory of Evidence. Princeton University Press, Princeton, N.J. (1976).

[14] Siegel, S., Castellan, N.J.: Nonparametric Statistics for the Behavioral Sciences, McGraw-Hill (1988).

[15] Teigen, K.H.: The language of uncertainty. Acta Psychologica, 68 (1988) 27-38.

[16] Teigen, K.H.: When are low-probability events judged to be 'probable'? Effects of outcome-set characteristic on verbal probability estimates. Acta Psychologica, 68 (1988) 157-174.

[17] Tversky, A., Kahneman, D.: Extensional vs. intuitive reasoning: The conjunction fallacy in probability judgment. Psychological Review, 91, 293-315, (1983).

[18] Wallsten, T.S., Budescu, D.V., Erev, I.: Understanding and using linguistic uncertainties. Acta Psychologica, 68 (1988) 39-52.

[19] Zadeh, L.A.: Fuzzy sets as a basis for a theory of possibility. Fuzzy Sets and Systems, **1** (1978) 3-28

[20] Zimmer Alf C.: Verbal versus Numerical Processing of Subjective Probabilities, in: Sholz, R.W. (Ed.), Decision Making Under Uncertainty (Nort-Holland, Amsterdam) 1983, pp. 159-182..

How to Doubt about a Conditional

Guy Politzer

CNRS - Laboratoire Cognition et Activités Finalisées
Université de Paris VIII, 2 rue de la Liberté
93526 Saint-Denis, France
politzer@univ-paris8.fr

Abstract. Psychological studies of reasoning with simple conditional arguments have shown that about one half of the participants do not consider the conclusion as certain when some specific information is added to the premises, explicitly or implicitly. This nonmonotonic effect is explained by generalising Mackie's [8] analysis of conditionals within the framework of Relevance theory (Sperber & Wilson [12]): Conditionals are uttered with a *ceteris paribus* assumption of normality; calling in question this assumption induces doubt in the conditional: This is what characterises additional premises used in the experiments mentioned above as well as in ordinary conversation.

1 Introduction

In the past twelve years or so, a number of psychological studies of deduction using essentially the simple arguments Modus Ponendo Ponens and Modus Tollendo Tollens have shown the following phenomenon. After the explicit or implicit addition of a piece of information to the premises by various experimental procedures (a few of which will be described succintly), the proportion of people who endorse the conclusion as certainly true is typically cut by one half, as compared to the usual rate of endorsement. This effect can be qualified as nonmonotonic as the major premise of the original argument operates like a general rule and the additional information like a specification leading to an apparent inconsistency, which results in participants' retractation. A general hypothesis on knowledge representation associated with conditionals will be outlined, on the basis of which a pragmatic explanation of the effect will be proposed.

S. Benferhat and P. Besnard (Eds.): ECSQARU 2001, LNAI 2143, pp. 659–667, 2001.

2 Some Psychological Studies of NonMonotonic Reasoning

2.1 Adding Premises Explicitly

Byrne [2] asked one control group of participants to solve standard arguments such as, for Modus Ponendo Ponens (MP): *If she meets her friend, then she will go to a play; she meets her friend;* therefore: (a) *she will go to a play;* (b) *she will not go to a play;* (c) *she may or may not go to a play.* As is commonly observed, over 95 percent of the participants chose option (a). An experimental group was asked to solve the same arguments modified by the addition of a third premise, *if she has enough money, then she will go to a play.* The result is that fewer than 40 percent in this group chose option (a). A similar effect was observed with Modus Tollendo Tollens (MT). Notice the special structure of the argument: the third (additional) premise was a conditional that had a necessary condition in its antecedent; since it had the same consequent as the major premise, it contained, in fact, a necessary condition for the consequent of the major premise and served as a means of introducing it in the context.

Chan & Chua [3] introduced a refinement on Byrne's [2] paradigm. Using various non causal conditional rules as premises, for each of them they defined three necessary conditions for the consequent to hold; these conditions varied in importance (that is, in degree of necessity independently estimated by judges). For example, with a MP whose major premise was *If Steven is invited then he will attend the party* the three degrees of necessity were introduced each time by an additional premise: *If Steven knows the host well then he will attend the party* (low degree), or *If Steven knows at least some people well then he will attend the party* (intermediate degree), or *If Steven completes the report to night then he will attend the party* (high degree). The response options were (a) *he will attend the party;* (b) *he will not attend the party;* (c) *he may or may not attend the party.* It was observed that the rate of (a) answers to these three-premise arguments was a decreasing function of the degree of necessity. Similar results were obtained for MT. In brief, the statement of an additional conditional premise which contained in its antecedent a necessary condition for the consequent to occur diminished the rate of endorsement of the conclusion all the more sharply as the condition was rated as more important.

Stevenson and Over's [13] first experiment had two controls and five experimental conditions. The first control was a standard argument, e. g. (for MP), *If John goes fishing, he will have a fish supper; John goes fishing* whose conclusion was evaluated on a five-option scale: *John will have a fish supper; . . will probably have. . ; . . may or may not have. . ; probably won't have. . ; won't have. . .* The second control was similar to Byrne's [2] experimental condition: There was a third premise, a conditional whose antecedent was a necessary condition for the consquent of the major premise: *if John catches a fish, he will have a fish supper.* The five experimental conditions had a fourth premise that informed the participant about the likelihood of the satisfaction of the necessary condition in the third premise: *John is always lucky; . . almost always. . ; . . sometimes. . ; . . rarely. . ; . . very rarely. .* While in the second control condition Byrne's results were replicated, the effect of the fourth premise on both MP and MT was to decrease the rate of endorsement of the conclusion and correlatively to increase the uncertainty ratings on the five-point scale in a near-monotonic fashion across conditions. In brief, the manipulation of degrees of necessity resulted in functionally related degrees of belief in the conclusion of the arguments.

In their second experiment the same authors used three-premise arguments in which the second premise was a categorical sentence that introduced various levels of frequency directly into the necessary condition. For example, given the major premise *If John goes fishing, he will have a fish supper,* there were five levels in the second premise: *John always catches a fish when he goes fishing; . . almost always. . ; . . sometimes. . ; . . almost never. . ; . . never. . .* For both MP and MT the rate of endorsement of the conclusion decreased monotonically as the frequency mentioned in the second (categorical) premise decreased (with a floor effect on the two smallest frequencies). In brief, the denial, and the explicit introduction of various degrees of doubt in the satisfaction of a condition necessary for the consequent to occur diminished the rate of endorsement of the conclusion and the greater the doubt, the greater the decrease.

Manktelow and Fairley [9] manipulated the extent to which a necessary condition is satisfied: with a low degree of satisfaction the consequent is less likely to occur and with a high degree it is more likely to occur. The control argument was a standard MP with the major premise *If you pass your exams, you will get a good job* and there were four experimental arguments made of this MP augmented with one of the following premises: (i) *got very low grade;* (ii) *got low grade;* (iii) *got respectable grade;* (iv) *got excellent grade.* The conclusion had to be assessed on a 7-point scale (from very low to very high certainty to be offered a good job). For the first two experimental arguments the certainty ratings were below the control (and lower for the *very low grade* condition than for the *low grade* condition). For the last two, the certainty ratings were above the control (and higher for the *excellent grade* condition than for the *respectable grade* condition). In brief, they found that the degree of certainty of the conclusion was an increasing function of the degree to which a necessary condition is satisfied.

Politzer & Bourmaud [11] used five different MT arguments such as *If somebody touches an object on display then the alarm is set off; the alarm was not set off;* conclusion: *nobody touched an object on display* (to be evaluated on a five-point scale ranging from certainly true to certainly false). This was a control; in the three experimental conditions, degrees of credibillity in the conditional were defined by way of an additional premise that provided information on a necessary condition for the consequent to occur: High credibility: *there was no problem with the equipment;* Low: *there were some problems with the equipment;* Very low: *the equipment was totally out of order.* The coefficients of corrrelation between level of credibility and belief in the truth of the conclusion ranged between .48 and .71 and were highly significant. This result provides a wide generalisation for the previous investigations to the extent that (i) the kind of rule used was not limited to causals but included also means-end, remedial, and decision rules, (ii) there were several degrees of credibility, (iii) the major and minor premises were kept constant across levels of credibility, and (iv) the format of evaluation of the conclusion was sensitive enough to enable the expression of various degrees of belief.

In summary, the studies reviewed so far show that with simple conditional arguments (MP or MT) a majority of people become less certain of the conclusion, and consequently are reluctant to rate the conclusion as true, when a premise which has the following property is added: That premise questions the truth of a condition which (i) is necessary for the consequent of the major conditional premise to be true, and (ii) at the same time, must be assumed to be true if the major conditional is to be credible. The next few studies differ slightly in that they show that similar effects can be obtained without explicit additional information.

2.2 Adding Premises Implicitly

Studies by Cummins [4] and Cummins, Lubart, Alksnis, and Rist [5] were focused on MP and MT arguments with causal conditionals. They demonstrated that the acceptance rate of the conclusion was a decreasing function of the number of disabling conditions available, that is, conditions whose satisfaction is sufficient to prevent an effect from occurring (and whose non satisfaction is therefore necessary for the effect to occur). For example, of the following two MP arguments, *If the match was struck, then it lit; the match was struck / it lit* and *If Joe cut his finger, then it bled; Joe cut his finger / it bled,* people are less prone to accept the conclusion of the first, which has many disabling conditions, than the conclusion of the second, which has few. Thompson [14] obtained similar results with causals and also non causal rules such as obligations, permissions and definitions by using conditionals that varied in 'perceived sufficiency' (independently rated by judges). A sufficient relationship was defined as one in which the consequent always happens when the antecedent does. It was observed that the endorsement rate of the conclusion was an increasing function of the level of sufficiency. This manipulation can also be described by saying that the conditional premises differed by the number of necessary conditions, whether negative (disabling conditions) or positive (called 'enabling' conditions, that is, conditions whose satisfaction is necessary for an effect to occur). Clearly these conditions are less likely to be all satisfied when this number is high than when it is low, hence the difference in the acceptance rate of the valid conclusion, assuming that participants in these experiments were aware of this fact.

George [7] manipulated directly the credibility of the conditional premise of MP arguments. Two groups of participants received contrasted instructions. One group was asked to assume the truth of debatable conditionals such as *If a painter is talented, then his/her works are expensive* but the other group was reminded of the uncertain status of such statements. While 60 percent in the first group endorsed the conclusion of at least three of the four MP arguments, only 25 percent did in the second group. By asking to asssume the truth of such conditionals, participants were invited to dismiss possible objections (necessary conditions) like *the painter must be famous,* whereas stressing the uncertainty of the statement is a way to invite them to take such objections into account.

Newstead, Ellis, Evans, and Dennis [10] and Evans and Twyman-Musgrove [6] studied MP and MT arguments whose major conditional premise differed from the point of view of the 'speech act' they conveyed; they observed differences in the rate of endorsement of the conclusion: promises and threats on the one hand, and tips and warnings on the other hand seem to constitute two contrasted groups, the former giving rise to more frequent endorsements of the conclusion than the latter. The authors note that the key factor seems to be the extent to which the speaker has control over the occurrence of the consequent, which is higher for promises and threats than for tips and warnings. Weaker control implies greater difficulty to ensure the satisfaction of the necessary condition for the consequent to occur, hence less certainty that it will follow.

3 The Representation of Conditionals in Relation with the Knowledge Base

The following three related claims are made:

(i) conditionals are uttered in a background knowledge, of which they explicitly link two units (the antecedent and the consequent), keeping implicit the rest of it, which will be called a *conditional field;*

(ii) the conditional field has the structure of a disjunctive form, as proposed by Mackie [8] for causals. The mental representation of a conditional *if A then C* (excluding analytically true conditionals) in its conditional field can be formulated as follows :

$$[(A_m \& \ldots \& A_1 \& A) \vee (B_n \& \ldots \& B_1 \& B) \vee \ldots] \dashrightarrow C \quad (1)$$

A is the antecedent of the conditional under consideration; B is an alternative condition that could justify the assertion of *if B then C* in an appropriate context. Although such alternative antecedents may play an important role, B and its conjuncts will not be considered further here. We focus on the abridged form,

$$(A_m \&\ldots \& A_1 \& A) \dashrightarrow C \tag{2}$$

While (A_m &. . . & A_1& A) is a sufficient condition as a whole, each conjunct A_m , . . , A_1 separately is necessary *with respect to A*. These conjuncts will be called *complementary necessary conditions* (henceforth CNC).

(iii) it is hypothesised that in asserting the conditional *if A then C,* the speaker assumes that the necessity status of the conditions A_m , . . , A_1 is part of the shared knowledge, and most importantly that *these conditions are satisfied.*

This is justified on the basis of relevance. According to relevance theory (Sperber and Wilson [12]), in uttering the conditional sentence, the speaker guarantees that the utterance is worth paying attention to, that is, it will enable the hearer to derive a new piece of knowledge. But this in turn requires that the CNC's be satisfied, failing which the conclusion would not follow. The assumption of satisfaction of CNC's can be characterised as an epistemic implicature. In brief, conditionals are typically uttered with an implicit *ceteris paribus* assumption to the effect that the normal conditions of the world (the satisfaction of the CNC's that belong to shared knowledge) hold.

An important consequence is that if further information denies or just raises doubt on the assumption of satisfaction of the CNC's, (technically, the cancellation of an implicature), the conditional sentence no longer conveys a sufficient condition.

In terms of processing cost, the epistemic implicature attached to the utterance of the conditional has the advantage that in normal circumstances there is no need to explore the knowledge base in order to check whether all CNC's are satisfied: their satisfaction is assumed or guaranteed by the speaker (to the best of her knowledge). But if the hearer has reasons to be cautious about a conditional, he will search in the conditional field for non satisfied CNC's. Such reasons are typically based on the level of confidence of the hearer in the speaker, on the possible existence of alternative sources of information which the hearer believes to be unknown to the speaker, etc.

The experimental data reviewed earlier can now be explained by the following common mechanism. These manipulations amount to intoducing a CNC in the context together with a degree of belief in it; this introduction often comes explicitly in the form of a third premise [2], [3], [9], [11], [13]. The satisfaction of the CNC can be denied [11] or a doubt about a CNC can be expressed explicitly [13] or implicitly [9]; in the latter case, it can be expressed through an implicature triggered by the use of an additional conditional whose antecedent precisely is a CNC [2], [3]; sometimes it is the result of a search in the conditional field triggered by the instructions, or more generally, the representation of the task [4], [5], [6], [7], [10], [14]. Recall that CNC's (which are necessary conditions for the consequent to occur) complement the antecedent of the conditional to make it an actual sufficient condition. It follows that the degree of belief in the satisfaction of those CNC's acts as a mediator for the credibility of the conditional (and subsequently, by inheritance, for the degree of belief in the conclusion of the argument). The truth status of the conclusion is then treated by degree rather than in an all-or-nothing manner and this degree is closely correlated to the degree of belief in the conditional premise.

Consider, for instance, *If somebody touches an object on display then the alarm is set off.* That the equipment be in working condition is one of the CNC's for the alarm to be set off, a condition whose satisfaction is implicitly warranted by the speaker (say, a technician who has just revised the equipment). There is no doubt in the conditional as long as a doubt in the CNC is not expressed, explicitly or implicitly. This example shows that belief in the conditional crucially depends on the belief in the satisfaction of a CNC, and in particular, doubt in the conditional is an increasing function of the doubt about the satisfaction of the CNC. If there is a doubt about the equipment's being in working condition, that somebody touches an object on display can no longer be a sufficient condition for the alarm to be set off, which is why upon hearing about the state of the equipment one may withdraw full belief in the conditional. In order to restore full belief in it, the antecedent would have to be complemented with the necessary condition, *the equipment is in working condition,* yielding: *If somebody touches an object on display and the equipment is in working condition, then the alarm is set off.* In case there is a doubt about this condition, the conclusion of the MP, *the alarm is set off* is uncertain and it inherits the degree of belief in the equipment's being in working condition, while the conclusion of the MT, *nobody touched an object on display,* knowing that the alarm was not set off, is also uncertain.

It is remarkable that in all the experiments reported participants are split into two groups: an (often strong) minority endorse the conclusion of the argument while a majority do not. In the former case, they seem to have a standard logical understanding of the premises: the major conditional premise is understood as conveying a sufficient condition and the additional information is disregarded. In the latter case, the additional information, which has the status of a necessary condition, is treated as if its fulfilment were not warranted; consequently the major conditional premise does not convey a sufficient condition any more.

4 Conclusion

The nonmonotonic effects observed in experiments on reasoning from conditional premises, namely the reluctance to endorse the conclusion or the expression of a doubt about it result from the addition of a premise whose communicated meaning questions the satisfaction of what has been called earlier a complementary necessary condition, (that is a tacit condition whose satisfaction is necessary for the consequent to occur), and therefore for the antecedent to be regarded as sufficient. In investigating the nature of the credibility of conditionals, researchers have traditionally focused their attention on the relation between antecedent and consequent; the present approach shows that there is advantage in going one step further, analysing the structure of the knowledge base (the conditional field).

The widely shared view [1] that the credibility of *if A, then C* is measured by the conditional probability of the consequent on the antecedent p(C/A) is a global approach which is entirely compatible with the analytic approach taken here: it can easily be demonstrated (but space is lacking here) that when the satisfaction of a CNC hitherto implicitly assumed becomes questioned, p(C/A) decreases. In brief, doubting about a conditional is due to a doubt about a CNC, and the doubt in the former is an increasing function of the doubt in the latter.

A last point worth noticing is that in human communication the existence of possible defaults (the non satisfaction of CNC's) does not necessitate the inspection of the knowledge base; the 'burden of the proof' does not concern normality, but rather abnormality: as noticed earlier, because of the guarantee of relevance, a conditional is normally accepted and the knowledge base is inspected only if there are good reasons to do so.

References

1. Adams, E. W.: The logic of conditionals. Reidel, Dordrecht (1975).
2. Byrne, R.M.J.: Suppressing Valif Inferences with Conditionals. Cognition, 31 (1989) 61-83.
3. Chan, D., Chua, F.: Suppression of Valid Inferences: Syntactic Views, Mental Models, and Relative Salience. Cognition, 53 (1994) 217-238.
4. Cummins, D.D.: Naive Theories and Causal Deduction. Memory and Cognition, 23 (1995) 646-658.
5. Cummins, D.D., Lubart, T., Alksnis, O., Rist, R.: Conditional Reasoning and Causation. Memory and Cognition, 19 (1991) 274-282.
6. Evans, J. St. B. T., Twyman-Musgrove, J.: Conditional Reasoning with Inducements and Advice. Cognition, 69 (1998) B11-B16.
7. George, C.: The Endorsement of the Premises: Assumption-based or Belief-based Reasoning. British J. of Psychol. 86 (1995) 93-111.
8. Mackie, J.L.: The Cement of the Universe. Clarendon Press, Oxford (1974).

9. Manktelow, K.I., Fairley, N.: Superordinate Principles in Reasoning with Causal and Deontic Conditionals. Thinking and Reasoning, 6 (2000) 41-65.
10. Newstead, S.E., Ellis, M.C., Evans, J.St.B.T., Dennis,I.: Conditional Reasoning with Realistic Material. Thinking and Reasoning, 3 (1997) 49-76.
11. Politzer, G., Bourmaud, G.: Deductive Reasoning from Uncertain Conditionals. Manuscript submitted for publication (2001).
12. Sperber, D., Wilson, D.: Relevance: Communication and Cognition. 2nd edn. Basil Blackwell, Oxford (1995).
13. Stevenson, R.J., Over,D.E.: Deduction from Uncertain Premises. Quarterly J. Exp. Psychol. 48A (1995) 613-643.
14. Thompson, V.: Interpretational Factors in Conditional reasoning. Memory and Cognition, 22 (1994) 742-758.

Dialectical Proof Theories for the Credulous Preferred Semantics of Argumentation Frameworks

Claudette Cayrol, Sylvie Doutre, and Jérôme Mengin

Institut de Recherche en Informatique de Toulouse
Université Paul Sabatier - 118 route de Narbonne - F 31062 Toulouse Cedex 4
{ccayrol,doutre,mengin}@irit.fr

Abstract. Argumentation is a natural form of reasoning, in which two agents cooperate in order to establish the validity of a given argument that could be used to deduce some conclusion of interest. An interesting semantics for logical systems of argumentation is Dung's "preferred semantics", which ameliorates in some ways the better-known stable semantics. In this paper, we present proof theories for the credulous decision problem associated with the preferred semantics: is a given argument in at least one extension of a given argumentation framework? Our proof theories improve on the one by [VP00], in the sense that a proof for a given argument is usually shorter with our system.

1 Introduction

Argumentation is a natural form of reasoning, in which two agents cooperate in order to establish the validity of a given argument that could be used to deduce some conclusion of interest. During the process of argumentation, each agent forms and asserts arguments that contradict or undermine arguments proposed by the other agent. This dialogue normally goes on until one of the agents cannot reply anything new: the original argument is then considered valid or not, depending on which agent won the dispute, the proponent or the opponent. The connection between dialogue and argument games has been studied by many researchers (see e.g. [CML00] for further references). The formalization of this form of reasoning has recently captured the interest of many researchers in the Artificial Intelligence community. For example, logics of argumentation are used in the construction of systems for legal reasoning, collective decision making or negotiation.

Besides being interesting because they capture this natural form of reasoning, logics of argumentation have also turned out to generalize in some way non-monotonic logics (that had themselves been designed as extensions of classical logic that do not collapse in the presence of inconsistencies). The first formulation of a decision problem related to Reiter's default logic in terms of a dialogue between two agents is probably due to Poole [Poo89]. Similar ideas have been used for building theorem provers for circumscription [Prz89,Gin89]. The close connection between non-monotonic logics and argumentation has been formally established in [BDKT97].

S. Benferhat and P. Besnard (Eds.): ECSQARU 2001, LNAI 2143, pp. 668–679, 2001.

In both non-monotonic logics and logics of argumentation, one has to evaluate a set of pieces of knowledge (defaults or arguments) that can contradict each other. The computation of these contradictions can normally be performed by some classical theorem prover. Then, the evaluation of the defaults or of the arguments can often be based solely on the contradiction graph, where the vertices are the defaults or arguments, and where the directed edges represent the contradictions. One way to formalize this evaluation is to define acceptable sets of pieces of knowledge: usually, one would say that acceptable sets do not contain any contradiction, and are "strong enough" in some sense.

The most widespread definition of acceptability associated with non-monotonic logics or logic programs considers that the acceptable sets are the "stable extensions", which correspond to kernels of the contradiction graph [DMP97, Ber73]. However, the stable semantics has some features that can be undesirable in some contexts: notably, it can happen that no set of pieces of knowledge is stable. [Dun95] defines an abstract framework for studying argumentation, and proposes several semantics. In particular, Dung's preferred semantics seems to capture well the intuition of "strong enough", and avoids several drawbacks of the stable semantics. In the preferred semantics, acceptable sets of arguments are called "preferred extensions".

An important problem related to argumentation systems is the credulous decision problem: given an argument and an argumentation framework, is the argument in at least one acceptable set of arguments? Proof theories for that problem have been described by [KT99] for the preferred semantics but for a slightly different form of argumentation systems. Proof theories in the form of argument games have also been described for the grounded semantics by [PS97, AC00], and by [VP00] for the preferred semantics. [VP00] propose argument games to answer credulous queries, and also to answer sceptical queries in a particular case. In these argument games, proofs that an argument belongs to some extension of an argumentation framework have the form of dialogues between a proponent and an opponent. An important aspect of such proofs is that they give an easy way to understand the implications of the underlying notions of acceptability.

On the algorithmic side, [DM01] show how to optimize the enumeration of the subsets of the set of arguments in order to efficiently answer questions related to the preferred semantics: what are the extensions, is an argument in all or some extensions? A careful study of the algorithm designed to answer the credulous decision problem shows that it can also be seen as a dialogue between an opponent and a proponent. Moreover, it appeared to us that the dialogue performed by the algorithm seems to be usually shorter than the proofs as defined by [VP00]. This prompted us to design another proof theory for the credulous decision problem related to the preferred semantics.

We present below two proof theories for that problem, based on the dialectical framework of [JV99]. They both improve on the one by [VP00] in the sense that proofs for a given argument are usually shorter with our system.

The paper is built as follows: the next section presents Dung's basic definitions and the preferred semantics. Section 3 presents a general framework for defining dialectical proofs. Our proof theories for the credulous decision problem associated with the preferred semantics are defined in Sect. 4. We show in Sect. 5 that the algorithm in [DM01] can compute our proofs, and we explain why they are usually shorter than the ones by [VP00]. Proofs of the propositions are available in [CDM01].

2 The Preferred Semantics

Definition 1. [Dun95] An argumentation framework is a pair (A,R) where A is a set of arguments and R is a binary relation over arguments, i.e. $R \subseteq A \times A$. Given two arguments a and b, $(a,b) \in R$ or aRb means a attacks b (a is said to be an attacker of b). Moreover we say that a set $S \subseteq A$ of arguments attacks an argument a if some argument b in S attacks a. An argument $a \in R$ is self-attacking if $(a,a) \in R$. The set of the self-attacking arguments of (A,R) is denoted by Refl(A,R) (or Refl for short).

An argumentation framework can be simply represented as a directed graph where vertices are the arguments and edges correspond to the elements of R. Figure 1 shows an example of argumentation framework. Given an argument $a \in A$, we denote the set of the successors of a by $R^+(a) = \{b \in A \mid (a,b) \in R\}$, the set of its predecessors by $R^-(a) = \{b \in A \mid (b,a) \in R\}$, and the set $R^+(a) \cup R^-(a)$ by $R^{\pm}(a)$. Moreover, given a set $S \subseteq A$ of arguments and $\varepsilon \in \{+, -, \pm\}$, $R^{\varepsilon}(S) = \cup_{a \in S} R^{\varepsilon}(a)$.

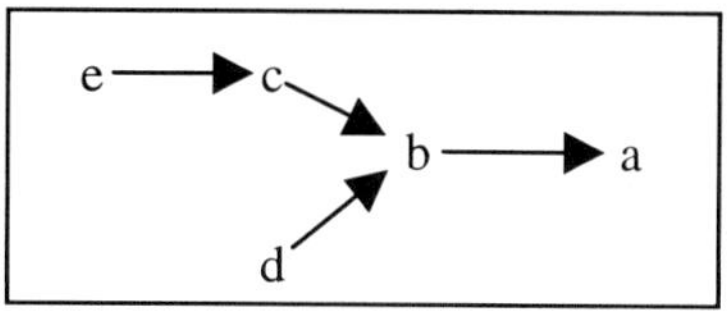

Fig. 1. The graph representation of an argumentation framework called AF1

Definition 2. Let (A,R) be an argumentation framework. An argument $a \in A$ is defended by a set $S \subseteq A$ of arguments (or S defends a) if and only if $\forall b \in A$, if bRa then S attacks b, i.e. $\exists c \in S$ such that cRb. A set $S \subseteq A$ is conflict-free if and only if there are no arguments a and b in S such that a attacks b. A set $S \subseteq A$ is admissible if S is conflict-free and $\forall x \in S$, S defends x.

Dung defines the preferred semantics of an argumentation framework by the set of preferred extensions. Precisely, a preferred extension is a maximal (with respect to set inclusion) admissible set of arguments. We characterise the preferred extensions on the graph representation of the argumentation framework.

Proposition 1. Given an argumentation framework (A,R), a subset S of A is a preferred extension if and only if the following conditions hold: 1) $R^+(S) \cap S = \varnothing$ (S is conflict-free); 2) $R^-(S) \subseteq R^+(S)$ (S defends every element it contains); 3) for every non-empty $X \subseteq A \setminus S$, $X \cap R^+(S \cup X) \neq \varnothing$ or $R^-(S) \not\subseteq R^+(S \cup X)$ (S is $\subseteq$-maximal such that 1 and 2). The set of the preferred extensions of (A,R) is denoted by Pref(A,R).

Dung exhibits interesting properties of the preferred semantics: in particular, every admissible set is contained in a preferred extension and every argumentation framework possesses at least one preferred extension.

The purpose of this paper is to answer an important question on preferred extensions: given an argument and an argumentation framework (A,R), is the argument in at least one preferred extension of (A,R), or equivalently, is the argument a credulous consequence of (A,R)? We define formally this notion:

Definition 3. Given an argumentation framework (A,R) and an argument a ∈ A, a is a credulous consequence of (A,R) under the preferred semantics if and only if a is contained in the union of the preferred extensions of (A,R).

Example. Given AF1, argument a is defended by S={a,d,e} against b. S is conflict-free and defends all its elements, so it is an admissible set, just like the sets ∅, {d}, {e}, {a,d}, {d,e} and {b,e}. The preferred extensions of AF1 are {a,d,e} and {b,e}. a, b, d and e are credulous consequences of AF1 under the preferred semantics, c is not.

Since a preferred extension is a maximal admissible set, deciding if an argument a is contained in a preferred extension of (A,R), amounts to deciding if it is contained in an admissible set. A procedure to solve this decision problem can take the form of a game between two players, one trying to build an admissible set containing a (the proponent), the other one trying to show it is not possible (the opponent).

Example. We want to decide if a is a credulous consequence of AF1. The proponent starts trying to build an admissible set containing a by advancing a. The opponent says that a is attacked by b. The proponent defends a by advancing c. But the opponent replies that c is attacked by e. The proponent cannot defend c against e, so he advances d another defender of a. The opponent has nothing to say since d is not attacked. The proponent has built an admissible set: {a,d}, so a is a credulous consequence of AF1.

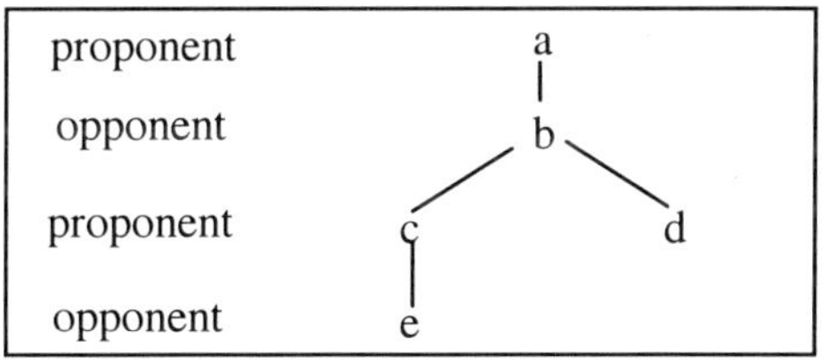

Fig. 2. Argument game to decide if a is a credulous consequence of AF1

3 The Dialectical Framework

Our purpose is to define a dialectical proof theory for the credulous preferred semantics, which takes into account the ideas of the credulous query answering algorithm of [DM01]. A general method for answering such a query takes the form of an argument game between a proponent (PRO) and an opponent (OPP). The proponent starts with the argument to be tested, and attempts to defend that argument against any attack coming from the opponent. The precise rules of the argument game depend on the semantics to be captured.

Argument games have been formalised in [JV99], where a general framework is proposed which enables to define dialectical proofs for winning positions in argumentation frameworks. The formalism developed by [JV99] encompasses the argument games of [PS97] and provides proof theories for two interesting semantics : the "robust" and the "defensible" semantics.

Following the methodological approach of [VP99], but with slightly different definitions, we propose in this section a dialectical framework which will enable us to provide two original proof theories for the credulous preferred semantics, in section 4.

3.1 Dialogue Type

An argument game is formalised by a dialogue between two players PRO and OPP. A dialogue takes place in a given argumentation framework and is governed by rules expressed in a so-called "legal-move" function.

Definition 4. A move in A is a pair [P,X] where P $\in$ {PRO, OPP} and X $\in$ A. For a move m = [P, X], we use pl(m) to denote P and arg(m) to denote X. A dialogue type is a tuple (A,R,Φ) where (A,R) is an argumentation framework and Φ : A* -> 2^A is a function[1] (called "legal-move" function). A dialogue d in (A,R,Φ) (or Φ-dialogue for short) is a countable sequence $m_0 m_1$,... of moves in A such that :

(i) $pl(m_0) = PRO$
(ii) $pl(m_i) \bullet pl(m_{i+1})$
(iii) $arg(m_{i+1}) \in \Phi(arg(m_0) \ldots arg(m_i))$

d is about the argument $arg(m_0)$.

So, each player plays in turn and PRO plays first. The next move is legal with respect to the preceding moves.

Remark. In [JV99], a conflict-free set of arguments may appear in a move. However, an additional requirement is that $arg(m_{i+1})$ must attack $arg(m_i)$.

Notations. Let d = $m_0 m_1$,... m_i a finite Φ-dialogue.
m_i is denoted by last(d).
$\Phi(arg(m_0) \ldots arg(m_i))$ is denoted by $\Phi(d)$.
PRO(d) will denote the set of arguments advanced by PRO during d.
Let m be a move in A such that $m_0 m_1$,... $m_i m$ is a Φ-dialogue. The extension of d with m is denoted by the juxtaposition d m.

Any restriction can be included in the "legal-move" function as for instance: an argument advanced in a move attacks the argument advanced in the previous move; PRO cannot repeat himself; no player can introduce a self-attacking argument.

---

[1] A* denotes the set of finite sequences of elements from A.

3.2 Proof Theory

As in any game, we must give winning criteria in order to determine which argument can be successfully defended with Φ-dialogues. We consider two criteria among those proposed by [JV99]. A given dialogue about an argument x can be won, or there can be a winning strategy for x, that is a way for PRO to defend x against all attacks of OPP.

Definition 5. Let d be a Φ-dialogue. d is won by PRO iff d is finite, cannot be continued (that is Φ (d)= ∅), and last(d) is played by PRO.

The next definition is simpler but equivalent to the one proposed in [JV99].

Definition 6. A Φ–winning strategy for x is a non-empty finite set S of finite Φ-dialogues about x such that : ∀ d ∈ S, ∀ d' prefix[2] of d such that last(d') is played by PRO, ∀ y ∈ Φ(d'), ∃ d" ∈ S such that d" is won by PRO and d" is an extension of d'[OPP,y].

The following result provides another characterization of Φ–winning strategies in which only dialogues which cannot be continued are considered.

Proposition 2. There exists a Φ–winning strategy for x iff there exists a finite non-empty set S of finite Φ-dialogues about x won by PRO such that : ∀ d ∈ S, ∀ d' prefix of d such that last(d') is played by PRO, ∀ y ∈ Φ(d'), ∃ d" ∈ S such that d" is an extension of d'[OPP,y].

4 Proof Theories for Credulous Preferred Semantics

The combination of a dialogue type and a winning criterion determines a proof theory. In this section, we present two specific proof theories dedicated to the credulous decision problem for the preferred semantics. The problem is to decide if an argument x belongs to a preferred extension. The basic idea is to prove that an admissible set of arguments can be built around x, with appropriate strategies for choosing attackers and defenders of the argument x. So, the "legal-move" functions we propose are inspired by the strategies used in the [DM01] algorithm.

Let d be a finite Φ-dialogue. $R^{\pm}$(PRO(d)) contains the arguments which attack or which are attacked by an argument avanced by PRO during d. Since PRO attempts to build an admissible set of arguments, PRO cannot choose any argument in $R^{\pm}$(PRO(d)) for pursuing the dialogue d. Nor any self-attacking argument. Let POSS(d) denote the set of arguments which may be chosen by PRO for extending the admissible set PRO(d). Formally, POSS(d) = A \ (PRO(d) ∪ $R^{\pm}$(PRO(d)) ∪ Refl).

The role of OPP is to attack one of the previous arguments advanced by PRO in d. But it is useless for OPP to advance an argument which is attacked by PRO(d).

---

2 The sequence y is prefix of the sequence x, or x is an extension of y iff there exists a sequence z such that x is obtained by the concatenation of y and z, x = yz.

4.1 The Φ1–Proof Theory

Definition 7. Let Φ1 : A* -> 2^A defined by :

If d = $m_0 m_1, \dots m_{2i}$ $\Phi1(d) = R^-(PRO(d)) \setminus R^+(PRO(d))$

If d = $m_0 m_1, \dots m_{2i+1}$ $\Phi1(d) = R^-(arg(m_{2i+1})) \cap POSS(d)$

Combining Φ1 and the first winning criterion, we obtain Φ1 -proofs.

Definition 8. A Φ1 -proof for the argument x is a Φ1 -dialogue about x won by PRO.

The following results establish the soundness and the completeness of the Φ1 - proof theory.

Proposition 3. (Soundness) If d is a Φ1 -proof for the argument x, then PRO(d) is an admissible set containing x.

Proposition 4. (Completeness) If the argument x is in a preferred extension of the argumentation framework (A,R), then there exists a Φ1 -proof for x.

Example. Let AF2 as indicated on figure 3. Let us try to build a Φ1-proof for a. PRO plays a. OPP can respond with b, c or d, since these arguments are predecessors but not successors of a. Assume OPP responds with b. This argument has two attackers: i and j, which can be advanced by PRO. Assume PRO advances i. Since $R^-(\{a,i\}) \setminus R^+(\{a,i\})=\{c\}$, OPP can only advance c (Note that c attacks a). Then PRO responds with f. OPP cannot play anymore, since $R^-(\{a,i,f\}) \setminus R^+(\{a,i,f\})=\emptyset$. The dialogue cannot be continued, it is won by PRO, thus it constitutes a Φ1-proof for a.

4.2 The Φ2–Proof Theory

In order to compare our work with argument games, it is convenient to present proofs in a more traditional way, where at each stage of the proof, the advanced argument attacks the previous one. Such proofs are obtained via the following dialogue type.

Definition 9. Let Φ2 : A* -> 2^A defined by :

If d = $m_0 m_1, \dots m_{2i}$ $\Phi2(d) = R^-(arg(m_{2i})) \setminus R^+(PRO(d))$

If d = $m_0 m_1, \dots m_{2i+1}$ $\Phi2(d) = R^-(arg(m_{2i+1})) \cap POSS(d)$

Φ2 is a restriction of Φ1 since, according to Φ2, OPP must advance an argument which attacks the argument advanced in the previous move.

Combining Φ2 and the second winning criterion, we obtain Φ2 -proofs.

Definition 10. A Φ2 -proof for the argument x is a Φ2 -winning strategy S for x such that $\cup(PRO(d), d \in S)$ is conflict-free.

Both proof theories are equivalent as shown by the following result.

Proposition 5. There exists a Φ1 -proof for the argument x iff there exists a Φ2 -proof for x.

Example. Given AF2, let us try to build a Φ2-proof of a. PRO plays a. a has three attackers: b, c and d. Thus we have three Φ2–dialogues about a:

- in the first one (d1), OPP responds to a with b. Then PRO can advance i or j. Assume he advances i. Then OPP cannot respond since $R^-(\{i\}) \setminus R^+(\{a,i\})=\emptyset$.
- in the second one (d2), OPP responds to a with c. Then PRO can only advance f. OPP cannot respond since $R^-(\{f\}) \setminus R^+(\{a,f\})=\emptyset$.
- in the third one (d3), OPP responds to a with d. Then PRO can advance i or j. Assume he advances i. Then OPP cannot respond since $R^-(\{i\}) \setminus R^+(\{a,i\})=\emptyset$.

These three dialogues are finite, cannot be continued and are won by PRO. S = {d1, d2, d3} is a Φ2-winning strategy for a. $\cup$(PRO(d), d$\in$ S) = {a, i, f} is conflict-free. So S is a Φ2-proof for a.

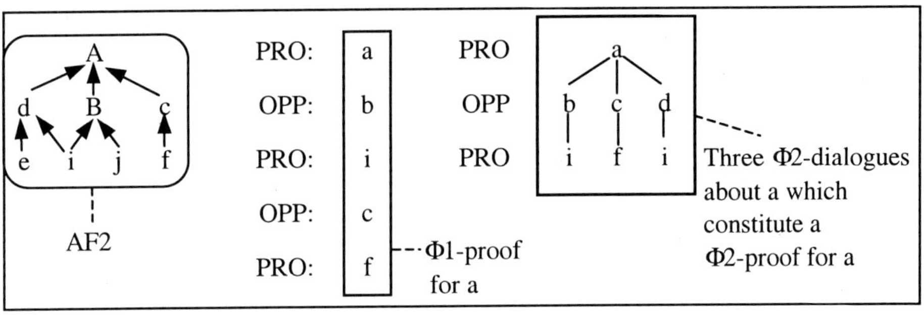

Fig. 3. The argumentation framework AF2, a Φ1-proof and a Φ2-proof for a

5 Related Works

5.1 The Credulous Query Answering Algorithm of [DM01]

We have proposed in [DM01] an algorithm to answer credulous queries related to the preferred semantics, of the form: given an argumentation framework (A,R) and an argument a in A, is a in at least one preferred extension of the framework? We have already mentionned that what prompted us to investigate a new proof theory is the fact that the proofs computed by our algorithm are in general shorter than the proofs of [VP00]. In this section, we show that our algorithm computes Φ1-proofs.

Let us first describe our algorithm. It is based on an enumeration of the subsets of A, which is performed by exploring a binary tree. Each node of the tree is labelled with a partition (I, O, U) of A: I is the set of arguments that have been put so far In the extension being built, O is the set of arguments that have been put Out of it, and U is the set of arguments that are still undecided at that stage. Since a preferred extension must be conflict free, the tree explores only nodes such that $R^{\pm}(I)\subseteq O$; in this case we say that (I,O,U) is an R-candidate. Normally, a node labelled with an R-candidate C=(I,O,U) such that U•∅ has two children: one is labelled with C+x=(I$\cup${x}, O$\cup R^{\pm}$(x), U\({x}$\cup R^{\pm}$(x))), the other one labelled with C–x=(I, O$\cup${x}, U\{x}), for some x∈U. Since we look for a preferred extension containing a, the root of the tree is labelled with the partition ({a}, $R^{\pm}$(a), A \ ({a} ∪ $R^{\pm}$(a))).

The set Op = R^{-}(I) \ R^{+}(I) denotes the set of arguments which are predecessors but not successors of I, that is, these arguments attack I and I cannot defend itself against them. When a partition associated to a node n is such that Op is empty, then I is an admissible set: the computation has proved that a is in at least one preferred extension. When the partition is such that there is some y ∈ Op which has no more undecided predecessor, then no preferred extension can be found on that branch, because an argument in I will never be defended by (I ∪ U): the exploration of that branch can be stopped. Thus the algorithm can be sketched in a functional programming style as follows:

function PrefEnum(R,C)
parameters: a binary relation R, and an R-candidate C=(I,O,U)
result: T if I is contained in at least one preferred extension, ⊥ otherwise
if Op=∅ **then** T
elseif there exists x∈Op **such that** R^{-}(x)⊆O **then** ⊥
elseif there exists y∈R^{-}(Op) **such that** yRy **then** PrefEnum(R,C−y)
else for some x∈Op **such that** R^{-}(x)⊄O **do**
    select some y∈R^{-}(x) \ O
    return(PrefEnum(R,C+y) **or** PrefEnum(R,C−y))

It is often possible to choose a "good" y such that only one branch has to be explored, but this is not relevant here. We will now show that when PrefEnum is called on ({a}, $R^{\pm}$(a), A \ ({a} ∪ $R^{\pm}$(a))), if the computation returns T then it is possible to extract a Φ1-proof for a from the successful branch.

Proposition 6. Let (A,R) be an argumentation framework, and let a be some element of the union of the preferred extensions of (A,R). Let C(0), C(1),…,C(n) be the sequence of R-candidates that label the nodes from the root to the success leaf of the tree explored by PrefEnum when called on ({a}, $R^{\pm}$(a), A \ ({a} ∪ $R^{\pm}$(a))). For 0•j•n, C(j) is of the form C(j) = (I(j),O(j),U(j)); let Op(j) = R^{-}(I(j)) \ R^{+}(I(j)). Let $(j_i)_{1•i•m}$ be the longest subsequence of (1,…,n) such that for every 1•i•m, C(j_i) is of the form C(j_i-1) + y(i), where y(i) ∈ R^{-}(x(i)) \ O(j_i-1) for some x(i) ∈ Op(j_i-1) with R^{-}(x(i)) ⊄ O(j_i-1). Let d=(c(0), …, c(2m)) be the dialogue defined by:

- c(0) = [PRO,a]
- c(2i-1) = [OPP,x(i)] and c(2i) = [PRO,y(i)] for 1•i•m.

Then d is a Φ1-proof for a.

Example. Let us illustrate the above algorithm on the argumentation framework AF2 of figure 3. We look for a preferred extension containing a, so the root of the tree is labelled with the partition C(0)=({a},{b,c,d},{e,f,i,j}). We have Op(0)={b,c,d}. We select i∈R^{-}(b) and we build two branches. One child of the root is labelled with C(0)+i, the other one is labelled with C(0)−i. We look at the one labelled with C(0)+i = C(1) = ({a,i}, {b,c,d}, {e,f,j}). In this case, Op(1)={c}. We select f ∈ R^{-}(c) and we build two branches. One child of the node associated with the partition C(1) is labelled with C(1)+f = C(2) = ({a,i,f}, {b,c,d}, {e,j}). Op(2)=∅, this is a leaf of success. The Φ1-proof for a shown on figure 3 can be easily extracted from this successful branch, given that x(1)=b, y(1)=i, x(2)=c, y(2)=f.

5.2 Comparison with [VP00]

[VP00] have proposed an argument game for the credulous decision problem, related to the preferred semantics. The precise rules of that game are the following ones:

The argument advanced in a move (except the first one), attacks one of the previous arguments of the other player. A dispute is a succession of moves satisfying the following conditions: PRO plays first. A line of dispute is a succession of moves such that each player plays in turn and attacks the previous argument proposed by the other player. In a same line of dispute, OPP cannot repeat himself, but OPP can repeat an argument already advanced by PRO. Each player can backtrack; backtracking consists in opening a new line of dispute. OPP can repeat himself in different lines of dispute. PRO can repeat himself but he cannot repeat an argument already proposed by OPP.

OPP wins a dispute if PRO cannot respond to the last move of OPP, or if the last move of OPP is an argument already proposed by PRO and on which there were no backtrack. PRO wins a dispute if OPP does not win.

A given argument is contained in a preferred extension if and only if each dispute beginning with that argument is won by PRO.

Example. (from [VP00]) Let AF3 as indicated on figure 4. There are two disputes starting with f. Let us build one of them, as done in [VP00]. PRO plays f. OPP advances n. PRO can respond with i or j. Assume PRO responds with i. Then OPP attacks i with j. To defend i against j, PRO repeats i. According to the [VP00] rules, the dispute cannot be continued, it is won by PRO. Note that it reduces to a single line of dispute. The second dispute starting with f is obtained by exchanging i and j. So, it is also won by PRO.

Similarly, there are two Φ1-proofs for f, which are also Φ2-proofs. Each one is shorter than the corresponding dispute. The three first moves are the same. The Φ1-proof stops at the third move, since at that stage, $R^-(\{f,i\}) \setminus R^+(\{f,i\})=\emptyset$.

Example. (from [VP00]) Let AF4 as indicated on figure 5. Let us build a dispute lost by PRO, starting with m, as done in [VP00]. PRO plays m. OPP responds with l. PRO can advance p or k. Assume PRO advances p. Then OPP responds with h. PRO cannot respond to h since h has no predecessor. This line of dispute cannot be continued, but we can open another one where PRO proposes k in response to l. But then OPP attacks k with m and PRO cannot respond, since PRO is not allowed to repeat l, already proposed by OPP. Consequently, m is not a credulous consequence of AF4.

We reach this conclusion faster with our Φ2-proof theory. Actually, to respond to l advanced by OPP, PRO can only play p: k is attacked by m, an argument previously advanced by PRO. OPP attacks p with h and the dialogue cannot be continued. This dialogue is lost by PRO. It corresponds to the first line of dispute.

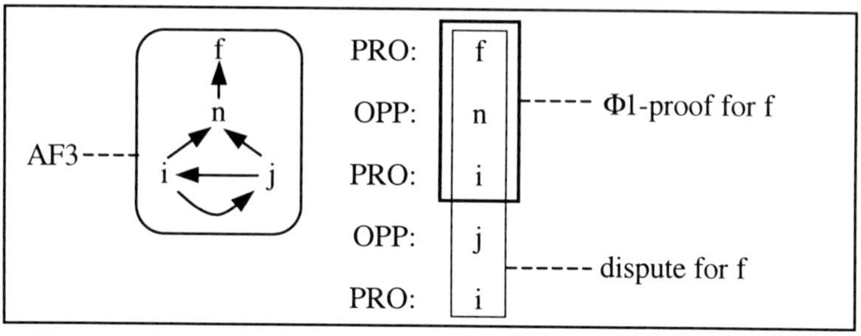

Fig. 4. The argumentation framework AF3, a dispute and a Φ1-proof for f

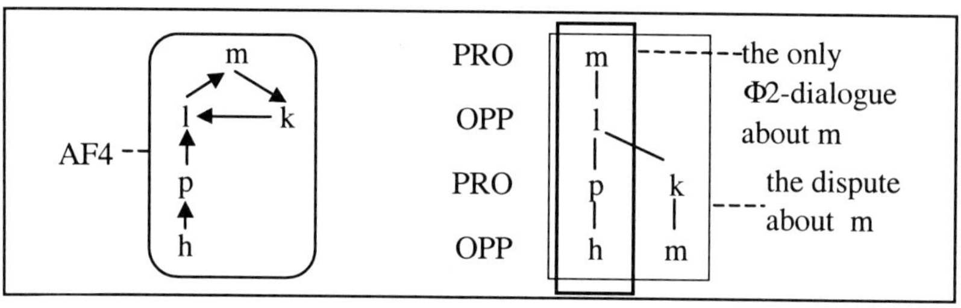

Fig. 5. The argumentation framework AF4, the Φ2-dialogue and the dispute about m

Our proofs are shorter than [VP00]'s proofs for a simple reason: we eliminate the arguments which are successors of PRO(d) from the possible moves of PRO and OPP. It is clear that such arguments are rejected from any admissible set containing PRO(d), so it is useless for OPP to advance these arguments (see figure 4). Moreover, such arguments are forbidden for PRO if we want PRO(d) to be contained in a conflict-free set (see figure 5).

6 Conclusion

The work reported in this paper concerns the credulous decision problem related to the preferred semantics. We have proposed two proof theories for that problem. These proof theories are presented in a dialectical framework, as done in [JV99]. Both proof theories improve on the work by [VP00] in the sense that our proofs for a given argument are usually shorter than the argument games proposed by [VP00].

Moreover, we have shown that our proofs can be computed by the credulous query answering algorithm of [DM01]. These results suggest to follow the same approach for the skeptical decision problem since [DM01] also present an efficient skeptical query answering algorithm. We project to design a dialectical proof theory for the skeptical preferred semantics.

References

[AC00] Amgoud, L., Cayrol, C.: A reasoning model based on the production of acceptable arguments. In Proceedings of the Workshop on Uncertainty Frameworks in Non-monotonic Reasoning, NMR 2000, Breckenbridge, Colorado, April 9-11, (2000).

[BDKT97] Bondarenko, A., Dung, P.M., Kowalski, R.A., Toni, F.: An abstract, argumentation-theoretic approach to default reasoning. Artificial Intelligence 93 (1997), 63-101.

[Ber73] Berge, C.: Graphs and Hypergraphs, vol.6 of North-Holland Mathematical Library, North-Holland (1973).

[CDM01] Cayrol, C., Doutre, S., Mengin, J.: Dialectical Proof Theories for the Credulous Preferred Semantics of Argumentation Frameworks. Research report, 2001-09-R, IRIT, May 2001.

[CML00] Chesñevar, C.I., Maguitman, A.G., Loui, R.P.: Logical Models of Argument. ACM Computing Surveys 32 (4) (2000), 337-383.

[DMP97] Dimopoulos, Y., Magirou, V., Papadimitriou, C.H.: On kernels, Defaults and Even Graphs. Annals of Mathematics and AI (1997).

[Dun95] Dung, P.M.: On the acceptability of arguments and its fundamental role in non-monotonic reasoning, logic programming and n-person games. Artificial Intelligence 77 (1995), 321-357.

[DM01] Doutre, S., Mengin, J.: Preferred Extensions of Argumentation Frameworks : Computation and Query Answering. In Proceedings of the Int. Joint Conf. on Automated Reasoning (IJCAR 2001), Siena, Italy, June 18-23 (2001).

[Gin89] Ginsberg, M.: A circumscriptive theorem prover. Artificial Intelligence, 39 (1989) 209-230.

[KT99] Kakas, A.C., Toni, F.: Computing Argumentation in Logic Programming. Journal of Logic and Computation 9 (4) (1999), 515-562.

[JV99] Jakobovits, H., Vermeir, D.: Dialectic Semantics for Argumentation Frameworks. In Proceedings of the 7th International Conference on Artificial Intelligence and Law, (ACM Press) (1999), 53-62.

[Poo89] Poole, D.: Explanation and prediction : an architecture for default and abductive reasoning. Computational Intelligence Journal 5 (1989) 97-110.

[Prz89] Przymusinski, T.: An algorithm to compute circumscription. Artificial Intelligence, 38 (1989) 49-73.

[PS97] Prakken, H., Sartor, G.: Argument-Based Extended logic Programming with Defeasible Priorities. Journal of Applied Non-classical Logics 7 (1997) 25-75.

[Rei80] Reiter, R.: A logic for default reasoning. Artificial Intelligence 13 (1980) 81-132.

[VP00] Vreeswijk, G., Prakken, H.: Credulous and Sceptical Argument Games for Preferred Semantics. In Proceedings of the European Workshop on Logics in Artificial Intelligence (JELIA 2000) LNA1 1919, Springer Verlag (2000).

Argumentation and Qualitative Probabilistic Reasoning Using the Kappa Calculus

Valentina Tamma and Simon Parsons

Department of Computer Science, University of Liverpool
Chadwick Building, Liverpool, L69 7ZF, UK
{V.A.M.Tamma,S.D.Parsons}@csc.liv.ac.uk

Abstract. This paper presents the *QRK* system for reasoning under uncertainty, which combines the building of logical arguments for formulae with infinitesimal probabilities of the kind handled by the kappa calculus. Each constituent of an argument has an associated κ-value which captures belief in that component, and these values are combined when arguments are constructed from the components. The paper is an extension of our previous work on systems of argumentation which reason with qualitative probabilities, providing a finer-grained approach to handling uncertainty.

1 Introduction

In the last few years there have been a number of attempts to build systems for reasoning under uncertainty that are of a qualitative nature—that is they use qualitative rather than numerical values, dealing with concepts such as increases in belief and the relative magnitude of values. Three main classes of system can be distinguished—systems of abstraction, infinitesimal systems, and systems of argumentation. In systems of abstraction, the focus is mainly on modelling how the probability of hypotheses changes when evidence is obtained. Such systems provide a qualitative abstraction of probabilistic networks, known as qualitative probabilistic networks (QPNs), which is sufficient for planning [14], explanation [3] and prediction [11] tasks. Infinitesimal systems deal with beliefs that are very nearly 1 or 0, providing formalisms that handle order of magnitude probabilities. Such systems may be used for diagnosis [2] and have been extended with infinitesimal utilities to give complete decision theories [12,15]. Systems of argumentation are based on the idea of constructing logical arguments for and against formulae. Such systems have been applied to problems such as diagnosis, protocol management and risk assessment [5], as well as handling inconsistent information [1], and providing a framework for default reasoning [4,9].

In this paper we provide a hybridisation of infinitesimal systems and systems of argumentation, by defining a system of argumentation which uses order of magnitude probabilities, in particular the values manipulated by the kappa calculus.

S. Benferhat and P. Besnard (Eds.): ECSQARU 2001, LNAI 2143, pp. 680–691, 2001.

2 Kappa Calculus

The kappa calculus is a formalism that makes it possible to handle order of magnitude probabilities, representing a state of belief by means of a ranking κ that maps propositions into class of ordinals. This mapping is such that:

$$\kappa(true) = 0 \tag{1}$$

$$\kappa(\phi \vee \psi) = \min(\kappa(\phi), \kappa(\psi)) \tag{2}$$

According to the kappa calculus, a proposition α is believed to degree s, if $\kappa(\neg\alpha) = s$; is disbelieved to degree s if $\kappa(\alpha) = s$; and is uncommitted if $\kappa(\alpha) = \kappa(\neg\alpha) = 0$. When accommodating disbelieved evidence, the choice about which beliefs have to be retracted depends on their strength.

The κ ranking also has the following properties, analogous to the familiar properties for probability distributions [7]:

$$\kappa(\phi) = \min_{\omega \models \phi} \kappa(\omega) \tag{3}$$

$$\kappa(\psi|\phi) = \kappa(\psi \wedge \phi) - \kappa(\phi) \tag{4}$$

Typically κ-values are assumed to be obtained from probabilities, by a form of order of magnitude abstraction in which all probabilities within a given order of magnitude are mapped to the same κ-value. Following Spohn [13], one can relate a probability p to κ-value k by:

$$\epsilon < \frac{p}{\epsilon^k} \leq 1$$

which of course is equivalent to:

$$\epsilon^{k+1} < p \leq \epsilon^k.$$

One procedure to map probabilities into κ values is [2]:

1. If $p = 0$ then print ∞;
2. $k \leftarrow 0$;
3. $p \leftarrow \frac{p}{\epsilon}$;
4. If $p > 1$, then print k otherwise $k \leftarrow k + 1$;
5. Goto 3;

and an alternative mapping has been suggested by Giang and Shenoy [6]. For this work we assume that either such a mapping has already been applied, or that the κ-values have been elicited directly—we just assume the existence of a set of κ-values for the propositions we are interested in.

3 The *QRK* System

Having introduced the kappa calculus, we can start to introduce the system of argumentation which will use κ-values.

3.1 Basic Concepts

We start with a set of atomic propositions $\mathcal{L}$. We also have a set of connectives $\{\neg, \rightarrow\}$, and the following set of rules for building the well-formed formulas (*wff*s) of the language.

1. If $l \in \mathcal{L}$ then l is a well-formed simple formula (*swff*).
2. If l is an *swff*, then $\neg l$ is an *swff*.
3. If l and m are *swff*s, then $l \rightarrow m$ is a well-formed implicational formula (*iwff*)

We denote the set of all *swff*s which can be derived using $\mathcal{L}$ by $\mathcal{S}_{\mathcal{L}}$, while $\mathcal{I}_{\mathcal{L}}$ denotes the corresponding set of *iwff*s. The set of *wff*s that can be defined using $\mathcal{L}$ is $\mathcal{W} = \mathcal{S}_{\mathcal{L}} \cup \mathcal{I}_{\mathcal{L}}$ may then be used to build up a database Δ where every item $d \in \Delta$ is a triple $(i : l : s)$ in which i is a token which uniquely identifies the database item (for convenience we will use the letter 'i' as an anonymous identifier), l is a *wff*, and s gives information about the degree of belief associated with l. In particular we distinguish two cases:

- l is an *swff*: In this case s is the pair expressing the degree of belief associated with l and the degree of disbelief associated with $\neg l$, that is $\langle \kappa(l), \kappa(\neg l) \rangle$;
- l is an *iwff*: In this case $\rightarrow$ does not represent material implication but that the antecedent of the *wff* has a probabilistic influence on the consequent. Therefore, the sign s indicates the belief in the consequent given the antecedent. Thus each *iwff* has associated with it a sign s which is the ordered set of four conditional κ-values: $\langle \kappa(m|l), \kappa(m|\neg l), \kappa(\neg m|l), \kappa(\neg m|\neg l) \rangle$.

Note that there is a notion of direction, similar to that in the directed arcs of probabilistic networks, associated with *iwff*s.

3.2 The Proof Theory

In the previous section we introduced a language for describing belief influences between formulae. For this to be useful we need to give a mechanism for taking sentences in that language and using them to derive new sentences. In particular we need to be able to take formulae with associated κ-values and use these to derive new formulae and their associated κ-values. This is done using the consequence relation $\vdash_{QRK}$ which is defined in Figure 1

The definition is in the form of Gentzen-style proof rules where the antecedents are written above the line and the consequent is written below. The consequence relation operates on a database of the kind of triples introduced in Section 3.1 and derives *arguments* about formulae from them. The concept of an argument is formally defined as follows:

Definition 1. *An* argument *for a well-formed formula p from a database Δ is a triple (p, G, Sg) such that $\Delta \vdash_{QRK} (p, G, Sg)$*

$$\text{Ax}\frac{}{\Delta \vdash_{QRK} (St, \{i\}, Sg)}\ (i : St : Sg) \in \Delta$$

$$\neg\text{-E}\frac{\Delta \vdash_{QRK} (\neg St, G, Sg)}{\Delta \vdash_{QRK} (St, G, \mathsf{neg}(Sg))}$$

$$\neg\text{-I}\frac{\Delta \vdash_{QRK} (St, G, Sg)}{\Delta \vdash_{QRK} (\neg St, G, \mathsf{neg}(Sg))}$$

$$\rightarrow\text{-E}\frac{\Delta \vdash_{QRK} (St, G, Sg) \quad \Delta \vdash_{QRK} (St \rightarrow St', G', Sg')}{\Delta \vdash_{QRK} (St', G \cup G', \mathsf{imp}_{\mathsf{elim}}(Sg, Sg'))}$$

$$\rightarrow\text{-R}\frac{\Delta \vdash_{QRK} (St', G, Sg) \quad \Delta \vdash_{QRK} (St \rightarrow St', G', Sg')}{\Delta \vdash_{QRK} (St, G \cup G', \mathsf{imp}_{\mathsf{rev}}(Sg, Sg'))}$$

Fig. 1. The consequence relation $\vdash_{QRK}$

The *sign* Sg of the argument denotes something about the degree of belief associated with the formula p, while the *grounds* G identify the elements of the database used in the derivation of p.

To see how the idea of an argument fits in with the proof rules in Figure 1, let us consider the rules Ax and $\rightarrow$-E. The first builds an argument from a triple $(i : St : Sg)$, which has a sign Sg and a set of grounds $\{i\}$, where the grounds identify which elements from the database are used in the derivation. This rule is a kind of bootstrap mechanism to allow the elements of the database to be turned into arguments to which other rules can be applied. The second, $\rightarrow$-E, can be thought of as analogous to modus ponens. From an argument for St and an argument for $St \rightarrow St'$ it is possible to build an argument for St' once the necessary book-keeping with grounds and signs has been carried out.

3.3 Combination Functions

In order to apply the proof rules of Figure 1 to build arguments, it is necessary to supply the functions used to combine signs. These are provided in this section.

The rules for handling negation are applicable only to *swff*s and permit negation to be either introduced or eliminated by altering the sign, for example allowing $(i : a : Sg)$ to be rewritten as $(i : \neg a : Sg')$. This leads to the definition of neg:

Definition 2. *The function neg:* $Sg \in [0, \infty[\times[0, \infty[\mapsto Sg' \in [0, \infty[\times[0, \infty[$ *is defined as follows:*

$$\begin{array}{ll} If & Sg = \langle s, s' \rangle \\ Then & Sg' = \langle s', s \rangle \end{array}$$

To deal with implication we need two elimination functions $\mathsf{imp}_{\mathsf{elim}}$ and $\mathsf{imp}_{\mathsf{rev}}$, where the former establishes the sign of formulae generated by the rule of inference $\rightarrow$-E, while the latter is used to establish the sign of formulae generated by

$\rightarrow$-R. We start by discussing $\mathsf{imp_{elim}}$. Let us suppose we have an implicational formula $(i : a \rightarrow b : Sg)$ where Sg is the quadruple of κ-values:

$$\langle \kappa(b|a), \kappa(b|\neg a), \kappa(\neg b|a), \kappa(\neg b|\neg a)\rangle$$

if we have the *swff*

$$(j : a : \langle \kappa(a), \kappa(\neg a)\rangle)$$

then by applying the rule $\mathsf{imp_{elim}}$ we can obtain b and the pair $\langle \kappa(b), \kappa(\neg b)\rangle$. In order to do so we have to combine $\langle \kappa(b|a), \kappa(b|\neg a), \kappa(\neg b|a), \kappa(\neg b|\neg a)\rangle$ with $\langle \kappa(a), \kappa(\neg a)\rangle$.

Definition 3. *The function* $\mathsf{imp_{elim}}$: $Sg \in [0,\infty[\times[0,\infty[\times Sg' \in [0,\infty[^4 \mapsto Sg'' \in [0,\infty[\times[0,\infty[$ *is defined as follows:*

$$\begin{aligned} If \quad & Sg = \langle s, s'\rangle \\ & Sg' = \langle r, r', t, t'\rangle \\ Then \; & Sg'' = \langle w, w'\rangle \end{aligned}$$

where:

$$w = \min(r + s, r' + s')$$
$$w' = \min(t + s, t' + s')$$

These two equalities are obtained by turning the probabilities in Jeffrey's rule [8] into κ-values.

The function $\mathsf{imp_{rev}}$ is obtained by computing $\Pr(a)$ by manipulating Jeffrey's rule for probabilities with Bayes' rule and then by mapping this expression into kappa calculus.

Definition 4. *The function* $\mathsf{imp_{rev}}$: $Sg \in [0,\infty[\times[0,\infty[\times Sg' \in [0,\infty[^4 \mapsto Sg'' \in [0,\infty[\times[0,\infty[$ *is defined as follows:*

$$\begin{aligned} If \quad & Sg = \langle s, s'\rangle \\ & Sg' = \langle r, r', t, t'\rangle \\ Then \; & Sg'' = \langle w, w'\rangle \end{aligned}$$

where:

$$w = \min\{s - \min(r, r' - 1), r' - 1 - \min(r, r' - 1)\}$$

and

$$w' = \begin{cases} \min\{s - \min(r', r - 1), r - 1 - \min(r', r - 1)\} & \text{if } w \neq 0 \\ \infty & \text{otherwise} \end{cases}$$

3.4 Soundness and Completeness

In order to prove soundness and completeness we first need to capture the kind of relationships that may hold between two formulae:

Definition 5. *A well-formed formula p is said to be a* cause *of a well-formed formula q if and only if it is possible to identify an ordered set of* iwffs $\{p \rightarrow c_1, c_1 \rightarrow c_2, \ldots, c_n \rightarrow q\}$.

That is, p is a cause of q if it is possible to build up a trail of (causally directed) implications linking p to q.

Definition 6. *A well-formed formula p is said to be an* effect *of a well-formed formula q if and only if q is a cause of p.*

Thus p is an effect of q if it is possible to build up a trail of (causally directed) implications linking q to p. Soundness will relate to ensuring that given information about the κ-value of a particular formula we can compute the correct κ-value of its causes and effects, and completeness will relate to ensuring that we can compute the κ-values of all such causes and effects.

Before proceeding to prove soundness and completeness, we need to take into account two problems which can arise when doing evidential reasoning, that is reasoning both in the direction of the implications and in the opposite direction. We are enabled to use evidential reasoning by having included the rule $\rightarrow$-R in the consequence relation. The first problem arises because when implications are reversed, then the proof procedure can loop and therefore build an infinite number of arguments. This is possible even if we have a single *iwff* since there is nothing to stop the proof procedure alternately applying $\rightarrow$-E and $\rightarrow$-R forever, building a new argument from each application. However, the problem can be easily solved by introducing the concept of a *minimal argument* as in [10]:

Definition 7. *A* minimal argument *is an argument in which no* iwff *appears more than once.*

We then reject non-minimal arguments, as we shall see below.

The second problem to deal with is caused by the need to handle conditional independence in the proper way. If proof rules are applied blindly then it is possible to build arguments which do not respect conditional independence. Such arguments would not be valid according to the kappa calculus, so they need to be eliminated. To identify arguments that are invalid because of conditional independence we introduce the notion of *d-separation* from probabilistic networks, suitably modified for κ-values. However, before proceeding any further we first need to introduce some additional definitions:

Definition 8. *A* source *of an argument* (p, G, Sg) *is an* swff *from G*

That is a source of an argument is one of the simple formula which grounds it, and therefore is the head of a chain of implications. In the same way we define the *destination* of an argument as:

Definition 9. *The* destination *of an argument* (p, G, Sg) *is p.*

We then define d-separation as follows:

Definition 10. *Two formulae p and q are* d-separated *if for all arguments which have p as their source and q as their destination, there is another formula r such that either:*

1. *p is a cause of r, r is a cause of q, and either r or $\neg r$ is known to be true; or*
2. *p is an effect of r, q is an effect of r, and either r or $\neg r$ is known to be true; or*
3. *p and q are both causes of r and there is no argument (r, G, Sg) such that all the* swffs *in G are effects of r.*

We are now in a position to define the subset of all arguments which do not suffer from the two problems we discussed above:

Definition 11. *An argument $A = (p, G, Sg)$ is invalid if any of the sources of A are d-separated from p.*

and consequently

Definition 12. *An argument $A = (p, G, Sg)$ is valid if it is not invalid.*

The set of minimal valid arguments are then the problem-free subset of all possible arguments which can be built from some database of triples.

Now, because arguments in *QRK* typically only indicate a degree of belief in a formula (rather than indicating that it is true or false), in general there will be several minimal valid arguments concerning it with differing degrees of belief. To combine these, we define a *flattening* function, and we do this in a way such that only minimal and valid arguments are taken into account. This function, $\mathsf{Flat}(\cdot)$ is a mapping from a set of arguments $\mathbf{A}^{\Delta}_{St}$ for a formula St built from a particular database Δ to the pair of that proposition and some overall measure of validity. Thus we have:

$$\mathbf{A}^{\Delta}_{St} = \{(St, G_i, Sg_i) | \Delta \vdash_{QRK} (St, G_i, Sg_i)\}$$

and then

$$\mathsf{Flat} : \{A \in \mathbf{A}^{\Delta}_{St} | A \text{ is minimal and valid}\} \mapsto \langle St, v\rangle$$

where v is a single pair of κ-values, $\langle \kappa(St), \kappa(\neg St)$. The value v is then the result of a suitable combination of all the signs of all the arguments for St:

$$v = \mathsf{MIN}_i(\{Sg_i | (St, G_i, Sg_i) \in \mathbf{A'}^{\Delta}_{St}\})$$

where each Sg_i is a pair $\langle \kappa(St), \kappa(\neg St)\rangle$, $\mathbf{A'}^{\Delta}_{St}$ is the set of all minimal, valid arguments in $\mathbf{A}^{\Delta}_{St}$, and the function MIN_i is defined as follows:

$$\mathsf{MIN}_i(\langle \kappa(a_i), \kappa(\neg a_i)\rangle) = \langle \min_i \kappa(a_i), \max_i \kappa(\neg a_i)\rangle$$

This definition of the flattening function is motivated by the fact that if we have different arguments, we want to consider the most plausible one—that is we tend to choose the one associated with the most normal world, therefore the one for which holds that a is highly believed while $\neg a$ is highly disbelieved.

Once the flattening function is established we can use it to provide a procedure to determine the overall procedure for determining the measure of belief in a formula q in which we are interested. This procedure is:

1. Add a triple $(i : p : s)$ for every formula p whose degree of belief is known;
2. Build $\mathbf{A}_q^{\Delta}$, the set of all arguments for q using the rules given in Figure 1;
3. Flatten this set to give $\langle q, \langle \kappa(q), \kappa(\neg q)\rangle\rangle$;

Given the previous definitions it is possible to show that, given information about the degree of belief in (that is the the κ-value associated with) some formula p, the rules of the consequence relation $\vdash_{QRK}$ may be used to soundly and completely compute arguments concerning the change in the degree of belief associated with the causes and effects of p.

Theorem 13. *The construction and flattening of arguments in* QRK *using the rules of* $\vdash_{QRK}$ *is sound with respect to the kappa calculus*

Proof. The proof is by showing the soundness of the combination functions. For $\mathsf{imp_{elim}}$: Let us consider the *iwff* $(i : a \to b : Sg)$, where Sg is quadruple of κ-values:

$$\langle \kappa(b|a), \kappa(b|\neg a), \kappa(\neg b|a), \kappa(\neg b|\neg a)\rangle$$

From the sign of $a \to b$ and the sign of a, which is $\langle \kappa(a), \kappa(\neg a)\rangle$ we want to be able to calculate the sign of the formula b, which is $\langle \kappa(b), \kappa(\neg b)\rangle$. Since κ-values are equivalent to probabilities, we manipulate Jeffrey's rule [8] and then map into κ-values in order to obtain $\kappa(b)$. Jeffrey's rule for probabilities is:

$$\Pr(b) = \Pr(b|a)\Pr(a) + \Pr(b|\neg a)\Pr(\neg a)$$

which can be mapped into the kappa calculus expression:

$$\kappa(b) = \min\{\kappa(b|a) + \kappa(a), \kappa(b|\neg a) + \kappa(\neg u)\}$$

In the same way we can use Jeffrey's rule to calculate the probability $\Pr(\neg b)$ from which we obtain the κ-value formulation for $\kappa(\neg b)$:

$$\kappa(\neg b) = \min\{\kappa(\neg b|a) + \kappa(a), \kappa(\neg b|\neg a) + \kappa(\neg a)\}$$

since this is exactly the combination function used, $\mathsf{imp_{elim}}$ is sound. $\mathsf{imp_{rev}}$ is slightly less straightforward and requires a few manipulations. This function calculates the sign of a formula a starting from the *iwff* $(i : a \to b : s)$ and the *swff* $(j : b : \langle \kappa(b), \kappa(\neg b)\rangle)$. We start by proving the formula for $\kappa(a)$. Jeffrey's rule is

$$\Pr(b) = \Pr(b|a)\Pr(a) + \Pr(b|\neg a)\Pr(\neg a)$$

which can be rewritten as:

$$\Pr(b) = \Pr(b|a)\Pr(a) + \Pr(b|\neg a)(1 - \Pr(a))$$

which is

$$\Pr(b) = \Pr(b|a)\Pr(a) - \Pr(b|\neg a) + \Pr(b|\neg a)\Pr(a)$$

therefore $\Pr(a)$ is obtained as:

$$\Pr(a)(\Pr(b|a) - \Pr(b|\neg a)) = \Pr(b) - \Pr(b|\neg a)$$

and so

$$\Pr(a) = \frac{\Pr(b) - \Pr(b|\neg a)}{\Pr(b|a) - \Pr(b|\neg a)}$$

which mapped into the kappa calculus becomes:

$$\kappa(a) = \min\{\kappa(b) - \min[\kappa(b|a), \kappa(b|\neg a) - 1], \kappa(b|\neg a) - 1 - \min[\kappa(b|a), \kappa(b|\neg a) - 1]\}$$

where the absolute value is added to make sure $\kappa(a) \geq 0$. In the same way the expression for $\kappa(\neg a)$ can be computed, thus obtaining:

$$\kappa(\neg a) = \min\{\kappa(b) - \min[\kappa(b|\neg a), \kappa(b|a) - 1], \kappa(b|a) - 1 - \min[\kappa(b|\neg a), \kappa(b|a) - 1]\}$$

neg is quite straightforward, following directly from the definition. The soundness of the flattening function can be proved by demonstrating that if we have two different arguments for a formula c, one from a to b and then to c and the second from d to b to c then the degree of belief which results from flattening the two arguments is the same that would be computed were there only one argument from a and d in combination to b, and then from b to c, where the combination is disjunctive, making something like the usual Noisy-Or assumption. In the first case we have the following chain of formulae:

1. $a \rightarrow b \rightarrow c$
2. $d \rightarrow b \rightarrow c$

and the two *swffs* $(i : a : \langle \kappa(a), \kappa(\neg a) \rangle)$ and $(j : d : \langle \kappa(d), \kappa(\neg d) \rangle)$ Let us denote with $\kappa_1(c)$ the degree of belief associated with the first argument and with $\kappa_2(c)$ the degree of belief associated with the second one. By applying $\rightarrow$-E twice we can compute:

$$\begin{aligned}\kappa_1(c) = \min\ \{&\kappa(c|b) + \min[\kappa(b|a) + \kappa(a), \kappa(b|\neg a) + \kappa(\neg a)],\\ &\kappa(c|\neg b) + \min[\kappa(\neg b|a) + \kappa(a), \kappa(\neg b|\neg a) + \kappa(\neg a)]\}\end{aligned}$$

where we have used the following substitutions:

$$\begin{aligned}\kappa(b) &= \min\{\kappa(b|a) + \kappa(a), \kappa(b|\neg a) + \kappa(\neg a)\}\\ \kappa(\neg b) &= \min\{\kappa(\neg b|a) + \kappa(a), \kappa(\neg b|\neg a) + \kappa(\neg a)\}\end{aligned}$$

Analogously we can compute $\kappa_2(c)$ as:

$$\begin{aligned}\kappa_2(c) = \min\{&\kappa(c|b) + \min[\kappa(b|d) + \kappa(d), \kappa(b|\neg d) + \kappa(\neg d)],\\ &\kappa(c|\neg b) + \min[\kappa(\neg b|d) + \kappa(d), \kappa(\neg b|\neg d) + \kappa(\neg d)]\}.\end{aligned}$$

In order to compute the degree of belief associated with c we need to flatten the two arguments by using the flattening function defined above. If we flatten them the resulting degree of belief will be

$$\langle \min(\kappa_1(c), \kappa_2(c)), \max(\kappa_1(\neg c), \kappa_2(\neg c)) \rangle$$

that is for c the overall κ-value is:

$$\min\{\min[\kappa(c|b) + \alpha, \kappa(c|\neg b) + \beta], \min[\kappa(c|b) + \gamma, \kappa(c|\neg b) + \delta]\}$$

where:

$$\alpha = \min[\kappa(b|a) + \kappa(a), \kappa(b|\neg a) + \kappa(\neg a)]$$
$$\beta = \min[\kappa(\neg b|a) + \kappa(a), \kappa(\neg b|\neg a) + \kappa(\neg a)]$$
$$\gamma = \min[\kappa(b|d) + \kappa(d), \kappa(b|\neg d) + \kappa(\neg d)]$$
$$\delta = \min[\kappa(\neg b|d) + \kappa(d), \kappa(\neg b|\neg d) + \kappa(\neg d)]$$

This can be rewritten as:

$$\min\{\kappa(c|b) + \min(\alpha, \gamma), \kappa(c|\neg b) + \min(\beta, \delta)\}$$

This result is the same as the degree of belief which would be computed were the degree of belief in b first computed from a disjunctive dependence on a and d and the result then propagated to c. Something very similar can be carried out for the κ-value of $\neg c$, but with max in place of the outer min, thus proving that QRK flattens arguments soundly. This concludes the proof. □

Having proved the soundness we can move on to prove completeness, but before giving such a proof we need to define what we mean by completeness.

Definition 14. *The construction and flattening of arguments is said to be* complete *with respect to some formula p if it is possible to use that system to compute all the κ-values of all the effects of p, all the causes of p and all the causes and effects of all the causes and effects of p.*

With this definition it is now possible to state and prove the following theorem:

Theorem 15. *The construction and flattening of arguments in* QRK *is complete with respect to any formula.*

Proof. The proof follows from the definition of $\vdash QRK$, that is the κ-value of all the causes and effects of any well-formed formula p which may be stated in QRK can be made by the application of the appropriate proof rules. In proving this we need to distinguish proof of completeness for causes from those for effects. We start from the latter. Let us consider the addition of the triple $(i : p : (\kappa(p), \kappa(\neg p)))$ where p contains no negation symbols, to a database that contains only formulae without negation symbols. We can have two types of of effect of p: The first are consequents of implications in which p forms the antecedent while the second are those effects that are related to p by two or more implications. In the first case the κ-values associated with the formula can be computed by applying the proof rule $\rightarrow$-E. In the latter case the degree of belief associated with the formula may be obtained by recursively applying the $\rightarrow$-E rule.

Analogously, we can recognise two types of causes of p, those which are antecedents of implications where p is the consequent and those which are causes that are related to p by two or more implications. In the first case the κ-value associated with the formula is computed by $\rightarrow$-R while in the second case the κ-value may be obtained by recursively applying $\rightarrow$-R.

Applying both $\rightarrow$-E and $\rightarrow$-R recursively is sufficient to ensure completeness for situations without negation, and the appropriate use of the rules $\neg$-I and $\neg$-E make it possible to deal with situations in which the negation symbol appears. □

4 Example

Let us suppose we have the following information about the health of a friend. The event that our friend has a cold (C) increases the belief that she is sneezing (S). But also the event R that she has an allergic reaction increases the belief that she is sneezing. The event T, that our friend has taken some antihistamine, however, reduces the belief that she is sneezing, while the event that she has an allergic reaction R increases the belief that she has taken an antihistamine. The event A, that our friend is allergic to cats increases the belief that she might have an allergic reaction. This information may be represented as:

$$\begin{array}{l}(r1 : C \rightarrow S : \langle\kappa(S|C) = 0, \kappa(\neg S|C) = 1, \kappa(S|\neg C) = 2, \kappa(\neg S|\neg C) = 1\rangle) \ \Delta \\ (r2 : R \rightarrow S : \langle\kappa(S|R) = 0, \kappa(\neg S|R) = 1, \kappa(S|\neg R) = 2, \kappa(\neg S|\neg R) = 1\rangle) \\ (r3 : T \rightarrow S : \langle\kappa(S|T) = 2, \kappa(\neg S|T) = 1, \kappa(S|\neg T) = 1, \kappa(\neg S|\neg T) = 1\rangle) \\ (r4 : R \rightarrow T : \langle\kappa(T|R) = 1, \kappa(\neg T|R) = 1, \kappa(T|\neg R) = 4, \kappa(\neg T|\neg R) = 1\rangle)\end{array}$$

If we believe that our friend is having an allergic reaction, then we can add the following fact to Δ:

$$(f1 : R : \langle\kappa(R) = 1, \kappa(\neg R) = 3\rangle).$$

Adding this fact permits us to build two minimal, valid arguments concerning our friend taking antihistamine:

$$\Delta \vdash_{QRK} (T,\ \{f1, r4\},\ \langle\kappa 1(T) = 3, \kappa 1(\neg T) = 3\rangle\rangle),$$

by applying $\rightarrow$-E once while if we first apply $\rightarrow$-E and then $\rightarrow$-R we obtain:

$$\Delta \vdash_{QRK} (T,\ \{f1, r2, r3\},\ \langle\kappa 2(T) = 0, \kappa 2(\neg T) = \infty\rangle)$$

By flattening these combine to give the pair $\langle T, \langle\kappa(T) = 0, \kappa(\neg T) = \infty\rangle\rangle$ to indicate that the event that our friend is not taking antihistamine warrants a much greater degree of disbelief than the event that she is taking antihistamine.

5 Conclusions

In this paper we have presented *QRK*, a system of argumentation in which uncertainty is handled using infinitesimal probability values, in particular values from the kappa calculus. The use of κ-values means that the system can be used when probabilistic knowledge of a domain is incomplete, and this makes it applicable to a wider range of situations with respect to systems based on complete probabilistic information. The system associates a κ-value with every logical formula, and combines these values as arguments are built in a way which is sound with respect to the kappa calculus. Thus the arguments which can be constructed in *QRK* come complete with an order of magnitude estimate of the probability of the formula supported by the argument, and the system thus supports qualitative probabilistic reasoning.

References

1. S. Benferhat, D. Dubois, and H. Prade. Argumentative inference in uncertain and inconsistent knowledge bases. In *Proceedings of the 9th Conference on Uncertainty in Artificial Intelligence*, 1993.
2. A. Darwiche and M. Goldszmidt. On the relation between kappa calculus and probabilistic reasoning. In *Proceedings of the 10th Conference on Uncertainty in Artificial Intelligence*, 1994.
3. M. J. Druzdzel. *Probabilistic reasoning in decision support systems: from computation to common sense.* PhD thesis, Carnegie Mellon University, 1993.
4. P. M. Dung. On the acceptability of arguments and its fundamental role in non-monotonic reasoning and logic programming. In *Proceedings of the 13th International Conference on Artificial Intelligence*, 1993.
5. J. Fox. A unified framework for hypothetical and practical reasoning (2): lessons from clinical medicine. In *Proceedings of the Conference on Formal and Applied Practical Reasoning*, 1996.
6. P. H. Giang and P. P. Shenoy. On transformations between probability and Spohnian disbelief functions. In K. B. Laskey and H. Prade, editors, *Proceedings of the 15th Conference on Uncertainty in Artificial Intelligence*, pages 236–244, San Francisco, CA, 1999. Morgan Kaufmann.
7. M. Goldszmidt and J. Pearl. Qualitative probabilistic for default reasoning, belief revision, and causal modelling. *Artificial Intelligence*, 84(1-2):57–112, 1996.
8. R. Jeffrey. *The logic of decision.* University of Chicago Press, Chicago, IL, 2nd edition, 1983.
9. R. Loui. Defeat among arguments: a system of defeasible inference. *Computational Intelligence*, 3:100–106, 1987.
10. S. Parsons. A proof theoretic approach to qualitative probabilistic reasoning. *International Journal od Approximate Reasoning*, 19:265–297, 1998.
11. S. Parsons. *Qualitative approaches to reasoning under uncertainty.* MIT Press, (to appear), Cambridge, MA, 1998.
12. J. Pearl. From conditional oughts to qualitative decision theory. In *Proceedings of the 9th Conference on Uncertainty in Artificial Intelligence*, 1993.
13. W. Spohn. Ordinal conditional functions: A dynamic theory of epistemic states. In W.L. Harper and B. Skyrms, editors, *Causation in Decision, Belief Change, and Statistics*, volume 2, pages 105–134. 1987.
14. M. P. Wellman. *Formulation of tradeoffs in planning under uncertainty.* Pitman, London, 1990.
15. N. Wilson. An order of magnitude calculus. In *Proceedings of the 11th Conference on Uncertainty in Artificial Intelligence*, 1995.

Importance Measures from Reliability Theory for Probabilistic Assumption-Based Reasoning

Bernhard Anrig*

Department of Informatics, University of Fribourg
CH–1700 Fribourg, Switzerland
Bernhard.Anrig@unifr.ch,
http://www-iiuf.unifr.ch/tcs

Abstract. Importance measures are a well-known concept developed in reliability theory. Here, we apply this concept to assumption-based reasoning, a field which in fact is quite close to reliability theory. Based on quasi-supporting and supporting arguments, we develop two concepts of importance measures and show how they are related to the ones from reliability theory.

1 Introduction

Consider a typical situation in model-based diagnostics as described in general in (Kohlas *et al.*, 1998, Anrig, 2000): given some knowledge about, for example, an electronic device in a propositional language over propositions and assumptions, sometimes together with some observations on the in- and outputs of the system, one can compute symbolic and numerical diagnoses and conflicts as well as support, doubt, etc. for the interesting hypotheses. In model-based diagnostics, we are especially interested in the symbolic and numerical values for the (minimal) conflicts and the (minimal) diagnoses. The question addressed in this paper is: which one(s) of the assumptions does influence the conflicts (or diagnoses) at most? Which assumptions are more relevant, which ones less relevant, and which are irrelevant? We will use the term *importance* instead of *relevance* inspired by reliability theory (Beichelt, 1993), see also Section 4.

The approach considered in this paper is based on computing symbolic arguments and only afterwards their respective probabilities. In Section 4 we consider some of the connections between computing conflicts and diagnoses and the computation of structure functions in reliability theory,

In the sequel, we will use the formalism of assumption-based reasoning as introduced in (Kohlas *et al.*, 1998, 2000); we refer also to these articles for a comparison with the work of Reiter (1987) as well as De Kleer & Williams, Provan, Laskey & Lehner, and others.

The following example will be used throughout this paper to illustrate the different concepts.

* Research supported by grant No. 2000-061454.00 of the Swiss National Foundation for Research.

S. Benferhat and P. Besnard (Eds.): ECSQARU 2001, LNAI 2143, pp. 692–703, 2001.

Example 1. A network with binary gates. Consider a network which consists of "or" gates or_1, or_2, or_3 and "exclusive-or" gates xor_1, xor_2 connected as in Fig. 1. The values of the in- and outputs of the system are assumed to be observed according to Fig. 1.

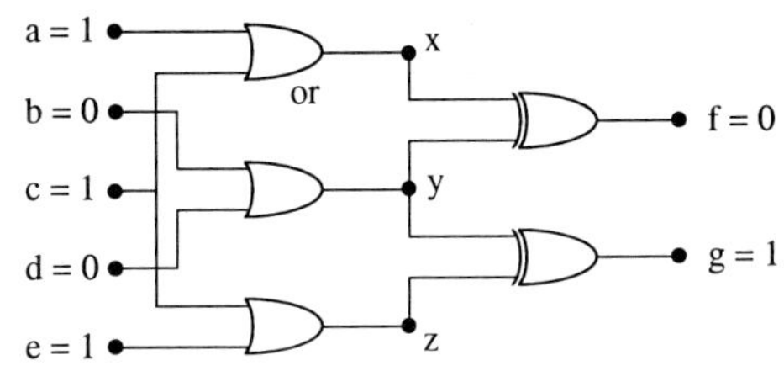

Fig. 1. An arithmetical network.

The behavior of each component is expressed by a material implication, so for example the or-gate or_1 is specified by

$$or_1 \rightarrow (out \leftrightarrow (in_1 \vee in_2))$$

i.e. if the or-gate is working correctly (or_1 true) then its output is on only if at least one of the inputs is so. Nothing is known about the behavior of a faulty component. An analogue modeling is given for the other gates. Assume that the probability of a component working correctly is 0.95 for xor-gates and 0.97 for or-gates. Apparently, the observations in Fig. 1 imply that the system is not working correctly, because the predicted output (1) at point f is in conflict with the observed one (0). The minimal conflicts and diagnoses can be computed using standard techniques (for example using a solver for ABEL, see Haenni *et al.*, 2000) as sets

$$qs(\bot) = \{xor_1 \wedge or_1 \wedge or_2,\ xor_1 \wedge xor_2 \wedge or_1 \wedge or_3\},$$
$$sp(\top) = \{\neg or_1,\ \neg xor_1,\ \neg or_2 \wedge \neg or_3,\ \neg xor_2 \wedge \neg or_2\}$$

of conjunctions over assumptions in $\{or_1, or_2, or_3, xor_1, xor_2\}$ and, for example, $p(qs(\bot)) = 0.919$. Now the question is: which assumption is important? Or, in more detail, which assumption does influence the probabilities of the diagnoses and/or conflicts at most? Which one has no importance? In this example, one can deduce from the graphical representation of the situation (Fig. 1), that the or-gate or_1 and the xor-gate xor_1 are more important than the other components but there is no component which has no influence at all. ⊖

In the remainder of this section, we will introduce the basic definitions for the concept of assumption-based reasoning; for further introductory literature see (Kohlas *et al.*, 2000).

A tuple (Σ, P, A, Π) is called a *probabilistic argumentation system* (Kohlas *et al.*, 2000) where P and $A = \{a_1, a_2, \ldots, a_n\}$ are sets of of propositional variables with $A \cap P = \emptyset$, the elements of P are called *propositions*, the elements of A *assumptions*. Let $N \subseteq A \cup P$, then $\mathcal{L}_N$ denotes the propositional language built over the atoms $N \cup \{\top, \bot\}$ using the connectors $\wedge$, $\vee$, $\neg$, $\rightarrow$, and $\leftrightarrow$, as well as parentheses. The element $\bot$ represent inconsistency and is therefore never true, and $\top$ represents tautology and is always true. Logical equivalence of formulas from this language is denoted by "$\equiv$". $C_N \subseteq \mathcal{L}_N$ is the set of all the conjunctions in $\mathcal{L}_N$. The consequence operator "$\models$" is defined in the usual way using sets of models.

The set of formulas $\Sigma \subseteq \mathcal{L}_{A \cup P}$ is called the *knowledge base* and models the information available, for example the behaviour of a complex system. We assume that this knowledge base is not contradictory, i.e. $\bigwedge \Sigma \not\equiv \bot$. Besides, there are formulas from $\mathcal{L}_P$ which are called *observations* and will be added to the knowledge base in some situations.

Π is a set of probabilities $\{p_{a_1}, \ldots, p_{a_n}\}$ such that $p(a) = p_a$ for every $a \in A$. Here, we assume that the p_a's are independent. These probabilities imply a probability $p : \mathcal{L}_A \to [0,1]$ on the propositional language $\mathcal{L}_A$ by

$$p(f) = \sum_{\substack{\xi_1 \wedge \xi_2 \wedge \cdots \wedge \xi_n \models f \\ \xi_i \in \{a_i, \neg a_i\}}} \prod_{\xi_i = a_i} p_{a_i} \cdot \prod_{\xi_i = \neg a_i} (1 - p_{a_i})$$

for $f \in \mathcal{L}_A$. Algorithms for efficiently computing the probability $p(f)$ are discussed in (Kohlas & Monney, 1995, Bertschy & Monney, 1996).

2 Importance Based on Differences of Probabilities of Conflicts

The first importance measure depends on the basic notions of conflict and quasi-support defined in probabilistic argumentation systems. For $f \in \mathcal{L}_{A \cup P}$ the quasi-support $qs(f, \Sigma)$ and the degree of quasi-support $dqs(f, \Sigma)$ relative to the knowledge base Σ are defined as

$$qs(f, \Sigma) = \{a \in C_A : a, \Sigma \models f\}, \qquad dqs(f, \Sigma) = p(qs(f, \Sigma)).$$

Often, we omit Σ and consider the sets $qs(f)$ as disjunctions of conjunctions, i.e. as disjunctive normal forms (DNF). The context will always indicate which representation is used.

The probability of a quasi-support for $a \in A$ can be computed as

$$dqs(a) = p(a \vee qs(\bot)) = p(a) + p(\neg a \wedge qs(\bot)), \tag{1}$$

where the first part depends only on a, the second only on $\neg a$. Consider now the formulas

$$qs_a(\bot) := (qs(\bot))[\top/a] = \{c \in qs(\bot) : a \text{ in } c \text{ is instantiated by } \top\}$$
$$qs_{\neg a}(\bot) := (qs(\bot))[\bot/a] = \{c \in qs(\bot) : a \text{ in } c \text{ is instantiated by } \bot\}$$

The formulas $qs_a(\bot)$ and $qs_{\neg a}(\bot)$ are independent of a and $\neg a$, because the variable a does not occur any more. This allows to write the degree of quasi support in the following form:

$$dqs(a) = p(a) + p(\neg a \wedge qs_{\neg a}(\bot)) = p_a + (1 - p_a)p(qs_{\neg a}(\bot)).$$

Consider now the quasi-support of a as a function of the probability p_a, i.e.

$$f_a(p_a) := p_a + (1 - p_a)p(qs_{\neg a}(\bot)).$$

This function is linearly dependent of the probability p_a and $f_a(0) = p(qs_{\neg a}(\bot))$ as well as $f_a(1) = 1$.

Using the above ideas, we can say that an assumption $a \in A$ is important, if the difference $|p(qs_a(\bot)) - p(qs_{\neg a}(\bot))|$ is large.

Definition 1. *The D-importance of* $a \in A$ *is* $I^{\mathrm{D}}(a) = |p(qs_a(\bot)) - p(qs_{\neg a}(\bot))|$.

This definition has a nice property, namely that $I^{\mathrm{D}}(a) = I^{\mathrm{D}}(\neg a)$ so that we can talk of *the* D-importance of the assumption a. We will reconsider this idea in Section 4, where we will show that this approach is related to reliability theory and we will argue why it is not our preferred approach. But first, an example:

Example 2. (Continuation of Example 1) First, the values $p(qs_x(\bot))$ are computed for $x \in \{xor_1, \neg xor_1, \ldots, or_3, \neg or_3\}$. This computation is addressed in Section 5. The results are:

x	xor_1	xor_2	or_1	or_2	or_3
$p(qs_x(\bot))$	0.9463	0.9192	0.9662	0.9215	0.9201
$p(qs_{\neg x}(\bot))$	0	0.8754	0	0.8492	0.8754

(2)

This allows then to compute the following D-importances:

Component	xor_1	xor_2	or_1	or_2	or_3
$I^{\mathrm{D}}(\cdot)$	**0.9463**	0.0438	**0.9662**	0.0723	0.0447

So, the components xor_1 and or_1 have the highest D-importance, which is exactly what we have noted in Example 1 using a graphical argumentation. ⊖

3 Importance Based on Distances of Degrees of Support

In the framework of probabilistic argumentation systems, the concept of quasi-support is considered as a computationally interesting aid for determining supports. For $f \in \mathcal{L}_{A \cup P}$ define the support $sp(f)$ and degree of support $dsp(f)$ by

$$sp(f) = \{a \in C_A : a, \Sigma \models f,\ a, \Sigma \not\models \bot\} = qs(f) - qs(\bot),$$

$$dsp(f) = \frac{p(sp(f))}{1-p(qs(\bot))} = \frac{p(qs(f))-p(qs(\bot))}{1-p(qs(\bot))}.$$

We refer to (Kohlas *et al.*, 1998, 2000) for further discussion of the interpretation of supports and degrees of supports. As above with qs, we often consider the sets $sp(f)$ as DNFs.

For the degree of support, $p_a = 0$ implies $dsp(a) = 0$ and $p_a = 1$ implies $dsp(a) = 1$, but $dsp(a)$ does not linearly depend on p_a. Again, we try to separate the probability $p(a)$ of a from the rest of the information, i.e. using definitions from above we get

$$dsp(a) = \frac{p(a \vee qs(\bot)) - p(qs(\bot))}{1 - p(qs(\bot))} = \frac{p_a - p_a p(qs_a(\bot))}{1 - p_a p(qs_a(\bot)) - (1 - p_a)p(qs_{\neg a}(\bot))}.$$

Using an analogue idea as in the previous section, we can define the degree of support of a as a function of the probability p_a:

$$g_a(p_a) := \begin{cases} 0 & \text{if } p_a = 0, \\ \frac{1-p(qs_a(\perp))}{\frac{1}{p_a}(1-p(qs_{\neg a}(\perp))-p(qs_a(\perp))+p(qs_{\neg a}(\perp))} & \text{otherwise.} \end{cases} \tag{3}$$

In the sequel, it is often more convenient to consider g_a as a function of three arguments, i.e. we define the function γ as

$$\gamma(x,p_1,p_2) = \begin{cases} 0 & \text{if } x = 0, \\ \frac{1-p_1}{\frac{1}{x}(1-p_2)-p_1+p_2} & \text{otherwise} \end{cases} \tag{4}$$

for every $0 \leq p_1, p_2 < 1$.[1] So we have $g_a(p_a) = \gamma(p_a, p(qs_a(\perp)), p(qs_{\neg a}(\perp)))$.

Lemma 1. *In the interval* $[0,1]$ *the function* g_a *is symmetric with respect to the function* $x \mapsto 1-x$, *i.e.* $g_a(1-g_a(p_a)) = 1-p_a$ *for* $p_a \in [0,1]$.

In the interval $]0,1[$ *the function* g_a *is monotone strict increasing.*

For proofs see (Anrig, 2001).

Let us now consider the situation, where two different assumptions a and b and their corresponding functions g_a and g_b are given.

Lemma 2. *Given two functions* g_a *and* g_b *as above, if there exists a point* $x \in]0,1[$ *for which* $g_a(x) > g_b(x)$, *then* $g_a > g_b$ *in the interval* $]0,1[$.

In other words, there is a complete order on the set of functions $\{g_a : a \in A\}$ in the interval $]0,1[$. This order will be formalized in the following.

Example 3. (Cont. of Ex. 2)
We compute the five functions g_{or_1}, g_{or_2}, g_{or_3}, g_{xor_1}, and g_{xor_2} using (2); this means that we have to compute the graph of γ for five different situations, so for example for xor_1 we have $g_{xor_1}(p_{xor_1}) = \gamma(p_{xor_1}, 0.9463, 0)$. See Fig. 2 for the graphs of these functions. ⊖

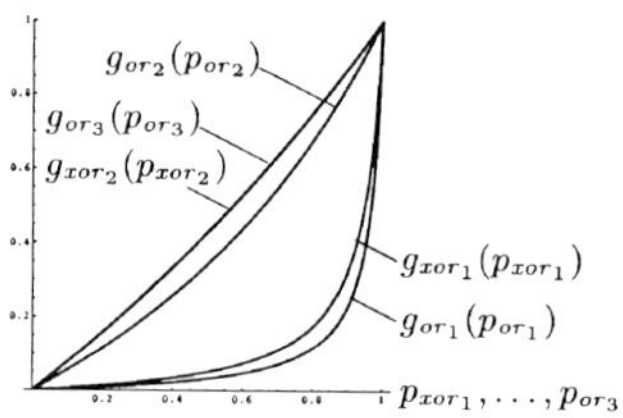

Fig. 2. (g_{xor_2} and g_{or_3} are nearly equal).

We will characterize in the sequel every function g_a by its maximal distance to the function $x \mapsto x$, i.e. we define

$$d_a := \max_{0<x<1} d\left((x, g_a(x)), (\frac{x+g_a(x)}{2}, \frac{x+g_a(x)}{2})\right)$$

or, using the definition of γ in (4) for $\gamma(\cdot, p_1, p_2) = g_a(\cdot)$,

$$d_{p_1,p_2} := \max_{0<x<1} d\left((x, \gamma(x,p_1,p_2)), (\frac{x+\gamma(x,p_1,p_2)}{2}, \frac{x+\gamma(x,p_1,p_2)}{2})\right)$$

where d is the usual euclidean distance function. The function $x \mapsto x$, which is equal to $\gamma(\cdot, p, p)$ for any $0 \leq p < 1$, has clearly distance 0.

[1] The case $p_1 = 1$ or $p_2 = 1$ is excluded here.

Lemma 3. *Let* $0 \leq p_1, p_2 < 1$*. Then*

$$d_{p_1,p_2} = d((0.5, 0.5), (x, 1-x)) = |x - 0.5|\sqrt{2}$$

where x *is the unique solution of* $\gamma(x, p_1, p_2) = 1 - x$ *in the interval* $]0, 1[$*, i.e.*

$$x = \begin{cases} 0.5 & \text{if } p_1 = p_2 \\ \frac{1-p_2-\sqrt{(1-p_1)(1-p_2)}}{p_1-p_2} & \text{otherwise} \end{cases} \tag{5}$$

The following lemma shows that this is indeed a unique characterization up to equivalence:

Lemma 4. *The mapping* $\gamma(\cdot, p_1, p_2) \mapsto d_{p_1,p_2}$ *is*

- injective *in the sense that for every pair of functions* $\gamma(\cdot, p_1, p_2)$, $\gamma(\cdot, p_1', p_2')$ *which satisfies* $\gamma(x, p_1, p_2) \neq \gamma(x, p_1', p_2')$ *for some* $x \in [0, 1]$*, we have* $d_{p_1,p_2} \neq d_{p_1',p_2'}$ *and*
- surjective *with respect to the interval* $[0, \frac{1}{2}\sqrt{2}[$*, i.e. for every* $\sigma \in [0, \frac{1}{2}\sqrt{2}[$ *there are parameters* $0 \leq p_1, p_2 < 1$ *so that* $d_{p_1,p_2} = \sigma$*.*

Corollary 1. *For* $0 \leq p_1, p_2 < 1$*, there is a* $0 \leq p < 1$ *so that* $d_{p_1,p_2} = d_{p,0}$*.*

For $a \in A$, we have $dsp(a) + dsp(\neg a) = 1$, which is a standard result of probabilistic argumentation systems (Kohlas *et al.*, 1998). This implies that $g_a(x) + g_{\neg a}(1-x) = 1$, which means that there is a symmetry between g_a and $g_{\neg a}$ with respect to the function $x \mapsto x$. So the distance depends in fact on the assumption and not on the literal. Therefore, we can speak of *the* distance d_a of an assumption a:

Lemma 5. *For every* $0 \leq p_1, p_2 < 1$*, we have* $d_{p_1,p_2} = d_{p_2,p_1}$*. For every* $a \in A$ *we have* $d_a = d_{\neg a}$*.*

Lemma 4 states that for a given d there are p_1 and p_2 with $d_{p_1,p_2} = d$, but there is no unique solution. Nevertheless, Corollary 1 states that for every pair (p_1, p_2), there is a uniquely defined p so that $d_{p_1,p_2} = d_{p,0}$, i.e. we have a normal form. Lemma 5 shows that in this case we even have $d_{p_1,p_2} = d_{p,0} = d_{0,p}$. This is recapitulated in the following corollary:

Corollary 2. *For* $0 \leq p_1, p_2 < 1$ *there is a uniquely defined parameter* p *with* $0 \leq p < 1$ *so that* $d_{p_1,p_2} = d_{p,0} = d_{0,p}$*.*

This corollary implies that the parameter space $[0, 1[\times[0, 1[$ has a class structure, i.e. every function $\gamma(\cdot, p_1, p_2)$ can be represented by a parameter $p \in [0, 1[$.

Consider an assumption $a \in A$ with probability $p_a = p(a)$ and the function $\gamma(p_a, p, p)$ for a fixed parameter $0 \leq p < 1$. This function represents a degree of support which depends only on the value p_a but not on $p(qs(\bot))$, because, for $x \neq 0$, clearly $\gamma(x, p, p) = x$, and using the definition of γ, also $\gamma(0, p, p) = 0$. This means that this assumption a does not influence the probability of the conflicts $p(qs(\bot))$ or of the diagnoses $p(sp(\top))$ at all. Furthermore, the degree of support of any formula which consists of assumptions in $A - \{a\}$ does not depend on p_a. The distance $d_a = d_{p,p}$ of this variable is zero. Therefore we say that this assumption a is *unimportant* to the present situation. The larger the distance d_a of an assumption a is, the more influence has the probability of this assumption on the probability of the conflicts $p(qs(\bot))$ (and therefore also the probability of the diagnoses). So we define the δ-importance as a normalization of the distance d to the interval $[0, 1]$:

Definition 2. *For $a \in A$ we define its δ-importance by $I^\delta(a) = d_a\sqrt{2}$.*

Example 4. (Continuation of Example 3) For the arithmetical network, we get the following δ-importances using the results from (2):

Component	xor_1	xor_2	or_1	or_2	or_3
$I^\delta(\cdot)$	**0.6236**	0.1078	**0.6894**	0.1618	0.1106

This result is qualitatively equal to the one computed in Example 2. ⊖

4 Importance Measures from Reliability Theory

4.1 Structure Functions versus Conflicts

In reliability theory, the concept of *structure function* is fundamental for importance measures. A structure function φ is a binary function which describes the state z_s of a system in dependence of the states z_i of the elements (or components) $i = 1, \ldots, n$, i.e. $z_s = \varphi(z_1, \ldots, z_n)$. The structure function is therefore a logical description of all system states $(z_1, \ldots, z_n) \in \{0, 1\}^n$ for which the system is functioning, i.e. for which $\varphi(z_1, \ldots, z_s) = 1$. Different methods for computing this function are known, see (Kohlas, 1987, Beichelt, 1993) for further literature.

A basic problem in reliability theory is to transform the structure function in a so-called disjoint form so that computing the reliability of the system becomes possible. This is very similar to the computations of probabilities of support in our context (cf. Section 1).

Consider the simple device in Fig. 3. The system consists of an input i, a component e_1 connected serially with two components e_2 and e_3 connected in parallel, and an output o. The connection between in- and output is established if e_1 and either e_2 or e_3 are working. Therefore, the structure function is $\varphi(z_1, z_2, z_3) = z_1 \wedge (z_2 \vee z_3)$, where z_i denotes the state of component e_i. Note that this structure function includes already the desired behaviour, namely that the input i is connected with the output o.

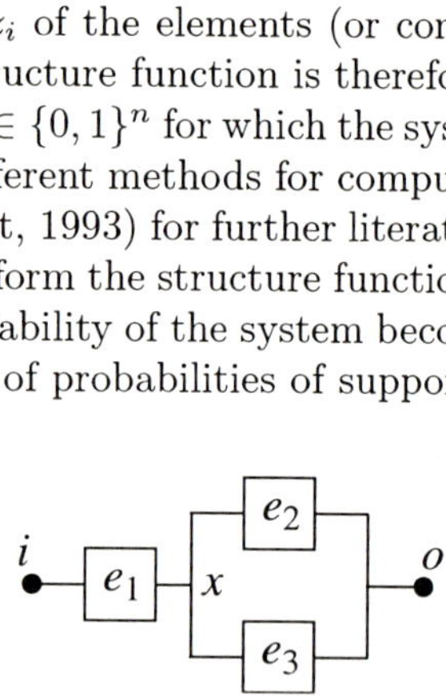

Fig. 3. A simple device

The same example, modeled in our logical framework reads as follows: we have three assumptions, i.e $A = \{ok_1, ok_2, ok_3\}$ and three propositions $P =$

$\{i, o, x\}$, where the assumption ok_i is true if the component e_i is functioning (i.e. if $z_i = 1$), and $\Sigma = \{ok_1 \to (i \leftrightarrow x),\ ok_2 \to (x \leftrightarrow o),\ ok_3 \to (x \leftrightarrow o)\}$. Now, this modeling does *not* contain the desired behavior, i.e. $i \leftrightarrow o$, because in our diagnostic environment, we are a priori interested not only in this problem. Nevertheless, this information can be taken into consideration in our approach. We just add the negation of this information to the knowledge base, i.e. we define the updated knowledge base by $\Sigma' = \Sigma \cup \{\neg(i \leftrightarrow o)\}$ and then, the diagnoses w.r.t Σ' are just the same as the structure function φ above, i.e.

$$sp(\top, \Sigma') = (ok_1 \wedge ok_2) \vee (ok_1 \wedge ok_3).$$

Note that $qs(i \leftrightarrow o, \Sigma) = sp(\top, \Sigma')$ allows another viewpoint of this situation.

So our framework of assumption-based reasoning is closely related to the framework of reliability theory and we can use our algorithms to compute structure functions, see (Kohlas *et al.*, 2000) for an overview and (Haenni, 2001) for new approximation techniques. Further, the implementation of ABEL (Haenni *et al.*, 2000) is capable of computing structure functions and therefore also the reliability of a system. For some further discussion and literature about the connections between model-based diagnosis and reliability theory see (Anrig, 2001).

4.2 Importance Measures in Reliability Theory

Importance measures are a well-known concept in reliability theory, where importance is understood as a measure of the criticality of a component. Several questions are addressed; for example (following Beichelt, 1993):

1. Which impact has a component on the reliability of a system?
2. How does the reliability of the system depend on the reliab. of a component?
3. Which component has the highest probab. to cause a failure of the system?
4. Which components have the highest probab. to cause a failure of the system?

In Section 4.3, we introduce the Birnbaum-Importance which gives answers for the first two questions. Questions 3 and 4 are not treated here, because their answer is given by what is known as degrees of support for components in our approach, yet see also (Kohlas *et al.*, 2001). In reliability theory, these two questions are usually answered by the Fussel-Vesley-Importance (Vesley, 1970, Viswanadham *et al.*, 1987). The idea of this importance measure is quite close to a degree of support, cf. Section 4.4. If no probabilities are known, then the structural importance can be used (Anrig, 2001). Note that in contrast to reliability theory, we will consider importances here independent of a time parameter.

4.3 Birnbaum-Importance

The Birnbaum-Importance was introduced in (Birnbaum, 1969); it is also called reliability importance (Barlow & Proschan, 1975). We follow here the description in (Beichelt, 1993). The Birnbaum-Importance of an element e_i is defined by

$$I(i, \mathbf{p}) = \frac{\partial h(\mathbf{p})}{\partial p_i}, \qquad (6)$$

where h is the structure function, $h(\mathbf{p})$ the availability of the system depending on the vector $\mathbf{p} = (p_1, p_2, \dots, p_n)$ of the probabilities of the element. This can also be written as $I(i, \mathbf{p}) = h((1_i, \mathbf{p})) - h((0_i, \mathbf{p}))$, where $(x_i, \mathbf{p})$ denotes the vector $\mathbf{p}$, where the i-th place is replaced by x.

This formula can be used in our context, where the structure function h is represented by the diagnoses $sp(\top) \equiv \neg qs(\bot)$ and $h(\mathbf{p})$ by $p(sp(\top)) = 1 - p(qs(\bot))$ with respect to the extended knowledge base (cf. Section 4.1). This implies that $h((1_i, \mathbf{p}))$ and $h((0_i, \mathbf{p}))$ are computed in our context by $1 - p(qs_a(\bot))$ and $1 - p(qs_{\neg a}(\bot))$ respectively.

Definition 3. *The Birnbaum-importance of an assumption $a \in A$ is*

$$I^{\mathrm{B}}(a) = \left| \frac{\partial p(sp(\top))}{\partial p(a)} \right| = \left| p(qs_a(\bot)) - p(qs_{\neg a}(\bot)) \right| .$$

Note that in the original definition (6), there is no need to take the absolute value because in reliability theory, the function h is monotone, but in the more general framework of assumption-based reasoning, this monotonicity property does not hold anymore. Nevertheless, considering that assumptions in our framework are a generalization of variables in reliability theory, it makes sense to take the absolute value, which implies the nice property $I^{\mathrm{B}}(a) = I^{\mathrm{B}}(\neg a)$ so that we can talk of *the Birnbaum-importance of the assumption a*.

The idea presented here is just the D-importance introduced in Section 2:

Lemma 6. $I^{\mathrm{D}}(a) = I^{\mathrm{B}}(a)$ *for every $a \in A$.*

4.4 Fussel-Vesley-Importance

The Fussel-Vesley-Importance was introduced by Vesley (1970) and used by Fussel (1973) in the context of fault trees. This importance measure depends on basic events, which, in our framework can be interpreted as *literals* of assumptions. Here we will not consider the time dependence of the importance, so for a basic event B_i, according to (Viswanadham *et al.*, 1987), the Fussel-Vesley is $I^{\mathrm{FV}}(B_i) = Q(B_i)/Q_s$, where $Q(B_i)$ denotes the probability that the structure function for the union of the cut sets containing B_i has value 1 and Q_s is the probability of a system failure.

In our framework, we will omit the factor Q_s because we only compare items with respect to the same knowledge, i.e. in a given situation the probability of a system failure is constant. The Fussel-Wesley importance can thus be defined in our framework by $I^{\mathrm{FV}}(a) = dsp(a)$ but note that in general $I^{\mathrm{FV}}(\neg a)$ is different from $I^{\mathrm{FV}}(a)$, i.e. we cannot speak of the importance of the assumption a. In reliability theory and especially in the framework of failure trees, where this importance measure was used by Fussel, the formulas are monotone, i.e. they contain only positive literals. Hence, there is no need to consider negated literals or their importance. Yet in the present more general context, we are mainly interested in an importance value defined with respect to the variable (and not to the literal). Clearly, in our framework we have $dsp(a) + dsp(\neg a) = 1$ because a

is an assumption, and therefore $I^{\mathrm{FV}}(a) = 1 - I^{\mathrm{FV}}(\neg a)$. But this does not tell us which one of these values we should take into consideration for the computation of *the* importance of a and we do not know how to combine these two pieces of information. So we will not consider this importance measure in the sequel.

5 Computation of Importances

For an assumption $a \in A$, the basic probabilities which have to be computed are $qs_a(\bot)$ and $qs_{\neg a}(\bot)$. In general, there are two situations to consider:

If the (minimal) conflicts $qs(\bot)$ are known, the probabilities we are interested in can be computed as follows: first, an equivalent, disjoint form of the formula $qs(\bot)$ is computed using the well-known inclusion-exclusion formula for computing probabilities of unions of events in probability theory or one of the much more efficient algorithms using disjoint forms (Kohlas & Monney, 1995, Bertschy & Monney, 1996). So given the conflicts $qs(\bot)$, these algorithms compute a set of formulas C so that $qs(\bot) = \sum C$, where the sum denotes the disjoint union. Then for $a \in A$ (and analogously for $\neg a$),

$$p(qs_a(\bot)) = p\left(\sum_{c \in C} c_a\right) = \sum_{c \in C} p(c_a)$$

where c_a denotes the formula c in which a is instantiated by $\top$. When using one of the efficient algorithms mentioned above, then the formulas c have a simple form and the computation of $p(c_a)$ can be done quite easily. This process is also called literal-conjoining (Darwiche, 2001) and can be applied to any logical structure for computing probabilities of formulas when a variable is instantiated.

If the conflicts $qs(\bot)$ have not yet been computed, there is another possibility to compute the probabilities $p(qs_a(\bot))$. Generalizing concepts of Lauritzen & Spiegelhalter (1988), Shenoy & Shafer developed a concept called *Computation in Hypertrees* (or Valuation Networks) for local computation (Shenoy & Shafer, 1990, Lauritzen & Shenoy, 1995). This concept has been used for several formalisms and here, we are especially interested in its application to belief function propagation. This subject and corresponding algorithms are in detail presented in (Lehmann, 2001) and we only outline the idea here. Consider the knowledge base Σ in the language $\mathcal{L}_{A \cup P}$. Now, a partition of this knowledge base is computed according to the assumptions A, i.e. the knowledge base is divided into several parts $\Sigma_1, \ldots, \Sigma_\ell$ so that $\Sigma_i \in \mathcal{L}_{P_i \cup A_i}$ and $A_i \cap A_j = \emptyset$ for every $i \neq j$ with $P_i \subseteq P$ and $A_i \subseteq A$. There are two main goals in this process of partitioning: first, the sets A_i should be small in order to keep the reasoning process in $\mathcal{L}_{P_i \cup A_i}$ feasible. Second, a "good" hypertree should be computable from the sets $P_1, \ldots, P_\ell$. Consider now the case where the set $\{P_1, \ldots, P_\ell\}$ is already a hypertree construction sequence (for the more general case see Lehmann, 2001). Then the knowledge Σ_i can be transformed into a belief function bel_i and these belief functions are propagated on the hypertree according to (Lehmann, 2001). This scheme allows efficient computation of $p(qs_a(\bot))$ and $p(qs_{\neg a}(\bot))$ for $a \in A$ by instantiating locally a to $\top$ or $\bot$ respectively.

Approximation techniques allow to determine upper and lower bounds for the beliefs we have to compute (Haenni & Lehmann, 2001, Lehmann, 2001). And clearly, for computing importances, approximated values of these beliefs are usually sufficient and therefore their computation quite fast.

6 Conclusions

The term *importance* is well-known in reliability theory. In this paper, we have introduced an analogue concept for the framework of assumption-based reasoning. Two different importance measures appear to be interesting for us: D-importance and δ-importance. The former is equivalent to the so-called Birnbaum-importance from reliability theory, whereas the latter is new and essentially based on supporting arguments. One has to be aware of the fact that the concept of importance of an assumption is different from the ideas of expressing the gain of testing the actual value of the assumption and also from the concept of likeliness of the assumption

A first conjecture was that in monotone situations, δ-importance and Birnbaum-importance yield qualitatively equal results, but this is not true. Several examples (see Anrig, 2001) show that the results of the two importance measures agree quite often qualitatively, but if they disagree, the new concept of δ-importance seems to reflect the "right" concept in our framework.

Consider the case where we are interested in symbolic results of the computation, for example the most important arguments for a given hypothesis. Further work has to be done in the direction of focusing the symbolic computation on important assumptions. This can be done by first computing numerically the importances of the assumptions and then focus the symbolic computation on the important assumptions using cost-bounded argumentation (Haenni, 2001). However, the integration of importance measures and approximation as well as the connections between reliability and probabilistic argumentation systems are subject to further research.

Acknowledgments. The author thanks the anonymous referees as well as Jürg Kohlas and Norbert Lehmann for their helpful comments.

References

Anrig, B. 2000. *Probabilistic Model-Based Diagnostics.* Ph.D. thesis, University of Fribourg, Institute of Informatics.

Anrig, B. 2001. *Importance Measures for Probabilistic Assumption-Based Reasoning.* Tech. rept. 01-02. University of Fribourg, Department of Informatics.

Barlow, R.E., & Proschan, R. 1975. *Statistical Theory of Reliability and Life Testing.* New York.

Beichelt, F. 1993. *Zuverlässigkeits- und Instandhaltungstheorie.* Teubner, Stuttgart.

Bertschy, R., & Monney, P.A. 1996. A Generalization of the Algorithm of Heidtmann to Non-Monotone Formulas. *J. of Computational and Applied Mathematics*, **76**, 55–76.

Birnbaum, Z.W. 1969. On the Importance of Different Components in a Multicomponent System. *In: Multivariate Analysis II.* Academic Press.

Darwiche, A. 2001. *Decomposable Negation Normal Form.* To appear in *J. of ACM.*

Fussel, B.J. 1973. How to Hand-Calculate System Reliability Characteristics. *IEEE Trans. on Reliability*, **24**.

Haenni, R. 2001. Cost-bounded Argumentation. *International Journal of Approximate Reasoning*, **26**(2), 101–127.

Haenni, R., & Lehmann, N. 2001. *Approximation Based on Incomplete Belief Functions.* Internal Paper, University of Fribourg, Department of Informatics.

Haenni, R., Anrig, B., Bissig, R., & Lehmann, N. 2000. *ABEL homepage.* `http://www-iiuf.unifr.ch/tcs/abel`.

Kohlas, J. 1987. *Zuverlässigkeit und Verfügbarkeit.* Teubner.

Kohlas, J., & Monney, P.A. 1995. *A Mathematical Theory of Hints. An Approach to the Dempster-Shafer Theory of Evidence.* Lecture Notes in Economics and Mathematical Systems, vol. 425. Springer.

Kohlas, J., Anrig, B., Haenni, R., & Monney, P.A. 1998. Model-Based Diagnostics and Probabilistic Assumption-Based Reasoning. *Artif. Intell.*, **104**, 71–106.

Kohlas, J., Haenni, R., & Lehmann, N. 2000. Probabilistic Argumentation Systems. *In:* Kohlas, J., & Moral, S. (eds), *Handbook of Defeasible Reasoning and Uncertainty Management Systems*, vol. 5: Algorithms for Uncertainty and Defeasible Reasoning. Kluwer, Dordrecht.

Kohlas, J., Anrig, B., & Bissig, R. 2001. Reliability and Diagnostic of Modular Systems. *South African J. on Operations Research ORiON.*

Lauritzen, S.L., & Shenoy, P.P. 1995. *Computing Marginals Using Local Computation.* Working Paper 267. School of Business, University of Kansas.

Lauritzen, S.L., & Spiegelhalter, D.J. 1988. Local Computations with Probabilities on Graphical Structures and their Application to Expert Systems. *J. of Royal Stat. Soc.*, **50**(2), 157–224.

Lehmann, N. 2001. *Probabilistic Approaches to Assumption-Based Reasoning.* Ph.D. thesis, University of Fribourg, Department of Informatics.

Reiter, R. 1987. A Theory of Diagnosis From First Principles. *Artif. Intell.*, **32**, 57–95.

Shenoy, P.P., & Shafer, G. 1990. Axioms for Probability and Belief Functions Propagation. *In:* Shachter, R.D., Levitt, T.S., Kanal, L.N., & Lemmer, J.F. (eds), *Uncertainty in Artif. Intell. 4.* North Holland.

Vesley, W. 1970. A Time-Dependent Methodology for Fault Tree Evaluation. *Nuclear Engineering and Design*, **13**, 339–360.

Viswanadham, N., Sarma, V.V.S., & Singh, M.G. 1987. *Reliability of Computer and Control Systems.* North Holland.

Ramification in the Normative Method of Causality

Mahat Khelfallah[1] and Aïcha Mokhtari[2]

Institut d'Informatique, USTHB, BP 32, El-Alia, Alger, Algeria
[1] mahat_k@hotmail.com,
[2] mokhtari@wissal.dz

Abstract. We present a method to tackle indirect effects in the context of reasoning about actions. The framework is based on the normative theory of causality. The method we propose, is close to Thielscher's method. To represent ramifications, we use directed relations between two single effects called indirect effects relationships, stating under which conditions the occurrence of the second effect follows the occurrence of the first. Our relationships represent both instantaneous and delayed indirect effects.

1. Introduction

The ramification problem has aroused interest of researchers community in the earlier 90's [2], [3], [6], [7], [10], [12]. It was defined, in the context of reasoning about actions, as the problem of describing all the indirect effects of actions. By indirect effects we mean the overflow effects that appear after performing an action. As an example, we consider the action "to win in lotto" which has as direct effect the fact "to become rich". This effect raises other (indirect) effects like "move to another house", "buy a new car", "pay more taxes", etc. To handle this kind of effects, many methods were proposed in the literature. Most of them used the domain constraints which are formulas that represent static dependencies existing between world components. These formulas are verified in every valid state of the world. The use of domain constraints is not sufficient to generate the expected indirect effects, as it was shown in [6], [7], and [12].
In this paper, we deal with the ramification problem in the framework of the normative method of causality [5], [9]. The solution we propose to compute all the indirect effects of actions uses relations called "indirect effect relationships". These relationships are inspired by Thielscher's causal relationships [12]. As for the former, indirect effect relationships are systematically generated from domain constraints and influence information. However, our method differ from Thielscher's one in that it handles delayed indirect effects. Moreover, indirect effects relationships are not applied randomly but according to the order of effects generation. This order allows to handle correctly examples like the stain cloth-table one [13].

In the next section, we give briefly fundamentals of normative method of causality, on which is based our framework. We then present our method to handle ramifications. Thereafter, we give the systematic generation algorithm of indirect effect relationships. We conclude with a brief related work and a summary.

S. Benferhat and P. Besnard (Eds.): ECSQARU 2001, LNAI 2143, pp. 704–713, 2001.

2. Normative Method of Causality Basics

The normative method of causality [5], [9] is based on an interventionist concept of causality where an agent has the choice to perform or not an action (free will). It is based also, on the principle which stipulates that "an action may cause one or many effects". We introduce some definitions.[1]

Time has been explicitly defined by means of time points.

A *time point* is defined by a subset of propositions and by a date. A time point is a universe snapshot where the propositions of the point are true at the date of the snapshot. Let T be the set of all time points.

The *date* of a time point is defined by the following function :

$date : T \rightarrow \mathbb{R}$, where $date(t) = d$ (noted d_t) means that d is the date of the time point t.

A *time line* is a set of time points which are in bijection with a set of dates. It represents a possible evolution of universe. Let L be the set of all time lines.

The time points of a time line are totally ordered by the precedence relation noted "$\leq$", where $t_1 \leq t_2$ means that t_2 doesn't precede t_1. Whenever $t_1 \leq t_2$ we have $d_{t1} \leq d_{t2}$. The precedence relation expresses the principle "no effect precedes its cause".

The representation of the notion of free will required a structure of time with a branching in the future. A branching in the past has been also required to examine different courses of events leading to the same situation.

Two time lines l_1 and l_2 *coincide* until a time point t (noted $coincide(l_1,l_2,t)$) iff $\forall t' \leq t, t' \in l_1 \equiv t' \in l_2$.

The set of *preferred time lines* for line l at time point t (noted $Lp(l,d_t)$) is defined as a function :

$$Lp : L \times \mathbb{R} \rightarrow 2^L$$

such that : $\forall l' (l' \in Lp(l,d_t) \supset coincide(l,l',t))$.

The proposed language is defined on two levels :

1. The first level represents *static information*. It's a plain propositional language in which : P is a set of propositions we are interested in, A is a set of actions, E is a set of effects (facts, events, ...), with $A \cap E = \emptyset$ and $P = A \cup E$.

A first level formula is either an action formula, or an effect formula.

Let $FOR(A)$ (respectively $FOR(E)$) be the set of *action* (respectively *effect*) *formulas*. An *effect literal* is either an effect, or an effect negation. The set of effect literal is noted $LIT(E)$. It is defined as: $LIT(E) = E \cup \{\neg e : e \in E\}$.

2. The second expresses *dynamic information* represented by formulas of the form: $v(p,l,d)$, which means that formula p is true in time line l at date d.

Causality is expressed by "*normal causality*" operator, noted "$\Rightarrow$". $a \Rightarrow e[\Delta]$ expresses that action a normally implies effect e in the delay Δ, unless there is an occurrence of an event inhibiting the effect e. The formalisation of such notion needs nonmonotonic reasoning which is expressed by means of action norm and inhibiting events.

Action norm is defined as the set of propositions which must normally be true in order to perform the action. Formally, the norm is defined as a function :

---

[1] More details can be found in [5] and [9].

$$norm : A \rightarrow 2^{FOR(E)}$$

where *norm*(a) contains the qualifications of action a.

The set of the external events that are susceptible to inhibit the effect of the action a is defined as a function :

$$inhibit : LIT(E) \times A \rightarrow 2^{LIT(E)}.$$

where $e' \in inhibit(e,a)$ iff e' inhibits the effect e of action a.

3. Ramification in Normative Method of Causality

In this section, we present an approach to tackle action ramifications in the normative method of causality. To compute indirect effects, we introduce directed relations between two single effects called indirect effect relationships. Before defining these relationships, we augment the language of the normative method of causality with a new predicate :

$occ(e,l,d)$, with the intented meaning that the effect e has been generated in time line l at the date d. We have : $\forall\, e,l,d : occ(e,l,d) \supset v(e,l,d)$.

After defining *occ*, we define formally normal implication.

Definition 1. Action a *implies normally* effect e ($e \in LIT(E)$), in a delay Δ (noted $a \Rightarrow e[\Delta]$) iff : $(\forall\, l,t)\ (t \in l \supset (C1 \wedge C2))$
where C1 and C2 are abbreviation of the following conditions :

C1 $\{\ [v(a,l,d_t) \wedge \forall p\ (p \in norm(a) \supset v(p,l,d_t))] \supset (\forall l')(l' \in Lp(l,d_t) \supset C11 \vee C12)\}$

with : C11 $\{(\exists t')\ (t' \in l' \wedge d_t \leq d_{t'} \leq d_t + \Delta \wedge occ(e,l',d_{t'}))\}$

C12 $\{(\exists e', t'')\ (e' \in inhibit(e,a) \wedge t'' \in l' \wedge v(e',l',d_{t''}) \wedge d_t \leq d_{t''} \leq d_t + \Delta)\}$

C2 $\{\ v(\neg a,l,d_t) \supset (\exists l')(l' \in Lp(l,d_t) \wedge (\forall d)\ (d_t \leq d \leq d_t + \Delta \supset \neg v(e,l',d)))\}$

C1 expresses that whenever a is performed under normal conditions (i.e., all the propositions in *norm*(a) are true), (C11) either e occurs in all preferred futures during the delay Δ, (C12) or there has been an event e' after t and within delay Δ which has inhibited effect e of action a. C2 means that if a is not performed, there exists at least a preferred future where e does not occur during the delay Δ.

Definition 2. Rules $a \Rightarrow e[\Delta]$ is called *causal rule.* Causal rules are gathered in a rule base called *BR*.

We introduce a new operator called "*indirect implication*" operator, denoted "$\mapsto$". "$(e_1, e_2) \mapsto e\ [\Delta]$" expresses that the occurrence of effect e_1, in a situation in which formula e_2 is true, indirectly implies the occurrence of effect e within a delay Δ. We define formally our new implication as follows.

Definition 3. Effect e_1 *indirectly implies* effect e in a situation in which formula e_2 is true, within a delay Δ (noted $(e_1, e_2) \mapsto e\ [\Delta]$) iff

$$(\forall l, d)\ (occ(e_1,l,d) \wedge v(e_2,l,d) \supset (\exists\, d')\ (d \leq d' \leq d + \Delta \wedge occ(e,l,d')))$$

Definition 4. An *indirect effect relationship* is an expression of the form :

$$(e_1, e_2) \mapsto e\ [\Delta]$$

where e_1 and e are effect literals, e_2 is an effect formula, and Δ is a real.
Indirect effect relationships are gathered in a relationships base noted *BEI*.
If the delay $\Delta = 0$, the generated indirect effect e is said *instantaneous*.

Example 5. In a tennis match, if a player fails his service two time in succession, he loses the point.

Consider the facts *Service1Lost, Service2Lost and PointLost*. The game rule can be expressed by the following indirect effect relationship :

$$(Service2Lost, Service1Lost) \mapsto PointLost$$

which means that the fact failing in the second service implies losing the point, if the first service was lost too.

Before computing actions effects, we need to define the notion of effect persistence which is defined as a duration which is independent of *e*'s change causes.

Definition 6. *Persist(e,δ)*, where $e \in LIT(E)$[2] and $\delta \in \mathbb{R}$, means that the effect *e* normally persists during the delay *δ*.

This definition is not sufficient to deduce the truth value of the effect *e* during the delay *δ*. To do it, we need further information which describe time lines.

Let *DL* be the set of formulas of the form *v(e,l,d)* or *occ(e,l,d)* which describe time lines. *DL* represents the set of world observations at particular moments.

We introduce a new function called *Closure*, which generates the closure of a set of formulas of the form *v(e,l,d)* or *occ(e,l,d)*, by exploiting persistence delays.
Let $D = \{v(e,l,d) : e \in FOR(E) \wedge l \in L \wedge d \in \mathbb{R}\}$ and
$F = \{occ(e,l,d) : e \in FOR(E) \wedge l \in L \wedge d \in \mathbb{R}\}$.

Definition 7. The *closure* of a set of observations *DL* is defined by the function :

$$Closure : 2^{D \cup F} \rightarrow 2^{D},$$

Let $DL \in 2^{D \cup F}$ be a set of observations. The set *Closure(DL)* is defined by:

1. $\forall e \in LIT(E),\ l \in L,\ d \in \mathbb{R} : v(e,l,d) \in Closure(DL)$ iff one of the following conditions is verified :
   i. $v(e,l,d) \in DL$, or
   ii. $\exists d', \delta\, [\delta > d - d' \wedge v(e,l,d') \in Closure(DL) \wedge Persist(e,\delta)$
   $\wedge\, \forall d''(d' \le d'' < d \supset v(\neg e,l,d'') \notin Closure(DL))\,]$,
   iii. $\exists l'(l' \in L \wedge v(e,l',d) \in Closure(DL) \wedge Coincide(l,l',d))$,
   iv. $occ(e,l,d) \in DL$.
2. $\forall e \in FOR(E),\ l \in L,\ d \in \mathbb{R}: v(e,l,d) \in Closure(DL)$ if $v(e,l,d) \in DL$,
3. $\forall e_1, e_2 \in FOR(E),\ l \in L,\ d \in \mathbb{R}: (v(e_1 \wedge e_2, l, d) \in Closure(DL))$ if $(v(e_1, l, d) \in Closure(DL))$ ***and*** [3] $(v(e_2, l, d) \in Closure(DL))$.

---

[2] Persistence duration of the effect *e* is different from *¬e's* one. For example, the effect *¬Alive* persists indefinitely whereas the effect *Alive* persists during a limited period.

Point (1) treats only the case of effect literal. Intuitively, condition (1.i) means that if an effect is true in *DL*, it is also in *Closure*(*DL*). (1.ii) means that if an effect is true in *DL*, it will be true in *Closure(DL)*, during its persistence delay, unless its opposite occurs. (1.iii) copies out line contents on all the lines that coincide with it. (1.iv) uses relation between *occ* and *v*.
Points (2) and (3) treat the case of effect formulas. Point (2) copies out *DL* contents, and (3) closes *Closure*(*DL*) by using the definition of the *and* operator.

This function allows having a complete knowledge of the world from a set of observations. Intuitively, the set *DL* contains relevant information and *Closure(DL)* represents all the information we can deduce from *DL* by exploiting persistence delays.

$\forall\, e \in FOR(E), l \in L, d \in \mathcal{R}$: *e* is true in the time line *l* at the date *d*, in a world described by the observations set *DL* iff $v(e,l,d) \in Closure(DL)$.

The function *Closure* defined, we have to define *DL* the set of time lines descriptions. Computing *DL* depends on executed actions, because the latter are the only things that can change world state.

We are interested in computing all the (direct or indirect) effects of an action *a* which is performed in a state described by a set of observations *DL*. Action *a* is accomplished in the time line *l* at the date *d*. The (direct or indirect) generated effects are gathered in the set *EG*.

Definition 8. *Execution context* of an action *a* is defined by the tuple <*DL, l, d, EG*> where :

- *DL* a the set of formulas $v(e,l,d)$: observations on the state in which action *a* is performed,
- $l \in L$, is the time line in which *a* is performed,
- $d \in \mathcal{R}$, is the date at which *a* is performed,
- *EG* is a set of formulas of the form $occ(e,l,d)$ which represent the generated effects in the time line *l*, at the date *d*.

Informally, the generation of action *a* effects consists in applying sequentially causal rules and indirect effects relationships associated to *a*. The order of rules or relationships application is not arbitrary. It depends on the effects generation date, i.e., a rule or a relationship is applied only if all the effects, which should occur before its effect, were generated. [4] According to this criteria, effects are generated in the exact order of their appearance. The generation stops if no new effect is generated.
We define formally the notion of causal rule and indirect effect relationship applicability.

---

[3] Formulas including other logical operators can be transformed into formulas containing only $\neg$ and $\wedge$ operators.

[4] In the particular case where two rules generate effects at the same moment, they are applied sequentially without any priority (nondeterministic order). We suppose that the generated effects are not contradictory. This hypothesis is necessary to guarantee the safeness of the set of generated effects.

Definition 9. The rule $a \Rightarrow e\ [\Delta]$ is *applicable* in the context $< DL\ ,\ l\ ,\ d\ ,\ EG >$ with d_e the appearance date of the effect e iff the following conditions are verified :

1. $v(a,l,d)$,
2. $d_e = d + \Delta$,
3. $\forall p\ (p \in Norm(a) \supset v(p,l,d) \in Closure(DL \cup EG))$,
4. $(\forall e')(e' \in Inhibit(e,a) \supset (\forall d')\ (d \leq d' \leq d+\Delta : v(e',l,d') \notin Closure(DL \cup EG)))$,
5. $(a \Rightarrow e'[\Delta]) \in BR$ {respectively, $((e_1\ ,\ e_2) \mapsto e'[\Delta]) \in BEI$} applicable *in the context* $< DL\ ,\ l\ ,\ d\ ,\ EG >$ with d' is the appearance date of the effect e' $\supset d' \geq d$,
6. this rule was not already applied in the same context.

(1) means that action a occurs in the time line l at the date d,
(2) means that the effect e occurs at the least at the date $d + \Delta$,
(3) means that all a's preconditions, listed in $Norm(a)$, are verified in the context,
(4) expresses that inhibiting events of effect e must not occur in line l from a's execution date during the delay Δ.
(5) expresses that all effects appearing before the effect e, were generated (by applying the associated rules or relationships), and
(6) means that this causal rule is applied at most once for each execution of action a.

Definition 10. The relationship $(e_1\ ,\ e_2) \mapsto e\ [\Delta]$ is *applicable* in the context $< DL\ ,\ l\ ,\ d\ ,\ EG >$ with d_e the appearance date of the effect e iff the following conditions are verified :

1. $(\forall\ l',d')\ (l' \in Lp(l,d) \wedge d \leq d' \supset occ(e,l',d') \notin EG)$,
2. $(\exists\ l',d')(l' \in Lp(l,d) \wedge d \leq d' \wedge occ(e_1,l',d') \in EG \wedge v(e_2,l',d') \in Closure(DL \cup EG))$
3. $d_e = d + \Delta$.
4. $\forall\ (a \Rightarrow e'[\Delta]) \in BR$ {respectively, $((e_1\ ,\ e_2) \mapsto e'[\Delta]) \in BEI$} applicable *in the context* $< DL\ ,\ l\ ,\ d\ ,\ EG >$ with d' is the appearance date of the effect e' $\supset d' \geq d$.

Condition (1) checks if the effect has been already generated. This condition guarantees also that the indirect effects relationship is applied at most once for each execution of action a. (2) checks that the effect e_1 has been generated and e_2 is true in the context. (3) means that the effect e occurs after a maximum delay Δ.

Example 11. [12] We have a circuit with 3 switches (Sw_1, Sw_2, Sw_3), a light (*Light*), a relay (Relay), and a light detector (Detect). The light is activated iff the first and the second switches are closed. The relay is activated only if the first and the third switch are closed. Moreover, if the relay is activated, the second switch is opened. The detector is activated if the light is activated.[5]

Indirect effects are represented by the following relationships.[6]

---

[5] We suppose that the light and the detector are faster than the relay. Other cases can be easily considered, such the case where the relay is first activated (before the light), ...

[6] We give only the relationships we are interested in.

$$(\mathrm{Sw}_1, Sw_2) \mapsto Light\ [1s] \tag{1}$$

$$(\neg Sw_2, True) \mapsto \neg\ Light\ [1s] \tag{2}$$

$$(Sw_1, Sw_3) \mapsto Relay\ [2s] \tag{3}$$

$$(Relay, True) \mapsto \neg\ Sw_2\ [2s] \tag{4}$$

$$(Light, True) \mapsto Detect\ [1s] \tag{5}$$

Action which closes the first switch is represented by the rule $Close_1 \rightarrow Sw_1$ [1s].

We close the first switch in a state where both second and third switches are closed and light, relay and detector are deactivated, i.e., $Close_1$ is executed in the context $< DL , l , d , \varnothing >$ where $DL = \{v(\neg Sw_1,l,d), v(Sw_2,l,d), v(Sw_3,l,d), v(\neg Light,l,d), v(\neg Relay,l,d), v(\neg Detect,l,d)\}$.

The first rule to be applied is the causal rule. It generates $occ(Sw_1, l, d + 1s)$.[7]
The next to be applied is the relationship (1) because its effect, *Light,* is generated before the effects of the other relationships. The generated effect is $occ(Light, l, d + 2s)$.
(3) and (5) are both applicable. So the choice to apply one before the other is completely nondeterministic.
We choose to apply first relationship (3) which generates $occ(Relay, l, d + 3s)$. Then relationship (5) which generate $occ(Detect, l, d + 3s)$.
Thereafter, relationships (4) and (2) are applied in this order to generate respectively $occ(\neg Sw_2, l, d + 5s)$ and $occ(\neg Light, l, d + 6s)$.

In the (deterministic) obtained state, the light detector is activated although there is no light.

4. Systematic Generation of Indirect Effect Relationships

Our method computes successfully action ramifications (i.e., does not generate unexpected effects) thanks to an adequate set of indirect effect relationships. The latter are not written by a reasoning system designer but they are generated automatically from domain constraints and influence information which is useful to limit the changes deduced from domain constraints to the desired ones.

Domain constraints are effect formulas which represent static dependencies that exist between domain effects. In addition to the fact that they are concise, they are written in a natural and easy manner. Domain constraints are gathered in a set noted *CD*.

---

[7] We suppose that effects appear at the date $d + delay$.

Definition 12. Influence information is defined on LIT(E)×LIT(E)× ℝ, where $(e_1, e_2, \Delta) \in I$ means that the change of e_1's value potentially changes e_2's value, in a maximum delay Δ. The set of all influence information is noted I.

Indirect Effect Relationships Automatic Generation Algorithm

Input : the set of influence information *I* ;

disjunctive normal form $D_1 \wedge \ldots \wedge D_n$ of the conjunction of domain constraints of *CD*, CNF(*CD*).

Output : the set *BEI* of indirect effect relationships

BEI := { };

For each constraint $D_i = e_1 \vee \ldots \vee e_{mi} \in$ CNF(*CD*), $i = 1, \ldots, n$

For each $j = 1, \ldots, m_i$

For each $k = 1, \ldots, m_i$, $k \neq j$

If $(\neg e_j, e_k, \Delta) \in I$, add to *BEI* the relationship : $(\neg e_j , \bigwedge_{\substack{l=1,\ldots m_i \\ l \neq j, l \neq k}} \neg e_l) \mapsto e_k.[\Delta]$.

Actually, this algorithm is an extension of the Thielscher's algorithm for automatic generation of causal relationships [12].

First, the extension consists in introducing the notion of delay in influence information which allows us to handle delayed indirect effects.

The second extension is that influence information is defined on the set of effect literals instead of the set of effects. This extension allows us to deal with examples like Toulouse's suitcase [1].

Example 13. Toulouse's suitcase is an enhancement of Lin's suitcase [6] which is opened if and only if its two latches are opened. In addition, there is an automatic mechanism which ties the two latches, where the opening of the first leads to the second's one.

We have the following domain constraints:

$$L_1 \wedge L_2 \equiv Open,$$
$$L_1 \supset L_2.$$

$I = \{ (L_1, Open, 2s), (\neg L_1, \neg Open, 2s), (L_2, Open, 2s), (\neg L_2, \neg Open, 2s), (L_1, L_2, 1s) \}$.

From domain constraints and the set of influence information *I*, the algorithm described above generates intuitive indirect effect relationships. In particular, the undesirable relationship (generated in Thielscher's method) "$(L_1, \neg Open) \mapsto \neg L_2$ [1s]" is not generated. It is due to the absence of the influence information $(L_1, \neg L_2, 1s)$, because L_1 cannot close L_2.

5. Related Work

We have presented a method to compute action ramifications. To this purpose, we introduced indirect effect relationships which are inspired from Thielscher's causal relationships [12]. However, our method is more general than the latter. In particular, in handling delayed effects.

Influence information we used in the systematic generation of indirect effect relationships, is defined on the set of effect literal, whereas Thielscher's one is defined on the set of effects. This difference allows to tackle correctly the Toulouse's suitcase example [1].

By imposing a priority in the effects generation, our method gets closer to the method of Van Belleghem et al. [14] which is based in induction principle. It computes action effects in their appearance order by stratifying (direct and indirect) effect rules. An effect is generated only if all the effects of the previous stratum are computed. The equivalent rule of this law in our approach is the priority imposed on causal rules and indirect effect relationships application. This priority is based on effect appearance order.

Like the method ƐR [14], many other methods [8], [11] are based on induction principle. Nevertheless, the former requires syntactical restrictions to guarantee the stratification.

Shanahan [10] has introduced in a natural way ramifications in event calculus. In spite of the likeness of his method with [14]'s one, it is less general, because it does not handle mutually dependant effects.

Delayed effects in [4] are handled in a different manner than here. They are represented by means of direct effects and causal rules which provide indirect effects.

Generally, our method tackles concurrent actions without any extension. The only condition to guarantee the consistency of the obtained results is the *non existence of actions with opposite effects executed simultaneously in the same time line.* No extension is needed, due to the priority we impose in applying rules and relationships.

6. Conclusion

We have presented a method to tackle indirect effects of actions in the context of the normative method of causality. To this end, we have introduced directed relations defined between effect literals, called indirect effect relationships.

As is suggested by their name, indirect effect relationships are used to generate indirect effects of actions. These effects are generally delayed ones, i.e., their occurrence is not necessarily instantaneous. To represent this property, indirect effect relationships are of the form : $(e_1 , e_2) \mapsto e\ [\Delta]$, which means that the occurrence of the effect e_1, in a situation in which the formula e_2 is true, provokes the occurrence of the effect e in a maximum delay Δ.

We propose an algorithm which permits to systematically generate such relationships from domain constraints and further information called influence information.

For lack of space, we have not addressed an important part of our method. It concerns implicit qualifications and incomplete descriptions of the world. Implicit qualifications are deduced by exploiting domain constraints as qualification constraints [7], [12]. Domain constraints are also used to complete the set of observations about the world as it is done in [3].

We handle neither actions with non deterministic effects nor complex actions. A subset of concurrent actions is tackled. It is the set of actions with independent effects.

Thus, we plan to extend our method to handle a larger domain, which could contain non-deterministic, concurrent actions and continuous change.

References

1. M. A. Castilho, O. Gasquet, A. Herzig. Formalizing action and change in modal logic I : the frame problem. In *Journal of Logic and Computation*, 9(5) : 701-735, 1999.
2. L. Giordano, A. Martelli and C. Schwind. Ramification and Causality in a Modal Action Logic. Journal of Logic and Computation, 2000.
3. A. Kakas and R. Miller. Reasoning about actions, narratives and ramification. Electronic Transactions on Artificial Intelligence, vol 1 : 39-72, 1997. (http://www.ep.liu.se/ej/etai/1997/003/).
4. L. Karlsson, J. Gustafsson and P. Doherty. Delayed effects of actions. In proceedings of ECAI'98, 1998.
5. D. Kayser and A. Mokhtari. Time in a causal theory. Annals of Mathematics and Artificial Intelligence 22, pages 117-138, 1998.
6. F. Lin. Embracing causality in specifying the indirect effects of actions. In Proc. of IJCAI'95, 1995.
7. N. McCain and H. Turner. A causal theory of ramifications and qualifications. In Proc. of IJCAI'95, 1995.
8. S. McIlraith. A closed-form solution to the ramification problem (sometimes). Artificial Intelligence, 116:87-121, 2000.
9. A. Mokhtari. Action-based causal reasoning. Applied Intelligence, 7(2):99-112, 1997.
10. M. Shanahan. The ramification problem in the event calculus. In proc. of IJCAI'99, 1999.
11. E. Ternovskaia. Causality via Inductive Definitions. Working Notes of "Prospects for a Commonsense Theory of Causation", AAAI Spring Symposium Series : 94-100, 1998.
12. M. Thielscher. Ramification and causality. Artificial Intelligence, 89:317-364, 1997.
13. M. Thielscher. Steady versus stabilizing state constraints. Formalizing Common Sense (FCS'98), 1998.
14. K. Van Belleghem, M. Denecker and D. Theseider Dupré. Representing ramifications in an event-based language. Technical report, Leuven University, dec 1997.

Simultaneous Events: Conflicts and Preferences

John Bell

Applied Logic Group
Department of Computer Science
Queen Mary, University of London
London E1 4NS
jb@dcs.qmw.ac.uk

Abstract. Existing methods for representing conflicting simultaneous events employ the notion of *cancellations*; which are used in order to stipulate that the effects of certain events cancel the effects of other, conflicting, events. However it is argued that this technique is inadequate when it comes to the representation of conflicting defeasible events. Consequently *event preferences* are suggested. These can be used to indicate which of two conflicting events *normally* succeeds; and thus, in effect, which of the two conflicting events *normally* cancels the effects of the other.

1 Introduction

This paper is concerned with conflicts which arise between simultaneous defeasible events. Previous work, notably that of Gelfond, Lifschitz and Rabinov [3], and Lin and Shoham [5], which has been summarized by Shanahan [6, Sec. 10.4], has dealt with simultaneous events which are generally not defeasible but whose effects may be *cancelled* by other events. The notion of cancellation is motivated by the example of lifting a bowl full of soup. Thus, if only one side (the "left" side or the "right" side) of the bowl is lifted, then the soup is spilt. However, if both sides of the bowl are lifted simultaneously, then the soup is not spilt. Thus the complex lift-both-sides action cancels the effects of its component, elementary, lift-left and lift-right actions. Cancellations are realized in the Situation Calculus by introducing and minimizing a *Cancels* predicate, together with explicit cancellation axioms. Thus, in the example, a lift-left action has the effect of spilling the soup, but if it occurs as part of a complex lift-both-sides action, then the lift-right component cancels this effect; and similarly for a lift-right action.

However this approach is limited by the assumption that events are otherwise not defeasible; that is, that, cancellations aside, if the preconditions of an event hold when it occurs, then it always succeeds and its effects are guaranteed. In order to see the problems which arise when this assumption is lifted, suppose that one of the components of the complex lift-both-sides action fails; because a hand slips, etc. Then the failing component action should not cancel the effects of the other component action, and the soup should still be spilt. But how can a cancellation be cancelled? It may be argued that this can be done by introducing

S. Benferhat and P. Besnard (Eds.): ECSQARU 2001, LNAI 2143, pp. 714–725, 2001.

a more complex lift-both-sides-with-one-slip action, which has an additional slip-left or slip-right component action. But to do so is to embark on an endless task. What happens if both hands slip; what if another agent interferes; what if the soup bowl is being lifted on a ship which may pitch or roll in such a way that, regardless of which lift events occur, the soup is (is not) spilt, etc?

Clearly a more sophisticated approach is required for simultaneous defeasible events. Consider an example which involves two conflicting elementary events occurring simultaneously. Two agents, Stan and Ollie, attempt to move to the same location simultaneously but only one of them can succeed. Suppose further that Ollie's success is more likely than Stan's, say because he is bigger. Then we want to say that when these events conflict it is *normally* the case that Ollie succeeds and Stan fails, and consequently it is *normally* the case that the move-Ollie event effectively cancels the effects of the move-Stan event. However, if Ollie fails for some independent reason, if he slips say, then the move-Ollie event should not prevent the move-Stan event from succeeding; although, of course, Stan may also slip, etc. Similarly, if a complex action, such as lifting the soup bowl with both hands simultaneously, occurs, then we want to say that this normally succeeds and effectively cancels any conflicting effects of its component events. Consequently this paper suggests the notion of *event preferences*, which can be used to indicate which of two events should normally succeed when they conflict.

Event preferences are introduced as an extension of the *causal theories* developed in [1]. Consequently, in order to set the scene, a brief account of causal theories is given in Section 2. Event preferences are then added in Section 3, where a suitable pragmatics is defined and examples are given.

2 Causal Theories

The causal theories developed in [1] provide a unified means for representing predictive common sense reasoning about actual events and their effects (including the representation of inertia, qualifications, ramifications, and non-determinism) and they can be used as the basis of a theory of counterfactual events, which in turn can be used to represent explanatory common sense reasoning [2].

Causal theories are expressed in a language called the Temporal Calculus, or simply $\mathcal{TC}$. The formal syntax and semantics of $\mathcal{TC}$ are presented in [2], consequently the language will be introduced informally as required in this paper. $\mathcal{TC}$ is a three-valued, temporal language which permits first-order and limited higher-order quantification. Its propositional basis is provided by Kleene's strong three-valued language [4], which is given an epistemic, resource-bounded, interpretation. Accordingly, a sentence can be true (established by the reasoner(s) as being true), false (established by the reasoner(s) as being false) or undefined (ignored by the reasoner(s) as irrelevant, or unestablishable within the reasoner(s) resource limitations). In keeping with these intuitions the truth conditions for the logical constants yield a Boolean truth value wherever possible. For example, the sentence $\neg\phi$ is true if ϕ is false, is false if ϕ is true, and is undefined otherwise.

Similarly, the sentence $\phi \wedge \psi$ is true if ϕ and ψ are both true, is false if either is false, and is undefined otherwise. The analogues of classical disjunction, $\vee$, and material implication, $\supset$, can be defined in the usual way; thus $\phi \vee \psi$ is defined as $\neg(\neg\phi \wedge \neg\psi)$, and $\phi \supset \psi$ is defined as $\neg\phi \vee \psi$. In order to increase the expressiveness of Kleene's language the *undefined* operator, ?, is added. Informally the sentence $?\phi$ states that the truth value of ϕ is undefined; that is, that neither the truth nor the falsity of ϕ is established. The following additional operators can now be defined:

$$\circ\phi \stackrel{def}{=} ?\phi \vee \phi \qquad \phi \rightarrow \psi \stackrel{def}{=} \bullet\phi \vee \neg\bullet\psi$$
$$\bullet\phi \stackrel{def}{=} ?\phi \vee \neg\phi \qquad \phi \equiv \psi \stackrel{def}{=} (\neg\bullet\phi \wedge \neg\bullet\psi) \vee (\neg\circ\phi \wedge \neg\circ\psi) \vee (?\phi \wedge ?\psi)$$
$$!\phi \stackrel{def}{=} \neg?\phi$$

Thus $\circ\phi$ states that ϕ is not false, $\bullet\phi$ states that ϕ is not true, $!\phi$ states that ϕ is defined (is not undefined), $\phi \rightarrow \psi$ is a resource-bounded conditional which is true if ψ is true or ϕ is not, and $\phi \equiv \psi$ states that ϕ and ψ are equivalent (are both true, or both false, or both undefined).

As space is limited, the treatment of causal theories will be restricted to the theory of *primary events*. These can be thought of as defeasible STRIPS events. Thus they are defined by specifying their preconditions and postconditions; for example a *Move* event is defined by axioms (7) and (8) in the next section. The axiom of change then states that if event e occurs at time t and the preconditions of e are true at t and it is not true that e is qualified at t, then the postconditions of e are true at $t + 1$:[1]

$$Pre(e)(t) \wedge Occ(e)(t) \wedge \bullet Qual(e)(t) \rightarrow Post(e)(t+1) \tag{1}$$

Intuitively, e is qualified at t if there is some reason why e should not succeed at t. The intention is to use this axiom positively whenever possible: given $Pre(e)(t)$ and $Occ(e)(t)$, $?Qual(e)(t)$ should be assumed and the axiom used to conclude $Post(e)(t+1)$, if doing so is consistent. Thus, on the intended interpretation of the axiom, events normally succeed if their preconditions are true when they occur. Qualifications apply only to events which would otherwise succeed:

$$Qual(e)(t) \rightarrow Pre(e)(t) \wedge Occ(e)(t) \tag{2}$$

Thus assumptions of the form $?Qual(e)(t)$ are called *change assumptions*, and the distinction between the occurrence of an event and its success is underlined by the following axiom:

$$Succ(e)(t) \equiv Pre(e)(t) \wedge Occ(e)(t) \wedge \bullet Qual(e)(t) \tag{3}$$

[1] As is customary, terms starting with upper case letters are used for constants and terms starting with lower case letters are used for variables. Customary abbreviations are also used. In particular universal quantifiers are omitted. Free variables should thus be understood as being bound by universal quantifiers with wide scope.

Inertia is represented by means of a common sense inertia axiom. Elementary facts concerning the domain are represented by *first-order* atomic sentences of the form $r(u_1, \ldots, u_n)(t)$; where the u_i are terms denoting domain objects, and t denotes a time point. Thus, if the relation $r(u_1, \ldots, u_n)$ is true (false) at time t and there is no reason to doubt that its truth (falsity) persists, then we should conclude by default that it does so; that is, that $r(u_1, \ldots, u_n)(t+1)$ is true (false). In order to formalize this intuition, the non-temporal component $r(u_1, \ldots, u_n)$ of a first-order atom $r(u_1, \ldots, u_n)(t)$ is called a *Kleene atom*, and a *Kleene literal* is either a Kleene atom or its negation. Then, for Kleene literal ℓ and time point t, $\mathit{Aff}(\ell)(t)$ states that ℓ is affected at t; that is, that there is reason to doubt that that the truth value of ℓ persists beyond t. The inertia axiom can now be stated as follows:

$$\ell(t) \wedge \bullet \mathit{Aff}(\ell)(t) \rightarrow \ell(t+1) \tag{4}$$

Thus the axiom states that if the Kleene literal ℓ is true at time t and it is not true that ℓ is affected at t, then ℓ remains true at $t+1$. The intention is that the axiom should be used positively whenever possible: given $\ell(t)$, $?\mathit{Aff}(\ell)(t)$ should be assumed and the axiom used to conclude $\ell(t+1)$ if doing so is consistent. In keeping with this interpretation, assumptions of the form $?\mathit{Aff}(\ell)(t)$ are called *inertia assumptions.*

Definition 1. *The* theory of primary events, Θ_P, *consists of the axioms* {(*1*), ..., (*4*)}. *Theories which contain* Θ_P *are called* causal theories.

The intended interpretation of causal theories, and particularly of the defeasible change and inertia axioms occurring in them, is given by their formal pragmatics; which specifies a selected subset of the models of each causal theory, and which is appropriate to the extent that the selected models of the theory coincide with the intended models of the theory. The pragmatics is based on the principle of chronological minimization, suggested by Shoham [7], but refines this to what might be called *prioritized chronological minimization*; the minimization is still chronological, however, at each time point, facts and events are minimized before qualifications which in turn are minimized before affectations. As the pragmatics is intended for causal theories and these contain the theory of primary events, Θ_P, the models it selects will be referred to as P-preferred models.

For $\mathcal{TC}$-model M and time point t, let $M_{\mathcal{R}}/t$ ($M_{\mathcal{O}}/t$, $M_{\mathcal{Q}}/t$, $M_{\mathcal{A}}/t$) be the set of first-order (*Occ*, *Qual*, *Aff*) atomic sentences which are defined in M up to t:

$$\begin{aligned}
M_{\mathcal{R}}/t &= \{r(u_1, \ldots, u_n)(t') : t' \leq t \text{ and } M \models\, !r(u_1, \ldots, u_n)(t')\}, \\
M_{\mathcal{O}}/t &= \{\mathit{Occ}(e)(t') : t' \leq t \text{ and } M \models\, !\mathit{Occ}(e)(t')\}, \\
M_{\mathcal{Q}}/t &= \{\mathit{Qual}(e)(t') : t' \leq t \text{ and } M \models\, !\mathit{Qual}(e)(t')\}, \\
M_{\mathcal{A}}/t &= \{\mathit{Aff}(\ell)(t') : t' \leq t \text{ and } M \models\, !\mathit{Aff}(\ell)(t')\}.
\end{aligned}$$

For convenience, unions formed from these sets will be denoted by the juxtaposition of their subscripts; thus, for example, $M_{\mathcal{ROQ}}/t$ denotes the set $M_{\mathcal{R}}/t \cup M_{\mathcal{O}}/t \cup M_{\mathcal{Q}}/t$.

Definition 2. *Let M and M' be $\mathcal{TC}$-models which differ only on the interpretation of first-order relations and the Occ, Aff and Qual predicates. Then M is* P-preferred *to M' (written $M \prec_P M'$) if and only if there exists a time point t such that:*

- $M_{\mathcal{RO}}/t \subset M'_{\mathcal{RO}}/t$,
- *or* $M_{\mathcal{RO}}/t = M'_{\mathcal{RO}}/t$ *and* $M_{\mathcal{Q}}/t \subset M'_{\mathcal{Q}}/t$,
- *or* $M_{\mathcal{ROQ}}/t = M'_{\mathcal{ROQ}}/t$ *and* $M_{\mathcal{A}}/t \subset M'_{\mathcal{A}}/t$.

A model M is a P-preferred model of *a sentence ϕ if and only if $M \models \phi$ and there is no other model M' such that $M' \models \phi$ and $M' \prec_P M$. M is a P-preferred model of a set of sentences Θ if and only if $M \models \Theta$ and there is no other model M' such that $M' \models \Theta$ and $M' \prec_P M$. A causal theory Θ P*-predicts *a sentence ϕ, written $\Theta \approx_P \phi$, if and only if ϕ is true in all P-preferred models of Θ.*

The pragmatics seems natural. At each time point, the facts and events which follow from the pragmatic interpretation of the theory at earlier time points are fixed before any assumptions are made regarding the future. This has the effect that speculating about the future cannot alter the present (or the past). Then qualifications are minimized (change assumptions are maximized) before minimizing affectations (maximizing inertia assumptions). This has the effect that if (instances of) the change and inertia axioms conflict, then preference is given to the change axiom, and consequently, where there is a conflict, change is preferred to inertia.

3 Simultaneous Events

We are now in a position to consider simultaneous defeasible events. Recall the introductory example where two agents, Stan and Ollie, attempt to move to the same location simultaneously. Other things being equal, the two events conflict, and the result is chaos; that is, it is impossible to predict the outcome.

Example 1. (Two stooges) At time 1: Ollie is at location $L1$, Stan is at location $L3$ and both attempt to move to location $L2$:

$$At(O, L1)(1) \wedge At(S, L3)(1) \tag{5}$$
$$Occ(Move(O, L1, L2))(1) \wedge Occ(Move(S, L3, L2))(1) \tag{6}$$
$$Pre(Move(x, l, l'))(t) \equiv At(x, l)(t) \tag{7}$$
$$Post(Move(x, l, l'))(t) \equiv At(x, l')(t) \wedge \neg At(x, l)(t) \tag{8}$$
$$At(x, l)(t) \wedge x \neq y \rightarrow \neg At(y, l)(t) \tag{9}$$
$$UNA[S, O, L1, L2, L3] \tag{10}$$

Here (9) is a domain axiom which states that two different objects cannot be at the same location at the same time, and (10) states that the names S, O, $L1$, $L2$ and $L3$ are unique; formally, $UNA[u_1, \ldots u_n] \stackrel{def}{=} \bigwedge u_i \neq u_j$ for $1 \leq i < j \leq n$.

Let $\Theta_1 = \Theta_P \cup \{(5), \ldots, (10)\}$. Then there are P-preferred models of Θ_1 in which Ollie succeeds in getting to $L2$ at time 2 and Stan remains at $L3$. There are also P-preferred models of Θ_1 in which Stan succeeds in getting to $L2$ at time 2, and Ollie remains at $L1$. Consequently neither $\Theta_1 \approx_P At(O, L2)(2)$ nor $\Theta_1 \approx_P At(S, L2)(2)$.

Proof. The two move events which occur at time 1 conflict. If $Occ(Move(O, L1, L2))(1)$ succeeds, then it follows from the change axiom and axiom (8) that $At(O, L2)(2)$ is true. Similarly if $Occ(Move(S, L3, L2))(1)$ succeeds, then it follows from the change axiom and axiom (8) that $At(S, L2)(2)$ is true. However, in view of axioms (9) and (10), if $At(O, L2)(2)$ is true, then $At(S, L2)(2)$ is false, and vice-versa. Thus at least one of the two events fails, and it follows from the contrapositive of the change axiom at least one of $Qual(Move(O, L1, L2))(1)$ and $Qual(Move(S, L3, L2))(1)$ is true in any model of Θ_1.

Clearly also there are models Θ_1 in which one of the change assumptions $?Qual(Move(O, L1, L2))(1)$ and $?Qual(Move(S, L3, L2))(1)$ is true. Indeed, as qualifications are minimized before affectations (as change is preferred to inertia) at each time point in P-preferred models, one of these change assumptions is true in any P-preferred model of Θ_1.

So, let M be a P-preferred model of Θ_1 in which $?Qual(Move(O, L1, L2))(1)$ is true. Then it follows, by the success axiom and (5)-(7), that $Succ(Move(O, L1, L2))(2)$ is true in M. And it follows by (5)-(8) and the change axiom that $At(O, L2)(2)$ is true in M. Consequently it follows, by the argument above, that $Qual(Move(S, L3, L2))(1)$ is true in M. As M is a P-preferred model of Θ_1, the inertia assumption $?Aff(At(S, L3))(1)$ is true in M, so it follows by the inertia axiom that $At(Stan, L3)(2)$ is true in M.

Analogous reasoning shows that there are also P-preferred models of Θ_1 in which $At(S, L2)(2)$ and $At(O, L1)(2)$ are true. □

Example 1 can be elaborated by stating that when conflicting move events occur Ollie succeeds, say because he is bigger:

Example 2. Let $\Theta_2 = \Theta_1 \cup \{(11)\}$ where:

$$Occ(Move(O, l, l'))(t) \wedge Occ(Move(S, l'', l'))(t) \rightarrow \bullet Succ(Move(S, l'', l'))(t) \tag{11}$$

Then, as Stan's attempt to move fails in all models of Θ_2, Ollie's attempt to move succeeds in all P-preferred models of Θ_2: $\Theta_2 \approx_P At(O, L2)(2)$. □

In this example axiom (11) has the desired effect. If Stan and Ollie both attempt to move to the same location, then Stan fails and Ollie succeeds, and so the conflict is resolved in Ollie's favour; thus, in the terminology used in the introduction, the axiom cancels Stan's movement. However if there is some independent reason why Ollie fails, say because he slips, then the axiom has the unfortunate consequence that Stan also fails; as the cancellation of Stan's movement is uncancellable. Clearly what is needed is some means of saying that

Ollie's success is preferred to Stan's success, without it being the case that Stan's failure is prohibited should Ollie fail for some independent reason.

In order to be able to do so the relation *Pref* is introduced. Thus the *event preference* $Pref(e, e')(t)$ should be thought of as stating that if events e and e' occur at time t, then the success of e is preferred to the success of e' at t; that if e and e' conflict at t, then the success of e is more likely than the success of e'. Thus if there is no independent reason why e should fail (if there is no reason other than the occurrence of e'), then e should succeed and e' should fail. However, if e does fail for some independent reason, then the occurrence of e should not, of itself, prevent e' from succeeding. The conflict resolution axiom (11) can thus be replaced by the following one:

$$Occ(Move(O,l,l'))(t) \wedge Occ(Move(S,l'',l'))(t) \rightarrow \\ Pref(Move(O,l,l'), Move(S,l'',l'))(t)$$

Event preferences are required to be asymmetric:

$$Pref(e,e')(t) \rightarrow \neg Pref(e',e)(t) \tag{12}$$

However, in the interests of generality, no further conditions are imposed; although conditions such as transitivity can, of course, be added when they are appropriate.

Definition 3. *The* theory of event preferences, Θ_Q, *consists of the axiom (12), and the* theory of primary events with event preferences, Θ_{PQ}, *is* $\Theta_P \cup \Theta_Q$.

When causal theories contain Θ_Q and event preferences their pragmatics needs to be refined further. In particular, if models M and M' disagree on qualifications at time t, then M may be preferred to M' on the basis of event preferences. This may be because fewer event preferences are defined in M than in M' at t, or because M satisfies the event preferences which are applicable at t better than M' does. This better-satisfies relation on applicable event preferences is defined next.

For any model M and time point t, let $M_P(t)$ be the set of event preferences which are *applicable (in M at t)*:

$$M_P(t) = \{Pref(e,e')(t) : M \models Pref(e,e')(t) \wedge Pre(e)(t) \wedge Occ(e)(t) \\ \wedge Pre(e')(t) \wedge Occ(e')(t)\},$$

and call the events referred to in these event preferences the *preferential events (in M at t)*. Then the degree of each of the applicable event preferences can be defined in terms of the degree of the leftmost preferential event referred to in it. The ordering on preferential events is indicated as follows:

$$e \prec_q e' \text{ iff } Pref(e,e')(t) \in M_P(t),$$
$$e \prec_q^1 e' \text{ iff } e \prec_q e' \wedge \neg\exists e''(e \prec_q e'' \wedge e'' \prec_q e').$$

Let:

$$E_1 = \{e : \exists e' e \prec_q e' \wedge \neg\exists e' e' \prec_q e\} \text{ and, for } n > 1, \text{ let:}$$

$$E_n = \{e : \exists e'(e' \in E_{n-1} \wedge e' \prec_q^1 e \wedge e \notin \bigcup_{i=1}^{n-1} E_i)\}.$$

Then the degree of preferential event $e \in E_i$ is i and, for any e' such that $e \prec_q e'$, the degree of the corresponding event preference $\mathit{Pref}(e, e')(t)$ is also i. Now, an applicable event preference $\mathit{Pref}(e, e')(t)$ is *satisfied* if $\bullet \mathit{Qual}(e)(t)$ is true and is *violated* if $\mathit{Qual}(e)(t)$ is true. Consequently, if:

$$M_Q(t) = \{\mathit{Qual}(e)(t) \in M_Q/t : \\ \mathit{Pref}(e, e')(t) \in M_p(t) \vee \mathit{Pref}(e', e)(t) \in M_p(t)\}$$

is the set of preferential events which are qualified in M at t, then the set:

$$M_P(t)/n = \bigcup_{i=1}^{n} E_i \cap \{e : \mathit{Qual}(e)(t) \in M_Q(t)\}$$

consists of those preferential events of degree $n \geq 1$ whose corresponding event preferences of degree $n \geq 1$ are violated in M at t. So, suppose that M and M' are models which agree on which event preferences are applicable at some time t; suppose, that is, that $M_P(t) = M'_P(t)$. Then M satisfies the applicable event preferences at t better than M' does if and only if, for some n, more of the applicable event preferences of degree $m \leq n$ are satisfied in M than in M':

$$M_Q(t) \prec_Q M'_Q(t) \text{ iff there is some } n \text{ such that } M_P(t)/n \subset M'_P(t)/n.$$

Moreover, M satisfies the applicable event preferences at t at least as well as M' does if and only if either M satisfies these event preferences better than M' does, or M and M' agree on the qualification of preferential events at t:

$$M_Q(t) \preceq_Q M'_Q(t) \text{ iff } M_Q(t) \prec_Q M'_Q(t) \text{ or } M_Q(t) = M'_Q(t).$$

Now, let:

$$M_{\mathcal{P}}/t = \{\mathit{Pref}(e, e')(t') : t' \leq t \text{ and } M \models\, !\mathit{Pref}(e, e')(t)\}$$

be the set of atomic event preference sentences which are defined in M up to time t. Then the definition of P-preferred model is extended to that of PQ-preferred model as follows:

Definition 4. *Let M and M' be $\mathcal{TC}$-models which differ at most on the interpretation of first-order relations and the Occ, Aff, Pref and Qual relations. Then M is PQ-preferred to M' (written $M \prec_{PQ} M'$) if there exists a time point t such that:*

- $M_{\mathcal{RO}}/t \subset M'_{\mathcal{RO}}/t$,

- *or* $M_{\mathcal{RO}}/t = M'_{\mathcal{RO}}/t$ *and* $M_{\mathcal{P}}/t \subset M'_{\mathcal{P}}/t$,
- *or* $M_{\mathcal{ROP}}/t = M'_{\mathcal{ROP}}/t$ *and either*
  - $M_Q/t - M_Q(t) \subset M'_Q/t - M'_Q(t)$ *and* $M_Q(t) \preceq_Q M'_Q(t)$,
  - *or* $M_Q/t - M_Q(t) \subseteq M'_Q/t - M'_Q(t)$ *and* $M_Q(t) \prec_Q M'_Q(t)$,
- *or* $M_{\mathcal{ROPQ}}/t = M'_{\mathcal{ROPQ}}/t$ *and* $M_{\mathcal{A}}/t \subset M'_{\mathcal{A}}/t$.

Thus model M is preferred to model M' on the basis of event preferences at time t if and only if either fewer event preferences are defined in M up to t, or M and M' agree on defined event preferences up to t (and thus on applicable event preferences at t: $M_P(t) = M'_P(t)$) and either:

- fewer events are qualified in M up to t if the preferential events at t are set aside, and M satisfies the applicable event preferences at t at least as well as M' does,
- no more events are qualified in M up to t if the preferential events at t are set aside, and M satisfies the applicable event preferences at t better than M' does.

It is easy to check that $\prec_{PQ}$ is a partial order, and that PQ-preference reduces to P-preference in the absence of event preferences.

Definition 5. *A model M is a PQ-preferred model of a sentence ϕ if $M \models \phi$ and there is no other model M' such that $M' \models \phi$ and $M' \prec_{PQ} M$. M is a PQ-preferred model of a set of sentences Θ if $M \models \Theta$ and there is no other model M' such that $M' \models \Theta$ and $M' \prec_{PQ} M$. If Θ is a theory which contains Θ_{PQ}, then Θ PQ-predicts a sentence ϕ, written $\Theta \approx_{PQ} \phi$, if and only if ϕ is true in all PQ-preferred models of Θ.*

The following three examples illustrate various aspects of the formal definitions, particularly the better-satisfies relation on event preferences. The first example illustrates the fact that event preferences are interpreted transitively wherever possible.

Example 3. (Three stooges) Suppose that initially Ollie is at location $L1$, Stan is at location $L2$, and Charlie is at location $L3$. Suppose also that they simultaneously attempt to move to location $L4$ and that only one of them can succeed. If size is taken as the deciding factor, then as Ollie is bigger than Stan and Stan is bigger than Charlie, Ollie's success is more likely than Stan's and Stan's success is more likely than Charlie's.

This scenario can be represented by the causal theory $\Theta_3 = \Theta_{PQ} \cup \{(7), \ldots, (9), (13), \ldots, (17)\}$, where:

$$At(O, L1)(1) \wedge At(S, L2)(1) \wedge At(C, L3)(1) \quad (13)$$

$$Occ(Move(O, L1, L4))(1) \wedge Occ(Move(S, L2, L4))(1) \wedge Occ(Move(C, L3, L4))(1) \quad (14)$$

$$Pref(Move(O, L1, L4), Move(S, L2, L4))(1) \quad (15)$$

$$Pref(Move(S, L2, L4), Move(C, L3, L4))(1) \quad (16)$$

$$UNA[S, O, C, L1, L2, L3, L4] \quad (17)$$

Then, as desired, Θ_3 *PQ*-predicts that Ollie succeeds and that Stan and Charlie both fail; $\Theta_3 \approx_{PQ} At(O, L4)(2) \wedge At(S, L2)(2) \wedge At(C, L3)(2)$.

Proof. Suppose that M, M' and M'' are models of Θ_3 which agree on the minimal set of facts, events and event preferences up to time 1. Suppose, that is, that:

$$\begin{aligned} M_{\mathcal{ROP}}/1 = \{&At(O, L1)(1), At(S, L2)(1), At(C, L3)(1)\} \\ &\cup \{Occ(Move(O, L1, L4))(1), Occ(Move(S, L2, L4))(1), \\ &\quad Occ(Move(C, L3, L4))(1)\} \\ &\cup \{Pref(Move(O, L1, L4), Move(S, L2, L4))(1), \\ &\quad Pref(Move(S, L2, L4), Move(C, L3, L4))(1)\}, \end{aligned}$$

and that $M_{\mathcal{ROP}}/1 = M'_{\mathcal{ROP}}/1 = M''_{\mathcal{ROP}}/1$. Suppose also that, preferential events aside, the three models agree on the minimal set of qualifications up to time 1; thus $M_Q/1 - M_Q(1) = M'_Q/1 - M'_Q(1) = M''_Q/1 - M''_Q(1) = \emptyset$. Suppose finally that the three models disagree on the qualification of preferential events at time 1; thus:

$$\begin{aligned} M_Q(1) &= \{Qual(Move(S, L2, L4))(1), Qual(Move(C, L3, L4))(1)\}, \\ M'_Q(1) &= \{Qual(Move(O, L1, L4))(1), Qual(Move(C, L3, L4))(1)\}, \\ M''_Q(1) &= \{Qual(Move(O, L1, L4))(1), Qual(Move(S, L2, L4))(1)\}. \end{aligned}$$

This is in keeping with the assumption of minimality; as axioms (8), (9) and (17) require that two of the three preferential events are qualified in any model of Θ_3. Now, as the three models agree on $M_{\mathcal{ROP}}/1$ they also agree on which event preferences are applicable at time 1. Thus:

$$\begin{aligned} M_P(1) = \{&Pref(Move(O, L1, L4), Move(S, L2, L4))(1), \\ &Pref(Move(S, L2, L4), Move(C, L3, L4))(1)\}, \end{aligned}$$

and $M_P(1) = M'_P(1) = M''_P(1)$. Consequently the three models can be ordered according to the better-satisfies relation. The degree of each of the preferential events at time 1 is indicated as follows:

$$E_1 = \{Move(O, L1, L4)\}, E_2 = \{Move(S, L2, L4)\}, E_3 = \{Move(C, L3, L4)\}.$$

So $M_P(1)/1 = \emptyset$ and $M'_P(1)/1 = M''_P(1)/1 = \{Move(O, L1, L4)\}$. Consequently $M_Q(1) \prec_Q M'_Q(1)$ and $M_Q(1) \prec_Q M''_Q(1)$. (Similarly, as $M'_Q(1)/2 = \{Move(O, L1, L4)\}$ and $M''_Q(1)/2 = \{Move(O, L1, L4), Move(S, L2, L4)\}$, $M'_Q(1) \prec_Q M''_Q(1)$.) So $M \prec_{PQ} M'$ and $M \prec_{PQ} M''$. Consequently M' is not a *PQ*-preferred model of Θ_3 and neither is M''. Moreover, assuming that $M_{\mathcal{A}}/1$ is minimal, assuming that is that $M_{\mathcal{A}}/1 = \{Aff(At(O, L1))(1)\}$, M is a *PQ*-preferred model of Θ_3, and the desired conclusions follow in M by the change and inertia axioms and the definition of the move event. □

The following extension of Example 3 illustrates the success of a less preferred event when the more preferred event fails for some independent reason.

Example 4. Suppose that, in the scenario of Example 3, Ollie slips when attempting to move to location $L4$. As a result his attempt to move should fail and he should remain at $L1$. However, as Ollie fails, Stan should now succeed in his attempt to move to $L4$.

Let $\Theta_4 = \Theta_3 \cup \{(18), (19)\}$ where:

$$Slippery(L1)(1) \tag{18}$$

$$Occ(Move(x,l,l'))(t) \wedge Slippery(l)(t) \rightarrow \bullet Succ(Move(x,l,l'))(t) \tag{19}$$

Then, as desired, $\Theta_4 \approx_{PQ} At(O,L1)(2) \wedge At(S,L4)(2) \wedge At(C,L3)(2)$.

Proof. Let M be a model of Θ_4 which is minimal on facts, events and event preferences up to time 1. Then $M_{\mathcal{ROP}}/1$ consists of its namesake from the previous proof and the additional fact $Slippery(L1)(1)$, and $M_P(1)$ agrees with its namesake from the previous proof. Suppose finally that the only events which are qualified in M are those in the set $M'_Q(1)$ of the previous proof. Then clearly M is $\prec_{PQ}$-preferred to any model M'' of Θ_4 which agrees with M on $M_{\mathcal{ROP}}/1$ and $M_P(1)$ but which disagrees with M on qualifications; in particular, if $M''_Q(1)$ is as in the previous proof, then $M \prec_Q M''$ and $\emptyset \subseteq M''_Q/1 - M''_Q(1)$, so $M \prec_{PQ} M'$. □

The final example illustrates what happens when the event preferences cannot be interpreted transitively in a coherent way.

Example 5. Suppose that, in the scenario of Example 3, the event preferences are extended to take account of speed as well as size. Thus a preference is added to the effect that if Ollie and Charlie both attempt to move to the same location simultaneously, then Charlie, being quicker, should succeed. Clearly, if any two of the move events occur, then the preferences can be interpreted coherently; as in previous examples. However, if all three events occur simultaneously, then it is not possible to determine their outcome on the basis of the event preferences.

Let $\Theta_5 = \Theta_3 \cup \{Pref(Move(C,L3,L4), Move(O,L1,L4))(1)\}$. Then there are PQ-preferred models of Θ_5 in which $At(O,L4)(2)$ is true, but there are PQ-preferred models of Θ_5 in which $At(S,L4)(2)$ is true, and PQ-preferred models of Θ_5 in which $At(C,L4)(2)$ is true.

Proof. The models of Θ_5 which are minimal in facts, events, event preferences and qualifications at time 1 all have the following event preferences applicable in them:

$$\{Pref(Move(O,L1,L4), Move(S,L2,L4))(1),$$
$$Pref(Move(S,L2,L4), Move(C,L3,L4))(1),$$
$$Pref(Move(C,L3,L4), Move(O,L1,L4))(1)\}.$$

But, as these preferences are cyclical, the preferential events they refer to do not have a defined degree: for any $i \geq 1$, $E_i = \emptyset$. Consequently, these models cannot be ordered by the $\prec_Q$ relation. Thus there are PQ-preferred models in which each of the preferential events succeeds and the other two fail. □

4 Concluding Remarks

The treatment of event preferences has been at the level of elementary events; but the extension to complex events is straightforward. Indeed, a defeasible version of the introductory soup-bowl example can be represented without further ado by means of definitions such as the following:

$$\begin{aligned}
&\mathit{Pre}(LiftL)(t) \equiv \mathit{OnTable}(t) \wedge \neg HoldingL(t)\\
&\mathit{Post}(LiftL)(t) \equiv HoldingL(t) \wedge \mathit{Empty}(t)\\
&\mathit{Pre}(Lift)(t) \equiv \mathit{Pre}(LiftL)(t) \wedge \mathit{Occ}(LiftL)(t)\\
&\qquad\qquad \wedge \mathit{Pre}(LiftR)(t) \wedge \mathit{Occ}(LiftR)(t)\\
&\mathit{Post}(Lift)(t) \equiv HoldingL(t) \wedge HoldingR(t) \wedge \neg \mathit{Empty}(t)\\
&\mathit{Pref}(Lift, LiftL)(t) \wedge \mathit{Pref}(Lift, LiftR)(t)
\end{aligned}$$

The treatment has also been based on the theory of primary events. However, the inclusion of secondary events is straightforward; as the pragmatic refinements required for secondary events and event preferences are readily combined.

As event preferences have a temporal index it is also possible to represent changing event preferences over time; for example, a fast horse may be favourite to win next week's big race if the racecourse remains dry, while a sturdy horse may be favourite if the course becomes wet. In order to represent the default persistence of event preferences an *AffP*-predicate can be added (where, intuitively, $\mathit{AffP}(Pref(e,e'))(t)$ states that the event preference $\mathit{Pref}(e,e')$ is affected at time t) together with an appropriate inertia axiom. Definition 4 would also need to be extended with the effect that *AffP*-atoms are minimized with lowest priority at each time point.

References

1. J. Bell (2001) Primary and Secondary Events. Second version, May 2001. Submitted to *Electronic Transactions on Artificial Intelligence.* (www.ida.liu.se/ext/etai/rac/)
2. J. Bell (2001) Causal Counterfactuals. Working notes of *Common Sense 2001.* E. Davis et al. (Eds.), pp. 25-35. (www.cs.nyu.edu/faculty/davise/commonsense01)
3. M. Gelfond, V. Lifschitz and A. Rabinov (1991) What are the limitations of the Situation Calculus? In: *Essays in Honour of Woody Bledsoe.* R. Boyer (Ed.), Kluwer Academic Publishers, Amsterdam, 1991, pp. 167-179.
4. S.C. Kleene (1952) *Introduction to Metamathematics.* North-Holland, Amsterdam.
5. F. Lin and Y. Shoham (1992) Concurrent actions in the Situation Calculus. Proc. *AAAI'92*, pp. 590-595.
6. M. Shanahan (1997) *Solving the Frame Problem.* M.I.T. Press, Cambridge Mass.
7. Y. Shoham (1988) *Reasoning About Change.* M.I.T. Press, Cambridge Mass.

Orthogonal Relations for Reasoning about Abstract Events

Ajay Kshemkalyani[1] and Roshan Kamath[2]

[1] EECS Department, University of Illinois at Chicago, Chicago, IL 60607-7053, USA.
ajayk@eecs.uic.edu

[2] Motorola Inc. 1501 W. Shure Drive, IL27-1L20, Arlington Heights, IL 60004, USA.
Roshan.Kamath@motorola.com

Abstract. As systems become increasingly complex, event abstraction becomes an important issue in order to represent interactions and reason at the right level of abstraction. Abstract events are collections of more elementary events, that provide a view of the system execution at an appropriate level of granularity. Understanding how two abstract events relate to each other is a fundamental problem for knowledge representation and reasoning in a complex system. In this paper, we study how two abstract events in a distributed system are related to each other in terms of the more elementary causality relation. Specifically, we analyze the ways in which two abstract events can be related to each other *orthogonally*, that is, identify all the possible mutually independent relations by which two such events could be related to each other. Such an analysis is important because all possible relationships between two abstract events that can exist in the face of uncertain knowledge can be expressed in terms of the irreducible orthogonal relationships.

1 Introduction

As systems become increasingly complex, event abstraction becomes an important issue in order to represent interactions and reason at the right level of abstraction. Abstract events are collections of more elementary events, that provide a view of the system execution at an appropriate level of granularity. Understanding how two abstract events relate to each other is a fundamental problem for knowledge representation and reasoning in such a complex distributed system. This problem is of interest across philosophy, physics, artificial intelligence, computer science, and psychology [2].

Hamblin [10] and Allen [2] have shown that two linear time durations or *intervals* that are colocated can be related in one of 13 possible ways. These 13 relations form an *orthogonal* set of relations, i.e., the intervals must be related by one and only one of these relations, implying that the conjunction of any two relations is the empty relation. Orthogonal relations are important because they identify all possible mutually exclusive relations that can possibly hold between any given pair of intervals and because all possible relationships between two intervals that can exist in the face of uncertain knowledge can be expressed

S. Benferhat and P. Besnard (Eds.): ECSQARU 2001, LNAI 2143, pp. 726–735, 2001.

in terms of the irreducible orthogonal relationships. The set of 13 orthogonal relations between a pair of colocated linear intervals has been used extensively in the literature on artificial intelligence. For example, [8] developed a theory of temporal reasoning using semi-intervals which arise when there is uncertain and imprecise knowledge of intervals, using the 13 orthogonal relations of Allen. Examples of other uses of the 13 orthogonal relations between colocated linear intervals include [3,4,5,9,14,15,16].

The literature surveyed above considered the interactions and relative placement of time intervals, each of which can be viewed as a *linearly ordered* set of time instants. An additional assumption was that time was continuous, and hence the time intervals satisfy the density axiom (refer van Benthem [6] for the formal definitions and a detailed discussion of continuity and density).

Our objective is to study how two abstract events in a distributed system are related to each other in terms of the causality relation. The relativistic space-time model is an appropriate model of a distributed system execution for this study. We analyze the ways in which two abstract events can be related to each other orthogonally, that is, identify all the possible mutually independent relations by which two such events could be related to each other. The results of this paper differ from the work surveyed above in the following aspects. Each of the abstract events we consider is a partial order of more elementary events, unlike the time intervals which linearly order the component time instants. Additionally, the system model explicitly models individual events/actions/statement executions that occur at different processes in the execution of a complex distributed system, and hence models discrete events explicitly.

The work is motivated by the fact that in a distributed system, *abstract* events, wherein at least some of the component elementary events of the abstract event occur concurrently, are of great interest in simplifying the reasoning about distributed executions [12,13]. Henceforth, we also term such abstract events as *poset (partially ordered set) events*. Such poset events accurately model collaborative activity among multiple CPU subsystems in a distributed system, for various applications like navigation, planning, robotics, mobile computing, coordination among multiple participants in a virtual reality environment, and agent-based distributed cooperating programs. As a specific example, multiple autonomous robots need to cooperate to jointly solve a task such as to focus laser beams on a target so that the beams arrive at the target at a fixed moment. As another example, multiple roving mobile agents that can communicate only by message passing need to synchronize their actions in an adversarial environment. Causality between poset events has been studied in [12] wherein a spectrum of fine-grained causality relations between poset events was presented, along with an axiom system to reason with such relations. These relations provide a precise handle to express and represent a naturally occurring or enforce a desired fine-grained level of causality or synchronization among the cooperating agents. However, these relations are not orthogonal relations. In this paper, we present a methodology for deriving orthogonal relations between poset events. Section 2 gives the system model. Section 3 gives the main results. Section 4 concludes.

2 System Model and Preliminaries

A poset event structure model $(E, \prec)$, where $\prec$ is an irreflexive partial ordering representing the causality relation on the possibly infinite event set E, is used as the space-time model for a system execution, as in [12]. $(E, \prec)$ can follow either the discreteness or the density axioms [6]. E is partitioned into local executions at coordinates in the space dimensions. Each E_i is a linearly ordered set of events in partition i and corresponds to the execution of events by a distinct process i. An event e in partition i is denoted e_i. The causality relation on E is the transitive closure of the local ordering relation on each E_i and the ordering imposed by message send events and message receive events. In [11,12], poset events are defined as follows. Let $\mathcal{E}$ denote the power set of E. Let $\mathcal{A}$ $(\neq \emptyset)$ $\subseteq (\mathcal{E} - \emptyset)$. $\mathcal{A}$ is the set of all those sets that represent a higher level grouping of the events of E of interest to an application. Each element A of $\mathcal{A}$ is a subset of E, and is termed an *abstract event* or a *poset event*.

Table 1. The six basic relations, see [11,12].

Relation r	Expression for $r(X, Y)$
$R1$	$\forall x \in X \forall y \in Y, x \prec y$ $(= \forall y \in Y \forall x \in X, x \prec y)$
$R2$	$\forall x \in X \exists y \in Y, x \prec y$
$R2'$	$\exists y \in Y \forall x \in X, x \prec y$
$R3$	$\exists x \in X \forall y \in Y, x \prec y$
$R3'$	$\forall y \in Y \exists x \in X, x \prec y$
$R4$	$\exists x \in X \exists y \in Y, x \prec y$ $(= \exists y \in Y \exists x \in X, x \prec y)$

The causality relations between a pair of poset events were formulated in [12] using the notion of *proxies*. Each poset event X was defined to have two proxies – the set of its least elements L_X, and the set of its greatest elements U_X. These proxies were the equivalents of the beginning and end instants of the linearly ordered interval. Two alternate definitions of proxies were given:

- Definition 4 [12], viz., $L_X = \{e_i \in X \mid \forall e'_i \in X, e_i \preceq e'_i\}$ and $U_X = \{e_i \in X \mid \forall e'_i \in X, e_i \succeq e'_i\}$, and
- Definition 5 [12], viz., $L_X = \{e \in X \mid \forall e' \in X, e \not\succ e'\}$ and $U_X = \{e \in X \mid \forall e' \in X, e \not\prec e'\}$

Figure 1 depicts the proxies of X and shows the difference between the two definitions. In the figure, the time axis goes from left to right, and the lines with arrows denote the messages that impose causality across different processes (points in space). Depending on the problem domain, an application chooses and consistently uses one definition of proxy. For example, for events in a distributed sensor/robot system, where the various sensors/robots cooperate to perform loosely synchronized actions, the former definition is more suitable to represent the start and end of interactions. When different mobile agents invoke services offered by other agents/servers in a nested Remote Procedure Call (RPC) form, the latter definition is more suitable to represent the start and end of interactions.

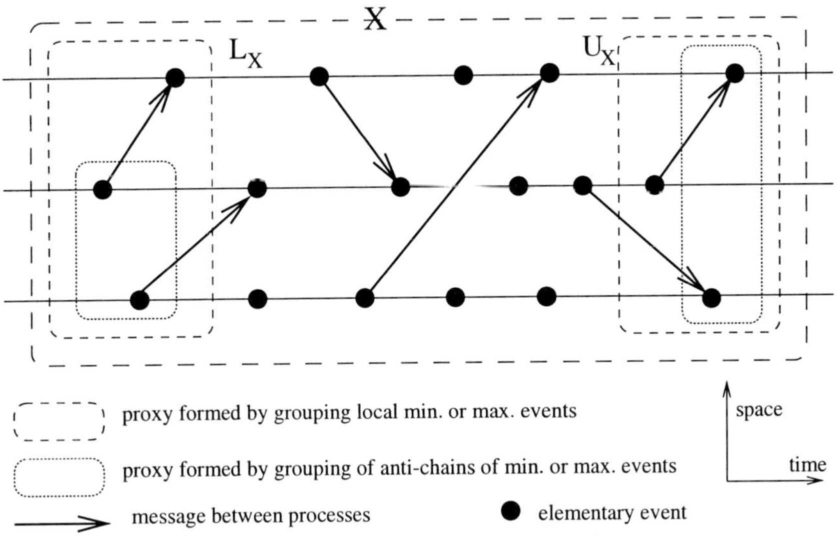

Fig. 1. Poset event X and its proxies L_X and U_X. The proxies defined by Definition 4 are shown by the closely spaced dashed lines. The proxies defined by Definition 5 are shown by dotted lines.

The causality relations in [12] were defined using the following two aspects of specifying the relations, based on the concept of proxies. (i) As there is a choice of two proxies of X and a choice of two proxies of Y, there are four combinations between the proxies. (ii) The six causality relations in Table 1 can be specified for each combination, thus yielding 24 relations between X and Y. The set of these causality relations is denoted $\mathcal{R}$. The following nomenclature was adopted to name the relations in $\mathcal{R}$. Relation $R?\#(X,Y)$ was such that $R?$ was a value from $\{R1, R2, R3, R4\}$ and indicated the choice of proxies of X and Y, whereas $\#$ indicated how the chosen proxies were related to each other, and took a value from $\{\ a, b, b', c, c', d\ \}$, where $R1$, $R2$, $R2'$, $R3$, $R3'$, $R4$ were renamed a, b, b', c, c', d, respectively, to avoid confusion with the previous usage of the relations $R1$ - $R4$. The set of relations $\mathcal{R}$ between poset events was complete using first-order predicate logic and only the $\prec$ relation between elementary events. The relation algebra given in [12] can be viewed as a power algebra [7].

In this paper, the label $\mathcal{R}$ is used to denote the set of the above relations when the discussion is common to the relations defined using either definition of proxies, viz., Definition 4 or 5 [12]. If the distinction matters, the notations $\mathcal{R}^{\prec_i}$ and $\mathcal{R}^{\prec}$ are used to denote the sets of relations that result when Definition 4 and 5 of proxies, respectively, are used. Intuitively, $\mathcal{R}^{\prec_i}$ indicates the set of relations resulting when the proxies are defined using the $\prec$ relation on each E_i, and $\mathcal{R}^{\prec}$

indicates the set of relations resulting when the proxies are defined using the $\prec$ relation on E. Each of $\mathcal{R}^{\prec}$ and $\mathcal{R}^{\prec_i}$ forms a hierarchy of *dependent* relations as shown in Figure 2. The relative hierarchy among relations in $\mathcal{R}^{\prec}$ and relations in $\mathcal{R}^{\prec_i}$ is given in [12].

A set of axioms to reason with the relations in $\mathcal{R}^{\prec}$ was given in [12]. The set of axioms was complete in the sense that (i) given any $R(X,Y)$, the axioms gave all enumerations of valid relations $r(X,Y)$ and $r'(Y,X)$, for $r, r', R \in \mathcal{R}^{\prec}$, and (ii) given $r_1(X,Y) \wedge r_2(Y,Z)$, the axioms gave all relations $r(X,Z)$ (and from (i), all $r'(Z,X)$), for $r, r', r_1, r_2 \in \mathcal{R}^{\prec}$. Hence, the axioms could be used to derive all possible implications from any given predicates on relations in $\mathcal{R}^{\prec}$.

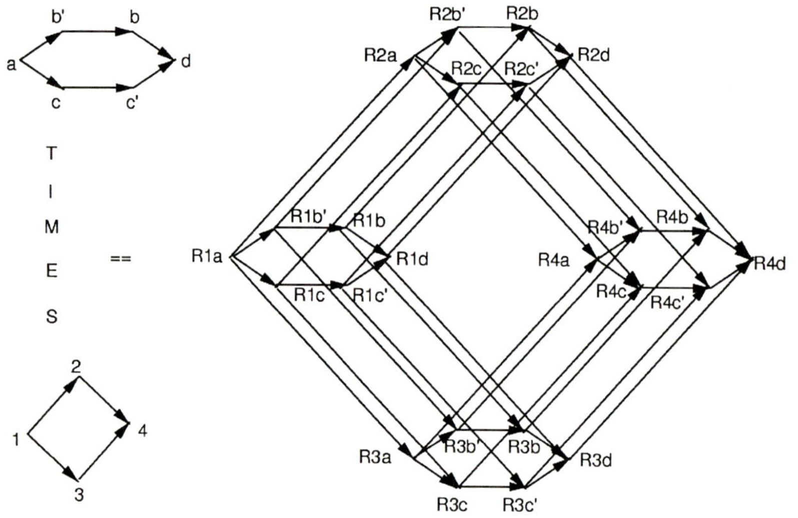

Fig. 2. Hierarchy of causality relations, ordered by "is a subrelation of" [12]. An edge from $r1$ to $r2$ indicates that $r1$ is a subrelation of $r2$.

In the next section, we give a methodology to enumerate the set of orthogonal relations for $\mathcal{R}$. The results of implementing this methodology for $\mathcal{R}^{\prec}$ using the axioms of [12] are then given. In this paper, we also modify the axiom system to make it applicable to $\mathcal{R}^{\prec_i}$. We then apply the above methodology to enumerate the set of orthogonal relations for $\mathcal{R}^{\prec_i}$ and give the results.

3 Orthogonal Relations

We now propose a method to derive and enumerate the orthogonal relations between any pair of poset events, using the set of dependent relations $\mathcal{R}$. We also present the numerical results of enumerating the orthogonal relations for $\mathcal{R}^{\prec}$ and $\mathcal{R}^{\prec_i}$ based on the appropriate axiom system. Specifically, for $\mathcal{R}^{\prec}$, we use axioms XP1-XP14 given in [12]. For $\mathcal{R}^{\prec_i}$, we use axioms XP1-XP6 and eight new axioms XP7$^{\prec_i}$-XP14$^{\prec_i}$. The results of the two enumerations were obtained by implementing the methodology in XSB Prolog.

The algorithm proposed here has the following two steps to create a (complete and mutually independent) set of orthogonal relations from the set of dependent relations $\mathcal{R}$.

1. Identify all possible combinations of relations $r(X,Y) \in \mathcal{R}$ that can hold simultaneously for a given X and Y.
2. For each of the identified combinations of relations $r(X,Y)$, identify all combinations of $r(Y,X)$ that can simultaneously hold for the same X and Y.

3.1 Step 1: All Possible Relations $r(X,Y)$

As a first step, we identify all the combinations of relations $r(X,Y)$, for $r \in \mathcal{R}$, that hold between poset events X and Y. Note that by construction, $(\mathcal{R}, \sqsubseteq)$, where $\sqsubseteq$ is the relation "is a subrelation of", is a lattice as illustrated in Figure 2. For a given pair of posets X and Y, it may be the case that a combination of the relations in $\mathcal{R}$ may hold. Specifically, if $R(X,Y)$ holds, then $\forall R' \mid R \sqsubseteq R'$, $R'(X,Y)$ holds. Thus, if $R(X,Y)$ holds, then for each R' in the upward-closed subset[1] of $\mathcal{R}$, $R'(X,Y)$ holds. In the partial order $(\mathcal{R}, \sqsubseteq)$, all upward-closed subsets of $\mathcal{R}$ correspond exactly to the combinations of relations in $\mathcal{R}$ that can hold concurrently for a given pair of poset events. It follows from the result on page 400 [1] that there is a 1-1 correspondence between the set of all upward-closed subsets of a partial order and the set of antichains[2] in the partial order. Therefore, an enumeration of the antichains in $(\mathcal{R}, \sqsubseteq)$ gives an enumeration of the upward-closed subsets of $(\mathcal{R}, \sqsubseteq)$, which corresponds to all the combinations of the relations in $\mathcal{R}$ that can hold for a pair of poset events. Let $\mathcal{RAC}$ be the set of all such antichains. A member of $\mathcal{RAC}$, denoted $rac(X,Y)$, is an antichain of $\mathcal{R}$ and can be expressed as the conjunction of the members of the antichain, each of which is a member of $\mathcal{R}$, i.e., $rac(X,Y)$ can be viewed as $\bigwedge_{r \in rac(X,Y)} r(X,Y)$. The number of antichains in $\mathcal{RAC}$ was computed by the implementation of axioms XP1-XP6 (given below), to be as follows. There are 1, 24, 147, 350, 341, 168, 44, 2, and 0 antichains of size 0 through 8, respectively, giving a total of 1077 antichains. The antichain of size 0 denotes the empty-set upward-closed subset of $\mathcal{R}$, equivalent to $\overline{R4d}(X,Y)$, where $\overline{R4d}(X,Y)$ denotes that $R4d(X,Y)$ is false. Observe from Figure 2 that the size of the largest antichain is 7.

The axioms XP1 - XP6 from [12] are reproduced here. The relation $||(r_1, r_2)$ stands for $\not\sqsubseteq (r_1, r_2) \wedge \not\sqsubseteq (r_2, r_1)$. V_1 denotes the set $\{1, 2, 3, 4\}$ and V_2 denotes the set $\{a, b, b', c, c', d\}$.

XP1. $R1? \sqsubseteq R2? \sqsubseteq R4?$, where ? is instantiated from V_2
XP2. $R1? \sqsubseteq R3? \sqsubseteq R4?$, where ? is instantiated from V_2
XP3. $R2?||R3\#$, where ? and # are separately instantiated from V_2

[1] A set $\Re \subseteq \mathcal{R}$ is upward-closed iff for every $r, r' \in \mathcal{R}$, $(r \in \Re \bigwedge r \sqsubseteq r') \implies r' \in \Re$.
[2] A set $\Re$ is an anti-chain iff for every r and r' in $\Re$, $r \not\sqsubseteq r' \wedge r' \not\sqsubseteq r$.

XP4. $R?a \sqsubseteq R?b' \sqsubseteq R?b \sqsubseteq R?d$, where ? is instantiated from V_1
XP5. $R?a \sqsubseteq R?c \sqsubseteq R?c' \sqsubseteq R?d$, where ? is instantiated from V_1
XP6. $R?b||R?c'$, $R?b'||R?c'$, $R?b||R?c$, $R?b'||R?c$, where ? is instantiated from V_1

3.2 Step 2: Relations $r(Y, X)$, Given That Certain $r(X, Y)$ Hold

The computed combinations of relations in $\mathcal{R}$, viz., antichains in $(\mathcal{R}, \sqsubseteq)$, are useful to determine all the orthogonal relations that can exist between any two poset events. For each of the $|\mathcal{RAC}|$ antichains that hold between X and Y, there are potentially $|\mathcal{RAC}|$ antichains that hold between Y and X, thus leading to a potential $|\mathcal{RAC}|^2$ orthogonal relations between X and Y. Several of these relations will be illegal because they contradict the relations $r(X, Y)$. The objective is to determine exactly all the orthogonal relations that are admissible by the axiom system. For each $rac1(X, Y)$, where $rac1 \in \mathcal{RAC}$, determine which $rac2(Y, X)$ can hold, where $rac2 \in \mathcal{RAC}$, using the axiom system which allows the derivation of all $r'(Y, X)$ from any $r(X, Y)$, where r, $r' \in \mathcal{R}$. Then each conjunction of an antichain $rac1(X, Y)$ and a compatible antichain $rac2(Y, X)$ is orthogonal from every other such conjunction; denote this set of conjunctions as $\mathcal{RO}$, which then represents all the possible orthogonal relations between two posets, based on the $\prec$ relation among elementary events.

Let us denote the sets of orthogonal relations obtained for relations in $\mathcal{R}^{\prec}$ and $\mathcal{R}^{\prec_i}$ by $\mathcal{RO}^{\prec}$ and $\mathcal{RO}^{\prec_i}$, respectively.

Table 2. Number of orthogonal relations in $\mathcal{RO}^{\prec}$, classified based on size of antichains.

Size/Number of $rac(X, Y)$ antichains	Number of antichains $rac(Y, X)$ of size $s = 0 \ldots 7$								$\sum_{s=0}^{7} col_s$
	$s = 0$	$s = 1$	$s = 2$	$s = 3$	$s = 4$	$s = 5$	$s = 6$	$s = 7$	
0 / 1	1	24	147	350	341	168	44	2	1077
1 / 24	24	261	898	1285	822	264	34	1	3589
2 / 147	147	898	1911	1683	642	130	4	0	5415
3 / 350	350	1285	1683	937	180	8	0	0	4443
4 / 341	341	822	642	180	18	0	0	0	2003
5 / 168	168	264	130	8	0	0	0	0	570
6 / 44	44	34	4	0	0	0	0	0	82
7 / 2	2	1	0	0	0	0	0	0	3

Relations $\mathcal{RO}^{\prec}$. Axioms XP7-XP14 along with XP1-XP6 were used to determine all the orthogonal relations $\mathcal{RO}^{\prec}$, counted in Table 2. Axioms XP7-XP14 are reproduced below with labels XP7$^{\prec}$ - XP14$^{\prec}$, respectively.

XP7$^{\prec}$. $R1a(X,Y) \bigvee R1b(X,Y) \bigvee R1b'(X,Y) \bigvee R1c(X,Y) \bigvee R1c'(X,Y) \Longrightarrow \overline{R4d}(Y,X)$.
XP8$^{\prec}$. $R1d(X,Y) \Longrightarrow \overline{R4b}(Y,X) \bigwedge \overline{R4c'}(Y,X)$.
XP9$^{\prec}$. $R2a(X,Y) \bigvee R2b(X,Y) \bigvee R2b'(X,Y) \bigvee R2c(X,Y) \bigvee R2c'(X,Y) \Longrightarrow \overline{R2d}(Y,X)$.

XP10$^{\prec}$. $R2d(X,Y) \Longrightarrow \overline{R2b}(Y,X) \bigwedge \overline{R2c'}(Y,X)$.
XP11$^{\prec}$. $R3a(X,Y) \bigvee R3b(X,Y) \bigvee R3b'(X,Y) \bigvee R3c(X,Y) \bigvee R3c'(X,Y) \Longrightarrow \overline{R3d}(Y,X)$.
XP12$^{\prec}$. $R3d(X,Y) \Longrightarrow \overline{R3b}(Y,X) \bigwedge \overline{R3c'}(Y,X)$.
XP13$^{\prec}$. $R4a(X,Y) \bigvee R4b(X,Y) \bigvee R4b'(X,Y) \bigvee R4c(X,Y) \bigvee R4c'(X,Y) \Longrightarrow \overline{R1d}(Y,X)$.
XP14$^{\prec}$. $R4d(X,Y) \Longrightarrow \overline{R1b}(Y,X) \bigwedge \overline{R1c'}(Y,X)$.

Table 2 consists of three parts, separated by vertical double-lines. The first part categorizes the $|\mathcal{RAC}(X,Y)|$ antichains of Figure 2, based on size which ranges from 0 to 7. Each row i, $i \in [0 \ldots 7]$, in the entire table is used to compute the orthogonal relations in which antichains $rac(X,Y)$ have size i. Consider any row i. For each antichain $rac(X,Y)$ of size i, the number of the corresponding legal (as per XP7$^{\prec}$–XP14$^{\prec}$) antichains $rac(Y,X)$ of size s, $s \in [0,\ldots,7]$, are added to column s in the second part of the table. The entry in row i in the last part of the table sums up the row entires of columns $s = 0$ through $s = 7$ of that row, and gives the total number of orthogonal relations in which antichains $rac(X,Y)$ have size i. The sum of the last column is 17,185 $= |\mathcal{RO}^{\prec}|$.

Note that $\mathcal{RAC}$ needs to consider all the antichains in $\mathcal{R}$, not just the maximal antichains, because even a subset of a maximal antichain identifies a different upward-closed subset of $\mathcal{R}$ than does the maximal antichain, indicating a different set of relations that hold. Also note that for any $rac1(X,Y)$, all relations in the upward-closed subset of $\mathcal{R}$ hold and those not in the upward-closed subset do not hold. Thus, for any $rac1(X,Y)$, there is a bit-vector of size 24 where each bit corresponds to a relation in $\mathcal{R}$, such that there is a "1" for each relation in the upward-closed subset of $rac1(X,Y)$ and a "0" for each relation not in the upward-closed subset of $rac1(X,Y)$. Analogously, for any $rac2(Y,X)$ that is compatible with $rac1(X,Y)$ as per the axioms, there is a bit-vector of size 24 where each bit corresponds to a relation in $\mathcal{R}$, such that there is a "1" for each relation in the upward-closed subset of $rac2(Y,X)$ and a "0" for each relation not in the upward-closed subset of $rac2(Y,X)$. Each orthogonal relation can thus be represented by a 48-bit vector.

Example: For the $rac1(X,Y)$ antichain $R2b(X,Y) \bigwedge R2c(X,Y) \bigwedge R3a(X,Y)$ of size three, the axioms XP7$^{\prec}$-XP14$^{\prec}$ give $\overline{R2d}(Y,X) \bigwedge \overline{R3d}(Y,X)$. The only possible antichains $rac2(Y,X)$ can be from the set of relations $\{\ R4*(Y,X)\ \}$ – this gives 11 possible antichains $rac2(Y,X)$, counting the antichain of size 0, that are compatible with $rac1(X,Y)$. Each of these 11 combinations of $rac2(Y,X)$ with $rac1(X,Y)$ yields a unique 48-bit vector.

Relations $\mathcal{RO}^{\prec_i}$. Observe that the axioms XP7-XP14 given in [12] are applicable only to relations in $\mathcal{R}^{\prec}$ which use Definition 5 of proxies [12], and not to relations in $\mathcal{R}^{\prec_i}$ which use Definition 4 of proxies [12]. If proxies are defined by Definition 4 and not Definition 5, then the axioms XP7-XP14 need to be replaced by the following axioms XP7$^{\prec_i}$–XP14$^{\prec_i}$ to obtain all the orthogonal relations $\mathcal{RO}^{\prec_i}$.

XP7$^{\prec_i}$. $R1a(X,Y) \Longrightarrow \overline{R4d}(Y,X)$;
$R1b(X,Y) \bigvee R1b'(X,Y) \Longrightarrow \overline{R4b}(Y,X)$;
$R1c(X,Y) \bigvee R1c'(X,Y) \Longrightarrow \overline{R4c'}(Y,X)$.
XP8$^{\prec_i}$. $R1d(X,Y) \Longrightarrow \overline{R4a}(Y,X)$.
XP9$^{\prec_i}$. $R2a(X,Y) \Longrightarrow \overline{R2d}(Y,X)$;
$R2b(X,Y) \bigvee R2b'(X,Y) \Longrightarrow \overline{R2b}(Y,X)$;
$R2c(X,Y) \bigvee R2c'(X,Y) \Longrightarrow \overline{R2c'}(Y,X)$.
XP10$^{\prec_i}$. $R2d(X,Y) \Longrightarrow \overline{R2a}(Y,X)$.
XP11$^{\prec_i}$. $R3a(X,Y) \Longrightarrow \overline{R3d}(Y,X)$;
$R3b(X,Y) \bigvee R3b'(X,Y) \Longrightarrow \overline{R3b}(Y,X)$;
$R3c(X,Y) \bigvee R3c'(X,Y) \Longrightarrow \overline{R3c'}(Y,X)$.
XP12$^{\prec_i}$. $R3d(X,Y) \Longrightarrow \overline{R3a}(Y,X)$.
XP13$^{\prec_i}$. $R4a(X,Y) \Longrightarrow \overline{R1d}(Y,X)$;
$R4b(X,Y) \bigvee R4b'(X,Y) \Longrightarrow \overline{R1b}(Y,X)$;
$R4c(X,Y) \bigvee R4c'(X,Y) \Longrightarrow \overline{R1c'}(Y,X)$.
XP14$^{\prec_i}$. $R4d(X,Y) \Longrightarrow \overline{R1a}(Y,X)$.

Axioms XP1-XP6 and XP7$^{\prec_i}$-XP14$^{\prec_i}$ are used to derive the orthogonal relations $\mathcal{RO}^{\prec_i}$, instead of axioms XP1-XP6 and XP7$^{\prec}$-XP14$^{\prec}$ that were used to obtain $\mathcal{RO}^{\prec}$. Results analogous to those in Table 2 for $\mathcal{RO}^{\prec}$ are obtained for $\mathcal{RO}^{\prec_i}$ and shown in Table 3. The sum of the last column is 123,474 = $|\mathcal{RO}^{\prec_i}|$.

Table 3. Number of orthogonal relations in $\mathcal{RO}^{\prec_i}$, classified based on size of antichains.

Size/Number of $rac(X,Y)$ antichains	Number of antichains $rac(Y,X)$ of size $s = 0 \ldots 7$								$\sum_{s=0}^{7} col_s$
	$s=0$	$s=1$	$s=2$	$s=3$	$s=4$	$s=5$	$s=6$	$s=7$	
0 / 1	1	24	147	350	341	168	44	2	1077
1 / 24	24	405	1926	3695	3084	1326	293	11	10764
2 / 147	147	1926	7097	11493	7963	2768	527	18	31939
3 / 350	350	3695	11493	16469	9406	2654	469	16	44552
4 / 341	341	3084	7963	9406	4158	802	132	4	25890
5 / 168	168	1326	2768	2654	802	18	0	0	7736
6 / 44	44	293	527	469	132	0	0	0	1465
7 / 2	2	11	18	16	4	0	0	0	51

4 Conclusions

Orthogonal relations between events provide an understanding of all possible mutually exclusive relations that can hold between the events when complete and precise knowledge is available. These form the basis of relation algebras, and allow the derivation of relations to represent knowledge when imprecise and incomplete information is available. Abstract events, each of which is a partially ordered collection of elementary events, are important when reasoning and representing actions in complex distributed systems. We derived orthogonal relations $\mathcal{RO}$ between abstract events using the space-time model for a distributed system execution. Relations in $\mathcal{RO}$ are analogous to the 13 orthogonal relations between linear intervals at a point in space [2]. Relations in $\mathcal{RO}$ are also analogous to the following sets of orthogonal relations based on the elementary causality relation: (i) the three orthogonal relations between two points in space-time ($a \prec b$, $b \prec a$, $a \not\prec b \wedge b \not\prec a$), (ii) the six orthogonal relations between a linear interval and a point in space-time [11], (iii) the 29 orthogonal relations between two linear intervals in space-time using the dense model of time [11], and (iv) the 40 orthogonal relations between two linear intervals in space-time using the nondense model of time [11]. We expect that as distributed agent-based programs and applications become more common, specific uses for these orthogonal relations between abstract events will emerge, similar to the uses of the 13 orthogonal relations between colocated linear intervals.

Acknowledgements. This work was supported by the U.S. National Science Foundation grants CCR-9875617 and EIA-9871345.

References

1. M. Aigner, *Combinatorial Theory,* Springer-Verlag, 1979.
2. J. Allen, Maintaining knowledge about temporal intervals, *Communications of the ACM*, 26(11):832-843, 1983.
3. J. Allen, Towards a general theory of action and time, *Artificial Intelligence*, 23:123-154, 1984.
4. P. van Beek, Reasoning about qualitative temporal information, *Artificial Intelligence*, 58:297-326, 1992.
5. P. van Beek, R. Cohen, Exact and approximate reasoning about temporal relations, *Computational Intelligence*, 6:132-144, 1990.
6. J. van Benthem, *The Logic of Time*, Kluwer Academic Publishers, (1ed. 1983), 2ed. 1991.
7. C. Brink, Power structures, *Algebra Universalis,* Vol. 30, 177-216, 1993.
8. C. Freksa, Temporal reasoning based on semi-intervals, *Artificial Intelligence*, 54: 199-227, 1992.
9. A. Gerevini, L. Schubert, Efficient algorithms for qualitative reasoning about time, *Artificial Intelligence*, 74: 207-248, 1995.
10. C. L. Hamblin, Instants and intervals, In *The Study of Time*, pp. 324-332, Springer-Verlag, 1972.
11. A. Kshemkalyani, Temporal interactions of intervals in distributed systems, *Journal of Computer and System Sciences*, 52(2), 287-298, April 1996.
12. A. Kshemkalyani, Reasoning about causality between distributed nonatomic events, *Artificial Intelligence*, 92(2): 301-315, May 1997.
13. L. Lamport, On interprocess communication, Part I: Basic formalism, *Distributed Computing*, 1:77-85, 1986.
14. B. Nebel, H. -J. Buerckert, Reasoning about temporal relations: A maximal tractable subclass of Allen's interval algebra, *Journal of the ACM*, 42(1): 43-66, Jan. 1995.
15. R. Rodriguez, F. Anger, K. Ford, Temporal reasoning: a relativistic model, *International Journal of Intelligent Systems*, 11: 237-254, 1991.
16. P. Terenziani, P. Torasso, Time, action-types, and causation, *Computational Intelligence*, 11(3):529-552, 1995.

Explanatory Relations Based on Mathematical Morphology

Isabelle Bloch[1], Ramón Pino-Pérez[2,3], and Carlos Uzcátegui[2]

[1] Ecole Nationale Supérieure des Télécommunications - Dept TSI - CNRS URA 820
46 rue Barrault, Paris, France - Isabelle.Bloch@enst.fr
[2] Facultad de Ciencias - Universidad de Los Andes
Mérida, Venezuela - pino@ciens.ula.ve, uzca@ciens.ula.ve
[3] CRIL, Université d'Artois
Rue Jean Souvraz, 62307 Lens, France - pino@cril.univ-artois.fr

Abstract. Using mathematical morphology on formulas introduced recently by Bloch and Lang (*Proceedings of IPMU'2000*) we define two new explanatory relations. Their logical behavior is analyzed. The results show that these natural ways for defining preferred explanations are robust because these relations satisfy almost all postulates of explanatory reasoning introduced by Pino-Pérez and Uzcátegui (*Artificial Intelligence,* 111:131–169, 1999). Actually, the first explanatory relation is Explanatory-Rational. The second one is not even Explanatory-Cumulative but it satisfies new weak postulates.

1 Introduction

The process of inferring the best explanation of an observation is usually known as *abduction.* In the logic-based approach to abduction, the background theory is given by a consistent set of formulas Σ. The notion of a *possible explanation* is defined by saying that a formula γ is an explanation of α if $\Sigma \cup \{\gamma\} \vdash \alpha$. An explanatory relation is a binary relation $\rhd$ where the intended meaning of $\alpha \rhd \gamma$ is "γ is a *preferred explanation* of α".

In [4], a set of postulates that should be satisfied by preferred explanatory relations is proposed and discussed.

The aim of this work is at least threefold. First, to propose very natural explanatory relations that in some cases are computationally practicable. Second, to examine the adequacy of logical postulates proposed in [4] and third, the discovery of new logical properties for the explanatory reasoning.

In order to accomplish our goals we propose concrete definitions of preferred explanations based on mathematical morphology. The starting point is a very general setting: a relation between worlds that in most of the cases can be viewed as a graph connecting worlds.

Mathematical morphology operators on logical formulas have been introduced recently in [1]. These ideas allow us to define the *most central part* of a formula, according to the fundamental principles of this theory (see e.g. [6,7]). Using this notion we define two explanatory relations. The first one, $\rhd^{\ell ne}$, has

S. Benferhat and P. Besnard (Eds.): ECSQARU 2001, LNAI 2143, pp. 736–747, 2001.

the following intended meaning: γ is a preferred explanation of α if γ is a formula entailing the *most central part* of the conjunction of Σ with α. For the second one, $\rhd^{\ell c}$, we define a sequence which approximates the most central part of Σ; then we say that γ is a preferred explanation of α if γ implies the conjunction of α with the closest element of the sequence which is consistent with α.

2 Preliminaries

Let us recall here the basic principles of morpho-logics. Let PS be a finite set of propositional symbols. The language is generated by PS and the usual connectives. Well-formed formulas will be denoted by Greek letters φ, ψ... Worlds will be denoted by ω, ω'... and the set of all worlds by Ω. $Mod(\varphi) = \{\omega \in \Omega \mid \omega \models \varphi\}$ is the set of all worlds where φ is satisfied. Dilation and erosion (the two fundamental operations of mathematical morphology [6]) of a formula φ by a structuring element B have been defined in [1] as follows:

$$Mod(D_B(\varphi)) = \{\omega \in \Omega \mid B(\omega) \cap Mod(\varphi) \neq \emptyset\}, \tag{1}$$

$$Mod(E_B(\varphi)) = \{\omega \in \Omega \mid B(\omega) \models \varphi\}. \tag{2}$$

In these equations, the structuring element B represents a relationship between worlds, i.e. $\omega' \in B(\omega)$ iff ω' satisfies some relationship with ω. The condition in Equation 1 expresses that the set of worlds in relation to ω should be consistent with φ, i.e.: $\exists \omega' \in B(\omega),\ \omega' \models \varphi$. The condition in Equation 2 is stronger and expresses that φ should be satisfied in all worlds which stand in relation to ω .

2.1 Properties

The properties of these basic operations and of other derived operations are detailed in [1]. The fundamental properties of erosion, that will be used intensively in the following, can be summarized as:

- Independence of the syntax (follows directly from the definition through the models).
- Monotonicity: erosion is increasing with respect to φ, i.e.

  $$\varphi \vdash \psi \ \Rightarrow\ E_B(\varphi) \vdash E_B(\psi), \tag{3}$$

  for any structuring element B. Erosion is decreasing with respect to the structuring element, i.e.

  $$\forall \omega \in \Omega, B_\omega \subset B'_\omega \ \Rightarrow\ E_{B'}(\varphi) \vdash E_B(\varphi). \tag{4}$$

- Anti-extensivity[1]: if B is derived from a reflexive relation, i.e. such that $\forall \omega \in \Omega, \omega \in B_\omega$, the erosion is anti-extensive, i.e.

  $$E_B(\varphi) \vdash \varphi. \tag{5}$$

[1] In set theoretical mathematical morphology an operation Ψ is said anti-extensive iff for any set X, $\Psi(X) \subset X$.

We will only deal with such cases in what follows. We will also consider symmetrical relations, i.e. $\forall(\omega,\omega') \in \Omega^2, \omega \in B_{\omega'} \Leftrightarrow \omega' \in B_\omega$.

- Iteration: Erosion satisfies an iteration property, which is expressed for symmetrical structuring elements as:

$$E_B[E_{B'}(\varphi)] = E_{D_B(B')}(\varphi). \tag{6}$$

For instance if $B = B'$, and if we denote by E^n the erosion by B dilated $(n-1)$ times by itself (this is typically the case for distance based operations where the structuring element is a ball of distance, as will be seen in Section 2.2), we have:

$$E^{n+n'}(\varphi) = E^{n'}[E^n(\varphi)] = E^n[E^{n'}(\varphi)], \tag{7}$$

where n, n' denote the size of the erosion (i.e. the "radius" of the structuring element).

- Commutativity with conjunction:

$$E_B(\wedge_{i=1}^m \varphi_i) = \wedge_{i=1}^m E_B(\varphi_i). \tag{8}$$

- Erosion of a disjunction: erosion and disjunction do not commute, but we have a partial relation:

$$E_B(\varphi) \vee E_B(\psi) \vdash E_B(\varphi \vee \psi). \tag{9}$$

2.2 Illustrative Example

In all what follows, we will consider as an illustrative example the case where the structuring element is defined as a ball of the Hamming distance between worlds d_H, where $d_H(\omega,\omega')$ is the number of propositional symbols that are instantiated differently in both worlds. Then dilation and erosion of size n are defined from Equations 1 and 2 by using the distance balls of radius n as structuring elements:

$$Mod(D^n(\varphi)) = \{\omega \in \Omega \mid \exists \omega' \in \Omega, \omega' \models \varphi \textit{ and } d_H(\omega,\omega') \leq n\}, \tag{10}$$

$$Mod(E^n(\varphi)) = \{\omega \in \Omega \mid \forall \omega' \in \Omega, d_H(\omega,\omega') \leq n \Rightarrow \omega' \models \varphi\}. \tag{11}$$

We make use of a graph representation of worlds, where each node represents a world and a link represents an elementary connection between two worlds, i.e. being at distance 1 from each other. A ball of radius 1 centered at ω is constituted by ω and the extremities of the arcs originating in ω. This allows for an easy visualization of the effects of transformations.

Let us consider an example with three propositional symbols a, b, c. The possible worlds are represented in Figure 1.

Let us consider $\varphi = \neg a \wedge b \wedge c$. Then we have:

$$D^1(\varphi) = (\neg a \wedge b) \vee (\neg a \wedge c) \vee (b \wedge c),$$

$$D^2(\varphi) = \neg a \vee b \vee c = \neg(a \wedge \neg b \wedge \neg c).$$

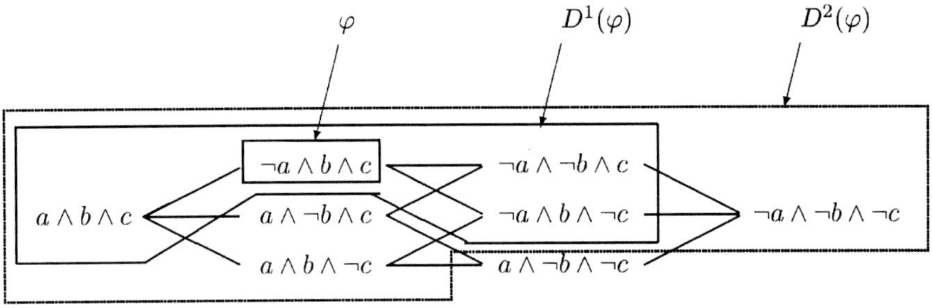

Fig. 1. Graph representation of possible worlds with 3 symbols and an example of φ and two successive dilations. An arc between two nodes means that the corresponding nodes are at a distance to each other equal to 1.

These results are illustrated in Figure 1. Notice that in this kind of figures the formula defined by a border is the disjunction of the formulas in the interior of the border.

Erosion can be computed very easily from any conjunctive normal form. Indeed, if φ is a disjunction of literals, i.e., $\varphi = l_1 \vee l_2 \vee ... \vee l_n$, then we have:

$$E^1(\varphi) = \wedge_{j=1}^{n}(\vee_{i \neq j} l_i). \tag{12}$$

This property, along with the commutativity of erosion with conjunction, allows to compute easily the erosion of any formula expressed as a CNF.

3 Explanatory Relations Based on Erosion

In this section we define precisely the concept of *most central part* of a formula with the help of the erosion operator. Then, based on this concept, we define two explanatory relations.

3.1 Last Non-empty Erosion

We denote by $E_\ell(\varphi)$ the last erosion of φ, i.e. the erosion of φ of the largest possible size such that the set of worlds where $E_\ell(\varphi)$ is satisfied is not empty:

$$E_\ell(\varphi) = E^n(\varphi) \Leftrightarrow \begin{cases} E^n(\varphi) \nvdash \bot, \\ \text{and } \forall m > n,\ E^m(\varphi) \vdash \bot. \end{cases} \tag{13}$$

By convention, we set $E^0(\varphi) = \varphi$. Note that last erosion is different from the classical notion of ultimate erosion in mathematical morphology[2]. We define the most central part of a formula as its last erosion. This concept is similar to one used in preference modeling in [3].

[2] The ultimate eorsion is obtained by successive erosions, and is defined as the union of the connected components that disappear from one step to the other.

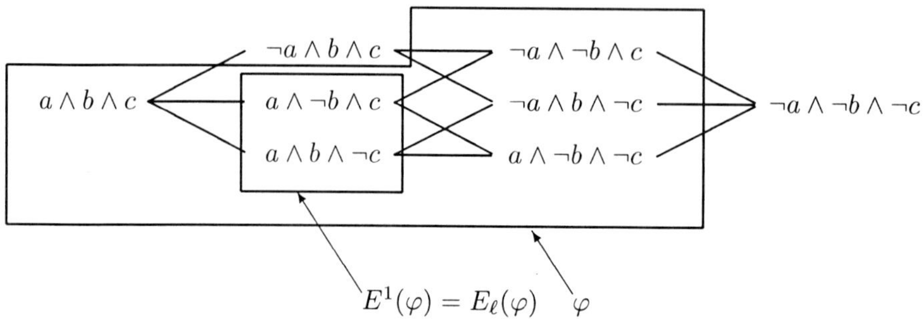

Fig. 2. An example of φ and its last erosion.

Let us consider the illustrative example of Section 2.2. Let us take (see Figure 2):

$$\varphi = (a \vee \neg b \vee \neg c) \wedge (a \vee b \vee c).$$

Using Equations 8 and 12, we derive:

$$E^1(\varphi) = (a\vee\neg b)\wedge(a\vee\neg c)\wedge(\neg b\vee\neg c)\wedge(a\vee b)\wedge(a\vee c)\wedge(b\vee c) = (a\wedge\neg b\wedge c)\vee(a\wedge b\wedge\neg c).$$

Since $E^2(\varphi) \vdash_\Sigma \perp$, we have $E^1(\varphi) = E_\ell(\varphi)$.

A preferred explanation of α is then defined from this operator applied on $\Sigma \wedge \alpha$, more precisely:

$$\alpha \rhd^{\ell ne} \gamma \overset{def}{\Leftrightarrow} \gamma \vdash E_\ell(\Sigma \wedge \alpha). \tag{14}$$

The idea of taking the last erosion of $\Sigma \wedge \alpha$ can be interpreted in terms of robustness. An erosion of size n of a formula is a formula that can be changed while still proving the initial formula. If at most n symbols are changed in $E^n(\varphi)$ then φ is always satisfied. Here, considering $E_\ell(\Sigma\wedge\alpha)$ means that we are looking at the most reduced formula that satisfies $\Sigma\wedge\alpha$, i.e. the one that can be changed the most while satisfying $\Sigma \wedge \alpha$.

Let us take $\Sigma \wedge \alpha = \varphi$ where φ is defined as in the previous example (Figure 2). For Definition 14, if we denote $PE_{\rhd^{\ell ne}}(\alpha) = \{\gamma \,:\, \alpha \rhd^{\ell ne} \gamma\}$ (the preferred explanations of α), we have:

$$PE_{\rhd^{\ell ne}}(\alpha) = \{(a \wedge \neg b \wedge c), (a \wedge b \wedge \neg c), (a \wedge \neg b \wedge c) \vee (a \wedge b \wedge \neg c)\}.$$

One potential problem with last erosion is that it does not represent all "parts" of a formula. Let us take for instance: $\Sigma \wedge \alpha = (a \vee b) \wedge (a \vee c) \wedge (b \vee c)$ and $\Sigma \wedge \beta = ((a \vee b) \wedge (a \vee c) \wedge (b \vee c)) \vee (\neg a \wedge \neg b \wedge \neg c)$. Then we have: $E_\ell(\Sigma \wedge \alpha) = E_\ell(\Sigma \wedge \beta) = a \wedge b \wedge c$ and $PE_{\rhd^{\ell ne}}(\alpha) = PE_{\rhd^{\ell ne}}(\beta)$. The set of worlds satisfying $\Sigma\wedge\beta$ is disconnected, and the connected component containing only $(\neg a\wedge\neg b\wedge\neg c)$ is not represented in the explanations of β. If this is considered to be a problem, it can be avoided by considering the ultimate erosion instead of the last erosion.

3.2 Last Consistent Erosion

Another idea consists in eroding Σ as much as possible but still under the constraint that it remains consistent with α:

$$E_{\ell c}(\Sigma, \alpha) = E^n(\Sigma) \text{ where } n = \max\{k : E^k(\Sigma) \wedge \alpha \not\vdash \bot\}. \tag{15}$$

From this operator, we define the following explanatory relation:

$$\alpha \rhd^{\ell c} \gamma \stackrel{def}{\Leftrightarrow} \gamma \vdash E_{\ell c}(\Sigma, \alpha) \wedge \alpha, \tag{16}$$

This definition has a different interpretation. Here we consider erosion of Σ alone, which means that we are looking at the formulas that satisfy α while being the most in the theory, i.e. that can be changed while remaining in the theory (but not necessary satisfying α after the changes).

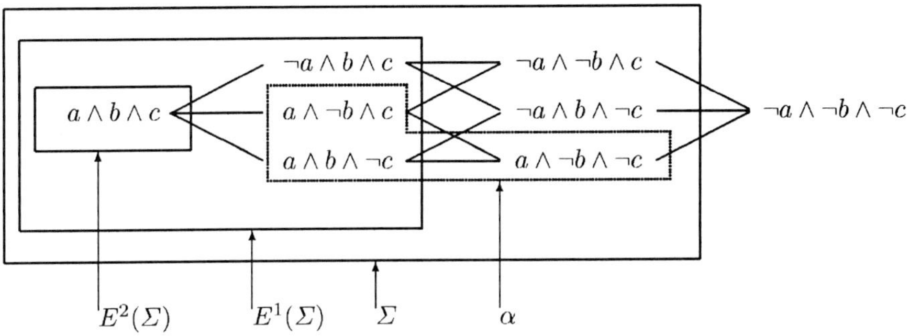

Fig. 3. An example of last consistent erosion.

Let us come back to the illustrative example, and take (see Figure 3): $\Sigma = a \vee b \vee c$, and $\alpha = (a \wedge \neg b \wedge c) \vee (a \wedge b \wedge \neg c) \vee (a \wedge \neg b \wedge \neg c)$. We have: $E^1(\Sigma) = (a \vee b) \wedge (a \vee c) \wedge (b \vee c)$, $E^2(\Sigma) = a \wedge b \wedge c$, and finally $E^3(\Sigma) \vdash \bot$. Therefore:

$$E^1(\Sigma) \wedge \alpha = (a \wedge \neg b \wedge c) \vee (a \wedge b \wedge \neg c)$$

and $E^2(\Sigma) \wedge \alpha \vdash \bot$. Therefore the value of n in Definition 16 is equal to 1. For Definition 16, γ can be anything in the set

$$PE_{\rhd^{\ell c}}(\alpha) = \{(a \wedge \neg b \wedge c), (a \wedge b \wedge \neg c), (a \wedge \neg b \wedge c) \vee (a \wedge b \wedge \neg c)\}.$$

There is an alternative way of looking at $\rhd^{\ell c}$ which will be particularly useful in the next section. The iteration of the erosion operator provides a method of linearly pre-ordering the models of Σ. Consider the following relation among models.

$$\omega \leq \omega' \stackrel{def}{\Leftrightarrow} \forall k \; (\omega' \in E^k(\Sigma) \rightarrow \omega \in E^k(\Sigma)).$$

It is clear that $\leq$ is a total pre-order and it is not difficult to verify that the following holds:

$$\alpha \rhd^{\ell c} \gamma \iff \text{mod}(\Sigma \cup \{\gamma\}) \subseteq \min(\text{mod}(\Sigma \cup \{\alpha\}), \leq). \tag{17}$$

4 Rationality Postulates

In this section we study the properties of the two proposed explanatory relations according to the postulates introduced in [4]. The basic rationality postulates for explanatory relations are the following (we use the notation $\alpha \vdash_\Sigma \beta$ instead of $\Sigma \cup \{\alpha\}$):

LLE$_\Sigma$: $$\frac{\vdash_\Sigma \alpha \leftrightarrow \alpha' \ , \ \alpha \rhd \gamma}{\alpha' \rhd \gamma}$$

RLE$_\Sigma$: $$\frac{\vdash_\Sigma \gamma \leftrightarrow \gamma' \ ; \ \alpha \rhd \gamma}{\alpha \rhd \gamma'}$$

E-CM: $$\frac{\alpha \rhd \gamma \ ; \ \gamma \vdash_\Sigma \beta}{(\alpha \wedge \beta) \rhd \gamma}$$

E-C-Cut: $$\frac{(\alpha \wedge \beta) \rhd \gamma \ , \ \forall \delta \, [\alpha \rhd \delta \Rightarrow \delta \vdash_\Sigma \beta]}{\alpha \rhd \gamma}$$

RA: $$\frac{\alpha \rhd \gamma \ ; \ \gamma' \vdash_\Sigma \gamma \ ; \ \gamma' \not\vdash_\Sigma \bot}{\alpha \rhd \gamma'}$$

E-RW: $$\frac{\alpha \rhd \gamma \ ; \ \alpha \rhd \delta}{\alpha \rhd (\gamma \vee \delta)}$$

LOR: $$\frac{\alpha \rhd \gamma \ ; \ \beta \rhd \gamma}{(\alpha \vee \beta) \rhd \gamma}$$

E-DR: $$\frac{\alpha \rhd \gamma \ ; \ \beta \rhd \delta}{(\alpha \vee \beta) \rhd \gamma \text{ or } (\alpha \vee \beta) \rhd \delta}$$

E-R-Cut: $$\frac{(\alpha \wedge \beta) \rhd \gamma \ ; \ \exists \delta \, [\alpha \rhd \delta \ \& \ \delta \vdash_\Sigma \beta]}{\alpha \rhd \gamma}$$

E-Reflexivity : $$\frac{\alpha \rhd \gamma}{\gamma \rhd \gamma}$$

E-Con$_\Sigma$: $\not\vdash_\Sigma \neg\alpha$ iff there is γ such that $\alpha \rhd \gamma$

The intended meaning and motivation for these postulates can be found in [4].

It is immediate from the definition of $\rhd^{\ell c}$ and $\rhd^{\ell ne}$ that LLE$_\Sigma$, RLE$_\Sigma$, RA, E-RW, and E-Con$_\Sigma$ are satisfied. Moreover, from the representation of $\rhd^{\ell c}$ given by equation 17 and some general results of [4] we get the following proposition.

Proposition 1. *$\rhd^{\ell c}$ is a causal E-rational explanatory relation. In particular, it satisfies* LLE$_\Sigma$, RLE$_\Sigma$, RA, E-RW, E-Con$_\Sigma$, E-CM *and* E-R-Cut.

From the results in [4] we also know that by being E-rational, $\rhd^{\ell c}$ also satisfies E-C-Cut, E-Reflexivity, E-DR and LOR. However, the situation for $\rhd^{\ell ne}$ is quite different since, as we will see below, the basic postulates E-CM and E-C-Cut do not hold.

We will provide now a counter-example of E-CM for $\rhd^{\ell ne}$. Let us consider our illustrative example (see Section 2.2), and take the following formulas (see Figure 4):

$$\Sigma \wedge \alpha = \neg a \vee b \vee c,$$

$$\Sigma \wedge \alpha \wedge \beta = \neg[(a \wedge b \wedge c) \vee (a \wedge \neg b \wedge c) \vee (a \wedge \neg b \wedge \neg c)] = (\neg a \vee \neg b \vee \neg c) \wedge (\neg a \vee b \vee \neg c) \wedge (\neg a \vee b \vee c).$$

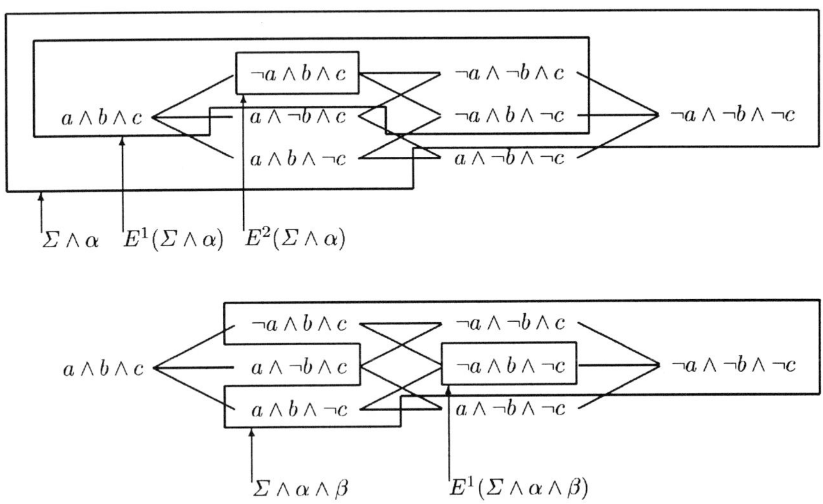

Fig. 4. A counter-example for **E-CM**.

Using the computation formulas for erosion of a formula under CNF (Equations 8 and 12), we get:

$$E^1(\Sigma \wedge \alpha) = (\neg a \vee b) \wedge (\neg a \vee c) \wedge (b \vee c),$$

$$E^2(\Sigma \wedge \alpha) = \neg a \wedge b \wedge c = E_\ell(\Sigma \wedge \alpha).$$

A unique world satisfies this formula, and therefore no further erosion can be performed ($E^3(\Sigma \wedge \alpha) \vdash_\Sigma \bot$). Similarly, we have:

$$E^1(\Sigma \wedge \alpha \wedge \beta) = \neg a \wedge b \wedge \neg c = E_\ell(\Sigma \wedge \alpha \wedge \beta)$$

which is the last non-empty erosion. It follows that $\alpha \rhd^{\ell ne} (\neg a \wedge b \wedge c)$ but clearly $\neg a \wedge b \wedge c$ is not a preferred explanation of $\alpha \wedge \beta$.

Now we will present a counterexample of E-C-Cut for $\rhd^{\ell ne}$. Consider

$$\Sigma \wedge \alpha = a \vee b \vee c,$$

$$\Sigma \wedge \beta = a \vee \neg b \vee \neg c.$$

We have then:

$$E^1(\Sigma \wedge \alpha) = (a \vee b) \wedge (a \vee c) \wedge (b \vee c),$$

$$E^2(\Sigma \wedge \alpha) = a \wedge b \wedge c = E_\ell(\Sigma \wedge \alpha),$$

$$E^1(\Sigma \wedge \beta) = (a \vee \neg b) \wedge (a \vee \neg c) \wedge (\neg b \vee \neg c),$$

$$E^2(\Sigma \wedge \beta) = a \wedge \neg b \wedge \neg c = E_\ell(\Sigma \wedge \beta),$$

$$\Sigma \wedge \alpha \wedge \beta = (a \vee b \vee c) \wedge (a \vee \neg b \vee \neg c),$$

$$E(\Sigma \wedge \alpha \wedge \beta) = (a \wedge b \wedge \neg c) \vee (a \wedge \neg b \wedge c) = E_\ell(\Sigma \wedge \alpha \wedge \beta).$$

Let us now put $\gamma = (a \wedge b \wedge \neg c) \vee (a \wedge \neg b \wedge c)$, then $(\alpha \wedge \beta) \rhd^{\ell ne} \gamma$. Then it is clear that $\alpha \not\rhd^{\ell ne} \gamma$. On the other hand, we have that $\alpha \rhd^{\ell ne} \delta$ iff $\delta \equiv a \wedge b \wedge c$. Thus if $\alpha \rhd^{\ell ne} \delta$, then $\delta \vdash_\Sigma \beta$.

We introduce a weaker form of these postulates:

E-W-CM: $$\frac{\alpha \rhd \gamma \ ; \ \beta \rhd \gamma}{(\alpha \wedge \beta) \rhd \gamma}$$

E-W-C-Cut: $$\frac{(\alpha \wedge \beta) \rhd \gamma \ , \ \forall \delta \, [\alpha \rhd \delta \Rightarrow \beta \rhd \delta\,]}{\alpha \rhd \gamma}$$

These new postulates might look even more natural than the original version E-CM and E-C-Cut. However, $\rhd^{\ell ne}$ is the first natural non trivial example known in the literature that satisfies E-W-CM and E-W-C-Cut but neither E-CM nor E-C-Cut[3]. There is a natural weakening of E-R-Cut which can be considered but we do not have any example for it in which the preferred explanations are not unique.

The next proposition collects all the facts we know about $\rhd^{\ell ne}$.

Proposition 2. *The explanatory relation* $\rhd^{\ell ne}$ *satisfies* LLE$_\Sigma$, RLE$_\Sigma$, RA, E-RW, E-W-CM, E-W-C-Cut, E-Reflexivity *and* E-Con$_\Sigma$.

Proof: (i) E-W-CM. Let us assume that $\gamma \vdash_\Sigma E_\ell(\Sigma \wedge \alpha)$ with $E_\ell(\Sigma \wedge \alpha) = E^n(\Sigma \wedge \alpha)$ and $\gamma \vdash_\Sigma E_\ell(\Sigma \wedge \beta)$ with $E_\ell(\Sigma \wedge \beta) = E^m(\Sigma \wedge \beta)$. Let us assume that the last non-empty erosion of $\Sigma \wedge \alpha \wedge \beta$ is obtained for k. We have, due to Equation 8: $E_\ell(\Sigma \wedge \alpha \wedge \beta) = E^k(\Sigma \wedge \alpha \wedge \beta) = E^k(\Sigma \wedge \alpha) \wedge E^k(\Sigma \wedge \beta)$.

[3] E-W-CM in fact was already considered by Flach [2] but he did not provide any example for it not satisfying already the stronger version E-CM

We necessarily have $k \leq n$ and $k \leq m$ since otherwise either $E^k(\Sigma \wedge \alpha)$ or $E^k(\Sigma \wedge \beta)$ would be inconsistent. This implies, due to the monotonicity property of erosion (Equation 4) that: $\vdash_\Sigma E^n(\Sigma \wedge \alpha) \rightarrow E^k(\Sigma \wedge \alpha)$ and $\vdash_\Sigma E^m(\Sigma \wedge \beta) \rightarrow E^k(\Sigma \wedge \beta)$ from which we derive:

$$\vdash_\Sigma E_\ell(\Sigma \wedge \alpha) \wedge E_\ell(\Sigma \wedge \beta) \rightarrow E_\ell(\Sigma \wedge \alpha \wedge \beta).$$

This interesting general result proves that $\gamma \vdash_\Sigma E_\ell(\Sigma \wedge \alpha \wedge \beta)$.

(ii) E-W-C-Cut. Let $\gamma \vdash_\Sigma E_\ell(\Sigma \wedge \alpha \wedge \beta) = E^n(\Sigma \wedge \alpha \wedge \beta)$. For all δ such that $\alpha \rhd \delta$, $\delta \vdash_\Sigma E_\ell(\Sigma \wedge \alpha) = E^m(\Sigma \wedge \alpha)$. Since $\Sigma \wedge \alpha \wedge \beta \vdash_\Sigma \Sigma \wedge \alpha$ we have:

$$E^n(\Sigma \wedge \alpha \wedge \beta) \not\vdash_\Sigma \perp \Rightarrow E^n(\Sigma \wedge \alpha) \not\vdash_\Sigma \perp.$$

Therefore $n \leq m$.

Let us first assume that $n < m$. For all δ such that $\alpha \rhd \delta$, we have $\beta \rhd \delta$, i.e. $\delta \vdash_\Sigma E_\ell(\Sigma \wedge \beta) = E^k(\Sigma \wedge \beta)$. For the same reason as before, we necessarily have $n \leq k$. Since the set of preferred explanations of α is included in the one of β, we have: $E^m(\Sigma \wedge \alpha) \vdash_\Sigma E^k(\Sigma \wedge \beta)$. Since $m > n$, we have:

$$E^m(\Sigma \wedge \alpha \wedge \beta) = E^m(\Sigma \wedge \alpha) \wedge E^m(\Sigma \wedge \beta) \vdash_\Sigma \perp.$$

Let us now assume $n < k$. Then similarly, we have:

$$E^k(\Sigma \wedge \alpha \wedge \beta) = E^k(\Sigma \wedge \alpha) \wedge E^k(\Sigma \wedge \beta) \vdash_\Sigma \perp.$$

If $k > m$, we have: $E^m(\Sigma \wedge \beta) \not\vdash_\Sigma \perp$, and, due to Equation 4: $E^k(\Sigma \wedge \beta) \vdash_\Sigma E^m(\Sigma \wedge \beta)$. Therefore: $E^m(\Sigma \wedge \alpha) \vdash_\Sigma E^k(\Sigma \wedge \beta) \vdash_\Sigma E^m(\Sigma \wedge \beta)$, which implies: $E^m(\Sigma \wedge \alpha \wedge \beta) \not\vdash_\Sigma \perp$ which leads to a contradiction.

Similarly, if $k < m$, we have: $E^k(\Sigma \wedge \alpha) \not\vdash_\Sigma \perp$, and $E^m(\Sigma \wedge \alpha) \vdash_\Sigma E^k(\Sigma \wedge \alpha)$. Therefore, since we had $E^m(\Sigma \wedge \alpha) \vdash_\Sigma E^k(\Sigma \wedge \beta)$, we have:

$$E^k(\Sigma \wedge \alpha \wedge \beta) = E^k(\Sigma \wedge \alpha) \wedge E^k(\Sigma \wedge \beta) \not\vdash_\Sigma \perp$$

which also leads to a contradiction. From these two contradictions, we can conclude that necessarily $k = m$. Then $E^m(\Sigma \wedge \alpha) \vdash_\Sigma E^k(\Sigma \wedge \beta)$ becomes $E^m(\Sigma \wedge \alpha) \vdash_\Sigma E^m(\Sigma \wedge \beta)$ and therefore we have:

$$E^m(\Sigma \wedge \alpha \wedge \beta) = E^m(\Sigma \wedge \alpha) \not\vdash_\Sigma \perp$$

which is in contradiction with $n < m$. Therefore we also have $n = m$.

Finally the only possibility is to have $k = n = m$. In this case, we have:

$$E^n(\Sigma \wedge \alpha \wedge \beta) \vdash_\Sigma E^n(\Sigma \wedge \alpha) = E^m(\Sigma \wedge \alpha) \vdash_\Sigma E^k(\Sigma \wedge \beta),$$

and therefore:

$$\gamma \vdash_\Sigma E^n(\Sigma \wedge \alpha \wedge \beta) \Rightarrow \gamma \vdash_\Sigma E^n(\Sigma \wedge \alpha),$$

i.e. $\alpha \rhd \gamma$.

(iii) E-Reflexivity. The definition of $\rhd^{\ell ne}$ is based on the notion of largest possible erosion, and therefore no further erosion can be performed. More precisely, let $\alpha \rhd^{\ell ne} \gamma$ and suppose that the last non empty erosion of $\Sigma \wedge \alpha$ is $E^n(\Sigma \wedge \alpha)$. Then we have:

$$E^0(\Sigma \wedge \gamma) = \Sigma \wedge \gamma = \gamma$$

and

$$E^1(\Sigma \wedge \gamma) = E^{n+1}(\Sigma \wedge \alpha)$$

which is inconsistent. Therefore $\gamma \rhd^{\ell ne} \gamma$. □

We end this section by considering the postulate LOR. We will give a counter-example of it for $\rhd^{\ell ne}$. Consider

$$\Sigma \wedge \alpha = (a \vee b \vee c) \wedge (a \vee \neg b \vee \neg c)$$

and

$$\Sigma \wedge \beta = (\neg a \vee \neg b \vee c) \wedge (a \vee \neg b \vee c) \wedge (a \vee b \vee c).$$

We have:

$$\begin{aligned} E^1(\Sigma \wedge \alpha) &= (a \wedge b \wedge \neg c) \vee (a \wedge \neg b \wedge c) = E_\ell(\Sigma \wedge \alpha), \\ E^1(\Sigma \wedge \beta) &= a \wedge \neg b \wedge c = E_\ell(\Sigma \wedge \alpha), \\ \Sigma \wedge (\alpha \vee \beta) &= a \vee b \vee c, \\ E^1(\Sigma \wedge (\alpha \vee \beta)) &= (a \vee b) \wedge (a \vee c) \wedge (b \vee c), \\ E^2(\Sigma \wedge (\alpha \vee \beta)) &= a \wedge b \wedge c = E_\ell(\Sigma \wedge (\alpha \vee \beta)). \end{aligned}$$

Let $\gamma = a \wedge \neg b \wedge c$. Then $\alpha \rhd^{\ell ne} \gamma$ and $\beta \rhd^{\ell ne} \gamma$, but $(\alpha \vee \beta) \not\rhd^{\ell ne} \gamma$.

Since E-DR implies LOR [4], then we already know that E-DR fails for $\rhd^{\ell ne}$.

Table 1 summarizes the results we obtained so far.

5 Conclusion

We have proposed in this paper two definitions of explanatory relations based on morphological erosion. Several other definitions could be developed based on mathematical morphology. For instance if we replace $\vdash$ by $=$ in Equations 14 and 16, we come up with definitions that have slightly different properties (in particular RA is not satisfied). More importantly, it is natural to use other morphological operators instead of erosion, for example the ultimate erosion.

It is important to observe that erosion provides a geometrical way to totally pre-order the models of a formula and this is the underlying idea behind the definition of $\rhd^{\ell c}$.

Another interesting feature of this work is that it reveals new properties as E-W-C-Cut and new aspects of E-W-CM. These two postulates are very natural; they are the weakening of the well known E-CM and E-C-Cut. But until now the methods used to define explanatory relations always yield relations satisfying the strongest ones. So the method presented here to construct $\rhd^{\ell ne}$ is indeed a new way of approaching the problem of selecting preferred explanations of an observation.

Table 1. Properties of the proposed relations.

Property	$\rhd^{\ell ne}$ (Equation 14)	$\rhd^{\ell c}$ (Equation 16)
LLE	√	√
RLE	√	√
E-CM	×	√
E-W-CM	√	√
E-C-Cut	×	√
E-R-Cut	×	√
E-W-C-Cut	√	√
E-Reflexivity	√	√
E-RW	√	√
RA	√	√
LOR	×	√
E-DR	×	√
E-Con$_\Sigma$	√	√

References

1. I. Bloch and J. Lang. Towards Mathematical Morpho-Logics. In *8th International Conference on Information Processing and Management of Uncertainty in Knowledge based Systems IPMU 2000*, volume III, pages 1405–1412, Madrid, Spain, jul 2000.
2. P. A. Flach. Rationality postulates for induction. In Yoav Shoham, editor, *Proc. of the Sixth Conference of Theoretical Aspects of Rationality and Knowledge (TARK96)*, pages 267–281, The Netherlands, March 17-20, 1996.
3. C. Lafage and J. Lang. Représentation logique de préférences pour la décision de groupe. In *RFIA 2000*, volume III, pages 267–276, Paris, France, February 2000.
4. R. Pino-Pérez and C. Uzcátegui. Jumping to Explanations versus jumping to Conclusions. *Artificial Intelligence*, 111:131–169, 1999.
5. R. Pino-Pérez and C. Uzcátegui. Ordering Explanations and the Structural Rules for Abduction. In A. G. Cohn, F. Giunchiglia, and B. Selman, editors, *7th International Conference on Principles of Knowledge Representation and Reasoning KR 2000*, pages 637–646, Breckenridge, CO, 2000. Morgan Kaufmann,
6. J. Serra. *Image Analysis and Mathematical Morphology.* Academic Press, London, 1982.
7. J. Serra. *Image Analysis and Mathematical Morphology Part II: Theoretical Advances.* Academic Press (J. Serra Ed.), London, 1988.

Monotonic and Residuated Logic Programs

Carlos Viegas Damásio and Luís Moniz Pereira

Centro de Inteligência Artificial (CENTRIA)
Departamento de Informática, Universidade Nova de Lisboa
2829-516 Caparica, Portugal. {cd|lmp}@di.fct.unl.pt

Abstract. In this paper we define the rather general framework of Monotonic Logic Programs, where the main results of (definite) logic programming are validly extrapolated. Whenever defining new logic programming extensions, we can thus turn our attention to the stipulation and study of its intuitive algebraic properties within the very general setting. Then, the existence of a minimum model and of a monotonic immediate consequences operator is guaranteed, and they are related as in classical logic programming. Afterwards we study the more restricted class of residuated logic programs which is able to capture several quite distinct logic programming semantics. Namely: Generalized Annotated Logic Programs, Fuzzy Logic Programming, Hybrid Probabilistic Logic Programs, and Possibilistic Logic Programming. We provide the embedding of possibilistic logic programming.

Keywords. Logic Programming, Possibilistic Logic, Many-valued logics.

1 Introduction

The literature on logic programming theory is brimming with proposals of languages and semantics for extensions of definite logic programs (e.g. [6,19,4,10]), i.e. those without non-monotonic or default negation. Usually, the authors characterize their programs with a model theoretic semantics, where a minimum model is guaranteed to exist, and a corresponding monotonic fixpoint operator (continuous or not). In many case the semantics is many-valued.

In this paper we abstract out all the details and define a rather general framework of Monotonic Logic Programs to capture the core "spirit" of logic programming. For this purpose we follow an algebraic approach to both the language and the semantics of logic programs. We were inspired by the deep theoretical results of many-valued logics and fuzzy logic (see [1,9] for excellent accounts) and applied these ideas to logic programming. In fact, a preliminary work in this direction is [19], but the authors restrict themselves to a linearly ordered set of truth-values (the real closed interval $[0, 1]$) and to a very limited syntax: the head of a rule is a literal and the body is a multiplication (t-norm) of literals. We start by defining the notion of an implication symbol, sufficient to guarantee the validity of the standard logic programming results. Later on we resort to residuated lattices (c.f. [1,9]), where a generalized modus ponens

S. Benferhat and P. Besnard (Eds.): ECSQARU 2001, LNAI 2143, pp. 748–759, 2001.

rule is defined. This characterizes the essence of logic programming: from the truth-value of bodies of rules for an atom we can determine the truth-value of that atom, depending on the degree of confidence in each of the rules.

Our paper proceeds as follows. In Section 2 we introduce the language of Monotonic Logic Programs and associated implication algebras. In the section after that we present our main theoretical results. Then we set forth the definitions of residual lattices and show that the Residuated Logic Programs of [2] are a special instance of Monotonic Logic Programs, where one associates with each rule a weight or confidence factor. Lastly, we show the embedding of Possibilistic Logic Programming into Residuated Logic Programs, and terminate with some conclusions and future directions.

2 Monotonic Logic Programs

The theoretical foundations of logic programming were clearly established in [11, 16] for definite logic programs (see also [12]), i.e. programs made up of rules of the form $A_0 \subset A_1 \wedge \ldots \wedge A_n (n \geq 0)$ where each $A_i (0 \leq i \leq n)$ is a propositional symbol (an atom), $\subset$ is classical implication, and $\wedge$ the usual Boolean conjunction. In this section we generalize the language of definite logic programs in order to encompass more complex bodies and heads and, evidently, many-valued logics. For simplicity, we consider only the propositional (ground) case.

When defining a (new) logic it is necessary to address the following two distinct but related aspects: the syntax and the corresponding interpretation of the logical symbols in the language. In this paper we adopt an algebraic characterization of both the language and interpretation of operators. This is a very general and powerful framework, allowing for a simple relation between the two. For lack of space, we reduce the presentation to the essentials. For more details consult for instance [8].

The main assumptions of the paper are collected in the next two definitions.

Definition 1 (Implication Algebra). *Let $\mathfrak{T} =< \mathcal{T}, \preceq >$ be a complete upper semilattice*[1] *and consider an algebra $\mathfrak{A}$ on the carrier set $\mathcal{T}$. We say that $\mathfrak{A}$ is an implication algebra with respect to $\mathfrak{T}$ iff it has defined an operator $\leftarrow$ on $\mathfrak{A}$ such that $\forall_{a_1, a_2 \in \mathfrak{T}}$ $(a_1 \leftarrow a_2) = \top$ iff $a_1 \succeq a_2$ where $\top$ is the top element of $\mathfrak{T}$.*

Example 1. The closed real interval $[0, 1]$ with the usual ordering is a complete lattice. The algebra $\mathfrak{G}$ on $[0, 1]$ with Gödel implication $x \Leftarrow y = 1$ (if $x \geq y$), and $x \Leftarrow y = x$ otherwise, is an implication algebra. It is obvious that if $x < y$ then $x \Leftarrow y < 1$.

Mark that some many-valued logics have implication connectives which do not obey the property of implication algebras. We shall illustrate this in the next section.

[1] The original formulation of this definition assumed a complete lattice. As shown in [13], we can easily generalize to complete upper semilattices since the meet operation over infinite sets is never used. This is also the case for GAPs [10].

Our Monotonic and Residuated Logic Programs will be constructed from the abstract syntax induced by an implication algebra and a set of propositional symbols. The method of relating syntax and semantics in such an algebraic setting is well-known and we defer again to [8] for more details.

Definition 2 (Monotonic Logic Programs). *Let* $\mathfrak{A}$ *be an implication algebra with respect to a complete lattice* $\mathfrak{T}$. *Let* Π *be a set of propositional symbols and* $FORM_{\mathfrak{A}}(\Pi)$ *the corresponding algebra of formulae freely generated from* Π *and the "symbols" of operators in* $\mathfrak{A}$. *A monotonic logic program is a set of rules of the form* $A \leftarrow \Psi$ *such that:*

1. *The rule* $(A \leftarrow \Psi)$ *is a formula of* $FORM_{\mathfrak{A}}(\Pi)$*;*
2. *The head of the rule* A *is a propositional symbol of* Π.
3. *The body formula* Ψ *with propositional symbols* $B_1, \ldots, B_n$ $(n \geq 0)$ *corresponds to an isotonic function having those symbols as arguments.*

As usual we shall represent binary connectives in infix notation.

A rule of a monotonic logic program expresses a (monotonic) computation rule of the truth-value of the head propositional symbol from the truth-values of the symbols in the body. The monotonicity of the rule is guaranteed by the isotonicity of the function corresponding to formula Ψ: if an argument of Ψ is monotonically increased then the truth-value of Ψ also monotonically increases. The unique homomorphic extension theorem, guarantees that for every interpretation of propositional symbols there is an unique associated valuation function.

Example 2. Consider the set of propositional symbols $\Pi = \{a, b, c\}$ and the implication algebra of Example 1 with the additional operator $x \wedge y = min(x, y)$. As common, we denote the algebra by $\mathfrak{G}([0,1], \Leftarrow, \wedge)$. The arity of the operators is implicit. Mark that $\wedge$ is the meet in $[0,1]$. The formulas $b \wedge c$ and $a \Leftarrow b \wedge c$ correspond to the functions $\lambda bc. \wedge (b, c)$ and $\lambda abc. \Leftarrow (a, \wedge(b, c))$, respectively. Variables range over the interval $[0,1]$.

Mark too that we employ the same symbol to represent a connective at the syntactic level (formulas) and the corresponding operator in the underlying algebra. This simplifies presentation. A simple analysis easily concludes that $a \Leftarrow b \wedge c$ is a correct monotonic logic program rule, since $\lambda bc. \wedge (b, c) = \lambda bc.min(b, c)$ is an isotonic function.

3 Model and Fixpoint Theory for Monotonic Logic Programs

In this section we define a model and a fixpoint theory for Monotonic Logic Programs, and extend to them the classical results of logic programming. The important point to realize is that all the fundamental results of logic programming depend only on the monotonicity of the body of the rule and on the fact that it is possible to determine the truth-value of the proposition in the head from the truth-value of the rule body. Also notice that we demand all the rules to be satisfied: every implication should evaluate to $\top$.

Let us start by defining the notion of interpretation. An interpretation is simply an assignment of truth-value to each propositional symbol in the language. We assume, in the remainder of this section, an implication algebra $\mathfrak{A}$ with respect to a complete lattice $\mathfrak{T} =< \mathcal{T}, \preceq>$. The operator and implication symbol will be denoted by $\leftarrow$. Consider also that a set Π of propositional symbols is given, as well as the corresponding algebra $FORM_{\mathfrak{A}}(\Pi)$ of formulae over Π. Forthwith, the notion of interpretation is straightforward:

Definition 3 (Interpretation). *An interpretation is a mapping $I : \Pi \to \mathcal{T}$. By the unique homomorphic extension theorem, the interpretation extends uniquely to a valuation function $\hat{I} : FORM_{\mathfrak{A}}(\Pi) \to \mathcal{T}$. The set of all interpretations with respect to the implication algebra $\mathfrak{A}$ is denoted by $\mathcal{I}_{\mathfrak{A}}$.*

The ordering $\preceq$ on the truth-values in $\mathfrak{T}$ is extended to the set of interpretations as follows:

Definition 4 (Lattice of interpretations). *Consider $\mathcal{I}_{\mathfrak{A}}$ the set of all interpretations with respect to implication algebra $\mathfrak{A}$, and two arbitrary interpretations $I_1, I_2 \in \mathcal{I}_{\mathfrak{A}}$. Then, $< \mathcal{I}_{\mathfrak{A}}, \sqsubseteq>$ is a complete lattice where $I_1 \sqsubseteq I_2$ iff $\forall_{p \in \Pi}\, I_1(p) \preceq I_2(p)$. The least interpretation $\triangle$ maps every propositional symbol to the least element of $\mathcal{T}$, and the greatest interpretation ∇ maps every propositional symbol to the top element of the complete lattice of truth values $\mathcal{T}$.*

A rule of a monotonic logic program is satisfied whenever the truth-value of the rule is $\top$. A model is an interpretation which satisfies every rule in the program. Formally:

Definition 5 (Model of a program). *Consider an interpretation $I \in \mathcal{I}_{\mathfrak{A}}$. A monotonic logic program rule $A \leftarrow \Psi$ is satisfied by I iff $\hat{I}((A \leftarrow \Psi)) = \top$. Interpretation I is a model of a monotonic logic program P iff all rules in P are satisfied by I.*

We proceed by showing that every monotonic logic program has a least model which is the least fixpoint of a monotonic operator, along with other standard logic programming results. One such result is the immediate consequences operator, extending the results of van Emden and Kowalski [16] to the general theoretical setting of implication algebras:

Definition 6 (Immediate consequences operator). *Let P be a monotonic logic program. Define the immediate consequences operator $T_P^{\mathfrak{A}} : \mathcal{I}_{\mathfrak{A}} \to \mathcal{I}_{\mathfrak{A}}$, mapping interpretations to interpretations, as:*

$$T_P^{\mathfrak{A}}(I)(A) = lub\left\{\hat{I}(\Psi) \text{ such that } A \leftarrow \Psi \in P\right\}$$

where A is a propositional symbol.

The immediate consequences operator evaluates the body of every rule for a propositional symbol A. The truth-value of A is simply the least upper bound of the truth-values of all the bodies of the rules for it.

Theorem 1 (Monotonicity of the immediate consequences operator). *Let I_1 and I_2 be two interpretations in $\mathcal{I}_{\mathfrak{A}}$, and P a monotonic logic program. Operator $T_P^{\mathfrak{A}}$ is monotonic, i.e. if $I_1 \sqsubseteq I_2$ then $T_P^{\mathfrak{A}}(I_1) \sqsubseteq T_P^{\mathfrak{A}}(I_2)$.*

As usual, the set of models of P is characterized by the post-fixpoints of $T_P^{\mathfrak{R}}$:

Theorem 2. *An interpretation I of $\mathcal{I}_{\mathfrak{A}}$ is a model of a monotonic logic program P iff $T_P^{\mathfrak{A}}(I) \sqsubseteq I$.*

By the Knaster-Tarski fixpoint theorem, $T_P^{\mathfrak{A}}$ has a least fixpoint. Thus:

Definition 7 (Semantics of Monotonic Logic Programs). *Let P be a monotonic logic program and M_P the least fixpoint of $T_P^{\mathfrak{A}}$. The semantics of a monotonic logic program is given by M_P, being its least model.*

Theorem 3 (Fixpoint Semantics). *Let P be a monotonic logic program, and consider the transfinite sequence of interpretations of $\mathcal{I}_{\mathfrak{A}}$:*

$$\begin{aligned} T_P^{\mathfrak{A}}\uparrow^0 &= \Delta \\ T_P^{\mathfrak{A}}\uparrow^{n+1} &= T_P^{\mathfrak{A}}(T_P^{\mathfrak{R}}\uparrow^n), \text{ if } n+1 \text{ is a successor ordinal} \\ T_P^{\mathfrak{A}}\uparrow^\alpha &= \bigsqcup_{\beta<\alpha} T_P^{\mathfrak{A}}\uparrow^\beta, \text{ if } \alpha \text{ is a limit ordinal} \end{aligned}$$

Then, there is an ordinal λ such that $T_P^{\mathfrak{A}}\uparrow^{\lambda+1}= T_P^{\mathfrak{A}}\uparrow^\lambda$, and the least model of P is $M_P = T_P^{\mathfrak{A}}\uparrow^\lambda$.

The major difference from standard classical logic programming is that our $T_P^{\mathfrak{A}}$ operator might not be continuous, and therefore more than ω iterations may be necessary to "reach" the least fixpoint. All the other important results carry over to our general framework. This possibility is unavoidable if one wants to retain generality. For the study of sufficient conditions to guarantee the continuity of the $T_P^{\mathfrak{A}}$, see [13].

We now illustrate the importance of the provisions of Definition 1 with an example:

Example 3. Reichenbach [15] devised a calculus for addressing the logical problems raised by quantum mechanics. He defined three implications, three negations, two equivalences, a conjunction and a disjunction. For our example, the three implication operators and conjunction will suffice. The set of truth-values is $\{0, 1, 2\}$ with the usual ordering. The truth-tables[2] are:

$\subset$	0	1	2
0	2	1	0
1	2	2	1
2	2	2	2

$\Leftarrow$	0	1	2
0	2	2	0
1	2	2	0
2	2	2	2

$\leftarrow$	0	1	2
0	1	1	0
1	1	1	1
2	1	1	2

$\wedge$	0	1	2
0	0	0	0
1	0	1	1
2	0	1	2

[2] For the implication connectives, the consequent truth-value appears in rows and the antecedent one in columns.

Consider the three programs below:

$$\begin{array}{lll} a \subset b \wedge c & a \Leftarrow b \wedge c & a \leftarrow b \wedge c \\ b \subset 1 & b \Leftarrow 1 & b \leftarrow 1 \\ c \subset 1 & c \Leftarrow 1 & c \leftarrow 1 \end{array}$$

The least fixpoint of the immediate consequences operator when applied to the above programs results in the same interpretation, mapping propositions a, b, and c to truth-value 1. The first implication ($\subset$) complies with the provisions of Definition 1. Therefore the interpretation so obtained is the least model of the program on the left, as can be checked easily .

For the middle program, we know that $t_1 \geq t_2$ implies $(t_1 \Leftarrow t_2) = 2$, for $t_1, t_2 \in \{0, 1, 2\}$ but the converse does not hold. In general, the least fixpoint is a model of the program but might not be minimal, as in this case: the interpretation mapping every proposition to 0 is a model.

Finally, for the program on the right, we have that $(t_1 \leftarrow t_2) = 2$ entails $t_1 \geq t_2$ but not conversely. This situation is more problematic, since the least fixpoint might not be a model of the program, as per the example. In fact, this program has no model because the implications will always be evaluated to a truth-value different from 2.

4 Residuated Logic Programs

In a non-classical setting the intended truth-value of a given rule might possibly not be absolute truth. So, a generalization of *Modus Ponens* is required to reason logically with confidence factors. In many-valued logics this issue is very well understood, namely in Fuzzy Propositional Logics [14,1,9]. Since one of our initial goals was to capture Fuzzy Logic Programming [5,19], it is natural to adopt as the semantical basis the *residuated lattices* (see for instance [1]).

Definition 8 (Adjoint pair). *Let $< P, \preceq_P >$ be a partially ordered set and $(\leftarrow, \otimes)$ a pair of binary operations in P. We say that $(\leftarrow, \otimes)$ forms an adjoint pair in $< P, \preceq_P >$ iff:*

- (a_1) *Operation $\otimes$ is isotonic, i.e. if $x_1, x_2, y \in P$ such that $x_1 \preceq_P x_2$ then $(x_1 \otimes y) \preceq_P (x_2 \otimes y)$ and $(y \otimes x_1) \preceq_P (y \otimes x_2)$;*
- (a_2) *Operation $\leftarrow$ is isotonic in the first argument (the consequent) and antitonic in the second argument (the antecedent), i.e. if $x_1, x_2, y \in P$ such that $x_1 \preceq_P x_2$ then $(x_1 \leftarrow y) \preceq_P (x_2 \leftarrow y)$ and $(y \leftarrow x_2) \preceq_P (y \leftarrow x_1)$;*
- (a_3) *For any $x, y, z \in P$, we have that $x \preceq_P (y \leftarrow z)$ holds if and only if $(x \otimes z) \preceq_P y$ holds.*

The intuition for the two above properties is immediate, the third one may be more difficult to grasp. In one direction, it is simply asserting that the following *Fuzzy Modus Ponens* rule is valid (cf. [9]):

> If x is a lower bound of $\psi \leftarrow \varphi$, and z is a lower bound of φ then a lower bound y of ψ is $x \otimes z$.

The other direction ensures that the truth-value of $y \leftarrow x$ is in fact the maximal z satisfying $x \otimes z \preceq_P y$. Mark that the implication symbol in an adjoint pair must obey the provisions of Definition 1.

Besides (a_1)–(a_3), it is necessary to assume the existence of a bottom and a top element in the lattice of truth-values, and that $\top$ is an unit element of $\otimes$. It is also usual to assume, additionally, extra conditions on the multiplication operation ($\otimes$), namely associativity, commutativity.

Definition 9 (Residuated Lattice). *Consider the lattice $\mathfrak{L} =< L, \preceq_L>$. We say that $(\mathfrak{L}, \leftarrow, \otimes)$ is a residuated lattice whenever the following three conditions are met:*

(l_1) *$\mathfrak{L}$ is a bounded lattice: it has a bottom ($\bot$) and a top element ($\top$);*
(l_2) *$(\leftarrow, \otimes)$ is an adjoint pair in $\mathfrak{L}$;*
(l_3) *$(L, \otimes, \top)$ is a commutative monoid*[3]*.*

We say that the residuated lattice is complete whenever $< L, \preceq_L>$ is complete. In this case condition (l_1) is immediately satisfied.

For residuated logic programs we resort to special implication algebra where a multiplication operation is defined, and the corresponding residuum operation (or implication), plus a constant representing the top element of the lattice of truth-values (whose set is the carrier of the algebra). Together they must define a complete residuated lattice since we intend to deal with infinite programs (theories). Obviously, a residuated algebra may have additional operators. Formally:

Definition 10 (Residuated Algebra). *Let $(\mathfrak{L}, \leftarrow, \otimes)$ be a complete residuated lattice. The implication algebra $\mathfrak{A}$ defining operators $\leftarrow, \otimes$ with respect to $\mathfrak{L}$ is a residuated algebra.*

From the example at the beginning of this section, it should be clear that in order to define the syntax of residuated logic programs it is necessary to know beforehand the underlying truth-value residuated algebra, given that each program rule must be associated with a truth-value. Thus, it is natural to generalize the language of monotonic logic programs as follows (for a particular instance see [19]):

Definition 11 (Residuated Logic Programs). *Let $\mathfrak{R}$ be a residuated algebra with respect to a residuated lattice $(\mathfrak{T}, \leftarrow, \otimes)$. A residual logic program is a monotonic logic program over $\mathfrak{R}$ with rules of the form $A \leftarrow \vartheta \otimes \Psi$ where ϑ is a truth-value in $\mathfrak{T}$, and Ψ an arbitrary isotonic formula. A (weighted) rule $A \leftarrow \vartheta \otimes \Psi$ is represented*[4] *by $A \stackrel{\vartheta}{\longleftarrow} \Psi$.*

[3] It is shown in [13] that (l_3) can be substituted by the weaker condition $\top \otimes \vartheta = \vartheta \otimes \top = \vartheta$.

[4] We are assuming that every truth-value has a corresponding constant mapping in $\mathfrak{R}$.

Consequently, residuated logic programs are a special class of monotonic ones. The important result is the following:

Theorem 4 (Model of a Residuated Logic Program). *An interpretation* $I \in \mathcal{I}_{\mathfrak{R}}$ *is a model of a residuated logic program* P *iff* $\hat{I}\,(A \leftarrow \Psi) \succeq \vartheta$ *for every weighted rule* $A \overset{\vartheta}{\longleftarrow} \Psi$ *in* P.

Therefore, all the theorems of monotonic logic programs carry over directly to residuated ones, under the notion of model portrayed in the above theorem. In [13] several implication operators can be put to use. However, it is easily seen that the embedding of Definition 11 can be trivially adapted to handle several adjoint pairs in the lattice of truth-values, and so the corresponding notion of model is the same. Thus Multi-Adjoint Logic Programs are indeed an instance of Monotonic ones.

5 Possibilistic Logic Programming

As summarized in [7], possibilistic logic is a logic of uncertainty tailored for reasoning under incomplete evidence and partially inconsistent knowledge. Each formula in the language is assigned a weight in a totally ordered set, corresponding to a lower bound on the degree of necessity or possibility of the formula. The degree of necessity of a formula states to what extent the available evidence entails the truth of the formula, while the degree of possibility expresses to what extent the truth of a formula is not incompatible with the available evidence. The theory is built upon the notion of possibility measure Π [20], obeying the following axioms:

$$\Pi(\bot) = 0 \quad \Pi(\top) = 1 \quad \forall_{p,q}\ \Pi(p \vee q) = max(\Pi(p), \Pi(q))$$

The logic is not truth-functional since in general it is only guaranteed that $\Pi(p \wedge q) \leq \min(\Pi(p), \Pi(q))$. We base our presentation on [6] and consider as well only propositional clauses. For the full theory the reader is referred to the excellent overview of [7].

A propositional possibilistic clause is either a pair $(c\ (N\alpha))$ or a pair $(c\ (\Pi\beta))$, where c is a propositional clause, $\alpha \in]0,1]$ and $\beta \in [0,1]$. In general terms, the semantics is engendered from the possibility measures which satisfy the set of possibilistic clauses:

- The formula $(c\ (N\alpha))$ states that c is certain at least to degree α, i.e. $N(c) \geq \alpha$ which is equivalent to $\Pi(\neg c) \leq 1 - \alpha$.
- The expression $(c\ (\Pi\beta))$ states that c is possible in some world at least to degree β, i.e. $\Pi(c) \geq \beta$.

Notice that Π and N are dual measures of necessity and possibility governed by the equation $N(c) = 1 - \Pi(\neg c)$. The truth-values $(\Pi 0), \ldots, (\Pi\beta), \ldots, (\Pi 1), \ldots, (N\alpha), \ldots, (N1)$ are totally ordered. We denote the complete lattice formed this way by $\mathcal{P}$. The semantics of a possibilistic set of clauses $\mathcal{F}$ is given by a consequence relation. We say that $(c\ w)$ is a logical consequence of $\mathcal{F}$ (denoted by $\mathcal{F} \models (c\ w)$) if every possibility measure that satisfies $\mathcal{F}$ also satisfies $(c\ w)$.

There is a formal system [7] which is sound and complete with respect to the above inconsistency-tolerant semantics of possibilistic logic. The inference rules for the propositional case are:

$$\begin{array}{ll} (GMP) & (\varphi\ w_1), (\varphi \rightarrow \psi\ w_2) \vdash (\psi\ w_1 * w_2) \\ (S) & (\varphi\ w_1) \vdash (\varphi\ w_2), \forall w_2 \leq w_1 \end{array}$$

where operation $*$ is defined by

$$\begin{aligned} (N\alpha) * (N\beta) &= (N\ \min(\alpha, \beta)) \\ (N\alpha) * (\Pi\beta) &= \begin{cases} (\Pi\beta) \text{ if } \alpha + \beta > 1 \\ (\Pi 0) \text{ if } \alpha + \beta \leq 1 \end{cases} \\ (\Pi\alpha) * (\Pi\beta) &= (\Pi 0) \end{aligned}$$

The important point for our discussion is that $*$ is a multiplication operation and therefore we can define an appropriate residuum operator ($\twoheadleftarrow$) such that jointly they form an adjoint pair. In our setting, and given an interpretation I such that $\hat{I}(\varphi) = w_1$ we know that

$$\hat{I}(\psi \twoheadleftarrow \varphi) \geq w_2 \text{ iff } \hat{I}(\psi) \geq \hat{I}(\varphi) * w_2 \text{ iff } \hat{I}(\psi) \geq w_1 * w_2$$

similarly to the above inference rule (GMP). Notice that our interpretations might not be models of the possibilistic theory. However, we are able to extract some information regarding the possibility or necessity degree of propositional symbols. This is a technique quite similar to the one employed by Kifer and Subrahmanian [10] for embedding van Emden's quantitative rules into GAPs [17].

To simplify the presentation we map the truth values in $\mathcal{P}$ to the real interval $[0, 1]$, as follows: truth-value $(\Pi\ \beta)$ is mapped to $\frac{\beta}{2}$ and truth-value $(N\ \alpha)$ corresponds to $\frac{1+\alpha}{2}$. This is a bijection. The multiplication operator $*$ is isomorphic to operator $\times$ in the definition next:

Definition 12 (Possibilistic Residuated Algebra). *Let $\mathfrak{P}$ be the residuated algebra on $[0, 1]$ with multiplication $\times$ and implication $\twoheadleftarrow$ operators defined by:*

$$p_1 \times p_2 = \begin{cases} 0 & \text{if } p_1 + p_2 \leq 1 \\ \min(p_1, p_2) & \text{if } p_1 + p_2 > 1 \end{cases}$$

$$p_1 \twoheadleftarrow p_2 = \begin{cases} 1 & \text{if } p_1 \geq p_2 \\ p_1 & \text{if } p_1 < p_2 \text{ and } p_1 + p_2 > 1 \\ 1 - p_2 & \text{if } p_1 < p_2 \text{ and } p_1 + p_2 \leq 1 \end{cases}$$

A Possibilistic Logic Program [6] is a finite set of (first-order) possibilistic Horn Clauses annotated only with necessity degrees. We consider just the case of propositional Possibilistic Logic Programs. We have the following expected result:

Theorem 5. *Let $\mathcal{F}$ be a propositional possibilistic logic program, a set of possibilistic Horn clauses $(B_1 \wedge \ldots \wedge B_n \;\rightarrow A\; w)$ where $A, B_1, \ldots B_n$ are propositional symbols and w is a weight of the form $(N\alpha)$. We construct monotonic logic program P over $\mathfrak{P}$ by translating each possibilistic Horn clause to the attendant monotonic logic program rule $A \twoheadleftarrow p \times B_1 \times \ldots \times B_n$ where $p = \frac{1+\alpha}{2}$ is the real number in $[0,1]$ corresponding to weight w. Then $\mathcal{F} \models (A\; w)$ iff $w \leq (\mathrm{lfp}\; T_P^{\mathfrak{P}})(A)$.*

For the case of possibilistic Horn clauses annotated with possibility degrees which is not addressed in [6], our own translation is sound but not complete, as discussed in the next example:

Example 4. Consider the possibilistic theory:

$$(a \wedge b \rightarrow \; q(N1)) \quad (p \rightarrow a\; (N1)) \quad (p \rightarrow b\; (N1)) \quad (p\; (\Pi 1))$$

Translating the above to a residual logic program we surmise in the least fixpoint of the immediate consequences operator that q is provable with degree $(\Pi 0)$. However, in possibilistic logic we conclude $(q\; (\Pi 1)$. The problem is that our $T_P^{\mathfrak{P}}$ operator is not aware that the proofs for $(a\; (\Pi 1)$ and $(b\; \Pi 1)$ depend on the same proposition p.

We conjecture, however, that in situations where the proof does not depend on multiple uses of the same proposition, we extract the correct conclusions:

Example 5 (adapted from [6]). Consider the knowledge base:

$$\begin{array}{l}
works(john, paris) \rightarrow lives(john, paris)\; (N\; 0.7) \\
works(mary, paris) \rightarrow lives(mary, paris)\; (N\; 0.7) \\
works(henry, paris) \rightarrow lives(henry, paris)\; (N\; 0.7) \\
lives(mary, paris) \rightarrow lives(john, paris)\; (N\; 0.6) \\
works(henry, paris) \rightarrow works(john, paris)\; (\Pi\; 0.8) \\
works(mary, paris)\; (N1) \\
works(henry, paris)\; (N1)
\end{array}$$

It translates to the monotonic logic program:

$$\begin{array}{l}
lives(john, paris) \twoheadleftarrow 0.85 \times works(john, paris) \\
lives(mary, paris) \twoheadleftarrow 0.85 \times works(mary, paris) \\
lives(henry, paris) \twoheadleftarrow 0.85 \times works(henry, paris) \\
lives(john, paris) \twoheadleftarrow 0.8 \times lives(mary, paris) \\
works(john, paris) \twoheadleftarrow 0.4 \times works(henry, paris) \\
works(mary, paris) \twoheadleftarrow 1 \\
works(henry, paris) \twoheadleftarrow 1
\end{array}$$

We gather from the least model of the above monotonic logic program that $works(mary, paris)$ and $works(henry, paris)$ have confidence 1.0, i.e. necessity degree $(N\; 1)$. Moreover, both Henry and Mary live in Paris with necessity degree $(N\; 0.7)$. Regarding John, the proposition $works(john, paris)$ is ascribed the truth-value 0.4 corresponding to possibility degree $(\Pi\; 0.8)$, and $lives(john, paris)$ receives value 0.8, meaning that it is necessary that John lives in Paris with at least degree 0.6. Such results are in accordance with Possibilistic Logic.

6 Conclusions and Further Work

The strong point of this paper is the generality of our setting, both at the language and at the semantical level. We have presented an algebraic characterization of Monotonic Logic Programs. Program rules are arbitrary monotonic body functions where the heads are propositional symbols. Our semantic structures are implication algebras where an appropriate implication operator is imposed. We then obtain a logic programming semantics with corresponding model and fixpoint theory. The major construction is a generalized immediate consequences operator, in the spirit of van Emden and Kowalski's T_p operator. The operator is monotonic and the models of a Monotonic Logic Program are its post-fixpoints. Therefore a minimum model is guaranteed to exist, it being the least fixpoint of the immediate consequences operator. Thus, when defining a new logic programming semantics we can shift attention to the stipulation and study of its intuitive semantical algebraic properties because the main results of definite logic programming carry over for free to this very general setting.

We have studied residual lattices and algebras, where a generalized form of *Modus Ponens Rule* is valid. Having defined an implication (or residuum operator), and the associated multiplication, we can assign to program rules a confidence factor, thereby defining residuated logic programs. We show that the results of Monotonic Logic Programs carry over immediately to Residuated ones.

We provide a simple translation of Possibilistic Logic Programming into Residuated Logic Programs, and discuss the issues arising from the introduction of possibility degrees. In [2] we have previously shown that our framework can capture Hybrid Probabilistic Logic Programs [4]. Both ground Generalized Annotated Logic Programs [10] and Fuzzy Logic Programming [19] are also special cases of our setting.

The embedding of c-annotated ground GAP rules under the restricted semantics is direct, and uses a technique similar to the one presented in [2]. More interestingly, we devised a way for translating ground GAPs rules with arbitrary annotations (constant, variable, or term annotated) into a single Monotonic Logic Programming rule without occurrences of variables. This translation only assumes that (finite) meets are defined in the truth-value complete upper semi-lattice. The converse is also possible, using an extension of the embedding of Fuzzy Logic Programs into Annotated Logic Programming [18]. It shall be the subject of forthcoming work.

Our incursion paves the way to combine and integrate several forms of reasoning into a uniform framework, namely fuzzy, probabilistic, uncertain, and paraconsistent reasoning. We have defined too [3] another class of logic programs, extending the Monotonic one, where rule bodies may be anti-monotonic functions, with well-founded and Stable Model like semantics. This brings together non-monotonic and incomplete forms of reasoning with those listed before.

Acknowledgements. Work partially supported by PRAXIS projects MENTAL and FLUX. We thank V. S. Subrahmanian, J. Dix, T. Eiter, J. Alferes and

L. Caires for helpful discussions. Special thanks to Manuel Ojeda-Aciego for his insightful comments and for sending us a preliminary version of the paper [13]. We also thank Peter Vojtás for letting us know of the existence of [18].

References

1. L. Bolc and P. Borowik. *Many-Valued Logics. Theoretical Foundations.* Springer–Verlag, 1992.
2. C. V. Damásio and L. M. Pereira. Hybrid probabilistic logic programs as residuated logic programs. In M. O. Aciego, I. P. de Guzmán, G. Brewka, and L. M. Pereira, editors, *Logics in AI, Proceedings of JELIA'00*, pages 57–72. LNAI 1919, Springer–Verlag, September 2000.
3. C. V. Damásio and L. M. Pereira. Antitonic logic programs. In *Proc. LPNMR'01*, September 2001. To appear.
4. A. Dekhtyar and V. S. Subrahmanian. Hybrid probabilistic programs. *Journal of Logic Programming*, 43(3):187–250, 2000.
5. D. Dubois, J. Lang, and H. Prade. Fuzzy sets in approximate reasoning, part 2: Logical approaches. *Fuzzy Sets and Systems*, 40:203–244, 1991.
6. D. Dubois, J. Lang, and H. Prade. Towards possibilistic logic programming. In *Proc. of ICLP'91*, pages 581–598. MIT Press, 1991.
7. D. Dubois, J. Lang, and H. Prade. Possibilistic logic. In D.M. Gabbay, C. J. Hogger, and J. A. Robinson, editors, *Handbook of Logic in Artificial Intelligence and Logic Programming*, volume 3, pages 439–513. Oxford University Press, 1994.
8. J. H. Gallier. *Logic for Computer Science.* John Wiley & Sons, 1987.
9. P. Hájek. *Metamathematics of Fuzzy Logic.* Trends in Logic. Studia Logica Library. Kluwer Academic Publishers, 1998.
10. M. Kifer and V. S. Subrahmanian. Theory of generalized annotated logic programming and its applications. *J. of Logic Programming*, 12:335–367, 1992.
11. R. Kowalski. Predicate logic as a programming language. In *Proceedings of IFIP'74*, pages 569–574. North Holland Publishing Company, 1974.
12. J. W. Lloyd. *Foundations of Logic Programming.* Springer–Verlag, 1987. 2nd. edition.
13. J. Medina, M. Ojeda-Aciego, and P. Vojtas. Multi-adjoint logic programming with continuous semantics. In *Proc. LPNMR'01*, September 2001. To appear.
14. J. Pavelka. On fuzzy logic I, II, III. *Zeitschr. f. Math. Logik und Grundl. der Math.*, 25, 1979.
15. H. Reichenbach. Reply to Ernest Nagel's criticism of my views on quantum mechanics. *Journal of Philosophy*, 43:239–247, 1946.
16. M. van Emden and R. Kowalski. The semantics of predicate logic as a programming language. *Journal of ACM*, 4(23):733–742, 1976.
17. M. H. van Emden. Quantitative deduction and its fixpoint theory. *Journal of Logic Programming*, 3(1):37–53, 1986.
18. P. Vojtas. Annotated and fuzzy logic programs - relationship and comparison of expressive power. Technical report, Safárik University, Slovakia, 2001.
19. P. Vojtás and L. Paulík. Soundness and completeness of non-classical extended SLD-resolution. In *Proc. of the Ws. on Extensions of Logic Programming (ELP'96)*, pages 289–301. LNCS 1050, Springer–Verlag., 1996.
20. L. A. Zadeh. Fuzzy sets as a basis for a theory of possibility. *Fuzzy Sets and Systems*, 1:3–28, 1978.

A Proof Procedure for Possibilistic Logic Programming with Fuzzy Constants*

Teresa Alsinet[1] and Lluís Godo[2]

[1] Departament d'Informàtica
Universitat de Lleida (UdL)
Jaume II, 69, E-25001 Lleida, Spain
tracy@eup.udl.es

[2] Institut d'Investigació en Intel·ligència Artificial (IIIA)
Consejo Superior de Investigaciones Científicas (CSIC)
Campus UAB, E-08193 Bellaterra, Spain
godo@iiia.csic.es

Abstract. In a recent work we defined a possibilistic logic programming language, called PGL$^+$, dealing with fuzzy propositions and with a fuzzy unification mechanism. The proof system, modus ponens-style, was shown to be complete when restricted to a class of Horn clauses satisfying two types of constraints. In this paper we complete the definition of the logic programming system. In particular, we first formalize a notion of PGL$^+$ program and discuss the two types of constraints (called modularity and context constraints) we argue they must satisfy; second, we extend the PGL$^+$ calculus with a chaining and fusion mechanism whose application ensures the fulfillment of the modularity constraint; and finally, we define an efficient (as much as possible) proof procedure oriented to goals which is complete for PGL$^+$ programs satisfying the context constraint.

1 Introduction

In the recent past, *fuzzy* logic programming has received increasing interest in areas such as Artificial Intelligence or deductive databases. This interest is due to the fact that both subfields of computer science need to produce systems exhibiting knowledge representation and reasoning models, more flexible than purely symbolic deduction.

In the literature, most proposals for logic programming in logics of uncertainty and fuzziness are mostly reduced to the question of how some generalization of the resolution principle can be formulated and how the automated deduction can be realized. The *fuzzy resolution principle* roots to 1972 when the paper of Lee [16] was published. From then, a number of systems have been proposed based on a variety of non-classical logics such as multiple-valued logics [15, 19], possibilistic logic [8], probabilistic logic [17], evidential support logic [6], or

* The authors acknowledge partial support of the Spanish CICYT project SMASH TIC96-1038-C04-01/03.

S. Benferhat and P. Besnard (Eds.): ECSQARU 2001, LNAI 2143, pp. 760–771, 2001.

fuzzy operator logic [20]. Depending on the underlying logic, some systems are more suitable for dealing with vague knowledge, while others are more appropriate for reasoning under uncertainty. And, although there exist some attempts to handle fuzzy unification [5,12,18] in the framework of fuzzy logic programming, only the inference systems defined by Baldwin et al. [7] for evidential reasoning, and Dubois et al. [11] and Godo and Vila [13] for possibilistic logic, provide a unified framework for the treatment of vagueness and uncertainty.

The necessity-valued fragment of Possibilistic logic [9] is a logic of uncertainty to reason with classical (propositional or first-order) formulas under incomplete information. To enhance the knowledge representation power, Dubois et al. [11] defined a syntactic extension of first-order possibilistic logic (called PLFC) to deal with fuzzy constants and fuzzily restricted quantifiers inside the language, for which Alsinet et al. [4] defined a formal semantics and a sound proof method for general clauses. PLFC provides a powerful framework representing disjunctive and conjunctive fuzzy information, but has some computational limitations [4]. On the one hand, the current proof method for PLFC (refutation through a generalized resolution rule, a fusion rule and a merging rule) is not complete. On the other hand, during the proof process, the merging rule must be applied after every resolution step, and thus the search space consists of all possible orderings of the literals in the knowledge base.

Due to these limitations, we have turned our attention to a possibilistic logic programming language, Horn-rule style, allowing only disjunctive fuzzy constants. Within this restricted framework our final aim is to fully define a logical system for reasoning under possibilistic uncertainty and disjunctive vague knowledge with an efficient and complete proof procedure oriented to goals. To achieve this objective, we first defined in [1] a possibilistic logic programming language of Horn rules with fuzzy propositional variables, called PGL, and we provided it with a complete modus ponens-style calculus. After, in [2], we extended this language with disjunctive fuzzy constants (called PGL^+) and the proof method with a semantical unification mechanism of disjunctive fuzzy constants and three other inference patterns. We proved that this extension was still complete for atomic deduction when clauses fulfill two kinds of constraints.

In this paper we complete the definition of the possibilistic logic programming language PGL^+ by (i) formalizing a notion of suitable PGL^+ program and discussing the need of the modularity and context constraints; (ii) extending the proof method with a chaining and fusion mechanism whose application in a pre-processing step ensures the satisfaction of the modularity constraint of PGL^+ programs; and (iii) defining an efficient as possible proof procedure for determining the maximum necessity degree of a goal from a PGL^+ program satisfying the context constraint. The paper is organized as follows. In Section 2 we present the syntax, the semantics and the inference machinery of PGL^+. In Section 3 we formalize a suitable notion of PGL^+ program, while in Section 4 we discuss the modularity and context constraints. Finally, in Section 5 we provide the basis for automating the deductive proof method. Proofs and algorithms of the results presented in this paper can be found in [3].

2 The Language PGL$^+$

We start by briefly recalling from [2] which is the syntax, the many-valued and the possibilistic semantics of PGL$^+$. Then, we present the logical inference, which basically consists of a resolution (chaining), a fusion and a fuzzy unification mechanisms.

The *basic components* of PGL$^+$ formulas are: a set of primitive propositions *Var*; *sorts* of constants; a set C of object *constants* (crisp and fuzzy constants), each having its sort; a set *Pred* of *unary*[1] *regular* predicates, each one having a type (a *type* is a tuple of sorts); and *connectives* $\wedge$, $\rightarrow$.

An *atomic formula* is either a primitive proposition from *Var* or of the form $p(A)$, where p is a predicate symbol from *Pred*, A is an object constant from C and the sort of A corresponds to the type of p.

Formulas are Horn-rules of the form $p_1 \wedge \cdots \wedge p_k \rightarrow q$ with $k \geq 0$, where $p_1, \ldots, p_k, q$ are atomic formulas. A (weighted) *clause* is a pair of the form (φ, α), where φ is a Horn-rule and $\alpha \in [0, 1]$.

Our intended interpretation is that a fuzzy constant represents a vague, ill-defined property, and weights denote lower bounds on the belief degree, in terms of necessity measures, with which events can be attached with. For instance, the statement "it is almost sure that he has a low salary" can be represented in this framework by the clause $(salary(low), 0.9)$, where $salary(\cdot)$ is a classical predicate of type $(\texttt{euros})$; low is a fuzzy constant of sort $\texttt{euros}$; and the degree 0.9 express how much is believed the formula $salary(low)$ in terms of a necessity measure. In case low denotes a crisp interval of salaries, the clause $(salary(low), 0.9)$ is interpreted as the sentence "$\exists x \in low$ such that $salary(x)$" being certain with a necessity of at least 0.9. In the case low denotes a fuzzy interval with a membership function μ_{low}, the above clause is interpreted in possibilistic terms as if, for each $\alpha \in [0, 1]$, the sentence "$\exists x \in [\mu_{low}]_\alpha$ such that $salary(x)$" is certain with a necessity of at least $\min(0.9, 1 - \alpha)$, where $[\mu_{low}]_\alpha$ denotes the α-cut of μ_{low}. So, fuzzy constants can be seen as (flexible) restrictions on an existential quantifier. Moreover, it is natural that the truth-value of $salary(low)$, under a given interpretation in which the salary is x_0 $\texttt{euros}$, be the degree in which the salary x_0 is considered to be low, i.e. $\mu_{low}(x_0)$. Therefore, instead of Boolean (two-valued), PGL$^+$ formulas are many-valued in nature, and we shall take the whole unit interval $[0, 1]$ as set of truth-values.

A many-valued *interpretation* for the language is a structure $I = (U, i, m)$ which maps each basic sort σ into a non-empty domain U_σ; a primitive proposition q into a value $i(q) \in [0, 1]$; a predicate p of type (σ) into a value $i(p) \in U_\sigma$; and an object constant A (crisp or fuzzy constant) of sort σ into a normalized fuzzy set $m(A)$ with membership function $\mu_{m(A)} : U_\sigma \rightarrow [0, 1]$. Remark that interpretations are *disjunctive* in the sense that, for each predicate symbol p, $i(p)$

[1] We restrict ourselves to unary predicates for the sake of simplicity. However, since variables and function symbols are not allowed, the language still remains propositional.

is a unique value of the domain. Indeed, in contrast to PLFC, fuzzy constants in PGL$^+$ always express disjunctive fuzzy knowledge.

The *truth value* of an atomic formula φ under an interpretation $I = (U, i, m)$, denoted by $I(\varphi)$, is just $i(q)$ if φ is a primitive proposition q, and it is computed as $\mu_{m(A)}(i(p))$ if φ is of the form $p(A)$. This truth value extends to rules by means of the min-conjunction and Gödel's many-valued implication:

$$I(p_1 \wedge \cdots \wedge p_k \to q) = \begin{cases} 1, & \text{if } \min(I(p_1), \ldots, I(p_k)) \leq I(q) \\ I(q), & \text{otherwise} \end{cases}$$

As it is usual in uncertainty logics, the belief on propositions is measured by means of an uncertainty measure on the set of interpretations. In a possibilistic logic, the measure is obviously related to Possibility Theory. In classical possibilistic logic, a necessity measure is used on top of the classical (Boolean) interpretations of the language. Here we have many-valued interpretations, and this means that each formula does not induce a crisp but a fuzzy set of interpretations, hence the uncertainty measure has to be defined for these fuzzy sets. Moreover we may choose multiple domains where to interpret fuzzy constants. Thus, in order to define a possibilistic semantics for PGL$^+$, we need to fix a meaning for the fuzzy constants and to consider some extension of the standard notion of necessity measure for fuzzy events (cf. [1]). The first is achieved by fixing what we call a *context*. Basically, a context is the set of interpretations sharing a common domain and a common interpretation of object constants. We denote by $\mathcal{I}_{U,m}$ the context of interpretations sharing a domain U and an interpretation of constants m. Notice that, in a given context $\mathcal{I}_{U,m}$ we can define which is the fuzzy set $[\varphi]$ of models for a formula φ, just by taking $\mu_{[\varphi]}(I) = I(\varphi)$, for all $I \in \mathcal{I}_{U,m}$.

Now, in a fixed context $\mathcal{I}_{U,m}$, a belief state (or *possibilistic model*) is determined by a normalized possibility distribution on $\mathcal{I}_{U,m}$, $\pi : \mathcal{I}_{U,m} \to [0, 1]$. Then, we say that π *satisfies* a clause (φ, α), written $\pi \models (\varphi, \alpha)$, iff the necessity measure of the fuzzy set of models of φ with respect to π, denoted $N([\varphi] \mid \pi)$, is indeed at least α. Here we take

$$N([\varphi] \mid \pi) = \inf_{I \in \mathcal{I}_{U,m}} \pi(I) \Rightarrow \mu_{[\varphi]}(I)$$

where $\Rightarrow$ is the reciprocal of Gödel's many-valued implication, defined as $x \Rightarrow y = 1$ if $x \leq y$ and $x \Rightarrow y = 1 - x$, otherwise. This necessity measure for fuzzy sets was proposed and discussed by Dubois and Prade in [10]. As usual, a set of clauses P is said to *entail* another clause (φ, α), written $P \models (\varphi, \alpha)$, iff every possibilistic model π satisfying all the clauses in P also satisfies (φ, α). Finally, still in a context $\mathcal{I}_{U,m}$, the *degree of possibilistic entailment* of an atomic formula (or goal) φ by a set of clauses P, denoted by $\|\varphi\|_P$, is the greatest $\alpha \in [0, 1]$ such that $P \models (\varphi, \alpha)$. In [2], we proved that $\|\varphi\|_P = \inf\{N([\varphi] \mid \pi) \mid \pi \models P\}$.

Notation convention: Since we need to fix a context $\mathcal{I}_{U,m}$ in order to perform deduction, we can identify a fuzzy constant A with its interpreted fuzzy set $m(A)$ and also with its membership function $\mu_{m(A)}$. Hence, for the sake of a simpler notation we shall consider fuzzy constants simply as fuzzy sets. Further, if A and B are fuzzy constants, $A \cap B$ and $A \cup B$ will refer to their fuzzy set min-intersection and max-union, respectively.

The calculus for PGL$^+$ in a given context $\mathcal{I}_{U,m}$ is defined by the following set of inference rules:

Generalized resolution:

$$\frac{\begin{array}{c}(p \wedge s \to q(A), \alpha)\\ (q(B) \wedge t \to r, \beta)\end{array}}{(p \wedge s \wedge t \to r, \min(\alpha, \beta))}\ [\mathrm{GR}], \quad \text{if } A \leq B$$

Fusion:

$$\frac{\begin{array}{c}(p(A) \wedge s \to q(D), \alpha)\\ (p(B) \wedge t \to q(E), \beta)\end{array}}{(p(A \cup B) \wedge s \wedge t \to q(D \cup E), \min(\alpha, \beta))}\ [\mathrm{FU}]$$

Intersection:

$$\frac{(p(A), \alpha) \quad (p(B), \beta)}{(p(A \cap B), \min(\alpha, \beta))}\ [\mathrm{IN}]$$

Resolving uncertainty:

$$\frac{(p(A), \alpha)}{(p(A'), 1)}\ [\mathrm{UN}], \quad \text{for } A' = \max(1 - \alpha, A)$$

Semantical unification:

$$\frac{(p(A), \alpha)}{(p(B), \min(\alpha, N(B \mid A)))}\ [\mathrm{SU}], \ \text{where } N(B \mid A) = \inf_{u \in U_\omega} A(u) \Rightarrow B(u)$$

For each context $\mathcal{I}_{U,m}$, the above GR, FU, SU, IN and UN inference rules can be proved to be *sound* with respect to the possibilistic entailment of clauses. Moreover we shall also refer to the following weighted **modus ponens** rule, which can be seen as particular case of the GR rule

$$\frac{\begin{array}{c}(p_1 \wedge \ldots \wedge p_n \to q, \alpha)\\ (p_1, \beta_1), \ldots, (p_n, \beta_n)\end{array}}{(q, \min(\alpha, \beta_1, \ldots, \beta_n))}\ [\mathrm{MP}]$$

Finally, the notion of *proof* in PGL$^+$, denoted by $\vdash$, is as in classical logic programming languages, i.e. deduction by means of the triviality axiom and the PGL$^+$ inference rules. Then, given a context $\mathcal{I}_{U,m}$, the *degree of deduction* of a goal φ from a set of clauses P, denoted $|\varphi|_P$, is the greatest $\alpha \in [0, 1]$ for which $P \vdash (\varphi, \alpha)$.

3 PGL$^+$ Programs

A *program* is a triple $\mathcal{P} = (P, U, m)$, where P is a finite set of PGL$^+$ clauses; U is a collection of non-empty domains; and m is an interpretation of object constants over U such that for each object constant B appearing in P there exist $u, v \in U_\sigma$, σ being the sort of B, such that $B(u) = 0$ and $B(v) = 1$. Notice that a program $\mathcal{P} = (P, U, m)$ determines a particular context $\mathcal{I}_{U,m}$ in the sense of the previous section. Further, we say that $\mathcal{P} = (P, U, m)$ is a *non-recursive* program if P does not contain recursive formulas[2] and is *satisfiable* if there exists a normalized possibility distribution $\pi : \mathcal{I}_{U,m} \to [0,1]$ that satisfies all the clauses in P. The idea is that we shall restrict ourselves to non-recursive and satisfiable programs. Next we justify this choice.

Given a context $\mathcal{I}_{U,m}$, it is easy to check that in PGL$^+$ the sets of clauses $P = \{(p(A), \alpha), (p(A) \to q(B), \beta)\}$ and $P' = \{(q(B), \min(\beta, \alpha))\}$ are equivalent as far as we are interested in the entailment degree of a goal $q(C)$, i.e. $\|q(C)\|_P = \|q(C)\|_{P'}$. However, this intuitive behavior may be lost when we consider programs with recursive formulas. For instance, consider the set of clauses

$$Q = \{(age(young) \wedge study\_university \to age(btw\_19\_26), 0.6), \\ (study\_university, 1)\},$$

in a particular context. The Horn-rule in Q is intended to express that "somebody can be assumed to be between 19 and 26 years old (with a necessity ≥ 0.6) whenever we know both he/she is young (in a broad sense) and he/she is studying at the university". Hence, since Q has no clause about whether the student is young, one would expect from Q to infer nothing about his age from the only fact that he/she is a university student. But it turns out that from Q one can logically derive the clause $(age(not\_young\text{-or-}btw\_19\_26), 0.6)$, where

$$not\_young\text{-or-}btw\_19\_26(u) = young(u) \Rightarrow_G btw\_19\_26(u)$$

with $\Rightarrow_G$ being Gödel's implication. The reason is that a recursive Horn-rule like $p(A) \wedge q \to p(B)$ is logically equivalent, in Gödel's logic, to the formula $q \to (p(A) \to p(B))$, and in our framework this is equivalent to $q \to p(C)$, where the fuzzy constant C is point-wisely defined as $C(u) = A(u) \Rightarrow_G B(u)$. Therefore, even though it would be possible to define an inference pattern for transforming recursive formulas into non-recursive ones, the system user could be negatively surprised by some of the computations done by the system, as we have seen above.

On the other hand, in contrast to the classical case, PGL$^+$ programs are not always satisfiable, and moreover, the satisfiability of a set of clauses depends on the interpretation of object constants. Therefore, in order to define a sound and coherent logic programming system, we shall restrict ourselves to non-recursive and satisfiable programs, simply referred in the rest of the paper as PGL$^+$ programs.

---

[2] A recursive formula is of the form $p \wedge q(B) \to q(C)$ or is the result of combining two or more formulas of the form $s \wedge p(A) \to q(B)$ and $r \wedge q(C) \to p(D)$.

4 The Modularity and Context Constraints

In this section we describe and discuss two kinds of constraints we argue our PGL$^+$ programs must satisfy in order the proof method to be complete. First we focus on what we call *modularity* constraint, which, in contrast to PLFC, we show it can be fulfilled by a pre-processing step of the program by means of the GR and FU rules. Then, we establish the bases for defining an efficient and complete proof procedure for PGL$^+$ programs satisfying what we call *context* constraint.

4.1 Modularity Constraint

The satisfaction of the modularity constraint by a PGL$^+$ program ensures that all (explicit and hidden) clauses of programs are considered. Indeed, since fuzzy constants are interpreted as (flexible) restrictions on an existential quantifier, atomic formulas clearly express disjunctive information. For instance, when $A = \{a_1, \ldots, a_n\}$, $p(A)$ is equivalent to the disjunction $p(a_1) \vee \ldots \vee p(a_n)$. Therefore, when parts of this (hidden) disjunctive information occur in the body of several formulas of a program, and we don't want to loose them, we are led to perform a completion process of the program, as a pre-processing step, based on the GR and FU rules. Let us briefly discuss this requirement by means of one example.

Example 1. Let $\mathcal{P} = (P, U, m)$ be a PGL program with

$$P = \{(p(A) \to q, 1), (p(B) \to r(C), 1), (r(C') \to q, 1), (p(D), 1)\},$$

and with m such that $A = \{a_1, a_2\}, B = \{b_1, b_2\}, C = \{c_1, c_2\}, C' = \{c_1, c_2, c_3\}$ and $D = \{a_1, b_1\}$. We can easily check that, using only MP and SU rules, the goal q cannot be deduced from P with a strictly positive degree. However, it is not difficult to also check that $(p(A \cup B) \to q, 1)$ is indeed a clause which logically follows from P and which can be proved from P if the GR and FU rules are used. Therefore, if we first complete P with $(p(A \cup B) \to q, 1)$, then $(q, 1)$ will be also provable by using the MP and SU rules. □

At this point we are ready to formalize the *modularity constraint* of PGL$^+$ program. Let $\mathcal{P} = (P, U, m)$ be a PGL$^+$ program. We recursively define the set of *valid clauses* of P, denoted by P^+, in the following way:

1. $P \subseteq P^+$.
2. If $(\varphi \to q(A), \alpha)$ and $(\psi \wedge q(B) \to r(C), \beta) \in P^+$ are such that $A \leq B$, then $(\varphi \wedge \psi \to r(C), \min(\alpha, \beta)) \in P^+$ as well.
3. If $(p(A) \wedge \varphi \to q(D), \alpha)$ and $(p(B) \wedge \psi \to q(E), \beta) \in P^+$ are such that $A \not\leq B$ and $B \not\leq A$, then $(p(A \cup B) \wedge \varphi \wedge \psi \to q(D \cup E), \min(\alpha, \beta)) \in P^+$ as well.
4. Only the clauses obtained by 1, 2 or 3 belong to P^+ .

Then, we say that P satisfies the *modularity constraint* if $P = P^+$. Moreover, we say that a clause $(\varphi, \alpha) \in P$ is a *basic* clause if $(P^+ \backslash \{(\varphi, \alpha)\})^+ = P^+ \backslash \{(\varphi, \alpha)\}$.

The following facts shed light on the relationship between a PGL$^+$ program P and its set of valid clauses P^+: (i) if $(\varphi, \alpha) \in P^+$, then $P \vdash (\varphi, \alpha)$; (ii) for any goal $q(C)$, $\|q(C)\|_P = \|q(C)\|_{P+}$; and (iii) for any predicate q appearing in P in the head of a formula, there exists a clause $(\varphi, \alpha) \in P$ such that the head of φ is q and (φ, α) is a basic clause of P.

4.2 Context Constraint

Now let us consider another kind of constraint we want our programs satisfy. The idea is that in a PGL$^+$ program satisfying the so-called *context* constraint the use of the SU and MP inference is enough to attain a degree of deduction equal to the degree of possibilistic entailment. And for this we need that

- the SU and MP rules work in a, say, locally complete way, and that
- the possibilistic entailment degree of a goal be univocally determined by those clauses in the program having the goal in their head or leading to one of these clauses by resolving them with other clauses.

Next we argue the need for these requirements.

As for the first one, it is indeed needed to avoid problems of weakening of the deduction power in simple modus ponens inference steps involving a unification process. For instance, given a context $\mathcal{I}_{U,m}$, we can prove $\|p(A)\|_{\{(p(E),\alpha)\}} = \min(\alpha, \delta)$, where $\delta = N(A \mid E)$, and $\|q(C)\|_{\{(p(A),\min(\alpha,\delta)),(p(A)\to q(B),\beta)\}} = \|q(C)\|_{\{(q(B),\min(\alpha,\delta,\beta))\}}$. However, due to the necessity measure used for computing the partial matching between fuzzy constants, the expected equality $\|q(C)\|_{\{(p(E),\alpha),(p(A)\to q(B),\beta)\}} = \|q(C)\|_{\{(q(B),\min(\alpha,\delta,\beta))\}}$ may not hold. Actually, it strongly depends on how m interprets each object constant. Indeed, it can be proved that the equality holds iff either $\min(\alpha, \beta) \leq \delta$ or, for some $v \in U_\sigma$, $A(v) = 0$ and $E(v) = 1 - \delta$, σ being the type of p.

Example 2. Let $\mathcal{P} = (P, U, m)$ be a PGL$^+$ program with

$$P = \{(age(btw\_19\_21) \to weight(about\_50), 0.4), (age(about\_20), 0.9)\},$$

and with m attaching to constants the following trapezoidal[3] fuzzy sets: $btw\_19\_21 = [18; 19; 21; 22]$(years), $about\_20 = [15; 20; 20; 25]$(years), and $about\_50 = [45; 50; 50; 55]$(kilograms). Then, $N(btw\_19\_21 \mid about\_20) = 0.25 < \min(0.9, 0.4)$ and, for all $u \in$ years such that $btw\_19\_21(u) = 0$ it is $about\_20(u) < 0.75$. And, one can check that, for any fuzzy constant C, $\|weight(C)\|_P = \|weight(C)\|_{\{(weight(D),1)\}}$, where

$$D(u) = \begin{cases} about\_50(u), & \text{if } u \in [48, 52] \\ 0.6, & \text{otherwise} \end{cases}$$

Therefore, $\|weight(about\_50)\|_{\{(weight(D),1)\}} = 0.4$, and hence, although $\|age(btw\_19\_21)\|_P < 0.4$, we get that $\|weight(about\_50)\|_P = 0.4$. However, our indeed intention was to express that "people can be assumed to weight about 50 kilos (with a necessity ≥ 0.4) whenever we know they are between 19 and 21 years old ". □

[3] We represent a trapezoidal fuzzy set as $[t_1; t_2; t_3; t_4]$, where the interval $[t_1, t_4]$ is the support and the interval $[t_2, t_3]$ is the core.

Again, it would be possible to define an inference pattern for transforming clauses as we have done in Example 2. However, the logic programming system would have some important computational limitations, besides of probably surprising an unaware user with some results computed by the system. In fact, after each resolution step, the membership function of the fuzzy constant in the resolvent clause should be recomputed from the interpretation of all fuzzy constants in the body of the resolved clause. Moreover, at this point, some new valid clauses should be considered since they could not be computed in a pre-processing step (see Section 5). Therefore, in order to define a sound and efficient proof procedure, we have to consider PGL$^+$ programs with well-behaved (in the above sense) interpretations of fuzzy constants.

As for the second requirement, the objective of the context constraint is to ensure that, for any goal $q(C)$, $\|q(C)\|_P$ can be determined only from the subset P_q of clauses (φ, α) in P for which either q is in the head of φ or q *depends*[4] on the head of φ. Roughly speaking, with this requirement one wants to avoid having formulas of the form $(q(A) \rightarrow t(\overline{B}), \alpha)$ and $(t(B), \beta)$ together in a program since, due to the disjunctive interpretation of fuzzy constants, we would have that a formula like $(q(\overline{A}), \delta)$ should be derivable, where $\overline{A}$ and $\overline{B}$ denote the complement of A and B, respectively, and thus we should enable a kind of *modus tollens* inference mechanism.

Example 3. Consider the set of clauses

$$P = \{(age(btw\_17\_20), 1),\ (weight(49), 1),\\ (age(btw\_18\_20) \rightarrow weight(btw\_50\_55), 1)\},$$

the goal $age(17)$, and a particular context in which the object constants btw_17_20, btw_18_20 and btw_50_55 are interpreted as the crisp intervals $[17, 20]$`(years)`, $[18, 20]$`(years)` and $[50, 55]$`(kilograms)`, respectively. One can check that $\|age(17)\|_P = \|age(17)\|_{\{(age(17),1)\}} = 1$. However, in P there is no explicit information expressing that "he or she is 17 years old", and thus, $\|age(17)\|_P$ should be determined just from $(age(btw\_17\_20), 1)$. □

In order to formalize the context constraint we need the following result, already stated in [2]. Let $\mathcal{P} = (P, U, m)$ be a PGL$^+$ program, let q be a predicate symbol of type σ appearing in P, and let us denote by D_q the object constant (of sort σ) such that, for all $u \in U_\sigma$,

$$D_q(u) = \inf\{D(u) \mid P \models (q(D), 1)\}\ .$$

Then, it holds that $P \models (q(D_q), 1)$ and $\|q(C)\|_P = \|q(C)\|_{\{(q(D_q),1)\}}$.

At this point we are ready to formalize the *context constraint*. Let $\mathcal{P} = (P, U, m)$ be a PGL$^+$ program and let $I_{\text{sat}} = (U, i_{\text{sat}}, m)$ be an interpretation of $\mathcal{I}_{U,m}$ such that $I_{\text{sat}}(\phi) = 1$, for each $(\phi, \gamma) \in P$ with $\gamma > 0$. Further, for each

[4] We say that q *depends* on p in P if P contains a set of clauses $\{(\varphi_1, \alpha_1), \ldots, (\varphi_k, \alpha_k)\}$, with $k \geq 1$, such that p appears in the body of φ_1, the head of φ_k is q, and the head of φ_i appears in the body of φ_{i+1}, with $i \in \{1, \ldots, k-1\}$.

predicate symbol q appearing in P, denote by P_q the set of clauses $\{(\varphi, \alpha)\} \subseteq P$ such that the head of φ is q or q depends on the head of φ in P; and denote by P_q^+ the set of valid clauses of P_q. Then, we say that $\mathcal{P}$ satisfies the context constraint if, for each predicate q appearing in P, it holds that

C1: for each clause of the form $(p(E) \rightarrow q(F), \delta) \in P_q^+$, either $\delta \leq \|p(E)\|_{P_p}$ or, for some v, $E(v) = 0$ and $D_p(v) = 1 - \|p(E)\|_{P_p}$; and

C2: for each clause of the form $(q(A) \rightarrow t(B), \beta) \in P \backslash P_q$, for each u either $A(u) \leq \alpha$ or $D_q(u) \leq \max(1 - \beta, \alpha)$, with $\alpha = B(i_{\mathrm{sat}}(t))$.

Then it can be proved that C1 ensures the degree of deduction obtained from P_q^+ by applying the SU and MP rules to be exactly the degree possibilistic entailment, and C2 ensures $\|q\|_P = \|q\|_{P_q}$ for any q.

The most important feature of the context constraint is that, in each deduction step, it can be checked from the previously computed information. However, the bad news is that the constraint C2 is actually stronger than the second requirement listed above. Indeed, if a PGL$^+$ program $\mathcal{P} = (P, U, m)$ does not satisfy C2 for some predicate q appearing in P, we cannot know whether $\|q\|_P = \|q\|_{P_q}$, and thus, in that case we should check whether, for all u,

$$D_q(u) \leq \sup_{I \in \mathcal{I}_{U,m}} \{ \min_{(\phi,\gamma) \in P} \{\max(1 - \gamma, I(\phi))\} \mid I = (U, i, m), i(q) = u\},$$

which in turn it is equivalent to determine whether $D_q(u) \leq \inf\{D(u) \mid P \models (q(D), 1)\}$. Thus, to strongly ensure the equality $\|q\|_P = \|q\|_{P_q}$ is equivalent to extend the PGL$^+$ proof method for determining $\|q\|_{P \backslash P_q}$. Hence, our current context constraint is a useful approach for ensuring that $\|q\|_P$ can be computed just from the clauses of P_q, and allowing us to define an efficient (as much as possible) proof procedure. Moreover, the context constraint can be checked for each predicate in an incremental way, and thus, for each goal the proof procedure can determine if the computed degree of deduction is in fact the degree of possibilistic entailment.

5 Automated Deduction

The proof procedure for PGL$^+$ can be divided in three algorithms which have to be applied sequentially. A completion algorithm, based on the GR and FU rules, which extends a PGL$^+$ program with all valid clauses. A translation algorithm, based on the MP, SU, UN and IN rules, which translates a PGL$^+$ program satisfying the modularity constraint into a semantically equivalent set of 1-weighted facts, whenever the program satisfied the context constraint. And, finally, a deduction algorithm, based on the SU rule, which computes the maximum degree of possibilistic entailment of a goal from the equivalent set of 1-weighted facts. Next we briefly describe the bases for designing each algorithm.

Given a PGL$^+$ program $\mathcal{P} = (P, U, m)$, the completion algorithm first computes the set of valid clauses that can be derived from P by applying the GR rule (i.e. by chaining clauses). Then, from this new set of valid clauses, the algorithm computes all valid clauses that can be derived by applying the FU rule (i.e. by fusing clauses). As the FU rule stretches the body of rules and the GR rule modifies the body or the head of rules, the chaining and fusion steps have to be performed while new valid clauses are derived. As the chaining and fusion steps cannot produce infinite loops and each valid clause of P is either a basic clause or can be derived at least from two clauses of P, in the worst-case each combination of clauses of P derives a different valid clause. Hence, as P is a finite set of clauses, denoting by N the number of clauses of P, in the worst-case the number of valid clauses is $N + \sum_{i=2}^{N} \binom{N}{i} \in \Theta(\frac{N^{N/2}}{N/2})$. However, in general, only a reduced set of clauses can be combined to derive new valid clauses. Indeed, c_1, c_2 and c_3 can derive a new valid clause if c_1 and c_2, c_1 and c_3, or c_2 and c_3 derive a valid clause different to c_1, c_2 and c_3.

The algorithm for translating a PGL$^+$ program $\mathcal{P} = (P, U, m)$ into a set of 1-weighted facts is based on the following result: $\|q(C)\|_P = \|q(C)\|_{\{(q(D_q),1)\}}$, where $D_q(u) = \inf\{D(u) \mid P \models (q(D), 1)\}$. Then, as $\|q(C)\|_P = \|q(C)\|_{P^+}$, if (P^+, U, m) satisfies the context constraint, the D_q can be determined just from P_q^+ (i.e. the clauses of P^+ whose heads are q or q depends on their heads), and each rule in P_q^+ can be be replaced by a fact applying the SU and MP rules: each clause $(p_1 \wedge \ldots \wedge p_n \to q, \alpha) \in P_q^+$ can be replaced by $(q, \min(\alpha, \min_{i=1,\ldots,n} \|p_i\|_P))$. At this point, D_q can be computed from this finite set of facts by applying the UN and IN rules. As we only consider non-recursive programs, the above mechanism can be recursively applied for determining $\|p\|_P$ for each predicate p such that q depends on p in P, and thus, the time complexity of the translation algorithm is linear in the total number of occurrences of predicates symbols in $(P)^+$.

Finally, if $(q(D_q), 1)$ is the 1-weighted fact computed by the translation algorithm for q, we have that $|q(C)|_P = N(C \mid D_q)$, and thus, after applying the completion and translation algorithms to a PGL$^+$ program, $|q(C)|_P$ can be computed in a constant time complexity in the sense that it is equivalent to compute the partial matching between two fuzzy constants. Moreover, if the program satisfies the context constraint, we can ensure that $|q(C)|_P = \|q(C)\|_P$.

One of the most important features of PGL$^+$ is that when extending a program with new facts only the set of 1-weighted facts must be computed again, and thus, the set of hidden clauses of a program, which from a computational point of view is the hard counterpart of dealing with fuzzy constants, must be computed again only if new rules are added to the knowledge base.

6 Conclusions

In the present paper we have completed the definition, already started in two previous works [1,2], of PGL$^+$, a possibilistic logic programming language with fuzzy constants and a fuzzy unification mechanism. Namely, we have identified and formalized a class of well-behaved programs and have provided this class of programs with a chaining (resolution) and fusion mechanism that, together with the fuzzy unification mechanism, has allowed us to design an efficient and complete proof procedure oriented to goals. In our opinion, this is a key feature that justifies by itself the interest of such a logic programming system. Future work will address the issue of checking the satisfiability of programs.

References

1. T. Alsinet and L. Godo. A complete calculus for possibilistic logic programming with fuzzy propositional variables. In *Proc. of UAI-2000*, 1–10, Stanford, CA, 2000.
2. T. Alsinet and L. Godo. A complete proof method for possibilistic logic programming with semantical unification of fuzzy constants. In *Proc. of ESTYLF-2000*, 279–284, Sevilla, Spain, 2000.
3. T. Alsinet and L. Godo. A proof procedure for possibilistic logic programming with fuzzy constants (extended version). Technical Report DIEI-01-RT-1, 2001. Available at http://fermat.eup.udl.es/~tracy/report011.ps.
4. T. Alsinet, L. Godo, and S. Sandri. On the semantics and automated deduction for PLFC, a logic of possibilistic uncertainty and fuzziness. In *Proc. of UAI-99*, 3–12, Stockholm, Sweden, 1999.
5. F. Arcelli, F. Formato, and G. Gerla. Fuzzy unification as a foundation of fuzzy logic programming. In *Logic Programming and Soft Computing*, (Arcelli and Martin eds.), 51–68. Research Studies Press, 1998.
6. J. Baldwin. Support logic programming. *International Journal of Intelligent Systems*, 1:73–104, 1986.
7. J. Baldwin, T. Martin, and B. Pilsworth. *Fril - Fuzzy and Evidential Reasoning in Artificial Intelligence*. Research Studies Press, 1995.
8. D. Dubois, J. Lang, and H. Prade. Towards possibilistic logic programming. In *Proc. of the Joint Intl. Conf. on Logic Programming*, 581–595, Paris, France, 1991.
9. D. Dubois, J. Lang, and H. Prade. Possibilistic logic. In *Handbook of Logic in Artificial Intelligence and Logic Programming* (Gabbay et al. eds.) Vol. 3, 439–513. Oxford Univ. Press, 1994.
10. D. Dubois and H. Prade. Fuzzy sets in approximate reasoning - Part 1: Inference with possibility distributions. *Fuzzy Sets and Systems*, 40(1):143–202, 1991.
11. D. Dubois, H. Prade, and S. Sandri. Possibilistic logic with fuzzy constants and fuzzily restricted quantifiers. In *Logic Programming and Soft Computing* (Arcelli and Martin eds.), 69–90. Research Studies Press, 1998.
12. F. Formato, G. Gerla, and M. Sessa. Similarity-based unification. *Fundamenta Informaticae*, 40:1–22, 2000.
13. L. Godo and L. Vila. Possibilistic temporal reasoning based on fuzzy temporal constraint. In *Proc. of IJCAI-95*, pages 1916–1922, Montreal, Canada, 1995.
14. P. Hájek. *Metamathematics of Fuzzy Logic*. Kluwer, 1998.
15. F. Klawonn and R. Kruse. A Łukasiewicz logic based Prolog. *Mathware and Soft Computing*, 1:5–29, 1994.
16. R. Lee. Fuzzy logic and the resolution principle. *Journal of the ACM*, 19(1):109–119, 1972.
17. T. Lukasiewicz. Probabilistic logic programming. In *Proceedings of ECAI-98 Conference*, pages 388–392, Brighton, UK, 1998.
18. H. Virtanen. Linguistic logic programming. In F. Arcelli and T. Martin, editors, *Logic Programming and Soft Computing*, 91–128. Research Studies Press, 1998.
19. P. Vojtáš. Fuzzy reasoning with tunable *t*-operators. *Journal for Advanced Computer Intelligence*, 2:121–127, 1998.
20. T. Weigert, J. Tsai, and X. Liu. Fuzzy operator logic and fuzzy resolution. *Journal of Automated Reasoning*, 10:59–78, 1993.

First-Order Characterization and Modal Analysis of Indiscernibility and Complementarity in Information Systems

Philippe Balbiani[1] and Dimiter Vakarelov[2]

[1] Institut de recherche en informatique de Toulouse
118 route de Narbonne, 31062 Toulouse Cedex 4, France
[2] Department of Mathematical Logic with Laboratory for Applied Logic
Faculty of Mathematics and Computer Science, Sofia University
blvd James Bouchier 5, 1126 Sofia, Bulgaria

Abstract. In this paper, we study indiscernibility relations and complementarity relations in information systems. The first-order characterization of indiscernibility and complementarity is obtained through a duality result between information systems and certain structures of relational type characterized by first-order conditions. The modal analysis of indiscernibility and complementarity is performed through a modal logic which modalities correspond to indiscernibility relations and complementarity relations in information systems.

1 Introduction

Information systems are knowledge-based systems which describe properties of objects in terms of attributes. They provide an effective and broadly applicable framework for the management and the processing of uncertainty, a crucial issue in the development of reasoning systems that are concerned with incomplete information. The increasing number of knowledge-based systems that manage and process incomplete information leads us to develop formal methods for reasoning about uncertain knowledge discovered from information systems. Initiated by Pawlak [8] and furthered by Demri [2], Demri, Orłowska and Vakarelov [3], Orłowska [5,6], Orłowska and Pawlak [7] and Vakarelov [9,10,11,12], the theoretical foundations of information systems investigate the relationships between objects determined by their properties. All the relations defined in this context are either indistinguishability relations or distinguishability relations. Indistinguishability relations indicate the way objects share properties whereas distinguishability relations indicate the way properties differentiate objects. Typical issues are the following: first-order characterization and modal analysis of various classes of indistinguishability relations and distinguishability relations. To obtain the first-order characterization of a class of indistinguishability relations and distinguishability relations, one has to find first-order conditions such that relations satisfying these conditions correspond to the indistinguishability relations and the distinguishability relations of this class derived from information

S. Benferhat and P. Besnard (Eds.): ECSQARU 2001, LNAI 2143, pp. 772–781, 2001.

systems. To perform the modal analysis of a class of indistinguishability relations and distinguishability relations, one has to address the questions of axiomatization/completeness and decidability/complexity of a modal logic which modalities correspond to the indistinguishability relations and the distinguishability relations of this class. In this paper, extending the line of reasoning suggested by Demri, Orłowska and Vakarelov [3], we study indiscernibility relations and complementarity relations in information systems. The first-order characterization of indiscernibility and complementarity is obtained through a duality result between certain structures of relational type characterized by first-order conditions and information systems. The modal analysis of indiscernibility and complementarity is performed through a modal logic which modalities correspond to indiscernibility relations and complementarity relations in information systems.

2 Indiscernibility and Complementarity

Adapted from Pawlak [8], an information system will be any structure $(Att, Obj, \{Val_a \mid a \in Att\}, f)$ where:

- Att is a nonempty set of attributes;
- Obj is a nonempty set of objects;
- For all $a \in Att$, Val_a is a nonempty subset of a fixed nonempty set Val of properties;
- f is a function with domain $Att \times Obj$ and range the power set of Val such that for all $a \in Att$ and for all $x \in Obj$, $f(a, x) \subseteq Val_a$.

We should consider, for example, the information system $S = (Att, Obj, \{Val_a \mid a \in Att\}, f)$ defined as follows. Define:

- Att is $\{Languages, Sports\}$;
- Obj is $\{Ann, Bob, Cindy, Daniel, Emma\}$;
- $Val_{Languages}$ is $\{Arabic, Bulgarian, Castilian, Dutch\}$;
- Val_{Sports} is $\{athletics, basketball, cycling\}$;
- f is the function defined by table 1.

In this information system, the object *Bob* possesses the properties *Arabic* and *Bulgarian* of mastering Arabic and Bulgarian whereas the object *Daniel* possesses the properties *athletics* and *cycling* of practising in athletics and cycling. Information systems constitute the starting point for the formal examination of sentences of the form "object x is indistinguishable from object y" or sentences of the form "object x is distinguishable from object y". In this respect, indiscernibility relations and complementarity relations play an important role. Let $S = (Att, Obj, \{Val_a \mid a \in Att\}, f)$ be an information system. For all $x, y \in Obj$, define:

Strong indiscernibility: $x \equiv_S y$ iff for all $a \in Att$, $f(a, x) = f(a, y)$;
Strong complementarity: $xR_S y$ iff for all $a \in Att$, $f(a, x) = (Val_a \setminus f(a, y))$.

Table 1. Example of an information system.

f	Ann	Bob	Cindy	Daniel	Emma
Languages	{*Arabic*, *Bulgarian*}	{*Arabic*, *Bulgarian*}	{*Castilian*, *Dutch*}	{*Arabic*, *Bulgarian*}	{*Arabic*, *Castilian*}
Sports	{*athletics*, *basketball*}	{*athletics*, *basketball*}	{*cycling*}	{*athletics*, *cycling*}	{*cycling*}

Intuitively, two objects are strongly indiscernible if all their respective sets of properties determined by the attributes are indiscernible whereas two objects are strongly complementary if all their respective sets of properties determined by the attributes are complementary. The information system of table 1 is such that $Ann \equiv_S Bob$ and $Ann R_S Cindy$. For all $x, y \in Obj$, define:

Weak indiscernibility: $x \cong_S y$ iff there is $a \in Att$ such that $f(a, x) = f(a, y)$;
Weak complementarity: $x \rho_S y$ iff there is $a \in Att$ such that $f(a, x) = (Val_a \setminus f(a, y))$.

Intuitively, two objects are weakly indiscernible if some of their respective sets of properties determined by the attributes are indiscernible whereas two objects are weakly complementary if some of their respective sets of properties determined by the attributes are complementary. The information system of table 1 is such that $Ann \cong_S Daniel$ and $Ann \rho_S Emma$. The structure $(Obj, \equiv_S, R_S, \cong_S, \rho_S)$ is called abstract structure derived from S. We leave it to the reader to prove the following lemmas.

Lemma 1. *For all* $x, y, z \in Obj$*:*

$x \equiv_S x$; $x\overline{R_S}x$;
If $x \equiv_S y$ *then* $y \equiv_S x$; *If* xR_Sy *then* yR_Sx;
If $x \equiv_S y$ *and* $y \equiv_S z$ *then* $x \equiv_S z$; *If* xR_Sy *and* $y \equiv_S z$ *then* xR_Sz;
If $x \equiv_S y$ *and* yR_Sz *then* xR_Sz; *If* xR_Sy *and* yR_Sz *then* $x \equiv_S z$.

Lemma 2. *For all* $x, y, z \in Obj$*:*

$x \cong_S x$; $x\overline{\rho_S}x$;
If $x \cong_S y$ *then* $y \cong_S x$; *If* $x\rho_Sy$ *then* $y\rho_Sx$;
If $x \cong_S y$ *and* $y \equiv_S z$ *then* $x \cong_S z$; *If* $x\rho_Sy$ *and* $y \equiv_S z$ *then* $x\rho_Sz$;
If $x \cong_S y$ *and* yR_Sz *then* $x\rho_Sz$; *If* $x\rho_Sy$ *and* yR_Sz *then* $x \cong_S z$.

Lemma 1 and lemma 2 motivate the following definition. An abstract structure is a structure $(W, \equiv, R, \cong, \rho)$ where:

- W is a nonempty set of possible worlds;
- $\equiv$ and R are binary relations on W subject to the conditions of lemma 1;
- $\cong$ and ρ are binary relations on W subject to the conditions of lemma 2.

In section 3, the concept of abstract structure will be of use to us for the purpose of giving a first-order characterization of indiscernibility relations and complementarity relations in information systems. In section 4, the concept of abstract structure will be of use to us for the purpose of giving a modal analysis of indiscernibility relations and complementarity relations in information systems.

3 First-Order Characterization

The concept of abstract structure is of use to us for the purpose of giving a first-order characterization of indiscernibility relations and complementarity relations in information systems. The following important theorem explains the connection between abstract structures and information systems. All the section 3 is devoted to its proof.

Theorem 3. *Let $F = (W, \equiv, R, \cong, \rho)$ be an abstract structure. There is an information system $S = (Att, Obj, \{Val_a \mid a \in Att\}, f)$ such that $Obj = W$ and for all $x, y \in Obj$:*

$x \equiv_S y$ *iff* $x \equiv y$;	$x \cong_S y$ *iff* $x \cong y$;
$xR_S y$ *iff* xRy;	$x\rho_S y$ *iff* $x\rho y$.

As a consequence, abstract structures and information systems have equal mathematical content as far as indiscernibility relations and complementarity relations are concerned. Holding the proof of theorem 1 in abeyance for a while, we proceed to introduce the concepts of indiscernibility set, positive set, negative set and good set. Two subsets A and B of W are called comparable if $A \subseteq B$ or $B \subseteq A$. A set of pairwise comparable subsets of W is called a chain. A subset A of W such that for all $x, y \in W$:

- If $x \equiv y$ and $x \in A$ then $y \in A$;
- If $x \equiv y$ and $x \notin A$ then $y \notin A$;

will be defined to be an indiscernibility set. An indiscernibility set A such that for all $x, y \in W$:

- If xRy and $x \in A$ then $y \notin A$;

will be defined to be a positive set. An indiscernibility set A such that for all $x, y \in W$:

- If xRy and $x \notin A$ then $y \in A$;

will be defined to be a negative set. An indiscernibility set A such that A is a positive set and A is a negative set will be defined to be a good set. The proof of the following lemmas is left as an exercise for the reader.

Lemma 4. – *$\emptyset$ and W are indiscernibility sets.*
- *For all $x \in W$, $\equiv(x)$ is an indiscernibility set.*
- *For all $x, y \in W$, $\equiv(x) \cup \equiv(y)$ is an indiscernibility set.*

- *For all indiscernibility sets A, $(W \setminus A)$ is an indiscernibility set.*
- *For all families $(A_i \mid i \in I)$ of indiscernibility sets, $\bigcup(A_i \mid i \in I)$ is an indiscernibility set and $\bigcap(A_i \mid i \in I)$ is an indiscernibility set.*

Lemma 5. – *$\emptyset$ is a positive set.*
- *For all $x \in W$, $\equiv (x)$ is a positive set.*
- *For all $x, y \in W$, if $x\overline{R}y$ then $\equiv (x) \cup \equiv (y)$ is a positive set.*
- *For all positive sets A, $(W \setminus A)$ is a negative set.*
- *For all chains $(A_i \mid i \in I)$ of positive sets, $\bigcup(A_i \mid i \in I)$ is a positive set.*

Lemma 6. – *W is a negative set.*
- *For all $x \in W$, $\not\equiv (x)$ is a negative set.*
- *For all $x, y \in W$, if $x\overline{R}y$ then $\not\equiv (x) \cap \not\equiv (y)$ is a negative set.*
- *For all negative sets A, $(W \setminus A)$ is a positive set.*
- *For all chains $(A_i \mid i \in I)$ of negative sets, $\bigcap(A_i \mid i \in I)$ is a negative set.*

Lemma 7. *Let A be a positive set and $x \in W$ be such that $A \cup \equiv (x)$ is not a positive set. Then there is $y \in W$ such that $y \in A$ and xRy.*

Lemma 8. *Let A be a negative set and $x \in W$ be such that $A \cap \not\equiv (x)$ is not a negative set. Then there is $y \in W$ such that $y \notin A$ and xRy.*

A more important further consequence is the following lemma.

Lemma 9. *Let A be a positive set, B be a negative set and $x \in W$ be such that $A \subseteq B$. Then ($A \cup \equiv (x)$ is a positive set and $A \cup \equiv (x) \subseteq B$) or ($B \cap \not\equiv (x)$ is a negative set and $A \subseteq B \cap \not\equiv (x)$).*

Proof. See Balbiani and Vakarelov [1] for details.

An important related result is the following proposition.

Proposition 10. *Let A be a positive set and B be a negative set such that $A \subseteq B$. Then there is a good set C such that $A \subseteq C$ and $C \subseteq B$.*

Proof. See Balbiani and Vakarelov [1] for details.

A set a of good sets such that for all $x, y \in W$:

- If $x \not\equiv y$ then there is $A \in a$ such that $x \in A$ iff $y \notin A$;
- If $x\bar{p}y$ then there is $A \in a$ such that $x \in A$ iff $y \in A$;

will be defined to be a nice set. The following lemma is easy to check.

Lemma 11. *The set of all good sets is a nice set.*

Proof. See Balbiani and Vakarelov [1] for details.

A less obvious result is the following lemma.

Lemma 12. *For all $x, y \in W$:*

- $x \equiv y$ *iff for all nice sets a and for all $A \in a$, $x \in A$ iff $y \in A$;*
- xRy *iff for all nice sets a and for all $A \in a$, $x \in A$ iff $y \notin A$;*
- $x \cong y$ *iff there is a nice set a such that for all $A \in a$, $x \in A$ iff $y \in A$;*
- $x\rho y$ *iff there is a nice set a such that for all $A \in a$, $x \in A$ iff $y \notin A$.*

Proof. See Balbiani and Vakarelov [1] for details.

Referring to lemma 10, we easily obtain a proof of theorem 1. Let $S = (Att, Obj, \{Val_a \mid a \in Att\}, f)$ be the information system defined as follows. Define:

- Att is the set of all nice sets;
- Obj is the set of all possible worlds;
- For all $a \in Att$, Val_a is the set of all good sets A such that $A \in a$;
- For all $a \in Att$ and for all $x \in Obj$, $f(a, x)$ is the set of all good sets A such that $A \in a$ and $x \in A$.

The reader may easily verify that for all $x, y \in Obj$:

$x \equiv_S y$ iff $x \equiv y$; $\quad$ $x \cong_S y$ iff $x \cong y$;
$xR_S y$ iff xRy; $\quad$ $x\rho_S y$ iff $x\rho y$.

4 Modal Analysis

The concept of abstract structure is of use to us for the purpose of giving a modal analysis of indiscernibility relations and complementarity relations in information systems. The reader is assumed to be familiar with the general concepts of modal logic, see Hughes and Cresswell [4] for details. Seeing that the condition $x\overline{R}x$ of lemma 1 and the condition $x\overline{\rho}x$ of lemma 2 are not modally definable, we need to introduce the concept of nonstandard abstract structure. A nonstandard abstract structure is a structure $(W, \equiv, R, \cong, \rho)$ where:

- W is a nonempty set of possible worlds;
- $\equiv$ and R are binary relations on W subject to the conditions of lemma 1 but the condition $x\overline{R}x$;
- $\cong$ and ρ are binary relations on W subject to the conditions of lemma 2 but the condition $x\overline{\rho}x$.

The linguistic basis of our modal logic is the propositional calculus enlarged with the modalities $[\equiv]$, $[R]$, $[\cong]$ and $[\rho]$ corresponding to the indiscernibility relations and the complementarity relations in information systems. We define the set of all formulas as follows:

- $A ::= p \mid \neg A \mid (A \vee B) \mid [\equiv]A \mid [R]A \mid [\cong]A \mid [\rho]A;$

where p ranges over a countably infinite set of propositional variables. The other standard connectives are defined by the usual abbreviations. In particular, $\langle\equiv\rangle A$ is $\neg[\equiv]\neg A$, $\langle R\rangle A$ is $\neg[R]\neg A$, $\langle\cong\rangle A$ is $\neg[\cong]\neg A$ and $\langle\rho\rangle A$ is $\neg[\rho]\neg A$. We follow the standard rules for omission of the parentheses. A model (respectively: a nonstandard model) is a structure $(W, \equiv, R, \cong, \rho, V)$ where:

- $(W, \equiv, R, \cong, \rho)$ is an abstract structure (respectively: a nonstandard abstract structure);
- V is a function with domain the set of all propositional variables and range the power set of W.

Let $M = (W, \equiv, R, \cong, \rho, V)$ be either a model or a nonstandard model. We define the relation "formula A is true at possible world x in M", denoted $M, x \models A$, as follows:

- $M, x \models p$ iff $x \in V(p)$;
- $M, x \models \neg A$ iff $M, x \not\models A$;
- $M, x \models A \vee B$ iff $M, x \models A$ or $M, x \models B$;
- $M, x \models [\equiv]A$ iff for all $y \in W$, if $x \equiv y$ then $M, y \models A$;
- $M, x \models [R]A$ iff for all $y \in W$, if xRy then $M, y \models A$;
- $M, x \models [\cong]A$ iff for all $y \in W$, if $x \cong y$ then $M, y \models A$;
- $M, x \models [\rho]A$ iff for all $y \in W$, if $x\rho y$ then $M, y \models A$.

An alternative formulation is "M satisfies formula A at possible world x". The following lemma is basic.

Lemma 13. *The following conditions are equivalent.*

1. *A is true at some possible world in some finite model;*
2. *A is true at some possible world in some model;*
3. *A is true at some possible world in some nonstandard model;*
4. *A is true at some possible world in some finite nonstandard model.*

Proof. (1 implies 2): Obvious.
(2 implies 3): Obvious.
(3 implies 4): Let $M = (W, \equiv, R, \cong, \rho, V)$ be a nonstandard model and $M' = (W', \equiv', R', \cong', \rho', V')$ be the finite nonstandard model defined as follows. Let Γ_A be the smallest set of formulas containing the set $Sf(A)$ of all subformulas of A and such that for all formulas B, if $[\equiv]B \in \Gamma_A$ or $[R]B \in \Gamma_A$ or $[\cong]B \in \Gamma_A$ or $[\rho]B \in \Gamma_A$ then $[\equiv]B \in \Gamma_A$ and $[R]B \in \Gamma_A$ and $[\cong]B \in \Gamma_A$ and $[\rho]B \in \Gamma_A$. It should be remarked that $Card(\Gamma_A) < 4 \times Card(Sf(A))$. Let $=_{\Gamma_A}$ be the equivalence relation on W defined as follows. For all $x, y \in W$, define:

- $x =_{\Gamma_A} y$ iff for all formulas B, if $B \in \Gamma_A$ then $M, x \models B$ iff $M, y \models B$.

For all $x \in W$, the equivalence class of x modulo $=_{\Gamma_A}$ is denoted $\mid x \mid$. The quotient set of W modulo $=_{\Gamma_A}$ is denoted by $W_{|=_{\Gamma_A}}$. Define:

- W' is $W_{|=_{\Gamma_A}}$;
- For all $x, y \in W$, $\mid x \mid \equiv' \mid y \mid$ iff for all formulas B, if $[\equiv]B \in \Gamma_A$ then:

If $M, x \models [\equiv]B$ then $M, y \models [\equiv]B$;	If $M, x \models [\cong]B$ then $M, y \models [\cong]B$;
If $M, y \models [\equiv]B$ then $M, x \models [\equiv]B$;	If $M, y \models [\cong]B$ then $M, x \models [\cong]B$;
If $M, x \models [R]B$ then $M, y \models [R]B$;	If $M, x \models [\rho]B$ then $M, y \models [\rho]B$;
If $M, y \models [R]B$ then $M, x \models [R]B$;	If $M, y \models [\rho]B$ then $M, x \models [\rho]B$;

- For all $x, y \in W$, $| x | R' | y |$ iff for all formulas B, if $[R]B \in \Gamma_A$ then:

$$\begin{array}{ll} \text{If } M, x \models [\equiv]B \text{ then } M, y \models [R]B; & \text{If } M, x \models [\cong]B \text{ then } M, y \models [\rho]B; \\ \text{If } M, y \models [\equiv]B \text{ then } M, x \models [R]B; & \text{If } M, y \models [\cong]B \text{ then } M, x \models [\rho]B; \\ \text{If } M, x \models [R]B \text{ then } M, y \models [\equiv]B; & \text{If } M, x \models [\rho]B \text{ then } M, y \models [\cong]B; \\ \text{If } M, y \models [R]B \text{ then } M, x \models [\equiv]B; & \text{If } M, y \models [\rho]B \text{ then } M, x \models [\cong]B; \end{array}$$

- For all $x, y \in W$, $| x |\cong'| y |$ iff for all formulas B, if $[\cong]B \in \Gamma_A$ then:

$$\begin{array}{ll} \text{If } M, x \models [\cong]B \text{ then } M, y \models [\equiv]B; & \text{If } M, x \models [\rho]B \text{ then } M, y \models [R]B; \\ \text{If } M, y \models [\cong]B \text{ then } M, x \models [\equiv]B; & \text{If } M, y \models [\rho]B \text{ then } M, x \models [R]B; \end{array}$$

- For all $x, y \in W$, $| x | \rho' | y |$ iff for all formulas B, if $[\rho]B \in \Gamma_A$ then:

$$\begin{array}{ll} \text{If } M, x \models [\cong]B \text{ then } M, y \models [R]B; & \text{If } M, x \models [\rho]B \text{ then } M, y \models [\equiv]B; \\ \text{If } M, y \models [\cong]B \text{ then } M, x \models [R]B; & \text{If } M, y \models [\rho]B \text{ then } M, x \models [\equiv]B; \end{array}$$

- For all propositional variables p, $V'(p)$ is $V(p)_{|=_{\Gamma_A}}$.

It follows immediately that M' is a filtration of M. As a consequence, if A is true at some possible world in M then A is true at some possible world in M'.
(4 implies 1): Let $M = (W, \equiv, R, \cong, \rho, V)$ be a finite nonstandard model and $M' = (W', \equiv', R', \cong', \rho', V')$ be the finite model defined as follows. Define:

- W' is $W \times \{0, 1\}$;
- For all $x, y \in W$ and for all $i, j \in \{0, 1\}$, $(x, i) \equiv' (y, j)$ iff $x \equiv y$ and $i = j$;
- For all $x, y \in W$ and for all $i, j \in \{0, 1\}$, $(x, i)R'(y, j)$ iff xRy and $i = 1 - j$;
- For all $x, y \in W$ and for all $i, j \in \{0, 1\}$, $(x, i) \cong' (y, j)$ iff $x \cong y$ and $i = j$;
- For all $x, y \in W$ and for all $i, j \in \{0, 1\}$, $(x, i)\rho'(y, j)$ iff $x\rho y$ and $i = 1 - j$;
- For all propositional variables p, $V'(p)$ is $V(p) \times \{0, 1\}$.

It follows immediately that M is a p-morphic image of M'. As a consequence, if A is true at some possible world in M then A is true at some possible world in M'. □

Now we turn to the axiomatization of the set of all formulas true at all possible worlds in all models. Let *LSWIC* — logic of strong and weak indiscernibility and complementarity — be the smallest normal modal logic that contains the axioms of table 2. A typical result is the following.

Theorem 14. *LSWIC is complete with respect to the class of all models and the class of all nonstandard models, i.e. the following conditions are equivalent.*

1. *A is true at all possible worlds in all models;*
2. *A is true at all possible worlds in all nonstandard models;*
3. *A is a theorem of LSWIC.*

Proof. (1 implies 2): By lemma 11.
(2 implies 1): By lemma 11.
(2 implies 3): The proof can be obtained by the canonical model construction.
(3 implies 2): The proof is trivial because nonstandard models satisfy the conditions which are needed to verify the axioms of *LSWIC*. □

Table 2. Axioms of $LSWIC$.

$[\equiv]A \rightarrow A$	$[\cong]A \rightarrow A$
$A \rightarrow [\equiv]\langle\equiv\rangle A$	$A \rightarrow [\cong]\langle\cong\rangle A$
$[\equiv]A \rightarrow [\equiv][\equiv]A$	$[\cong]A \rightarrow [\cong][\equiv]A$
$[R]A \rightarrow [\equiv][R]A$	$[\rho]A \rightarrow [\cong][R]A$
$A \rightarrow [R]\langle R\rangle A$	$A \rightarrow [\rho]\langle\rho\rangle A$
$[R]A \rightarrow [R][\equiv]A$	$[\rho]A \rightarrow [\rho][\equiv]A$
$[\equiv]A \rightarrow [R][R]A$	$[\cong]A \rightarrow [\rho][R]A$

We now turn our attention to the decidability of the problem of determining of any given formula whether it is a theorem of $LSWIC$ or not.

Theorem 15. *Determining of any given formula whether it is a theorem of $LSWIC$ or not is decidable.*

Proof. By lemma 11 and theorem 2, $LSWIC$ is a finitely axiomatizable normal modal logic which has the finite model property. As a consequence, determining of any given formula whether it is a theorem of $LSWIC$ or not is decidable. □

5 Conclusion

We have addressed the issues of first-order characterization and modal analysis of indiscernibility and complementarity in information systems. Previous first-order characterizations and modal analyses have been given by Demri [2], Demri, Orłowska and Vakarelov [3], Orłowska [5,6], Orłowska and Pawlak [7] and Vakarelov [9,10,11,12] who consider indistinguishability relations and distinguishability relations like the similarity relations defined as follows. Let $S = (Att, Obj, \{Val_a \mid a \in Att\}, f)$ be an information system. For all $x, y \in Obj$, define:

Strong positive similarity: $x\sigma_S y$ iff for all $a \in Att$, $f(a,x) \cap f(a,y) \neq \emptyset$;
Strong negative similarity: $x\nu_S y$ iff for all $a \in Att$, $(Val_a \setminus f(a,x)) \cap (Val_a \setminus f(a,y)) \neq \emptyset$;
Weak positive similarity: $x\Sigma_S y$ iff there is $a \in Att$ such that $f(a,x) \cap f(a,y) \neq \emptyset$;
Weak negative similarity: $xN_S y$ iff there is $a \in Att$ such that $(Val_a \setminus f(a,x)) \cap (Val_a \setminus f(a,y)) \neq \emptyset$;

It should be remarked that the strong complementarity relation is definable by means of the strong similarity relations as follows:

- $R_S = \overline{\sigma_S} \cap \overline{\nu_S}$;

whereas the weak complementarity relation is definable neither by means of the strong similarity relations nor by means of the weak similarity relations.

First-order characterizations and modal analyses of indiscernibility relations and complementarity relations in information systems together with other indistinguishability relations or distinguishability relations like similarity relations are not known.

References

1. Balbiani, P., Vakarelov, D.: A modal logic for indiscernibility and complementarity in information systems. To appear.
2. Demri, S.: The nondeterministic information logic NIL is PSPACE-complete. Fundamenta Informaticæ**42** (2000) 211–234.
3. Demri, S., Orłowska, E., Vakarelov, D.: Indiscernibility and complementarity relations in information systems. In Gerbrandy, J., Marx, M., de Rijke, M., Venema, Y. (Editors): JFAK: Essays Dedicated to Johan van Benthem on the Occasion of his 50th Birthday. Amsterdam University Press (1999) http://turing.wins.uva.nl/ j50/cdrom/contribs/demri/index.html.
4. Hughes, G., Cresswell, M.: A Companion to Modal Logic. Methuen (1984).
5. Orłowska, E.: Logic of nondeterministic information. Studia Logica **44** (1985) 91–100.
6. Orłowska, E.: Kripke semantics for knowledge representation logics. Studia Logica **49** (1990) 255–272.
7. Orłowska, E., Pawlak, Z.: Representation of nondeterministic information. Theoretical Computer Science **29** (1984) 27–39.
8. Pawlak, Z.: Information systems — theoretical foundations. Information Systems **6** (1981) 205–218.
9. Vakarelov, D.: A modal logic for similarity relations in Pawlak knowledge representation systems. Fundamenta Informaticæ**15** (1991) 61–79.
10. Vakarelov, D.: Modal logics for knowledge representation systems. Theoretical Computer Science **90** (1991) 433–456.
11. Vakarelov, D.: A duality between Pawlak's knowledge representation systems and BI-consequence systems. Studia Logica **55** (1995) 205–228.
12. Vakarelov, D.: Information systems, similarity relations and modal logics. In Orłowska, E. (Editor): Incomplete Information: Rough Set Analysis. Physica-Verlag, Studies in Fuzziness and Soft Computing **13** (1998) 492–550.

Complete and Incomplete Knowledge in Logical Information Systems

Sébastien Ferré*

IRISA, Campus Universitaire de Beaulieu, 35042 RENNES cedex,
ferre@irisa.fr

Abstract. We present a generalization of logic All I Know by presenting it as an extension of standard modal logics. We study how this logic can be used to represent complete and incomplete knowledge in Logical Information Systems. In these information systems, a knowledge base is a collection of objects (e.g., files, bibliographical items) described in the same logic as used for expressing queries. We show that usual All I Know (transitive and euclidean accessibility relation) is convenient for representing complete knowledge, but not for incomplete knowledge. For this, we use *serial* All I Know (serial accessibility relation).

1 Introduction

Most common paradigms of information systems are *hierarchical systems* (e.g., File Systems), *relational databases*, and *deductive databases*. While the first paradigm is based on *navigation* in a hierarchy built by hand, the other ones are based on a *querying* language (e.g., SQL, first-order logic). However, it appears in practice that both navigation and querying are needed in information retrieval [GMA93], which none of the three above paradigms offers simultaneously. A new paradigm of information system was proposed [GMA93] for tightly combining navigation and querying, which is based on Concept Analysis [Wil82]. Recently, we presented a logical generalization of this new paradigm, that we call *Logical Information System* (LIS) [FR00], in which an almost arbitrary logic can be used to describe individual objects.

As for deductive databases, a LIS knowledge base is expressed in a logical way. A first difference is that this knowledge base is composed of objects (e.g., files, bibliographic items, web pages) described by formulas, rather than composed of relations. It is called a *logical context* by reference to Concept Analysis that serves as a framework for LIS. On this point, a logical context is similar to an ABox in description logics [DJ94,DNR97], except the logic used is almost arbitrary. A second difference is that the answers are formulas expressed in the same logic as queries, and not set of objects or values as it is usually the case. This enables a "dialogue" between a LIS and a user because they use the same logical language. This dialogue acts as a logical, automatic, and relevant navigation, that helps the user in the information retrieval process. Moreover, this navigation makes it

* This author is supported by a scholarship from CNRS and Région Bretagne

S. Benferhat and P. Besnard (Eds.): ECSQARU 2001, LNAI 2143, pp. 782–791, 2001.

possible to start with no knowledge of the contents of a LIS, neither the objects, nor the logic in use. It is the logical answers that informs gradually the user on both the logic and the objects.

We realized a prototype and made some experiments. They rapidly showed that deduction capabilities in propositional logic were not fully satisfying. For instance, in a bibliographic application, the query $\neg Jones$ releases no answer because bibliographic items are described by the authors they have (e.g., $Smith \wedge Bond$), and not by the authors they do not have: i.e., negative facts are not explicitly represented. Thus, following Levesque and Reiter [Rei92], we argue that the logic must be equipped with epistemic features to enhance the expressiveness of queries. This would allow to describe what is known about the external world, and to query what is known by the information system.

This paper aims at showing how complete and incomplete knowledge can be represented in a LIS. Section 2 shows that Levesque's logic All I Know (noted $\mathcal{ONL}$) is a well suited formalism among non-monotonic ones for representing complete knowledge. Section 3 explains why $\mathcal{ONL}$ has to be modified for representing incomplete knowledge. The modification consists in replacing the transitive and euclidean accessibility relation by a serial one. Both these sections also present some idiomatics that characterize new notions of truth and make the use of $\mathcal{ONL}$ easier for LIS end users that are unaware about modal logic. Finally, Section 4 concludes the paper and draws some perspectives.

2 Expressing Complete Knowledge

When we have a complete knowledge about objects, we want to deduce negative facts about objects, without having to assert them in object descriptions. For instance, we do not want to mention the fact that an object satisfies $\neg Jones$, while we want that this fact be deducible from its description because we have a *complete knowledge* on this object. This is obviously a formulation of the well-known *Closed World Assumption* (CWA), which led to many formalisms for non-monotonic reasoning (e.g., Minimal Belief and Negation as Failure [Lif91,DNR97], Auto-Epistemic Logic [Moo85], Circumscription [McC86], All I Know [Lev90]). However, logics used in LIS must have a monotonic deduction relation because of the framework on which it is based, i.e., Concept Analysis. In fact, this framework requires that the logic has a deduction relation that forms a lattice. In other words, we need to apply CWA locally in formulas (especially in object descriptions) rather than globally in the deduction relation. Levesque's logic All I Know (noted $\mathcal{ONL}$) is precisely a formalism that defines such an operation. Moreover, logic $\mathcal{ONL}$ is proved to encompass all these non-monotonic formalisms (see [Che94] for mappings between these formalisms), and there exists a proof method for it [Ros00].

2.1 Logic $\mathcal{ONL}$

In this section, we recall the formalization of logic $\mathcal{ONL}$ (here, we consider its semantics [Ros00], but there also exists an axiomatics [Lev90]). The logical language $\mathcal{ONL}$ is defined as a propositional language with connectives $\wedge$, $\neg$ ($\vee$ and $\Rightarrow$ are defined as abbrevations), whose atomic propositions belong to an infinite set $\mathcal{A}$, and that is extended with modal operators K, N, O. Logic $\mathcal{ONL}$ can be given a Kripke semantics: the *worlds* are valuations of $\mathcal{A}$ in $\{TRUE, FALSE\}$ extended in the usual way to propositional formulas, and the *accessibility relation* is defined as a relation between these worlds.

Definition 1 *Let w be a world, and let R be a* transitive[1] *and* euclidean[2] *accessibility relation. We say that a structure (w, R) is a* model *of a formula $\phi \in \mathcal{ONL}$, and we note $(w, R) \models \phi$, iff the following conditions hold ($R(w)$ denotes the set of successor worlds of w through R):*
1. if $\phi \in \mathcal{A}$, then $(w, R) \models \phi$ iff $w(\phi) = TRUE$;
2. if $\phi = \neg\phi_1$, then $(w, R) \models \phi$ iff $(w, R) \not\models \phi_1$;
3. if $\phi = \phi_1 \wedge \phi_2$, then $(w, R) \models \phi$ iff $(w, R) \models \phi_1$ and $(w, R) \models \phi_2$;
4. if $\phi = K\phi_1$, then $(w, R) \models \phi$ iff for every $w' \in R(w)$, $(w', R) \models \phi_1$;
5. if $\phi = N\phi_1$, then $(w, R) \models \phi$ iff for every $w' \notin R(w)$, $(w', R) \models \phi_1$;
6. if $\phi = O\phi_1$, then $(w, R) \models \phi$ iff for every w', $w' \in R(w)$ iff $(w', R) \models \phi_1$.

We remark here that for every worlds w, w' such that wRw', we have $R(w) = R(w')$ because the accessibility relation is both transitive and euclidean. This means for a structure (w, R) that every world accessible from w (in zero, one or more steps) has the same set of successor worlds $R(w)$. Therefore, we can use instead a structure (w, W) where $W = R(w)$ [Lev90,Ros00]. We do not do so because this statement is not right in all the rest of this paper.

Logic $\mathcal{ONL}$ is equipped with a monotonic deduction relation $\models_{\mathcal{ONL}}$, that enables to compare object descriptions with queries, but also queries themselves.

Definition 2 *A formula $\phi \in \mathcal{ONL}$ entails a formula $\psi \in \mathcal{ONL}$ (denoted as $\phi \models_{\mathcal{ONL}} \psi$) iff $\phi \Rightarrow \psi$ is $\mathcal{ONL}$-valid, i.e., for every Kripke structure (w, R) where R is transitive and euclidean, $(w, R) \models \phi \Rightarrow \psi$.*

In order to better understand modal operators, we prove the following lemma.

Lemma 1 *If ϕ is a $\mathcal{ONL}$-formula and $W_R(\phi) = \{w | (w, R) \models \phi\}$ is the set of worlds where ϕ is true, then for every structure (w, R)*
1. $(w, R) \models K\phi$ iff $R(w) \subseteq W_R(\phi)$;
2. $(w, R) \models N\neg\phi$ iff $R(w) \supseteq W_R(\phi)$;
3. $(w, R) \models O\phi$ iff $R(w) = W_R(\phi)$.

Proof 1 *Proofs for each item is directly obtained from Definition 1, and are similar. So, we detail the proof only for modality K.*
(1) $(w, R) \models K\phi \iff \forall w' \in R(w) : (w', R) \models \phi$
$\iff \forall w' : w' \in R(w) \Rightarrow w' \in W_R(\phi) \iff R(w) \subseteq W_R(\phi)$. ■

---

[1] A relation R is transitive iff $\forall w, w', w'' : wRw'$ and $w'Rw''$ implies wRw''.
[2] A relation R is euclidean iff $\forall w, w', w'' : wRw'$ and wRw'' implies $w'Rw''$.

This lemma shows that in a model (w, R) of a modal formula, what is important is not the initial world w, neither the accessibility relation itself, but the set of successor worlds $R(w)$. Therefore, these modal formulas $M\phi$ ($M \in \{K, N\neg, O\}$) describe sets of models of ϕ, rather than individual models of ϕ. For instance, modal formula $K\phi$ describes some subsets of $W_R(\phi)$, in which ϕ is always true but not only ϕ. So, $K\phi$ can be read as "at least ϕ". Dualy, modal formula $N\neg\phi$ can be read as "at most ϕ", and modal formula $O\phi$, which is semantically equivalent to $K\phi \wedge N\neg\phi$ according to Definition 1, can be read as "exactly ϕ" or "all I know is ϕ" (hence, the original name of logic $\mathcal{ONL}$ [Lev90]).

2.2 Completing Knowledge with Logic $\mathcal{ONL}$

We now consider the representation of complete knowledge with logic $\mathcal{ONL}$. For instance, in the context of a bibliography, we want to represent the authors of a document o. If A and B are authors (represented as independant atoms), we can logically describe this document with the propositional formula $d(o) = A \wedge B$. Then, o is an answer of the query $q = A$ (because $d(o)$ entails q), but is not an answer of the query $q' = \neg C$ (because $d(o)$ does not entail q'). But, if the knowledge expressed in $d(o)$ is complete, we want to deduce from it that C is not an author of the considered document.

For this, we propose to complete object decriptions by embedding them in modal operator O (this idea has already been proposed, e.g., in the conclusion of [Rei92]). In our example, we establish the following entailments (by the mean of a tableau calculus [Ros00])

$$O(A \wedge B) \models_{\mathcal{ONL}} K(A), \quad O(A \wedge B) \models_{\mathcal{ONL}} \neg K(C),$$

which can be translated in English as "if A and B are authors and the only ones, then A is an author and C is not".

2.3 Idiomatics for Complete Knowledge

Following Reiter [Rei92], we think that modal operators are not convenient for naive end users, which tend to reason on non-modal formulas. For this, we introduce some idiomatics for expressing descriptions and queries in an easier way:

description: $[d] \equiv Od$, where d is a non-modal formula describing an object: ex., $[A \wedge \neg B]$;

query: proposition whose atoms are either $+q \equiv Kq$ or $-q \equiv \neg Kq$, q being a non-modal formula: ex., $(+(A \wedge B) \vee +\neg B) \wedge -C$.

These idiomatics are not arbitrary and characterize the deducibility of some properties in propositional logic, as proved by the following lemma.

Lemma 2 *Let $\models_{\mathcal{L}}$ be a deduction relation on non-modal formulas (propositions). For every non-modal formulas d, q*

1. *$[d] \models_{\mathcal{ONL}} +q$ iff $d \models_{\mathcal{L}} q$;*
2. *$[d] \models_{\mathcal{ONL}} -q$ iff $d \not\models_{\mathcal{L}} q$.*

Proof 2
(1) $[d] \models_{\mathcal{ONL}} +q \iff (Od \Rightarrow Kq)$ *is valid (Definition 2)*
$\iff \forall(w,R) : (w,R) \models Od) \Rightarrow (w,R) \models Kq)$ *(Definition 1)*
$\iff \forall(w,R) : R(w) = W_R(d) \Rightarrow R(w) \subseteq W_R(q)$ *(Lemma 1)*
$\iff \forall R : W_R(d) \subseteq W_R(q) \iff d \models_{\mathcal{L}} q$ *$(d, q$ are non-modal formulas).*
(2) similar to proof (1). ∎

If a non-modal formula d represents the knowledge we have about an object, then $[d] \models_{\mathcal{ONL}} +q$ means "one knows q" because this is equivalent to $d \models_{\mathcal{L}} q$ (Lemma 2). Conversely, $[d] \models_{\mathcal{ONL}} -q$ means "one does not know q". Now, if we use $[d]$ to represent a complete knowledge, i.e., everything unknown is considered as false, we must read $+q$ as "q is *true*", and $-q$ as "q is *false*". Here, truth and falsity are expressed from a *knowledge point of view*, whereas from a *real world point of view*, they would be expressed by q and $\neg q$.

Lemma 2 shows how a subset of logic $\mathcal{ONL}$ can be used to represent complete knowledge. While this subset is simple, it enables some fine distinctions. First, $+q_1 \vee +q_2 \models_{\mathcal{ONL}} +(q_1 \vee q_2)$ while the converse is false ($[q_1 \vee q_2]$ is a counter-example): $+q_1 \vee +q_2$ represents determination (at least q_1 or q_2 is known as true), whereas $+(q_1 \vee q_2)$ represents some indetermination in knowledge ($q_1 \vee q_2$ is known as true, but which part is true can be unknown). Second, $+\neg q \models_{\mathcal{ONL}} -q$ while the converse is false ($[d]$ is a counter-example if $d \not\models_{\mathcal{L}} q$): $+\neg q$ represents explicit falsity (q is known as false), whereas $-q$ represents absence of truth (q is not known as true, but it is not necessary known as false either).

In the following section, we show that even finer knowledge distinctions can be made by means of logic $\mathcal{ONL}$, e.g., taking into account incomplete knowledge.

3 Expressing Incomplete Knowledge

From Lemma 2, it follows that for every non-modal description d, and every non-modal query q, $[d] \equiv Od$ always entails either $+q \equiv Kq$ or $-q \equiv \neg Kq$, i.e., we have a complete knowledge with descriptions embedded by modal operator O. We recall that for every formula $d \in \mathcal{ONL}$, Od can be defined as $Kd \wedge N\neg d$, which can be read as "at least d and at most d". Each part of this definition expresses an incomplete knowledge, and this is the conjunction of the application of both parts to a *same* formula that forms a complete knowledge. The issue of this section is to find how expressing incomplete knowledge by using modalities K and N in a less tight combination than in the definition of modality O. For this, we consider different formulas for the *at least* and *at most* parts, where the later must entails the former for consistency reasons (see Lemma 1). So, incomplete descriptions are in the form $Kd \wedge N\neg(d \wedge d')$, which we note $[d, d']$.

3.1 Examples and Problems

As in Section 2, we consider some examples about the representation of authors in a bibliographic application. Authors are simply represented by independant atoms $(A, B, C, D, \ldots)$. We present some modal formulas with an expected meaning:

1. $d(o_1) = [A \wedge B, \perp] \equiv K(A \wedge B)$: "at least $A \wedge B$", i.e., "A and B are certainly authors, but there are possibly other ones";
2. $d(o_2) = [\top, A \wedge B \wedge C] \equiv N\neg(A \wedge B \wedge C)$: "at most $A \wedge B \wedge C$", i.e., "A, B, and C are the only possible authors, but we do not know exactly which ones are effectively";
3. $d(o_3) = [A \wedge B, C] \equiv K(A \wedge B) \wedge N\neg(A \wedge B \wedge C)$: "A and B are certainly authors, C is possibly also, but there are no other one".

In order to know if these formulas meet their expected meaning, we look at what can be deduced from them in $\mathcal{ONL}$. The following table summaries some entailments for each example. For instance, it shows that $d(o_3)$ entails $+A$, $-D$, and that neither $+C$, nor $-C$ is deducible.

$\models_{\mathcal{ONL}}$	A	$\neg A$	C	D
$d(o_1)$	$+$			
$d(o_2)$		$-$		$-$
$d(o_3)$	$+$	$-$		$-$

Two problems are revealed by these examples. The first one is that half of the above table is empty, which corresponds to an extra-logical property ($d(o_3) \not\models_{\mathcal{ONL}} +C$ and $d(o_3) \not\models_{\mathcal{ONL}} -C$). This means that we can not ask for documents where author C is *possible*, that is where C is neither true, nor false. This notion of possibility is necessary with an incomplete knowledge, which we try to represent, but we want to express it in the logic itself.

The second problem is that $\neg A$ is possible in $d(o_1)$, whereas A is true. This means that a model (w, R) where $R(w) = \emptyset$ is considered. In this model, object o_1 is considered as an impossible object. As objects do exist in the real world, we want to exclude this possibility, and to deduce that $\neg A$ is false like in $d(o_2)$. These two problems are addressed in the next section.

3.2 Generalization of Logic $\mathcal{ONL}$

The first problem revealed in previous section is about expressing a *possible* fact q, that is a fact which is neither true ($[d, d'] \not\models_{\mathcal{ONL}} +q$), nor false ($[d, d'] \not\models_{\mathcal{ONL}} -q$), where $[d, d']$ is an incomplete description. This problem is in fact similar to the one of Section 2.2 about complete knowledge, and it is tempting to adopt a similar solution, i.e., to embed object description of Section 3.1 in modal operator O and to embed undeducible facts by modality $\neg K$ (see Lemma 2). Therefore, the description becomes $O[d, d'] \equiv O(Kd \wedge N\neg(d \wedge d'))$, and we expect to express that proposition q is possible by:

$$O[d, d'] \models_{\mathcal{ONL}} \neg K(+q) \wedge \neg K(-q),$$
$$O(Kd \wedge N\neg(d \wedge d')) \models_{\mathcal{ONL}} \neg K(Kq) \wedge \neg K(\neg Kq).$$

Unfortunately, formulas in the form $O[d, d']$ are not $\mathcal{ONL}$-satisfiable (see Example 2 of Section 2 in [Ros00]). For explaining this, we first need to recall that a structure (w, R) can be replaced by a structure (w, W) where W is the constant world set $R(w)$ (see Section 2.1). Now, let (w, W) be a model of $O[A \wedge B, \perp] \equiv OK(A \wedge B)$. If $W \subseteq W(A \wedge B)$, then for every world w', (w', W) is a model of $K(A \wedge B)$ as $W = R(w')$ (Definition 1). Then, from semantics of modality O, every world w' belongs to W since $R(w) = W$. This is contradictory because $A \wedge B$ is not a tautology. However, $W \not\subseteq W(A \wedge B)$ contradicts that (w, W) is a model of $OK(A \wedge B)$.

In the same way as formula $O(A \wedge B)$ enables us to reason on all models of $A \wedge B$, we would like that formula $OK(A \wedge B)$ enables us to reason on all models of $K(A \wedge B)$, i.e., on all structure (w, R) such that $R(w) \subseteq W_R(A \wedge B)$ (see Lemma 1). For this, it is necessary that $R(w)$ does depend on world w, in order to keep the meaning of an incomplete knowledge. This is why we propose to generalize logic $\mathcal{ONL}$ by removing transitive and euclidean conditions on the accessibility relation from Definition 1. Therefore, we can see logic $\mathcal{ONL}$ as an ordinary modal logic where K is the main modal operator defined on accessible worlds $R(w)$, whereas N is a dual modal operator defined on unaccessible worlds $\overline{R(w)}$, and O is simply defined as a combination of K and N ($O\phi \equiv K\phi \wedge N\neg\phi$). Then, a whole family of $\mathcal{ONL}$-logic can be derived by applying various conditions on the accessibility relation, as it is done for usual modal logics [Bow79]. For instance, usual logic $\mathcal{ONL}$ has a transitive and euclidean accessibility relation and can so be renamed as K45-$\mathcal{ONL}$, whereas our generalization leads to an arbitrary accessibility relation and can be named as K-$\mathcal{ONL}$.

Definition 3 *Semantics and entailment of logic K-$\mathcal{ONL}$ are defined as in Definitions 1 and 2, except there are no condition on the accessibility relation.*

With logic K-$\mathcal{ONL}$, the knowledge is stratified because the accessibility relation is neither transitive, nor euclidean. Object description $Od(o_1) = OK(A \wedge B)$ is now satisfiable and can be read as three levels of knowledge: a model of

1. $A \wedge B$ is a world w satisfying both A and B;
2. $K(A \wedge B)$ is a world w whose $R(w)$ is a set of models of $A \wedge B$;
3. $OK(A \wedge B)$ is a world w whose $R(w)$ collects all models of $K(A \wedge B)$.

This description represents a complete knowledge about an incomplete knowledge about object o_1: "All I know about object o_1 is that it has at least authors A and B". It allows the following entailment with idiomatics of Section 2.3.

Proposition 1 $O[A \wedge B, \bot] \models_{K-\mathcal{ONL}}$
$$K(+A) \wedge (\neg K(+\neg A) \wedge \neg K(-\neg A)) \wedge (\neg K(+C) \wedge \neg K(-C)).$$

This means that $Od(o_1)$ entails "one knows that A is true" (i.e., is an author), and also "one does not know about $\neg A$ and C". So, the fact that C is a possible author is correctly expressed by $(\neg K(+C) \wedge \neg K(-C))$, which solves the first problem presented in Section 3.1.

On the contrary, the second problem is not solved because $\neg A$ is proved possible rather than false as expected. The reason is that a Kripke structure (w, R) where $R(w) = \emptyset$ is considered as a model of $K(A \wedge B)$, which means that an impossible object is considered. This is not convenient in our Logical Information System where objects do exist in the real world. To exclude these empty models, we just add a condition of *seriality*[3] on the accessibility relation [Bow79], which forces any world to have at least one successor: we obtain logic KD-$\mathcal{ONL}$.

[3] A relation R is serial iff $\forall w : \exists w' : wRw'$.

Definition 4 *Semantics and entailment of logic KD-$\mathcal{ONL}$ are defined as in Definitions 1 and 2, except the accessibility relation must only be serial.*

This time, we get the expected entailment: "one knows that $\neg A$ is false".

Proposition 2 $O[A \wedge B, \perp] \models_{KD-\mathcal{ONL}}$
$K(+A) \wedge K(-\neg A) \wedge (\neg K(+C) \wedge \neg K(-C))$.

3.3 Idiomatics for Incomplete Knowledge

As for complete knowledge, we introduce some idiomatics, by extending idiomatics of Section 2.3:

description: $[d, d'] \equiv O[d, d'] \equiv O(Kd \wedge N\neg(d \wedge d'))$, where d and d' are non-modal formulas, represents a kind of knowledge interval where d represents what is known as true, and d' represents what is known as possible, all the rest being considered as implicitly false. A complete knowledge d can also be represented as $[d] = [d, \top] \equiv OOd$.

query: a proposition whose atoms are either $+q \equiv K(+q)$, or $-q \equiv K(-q)$, or $?q \equiv (\neg K(+q) \wedge \neg K(-q))$, q being a non-modal formula: ex., $(+(A \wedge \neg B) \vee ?C) \wedge -D$.

In the following, we use only these new definitions of idioms. The following lemma characterizes the meaning of these idiomatics by relating them to the non-modal propositional logic.

Lemma 3 *Let $\models_{\mathcal{L}}$ be a deduction relation on non-modal formulas (propositions). For every non-modal formulas d, d', q*
1. $[d, d'] \models_{KD-\mathcal{ONL}} +q$ iff $d \models_{\mathcal{L}} q$;
2. $[d, d'] \models_{KD-\mathcal{ONL}} -q$ iff $d \wedge q \models_{\mathcal{L}} \perp$ or $d \wedge d' \not\models q$;
3. $[d, d'] \models_{KD-\mathcal{ONL}} ?q$ otherwise.

Proof 3
(1) $[d, d'] \models_{KD-\mathcal{ONL}} +q \iff O(Kd \wedge N\neg(d \wedge d')) \models_{KD-\mathcal{ONL}} KKq$
$\iff \forall(w, R) : (w, R) \models O(Kd \wedge N\neg(d \wedge d')) \Rightarrow (w, R) \models KKq$ (Definition 2)
$\iff \forall(w', R) : (w', R) \models Kd$ and $(w', R) \models N\neg(d \wedge d') \Rightarrow (w', R) \models Kq$ (semantics of O, K, and $\wedge$)
$\iff \forall(w', R) : R(w') \subseteq W_R(d)$ and $R(w') \supseteq W_R(d \wedge d') \Rightarrow R(w') \subseteq W_R(q)$ (Lemma 1)
$\iff \forall R : W_R(d) \subseteq W_R(q)$ (take $R(w') = W_R(d)$)
$\iff d \models_{\mathcal{L}} q$ (d, q are non-modal formulas).
(2) similar to proof (1).
(3) $[d, d'] \models_{KD-\mathcal{ONL}} ?q \iff O(Kd \wedge N\neg(d \wedge d')) \models_{KD-\mathcal{ONL}} \neg KKq \wedge \neg K\neg Kq$
$\iff \forall(w, R) : (w, R) \models O(Kd \wedge N\neg(d \wedge d')) \Rightarrow (w, R) \not\models KKq$ and $(w, R) \not\models K\neg Kq$ (Definitions 2 and 1)
$\iff \forall(w, R) : (w, R) \models O(Kd \wedge N\neg(d \wedge d')) \Rightarrow \exists w'_1 \in R(w) : (w'_1, R) \not\models Kq$ and $\exists w'_2 \in R(w) : (w'_2, R) \models K$ (semantics of K and $\neg$)

$\iff \forall w : \exists (w_1', R_1) : (w_1', R_1) \models Kd, (w_1', R_1) \models N\neg(d \wedge d'), (w_1', R_1) \not\models Kq$ *and* $\exists (w_2', R_2) : (w_2', R_2) \models Kd, (w_2', R_2) \models N\neg(d \wedge d'), (w_2', R_2) \models Kq$ *(take* $R_i(w) = \{w' | (w', R_i) \models Kd \wedge N\neg(d \wedge d')\}$*, for* $i \in \{1, 2\}$*)*
$\iff \exists (w_1', R_1) : R_1(w_1') \subseteq W_{R_1}(d), R_1(w_1') \supseteq W_{R_1}(d \wedge d'), R_1(w_1') \not\subseteq W_{R_1}(q)$ *and* $\exists (w_2', R_2) : R_2(w_2') \subseteq W_{R_2}(d), R_2(w_2') \supseteq W_{R_2}(d \wedge d'), R_2(w_2') \subseteq W_{R_2}(q)$ *(Lemma 1)*
$\iff \forall R : W_R(d) \not\subseteq W_R(q)$ *and* $W_R(d) \cap W_R(q) \not\subseteq \emptyset$ *and* $W_R(d \wedge d') \subseteq W_R(q)$ *((*$\Rightarrow$*) use seriality for* $W_R(d) \cap W_R(q) \not\subseteq \emptyset$ *and non-modality of* d, d', q*; (*$\Leftarrow$*) take* $R_1(w_1') = W_R(d)$ *and* $R_2(w_2') = W_R(d) \cap W_R(q)$ *which are non empty because of seriality)*
$\iff d \not\models_{\mathcal{L}} q$ *and* $d \wedge q \not\models_{\mathcal{L}} \bot$ *and* $d \wedge d' \models_{\mathcal{L}} q$
$\iff [d, d'] \not\models_{KD-\mathcal{ONL}} +q$ *and* $[d, d'] \not\models_{KD-\mathcal{ONL}} -q$. ∎

Lemma 3 proves that the above idiomatics are exhaustive because a query q is always either true ($+q$), false ($-q$), or possible ($?q$) with regard to a description in the form $[d, d']$. We see also that ? is disjoint from + and −, but a query can be both true and false in the special case where $d \models_{\mathcal{L}} \bot$, i.e., the description is contradictory. In fact, in information systems, object descriptions are kept consistent by *integrity constraints*. Finally, idiomatics presented in this section offers a simple way to implement logic KD-$\mathcal{ONL}$ by relying only on a non-modal propositional prover.

4 Conclusion and Future Work

Section 3.2 presents a generalized form of logic $\mathcal{ONL}$ that is parallel to standard modal logics: a logic $\mathcal{ONL}$ is a modal logic extended with a new modal operator N that enables to reason on unaccessible worlds, whereas the usual modal operator K enables to reason on accessible worlds. Thus, as there are a whole family of modal logics depending on various conditions on the accessibility relation (AR), we get a whole family of $\mathcal{ONL}$-logics. Even if it is already known that logic $\mathcal{ONL}$ can be defined like a modal logic [Ros00], to our knowledge only K45-$\mathcal{ONL}$ (transitive and euclidean AR) has been studied. In this paper, we have studied K-$\mathcal{ONL}$ (any AR), then KD-$\mathcal{ONL}$ (serial AR), and we have showed they are more convenient for representing incomplete knowledge by enabling several levels of knowledge. Future work is to explore more deeply logic $\mathcal{ONL}$ both in its general and specific forms.

Recently, a tableau calculus has been proposed for logic K45-$\mathcal{ONL}$ [Ros00]. We think it would not be too difficult to extend it to any logic $\mathcal{ONL}$ by taking inspiration of what is done for modal logics with tableaux [Mas94].

In Section 1, we present the arbitrarity of the logic used as an important feature of our Logical Information Systems. A problem is that logic $\mathcal{ONL}$ sets the logic as soon as we want to represent knowledge. To combine $\mathcal{ONL}$ features with genericity, our idea is to build an abstraction of logic $\mathcal{ONL}$ by making the logic $\langle \mathcal{L}; \models_{\mathcal{L}} \rangle$ appearing in Lemmas 2 and 3 a logical parameter. We call such an abstraction a *logic functor*, and we already did this work for several logics such as the propositional logic that we abstracted over atoms. An $\mathcal{ONL}$ logic functor would allow to represent complete and incomplete knowledge as presented in this paper, but with the non-modal part of descriptions and queries expressed in a dedicated logic (e.g., regular expressions, intervals for dates, sets of valued attributes for the bibliographical application).

Finally, we intend to study how to express integrity constraints in logic $\mathcal{ONL}$ itself [Rei92], and how to design declarative revisions and updates in order to integrate in the description of an object new knowledge facts about it, while preserving its consistency, and without having to edit it by hand.

Acknowledgements. A warm thank goes to Olivier Ridoux for insightful discussions and advices. His expertise in logic has been helpful to the highest point. I am also thankful to Philippe Besnard who make me know about logic All I Know and has supported my work.

References

[Bow79] K. A. Bowen. *Model Theory for Modal Logic.* D. Reidel, London, 1979.

[Che94] Chen. The logic of only knowing as a unified framework for non-monotonic reasoning. *FUNDINF: Fundamenta Informatica*, 21, 1994.

[DJ94] P. T. Devanbu and M. A. Jones. The use of description logics in KBSE systems. In Bruno Fadini, editor, *Proceedings of the 16th International Conference on Software Engineering*, pages 23–38, Sorrento, Italy, May 1994. IEEE Computer Society Press.

[DNR97] F. M. Donini, D. Nardi, and R. Rosati. Autoepistemic description logics. In *IJCAI*, 1997.

[FR00] Sébastien Ferré and Olivier Ridoux. A file system based on concept analysis. In Yehoshua Sagiv, editor, *International Conference on Rules and Objects in Databases*, LNCS 1861, pages 1033–1047. Springer, 2000.

[GMA93] R. Godin, R. Missaoui, and A. April. Experimental comparison of navigation in a Galois lattice with conventional information retrieval methods. *International Journal of Man-Machine Studies*, 38(5):747–767, 1993.

[Lev90] Hector Levesque. All I know: a study in autoepistemic logic. *Artificial Intelligence*, 42(2), March 1990.

[Lif91] V. Lifschitz. Nonmonotonic databases and epistemic queries. In *12th International Joint Conference on Artificial Intelligence*, pages 381–386, 1991.

[Mas94] Fabio Massacci. Strongly analytic tableaux for normal modal logics. In Alan Bundy, editor, *Proceedings of the 12th International Conference on Automated Deduction*, LNAI 814, pages 723–737, Berlin, 1994. Springer.

[McC86] John McCarthy. Applications of circumscription to formalizing common sense knowledge. *Artificial Intelligence*, 28(1), 1986.

[Moo85] Robert C. Moore. Semantical considerations on nonmonotonic logic. *Artificial Intelligence*, 25(1):75–94, 1985.

[Rei92] Raymond Reiter. What should a database know? *Journal of Logic Programming*, 14(1-2):127–153, October 1992.

[Ros00] Riccardo Rosati. Tableau calculus for only knowing and knowing at most. In Roy Dickhoff, editor, *TABLEAUX*, LNCS 1847. Springer, 2000.

[Wil82] Rudolf Wille. *Ordered Sets*, chapter Restructuring lattice theory: an approach based on hierarchies of concepts, pages 445–470. Reidel, Dordrecht Boston, 1982.

Extending Polynomiality to a Class of Non-clausal Many-Valued Horn-Like Formulas

E. Altamirano and G. Escalada-Imaz

Artificial Intelligence Research Institute (IIIA)
Spanish Scientific Research Council (CSIC)
Campus UAB, s/n, 08193 Bellaterra, Barcelona (Spain)
{ealtamir,gonzalo}@iiia.csic.es

Abstract. In this paper we deal with the SAT problem in many-valued logics which is of relevant interest in many areas of Artificial Intelligence and Computer Science. Regarding tractability issues, several works have been previously published solving polynomially some clausal many-valued SAT problems. Thus, our aim is to show that certain non-clausal many-valued SAT problems can be solved in polynomial time too, extending in this way, earlier results from the clausal framework to the more general non-clausal one.

1 Introduction

Solving the SAT problem in many-valued logics is an important challenge due to the repercussions in many different areas of Computer Science such as Approximated Reasoning, Hardware Design, Deductive Data Bases, Automated Software Validation, Logic Programming, Knowledge Rule-Based System, etc. The interest of considering many-valued logics instead of classical logic lies mainly in the fact that many-valued logics can cope with certain uncertainty aspects existing almost always in real world applications. For a survey on Many-valued Automated Deduction issues the reader can see [15].

In this paper we will deal with the non clausal signed logic SAT problem. Signed logic is a kind of many-valued logic that is an extension of the classical logic in the following sense. Atoms in propositional bi-valued logic are noted by p and $\neg p$. Knowing that the set of truth values is $\{0,1\}$, these atoms could be written differently as $\{1\}:p$ and $\{0\}:p$ respectively. Thus, in a general case, if N is the set of truth values an atom in signed logic is denoted by $S:p$, where $S \subseteq N$, and its negated by $N/S:p$.

Regular logic is a particular case of signed logic with two assumptions 1) N is a total ordered set $\{0, \frac{1}{N-1}, \frac{2}{N-1}, \ldots, 1\}$ and, 2) the set S can be either of positive polarity or negative polarity. Positive (resp. negative) polarity means that S takes the interval of values comprised between a given value $j \in N$ and 1 (resp. 0 and the given value j).

The satisfiability relation varies only w.r.t. the literal level. Namely, an interpretation I satisfies $S : p$ iff $I(p) \in S$ and it satisfies a conjunction (resp.

S. Benferhat and P. Besnard (Eds.): ECSQARU 2001, LNAI 2143, pp. 792–804, 2001.

disjunction) of formulas iff it satisfies each (resp. at least one) formula of the conjunction (resp. disjunction).

The signed SAT problem keeps a particular relevance with respect to any other many-valued SAT problem. This is because in [13] has been proved that a SAT problem expressed in any finite many-valued logic can be transformed into an equivalent signed SAT problem in polynomial time. This means that a solver of the signed SAT problem can act as a general many-valued SAT solver. Indeed, in order to solve a many-valued SAT problem first one could transform the problem into a signed SAT problem and then applying the signed SAT solver. Thus, advances in solving the signed SAT problem have direct consequences on solving any finite many-valued SAT problem.

Our work. Our purpose is to prove the polynomiality of the satisfiability problem in non-clausal regular formulas of kind $\Gamma = \Delta_1 \wedge \Delta_2 \wedge \ldots \wedge \Delta_m$ where the Δ's are more general formulas than simple clauses.

Thus, if we denote by D^- (resp C^+) a disjunction (resp. conjunction) of regular literals with negative (resp. positive) polarity and DNF^- (resp. CNF^-) a disjunctive (resp. conjunctive) normal form formula composed by regular literals with negative polarity, then the Δ's elements of Γ are Negation Normal Form formulas of kind $\Delta = DNF^- \vee CNF^- \vee C^+$.

For the previous class of formulas, we provide a refutation complete calculus and an efficient almost linear algorithm. Indeed, we prove that the mentioned problem can be solved in $O(n.log(n))$ time.

It can be noticed that the considered formulas present a Horn-like structure. Indeed the identified formulas are compact representations of Horn theories in the sense that they represent the same logical theory that could be represented by Horn formulas but, with considerable less symbols. In a favourable case, the reduction rate can be exponential. Thus, the identified formulas are of relevant interest for instance, in applications issued from the Knowledge Rule-Based Systems where non-clausal formulas are a natural expression of the real problems.

To solve the SAT problem in non-clausal form a known general principle is to translate the problem to a clausal form. However, this method is not exempt of severe drawbacks pointed out already in the literature related to this topic. Indeed two transformations are known, one preserve the logical equivalence and the other only the satisfiability equivalence.

1. In the first case, the translation cannot skip the explosion of the number of symbols due to the $\wedge/\vee$ distribution operation and thus the size of the resulting CNF formula can increase exponentially.
2. The other approach consists in modifying the formula by introducing artificial literals [13] aiming at preserving the satisfiability relation. This second line of solution has two strong drawbacks: first, the logical equivalence relation is lost which could be invalid for certain applications and second, the size of the derived formula increases polynomially [13] reducing significantly the efficiency of the approach.

Hence, processing directly the non-clausal formula in an appropriated way arises as the most efficient approach of solving non-clausal many-valued SAT problems.

This paper is structured as follows. Firstly, we define the syntax and semantics of the non-clausal regular formulas dealt with here. Afterwards, we define the Logical Calculus. In section three, we give a quadratic correct algorithm. Next, we design an almost linear algorithm for the non-clausal regular SAT problem. Finally, we review the related work.

2 Regular Many-Valued Γ-Formulas

The first four definitions describe the syntax and semantics of regular formulas. A more detailed description about these concepts can be found in [8,12,14].

Definition 1. Signed formulas. *Let N be a finite set of truth values, S a subset of N ($S \subseteq N$) and p a proposition. An expression of the form $S\!:\!p$ is a signed literal and S is its sign. Given a signed literal $S\!:\!p$ and a set of truth values N, $(N \setminus S)\!:\!p$ denotes the complement of $S\!:\!p$. A signed clause is a disjunction of signed literals. A signed formula is a conjunction of signed clauses.*

Definition 2. Interpretation and satisfiability. *An interpretation* **I** *is a mapping that assigns to every proposition a value in the set of truth values N. An interpretation* **I** *satisfies a signed literal $S\!:\!p$ iff $\mathbf{I}(p) \in S$. An interpretation* **I** *satisfies a signed clause iff* **I** *satisfies at least one of its signed literals. A signed formula Γ is satisfiable iff there exists at least one interpretation that satisfies all the signed clauses in Γ. A signed formula that is not satisfiable is unsatisfiable. The empty signed clause $\Box$ is unsatisfiable and the empty signed formula $\Gamma = \{\}$ is satisfiable.*

Definition 3. Regular sign. *Let $\uparrow i$ denote the set $\{j \in N \mid j \geq i\}$ and $\downarrow i$ the set $\{j \in N \mid j \leq i\}$, where N is the set of truth values, $\leq$ a linear order on N and $i \in N$. If a sign S is equal to either $\uparrow i$ or $\downarrow i$, then it is a regular sign. A signed literal $S\!:\!p$ has positive (resp. negative) polarity if $S = \uparrow i$ (resp. $S = \downarrow i$).*

Definition 4. Regular formulas. *Let R be a regular sign. A regular literal is a signed literal whose sign is regular. A regular clause C is a disjunction of regular literals $C = R_1 : p_1 \vee R_2 : p_2 \vee \ldots \vee R_m : p_m$. A regular Horn clause is a regular clause with at most one regular literal with positive polarity. A regular unit clause is a regular clause containing only one literal. A regular formula is a conjunction of regular clauses.*

Now, we can describe the many-valued non-clausal formulas called Γ-formulas that are a non-clausal extension of the regular Horn formulas. They allow to represent the same theories that regular Horn formulas but with less number of literals. It can be easily proved that the reduction in the number of symbols can be of exponential rate. Thus, the proposed algorithm running with an almost linear complexity with non-clausal formulas is exponentially faster for the same problems than the polynomial algorithms [8,14] computing Horn regular formulas due to the exponential rate between the sizes of the inputs.

Definition 5. *A negative disjunction, noted* $D^- = (\downarrow i_1 : p_1 \vee \downarrow i_2 : p_2 \vee \ldots \vee \downarrow i_n : p_n)$*, is a disjunction of literals with negative polarity. A negative conjunctive normal form, noted* CNF^-*, is a conjunction of negative disjunctions. A negative conjunction* $C^- = (\downarrow i_1 : p_1 \wedge \downarrow i_2 : p_2 \wedge \ldots \wedge \downarrow i_n : p_n)$ *is a conjunction of literals with negative polarity. A negative disjunctive normal form* DNF^- *is a disjunction of negative conjunctions.*

Definition 6. **Γ-formulas** *A subformula* Δ *is a disjunction of three optional terms* $\Delta = DNF^- \vee CNF^- \vee C^+$ *where* $DNF^- = C_1^- \vee C_2^- \vee \ldots \vee C_n^-$ *is a negative disjunctive normal form,* $CNF^- = D_1^- \wedge D_2^- \wedge \ldots \wedge D_n^-$ *is a negative conjunctive normal form and* $C^+ = (\uparrow i_1 : p_1 \wedge \ldots \wedge \uparrow i_n : p_n)$ *is a regular conjunction with positive polarity. A* Γ*-formula is a finite conjunction of formulas* Δ*.* $\Gamma_\Box$ *denotes any* Γ*-formula containing the empty clause and hence it is unsatisfiable.*

Example 1. The formula here below is an unsatisfiable Γ-formula:

$$
\begin{aligned}
\Gamma = \{ \Delta_1 &= (\uparrow 0.7 : p_1), \\
\Delta_2 &= (\uparrow 0.6 : p_3), \\
\Delta_3 &= (\uparrow 0.8 : p_6), \\
\Delta_4 &= (((\downarrow 0.2 : p_1 \wedge \downarrow 0.1 : p_2) \vee \downarrow 0.15 : p_3) \vee \\
&\quad ((\downarrow 0.25 : p_4 \vee \downarrow 0.4 : p_5) \wedge \downarrow 0.2 : p_6) \vee \\
&\quad (\uparrow 0.8 : p_7 \wedge \uparrow 0.7 : p_8)), \\
\Delta_5 &= (\downarrow 0.1 : p_8)\}
\end{aligned}
$$

The formula can be rewritten more intuitively, as a Knowledge Rule-based System (KBRS). Thus, Δ_1 to Δ_3 are the facts, Δ_4 is the unique implication rule and Δ_5 comes from the query. Hence, Δ_4 can be stated as:

$$
\begin{aligned}
(\uparrow 0.2 : p_1 \vee \uparrow 0.1 : p_2) \wedge (\uparrow 0.15 : p_3) \wedge ((\uparrow 0.25 : p_4 \wedge \uparrow 0.4 : p_5) \vee (\uparrow 0.2 : p_6)) \\
\Rightarrow (\uparrow 0.8 : p_7 \wedge \uparrow 0.7 : p_8))
\end{aligned}
$$

It can be checked that Δ_4 is equivalent to 8 regular Horn clauses or what is the same, to 8 simple impicational rules. For instance, two of them are:

$$
\begin{aligned}
&\uparrow 0.2 : p_1 \wedge \uparrow 0.15 : p_3 \wedge \uparrow 0.25 : p_4 \wedge \uparrow 0.4 : p_5 \Rightarrow \uparrow 0.8 : p_7 \\
&\uparrow 0.1 : p_2 \wedge \uparrow 0.15 : p_3 \wedge \uparrow 0.2 : p_6 \Rightarrow \uparrow 0.7 : p_8
\end{aligned}
$$

This simple example shows how our richer language enable to reduce up to an exponential order the size of the KBRS. Later on, we will show that the required time to solve the associated SAT problem can be reduced exponentially also compared to its counterpart clausal regular SAT problem [8,14].

3 Logical Calculus

Here below we give the four inferences rules forming our logical calculus. The first three ones are generalisations of the Regular Unit Resolution (GRUR) to our non-clausal Horn-like language and the fourth one is related to the And-Elimination rule of the Natural Deduction Calculus extended to the Regular language (RAE). Our regular non-clausal unit resolution rules can be seen either as generalisations of the regular clausal unit resolution rule [5,16] or as particular cases of the extension to the regular language of the non-clausal propositional resolution given in [17].

Definition 7. Logical Calculus. *For $i > j$, the inference rules are:*

$$\frac{(\uparrow i : p), ((\downarrow j : p \wedge \downarrow j_1 : p \wedge \ldots \wedge \downarrow j_n : p) \vee C_2^- \vee \ldots \vee C_m^- \vee CNF^- \vee C^+)}{(C_2^- \vee \ldots \vee C_m^- \vee CNF^- \vee C^+)} \; (GRUR1)$$

$$\frac{(\uparrow i : p), (((\downarrow j : p \vee \downarrow j_1 : p \vee \ldots \vee \downarrow j_n : p) \wedge D_2^- \wedge \ldots \wedge D_m^-) \vee DNF^- \vee C^+)}{(((\downarrow j_1 : p \vee \ldots \vee \downarrow j_n : p) \wedge D_2^- \wedge \ldots \wedge D_m^-) \vee DNF^- \vee C^+)} \; (GRUR2)$$

$$\frac{(\uparrow i : p), (((\downarrow j : p) \wedge D_2^- \wedge \ldots \wedge D_m^-) \vee DNF^- \vee C^+)}{(DNF^- \vee C^+)} \; (GRUR3)$$

$$\frac{(\uparrow i_1 : p_1 \wedge \ldots \wedge \uparrow i_j : p_j \wedge \ldots \wedge \uparrow i_n : p_n)}{(\uparrow i_1 : p_1), \ldots, (\uparrow i_j : p_j), \ldots, (\uparrow i_n : p_n)} \; (RAE)$$

As it can be checked, the GRURi rules simplify the sub-formulas because some factors are removed from them. The removals could transform a subformula $\Delta = CNF^- \vee DNF^- \vee C^+$ in a positive formula $\Delta = C^+$. If that happens the RAE rule is applied. In the particular case where $C^+ = \{\}$, the unsatisfiability of the formula is detected.

Theorem 1. Soundness. *GRUR1, GRUR2, GRUR3 and RAE are sound, namely $\Gamma \vdash_{GRURi_{i\in 1,2,3}} \Gamma' \Rightarrow \Gamma \models \Gamma'$ and $\Gamma \vdash_{RAE} \Gamma' \Rightarrow \Gamma \models \Gamma'$.*

Definition 8. Refutation. *A* refutation *of a formula Γ, is a succession of formulas $< \Gamma_1, \Gamma_2, \ldots, \Gamma_n >$ such that $\Gamma_1 = \Gamma, \Gamma_n = \Gamma_\Box$ and for each $1 \leq i \leq n-1$, $\Gamma_{i+1} = \Gamma_i \wedge \Delta_i$ where Δ_i is a subformula deduced by the application of GRUR1, GRUR2 or GRUR3 or a conjunction of unit clauses derived by the application of the RAE inference rule.*

Theorem 2. Refutation Completeness. *Γ is unsatisfiable $\Rightarrow \Gamma \vdash \Gamma_\Box$.*

The next steps of this section intend to show that the Logical Calculus can be rewritten in a more algorithmic way with the twofold advantage:

- there exists an efficient implementation of the Logical Calculus;
- the correctness of the SAT algorithm is strightforward from the correctnes of the Logical Calculus.

Thus, rewriting progressively and appropriately the Logical Calculus, the proof of the correctness of the complex resulting SAT algorithm can be avoided using instead of, the correctness proof of the Logical Calculus which is quite standard and considerably easier.

If some abstraction is introduced in the form of the subformulas appearing in the inference rules, the three GRUR rules can be rewritten in only two rules by merging GRUR1 and GRUR3 in the new GRUR1 rule as follows:

Definition 9. Logical Calculus.

$$(\uparrow i : p), ((\downarrow j : p \wedge \Delta_1) \vee \Delta_2), i > j \vdash_{GUR1} \Delta_2$$
$$(\uparrow i : p), (((\downarrow j : p \vee \Delta_1) \wedge \Delta_2) \vee \Delta_3), i > j \vdash_{GRUR2} ((\Delta_1 \wedge \Delta_2) \vee \Delta_3)$$

Although the Logical Calculus given above is sound and complete, observe that the deduced subformulas should be copied and this provokes a computational cost increasing quadratically with the number of Generalised Unit Resolutions. Thus, the next step trends to formalise the Logical Calculus algorithm by avoiding copies of subformulas. We note by $\Gamma.\{\Delta_1 \leftarrow \Delta_2\}$ the formula resulting of substituting in Γ a subformula Δ_1 by another subformula Δ_2.

Definition 10. Logical calculus.

$$(\uparrow i : p), \Gamma, i > j \vdash_{GUR1} \Gamma.\{(\downarrow j : p \wedge \Delta_1) \vee \Delta_2) \leftarrow \Delta_2\}$$
$$(\uparrow i : p), \Gamma, i > j \vdash_{GUR2} \Gamma.\{(((\downarrow j : p \vee \Delta_1) \wedge \Delta_2) \vee \Delta_3) \leftarrow ((\Delta_1 \wedge \Delta_2) \vee \Delta_3)\}$$

Notice that now the Logical Calculus expressed in the previous format allows to perform the inferences without adding any copy of the subformulas of the original formula. Contrarily to this, one can check that the size of the formula decreases. From a logical point of view, nothing has changed and thus refutation correctness is still warranted by the rewritten calculus.

Looking closer at the previous calculi, one can see that it could be expressed in a more algorithmic. Thus, the next definition of the inference rules is closed on the one hand, to the previous Logical Calculus and on the other hand, to the first description of the SAT algorithm.

Definition 11. Logical calculus. *We note Remove(Γ,Δ) a function that returns the formula Γ after removing its subformula Δ.*

$$(\uparrow i : p), \Gamma, i > j \vdash_{GUR1} \Gamma \leftarrow Remove(\Gamma, (\downarrow j : p \wedge \Delta))$$
$$(\uparrow i : p), \Gamma, i > j \vdash_{GRU2} \Gamma \leftarrow Remove(\Gamma, (\downarrow j : p))$$

Example 2. A proof of the unsatisfiability of the formula in the first example is:

$\Gamma = \{\Delta_1, \Delta_2, \Delta_3, \Delta_4, \Delta_5\} =$
$= \{(\uparrow 0.7 : p_1), \Delta_2, \Delta_3, (((\downarrow 0.2 : p_1 \wedge \downarrow 0.1 : p_2) \vee \downarrow 0.15 : p_3) \vee$
$((\downarrow 0.25 : p_4 \vee \downarrow 0.4 : p_5) \wedge \downarrow 0.2 : p_6) \vee (\uparrow 0.8 : p_7 \wedge \uparrow 0.7 : p_8)), \Delta_5\}$
$\vdash_{GRUR1} \{(\uparrow 0.7 : p_1), \Delta_2, \Delta_3, ((\downarrow 0.15 : p_3) \vee$
$((\downarrow 0.25 : p_4 \vee \downarrow 0.4 : p_5) \wedge \downarrow 0.2 : p_6)) \vee (\uparrow 0.8 : p_7 \wedge \uparrow 0.7 : p_8)), \Delta_5\} =$

$= \{(\uparrow 0.7 : p_1), (\uparrow 0.6 : p_3), \Delta_3, ((\downarrow 0.15 : p_3) \vee$
$((\downarrow 0.25 : p_4 \vee \downarrow 0.4 : p_5) \wedge \downarrow 0.2 : p_6)) \vee (\uparrow 0.8 : p_7 \wedge \uparrow 0.7 : p_8)), \Delta_5\}$
$\vdash_{GRUR2} \{(\uparrow 0.7 : p_1), (\uparrow 0.6 : p_3), \Delta_3,$
$(((\downarrow 0.25 : p_4 \vee \downarrow 0.4 : p_5) \wedge \downarrow 0.2 : p_6) \vee (\uparrow 0.8 : p_7 \wedge \uparrow 0.7 : p_8)), \Delta_5\} =$
$= \{(\uparrow 0.7 : p_1), (\uparrow 0.6 : p_3), (\uparrow 0.8 : p_6),$
$(((\downarrow 0.25 : p_4 \vee \downarrow 0.4 : p_5) \wedge \downarrow 0.2 : p_6) \vee (\uparrow 0.8 : p_7 \wedge \uparrow 0.7 : p_8)), \Delta_5\}$
$\vdash_{GRUR1} \{(\uparrow 0.7 : p_1), (\uparrow 0.6 : p_3), (\uparrow 0.8 : p_6)(\uparrow 0.8 : p_7 \wedge \uparrow 0.7 : p_8), \Delta_5\}$
$\vdash_{RAE} \{(\uparrow 0.7 : p_1), (\uparrow 0.6 : p_3), (\uparrow 0.8 : p_6), (\uparrow 0.8 : p_7), (\uparrow 0.7 : p_8), \Delta_5\}$
$= \{(\uparrow 0.7 : p_1), (\uparrow 0.6 : p_3), (\uparrow 0.8 : p_6), (\uparrow 0.8 : p_7), (\uparrow 0.7 : p_8), (\downarrow 0.1 : p_8)\}$
$\vdash_{GRUR1} \{(\uparrow 0.7 : p_1), (\uparrow 0.6 : p_3), (\uparrow 0.8 : p_6), (\uparrow 0.8 : p_7), (\uparrow 0.7 : p_8), (\downarrow 0.1 : p_8), \Box\}$
$= \Gamma_{\Box}$

4 Algorithm Description

When the formula Γ has no positive subformulas then Γ is trivially satisfiable. So assume that some positive subformulas C^+ are present in Γ. Thus, applying the RAE rule over the positive subformulas C^+ in Γ produces positive literals $(\uparrow j : p)$. Then, this leads to the statement that the formula Γ is satisfiable or otherwise, some unit positive literals can be deduced. Thus, the next step is to apply the GRURi inference rules with the unit formulas. This process is repeated until no more unit formulas are generated, or an empty clause is produced. In the first case, the formula is satisfiable and in the second unsatisfiable.

The principle of the algorithm is the following. First the regular literals in the unit formulas are pushed in a stack (function $ApplyRAE(\Gamma, Stack)$). For each regular literal in the Stack, the GRURi rules are applied iteratively (*While* loop). If as a consequence of the GRURi applications some subformulas become positive conjunctions, the RAE rule is applied adding new literals to the Stack. The process finishes when there are no more unit formulas in the stack or when an empty clause is deduced. In the first case, the formula is satisfiable and in the second it is unsatisfiable.

Algorithm 1
Apply-GRURi-RAE(Γ)
1 ApplyRAE(Γ, Stack)
2 While $Stack \neq \{\}$ do:
3 $\quad(\uparrow i : p) \leftarrow pop(Stack)$
4 $\quad$Remove all conjunctions $(\downarrow j : p \wedge \Delta)$ s.t. $i > j$ from Γ
5 $\quad$Remove all literals $(\downarrow i : p)$ s.t. $i > j$ from Γ
6 $\quad$ApplyRAE(Γ, Stack)
7 EndWhile
8 If $\{\} \in \Gamma$ then return (UNSAT) else return (SAT)

The lines 4 and 5 are straightforward applications of the GRUR1 and GRUR2 inference rules described in definition 11, and the lines 1 and 6 represent a direct application of the RAE rule defined in 7.

Theorem 3. Correctness. *Alg. 1 returns "UNSAT" iff Γ is unsatisfiable.*

This proof is a direct consequence of the correctness of the Logical Calculus.

The next goal is to optimise the complexity of the algorithm. For this purpose, we need first to precise the data structure.

Data Structure. We note [X] a pointer to the object X. To each proposition, we associate two sets of pointers $Neg.C(p)$ and $Neg.D(p)$. Each element in $Neg.C(p)$ is a list of triplets $(j, [C], [\Delta])$ such that $(\downarrow j : p)$ is a regular literal in the conjunction C of the subformula Δ. Similarly $Neg.D(p)$ stocks triplets $(j, [D], [\Delta])$ corresponding to disjunctions containing a literal $(\downarrow j : p)$.

For each subformula Δ, a counter Counter.DNF(Δ) is provided. Each decrement of Counter.DNF(Δ) represents a removal of a falsified conjunction in Δ.

For each disjunction D^- in the CNF^- terms, a counter Counter(D) is provided. A decrement of Counter(D) indicates the removal of a falsified literal in D^-. If one of these counters is set to 0 means that the whole CNF^- term is falsified.

Remark Notice that we do not need to know which conjunction has been removed, what we need to know is only how many conjunctions have been removed in order to detect when the whole DNF^- term has been removed. Similarly for the removal of literal in disjunctions D^-.

Algorithm 2

Apply-GRURi-RAE(Γ)
1 $\forall(\uparrow k : q) \in C^+ \in \Gamma$ $push((\uparrow k : q), Stack)$
2 While $Stack \neq \{\}$ do:
3 $(\uparrow i : p) \leftarrow pop(Stack)$
4 $\forall(j, [C], [\Delta]) \in Neg.C(p)$ do: If $i > j$ then decrement Counter.DNF(Δ)
5 $\forall(j, [D], [\Delta]) \in Neg.D(p)$ do: If $i > j$ decrement $Counter(D, \Delta)$
6 $\forall(j, [D], [\Delta]) \in Neg.D(p)$ do:
7 If $Counter(D, \Delta) = 0$ and $Counter.DNF(\Delta) = 0$ then:
8 $\forall(\uparrow k : q) \in C^+ \in \Gamma$ do: $push((\uparrow k : q), Stack)$
9 Endwhile
10 If $\{\} \in \Gamma$ then return(UNSAT) Else return(SAT)

Remark. For reasons of clarity, in the design of the algorithm we have assumed that the CNF^- term of each subformula Δ exists. The consideration of other cases is a mere question of implementation details regarding only line 6.

It can be proved that the complexity of the algorithm is quadratic, but the algorithm is not correct yet. Actually, each decrement of the Counter.DNF(Δ) must correspond to the falsification of one conjunct of the DNF^- term. This counter should be set to 0 only when all the conjuncts are falsified. However, in the previous algorithm the deduction of n literals that could belong to a same conjunct of the DNF^- term implies n decrements of Counter.DNF(Δ). Thus, the counter could be set to 0, indicating that the DNF^- term has been removed, without having falsified all the conjuncts in the DNF^-.

To overcome this problem we use a flag call First(C) for each conjunct C^- in the DNF^-. This flag is set to True initially and after the first falsification of a literal in C^-, the flag is set to False. In this way, only one decrement of Counter.DNF for each conjunct C^- in DNF^- is allowed.

Thus, to correct the previous algorithm only its line 4 should be changed including the test of the flag First(C) as follows:

4 $\forall(j, [C], [\Delta]) \in Neg.C(p)$ do:
    If $i > j$ and First(C)= True
    then decrement Counter.DNF(Δ)
        First(C) $\leftarrow$ False

Now, we can ensure the correctness of the algorithm.

Theorem 4. Correctness. *The algorithm Apply-RURi-RAE(Γ) returns "UN-SAT" iff Γ is satisfiable.*

The proof is a consequence of the correctness of the algorithm 1 that in turn is a consequence of the soundness and completeness of the Logical Calculus.

Concerning the algorithms' complexity, the last algorithm is of course more efficient than the previous one, but nevertheless, it is still quadratic.

Theorem 5. *The complexity of the previous procedure is in $O(k \cdot m)$, where k is the maximum number of subformulas including positive literals ($\uparrow i : p$) with the same proposition p and m is the maximum number of subformulas sharing negative literals ($\downarrow j : p$) with the same proposition p.*

5 An Almost Linear Algorithm

The aim of the following optimisation is to design a strictly linear main procedure. The non-linear complexity factor will be confined to only the Pre-process step.

Ordering $Neg.C(p)$ and $Neg.D(p)$. Once the $Neg.C(p)$ lists are obtained, we sort them based on the i value from each pair ($\downarrow i : p$) and in ascending order. This is done with a call to the well known procedure MergeSort, namely $Neg.C(p) \leftarrow MergeSort(Neg.C(p))$. An identical process is made with the $Neg.D(p)$ list. Once the $Neg.C(p)$ and $Neg.D(p)$ lists are ordered, the removals of subformulas can be performed in a more efficient way.

When a multi-valued literal ($\downarrow i : p$) is deduced, the first pointer $(j, [C^-][\Delta])$ to a subformula Δ in $Neg.C(p)$ is considered checking whether $i > j$. In the affirmative case, the pointer is removed from $Neg.C(p)$, the counter decrements are executed and the same check is carried out with the second clause pointer in $Neg.C(p)$.

Apply-GRURi-RAE(Γ)
1 **Initialization(Γ)**
2 While $Stack \neq \{\}$ do:

3 $(\uparrow i : p) \leftarrow pop(Stack)$
4 **while** $i > Val(First.conjunction(Neg.C(p)))$ and First(C)=True **do:**
Remove $First.conjunction(Neg.C(p))$ from Neg.C(p)
Decrement Counter.DNF(Δ)
First(C) $\leftarrow$ False
5 **while** $i > Val(First.disjunction(Neg.D(p)))$ **do:**
Remove $First.disjunction(Neg.D(p))$ from Neg.D(p)
Decrement $Counter(D, \Delta)$
6 If $Counter(D, \Delta) = 0$ and $Counter.DNF(\Delta) = 0$ then:
7 $\forall (\uparrow k : q) \in C^{+} \in \Gamma$ $push((\uparrow k : q), Stack)$
8 Endwhile
9 If $\{\} \in \Gamma$ return(UNSAT) else return(SAT)

These operations are repeated till a certain check is negative and at that moment, the removal of pointers from $Neg.C(p)$ is stopped. This process ensures that the list $Neg.C(p)$ is revised at most once. Identical process for the list $Neg.D(p)$ is performed.

The definitive algorithm is given avove.

The correctness of this algorithm follows directly from that of the previous algorithm.

The Initialisation algorithm is not given because it does not present any particular difficulty: it only initialises the mentioned data structure to be used by the main procedure. The only point to be stressed is that its complexity is in $O(n \cdot log(m))$ which is the worst case complexity of the well-known algorithm MergeSort which is required to have initially ordered the lists $Neg.C(p)$ and $Neg.D(p)$.

Theorem 6. *The complexity of the main procedure is in $O(n)$.*

The proof follows from the previous explained optimisations of the steps of this procedure.

Thus, the main procedure is strictly linear and the non-linear factor has been confined only to the initialization step.

6 Related Work

We review successively the main works concerning non-clausal tractability and many-valued tractability.

Non-clausal Tractability. Tractability has attracted much attention, specially in classical logic. As far as we know, the first published results concerning non-clausal tractability comes from [6,7,10] where a strictly linear bottom-up algorithm to test the satisfiability of a subclass of non-clausal formulas is detailed. Such a class embeds the Horn case as a particular case. In [11] a linear top-down algorithm is given for the same non-clausal subclass of formulas.

New results concerning non-clausal tractability are reported in [18] where a method called Restricted Fact Propagation is presented which is a quadratic, incomplete non-clausal inference procedure.

More recently, in [19,20] a significant advance in non-clausal tractability has been accomplished. The author defines a class of formulas by extending the Horn formulas to the field of non-clausal formulas. Such extension relies on the concept of polarity. In [19], a SLD-resolution variant with the property of being refutationally complete is showed, although its computational complexity is not studied. In [20] a method for propositional and some many-valued non-clausal Horn-like formulas is described and it is stated that the method is sound, incomplete and linear. However, concerning the last issue, no algorithm is specified, indeed the steps of the method are described as different propagations of some truth values in a sparse tree. Then, although it seems that the number of inferences of the proposed method is linear, it is not proved the resulting complexity (w.r.t. the number of computer instructions) of a linear number of truth value propagations on the employed sparse trees.

In [1,4,3] some non-clausal SAT problems are proved to be strictly linear. These linearities are proved providing complete logical calculi and correct linear algorithms.

Many-valued tractability. The earliest work on this topic is due to [8] where the SAT problem and other related problems for a sub-class of the Horn regular logic is proved to be almost linear. In [14] the regular Horn problem is proved to be also almost linear. Then, in [9] the 2-SAT problem is analysed proving that the regular 2-SAT and the special case of the signed 2-SAT in which all the signs are singletons are polynomial ones. In [5] the regular Horn SAT problem where the truth values form a finite lattice is proved to be polynomial.

In [20] the first many-valued non-clausal SAT problem that can be determined in polynomial time has been defined. Recently, another many-valued non-clausal SAT problem with a polynomial complexity has been identified [2]. The many-valued logic and the non-clausal form studied there are sub-cases respectively of the non-clausal form and the regular logic analysed in this paper.

7 Conclusions

Advances in the efficient solution of the many-valued SAT problem have important repercussions in many areas of Computer Science. In this paper we have proved that some non-clausal many-valued SAT problems can be solved efficiently in $O(n{\cdot}log(n))$ time. Thus we have generalised some existing results about clausal tractability to the more general non-clausal framework. The non-clausal formulas considered here could be of significant interest in applications because of they present a Horn-like structure. An important advantage of the proposed method is that it does not need to transform the original formula. Indeed, it processes the original formula preserving in this way all its logical properties contrarily to what happens when the formula is transformed to clausal forms by introducing artificial literals.

Acknowledgements This work was developed under a bilateral collaboration between the IIIA-CSIC and the CINVESTAV-CONACYT and was partially financed by the Universidad Autónoma de Guerrero (Mexico) and the Spanish MCyT project with reference BFM2000-1054-C02. Some modifications asked by the constructive comments of the anonymous referees could not be inserted only by lack of space.

References

1. E. Altamirano and G. Escalada-Imaz. Algoritmos óptimos para algunas teorías de Horn factorizadas. In *II Congrés Català d'Intel-ligència Artificial*, CCIA'99, pages 31–38, Girona, Spain, october 1999.
2. E. Altamirano and G. Escalada-Imaz. An almost linear class of multiple-valued non-clausal Horn formulas. In *X Congreso Español sobre Tecnologías y Lógica Fuzzy*, ESTYLF'00, pages 145–150, Sevilla, Spain, September 2000.
3. E. Altamirano and G. Escalada-Imaz. An efficient proof method for non-clausal reasoning. In *XII International Symposium on Methodologies for Intelligent Systems*, volume 1932 of *LNAI*, pages 534–542, Charlotte, USA, October 2000. Springer-Verlag.
4. E. Altamirano and G. Escalada-Imaz. Finding tractable formulas in NNF. In *I International Conference on Computational Logic*, volume 1861 of *LNAI*, pages 493–507, London, UK, July 2000. Springer-Verlag.
5. B. Beckert, R. Hähnle, and F. Manya. Transformations between signed and classical clause logic. In *Proc. Int. Symp. on Multiple Valued Logics, ISMVL'99*, Freiburg, Germany, 1999.
6. G. Escalada-Imaz. Moteurs d'Inférence Lineaires en Chaînage-Avant pour une classe de Systèmes de Règles. Technical Report LAAS-89172, Laboratoire D'Automatique et Analyse des Systemes, Toulouse, France, 1989.
7. G. Escalada-Imaz. *Optimisation d'algorithmes d'inference monotone en logique des propositions et du premier ordre.* PhD thesis, Université Paul Sabatier, Toulouse, France, 1989.
8. G. Escalada-Imaz and F. Manya. The satisfiability problem for multiple-valued horn formulae. In *Proc. International Symposium on Multiple-Valued Logics, ISMVL'94*, pages 250–256, Boston/MA, USA, 1994. IEEE Press, Los Alamitos.
9. G. Escalada-Imaz and F. Manya. On the 2-SAT problem for signed formulas. In *Proc. Workshop/Conference on Many-Valued Logics for Computer Science Applications, COST Action 15.*, Barcelona, Spain, 1996.
10. G. Escalada-Imaz and A.M. Martínez-Enríquez. Motores de Inferencia de Complejidad Optima de encadenamiento hacia adelante para diversas clases de sistemas de reglas. *Informática y Automática*, 27(3):23–30, 1994.
11. M. Ghallab and G. Escalada-Imaz. A linear control algorithm for a class of rule-based systems. *Journal of Logic Programming*, (11):117–132, 1991.
12. R. Hähnle. *Automated deduction in multiple-valued logics*, volume 10 of *International Series of Monographs in Computer Sciences.* Oxford University Press, 1993.
13. R. Hähnle. Short conjunctive normal forms in finitely-valued logics. *Journal of Logic and Computation*, 4(6):905–927, 1994.
14. R. Hähnle. Exploiting data dependencies in many-valued logics. *Journal of Applied Non-classical Logics*, (6):49–69, 1996.

15. R. Hahnle and G. Escalada-Imaz. Deduction in many-valued logics: A survey. *Mathware and Soft Computing*, 4(2):69–97, 1997.
16. F. Manya. *Proof Procedures for Multiple-Valued Propositional Logics*. PhD thesis, Universidad Autónoma de Barcelona, 1996.
17. N.V. Murray. Completely Non-Clausal Theorem Proving. *Artificial Intelligence*, 18(1):67–85, 1982.
18. R. Roy-Chowdhury-Dalal. Model theoretic semantics and tractable algorithm for CNF-BCP. In *Proc. of the AAAI-97*, pages 227–232, 1997.
19. Z. Stachniak. Non-clausal reasoning with propositional definite theories. In *International Conferences on Artificial Intelligence and Symbolic Computation*, volume 1476 of *Lecture Notes in Computer Science*, pages 296–307. Springer Verlag, 1998.
20. Z. Stachniak. Polarity guided tractable reasoning. In *International American Association on Artificial Intelligence, AAAI-99*, pages 751–758, 1999.

A Genetic Algorithm for Satisfiability Problem in a Probabilistic Logic: A First Report

Zoran Ognjanović, Jozef Kratica, and Miloš Milovanović

Matematički Institut
Kneza Mihaila 35, 11000 Beograd, Yugoslavia
zorano@mi.sanu.ac.yu jkratica@mi.sanu.ac.yu

Abstract. This paper introduces a genetic algorithm for satisfiability problem in a probabilistic logic. A local search based improvement procedure is integrated in the algorithm. A test methodology is presented and some results are given. The results indicate that this approach could work well. Some directions for further research are described.

1 Introduction

Probabilistic logics are used to reason about uncertainty expressed in terms of probability. Since the paper [19] many such logics have been developed (see [6, 7,20,21,22], and the references given therein). In those logics classical propositional language is expanded by expressions that speak about probability, while formulas remain true or false. Some of the logics allow making statements about higher order probabilities [7,21], while in the other [6,20,21] only probabilities of classical formulas can be expressed. In this paper we consider a logic of the later type which is the probabilistic logic about measurable events from [6]. A sound and complete axiomatization and a decision procedure for satisfiability problem are given there (see also [20,21] for an alternative approach). Satisfiability of a probabilistic formula can be reduced to linear programming problem. However, the number of variables in the linear system corresponding to a formula is exponential in the number of primitive propositions from the formula. It makes any standard linear system solving procedure (Fourier-Motzkin elimination, for example) not suitable in practice when scaling up to larger formulas. That statement was already argued, for example in [8] where a procedure for probabilistic deduction which can be stopped at any time to yield partial information was suggested.

Genetic algorithms (GA, for short) are general problem solving methods inspired by processes of natural evolution. First GA's appeared in early 1970s and were rigorously stated in [13]. GA's can be applied in many areas [2,10]. For example, GA's are used to solve SAT, satisfiability problem for classical propositional logic (see [1,5,18], and the references given therein) which is an NP-complete problem. We note that pure GA's are incomplete procedures for SAT. It is customary to combine GA's with some heuristic procedures to obtain more powerful (but still incomplete) methods. Such an integration of a local search procedure into a GA for SAT is presented in [17].

S. Benferhat and P. Besnard (Eds.): ECSQARU 2001, LNAI 2143, pp. 805–816, 2001.

In this paper we try to apply similar ideas to attack satisfiability problem for the mentioned probabilistic logic which is also NP-complete [6]. We describe here the first step in developing of a satisfiability checker for the probabilistic logic based on the GA-approach as well as on a heuristic procedure for local search. If the checker finds that a formula is satisfiable, it also gives an actual model in which the formula holds. Our aim is to obtain an efficient checker. Thus, even if the underline procedure is semi decidable, it may still be preferable to a slow decision procedure which guarantees to find a solution if one exists. We use a set of formulas that are known to be satisfiable and measure the performance of the algorithm by the percentage of solved formulas.

The rest of the paper is organized as follows. In Section 2 we give a brief description of the mentioned probabilistic logic. In Section 3 the paradigm of GA's is presented, while in Section 4 we summarize how the general GA-approach is adapted to check satisfiability in the probabilistic logic. Section 5 contains some experimental results. We give concluding remarks and directions for further investigations in Section 6.

2 Probabilistic Logic

Starting from the set $\phi = \{p, q, r, \ldots\}$ of primitive propositions the set of classical propositional formulas is obtained in the usual way. We use α, β, ..., to denote classical propositional formulas. A literal is a primitive proposition or a negation of a primitive proposition. A weight term is an expression of the form $a_1 w(\alpha_1) + \ldots + a_n w(\alpha_n)$, where a_i's are rational numbers, and α_i's are classical propositional formulas. The intended meaning of $w(\alpha)$ is probability of α. A basic weight formula has the form $t \geq c$, where t is a weight term, and c is a rational number. Finally, the set of all weight formulas contains all basic weight formulas, and it is closed under Boolean operations. We use f, g, ..., to denote weight formulas. The other forms of weight formulas can be defined as abbreviations. For example, $(t < c) \stackrel{\text{def}}{=} \neg(t \geq c)$. An expression of the form $t \geq c$ or $t < c$ is called a weight literal.

Let α be a classical propositional formula and $\{p_1, \ldots, p_k\}$ be the set of all primitive propositions that appear in α. An atom of α is defined as a formula $at = \pm p_1 \wedge \ldots \wedge \pm p_k$ where $\pm p_i$ is used to denote either p_i or $\neg p_i$. There are 2^k different atoms of a formula containing k primitive propositions. Let At denote the set $\{at_1, \ldots, at_{2^k}\}$ of all atoms of α. Every classical propositional formula α is equivalent to formulas DNF(α) and CDNF$(\alpha) = \vee_{i=1}^{m} at_i$, called disjunctive normal form and complete disjunctive normal form of α, respectively. We use $at \in$ CDNF(α) to denote that the atom at appears in CDNF(α).

Semantics of the logic is given using models similar to Kripke models. That allows that probability formulas are not truth-functional, i.e., that $w(\alpha) \geq c$ is not equivalent to any truth-function of α.

Definition 1. *A probabilistic model is a structure $M = \langle W, H, \mu, v \rangle$ where:*

- *W is a set of elements called worlds,*

- *H is a σ-algebra of subsets of W,*
- *$\mu : H \to [0,1]$ is a σ-additive probabilistic measure, and*
- *$v : W \times \phi \to \{\top, \bot\}$ is a valuation which associated with every world $w \in W$ a truth assignment $v(w)$ on the primitive propositions.*

The valuation v is extended to a truth assignment on all classical propositional formulas. Let $M = \langle W, H, \mu, v \rangle$ and α be a probabilistic model and a classical formula, respectively. The set $\{w \in W : v(w)(\alpha) = \top\}$ is denoted by $[\alpha]_M$. A probabilistic model M is measurable if H contains sets of the form $[\alpha]_M$ only, i.e., if $[\alpha]_M$ is measurable for every classical formula α and only sets of worlds definable by classical formulas are measurable. In the sequel we shall consider the class of all measurable probabilistic models, and omit the word measurable.

Definition 2. *The satisfiability relation $\models$ fulfills the following conditions for every probabilistic model $M = \langle W, H, \mu, v \rangle$:*

1. *if α is a classical formula, $M \models \alpha$ if for every world $w \in W$, $v(w)(\alpha) = \top$,*
2. *$M \models a_1 w(\alpha_1) + \ldots + a_n w(\alpha_n) \geq c$ if $\sum_{i=1}^{n} a_i \mu([\alpha_i]_M) \geq c$,*
3. *for every weight formula f, $M \models \neg f$ if $M \not\models f$, and*
4. *for all weight formulas f, and g, $M \models f \wedge g$ if $M \models f$, and $M \models g$.*

A set of formulas is satisfiable if there is a probabilistic model M such that $M \models A$ for every formula A from the set. A formula A is satisfiable if the set $\{A\}$ is, while A is valid if for every probabilistic model M, $M \models A$. Every weight formula f is equivalent to a disjunctive normal form

$$\mathrm{DNF}(f) = \bigvee_{i=1}^{m} \bigwedge_{j=1}^{k_i} (a_1^{i,j} w(\alpha_1^{i,j}) + \ldots + a_{n_{i,j}}^{i,j} w(\alpha_{n_{i,j}}^{i,j}) \ \rho_i \ c_{i,j}) \tag{1}$$

where disjuncts are conjunctions of weight literals, and ρ_i is either $\geq$ or $<$. Thus, f is satisfiable iff at least one such conjunction of weight literals is satisfiable. Note that f can be transformed to DNF(f) in polynomial time. We say that a formula f is in the weight conjunctive form (wfc-form, for short) if it is a conjunction of weight literals. Now, Probabilistic Satisfiability Problem (PrSAT, for short) is the following problem: given a formula f in wfc-form, is it satisfiable?

It is proved that PrSAT is decidable [6]. The main idea of the proof is that PrSAT can be reduced to linear programming problem. Namely, every weight formula f in wfc-form can be transformed to a system of linear equalities and inequalities containing:

$$\sum_{at \in \mathrm{At}(f)} \mu(at) = 1$$
$$\mu(at) \geq 0, \text{ for every } at \in \mathrm{At}(f),$$

as well as an inequality of the form

$$a_1 \sum_{at \in \mathrm{CDNF}(\alpha_1)} \mu(at) + \ldots + a_n \sum_{at \in \mathrm{CDNF}(\alpha_n)} \mu(at) \ \rho \ c$$

for every weight literal $a_1 w(\alpha_1) + \ldots + a_n w(\alpha_n)\ \rho\ c$ which appears in f such that f is satisfiable iff the system is. Note that any solution of the system defines a probability distribution over the set of atoms $\mathrm{At}(f)$. It is enough to guarantee that the probabilistic model whose worlds are identified with atoms from $\mathrm{At}(f)$ that hold in the worlds is measurable. In [6] it is proved even more, i.e., that PrSAT is NP-complete. That follows from the statement that a system of L linear equalities and inequalities has a nonnegative solution if it has a nonnegative solution with at most L entries positive such that the sizes of entries are bounded by a polynomial function of the size of the longest coefficient from the system.

3 Genetic Algorithms

GA's use populations of individuals. Each individual (also called chromosome) is seen as a possible solution in the search space for the particular problem. Thus, a GA can be seen as a searching procedure for the global optima of the corresponding problem. Individuals are represented by genetic code over a finite alphabet. An evaluation function assigning fitness values to individuals has to be defined. Fitness values indicate quality of the corresponding individuals, while average fitness of entire populations may be good measures of obtained quality of the procedures. GA's consist of applications of the genetic operators to populations that must ensure that average fitness values are continually improved from each generation to subsequent. Basic genetic operators are selection, crossover and mutation, but some additional operators such as inversion, local search, etc., may be used.

Selection mechanism favourizes highly fitted individuals (as well as parts of genetic code of individuals, i.e. genes) to have better chances for reproduction into next generations. On the other hand, chances for reproduction for less fitted members are reduced, and they are gradually wiped out from populations. Crossover operator partitions a population into a set of pairs of individuals named parents. For each pair a recombination of their genetic material is performed with some probability. In that way nondeterministic exchange of genetic material in populations is obtained. Multiple usage of selection and crossover operators may produce that the variety of genetic materials is lost. It means that some areas of search spaces become not reachable. This usually causes the convergence in local optimums far from the global optimal values. Mutation operator can help to avoid this shortcoming. Parts of individuals (genes) can be changed with some small probability to increase diversibility of genetic material. An initial population is usually generated by random, although sometimes it may be fully or partially produced by an initial heuristic. A general description of GA's is given in Figure 1, where N_{pop} and p_i denote the number of individuals and their objective values, respectively. The objective value of an individual corresponds to the value which the individual owns in the case of the considered problem. The for-loop is repeated until a finishing criterion (the global optima is found, the maximal number of iterations is reached, ...) is satisfied. Since the procedure is not complete, if the maximal number of iterations is reached, we do not know whether the considered problem is solvable. HeuristicImprovement() can be optionally included to improve efficiency of GA and/or to help the procedure to escape from local optima.

```
InputData();
PopulationInit();
while ( not FinishedGA() ) {
      for ( i = 0 ; i < N_pop ; i++) p_i = ObjectiveFunction();
      HeuristicImprovement();
      ComputeFitnesses();
      Selection();
      Crossover();
      Mutation();
}
OutputResults();
```

Fig. 1. A general description of GA's

The idea of caching is used to avoid permanent attempts to compute the same objective value [15]. It is especially important when computing is time expensive. If the value of an individual has to be computed, and it is already cached, we just read it from the cache. In this paper a simple but efficient strategy called Least Recently Used (LRU) strategy for caching is used. It is implemented by a hash-queue data structure which saves the individuals and the corresponding values. The queue size is a parameter which depends on memory size and other performance constraints. A basic description of LRU is given in Figure 2. It can bee seen that after LRU caches a value, the value cannot be removed until all other values in the cache have been used more recently. LRU replaces ObjectiveFunction() from Figure 1.

```
if Belong( individual, CacheMemory ) SetValue( individual, CacheBlock );
else {
  p_i = ObjectiveFunction();
  if Full( CacheMemory ) Remove( CacheMemory, LRUCacheBlock );
  Put( CacheMemory, p_i );
}
```

Fig. 2. Description of LRU strategy

4 A Genetic Algorithm for PrSAT

We have implemented our GA for PrSAT on top of a program which is a general GA's simulator [16]. The input of the program is a weight formula f in wfc-form with L weight literals of the form $t_i \rho c_i$. Without loss of generality, we demand that classical formulas appearing in weight terms are in disjunctive normal form. Let $\phi(f) = \{p_1, \ldots, p_N\}$ denote the set of all primitive propositions from f, and $|\phi(f)| = N$. Recall that our goal is to find a probabilistic model M such that $M \models f$. As we already noted, that model can be described as a probability distribution defined over the set of atoms $\mathrm{At}(f)$.

An individual M from the population consists of L pairs of the form (atom, probability) that describe a probabilistic model. The first coordinate is given as a bit string of length N, where 0 at the position i denotes $\neg p_i$, while 1 denotes p_i. The second coordinate is a floating point number representing the probability of the corresponding atom. The internal representation of an individual is a bit string obtained by concatenation of the mentioned pairs.

We define two evaluation functions that rank individuals. The first function (t) gives the total number of weight literals in f that are true for an individual M. If $t(M)$ is equal to L, the individual M is a solution. The second function (d) measures a degree of unsatisfiability of an individual M. The degree is defined as the distance between left side values of the weight literals of the form $a_1^i w(\alpha_1^i) + \ldots + a_{n_i}^i w(\alpha_{n_i}^i)\ \rho_i\ c_i$ that are not satisfied in the model described by an individual M, and the corresponding right side values:

$$d(M) = \sqrt{\sum_{M \not\models t_i\ \rho_i\ c_i} (a_1^i \sum_{at \in \mathrm{CDNF}(\alpha_1^i)} \mu(at) + \ldots + a_{n_i}^i \sum_{at \in \mathrm{CDNF}(\alpha_{n_i}^i)} \mu(at) - c_i)^2}.$$

Our program allows that the size of a population, and the types of genetic operators and the corresponding probabilities, etc. can be given as input parameters. The main features of our GA are as follows:

- the population consists of 10 individuals,
- selection is performed using the rank-based operator, with the rank from 2.5 for the best individual to 1.6 for the worst individual (the step is 0.1),
- the crossover operator is one-point, with the probability 0.85,
- the simple mutation operator is used with the probability 0.03,
- the elitist strategy with one elite individual is used in the generation replacement scheme,
- multiple occurrences of an individual is removed from the population,
- as an additional finishing criterion a measure of population homogenity is used, and when that measure exceeds, the trial is finished, and
- the LRU strategy with the buffer containing at most 5000 individuals is used for caching.

The initial population can be generated in one of the following ways:

- randomly or
- for each individual ith atom is chosen such that it satisfies at least one classical formula appearing in ith weight literal.

We use local search as a HeuristicImprovement() procedure in our GA. It consists of the following steps:

- for an individual M all the weight literals are divided into two sets; the first set (denoted B) contains all satisfied formulas, while the second one (denoted W) contains all the remained formulas,
- from the set B the formula $t_B\ \rho_B\ c_B$ (called the best one) with the biggest difference $|\mu(t_B) - c_B|$ between the left and the right side is found,
- similarly, from the set W the formula $t_W\ \rho_W\ c_W$ (the worst one) with the biggest difference $|\mu(t_W) - c_W|$ is found,
- two sets of atoms are determined; the first set $B_{\mathrm{At}(f)}$ contains all the atoms from M satisfying at least one classical formula α_i^B from $t_B = a_1^B w(\alpha_1^B) + \ldots + a_n^B w(\alpha_k^B)$, while the second one $W_{\mathrm{At}(f)}$ contains all the atoms from M satisfying at least one classical formula α_i^W from $t_W = a_1^W w(\alpha_1^W) + \ldots + a_n^W w(\alpha_k^W)$,
- the probabilities of atoms from $B_{\mathrm{At}(f)} \setminus W_{\mathrm{At}(f)}$ are changed such that $t_B\ \rho_B\ c_B$ remains satisfied, although the distance $|\mu(t_B) - c_B|$ is decreased, and
- the probabilities of atoms from $W_{\mathrm{At}(f)} \setminus B_{\mathrm{At}(f)}$ are changed trying to satisfy $t_W\ \rho_W\ c_W$.

We have experimented with the following choices in the above local search procedure:

1. probabilities of only one atom from $B_{\mathrm{At}(f)} \setminus W_{\mathrm{At}(f)}$ and only one atom from $W_{\mathrm{At}(f)} \setminus B_{\mathrm{At}(f)}$ are changed,
2. probabilities of all atoms from $B_{\mathrm{At}(f)} \setminus W_{\mathrm{At}(f)}$ and all atoms from $W_{\mathrm{At}(f)} \setminus B_{\mathrm{At}(f)}$ arc changed,
3. the procedure is applied on the best individual M only,
4. the procedure is applied on all individuals from the population,
5. the procedure is performed only once, and
6. the procedure is repeated until no improvement of degrees of unsatisfiability is obtained.

As a starting point of our work, a program which randomly generates satisfiable weight formulas in wfc-form (with classical formulas in disjunctive normal form) was developed. It allows us to measure the success rate of the algorithm, i.e. the percentage of solved problem instances. The corresponding input parameters are: an integer used as a seed for initialization of the random number generator, the number of primitive propositions N, the number of atoms L, the maximal number S of summands in weight terms, and the maximal number D of disjuncts in disjunctive normal forms of classical formulas appearing in weight terms.

Two kinds of the problem instances are generated. In the first one, having the above parameters, the program randomly generated L atoms and their probabilities (with the constraint that the sum of probabilities must be equal to 1) representing a model M. Next, a weight formula f containing L basic weight formulas is generated. It contains primitive propositions from the set $\{p_1, \ldots, p_N\}$ only. Every weight literal contains at most S summands in its weight term. Every classical formula is in disjunctive normal form with at most D disjuncts, while every disjunct is a conjunction of at most N literals. For every weight term coefficients are chosen, and the probability of the weight term is computed. Next, the sum $sp(t)$ of positive coefficients and the sum $sn(t)$ of negative coefficients are computed. Finally, the right side value of the weight literals between $sp(t)$ and $sn(t)$, and the relation sign are chosen such that $M \models f$. In the second kind of the problem instances, there is an additional parameter δ. For every weight term t the probability $\mu_M(t)$ is computed. A lower and a upper bound ($lb(t) = \mu_M(t) - \delta$ and $ub(t) = \mu_M(t) + \delta$) of the probability of t are chosen, and two basic weight formulas of form $t \geq lb(t)$ and $t \leq up(t)$ are produced. In that way a weight formula with $2L$ basic weight formulas is obtained.

A description of our file format for PrSAT problems as well as the problem generator and used problem instances can be found at *www.mi.sanu.ac.yu/˜zorano/prsat/prsat.html*.

5 Experimental Results

All of our experiments were done under Linux operating system running on IBM-PC compatible computers with an Intel processor (Pentium III/800MHz), and 256MB of RAM. The 10 problem instances of the first kind were generated for $N = 15$ and $L = 15$, $N = 15$ and $L = 30$, $N = 30$ and $L = 30$, $N = 30$ and $L = 60$, and $N = 60$ and $L = 60$. For every instance $S = 5$, and $D = 5$. For every fixed combination of N and L there were 2 different instances numbered from 1 (for $N = 15$ and $L = 15$) to 10 (for $N = 60$ and $L = 60$). Also, the 3 problem instances of the second kind were generated for $N = 15$ and $2L = 16$, $N = 15$ and $2L = 30$, and $N = 30$ and $2L = 30$, numbered from 11 to 13. In those instances $\delta = 0.1$.

We investigated several variants of our algorithm. They differ in the mutation probability and the type of the applied local search procedure. Abbreviations of the various tested variants of our GA, as well as the corresponding parameters, are given in Table 1. '2, random' in the column 'local search procedure, atoms' means that the probabilities of only one randomly chosen atom from $B_{\mathrm{At}(f)} \setminus W_{\mathrm{At}(f)}$ and only one randomly chosen atom from $W_{\mathrm{At}(f)} \setminus B_{\mathrm{At}(f)}$ are changed. 'repeat' in the column 'local search procedure, performed' means that the procedure is repeated until no improvement of degrees of unsatisfiability is obtained. Since the number of trials required to find a solution can vary, all the presented results represent data average over 5 independent trials. The maximal number of generations was set to be 2000. The results are summarized in tables 2 and 3.

Table 2 contains results for the first set of the problem instances (numbered 1 to 10), and Table 3 contains results for the second set of the problem instances (numbered 11 to 13). Each table entry contains the number of successful trials (if it is not 5), the average number of generations and the average running time (in seconds) in trials where a solution was found.

Comparing the performance of the variants shows that the algorithm based on the local search procedure without the mutation operator give the worst results.

Table 1. Parameters of the tested variants of GA

	mutation	initial population	local search procedure individual(s)	atoms	performed
GA	+	random	not applied		
CHAAR	+	chosen	all	all	repeat
CHRA	+	chosen	all	2, random	only once
CHAA	+	chosen	all	all	only once
CHRAR	+	chosen	all	2, random	repeat
RHAAR	+	random	all	all	repeat
RHRA	+	random	all	2, random	only once
RHAA	+	random	all	all	only once
RHRAR	+	random	all	2, random	repeat
RHBA	+	random	the best one	all	only once
CHBA	+	chosen	the best one	all	only once
RHBR	+	random	the best one	2, random	only once
CHBR	+	chosen	the best one	2, random	only once
RHBAR	+	random	the best one	all	repeat
CHBAR	+	chosen	the best one	all	repeat
RHBRR	+	random	the best one	2, random	repeat
CHBRR	+	chosen	the best one	2, random	repeat
RHABRWM	-	random	all	2, random	repeat

Table 2. Results on the first set of problem instances

	1	2	3	4	5	6	7	8	9	10
GA	1/0.01	1/0.01	186/2.81	12/0.22	4/0.19	33/1.6	22/3.87	749/136.6	3/1.71	21/13.57
CHAAR	1/0.14	1/0.19	25/29.56	4/3.77	1/5.68	1/4.75	18/371.7	74/1827,92	1/95,82	1/196,86
CHRA	2/0.03	3/0.04	600/29.97	10/0.6	4/0.5	14/2.27	32/17.88	3/961/581.85	2/3.93	15/30.75
CHAA	1/0.06	1/0.07	88/112.92	4/1.4	4/2/1.12	6/78.5	8/91.72	271/2710.48	1/27.55	4/136.42
CHRAR	2/0.02	2/0.02	197/11.29	9/0.5	5/0.87	6/1.1	30/18.67	3/1088/707.8	2/3.76	8/16.07
RHAAR	1/0.01	51/0.01	40/47.64	4/3.02	1/3.73	3/11.72	7/149.93	30/784.78	1/85.41	1/123.11
RHRAR	1/0.01	1/0.01	205/12.0	8/0.44	2/0.44	12/2.55	17/10.23	3/546/360.14	2/5.2	14/28.74
RHAA	1/0.01	1/0.01	83/27.91	8/2.65	1/1.3	4/5.85	10/124.72	883/9045.75	1/34.84	2/74.55
RHRA	1/0.01	1/0.01	179/8.44	9/0.5	3/0.46	10/1.66	12/6.86	3/269/160.87	2/3.63	11/22.46
RHBA	1/0.01	1/0.01	315/13.77	10/0.65	1/0.16	21/5.0	14/10.61	1/316/422.35	1/2.67	6/22.11
CHBA	3/0.03	4/0.04	298/15.53	14/0.85	4/0.54	66/9.18	24/28.05	3/415/542.12	2.4.6	7/39.98
RHBR	1/0.01	1/0.01	330/6.07	10/0.25	7/0.36	36/2.1	17/3.61	4/980/175.53	2/1.46	22/17.55
CHBR	3/0.02	4/0.02	519/9.61	8/0.18	4/0.23	45/2.65	38/8.17	3/831/185.80	3/2.1	16/12.7
RHBAR	1/0.01	1/0.01	191/10.24	8/0.66	1/0.28	31/10.06	18/19.62	2/740/1341.7	1/7.63	8/61.7
CHBAR	3/0.03	3/0.04	93/4.77	8/0.76	6/1.7	31/9.66	26/30.57	1/664/1004.68	2/17.75	9/75.15
RHBRR	1/0.01	1/0.01	353/6.53	8/0.17	4/0.21	47/2.7	22/4.88	3/237/53.4	2/1.76	22/17.78
CHBRR	2/0.01	4/0.02	263/4.89	14/0.29	5/0.28	17/1.05	30/6.54	803/179.8	3/2.47	19/15.03
RHABRWM	1/0.01	1/0.01	1/21/1.15	4/10/3.98	4/0.61	4/8/1.46	2/45/23.04	0	2/3.64	3/40/76.23

Almost all unsuccessful trials of that variant finish because of the premature convergence (i.e. a high population homogenity is obtained). On the other hand, the pure GA, as well as various combinations of the local search variants and the GA are more successful. An interesting observation is that the success rates in those variants are more or less similar. It means that in almost all cases neither the way in which the initial population is generated nor the chosen variant of the local search procedure influence the results significantly. However, the variants that apply the local search procedure on the best individual only, perform worse than the other variants while solving the problem 8.

Table 3. Results on the second set of problem instances

	11	12	13
GA	236/1.04	3/963/14.66	1/1055/46.51
CHAAR	348/3.36	3/1298/42.49	2/945/91.79
CHRA	230/3.28	1/1681/82.58	3/1557/227.17
CHAA	384/3.7	0	2/880/85.9
CHRAR	286/6.69	3/1063/52.13	1/1359/198.26
RHAAR	182/1.75	3/1104/36.2	3/1246/121.3
RHRAR	318/4.5	3/1430/69.98	3/1293/188.21
RHAA	232/2.25	3/1091/35.66	2/1111/108.33
RHRA	151/2.12	2/1338/64.24	2/1725/252.09
RHBA	174/0.84	2/963/16.37	4/1669/82.26
CHBA	358/1.73	2/1138/19.33	0
RHBR	191/1.01	4/1185/22.1	0
CHBR	287/1.5	3/1250/23.31	2/1411/76.57
RHBAR	364/1.77	2/590/9.87	2/1279/63.22
CHBAR	428/2.08	2/1136/19.18	2/1242/61.55
RHBRR	288/1.52	2/1025/19.01	0
CHBRR	683/3.62	4/1030/19.17	2/1206/65.28
RHABRWM	0	0	0

The pure GA is the fastest variant because it does not contain the local search procedure. However, Table 2 shows that enriching our GA with the local search procedure increases the success rates at the cost of more evaluation. In the column '13' which corresponds to the biggest instance the pure GA have only one success, while the majority of the enriching GA's have better results. We expect that on the larger test cases the difference between those two approaches will be even greater.

6 Conclusion

We have described a genetic algorithm for solving satisfiability problem in a probabilistic logic. Since the problem is NP-complete, we have tried to develop a semi decidable but fast procedure, and to make a tradeoff between completeness and computation time. To the best of our knowledge, this is the first paper which studies PrSAT using such an approach. Although it is clear that far more tests and an exhaustive study should be done, our preliminary results indicates that the genetic approach for PrSAT works well.

Besides testing of numerous problem instances and tuning parameters of the algorithm, there are many other directions for further investigations. In the case of SAT, as a general method for increasing quality of GA's, researchers developed algorithms that redefine their fitness functions while running [1] to guide search in the right directions. It is interesting to see whether such an idea is suitable for PrSAT. Since GA's are semi decidable procedures, we can ask what can we do if we do not know whether a given formula is or is not satisfiable, and a maximal number of generations is reached. One possibility is to decrease the allowed number of steps and to restart the procedure from another random initial point instead of continuing an unsuccessful search. Obviously, the problem is to determine when to restart. It is already reported that in the case of classical propositional formulas in conjunctive normal form, each clause consisting of 3 literals, particularly hard instances for satisfiability problem have a ratio of 4.3 for clause/literals [4]. Although there are more parameters that are important in the case of PrSAT and formulas in wfc-form, it would be interesting to explore whether such an phase transition phenomenon exists there. Also, it must be checked whether our tests generation methodology is fair and adequate.

In summary, we feel that the experimental results reported here are encouraging, and that the future work along these lines should yield new insights into the field of probabilistic satisfiability.

A note added in the proof. We have been informed by the anonymous referee about papers [3,9,12,14]. In [9,12,14] the powerful column generation technique of linear programming were applied to PrSAT (which was denoted by PSAT in those papers). In [3] a version of genetic algorithms was used to calculate intervals of propagated probabilities in causal networks. We plan to consider those results and compare them to ours in a future work.

Acknowledgements. This work was supported by the Ministarstvo za nauku, tehniologiju i razvoj Republike Srbije, through Matematički Institut. We would like to thank to the anonymous referees for their careful reading of the paper and useful comments.

References

1. T. Bäck, A. E. Eiben, and M. E. Vink. A superior evolutionary algorithm for 3-SAT. In *Proc. of the 7th Annual Conference on Evolutionary Programming*, LNCS 1744, 125 – 136, 1998.
2. D. Beasley, D. R. Bull, and R. R. Martin. An Overview of Genetic Algorithms, Part 1: Fundamentals. *University Computing*, Vol. 15, No. 2, pp. 58–69, 1993.
3. A. Cano and S. Moral. A genetic algorithm to approximate convex sets of probabilities. In *Proc. of the IPMU-96*, Vol. 2, 859–864, 1996.
4. P. Cheeseman, B. Kanefsky, and W. M. Taylor. Where the really hard problems are. In *Proc. of the IJCAI-91*. 331–337,1991.
5. K. A. De Jong and W. M. Spears. Using genetic algorithms to solve NP-complete problems. In *3th International Conference on Genetic Algorithms*, 124–132. 1989.
6. R. Fagin, J. Halpern, and N. Megiddo. A logic for reasoning about probabilities. *Information and Computation*, 87:78–128, 1990.
7. R. Fagin and J. Halpern. Reasoning about knowledge and probability. *JACM*, 41(2):340–367, 1994.
8. A. Frish and P. Haddawy. Anytime deduction for probabilistic logic. *Artificial Intelligence*, 69:93–122, 1994.

9. G. Georgakopoulos, D. Kavvadias, and C. Papadimitriou. Probabilistic satisfiability. *Journal of Complexity*, 4(1):1-11, 1988.
10. D. E. Goldberg. Genetic Algorithms in Search, Optimization and Machine Learning. Addison-Weseley Publ. Comp., Reading, Mass., 412p, 1989.
11. J. Y. Halpern. A logical approach to reasoning about uncertainty: A tutorial. In X. Arrazola, K. Korta, and F. J. Pelletier, editors, *Discourse, Interaction, and Communication.* Kluwer, 1997.
12. P. Hansen, B. Jaumard, G.-B. D. Nguetse, and M. P. de Aragao. Models and algorithms for probabilistic and Bayesian logic. In *Proceedings IJCAI-95*, 1862–1868, 1995.
13. J. H. Holland. Adaptation in Natural and Artificial Systems. The University of Michigan Press, Ann Arbor 1975.
14. B. Jaumard, P. Hansen, and M. P. de Aragao. Column generation methods for probabilistic logic. *ORSA Journal on Computing*, 3:135–147, 1991.
15. J. Kratica. Improving Performances of the Genetic Algorithm by Caching. *Computers and Artificial Intelligence*, Vol. 18, No. 3, pp. 271–283, 1999.
16. J. Kratica. Parallelization of Genetic Algorithms for Solving Some NP-Complete Problems. Ph.D. thesis, University of Belgrade, Faculty of Mathematics, 2000. (in Serbian)
17. E. Marchiori, and C. Rossi. A flipping genetic algorithm for hard 3-SAT problems. In *Proc. of the Genetic and Evolutionary Computation Conference*, 1999.
18. E. Marchiori, and A. Steenbeek. A genetic local search algorithm for random binary constraint satisfaction problems. In *Proc. of the SAC2000.*
19. N. Nilsson. Probabilistic logic. *Artificial Intelligence*, 28:71–87, 1986.
20. Z. Ognjanović and M. Rašković. Some probability logics with new types of probability operators. *Journal of Logic and Computation*, 9(2):181–195, 1999.
21. Z. Ognjanović and M. Rašković. Some first-order probability logics. *Theoretical Computer Science*, 247(1-2):191–212, 2000.
22. M. Rašković. Classical logic with some probability operators. *Publications de l'Institut Mathématique, Nouvelle Série, Beograd*, 53(67):1–3, 1993.

Author Index

Lecture Notes in Artificial Intelligence (LNAI)

Vol. 1968: H. Arimura, S. Jain, A. Sharma (Eds.), Algorithmic Learning Theory. Proceedings, 2000. XI, 335 pages. 2000.

Vol. 1972: A. Omicini, R. Tolksdorf, F. Zambonelli (Eds.), Engineering Societies in the Agents World. Proceedings, 2000. IX, 143 pages. 2000.

Vol. 1979: S. Moss, P. Davidsson (Eds.), Multi-Agent-Based Simulation. Proceedings, 2000. VIII, 267 pages. 2001.

Vol. 1986: C. Castelfranchi, Y. Lespérance (Eds.), Intelligent Agents VII. Proceedings, 2000. XVII, 357 pages. 2001.

Vol. 1991: F. Dignum, C. Sierra (Eds.), Agent Mediated Electronic Commerce. VIII, 241 pages. 2001.

Vol. 1994: J. Lind, Iterative Software Engineering for Multiagent Systems. XVII, 286 pages. 2001.

Vol. 1996: P.L. Lanzi, W. Stolzmann, S.W. Wilson (Eds.), Advances in Learning Classifier Systems. Proceedings, 2000. VIII, 273 pages. 2001. (Subseries LNAI).

Vol. 2003: F. Dignum, U. Cortés (Eds.), Agent-Mediated Electronic Commerce III. XII, 193 pages. 2001.

Vol. 2007: J.F. Roddick, K. Hornsby (Eds.), Temporal, Spatial, and Spatio-Temporal Data Mining. Proceedings, 2000. VII, 165 pages. 2001.

Vol. 2014: M. Moortgat (Ed.), Logical Aspects of Computational Linguistics. Proceedings, 1998. X, 287 pages. 2001.

Vol. 2019: P. Stone, T. Balch, G. Kraetzschmar (Eds.), RoboCup 2000: Robot Soccer World Cup IV. XVII, 658 pages. 2001.

Vol. 2033: J. Liu, Y. Ye (Eds.), E-Commerce Agents. VI, 347 pages. 2001.

Vol. 2035: D. Cheung, G.J. Williams, Q. Li (Eds.), Advances in Knowledge Discovery and Data Mining – PAKDD 2001. Proceedings, 2001. XVIII, 596 pages. 2001.

Vol. 2036: S. Wermter, J. Austin, D. Willshaw (Eds.), Emergent Neural Computational Architectures Based on Neuroscience. X, 577 pages. 2001.

Vol. 2039: M. Schumacher, Objective Coordination in Multi-Agent System Engineering. XIV, 149 pages. 2001.

Vol. 2049: G. Paliouras, V. Karkaletis, C.D. Spyropoulos (Eds.), Machine Learning and Its Applications. VIII, 325 pages. 2001.

Vol. 2056: E. Stroulia, S. Matwin (Eds.), Advances in Artificial Intelligence. Proceedings, 2001. XII, 366 pages. 2001.

Vol. 2062: A. Nareyek, Constraint-Based Agents. XIV, 178 pages. 2001.

Vol. 2070: L. Monostori, J. Váncza, M. Ali (Eds.), Engineering of Intelligent Systems. Proceedings, 2001. XVIII, 951 pages. 2001.

Vol. 2080: D.W. Aha, I. Watson (Eds.), Case-Based Reasoning Research and Development. Proceedings, 2001. XII, 758 pages. 2001.

Vol. 2083: R. Goré, A. Leitsch, T. Nipkow (Eds.), Automated Reasoning. Proceedings, 2001. XV, 708 pages. 2001.

Vol. 2086: M. Luck, V. Mařík, O. Štěpánková, R. Trappl (Eds.), Multi-Agent Systems and Applications. Proceedings, 2001. X, 437 pages. 2001.

Vol. 2087: G. Kern-Isberner, Conditionals in Nonmonotonic Reasoning and Belief Revision. X, 190 pages. 2001.

Vol. 2099: P. de Groote, G. Morrill, C. Retoré (Eds.), Logical Aspects of Computational Linguistics. Proceedings, 2001. VIII, 311 pages. 2001.

Vol. 2100: R. Küsters, Non-Standard Inferences in Description Logics. X, 250 pages. 2001.

Vol. 2101: S. Quaglini, P. Barahona, S. Andreassen (Eds.), Artificial Intelligence in Medicine. Proceedings, 2001. XIV, 469 pages. 2001.

Vol. 2103: M. Hannebauer, J. Wendler, E. Pagello (Eds.), Balancing Reactivity and Social Deliberation in Multi-Agent Systems. VIII, 237 pages. 2001.

Vol. 2109: M. Bauer, P.J. Gmytrasiewicz, J. Vassileva (Eds.), User Modeling 2001. Proceedings, 2001. XIII, 318 pages. 2001.

Vol. 2111: D. Helmbold, B. Williamson (Eds.), Computational Learning Theory. Proceedings, 2001. IX, 631 pages. 2001.

Vol. 2116: V. Akman, P. Bouquet, R. Thomason, R.A. Young (Eds.), Modeling and Using Context. Proceedings, 2001. XII, 472 pages. 2001.

Vol. 2117: M. Beynon, C.L. Nehaniv, K. Dautenhahn (Eds.), Cognitive Technology: Instruments of Mind. Proceedings, 2001. XV, 522 pages. 2001.

Vol. 2120: H.S. Delugach, G. Stumme (Eds.), Conceptual Structures: Broadening the Base. Proceedings, 2001. X, 377 pages. 2001.

Vol. 2123: P. Perner (Ed.), Machine Learning and Data Mining in Pattern Recognition. Proceedings, 2001. XI, 363 pages. 2001.

Vol. 2132: S.-T. Yuan, M. Yokoo (Eds.), Intelligent Agents: Specification, Modeling, and Application. Proceedings, 2001. X, 237 pages. 2001.

Vol. 2143: S. Benferhat, P. Besnard (Eds.), Symbolic and Quantitative Approaches to Reasoning with Uncertainty. Proceedings, 2001. XIV, 818 pages. 2001.

Lecture Notes in Computer Science